Lecture Notes in Computer Science 14082

Founding Editors

Gerhard Goos
Juris Hartmanis

Editorial Board Members

The series Lecture Notes in Computer Science (LNCS), including its subseries Lecture Notes in Artificial Intelligence (LNAI) and Lecture Notes in Bioinformatics (LNBI), has established itself as a medium for the publication of new developments in computer science and information technology research, teaching, and education.

LNCS enjoys close cooperation with the computer science R & D community, the series counts many renowned academics among its volume editors and paper authors, and collaborates with prestigious societies. Its mission is to serve this international community by providing an invaluable service, mainly focused on the publication of conference and workshop proceedings and postproceedings. LNCS commenced publication in 1973.

Helena Handschuh · Anna Lysyanskaya
Editors

Advances in Cryptology – CRYPTO 2023

43rd Annual International Cryptology Conference, CRYPTO 2023
Santa Barbara, CA, USA, August 20–24, 2023
Proceedings, Part II

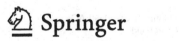 Springer

Editors
Helena Handschuh
Rambus Inc.
San Jose, CA, USA

Anna Lysyanskaya
Brown University
Providence, RI, USA

ISSN 0302-9743   ISSN 1611-3349 (electronic)
Lecture Notes in Computer Science
ISBN 978-3-031-38544-5   ISBN 978-3-031-38545-2 (eBook)
https://doi.org/10.1007/978-3-031-38545-2

This Springer imprint is published by the registered company Springer Nature Switzerland AG
The registered company address is: Gewerbestrasse 11, 6330 Cham, Switzerland

Preface

The 43rd International Cryptology Conference (CRYPTO 2023) was held at the University of California, Santa Barbara, California, USA, from August 20th to August 24th, 2023. It is an annual conference organized by the International Association for Cryptologic Research (IACR).

A record 479 papers were submitted for presentation at the conference, and 124 were selected, including two pairs of soft merges, for a total of 122 speaking slots. As a result of this record high, CRYPTO 2023 had three tracks for the first time in its history.

For the first time in its history as well, CRYPTO benefited from the great advice and tremendous help from six area chairs, covering the main areas of focus for the conference. These were Lejla Batina for Efficient and Secure Implementations, Dan Boneh for Public Key Primitives with Advanced Functionalities, Orr Dunkelman for Symmetric Cryptology, Leo Reyzin for Information-Theoretic and Complexity-Theoretic Cryptography, Douglas Stebila for Public-Key Cryptography and Muthuramakrishnan Venkitasubramaniam for Multi-Party Computation. Each of them helped lead discussions and decide which ones of the approximately 80 submissions in their area should be accepted. Their help was invaluable and we could not have succeeded without them.

To evaluate the submissions, we selected a program committee that consisted of 102 top cryptography researchers from all over the world. This was the largest program committee that CRYPTO has ever had, as well. Each paper was assigned to three program committee members who reviewed it either by themselves or with the help of a trusted sub-referee. As a result, we benefited from the expertise of almost 500 sub-referees. Together, they generated a staggering 1500 reviews. We thank our program committee members and the external sub-referees for the hard work of peer review which is the bedrock of scientific progress.

The review process was double-blind and confidential. In accordance with the IACR conflict-of-interest policy, the reviewing software we used (HotCRP) kept track of which reviewers had a conflict of interest with which authors (for example, by virtue of being a close collaborator or an advisor) and ensured that no paper was assigned a conflicted reviewer.

In order to be considered, submissions had to be anonymous and their length was limited to 30 pages excluding the bibliography and supplementary materials. After the first six or so weeks of evaluation, the committee chose to continue considering 330 papers; the remaining 149 papers were rejected, including five desk rejects. The majority of these received three reviews, none of which favored acceptance, although in limited cases the decision was made based on only two reviews that were in agreement. The papers that remained under consideration were invited to submit a response (rebuttal) to clarifications requested from their reviewers. Two papers were withdrawn during this second phase. Each of the 328 remaining papers received at least three reviews. After around five weeks of additional discussions, the committee made the final selection of the 124 papers that appear in these proceedings.

We would like to thank all the authors who submitted their papers to CRYPTO 2023. The vast majority of the submissions, including those that were ultimately not selected, were of very high quality, and we are very honored that CRYPTO was the venue that the authors chose for their work. We are additionally grateful to the authors of the accepted papers for the extra work of incorporating the reviewers' feedback and presenting their papers at the conference.

This year the Best Paper Award was awarded to Keegan Ryan and Nadia Heninger for their paper "Fast Practical Lattice Reduction Through Iterated Compression." The Best Early Career Paper Award went to Elizabeth Crites, Chelsea Komlo and Mary Maller for their paper "Fully Adaptive Schnorr Threshold Signatures." The runner up Best Early Career Paper was by Ward Beullens on "Graph-Theoretic Algorithms for the Alternating Trilinear Form Equivalence Problem." These three papers were subsequently invited to be submitted to the IACR Journal of Cryptology.

In addition to the presentations of contributed papers included in these proceedings, the conference also featured two plenary talks: Hugo Krawczyk delivered the IACR Distinguished Lecture, and Scott Aaronson gave an invited talk titled "Neurocryptography." The traditional rump session, chaired by Allison Bishop, took place on Tuesday, August 22nd, and featured numerous short talks.

Co-located cryptography workshops were held in the preceding weekend; they included the following seven events, "Crypto meets Artificial Intelligence—The Glowing Hot Topics in Cryptography," "MathCrypt—The Workshop on Mathematical Cryptology," "CFAIL—The Conference for Failed Approaches and Insightful Losses in Cryptography," "PPML—The Privacy-Preserving Machine Learning Workshop," "WAC6—The Workshop on Attacks in Cryptography 6," "ACAI—Applied Cryptology and Artificial Intelligence," and "RISE—Research Insights and Stories for Enlightenment." We gladly thank Alessandra Scafuro for serving as the Affiliated Events Chair and putting together such an enticing program.

All of this was possible thanks to Kevin McCurley and Kay McKelly without whom all of our review software would be crashing non-stop, and all of the Crypto presentations would be nothing but static. They are the true pillars of all of our IACR Crypto events and conferences. Last but not least we thank Britta Hale for serving as our General Chair and making sure the conference went smoothly and attendees had a great experience. Thank you to our industry sponsors, including early sponsors a16z, AWS, Casper, Google, JPMorgan, Meta, PQShield, and TII for their generous contributions, as well as to the NSF Award 2330160 for supporting Ph.D. student participants.

August 2023

Helena Handschuh
Anna Lysyanskaya

Organization

General Chair

Britta Hale   Naval Postgraduate School, USA

Program Co-chairs

Helena Handschuh   Rambus Inc., USA
Anna Lysyanskaya   Brown University, USA

Area Chairs

Lejla Batina *(for Efficient and*   Radboud University, the Netherlands
Secure Implementations)
Dan Boneh *(for Public Key*   Stanford University, USA
Primitives with Advanced
Functionalities)
Orr Dunkelman *(for Symmetric*   University of Haifa, Israel
Cryptology)
Leo Reyzin *(for*   Boston University, USA
Information-Theoretic and
Complexity-Theoretic
Cryptography)
Douglas Stebila *(for Public-Key*   University of Waterloo, Canada
Cryptography)
Muthu Venkitasubramaniam *(for*   Georgetown University, USA
Multi-Party Computation)

Program Committee

Shweta Agrawal   IIT Madras, India
Ghada Almashaqbeh   University of Connecticut, USA
Benny Applebaum   Tel-Aviv University, Israel
Marshall Ball   New York University, USA
Fabrice Benhamouda   Algorand Foundation, USA

Anja Lehmann	Hasso-Plattner-Institute, University of Potsdam, Germany
Tancrède Lepoint	Amazon, USA
Benjamin Lipp	Max Planck Institute for Security and Privacy, Germany
Feng-Hao Liu	Florida Atlantic University, USA
Tianren Liu	Peking University, China
Patrick Longa	Microsoft Research, USA
Julian Loss	CISPA Helmholtz Center for Information Security, Germany
Fermi Ma	Simons Institute and UC Berkeley, USA
Mary Maller	Ethereum Foundation and PQShield, UK
Chloe Martindale	University of Bristol, UK
Alexander May	Ruhr-University Bochum, Germany
Florian Mendel	Infineon Technologies, Germany
Bart Mennink	Radboud University, the Netherlands
Brice Minaud	Inria and ENS, France
Kazuhiko Minematsu	NEC and Yokohama National University, Japan
Pratyush Mishra	Aleo Systems, USA
Tarik Moataz	MongoDB, USA
Jesper Buus Nielsen	Aarhus University, Denmark
Kaisa Nyberg	Aalto University, Finland
Miyako Ohkubo	NICT, Japan
Eran Omri	Ariel University, Israel
David Oswald	University of Birmingham, UK
Omkant Pandey	Stony Brook University, USA
Omer Paneth	Tel-Aviv University, Israel
Alain Passelègue	Inria and ENS Lyon, France
Arpita Patra	IISc Bangalore and Google Research, India
Léo Perrin	Inria, France
Thomas Peters	UCLouvain and FNRS, Belgium
Thomas Peyrin	Nanyang Technological University, Singapore
Stjepan Picek	Radboud University, the Netherlands
David Pointcheval	École Normale Supérieure, France
Antigoni Polychroniadou	J.P. Morgan AI Research, USA
Bart Preneel	University of Leuven, Belgium
Mariana Raykova	Google, USA
Christian Rechberger	TU Graz, Austria
Oscar Reparaz	Block, Inc., USA
Matthieu Rivain	CryptoExperts, France
Mélissa Rossi	ANSSI, France
Guy Rothblum	Apple, USA

Alexander Russell	University of Connecticut, USA
Paul Rösler	FAU Erlangen-Nürnberg, Germany
Kazue Sako	Waseda University, Japan
Alessandra Scafuro	North Carolina State University, USA
Patrick Schaumont	Worcester Polytechnic Institute, USA
Thomas Schneider	TU Darmstadt, Germany
André Schrottenloher	Inria, Univ. Rennes, CNRS, IRISA, France
Dominique Schröder	FAU Erlangen-Nürnberg, Germany
Benjamin Smith	Inria and École Polytechnique, France
Ling Song	Jinan University, China
Mehdi Tibouchi	NTT Social Informatics Laboratories, Japan
Yosuke Todo	NTT Social Informatics Laboratories, Japan
Alin Tomescu	Aptos Labs, USA
Dominique Unruh	University of Tartu, Estonia
Gilles Van Assche	STMicroelectronics, Belgium
Damien Vergnaud	Sorbonne Université, France
Jiayu Xu	Oregon State University, USA
Arkady Yerukhimovich	George Washington University, USA
Yu Yu	Shanghai Jiao Tong University, China

Additional Reviewers

Kasra Abbaszadeh
Behzad Abdolmaleki
Masayuki Abe
Ittai Abraham
Hamza Abusalah
Amit Agarwal
Akshima
Gorjan Alagic
Martin Albrecht
Bar Alon
Miguel Ambrona
Prabhanjan Ananth
Megumi Ando
Yoshinori Aono
Paula Arnold
Gal Arnon
Arasu Arun
Gilad Asharov
Renas Bacho
Matilda Backendal

Christian Badertscher
Shi Bai
David Balbás
Paulo Barreto
James Bartusek
Andrea Basso
Jules Baudrin
Balthazar Bauer
Carsten Baum
Josh Beal
Hugo Beguinet
Amos Beimel
Sana Belguith
Thiago Bergamaschi
Olivier Bernard
Sebastian Berndt
Ward Beullens
Tim Beyne
Rishiraj Bhattacharyya
Ritam Bhaumik

Mengda Bi

Alexander Bienstock

Bruno Blanchet

Olivier Blazy

Maxime Bombar

Xavier Bonnetain

Jonathan Bootle

Samuel Bouaziz-Ermann

Katharina Boudgoust

Alexandre Bouez

Charles Bouillaguet

Christina Boura

Clémence Bouvier

Ross Bowden

Pedro Branco

Anne Broadbent

Olivier Bronchain

Andreas Brüggemann

Anirudh Chandramouli

Eleonora Cagli

Matteo Campanelli

Pedro Capitão

Eliana Carozza

Kévin Carrier

Wouter Castryck

Pyrros Chaidos

Andre Chailloux

Suvradip Chakraborty

Gowri Chandran

Rohit Chatterjee

Albert Cheu

Céline Chevalier

Nai-Hui Chia

Arka Rai Choudhuri

Hien Chu

Hao Chung

Michele Ciampi

Valerio Cini

James Clements

Christine Cloostermans

Benoît Cogliati

Andrea Coladangelo

Jean-Sébastien Coron

Henry Corrigan-Gibbs

Craig Costello

Elizabeth Crites

Eric Crockett

Jan-Pieter D'Anvers

Antoine Dallon

Poulami Das

Gareth Davies

Hannah Davis

Dennis Dayanikli

Leo de Castro

Paola De Perthuis

Rafael del Pino

Cyprien Delpech de Saint Guilhem

Jeroen Delvaux

Patrick Derbez

Zach DeStefano

Lalita Devadas

Julien Devevey

Henri Devillez

Jean-François Dhem

Adam Ding

Yevgeniy Dodis

Xiaoyang Dong

Nico Döttling

Benjamin Dowling

Leo Ducas

Clément Ducros

Céline Duguey

Jesko Dujmovic

Christoph Egger

Maria Eichlseder

Reo Eriguchi

Andreas Erwig

Daniel Escudero

Thomas Espitau

Andre Esser

Simona Etinski

Thibauld Feneuil

Pouria Fallahpour

Maya Farber Brodsky

Pooya Farshim

Joël Felderhoff

Rex Fernando

Matthias Fitzi

Antonio Flórez-Gutiérrez

Cody Freitag

Sapir Freizeit
Benjamin Fuller
Phillip Gajland
Tarek Galal
Nicolas Gama
John Gaspoz
Pierrick Gaudry
Romain Gay
Peter Gaži
Yuval Gelles
Marilyn George
François Gérard
Paul Gerhart
Alexandru Gheorghiu
Ashrujit Ghoshal
Shane Gibbons
Benedikt Gierlichs
Barbara Gigerl
Noemi Glaeser
Aarushi Goel
Eli Goldin
Junqing Gong
Dov Gordon
Lénaïck Gouriou
Marc Gourjon
Jerome Govinden
Juan Grados
Lorenzo Grassi
Sandra Guasch
Aurore Guillevic
Sam Gunn
Aldo Gunsing
Daniel Günther
Chun Guo
Siyao Guo
Yue Guo
Shreyas Gupta
Hosein Hadipour
Mohammad Hajiabadi
Shai Halevi
Lucjan Hanzlik
Aditya Hegde
Rachelle Heim
Lena Heimberger
Paul Hermouet

Julia Hesse
Minki Hhan
Taiga Hiroka
Justin Holmgren
Alex Hoover
Akinori Hosoyamada
Kristina Hostakova
Kai Hu
Yu-Hsuan Huang
Mi-Ying Miryam Huang
Pavel Hubáček
Andreas Hülsing
Akiko Inoue
Takanori Isobe
Akira Ito
Ryoma Ito
Tetsu Iwata
Jennifer Jackson
Joseph Jaeger
Zahra Jafargholi
Jonas Janneck
Stanislaw Jarecki
Zhengzhong Jin
David Joseph
Daniel Jost
Nathan Ju
Seny Kamara
Chetan Kamath
Simon Holmgaard Kamp
Gabriel Kaptchuk
Vukašin Karadžić
Ioanna Karantaidou
Harish Karthikeyan
Mustafa Khairallah
Mojtaba Khalili
Nora Khayata
Hamidreza Khoshakhlagh
Eda Kirimli
Elena Kirshanova
Ágnes Kiss
Fuyuki Kitagawa
Susumu Kiyoshima
Alexander Koch
Dmitry Kogan
Konrad Kohbrok

Sreehari Kollath
Yashvanth Kondi
Venkata Koppula
Marina Krcek
Maximilian Kroschewski
Daniël Kuijsters
Péter Kutas
Qiqi Lai
Yi-Fu Lai
Philip Lazos
Jason LeGrow
Gregor Leander
Ulysse Léchine
Yi Lee
Charlotte Lefevre
Jonas Lehmann
Antonin Leroux
Baiyu Li
Chaoyun Li
Hanjun Li
Wenjie Li
Xin Li
Xingjian Li
Zhe Li
Mingyu Liang
Xiao Liang
Damien Ligier
Wei-Kai Lin
Helger Lipmaa
Guozhen Liu
Jiahui Liu
Linsheng Liu
Meicheng Liu
Qipeng Liu
Zeyu Liu
Chen-Da Liu-Zhang
Alex Lombardi
Johanna Loyer
Ji Luo
Vadim Lyubashevsky
Yiping Ma
Varun Madathil
Bernardo Magri
Luciano Maino
Monosij Maitra

Christian Majenz
Jasleen Malvai
Marian Margraf
Mario Marhuenda Beltrán
Erik Mårtensson
Ange Martinelli
Daniel Masny
Loïc Masure
Takahiro Matsuda
Kotaro Matsuoka
Christian Matt
Krystian Matusiewicz
Noam Mazor
Matthias Meijers
Fredrik Meisingseth
Pierre Meyer
Daniele Micciancio
Elena Micheli
Marine Minier
Helen Möllering
Charles Momin
Atsuki Momose
Hart Montgomery
Tal Moran
Tomoyuki Morimae
Kirill Morozov
Fabrice Mouhartem
Koksal Mus
Saachi Mutreja
Michael Naehrig
Marcel Nageler
Rishub Nagpal
Yusuke Naito
Anand Kumar Narayanan
Shoei Nashimoto
Ky Nguyen
Georgio Nicolas
Raine Nieminen
Valeria Nikolaenko
Oded Nir
Ryo Nishimaki
Olga Nissenbaum
Anca Nitulescu
Julian Nowakowski
Adam O'Neill

Sai Lakshmi Bhavana Obbattu
Maciej Obremski
Arne Tobias Ødegaard
Morten Øygarden
Cavit Özbay
Erdinc Ozturk
Jiaxin Pan
Dimitrios Papachristoudis
Aditi Partap
Anat Paskin-Cherniavsky
Rafael Pass
Sikhar Patranabis
Stanislav Peceny
Chris Peikert
Angelos Pelecanos
Alice Pellet-Mary
Octavio Perez-Kempner
Guilherme Perin
Trevor Perrin
Giuseppe Persiano
Pessl Peter
Spencer Peters
Duong Hieu Phan
Benny Pinkas
Bertram Poettering
Guru Vamsi Policharla
Jason Pollack
Giacomo Pope
Alexander Poremba
Eamonn Postlethwaite
Thomas Prest
Robert Primas
Luowen Qian
Willy Quach
Håvard Raddum
Shahram Rasoolzadeh
Divya Ravi
Michael Reichle
Jean-René Reinhard
Omar Renawi
Joost Renes
Nicolas Resch
Mahshid Riahinia
Silas Richelson
Jan Richter-Brockmann

Doreen Riepel
Peter Rindal
Bhaskar Roberts
Wrenna Robson
Sondre Rønjom
Mike Rosulek
Yann Rotella
Lior Rotem
Ron Rothblum
Adeline Roux-Langlois
Joe Rowell
Lawrence Roy
Keegan Ryan
Mark Ryan
Sherman S. M. Chow
Eric Sageloli
Antonio Sanso
Practik Sarkar
Yu Sasaki
Robert Schaedlich
Jan Schlegel
Martin Schläffer
Markus Schofnegger
Peter Scholl
Jan Schoone
Phillipp Schoppmann
Jacob Schuldt
Mark Schultz
Marek Sefranek
Nicolas Sendrier
Jae Hong Seo
Karn Seth
Srinath Setty
Yannick Seurin
Dana Shamir
Devika Sharma
Yaobin Shen
Yixin Shen
Danping Shi
Sina Shiehian
Omri Shmueli
Ferdinand Sibleyras
Janno Siim
Mark Simkin
Jaspal Singh

Amit Singh Bhati
Sujoy Sinha Roy
Naomi Sirkin
Daniel Slamanig
Christopher Smith
Tomer Solomon
Fang Song
Yifan Song
Pratik Soni
Jesse Spielman
Srivatsan Sridhar
Damien Stehlé
Marc Stevens
Christoph Striecks
Patrick Struck
Adam Suhl
Chao Sun
Siwei Sun
Berk Sunar
Ajith Suresh
Moeto Suzuki
Erkan Tairi
Akira Takahashi
Katsuyuki Takashima
Abdul Rahman Taleb
Quan Quan Tan
Er-Cheng Tang
Qiang Tang
Stefano Tessaro
Justin Thaler
Yan Bo Ti
Tyge Tiessen
Junichi Tomida
Dilara Toprakhisar
Andreas Trügler
Daniel Tschudi
Yiannis Tselekounis
Ida Tucker
Balazs Udvarhelyi
Rei Ueno
Florian Unterstein
Annapurna Valiveti
Gijs Van Laer
Wessel van Woerden
Akhil Vanukuri
Karolin Varner

Javier Verbel
Tanner Verber
Frederik Vercauteren
Corentin Verhamme
Psi Vesely
Fernando Virdia
Quoc-Huy Vu
Benedikt Wagner
Roman Walch
Hendrik Waldner
Han Wang
Libo Wang
William Wang
Yunhao Wang
Zhedong Wang
Hoeteck Wee
Mor Weiss
Weiqiang Wen
Chenkai Weng
Luca Wilke
Mathias Wolf
David Wu
Lichao Wu
Zejun Xiang
Tiancheng Xie
Alex Xiong
Anshu Yadav
Sophia Yakoubov
Hossein Yalame
Shota Yamada
Avishay Yanai
Kang Yang
Qianqian Yang
Tianqi Yang
Yibin Yang
Kan Yasuda
Eylon Yogev
Yang Yu
Arantxa Zapico
Hadas Zeilberger
Bin Zhang
Jiang Zhang
Ruizhe Zhang
Zhenda Zhang
Chenzhi Zhu
Jens Zumbraegel

Contents – Part II

Succinctness

Revisiting Cycles of Pairing-Friendly Elliptic Curves 3
  Marta Bellés-Muñoz, Jorge Jiménez Urroz, and Javier Silva

Non-interactive Zero-Knowledge from Non-interactive Batch Arguments 38
  Jeffrey Champion and David J. Wu

Lattice-Based Succinct Arguments from Vanishing Polynomials:
(Extended Abstract) 72
  Valerio Cini, Russell W. F. Lai, and Giulio Malavolta

Orbweaver: Succinct Linear Functional Commitments from Lattices 106
  Ben Fisch, Zeyu Liu, and Psi Vesely

Non-interactive Universal Arguments 132
  Nir Bitansky, Omer Paneth, Dana Shamir, and Tomer Solomon

Succinct Arguments for RAM Programs via Projection Codes 159
  Yuval Ishai, Rafail Ostrovsky, and Akash Shah

Brakedown: Linear-Time and Field-Agnostic SNARKs for R1CS 193
  Alexander Golovnev, Jonathan Lee, Srinath Setty, Justin Thaler,
  and Riad S. Wahby

Lattice-Based Succinct Arguments for NP with Polylogarithmic-Time
Verification 227
  Jonathan Bootle, Alessandro Chiesa, and Katerina Sotiraki

SNARGs for Monotone Policy Batch NP 252
  Zvika Brakerski, Maya Farber Brodsky, Yael Tauman Kalai,
  Alex Lombardi, and Omer Paneth

TreePIR: Sublinear-Time and Polylog-Bandwidth Private Information
Retrieval from DDH 284
  Arthur Lazzaretti and Charalampos Papamanthou

Multi-party Homomorphic Secret Sharing and Sublinear MPC from Sparse
LPN 315
  Quang Dao, Yuval Ishai, Aayush Jain, and Huijia Lin

Anonymous Credentials

Lattice Signature with Efficient Protocols, Application to Anonymous
Credentials 351
   Corentin Jeudy, Adeline Roux-Langlois, and Olivier Sanders

A Framework for Practical Anonymous Credentials from Lattices 384
   Jonathan Bootle, Vadim Lyubashevsky, Ngoc Khanh Nguyen,
   and Alessandro Sorniotti

Anonymous Tokens with Stronger Metadata Bit Hiding from Algebraic
MACs 418
   Melissa Chase, F. Betül Durak, and Serge Vaudenay

New Paradigms and Foundations

Revisiting Time-Space Tradeoffs for Function Inversion 453
   Alexander Golovnev, Siyao Guo, Spencer Peters,
   and Noah Stephens-Davidowitz

The Query-Complexity of Preprocessing Attacks 482
   Ashrujit Ghoshal and Stefano Tessaro

Random Oracle Combiners: Breaking the Concatenation Barrier
for Collision-Resistance 514
   Yevgeniy Dodis, Niels Ferguson, Eli Goldin, Peter Hall,
   and Krzysztof Pietrzak

Individual Cryptography 547
   Stefan Dziembowski, Sebastian Faust, and Tomasz Lizurej

Extractors: Low Entropy Requirements Colliding with Non-malleability 580
   Divesh Aggarwal, Eldon Chung, and Maciej Obremski

PAC Privacy: Automatic Privacy Measurement and Control of Data
Processing 611
   Hanshen Xiao and Srinivas Devadas

One-Way Functions and the Hardness of (Probabilistic) Time-Bounded
Kolmogorov Complexity w.r.t. Samplable Distributions 645
   Yanyi Liu and Rafael Pass

Universal Amplification of KDM Security: From 1-Key Circular
to Multi-Key KDM 674
   Brent Waters and Daniel Wichs

Improved Multi-user Security Using the Squared-Ratio Method 694
  Yu Long Chen, Wonseok Choi, and Changmin Lee

The Power of Undirected Rewindings for Adaptive Security 725
  Dennis Hofheinz, Julia Kastner, and Karen Klein

Anamorphic Signatures: Secrecy from a Dictator Who Only Permits
Authentication! 759
  *Mirosław Kutyłowski, Giuseppe Persiano, Duong Hieu Phan,
  Moti Yung, and Marcin Zawada*

Author Index 791

Succinctness

Revisiting Cycles of Pairing-Friendly Elliptic Curves

Marta Bellés-Muñoz[1,2], Jorge Jiménez Urroz[3,4], and Javier Silva[1(✉)]

[1] Dusk Network, Amsterdam, The Netherlands
{marta,javier}@dusk.network
[2] Pompeu Fabra University, Barcelona, Spain
[3] Polytechnic University of Catalonia, Barcelona, Spain
jorge.urroz@upc.edu
[4] Technical University of Madrid, Madrid, Spain

Abstract. A recent area of interest in cryptography is recursive composition of proof systems. One of the approaches to make recursive composition efficient involves cycles of pairing-friendly elliptic curves of prime order. However, known constructions have very low embedding degrees. This entails large parameter sizes, which makes the overall system inefficient. In this paper, we explore 2-cycles composed of curves from families parameterized by polynomials, and show that such cycles do not exist unless a strong condition holds. As a consequence, we prove that no 2-cycles can arise from the known families, except for those cycles already known. Additionally, we show some general properties about cycles, and provide a detailed computation on the density of pairing-friendly cycles among all cycles.

Keywords: pairing-friendly elliptic curves · cycles of elliptic curves · proof systems

1 Introduction

A *proof system* is an interactive protocol between two parties, called the *prover* and the *verifier*. The prover aims to convince the verifier of the truth of a certain statement u, which is an element of a language $\mathcal{L}$ in NP. Associated to a statement is a *witness*, which is a potentially secret input w that the prover uses to produce the proof of $u \in \mathcal{L}$. A recent area of interest is *recursive composition* of proof systems [7,44], since it leads to *proof-carrying data (PCD)* [16], a cryptographic primitive that allows multiple untrusted parties to collaborate on a computation that runs indefinitely, and has found multiple applications [10,17,30,37]. In recursive composition of proof systems, each prover in a sequence of provers takes the previous proof and verifies it, and performs some computations on their own, finally producing a proof that guarantees that (a) the previous proof verifies correctly, and (b) the new computation has been

Authors are listed in alphabetical order (https://www.ams.org/profession/leaders/CultureStatement04.pdf).

H. Handschuh and A. Lysyanskaya (Eds.): CRYPTO 2023, LNCS 14082, pp. 3–37, 2023.
https://doi.org/10.1007/978-3-031-38545-2_1

performed correctly. This way, the verifier, who simply verifies the last proof produced in the sequence, can be sure of the correct computation of every step.

We require two things from the proof system for recursive composition to work. First, that it is expressive enough to be able to accept its own verification algorithm as something to prove statements about, and second, that the verification algorithm is small enough so that the prover algorithm does not grow on each step. In the literature we can find several proof systems that differ on their cryptographic assumptions and performance. *Succinct non-interactive arguments of knowledge* (SNARKs) are of particular interest, since they provide a computationally sound proof of small size compared to the size of the statement [8]. In particular, we focus on pairing-based SNARKs [25, 27, 29, 38], which make use of elliptic-curve pairings for verification of proofs, achieving verification time that does not depend on the size of the statement being proven. One downside of SNARKs is that they require a set of public parameters, known as the *common reference string (CRS)*, that is at best linear in the size of the statement. We note that there is a way to achieve recursive composition with a linear-time verifier, as long as the proof system is compatible with an efficient accumulator scheme [9, 11–13]. However, we focus on the case of pairing-based SNARKs, due to the appeal of constant verification time.

1.1   Avoiding Non-native Arithmetic with Cycles

A pairing-based SNARK relies on an elliptic curve $E/\mathbb{F}_q$ for some prime q, and such that $E(\mathbb{F}_q)$ has a large subgroup of prime order p. With this setting, the SNARK is able to prove satisfiability of arithmetic circuits over $\mathbb{F}_p$. However, the proof will be composed of elements in $\mathbb{F}_p$ and, crucially, elements in $E(\mathbb{F}_q)$. Each of these latter elements, although they belong to a group of order p, are represented as a pair of elements in $\mathbb{F}_q$. Moreover, the verification involves operations on the curve, which have formulas that use $\mathbb{F}_q$-arithmetic. Therefore, recursive composition of SNARK proofs requires to write the $\mathbb{F}_q$-arithmetic, derived from the verification algorithm, with an $\mathbb{F}_p$-circuit. Since $\mathbb{F}_p$-circuit satisfiability is an NP complete problem, it is possible to simulate $\mathbb{F}_q$-arithmetic via $\mathbb{F}_p$-operations, but this solution incurs into an efficiency blowup of $O(\log q)$ compared to native arithmetic [7, Section 3.1].

Ideally, we would like $q = p$. However, there is a linear-time algorithm for solving the discrete logarithm problem on curves of this kind [42]. Therefore, we shall assume that $p \neq q$. In this case, one approach is to instantiate a new copy of the SNARK with another elliptic curve E' to deal with $\mathbb{F}_q$-circuits. In [18], the authors propose to use a *2-chain* of pairing-friendly elliptic curves to achieve bounded recursive proof composition. A 2-chain of (pairing-friendly) elliptic curves is a tuple of pairing-friendly elliptic curves (E_1, E_2), defined over $\mathbb{F}_{p_1}$ and $\mathbb{F}_{p_2}$, where $p_1 \mid \#E_2(\mathbb{F}_{p_2})$ [2].

A more ambitious approach, proposed in [7], is to use pairs of curves that also satisfy that $p_2 \mid \#E_1(\mathbb{F}_{p_1})$. In this case, the pair of curves is called a *2–cycle*. By alternating the instantiation of the SNARK with the two curves of the cycle, it is possible to allow unbounded recursive composition of the SNARK without incurring into non-native arithmetic simulation. Although this idea can also be used with longer cycles, 2-cycles are the optimal choice for recursive SNARKs, because they only require the generation and maintenance of two CRS.

1.2 State of the Art

Silverman and Stange [41] introduced and did a systematic study on 2-cycles of elliptic curves. As they show in their paper, in general, cycles of elliptic curves are easy to find. However, for recursive composition of pairing-based SNARKs, we need to be able to compute a pairing operation on the curves of the cycle. For this reason, curves need to have a *low* embedding degree, so that the pairing can be computed in a reasonable amount of time. Such curves are called *pairing-friendly* curves.

In [15], Chiesa, Chua, and Weidner focused on cycles of pairing-friendly curves. In particular, they showed that only prime-order curves can form cycles. The only known method to produce prime-order curves is via families of curves parameterized by polynomials, and currently there are only five that are known. The first three of these families were introduced by Miyaji, Nakabayashi, and Takano [35], who characterized all prime-order curves with embedding degrees 3, 4, and 6. These are called MNT curves. Based on the work from [26], Barreto and Naehrig [5] found a new family of curves with embedding degree 12, and later Freeman [22] found another one with embedding degree 10. The only known cycles are formed by alternating MNT curves of embedding degrees 4 and 6 [15, 28]. As proposed in [7], these cycles can be used to instantiate recursive composition of SNARKs, but due to their very low embedding degree, the parameter sizes need to be very large to avoid classical discrete-logarithm attacks [33], making the whole construction slow. Furthermore, the fact that the embedding degrees are different leads to an unbalance in the parameters, making one curve larger than necessary. Therefore, it would be desirable to have 2-cycles in which both curves have the same embedding degree k, for k a bit larger than in MNT curves. For instance, [15] suggests embedding degrees 12 or 20. This would allow for more efficient instantiations of protocols that make use of recursive composition of pairing-friendly SNARKs.

A characterization of all the possible cycles consisting of MNT curves is given in [15]. They also showed that there are no cycles consisting of curves from only the Freeman or Barreto–Naehrig (BN) families. They also gave some properties and impossibility results about pairing-friendly cycles, suggesting that adding the condition of pairing-friendliness to the curves of a cycle is a strong requirement: while cycles of curves are easy to find, cycles of pairing-friendly curves are not.

Recent progress has focused on chains of elliptic curves [20] but there are still some interesting problems in the direction of cycles. In particular, [15] lists some open problems, such as studying 2-cycles where the two curves have the same embedding degree or finding a cycle by combining curves from different families.

1.3   Contributions and Organization

In this paper, we continue with the line of research of [15] and tackle some of the open problems suggested by the authors. In Sect. 2, we review the background material on elliptic curves, focusing on families of pairing-friendly curves with prime order. In Sect. 3, we recall the notion of cycles of elliptic curves, and what is known about them. We also present some new results, in particular a lower bound on the trace of curves involved in a 2-cycle, when both curves have the same (small) embedding degree. In Sect. 4 we study whether a combination of curves from different families can form a 2-cycle. This answers one of the open questions from [15], for the case of 2-cycles.

Theorem 4.5 (informal). *Parametric families either form 2-cycles as polynomials or only form finitely many pairing-friendly 2-cycles, and these can be explicitly bounded.*

   Moreover, we show that no curve from any of the known families can be in a 2-cycle in which the other curve has embedding degree $\ell \leq 22$, even going a bit further in some cases. This is achieved by combining the previous theorem with explicit computations for each of the families. These results shed some light over the difficulty of finding new cycles of elliptic curves, considering the fact that polynomial families are the only known way to produce pairing-friendly elliptic curves with prime order. Finally, in Sect. 5 we estimate the density of pairing-friendly cycles among all cycles. In [3], Balasubramanian and Koblitz estimated the density of pairing-friendly curves. We generalize their result to cycles of pairing-friendly curves. We conclude the paper in Sect. 6. Appendices A, B, C include additional computations and SageMath code, which can also be found in [1].

2   Pairing-Friendly Elliptic Curves

Notation. Throughout this document, we assume that $p, q, q_i > 3$ are prime numbers. We denote by $\mathbb{F}_q$ the finite field with q elements. For $n \in \mathbb{N}$, we denote by $\varphi(n)$ the Euler's totient function on n, and by Φ_n the n-th cyclotomic polynomial, which has degree $\varphi(n)$. A polynomial $g \in \mathbb{Q}[X]$ is *integer-valued* if $g(x) \in \mathbb{Z}$ for all $x \in \mathbb{Z}$.

2.1   Elliptic Curves

An *elliptic curve* E over $\mathbb{F}_q$ (denoted $E/\mathbb{F}_q$) is a smooth algebraic curve of genus 1, defined by the equation

$$Y^2 = X^3 + aX + b,$$

for some $a, b \in \mathbb{F}_q$ such that $4a^3 - 27b^2 \neq 0$. We denote the group of $\mathbb{F}_q$-rational points by $E(\mathbb{F}_q)$, and refer to $\#E(\mathbb{F}_q)$ as the *order* of the curve. The neutral point is denoted by O. Given $m \in \mathbb{N}$, the *m-torsion group* of E is $E[m] = \{P \in$

$E(\overline{\mathbb{F}}_q) \mid mP = O\}$, where $\overline{\mathbb{F}}_q$ is the algebraic closure of $\mathbb{F}_q$. When $q \nmid m$, we have that $E[m] \cong \mathbb{Z}_m \times \mathbb{Z}_m$. The *trace of Frobenius* (often called just *trace*) of E is

$$t = q + 1 - \#E(\mathbb{F}_q).$$

Hasse's theorem [40, Theorem V.1.1] states that $|t| \le 2\sqrt{q}$, and Deuring's theorem [19, Theorem 14.18] states that, for any $t \in \mathbb{Z}$ within the Hasse bound, there exists an elliptic curve $E/\mathbb{F}_q$ with trace t.

A curve is said to be *supersingular* when $q \mid t$, and *ordinary* otherwise. Since we work with $q > 3$ prime, the Hasse bound implies that the only supersingular curves are those with $t = 0$. In the case of ordinary curves, the endomorphism ring will be an order $\mathcal{O} \subseteq \mathbb{Q}(\sqrt{d})$, where d is the square-free part of $t^2 - 4q$. The value d is called the *discriminant* of the curve E, and we say that E has *complex multiplication* by $\mathcal{O}$. Note that the Hasse bound implies that $d < 0$.[1]

Pairings and the Embedding Degree. Let $E/\mathbb{F}_q$ be an elliptic curve. Then, for m such that $q \nmid m$, we can build a *pairing*

$$e : E[m] \times E[m] \to \mu_m,$$

where $E[m] \cong \mathbb{Z}_m \times \mathbb{Z}_m$ is the m-torsion group of the curve and μ_m is the group of mth roots of unity. The map e is bilinear, i.e. $e(aP, bQ) = e(P, Q)^{ab}$ for any $P, Q \in E[m]$. Various instantiations of this map exist, e.g. the Weil pairing [40, §III.8]. Since $\mu_m \subset \mathbb{F}_{q^k}^*$ for some $k \in \mathbb{N}$ and is a multiplicative subgroup, it follows that $m \mid q^k - 1$. The smallest k satisfying this property is called the *embedding degree* of $E[m]$. When $m = \#E(\mathbb{F}_q)$, we refer to this k as the embedding degree of E.

Proposition 2.1. *Let $E/\mathbb{F}_q$ be an elliptic curve of prime order p. The following conditions are equivalent:*

- *E has embedding degree k.*
- *k is minimal such that $p \mid \Phi_k(q)$ [35, Remark 1].*
- *k is minimal such that $p \mid \Phi_k(t - 1)$ [4, Lemma 1].*

Most curves have a very large embedding degree [3, Theorem 2]. This has a direct impact on the computational cost of computing the pairing. On the one hand, we want small embedding degrees to ensure efficient arithmetic. On the other hand, however, small embedding degrees open an avenue for attacks, more precisely the [24,33] reductions. These translate the discrete logarithm problem on the curve to the discrete logarithm problem on the finite field $\mathbb{F}_{q^k}$, where faster (subexponential) algorithms are known. With a small embedding degree, we are forced to counteract the reduction to finite field discrete logarithms by increasing our parameter sizes. Therefore, a balanced embedding degree is preferred when using pairing-friendly curves.

We note the following result, useful for finding curves with small embedding degree.

---

[1] Other works take $|d|$ as the discriminant.

Proposition 2.2. *Let $E/\mathbb{F}_q$ be an elliptic curve with prime order p and embedding degree k such that $p \nmid k$. Then $p \equiv 1 \pmod{k}$.*

Proof. The embedding degree condition is equivalent to k being minimal such that $q^k \equiv 1 \pmod{p}$. Since p is prime, by Lagrange's theorem we have that $k \mid p - 1$. □

The Complex Multiplication (CM) Method. Let $E/\mathbb{F}_q$ be an elliptic curve with prime order p and trace t. The embedding degree condition is determined by p and q alone, so the actual coefficients of the curve equation do not play any role. Because of this, the main approach to finding pairing-friendly curves tries to find (t, p, q) first, and then curve coefficients that are compatible with these values.

Given (t, p, q) such that $p = q + 1 - t$ and $t \leq 2\sqrt{q}$, Deuring's theorem ensures that a curve exists, but that does not mean that it is easy to find. The algorithm that takes (t, p, q) and produces the curve coefficients is known as the *complex multiplication (CM) method*, and its complexity strongly depends on the discriminant d of the curve. Currently, this is considered feasible up to $|d| \approx 10^{16}$ [43].

Because of our focus on finding *good* triples (t, p, q), we will identify curves with them. That is, we write $E \leftrightarrow (t, p, q)$ as shorthand for an elliptic curve $E/\mathbb{F}_q$ with order p and trace t. This curve might not be unique, but any of them will have the same embedding degree and discriminant, so they are indistinguishable for our purposes.

2.2 Pairing-Friendly Polynomial Families

The idea of considering families of elliptic curves parameterized by low-degree polynomials is already present in [5, 35], but is studied in a more systematic way in [21, 23]. We will consider triples of polynomials $(t, p, q) \in \mathbb{Q}[X]^3$ such that, given $x \in \mathbb{Z}$, there is an elliptic curve $E \leftrightarrow (t(x), p(x), q(x))$.

We are interested in prime-order elliptic curves, so we require that the polynomials p, q represent primes.

Definition 2.3. *Let $g \in \mathbb{Q}[X]$. We say that g represents primes if:*

- *$g(X)$ is irreducible, non-constant and has a positive leading coefficient,*
- *$g(x) \in \mathbb{Z}$ for some $x \in \mathbb{Z}$ (equivalently, for infinitely many such x), and*
- *$\gcd\{g(x) \mid x, g(x) \in \mathbb{Z}\} = 1$.*

The Bunyakovsky conjecture [39] states that a polynomial in the conditions of the definition above takes prime values for infinitely many $x \in \mathbb{Z}$. We now formally define polynomial families of pairing-friendly elliptic curves.

Definition 2.4. *Let $k, d \in \mathbb{Z}$ with $d < 0 < k$. We say that a triple of polynomials $(t, p, q) \in \mathbb{Q}[X]^3$ parameterizes a family of elliptic curves with embedding degree k and discriminant d if:*

1. $p(X) = q(X) + 1 - t(X)$,
2. p is integer-valued (even if its coefficients are in $\mathbb{Q} \setminus \mathbb{Z}$),
3. p and q represent primes,
4. $p(X) \mid \Phi_k(t(X) - 1)$, and
5. the equation $4q(X) = t(X)^2 + |d|Y^2$ has infinitely-many integer solutions (x, y).

We naturally extend the notation $E \leftrightarrow (t, p, q)$ to polynomial families.

Conditions 1–3 ensure that the polynomials represent infinitely many sets of parameters compatible with an elliptic curve. Condition 4 ensures that the embedding degree is at most k, where ideally k is small. Condition 5 ensures that there are infinitely many curves in the family with the same discriminant d. If this d is not too large, we will be able to use the CM method to find the curves corresponding to these parameters. If we ignore condition 5, such families are not too hard to find, as illustrated by the following lemma.[2]

Lemma 2.5. *For any integer $k \geq 3$ there are infinitely many pairs (q, E_q) with embedding degree k, and such that $|E(\mathbb{F}_q)|$ is prime, under the Bunyakovsky conjecture.*

Proof. Infinite families are known for $k = 3, 4, 6$, as detailed below in Table 1. We can then assume $\varphi(k) \geq 4$. We will construct a family represented by the polynomial tuple (t, p, q) as follows.

Let $p(X) = \Phi_{rk}(X)$, for some prime number r such that $r \nmid k$. Then, it holds that $\varphi(kr) \geq 4(r - 1) \geq 2r$. We set $q(X) = p(X) + X^r$. Then

$$p(X) \mid X^{rk} - 1 = (X^r)^k - 1 = (q(X) - p(X))^k - 1,$$

so $p(X) \mid q(X)^k - 1$. In this case $p(X) = q(X) - X^r$, so the trace is given by $t(X) = 1 + X^r$, and $\deg(t) \leq \deg(p)/2$. Also, the cyclotomic polynomial is irreducible, so it represents infinitely many prime values. $\square$

Let $f(X) = 4q(X) - t(X)^2$. Freeman [21] observed that condition 5 in Definition 2.4 is strongly related to the form of this polynomial.

Proposition 2.6. *Fix $k \in \mathbb{N}$, and let $(t, p, q) \in \mathbb{Z}[X]^3$ satisfying conditions (1–4) in the previous definition. Assume that one of these holds:*

- *$f(X) = aX^2 + bX + c$, with $a, b, c \in \mathbb{Z}$, $a > 0$ and $b^2 - 4ac \neq 0$. There exists a discriminant d such that ad is not a square. Also, the CM equation has an integer solution.*
- *$f(X) = (\ell X + |d|)g(X)^2$ for some discriminant d, $\ell \in \mathbb{Z}$, and $g \in \mathbb{Z}[X]$.*

Then, we have that (t, p, q) parameterizes a family of elliptic curves with embedding degree k and discriminant d.

---

[2] Furthermore, numerical experiments easily find many tuples (t, p, q) with low degree and small coefficients satisfying conditions 1–4, but unfortunately not condition 5.

On the other hand, if $\deg f \geq 3$, it is unlikely to produce a family of curves, as highlighted by the following result, which is a direct consequence of Siegel's theorem [40, Corollary IX.3.2.2].

Proposition 2.7. *Fix $k \in \mathbb{N}$, and let (t, p, q) as above, and satisfying conditions (1–4) in the previous definition. Assume that $f(X)$ is square-free and $\deg f \geq 3$. Then (t, p, q) cannot represent a family of elliptic curves with embedding degree k.*

Finally, [21] also proves some results on the relations between the degrees of the polynomials involved in representing a family of curves.

Proposition 2.8. *Let $t \in \mathbb{Q}[X]$. Then, for any k and any irreducible factor $p \mid \Phi_k(t - 1)$, we have that $\varphi(k) \mid \deg p$.*

Proposition 2.9. *Let (t, p, q) represent a family of curves with embedding degree k, with $\varphi(k) \geq 4$. If $f = 4q - t^2$ is square-free, then:*

- $\deg p = \deg q = 2\deg t$.
- *If a is the leading coefficient of $t(X)$, then $a^2/4$ is the leading coefficient of $p(X), q(X)$.*

Known Pairing-Friendly Families with Prime Order. Only a few polynomial families of elliptic curves with prime order and low embedding degree are known. The first work in this direction is due to Miyaji, Nakabayashi, and Takano, [35], who characterized all prime-order curves with embedding degrees $k = 3, 4, 6$ (these correspond to $\varphi(k) = 2$). Based on the work of Galbraith, McKee and Valença [26], two additional families were found: Barreto and Naehrig [5] found a family with $k = 12$, and Freeman [21] found another one with $k = 10$ (both cases have $\varphi(k) = 4$). Note, however, that their results are not exhaustive, meaning that there could still be other families with these embedding degrees that have not been found, unlike in the MNT case. We summarize the polynomial descriptions of these families in Table 1.

Table 1. Polynomial descriptions of MNT, Freeman and BN curves, where k corresponds to the embedding degree, $t(X)$ is the trace, $p(X)$ is the order, and $q(X)$ is the order of the base field.

Family	k	$t(X)$	$p(X)$	$q(X)$
MNT3	3	$6X - 1$	$12X^2 - 6X + 1$	$12X^2 - 1$
MNT4	4	$-X$	$X^2 + 2X + 2$	$X^2 + X + 1$
MNT6	6	$2X + 1$	$4X^2 - 2X + 1$	$4X^2 + 1$
Freeman	10	$10X^2 + 5X + 3$	$25X^4 + 25X^3 + 15X^2 + 5X + 1$	$25X^4 + 25X^3 + 25X^2 + 10X + 3$
BN	12	$6X^2 + 1$	$36X^4 + 36X^3 + 18X^2 + 6X + 1$	$36X^4 + 36X^3 + 24X^2 + 6X + 1$

For completeness, we note that there are no elliptic curves with prime order and embedding degree $k \leq 2$, except for a few cases of no cryptographic interest.

Proposition 2.10. *Let $p, q \in \mathbb{Z}$ be prime numbers. If $q \geq 14$, then there is no elliptic curve $E/\mathbb{F}_q$ with $\#E(\mathbb{F}_q) = p$ and embedding degree $k \leq 2$.*

Proof. Suppose that such a curve exists.

- If $k = 1$, then $p \mid q - 1$. Clearly $p \neq q - 1$, since otherwise p, q cannot both be prime. Then $p \leq \frac{q-1}{2}$, and then $q - p \geq \frac{q+1}{2}$. But, at the same time, $q - p = t - 1 \leq 2\sqrt{q} - 1$, due to the Hasse bound. These two conditions are only compatible when $q \leq 9$, which is already ruled out by hypothesis.
- If $k = 2$, then $p \mid q^2 - 1 = (q-1)(q+1)$. We have that $p \nmid q - 1$ (otherwise $k = 1$), and thus $p \mid q + 1$ because p is prime. Again, $p \neq q + 1$, because otherwise p, q cannot both be prime. Then $p \leq \frac{q+1}{2}$, and thus $q - p \geq \frac{q-1}{2}$. By the Hasse bound, $q - p \leq 2\sqrt{q} - 1$, and these are only compatible for $q < 14$.

$\square$

3   Cycles of Elliptic Curves

3.1   Definition and Known Results

The notion of cycles of elliptic curves was introduced in [41].

Definition 3.1. *Let $s \in \mathbb{N}$. An s-cycle of elliptic curves is a tuple $(E_1, \ldots, E_s)$ of elliptic curves, defined over fields $\mathbb{F}_{q_1}, \ldots, \mathbb{F}_{q_s}$, respectively, and such that*

$$\#E_i(\mathbb{F}_{q_i}) = q_{i+1 \bmod s},$$

for all $i = 1, \ldots, s$.

Remark 3.2. Cycles of length 2 have some particular properties that are worth noting. Let E, E' be two curves forming a 2-cycle.

- If $E \leftrightarrow (t, p, q)$, then Definition 3.1 implies that $E' \leftrightarrow (2 - t, q, p)$.
- We have that $p = \#E(\mathbb{F}_q)$ is in the Hasse interval of $q = \#E'(\mathbb{F}_p)$ if and only if q is in the Hasse interval of p. Indeed, if the former holds, then

$$\sqrt{p} - 1 \leq \sqrt{q} \leq \sqrt{p} + 1,$$

which is equivalent to

$$\sqrt{q} - 1 \leq \sqrt{p} \leq \sqrt{q} + 1.$$

It is known that cycles of any length exist [41, Theorem 11]. We summarize in the following two propositions some facts about cycles. These results are due to [15].

Proposition 3.3. *Let $E_1, \ldots, E_s$ be an s-cycle of elliptic curves, defined over prime fields $\mathbb{F}_{q_1}, \ldots, \mathbb{F}_{q_s}$. Then:*

(i) $E_1, \ldots, E_s$ are ordinary curves.
(ii) If $q_1, \ldots, q_s > 12s^2$, then $E_1, \ldots E_s$ have prime order.

(iii) Let $t_1, \ldots, t_s$ be the traces of $E_1, \ldots, E_s$, respectively. Then

$$\sum_{i=1}^{s} t_i = s.$$

(iv) If $s = 2$, then the curves in the cycle have the same discriminant d.
(v) If the curves in the cycle have the same discriminant $|d| > 3$, then $s = 2$.
(vi) If $s > 2$ and $E_1, \ldots, E_s$ have the same discriminant d, then necessarily $s = 6$ and $|d| = 3$.

There are also some impossibility results.

Proposition 3.4. *We have the following.*

(i) There is no 2-cycle with embedding degree pairs $(5, 10)$, $(8, 8)$ or $(12, 12)$.
(ii) There is no cycle formed only by Freeman curves.
(iii) There is no cycle formed only by BN curves.

3.2   Some Properties of Cycles

In this section, we show some results about cycles, most of them about 2-cycles in which both curves have the same embedding degree. We start with a small result that rules out safe primes in 2-cycles with the same embedding degree.

Proposition 3.5. *Safe primes are not part of any 2-cycle in which both curves have the same embedding degree k.*

Proof. Let p, q be the orders of the curves in the cycle. Assume that p is a safe prime, i.e. $p = 1 + 2r$, with r prime. Since p, q are in a cycle, $q = p + 1 - t$ for some $|t| \leq 2\sqrt{p}$. Now, since $k \mid p - 1$ by Proposition 2.2, we have $k = 1, 2, r, 2r$. We already know that $k \neq 1, 2$, hence $k \in \{r, 2r\}$. Since q also has embedding degree k, again by Proposition 2.2 we have that $k \mid q - p$, and thus $r \mid q - p$. Therefore

$$|q - p| \geq r = \frac{p - 1}{2} > 2\sqrt{p} + 1$$

for any $p > 3$, which contradicts the fact that $|q - p| = |1 - t| < 2\sqrt{p} + 1$. $\square$

Proposition 3.6. *Let $s \in \mathbb{Z}$, and let $(t, p, q) \in \mathbb{Q}[X]^3$ parameterize a family of pairing-friendly elliptic curves, with $\deg t$ even. Then, there are only finitely many s-cycles such that all s curves in the cycle belong to the family.*

Proof. If s curves with traces $t_1, \ldots, t_s$, respectively, form a cycle, by Proposition 3.3.(iii) we have that $\sum_{i=1}^{s} t_i = s$. Since $\deg t \geq 2$ and s is fixed, necessarily there exist $a, b \in \{1, \ldots, s\}$ such that t_a, t_b have different signs. However, since $\deg t$ is even, there exists a lower bound b such that, for all $|x| > b$, we have that $t(x)$ has the same sign. Therefore, only finitely many cases can occur in which the traces have opposing sign. $\square$

Given an elliptic curve $E \leftrightarrow (t, p, q)$, Hasse's theorem gives us the bound $|t| \leq 2\sqrt{q}$, which in the polynomial case implies that $\deg t \leq \frac{1}{2}\deg q$. We now derive a lower bound for t in the case of 2-cycles in which both curves have the same small embedding degree. We require first the following technical lemma.

Lemma 3.7. *Let $k \in \mathbb{N}$ and $3 \leq k \leq 104$. We have that:*

(i) For any $|x| > 1$,

$$\Phi_k(x) \leq \frac{|x|}{|x| - 1} x^{\varphi(k)}.$$

(ii) For any $\varepsilon > 0$, there exists $B > 0$ such that, for all x with $|x| > B$,

$$\Phi_k(x - 1) \leq (1 + \varepsilon)\frac{|x|}{|x| - 1} x^{\varphi(k)}.$$

Proof. Clearly such bound exists for $|x|$ large enough, since $\Phi_k(x) = x^{\varphi(k)} + o\left(x^{\varphi(k)}\right)$. More precisely, for $k \leq 104$, the k-th cyclotomic polynomial has only 0 and ± 1 as coefficients [34]. Therefore

$$\Phi_k(x) \leq x^{\varphi(k)} + \sum_{i=0}^{\varphi(k)-1} |x|^i = x^{\varphi(k)} \left(1 + \sum_{i=1}^{\varphi(k)} \frac{1}{|x|^i}\right) \leq x^{\varphi(k)} \left(1 + \frac{1}{|x| - 1}\right) = \frac{|x|}{|x| - 1} x^{\varphi(k)},$$

using the fact that the geometric series converges when $|x| > 1$.

Part (ii) is now trivial when $x > 0$. For $x < 0$, we note that, since Φ_k is a polynomial with positive leading coefficient, for any $\varepsilon > 0$ there exists $B > 0$ such that, for all x with $|x| > B$,

$$\Phi_k(x - 1) \leq (1 + \varepsilon)\Phi_k(x),$$

since otherwise the function would grow exponentially fast when $x \to -\infty$. The result follows directly from applying part (i) to $\Phi_k(x)$. □

Remark 3.8. More precisely, for k such that $3 \leq k \leq 104$, we do not need to choose B too large to achieve a small constant. The following values have been obtained computationally.

$1 + \varepsilon$	2	1.1	1.01
B	146	1069	10250

Proposition 3.9. *Let $E \leftrightarrow (t, p, q)$ be an elliptic curve with embedding degree k, with $|t| > 1$ and $3 \leq k \leq 104$. Then, for any $\varepsilon > 0$ there exists $B > 0$ such that, for all t with $|t| > B$, we have*

$$|t| > \left(\frac{1}{1 + \varepsilon}\frac{|t| - 1}{|t|}q\right)^{\frac{1}{\varphi(k)}}.$$

Proof. We have that $p \mid \Phi_k(t-1)$, so $p \leq \Phi_k(t-1)$. Also, we have that $|t| < |\Phi_k(t) - \Phi_k(t-1)|$ for $|t|$ large enough, since Φ_k is at least quadratic in t. Assume first that $t > 1$. Then, combining these upper bounds on p and t, and using part (i) of the previous lemma, we obtain

$$q = p - 1 + t \leq p + t < \Phi_k(t) \leq \frac{t}{t-1} t^{\varphi(k)}.$$

Taking $\varphi(k)$-th roots,

$$t > \left(\frac{t-1}{t} q \right)^{\frac{1}{\varphi(k)}}.$$

The case $t < -1$ is completely analogous, using part (ii) of Lemma 3.7.   □

The result above deals with a single curve, but actually it can be strengthened for some 2-cycles.

Proposition 3.10. *Let $E \leftrightarrow (t, p, q)$ and $E' \leftrightarrow (2-t, q, p)$ be two elliptic curves with $|t| > 1$ and the same embedding degree $k \equiv 0 \pmod 4$, such that $3 \leq k \leq 104$. Then, for any $\varepsilon > 0$ there exists $B > 0$ such that, for all t with $|t| > B$, we have*

$$|t| > \left(\frac{1}{1+\varepsilon} \frac{|t|-1}{|t|} q \right)^{\frac{2}{\varphi(k)}}.$$

Proof. The case $k \equiv 0 \pmod 4$ corresponds to those cyclotomic polynomials such that $\Phi_k(x) = \Phi_k(-x)$ for all x. From the embedding degree conditions, we have

$$p \mid \Phi_k(t-1),$$
$$q \mid \Phi_k(1-t),$$

and therefore $pq \mid \Phi_k(t-1)$, since p, q are different primes. Assume, without loss of generality, that $q < p$. Then $q^2 \leq pq \leq \Phi_k(t-1)$, and proceeding as the proof of Proposition 3.9, we obtain

$$q^2 \leq (1+\varepsilon) \frac{|t|}{|t|-1} t^{\varphi(k)},$$

from which we obtain the desired bound.   □

Corollary 3.11. *Let $E \leftrightarrow (t, p, q)$ and $E' \leftrightarrow (2-t, q, p)$ be two elliptic curves with the same embedding degree $k \equiv 0 \pmod 4$, such that $3 \leq k \leq 104$. There exists B such that, if $|t| > B$, then*

$$\frac{1}{2} q^{\frac{2}{\varphi(k)}} < |t| \leq 2q^{\frac{1}{2}}.$$

Remark 3.12. The result above is particularly interesting in two cases:

– When $\varphi(k) = 2$, i.e. $k = 4$. In this case,

$$\frac{1}{2}q < |t| \le 2q^{\frac{1}{2}},$$

which cannot happen for $q > 15$. This shows that there are no $(4,4)$-cycles (which was already known from [15]).
– When $\varphi(k) = 4$, i.e. $k \in \{8, 12\}$. In this case,

$$\frac{1}{2}q^{\frac{1}{2}} < |t| \le 2q^{\frac{1}{2}},$$

which shows that t asymptotically behaves like $\sqrt{q}$, and therefore is on the outermost part of the Hasse interval. In particular, for polynomial families this means that $\deg t = \frac{1}{2}\deg p$, which improves on the inequality known before.

4   Cycles from Known Families

In this section, we prove our main result about 2-cycles of elliptic curves: given a family $(t, p, q) \in \mathbb{Q}[X]^3$ with embedding degree k, and $\ell \in \mathbb{N}$, one of two things can happen:

(a) $q \mid p^\ell - 1$, as polynomials. In this case, any curve in the family forms a 2-cycle with the corresponding curve in the family $(2-t, q, p)$, which has embedding degree ℓ (see Proposition 2.1). Observe that, due to Proposition 3.3, both families have the same discriminant.
(b) Only finitely many curves from the family form a 2-cycle with curves of embedding degree ℓ.

Furthermore, when we are in the second case we can explicitly find these cycles. For all known families (Table 1), we prove that no curve from them (except for a few anecdotal cases) is part of a 2-cycle with any curve with embedding degree $\ell \le L$. The bound L depends on the family, and in all cases at least $L \ge 22$.

4.1   Cycles from Parametric-Families

First, we show a technique that will help us rule out many cases from our main results, by performing a very simple check.

Proposition 4.1. *Let $(t, p, q) \in \mathbb{Q}[X]^3$ parameterize a family of pairing-friendly elliptic curves. Let a curve E from the family be in a cycle, and assume that the previous curve in the cycle has embedding degree ℓ. Then there exists $i \in \{0, \ldots, \ell - 1\}$ such that*

$$q(i) \equiv 1 \pmod{\ell}.$$

Proof. Let $x \in \mathbb{Z}$ such that $E \leftrightarrow (t(x), p(x), q(x))$, and let $E' \leftrightarrow (t', p', q')$ be the previous curve in the cycle with embedding degree ℓ. From the definition of cycle, $p' = q(x)$. Then, applying Proposition 2.2 to curve E', we deduce that

$$q(x \bmod \ell) \equiv q(x) \equiv p' \equiv 1 \pmod{\ell}.$$

$\square$

By testing the condition given by Proposition 4.1 for known families and $3 \le \ell \le 100$, we obtain the following results. Note that this not help for BN curves, since in that case $q(0) = 1$, and thus the condition holds for any ℓ.

Corollary 4.2. *An MNT3 curve cannot be preceded in a cycle by a curve with embedding degree ℓ, where*

$\ell \in \{3, 4, 6, 7, 8, 9, 11, 12, 13, 14, 15, 16, 17, 18, 20, 21, 22, 24, 26, 27, 28, 30, 31, 32, 33, 34, 35, 36,$
$\qquad 37, 39, 40, 41, 42, 44, 45, 48, 49, 51, 52, 54, 55, 56, 57, 59, 60, 61, 62, 63, 64, 65, 66, 68, 69, 70,$
$\qquad 72, 74, 75, 76, 77, 78, 79, 80, 81, 82, 83, 84, 85, 87, 88, 89, 90, 91, 92, 93, 96, 98, 99, 100\}.$

Corollary 4.3. *A Freeman curve cannot be preceded in a cycle by a curve with embedding degree ℓ, where*

$\ell \in \{4, 5, 8, 10, 11, 12, 15, 16, 20, 22, 24, 25, 28, 30, 32, 33, 35, 36, 40, 44, 45, 48, 50, 52, 53, 55, 56,$
$\qquad 59, 60, 61, 64, 65, 66, 68, 70, 72, 75, 76, 77, 79, 80, 83, 84, 85, 88, 90, 92, 95, 96, 97, 99, 100\}.$

Furthermore, even when we cannot rule out a certain ℓ, we obtain a condition on $x \bmod \ell$, which will help us later when we check by brute force all x in an interval. Also note that, despite the fact that we will use these corollaries to simplify our work in the next section, which deals with 2-cycles, these results work for cycles of any length.

4.2   2-cycles from Parametric Families

The goal here will be to start from a known family of pairing-friendly elliptic curves, and argue that they form no 2-cycles with other pairing-friendly curves. To do so, let (t, p, q) represent such family. For any curve $E \leftrightarrow (t(x), p(x), q(x))$, there is another curve $E' \leftrightarrow (2 - t(x), q(x), p(x))$ such that the two of them form a 2-cycle. Furthermore, if E' has a small embedding degree $\ell \in \mathbb{Z}$, then $q(x) \mid p(x)^\ell - 1$. Note that this is for a particular $x \in \mathbb{Z}$, not as polynomials.

Informally, our strategy will be the following. The embedding degree condition on E' can be reformulated in terms of integer division: the division of $p(x)^\ell$ by $q(x)$ has remainder 1. We will compare integer division and polynomial division, and show that, outside of a finite interval $[N_{\text{left}}, N_{\text{right}}]$, the remainders in both cases essentially agree. Therefore, by showing that the polynomial remainder $r(x)$ never takes the value 1, we will rule out any possibility of cycles outside of $[N_{\text{left}}, N_{\text{right}}]$. For known families of curves, we will deal with the cases $x \in [N_{\text{left}}, N_{\text{right}}]$ manually, as there are only a finite number of them, and show that none of them leads to a partner curve with small embedding degree.

Lemma 4.4. *Let $x \in \mathbb{Z}$, and let $a, b \in \mathbb{Q}[X]$ be two integer-valued polynomials. Assume that b has even degree and positive leading coefficient.*

- *Let $h, r \in \mathbb{Q}[X]$ be the quotient and remainder, respectively, of the polynomial division of a by b. Let $c > 0$ be the smallest integer such that $ch, cr \in \mathbb{Z}[X]$.*
- *Let $h_x, r_x \in \mathbb{Z}$ be the quotient and remainder, respectively, of the integer division of $ca(x)$ by $b(x)$.*

Then either $\deg r = 0$, or there exist $N_{\mathsf{left}}, N_{\mathsf{right}} \in \mathbb{Z}$ and $\delta_{\mathsf{left}}, \delta_{\mathsf{right}} \in \{0, 1\}$ such that:

- *For all $x < N_{\mathsf{left}}$, we have that $\mathrm{sign}(r(x))$ is constant, and $r_x = cr(x) + \delta_{\mathsf{left}} b(x)$.*
- *For all $x > N_{\mathsf{right}}$, we have that $\mathrm{sign}(r(x))$ is constant, and $r_x = cr(x) + \delta_{\mathsf{right}} b(x)$.*

Furthermore, let us denote $\sigma_{\mathsf{left}} = \mathrm{sign}\{r(x) \mid x < N_{\mathsf{left}}\}$ and $\sigma_{\mathsf{right}} = \mathrm{sign}\{r(x) \mid x > N_{\mathsf{right}}\}$. Then

$$\delta_{\mathsf{left}} = \frac{1 - \sigma_{\mathsf{left}}}{2}, \qquad \delta_{\mathsf{right}} = \frac{1 - \sigma_{\mathsf{right}}}{2}.$$

Proof. We observe that c is well-defined, as it can be taken as the least common multiple of all denominators occurring in the coefficients of h, r. Likewise, $\sigma_{\mathsf{left}}, \sigma_{\mathsf{right}}$ are well-defined, since r is a polynomial, and thus at most it changes sign $\deg r$ times. For the second part, we have that

$$ca(x) = b(x)h_x + r_x,$$
$$ca(x) = b(x)(ch(x)) + cr(x),$$

where $0 \le r_x < b(x)$, and $\deg r < \deg b$, and all these values are integer. Subtracting, we obtain

$$r_x - cr(x) = b(x)(ch(x) - h_x),$$

and thus $r_x \equiv cr(x) \pmod{b(x)}$. Since $0 \le r_x < b(x)$, we just need to find $cr(x) \bmod b(x)$, as this will necessarily be the same as r_x.

We illustrate the technique for the case $\sigma_{\mathsf{left}} = -1, \sigma_{\mathsf{right}} = 1$ (the other cases are completely analogous). Note that, if $\deg r > 0$, then r is not a constant polynomial.

- Let $N_{\mathsf{left}} \in \mathbb{Z}$ be the largest integer such that $0 < -cr(x) \le b(x)$ for all $x < N_{\mathsf{left}}$. Such N_{left} exists because both $b(x), -cr(x) \to \infty$ when $x \to -\infty$, and $\deg b > \deg(-cr)$. If $x < N_{\mathsf{left}}$, then $0 < -cr(x) \le b(x)$. Multiplying by (-1), we get that $-b(x) \le cr(x) < 0$, and adding $b(x)$, we get $0 \le cr(x) + b(x) < b(x)$. Therefore, $r_x = cr(x) + b(x)$.
- Let $N_{\mathsf{right}} \in \mathbb{Z}$ be the smallest integer such that $0 \le cr(x) < b(x)$ for all $x > N_{\mathsf{right}}$. Such N_{right} exists because both $b(x), cr(x) \to \infty$ when $x \to \infty$, and $\deg b > \deg(cr)$. If $x > N_{\mathsf{right}}$, then $0 \le cr(x) < b(x)$. Therefore, necessarily $r_x = cr(x)$.

We can now prove the main theorem of this section, from which the desired results will directly follow.

Theorem 4.5. *Let $k, \ell \in \mathbb{N}$. Let (t, p, q) be a triple of polynomials parameterizing a family of elliptic curves with embedding degree k. Then either $q \mid p^\ell - 1$ as polynomials, or there are at most finitely many 2-cycles formed by a curve from the family and a curve with embedding degree ℓ. Furthermore, in the second case, there exist efficiently computable bounds such that all cycles considered above are within those bounds.*

Proof. Due to Proposition 2.10, we can safely assume that $k, \ell \geq 3$. Assume that there exists a 2-cycle involving a curve E from the family and another curve E' with embedding degree ℓ. That is, assume that there exists $x \in \mathbb{Z}$ such that $E \leftrightarrow (t(x), p(x), q(x))$ is in a 2-cycle. Then $E' \leftrightarrow (2 - t(x), q(x), p(x))$. By the condition of the embedding degree, we have that

$$q(x) \mid p(x)^\ell - 1,$$

and thus there exists $h \in \mathbb{Z}$ such that

$$p(x)^\ell = q(x)h + 1.$$

We now wish to apply Lemma 4.4, with $a = p^\ell$ and $b = q$, so we must argue that q has even degree and positive leading coefficient. We distinguish two cases:

- For $k \in \{3, 4, 6\}$, all the prime-order families are the MNT families, which have $\deg q = 2$ and positive leading coefficient.
- For k with $\varphi(k) \geq 4$, we have from Proposition 2.8 that $\varphi(k) \mid \deg p$, and in this case $\varphi(k)$ is always even. Furthermore, since $p = q + 1 - t$ and $t = O(\sqrt{q})$ (due to the Hasse bound), necessarily $\deg q = \deg p$. Now, since q has even degree, it necessarily has positive leading coefficient, otherwise it could not represent infinitely many curves.

Let $h, r \in \mathbb{Q}[X]$ be the quotient and remainder, respectively, of the polynomial division of p^ℓ by q. If $q \nmid p^\ell - 1$ as polynomials, then $r \neq 1$. If r is another constant polynomial, then the embedding degree condition does not hold for any $x \in \mathbb{Z}$. If $\deg r > 0$, Lemma 4.4 gives us $c, N_{\mathsf{left}}, N_{\mathsf{right}} \in \mathbb{Z}, \delta_{\mathsf{left}}, \delta_{\mathsf{right}} \in \{0, 1\}$ such that, if $x < N_{\mathsf{left}}$,

$$cr(x) + \delta_{\mathsf{left}} b(x) = 1,$$

and, if $x > N_{\mathsf{right}}$, then

$$cr(x) + \delta_{\mathsf{right}} b(x) = 1.$$

The polynomials $cr(X)$ and $cr(X) + b(X)$ can only take the value 1 finitely many times. By enlarging $[N_{\mathsf{left}}, N_{\mathsf{right}}]$ if necessary, we can ensure that this only happens inside of $[N_{\mathsf{left}}, N_{\mathsf{right}}]$. Therefore, there are no cycles for $x \notin [N_{\mathsf{left}}, N_{\mathsf{right}}]$. $\square$

This result immediately yields the following consequences for concrete families of curves. Let (t, p, q) parametrize a family of curves. Given a certain value of ℓ, it is immediate to check whether $q \nmid p^\ell - 1$ as polynomials. If that is not the case (which happens most of the time), Theorem 4.5 ensures that there are at most finitely-many cycles formed by a curve from the family and a curve with embedding degree ℓ. For each candidate ℓ, we compute the values $c, N_{\text{left}}, N_{\text{right}}$ from Theorem 4.5 corresponding to the division of p^ℓ by q. Interestingly, $c = 1$ for all known families of pairing-friendly curves with prime order. The resulting values of $N_{\text{left}}, N_{\text{right}}$ are summarized in Table 3 for the MNT3, Freeman, and BN families. No tables are included for MNT4 and MNT6 families because, in these cases, we have $N_{\text{left}} = -1, N_{\text{right}} = 0$ and $N_{\text{left}} = N_{\text{right}} = 0$, respectively, regardless of ℓ.

Remark 4.6. Given arbitrary integer-valued polynomials $p, q \in \mathbb{Q}[X]$ and $\ell \in \mathbb{N}$, there is no guarantee that the polynomial remainder of p^ℓ by q will have integer coefficients, i.e. $c = 1$, or even be integer-valued. Nevertheless, this does happen for MNT, Freeman, and BN curves. We show this for Freeman curves, but the argument is very similar in all cases. For completeness, the other cases are included in Appendix A.

We proceed by induction on ℓ. For $\ell = 1$, we have that

$$p(X) \bmod q(X) = -10X^2 - 5X - 2.$$

This polynomial is of the form $25aX^3 + 5bX^2 + 5cX + d$, for some $a, b, c, d \in \mathbb{Z}$. We will now show that, if $p^\ell \bmod q$ is of this form, then $p^{\ell+1} \bmod q$ is also of this form. This will prove that all the remainder is actually in $\mathbb{Z}[X]$ for any $\ell \in \mathbb{N}$.

Hence, suppose that there exist $a, b, c, d \in \mathbb{N}$ such that

$$p(X)^\ell \bmod q(X) = 25aX^3 + 5bX^2 + 5cX + d.$$

Then

$$
\begin{aligned}
p(X)^{\ell+1} &\equiv p(X)^\ell p(X) \equiv \left(25aX^3 + 5bX^2 + 5cX + d\right)\left(-10X^2 - 5X - 2\right) \\
&\equiv -250aX^5 - (125a + 50b)X^4 - (50a + 25b + 50c)X^3 \\
&\quad -(10b + 25c + 10d)X^2 - (10c + 5d)X - 2d \\
&\equiv (75a + 25b - 50c)X^3 + (-25a + 40b - 25c - 10d)X^2 \\
&\quad +(-20a + 20b - 10c - 5d)X + (-15a + 6b - 2d) \pmod{q(X)}.
\end{aligned}
$$

Since the coefficient of degree 3 is divisible by 25, and the coefficients of degree 2 and 1 are divisible by 5, the induction step works.

Remark 4.7. The values of $N_{\text{left}}, N_{\text{right}}$ in MNT4 and MNT6 families are in stark contrast with the other families (shown in Appendix B), but can be easily explained. In MNT3, Freeman, and BN curves, the remainder r of the polynomial division q^k by p has coefficients that mostly increase with k. Because of this, we need to get further away from zero before the asymptotic behavior kicks in.

On the contrary, only a small number of remainders are possible in MNT4 and MNT6 curves. Let $(t, p, q) \in \mathbb{Q}[X]^3$ parameterize MNT4 curves. We have that $q \mid p^6 - 1$ (they form infinitely many cycles with MNT6 curves). That is, p has order 6 modulo q, and thus $p^k \bmod q$ can only take 6 possible values. Concretely, $p(X)^k \bmod q(X) \in \{\pm 1, \pm X, \pm(X + 1)\}$ for any $k \in \mathbb{N}$, and all of these yield the bounds $N_{\text{left}} = -1, N_{\text{right}} = 0$. Similarly, in the case of MNT6 curves, the remainder of p^k by q can only take 4 values. Concretely $p(X)^k \bmod q(X) \in \{\pm 1, \pm 2X\}$ for any $k \in \mathbb{N}$, which yield the bounds $N_{\text{left}} = N_{\text{right}} = 0$.

An exhaustive search in $[N_{\text{left}}, N_{\text{right}}]$ reveals no curves with embedding degree ℓ, for any of the values of ℓ considered, except for a few examples with no cryptographic interest (see Table 2). We consider MNT3, Freeman, and BN curves, since it is already known [15] that MNT4 and MNT6 curves are only in cycles with each other.

Corollary 4.8. *Let (E, E') be a 2-cycle of elliptic curves, and assume that E is not one of the curves described in Table 2.*

(i)   If E is an MNT3 curve, then E' has embedding degree $\ell \geq 23$.
(ii) If E is a Freeman curve, then E' has embedding degree $\ell \geq 26$.
(iii) If E is a BN curve, then E' has embedding degree $\ell \geq 33$.

Table 2. Instances of curves $E \leftrightarrow (t, p, q)$, with embedding degree k, from known cycles that form a pairing-friendly 2-cycle with another curve E' with embedding degree ℓ.

Family	k	ℓ	x	t	p	q
MNT3	3	10	−1	−7	19	11
MNT3	3	10	1	5	7	11
BN	12	18	−1	7	13	19

The computational check took a few hours on a standard computer, using the SageMath code from Appendix C. Theoretically, there is no reason to stop at a given embedding degree ℓ. However, the interval $[N_{\text{left}}, N_{\text{right}}]$ grow rapidly, making the brute force check inside of the interval a much more serious computing effort, requiring a more polished implementation. Still, the most interesting cases are those with smaller embedding degree, as the ideal cycles for recursive composition would be those in which the embedding degrees of both curves are as close as possible.

5   Density of Pairing-Friendly Cycles

So far, this work has been mostly an algebraic treatment of cycles. In this section, we look at cycles from a different angle, concerning ourselves with their density. The goal is to quantify in concrete terms the folklore notion that pairing-friendly cycles are hard to find. Our starting point is the following result of [3]. It proves an upper bound on the probability of a random elliptic curve being pairing-friendly.[3]

---

[3] In [3], the authors define pairing friendliness as having an embedding degree $k \leq (\log q)^2$. We will keep the bound as an unspecified parameter K.

Theorem 5.1 ([3], Theorem 2). *Let $M \in \mathbb{Z}$. Let $\mathfrak{p}$ be the probability of finding an elliptic curve $E/\mathbb{F}_q$ with prime order $p \in [M, 2M]$ and embedding degree $k \leq (\log q)^2$, by sampling uniformly from all the curves with orders in the interval $[M, 2M]$. Then*

$$\mathfrak{p} < c\frac{(\log M)^9 (\log \log M)^2}{M},$$

for some constant $c > 0$.

We generalize the result above to s-cycles of elliptic curves. In particular, an s-cycle is a collection of s primes $q_1, \ldots, q_s$ and s elliptic curves $E_1/\mathbb{F}_{q_1}, \ldots, E_s/\mathbb{F}_{q_s}$, such that $\#E_i(\mathbb{F}_{q_i}) = q_{i+1 \bmod s}$. Among these, we are interested in finding those with small embedding degrees. As s increases, the number of cycles also increases. However, since the embedding degree condition is imposed on every step of the cycle, the probability decreases dramatically with s, as this is a very strong requirement. We start by stating the main result of this section.

Theorem 5.2. *Let $s \geq 2$, $K > 0$, and $M \in \mathbb{Z}$. Let $\mathfrak{p}$ be the probability of finding an s-cycle of elliptic curves $E_1/\mathbb{F}_{q_1}, \ldots, E_s/\mathbb{F}_{q_s}$ with $q_i \in [M, 2M]$ and embedding degrees $k_i \leq K$ for all $i = 1, \ldots, s$, by sampling uniformly from all the s-cycles of elliptic curves with orders in the interval $[M, 2M]$. Then*

$$\mathfrak{p} < cK(K+1)\frac{(\log M)^{3s} (\log \log M)^{2s}}{M^{s/2}},$$

for some constant $c > 0$ depending on s.

We will prove our result above through a sequence of lemmas. The overall strategy is as follows: in Lemma 5.3, we count the number of s-tuples of primes within the interval $[M, 2M]$ that are compatible with the Hasse condition. In Lemma 5.5, we impose an upper bound K on the embedding degree. Finally, in Lemmas 5.7 and 5.8, we count the curves that are compatible with the primes counted in the previous two results.

We start by disregarding the curves and just looking at the primes. In order to get a cycle, we need an s-tuple of primes $q_1, \ldots, q_s$ that fit in the Hasse interval of each other, i.e. $|q_{i+1} - q_i - 1| \leq 2\sqrt{q_i}$. Thus, we first count the s-tuples of possible primes $q_1, \ldots, q_s$ that are not too far apart.

Lemma 5.3. *Let $s \geq 2$ be a fixed positive integer and $C > 0$ a constant depending on s. For any $M \geq 2$ we denote by $T_s(M)$ the number of s-tuples of primes in the interval $[M, 2M]$ with $|q_i - q_j| \leq C\sqrt{M}$. Then, there exist constants c_5, c_9 depending on s, such that*

$$c_5\frac{M^{(s+1)/2}}{(\log M)^s} \leq T_s(M) \leq c_9\frac{M^{(s+1)/2}}{(\log M)^s}.$$

Proof. We split the interval $[M, 2M]$ in subintervals $I_k = [M + (k-1)C\sqrt{M}, M + kC\sqrt{M})$ for $1 \leq k \leq \lfloor \sqrt{M}/C \rfloor$ and call π_k the number of primes on the interval

I_k. We denote $M_C = M + C \left\lfloor \frac{\sqrt{M}}{C} \right\rfloor \sqrt{M}$. Observe that $2M - M_C \leq C\sqrt{M}$ and, hence, the prime number theorem gives

$$\sum_{k=1}^{\lfloor \sqrt{M}/C \rfloor} \pi_k = \pi(M_C) - \pi(M) = \frac{M}{\log M} + e,$$

where $|e| < \varepsilon \frac{M}{\log M}$ for any $\varepsilon > 0$ and $M > M_\varepsilon$ sufficiently large, depending on ε. Then, a simple application of Hölder's inequality [6, Chapter 1, Theorem 2] for $p = s$ and $q = \frac{s}{s-1}$ gives us that, for $M > M_\varepsilon$,

$$(1-\varepsilon)\frac{M}{\log M} \leq \sum_{k=1}^{\lfloor \sqrt{M}/C \rfloor} \pi_k \leq \left(\sum_{k=1}^{\lfloor \sqrt{M}/C \rfloor} 1 \right)^{(s-1)/s} \left(\sum_{k=1}^{\lfloor \sqrt{M}/C \rfloor} \pi_k^s \right)^{1/s}$$

$$\leq c_1 M^{(s-1)/2s} \left(\sum_{k=1}^{\lfloor \sqrt{M}/C \rfloor} \pi_k^s \right)^{1/s}. \tag{1}$$

Hence,

$$\frac{c_2 M^{(s+1)/2}}{(\log M)^s} \leq \sum_{k=1}^{\lfloor \sqrt{M}/C \rfloor} \pi_k^s.$$

Finally, observe that every s-tuple of primes on each interval I_k is counted in $T_s(M)$, so we can use the above expression to get a lower bound on $T_s(M)$. Let A be the set of indices k such that the interval I_k has more than $(s+1)^2$ primes. Now, since for any $N_1 > 0$ and $N_2 > 1$ we have the following inequality [36, Corollary 2],

$$\pi(N_1 + N_2) - \pi(N_1) \leq \frac{2N_2}{\log N_2}, \tag{2}$$

we get that $\pi_k \leq c_3 \frac{\sqrt{M}}{\log M}$ for any k. Therefore,

$$\frac{M}{\log M} \sim \sum_{k \in A} \pi_k + \sum_{k \in \overline{A}} \pi_k < c_3 \frac{\sqrt{M}}{\log M} \#A + (s+1)^2(\sqrt{M} - \#A)$$

$$< c_3 \frac{\sqrt{M}}{\log M} \#A + (s+1)^2\sqrt{M},$$

which gives us the bound

$$\#A > c_4\sqrt{M}$$

for any M sufficiently large. Now, to get the lower bound, we look at the variations of s-tuples of primes in each interval I_k for $1 \leq k \leq \lfloor \sqrt{M}/C \rfloor$.

$$T_s(M) \geq \sum_{k=1}^{\lfloor \sqrt{M}/C \rfloor} \frac{\pi_k!}{(\pi_k - s)!} \geq \sum_{k \in A} \frac{\pi_k!}{(\pi_k - s)!} = \sum_{k \in A} \pi_k^s \prod_{j=0}^{s-1} \left(1 - \frac{j}{\pi_k}\right)$$

$$> \sum_{k \in A} \pi_k^s e^{-s(s+1)/\pi_k} > \frac{1}{e} \sum_{k \in A} \pi_k^s$$

$$= \frac{1}{e} \left(\sum_{k=1}^{\lfloor \sqrt{M}/C \rfloor} \pi_k^s - \sum_{k \in \overline{A}} \pi_k^s \right) \geq c_5 \frac{M^{(s+1)/2}}{(\log M)^s} - \frac{1}{e}(s+1)^{2s}\sqrt{M}$$

$$> c_6 \frac{M^{(s+1)/2}}{(\log M)^s}.$$

In order to prove the second inequality, we denote the primes in the interval $[M, 2M]$, in increasing order, as $q_1, \ldots, q_N$. If we have an s-tuple starting with q_i, then the rest of the $s - 1$ primes on the s-tuple will be in the interval $I_i = (q_i, q_i + C\sqrt{M}]$. Hence, letting $\pi_i = \sum_{q \in I_i} 1$, we can apply the inequality of Eq. (2) to obtain

$$T_s(M) \leq \sum_{i=1}^{N} \binom{\pi_i}{s-1} \leq c_7 \sum_{i=1}^{N} \pi_i^{s-1} \leq c_8 \frac{M^{\frac{s-1}{2}}}{(\log M)^{s-1}} N \leq c_9 \frac{M^{\frac{s+1}{2}}}{(\log M)^s}. \tag{3}$$

$\square$

Remark 5.4. For $s = 2$ and $C = 1$ we can get any constant $c_5 < 1/2$. Observe that, when $C = 1$, we have $c_1 = 1$ in (1), and thus it yields the inequality

$$\sum_{k=1}^{\lfloor \sqrt{M} \rfloor} \pi_k^s \geq (1 - \varepsilon) \frac{M^{(s+1)/2}}{(\log M)^s},$$

for any $\varepsilon > 0$. Then, we note that, for M large enough,

$$T_2(M) \geq \frac{1}{2} \sum_{k=1}^{\sqrt{M}} \pi_k(\pi_k - 1) = \frac{1}{2} \sum_{k=1}^{\sqrt{M}} \pi_k^2 - \frac{1}{2} \sum_{k=1}^{\sqrt{M}} \pi_k \geq \frac{1}{2} \frac{M^{3/2}}{(\log M)^2} - \frac{1}{2} \frac{M}{\log M} \geq \left(\frac{1}{2} - \varepsilon'\right) \frac{M^{3/2}}{(\log M)^2},$$

where in the last inequality we have used that the first term is asymptotically dominant. A different proof of the lower bound for the case $s = 2$ and $C = 1$, with a slightly worse constant, is given in [31, Lemma 1].

Now, let us impose the condition of having very small embedding degree.

Lemma 5.5. For any $M > 0$ and $K > 0$, let $T_{s,K}(M)$ be the number of s-tuples of primes in the interval $[M, 2M]$, with $|q_i - q_j| \leq C\sqrt{M}$, for some constant $C > 0$ and such that $q_{i+1} \mid q_i^{k_i} - 1$ for some $k_i \leq K$. Then

$$T_{s,K}(M) \leq c_2 K(K+1)\sqrt{M},$$

for some constant $c_2 > 0$.

Proof. We proceed similarly to [3]. First note that if $q_{i+1} \mid q_i^{k_i} - 1$, then $q_{i+1} \mid (q_i - q_{i+1})^{k_i} - 1$ and, since $|q_i - q_j| \leq C\sqrt{M}$, we have that for any i there exists an integer $|h_i| \leq C\sqrt{M}$ such that $q_{i+1} \mid h_i^{k_i} - 1$ for some $k_i \leq K$. Now, since $q_{i+1} > M \geq (Ch_i)^2$, we see that $h_i^{k_i} - 1$ has at most $c_1 \frac{k_i}{2}$ prime divisors on the interval $[M, 2M]$, for some constant $c_1 > 0$. Summing over the possible k and h we get

$$T_{s,K}(M) \leq \sum_{k \leq K} \sum_{|h| \leq C\sqrt{M}} \sum_{q | h^k - 1} 1 \leq c_2 K(K+1)\sqrt{M}.$$

$\square$

Finally, we bring curves back into the equation. Given an interval $[M, 2M]$, we will count the tuples of curves with orders in the intervals, and the subset of those such that every curve in the tuple is pairing-friendly. Theorem 5.2 will follow directly from these. We introduce the following result from [32], which we will require for the proof.

Lemma 5.6 ([32], **Proposition 1.9**). *Let $q > 3$ be a prime number, let $P \subset \mathbb{N}$ and let $N_{q,P}$ be the number of isomorphism classes of elliptic curves over $\mathbb{F}_q$ and order $\#E(\mathbb{F}_q) \in P$. Then:*

- *If $P \subset [q + 1 - 2\sqrt{q}, q + 1 + 2\sqrt{q}]$, then $N_{q,P} \leq c\#P(\log q)(\log \log q)^2 \sqrt{q}$ for some constant $c > 0$.*
- *If $P \subset [q - \sqrt{q}, q + \sqrt{q}]$ and $\#P \geq 3$, then $N_{q,P} \geq c(\#P - 2)\frac{\sqrt{q}}{\log q}$ for some constant $c > 0$.*

Lemma 5.7. *Let $M \geq 2$, and let $C_s(M)$ be the number of s-tuples of elliptic curves $E_1/\mathbb{F}_{q_1}, \ldots, E_s/\mathbb{F}_{q_s}$ forming a cycle of length s, where $q_i \in [M, 2M]$ for all $i = 1, \ldots, s$. Then there exist constants c_7, c_2, depending on s, such that*

$$c_7 \frac{M^{(2s+1)/2}}{(\log M)^{2s}} \leq C_s(M) \leq c_2 (\log \log M)^{2s} M^{(2s+1)/2}.$$

Proof. First, note that, if we have an s-cycle of curves, then the corresponding primes are as in Lemma 5.3 for any $C > s$. Without loss of generality, let us assume that cycles start at the smallest prime. Now, if we have an s-tuple in which the smallest prime is q_1, then the rest of the $s - 1$ primes on the s-tuple will be in the interval $I_i = (q_1, q_1 + s\sqrt{q_1} + (s/2)^2]$. To see this, we first prove a result by induction. Let $q_\ell, q_{\ell+1}$ be the ℓ-th and $(\ell + 1)$-th primes in the cycle, respectively. The induction hypothesis is that $q_\ell \leq (\sqrt{q_1} + \ell)^2$ (the base case is true due to the Hasse bound). Then,

$$q_{\ell+1} \leq q_\ell + 2\sqrt{q_\ell} + 1 \leq q_1 + 2\ell\sqrt{q_1} + \ell^2 + 2\sqrt{q_1 + 2\ell\sqrt{q_1} + \ell^2} + 1$$
$$= q_1 + 2(\ell+1)\sqrt{q_1} + (\ell+1)^2 = (\sqrt{q_1} + (\ell+1))^2,$$

concluding the induction step. From here, we deduce that, for any $\ell = 1, \ldots, s$, we have that

$$\sqrt{q_\ell} - \sqrt{q_1} \leq \ell.$$

Since they form a cycle, then it must be the case that $q_\ell \in I_i$ for all ℓ (note that there are at most $s/2$ primes between the largest and the smallest prime of a cycle).

Now, let us start by proving the upper bound for $C_s(M)$. Let P be a subset of primes p satisfying that $|p - (q + 1)| \le 2q$. By the first part of Lemma 5.6, we know that there are at most $c_1\sqrt{q}\log q(\log\log q)^2 \#P$ isomorphism classes over $\mathbb{F}_q$ of elliptic curves with $\#E(\mathbb{F}_q) \in P$ for some constant c_1. Taking P with $\#P = s$ and multiplying over each prime of an s-tuple we get that, on each s-tuple, there will be less than

$$c_2(\log M)^s(\log\log M)^{2s}M^{s/2}$$

isomorphism classes of elliptic curves with points on the s-tuple and, in particular, forming a cycle of length at most s. Note that the constant c_2 depends on s. Applying the second inequality of Lemma 5.3, we get the expected upper bound for cycles of length at most s, and in particular for $C_s(M)$.

To prove the lower bound for $C_s(M)$ we will use the second part of Lemma 5.6. In this case, for any q and any subset of primes $P \subset [q-\sqrt{q}, q+\sqrt{q}]$ with $\#P \ge 3$ there are more than $c_3(\#P-2)\frac{\sqrt{q}}{\log q}$ isomorphism classes over $\mathbb{F}_q$ of elliptic curves with $\#E(\mathbb{F}_q) \in P$ for some constant c_3. Hence, on each s-tuple with $s \ge 3$ we have more than $c_4\frac{M^{s/2}}{(\log M)^s}$ isomorphism classes of elliptic curves with points on the s-tuple and, in particular, forming a cycle of length at most s. Note that c_4 is a constant that depends on s. Observe that, in particular, all those primes lie on the Hasse interval for q, since $P \subset [q-\sqrt{q}, q+\sqrt{q}] \subset [q+1-2\sqrt{q}, q+1+2\sqrt{q}]$. Combining this with the first inequality of Lemma 5.3, we get the lower bound

$$c_5\frac{M^{(2s+1)/2}}{(\log M)^{2s}}.$$

Then, $C_s(M)$ will be cycles of isomorphism classes of elliptic curves of length at most s minus cycles of isomorphism classes of elliptic curves of length at most $s - 1$. In order to bound the number of cycles of length at most $s - 1$, we use the previous upper bound for $C_i(M)$, for $i = 1, \ldots, s - 1$, so we get

$$\sum_{i=1}^{s-1}(\log\log M)^{2i}M^{(2i+1)/2} \le c_6(\log\log M)^{2s-2}M^{(2s-1)/2}$$

for some constant c_6. Hence,

$$C_s(M) \ge c_5\frac{M^{(2s+1)/2}}{(\log M)^{2s}} - c_6(\log\log M)^{2s-2}M^{(2s-1)/2} \ge c_7\frac{M^{(2s+1)/2}}{(\log M)^{2s}},$$

for some constant c_7 and for M sufficiently large depending on s. $\qquad\square$

By mimicking the second part of the previous proof, but using Lemma 5.5 instead of Lemma 5.3, we obtain the following analogous result.

Lemma 5.8. *Let $M \geq 2$. Let $C_{s,K}(M)$ be the number of s-tuples in the same conditions as in Lemma 5.7, which additionally satisfy that E_i has embedding $k_i \leq K$ for all $i = 1, \ldots, s$. Then there exists a constant c, depending on s, such that*

$$C_{s,K}(M) \leq cK(K+1)(\log M)^s (\log\log M)^{2s} M^{(s+1)/2}.$$

Finally, from Lemmas 5.7 and 5.8, we get Theorem 5.2 by dividing $C_{s,K}(M)$ by $C_s(M)$.

6 Conclusions

Cycles of elliptic curves require the curves involved to be of prime order, and families of elliptic curves parameterized by low-degree polynomials are the only known approach at generating pairing-friendly curves with prime order. In this work, we have shown that this approach is unlikely to yield new cycles, beyond the MNT4-MNT6 cycles that are already known. In particular, we have shown that no known families are involved in a 2-cycle with any pairing-friendly curve of cryptographic interest. Along the way, we have developed our understanding of these mathematical objects, showing some new properties and a probability analysis.

While a lot is still unknown about pairing-friendly cycles, we highlight two avenues that we consider interesting for future research.

- Generalizing Theorem 4.5 and Corollary 4.8 to s-cycles, for $s > 2$. The case $s = 2$ is the most appealing from a practical perspective, due to the application to recursive composition of SNARKs, but it would be desirable to have the complete picture. The main hurdle here is that, whereas fixing a curve in a 2-cycle automatically determines the other, longer cycles have more degrees of freedom, so we do not have as much explicit information to work with in the proof.
- Consider a 2-cycle such that both curves $E \leftrightarrow (t, p, q)$ and $E' \leftrightarrow (2 - t, q, p)$ have the same embedding degree k. If we restrict ourselves to the case $k \equiv 0 \pmod 4$, it is easy to argue (as in Proposition 3.10) that

$$pq \mid \Phi_k(t - 1).$$

This approach allows [15] to prove that said cycles cannot exist when $k \in \{8, 12\}$. However, the authors leave higher values of k as an open question. If we consider families of curves, Theorem 4.5 tells us that the above relation must hold as polynomials, or else only a finite number of cycles will exist. Thus, we wonder if considering the above condition as a relation between polynomials, and applying polynomial machinery, could help in answering this question.

Acknowledgements. The second author is partially supported by Dusk Network and the Spanish grant PID2019-110224RB-I00.

A   Polynomial Division

In this section, we show that $p(X)^\ell \bmod q(X)$ is an integer-valued polynomial, when $E \leftrightarrow (t, p, q)$ are either the MNT3 or BN curves. This is completely analogous to the argument in Remark 4.6.

MNT3 Curves. In this case, $q(X) = 12X^2 - 1$. We proceed by induction on ℓ. For $\ell = 1$, we have that

$$p(X) \bmod q(X) = -6X + 2,$$

which is of the form $6aX + b$, for some $a, b \in \mathbb{Z}$. We show that, if $p^\ell \bmod q$ is of this form, then so is $p^{\ell+1} \bmod q$. Then all the remainders will actually be in $\mathbb{Z}[X]$.

Assume that there exist $a, b, c, d \in \mathbb{N}$ such that

$$p(X)^\ell \bmod q(X) = 6aX + b.$$

Then

$$\begin{aligned}
p(X)^{\ell+1} &\equiv p(X)^\ell p(X) \equiv (6aX + b)(-6X + 2) \\
&\equiv -36aX^2 + (12a - 6b)X + 2b \\
&\equiv (12a - 6b)X + (-3a + 2b) \pmod{q(X)}.
\end{aligned}$$

Since the coefficient of degree 1 is divisible by 6, the induction step works.

BN Curves. In this case, $q(X) = 36X^4 + 36X^3 + 24X^2 + 6X + 1$. Assume that there exist $a, b, c, d \in \mathbb{N}$ such that

$$p(X)^\ell \bmod q(X) = 36aX^3 + 6bX^2 + 6cX + d,$$

for some $a, b, c, d \in \mathbb{Z}$. Then

$$\begin{aligned}
p(X)^{\ell+1} &\equiv p(X)^\ell p(X) \equiv \left(36aX^3 + 6bX^2 + 6cX + d\right)\left(-6X^2\right) \\
&\equiv -216aX^5 - 36bX^4 - -36cX^3 - 6dX^2 \\
&\equiv (-72a + 36b - 36c)X^3 + (-108a + 24b - 6d)X^2 \\
&\quad + (-30a + 6b)X + (-6a + b) \pmod{q(X)}.
\end{aligned}$$

Since the coefficient of degree 3 is divisible by 36, and the coefficients of degree 2 and 1 are divisible by 6, the induction step works.

B   Tables

Table 3. Bounds $N_{\mathsf{left}}, N_{\mathsf{right}}$ from Lemma 4.4 for different embedding degrees ℓ of the potential partner curve of MNT3, Freeman, and BN curves. The remaining intermediate values of ℓ are covered by Corollaries 4.2 and 4.3 for MNT3 and Freeman curves, respectively.

Bounds for BN

ℓ	N_{left}	N_{right}
3	-1	0
4	-3	4
5	-12	11
6	-15	4
7	-65	64
8	-104	103
9	-167	168
10	-831	830
11	-513	508
12	-3523	3524
13	-8620	8619
14	-4092	4097
15	-52351	52350
16	-66417	66414
17	-164463	164464
18	-626817	626816
19	-186373	186364
20	-2992820	2992819
21	-6014684	6014683
22	-5673471	5673474
23	-41263041	41263040
24	-39448697	39448694
25	-151319223	151319224
26	-462478015	462478014
27	-20593636	20593693
28	-2473968276	2473968275
29	-4050737756	4050737755
30	-6238668798	6238668799
31	-31854421247	31854421246
32	-20649322466	20649322461

Bounds for MNT3

ℓ	N_{left}	N_{right}
5	-104	104
10	-75658	75657
19	-10626317415	10626317415

Bounds for Freeman

ℓ	N_{left}	N_{right}
3	-2	4
6	-164	161
7	-686	685
9	-10608	10607
13	-1805067	1805066
14	-6158596	6158595
17	-210958904	210958905
18	-643610018	643610019
19	-1875810507	1875810508
21	-12522961240	12522961243
23	-15125575810	15125575853

C SageMath Code

This code is available at [1].

Setup

MNT3(), MNT4(), MNT6(), Freeman(), BN()

These functions return the set of polynomials that define the families of curves MNT3, MNT4, MNT6, Freeman, and BN, respectively.

The expected outputs are:

- t: polynomial $t(X) \in \mathbb{Q}[X]$ that parameterizes the trace.
- p: polynomial $p(X) \in \mathbb{Q}[X]$ that parameterizes the order of the curves.
- q: polynomial $q(X) \in \mathbb{Q}[X]$ that parameterizes the order of the finite field over which the curve is defined.

```
# SETUP

# Polynomial rings over the reals and rationals.
R.<X> = PolynomialRing(RR, 'X')
Q.<X> = PolynomialRing(QQ, 'X')

# Curve families.
def MNT3():
    t = Q(6*X -1)
    q = Q(12*X^2 - 1)
    p = q + 1 - t
    return(t, p, q)

def MNT4():
    t = Q(-X)
    q = Q(X^2 + X + 1)
    p = q + 1 - t
    return(t, p, q)

def MNT6():
    t = Q(2*X + 1)
    q = Q(4*X^2 + 1)
    p = q + 1 - t
    return(t, p, q)

def Freeman():
    t = Q(10*X^2 + 5*X + 3)
    q = Q(25*X^4 + 25*X^3 + 25*X^2 + 10*X + 3)
    p = q + 1 - t
    return(t, p, q)

def BN():
    t = Q(6*X^2 + 1)
    q = Q(36*X^4 + 36*X^3 + 24*X^2 + 6*X + 1)
    p = q + 1 - t
    return(t, p, q)
```

Code for Proposition 4.1

`candidate_embedding_degrees(Family, K_low, K_high)`

Given a family of curves, this function computes the possible embedding degrees of curves that may form 2-cycles with a curve of the given family.
The expected inputs are:

- `Family`: a polynomial parameterization $(t(X), p(X), q(X))$ of a family of pairing-friendly elliptic curves with prime order.
- `K_low`, `K_high`: lower and upper bounds on the embedding degree to look for.

The expected outputs are:

- `embedding_degrees`: a list of potential embedding degrees k such that `K_low` $\leq k \leq$ `K_high` and a curve from the family *might* form a cycle with a curve with embedding degree k.
- `modular_conditions`: conditions on $x \bmod k$ for each of these k.

```
1  def candidate_embedding_degrees(Family, K_low, K_high):
2
3      (t, p, q) = Family()
4      # Create an empty list to store the candidate embedding
       degrees
5      embedding_degrees = []
6      # Create an empty list to store the lists of modular
       conditions for each k
7      modular_conditions = [None] * (K_high + 1)
8
9      # Embedding degree k implies that q(x) = 1 (mod k).
10     # We check this condition in 0, ..., k-1 and build a list
       of candidates
11     # such that any x has to be congruent to one of them modulo
        k.
12     for k in range(K_low, K_high + 1):
13
14         candidate = False
15
16         for i in range(k):
17             if ((q(i) % k) == 1):
18                 # First time a candidate k is discovered, add
       it to the list and
19                 # create a list within modular_conditions to
       store the values i.
20                 if (not candidate):
21                     candidate = True
22                     embedding_degrees.append(k)
23                     modular_conditions[k] = []
24                 modular_conditions[k].append(i)
25
26     return embedding_degrees, modular_conditions
```

Auxiliary functions

`is_integer_valued(g)`

This function checks whether a given polynomial `g` is integer-valued. It returns `True` if so, and `False` otherwise. The test is based on the fact that a polynomial $g \in \mathbb{Q}[X]$ is integer-valued if and only if $g(x) \in \mathbb{Z}$ for $\deg g + 1$ consecutive $x \in \mathbb{Z}$ [14, Corollary 2].

```
def is_integer_valued(g):

    # Check if evaluation is integer in deg(g) + 1 consecutive
    points.
    for x in range(g.degree()+1):
        if (not g(x) in ZZ):
            print(str(g) + " is not integer-valued.")
            return False
    return True
```

find_relevant_root(w, b, side)

This function finds the left-most or right-most root of a polynomial $b(X) \in \mathbb{Q}[X]$.

The expected inputs are:

– w: positive integer.
– b: polynomial $b(X) \in \mathbb{Q}[X]$.
– side: this parameter specifies which root to keep. If side = -1, then the function takes the left-most root, and if side = 1, it returns the right-most root.

The expected output is the relevant extremal root.

```
def find_relevant_root(w, b, side):
    # Decide whether to keep the left-most or right-most root.
    i = -(1 + side) / 2
    # 0 <= w(x)
    C_1 = 0
    w_roots = R(w).roots()
    if (w_roots != []):
        C_1 = w_roots[i][0]
    # w(x) < b(x)
    C_2 = 0
    bw_roots = R(b - w).roots()
    if (bw_roots != []):
        C_2 = bw_roots[i][0]
    # Return the relevant extremal root.
    if (side == -1):
        return ceil(min(C_1, C_2))
    else:
        return floor(max(C_1, C_2))
```

check_embedding_degree(px, qx, k)

This function determines whether k is the smallest positive integer such that $(\text{px}^k - 1) \pmod{\text{qx}} = 1$, and outputs True/False.

```
1  def check_embedding_degree(px, qx, k):
2      # Checks divisibility condition
3      if ((px^k - 1) % qx != 0): return False
4      # Checks that divisibility conditions does not happen for
       smaller exponents
5      div = divisors(k)
6      div.remove(k)
7      for j in div:
8          if ((px^j - 1) % qx == 0):
9              return False
10     return True
```

Code for Table 3

compute_bounds(a, b)

This function computes the bounds $N_{\text{left}}, N_{\text{right}}$ of Lemma 4.4. This function has been used to produce the results of tables from Table 3. It uses the auxiliary functions from Appendix C.

The expected inputs are:

- a, b: two integer-valued polynomials in $\mathbb{Q}[X]$.

The expected outputs are:

- N_left, N_right: integer bounds $N_{\text{left}}, N_{\text{right}}$ described in Lemma 4.4.

```
1  def compute_bounds(a, b):
2
3      # Check that b has even degree and positive leading coefficient
4      if (b.degree() % 2 == 1 or b.leading_coefficient() < 0):
5          print("Invalid divisor.")
6          return
7
8      # Check that a, b are integer valued.
9      if (not is_integer_valued(a) or not is_integer_valued(b)):
10         return
11
12     # Polynomial division
13     (h, r) = a.quo_rem(b)
14
15     # Compute c so that ch, cr are in Z[X]
16     denominators = [i.denominator() for i in (h.coefficients() + r.coefficients())]
17     c = lcm(denominators)
18
19     # Compute signs
20     sigma_right = sign(r.leading_coefficient())
21     sigma_left = sigma_right * (-1)^(r.degree())
22
23     # We compute the polynomials w_left, w_right such that
24     # 0 <= w_left < b(x) for all x < N_left, and
25     # 0 <= w_right < b(x) for all x > N_right.
26     w_left = c * r + ((1 - sigma_left) / 2) * b
27     w_right = c * r + ((1 - sigma_right) / 2) * b
28
29     # Compute N_left, N_right
30     N_left = find_relevant_root(w_left, b, -1)
31     N_right = find_relevant_root(w_right, b, 1)
32
33     return (N_left, N_right)
```

Code for Corollary 4.8

`exhaustive_search(Family, k, N_left, N_right, mod_cond)`

This function performs the exhaustive search from Corollary 4.8 within the intervals $[N_{\text{left}}, N_{\text{right}}]$.

The expected inputs are:

- Family: a polynomial parameterization $(t(X), p(X), q(X))$ of a family of pairing-friendly elliptic curves with prime order.
- k: an embedding degree.
- N_left, N_right: upper and lower integer bounds.
- mod_cond: conditions on $x \bmod k$ for every x in the interval [N_left, N_right].

The expected output is:

- curves: a list of curve descriptions $(x, k, t(x), p(x), q(x))$ such that $x \in$ [N_left, N_right], and the curve parameterized by $(t(x), p(x), q(x))$ forms a cycle with a curve with embedding degree k.

```
1  def exhaustive_search(Family, k, N_left, N_right, mod_cond):
2
3     (t, p, q) = Family()
4     curves   = []
5
6     for x in range(N_left, N_right+1):
7        # We skip those values that will never yield q(x) = 1 (
          mod k), as precomputed above.
8        if (not (x % k) in mod_cond): continue
9        # Check the embedding degree condition
10       if (check_embedding_degree(p(x), q(x), k)):
11          curves.append((x, k, t(x), p(x), q(x)))
12
13    return curves
```

Main function

`search_for_cycles(Family, K_low, K_high)`

This function looks for 2-cycles formed by a curve belonging to a given parameterized family of curves and a prime-order curve with an embedding degree between two given bounds.

The expected inputs are:

- Family: a polynomial parameterization $(t(X), p(X), q(X))$ of a family of pairing-friendly elliptic curves with prime order.
- K_low, K_high: integer lower and upper bounds on the embedding degree to look for.

The function prints to a file all 2-cycles involving a curve from the family and a prime-order curve with embedding degree $K\_low \leq k \leq K\_high$.

```
 1  import time
 2
 3  def search_for_cycles(Family, K_low, K_high):
 4
 5      file_name = 'output_' + Family.__name__ + '.txt'
 6      f = open(file_name, 'w')
 7      start = time.time()
 8
 9      # Instantiate the family
10      (t, p, q) = Family()
11      print("Starting family: " + str(Family.__name__), file=f)
12      print("t(X) = " + str(t), file=f)
13      print("p(X) = " + str(p), file=f)
14      print("q(X) = " + str(q), file=f)
15
16      # Find the candidate embedding degrees up to K that are
        compatible with this family
17      (embedding_degrees, modular_conditions) =
        candidate_embedding_degrees(Family, K_low, K_high)
18      print("Candidate embedding degrees: " + str(
        embedding_degrees), file=f)
19      for k in embedding_degrees:
20          print(("For k = " + str(k) + ", necessarily x = " +str(
        modular_conditions[k])) + " (mod " + str(k) + ")", file=f)
21      print("========================", file=f)
22
23      # For each potential embedding degree, find the bounds
        N_left, N_right and perform exhaustive search within [
        N_left, N_right].
24      for k in embedding_degrees:
25
26          f.close()
27          f = open(file_name, 'a')
28          start_k = time.time()
29
30          print("k = " + str(k), file=f)
31          (N_left, N_right) = compute_bounds(p^k, q)
32          print("N_left = " + str(N_left) + ", N_right = " + str(
        N_right), file=f)
33
34          curves = exhaustive_search(Family, k, N_left, N_right,
        modular_conditions[k])
35          print("Curves with embedding degree " + str(k) + " that
         form a cycle with a curve from the " + str(Family.__name__
        ) + " family: " + str(len(curves)), file=f)
36
37          for curve in curves:
38              (x, k, tx, px, qx) = curve
39              print("x = " + str(x), file=f)
40              print("embedding degree = " + str(k), file=f)
41              print("t(x) = " + str(tx), file=f)
42              print("p(x) = " + str(px), file=f)
43              print("q(x) = " + str(qx), file=f)
44              print("------------", file=f)
45
46          end_k = time.time()
47          print('Computations for embedding degree ' + str(k) + '
         took', round(end_k - start_k, 2), 'seconds.', file=f)
48          print("------------------------", file=f)
49
50      end = time.time()
51      print("========================", file=f)
52      print('Overall computation took', round(end - start, 2), '
        time', file=f)
53
54      f.close()
```

References

1. SageMath code from Appendix C. GitHub repository (2022). https://github.com/pairingfriendlycycles/pairing-friendly-cycles/tree/main
2. Aranha, D.F., Housni, Y.E., Guillevic, A.: A survey of elliptic curves for proof systems. Cryptology ePrint Archive, Paper 2022/586 (2022)
3. Balasubramanian, R., Koblitz, N.: The improbability that an elliptic curve has subexponential discrete log problem under the Menezes-Okamoto-Vanstone algorithm. J. Cryptol. **11**(2), 141–145 (1998)
4. Barreto, P.S.L.M., Lynn, B., Scott, M.: Constructing elliptic curves with prescribed embedding degrees. In: Cimato, S., Persiano, G., Galdi, C. (eds.) SCN 2002. LNCS, vol. 2576, pp. 257–267. Springer, Heidelberg (2003). https://doi.org/10.1007/3-540-36413-7_19
5. Barreto, P.S.L.M., Naehrig, M.: Pairing-friendly elliptic curves of prime order. In: Preneel, B., Tavares, S. (eds.) SAC 2005. LNCS, vol. 3897, pp. 319–331. Springer, Heidelberg (2006). https://doi.org/10.1007/11693383_22
6. Beckenbach, E.F., Bellman, R.: Inequalities (1961)
7. Ben-Sasson, E., Chiesa, A., Tromer, E., Virza, M.: Scalable zero knowledge via cycles of elliptic curves. Algorithmica **79**(4), 1102–1160 (2017)
8. Bitansky, N., Canetti, R., Chiesa, A., Tromer, E.: From extractable collision resistance to succinct non-interactive arguments of knowledge, and back again. In: Proceedings of the 3rd Innovations in Theoretical Computer Science Conference, pp. 326–349 (2012)
9. Boneh, D., Drake, J., Fisch, B., Gabizon, A.: Halo Infinite: recursive zk-SNARKs from any additive polynomial commitment scheme. Cryptology ePrint Archive (2020)
10. Bonneau, J., Meckler, I., Rao, V., Shapiro, E.: Mina: decentralized cryptocurrency at scale. New York Univ. O(1) Labs, New York, NY, USA, Whitepaper, pp. 1–47 (2020)
11. Bowe, S., Grigg, J., Hopwood, D.: Recursive proof composition without a trusted setup. Cryptology ePrint Archive (2019)
12. Bünz, B., Chiesa, A., Lin, W., Mishra, P., Spooner, N.: Proof-carrying data without succinct arguments. In: Malkin, T., Peikert, C. (eds.) CRYPTO 2021. LNCS, vol. 12825, pp. 681–710. Springer, Cham (2021). https://doi.org/10.1007/978-3-030-84242-0_24
13. Bünz, B., Chiesa, A., Mishra, P., Spooner, N.: Proof-carrying data from accumulation schemes. Cryptology ePrint Archive (2020)
14. Cahen, P.J., Chabert, J.L.: What you should know about integer-valued polynomials. Am. Math. Mon. **123**(4), 311–337 (2016)
15. Chiesa, A., Chua, L., Weidner, M.: On cycles of pairing-friendly elliptic curves. SIAM J. Appl. Algebra Geometry **3**(2), 175–192 (2019)
16. Chiesa, A., Tromer, E.: Proof-carrying data and hearsay arguments from signature cards. In: ICS, vol. 10, pp. 310–331 (2010)
17. Chiesa, A., Tromer, E., Virza, M.: Cluster computing in zero knowledge. In: Oswald, E., Fischlin, M. (eds.) EUROCRYPT 2015. LNCS, vol. 9057, pp. 371–403. Springer, Heidelberg (2015). https://doi.org/10.1007/978-3-662-46803-6_13
18. Costello, C., et al.: Geppetto: versatile verifiable computation. In: 2015 IEEE Symposium on Security and Privacy, pp. 253–270 (2015). https://doi.org/10.1109/SP.2015.23

19. Cox, D.A.: Primes of the Form $x^2 + ny^2$: Fermat, Class Field Theory, and Complex Multiplication. Wiley, Hoboken (1989)
20. El Housni, Y., Guillevic, A.: Families of SNARK-friendly 2-chains of elliptic curves. In: Dunkelman, O., Dziembowski, S. (eds.) EUROCRYPT 2022. LNCS, vol. 13276, pp. 367–396. Springer, Cham (2022). https://doi.org/10.1007/978-3-031-07085-3_13
21. Freeman, D.: Constructing pairing-friendly elliptic curves with embedding degree 10. In: Hess, F., Pauli, S., Pohst, M. (eds.) ANTS 2006. LNCS, vol. 4076, pp. 452–465. Springer, Heidelberg (2006). https://doi.org/10.1007/11792086_32
22. Freeman, D.: Constructing pairing-friendly elliptic curves with embedding degree 10 (2006). https://theory.stanford.edu/dfreeman/talks/ants.pdf, presentation slides from ANTS-VII
23. Freeman, D., Scott, M., Teske, E.: A taxonomy of pairing-friendly elliptic curves. J. Cryptol. 23(2), 224–280 (2010)
24. Frey, G., Rück, H.G.: A remark concerning m-divisibility and the discrete logarithm in the divisor class group of curves. Math. Comput. 62(206), 865–874 (1994)
25. Gabizon, A., Williamson, Z.J., Ciobotaru, O.: PlonK: permutations over Lagrange-bases for oecumenical noninteractive arguments of knowledge. Cryptology ePrint Archive (2019)
26. Galbraith, S.D., McKee, J.F., Valença, P.C.: Ordinary abelian varieties having small embedding degree. Finite Fields Appl. 13(4), 800–814 (2007)
27. Groth, J.: On the size of pairing-based non-interactive arguments. In: Fischlin, M., Coron, J.-S. (eds.) EUROCRYPT 2016. LNCS, vol. 9666, pp. 305–326. Springer, Heidelberg (2016). https://doi.org/10.1007/978-3-662-49896-5_11
28. Karabina, K., Teske, E.: On prime-order elliptic curves with embedding degrees $k = 3$, 4, and 6. In: van der Poorten, A.J., Stein, A. (eds.) ANTS 2008. LNCS, vol. 5011, pp. 102–117. Springer, Heidelberg (2008). https://doi.org/10.1007/978-3-540-79456-1_6
29. Kate, A., Zaverucha, G.M., Goldberg, I.: Constant-size commitments to polynomials and their applications. In: Abe, M. (ed.) ASIACRYPT 2010. LNCS, vol. 6477, pp. 177–194. Springer, Heidelberg (2010). https://doi.org/10.1007/978-3-642-17373-8_11
30. Kattis, A., Bonneau, J.: Proof of necessary work: succinct state verification with fairness guarantees. Cryptology ePrint Archive (2020)
31. Koblitz, N.: Elliptic curve implementation of zero-knowledge blobs. J. Cryptol. 4(3), 207–213 (1991). https://doi.org/10.1007/BF00196728
32. Lenstra Jr., H.W.: Factoring integers with elliptic curves. Ann. Math. (2) 126(3), 649–673 (1987)
33. Menezes, A.J., Okamoto, T., Vanstone, S.A.: Reducing elliptic curve logarithms to logarithms in a finite field. IEEE Trans. Information Theory 39(5), 1639–1646 (1993)
34. Migotti, A.: Zur Theorie der Kreisteilungsgleichung. B. der Math.-Naturwiss, Classe der Kaiserlichen Akademie der Wissenschaften, Wien 87, 7–14 (1883)
35. Miyaji, A., Nakabayashi, M., Takano, S.: New explicit conditions of elliptic curve traces for FR-reduction. IEICE Trans. Fundam. Electron. Commun. Comput. Sci. 84(5), 1234–1243 (2001)
36. Montgomery, H.L., Vaughan, R.C.: The large sieve. Mathematika 20(2), 119–134 (1973)
37. Naveh, A., Tromer, E.: PhotoProof: cryptographic image authentication for any set of permissible transformations. In: 2016 IEEE Symposium on Security and Privacy (SP), pp. 255–271. IEEE (2016)

38. Parno, B., Howell, J., Gentry, C., Raykova, M.: Pinocchio: Nearly Practical Verifiable Computation, vol. 59, pp. 238–252 (2013). https://doi.org/10.1109/SP.2013.47

39. Pegg, E.J.: Bouniakowsky conjecture. MathWorld-A Wolfram Web Resource, created by Eric W. Weisstein. https://mathworld.wolfram.com/BouniakowskyConjecture.html

40. Silverman, J.H.: The Arithmetic of Elliptic Curves, vol. 106. Springer, New York (2009). https://doi.org/10.1007/978-0-387-09494-6

41. Silverman, J.H., Stange, K.E.: Amicable pairs and aliquot cycles for elliptic curves. Exp. Math. **20**(3), 329–357 (2011)

42. Smart, N.P.: The discrete logarithm problem on elliptic curves of trace one. J. Cryptol. **12**, 193–196 (1999)

43. Sutherland, A.V.: Accelerating the CM method. LMS J. Comput. Math. **15**, 172–204 (2012)

44. Valiant, P.: Incrementally verifiable computation or proofs of knowledge imply time/space efficiency. In: Canetti, R. (ed.) TCC 2008. LNCS, vol. 4948, pp. 1–18. Springer, Heidelberg (2008). https://doi.org/10.1007/978-3-540-78524-8_1

Non-interactive Zero-Knowledge
from Non-interactive Batch Arguments

Jeffrey Champion[✉] and David J. Wu

University of Texas at Austin, Austin, TX, USA
jchampion@utexas.edu

Abstract. Zero-knowledge and succinctness are two important properties that arise in the study of non-interactive arguments. Previously, Kitagawa et al. (TCC 2020) showed how to obtain a non-interactive zero-knowledge (NIZK) argument for NP from a succinct non-interactive argument (SNARG) for NP. In particular, their work demonstrates how to leverage the succinctness property from an argument system and transform it into a zero-knowledge property.

In this work, we study a similar question of leveraging succinctness for zero-knowledge. Our starting point is a batch argument for NP, a primitive that allows a prover to convince a verifier of T NP statements $x_1, \ldots, x_T$ with a proof whose size scales sublinearly with T. Unlike SNARGs for NP, batch arguments for NP can be built from group-based assumptions in both pairing and pairing-free groups and from lattice-based assumptions. The challenge with batch arguments is that the proof size is only amortized over the number of instances, but can still encode full information about the witness to a small number of instances.

We show how to combine a batch argument for NP with a local pseudorandom generator (i.e., a pseudorandom generator where each output bit only depends on a small number of input bits) and a dual-mode commitment scheme to obtain a NIZK for NP. Our work provides a new *generic* approach of realizing zero-knowledge from succinctness and highlights a new connection between succinctness and zero-knowledge.

1 Introduction

In a non-interactive argument system for an NP language $\mathcal{L}$, a prover sends a single message π to try and convince an efficient verifier that an NP statement x is true (i.e., $x \in \mathcal{L}$). In an argument system [BCC88], we require soundness to hold against *computationally-bounded* provers (i.e., a computationally-bounded prover should not be able to convince the verifier of a false statement). Two of the most important properties considered in the context of cryptographic argument systems are zero-knowledge and succinctness:

- **Zero-knowledge**: We say a non-interactive argument satisfies zero-knowledge [GMR85] if the proof π for an NP statement x reveals nothing more about x other than the fact that the statement is true. We refer to such arguments as non-interactive zero-knowledge (NIZK) arguments [BFM88]. While NIZKs for NP are unlikely to exist in the plain

© International Association for Cryptologic Research 2023
H. Handschuh and A. Lysyanskaya (Eds.): CRYPTO 2023, LNCS 14082, pp. 38–71, 2023.
https://doi.org/10.1007/978-3-031-38545-2_2

model (unless $NP \subseteq BPP$), a long line of works have constructed NIZKs in the common reference string (CRS) model from a broad range of algebraic assumptions including factoring [FLS90], assumptions on pairing groups [CHK03, GOS06, GOS12, LPWW20] and pairing-free groups [JJ21], lattice-based assumptions [CCH+19, PS19], and combinations of multiple assumptions [BKM20].

- **Succinctness:** A second property of interest is the length of the proof (and by correspondence, the verification complexity). We say that an argument system for $\mathcal{L}$ is succinct if the length of the proof and the running time of the verifier is sublinear (or more commonly, polylogarithmic) in the size of the NP relation associated with $\mathcal{L}$. Such arguments are referred to as *succinct non-interactive arguments*, or SNARGs [GW11]. We refer to [Mic95, Gro10, BCCT12, DFH12, Lip13, PHGR13, GGPR13, BCI+13, BCPR14, Gro16, BISW17, BCC+17, BISW18, BBHR18, COS20, CHM+20, Set20, ACL+22, BS23, CBBZ23] and the references therein for a survey of succinct arguments.

Many applications require non-interactive arguments that are simultaneously succinct and zero-knowledge (i.e., zkSNARGs). Given a SNARG and a NIZK (argument of knowledge), it is straightforward to obtain a zkSNARG by direct composition (i.e., the zkSNARG is a NIZK argument of knowledge of a SNARG proof of the statement). A natural question is whether there is a formal connection between these two fundamental properties of cryptographic arguments. Previously Kitagawa et al. [KMY20] showed that SNARGs for NP and one-way functions together imply NIZKs for NP (and by composition, a zkSNARG).[1] The intuition underlying this result is that since the length of a SNARG proof for an NP statement x is much shorter than the length of the associated witness w, the SNARG proof simply cannot reveal too many bits of the witness information-theoretically. Then, by composing the SNARG with leakage-resilient cryptography, this intuition can be leveraged to obtain a NIZK.

Batch Arguments and Zero Knowledge. In this work, we continue this line of inquiry of studying the relationship between succinctness and zero-knowledge. Instead of focusing on SNARGs for NP, which have a very strong succinctness property and necessitates constructions in either idealized models or based on non-falsifiable assumptions [GW11], we start with the weaker notion of SNARGs for *batch* NP languages. This is a notion that has received extensive study recently [KVZ21, CJJ21a, CJJ21b, HJKS22, WW22, DGKV22, GSWW22, CGJ+22, KLVW23] and can be realized from *standard* cryptographic assumptions. At a high level, in a non-interactive batch argument (BARG), a prover can convince a verifier of a collection of T NP statements $(x_1, \ldots, x_T)$ with a proof of size $\text{poly}(\lambda, s) \cdot o(T)$, where s is the size of the circuit computing the NP relation. In particular, a batch argument amortizes the cost of NP verification across multiple instances. While this amortization still confers some succinctness,

---

[1] More recently, Chakraborty et al. [CPW23] showed a similar implication holds starting from a mildly-compact computational witness map (a simpler primitive that is implied by a SNARG for NP).

it is certainly possible for a BARG proof to leak one or more of the underlying witnesses associated with the statements used to construct it. Thus, we ask the question:

Can we construct a NIZK argument for NP
from a non-interactive batch argument for NP?

Our Results. In this work, we give a generic construction of NIZKs for NP from a non-interactive batch argument for NP in conjunction with a dual-mode commitment scheme and a (sub-exponentially-hard) low-locality pseudorandom generator (PRG) with super-linear stretch. Dual-mode commitment schemes can be built from any lossy/dual-mode public-key encryption scheme, which is known from most standard assumptions [PW08, HLOV11, AFMP20]. A low-locality PRG is a PRG where each output bit only depends on a small number of the seed bits. PRGs with constant locality and super-linear stretch are a notable ingredient in the recent constructions of indistinguishability obfuscation from well-studied assumptions [JLS21, JLS22]. Our instantiations can rely on locality as high as $c \log \lambda$, where $c < 1$ is a constant and λ is the seed length; this is a much weaker requirement compared to the constant locality PRGs required for indistinguishability obfuscation. The local PRG can in turn be instantiated using Goldreich's family of PRGs [Gol00, CM01].

While the additional ingredients we rely on for constructing a NIZK for NP are (much) stronger than one-way functions, we emphasize that no combination of the underlying primitives by themselves are known to imply NIZKs for NP. We summarize our main result with the following theorem (see Corollary 3.15 for a formal description and parameter specification):

Theorem 1.1 (Informal). *Let $G: \{0,1\}^\lambda \to \{0,1\}^{\lambda^\delta}$ be a PRG with locality $c \log \lambda$ and super-linear stretch $\delta > 1$ for a (sufficiently-small) constant $c < 1$ and (sufficiently-large) $\delta > 1$. Then, assuming the existence of a dual-mode commitment scheme, a non-interactive batch argument for NP with (sufficiently-small) proof size,[2] and sub-exponential hardness of G, there exists a NIZK for NP.*

Our work highlights a new connection between the succinctness of an argument system and zero-knowledge. It also provides a new *generic* approach for constructing NIZKs for NP. Finally, by composing a batch argument satisfying certain efficiency properties (satisfied by most existing constructions [CJJ21b, WW22, CGJ+22]) with a NIZK for NP, we obtain a zero-knowledge batch argument. Thus, our approach can also be used to generically upgrade a non-interactive batch argument for NP into a zero-knowledge batch argument by relying only on a low-locality PRG and a dual-mode commitment (neither of which are known to imply NIZKs for NP).

---

[2] For instance, this is satisfied if the length of the proof scales polylogarithmically in the number of instances. More generally, we can instantiate the theorem even if the proof size scales with $T^{1/2-\varepsilon}$, where T is the number of instances and $\varepsilon > 0$ is a constant. We refer to Corollary 3.15 for the precise characterization.

1.1 Technical Overview

Our starting point is the generic approach of Kitagawa et al. [KMY20] who show how to generically transform a SNARG for NP into a NIZK for NP. The approach of [KMY20] instantiates the hidden-bits paradigm of Feige et al. [FLS90] of combining a NIZK in the idealized hidden-bits model with a hidden-bits generator (HBG) [QRW19].

NIZKs in the Hidden-Bits Model. The hidden-bits model is an *idealized* model for constructing non-interactive zero-knowledge proofs. In this model, a trusted party first generates a string of uniformly random bits $r_1, \ldots, r_m \xleftarrow{R} \{0, 1\}$ and gives them to the prover. To construct a proof for a statement x, the prover selects a subset of indices $I \subseteq [m]$ along with a proof π. The verifier then receives $\{r_i\}_{i \in I}$ and π from the trusted party. The model ensures that the prover cannot influence the choice of bits $r_1, \ldots, r_m$ and that the verifier cannot learn the value of any unrevealed bit r_i for $i \notin I$. Feige et al. [FLS90] previously showed how to construct a NIZK with statistical soundness and perfect zero-knowledge in the hidden-bits model for the NP-complete problem of graph Hamiltonicity.

Hidden-Bits Generators. Given a NIZK in the idealized hidden-bits model, a number of works have shown how to transform it into a NIZK in the CRS model through a cryptographic compiler [FLS90, BY92, CHK03, GR13, CL18, QRW19, LPWW20, KMY20]. In this work, we focus on the abstraction based on hidden-bits generators introduced by Quach et al. [QRW19]. At a high-level, a hidden-bits generator is a cryptographic primitive that generates a (pseudorandom) sequence of hidden bits. The prover can then open up a subset of the bits while ensuring the unopened bits remain hidden. Moreover, the hidden-bits generator ensures that the prover has limited control over the output sequence of bits. In a sense, hidden-bits generators provide a cryptographic realization of the trusted sampling of the hidden-bits string in the hidden-bits model. Thus, combined with the (unconditional) NIZK for NP in the hidden-bits model, a hidden-bits generator immediately implies a NIZK for NP in the CRS model. We now describe the syntax of a hidden-bits generator more formally; we specifically consider the adaptation from [KMY20]:

- The setup algorithm Setup takes as input the security parameter λ and an output length m and outputs a common reference string crs.
- The generator algorithm GenBits takes the common reference string crs and outputs a bit-string $\mathbf{r} \in \{0, 1\}^m$ of length m along with a generator state st. Here, $\mathbf{r}$ is the "hidden-bits string."
- The prove algorithm Prove takes the generator state st and a subset of indices $I \subseteq [m]$, and outputs a *succinct* proof π. The proof π is an "opening" to the bits of $\mathbf{r}$ indexed by I; we denote these bits by $\mathbf{r}_I \in \{0, 1\}^{|I|}$.
- The verification algorithm Verify takes as input the common reference string crs, a set of indices $I \subseteq [m]$, a collection of bits $\mathbf{r}_I \in \{0, 1\}^{|I|}$, and an opening π. The verification algorithms decides whether π is a valid opening or not to the bits indexed by I (with respect to crs).

The hidden-bits generator must in turn satisfy the following properties:

- **Correctness:** Correctness says that if $\mathsf{crs} \leftarrow \mathsf{Setup}(1^\lambda, 1^m)$ and $(\mathbf{r}, \mathsf{st}) \leftarrow \mathsf{GenBits}(\mathsf{crs})$, then for all sets of indices $I \subseteq [m]$, the opening π output by $\mathsf{Prove}(\mathsf{st}, I)$ is valid with respect to Verify.
- **Binding:** The binding property restricts the set of possible openings that can be computed by a computationally-bounded algorithm. Namely, for each crs in the support of Setup, there exists a subset $\mathcal{V}^{\mathsf{crs}} \subset \{0,1\}^m$ of "valid" hidden-bits strings. Namely, no efficient adversary can come up with an accepting proof π for a set of indices $I \subseteq [m]$ and an assignment $\mathbf{r}_I \in \{0,1\}^{|I|}$ that is inconsistent with every $\mathbf{r}' \in \mathcal{V}^{\mathsf{crs}}$ (i.e., an assignment $\mathbf{r}_I$ such that for all $\mathbf{r}' \in \mathcal{V}^{\mathsf{crs}}$, $\mathbf{r}'_I \neq \mathbf{r}_I$). Moreover, the set of possible hidden-bits strings induced by a particular CRS must be *sparse*: $|\mathcal{V}^{\mathsf{crs}}| \leq 2^{m^\gamma \mathsf{poly}(\lambda)}$ for some constant $\gamma < 1$ and where λ is a security parameter.
- **Hiding:** The hiding property says that the *unopened* bits of $\mathbf{r}$ are pseudorandom. Namely, for any set $I \subseteq [m]$ and honestly-generated $\mathbf{r}$ and π, the distribution $(\mathsf{crs}, I, \mathbf{r}_I, \mathbf{r}_{\bar{I}}, \pi)$ is computationally indistinguishable from the distribution $(\mathsf{crs}, I, \mathbf{r}_I, \hat{\mathbf{r}}_{\bar{I}}, \pi)$ where $\hat{\mathbf{r}} \xleftarrow{\mathrm{R}} \{0,1\}^m$ and $\bar{I} = [m] \setminus I$.

Kitagawa et al. [KMY20] show how to construct a hidden-bits generator satisfying the above properties by combining a SNARG for NP with a leakage-resilient (weak) pseudorandom function (PRF):

- The CRS contains m random points in the domain of the PRF $x_1, \ldots, x_m$ and the CRS for the SNARG.
- The hidden-bits string is constructed by sampling a PRF key k and setting $r_i \leftarrow \mathsf{PRF}(k, x_i)$ for each $i \in [m]$.
- The opening for a subset $I \subseteq [m]$ is a SNARG proof that there exists k such that for all $i \in I$, $r_i = \mathsf{PRF}(k, x_i)$.

In this case, binding follows from security of the (weak) PRF (as long as the length of the PRF key is smaller than the output length m) in conjunction with soundness of the SNARG (i.e., the only possible openings are to those consistent with an evaluation under a PRF key k on the inputs $x_1, \ldots, x_m$). The hiding property follows by treating the SNARG proof in the opening as "leakage" on the PRF key and then appealing to leakage-resilient pseudorandomness of the underlying PRF. Critically, this latter step relies on the length of the SNARG being *sublinear* in the length of the PRF key.

Replacing the SNARG with a Batch Argument. We first observe that the SNARG proof in the opening is *almost* a *batch* language. Namely, the proof is showing that for each index $i \in I$, the bit r_i satisfies $r_i = \mathsf{PRF}(k, x_i)$. Each instance is described by a tuple (i, x_i, r_i) and the witness is the PRF key k. The caveat is that in a batch language, there is no requirement that the prover uses the *same* witness (i.e., the PRF key k) for each instance. Namely, if we use replace the SNARG in the [KMY20] construction with a BARG, then the proof only suffices to argue "local consistency" (i.e., there exists some key k_i that explains each output bit r_i) rather than "global consistency" (i.e., there exists a *single* key k that explains each output bit r_i). Certainly, local consistency is insufficient as it is trivial to find a tuple of keys $(k_1, \ldots, k_m)$ that explains *any* candidate hidden-bits string $\mathbf{r} \in \{0,1\}^m$.

Enforcing Consistency. To force the prover to use a consistent PRF key k across all of the instances when constructing the batch argument, we have the prover include a commitment c to the PRF key k as part of the opening. Each instance of the batch NP language is now

$$\exists k : c \text{ is a commitment to } k \text{ and } \mathsf{PRF}(k, x_i) = r_i.$$

In fact, we note that we can replace the PRF with a pseudorandom generator $\mathsf{PRG} \colon \{0,1\}^\lambda \to \{0,1\}^m$, and indeed, the (weak) PRF in the [KMY20] construction is essentially used as a PRG. We will write $\mathsf{PRG}_i \colon \{0,1\}^\lambda \to \{0,1\}$ to denote the function that takes as input the seed $\mathbf{s} \in \{0,1\}^\lambda$ and outputs the ith bit of $\mathsf{PRG}(\mathbf{s})$. To generate the hidden-bits string, the generator now samples $\mathbf{s} \xleftarrow{R} \{0,1\}^\lambda$ and commits to $\mathbf{s}$ with a commitment c. The hidden-bits string is $\mathbf{r} \leftarrow \mathsf{PRG}(\mathbf{s})$ and the opening to $\mathbf{r}_I$ is a batch argument π for the following language:

$$\forall i \in I, \exists \mathbf{s} \in \{0,1\}^\lambda : c \text{ is a commitment to } \mathbf{s} \text{ and } \mathsf{PRG}_i(\mathbf{s}) = r_i.$$

As long as the commitment is *statistically* binding (i.e., the commitment c can be opened to at most one seed $\mathbf{s}$) and the batch argument is computationally sound, the scheme satisfies the binding requirement. In our security analysis (Theorem 3.3), we technically require a stronger extractability property on the commitment, which allows us to base binding on *semi-adaptive* soundness of the underlying BARG; this is the notion achieved by most recent constructions from standard assumptions [CJJ21b, WW22, HJKS22, DGKV22, HJKS22].[3] In contrast, the construction of [KMY20] relied on a SNARG with *adaptive* soundness. This is a stronger requirement that cannot be proven under a black-box reduction to a falsifiable assumption [GW11]. However, this approach for constructing a hidden bits generator does not satisfy hiding. There are two issues:

– **Length of the commitment:** The opening now contains a commitment c to the PRG seed $\mathbf{s}$. Since c is *statistically binding*, the length of c is at least as long as the seed $\mathbf{s}$.
– **Length of the proof:** Succinctness of the batch argument says that the length of the proof π satisfies $|\pi| = \mathsf{poly}(\lambda, |C|, \log |I|)$, where C is the circuit that takes as input $(i, \mathbf{s}, r_i)$ and checks that c is a commitment to $\mathbf{s}$ and $\mathsf{PRG}_i(\mathbf{s}) = r_i$. Unlike the case of a SNARG, the length of π scales *polynomially* with the size of the circuit $|C|$. Since C takes the PRG seed as input, $|C| \geq |\mathbf{s}|$, so the length of π is at least as long as the seed $\mathbf{s}$.

---

[3] Semi-adaptive soundness for a batch argument says that the adversary must first commit to the index i of the false statement in the soundness game. It can adaptively choose the statements $x_1, \ldots, x_T$ *after* seeing the CRS, with the restriction that instance x_i must be false.

The [KMY20] construction argues hiding by relying on leakage resilience of the underlying weak PRF. In their setting, the only leakage on the PRF key is from the SNARG, whose length is *smaller* than the length of the PRF key. As such, the analysis reduces to a standard leakage-resilience argument. In our setting, both the commitment to the PRG seed and the length of the BARG proof potentially leak too much information about the PRG seed, and we cannot directly leverage leakage resilience to argue hiding.

Leveraging Locality. Our first observation is that each individual instance in the batch language is checking a *single* output bit of the PRG. Since the length of the BARG proof scales with the size of the circuit checking a single instance, this means that if the circuit for validating a single output bit of the PRG is much smaller than the length of the overall PRG seed, we can rely on BARG succinctness. One way to construct PRGs with this property is by relying on locality. We say that a PRG is k-local if each output bit only depends on at most k bits of the seed. If a PRG is k-local, then each output bit can be verified with a circuit of size at most $2^k \cdot \text{poly}(\lambda)$. In this case, to check that output bit i is correctly computed, the relation only needs to check (local) openings for the k bits of $\mathbf{s}$ that determine $\text{PRG}_i(\mathbf{s})$. For instance, if the PRG has constant locality [Gol00, CM01], and we take the commitment c to be a bit-by-bit commitment to the bits of $\mathbf{s}$, then verifying a single output bit only requires a circuit of size λ^δ, for some fixed constant $\delta > 0$ that depends on the BARG scheme and the commitment scheme (but *not* the seed length of the PRG). Here λ is the main security parameter (for the BARG and for the commitment scheme). If we set the length of the PRG seed to be at least $n > \lambda^\delta$, then we can hope to rely on leakage resilience of the PRG to argue that the output still has high min-entropy even given the BARG proof. In our constructions (Theorem 1.1 and Corollary 3.15), we can use k-local PRGs with locality as high as $k = c \log \lambda$ for some constant $c < 1$.

We additionally require that our k-local PRGs be leakage resilient. Here, we rely on sub-exponential hardness and the Gentry-Wichs leakage-simulation lemma [GW11]. Roughly speaking, it says that if $\text{PRG}(\mathbf{s})$ is computationally indistinguishable from $\mathbf{t} \xleftarrow{R} \{0,1\}^m$ against (non-uniform) adversaries of size at most s, then there exists an auxiliary distribution over strings $(\mathbf{t}, \text{aux}^*)$ such that $(\text{PRG}(\mathbf{s}), \text{aux})$ is computationally indistinguishable from $(\mathbf{t}, \text{aux}^*)$ against (non-uniform) adversaries of size at most $s/2^{|\text{aux}|}$. Here aux is a string that can be arbitrarily correlated with $\mathbf{s}$. Thus, as long as the leakage aux is sufficiently short (as a function of the seed length) and the PRG satisfies sub-exponential security, we can argue that the outputs are still pseudorandom. Finally, we can apply a standard randomness extractor to $\mathbf{t}$ to obtain a sequence of bits that are statistically close to uniform (even given aux^*).

Dual-Mode Commitments. The only remaining challenge is to ensure that the (statistically-binding) commitment to the PRG seed $\mathbf{s}$ does not leak information about the seed. While it is tempting to rely on computational hiding of the commitment scheme and replace the commitment to the seed with a commitment to the all-zeroes string, this hybrid strategy does not work. The BARG proof (in the opening) is generated using the *openings* to the commitment scheme (i.e., the openings to the commitment are part of the witness for the BARG). Alternatively, we can apply the Gentry-Wichs leakage lemma to argue that the joint distribution $(\mathsf{Commit}(\mathbf{s}), \mathsf{PRG}(\mathbf{s}), \mathsf{aux})$ is computationally indistinguishable from $(\mathsf{Commit}(\mathbf{0}), \mathbf{t}, \mathsf{aux}^*)$. As long as the commitment scheme is hiding even for adversaries of size $2^{|\mathsf{aux}|}$, then security follows. However, there is a circular dependency here, as the length of aux is the length of the BARG proof, which is at least as long as the commitment (since the commitment is an input to the BARG relation). As a result, we cannot use complexity leveraging on the commitment as we could with the PRG.

We instead take a different "dual-mode" strategy [GOS06, PW08]. Specifically, we consider a dual-mode commitment scheme where the CRS can be sampled in one of two (computationally indistinguishable) modes: (1) an extractable mode which we use to argue binding; and (2) a statistically hiding mode where the commitments now *statistically* hide the input. Dual-mode commitments can be constructed from a lossy public-key encryption scheme, which is implied by most number-theoretic intractability assumptions [PW08, HLOV11, AFMP20].

The idea in the hiding proof then is to first switch the dual-mode commitment from binding mode into hiding mode. Observe that this step only changes the public parameters in the scheme. Once the CRS is in hiding mode, the commitments to the PRG seed $\mathbf{s}$ *statistically* hide $\mathbf{s}$, regardless of the size of the adversary. In this case, we can appeal to the Gentry-Wichs leakage lemma to argue that the joint distribution $(\mathsf{Commit}(\mathbf{s}), \mathsf{PRG}(\mathbf{s}), \mathsf{aux})$ is computationally indistinguishable from $(\mathsf{Commit}(\mathbf{0}), \mathbf{t}, \mathsf{aux}^*)$ assuming only sub-exponential hardness of the PRG. This means the unopened bits in the hidden-bits string are uniformly random and hiding holds. We provide the full details in Sect. 3 (Theorem 3.4).

Upgrading BARGs to zkBARGs. For completeness, we conclude with a few remarks on using a NIZK for NP to generically upgrade a batch argument to a zero-knowledge batch argument (zkBARG). First, we note that the naïve approach of giving a NIZK proof of knowledge of a BARG proof does *not* work out of the box. The issue is that the verification algorithm for the BARG needs to read the statements $(x_1, \ldots, x_T)$, and thus, the size of the verification circuit scales linear with T. Since the size of a NIZK proof can scale polynomially with the size of the verification circuit, the size of the NIZK proof of knowledge of a valid BARG proof for $(x_1, \ldots, x_T)$ can scale polynomially with T. Nonetheless, we can still apply this general approach in the following settings:

- **Index BARGs:** An index BARG for an NP language is one where the statements are always fixed to be the integers $1, \ldots, T$ [CJJ21b]. In an index BARG, the verification algorithm only takes the upper bound T as input and is required to run in time that is polylogarithmic in T. We can generically compose an index BARG with a NIZK to obtain a zero-knowledge index BARG. We can then apply the index-BARG-to-BARG transformation from [CJJ21b] to the zero-knowledge index BARG for NP to obtain a zkBARG for NP; note here that the [CJJ21b] transformation preserves zero-knowledge.

- **BARGs with split verification:** A BARG satisfies "split verification" [CJJ21b, WW22, CGJ+22] if the verification algorithm decomposes into a (non-succinct) statement-dependent preprocessing step that outputs a short verification key vk and a (succinct) online verification step that takes the preprocessed key vk and the proof π and decides whether to accept or reject the proof. Importantly, the online verification step can be implemented by a circuit whose size is polylogarithmic in the number of instances T. Given a BARG with a split verification property, it suffices to use a NIZK to prove knowledge of a BARG proof that satisfies the online verification check. This yields a zkBARG with split verification.

2   Preliminaries

We write λ to denote the security parameter. For a positive integer $n \in \mathbb{N}$, we write $[n]$ to denote the set $\{1, \ldots, n\}$. We use boldface letters (e.g., $\mathbf{x}$) to denote vectors. We write $\mathsf{poly}(\lambda)$ to denote a fixed function that is $O(\lambda^c)$ for some $c \in \mathbb{N}$ and $\mathsf{negl}(\lambda)$ to denote a function that is $o(\lambda^{-c})$ for all $c \in \mathbb{N}$. We say an event occurs with overwhelming probability if its complement occurs with negligible probability. We say an algorithm on λ-bit inputs is efficient if it can be computed by a Boolean circuit of size $\mathsf{poly}(\lambda)$, or equivalently, if it can be computed by a Turing machine in $\mathsf{poly}(\lambda)$ time with $\mathsf{poly}(\lambda)$ bits of advice.

Let $\mathcal{D}_1 = \{\mathcal{D}_{1,\lambda}\}_{\lambda \in \mathbb{N}}$ and $\mathcal{D}_2 = \{\mathcal{D}_{2,\lambda}\}_{\lambda \in \mathbb{N}}$ be two ensembles of distributions. For functions $s = s(\lambda)$ and $\varepsilon = \varepsilon(\lambda)$, we say that $\mathcal{D}_1$ and $\mathcal{D}_2$ are (s, ε)-indistinguishable if for all non-negative polynomials $\mathsf{poly}(\cdot)$ and all adversaries $\mathcal{A}$, modeled as Boolean circuits of size at most $s(\lambda) \cdot \mathsf{poly}(\lambda)$, and all sufficiently large $\lambda \geq \lambda_{\mathcal{A}}$,

$$|\Pr[\mathcal{A}(x) = 1 : x \leftarrow \mathcal{D}_{1,\lambda}] - \Pr[\mathcal{A}(x) = 1 : x \leftarrow \mathcal{D}_{2,\lambda}]| \leq \varepsilon(\lambda).$$

We say that $\mathcal{D}_1$ and $\mathcal{D}_2$ are computationally indistinguishable if there exists a negligible function $\varepsilon(\lambda) = \mathsf{negl}(\lambda)$ such that $\mathcal{D}_1$ and $\mathcal{D}_2$ are $(1, \varepsilon)$-indistinguishable. We say that $\mathcal{D}_1$ and $\mathcal{D}_2$ are statistically indistinguishable if the statistical distance $\Delta(\mathcal{D}_1, \mathcal{D}_2)$ is bounded by a negligible function $\mathsf{negl}(\lambda)$.

Min-entropy. We recall some basic definitions on min-entropy. Our definitions are adapted from those in [DRS04]. For a (discrete) random variable X, we write $\mathbf{H}_\infty(X) = -\log(\max_x \Pr[X = x])$ to denote its min-entropy. For two (possibly correlated) discrete random variables X and Y, we define the average min-entropy of X given Y to be $\mathbf{H}_\infty(X \mid Y) = -\log(\mathbb{E}_{y \leftarrow Y} \max_x \Pr[X = x \mid Y = y])$. The optimal probability of an unbounded adversary guessing X given the correlated value Y is $2^{-\mathbf{H}_\infty(X|Y)}$.

Lemma 2.1 (Conditional Min-Entropy [DRS04, Lemma 2.2]). *Let A, B be random variables and suppose there are at most 2^λ elements in the support of B. Then $\mathbf{H}_\infty(A \mid B) \geq \mathbf{H}_\infty(A, B) - \lambda \geq \mathbf{H}_\infty(A) - \lambda$.*

Gentry-Wichs Leakage Lemma. Our analysis will rely on the following "leakage lemma" from [GW11]:

Lemma 2.2 (Indistinguishability with Auxiliary Information [GW11, Lemma 3.1]). *Let λ be a security parameter. There exists a polynomial $\mathsf{poly}(\cdot)$ such that the following property holds. Let $\mathcal{X} = \{\mathcal{X}_\lambda\}_{\lambda \in \mathbb{N}}$ and $\mathcal{Y} = \{\mathcal{Y}_\lambda\}_{\lambda \in \mathbb{N}}$ be arbitrary distributions that are (s, ε)-indistinguishable for some $s = s(\lambda)$ and $\varepsilon = \varepsilon(\lambda)$. Let $\mathcal{X}_\lambda^* = \{\mathcal{X}_\lambda^*\}_{\lambda \in \mathbb{N}}$ be an augmented distribution where $\mathcal{X}_\lambda^*$ is a distribution on pairs (x_λ, π_λ) where $x_\lambda \leftarrow \mathcal{X}_\lambda$ and $\pi \in \{0,1\}^{\ell(\lambda)}$ can be arbitrarily correlated with x_λ. Then, there exists a distribution $\mathcal{Y}^* = \{\mathcal{Y}_\lambda^*\}_{\lambda \in \mathbb{N}}$ with the following properties:*

- *Each $\mathcal{Y}_\lambda^*$ is a distribution on tuples $(y_\lambda, \hat{\pi}_\lambda)$, where $y_\lambda \leftarrow \mathcal{Y}_\lambda$ and $\pi_\lambda \in \{0,1\}^{\ell(\lambda)}$.*
- *The distributions $\mathcal{X}^*$ and $\mathcal{Y}^*$ are (s', ε')-indistinguishable, where $s'(\lambda) = s(\lambda) \cdot \mathsf{poly}(\varepsilon(\lambda)/2^{\ell(\lambda)})$ and $\varepsilon'(\lambda) = 2\varepsilon(\lambda)$.*

Leftover Hash Lemma. Our construction will also rely on the generalized leftover hash lemma (LHL) from [BDK+11]:

Theorem 2.3 (LHL with Conditional Min-Entropy [BDK+11, Theorem 3.2, adapted]). *Let (X, Z) be random variables sampled from some joint distribution $\mathcal{D}$ over $\mathcal{X} \times \mathcal{Z}$. Let $\mathcal{H} = \{h \colon \mathcal{X} \to \{0,1\}^v\}$ be a family of universal hash functions, and let $L = \mathbf{H}_\infty(X \mid Z) - v$ be the entropy loss. Let $\mathcal{A}(r, h, z)$ be a (possibly probabilistic) distinguisher where*

$$\Pr[\mathcal{A}(r, h, z) = 1 : r \xleftarrow{\text{R}} \{0,1\}^v, h \xleftarrow{\text{R}} \mathcal{H}, (x, z) \leftarrow \mathcal{D}] \leq \varepsilon.$$

Then, the statistical distance between the following distributions is at most $\sqrt{\varepsilon/2^L}$:

$$\left\{ (h(x), h, z) : \begin{matrix} (x, z) \leftarrow \mathcal{D} \\ h \xleftarrow{\text{R}} \mathcal{H} \end{matrix} \right\} \quad and \quad \left\{ (r, h, z) : \begin{matrix} (x, z) \leftarrow \mathcal{D} \\ r \xleftarrow{\text{R}} \{0,1\}^v, h \xleftarrow{\text{R}} \mathcal{H} \end{matrix} \right\}$$

Corollary 2.4 (LHL with Conditional Min-Entropy). *Let (X, Z) be random variables sampled from some joint distribution $\mathcal{D}$ over $\mathcal{X} \times \mathcal{Z}$. Let $\mathcal{H} = \{h \colon \mathcal{X} \to \{0,1\}^v\}$ be a family of universal hash functions. Let $L = \mathbf{H}_\infty(X \mid Z) - v$ be the entropy loss. Then the statistical distance between the following distributions is at most $2^{-L/2}$:*

$$\left\{ (h(x), h, z) : \begin{matrix} (x, z) \leftarrow \mathcal{D} \\ h \xleftarrow{\text{R}} \mathcal{H} \end{matrix} \right\} \quad and \quad \left\{ (r, h, z) : \begin{matrix} (x, z) \leftarrow \mathcal{D} \\ r \xleftarrow{\text{R}} \{0,1\}^v, h \xleftarrow{\text{R}} \mathcal{H} \end{matrix} \right\}$$

Proof. Follows by setting $\varepsilon = 1$ in Theorem 2.3 (which captures *all* distinguishers). ∎

Pseudorandom Generators. We recall the definition of a pseudorandom generator.

Definition 2.5 (Pseudorandom Generator). *Let λ be a security parameter. A pseudorandom generator with output length $m = m(\lambda)$ is an efficiently-computable function family* $\mathsf{PRG} = \{\mathsf{PRG}_\lambda\}_{\lambda \in \mathbb{N}}$ *where* $\mathsf{PRG}_\lambda \colon \{0,1\}^\lambda \to \{0,1\}^{m(\lambda)}$. *For functions $s = s(\lambda)$ and $\varepsilon = \varepsilon(\lambda)$, we say that* PRG *is* (s, ε)-*secure if the following two distributions are* (s, ε)-*indistinguishable:*

$$\left\{\mathsf{PRG}_\lambda(x) : x \xleftarrow{\mathrm{R}} \{0,1\}^\lambda\right\} \quad and \quad \left\{y \xleftarrow{\mathrm{R}} \{0,1\}^{m(\lambda)}\right\}.$$

We say that PRG *is sub-exponentially secure if there exists a constant $\alpha > 0$ and a negligible function $\varepsilon = \mathsf{negl}(\lambda)$ such that* PRG *is* $\left(2^{\lambda^\alpha}, \varepsilon\right)$-*secure.*

Definition 2.6 (Locality of a PRG). *We say a* $\mathsf{PRG} \colon \{0,1\}^\lambda \to \{0,1\}^m$ *has locality $k = k(\lambda)$ if each output bit of* $\mathsf{PRG}(x)$ *is a function of at most k bits of the seed x. We say that* PRG *is computable in* NC^0 *if* PRG *has constant locality $k = O(1)$.*

Local PRGs Constructions. Goldreich [Gol00, MST03] gave the first candidate local PRG construction (with constant locality) based on constraint-satisfiability problems over expander graphs. A long line of subsequent works have studied variants of Goldreich's construction [CM01, MST03, CEMT09, App12, ABR12, OW14, AL16, AK19]; we refer to [App15] for an excellent survey of the state of the art. Notably, PRGs with constant locality and super-linear stretch have featured prominently in constructions of indistinguishability obfuscation [Lin17, LT17, JLS21, JLS22].

There has also been an extensive line of works studying attacks and ruling out certain instantiations of local PRGs [MST03, CEMT09, BQ09, OW14, App15, AL16, CDM+18, Üna23]. For local PRGs with super-linear stretch $\lambda^{1+\delta}$, the most recent attacks [BQ09, Üna23] run in time roughly $\lambda^{O(\lambda^{1-\delta/k})}$ where k is the locality.

Dual-Mode Commitments. Next, we recall the notion of a "dual-mode" commitment (also called a "mixed commitment") [DN02]. At a high-level, these are non-interactive commitment schemes in the common reference string (CRS) model where the CRS can be sampled from one of two computationally indistinguishable distributions. In one distribution (or mode), the commitment scheme is extractable (i.e., given trapdoor information, one can efficiently extract the committed value from a commitment), and in the other distribution (or mode), the commitment scheme is statistically hiding.[4] We give the formal definition below:

Definition 2.7 (Dual-Mode Bit Commitment [DN02]). *A dual-mode bit commitment scheme is a tuple of efficient algorithms* $\Pi_{\mathsf{BC}} = (\mathsf{Setup}, \mathsf{Commit}, \mathsf{Verify})$ *with the following syntax:*

---

[4] In some settings, we can require a stronger "equivocation" property in hiding mode where given trapdoor information, one can sample a commitment c and openings for c to *any* value. Our constructions do not require equivocation.

- Setup(1^λ, mode) $\rightarrow$ (crs, td): *On input the security parameter λ and* mode $\in$ *{bind, hide}, the setup algorithm outputs a common reference string* crs *and a trapdoor* td *(possibly empty).*
- Commit(crs, b) $\rightarrow$ (c, σ): *On input the common reference string* crs *and a bit $b \in \{0, 1\}$, the commit algorithm outputs a commitment c and an opening σ.*
- Verify(crs, c, b, σ) $\rightarrow \{0, 1\}$: *On input the common reference string* crs, *a commitment c, a bit $b \in \{0, 1\}$, and an opening σ, the verification algorithm outputs a bit $b' \in \{0, 1\}$.*

Moreover, Π_{BC} should satisfy the following properties:

- **Correctness:** *For all security parameters $\lambda \in \mathbb{N}$, all bits $b \in \{0, 1\}$, all modes* mode $\in$ *{bind, hide},*

$$\Pr\left[\mathsf{Verify}(\mathsf{crs}, c, b, \sigma) = 1 : \begin{array}{l} (\mathsf{crs}, \mathsf{td}) \leftarrow \mathsf{Setup}(1^\lambda, \mathsf{mode}); \\ (c, \sigma) \leftarrow \mathsf{Commit}(\mathsf{crs}, b) \end{array}\right] = 1.$$

- **Mode indistinguishability:** *For all efficient adversaries $\mathcal{A}$, and sampling* $(\mathsf{crs}_{\mathsf{bind}}, \mathsf{td}) \leftarrow \mathsf{Setup}(1^\lambda, \mathsf{bind})$, $(\mathsf{crs}_{\mathsf{hide}}, \mathsf{td}') \leftarrow \mathsf{Setup}(1^\lambda, \mathsf{hide})$, *we have that*

$$\left| \Pr\left[\mathcal{A}(1^\lambda, \mathsf{crs}_{\mathsf{bind}}) = 1\right] - \Pr\left[\mathcal{A}(1^\lambda, \mathsf{crs}_{\mathsf{hide}}) = 1\right]\right| = \mathsf{negl}(\lambda).$$

- **Extractable in binding mode:** *There exists an efficient algorithm* Extract *that takes as input a trapdoor* td *and a string $c \in \{0, 1\}^*$, and outputs a bit $b \in \{0, 1\}$. Then, for all adversaries $\mathcal{A}$,*

$$\Pr\left[\mathsf{Verify}(\mathsf{crs}, c, b, \sigma) = 1 \wedge b \neq b' : \begin{array}{l} (\mathsf{crs}, \mathsf{td}) \leftarrow \mathsf{Setup}(1^\lambda, \mathsf{bind}); \\ (c, \sigma, b) \leftarrow \mathcal{A}(\mathsf{crs}); \\ b' \leftarrow \mathsf{Extract}(\mathsf{td}, c) \end{array}\right] = \mathsf{negl}(\lambda).$$

- **Statistically hiding in hiding mode:** *For a security parameter λ and a bit $\beta \in \{0, 1\}$, we define the hiding game between an adversary $\mathcal{A}$ and a challenger as follows:*
  1. *The challenger starts by sampling* $(\mathsf{crs}, \mathsf{td}) \leftarrow \mathsf{Setup}(1^\lambda, \mathsf{hide})$ *and gives* crs *to $\mathcal{A}$.*
  2. *Algorithm $\mathcal{A}$ outputs two messages $b_0, b_1 \in \{0, 1\}$.*
  3. *The challenger computes $(c, \sigma) \leftarrow \mathsf{Commit}(\mathsf{crs}, b_\beta)$ and replies to $\mathcal{A}$ with c.*
  4. *Algorithm $\mathcal{A}$ outputs a bit $b' \in \{0, 1\}$, which is the output of the experiment.*

  Then Π_{BC} is statistically hiding in hiding mode if there exists a negligible function $\mathsf{negl}(\cdot)$ such that for all adversaries $\mathcal{A}$ in the above hiding experiment,

$$|\Pr[b' = 1 \mid \beta = 0] - \Pr[b' = 1 \mid \beta = 1]| = \mathsf{negl}(\lambda).$$

Constructions of Dual-Mode Commitments. Dual-mode commitments (with extraction) can be built from any lossy public-key encryption scheme [BHY09], which can in turn be constructed from most standard algebraic assumptions [PW08, HLOV11, AFMP20]. In particular, a commitment to an input x is just a public-key encryption of x and the opening is the corresponding encryption randomness. In extracting mode, the extraction trapdoor is the decryption key.

2.1   Non-Interactive Zero-Knowledge Arguments for NP

We recall the notion of a non-interactive zero-knowledge argument for NP [GMR85, BFM88]. We specifically consider the NP-complete language of Boolean circuit satisfiability. Namely, for a Boolean circuit $C \colon \{0,1\}^n \times \{0,1\}^h \to \{0,1\}$, we say that a statement $\mathbf{x} \in \{0,1\}^n$ is a YES instance if there exists a witness $\mathbf{w} \in \{0,1\}^h$ such that $C(\mathbf{x}, \mathbf{w}) = 1$.

Definition 2.8 (NIZK Argument for NP). *A non-interactive zero-knowledge argument for Boolean circuit satisfiability is a tuple of efficient algorithms $\Pi_{\mathsf{NIZK}} = (\mathsf{Setup}, \mathsf{Prove}, \mathsf{Verify})$ with the following syntax:*

- $\mathsf{Setup}(1^\lambda) \to \mathsf{crs}$: *On input the security parameter $\lambda \in \mathbb{N}$, the setup algorithm outputs a common reference string crs.*
- $\mathsf{Prove}(\mathsf{crs}, C, \mathbf{x}, \mathbf{w}) \to \pi$: *On input the common reference string crs, a Boolean circuit $C \colon \{0,1\}^n \times \{0,1\}^h \to \{0,1\}$, a statement $\mathbf{x} \in \{0,1\}^n$, and a witness $\mathbf{w} \in \{0,1\}^h$, the prove algorithm outputs a proof π.*
- $\mathsf{Verify}(\mathsf{crs}, C, \mathbf{x}, \pi) \to b$: *On input the common reference string crs, the Boolean circuit $C \colon \{0,1\}^n \times \{0,1\}^h \to \{0,1\}$, a statement $\mathbf{x} \in \{0,1\}^n$, and a proof π, the verification algorithm outputs a bit $b \in \{0,1\}$.*

Moreover, Π_{NIZK} should satisfy the following properties:

- **Completeness:** *For all $\lambda \in \mathbb{N}$, all Boolean circuits $C \colon \{0,1\}^n \times \{0,1\}^h \to \{0,1\}$, all statements $\mathbf{x} \in \{0,1\}^n$, and all witnesses $\mathbf{w} \in \{0,1\}^h$ where $C(\mathbf{x}, \mathbf{w}) = 1$,*

$$\Pr\left[\mathsf{Verify}(\mathsf{crs}, C, \mathbf{x}, \pi) = 1 : \begin{array}{l} \mathsf{crs} \leftarrow \mathsf{Setup}(1^\lambda); \\ \pi \leftarrow \mathsf{Prove}(\mathsf{crs}, C, \mathbf{x}, \mathbf{w}) \end{array}\right] = 1.$$

- **Computational soundness:** *For all efficient adversaries $\mathcal{A}$,*

$$\Pr\left[\mathbf{x} \notin \mathcal{L}_C \wedge \mathsf{Verify}(\mathsf{crs}, C, \mathbf{x}, \pi) = 1 : \begin{array}{l} \mathsf{crs} \leftarrow \mathsf{Setup}(1^\lambda) \\ (C, \mathbf{x}, \pi) \leftarrow \mathcal{A}(1^\lambda, \mathsf{crs}) \end{array}\right] = \mathsf{negl}(\lambda),$$

where for a circuit $C \colon \{0,1\}^n \times \{0,1\}^h \to \{0,1\}$, we define $\mathcal{L}_C$ to be the language of Boolean circuit satisfiability:

$$\mathcal{L}_C := \left\{\mathbf{x} \in \{0,1\}^n : \exists \mathbf{w} \in \{0,1\}^h, C(\mathbf{x}, \mathbf{w}) = 1\right\}.$$

- **Computational zero-knowledge:** *For every efficient adversary $\mathcal{A}$, there exists an efficient simulator $\mathcal{S} = (\mathcal{S}_1, \mathcal{S}_2)$ such that for $\mathsf{crs} \leftarrow \mathsf{Setup}(1^\lambda)$ and $(\widetilde{\mathsf{crs}}, \mathsf{st}_{\mathcal{S}}) \leftarrow \mathcal{S}_1(1^\lambda)$, we have that*

$$\left|\Pr\left[\mathcal{A}^{\mathcal{O}_0(\mathsf{crs}, \cdot, \cdot, \cdot)}(1^\lambda, \mathsf{crs}) = 1\right] - \Pr\left[\mathcal{A}^{\mathcal{O}_1(\mathsf{st}_{\mathcal{S}}, \cdot, \cdot, \cdot)}(1^\lambda, \widetilde{\mathsf{crs}}) = 1\right]\right| = \mathsf{negl}(\lambda),$$

where the oracles $\mathcal{O}_0$ and $\mathcal{O}_1$ are defined as follows:
  - $\mathcal{O}_0(\mathsf{crs}, C, \mathbf{x}, \mathbf{w})$: *On input crs, a circuit $C \colon \{0,1\}^n \times \{0,1\}^h \to \{0,1\}$, a statement $\mathbf{x} \in \{0,1\}^n$, and a witness $\mathbf{w} \in \{0,1\}^h$, the oracle outputs $\perp$ if $C(\mathbf{x}, \mathbf{w}) = 0$. If $C(\mathbf{x}, \mathbf{w}) = 1$, it outputs $\mathsf{Prove}(\mathsf{crs}, C, \mathbf{x}, \mathbf{w})$.*
  - $\mathcal{O}_1(\mathsf{st}_{\mathcal{S}}, C, \mathbf{x}, \mathbf{w})$: *On input the simulator state $\mathsf{st}_{\mathcal{S}}$, a circuit $C \colon \{0,1\}^n \times \{0,1\}^h \to \{0,1\}$, a statement $\mathbf{x} \in \{0,1\}^n$, and a witness $\mathbf{w} \in \{0,1\}^h$, the oracle outputs $\perp$ if $C(\mathbf{x}, \mathbf{w}) = 0$. If $C(\mathbf{x}, \mathbf{w}) = 1$, it outputs $\mathcal{S}_2(\mathsf{st}_{\mathcal{S}}, C, \mathbf{x})$.*

2.2   Non-Interactive Batch Arguments for NP

The main cryptographic primitive we consider in this work is a non-interactive batch argument for NP. As before, we consider the NP-complete language of Boolean circuit satisfiability. We now recall the definition of a non-interactive batch argument for NP from [KPY19, CJJ21a]. Our construction relies on the notion of semi-adaptive soundness used in [CJJ21b, WW22, DGKV22, KLVW23, CGJ+22].

Definition 2.9 (Batch Argument for NP [CJJ21b, adapted]). *A non-interactive batch argument (BARG) for Boolean circuit satisfiability is a tuple of three efficient algorithms $\Pi_{\mathsf{BARG}} = (\mathsf{Setup}, \mathsf{Prove}, \mathsf{Verify})$ with the following syntax:*

- $\mathsf{Setup}(1^\lambda, 1^T, 1^s) \to \mathsf{crs}$: *On input the security parameter $\lambda \in \mathbb{N}$, the number of instances $T \in \mathbb{N}$, and a bound on the circuit size $s \in \mathbb{N}$, the setup algorithm outputs a common reference string crs.*
- $\mathsf{Prove}(\mathsf{crs}, C, (\mathbf{x}_1, \dots, \mathbf{x}_T), (\mathbf{w}_1, \dots, \mathbf{w}_T)) \to \pi$: *On input the common reference string crs, a Boolean circuit $C \colon \{0,1\}^n \times \{0,1\}^h \to \{0,1\}$, statements $\mathbf{x}_1, \dots, \mathbf{x}_T \in \{0,1\}^n$, and witnesses $\mathbf{w}_1, \dots, \mathbf{w}_T \in \{0,1\}^h$, the prove algorithm outputs a proof π.*
- $\mathsf{Verify}(\mathsf{crs}, C, (\mathbf{x}_1, \dots, \mathbf{x}_T), \pi) \to b$: *On input the common reference string crs, the Boolean circuit $C \colon \{0,1\}^n \times \{0,1\}^h \to \{0,1\}$, statements $\mathbf{x}_1, \dots, \mathbf{x}_T \in \{0,1\}^n$ and a proof π, the verification algorithm outputs a bit $b \in \{0,1\}$.*

Moreover, Π_{BARG} should satisfy the following properties:

- **Completeness:** *For all $\lambda, T, s \in \mathbb{N}$, all circuits $C \colon \{0,1\}^n \times \{0,1\}^h \to \{0,1\}$ of size at most s, all statements $\mathbf{x}_1, \dots, \mathbf{x}_T \in \{0,1\}^n$, and all witnesses $\mathbf{w}_1, \dots, \mathbf{w}_T \in \{0,1\}^h$ where $C(\mathbf{x}_i, \mathbf{w}_i) = 1$ for all $i \in [T]$,*

$$\Pr\left[\mathsf{Verify}(\mathsf{crs}, C, \mathbf{x}, \pi) = 1 : \begin{array}{l} \mathsf{crs} \leftarrow \mathsf{Setup}(1^\lambda, 1^T, 1^s); \\ \pi \leftarrow \mathsf{Prove}(\mathsf{crs}, C, \mathbf{x}, \mathbf{w}) \end{array}\right] = 1,$$

  where $\mathbf{x} = (\mathbf{x}_1, \dots, \mathbf{x}_T)$ and $\mathbf{w} = (\mathbf{w}_1, \dots, \mathbf{w}_T)$.
- **Succinct proof size:**[5] *There exists a polynomial $\mathsf{poly}(\cdot, \cdot, \cdot)$ such that for all $\lambda, T, s \in \mathbb{N}$, all crs in the support of $\mathsf{Setup}(1^\lambda, 1^T, 1^s)$, and all Boolean circuits $C \colon \{0,1\}^n \times \{0,1\}^h \to \{0,1\}$ of size at most s, the size of the proof π output by $\mathsf{Prove}(\mathsf{crs}, C, \cdot, \cdot)$ satisfies $|\pi| \leq \mathsf{poly}(\lambda, \log T, s)$.*
- **Semi-adaptive soundness:** *For a security parameter λ, we define the semi-adaptive soundness game between an adversary $\mathcal{A}$ and a challenger as follows:*
  1. *Algorithm $\mathcal{A}$ starts by outputting the number of instances 1^T, the bound on the circuit size 1^s, and an index $i \in [T]$.*
  2. *The challenger samples a common reference string $\mathsf{crs} \leftarrow \mathsf{Setup}(1^\lambda, 1^T, 1^s)$ and gives crs to $\mathcal{A}$.*

---

[5] Previous works [KPY19, CJJ21a, CJJ21b, WW22, DGKV22, CGJ+22] also impose requirements on the size of the CRS and the running time of the verifier. These additional properties are not needed in our work.

3. *Algorithm $\mathcal{A}$ outputs a Boolean circuit $C\colon \{0,1\}^n \times \{0,1\}^h \to \{0,1\}$ of size at most s, statements $(\mathbf{x}_1, \ldots, \mathbf{x}_T)$ where each $\mathbf{x}_i \in \{0,1\}^n$, and a proof π.*
4. *The output of the experiment is $b = 1$ if $\mathsf{Verify}(\mathsf{crs}, C, (\mathbf{x}_1, \ldots, \mathbf{x}_T), \pi) = 1$ and for all $\mathbf{w}_i \in \{0,1\}^h$, $C(\mathbf{x}_i, \mathbf{w}_i) = 0$. Otherwise, the output is $b = 0$.*

Then Π_{BARG} satisfies semi-adaptive soundness if for all efficient adversaries $\mathcal{A}$, $\Pr[b = 1] = \mathsf{negl}(\lambda)$ in the semi-adaptive soundness game.

Constructions of batch arguments for NP *.* Batch arguments for NP have recently been realized from a broad range of standard assumptions including lattice-based assumptions [CJJ21b, DGKV22] as well as assumptions over pairing groups [KVZ21, WW22] and pairing-free groups [CGJ+22].

2.3 Hidden-Bits Generator

We recall the notion of a hidden-bits generator with subset-dependent proofs from [KMY20]. For a bitstring $\mathbf{r} \in \{0,1\}^n$ and a set of indices $I \subseteq [n]$, we write $\mathbf{r}_I \in \{0,1\}^{|I|}$ to denote the substring corresponding to the bits of $\mathbf{r}$ indexed by I.

Definition 2.10 (Hidden-Bits Generator [KMY20, Definition 11]). *A hidden-bits generator with subset-dependent proofs is a tuple of efficient algorithms $\Pi_{\mathsf{HBG}} = (\mathsf{Setup}, \mathsf{GenBits}, \mathsf{Prove}, \mathsf{Verify})$ with the following syntax:*

- $\mathsf{Setup}(1^\lambda, 1^m) \to \mathsf{crs}$: *On input the security parameter λ, and the output length m, the setup algorithm outputs a common reference string crs.*
- $\mathsf{GenBits}(\mathsf{crs}) \to (\mathbf{r}, \mathsf{st})$: *On input the the common reference string crs, the generator algorithm outputs a string $\mathbf{r} \in \{0,1\}^m$ and a state st.*
- $\mathsf{Prove}(\mathsf{st}, I) \to \pi$: *On input the state st and a subset $I \subseteq [m]$, the prove algorithm outputs a proof π.*
- $\mathsf{Verify}(\mathsf{crs}, I, \mathbf{r}_I, \pi) \to b$: *On input a common reference string crs, a subset $I \subseteq [m]$, a string $\mathbf{r}_I \in \{0,1\}^{|I|}$, and a proof π, the verification algorithm outputs a bit $b \in \{0,1\}$.*

We require Π_{HBG} to satisfy the following properties:

- **Correctness:** *For all $m, \lambda \in \mathbb{N}$ and all subsets $I \subseteq [m]$, we have*

$$\Pr\left[\mathsf{Verify}(\mathsf{crs}, I, \mathbf{r}_I, \pi) = 1 : \begin{array}{l} \mathsf{crs} \leftarrow \mathsf{Setup}(1^\lambda, 1^m); \\ (\mathbf{r}, \mathsf{st}) \leftarrow \mathsf{GenBits}(\mathsf{crs}); \\ \pi \leftarrow \mathsf{Prove}(\mathsf{st}, I) \end{array}\right] = 1.$$

- **Somewhat computational binding:** *For every crs in the support of the algorithm $\mathsf{Setup}(1^\lambda, 1^m)$, there exists a set $\mathcal{V}^{\mathsf{crs}}$ with the following properties:*
  (i) **Output sparsity.** *There exists a universal constant $\gamma < 1$ and a fixed polynomial $p(\cdot)$ such that for every polynomial $m = m(\lambda)$, and every crs in the support of $\mathsf{Setup}(1^\lambda, 1^m)$, $|\mathcal{V}^{\mathsf{crs}}| \leq 2^{m^\gamma \cdot p(\lambda)}$*

(ii) **Computational binding.** *For every efficient and stateful adversary $\mathcal{A}$,*

$$\Pr\left[\mathbf{r}_I \notin \mathcal{V}_I^{\mathsf{crs}} \wedge \mathsf{Verify}(\mathsf{crs}, I, \mathbf{r}_I, \pi) = 1 : \begin{array}{l} 1^m \leftarrow \mathcal{A}(1^\lambda); \\ \mathsf{crs} \leftarrow \mathsf{Setup}(1^\lambda, 1^m); \\ (I, \mathbf{r}_I, \pi) \leftarrow \mathcal{A}(\mathsf{crs}) \end{array}\right] = \mathsf{negl}(\lambda),$$

where $\mathcal{V}_I^{\mathsf{crs}} := \{\mathbf{r}_I : \mathbf{r} \in \mathcal{V}^{\mathsf{crs}}\}$.

– *Computationally hiding: For every polynomial $m = m(\lambda)$, every subset $I \subseteq [m]$, and all efficient adversaries $\mathcal{A}$, we have*

$$\left|\Pr[\mathcal{A}(\mathsf{crs}, I, \mathbf{r}_I, \pi, \mathbf{r}_{\bar{I}}) = 1] - \Pr[\mathcal{A}(\mathsf{crs}, I, \mathbf{r}_I, \pi, \mathbf{r}'_{\bar{I}}) = 1]\right| = \mathsf{negl}(\lambda),$$

where $\mathsf{crs} \leftarrow \mathsf{Setup}(1^\lambda, 1^m)$, $(\mathbf{r}, \mathsf{st}) \leftarrow \mathsf{GenBits}(\mathsf{crs})$, $\pi \leftarrow \mathsf{Prove}(\mathsf{st}, I)$, $\mathbf{r}' \xleftarrow{\text{R}} \{0, 1\}^m$, and $\bar{I} = [m] \setminus I$.

Theorem 2.11 (NIZK from Hidden-Bits Generator [KMY20, Theorem 5]). *If there exists a hidden-bits generator with subset-dependent proofs, then there exists a computational NIZK argument for NP.*

3 Hidden-Bits Generator from Batch Arguments

In this section, we show how to construct a hidden-bits generator with subset-dependent proofs using a batch argument for NP together with a dual-mode commitment and a low-complexity PRG. Then combined with Theorem 2.11, we obtain a NIZK for NP from the same underlying set of assumptions.

Construction 3.1 (Hidden-Bits Generator from Batch Arguments). Let $\lambda \in \mathbb{N}$ be a security parameter and m be an output length parameter. Let $n = n(\lambda, m)$ be a PRG seed length parameter and let $B = B(\lambda, m)$ be a block length parameter. These parameters will be determined in the security analysis. Our construction relies on the following primitives:

– Let $G_\lambda \colon \{0, 1\}^\lambda \to \{0, 1\}^{\ell(\lambda)}$ be a family of PRGs. Let $k = k(\lambda)$ be the locality of the PRG (i.e., each output bit of G_λ depends on at most k input bits). In the following description, we require that $\ell(n) \geq mB$.
– Let $\Pi_{\mathsf{BC}} = (\mathsf{BC.Setup}, \mathsf{BC.Commit}, \mathsf{BC.Verify})$ be a dual-mode bit commitment scheme.
– Let $\Pi_{\mathsf{BARG}} = (\mathsf{BARG.Setup}, \mathsf{BARG.Prove}, \mathsf{BARG.Verify})$ be a batch argument for NP with proof length $\ell_{\mathsf{BARG}} = \ell_{\mathsf{BARG}}(\lambda, T, s)$, where s denotes the size of the underlying NP relation and T denotes the number of instances.
– For an index $i \in [\ell]$ where $\ell = \ell(n)$, let $i_1, \ldots, i_k \in [n]$ be the indices of the k seed bits on which the ith output bit of $G_n(\cdot)$ depends. Let $\mathbf{s} \in \{0, 1\}^n$ be a seed for the PRG, and let $G_n^{(i)} \colon \{0, 1\}^k \to \{0, 1\}$ be the circuit that takes as input the seed bits $s_{i_1}, \ldots, s_{i_k} \in \{0, 1\}$ and outputs the ith bit of $G_n(\mathbf{s})$. Then, for a common reference string $\mathsf{crs}_{\mathsf{BC}}$ for the bit commitment scheme, define the NP relation $\mathcal{R}[n, \mathsf{crs}_{\mathsf{BC}}]$ as follows:

Hard-wired: PRG seed length n, common reference string $\mathsf{crs_{BC}}$
Statement: circuit $G_n^{(i)} : \{0,1\}^k \to \{0,1\}$, commitments $c_1, \ldots, c_k$, output $t \in \{0,1\}$
Witness: bits $s_1, \ldots, s_k \in \{0,1\}$, openings $\sigma_1, \ldots, \sigma_k$

Output 1 if all of the following conditions hold:

- For each $i \in [k]$, $\mathsf{BC.Verify}(\mathsf{crs_{BC}}, c_i, s_i, \sigma_i) = 1$;
- $t = G_n^{(i)}(s_1, \ldots, s_k)$.

Otherwise, output 0.

Fig. 1. Relation $\mathcal{R}[n, \mathsf{crs_{BC}}]\big((G_n^{(i)}, c_1, \ldots, c_k, t), (s_1, \ldots, s_k, \sigma_1, \ldots, \sigma_k)\big)$.

We now construct our hidden-bits generator $\Pi_{\mathsf{HBG}} = (\mathsf{Setup}, \mathsf{GenBits}, \mathsf{Prove}, \mathsf{Verify})$ as follows:

- $\mathsf{Setup}(1^\lambda, 1^m)$: On input the security parameter λ and the output length m, the setup algorithm proceeds as follows:
  1. Sample a CRS for the dual-mode commitment scheme: $(\mathsf{crs_{BC}}, \mathsf{td}) \leftarrow \mathsf{BC.Setup}(1^\lambda, \mathsf{bind})$.
  2. Let $n = n(\lambda, m)$ be the PRG seed length. Let C be the circuit that computes the NP relation $\mathcal{R}[n, \mathsf{crs_{BC}}]$. Sample a common reference string $\mathsf{crs_{BARG}} \leftarrow \mathsf{BARG.Setup}(1^\lambda, 1^{mB}, 1^{|C|})$.
  3. Let $B = B(\lambda, m)$ be the block size and sample $\mathbf{v}_1, \ldots, \mathbf{v}_m \xleftarrow{\mathbb{R}} \{0,1\}^B$.

  Output the common reference string $\mathsf{crs} = (n, \mathsf{crs_{BARG}}, \mathsf{crs_{BC}}, \mathbf{v}_1, \ldots, \mathbf{v}_m)$.
- $\mathsf{GenBits}(\mathsf{crs})$: On input $\mathsf{crs} = (n, \mathsf{crs_{BARG}}, \mathsf{crs_{BC}}, \mathbf{v}_1, \ldots, \mathbf{v}_m)$, the generator algorithm proceeds as follows:
  1. Sample a PRG seed $\mathbf{s} \xleftarrow{\mathbb{R}} \{0,1\}^n$, and compute $\mathbf{t} = \{0,1\}^{mB} \leftarrow G_n(\mathbf{s})$.[6] For each $i \in [n]$, compute a commitment $(c_i, \sigma_i) \leftarrow \mathsf{BC.Commit}(\mathsf{crs_{BC}}, s_i)$ to the bits of the seed.
  2. Split $\mathbf{t} = \mathbf{t}_1 \| \mathbf{t}_2 \| \cdots \| \mathbf{t}_m$ into blocks where each $\mathbf{t}_i \in \{0,1\}^B$ for each $i \in [m]$. Next, for each $i \in [m]$, compute $r_i \leftarrow \mathbf{v}_i^\mathsf{T} \mathbf{t}_i$ (where the vectors $\mathbf{v}_i$ and $\mathbf{t}_i$ are interpreted as vectors in $\mathbb{Z}_2^B$).

  The algorithm outputs the hidden-bits string $\mathbf{r} = r_1 \| r_2 \| \cdots \| r_m \in \{0,1\}^m$ together with the generator state $\mathsf{st} = (n, \mathsf{crs_{BARG}}, \mathsf{crs_{BC}}, \mathbf{s}, c_1, \ldots, c_n, \sigma_1, \ldots, \sigma_n)$.
- $\mathsf{Prove}(\mathsf{st}, I)$: On input $\mathsf{st} = (n, \mathsf{crs_{BARG}}, \mathsf{crs_{BC}}, \mathbf{s}, c_1, \ldots, c_n, \sigma_1, \ldots, \sigma_n)$ and a set of indices $I \subseteq [m]$, the prove algorithm proceeds as follows:
  1. Let $\mathbf{t} = G_n(\mathbf{s})$ and parse $\mathbf{t} = \mathbf{t}_1 \| \mathbf{t}_2 \| \cdots \| \mathbf{t}_m$ where each $\mathbf{t}_i \in \{0,1\}^B$. We will also use the notation $\mathbf{t}[i] := \mathbf{t}_i$ to refer to the ith block of $\mathbf{t}$ and $G_n[i] := G_n^{(i)}$ to refer to the circuit computing the ith bit of $G_n(\mathbf{s})$. In the analysis, we will often associate an index $i \in [mB]$ with a pair $(j, \beta) \in [m] \times [B]$ and vice versa (where $i = (j-1)B + \beta$).

---

[6] As noted above, we require that $\ell(n) \geq mB$. If $\ell(n) > mB$, we truncate the output of G_n to output a string of length exactly mB.

2. Let $I = \{i^{(1)}, \ldots, i^{(L)}\}$, where the indices $i^{(1)}, \ldots, i^{(L)} \in [m]$ are in sorted order. For each $j \in [L], \beta \in [B]$, let $\mathbf{t}[i^{(j)}, \beta] \in \{0, 1\}$ denote the βth bit of $\mathbf{t}[i^{(j)}]$.

3. By construction, the value of $\mathbf{t}[i^{(j)}, \beta]$ depends on at most k bits of $\mathbf{s}$. We define $G_n[i^{(j)}, \beta]$ to denote the circuit that reads up to k bits of $\mathbf{s}$ and outputs $\mathbf{t}[i^{(j)}, \beta]$. Next, we define the function $\mathsf{idx} \colon [L] \times [B] \times [k] \to [n]$ where $\mathsf{idx}(i^{(j)}, \beta, \gamma)$ outputs the γth input bit of $\mathbf{s}$ on which the output bit $\mathbf{t}[i^{(j)}, \beta]$ depends. In particular, the inputs to the circuit $G_n[i^{(j)}, \beta]$ consist of bits $\mathsf{idx}(i^{(j)}, \beta, 1), \ldots, \mathsf{idx}(i^{(j)}, \beta, k)$ of $\mathbf{s}$.

4. For each $j \in [L]$ and $\beta \in [B]$, define the statement $x_{j,\beta}$ and associated witness $w_{j,\beta}$ as follows:

$$x_{j,\beta} = \left(G_n[i^{(j)}, \beta], c_{\mathsf{idx}(i^{(j)}, \beta, 1)}, \ldots, c_{\mathsf{idx}(i^{(j)}, \beta, k)}, \mathbf{t}[i^{(j)}, \beta] \right) \tag{3.1}$$

$$w_{j,\beta} = \left(s_{\mathsf{idx}(i^{(j)}, \beta, 1)}, \ldots, s_{\mathsf{idx}(i^{(j)}, \beta, k)}, \sigma_{\mathsf{idx}(i^{(j)}, \beta, 1)}, \ldots, \sigma_{\mathsf{idx}(i^{(j)}, \beta, k)} \right). \tag{3.2}$$

Let C be the circuit that computes the NP relation in Fig. 1. Then, compute the proof

$$\pi_{\mathsf{BARG}} \leftarrow \mathsf{BARG.Prove}(\mathsf{crs}_{\mathsf{BARG}}, C, (x_{1,1}, \ldots, x_{L,B}), (w_{1,1}, \ldots, w_{L,B})).$$

5. Output $\pi = \left(\pi_{\mathsf{BARG}}, (c_1, \ldots, c_n), (\mathbf{t}_{i^{(1)}}, \ldots, \mathbf{t}_{i^{(L)}}) \right)$.

– Verify$(\mathsf{crs}, I, \mathbf{r}_I, \pi)$: On input $\mathsf{crs} = (n, \mathsf{crs}_{\mathsf{BARG}}, \mathsf{crs}_{\mathsf{BC}}, \mathbf{v}_1, \ldots, \mathbf{v}_m)$, a set of indices $I = \{i^{(1)}, \ldots, i^{(L)}\} \subseteq [m]$ (in sorted order), a string $\mathbf{r}_I \in \{0, 1\}^L$, and a proof $\pi = \left(\pi_{\mathsf{BARG}}, (c_1, \ldots, c_n), (\mathbf{t}_{i^{(1)}}, \ldots, \mathbf{t}_{i^{(L)}}) \right)$, the verification algorithm proceeds as follows:

1. For each $j \in [L]$, let $r_{i^{(j)}} \in \{0, 1\}$ be the bit of $\mathbf{r}_I$ associated with index $i^{(j)}$. Then, for each $j \in [L]$, check that $r_{i^{(j)}} = \mathbf{v}_{i^{(j)}}^{\mathsf{T}} \mathbf{t}_{i^{(j)}}$. Output 0 if any check fails.

2. Using the commitments $c_1, \ldots, c_n$ and the bits of $\mathbf{t}_{i^{(1)}}, \ldots, \mathbf{t}_{i^{(L)}}$, construct the statements $x_{j,\beta}$ for each $j \in [L]$ and $\beta \in [B]$ according to Eq. 3.1. Let C be the circuit that computes the NP relation $\mathcal{R}[n, \mathsf{crs}_{\mathsf{BC}}]$ in Fig. 1.

3. Output $\mathsf{BARG.Verify}(\mathsf{crs}_{\mathsf{BARG}}, C, (x_{1,1}, \ldots, x_{L,B}), \pi_{\mathsf{BARG}})$.

Theorem 3.2 (Correctness). *If Π_{BARG} is complete and Π_{BC} is correct, then Construction 3.1 is correct.*

Proof. Take any security parameter λ, output length m, and set of indices $I \subseteq [m]$. Let $\mathsf{crs} \leftarrow \mathsf{Setup}(1^\lambda, 1^m)$ where $\mathsf{crs} = (n, \mathsf{crs}_{\mathsf{BARG}}, \mathsf{crs}_{\mathsf{BC}}, \mathbf{v}_1, \ldots, \mathbf{v}_m)$. Let $(\mathbf{r}, \mathsf{st}) \leftarrow \mathsf{GenBits}(\mathsf{crs})$ and $\pi \leftarrow \mathsf{Prove}(\mathsf{st}, I)$. Consider the output of Verify$(\mathsf{crs}, I, \mathbf{r}_I, \pi)$.

– By construction of GenBits, $r_i = \mathbf{v}_i^{\mathsf{T}} \mathbf{t}_i$ for all $i \in [L]$. Thus, the first set of checks in Verify pass.

– Next, for each $j \in [L]$ and $\beta \in [B]$, let $x_{j,\beta}$ and $w_{j,\beta}$ be the statement and witness defined as in Eqs. (3.1) and (3.2). By correctness of Π_{BC}, it follows that $(x_{j,\beta}, w_{j,\beta}) \in \mathcal{R}[n, \mathsf{crs}_{\mathsf{BC}}]$.

– Let $\pi = (\pi_{\mathsf{BARG}}, (c_1, \ldots, c_n), (\mathbf{t}_{i^{(1)}}, \ldots, \mathbf{t}_{i^{(L)}}))$. Since $(x_{j,\beta}, w_{j,\beta}) \in \mathcal{R}[n, \mathsf{crs_{BC}}]$ for all $j \in [L]$ and $\beta \in [B]$, completeness of Π_{BARG} implies that

$$\mathsf{BARG.Verify}(\mathsf{crs_{BARG}}, C, (x_{1,1}, \ldots, x_{1,B}, \ldots, x_{L,1}, \ldots, x_{L,B}), \pi_{\mathsf{BARG}}) = 1.$$

Correspondingly, $\mathsf{Verify}(\mathsf{crs}, I, \mathbf{r}_I, \pi) = 1$, as required.   □

Theorem 3.3 (Somewhat Computational Binding). *Let λ be a security parameter. Suppose there exists a universal constant $\delta < 1$ and a fixed polynomial $p(\cdot)$ such that for every polynomial $m = m(\lambda)$, it follows that $n = n(\lambda, m) \leq m^\delta \cdot p(\lambda)$. Suppose also that Π_{BARG} satisfies semi-adaptive soundness, Π_{BC} is extractable in binding mode, and that $B = B(\lambda, m)$ is polynomially bounded. Then, Construction 3.1 satisfies somewhat computational binding.*

Proof. Let $\mathsf{crs} = (n, \mathsf{crs_{BARG}}, \mathsf{crs_{BC}}, \mathbf{v}_1, \ldots, \mathbf{v}_m)$ be a common reference string in the support of $\mathsf{Setup}(1^\lambda, 1^m)$. We define the set $\mathcal{V}^{\mathsf{crs}} \subset \{0,1\}^m$ as follows:

$$\mathcal{V}^{\mathsf{crs}} := \{(\mathbf{v}_1^\mathsf{T} \mathbf{t}_1, \ldots, \mathbf{v}_m^\mathsf{T} \mathbf{t}_m) \mid \exists \mathbf{s} \in \{0,1\}^n : \mathbf{t}_1 \| \cdots \| \mathbf{t}_m = G_n(\mathbf{s})\}.$$

We now show that each of the requirements in Definition 2.10 is satisfied:

Output Sparsity. This is immediate from the construction: $|\mathcal{V}^{\mathsf{crs}}| \leq 2^n \leq 2^{m^\delta \cdot p(\lambda)}$.

Computational Binding. To argue computational binding, we appeal to the fact that Π_{BC} is extractable in binding mode and to semi-adaptive soundness of Π_{BARG}. Formally, suppose there is an efficient adversary $\mathcal{A}$ that breaks computational binding of Construction 3.1 with non-negligible advantage ε. We construct an adversary $\mathcal{B}$ that breaks semi-adaptive soundness of the BARG as follows:

1. Algorithm $\mathcal{B}$ starts running $\mathcal{A}$ on input the security parameter 1^λ. Algorithm $\mathcal{A}$ chooses the output length 1^m.
2. Algorithm $\mathcal{B}$ then samples $(\mathsf{crs_{BC}}, \mathsf{td}) \leftarrow \mathsf{BC.Setup}(1^\lambda, \mathsf{bind})$ as well as an index $i^* \xleftarrow{\mathsf{R}} [mB]$. It outputs 1^{mB} as the number of instances, 1^s as the size of the circuit (for computing the relation $\mathcal{R}[n, \mathsf{crs_{BC}}]$ in Fig. 1), and the chosen index i^*.
3. Algorithm $\mathcal{B}$ receives $\mathsf{crs_{BARG}}$ from its challenger. Then, it samples the strings $\mathbf{v}_1, \ldots, \mathbf{v}_m \xleftarrow{\mathsf{R}} \{0,1\}^B$. It gives $\mathsf{crs} = (n, \mathsf{crs_{BARG}}, \mathsf{crs_{BC}}, \mathbf{v}_1, \ldots, \mathbf{v}_m)$ to $\mathcal{A}$.
4. Algorithm $\mathcal{A}$ outputs an opening $(I, \mathbf{r}_I, \pi)$.
5. $\mathcal{B}$ parses $I = \{i^{(1)}, \ldots, i^{(L)}\}$ and $\pi = (\pi_{\mathsf{BARG}}, (c_1, \ldots, c_n), (\mathbf{t}_{i^{(1)}}, \ldots, \mathbf{t}_{i^{(L)}}))$. It constructs the statement $\mathbf{x} = (x_{1,1}, \ldots, x_{1,B}, \ldots, x_{L,1}, \ldots, x_{L,B})$ from $c_1, \ldots, c_m$ and $\mathbf{t}_{i^{(1)}}, \ldots, \mathbf{t}_{i^{(L)}}$ according to Eq. (3.1) and defines C to be the circuit that computes the NP relation $\mathcal{R}[n, \mathsf{crs_{BC}}]$ from Fig. 1.
6. Now, for each $i \in [n]$, algorithm $\mathcal{B}$ runs $s_i \leftarrow \mathsf{BC.Extract}(\mathsf{td}, c_i)$. Let $\mathbf{s} = s_1 \| \cdots \| s_n \in \{0,1\}^n$ be the extracted seed. $\mathcal{B}$ now outputs $(C, \mathbf{x}, \pi_{\mathsf{BARG}})$ if the index i^* satisfies $i^* \in I$ and $t_{i^*} \neq t'_{i^*}$, where $\mathbf{t}' = G_n(\mathbf{s})$. Otherwise algorithm $\mathcal{B}$ outputs $\perp$.

First, we argue that algorithm $\mathcal{B}$ is admissible.

- Suppose that $t_{i^*} \neq t'_{i^*}$ where $\mathbf{t}' = G_n(\mathbf{s})$. Write $i^* = (i^{(j)}, \beta) \in [m] \times [B]$. Then,

$$\mathbf{t}[i^{(j)}, \beta] = t_{i^*} \neq G_n^{(i^*)}(\mathbf{s}) = G_n[i^{(j)}, \beta]\left(s_{\mathsf{idx}(i^{(j)},\beta,1)}, \ldots, s_{\mathsf{idx}(i^{(j)},\beta,k)}\right).$$

- Consider the instance

$$x_{i^{(j)},\beta} = \left(G_n[i^{(j)}, \beta], c_{\mathsf{idx}(i^{(j)},\beta,1)}, \ldots, c_{\mathsf{idx}(i^{(j)},\beta,k)}, \mathbf{t}[i^{(j)}, \beta]\right),$$

and any candidate witness

$$w_{i^{(j)},\beta} = \left(s'_{\mathsf{idx}(i^{(j)},\beta,1)}, \ldots, s'_{\mathsf{idx}(i^{(j)},\beta,k)}, \sigma_{\mathsf{idx}(i^{(j)},\beta,1)}, \ldots, \sigma_{\mathsf{idx}(i^{(j)},\beta,k)}\right).$$

We consider two possibilities:

- Suppose there exists $\gamma \in [k]$ where $s'_{\mathsf{idx}(i^{(j)},\beta,\gamma)} \neq s_{\mathsf{idx}(i^{(j)},\beta,\gamma)}$. By extractability of Π_{BC}, with overwhelming probability over the choice of $\mathsf{crs}_{\mathsf{BC}}$,

$$\mathsf{BC.Verify}\left(\mathsf{crs}_{\mathsf{BC}}, c_{\mathsf{idx}(i^{(j)},\beta,\gamma)}, s'_{\mathsf{idx}(i^{(j)},\beta,\gamma)}, \sigma_{\mathsf{idx}(i^{(j)},\beta,\gamma)}\right) = 0.$$

Correspondingly, $\mathcal{R}[\mathsf{crs}_{\mathsf{BC}}](x_{i^{(j)},\beta}, w_{i^{(j)},\beta}) = 0$.

- Suppose that for all $\gamma \in [k]$, $s'_{\mathsf{idx}(i^{(j)},\beta,\gamma)} = s_{\mathsf{idx}(i^{(j)},\beta,\gamma)}$. In this case,

$$G_n[i^{(j)}, \beta]\left(s'_{\mathsf{idx}(i^{(j)},\beta,1)}, \ldots, s'_{\mathsf{idx}(i^{(j)},\beta,k)}\right) =$$
$$G_n[i^{(j)}, \beta]\left(s_{\mathsf{idx}(i^{(j)},\beta,1)}, \ldots, s_{\mathsf{idx}(i^{(j)},\beta,k)}\right) \neq \mathbf{t}[i^{(j)}, \beta].$$

Once again, $\mathcal{R}[\mathsf{crs}_{\mathsf{BC}}](x_{i^{(j)},\beta}, w_{i^{(j)},\beta}) = 0$.

Thus, we conclude that if $t_{i^*} \neq t'_{i^*}$, then instance $x_{i^{(j)},\beta} = x_{i^*}$ is false with all but negligible probability over the choice of $\mathsf{crs}_{\mathsf{BC}}$. Algorithm $\mathcal{B}$ only produces an output when $t_{i^*} \neq t'_{i^*}$ (i.e., when x_{i^*} is false), so algorithm $\mathcal{B}$ is admissible for the semi-adaptive soundness game. To conclude the proof, we compute the advantage of $\mathcal{B}$. In the semi-adaptive soundness game, the challenger constructs $\mathsf{crs}_{\mathsf{BARG}}$ using $\mathsf{BARG.Setup}(1^\lambda, 1^{mB}, 1^{|C|})$, which is identical to the distribution in computational binding game. Thus, algorithm $\mathcal{B}$ perfectly simulates an execution of the binding game for $\mathcal{A}$. This means that with probability ε, algorithm $\mathcal{A}$ outputs (I, r_I, π) where $\pi = (\pi_{\mathsf{BARG}}, (c_1, \ldots, c_n), (\mathbf{t}_{i^{(1)}}, \ldots, \mathbf{t}_{i^{(L)}}))$ with the following two properties:

- Let $\mathbf{x} = (x_{1,1}, \ldots, x_{1,B}, \ldots, x_{L,1}, \ldots, x_{L,B})$ be the statement constructed from $c_1, \ldots, c_n$ and $\mathbf{t}_{i^{(1)}}, \ldots, \mathbf{t}_{i^{(L)}}$ according to Eq. (3.1). Then, we have $\mathsf{BARG.Verify}(\mathsf{crs}_{\mathsf{BARG}}, C, \mathbf{x}, \pi_{\mathsf{BARG}}) = 1$, where C is the circuit computing the NP relation $\mathcal{R}[\mathsf{crs}_{\mathsf{BC}}]$ from Fig. 1.
- The bits r_I satisfy $r_I \notin \mathcal{V}_I^{\mathsf{crs}}$. This means that for every seed $\mathbf{s} \in \{0,1\}^n$, there must exist some output index $i \in [mB]$ such that $t_i \neq G_n^{(i)}(\mathbf{s})$.

Thus, with probability ε, both of the above conditions hold. In particular, this means that $\mathcal{A}$ outputs $(I, \mathbf{r}_I, \pi)$ such that there exists some index $\hat{i} \in [mB]$ where $t_{\hat{i}} \neq t'_{\hat{i}} = G_n^{(\hat{i})}(\mathbf{s})$. Now, algorithm $\mathcal{B}$ samples $i^* \xleftarrow{R} [mB]$ and moreover i^* is independent of $\mathcal{A}$'s view. Thus, $\hat{i} = i^*$ with probability at least $1/mB$, in which case, algorithm $\mathcal{B}$ outputs the instance $(C, \mathbf{x})$ with the proof π_{BARG}. Again from the above conditions, $\mathsf{BARG.Verify}(\mathsf{crs}_{\mathsf{BARG}}, C, \mathbf{x}, \pi_{\mathsf{BARG}}) = 1$, and algorithm $\mathcal{B}$ succeeds in breaking semi-adaptive soundness of Π_{BARG}. We conclude that algorithm $\mathcal{B}$ breaks semi-adaptive soundness of Π_{BARG} with advantage $\varepsilon/mB - \mathsf{negl}(\lambda)$, and the claim follows.

Theorem 3.4 (Computational Hiding). *Suppose the following conditions hold:*

- *The PRG G_λ is sub-exponentially secure (i.e., there exists a constant $\alpha > 0$ and a negligible function $\varepsilon_{\mathsf{PRG}} = \mathsf{negl}(\lambda)$ such that G_λ is $\left(2^{\lambda^\alpha}, \varepsilon_{\mathsf{PRG}}\right)$-secure).*
- *The bit commitment scheme Π_{BC} satisfies mode indistinguishability and is statistically hiding in hiding mode.*
- *The length of the BARG proof $\ell_{\mathsf{BARG}} = \mathsf{poly}(\lambda, m)$ is polynomially-bounded.*
- *The length of the PRG seed satisfies $n = n(\lambda, m) \geq \max(\lambda, \ell_{\mathsf{BARG}}^c)$ for some constant $c > 1/\alpha$, and the block size satisfies $B = B(\lambda, m) \geq \omega(\log \lambda) + \ell_{\mathsf{BARG}}$.*

Then, for all polynomially-bounded $m = m(\lambda)$, Construction 3.1 is computationally hiding.

Proof. Let $I \subseteq [m]$ be an arbitrary subset. We start by defining two distributions $\mathcal{D}_{\mathsf{real}}$ and $\mathcal{D}_{\mathsf{ideal}}$ that will be helpful for our analysis:

- $\mathcal{D}_{\mathsf{real}}(1^\lambda)$: On input the security parameter $\lambda \in \mathbb{N}$, the real distribution constructs the output as follows:
  - Sample $(\mathsf{crs}_{\mathsf{BC}}, \mathsf{td}) \leftarrow \mathsf{BC.Setup}(1^\lambda, \mathsf{hide})$.
  - Sample $\mathsf{crs}_{\mathsf{BARG}} \leftarrow \mathsf{BARG.Setup}(1^\lambda, 1^{mB}, 1^{|C|})$.
  - Let $n = n(\lambda, m)$ and sample $\mathbf{s} \xleftarrow{R} \{0,1\}^n$ and compute $(c_i, \sigma_i) \leftarrow \mathsf{BC.Commit}(\mathsf{crs}_{\mathsf{BC}}, s_i)$ for each $i \in [n]$.
  - Compute $\mathbf{t} \leftarrow G_n(\mathbf{s})$ and output $(I, \mathsf{crs}_{\mathsf{BARG}}, \mathsf{crs}_{\mathsf{BC}}, c_1, \ldots, c_n, \mathbf{t})$.
- $\mathcal{D}_{\mathsf{ideal}}(1^\lambda)$: Same as $\mathcal{D}_{\mathsf{real}}(1^\lambda)$ except we replace each c_i with a commitment to 0 and $\mathbf{t}$ with a uniformly random string: $(c_i, \sigma_i) \leftarrow \mathsf{BC.Commit}(\mathsf{crs}_{\mathsf{BC}}, 0)$ for each $i \in [n]$ and $\mathbf{t} \xleftarrow{R} \{0,1\}^{mB}$.

We now show that if G_n is sub-exponentially secure (and the commitment scheme is statistically hiding), then $\mathcal{D}_{\mathsf{real}}$ and $\mathcal{D}_{\mathsf{ideal}}$ are also indistinguishable to a sub-exponential time algorithm.

Lemma 3.5. *Suppose G_λ is $\left(2^{\lambda^\alpha}, \varepsilon_{\mathsf{PRG}}\right)$-secure for some constant $\alpha > 0$ and negligible function $\varepsilon_{\mathsf{PRG}} = \mathsf{negl}(\lambda)$ and that Π_{BC} is statistically hiding in hiding mode. Suppose also that $\ell_{\mathsf{BARG}} = \mathsf{poly}(\lambda, m)$, and $B \geq \omega(\log \lambda) + \ell_{\mathsf{BARG}}$, $n \geq \max(\lambda, \ell_{\mathsf{BARG}}^c)$ for some constant $c > 1/\alpha$. Then, there exists a negligible function $\varepsilon_{\mathsf{ideal}} = \mathsf{negl}(\lambda)$ such that for all subsets $I \subseteq [m]$, $\mathcal{D}_{\mathsf{real}}$ and $\mathcal{D}_{\mathsf{ideal}}$ are $\left(2^{n^\alpha}, \varepsilon_{\mathsf{ideal}}\right)$-indistinguishable*

Proof. We start by defining a sequence of hybrid experiments:

- Hyb_0: This is the real distribution $\mathcal{D}_{\mathsf{real}}$.
- Hyb_i: Same as Hyb_0 except for all $j \leq i$, we now sample commitments $(c_j, \sigma_j) \leftarrow \mathsf{BC.Commit}(\mathsf{crs}_{\mathsf{BC}}, 0)$. The commitments for $j > i$ are sampled as in Hyb_0.
- Hyb_{n+1}: Same as Hyb_n except $t \xleftarrow{\text{R}} \{0,1\}^{mB}$. This is the ideal distribution $\mathcal{D}_{\mathsf{ideal}}$.

We now show that each adjacent pair of experiments are indistinguishable.

Claim 3.6. *Suppose Π_{BC} is statistically hiding in hiding mode. Then, there exists a negligible function $\varepsilon_0 = \mathsf{negl}(\lambda)$ such that for all (possibly super-polynomial) functions $s_0 = s_0(\lambda)$ and all $i \in [n]$, the distributions Hyb_{i-1} and Hyb_i are (s_0, ε_0)-indistinguishable.*

Proof. Suppose there exists an adversary $\mathcal{A}$ of size s_0 that can distinguish Hyb_{i-1} and Hyb_i with non-negligible advantage δ. We use $\mathcal{A}$ to construct an adversary $\mathcal{B}$ that breaks hiding of Π_{BC} as follows:

1. Algorithm $\mathcal{B}$ receives $\mathsf{crs}_{\mathsf{BC}}$ from its challenger. The algorithm samples $\mathsf{crs}_{\mathsf{BARG}} \leftarrow \mathsf{BARG.Setup}(1^\lambda, 1^{mB}, 1^{|C|})$, $\mathbf{s} \xleftarrow{\text{R}} \{0,1\}^n$, and computes $\mathbf{t} \leftarrow G_n(\mathbf{s})$.
2. Then, for $j < i$, algorithm $\mathcal{B}$ computes $(c_j, \sigma_j) \leftarrow \mathsf{BC.Commit}(\mathsf{crs}_{\mathsf{BC}}, 0)$ and for $j > i$, it computes $(c_j, \sigma_j) \leftarrow \mathsf{BC.Commit}(\mathsf{crs}_{\mathsf{BC}}, s_j)$. Algorithm $\mathcal{B}$ submits $(s_i, 0)$ as its challenge and sets c_i to be the challenger's response.
3. Algorithm $\mathcal{B}$ gives $(I, \mathsf{crs}_{\mathsf{BARG}}, \mathsf{crs}_{\mathsf{BC}}, c_1, \ldots, c_n, \mathbf{t})$ to $\mathcal{A}$ and outputs whatever $\mathcal{A}$ outputs.

If c_i is a commitment to s_i, then algorithm $\mathcal{B}$ perfectly simulates distribution Hyb_{i-1} and if c_i is a commitment to 0, then algorithm $\mathcal{B}$ perfectly simulates distribution Hyb_i. Thus, algorithm $\mathcal{B}$ also succeeds with advantage δ, and the claim follows.

Claim 3.7. *Suppose G_λ is $\left(2^{\lambda^\alpha}, \varepsilon_{\mathsf{PRG}}\right)$-secure for some constant $\alpha > 0$ and negligible function $\varepsilon_{\mathsf{PRG}} = \varepsilon_{\mathsf{PRG}}(\lambda) = \mathsf{negl}(\lambda)$. Then, Hyb_n and Hyb_{n+1} are $\left(2^{n^\alpha}, \varepsilon'_{\mathsf{PRG}}\right)$-indistinguishable, where $\varepsilon'_{\mathsf{PRG}} = \varepsilon_{\mathsf{PRG}}(n)$.*

Proof. Suppose there exists an adversary $\mathcal{A}$ of size $s_\mathcal{A} \leq 2^{n^\alpha}$ that can distinguish $\mathsf{Hyb}_n(1^\lambda)$ and $\mathsf{Hyb}_{n+1}(1^\lambda)$ with advantage $\delta > \varepsilon'_{\mathsf{PRG}}$. We use $\mathcal{A}$ to construct an adversary $\mathcal{B}$ that breaks PRG security with seed length n:

1. At the beginning of the experiment, algorithm $\mathcal{B}$ receives a challenge $\mathbf{t} \in \{0,1\}^{mB}$.
2. $\mathcal{B}$ samples $\mathsf{crs}_{\mathsf{BC}} \leftarrow \mathsf{BC.Setup}(1^\lambda, \mathsf{hide})$, $\mathsf{crs}_{\mathsf{BARG}} \leftarrow \mathsf{BARG.Setup}(1^\lambda, 1^{mB}, 1^{|C|})$. For each $i \in [n]$, it computes $(c_i, \sigma_i) \leftarrow \mathsf{BC.Commit}(\mathsf{crs}_{\mathsf{BC}}, 0)$.
3. Algorithm $\mathcal{B}$ gives $(I, \mathsf{crs}_{\mathsf{BARG}}, \mathsf{crs}_{\mathsf{BC}}, c_1, \ldots, c_n, \mathbf{t})$ to $\mathcal{A}$ and outputs whatever $\mathcal{A}$ outputs.

By construction, the size of algorithm $\mathcal{B}$ is $s_{\mathcal{A}} + \mathsf{poly}(\lambda, m, B, |C|) \leq s_{\mathcal{A}} \cdot \mathsf{poly}(n)$, where the inequality holds since $m, B, |C|$ are all polynomially-bounded (in both λ and n). If $\mathbf{t} = G_n(\mathbf{s})$ for some $\mathbf{s} \xleftarrow{R} \{0,1\}^n$, then $\mathcal{B}$ perfectly simulates $\mathsf{Hyb}_n(1^\lambda)$ for $\mathcal{A}$. Otherwise, if $\mathbf{t} \xleftarrow{R} \{0,1\}^{mB}$, then $\mathcal{B}$ perfectly simulates $\mathsf{Hyb}_{n+1}(1^\lambda)$ for $\mathcal{A}$. Thus, algorithm $\mathcal{B}$ breaks security of G_n with the same advantage $\delta > \varepsilon'_{\mathsf{PRG}} = \varepsilon_{\mathsf{PRG}}(n)$.

By Claims 3.6 and 3.7, we can set $\varepsilon_{\mathsf{ideal}} = n \cdot \varepsilon_0 + \varepsilon_{\mathsf{PRG}}(n(\lambda, m)) = \mathsf{negl}(\lambda)$. The latter equality follows since $n(\lambda, m) \geq \lambda$. The lemma now follows by a hybrid argument.

To complete the proof, we start by appealing to the Gentry-Wichs leakage simulation lemma (Lemma 2.2). Take any subset $I \subseteq [m]$. We start by defining the augmented distribution $\mathcal{D}^*_{\mathsf{real}} = \mathcal{D}^*_{\mathsf{real}}(1^\lambda)$:

- Sample $(I, \mathsf{crs}_{\mathsf{BARG}}, \mathsf{crs}_{\mathsf{BC}}, c_1, \ldots, c_n, \mathbf{t}) \leftarrow \mathcal{D}_{\mathsf{real}}(1^\lambda)$ according to the real distribution. Each commitment c_i is computed as $(c_i, \sigma_i) \leftarrow \mathsf{BC.Commit}(\mathsf{crs}_{\mathsf{BC}}, s_i)$ where $\mathbf{s} \xleftarrow{R} \{0,1\}^n$ and $\mathbf{t} = G_n(\mathbf{s})$.
- Let $\mathsf{st} = (n, \mathsf{crs}_{\mathsf{BARG}}, \mathsf{crs}_{\mathsf{BC}}, \mathbf{s}, c_1, \ldots, c_n, \sigma_1, \ldots, \sigma_n)$, and compute the proof $\pi = (\pi_{\mathsf{BARG}}, (c_1, \ldots, c_n), (\mathbf{t}_{i^{(1)}}, \ldots, \mathbf{t}_{i^{(L)}})) \leftarrow \mathsf{Prove}(\mathsf{st}, I)$.
- Output $(I, \mathsf{crs}_{\mathsf{BARG}}, \mathsf{crs}_{\mathsf{BC}}, c_1, \ldots, c_n, \mathbf{t})$ and the auxiliary information $\mathsf{aux} = \pi_{\mathsf{BARG}}$. By definition, $|\mathsf{aux}| = |\pi_{\mathsf{BARG}}| = \ell_{\mathsf{BARG}}$.

By Lemma 3.5, the distributions $\mathcal{D}_{\mathsf{real}}$ and $\mathcal{D}_{\mathsf{ideal}}$ are $(s_{\mathsf{ideal}}, \varepsilon_{\mathsf{ideal}})$-indistinguishable for $s_{\mathsf{ideal}} = 2^{n^\alpha}$ and a negligible function $\varepsilon_{\mathsf{ideal}} = \mathsf{negl}(\lambda)$. Without loss of generality, we can assume that $\varepsilon_{\mathsf{ideal}} \geq 2^{-n^{\alpha/2}}$ (e.g., we can set $\varepsilon_{\mathsf{ideal}} = \max(\varepsilon'_{\mathsf{ideal}}, 2^{-n^{\alpha/2}})$, where $\varepsilon'_{\mathsf{ideal}}$ is the negligible function from Lemma 3.5). By Lemma 2.2, there exists an augmented distribution $\mathcal{D}^*_{\mathsf{ideal}} = \mathcal{D}^*_{\mathsf{ideal}}(1^\lambda)$ over tuples

$$((I, \mathsf{crs}_{\mathsf{BARG}}, \mathsf{crs}_{\mathsf{BC}}, c_1, \ldots, c_n, \mathbf{t}), \mathsf{aux}')$$

where $(I, \mathsf{crs}_{\mathsf{BARG}}, \mathsf{crs}_{\mathsf{BC}}, c_1, \ldots, c_n, \mathbf{t}) \leftarrow \mathcal{D}_{\mathsf{ideal}}(1^\lambda)$ and $\mathsf{aux}' \in \{0,1\}^{\ell_{\mathsf{BARG}}}$. Moreover, the distributions $\mathcal{D}^*_{\mathsf{real}}$ and $\mathcal{D}^*_{\mathsf{ideal}}$ are $(s_{\mathsf{aug}}, \varepsilon_{\mathsf{aug}})$-indistinguishable where

$$s_{\mathsf{aug}} = s_{\mathsf{ideal}} \cdot \mathsf{poly}(\varepsilon_{\mathsf{ideal}}/2^{\ell_{\mathsf{BARG}}}) = 2^{n^\alpha} \cdot \mathsf{poly}(\varepsilon_{\mathsf{ideal}}/2^{\ell_{\mathsf{BARG}}})$$

and $\varepsilon_{\mathsf{aug}} = 2 \cdot \varepsilon_{\mathsf{ideal}} = \mathsf{negl}(\lambda)$. Since $\varepsilon_{\mathsf{ideal}} \geq 2^{-n^{\alpha/2}}$ and $n \geq \ell_{\mathsf{BARG}}^c$ for some constant $c > 1/\alpha$, this means that $s_{\mathsf{aug}} = 2^{\Omega(n^\alpha)}$. We summarize this in the following claim:

Claim 3.8. *Under the same conditions as in the statement of Lemma 3.5, the distributions $\mathcal{D}^*_{\mathsf{real}}$ and $\mathcal{D}^*_{\mathsf{ideal}}$ are $(s_{\mathsf{aug}}, \varepsilon_{\mathsf{aug}})$-indistinguishable where $s_{\mathsf{aug}} = 2^{\Omega(n^\alpha)}$ and $\varepsilon_{\mathsf{aug}} = \mathsf{negl}(\lambda)$.*

To complete the proof, we proceed via a sequence of hybrid experiments:

- Hyb_0: This is the real distribution where the challenger samples the bits $\mathbf{r}$ and the proof π as in the real scheme:

- The challenger first samples $\mathsf{crs} \leftarrow \mathsf{Setup}(1^\lambda, 1^m)$. In particular, $\mathsf{crs} = (n, \mathsf{crs}_{\mathsf{BARG}}, \mathsf{crs}_{\mathsf{BC}}, \mathbf{v}_1, \ldots, \mathbf{v}_m)$, where $(\mathsf{crs}_{\mathsf{BC}}, \mathsf{td}) \leftarrow \mathsf{BC.Setup}(1^\lambda, \mathsf{bind})$, $\mathsf{crs}_{\mathsf{BARG}} \leftarrow \mathsf{BARG.Setup}(1^\lambda, 1^{mB}, 1^{|C|})$, C is the circuit that computes the NP relation $\mathcal{R}[n, \mathsf{crs}_{\mathsf{BC}}]$ from Fig. 1, and $\mathbf{v}_1, \ldots, \mathbf{v}_m \xleftarrow{\text{R}} \{0,1\}^B$.
- Next, the challenger samples the bits $\mathbf{r}$ by running $(\mathbf{r}, \mathsf{st}) \leftarrow \mathsf{GenBits}(\mathsf{crs})$ and a proof by computing $\pi \leftarrow \mathsf{Prove}(\mathsf{st}, I)$. In particular, the challenger first samples a seed $\mathbf{s} \xleftarrow{\text{R}} \{0,1\}^n$ and computes $\mathbf{t} \leftarrow G_n(\mathbf{s})$. It splits $\mathbf{t} = \mathbf{t}_1 \| \mathbf{t}_2 \| \cdots \| \mathbf{t}_m$ into blocks where each $\mathbf{t}_i \in \{0,1\}^B$ for each $i \in [m]$. For each $i \in [m]$, the challenger computes $r_i \leftarrow \mathbf{v}_i^\mathsf{T} \mathbf{t}_i$ and sets $\mathbf{r} = r_1 \| \cdots \| r_m \in \{0,1\}^m$.
- To construct the proof π, the challenger computes the commitments $(c_i, \sigma_i) \leftarrow \mathsf{BC.Commit}(\mathsf{crs}_{\mathsf{BC}}, s_i)$ for each $i \in [n]$. It then parses $I = \{i^{(1)}, \ldots, i^{(L)}\}$, where the indices $i^{(1)}, \ldots, i^{(L)} \in [m]$ are in sorted order. The challenger then constructs the statement $\mathbf{x} = (x_{1,1}, \ldots, x_{L,B})$ and witness $(w_{1,1}, \ldots, w_{1,B}, \ldots, w_{L,1}, \ldots, w_{L,B})$ according to Eq. (3.1) and Eq. (3.2). It constructs the BARG proof as in Prove:

$$\pi_{\mathsf{BARG}} \leftarrow \mathsf{BARG.Prove}(\mathsf{crs}_{\mathsf{BARG}}, C, (x_{1,1}, \ldots, x_{L,B}), (w_{1,1}, \ldots, w_{L,B})),$$

and sets $\pi = (\pi_{\mathsf{BARG}}, (c_1, \ldots, c_n), (\mathbf{t}_{i^{(1)}}, \ldots, \mathbf{t}_{i^{(L)}}))$.
- The challenger gives $(\mathsf{crs}, I, \mathbf{r}_I, \pi, \mathbf{r}_{\bar{I}})$ to $\mathcal{A}$. Algorithm $\mathcal{A}$ then outputs a bit $b \in \{0,1\}$ which is the output of the experiment.

- Hyb_1: Same as Hyb_0 except the challenger now samples the commitment CRS $(\mathsf{crs}_{\mathsf{BC}}, \mathsf{td}) \leftarrow \mathsf{BC.Setup}(1^\lambda, \mathsf{hide})$. In this experiment, the distribution of $((\mathsf{crs}_{\mathsf{BARG}}, \mathsf{crs}_{\mathsf{BC}}, c_1, \ldots, c_n, \mathbf{t}), \pi_{\mathsf{BARG}})$ is distributed according to $\mathcal{D}^*_{\mathsf{real}}$.
- Hyb_2: Same as Hyb_1 except the challenger samples components

$$((\mathsf{crs}_{\mathsf{BARG}}, \mathsf{crs}_{\mathsf{BC}}, c_1, \ldots, c_n, \mathbf{t}), \pi_{\mathsf{BARG}}) \leftarrow \mathcal{D}^*_{\mathsf{ideal}}.$$

Specifically, the experiment now proceeds as follows:

- The challenger samples $((\mathsf{crs}_{\mathsf{BARG}}, \mathsf{crs}_{\mathsf{BC}}, c_1, \ldots, c_n, \mathbf{t}), \pi_{\mathsf{BARG}}) \leftarrow \mathcal{D}^*_{\mathsf{ideal}}$, $\mathbf{v}_1, \ldots, \mathbf{v}_m \xleftarrow{\text{R}} \{0,1\}^B$, and sets $\mathsf{crs} = (n, \mathsf{crs}_{\mathsf{BARG}}, \mathsf{crs}_{\mathsf{BC}}, \mathbf{v}_1, \ldots, \mathbf{v}_m)$.
- Next, the challenger splits $\mathbf{t} = \mathbf{t}_1 \| \mathbf{t}_2 \| \cdots \| \mathbf{t}_m$ into blocks where each $\mathbf{t}_i \in \{0,1\}^B$ for each $i \in [m]$. For each $i \in [m]$, the challenger computes $r_i \leftarrow \mathbf{v}_i^\mathsf{T} \mathbf{t}_i$ and sets $\mathbf{r} = r_1 \| \cdots \| r_m \in \{0,1\}^m$.
- The challenger sets the proof $\pi = (\pi_{\mathsf{BARG}}, (c_1, \ldots, c_n), (\mathbf{t}_{i^{(1)}}, \ldots, \mathbf{t}_{i^{(L)}}))$ and gives $(\mathsf{crs}, I, \mathbf{r}_I, \pi, \mathbf{r}_{\bar{I}})$ to $\mathcal{A}$.

- Hyb_3: Same as Hyb_2 except the challenger samples $\mathbf{r}_{\bar{I}} \xleftarrow{\text{R}} \{0,1\}^{|\bar{I}|}$.
- Hyb_4: Same as Hyb_3 except the challenger samples

$$((\mathsf{crs}_{\mathsf{BARG}}, \mathsf{crs}_{\mathsf{BC}}, c_1, \ldots, c_n, \mathbf{t}), \pi_{\mathsf{BARG}}) \leftarrow \mathcal{D}^*_{\mathsf{real}}.$$

- Hyb_5: Same as Hyb_4 except the challenger samples $\mathsf{crs}_{\mathsf{BC}} \leftarrow \mathsf{BC.Setup}(1^\lambda, \mathsf{bind})$. Note that this coincides with the ideal distribution.

Lemma 3.9. *Suppose* Π_{BC} *satisfies mode indistinguishability. Then,* Hyb_0 *and* Hyb_1 *are computationally indistinguishable.*

Proof. Suppose there is an adversary $\mathcal{A}$ of size $s_0 = \mathsf{poly}(\lambda)$ that distinguishes the outputs of Hyb_0 and Hyb_1 with non-negligible probability δ. We use $\mathcal{A}$ to construct an adversary $\mathcal{B}$ that breaks mode indistinguishability:

1. At the beginning of the game, algorithm $\mathcal{B}$ receives the security parameter 1^λ and a common reference string $\mathsf{crs}_{\mathsf{BC}}$ from the challenger.
2. $\mathcal{B}$
   samples $\mathsf{crs}_{\mathsf{BARG}} \leftarrow \mathsf{BARG.Setup}(1^\lambda, 1^{mB}, 1^{|C|})$ and $\mathbf{v}_1, \ldots, \mathbf{v}_m \xleftarrow{\text{R}} \{0,1\}^B$. It constructs the common reference string $\mathsf{crs} = (n, \mathsf{crs}_{\mathsf{BARG}}, \mathsf{crs}_{\mathsf{BC}}, \mathbf{v}_1, \ldots, \mathbf{v}_m)$.
3. Algorithm $\mathcal{B}$ computes $(\mathbf{r}, \mathsf{st}) \leftarrow \mathsf{GenBits}(\mathsf{crs})$ and $\pi \leftarrow \mathsf{Prove}(\mathsf{st}, I)$.
4. Algorithm $\mathcal{B}$ gives $(\mathsf{crs}, I, \mathbf{r}_I, \pi, \mathbf{r}_{\bar{I}})$ to $\mathcal{A}$ and outputs whatever $\mathcal{A}$ outputs.

By construction, algorithm $\mathcal{B}$ has size $s_0 + \mathsf{poly}(\lambda, m, B, |C|) \leq s_0 \cdot \mathsf{poly}(\lambda)$ which holds due to $m, B, |C|$ all being $\mathsf{poly}(\lambda)$. When $\mathsf{crs}_{\mathsf{BC}}$ is sampled in binding mode, then algorithm $\mathcal{B}$ perfectly simulates Hyb_0 for $\mathcal{A}$. Alternatively, if $\mathsf{crs}_{\mathsf{BC}}$ is sampled in hiding mode, then algorithm $\mathcal{B}$ perfectly simulates Hyb_1 for $\mathcal{A}$. Critically, neither the GenBits nor the Prove algorithms require knowledge of the trapdoor td for the bit commitment scheme. Thus, algorithm $\mathcal{B}$ succeeds with the same advantage δ.

Lemma 3.10. *Under the same conditions as in the statement of Claim 3.8,* Hyb_1 *and* Hyb_2 *are* $(s_{\mathsf{aug}}, \varepsilon_{\mathsf{aug}})$-*indistinguishable for* $s_{\mathsf{aug}} = 2^{\Omega(n^\alpha)}$ *and* $\varepsilon_{\mathsf{aug}} = \mathsf{negl}(\lambda)$.

Proof. Suppose there is an adversary $\mathcal{A}$ with size s_{aug} that distinguishes Hyb_1 and Hyb_2 with advantage $\delta > \varepsilon_{\mathsf{aug}}$. We construct algorithm $\mathcal{B}$ that distinguishes the distributions $\mathcal{D}^*_{\mathsf{real}}(1^\lambda)$ and $\mathcal{D}^*_{\mathsf{ideal}}(1^\lambda)$ as follows:

1. Algorithm $\mathcal{B}$ receives $(I, \mathsf{crs}_{\mathsf{BARG}}, \mathsf{crs}_{\mathsf{BC}}, c_1, \ldots, c_n, \mathbf{t}, \pi_{\mathsf{BARG}})$ from the challenger. It parses $\mathbf{t} = \mathbf{t}_1 \| \cdots \| \mathbf{t}_m \in \{0,1\}^{mB}$ where each $\mathbf{t}_i \in \{0,1\}^B$. In addition, algorithm $\mathcal{B}$ samples $\mathbf{v}_1, \ldots, \mathbf{v}_m \xleftarrow{\text{R}} \{0,1\}^B$.
2. $\mathcal{B}$ computes $n = n(\lambda, m)$ and sets $\mathsf{crs} = (n, \mathsf{crs}_{\mathsf{BARG}}, \mathsf{crs}_{\mathsf{BC}}, \mathbf{v}_1, \ldots, \mathbf{v}_m)$. For each $i \in [m]$, it computes $r_i \leftarrow \mathbf{v}_i^{\mathsf{T}} \mathbf{t}_i$ and sets $\mathbf{r} = r_1 \| \cdots \| r_m$. Finally, it sets $\pi = (\pi_{\mathsf{BARG}}, (c_1, \ldots, c_n), (\mathbf{t}_{i^{(1)}}, \ldots, \mathbf{t}_{i^{(L)}}))$, where $I = \{i^{(1)}, \ldots, i^{(L)}\}$.
3. Algorithm $\mathcal{B}$ gives $(\mathsf{crs}, I, \mathbf{r}_I, \pi, \mathbf{r}_{\bar{I}})$ to $\mathcal{A}$ and outputs whatever $\mathcal{A}$ outputs.

Since algorithm $\mathcal{A}$ has size s_{aug}, the size of algorithm $\mathcal{B}$ is bounded by $s_{\mathsf{aug}} + \mathsf{poly}(\lambda, m, B) \leq s_{\mathsf{aug}} \cdot \mathsf{poly}(\lambda)$ since m and B are both polynomially-bounded. By construction, when the challenge is sampled from the real distribution $\mathcal{D}^*_{\mathsf{real}}$, algorithm $\mathcal{B}$ perfectly simulates the distribution in Hyb_1. Alternatively, if the challenge is sampled from the ideal distribution $\mathcal{D}^*_{\mathsf{ideal}}$, algorithm $\mathcal{B}$ perfectly simulates the distribution in Hyb_2. Correspondingly, algorithm $\mathcal{B}$ is able to distinguish $\mathcal{D}^*_{\mathsf{real}}(1^\lambda)$ and $\mathcal{D}^*_{\mathsf{ideal}}(1^\lambda)$ with advantage $\delta > \varepsilon_{\mathsf{aug}}$ which contradicts Claim 3.8.

Lemma 3.11. *Suppose* $B \geq \omega(\log \lambda) + \ell_{\mathsf{BARG}}$. *Then,* Hyb_2 *and* Hyb_3 *are statistically indistinguishable.*

Proof. Let $\bar{I} = \{i^{(1)}, i^{(2)}, \ldots, i^{(m-L)}\} \subseteq [m]$. We define a sequence of intermediate experiments $\mathsf{Hyb}_{2,j}$ for each $j \in \{0, \ldots, m-L\}$ as follows:

- $\mathsf{Hyb}_{2,0}$: Same as Hyb_2. In particular, the challenger samples

$$\left((I, \mathsf{crs}_{\mathsf{BARG}}, \mathsf{crs}_{\mathsf{BC}}, c_1, \ldots, c_n, \mathbf{t}), \pi_{\mathsf{BARG}}\right) \leftarrow \mathcal{D}^*_{\mathsf{ideal}},$$

$\mathbf{v}_1, \ldots, \mathbf{v}_m \xleftarrow{\mathsf{R}} \{0,1\}^B$ and sets $\mathsf{crs} = (n, \mathsf{crs}_{\mathsf{BARG}}, \mathsf{crs}_{\mathsf{BC}}, \mathbf{v}_1, \ldots, \mathbf{v}_m)$. It parses $\mathbf{t} = \mathbf{t}_1 \| \cdots \| \mathbf{t}_m$ where $\mathbf{t}_i \in \{0,1\}^B$ and computes $\mathbf{r} \leftarrow (\mathbf{v}_1^\mathsf{T}\mathbf{t}_1 \| \cdots \| \mathbf{v}_m^\mathsf{T}\mathbf{t}_m)$. Finally, it sets $\pi = \left(\pi_{\mathsf{BARG}}, (c_1, \ldots, c_n), (\mathbf{t}_{i^{(1)}}, \ldots, \mathbf{t}_{i^{(L)}})\right)$ and gives the tuple $(\mathsf{crs}, I, \mathbf{r}_I, \pi, \mathbf{r}_{\bar{I}})$ to the adversary.
- $\mathsf{Hyb}_{2,j}$: Same as $\mathsf{Hyb}_{2,j-1}$ except $r_{i^{(j)}} \xleftarrow{\mathsf{R}} \{0,1\}$. Note that $\mathsf{Hyb}_{2,m-L}$ is identical to Hyb_3.

We now appeal to the leftover hash lemma to show that for all $j \in [m-L]$, the statistical distance between $\mathsf{Hyb}_{2,j-1}(1^\lambda)$ and $\mathsf{Hyb}_{2,j}(1^\lambda)$ is negligible.

Claim 3.12. *Suppose $B \geq \omega(\log \lambda) + \ell_{\mathsf{BARG}}$. Then, for all $j \in [m-L]$, the statistical distance between $\mathsf{Hyb}_{2,j-1}(1^\lambda)$ and $\mathsf{Hyb}_{2,j}(1^\lambda)$ is negligible.*

Proof. The only difference between the two distributions is that in $\mathsf{Hyb}_{2,j-1}$, the challenger samples $r_{i^{(j)}} \leftarrow \mathbf{v}_{i^{(j)}}^\mathsf{T}\mathbf{t}_{i^{(j)}}$, whereas in $\mathsf{Hyb}_{2,j}$, the challenger samples $r_{i^{(j)}} \xleftarrow{\mathsf{R}} \{0,1\}$. First, define the random variable Z to be

$$Z = \left(n, \mathsf{crs}_{\mathsf{BARG}}, \mathsf{crs}_{\mathsf{BC}}, \{\mathbf{v}_i\}_{i \neq i^{(j)}}, I, \mathbf{r}_I, (\pi_{\mathsf{BARG}}, (c_1, \ldots, c_n), \{\mathbf{t}_i\}_{i \in I}), \mathbf{r}_{\bar{I} \setminus \{i^{(j)}\}}\right).$$

Observe that the adversary's view in the two experiments then consists of the tuple $\left(r_{i^{(j)}}, \mathbf{v}_{i^{(j)}}, Z\right)$. In both $\mathsf{Hyb}_{2,j-1}$ and $\mathsf{Hyb}_{2,j}$, the challenger samples $\mathbf{t} \xleftarrow{\mathsf{R}} \{0,1\}^{mB}$. By construction, $\mathbf{t}_{i^{(j)}}$ is independent of all of the components in Z other than π_{BARG}. In conjunction with Lemma 2.1, we can now write

$$\mathbf{H}_\infty\left(\mathbf{t}_{i^{(j)}} \mid Z\right) = \mathbf{H}_\infty\left(\mathbf{t}_{i^{(j)}} \mid \pi_{\mathsf{BARG}}\right) \geq \mathbf{H}_\infty(\mathbf{t}_{i^{(j)}}) - |\pi_{\mathsf{BARG}}| = B - \ell_{\mathsf{BARG}} \geq \omega(\log \lambda),$$

since $B \geq \omega(\log \lambda) + \ell_{\mathsf{BARG}}$. Then, by the (generalized) leftover hash lemma (Corollary 2.4), we can conclude that the statistical distance between the distributions

$$\left(\mathbf{v}_{i^{(j)}}^\mathsf{T}\mathbf{t}_{i^{(j)}}, \mathbf{v}_{i^{(j)}}, Z\right) \quad \text{and} \quad \left(r_{i^{(j)}}, \mathbf{v}_{i^{(j)}}, Z\right),$$

where $\mathbf{v}_{i^{(j)}} \xleftarrow{\mathsf{R}} \{0,1\}^B$ and $r_{i^{(j)}} \xleftarrow{\mathsf{R}} \{0,1\}$ is at most $2^{-(\omega(\log \lambda)-1)/2} = \mathsf{negl}(\lambda)$. Since the statistical distance between the two experiments is negligible, the claim holds.

The lemma now follows from Claim 3.12 and a standard hybrid argument (since $m = \mathsf{poly}(\lambda)$).

Lemma 3.13. *Under the same conditions as in the statement of Claim 3.8, Hyb_3 and Hyb_4 are $(s_{\mathsf{aug}}, \varepsilon_{\mathsf{aug}})$-indistinguishable for $s_{\mathsf{aug}} = 2^{\Omega(n^\alpha)}$ and $\varepsilon_{\mathsf{aug}} = \mathsf{negl}(\lambda)$.*

Proof. Follows by an analogous argument as the proof of Lemma 3.10.

Lemma 3.14. *Suppose Π_{BC} satisfies mode indistinguishability. Then, Hyb_4 and Hyb_5 are computationally indistinguishable.*

Proof. Follows by an analogous argument as the proof of Lemma 3.9.

Combining Lemmas 3.9 to 3.11, 3.13 and 3.14 yields the theorem.

Parameter Selection. We now describe one candidate approach for instantiating the parameters in Construction 3.1:

Corollary 3.15 (Hidden-Bits Generator from Batch Arguments). *Let $k = k(\lambda)$ be a locality parameter and suppose that $G_\lambda \colon \{0,1\}^\lambda \to \{0,1\}^{\ell(\lambda)}$ is a k-local PRG. Suppose Π_{BARG} is a non-interactive batch argument satisfying semi-adaptive soundness, Π_{BC} is a dual-mode commitment scheme, and that these underlying schemes satisfy the following conditions:*

- **PRG parameters:** *Suppose there exists a constant $\alpha \in (0,1)$ and a negligible function $\varepsilon_{\mathsf{PRG}} = \mathsf{negl}(\lambda)$ such that G_λ is $\left(2^{\lambda^\alpha}, \varepsilon_{\mathsf{PRG}}\right)$ secure. Moreover, suppose there exists a constant $\delta_1 \in (0,1)$ such that $k \leq \delta_1 \log \lambda$ and a constant $s > 1$ such that $\ell(\lambda) \geq \lambda^s$. In words, we assume that G_λ has super-linear stretch, logarithmic locality, and sub-exponential security.*
- **BARG succinctness:** *Suppose there exists constants $d > 0$, $\delta_2 \in (0,1)$ and a polynomial $q = q(\lambda)$ such that the proof length $\ell_{\mathsf{BARG}} = \ell_{\mathsf{BARG}}(\lambda, T, s)$ for Π_{BARG} satisfies*

$$\ell_{\mathsf{BARG}}(\lambda, T, s) \leq s^d \cdot T^{\delta_2} \cdot q(\lambda),$$

  where T denotes the number of instances and s denotes a bound on the size of the circuit.
- **Block size:** *Suppose $B = \lambda + \ell_{\mathsf{BARG}}$.*

Let $\delta_1' = (d \cdot \delta_1 + \varepsilon)/(1 - \delta_2)$ for an arbitrarily small constant $\varepsilon > 0$, $\delta_2' = \delta_2/(1 - \delta_2)$, and $q'(\lambda) = q(\lambda)^{1/(1-\delta_2)}$. Suppose moreover that the parameters satisfy the following properties:

- **Hardness parameter:** $\alpha > \delta_1' + \delta_2'$.
- **Seed length:** $n = \max(\lambda, (m^{\delta_2'} \cdot q'(\lambda) \cdot O(\lambda^{\delta_2'}))^{1/(\alpha - \delta_1' - \varepsilon')})$ *for an arbitrary constant $0 < \varepsilon' < \alpha - \delta_1' - \delta_2'$.*
- **Stretch:** $s \geq (\alpha - \delta_1' - \varepsilon')(1 + \delta_2')/\delta_2' + \delta_1'$.

Then Construction 3.1 is a hidden-bits generator with subset-dependent proofs.

Proof. Take any input length m. Let $\mathsf{crs} = (n, \mathsf{crs}_{\mathsf{BARG}}, \mathsf{crs}_{\mathsf{BC}}, \mathbf{v}_1, \ldots, \mathbf{v}_m) \leftarrow \mathsf{Setup}(1^\lambda, 1^m)$. We first bound the size of the circuit C that computes the relation $\mathcal{R}[n, \mathsf{crs}_{\mathsf{BC}}]$:

- By construction, $|\mathsf{crs}_{\mathsf{BC}}| = \mathsf{poly}(\lambda)$. Correspondingly, the size of the circuit computing $\mathsf{BC.Verify}$ is $\mathsf{poly}(\lambda)$.
- Next, $G_n^{(i)}$ is a function on k-bit inputs, so it can be computed by a circuit of size $2^k \cdot \mathsf{poly}(k)$. Since $k \leq \delta_1 \log n$, we can bound

$$|C| \leq n^{\delta_1} \cdot \mathsf{poly}(\log n) = O(n^{\delta_1 + \varepsilon/d}).$$

For this choice of parameters, the length ℓ_{BARG} of the BARG proof satisfies

$$\ell_{\mathsf{BARG}} = \ell_{\mathsf{BARG}}(\lambda, mB, |C|) \leq |C|^d \cdot (mB)^{\delta_2} \cdot q(\lambda) = n^{d\delta_1 + \varepsilon} \cdot m^{\delta_2} \cdot \ell_{\mathsf{BARG}}^{\delta_2} \cdot q(\lambda) \cdot O(\lambda^{\delta_2}).$$

Equivalently, this means

$$\ell_{\mathsf{BARG}} \leq (n^{d\delta_1 + \varepsilon} \cdot m^{\delta_2})^{1/(1-\delta_2)} \cdot q(\lambda)^{1/(1-\delta_2)} \cdot O(\lambda^{\delta_2/(1-\delta_2)}) = n^{\delta_1'} \cdot m^{\delta_2'} \cdot q'(\lambda) \cdot O(\lambda^{\delta_2'}),$$

We now consider the requirements of Theorem 3.3, Theorem 3.4 and the requirement on the PRG stretch:

- Theorem 3.4 requires that $n \geq \max(\lambda, \ell_{\mathsf{BARG}}^c)$ for some constant $c > 1/\alpha$. Let $c = 1/(\alpha - \varepsilon') > 1/\alpha$. By assumption, we now have

$$n^{\alpha - \delta_1' - \varepsilon'} \geq m^{\delta_2'} \cdot q'(\lambda) \cdot O(\lambda^{\delta_2'}).$$

In particular, this means that

$$n^{\alpha - \varepsilon'} \geq n^{\delta_1'} \cdot m^{\delta_2'} \cdot q'(\lambda) \cdot O(\lambda^{\delta_2'}) \geq \ell_{\mathsf{BARG}}.$$

Correspondingly, we have $(n^{\alpha - \varepsilon'})^c = n \geq \ell_{\mathsf{BARG}}^c$, as required.
- Theorem 3.3 requires that $n \leq m^{\delta} \cdot \mathsf{poly}(\lambda)$ for some (universal) constant $\delta \in (0, 1)$. Since $q = \mathsf{poly}(\lambda)$ and $\alpha, \delta_1', \varepsilon'$ are all constants, we currently have that $n \leq m^{\delta_2'/(\alpha - \delta_1' - \varepsilon')} \cdot \mathsf{poly}(\lambda)$. By construction, we have that $0 < \alpha - \delta_1' - \delta_2' - \varepsilon'$, so $\delta_2' < \alpha - \delta_1' - \varepsilon$. Thus, setting $\delta = \delta_2'/(\alpha - \delta_1' - \varepsilon') < 1$ satisfies the requirement.
- Finally, we require that $\ell(n) \geq mB$, or equivalently, $n^s \geq mB$. By construction,

$$\begin{aligned} n^s = n^{\delta_1'} n^{s - \delta_1'} &\geq n^{\delta_1'} \cdot \left(m^{\delta_2'} \cdot q'(\lambda) \cdot O(\lambda^{\delta_2'})\right)^{(s - \delta_1')/(\alpha - \delta_1' - \varepsilon')} \\ &\geq n^{\delta_1'} \cdot \left(m^{\delta_2'} \cdot q'(\lambda) \cdot O(\lambda^{\delta_2'})\right)^{(1 + \delta_2')/\delta_2'} \\ &\geq n^{\delta_1'} \cdot m^{1 + \delta_2'} \cdot (q'(\lambda))^{(1 + \delta_2')/\delta_2'} \cdot O(\lambda^{1 + \delta_2'}). \end{aligned}$$

Finally, we have

$$mB = m\lambda + m\ell_{\mathsf{BARG}} \leq m\lambda + n^{\delta_1'} \cdot m^{1 + \delta_2'} \cdot q'(\lambda) \cdot O(\lambda^{\delta_2'}) \leq n^s,$$

as required. $\qquad\square$

Candidate Instantiations. For illustrative purposes, we now describe some instantiations of Theorem 3.15.

- Suppose we instantiate Construction 3.1 and Corollary 3.15 with a batch argument where the proof size scales *polylogarithmically* with the number of instances:

$$\ell_{\mathsf{BARG}}(\lambda, T, s) \leq s^d \cdot \mathsf{polylog}(T) \cdot q(\lambda)$$

for some constant $d > 0$. This is satisfied by most existing BARG constructions [CJJ21b, WW22, DGKV22, KLVW23, CGJ+22]. In this case, the constant δ_2 in Corollary 3.15 can be made *arbitrarily* small. Then we can instantiate Corollary 3.15 with any k-local PRG that is secure against 2^{λ^α}-size adversaries with locality $k \leq \delta_1 \log \lambda$ and stretch $s > 1 + d\delta_1$, provided that $\alpha/\delta_1 > d$. For example, we can rely on sub-exponential hardness of Goldreich's local PRG [Gol00] with *logarithmic* locality.

- We can also instantiate Construction 3.1 and Corollary 3.15 with a "mildly-succinct" batch argument where the BARG proof size scales polynomially with the number of instances:[7]

$$\ell_{\mathsf{BARG}}(\lambda, T, s) \leq s^d \cdot T^{\delta_2} \cdot q(\lambda)$$

for constants $\delta_2 \in (0, 1/2)$ and $d > 0$. In this case, we can instantiate Corollary 3.15 with a k-local PRG that is secure against 2^{λ^α}-size adversaries with locality $k \leq \delta_1 \log \lambda$ and stretch $s > 1 + \delta_1' + \delta_2'$, as long as $\delta_1' < \alpha - \delta_2'$ (for δ_1', δ_2' as in Corollary 3.15). In particular, we can still rely on sub-exponential hardness of Goldreich's PRG with logarithmic locality, but the sub-exponential hardness parameter α increases as δ_2 increases.

NIZK from Batch Arguments. Combining Theorem 2.11 and Corollary 3.15, we now obtain a NIZK for NP from a batch argument for NP:

Corollary 3.16 (NIZK from Batch Arguments). *Suppose there exists a semi-adaptively-sound BARG, a dual-mode commitment scheme, and a sub-exponentially secure PRG with super-linear stretch and locality at most $k = c \log n$ with $c < 1$ and n-bit inputs. Then there exists a computational NIZK argument for NP.*

Remark 3.17 (Using Non-Local PRGs). We note that a local PRG is not strictly necessary for Construction 3.1. It is sufficient to construct a PRG where each output bit of the PRG can be *verified* by a circuit of size n^δ where n is the seed length and $\delta < 1$ is a constant. Any PRG with this local verification property suffices for our main transformation.

Acknowledgments. D. J. Wu is supported by NSF CNS-2151131, CNS-2140975, a Microsoft Research Faculty Fellowship, and a Google Research Scholar award.

References

[ABR12] Applebaum, B., Bogdanov, A., Rosen, A.: A dichotomy for local small-bias generators. In: Cramer, R. (ed.) TCC 2012. LNCS, vol. 7194, pp. 600–617. Springer, Heidelberg (2012). https://doi.org/10.1007/978-3-642-28914-9_34

---

[7] We note here that additionally assuming a rate-1 string oblivious transfer protocol [DGI+19], such a BARG can be transformed into a BARG where the proof size scales polylogarithmically with the number of instances [KLVW23]. In this case, we would be able to appeal to our previous instantiation.

[ACL+22] Albrecht, M.R., Cini, V., Lai, R.W.F., Malavolta, G., Thyagarajan, S.A.K.: Lattice-based SNARKs: publicly verifiable, preprocessing, and recursively composable. In: Dodis, Y., Shrimpton, T. (eds.) CRYPTO 2022. LNCS, vol. 13508, pp. 102–132. Springer, Cham (2022). https://doi.org/10.1007/978-3-031-15979-4_4

[AFMP20] Alamati, N., De Feo, L., Montgomery, H., Patranabis, S.: Cryptographic group actions and applications. In: Moriai, S., Wang, H. (eds.) ASI-ACRYPT 2020. LNCS, vol. 12492, pp. 411–439. Springer, Cham (2020). https://doi.org/10.1007/978-3-030-64834-3_14

[AK19] Applebaum, B., Kachlon, E.: Sampling graphs without forbidden subgraphs and unbalanced expanders with negligible error. In: FOCS (2019)

[AL16] Applebaum, B., Lovett, S.: Algebraic attacks against random local functions and their countermeasures. In: STOC (2016)

[App12] Applebaum, B.: Pseudorandom generators with long stretch and low locality from random local one-way functions. In: STOC (2012)

[App15] Applebaum, B.: The cryptographic hardness of random local functions - survey. IACR Cryptol. ePrint Arch. (2015)

[BBHR18] Ben-Sasson, E. Bentov, I., Horesh, Y., Riabzev, M.: Scalable, transparent, and post-quantum secure computational integrity. IACR Cryptol. ePrint Arch. 2018 (2018)

[BCC88] Brassard, G., Chaum, D., Crépeau, C.: Minimum disclosure proofs of knowledge. J. Comput. Syst. Sci., **37**(2) (1988)

[BCC+17] Bitansky, N., et al.: The hunting of the SNARK. J. Cryptol. **30**(4) (2017)

[BCCT12] Bitansky, N., Canetti, R., Chiesa, R., Tromer, E.: From extractable collision resistance to succinct non-interactive arguments of knowledge, and back again. In: ITCS 2012 (2012)

[BCI+13] Bitansky, N., Chiesa, A., Ishai, Y., Paneth, O., Ostrovsky, R.: Succinct non-interactive arguments via linear interactive proofs. In: Sahai, A. (ed.) TCC 2013. LNCS, vol. 7785, pp. 315–333. Springer, Heidelberg (2013). https://doi.org/10.1007/978-3-642-36594-2_18

[BCPR14] Bitansky, N., Canetti, R., Paneth, O., Rosen, A.: On the existence of extractable one-way functions. In: STOC (2014)

[BDK+11] Barak, B., et al.: Leftover hash lemma, revisited. In: Rogaway, P. (ed.) CRYPTO 2011. LNCS, vol. 6841, pp. 1–20. Springer, Heidelberg (2011). https://doi.org/10.1007/978-3-642-22792-9_1

[BFM88] Blum, M., Feldman, P., Micali, S.: Non-interactive zero-knowledge and its applications (extended abstract). In: STOC 1988 (1988)

[BHY09] Bellare, M., Hofheinz, D., Yilek, S.: Possibility and impossibility results for encryption and commitment secure under selective opening. In: Joux, A. (ed.) EUROCRYPT 2009. LNCS, vol. 5479, pp. 1–35. Springer, Heidelberg (2009). https://doi.org/10.1007/978-3-642-01001-9_1

[BISW17] Boneh, D., Ishai, Y., Sahai, A., Wu, D.J.: Lattice-based SNARGs and their application to more efficient obfuscation. In: Coron, J.-S., Nielsen, J.B. (eds.) EUROCRYPT 2017. LNCS, vol. 10212, pp. 247–277. Springer, Cham (2017). https://doi.org/10.1007/978-3-319-56617-7_9

[BISW18] Boneh, D., Ishai, Y., Sahai, A., Wu, D.J.: Quasi-optimal SNARGs via linear multi-prover interactive proofs. In: Nielsen, J.B., Rijmen, V. (eds.) EUROCRYPT 2018. LNCS, vol. 10822, pp. 222–255. Springer, Cham (2018). https://doi.org/10.1007/978-3-319-78372-7_8

[BKM20] Brakerski, Z., Koppula, V., Mour, T.: NIZK from LPN and trapdoor hash via correlation intractability for approximable relations. In: Micciancio, D., Ristenpart, T. (eds.) CRYPTO 2020. LNCS, vol. 12172, pp. 738–767. Springer, Cham (2020). https://doi.org/10.1007/978-3-030-56877-1_26

[BQ09] Bogdanov, A., Qiao, Y.: On the security of goldreich's one-way function. In: APPROX-RANDOM (2009)

[BS23] Beullens, W., Seiler, G.: Labrador: compact proofs for R1CS from modulesis. In: EUROCRYPT (2023)

[BY92] Bellare, M., Yung, M.: Certifying cryptographic tools: the case of trapdoor permutations. In: Brickell, E.F. (ed.) CRYPTO 1992. LNCS, vol. 740, pp. 442–460. Springer, Heidelberg (1993). https://doi.org/10.1007/3-540-48071-4_31

[CBBZ23] Chen, B., Bünz, B., Boneh, D., Zhang, Z.: Plonk with linear-time prover and high-degree custom gates. In: Hazay, C., Stam, M. (eds.) EUROCRYPT 2023. LNCS, vol. 14005, pp. 499–530. Springer, Cham (2023). https://doi.org/10.1007/978-3-031-30617-4_17

[CCH+19] Canetti, R., et al.: Fiat-shamir: from practice to theory. In: STOC 2019 (2019)

[CDM+18] Couteau, G., Dupin, A., Méaux, P., Rossi, M., Rotella, Y.: On the concrete security of goldreich's pseudorandom generator. In: Peyrin, T., Galbraith, S. (eds.) ASIACRYPT 2018. LNCS, vol. 11273, pp. 96–124. Springer, Cham (2018). https://doi.org/10.1007/978-3-030-03329-3_4

[CEMT09] Cook, J., Etesami, O., Miller, R., Trevisan, L.: Goldreich's one-way function candidate and myopic backtracking algorithms. In: Reingold, O. (ed.) TCC 2009. LNCS, vol. 5444, pp. 521–538. Springer, Heidelberg (2009). https://doi.org/10.1007/978-3-642-00457-5_31

[CGJ+22] Choudhuri, A.R., Garg, S., Jain, A., Jin, Z., Zhang, J.: Correlation intractability and SNARGs from sub-exponential DDH. IACR Cryptol. ePrint Arch. (2022)

[CHK03] Canetti, R., Halevi, S., Katz, J.: A forward-secure public-key encryption scheme. In: Biham, E. (ed.) EUROCRYPT 2003. LNCS, vol. 2656, pp. 255–271. Springer, Heidelberg (2003). https://doi.org/10.1007/3-540-39200-9_16

[CHM+20] Chiesa, A., Hu, Y., Maller, M., Mishra, P., Vesely, N., Ward, N.: Marlin: preprocessing zkSNARKs with universal and updatable SRS. In: Canteaut, A., Ishai, Y. (eds.) EUROCRYPT 2020. LNCS, vol. 12105, pp. 738–768. Springer, Cham (2020). https://doi.org/10.1007/978-3-030-45721-1_26

[CJJ21a] Choudhuri, A.R., Jain, A., Jin, Z.: Non-interactive batch arguments for NP from standard assumptions. In: Malkin, T., Peikert, C. (eds.) CRYPTO 2021. LNCS, vol. 12828, pp. 394–423. Springer, Cham (2021). https://doi.org/10.1007/978-3-030-84259-8_14

[CJJ21b] Choudhuri, A.R., Jain, A., Jin, Z.: SNARGs for P from LWE. In: FOCS 2021 (2021)

[CL18] Canetti, R., Lichtenberg, A.: Certifying trapdoor permutations, revisited. In: Beimel, A., Dziembowski, S. (eds.) TCC 2018. LNCS, vol. 11239, pp. 476–506. Springer, Cham (2018). https://doi.org/10.1007/978-3-030-03807-6_18

[CM01] Cryan, M., Miltersen, P.B.: On pseudorandom generators in NC^0. In: Sgall, J., Pultr, A., Kolman, P. (eds.) MFCS 2001. LNCS, vol. 2136, pp. 272–284. Springer, Heidelberg (2001). https://doi.org/10.1007/3-540-44683-4_24

[COS20] Chiesa, A., Ojha, D., Spooner, N.: FRACTAL: post-quantum and transparent recursive proofs from holography. In: Canteaut, A., Ishai, Y. (eds.) EUROCRYPT 2020. LNCS, vol. 12105, pp. 769–793. Springer, Cham (2020). https://doi.org/10.1007/978-3-030-45721-1_27

[CPW23] Chakraborty, S., Prabhakaran, M., Wichs, D.: A map of witness maps: new definitions and connections. In: Boldyreva, A., Kolesnikov, V. (eds.) PKC 2023. LNCS, vol. 13941, pp 635–662. Springer, Cham (2023). https://doi.org/10.1007/978-3-031-31371-4_22

[DFH12] Damgård, I., Faust, S., Hazay, C.: Secure two-party computation with low communication. In: Cramer, R. (ed.) TCC 2012. LNCS, vol. 7194, pp. 54–74. Springer, Heidelberg (2012). https://doi.org/10.1007/978-3-642-28914-9_4

[DGI+19] Döttling, N., Garg, S., Ishai, Y., Malavolta, G., Mour, T., Ostrovsky, R.: Trapdoor hash functions and their applications. In: Boldyreva, A., Micciancio, D. (eds.) CRYPTO 2019. LNCS, vol. 11694, pp. 3–32. Springer, Cham (2019). https://doi.org/10.1007/978-3-030-26954-8_1

[DGKV22] Devadas, L., Goyal, R., Kalai, Y., Vaikuntanathan, V.: Rate-1 non-interactive arguments for batch-NP and applications. In: FOCS 2022 (2022)

[DN02] Damgård, I., Nielsen, J.B.: Perfect hiding and perfect binding universally composable commitment schemes with constant expansion factor. In: Yung, M. (ed.) CRYPTO 2002. LNCS, vol. 2442, pp. 581–596. Springer, Heidelberg (2002). https://doi.org/10.1007/3-540-45708-9_37

[DRS04] Dodis, Y., Reyzin, L., Smith, A.: Fuzzy extractors: how to generate strong keys from biometrics and other noisy data. In: Cachin, C., Camenisch, J.L. (eds.) EUROCRYPT 2004. LNCS, vol. 3027, pp. 523–540. Springer, Heidelberg (2004). https://doi.org/10.1007/978-3-540-24676-3_31

[FLS90] Feige, U., Lapidot, D., Shamir, A.: Multiple non-interactive zero knowledge proofs based on a single random string (extended abstract). In: FOCS 1990 (1990)

[GGPR13] Gennaro, R., Gentry, C., Parno, B., Raykova, M.: Quadratic span programs and succinct NIZKs without PCPs. In: Johansson, T., Nguyen, P.Q. (eds.) EUROCRYPT 2013. LNCS, vol. 7881, pp. 626–645. Springer, Heidelberg (2013). https://doi.org/10.1007/978-3-642-38348-9_37

[GMR85] Goldwasser, S., Micali, S., Rackoff, C.: The knowledge complexity of interactive proof-systems (extended abstract). In: STOC 1985 (1985)

[Gol00] Goldreich, O.: Candidate one-way functions based on expander graphs. IACR Cryptol. ePrint Arch. (2000)

[GOS06] Groth, J., Ostrovsky, R., Sahai, A.: Perfect non-interactive zero knowledge for NP. In: Vaudenay, S. (ed.) EUROCRYPT 2006. LNCS, vol. 4004, pp. 339–358. Springer, Heidelberg (2006). https://doi.org/10.1007/11761679_21

[GOS12] Groth, J., Ostrovsky, R., Sahai, A.: New techniques for non-interactive zero-knowledge. J. ACM 59(3), 1–35 (2012)

[GR13] Goldreich, O., Rothblum, R.D.: Enhancements of trapdoor permutations. J. Cryptol. 26(3), 484–512 (2013)

[Gro10] Groth, J.: Short pairing-based non-interactive zero-knowledge arguments. In: Abe, M. (ed.) ASIACRYPT 2010. LNCS, vol. 6477, pp. 321–340. Springer, Heidelberg (2010). https://doi.org/10.1007/978-3-642-17373-8_19

[Gro16] Groth, J.: On the size of pairing-based non-interactive arguments. In: Fischlin, M., Coron, J.-S. (eds.) EUROCRYPT 2016. LNCS, vol. 9666, pp. 305–326. Springer, Heidelberg (2016). https://doi.org/10.1007/978-3-662-49896-5_11

[GSWW22] Garg, R., Sheridan, K., Waters, B., Wu, D.J.: Fully succinct batch arguments for np from indistinguishability obfuscation. In: Kiltz, E., Vaikuntanathan, V. (eds.) TCC 2022. LNCS, vol. 13747, pp. 526–555. Springer, Cham (2022). https://doi.org/10.1007/978-3-031-22318-1_19

[GW11] Gentry, C., Wichs, D.: Separating succinct non-interactive arguments from all falsifiable assumptions. In: STOC 2011 (2011)

[HJKS22] Hulett, J., Jawale, R., Khurana, D., Srinivasan, A.: SNARGS for P from sub-exponential DDH and QR. In: Dunkelman, O., Dziembowski, S. (eds.) EUROCRYPT 2022. LNCS, vol. 13276, pp. 520–549. Springer, Cham (2022). https://doi.org/10.1007/978-3-031-07085-3_18

[HLOV11] Hemenway, B., Libert, B., Ostrovsky, R., Vergnaud, D.: Lossy encryption: constructions from general assumptions and efficient selective opening chosen ciphertext security. In: Lee, D.H., Wang, X. (eds.) ASIACRYPT 2011. LNCS, vol. 7073, pp. 70–88. Springer, Heidelberg (2011). https://doi.org/10.1007/978-3-642-25385-0_4

[JJ21] Jain, A., Jin, Z.: Non-interactive zero knowledge from sub-exponential DDH. In: Canteaut, A., Standaert, F.-X. (eds.) EUROCRYPT 2021. LNCS, vol. 12696, pp. 3–32. Springer, Cham (2021). https://doi.org/10.1007/978-3-030-77870-5_1

[JLS21] Jain, A., Lin, H., Sahai, A.: Indistinguishability obfuscation from well-founded assumptions. In: STOC 2021 (2021)

[JLS22] Jain, A., Lin, H., Sahai, A.: Indistinguishability obfuscation from LPN over $\mathbb{F}_p$, DLIN, and PRGs in NC^0. In: Dunkelman, O., Dziembowski, S. (eds.) EUROCRYPT 2022. LNCS, vol. 13275, pp. 670–699. Springer, Cham (2022). https://doi.org/10.1007/978-3-031-06944-4_23

[KLVW23] Kalai, Y.T., Lombardi, A., Vaikuntanathan, V., Wichs, D.: Boosting batch arguments and RAM delegation. In: STOC (2023)

[KMY20] Kitagawa, F., Matsuda, T., Yamakawa, T.: NIZK from SNARG. In: Pass, R., Pietrzak, K. (eds.) TCC 2020. LNCS, vol. 12550, pp. 567–595. Springer, Cham (2020). https://doi.org/10.1007/978-3-030-64375-1_20

[KPY19] Kalai, Y.T., Paneth, O., Yang, L.: How to delegate computations publicly. In: STOC (2019)

[KVZ21] Kalai, Y.T., Vaikuntanathan, V., Zhang, R.Y.: Somewhere statistical soundness, post-quantum security, and SNARGs. In: Nissim, K., Waters, B. (eds.) TCC 2021. LNCS, vol. 13042, pp. 330–368. Springer, Cham (2021). https://doi.org/10.1007/978-3-030-90459-3_12

[Lin17] Lin, H.: Indistinguishability obfuscation from SXDH on 5-linear maps and locality-5 PRGs. In: Katz, J., Shacham, H. (eds.) CRYPTO 2017. LNCS, vol. 10401, pp. 599–629. Springer, Cham (2017). https://doi.org/10.1007/978-3-319-63688-7_20

[Lip13] Lipmaa, H.: Succinct non-interactive zero knowledge arguments from span programs and linear error-correcting codes. In: Sako, K., Sarkar, P. (eds.) ASIACRYPT 2013. LNCS, vol. 8269, pp. 41–60. Springer, Heidelberg (2013). https://doi.org/10.1007/978-3-642-42033-7_3

[LPWW20] Libert, B., Passelègue, A., Wee, H., Wu, D.J.: New constructions of statistical NIZKs: dual-mode DV-NIZKs and more. In: Canteaut, A., Ishai, Y. (eds.) EUROCRYPT 2020. LNCS, vol. 12107, pp. 410–441. Springer, Cham (2020). https://doi.org/10.1007/978-3-030-45727-3_14

[LT17] Lin, H., Tessaro, S.: Indistinguishability obfuscation from trilinear maps and block-wise local PRGs. In: Katz, J., Shacham, H. (eds.) CRYPTO 2017. LNCS, vol. 10401, pp. 630–660. Springer, Cham (2017). https://doi.org/10.1007/978-3-319-63688-7_21

[Mic95] Micali, S.: Computationally-sound proofs. In: Proceedings of the Annual European Summer Meeting of the Association of Symbolic Logic (1995)

[MST03] Mossel, E., Shpilka, A., Trevisan, L.: On ε-biased generators in NC^0. In: FOCS 2003 (2003)

[OW14] O'Donnell, R., Witmer, D.: Goldreich's PRG: evidence for near-optimal polynomial stretch. In: CCC 2014 (2014)

[PHGR13] Parno, B., Howell, J., Gentry, C., Raykova, M.: Pinocchio: nearly practical verifiable computation. In: IEEE Symposium on Security and Privacy (2013)

[PS19] Peikert, C., Shiehian, S.: Noninteractive zero knowledge for NP from (plain) learning with errors. In: Boldyreva, A., Micciancio, D. (eds.) CRYPTO 2019. LNCS, vol. 11692, pp. 89–114. Springer, Cham (2019). https://doi.org/10.1007/978-3-030-26948-7_4

[PW08] Peikert, C., Waters, B.: Lossy trapdoor functions and their applications. In: STOC 2008 (2008)

[QRW19] Quach, W., Rothblum, R.D., Wichs, D.: Reusable designated-verifier NIZKs for all NP from CDH. In: Ishai, Y., Rijmen, V. (eds.) EUROCRYPT 2019. LNCS, vol. 11477, pp. 593–621. Springer, Cham (2019). https://doi.org/10.1007/978-3-030-17656-3_21

[Set20] Setty, S.: Spartan: efficient and general-purpose zkSNARKs without trusted setup. In: Micciancio, D., Ristenpart, T. (eds.) CRYPTO 2020. LNCS, vol. 12172, pp. 704–737. Springer, Cham (2020). https://doi.org/10.1007/978-3-030-56877-1_25

[Üna23] Ünal, A.: Worst-case subexponential attacks on PRGs of constant degree or constant locality. In: Hazay, C., Stam, M. (eds.) EUROCRYPT 2023. LNCS, vol. 14004, pp. 25–54. Springer, Cham (2023). https://doi.org/10.1007/978-3-031-30545-0_2

[WW22] Waters, B., Wu, D.J.: Batch arguments for NP and more from standard bilinear group assumptions. In: Dodis, Y., Shrimpton, T. (eds.) CRYPTO, 2022, LNCS, vol. 13508, pp. 433–463. Springer, Cham (2022). https://doi.org/10.1007/978-3-031-15979-4_15

Lattice-Based Succinct Arguments
from Vanishing Polynomials
(Extended Abstract)

Valerio Cini[1]($\boxtimes$), Russell W. F. Lai[2], and Giulio Malavolta[3]

[1] AIT Austrian Institute of Technology, Vienna, Austria
valerio.cini@ait.ac.at
[2] Aalto University, Espoo, Finland
[3] Max Planck Institute for Security and Privacy, Bochum, Germany

Abstract. Succinct arguments allow a prover to convince a verifier of the validity of any statement in a language, with minimal communication and verifier's work. Among other approaches, lattice-based protocols offer solid theoretical foundations, post-quantum security, and a rich algebraic structure. In this work, we present some new approaches to constructing efficient lattice-based succinct arguments. Our main technical ingredient is a new commitment scheme based on *vanishing polynomials*, a notion borrowed from algebraic geometry. We analyse the security of such a commitment scheme, and show how to take advantage of the additional algebraic structure to build new lattice-based succinct arguments. A few highlights amongst our results are:
(i) The first recursive folding (i.e. Bulletproofs-like) protocol for linear relations with *polylogarithmic* verifier runtime. Traditionally, the verifier runtime has been the efficiency bottleneck for such protocols (regardless of the underlying assumptions).
(ii) The first verifiable delay function (VDF) based on lattices, building on a recently introduced sequential relation.
(iii) The first lattice-based *linear-time prover* succinct argument for NP, in the preprocessing model. The soundness of the scheme is based on (knowledge)-k-R-ISIS assumption [Albrecht et al., CRYPTO'22].

1 Introduction

A succinct non-interactive argument of knowledge (SNARK) [30,35] allows a prover to convince a verifier of the validity of an NP relation. The argument is said to be *succinct* if the size of the proof and the runtime of the verifier are sublinear in (or ideally independent of) the time needed to check the validity

V. Cini was funded by the Austrian Science Fund (FWF) and netidee SCIENCE grant P31621-N38 (PROFET).
G. Malavolta was partially funded by the German Federal Ministry of Education and Research (BMBF) in the course of the 6GEM research hub under grant number 16KISK038 and by the Deutsche Forschungsgemeinschaft (DFG, German Research Foundation) under Germany's Excellence Strategy - EXC 2092 CASA - 390781972.

H. Handschuh and A. Lysyanskaya (Eds.): CRYPTO 2023, LNCS 14082, pp. 72–105, 2023.
https://doi.org/10.1007/978-3-031-38545-2_3

of the witness. Due to these strong efficiency requirements, SNARKs for NP have become a cornerstone of modern cryptography: They count a large array of applications [8,11,14,18,27,31] and have recently found their way into real-world systems in the context of blockchain-based cryptocurrencies [8,11,14,18,27,31].

A promising approach for constructing efficient SNARKs is to leverage the algebraic structure offered by computational problems in lattice-based cryptography [2,3,5,12,13,16,24]. Compared to other approaches (see Sect. 1.2 for a detailed discussion), lattice-based SNARKs offer many desirable properties: (1) They are conjectured to be secure against quantum attacks, (ii) are based on computational problems with solid theoretical foundations, and (iii) have a rich algebraic structure, allowing to prove many interesting statements "natively", i.e. without needing to run the relation through an expensive Karp reduction.

In spite of these promising properties, lattice-based SNARKs are still somewhat limited compared to competing approaches. In particular, known lattice-based schemes suffer from (at least) one of the following limitations:

- They require the verifier to hold some information secret from the prover, i.e. they are in the designated-verifier settings [12,13,24].
- They have a non-succinct verifier, whose runtime is at least linear in the size of the relation [3,5,16].
- They have a slow prover runtime, i.e. quartic [2] in the size of the relation.

In this work, we propose new techniques for lattice-based SNARKs that allow us to overcome these barriers, making lattice-based SNARKs qualitatively closer (and, in some aspects, superior) to other approaches.

1.1   Our Results

We present new algebraic techniques that allow us to overcome traditional limitations of lattice-based SNARKs. Our central technical ingredient is a new lattice-based commitment scheme based on *vanishing polynomials*, an object borrowed from algebraic geometry. The security of our commitment is based on the vanishing Short Integer Solution (vSIS) problem, a variant of the well-known SIS problem that we introduce in this work. We then show how to exploit the additional algebraic structure of vSIS to obtain new results for lattice-based succinct arguments. In more details, our contributions can be summarized as follows.

(1) The Vanishing-SIS Problem. We introduce the vSIS problem, a variant of the standard SIS over rings, which asks to find a polynomial with short coefficients which vanishes at the given point(s). We show that vSIS is no easier than the k-R-ISIS problem, a recently introduced family of problems [2]. We also show that vSIS can be explained as a natural generalisation of the search NTRU problem. We propose a worst-case to average-case reduction and a reduction from search NTRU, both conditioning on the hardness of decision NTRU.

(2) New Commitments Based on vSIS. We show that the vSIS problem immediately implies the existence of a commitment scheme with useful algebraic properties which are key to our new results in succinct arguments:

- Succinct: The size of the commitment key and the commitment are logarithmic in the size of the input. In particular, this implies that the commitment is also a collision-resistant hash function with very short key.
- Homomorphic: The commitment is (bounded) linearly homomorphic and multiplicatively homomorphic for a constant number of multiplications.
- Foldable: We show that the commitment can be "folded" (in the sense of folding arguments, e.g. Bulletproofs [16]) in such a way that the folded commitment key retains a succinct representation. Loosely speaking, this allows us to combine the two halves of the committed value and simultaneously half the size of the input *and* the size of the commitment key.

(3) Simple Method for Proving Quadratic Relations. Exploiting the multiplicatively homomorphic property of vSIS commitments, we show a simple method for reducing the task of proving quadratic relations to that of proving linear relations, with only additive quasi-linear overhead in prover time. As an example, to prove that $\langle \mathbf{x}_0, \mathbf{x}_1 \rangle = y$, the prover commits to the polynomials $\bar{p}_{\mathbf{x}_0}(V) = \sum_i x_{0,i} \cdot V^{-i}$ and $p_{\mathbf{x}_1}(V) = \sum_j x_{1,j} \cdot V^j$ as $\bar{c}_{\mathbf{x}_0}$ and $c_{\mathbf{x}_1}$ respectively, and proves the linear relations that the commitments are well-formed. Then, the prover proves that the product $\bar{c}_{\mathbf{x}_0} \cdot c_{\mathbf{x}_1}$, which the verifier can compute themself, is a commitment to a polynomial whose constant term is y, which is again a linear relation. Instantiating with succinct arguments for linear relations with quasi-linear-time prover, we obtain succinct arguments for quadratic relations also with quasi-linear-time prover.

(4a) New Folding Protocols for Structured SIS. The first kind of linear relations that we consider are *structured SIS relations* (roughly) of the form

$$\begin{pmatrix} \mathbf{A} & & & & \\ \mathbf{B} & \mathbf{A} & & & \\ & \mathbf{B} & \ddots & & \\ & & \ddots & \mathbf{A} & \\ & & & \mathbf{B} & \\ \mathbf{C}_1 & \mathbf{C}_2 & \dots & \mathbf{C}_n \end{pmatrix} \cdot \mathbf{x} = \mathbf{y} \bmod q \qquad \text{and} \qquad ||\mathbf{x}|| \approx 0$$

where $\mathbf{C}_1, \dots, \mathbf{C}_n$ conform to certain foldable structure. For such relations, we obtain SNARKs with transparent setup, quasi-linear time prover, and poly-logarithmic time verifier (*without* preprocessing), in the random oracle model.[1] The main technical ingredient that enables this result is a new Bulletproof-like folding protocol for *foldable* linear relations, where the verifier runtime is *polylog-arithmic* in the length of the relation. Prior folding protocols had a *linear-time*

---

[1] The interactive variant can be proven secure without random oracles.

verifier [3,5,16], including those based on the discrete logarithm problem [15,19], with the exception of [20] where the verifier computation is proportional to the square root of the length of the relation.

(4b) Optimised Knowledge-based Protocols for SIS. Next, we consider *unstructured SIS relations* of the form "$\mathbf{M} \cdot \mathbf{x} = \mathbf{y} \bmod q$ and $\|\mathbf{x}\| \approx 0$". For these relations, we obtain SNARKs with quasi-linear time prover and polylogarithmic time verifier after preprocessing, based on the recently introduced (knowledge-)k-R-ISIS assumption [2]. This improves upon previous schemes which do not natively support proving modular arithmetic relations [2] and require at least a quadratic-time prover [2,7].

(5) Applications. Putting everything together, we obtain SNARKs for quadratic relations with quasi-linear-time prover and polylogarithmic-time verifier (after preprocessing for the unstructured case). We highlight two particular instances.

First, we obtain SNARKs for proving "$\mathbf{M} \cdot \mathbf{x} = \mathbf{y} \bmod q$ and $\mathbf{x}$ is *exactly binary*". In particular, applying the structured instantiation on the recently introduced SIS-based sequential relations [32], we obtain the first lattice-based verifiable delay functions (VDF). Prior lattice-based schemes [17,22,34,40] for exact SIS relations[2] are not succinct.

Second, we obtain SNARKs for rank-1 constraint satisfiability (R1CS). Prior lattice-based schemes [2,7] have at least quadratic-time prover.

1.2 Related Work

There is a vast amount of literature on SNARKs for different classes of relations. We do not attempt to survey all existing works here, but rather provide a high-level overview of various approaches and discuss in details those that are closely related to our work.

Pairing-based. To date, the most efficient and feature-rich SNARKs are constructed over *bilinear pairing groups* (e.g. [28]) with a trusted setup. Typically, they are publicly verifiable and have simple verification algorithms consisting of a constant amount of pairing-product equations. Moreover, pairing-based SNARKs offer a rich algebraic structures that is known to enable proof batching [20,33] and efficient recursive composition [10].

Hash-based. Another approach to build SNARKs is to compile an information-theoretic proof system, e.g. a probabilistically checkable proof (PCP) [30,35] or an interactive oracle proof (IOP), via a vector commitment scheme. Since the

---

[2] Not counting those for more general relations.

vector commitment is usually instantiated with a Merkle-hash tree in the random oracle (RO) model, we call this the hash-based approach. A major difference between pairing-based and hash-based SNARKs, from both theoretical and practical perspectives, is the algebraic structure of the verification algorithm. The reliance of hash-based SNARKs on an RO makes recursive composition challenging, since an RO is typically instantiated with a hash function of high multiplicative degree. On the flip side, hash-based SNARKs can be shown to be post-quantum secure [21].

Lattice-based. Finally, we discuss *lattice-based* approaches to build SNARKs. Until recently, lattice-based SNARKs required the verifier to keep a secret state hidden from the prover, i.e. they are in the designated verifier settings [24,29]. Excitingly, recent development sees two emerging paradigms for constructing publicly verifiable SNARKs, both of which we improve upon in this work.

The first line of work [3,5,16] studies lattice-based folding protocols which, as discussed above, give quasi-linear-time prover SNARKs in the random oracle model. However, due to lack of preprocessing support, the verifier complexity in folding protocols has always been *linear* in the size of the relation. In this work, we work around this barrier by considering structured relations which retain their foldable structures after folding, and obtain the first folding protocols with a polylogarithmic-time verifier.

Another line of work [2,7] constructs publicly verifiable SNARKs in the preprocessing model. At the core of these constructions are functional commitment schemes which allow to succinctly prove that a committed vector $\mathbf{x}$ satisfies $f(\mathbf{x}) = \mathbf{y}$ for low-degree polynomials [2] or even unbounded-depth circuits [7]. To this end, we propose a construction with *quasi-linear*-time prover using similar techniques, while in [2,7] the prover has at least quadratic complexity. We remark that while the recent work of Wee and Wu [39] constructs functional commitments for circuits, their scheme does not support preprocessing and therefore has inefficient verifier.

1.3 Subsequent Work

We have been informed that a recent result [4] shows a counterexample that morally invalidates the knowledge version of the assumption introduced in [2]. Although this is a strong indication that some algorithms may not be captured by the security model that some of our schemes (e.g. those presented in Sect. 7) are proven against, it does not imply a direct attack against any of our schemes. Furthermore, even in light of these recent findings, we believe that our security proofs are meaningful as *sanity checks*, for the same reason as proofs in other unsound models, such as the random oracle model or the generic group model, are also meaningful.

2   Technical Overview

We provide a high-level overview of the techniques that we develop in this work. First, we present our main new technical ingredient that is at the center of our results, namely a new commitment based on vanishing-SIS. Then we show how arguments for vanishing-SIS commitments can be efficiently composed into an argument for binary-satisfiability of both structured and unstructured linear relations. Finally, we describe our new succinct arguments in both the structured and unstructured settings, and present some immediate applications.

Throughout this overview, we will work with a cyclotomic field $\mathcal{K} = \mathbb{Q}(\zeta)$ where ζ is a root of unity of some prime order ρ, its ring of integers $\mathcal{R} = \mathbb{Z}[\zeta]$, and the quotient rings $\mathcal{R}_q := \mathcal{R}/q\mathcal{R}$ for different values of $q \in \mathbb{N}$. Ring elements will be represented by their coefficient embedding and the norm of a ring element is defined accordingly. Readers not familiar with these objects can treat $\mathcal{K} = \mathbb{Q}$ and $\mathcal{R} = \mathbb{Z}$, which suffices in most places.

2.1   Vanishing-SIS Commitments

The main technical ingredient behind of our results is a new family of commitment schemes for committing to short vectors $\mathbf{x} \in \mathcal{R}^d$ and companion argument systems for proving that the committed vector is in fact a bit string, i.e. $\mathbf{x} \in \{0, 1\}^d$. In their simplest form, the commitment key is a single random element $v \leftarrow_\$ \mathcal{R}_q^\times$, where $\mathcal{R}_q^\times$ is the set of invertible elements in $\mathcal{R}_q$. To commit to a short $\mathbf{x} \in \mathcal{R}^d$, we interpret $\mathbf{x}$ as the coefficients of a degree-d polynomial $p_\mathbf{x}(V)$ without a constant term, and compute the commitment as the evaluation of $p_\mathbf{x}$ at the point v modulo q, i.e.

$$p_\mathbf{x}(V) = \sum_{i=1}^{d} x_i \cdot V^i \qquad \text{and} \qquad c = p_\mathbf{x}(v) \bmod q.$$

We refer to this family of commitment schemes as the vanishing short integer solution (vSIS) commitments, for reasons that will become clear shortly. The binding property of the vSIS commitment above is based on the following vSIS assumption which we introduce in this work.

Definition 1 (vSIS, Informal). *Given a random point $v \leftarrow_\$ \mathcal{R}_q^\times$, it is hard to find a degree-d polynomial $p = \sum_{i=0}^{d} p_i \cdot V^i \in \mathcal{R}[V]$ with short coefficients such that $p(v) = 0 \bmod q$. In other words, p is a short element in $\mathcal{I}(v)$, the ideal (lattice) of polynomials vanishing at the given point v.*

In general, the vSIS assumption could be parametrised by a set $\mathcal{G}$ of (multivariate) monomials[3] over $\mathcal{R}$, where the task is to find a short linear combination $(p_g)_{g \in \mathcal{G}}$ such that $\sum_{g \in \mathcal{G}} p_g \cdot g(\mathbf{v}) = 0 \bmod q$. To gain confidence in its validity, we show that the vSIS assumptions are implied by the k-R-ISIS assumptions

---

[3] Or rational functions in general.

introduced in [2]. For certain parameter regimes (although *not* the ones that we need), we show that the vSIS problem is as hard as the search NTRU problem, conditioned on the hardness of the decision NTRU problem. For more details, we refer the reader to Sect. 4 and the full version of this work.

The vSIS commitment schemes have nice homomorphic properties. For starters, they are clearly linearly homomorphic, similarly to the standard SIS-based commitments. More importantly for us, they are also bounded *multiplicatively homomorphic*: If c_f and c_g commit to the polynomials f and g respectively, then $c_f \cdot c_g \mod q$ commits to the polynomial $f \cdot g$. An elementary fact that will be particularly useful later, is that if $g(V) = f(V^{-1})$, then the constant term of $f \cdot g$ is given by the inner-product of the coefficients of f and g.

Proof of Binary-Satisfiability of Linear Relations. As a warm-up, we outline the construction of a succinct argument system for a prover to convince a verifier that a vector $\mathbf{x} \in \mathcal{R}^d$ satisfies

$$\mathbf{M} \cdot \mathbf{x} = \mathbf{y} \mod q_0 \qquad \text{and} \qquad \mathbf{x} \in \{0,1\}^d.$$

As building blocks, we will use succinct argument systems for SIS relations with soundness gaps, i.e. they are complete and sound for relations of the form

$$\mathbf{M} \cdot \mathbf{x} = \mathbf{y} \mod q_0 \qquad \text{and} \qquad ||\mathbf{x}|| \approx 0$$

but the constraints on the shortness of $\mathbf{x}$ differ. That is, we will turn succinct arguments for showing that $\mathbf{x}$ satisfying a linear relation is short, into an argument for showing the $\mathbf{x}$ is *exactly binary*. While this may seem like a technicality, this *proof of binariness* will be crucial for our later applications, and can be generalised to prove arbitrary quadratic relations. Later in this overview, we will also show how to instantiate the required building blocks.

The common reference string of our argument system contains a random vector $\mathbf{h} \in \mathcal{R}_{q_1}^d$ and a vSIS commitment key $v \in \mathcal{R}_{q_2}^\times$, where $q_0 \ll q_1 \ll q_2$ and the purpose of $\mathbf{h}$ will become clear later. For $\mathbf{x} \in \mathcal{R}^d$ and $\mathbf{w} = (\mathbf{w}_-, \mathbf{w}_+) \in \mathcal{R}^{2d}$, define the (Laurent) polynomials

$$\bar{p}_{\mathbf{x}}(V) := p_{\mathbf{h}\circ\mathbf{x}}(V^{-1}) \qquad \text{and} \qquad \tilde{p}_{\mathbf{w}}(V) := p_{\mathbf{w}_-}(V^{-1}) + p_{\mathbf{w}_+}(V)$$

where $\mathbf{h} \circ \mathbf{x}$ denotes the Hadamard (component-wise) product of the two vectors. The argument proceeds as follows:

(i) The prover reveals the following "complementary" vSIS commitments to $\mathbf{x}$:

$$c_{\mathbf{x}} := p_{\mathbf{x}}(v) \mod q_2 \qquad \text{and} \qquad \bar{c}_{\mathbf{x}} := \bar{p}_{\mathbf{x}}(v) \mod q_2.$$

(ii) The prover then proves the following relations:

$$\mathbf{M} \cdot \mathbf{x} = \mathbf{y} \mod q_0,$$

$$\exists\, \mathbf{x} \in \mathcal{R}^d, \quad p_{\mathbf{x}}(v) = c_{\mathbf{x}} \mod q_2, \quad \text{and} \quad ||\mathbf{x}|| \approx 0. \qquad (1)$$

$$\bar{p}_{\mathbf{x}}(v) = \bar{c}_{\mathbf{x}} \mod q_2,$$

$$\exists\, \mathbf{w} \in \mathcal{R}^{2d}, \quad \tilde{p}_{\mathbf{w}}(v) = c_{\mathbf{x}} \cdot (\bar{c}_{\mathbf{x}} - \bar{p}_1(v)) \mod q_2 \quad \text{and} \quad ||\mathbf{w}|| \approx 0. \qquad (2)$$

Since $p_\mathbf{x}(v)$, $\bar{p}_\mathbf{x}(v)$, and $\tilde{p}_\mathbf{w}(v)$ can be computed as linear functions evaluated at the monomials expansion of v, Eqs. (6) and (2) can be proven by using argument systems for SIS relations, as required above.

The interesting bit of our protocols is that, even though the the underlying arguments for the SIS relation have soundness gaps, the verifier of our protocol will be convinced that $\mathbf{x}$ is *exactly* binary. First, from the knowledge soundness of the argument for Eq. (1), the verifier is convinced that there exists a candidate short vectors $\hat{\mathbf{x}}$ and $\hat{\mathbf{w}}$ satisfying Eq. (1) and Eq. 2 respectively. From $\hat{\mathbf{x}}$, one could derive a short vector $\hat{\mathbf{u}} = (\hat{\mathbf{u}}_-, \hat{u}_0, \hat{\mathbf{u}}_+) \in \mathcal{R}^{2d+1}$ encoding

$$\hat{p}_{\hat{\mathbf{u}}}(V) := p_\mathbf{x}(V) \cdot \bar{p}_{\mathbf{x}-\mathbf{1}}(V) = p_\mathbf{x}(V) \cdot p_{\mathbf{h}\circ(\mathbf{x}-\mathbf{1})}(V^{-1}).$$

Clearly, $\hat{p}_{\hat{\mathbf{u}}}(v) = c_\mathbf{x} \cdot (\bar{c}_\mathbf{x} - \bar{p}_\mathbf{1}(v)) \bmod q_2$. This means that $\tilde{p}_{\hat{\mathbf{w}}}(V) - \hat{p}_{\hat{\mathbf{u}}}(V)$ is a polynomial with short coefficients which vanishes at v. Furthermore, notice that $\tilde{p}_{\hat{\mathbf{w}}}$ does not have a constant term, while the constant term $\hat{u}_0$ of $\hat{p}_{\hat{\mathbf{u}}}$ is given by the inner-product

$$\hat{u}_0 = \langle \mathbf{x}, \mathbf{h} \circ (\mathbf{x}-\mathbf{1}) \rangle = \sum_{i=1}^{d} h_i \cdot \underbrace{x_i \cdot (x_i - 1)}_{=0 \text{ iff } x_i \in \{0,1\}}.$$

Let us first establish that $\hat{u}_0$ must indeed be 0. This is an easy reduction to the vSIS, since it would otherwise yield a non-zero short solution to a vSIS problem, which we assume to be hard to find. However, we are not yet done, since the fact that $\hat{u}_0 = 0$ *does not* imply that all of its summands are also zero (which is what we need to ensure that $\mathbf{x}$ is binary). This is where the vector $\mathbf{h}$ comes into play, using a technique first introduced in [2]: Suppose $\hat{u}_0 = 0$, then we also have $\hat{u}_0 = \sum_{i=1}^{d} h_i \cdot x_i \cdot (x_i - 1) = 0 \bmod q_1$. If $\mathbf{x}$ is not binary, the vector $\mathbf{x} \circ (\mathbf{x} - \mathbf{1})$ would be a short non-zero solution to the RingSIS instance given by $\mathbf{h}$ over $\mathcal{R}_{q_1}$.

2.2   Efficient Proofs for SIS Relations

In the above proof of binary-satisfiability of linear relations, the prover and verifier computation costs are dominated by the costs of the succinct arguments for SIS relations with soundness gaps. Here we discuss two approaches in the literature, and how we can improve on both fronts using the algebraic properties of our vSIS-based commitment scheme.

Approach I: Folding Protocols. (Lattice-based) Bulletproofs [3,5,16] are interactive arguments with quasi-linear time prover, and can be made non-interactive using the Fiat-Shamir transform in the random oracle model. It is based on the technique of iteratively "folding" the relation into a smaller one until a trivial relation is derived. Recall that in Bulletproofs the prover wants to convince the verifier that they know a short vector $\mathbf{x}$ satisfying

$$\mathbf{M} \cdot \mathbf{x} = \mathbf{y} \bmod q \qquad \text{and} \qquad \|\mathbf{x}\| \approx 0.$$

Let $(\mathbf{M}, \mathbf{x}, \mathbf{y}) = (\mathbf{M}^{(0)}, \mathbf{x}^{(0)}, \mathbf{y}^{(0)})$. The protocol consists of $\ell + 1$ rounds, where in the i-th round the two parties "fold" the relation represented by $(\mathbf{M}^{(i)}, \mathbf{y}^{(i)})$ into another represented by $(\mathbf{M}^{(i+1)}, \mathbf{y}^{(i+1)})$ where the dimension of $\mathbf{M}^{(i+1)}$ is half that of $\mathbf{M}^{(i)}$. Correspondingly, the prover folds its witness $\mathbf{x}^{(i)}$ into $\mathbf{x}^{(i+1)}$. After ℓ such folding steps, a constant-size relation $(\mathbf{M}^{(\ell)}, \mathbf{y}^{(\ell)})$ is reached and the prover simply sends the satisfying witness $\mathbf{x}^{(\ell)}$ over to the verifier.

In more detail, for $0 \leq i < \ell$, the i-th of the first ℓ rounds of the protocol goes as follows. The parties split $\mathbf{M}^{(i)}$ into two halves as $\mathbf{M}^{(i)} = (\mathbf{M}_L^{(i)}, \mathbf{M}_R^{(i)})$ and the prover splits $\mathbf{x}^{(i)} = (\mathbf{x}_L^{(i)}, \mathbf{x}_R^{(i)})$. The prover sends the cross terms

$$\mathbf{y}_{LR}^{(i)} = \langle \mathbf{M}_L^{(i)}, \mathbf{x}_R^{(i)} \rangle \bmod q \qquad \text{and} \qquad \mathbf{y}_{RL}^{(i)} = \langle \mathbf{M}_R^{(i)}, \mathbf{x}_L^{(i)} \rangle \bmod q.$$

The verifier sends a random challenge $r_i \leftarrow_{\!\$} S$ sampled from some challenge set $S \subseteq \mathcal{R}^\times$. Both parties fold $(\mathbf{M}^{(i)}, \mathbf{y}^{(i)})$ into

$$(\mathbf{M}^{(i+1)}, \mathbf{y}^{(i+1)}) := (\mathbf{M}_L^{(i)} + \mathbf{M}_R^{(i)} \cdot r_i^{-1}, \mathbf{y}_{RL}^{(i)} \cdot r_i^{-1} + \mathbf{y}_{LR}^{(i)}) \bmod q,$$

and the prover folds $\mathbf{x}$ into $\mathbf{x}^{(i+1)} = \mathbf{x}_L^{(i)} + \mathbf{x}_R^{(i)} \cdot r_i$. At the ℓ-th (i.e. last) round, the prover simply sends $\mathbf{x}^{(\ell)}$ and the verifier checks that $\mathbf{x}^{(\ell)}$ is short and satisfies $\langle \mathbf{M}^{(\ell)}, \mathbf{x}^{(\ell)} \rangle = \mathbf{y}^{(\ell)} \bmod q$.

It can been shown [3,5,6,16] that the protocol satisfies knowledge soundness, and furthermore it is easy to see that the prover runs in time quasi-linear in the length of the witness. However, a major drawback of this approach is that the verifier computation is also quasi-linear for general linear relations $\mathbf{M}$, and it cannot be preprocessed due to the interactive nature of the scheme.

Polylogarithmic Verifier for Structured Relations. In this work, we observe that, while we cannot hope to reduce the verifier complexity for general matrices $\mathbf{M}$, for suitably structured $\mathbf{M}$ the verification can be sped up to run in time polylogarithmic in the witness length. As an example, the simplest $\mathbf{M}$ with the required structure is a vector consisting of powers of an element $v \in \mathcal{R}_q^\times$, i.e.

$$\mathbf{M} = (v \ v^2 \ \ldots \ v^d) \bmod q.$$

Importantly, $\mathbf{M} \cdot \mathbf{x} = p_{\mathbf{x}}(v) \bmod q$ is the vSIS commitment of $\mathbf{x}$ with commitment key v. This observation allows us to prove the knowledge of a preimage of a vSIS commitment via the above protocol with polylogarithmic verifier complexity.

To see why this is the case, it suffices to observe that the verifier complexity is dominated by the computation of the matrix $\mathbf{M}^{(\ell)}$, which is obtained by successive foldings of the starting matrix $\mathbf{M}^{(0)}$. Plugging in the structured relation, we can see that at each iteration the matrix evolves into

$$\mathbf{M}^{(i+1)} = \mathbf{M}_L^{(i)} + \mathbf{M}_R^{(i)} \cdot r_i^{-1} = \left(v \ v^2 \ \ldots \ v^{d_i/2} \right) + \left(v^{d_i/2+1} \ v^{d_i/2+2} \ \ldots \ v^{d_i} \right) \cdot r_i^{-1}$$

$$= \left(v \ v^2 \ \ldots \ v^{d_i/2} \right) \cdot \left(1 + v^{d_i/2} \cdot r_i^{-1} \right) \bmod q$$

where d_i is the input length at the i-th iteration. Recursing over all iterations, we obtain that the final matrix $\mathbf{M}^{(\ell)}$ is defined as

$$\mathbf{M}^{(\ell)} = \prod_{i=0}^{\ell-1} \left(1 + v^{2^{\ell-i-1}} \cdot r_i^{-1}\right) \bmod q,$$

which can be computed in time polynomial in ℓ, i.e. polylogarithmic in d. In Sects. 5 and 6, we extend the above structured folding technique in three ways:

(i) We identify a general class of "foldable" (block-)matrices for which the verifier computation can be made polylogarithmic in the number of columns.

(ii) By modifying the Bulletproofs protocol with techniques borrowed from another folding protocol of Pietrzak [38], we are able to support foldable matrices with an arbitrary (i.e. non-power-of-2) number of columns, without breaking the foldable structure.[4]

(iii) Borrowing techniques from [38] again, we can make the verifier computation *also* polylogarithmic in the number of rows of $\mathbf{M}$, for $\mathbf{M}$ with repeating block-bidiagonals, if $\mathbf{y}$ is also foldable.

Approach II: Pre-Processing (Knowledge-Based) Protocols. The second approach for lattice-based arguments for SIS relation is the recent work of [2], which is based on a newly recently introduced (knowledge-)k-R-ISIS assumption. In this protocol, the verifier computation can be preprocessed such that the online verification time is polylogarithmic in the relation size. However, a major drawback of this approach is that the public parameters size and the prover complexity are at least quadratic in the relation size. Let us recall (a somewhat simplified version of) the commit-and-prove protocol of [2] specialised to the case of SIS (i.e. linear) relations. The public parameters consists of

$$\mathbf{A}, \mathbf{t}, \mathbf{v}, \mathbf{h}, \left(\mathbf{A}^{-1}(\mathbf{t} \cdot (g \cdot \bar{g}')(\mathbf{v}))\right)_{g,g' \in \mathcal{G}, g \neq g'}$$

for some set of monomials $\mathcal{G}$, where $\mathbf{A}, \mathbf{t}, \mathbf{v}$ are random over $\mathcal{R}_{q_2}$, $\mathbf{h}$ is a random vector over $\mathcal{R}_{q_1}$, $\bar{g} := 1/g$ denotes the complement of g, and $\mathbf{A}^{-1}(\mathbf{t} \cdot g(\mathbf{v}))$ denotes a short preimage $\mathbf{u}_g$ satisfying $\mathbf{A} \cdot \mathbf{u}_g = \mathbf{t} \cdot g(\mathbf{v}) \bmod q_2$. To prove that

$$\mathbf{M} \cdot \mathbf{x} = \mathbf{y} \text{ (without mod)} \qquad \text{and} \qquad \|\mathbf{x}\| \approx 0,$$

commit to $\mathbf{x}$ as $c_\mathbf{x} := \sum_{g \in \mathcal{G}} x_g \cdot g(\mathbf{v}) \bmod q_2$ and derive a short vector $\mathbf{u}$ satisfying

$$\mathbf{A} \cdot \mathbf{u} = \mathbf{t} \cdot \mathbf{h}^\mathsf{T} \cdot (\mathbf{M} \cdot \bar{\mathcal{G}}(\mathbf{v}) \cdot c_\mathbf{x} - \mathbf{y}) \bmod q_2,$$

where $\bar{\mathcal{G}}(\mathbf{v}) = (\bar{g}(\mathbf{v}))_{g \in \mathcal{G}}$. To compute such a short vector $\mathbf{u}$, the prover needs to perform a linear combination of $|\{g \cdot \bar{g}' : g, g' \in \mathcal{G}, g \neq g'\}|$ short vectors given in the public parameters. For $\mathcal{G} = \{V_1, \ldots, V_d\}$ chosen in [2], we have $|\{g \cdot \bar{g}' : g \neq g' \in \mathcal{G}\}| = O(d^2)$, hence the quasi-quadratic prover complexity.

---

[4] The usual technique of padding zero columns breaks the foldable structure.

Achieving Quasi-Linear Time Prover. A natural idea is to choose $\mathcal{G} = \{V, V^2, \ldots, V^d\}$ so $\mathbf{v}$ becomes a single element v. This makes

$$|\{g \cdot \bar{g}' : g, g' \in \mathcal{G}, g \neq g'\}| = |\{V^{-i}, V^i\}_{i=1}^{d-1}| = 2d - 2 = O(d).$$

Further exploiting fast multiplication algorithms for Toeplitz matrices allows us to achieve quasi-linear prover time. Notably, with this choice of $\mathcal{G}$ we have

$$c_{\mathbf{x}} = p_{\mathbf{x}}(v) \bmod q_2 \qquad \text{and} \qquad \mathbf{h}^{\mathsf{T}} \cdot \mathbf{M} \cdot (\bar{g}(v))_{g \in \mathcal{G}} = \bar{p}_{\mathbf{M}^{\mathsf{T}} \cdot \mathbf{h}}(v) \bmod q_2,$$

and $\mathbf{h}^{\mathsf{T}} \cdot \mathbf{M} \cdot (\bar{g}(V))_{g \in \mathcal{G}} \cdot c_{\mathbf{x}} - \mathbf{h}^{\mathsf{T}} \cdot \mathbf{y}$ being a polynomial with constant term 0. In the main body, we also show how to support natively modular arithmetic, by borrowing techniques from chainable functional commitments [7]. We refer the interested reader to Sect. 7 for more details.

2.3   Applications

To summarise, we have constructed succinct arguments for relations of the form

$$\mathbf{M} \cdot \mathbf{x} = \mathbf{y} \bmod q_0 \qquad \text{and} \qquad \mathbf{x} \in \{0,1\}^d$$

with quasi-linear time provers (in both the folding and the preprocessing settings). This gives a efficient and powerful building block for constructing advanced lattice-based cryptographic primitives which require proving relations of the above form. We provide a few examples below.

Lattice-based Verifiable Delay Functions. For the instantiation based on folding protocols, the verifier computation is polylogarithmic if the relation $(\mathbf{M}, \mathbf{y})$ conforms to a certain foldable structure. One example is the sequential-SIS relation proposed in a recent work [32], which was used to construct proofs of sequential work (PoSW). In more details, the sequential-SIS relation proposed in their work induces the following linear relation

$$\underbrace{\begin{pmatrix} \mathbf{G} & & & \\ \mathbf{A} & \mathbf{G} & & \\ & \mathbf{A} & \ddots & \\ & & \ddots & \mathbf{G} \\ & & & \mathbf{A} \end{pmatrix}}_{\mathbf{M}} \cdot \mathbf{x} = \underbrace{\begin{pmatrix} \mathbf{z}_0 \\ 0 \\ \vdots \\ 0 \\ \mathbf{z}_T \end{pmatrix}}_{\mathbf{y}} \bmod q \qquad \text{and} \qquad \mathbf{x} \in \mathcal{R}_2^{mT}$$

for a uniformly sampled $\mathbf{A}$ and $\mathbf{z}_0$. The PoSW construction in [32] falls short of giving verifiable delay functions (VDF) due to the soundness gap in lattice-based folding protocols. By embedding the $\mathbb{Z}_2$ coefficients of $\mathbf{x} \in \mathcal{R}_2^{mT}$ into $\mathbf{x}' \in \{0,1\}^{mT\varphi(\rho)}$, and plugging in the structured folding protocol constructed in this work, we immediately get the first construction of lattice-based VDFs.

Efficient Lattice-based SNARKs for NP. Recall that our results ultimately rely on the observation that the inner-product of $\mathbf{x}$ and $\mathbf{y}$ is encoded as the constant term of the polynomial $p_\mathbf{x} \cdot \bar{p}_\mathbf{y}$. In the above, we used this to encode the vectors $\mathbf{x}$ and $\mathbf{y} := \mathbf{h} \circ (\mathbf{x} - \mathbf{1})$ for proving binariness. The same idea can be used to prove general quadratic relations.

Consider the NP-complete rank-1 constraint satisfiability (R1CS) relation which is of the form

$$\exists\, \mathbf{x}, \ (\mathbf{A} \cdot \mathbf{x}) \circ (\mathbf{B} \cdot \mathbf{x}) = \mathbf{C} \cdot \mathbf{x} \bmod q$$

where some entries of $\mathbf{x}$ are publicly known. To prove knowledge of $\mathbf{x}$, the prover computation roughly goes as follows. First, they compute

$$\mathbf{a} := \mathbf{A} \cdot \mathbf{x}, \qquad \mathbf{b} := \mathbf{B} \cdot \mathbf{x}, \qquad \text{and} \qquad \mathbf{c} := \mathbf{C} \cdot \mathbf{x}.$$

They then commit to $(\mathbf{x}, \mathbf{h} \circ \mathbf{a}, \mathbf{b}, \mathbf{c})$ as $(c_\mathbf{x}, \bar{c}_\mathbf{a}, c_\mathbf{b}, c_\mathbf{c})$, and prove that the commitments are consistent. Finally, they prove that the constant term in (the polynomial underlying) $\bar{c}_\mathbf{a} \cdot c_\mathbf{b}$ is identical to $\langle \mathbf{h}, \mathbf{c} \rangle$ for $\mathbf{c}$ committed in $c_\mathbf{c}$.

3 Preliminaries

Let $\lambda \in \mathbb{N}$ denote the security parameter, and $\mathsf{poly}(\lambda)$ and $\mathsf{negl}(\lambda)$ the set of all polynomials and negligible functions in λ respectively. Denote the empty string by ϵ. For a function f which may depend on λ and other parameters, we write $O_\lambda(f) := f \cdot \mathsf{poly}(\lambda)$ to hide fixed polynomial factors in λ. For matrices $\mathbf{A}$ and $\mathbf{B}$ with the same dimensions, write $\begin{bmatrix} \mathbf{A} \\ \mathbf{B} \end{bmatrix}_{\backslash 3} := \begin{pmatrix} \mathbf{A} & & \\ \mathbf{B} & \mathbf{A} & \\ & \mathbf{B} & \mathbf{A} \\ & & \mathbf{B} \end{pmatrix}$ and define $\begin{bmatrix} \mathbf{A} \\ \mathbf{B} \end{bmatrix}_{\backslash n}$

analogously for $n \in \mathbb{N}$. If S is a set and $\mathcal{D}$ is a distribution over S, write $\mathcal{D} \sim S$.

3.1 Cyclotomic Rings

Let $\mathcal{K} = \mathbb{Q}(\zeta)$ be a cyclotomic field, where ζ is a root of unity of order $\rho = \mathsf{poly}(\lambda)$, and $\mathcal{R} = \mathbb{Z}[\zeta]$ be its ring of integers. If ρ is a power of 2 (resp. prime power), $\mathcal{R}$ is called a power-of-2 (resp. prime power) cyclotomic ring. For $q \in \mathbb{N}$, define the quotient ring $\mathcal{R}_q := \mathcal{R}/q\mathcal{R}$. We denote by $\mathcal{R}^\times$ and $\mathcal{R}_q^\times$ the sets of units in $\mathcal{R}$ and $\mathcal{R}_q$ respectively. An element $a = \sum_{i=0}^{\rho-1} a_i \cdot \zeta^i \in \mathcal{R}$ (or $\mathcal{R}_q$) is represented by its coefficients $(a_0, \ldots, a_{\rho-1}) \in \mathbb{Z}^\rho$ (or $\mathbb{Z}_q^\rho$). The (infinity) norm of $a \in \mathcal{R}$ (or $\mathcal{R}_q$) is taken as $||a|| := \max_{i=0}^{\rho-1}(|a_i|)$, where in the case of $a_i \in \mathbb{Z}_q$ the balanced representation is taken, i.e. $a_i \in \{-\lceil q/2 \rceil + 1, \ldots, \lfloor q/2 \rfloor\}$. For a vector $\mathbf{a} = (a_1, \ldots, a_n) \in \mathcal{R}^n$, $||\mathbf{a}|| := \max_{i=1}^n ||a_i||$. For a matrix $\mathbf{A} = (A_{i,j})_{i,j}$, the max-norm is taken, i.e. $||\mathbf{A}|| = \max_{i,j} ||A_{i,j}||$. The ring expansion factor of $\mathcal{R}$ is defined as $\gamma_\mathcal{R} := \max_{a,b \in \mathcal{R}} ||a \cdot b|| / (||a|| \cdot ||b||)$. For power-of-2 and prime-power $\mathcal{R}$, it is known that $\gamma_\mathcal{R} \leq 2\varphi(\rho)$, where φ is Euler's totient function. A set $S \subseteq \mathcal{R}$ is said to be subtractive if $a - b \in \mathcal{R}^\times$ for any distinct $a, b \in S$. For a prime-power $\mathcal{R}$, it is known that $S := \{(\zeta^i - 1)/(\zeta - 1) : i \in [\mathsf{rad}(\rho) - 1]\} \subset \mathcal{R}^\times$ is subtractive, where $\mathsf{rad}(\rho)$ denotes the radical. Note that $||r|| = 1$ for all $r \in S$.

3.2 Lattice Trapdoors

In our constructions based on the (knowledge-)k-R-ISIS assumption, we will make use of lattice trapdoor algorithms. Let η, m, q, β be functions of λ. Let (TrapGen, SampD, SampPre) be PPT algorithms parametrised by (η, m, q, β) with the following syntax and properties [23,25,36]:

- $(\mathbf{D}, \mathsf{td}) \leftarrow \mathsf{TrapGen}(1^\lambda)$ generates a matrix $\mathbf{D} \in \mathcal{R}_q^{\eta \times m}$ and a trapdoor td. The distribution of $\mathbf{D}$ is statistically close to the uniform distribution over $\mathcal{R}_q^{\eta \times m}$.
- $\mathbf{u} \leftarrow \mathsf{SampD}(1^\lambda)$ samples a vector $\mathbf{u} \in \mathcal{R}^m$. For any $(\mathbf{D}, \mathbf{v}) \in \mathcal{R}_q^{\eta \times m} \times \mathcal{R}_q^\eta$ and $\mathbf{u} \leftarrow \mathsf{SampD}(1^\lambda)$ subject to $\mathbf{D}\mathbf{u} = \mathbf{v} \bmod q$, it is guaranteed that $\|\mathbf{u}\| \le \beta$ with overwhelming probability. Furthermore, the following distributions are statistically close:

$$\left\{ \begin{array}{l} (\mathbf{D}, \mathbf{u}, \mathbf{v}) : \\ \quad \mathbf{D} \leftarrow_{\$} \mathcal{R}_q^{\eta \times m} \\ \quad \mathbf{u} \leftarrow \mathsf{SampD}(1^\lambda) \\ \quad \mathbf{v} = \mathbf{D}\mathbf{u} \bmod q \end{array} \right\} \quad \text{and} \quad \left\{ \begin{array}{l} (\mathbf{D}, \mathbf{u}, \mathbf{v}) : \\ \quad \mathbf{D} \leftarrow_{\$} \mathcal{R}_q^{\eta \times m} \\ \quad \mathbf{v} \leftarrow_{\$} \mathcal{R}_q^\eta \\ \quad \mathbf{u} \leftarrow \mathsf{SampD}(1^\lambda) : \mathbf{D}\mathbf{u} = \mathbf{v} \bmod q \end{array} \right\}$$

- $\mathbf{u} \leftarrow \mathsf{SampPre}(\mathsf{td}, \mathbf{v})$ inputs a target vector $\mathbf{v} \in \mathcal{R}_q^\eta$ and samples a vector $\mathbf{u} \in \mathcal{R}^m$. For $(\mathbf{D}, \mathsf{td}) \leftarrow \mathsf{TrapGen}(1^\lambda)$, it is guaranteed that $\mathbf{D} \cdot \mathbf{u} = \mathbf{v} \bmod q$ and $\|\mathbf{u}\| \le \beta$ with overwhelming probability. Furthermore, for any $\mathbf{v} \in \mathcal{R}_q^\eta$, the following distributions are statistically close:

$$\left\{ \begin{array}{l} (\mathbf{D}, \mathbf{u}) : \\ \quad (\mathbf{D}, \mathsf{td}) \leftarrow \mathsf{TrapGen}(1^\lambda) \\ \quad \mathbf{u} \leftarrow \mathsf{SampPre}(\mathsf{td}, \mathbf{v}) \end{array} \right\} \quad \text{and} \quad \left\{ \begin{array}{l} (\mathbf{D}, \mathbf{u}) : \\ \quad (\mathbf{D}, \mathsf{td}) \leftarrow \mathsf{TrapGen}(1^\lambda) \\ \quad \mathbf{u} \leftarrow \mathsf{SampD}(1^\lambda) : \mathbf{D}\mathbf{u} = \mathbf{v} \bmod q \end{array} \right\}$$

3.3 Presumed Hard Problems

The Short Integer Solution (SIS) problem was introduced in the seminal work of Ajtai [1]. It asks to find a short vector in the kernel of a given random matrix modulo q. In this work, we consider the generalisation of SIS over $\mathcal{R}$ and the k-R-ISIS problem introduced in [2].

Definition 2 (R-SIS Assumption). *Let $m, q, \beta^* \in \mathbb{N}$ depend on λ. The Ring-SIS (or R-SIS) problem, denoted $\text{R-SIS}_{\mathcal{R},m,q,\beta^*}$, is: Given $\mathbf{h} \leftarrow_{\$} \mathcal{R}_q^m$, find $\mathbf{u} \in \mathcal{R}^m$ such that $0 < \|\mathbf{u}\| \le \beta^*$ and $\mathbf{h}^\mathsf{T}\mathbf{u} \equiv \mathbf{0} \bmod q$. We write $\mathsf{Adv}_{\mathcal{R},m,q,\beta^*,\mathcal{A}}^{r\text{-}sis}(\lambda)$ for the advantage of any algorithm $\mathcal{A}$ in solving $\text{R-SIS}_{\mathcal{R},\eta,m,q,\beta^*}$. The $\text{R-SIS}_{\mathcal{R},\eta,m,q,\beta^*}$ assumption states that, for any PPT adversary $\mathcal{A}$, $\mathsf{Adv}_{\mathcal{R},m,q,\beta^*,\mathcal{A}}^{r\text{-}sis}(\lambda) \le \mathsf{negl}(\lambda)$.*

We state a streamlined version of the (knowledge) k-R-ISIS[5] assumptions defined in [2] with two main changes: (i) To improve readability, our definitions of the assumptions do not impose admissibility constraints on parameters. Instead,

---

[5] In [2], the assumptions over modules were separately called (knowledge-)k-M-ISIS.

we mention these admissibility parameters separately outside of the definitions. (ii) We assume that all preimages $\mathbf{u}_g$ given to the adversary are sampled from the same distribution conditioned on different constraints. The original definitions [2] are more general in that they allow a different distribution per constraint.

Definition 3 (k-R-ISIS Assumptions). *Let $\eta, m, q, \beta, \beta^* \in \mathbb{N}$, $\mathcal{G} \cup \{g^*\}$ be a set of w-variate Laurent monomials, $\mathcal{T} \sim \mathcal{R}_q^\eta$, and $\mathcal{D} \sim \mathcal{R}^m$, all dependent on λ. Write $\mathsf{pp} := (\mathcal{R}, \eta, m, w, q, \beta, \beta^*, \mathcal{G}, g^*, \mathcal{D}, \mathcal{T})$. The k-R-ISIS$_{\mathsf{pp}}$ assumption states that, for any PPT adversary $\mathcal{A}$, $\mathsf{Adv}_{\mathsf{pp},\mathcal{A}}^{k\text{-}r\text{-}sis}(\lambda) \leq \mathsf{negl}(\lambda)$, where $\mathsf{Adv}_{\mathsf{pp},\mathcal{A}}^{k\text{-}r\text{-}sis}(\lambda) :=$*

$$
\Pr \left[
\begin{array}{l}
\mathbf{D} \cdot \mathbf{u}_{g^*} \equiv \mathbf{t} \cdot s^* \cdot g^*(\mathbf{v}) \bmod q \\[4pt]
\wedge\ 0 < \|(\mathbf{u}_{g^*}, s^*)\| \leq \beta^*
\end{array}
\left|
\begin{array}{l}
\mathbf{D} \leftarrow_\$ \mathcal{R}_q^{\eta \times m};\ \mathbf{t} \leftarrow_\$ \mathcal{T};\ \mathbf{v} \leftarrow_\$ (\mathcal{R}_q^\times)^w \\[4pt]
\mathbf{u}_g \leftarrow_\$ \mathcal{D} : \mathbf{D} \cdot \mathbf{u}_g = \mathbf{t} \cdot g(\mathbf{v}) \bmod q,\ \forall\ g \in \mathcal{G} \\[4pt]
(s^*, \mathbf{u}_{g^*}) \leftarrow \mathcal{A}\left(\mathbf{D}, \mathbf{t}, \mathbf{v}, \{\mathbf{u}_g\}_{g \in \mathcal{G}}\right)
\end{array}
\right.
\right].
$$

Individual parameters are omitted when they are clear from the context.

Definition 4 (Knowledge k-R-ISIS Assumptions). *Let $\eta, m, q, \alpha^*, \beta, \beta^* \in \mathbb{N}$, $\mathcal{G}$ be a set of w-variate Laurent monomials, $\mathcal{T} \sim \mathcal{R}_q^\eta$, and $\mathcal{D} \sim \mathcal{R}^m$, all dependent on λ. Let $\mathcal{Z}$ be a PPT auxiliary input generator. Write $\mathsf{pp} := (\mathcal{R}, \eta, m, w, q, \alpha^*, \beta, \beta^*, \mathcal{G}, \mathcal{D}, \mathcal{T}, \mathcal{Z})$. The knowledge k-R-ISIS$_{\mathsf{pp}}$ assumption states that for any PPT adversary $\mathcal{A}$ there exists a PPT extractor $\mathcal{E}_\mathcal{A}$ such that $\mathsf{Adv}_{\mathsf{pp},\mathcal{A}}^{k\text{-}r\text{-}isis}(\lambda) \leq \mathsf{negl}(\lambda)$, where $\mathsf{Adv}_{\mathsf{pp},\mathcal{A}}^{k\text{-}r\text{-}isis}(\lambda) :=$*

$$
\Pr \left[
\begin{array}{l}
\mathbf{D} \cdot \mathbf{u} \equiv \mathbf{t} \cdot c \bmod q \\[4pt]
\wedge\ 0 < \|\mathbf{u}\| \leq \beta^* \\[4pt]
\wedge\ \neg \left(
\begin{array}{l}
c \equiv \sum_{g \in \mathcal{G}} x_g \cdot g(\mathbf{v}) \bmod q \\[4pt]
\wedge\ \|(x_g)_{g \in \mathcal{G}}\| \leq \alpha^*
\end{array}
\right)
\end{array}
\left|
\begin{array}{l}
\mathbf{D} \leftarrow_\$ \mathcal{R}_q^{\eta \times m};\ \mathbf{t} \leftarrow_\$ \mathcal{T};\ \mathbf{v} \leftarrow_\$ (\mathcal{R}_q^\times)^w \\[4pt]
\mathbf{u}_g \leftarrow_\$ \mathcal{D} : \mathbf{D} \cdot \mathbf{u}_g = \mathbf{t} \cdot g(\mathbf{v}) \bmod q,\ \forall\ g \in \mathcal{G} \\[4pt]
\mathsf{pp} := (\mathbf{D}, \mathbf{t}, \mathbf{v}, \{\mathbf{u}_g\}_{g \in \mathcal{G}});\ \mathsf{aux} \leftarrow \mathcal{Z}(\mathsf{pp}) \\[4pt]
\left((c, \mathbf{u}), (x_g)_{g \in \mathcal{G}}\right) \leftarrow (\mathcal{A} \| \mathcal{E}_\mathcal{A})\,(\mathsf{pp}, \mathsf{aux})
\end{array}
\right.
\right]
$$

where $(\mathcal{A} \| \mathcal{E}_\mathcal{A})$ means that $\mathcal{A}$ and $\mathcal{E}_\mathcal{A}$ are run on the same input including the randomness, and $(c, \mathbf{u})$ and $(x_g)_{g \in \mathcal{G}}$ are the outputs of $\mathcal{A}$ and $\mathcal{E}_\mathcal{A}$ respectively. Individual parameters are omitted when they are clear from the context.

For both assumptions to be meaningful, we always consider $m > \eta$.[6] For non-triviality, we want $g^* \notin \mathcal{G}$ and $\mathbf{t} \neq \mathbf{0}$ with overwhelming probability. To avoid complications of giving the adversary short vectors in the kernel of $\mathbf{D}$, we do not consider the case where $\mathcal{G}$ is a multiset – all monomials in $\mathcal{G}$ are distinct.[7] To avoid SIS attacks in the image space, we want $1/|\mathcal{R}_q^\times| = \mathsf{negl}(\lambda)$.

For the knowledge assumption to be plausible, we would like that $\alpha^* \geq \beta^*$, and for $\mathbf{t} \leftarrow_\$ \mathcal{T}$, $1/|\langle \mathbf{t} \rangle| = \mathsf{negl}(\lambda)$ and $|\langle \mathbf{t} \rangle|/|\mathcal{R}_q^\eta| = \mathsf{negl}(\lambda)$ with overwhelming probability. Furthermore, to avoid easy instances of ideal-SVP (relevant when $\eta = 1$), we would like the problem of finding short elements in $\{s \in \mathcal{R} : \mathbf{t} \cdot s = \mathbf{0} \bmod q\}$ to be hard.

---

[6] In [2], m is considered to be large enough so that the leftover hash lemma holds. However, smaller m only makes the problems harder.

[7] In [2, Definition 22], monomials in $\mathcal{G}$ and g^* are further required to be independent of $\mathcal{R}$. We discuss in Sect. 4.2 why we believe that this restriction can be lifted.

3.4   Argument Systems

We recall the definition of argument systems which allow a prover to convince a verifier that a relation is satisfiable. Formally, we define a (family of) relation(s) $\Psi (= (\Psi_\lambda)_{\lambda \in \mathbb{N}})$ to be polynomial-time-decidable triples of the form $(\mathsf{pp}, \mathsf{stmt}, \mathsf{wit})$, corresponding to the public parameters of the argument system, the statement, and the witness respectively. We consider a statement $\mathsf{stmt} = (\mathsf{stmt_{off}}, \mathsf{stmt_{on}})$ to consist an offline part $\mathsf{stmt_{off}}$ which is potentially preprocessable and an online part $\mathsf{stmt_{on}}$. For any fixed public parameters pp, we define the (sub-)relation $\Psi_{\mathsf{pp}} := \{ (\mathsf{stmt}, \mathsf{wit}) : (\mathsf{pp}, \mathsf{stmt}, \mathsf{wit}) \in \Psi \}$ and the corresponding language $\mathcal{L}_{\mathsf{pp}} := \{ \mathsf{stmt} : \exists \, \mathsf{wit}, (\mathsf{stmt}, \mathsf{wit}) \in \Psi_{\mathsf{pp}} \}$. We focus on relations where the public parameters pp can be efficiently generated, and denote such a generator by Gen_Ψ. We suppress pp when it is the empty string.

Definition 5 (Arguments). *A (preprocessing) argument system consists of PPT algorithms* (Setup, PreVerify) *and PPT interactive algorithms* (Prove, Verify) *with the following syntax:*

- $\mathsf{crs} \leftarrow \mathsf{Setup}(1^\lambda, \mathsf{pp})$: *Input some public parameters* pp *and generate a common reference string* crs.
- $\mathsf{crs_{stmt_{off}}} \leftarrow \mathsf{PreVerify}(\mathsf{crs}, \mathsf{stmt_{off}})$: *Preprocess the statement* $\mathsf{stmt_{off}}$. *Systems not supporting preprocessing are captured by having a trivial preverification, i.e.* $\mathsf{crs_{stmt_{off}}} = (\mathsf{crs}, \mathsf{stmt_{off}})$.
- $(\mathsf{tx}, b) \leftarrow \langle \mathsf{Prove}(\mathsf{crs}, \mathsf{stmt}, \mathsf{wit}), \mathsf{Verify}(\mathsf{crs_{stmt_{off}}}, \mathsf{stmt_{on}}) \rangle$: *An interactive protocol where the prover tries to convince the verifier about the statement* stmt. *The protocol produces a transcript* tx *and ends with the verifier outputting a bit* $b \in \{0, 1\}$. *The transcript* tx *is suppressed from the output when it is not needed. In the case where the protocol is non-interactive, i.e. the prover sends a single message, then we split the protocol into two PPT algorithms* $\pi \leftarrow \mathsf{Prove}(\mathsf{crs}, \mathsf{stmt}, \mathsf{wit})$ *and* $b \leftarrow \mathsf{Verify}(\mathsf{crs_{stmt_{off}}}, \mathsf{stmt_{on}}, \pi)$, *where* π *is referred to as a proof.*

Definition 6 (Completeness). *An argument system Π is said to be complete for Ψ if for all adversaries $\mathcal{A}$*

$$
\Pr \left[
\begin{array}{c|c}
(\mathsf{stmt}, \mathsf{wit}) \in \Psi_{\mathsf{pp}} & \mathsf{pp} \leftarrow \mathsf{Gen}_\Psi(1^\lambda); \; \mathsf{crs} \leftarrow \mathsf{Setup}(1^\lambda, \mathsf{pp}) \\
 & (\mathsf{stmt}, \mathsf{wit}) \leftarrow \mathcal{A}(\mathsf{pp}, \mathsf{crs}) \\
\wedge \; b = 0 & \mathsf{crs_{stmt_{off}}} \leftarrow \mathsf{PreVerify}(\mathsf{crs}, \mathsf{stmt_{off}}) \\
 & b \leftarrow \langle \mathcal{P}(\mathsf{crs}, \mathsf{stmt}, \mathsf{wit}), \mathcal{V}(\mathsf{crs_{stmt_{off}}}, \mathsf{stmt_{on}}) \rangle
\end{array}
\right] \leq \mathsf{negl}(\lambda) .
$$

Definition 7 (Special Soundness). *An argument system Π is said to be public-coin if each message sent by $\mathcal{V}$ is sampled from a public distribution independent of the messages sent by* Prove. *A transcript* tx *is said to be accepting for* $(\mathsf{pp}, \mathsf{stmt})$ *if* $(\mathsf{tx}, 1)$ *is in the output space of* $\langle \mathcal{P}, \mathcal{V}(\mathsf{crs_{stmt_{off}}}, \mathsf{stmt_{on}}) \rangle$ *where* $\mathsf{crs_{stmt_{off}}} \in \mathsf{PreVerify}(\mathsf{Setup}(1^\lambda, \mathsf{pp}), \mathsf{stmt})$. *Suppose $\mathcal{V}$ sends ℓ messages throughout the execution of* $\langle \mathcal{P}, \mathcal{V} \rangle$. *A tree T is said to be a $(k_1, \ldots, k_\ell)$-tree of accepting transcripts for* $(\mathsf{pp}, \mathsf{stmt})$ *if it is of (node-)depth $(\ell + 1)$, each node is labelled by* *a prover message, each depth-i node has exactly k_i children each connected by an edge labelled by a distinct verifier message, and the labels on each root-to-leaf path give an accepting transcript for (pp, stmt). The argument system Π is said to be $(k_1, \ldots, k_\ell)$-special-sound for Ψ if there exists a polynomial-time extractor $\mathcal{E}$ which on input a $(k_1, \ldots, k_\ell)$-tree of accepting transcripts for (pp, stmt) outputs* wit* *such that* (stmt, wit*) $\in \Psi_{pp}$.

Definition 8 (Knowledge Soundness). *Let $\kappa = \kappa(\lambda)$ denote the knowledge error. An argument system Π is said to be κ-knowledge-sound for Ψ if for all PPT $\mathcal{P}^*$ there exists an expected polynomial-time extractor $\mathcal{E}_{\mathcal{P}^*}$ such that for all PPT adversaries $\mathcal{A}$ the following is at most κ:*

$$
\Pr\left[
\begin{array}{c}
(\mathsf{stmt}, \mathsf{wit}^*) \notin \Psi_{\mathsf{pp}} \\
\wedge\ b = 1
\end{array}
\left|
\begin{array}{l}
\mathsf{pp} \leftarrow \mathsf{Gen}_\Psi(1^\lambda);\ \ \mathsf{crs} \leftarrow \mathsf{Setup}(1^\lambda, \mathsf{pp}) \\
(\mathsf{stmt}, \mathsf{wit}) \leftarrow \mathcal{A}(\mathsf{pp}, \mathsf{crs}) \\
\mathsf{crs}_{\mathsf{stmt}_{\mathsf{off}}} \leftarrow \mathsf{PreVerify}(\mathsf{crs}, \mathsf{stmt}_{\mathsf{off}}) \\
(\mathsf{wit}^*, b) \leftarrow \langle (\mathcal{P}^* | \mathcal{E}_{\mathcal{P}^*})(\mathsf{crs}, \mathsf{stmt}, \mathsf{wit}), \mathcal{V}(\mathsf{crs}_{\mathsf{stmt}_{\mathsf{off}}}, \mathsf{stmt}_{\mathsf{on}}) \rangle
\end{array}
\right.
\right]
$$

The argument system Π is said to be knowledge-sound for Ψ if it is κ-knowledge-sound for Ψ for some $\kappa = \mathsf{negl}(\lambda)$.

It is known that a parallel-repetition of a $(k_1, \ldots, k_\ell)$-special-sound protocol yields a knowledge-sound protocol [6].

Note that it is common for lattice-based argument systems to have a "soundness gap": They are complete for a relation Ψ, but special- or knowledge-sound for a relaxed relation $\Psi' \supseteq \Psi$, i.e. the extracted witness wit* for (pp, stmt) may not satisfy (stmt, wit*) $\in \Psi_{\mathsf{pp}}$ but only (stmt, wit*) $\in \Psi'_{\mathsf{pp}}$.

Definition 9 (Succinctness). *An argument system Π is said to have succinct proofs (resp. succinct verifier) for Ψ if for any $\mathsf{pp} \in \mathsf{Gen}_\Psi(1^\lambda)$, $\mathsf{crs} \in \mathsf{Setup}(1^\lambda, \mathsf{pp})$, (stmt, wit) $\in \Psi_{\mathsf{pp}}$, $\mathsf{crs}_{\mathsf{stmt}_{\mathsf{off}}} \in \mathsf{PreVerify}(\mathsf{crs}, \mathsf{stmt}_{\mathsf{off}})$, the communication complexity of $\langle \mathsf{Prove}(\mathsf{crs}, \mathsf{stmt}, \mathsf{wit}), \mathsf{Verify}(\mathsf{crs}_{\mathsf{stmt}_{\mathsf{off}}}, \mathsf{stmt}_{\mathsf{on}}) \rangle$ (resp. computation complexity of $\mathsf{Verify}(\mathsf{crs}_{\mathsf{stmt}_{\mathsf{off}}}, \mathsf{stmt}_{\mathsf{on}})$) is $\mathsf{polylog}(|\mathsf{stmt}| + |\mathsf{wit}|) \cdot \mathsf{poly}(\lambda)$ where the $\mathsf{poly}(\lambda)$ factor is independent of $|\mathsf{stmt}|$ and $|\mathsf{wit}|$.*

Argument systems which are succinct, non-interactive, and knowledge-sound are known as succinct non-interactive arguments of knowledge (SNARK). Arguments whose soundness holds even against adversaries given the randomness of Setup are said to have transparent setups.

4   Vanishing Short Integer Solutions

In this section, we formalise the vanishing-SIS problems and assumptions, and discuss their relations with existing problems and assumptions. We also discuss the properties of the collision-resistant hash functions obtained immediately from the vanishing-SIS assumptions.

4.1 Definition

Definition 10 (Vanishing-SIS). *Let* $n, d, w, q, \beta \in \mathbb{N}$ *and* $\mathcal{G}$, *a set of w-variate (Laurent) monomials of individual degree at most* d, *be functions of* λ. *The* $\mathsf{vSIS}_{\mathcal{R},\mathcal{G},n,q,\beta}$ *problem is the following: Given a set* $V = \{\mathbf{v}_i\}_{i=1}^n \in (\mathcal{R}_q^\times)^w$ *of n uniformly random points in* $(\mathcal{R}_q^\times)^w$, *find a non-zero polynomial* $p \in \mathcal{R}[X_1, \ldots, X_w]$ *with monomial support[8] over* $\mathcal{G}$ *such that*

$$\forall i \in [n], \qquad p(\mathbf{v}_i) = 0 \bmod q \qquad and \qquad ||p|| \le \beta$$

where $||p||$ *is the maximum of the norm of the coefficients of p. The* $\mathsf{vSIS}_{\mathcal{R},\mathcal{G},n,q,\beta}$ *assumption states that, for any PPT adversary* $\mathcal{A}$, *the probability of* $\mathcal{A}$ *solving a uniformly random instance of* $\mathsf{vSIS}_{\mathcal{R},\mathcal{G},n,q,\beta}$ *is negligible in* λ. *Individual parameters are omitted from the subscript when they are clear from the context. If* $\mathcal{G}$ *is the set of all w-variate (Laurent) monomials of individual degree at most* d, *we denote the problem by* $\mathsf{vSIS}_{\mathcal{R},d,w,n,q,\beta}$. *To emphasise certain parameters, e.g.* $n = n^*$ *and* $w = w^*$, *we sometimes write* $\mathsf{vSIS}_{(n,w)=(n^*,w^*)}$.

Another way to phrase the problem, borrowing terminologies from algebraic geometry, is that it asks to find an element of bounded norm and degree in the ideal $\mathcal{I}(V)$ of polynomials vanishing at the set of points V. Clearly, the subset of bounded-degree polynomials in $\mathcal{I}(V)$ forms a (module) lattice. Therefore a vanishing-SIS problem can also be seen as an average-case approximate shortest vector problem (SVP) over such lattices.[9]

The connection of the vanishing-SIS problem to the standard SIS problem stems from the following simple observation: If we interpret the coefficients of a solution p as a vector $\mathbf{p}$, and write the relation in matrix form, we obtain

$$\begin{pmatrix} 1 & v_{1,1} & \cdots & v_{1,w} & \cdots & \prod_{j=1}^w v_{1,j}^{e_j} & \cdots & \prod_{j=1}^w v_{1,j}^d \\ 1 & v_{2,1} & \cdots & v_{2,w} & \cdots & \prod_{j=1}^w v_{2,j}^{e_j} & \cdots & \prod_{j=1}^w v_{2,j}^d \\ \vdots & \vdots & \ddots & \vdots & \ddots & \vdots & \ddots & \vdots \\ 1 & v_{n,1} & \cdots & v_{n,w} & \cdots & \prod_{j=1}^w v_{n,j}^{e_j} & \cdots & \prod_{j=1}^w v_{n,j}^d \end{pmatrix} \cdot \mathbf{p} = \mathbf{0} \bmod q \quad and \quad ||\mathbf{p}|| \le \beta,$$

a SIS relation with respect to a (Vandermonde-like) structured matrix.

Note that since $v_{i,j} \in \mathcal{R}_q^\times$ for all i and j, it is not important for p to be a polynomial with only non-negative powers. Laurent polynomials can be captured scaling the each i-th row of the matrix by $\prod_{j=1}^w v_{i,j}^{-e_j}$ for any desired powers $(e_1, \ldots, e_w) \in \mathbb{Z}^w$. In fact, using the matrix formulation, the scaling factors for each row could be different.

It is easy to observe that the vanishing-SIS assumption is implied by the k-R-ISIS assumption with related parameters. In the full version, we discuss this implication in more detail, show that the converse holds conditioned on a related knowledge-k-R-ISIS assumption, and explore the connections of vanishing-SIS to more established assumptions, i.e. NTRU and RingLWE.

---

[8] e.g. the monomial support of $3X_1X_2 + 2X_2^2 + 1$ is $\{X_1X_2, X_2^2, 1\}$.

[9] Interestingly, after restricting to a bounded-degree subset, we no longer have an ideal. Therefore this approximate SVP problem is not over ideal-lattices.

4.2   On Choice of Parameters

On the modulus q. Note that, for some (preferable) parameters settings, it is important for $q > d$ for the vSIS assumption to be plausible. Indeed, for example, if q is prime and is such that $q\mathcal{R}$ splits completely into $\varphi(\rho)$ ideals, then we have $v^{q-1} - 1 = 0 \bmod q$ for any $v \in \mathcal{R}$. This gives rise to trivial solutions, e.g. $p(X) = X^{q-1} - 1$, to the vSIS problem.

On the space of V. It is also important for the set of points V to be chosen over $\mathcal{R}_q^\times$ instead of $\mathcal{R}_q$. For example, consider a power-of-2 $\mathcal{R}$ and $q = 2^\ell$. The ideal $q\mathcal{R}$ splits into $q\mathcal{R} = \mathcal{I}^{\ell \cdot \varphi(\rho)}$ for some ideal $\mathcal{I}$ of (algebraic) norm $\mathcal{N}(\mathcal{I}) = 2$. Therefore, with probability $1/2$, a random element $v \leftarrow_\$ \mathcal{R}_q$ satisfies $v = 0 \bmod \mathcal{I}$ and hence $v^{\ell \cdot \varphi(\rho)} = 0 \bmod q$. This means that $p(X) = X^{\ell \cdot \phi(\rho)}$ is a solution to any vanishing-SIS over $\mathcal{R}_q$ if instances were sampled from $\mathcal{R}_q$.[10]

On the cardinality $|\mathcal{R}_q^\times|$. It is crucial that the cardinality $|\mathcal{R}_q^\times|$ is large enough so that $1/|\mathcal{R}_q^\times| = \mathsf{negl}(\lambda)$. Suppose not, then there might exist small $e \in \mathbb{N}$ such that $\{ v, v^2, \dots, v^e \}$ contains a short element modulo q. Note that the set of elements in $\mathcal{R}$ of norm at most β has cardinality $(2\beta + 1)^{\varphi(\rho)}$. If we heuristically model the multiplication-by-v map $a \mapsto a \cdot v \bmod q$ as a random permutation for $v \leftarrow_\$ \mathcal{R}_q^\times$, and if $\mathcal{R}_q^\times$ is large enough, we have some confidence to believe that small powers of v modulo q will not be short.

  In general, it appears that $|\mathcal{R}_q^\times|$ is usually quite close to $q^{\varphi(\rho)}$. We calculate this cardinality for some specific choices of q and $\mathcal{R}$. For $q = 2^\ell$ and ρ being a power of 2, we have $|\mathcal{R}_q^\times| = q^{\varphi(\rho)}/2$. For arbitrary $\mathcal{R}$ and prime $q = 1 \bmod \varphi(\rho)$, we have $|\mathcal{R}_q^\times| = (q-1)^{\varphi(\rho)}$. In either case, if $\beta \le q/4$, we have $\Pr\left[\|x\| \le \beta \mid x \leftarrow_\$ \mathcal{R}_q^\times \right] < 2^{-\varphi(\rho)}$ which is negligible in ρ.

4.3   A Family of Hash Functions with Short Keys

Similar to the standard SIS-based hash function, the vanishing-SIS assumption immediately implies the existence of a collision-resistant hash function, except that in this case the keys are very small, and could potentially be *logarithmic* in the message size. Furthermore, the hash function satisfies many desirable properties, such as (approximate) ring homomorphism.

  In more detail, for any set of points $V = \{ \mathbf{v}_i \}_{i=1}^n \subseteq ((\mathcal{R}_q^\times)^w)^n$, define

$$\mathcal{H}_V : \mathcal{R}_\beta^{(d+1)w} \to \mathcal{R}_q^n, \; \mathcal{H}_V(p) = (p(\mathbf{v}_1), \dots, p(\mathbf{v}_n)) \bmod q$$

where an input $\mathbf{p} \in \mathcal{R}_\beta^{(d+1)w}$ is interpreted, for example, as a polynomial $p \in \mathcal{R}_\beta[X_1, \dots, X_w]$ of individual degree at most d.

---

[10] This is the reason why $\mathcal{G}$ was restricted to be independent of $\mathcal{R}$ in the definition of "k-R-ISIS-admissible" parameters in [2, Definition 22]. However, since [2, Definition 23] also restricts $\mathbf{v} \in (\mathcal{R}_q^\times)^w$, the restriction on $\mathcal{G}$ appears to be redundant.

It is easy to show that this function is collision resistant by observing that $\mathcal{H}_V(p) = \mathcal{H}_V(p')$ implies

$$\forall i \in [n], \ (p - p')(\mathbf{v}_i) = 0 \bmod q \qquad \text{and} \qquad ||p - p'|| \leq \beta,$$

i.e. $p - p'$ is a solution to the vSIS instance V.

Observe that each hash function can be described by a key of size $n \cdot w \log q$ bits, and can hash messages of length $(d + 1) \cdot w \cdot \log \beta$ bits to $n \cdot \log q$ bits, where n and w could be as small as 1. As discussed in Sect. 4.1, for the vSIS assumption to be plausible for the case where q fully splits, which is desirable for efficiency, it is necessary that $q > d$. For $q = O(d)$ and $n, w, \beta = \text{poly}(\lambda)$, the key size and the message length are $O_\lambda(\log d)$ and $O_\lambda(d)$ respectively.

Similar to the standard SIS-based hash function, $\mathcal{H}_V$ is almost linearly homomorphic in the sense that

$$\mathcal{H}_V(p) + \mathcal{H}_V(p') = \mathcal{H}_V(p + p') \bmod q \qquad \text{and} \qquad ||p + p'|| \leq ||p|| + ||p'||.$$

Different from the standard SIS-based hash function, however, is that $\mathcal{H}_V$ is also almost multiplicatively homomorphic in the sense that

$$\mathcal{H}_V(p) \cdot \mathcal{H}_V(p') = \mathcal{H}_V(p \cdot p') \bmod q \quad \text{and} \quad ||p \cdot p'|| \leq (d + 1)^w \cdot ||p|| \cdot ||p'|| \cdot \gamma_\mathcal{R},$$

with multiplications taken over $\mathcal{R}_q$ and $\mathcal{R}[\mathbf{X}]$ respectively.

For our purpose of construction linear-time succinct arguments, the univariate case (i.e. $w = 1$) is the most interesting due to the exponential dependency of various parameters on w. Moreover, we notice that if $p_0(X)$ and $p_1(X)$ encode the vectors $\mathbf{p}_0$ and $\mathbf{p}_1$ respectively as their coefficients, then the product polynomial $p(X) \cdot p(X^{-1})$ has norm at most $||\mathbf{p}_0|| \cdot ||\mathbf{p}_1|| \cdot \gamma_\mathcal{R}$, and its constant term encodes the inner product $\langle \mathbf{p}_0, \mathbf{p}_1 \rangle$.

5   Foldable Structures

We define a family of monomials, polynomials, vectors, and matrices that exhibit "foldable" structures.

Definition 11 (Foldable Polynomials).   *Let $\ell \geq 0$, $k_\ell > 0$, and $k_{\ell-1}, \ldots, k_0 \geq 0$ be integers. A sequence of (monic multivariate Laurent) monomials $\mathbf{m}$[11] of length $n = \sum_{i=0}^{\ell} 2^i \cdot k_i$ (where k_i are not necessarily binary) is said to be $(k_0, k_1, \ldots, k_\ell)$-foldable if the following properties are satisfied:*

- *$\mathbf{m} = \mathbf{m}_0$ can be generated from a "seed" $\mathbf{m}_\ell$ and a "generator" $(\ell_i, \mathbf{c}_i, r_i)_{i=0}^{\ell-1}$, where $\mathbf{m}_\ell$ is a sequence of monomials of length k_ℓ, $\mathbf{c}_i$ is a sequence of monomials of length k_i, and ℓ_i, r_i are monomials, in a recursive fashion:[12]*

$$\forall i \in [\ell], \ \mathbf{m}_{i-1}^\mathsf{T} := \left(\ell_{i-1} \cdot \mathbf{m}_i^\mathsf{T} \ || \ \mathbf{c}_{i-1}^\mathsf{T} \ || \ r_{i-1} \cdot \mathbf{m}_i^\mathsf{T} \right).$$

---

[11] That is, each entry of $\mathbf{m}$ is a monic multivariate Laurent monomial.

[12] In the recursive expression, "$\cdot$" denotes the symbolic multiplication of monomials. For example, $X \cdot (X^2, X^3) = (X^3, X^4)$.

- *For all $i \in \{0, \ldots, \ell\}$, $\mathbf{m}_i$ consists of distinct monomials.*

We say that $\mathbf{m}$ is foldable if it is $(k_0, k_1, \ldots, k_\ell)$-foldable for some $(k_0, k_1, \ldots, k_\ell)$. A foldable polynomial is a polynomial whose supporting monomials can be arranged into a foldable sequence of monomials.

Note that any sequence of monomials $\mathbf{m}$ of length n is trivially $(0, \ldots, 0, n)$-foldable. However, we are most interested in sequences which are $(k_0, k_1, \ldots, k_\ell)$-foldable for small constants k_i, e.g. $k_i \in \{0, 1, 2\}$, for all $i \in \{0, \ldots, \ell\}$. Below, we state some elementary properties satisfied by foldable monomials.

Lemma 1. *Let $\mathbf{m}$ of length n be $(k_0, \ldots, k_\ell)$-foldable. Let $k^* := \max_{i=0}^{\ell} k_i$. It holds that $\ell \leq \log n < \ell + \log 2 \cdot k^*$.*

The proof of Lemma 1 is deferred to the full version. The following properties follow immediately from the definition and are stated without proof.

Lemma 2 (Chaining/Decomposition). *If $\mathbf{m}$ is foldable with seed and generator $(\mathbf{m}', \mathbf{g}')$ and $\mathbf{m}'$ is foldable with seed and generator $(\mathbf{m}'', \mathbf{g}'')$, then $\mathbf{m}$ is foldable with seed and generator $(\mathbf{m}'', \mathbf{g}''\|\mathbf{g}')$.*

Lemma 3 (Closure under Hadamard Product). *If $\mathbf{m}$ and $\mathbf{m}'$ are both $(k_0, k_1, \ldots, k_\ell)$-foldable with, where $\mathbf{m}$ and $\mathbf{m}'$ are supported by disjoint sets of variables and have seeds and generators*

$$(\mathbf{s}, (\ell_i, \mathbf{c}_i, r_i)_{i=0}^{\ell-1}) \qquad and \qquad (\mathbf{s}', (\ell_i', \mathbf{c}_i', r_i')_{i=0}^{\ell-1})$$

respectively, then the Hadamard product $\mathbf{m} \circ \mathbf{m}'$ is also $(k_0, k_1, \ldots, k_\ell)$-foldable with seed and generator

$$(\mathbf{s} \circ \mathbf{s}', (\ell_i \cdot \ell_i', \mathbf{c}_i \circ \mathbf{c}_i', r_i \cdot r_i')_{i=0}^{\ell-1}).$$

Next, we extend the definition of foldable monomials and polynomials to that of (block-)foldable vectors and matrices. We then give examples of such objects. The formal analysis of the lemmas are deferred to the full version.

Definition 12 (Foldable Vectors and Matrices). *A vector $\mathbf{a} = (a_1, \ldots, a_n)$ is said to be $(k_0, k_1, \ldots, k_\ell)$-foldable if there exists a $(k_0, k_1, \ldots, k_\ell)$-foldable sequence of monomials $\mathbf{m} = (m_1, \ldots, m_n)$ and a point $\mathbf{v} \in (\mathcal{R}^\times)^k$ such that $a_i = m_i(\mathbf{v})$ for all $i \in [n]$, i.e. the i-th entry of $\mathbf{a}$ is obtained by evaluating the i-th monomial in $\mathbf{m}$ at the point $\mathbf{v}$. The point $\mathbf{v}$ is said to be the evaluation point of $\mathbf{a}$. A matrix is said to be foldable if every row of it is foldable with a common evaluation point $\mathbf{v}$. A block-matrix $\mathbf{A} = (\mathbf{A}_1, \ldots, \mathbf{A}_n)$ where $\mathsf{ncol}(\mathbf{A}_i) = w$ for all $i \in [n]$ is said to be block-foldable with block-size w if, for all (i, j), the vector formed by taking the (i, j)-th entry of each of $(\mathbf{A}_1, \ldots, \mathbf{A}_n)$ is foldable.*

Lemma 4 (Power Sequence). *For any $n \in \mathbb{N}$, express n uniquely[13] as $n = \sum_{i=0}^{\ell} 2^i \cdot k_i$ with $k_i \in \{1, 2\}$ for $i \in \{0, \ldots, \ell\}$. Then for any $v \in \mathcal{R}$, the vector $\mathbf{v}^{\mathsf{T}} = (v, v^2, \ldots, v^n)$. is $(k_0, k_1, \ldots, k_\ell)$-foldable. Generalising, for $w \in \mathbb{N}$, the vector $\mathbf{v}^{\mathsf{T}} = (v, v^2, \ldots, v^{wn})$ is $(k_0, k_1, \ldots, k_\ell)$-block-foldable with block-size w.*

Lemma 5 (Balanced Power Sequence). *For any $n \in \mathbb{N}$, express n uniquely as $n = \sum_{i=0}^{\ell} 2^i \cdot k_i$ with $k_\ell = 1$ and $k_i \in \{0, 1\}$ for all $i \in \{0, \ldots, \ell - 1\}$. Then for any $v \in \mathcal{R}$, the following vector is $(0, k_0, k_1, \ldots, k_\ell)$-foldable:*

$$\mathbf{v}^{\mathsf{T}} = (v^{-n}, \ldots, v^{-2}, v^{-1}, v, v^2, \ldots, v^n).$$

Lemma 6 (Compression Vector). *For any integers $\ell \geq 0$, $k_\ell > 0$ and $k_0, \ldots, k_{\ell-1} \geq 0$, let X_{i,j_i} be independent variables for $i \in \{0, \ldots, \ell\}$ and $j_i \in \{0, \ldots, k_i\}$. The seed and generator*

$$((X_{\ell,1}, \ldots, X_{\ell,k_\ell}), (1, (X_{i,1}, \ldots, X_{i,k_i}), X_{i,0})_{i=0}^{\ell-1})$$

generate a $(k_0, k_1, \ldots, k_\ell)$-foldable sequence of monomials $\mathbf{m}$. Furthermore, let $\mathbf{x} = (x_{i,j})_{i=0,j=1}^{\ell,k_i}$ be a vector over $\mathcal{R}$ with $\|\mathbf{x}\| \leq \alpha$. Let $\mathbf{h} := \mathbf{m}(\mathbf{x})$ be the foldable vector obtained by evaluating $\mathbf{m}$ at $\mathbf{x}$. It holds that $\|\mathbf{h}\| \leq \alpha^{\ell+1} \cdot \gamma_{\mathcal{R}}^\ell$.

6 Folding Protocols

We state two folding protocols Π_0^{fold} and Π_1^{fold} for bounded-norm satisfiability of (structured) linear relations which respect the foldable structures (Sect. 5) of the matrices and vectors defining the relations. Both protocols have trivial (hence transparent) setup and trivial pre-verification, i.e. $\mathsf{crs} = \Pi_b^{\mathsf{fold}}.\mathsf{Setup}(1^\lambda, \mathsf{pp}) = (1^\lambda, \mathsf{pp})$ and $\mathsf{crs}_{\mathsf{stmt}_{\mathsf{off}}} = \Pi_b^{\mathsf{fold}}.\mathsf{PreVerify}(\mathsf{crs}, \mathsf{stmt}_{\mathsf{off}}) = (\mathsf{crs}, \mathsf{stmt})$. We detail below the prove-verify protocols

$$\Pi_b^{\mathsf{fold}}.\langle \mathsf{Prove}(\mathsf{crs}, \mathsf{stmt}, \mathsf{wit}), \mathsf{Verify}(\mathsf{crs}_{\mathsf{stmt}_{\mathsf{off}}}, \mathsf{stmt}_{\mathsf{on}}) \rangle.$$

6.1 Type-0 Linear Relations

Define the relation $\Psi_0^{\mathsf{fold}} = \Psi_0^{\mathsf{fold}}[\mathcal{R}, h_0, h_1, w, n, q_0, q_1, \alpha]$:

$$\Psi_0^{\mathsf{fold}} := \left\{ (\mathsf{pp}, ((\mathbf{A}, \mathbf{B}, \mathbf{C}, \mathbf{y}), \mathbf{z}), \mathbf{x}) : \begin{bmatrix} \mathbf{A} \\ \mathbf{B} \end{bmatrix}_{\searrow n} \cdot \mathbf{x} = \mathbf{y} \bmod q_0, \quad \text{and} \quad \|\mathbf{x}\| \leq \alpha, \right\},$$
$$\mathbf{C} \cdot \mathbf{x} = \mathbf{z} \bmod q_1,$$

$\mathcal{R}$ is a prime-power ring for a prime ≥ 5, $\mathbf{A}, \mathbf{B} \in \mathcal{R}_{q_0}^{h_0 \times w}$, $\mathbf{C} = (\mathbf{C}_1, \ldots, \mathbf{C}_n) \in \mathcal{R}_{q_1}^{h_1 \times wn}$, $\mathbf{y} \in \mathcal{R}_{q_0}^{h_0 \cdot (n+1)}$, $\mathbf{z} \in \mathcal{R}_{q_1}^{h_1}$, and $\mathbf{x} \in \mathcal{R}^{wn}$. Note that the linear constraints

---

[13] Suppose the expression is not unique, let $n = \sum_{i=0}^{\ell} 2^i \cdot k_i = \sum_{i=0}^{\ell} 2^i \cdot k_i'$ with $k_i, k_i' \in \{1, 2\}$. Let $d_i = k_i - k_i' \in \{-1, 0, 1\}$. We have $\sum_{i=0}^{\ell} 2^i \cdot d_i = 0$, which means that $d_0 = 0$ or else the LHS is odd while the RHS is even. Dividing both sides by 2, we get $\sum_{i=0}^{\ell-1} 2^i \cdot d_{i+1} = 0$. By the same argument, we have $d_1 = 0$. Repeating this for all i yields $d_i = 0$ for all $i \in \{0, \ldots, \ell\}$, a contradiction.

consist of a sparse structured part represented by a block-bidiagonal matrix and a dense part. By default, we suppress all parameters of Ψ_0^{fold} except those that we highlight. Note that the above constraints are independent of pp, therefore Ψ_0^{fold} is compatible with any parameter generator Gen. We describe Π_0^{fold} which is complete for $\Psi_0^{\text{fold}}[\alpha]$ and knowledge sound for $\Psi_0^{\text{fold}}[\alpha^*]$ for some $\alpha^* > \alpha$.

Construction. The protocol Π_0^{fold} is essentially a merge between (the lattice analogue of) Pietrzak's folding protocol [38] and the lattice-based Bulletproofs protocol [16]. Consider $n > 2$ and let $n' = \lfloor (n-1)/2 \rfloor$. Our protocol hinges on the following observation: Depending on whether n is odd or even, we have

$$\begin{bmatrix} \mathbf{A} \\ \mathbf{B} \end{bmatrix}_{\searrow n} = \left(\begin{array}{c|c} \begin{bmatrix} \mathbf{A} \\ \mathbf{B} \end{bmatrix}_{\searrow n'} \mathbf{A} & \\ \hline & \mathbf{B} \begin{bmatrix} \mathbf{A} \\ \mathbf{B} \end{bmatrix}_{\searrow n'} \end{array} \right) \quad \text{or} \quad \left(\begin{array}{c|c} \begin{bmatrix} \mathbf{A} \\ \mathbf{B} \end{bmatrix}_{\searrow n'} \mathbf{A} & \\ \hline \mathbf{B} \ \mathbf{A} & \\ \mathbf{B} & \begin{bmatrix} \mathbf{A} \\ \mathbf{B} \end{bmatrix}_{\searrow n'} \end{array} \right).$$

The protocol $\Pi_0^{\text{fold}}.\langle \text{Prove}(\text{crs}, \text{stmt}, \text{wit}), \text{Verify}(\text{crs}_{\text{stmt}_{\text{off}}}, \text{stmt}_{\text{on}}) \rangle$ consists of $\ell + 1$ rounds and makes use of the subtractive set $S \subset \mathcal{R}^\times$ mentioned in Sect. 3.1. Denote $(\mathbf{C}^{(0)}, \mathbf{x}^{(0)}, \mathbf{y}^{(0)}, \mathbf{z}^{(0)}, \alpha^{(0)}) := (\mathbf{C}, \mathbf{x}, \mathbf{y}, \mathbf{z}, \alpha)$. Express n uniquely as $n = \sum_{j=0}^{\ell} 2^j \cdot k_j$ where $k_j \in \{1, 2\}$. Note that $\mathbf{y}$ consists of $n' := n + 1 = \sum_{j=0}^{\ell-1} 2^j \cdot (k_j - 1) + 2^\ell \cdot (k_\ell + 1)$ blocks. For $i \in \{0, \ldots, \ell\}$, define $n_i := \sum_{j=i}^{\ell} 2^{j-i} \cdot k_j$ and $n_i' := \sum_{j=i}^{\ell-1} 2^{j-i} \cdot (k_j - 1) + 2^{\ell-i} \cdot (k_\ell + 1)$. Then, for $i < \ell$, the i-th round of the protocol is as follows:

- Parse $(\mathbf{C}^{(i)}, \mathbf{x}^{(i)}, \mathbf{y}^{(i)})$ as

$$(\mathbf{C}_L^{(i)}, \mathbf{C}_c^{(i)}, \mathbf{C}_R^{(i)}), \qquad (\mathbf{x}_L^{(i)}, \mathbf{x}_c^{(i)}, \mathbf{x}_R^{(i)}), \quad \text{and} \quad (\mathbf{y}_L^{(i)}, \mathbf{y}_c^{(i)}, \mathbf{y}_R^{(i)})$$

respectively where $\text{ncol}(\mathbf{C}_L^{(i)}) = \text{ncol}(\mathbf{C}_R^{(i)}) = \text{nrow}(\mathbf{x}_L^{(i)}) = \text{nrow}(\mathbf{x}_R^{(i)}) = n_i \cdot w$ and $\text{nrow}(\mathbf{y}_L^{(i)}) = \text{nrow}(\mathbf{y}_R^{(i)}) = n_i' \cdot h_0$. Note that $\text{nrow}(\mathbf{x}_c^{(i)}) = k_i$ and $\text{nrow}(\mathbf{y}_c^{(i)}) = k_i - 1$, meaning that $\mathbf{y}_c^{(i)}$ is empty when $k_i = 1$.
- $\mathcal{P}$ sends

$$\mathbf{x}_c^{(i)}, \qquad \mathbf{z}_{LR}^{(i)} := \mathbf{C}_L^{(i)} \cdot \mathbf{x}_R^{(i)} \bmod q_1, \quad \text{and} \quad \mathbf{z}_{RL}^{(i)} := \mathbf{C}_R^{(i)} \cdot \mathbf{x}_L^{(i)} \bmod q_1.$$

- $\mathcal{V}$ checks that $\|\mathbf{x}_c^{(i)}\| \leq \alpha^{(i)}$. If $k_i = 2$, $\mathcal{V}$ further checks that $(\mathbf{B} \ \mathbf{A}) \cdot \mathbf{x}_c^{(i)} = \mathbf{y}_c^{(i)} \bmod q_0$. If any of these checks fails, $\mathcal{V}$ aborts.
- $\mathcal{V}$ samples $r_i \leftarrow_{\$} S$ and sends r_i to $\mathcal{P}$.
- $\mathcal{P}$ computes the compressed witness $\mathbf{x}^{(i+1)} := \mathbf{x}_L^{(i)} + \mathbf{x}_R^{(i)} \cdot r_i$.
- $\mathcal{P}$ and $\mathcal{V}$ compute the compressed statement

$$\mathbf{C}^{(i+1)} := \mathbf{C}_L^{(i)} + \mathbf{C}_R^{(i)} \cdot r_i^{-1} \bmod q_1$$

$$\mathbf{y}^{(i+1)} := \mathbf{y}_L^{(i)} + \mathbf{y}_R^{(i)} \cdot r_i - \begin{pmatrix} \mathbf{B} \cdot r_i \\ \mathbf{0} \\ \mathbf{A} \end{pmatrix} \cdot \mathbf{x}_c^{(i)} \bmod q_0$$

$$\mathbf{z}^{(i+1)} := \mathbf{z}^{(i)} - \mathbf{C}_c^{(i)} \cdot \mathbf{x}_c^{(i)} + \mathbf{z}_{RL}^{(i)} \cdot r_i^{-1} + \mathbf{z}_{LR}^{(i)} \cdot r_i \bmod q_1$$

$$\alpha^{(i+1)} := 2 \cdot \alpha^{(i)} \cdot \gamma_{\mathcal{R}}$$

In the ℓ-th (i.e. final) round, $\mathcal{P}$ sends $\mathbf{x}^{(\ell)}$ and $\mathcal{V}$ checks that

$$\begin{bmatrix} \mathbf{A} \\ \mathbf{B} \end{bmatrix}_{\searrow k_\ell} \cdot \mathbf{x}^{(\ell)} = \mathbf{y}^{(\ell)} \bmod q_0, \qquad \text{and} \qquad \|\mathbf{x}^{(\ell)}\| \le \alpha^{(\ell)} = (2\gamma_{\mathcal{R}})^\ell \cdot \alpha.$$

$$\mathbf{C}^{(\ell)} \cdot \mathbf{x}^{(\ell)} = \mathbf{z}^{(\ell)} \bmod q_1,$$

Analysis. We show that $\Pi_0^{\mathtt{fold}}$ is complete and (unconditionally) special-sound. We further show that $\Pi_0^{\mathtt{fold}}$ has short proofs, quasi-linear-time prover, and polylogarithmic-time verifier.

Due to limited space, we defer the proofs of these claims to the full version.

Theorem 1. $\Pi_0^{\mathtt{fold}}$ *is complete for* $\Psi_0^{\mathtt{fold}}[\alpha]$.

Theorem 2. *If* $\alpha^* \ge (8\gamma_{\mathcal{R}}^4)^{\log n}\alpha$, $\Pi_0^{\mathtt{fold}}$ *is* $(3,\dots,3)$-*special sound for* $\Psi_0^{\mathtt{fold}}[\alpha^*]$.

For the purpose of estimating the complexities of $\Pi_0^{\mathtt{fold}}$, let $h_0, h_1, w, \gamma_{\mathcal{R}} = \mathsf{poly}(\lambda)$ be fixed polynomials in λ. Pick α^* to be tight in Theorem 2 and set $q_0, q_1 = O_\lambda(\alpha^*) = \lambda^{O(\log n)}$. The following theorem states the complexities of $\Pi_0^{\mathtt{fold}}$ with the above parameter choices.

Theorem 3. *Let* $h_0, h_1, w, \gamma_{\mathcal{R}} = \mathsf{poly}(\lambda)$ *be fixed polynomials in* λ, *and* $q_0, q_1 = \lambda^{O(\log n)}$. $\Pi_0^{\mathtt{fold}}$ *has (i) prover time* $O_\lambda(n \cdot \log^2 n)$, *and (ii) proof size* $O_\lambda(\log^2 n)$. *If* $\mathbf{C}$ *is* $(k_0, \dots, k_\ell)$-*block-foldable with block-size* w *and* $\mathbf{y}$ *is* $(k_0 - 1, \dots, k_{\ell-1} - 1, k_\ell + 1)$-*block-foldable with block-size* h_0, *then the verifier time is* $O_\lambda(\log^3 n)$.

6.2 Type-1 Linear Relations

Define the relation $\Psi_1^{\mathtt{fold}} = \Psi_1^{\mathtt{fold}}[\mathcal{R}, h, w, n, q, \alpha]$:

$$\Psi_1^{\mathtt{fold}} := \left\{ (\mathsf{pp}, (\mathbf{A}, \mathbf{y}), \mathbf{x}) : \mathbf{A} \cdot \mathbf{x} = \mathbf{y} \bmod q \quad \text{and} \quad \|\mathbf{x}\| \le \alpha \right\},$$

$\mathcal{R}$ is a prime-power ring for a prime ≥ 5, $\mathbf{A} = (\mathbf{A}_1, \dots, \mathbf{A}_n)$, $\mathbf{A}_i \in \mathcal{R}_q^{h \times w}$, $\mathbf{y} \in \mathcal{R}_q^h$, and $\mathbf{x} \in \mathcal{R}^{wn}$. By default, we suppress parameters of $\Psi_1^{\mathtt{fold}}$ except those that we highlight. Note that the above constraints are independent of pp, therefore $\Psi_1^{\mathtt{fold}}$ is compatible with any parameter generator Gen. In the full version, we describe $\Pi_1^{\mathtt{fold}}$ which satisfies the following properties.

Theorem 4. $\Pi_1^{\mathtt{fold}}$ *is complete for* $\Psi_1^{\mathtt{fold}}[\alpha]$.

Theorem 5. *If* $\alpha^* \geq (8\gamma_{\mathcal{R}}^4)^{\log n}\alpha$, Π_1^{fold} *is* $(3, \ldots, 3)$-*special sound for* $\Psi_1^{\text{fold}}[\alpha^*]$.

Theorem 6. *Let* $h, w = \text{poly}(\lambda)$ *and* $q = \lambda^{O(\log n)}$. Π_1^{fold} *has (i) prover time* $O_\lambda(n \cdot \log^2 n)$, *and (ii) proof size* $O_\lambda(\log^2 n)$. *If* $\mathbf{A}$ *is* $(k_0, \ldots, k_\ell)$-*block-foldable with block-size* w, *then the verifier time is* $O_\lambda(\log^3 n)$.

7 Knowledge-Based Protocols

Mirroring the folding protocols constructed in Sect. 6, we present below two argument systems Π_0^{know} and Π_1^{know} for unstructured linear relations based on the (knowledge-)k-R-ISIS assumptions. Different from existing protocols based on the same family of assumptions and construction template, the constructions below feature quasi-linear-time provers.

7.1 Linear Relations

Define the relation $\Psi_0 = \Psi_0[\mathcal{R}, s, t, q_0, q_1, q_2, \alpha]$:

$$\Psi_0 := \left\{ ((\mathbf{v}, \mathbf{h}), ((\mathbf{M}, \mathbf{y}), (c_{\mathbf{x}}, \bar{c}_{\mathbf{x}})), \mathbf{x}) : \begin{array}{c} \mathbf{M} \cdot \mathbf{x} = \mathbf{y} \bmod q_0, \\ \mathbf{v}^{\mathsf{T}} \cdot \mathbf{x} = c_{\mathbf{x}} \bmod q_3, \quad \|\mathbf{x}\| \leq \alpha \\ (\bar{\mathbf{v}} \circ \mathbf{h})^{\mathsf{T}} \cdot \mathbf{x} = \bar{c}_{\mathbf{x}} \bmod q_3, \end{array} \right\}$$

where $\mathbf{M} \in \mathcal{R}_{q_3}^{t \times s}$, $\mathbf{y} \in \mathcal{R}_{q_3}^t$, $c_{\mathbf{x}}, \bar{c}_{\mathbf{x}} \in \mathcal{R}_{q_3}$, $\mathbf{x} \in \mathcal{R}^s$, $\mathbf{v} = (v, v^2, \ldots, v^s)$, and $\bar{\mathbf{v}} = (v^{-1}, v^{-2}, \ldots, v^{-s})$. Accompanying the relation, we define a parameter generator $\text{Gen}^{\text{unstr}}$ which samples $v \leftarrow_{\$} \mathcal{R}_{q_3}^{\times}$ and $\mathbf{h} \leftarrow_{\$} \mathcal{R}_{q_1}^s$ and outputs $(\mathbf{v}, \mathbf{h})$. Note that the compression vector $\mathbf{h}$ is unstructured. By default, we suppress all parameters of Ψ_0 except those that we highlight. We describe a protocol Π_0^{know} which is complete for $\Psi_0[\alpha]$ and knowledge sound for $\Psi_0[\alpha^*]$ for some $\alpha^* > \alpha$.

Construction. Let $\mathcal{R}, s, t, \eta, m, (q_i)_{i=0}^3, \beta, (\delta_i)_{i=0}^3, \mathcal{T}$ depend on λ. Using the lattice trapdoor algorithms (Sect. 3.2) parametrised by (η, m, q_3, β), in Fig. 1 we give a formal description of Π_0^{know}, which is based on the construction template of functional commitments in [2]. In particular, in Π_0^{know} the prover proves to the verifier that they know witnesses to the following relations

$$\begin{pmatrix} \mathbf{v}^{\mathsf{T}} \\ (\bar{\mathbf{v}} \circ \mathbf{h})^{\mathsf{T}} \end{pmatrix} \cdot \mathbf{x} = \begin{pmatrix} c_{\mathbf{x}} \\ \bar{c}_{\mathbf{x}} \end{pmatrix} \bmod q_3, \quad \text{and} \quad \|\mathbf{x}\| \leq \alpha, \tag{3}$$

$$\mathbf{v}_t^{\mathsf{T}} \cdot \mathbf{r} = c_{\mathbf{r}}, \quad \text{with} \quad \mathbf{r} \in \mathcal{R}^t, \tag{4}$$

and

$$\mathbf{M} \cdot \mathbf{x} = \mathbf{y} \bmod q_0 \quad \|\mathbf{x}\| \leq \alpha. \tag{5}$$

The prover will prove that $c_{\mathbf{x}}$, $\bar{c}_{\mathbf{x}}$, and $c_{\mathbf{r}}$ are well-formed by proving knowledge of a short opening of the commitments $c_{\mathbf{x}}$, $\bar{c}_{\mathbf{x}}$, and $c_{\mathbf{r}}$ with respect to the commitment key $(v^i)_{i \in [s]}$, $(v^{-i})_{i \in [s]}$, and $(v_i)_{i \in [t]}$ respectively. To prove consistency between c_x and $\bar{c}_x$, the prover proves knowledge of a short opening of the commitment $\bar{c}_I \cdot c_x - \bar{c}_x \cdot c_I$, where the values $\bar{c}_I$ and c_I can be precomputed by the

---

Setup(1^λ, pp)

$(\mathbf{v}, \mathbf{h}) \leftarrow$ pp

$\mathbf{f}_0 \leftarrow\!\!\$\; \mathcal{R}_{q_2}^t, \quad \mathbf{f}_1 \leftarrow\!\!\$\; \mathcal{R}_{q_2}^s$

$I_0 := \pm[\max\{s, t\}], \quad I_1 := [s]$

$I_2 := -[s], \quad I_3 := [t]$

for $i \in \{0, 1, 2, 3\}$ **do**

$\quad (\mathbf{D}_i, \mathsf{td}_i) \leftarrow \mathsf{TrapGen}(1^\lambda)$

$\quad t_i \leftarrow\!\!\$\; \mathcal{T}$

$\quad \mathbf{u}_{i,j} \leftarrow \mathsf{SampPre}(\mathsf{td}_i, t_i \cdot v^j), \; \forall j \in I_i$

$\mathsf{crs} := \begin{pmatrix} (\mathbf{D}_i, t_i, (\mathbf{u}_{i,j})_{j \in I_i})_{i=0}^3, \\ v \quad \mathbf{h} \quad \mathbf{f}_0, \; \mathbf{f}_1 \end{pmatrix}$

return crs

Prove(crs, $((\mathbf{M}, \mathbf{y}), (c_x, \bar{c}_x)), \mathbf{x}$)

$\mathbf{v}_t := (v, v^2, \dots, v^t)$

$c_r := \mathbf{v}_t^\mathsf{T} \cdot \mathbf{r} \bmod q_3$

$\mathbf{u}_{0,0} := \sum_{i \in [s], k \in [t]} f_{0,k} M_{k,i} \sum_{j \in [s] : j \neq i} \mathbf{u}_{0, j-i} x_j$

$\quad + \sum_{i, k \in [t]} f_{0,k} q_0 \sum_{j \in [t] : j \neq i} \mathbf{u}_{0, j-i} r_j$

$\mathbf{u}_{0,1} := \sum_{j \in [s]} h_j f_{1,j} \sum_{i \in [s] : i \neq j} \mathbf{u}_{0, i-j} x_i$

$\quad - \sum_{i \in [s]} f_{1,i} \sum_{j \in [s] : j \neq i} \mathbf{u}_{0, i-j} h_j \cdot x_j$

$\mathbf{u}_0 := \mathbf{u}_{0,0} + \mathbf{u}_{0,1}$

$\mathbf{u}_1 := \sum_{j \in [s]} \mathbf{u}_{1,j} \cdot x_j$

$\mathbf{u}_2 := \sum_{j \in [s]} \mathbf{u}_{2,-j} \cdot h_j \cdot x_j$

$\mathbf{u}_3 := \sum_{j \in [t]} \mathbf{u}_{3,j} \cdot r_j$

return $\pi := (c_x, \bar{c}_x, c_r, \mathbf{u}_0, \mathbf{u}_1, \mathbf{u}_2, \mathbf{u}_3)$

PreVerify(crs, $(\mathbf{M}, \mathbf{y})$)

$\mathbf{v} := (v, v^2, \dots, v^s)$

$\bar{\mathbf{v}} := (v^{-1}, v^{-2}, \dots, v^{-s})$

$\bar{\mathbf{v}}_t := (v^{-1}, v^{-2}, \dots, v^{-t})$

$\bar{c}_M := \mathbf{f}_0^\mathsf{T} \cdot \mathbf{M} \cdot \bar{\mathbf{v}} \bmod q_3$

$\bar{c}_{q0} := \mathbf{f}_0^\mathsf{T} \cdot q_0 \cdot \bar{\mathbf{v}}_t \bmod q_3$

$\bar{c}_I := \mathbf{f}_1^\mathsf{T} \cdot \mathbf{I} \cdot (\bar{\mathbf{v}} \circ \mathbf{h})$

$\quad = \mathbf{f}_1^\mathsf{T} \cdot (\bar{\mathbf{v}} \circ \mathbf{h}) \bmod q_3$

$c_I := \mathbf{v}^\mathsf{T} \cdot \mathbf{I} \cdot \mathbf{f}_1 = \mathbf{v}^\mathsf{T} \cdot \mathbf{f}_1 \bmod q_3$

$\hat{c}_y := \mathbf{f}_0^\mathsf{T} \cdot \mathbf{y} \bmod q_3$

$\mathsf{pp}_{\mathbf{M}, \mathbf{y}, c_x, \bar{c}_x} := \begin{pmatrix} (\mathbf{D}_i, t_i)_{i=0}^3, \\ \bar{c}_M, \bar{c}_{q0}, \bar{c}_I, c_I, \hat{c}_y \end{pmatrix}$

return $\mathsf{pp}_{\mathbf{M}, \mathbf{y}}$

Verify($\mathsf{crs}_{\mathbf{M}, \mathbf{y}}$, $(c_x, \bar{c}_x), \pi$)

$c_{0,0} := \bar{c}_M \cdot c_x + \bar{c}_{q0} \cdot c_r - \hat{c}_y \bmod q_3$

$c_{0,1} := \bar{c}_I \cdot c_x - \bar{c}_x \cdot c_I \bmod q_3$

$c_0 := c_{0,0} + c_{0,1} \bmod q_3$

$c_1 := c_x$

$c_2 := \bar{c}_x$

$c_3 := c_r$

for $i \in \{0, 1, 2, 3\}$ **do**

$\quad b_i := \begin{pmatrix} \mathbf{D}_i \cdot \mathbf{u}_i \overset{?}{\equiv} t_i \cdot c_i \bmod q_3 \\ \wedge \quad \|\mathbf{u}_i\| \overset{?}{\leq} \delta_i \end{pmatrix}$

return $b_0 \wedge b_1 \wedge b_2 \wedge b_3$

Fig. 1. Our argument system Π_0^{know}.

verifier. This is with respect to the commitment key $(v^k)_{k \in \pm[\max\{s,t\}]}$. Finally, to prove Eq. (5), the prover proves knowledge of a short opening of the commitment $\bar{c}_{\mathbf{M}} \cdot c_{\mathbf{x}} + \bar{c}_{q_0} \cdot c_{\mathbf{r}} - \hat{c}_{\mathbf{y}}$, where the values $\bar{c}_{\mathbf{M}}, \bar{c}_{q_0}$, and $\hat{c}_{\mathbf{y}}$ can be precomputed by the verifier. This is again with respect to the commitment key $(v^k)_{k \in \pm[\max\{s,t\}]}$.

We highlight a few crucial differences with [2]:

(i) The witness $\mathbf{x}$ is committed using a univariate vSIS commitment, i.e. the commitment key is $\mathbf{v} = (v, v^2, \ldots, v^s)$, while in [2] the commitment is an s-variate vSIS commitment. The fact that $|\{ v^{i-j} : i, j \in [s] \}|$ has cardinality $O(s)$ and that the prover computation consists of mainly Toeplitz-vector multiplications are crucial for obtaining a quasi-linear-time prover.

(ii) We support proving relations modulo q_0 natively[14] by introducing the auxiliary witness $\mathbf{r}$ satisfying $\mathbf{M} \cdot \mathbf{x} + q_0 \cdot \mathbf{r} = \mathbf{y}$. In [2], modular arithmetic is handled via generic and expensive bit-decomposition techniques.

(iii) To prove that values committed in multiple commitments, i.e. $c_{\mathbf{x}}$, $\bar{c}_{\mathbf{x}}$, and $c_{\mathbf{r}}$, satisfy some relation, we adapt techniques developed for the recent construction of chainable functional commitments [7].

Analysis. We show that Π_0^{know} is correct and knowledge-sound under (knowledge-)k-R-ISIS and R-SIS assumptions. We further show that Π_0^{know} has short CRS and proofs, quasi-linear-time prover and preprocessing, and polylogarithmic-time verifier after preprocessing. The proofs are deferred to the full version.

Theorem 7 (Completeness). *Let (η, m, q_3, β) be such that the properties of lattice trapdoor algorithms described in Sect. 3.2 hold. For*

$$\delta_0 \geq (s+t)^4 \cdot q_0 \cdot q_1 \cdot q_2 \cdot \alpha \cdot \beta \cdot \gamma_{\mathcal{R}}^3, \qquad \qquad \delta_1 \geq s \cdot \alpha \cdot \beta \cdot \gamma_{\mathcal{R}},$$
$$\delta_2 \geq s \cdot q_1 \cdot \alpha \cdot \beta \cdot \gamma_{\mathcal{R}}, \qquad and \qquad \delta_3 \geq s^2 \cdot \alpha \cdot \beta \cdot \gamma_{\mathcal{R}}^2,$$

Π_0^{know} in Fig. 1 is complete for $\Psi_0[\alpha]$.

Theorem 8 (Knowledge Soundness). *Let (η, m, q_3, β) be such that the properties of lattice trapdoor algorithms described in Sect. 3.2 hold. Let $w = 1$, $\mathcal{G}_0 = \{ X^i : i \in \pm[\max\{s,t\}] \}$, $\mathcal{G}_1 = \{ X^i : i \in [s] \}$, $\mathcal{G}_2 = \{ X^i : i \in -[s] \}$, and $\mathcal{G}_3 = \{ X^i : i \in [t] \}$ be sets of monomials in X. Let $\mathcal{D} = \mathsf{SampD}(1^\lambda)$. For $i \in \{1,2,3\}$, let $\mathcal{Z}_i(1^\lambda)$ be almost identical to $\mathsf{Setup}(1^\lambda, \mathsf{Gen}^{\text{unstr}}(1^\lambda))$, except that it inputs $(\mathbf{D}_i, \mathbf{t}_i, v, \{ \mathbf{u}_{i,j} \}_{j \in I_i})$ and generates the rest of crs. Let*

$$\alpha_i^* \geq \delta_i, \ \forall i \in [3], \qquad \alpha^* := \max\{ \alpha_1^*, \alpha_2^*, \alpha_3^* \}, \qquad q_2 \geq \beta_{q_2}^* \geq s \cdot q_0 \cdot q_1 \cdot \alpha^* \cdot \gamma_{\mathcal{R}},$$
$$q_3 \geq \beta_{q_3}^* \geq \max\{ 2\delta_0, (s+t)^3 \cdot q_0 \cdot q_1 \cdot q_2 \cdot \alpha^* \cdot \beta \cdot \gamma_{\mathcal{R}}^3 \}.$$

Π_0^{know} in Fig. 1 is knowledge-sound for $\Psi_0[\alpha_1^*]$ if the following assumptions hold:

Assumption 0. $k\text{-}R\text{-}\mathsf{ISIS}_{\mathcal{R}, \eta, m, w, q_3, \beta, \beta_{q_3}^*, \mathcal{G}_0, g^*=1, \mathcal{D}, \mathcal{T}},$

---

[14] Relations without modular reduction are captured by setting $q_0 = 0$.

Assumption 1. $knowledge\text{-}k\text{-}R\text{-}\mathsf{ISIS}_{\mathcal{R},\eta,m,w,q_3,\alpha_1^*,\beta,\delta_1,\mathcal{G}_1,\mathcal{D},\mathcal{T},\mathcal{Z}_1}$,
Assumption 2. $knowledge\text{-}k\text{-}R\text{-}\mathsf{ISIS}_{\mathcal{R},\eta,m,w,q_3,\alpha_2^*,\beta,\delta_2,\mathcal{G}_2,\mathcal{D},\mathcal{T},\mathcal{Z}_2}$,
Assumption 3. $knowledge\text{-}k\text{-}R\text{-}\mathsf{ISIS}_{\mathcal{R},\eta,m,w,q_3,\alpha_3^*,\beta,\delta_3,\mathcal{G}_3,\mathcal{D},\mathcal{T},\mathcal{Z}_3}$, and
Assumption 4. $R\text{-}\mathsf{SIS}_{\mathcal{R},s+t,q_2,\beta_{q_2}^*}$.

For the purpose of estimating complexities, we assume that the assumptions in Theorem 8 hold for moduli which are a fixed polynomial factor larger than their norm bounds, e.g. $q_2 \geq \beta_{q_2}^* \cdot \mathsf{poly}(\lambda)$ for the $R\text{-}\mathsf{SIS}_{\mathcal{R},s+t,q_2,\beta_{q_2}^*}$ assumption. For the k-R-ISIS assumptions, we assume that they hold for $m = O(\eta \cdot \log q)$.

Let $\eta, \alpha, \beta, \gamma_{\mathcal{R}} = \mathsf{poly}(\lambda)$ be fixed polynomials in λ. For our application in Sect. 8, we want $q_1 = O(s^2 \cdot \alpha^2) = O_\lambda(s^2)$. Pick $\delta_1, \delta_2, \delta_3, \alpha_1^*, \alpha_2^*, \alpha_3^*$ so that they match their lower bounds given in Theorem 7 and Theorem 8 respectively. Substituting q_1, we have $\alpha_1^* = \delta_1 = O_\lambda(s)$, $\alpha_2^* = \delta_2 = O_\lambda(s^3)$, and $\alpha_3^* = \delta_3 = O_\lambda(s^2)$. We therefore have $\alpha^* = O_\lambda(s^3)$. Pick $q_0 = O_\lambda(\alpha^*) = O_\lambda(s)$. Pick $\beta_{q_2}^*$ so that it matches its lower bound in Theorem 8, and set $q_2 = O_\lambda(\beta_{q_2}^*)$. Substituting (q_0, q_1, α^*), we have $q_2 = O_\lambda(s^7)$. Pick δ_0 so that it matches its lower bound given in Theorem 7. Substituting (q_0, q_1, q_2), we have $\delta_0 = O_\lambda((s+t)^{14})$. Pick $\beta_{q_3}^*$ so that it matches its lower bound in Thoerem 8, and set $q_3 = O_\lambda(\beta_{q_3}^*)$. Substituting $(q_0, q_1, q_2, \alpha^*)$, we have $q_3 = O_\lambda((s+t)^{16})$. Let $n = \max\{|\mathbf{M}|, s+t\}$, where $|\mathbf{M}|$ denote the number of non-zero entries in $\mathbf{M}$. Pick $m = O(\eta \cdot \log q) = O_\lambda(\log n)$. Theorem 9 states the complexities of Π_0^{know} with the above parameter choices.

Theorem 9 (Efficiency). *Let* $n = \max\{|\mathbf{M}|, s+t\}$, *where* $|\mathbf{M}|$ *denote the number of non-zero entries in* $\mathbf{M}$, $\eta, \alpha, \beta, \gamma_{\mathcal{R}} = \mathsf{poly}(\lambda)$ *be fixed polynomials in* λ, *and* $(m, q_0, q_1, q_2, q_3) = (\log n, s, s^2, s^7, (s+t)^{16}) \cdot \mathsf{poly}(\lambda)$. *Then* Π_0^{fold} *has (i) common reference string size* $O_\lambda(n \cdot \log n)$, *(ii) proof size* $O_\lambda(\log^2 n)$, *(iii) prover time* $O_\lambda(n \cdot \log^3 n)$, *(iv) preprocessing time* $O_\lambda(n \cdot \log^2 n)$, *and (v) verifier time* $O_\lambda(\log^3 n)$ *after preprocessing.*

7.2   Well-Formedness of vSIS Commitments

Define the relation $\Psi_1 = \Psi_1[\mathcal{R}, s, q_1, q_3, \alpha]$ equipped with the same parameter generator $\mathsf{Gen}^{\mathsf{unstr}}$ as Ψ_0:

$$\Psi_1 := \left\{ ((\mathbf{v}, \mathbf{h}), (\epsilon, c_{\mathbf{z}}), \mathbf{z}) : \left(\bar{\mathbf{v}}^{\mathsf{T}} \, \mathbf{v}^{\mathsf{T}} \right) \cdot \mathbf{z} = c_{\mathbf{z}} \bmod q_3 \ \wedge \ ||\mathbf{z}|| \leq \alpha \right\}$$

where $c_{\mathbf{z}} \in \mathcal{R}_{q_3}$, $\mathbf{z} \in \mathcal{R}^{2s}$, $\mathbf{v} = (v, v^2, \dots, v^s)$, and $\bar{\mathbf{v}} = (v^{-1}, v^{-2}, \dots, v^{-s})$. By default, we suppress all parameters of Ψ_1 except those that we highlight. In the full version, we describe Π_1^{know} which satisfies the following properties.

Theorem 10 (Completeness). *Let* (η, m, q_3, β) *be such that the properties of lattice trapdoor algorithms described in Sect. 3.2 hold. For* $\delta \geq 2s \cdot \alpha \cdot \beta \cdot \gamma_{\mathcal{R}}$ Π_1^{know} *in Fig. 1 is complete for* $\Psi_1[\alpha]$.

Theorem 11 (Knowledge Soundness). *Let* (η, m, q_3, β) *be such that the properties of lattice trapdoor algorithms described in Sect. 3.2 hold,* $w = 1$, $\alpha^* \geq \delta$, $\mathcal{G} = \{X^i : i \in \pm[s]\}$ *be a set of monomials in* X, $\mathcal{D}$ *denote the distribution*

$\mathsf{SampD}(1^\lambda)$, *and* $\mathcal{Z}$ *be trivial (i.e. it outputs* $\bot$*).* $\varPi_1^{\mathtt{know}}$ *in Fig. 1 is knowledge-sound for* $\varPsi_0[\alpha^*]$ *if the knowledge-k-R-*$\mathsf{ISIS}_{\mathcal{R},\eta,m,w,q_3,\alpha^*,\beta,\delta,\mathcal{G},\mathcal{D},\mathcal{T},\mathcal{Z}}$ *assumption holds.*

Theorem 12 (Efficiency). *Let parameters be as in Theorem 9.* $\varPi_1^{\mathtt{fold}}$ *has (i) common reference string size* $O_\lambda(n \cdot \log n)$*, (ii) proof size* $O_\lambda(\log^2 n)$*, (iii) prover time* $O_\lambda(n \cdot \log^2 n)$*, (iv) trivial preprocessing, and (v) verifier time* $O_\lambda(\log^3 n)$*.*

8 Applications

We show how to compose arguments obtain in Sects. 6 and 7 to build efficient arguments for more complex relations. In particular, we show how to construct arguments for the binary-satisfiability of (structured) linear equations and rank-1 constraint satisfiability (R1CS).

8.1 Proving Binary-Satisfiability of (Structured) Linear Equations

Recall that in Sect. 6 we built succinct arguments $\varPi_0^{\mathtt{fold}}$ and $\varPi_1^{\mathtt{fold}}$ for the relations $\varPsi_0^{\mathtt{fold}}$ and $\varPsi_1^{\mathtt{fold}}$ respectively, while in Sect. 7 we constructed $\varPi_0^{\mathtt{know}}$ and $\varPi_1^{\mathtt{know}}$ for the relations $\varPsi_0$ and $\varPsi_1$ respectively. By inspection, we see that $\varPsi_1$ is a special case of $\varPsi_1^{\mathtt{fold}}$, and thus $\varPi_1^{\mathtt{fold}}$ can be specialised to give a succinct argument for $\varPsi_1$. Similarly, $\varPi_0^{\mathtt{fold}}$ can be specialised as to give a succinct argument for the following special case of $\varPsi_0$ which we denote by $\varPsi_0^{\mathtt{str}} = \varPsi_0^{\mathtt{str}}[\mathcal{R}, h, w, n, q_0, q_1, q_3, \alpha]$, where $\mathbf{M}$ is restricted to be of the form

$$\mathbf{M} = \begin{bmatrix} \mathbf{A} \\ \mathbf{B} \end{bmatrix}_{\searrow n} \quad \text{succinctly represented by some } \mathbf{A}, \mathbf{B} \in \mathcal{R}_{q_0}^{h \times w}.$$

Accompanying $\varPsi_0^{\mathtt{str}}$, we define the parameter generator $\mathsf{Gen}^{\mathtt{str}}$ which samples $(\mathbf{v}, \mathbf{h})$ which are $(k_0, \ldots, k_\ell)$-block-foldable with block-size w where $n = \sum_{i=0}^\ell k_i$ for $k_i \in \{1, 2\}$. More concretely, $\mathsf{Gen}^{\mathtt{str}}$ does the following: (i) Sample $v \leftarrow_\$ \mathcal{R}_q^\times$ and $\tilde{\mathbf{h}} \leftarrow_\$ \mathcal{R}_{q_1}^{\tilde{n}}$. (ii) Set $\mathbf{v} := (v, \ldots, v^s) \bmod q_3$. (iii) Let $\tilde{n} := \sum_{i=0}^{\ell-1}(k_i + 1) + k_\ell$. (iv) Generate w copies of $\tilde{n}$-variate monomial sequences $\mathbf{m}_1, \ldots, \mathbf{m}_w$ according to Lemma 6, and concatenate them in an interleaved manner into a monomial sequence $\mathbf{m} = (m_{1,1}, m_{2,1}, \ldots, m_{w,1}, m_{1,2}, \ldots, m_{w,n})$. (v) Evaluate $\mathbf{m}$ at $\tilde{\mathbf{h}}$ to produce $\mathbf{h} = \mathbf{m}(\tilde{\mathbf{h}})$.

Equipped with succinct arguments for $\varPsi_0$ (or $\varPsi_0^{\mathtt{str}}$) and $\varPsi_1$, we construct a succinct argument $\varPi^{\mathtt{bin\text{-}sat}}$ for the binary-satisfiability of system of (structured) linear equations mod p. Formally, define the relation $\varPsi^{\mathtt{bin\text{-}sat}} = \varPsi^{\mathtt{bin\text{-}sat}}[\mathcal{R}, s, t, p]$:

$$\varPsi^{\mathtt{bin\text{-}sat}} := \left\{ (((\mathbf{M}, \mathbf{y}), \epsilon), \mathbf{x}) : \mathbf{M} \cdot \mathbf{x} = \mathbf{y} \bmod q_0 \ \wedge \ \mathbf{x} \in \{0, 1\}^s \right\},$$

with offline statement $(\mathbf{M}, \mathbf{y}) \in \mathcal{R}_{q_0}^{t \times s} \times \mathcal{R}_{q_0}^t$ and witness $\mathbf{x} \in \mathcal{R}^s$, and the corresponding structured variant $\varPsi^{\mathtt{str\text{-}bin\text{-}sat}} = \varPsi^{\mathtt{str\text{-}bin\text{-}sat}}[\mathcal{R}, h, w, n, p]$ where $\mathbf{M}$ is

of the form $\mathbf{M} = \begin{bmatrix} \mathbf{A} \\ \mathbf{B} \end{bmatrix}_{\searrow n}$ succinctly represented by some $\mathbf{A}, \mathbf{B} \in \mathcal{R}_{q_0}^{h \times w}$.

Let q_1, q_3 depend on λ. Let Π' and Π'' be argument systems for Ψ_0 (or Ψ_0^{str}) and Ψ_1 respectively, and let $\mathsf{Gen} = \mathsf{Gen}^{\mathrm{unstr}}$ (or $\mathsf{Gen}^{\mathrm{str}}$) be the accompanying parameter generator. The algorithms $\Pi^{\mathrm{bin\text{-}sat}}.(\mathsf{Setup}, \mathsf{PreVerify})$ are described in Fig. 2. The protocol $\Pi^{\mathrm{bin\text{-}sat}}.\langle \mathsf{Prove}(\mathsf{crs}, \mathsf{stmt}, \mathsf{wit}), \mathsf{Verify}(\mathsf{crs}_{(\mathbf{M},\mathbf{y})}, \epsilon)\rangle$ is below:

- Prove computes (i) $c_{\mathbf{x}} := \langle \mathbf{v}, \mathbf{x}\rangle \bmod q_3$, (ii) $\bar{c}_{\mathbf{x}} := \langle \bar{\mathbf{v}} \circ \mathbf{h}, \mathbf{x}\rangle \bmod q_3$, and (iii)
  $$\mathbf{z} := \left(\sum_{0 \leq i,j \leq s: i-j=k} h_j \cdot x_j \cdot (x_i - 1) \right)_{-s \leq k \leq s}.$$
- Prove sends $(c_{\mathbf{x}}, \bar{c}_{\mathbf{x}})$ to Verify.
- Prove and Verify compute:
  - $c_{\mathbf{z}} := \bar{c}_{\mathbf{x}} \cdot (c_{\mathbf{x}} - \langle \mathbf{v}, \mathbf{1}\rangle) \bmod q_3$.
  - $\mathsf{stmt}' := ((\mathbf{M}, \mathbf{y}), (c_{\mathbf{x}}, \bar{c}_{\mathbf{x}}))$, $\mathsf{stmt}'' := (\epsilon, c_{\mathbf{z}})$.
  - $(\mathsf{tx}', b') \leftarrow \Pi'.\langle \mathsf{Prove}(\mathsf{crs}', \mathsf{stmt}', \mathbf{x}), \mathsf{Verify}(\mathsf{crs}'_{(\mathbf{M},\mathbf{y})}, (c_{\mathbf{x}}, \bar{c}_{\mathbf{x}}))\rangle$.
  - $(\mathsf{tx}'', b'') \leftarrow \Pi''.\langle \mathsf{Prove}(\mathsf{crs}'', \mathsf{stmt}'', \mathbf{z}), \mathsf{Verify}(\mathsf{crs}''_{\epsilon}, c_{\mathbf{z}})\rangle$.
- Output (tx, b), where $\mathsf{tx} = (\mathsf{tx}', \mathsf{tx}'')$ and $b = b' \wedge b''$.

$\mathsf{Setup}(1^\lambda)$	$\mathsf{PreVerify}(\mathsf{crs}, (\mathbf{M}, \mathbf{y}))$
$\mathsf{pp} \leftarrow \mathsf{Gen}(1^\lambda)$	$\mathsf{crs}'_{(\mathbf{M},\mathbf{y})} \leftarrow \Pi'.\mathsf{PreVerify}(\mathsf{crs}', (\mathbf{M}, \mathbf{y}))$
$\mathsf{crs}' \leftarrow \Pi'.\mathsf{Setup}(1^\lambda, \mathsf{pp})$	$\mathsf{crs}''_\epsilon \leftarrow \Pi''.\mathsf{PreVerify}(\mathsf{crs}'', \epsilon)$
$\mathsf{crs}'' \leftarrow \Pi''.\mathsf{Setup}(1^\lambda, \mathsf{pp})$	$\mathbf{return}\ \mathsf{crs}_{(\mathbf{M},\mathbf{y})} := (\mathsf{crs}'_{(\mathbf{M},\mathbf{y})}, \mathsf{crs}''_\epsilon)$
$\mathbf{return}\ \mathsf{crs} := (\mathsf{crs}', \mathsf{crs}'')$	

Fig. 2. Setup and PreVerify algorithms of the argument system $\Pi^{\mathrm{bin\text{-}sat}}$.

We show that $\Pi^{\mathrm{bin\text{-}sat}}$ is complete and knowledge-sound, and that it has short proofs, quasi-linear-time prover, and polylogarithmic-time verifier (after preprocessing in the unstructured case), with proofs deferred to the full version.

Theorem 13. *If* $\mathsf{Gen} = \mathsf{Gen}^{\mathrm{str}}$ *(resp.* $\mathsf{Gen}^{\mathrm{unstr}}$*),* Π' *is complete for* $\Psi_0^{\mathrm{str}}[\alpha = 1]$*, and* Π'' *is complete for* $\Psi_1[\alpha = s \cdot (q_1/2)^{\ell+1} \cdot \gamma_{\mathcal{R}}^\ell]$ *(resp.* $\Psi_1[\alpha = s \cdot q_1/2]$*) then* $\Pi^{\mathrm{bin\text{-}sat}}$ *is complete for* $\Psi^{\mathrm{str\text{-}bin\text{-}sat}}$ *(resp.* $\Psi^{\text{-}bin\text{-}sat}$*).*

Theorem 14. *Let* $\mathsf{Gen} = \mathsf{Gen}^{\mathrm{str}}$ *(resp.* $\mathsf{Gen}^{\mathrm{unstr}}$*). Let* $\mathcal{G} := \{ X^j : -s \leq j \leq s\}$ *and* $\mathcal{G}_{\mathbf{h}}$ *be the set of monomials generated as in* $\mathsf{Gen}^{\mathrm{str}}$*. Let* $q_1, q_3, \alpha', \alpha'', \beta_{q_1}, \beta_{q_3}$ *be such that (i)* $\beta_{q_1} \geq (\alpha' + 1)^2 \cdot \gamma_{\mathcal{R}}$*, (ii)* $\beta_{q_3} \geq \alpha'' + s \cdot (q_1/2)^{\ell+1} \cdot (\alpha' + 1)^2 \cdot \gamma_{\mathcal{R}}^{\ell+2}$ *(resp.* $\alpha'' + s \cdot q_1/2 \cdot (\alpha' + 1)^2 \cdot \gamma_{\mathcal{R}}^2$*), (iii)* Π' *is knowledge-sound for* $\Psi_0^{\mathrm{str}}[\alpha']$ *(resp.* $\Psi_0^{\mathrm{unstr}}[\alpha']$*), and (iv)* Π'' *is knowledge-sound for* $\Psi_1[\alpha'']$*.* $\Pi^{\mathrm{bin\text{-}sat}}$ *is knowledge-sound for* $\Psi^{\mathrm{str\text{-}bin\text{-}sat}}$ *(resp.* $\Psi^{\text{-}bin\text{-}sat}$*), if the following assumptions hold:*

Assumption 0. $\mathsf{vSIS}_{\mathcal{R}, \mathcal{G}_{\mathbf{h}}, 1, q_1, \beta_{q_1}}$ *(resp.* $\mathsf{R\text{-}SIS}_{\mathcal{R}, s, q_1, \beta_{q_1}}$*), and*
Assumption 1. $\mathsf{vSIS}_{\mathcal{R}, \mathcal{G}, 1, q_3, \beta_{q_3}}$*.*

Below, we estimate the complexities of $\Pi^{\mathrm{bin\text{-}sat}}$ for parameters chosen in such a way that completeness and knowledge-soundness (are believed to) hold.

Theorem 15. *In the structured setting, let* $\mathsf{Gen} = \mathsf{Gen}^{\mathrm{str}}$, $\Pi' = \Pi_0^{\mathrm{fold}}$ *(specialised for* Ψ_0^{str}*),* $\Pi'' = \Pi_1^{\mathrm{fold}}$ *(specialised for* Ψ_1*),* $\gamma_{\mathcal{R}}, \alpha', \alpha'', h, w = \mathsf{poly}(\lambda)$ *be fixed polynomials in* λ*, and* $q_0, q_1, q_3 = \lambda^{O(\log n)}$*.* $\Pi^{\mathrm{bin\text{-}sat}}$ *has (i) common reference string size* $O_\lambda(\log^2 n)$*, (ii) prover time* $O_\lambda(n \cdot \log^3 n)$*, and (iii) proof size* $O_\lambda(\log^2 n)$*. If* $\mathbf{y}$ *is* $(k_0 - 1, \ldots, k_{\ell-1} - 1, k_\ell + 1)$*-block-foldable with block-size* h*, then the verifier time is* $O_\lambda(\log^3 n)$*.*

In the unstructured setting, let $\mathsf{Gen} = \mathsf{Gen}^{\mathrm{unstr}}$*,* $\Pi' = \Pi_0^{\mathrm{know}}$*,* $\Pi'' = \Pi_1^{\mathrm{know}}$*,* $\gamma_{\mathcal{R}} = \mathsf{poly}(\lambda)$ *be a fixed polynomial in* λ*,* $n = \max\{|\mathbf{M}|, s+t\}$ *where* $|\mathbf{M}|$ *denote the number of non-zero entries in* $\mathbf{M}$*,* $(q_0, q_1, q_3) = (s, s^2, (s+t)^{16}) \cdot \mathsf{poly}(\lambda)$ *and other internal parameters of* Π_0^{know} *and* Π_1^{know} *be chosen as in Theorem 9 and 12.* $\Pi^{\mathrm{bin\text{-}sat}}$ *has (i) common reference string size* $O_\lambda(n \cdot \log n)$*, (ii) proof size* $O_\lambda(\log^2 n)$*, (iii) prover time* $O_\lambda(n \cdot \log^3 n)$*, (iv) preprocessing time* $O_\lambda(n \cdot \log^2 n)$*, and (v) verifier time* $O_\lambda(\log^3 n)$ *after preprocessing.*

8.2   Rank-1 Constraint Systems

We show how to use the same ideas to construct an argument of knowledge, Π_{R1CS}, for the satisfiability of Rank-1 Constraint Systems. Formally, define the relation $\Psi^{\mathrm{R1CS}} = \Psi^{\mathrm{R1CS}}[\mathcal{R}, t, s_1, s_2, q_0, \alpha]$:

$$\Psi^{\mathrm{R1CS}} := \{((\mathbf{x}_1, \mathbf{E}, \mathbf{F}, \mathbf{G}), \mathbf{x}_2) : (\mathbf{E} \cdot \mathbf{x}) \circ (\mathbf{F} \cdot \mathbf{x}) = \mathbf{G} \cdot \mathbf{x} \bmod q_0 \ \wedge \ ||\mathbf{x}|| \leq \alpha\},$$

where $\mathbf{x} := (\mathbf{x}_1, \mathbf{x}_2) \in \mathcal{R}^{s_1} \times \mathcal{R}^{s_2}$, $\mathbf{E}, \mathbf{F}, \mathbf{G} \in \mathcal{R}_{q_0}^{t \times s}$, and $s = s_1 + s_2$. If we let $\mathbf{e} := \mathbf{E} \cdot \mathbf{x}$, $\mathbf{f} := \mathbf{F} \cdot \mathbf{x}$, and $\mathbf{g} := \mathbf{G} \cdot \mathbf{x}$, the above equation can be rewritten as $\mathbf{e} \circ \mathbf{f} + q_0 \cdot \mathbf{r} = \mathbf{g}$, for some $\mathbf{r} \in \mathcal{R}^t$. We informally describe here how the argument system works, and defer the formal description of Π^{R1CS} to the full version.

In Π_{R1CS}, the prover proves that they know witnesses to the following relations

$$\mathbf{v}_2^{\mathsf{T}} \cdot \mathbf{x}_2 = c_{\mathbf{x}_2} \bmod q_3, \quad \text{and} \quad ||\mathbf{x}_2|| \leq \alpha, \tag{6}$$

$$\begin{pmatrix} (\bar{\mathbf{v}}_t \circ \mathbf{h})^{\mathsf{T}} \cdot \mathbf{E} \\ \mathbf{v}_t^{\mathsf{T}} \cdot \mathbf{F} \\ \mathbf{v}_t^{\mathsf{T}} \cdot \mathbf{G} \end{pmatrix} \cdot \begin{pmatrix} \mathbf{x}_1 \\ \mathbf{x}_2 \end{pmatrix} = \begin{pmatrix} \bar{c}_{\mathbf{e}} \\ c_{\mathbf{f}} \\ c_{\mathbf{g}} \end{pmatrix} \bmod q_3, \quad \text{and} \quad ||(\mathbf{x}_2)|| \leq \alpha, \tag{7}$$

$$(\bar{\mathbf{v}}^{\mathsf{T}} || \mathbf{v}^{\mathsf{T}}) \cdot \mathbf{z} = c_{\mathbf{z}} \bmod q_3, \quad \text{and} \quad ||\mathbf{z}|| \leq \alpha', \tag{8}$$

where $\mathbf{v}_2 = (v^{s_1+1}, \ldots, v^s)$, $\mathbf{h} \in \mathcal{R}_{q_1}^t$, and $\mathbf{z} = (z_k)_{k \in \pm[s]}$, $z_k = \sum_{i,j,i-j=k} h_j \cdot e_j \cdot f_i + q_0 \cdot h_j \cdot r_i - g_i \cdot h_j$, $c_{\mathbf{z}} = \bar{c}_{\mathbf{e}} \cdot c_{\mathbf{f}} + q_0 \cdot c_{\mathbf{r}} \cdot \bar{c}_{\mathbf{I}} - c_{\mathbf{g}} \cdot \bar{c}_{\mathbf{I}}$, and $c_{\mathbf{r}} = \mathbf{v}_t^{\mathsf{T}} \cdot \mathbf{r}$.

The prover will prove that $c_{\mathbf{x}_2}$ is well-formed, i.e. relation in Eq. (6), by proving knowledge of a short opening of the commitment $c_{\mathbf{x}_2}$ with respect to the commitment key $(v^i)_{i \in [s_1+1;s]}$. To prove consistency between $c_{\mathbf{x}_2}$ and $\bar{c}_{\mathbf{e}}$, the prover proves knowledge of a short opening of the commitment $\bar{c}_{\mathbf{E}} \cdot c_{\mathbf{x}} - c_{\mathbf{I}} \cdot \bar{c}_{\mathbf{e}}$ where $c_{\mathbf{x}} := c_{\mathbf{x}_1} + c_{\mathbf{x}_2}$, and the values $c_{\mathbf{x}_1} := \mathbf{v}_1^{\mathsf{T}} \cdot \mathbf{x}_1$, $\bar{c}_{\mathbf{E}}$, and $c_{\mathbf{I}}$ can be precomputed by the verifier. This with respect to the commitment key $(v^{i-j})_{i-j=k,k \in \pm[s]}$. Proofs of consistency between $c_{\mathbf{x}_2}$ and $c_{\mathbf{f}}$, $c_{\mathbf{x}_2}$ and $c_{\mathbf{g}}$ are obtained similarly. This suffices to prove the relation in Eq. (7).

Finally, to prove that $\mathbf{e} \circ \mathbf{f} = \mathbf{g} \bmod q_0$, i.e. relation in Eq. (8), the prover will prove knowledge of a short opening of the commitment

$$c_{\mathbf{z}} = \bar{c}_{\mathbf{e}} \cdot c_{\mathbf{f}} + q_0 \cdot \bar{c}_{\mathbf{I}} \cdot c_{\mathbf{r}} - c_{\mathbf{g}} \cdot \bar{c}_{\mathbf{I}}$$

again with respect to the commitment key $(v^{i-j})_{i-j=k, k \in \pm[s]}$.

Analysis. In the full version we show that Π^{R1CS} is correct and knowledge-sound under (knowledge-)k-R-ISIS and R-SIS assumptions. We further show that Π^{R1CS} has short CRS and proofs, quasi-linear-time prover and preprocessing, and polylogarithmic-time verifier after preprocessing. For readability, we defer formal claims and relative proofs to the full version.

References

1. Ajtai, M.: Generating hard instances of lattice problems (extended abstract). In: 28th ACM STOC, pp. 99–108. ACM Press (May 1996). https://doi.org/10.1145/237814.237838
2. Albrecht, M.R., Cini, V., Lai, R.W.F., Malavolta, G., Thyagarajan, S.A.K.: Lattice-based SNARKs: publicly verifiable, preprocessing, and recursively composable - (extended abstract). In: Dodis, Y., Shrimpton, T. (eds.) CRYPTO 2022, Part II. LNCS, vol. 13508, pp. 102–132. Springer, Heidelberg (Aug 2022). https://doi.org/10.1007/978-3-031-15979-4_4
3. Albrecht, M.R., Lai, R.W.F.: Subtractive sets over cyclotomic rings - limits of Schnorr-like arguments over lattices. In: Malkin, T., Peikert, C. (eds.) CRYPTO 2021, Part II. LNCS, vol. 12826, pp. 519–548. Springer, Heidelberg, Virtual Event (Aug 2021). https://doi.org/10.1007/978-3-030-84245-1_18
4. Anonymous: Lattice-based functional commitments: fast verification and cryptanalysis. private communication (May 2023)
5. Attema, T., Cramer, R., Kohl, L.: A compressed Σ-protocol theory for lattices. In: Malkin, T., Peikert, C. (eds.) CRYPTO 2021, Part II. LNCS, vol. 12826, pp. 549–579. Springer, Heidelberg, Virtual Event (Aug 2021). https://doi.org/10.1007/978-3-030-84245-1_19
6. Attema, T., Fehr, S.: Parallel repetition of $(k_1, \ldots, k_\mu)$-special-sound multi-round interactive proofs. In: Dodis, Y., Shrimpton, T. (eds.) CRYPTO 2022, Part I. LNCS, vol. 13507, pp. 415–443. Springer, Heidelberg (Aug 2022). https://doi.org/10.1007/978-3-031-15802-5_15
7. Balbás, D., Catalano, D., Fiore, D., Lai, R.W.F.: Functional commitments for circuits from falsifiable assumptions. Cryptology ePrint Archive, Report 2022/1365 (2022). https://eprint.iacr.org/2022/1365
8. Ben-Sasson, E., et al.: Zerocash: decentralized anonymous payments from bitcoin. In: 2014 IEEE Symposium on Security and Privacy, pp. 459–474. IEEE Computer Society Press (May 2014). https://doi.org/10.1109/SP.2014.36
9. Ben-Sasson, E., Chiesa, A., Goldberg, L., Gur, T., Riabzev, M., Spooner, N.: Linear-size constant-query IOPs for delegating computation. In: Hofheinz, D., Rosen, A. (eds.) TCC 2019, Part II. LNCS, vol. 11892, pp. 494–521. Springer, Heidelberg (Dec 2019). https://doi.org/10.1007/978-3-030-36033-7_19

10. Ben-Sasson, E., Chiesa, A., Tromer, E., Virza, M.: Scalable zero knowledge via cycles of elliptic curves. In: Garay, J.A., Gennaro, R. (eds.) CRYPTO 2014, Part II. LNCS, vol. 8617, pp. 276–294. Springer, Heidelberg (Aug 2014). https://doi.org/10.1007/978-3-662-44381-1_16

11. Boneh, D., Drake, J., Fisch, B., Gabizon, A.: Halo Infinite: proof-carrying data from additive polynomial commitments. In: Malkin, T., Peikert, C. (eds.) CRYPTO 2021. LNCS, vol. 12825, pp. 649–680. Springer, Cham (2021). https://doi.org/10.1007/978-3-030-84242-0_23

12. Boneh, D., Ishai, Y., Sahai, A., Wu, D.J.: Lattice-Based SNARGs and their application to more efficient obfuscation. In: Coron, J.-S., Nielsen, J.B. (eds.) EURO-CRYPT 2017. LNCS, vol. 10212, pp. 247–277. Springer, Cham (2017). https://doi.org/10.1007/978-3-319-56617-7_9

13. Boneh, D., Ishai, Y., Sahai, A., Wu, D.J.: Quasi-optimal SNARGs via linear multi-prover interactive proofs. In: Nielsen, J.B., Rijmen, V. (eds.) EUROCRYPT 2018. LNCS, vol. 10822, pp. 222–255. Springer, Cham (2018). https://doi.org/10.1007/978-3-319-78372-7_8

14. Bonneau, J., Meckler, I., Rao, V., Shapiro, E.: Coda: decentralized cryptocurrency at scale. Cryptology ePrint Archive (2020)

15. Bootle, J., Cerulli, A., Chaidos, P., Groth, J., Petit, C.: Efficient zero-knowledge arguments for arithmetic circuits in the discrete log setting. In: Fischlin, M., Coron, J.-S. (eds.) EUROCRYPT 2016. LNCS, vol. 9666, pp. 327–357. Springer, Heidelberg (2016). https://doi.org/10.1007/978-3-662-49896-5_12

16. Bootle, J., Lyubashevsky, V., Nguyen, N.K., Seiler, G.: A non-PCP approach to succinct quantum-safe zero-knowledge. In: Micciancio, D., Ristenpart, T. (eds.) CRYPTO 2020. LNCS, vol. 12171, pp. 441–469. Springer, Cham (2020). https://doi.org/10.1007/978-3-030-56880-1_16

17. Bootle, J., Lyubashevsky, V., Seiler, G.: Algebraic techniques for short(er) exact lattice-based zero-knowledge proofs. In: Boldyreva, A., Micciancio, D. (eds.) CRYPTO 2019. LNCS, vol. 11692, pp. 176–202. Springer, Cham (2019). https://doi.org/10.1007/978-3-030-26948-7_7

18. Bowe, S., Grigg, J., Hopwood, D.: Halo: Recursive proof composition without a trusted setup. Cryptology ePrint Archive, Report 2019/1021 (2019), https://eprint.iacr.org/2019/1021

19. Bünz, B., Bootle, J., Boneh, D., Poelstra, A., Wuille, P., Maxwell, G.: Bulletproofs: Short proofs for confidential transactions and more. In: 2018 IEEE Symposium on Security and Privacy, pp. 315–334. IEEE Computer Society Press (May 2018). https://doi.org/10.1109/SP.2018.00020

20. Bünz, B., Maller, M., Mishra, P., Tyagi, N., Vesely, P.: Proofs for inner pairing products and applications. In: Tibouchi, M., Wang, H. (eds.) ASIACRYPT 2021. LNCS, vol. 13092, pp. 65–97. Springer, Cham (2021). https://doi.org/10.1007/978-3-030-92078-4_3

21. Chiesa, A., Manohar, P., Spooner, N.: Succinct arguments in the quantum random oracle model. In: Hofheinz, D., Rosen, A. (eds.) TCC 2019. LNCS, vol. 11892, pp. 1–29. Springer, Cham (2019). https://doi.org/10.1007/978-3-030-36033-7_1

22. Esgin, M.F., Nguyen, N.K., Seiler, G.: Practical exact proofs from lattices: new techniques to exploit fully-splitting rings. In: Moriai, S., Wang, H. (eds.) ASI-ACRYPT 2020. LNCS, vol. 12492, pp. 259–288. Springer, Cham (2020). https://doi.org/10.1007/978-3-030-64834-3_9

23. Genise, N., Micciancio, D.: Faster Gaussian sampling for trapdoor lattices with arbitrary modulus. In: Nielsen, J.B., Rijmen, V. (eds.) EUROCRYPT 2018. LNCS, vol. 10820, pp. 174–203. Springer, Cham (2018). https://doi.org/10.1007/978-3-319-78381-9_7

24. Gennaro, R., Minelli, M., Nitulescu, A., Orrù, M.: Lattice-based zk-SNARKs from square span programs. In: Lie, D., Mannan, M., Backes, M., Wang, X. (eds.) ACM CCS 2018, pp. 556–573. ACM Press (Oct 2018). https://doi.org/10.1145/3243734.3243845

25. Gentry, C., Peikert, C., Vaikuntanathan, V.: Trapdoors for hard lattices and new cryptographic constructions. In: Ladner, R.E., Dwork, C. (eds.) 40th ACM STOC, pp. 197–206. ACM Press (May 2008). https://doi.org/10.1145/1374376.1374407

26. Golub, G.H., Loan, C.F.V.: Matrix Computations, 3rd edn. Johns Hopkins University Press, USA (1996)

27. Green, M., Miers, I.: Bolt: Anonymous payment channels for decentralized currencies. In: Thuraisingham, B.M., Evans, D., Malkin, T., Xu, D. (eds.) ACM CCS 2017, pp. 473–489. ACM Press (Oct/Nov 2017). https://doi.org/10.1145/3133956.3134093

28. Groth, J.: On the size of pairing-based non-interactive arguments. In: Fischlin, M., Coron, J.-S. (eds.) EUROCRYPT 2016. LNCS, vol. 9666, pp. 305–326. Springer, Heidelberg (2016). https://doi.org/10.1007/978-3-662-49896-5_11

29. Ishai, Y., Su, H., Wu, D.J.: Shorter and faster post-quantum designated-verifier zkSNARKs from lattices. In: Vigna, G., Shi, E. (eds.) ACM CCS 2021, pp. 212–234. ACM Press (Nov 2021). https://doi.org/10.1145/3460120.3484572

30. Kilian, J.: A note on efficient zero-knowledge proofs and arguments (extended abstract). In: 24th ACM STOC, pp. 723–732. ACM Press (May 1992). https://doi.org/10.1145/129712.129782

31. Kosba, A.E., Miller, A., Shi, E., Wen, Z., Papamanthou, C.: Hawk: the blockchain model of cryptography and privacy-preserving smart contracts. In: 2016 IEEE Symposium on Security and Privacy, pp. 839–858. IEEE Computer Society Press (May 2016). https://doi.org/10.1109/SP.2016.55

32. Lai, R.W.F., Malavolta, G.: Lattice-based timed-cryptography. In: CRYPTO 2023, vol. 14085, pp. 782–804. Springer, Hidelberg (2023)

33. Lai, R.W.F., Malavolta, G., Ronge, V.: Succinct arguments for bilinear group arithmetic: Practical structure-preserving cryptography. In: Cavallaro, L., Kinder, J., Wang, X., Katz, J. (eds.) ACM CCS 2019. pp.2057–2074. ACM Press (Nov 2019)

34. Lyubashevsky, V., Nguyen, N.K., Plançon, M.: Lattice-based zero-knowledge proofs and applications: Shorter, simpler, and more general. In: Dodis, Y., Shrimpton, T. (eds.) CRYPTO 2022, Part II. LNCS, vol. 13508, pp. 71–101. Springer, Heidelberg (Aug 2022). https://doi.org/10.1007/978-3-031-15979-4_3

35. Micali, S.: CS proofs (extended abstracts). In: 35th FOCS. pp. 436–453. IEEE Computer Society Press (Nov 1994). https://doi.org/10.1109/SFCS.1994.365746

36. Micciancio, D., Peikert, C.: Trapdoors for lattices: simpler, tighter, faster, smaller. In: Pointcheval, D., Johansson, T. (eds.) EUROCRYPT 2012. LNCS, vol. 7237, pp. 700–718. Springer, Heidelberg (2012). https://doi.org/10.1007/978-3-642-29011-4_41

37. Pellet-Mary, A., Stehlé, D.: On the hardness of the NTRU Problem. In: Tibouchi, M., Wang, H. (eds.) ASIACRYPT 2021. LNCS, vol. 13090, pp. 3–35. Springer, Cham (2021). https://doi.org/10.1007/978-3-030-92062-3_1

38. Pietrzak, K.: Simple verifiable delay functions. In: Blum, A. (ed.) ITCS 2019. vol. 124, pp. 60:1–60:15. LIPIcs (Jan 2019). https://doi.org/10.4230/LIPIcs.ITCS.2019.60

39. Wee, H., Wu, D.J.: Succinct vector, polynomial, and functional commitments from lattices. In: EUROCRYPT 2023 (2023), to appear
40. Yang, R., Au, M.H., Zhang, Z., Xu, Q., Yu, Z., Whyte, W.: Efficient lattice-based zero-knowledge arguments with standard soundness: construction and applications. In: Boldyreva, A., Micciancio, D. (eds.) CRYPTO 2019. LNCS, vol. 11692, pp. 147–175. Springer, Cham (2019). https://doi.org/10.1007/978-3-030-26948-7_6

Orbweaver: Succinct Linear Functional Commitments from Lattices

Ben Fisch, Zeyu Liu, and Psi Vesely[✉]

Yale University, New Haven, USA
{benjamin.fisch,zeyu.liu,psi.vesely}@yale.edu

Abstract. We present Orbweaver, the first plausibly post-quantum functional commitment to achieve quasilinear prover time together with $O(\log n)$ proof size and $O(\log n \log \log n)$ verifier time. Orbweaver enables evaluation of linear maps on committed vectors over cyclotomic rings or the integers. It is extractable, preprocessing, non-interactive, structure-preserving, amenable to recursive composition, and supports logarithmic public proof aggregation. The security of our scheme is based on the k-R-ISIS assumption (and its knowledge counterpart), whereby we require a trusted setup to generate a universal structured reference string. We additionally use Orbweaver to construct a succinct polynomial commitment for integer polynomials.

1 Introduction

Over the last decade there has been tremendous progress in the development succinct non-interactive argument of knowledge protocols, called SNARKs [15]. For a public arithmetic circuit C and a public input x, these SNARKs enable a prover to convince a verifier that the prover knows a witness w such that $C(\mathsf{x}, \mathsf{w}) = 1$, where:

- the proof is short, its length is at most $\mathrm{poly}(\log|C|, |\mathsf{x}|, \lambda)$;
- the proof can be verified in time $\mathrm{poly}(\log|C|, |\mathsf{x}|, \lambda)$; and
- generating the proofs takes quasi-linear time in $|C|$.

Here $|C|$ is the number of gates in C, and λ is a security parameter. The logarithmic dependence on $|C|$ makes these proofs remarkably short and fast to verify. Since the verifier needs to at least read C, there is also a one-time pre-processing phase applied to the circuit C. Once pre-processed, the prover can provide proofs for many x.

Beyond knowledge of a witness, many of these proof systems can be efficiently extended to also provide zero-knowledge. This progress generated considerable real-world interest, and there are now implemented SNARKs and zkSNARKs capable of handling statements involving many millions of arithmetic gates that are now deployed in real-world applications (e.g., [13]).

There are multiple techniques for constructing a pre-processing SNARK. Some require a trusted setup [16,17,28,33,35,39–41,45,48,52] where a trusted

© International Association for Cryptologic Research 2023
H. Handschuh and A. Lysyanskaya (Eds.): CRYPTO 2023, LNCS 14082, pp. 106–131, 2023.
https://doi.org/10.1007/978-3-031-38545-2_4

party must honestly generate public parameters. This setup is called *universal* if it is not specific to the circuit C, i.e., it can be done once to generate parameters that can be used to preprocess any circuit C in a publicly verifiable way. Other systems, called transparent SNARKs, require no trusted setup [11,23,25,29]. Many of the existing SNARKs make use of a commitment scheme called a *polynomial commitment* [43], or PC. A polynomial commitment enables a prover to commit to a polynomial $f \in \mathbb{F}[x]$ of degree w using a short commitment. Later, given two public values $\alpha, \beta \in \mathbb{F}$, the prover can convince a verifier that the committed polynomial f satisfies $\beta = f(\alpha)$ and that f has degree at most w. Ideally, the prover can verifiably open the polynomial at any point $\alpha \in \mathbb{F}$ using a short proof that can be efficiently checked. In fact, it has been shown that given polynomial commitment scheme with proof size $S(w)$ and verification time $T(w)$ it is possible to construct SNARKs with the same complexity characteristics in w (the length of the witness), and additional complexity dependent only on a security parameter λ [26,28]. This compilation is in the random oracle model and relies on the Fiat-Shamir transform.

Polynomial commitment schemes are a special case of *linear functional commitments*, also known as *linear map vector commitments*, where the prover has a commitment $C = \mathsf{com}(\mathbf{x})$ to a vector $\mathbf{x} \in \mathbb{Z}_p^w$ and is able to open any linear form $f(\mathbf{x}) = \sum_{i=1}^{w} \mathbf{x}_i f_i \bmod p$. Polynomial commitments, and the more general linear functional commitments, have been built from bilinear pairings [43], groups of unknown order [25], proofs of proximity for Reed-Solomon codes [10], and to some degree from lattice-based assumptions [2]. However, thus far all lattice-based constructions have had significant drawbacks, and none have achieved asymptotically (in the polynomial's degree) a quasilinear prover time with logarithmic proof size and logarithmic verification time. There are lattice-based generalizations of Bulletproofs [18,24] based on the Ring-SIS assumption, which achieve quasilinear prover time and a polylogarithmic proof size, but have linear verification time [3,6,20]. Recently, [2] constructed general degree-d polynomial map vector commitments (which include linear maps $d = 1$ as a special case), which achieve logarithmic proof size and verification time, but have a CRS size and prover runtime that is at least $\Omega(w^{2d})$, and thus quadratic in the vector length for linear maps. This construction requires a trusted setup using lattice trapdoor sampling [50], and is based on k-R-ISIS, a new family of lattice-based knowledge assumptions related to Ring-SIS. Another recent work, LaBRADOR [14], uses recursion to achieve very compact proof sizes, but has verification time linear in w.

Polynomial commitment schemes based on codes and lattice assumptions are of particular importance due to their plausible post-quantum security. Constructions based on Reed-Solomon codes have quasilinear prover time and both polylogarithmic proof size and verifier time. So far they outperform any lattice-based construction not only asympotically, but also concretely by orders of magnitude in overall size and verification time, even when compared with recent lattice-based constructions that sacrifice prover performance for shorter proofs. Moreover, in the random oracle model, code-based constructions use weaker assumptions than lattice-based constructions. Nonetheless, we are optimistic that the additional structure lattices provide vs. generic (i.e., hash and code-based) constructions can be exploited such that lattice SNARKs eventually surpass these results. As a point of reference, hash-based signatures were originally more efficient, but after over a decade of development lattice-based signatures are an order of magnitude smaller and two faster.

A primary motivation of recent lattice-based constructions [2,53] of vector commitments supporting higher degree polynomial map openings is that, unlike linear map commitments, they can be used to build SNARKs more directly (e.g., by opening an R1CS form) without invoking the Fiat-Shamir transform. Unfortunately, current approaches to supporting higher degree polynomial maps seem to fundamentally require a quadratic prover time. Given the additional structure of lattices compared with code-based proof systems that rely only on hash functions, one might expect that it would be possible to obtain smaller proof sizes and faster verification times. The recent work LaBRADOR [14] was the first lattice-based system to achieve proof sizes smaller (both concretely and asymptotically) than code-based systems, but this has not yet been done for combined proof size and verification time. The results of this paper make progress in this direction.

1.1 Our Results

Building off of the techniques in [2], we present Orbweaver[1], the first linear-map vector commitment scheme from lattices that asymptotically has quasilinear prover time, logarithmic proof size, and quasi-logarithmic verifier time. The scheme supports commitments to vectors $\mathbf{x} \in \mathcal{R}^w$ over a cyclotomic ring $\mathcal{R}$ of degree n and openings of the form $\sum_{i=1}^{w} x_i \cdot f_i$ for any $\mathbf{f} \in \mathcal{R}^w$ mod q for a prime $q \gg \alpha$, where both $\mathbf{x}$ and $\mathbf{f}$ have norm bounded by α. The proof size and verification time are logarithmic and quasi-logarithmic in both w and α, respectively[2].

We also provide concrete performance comparisons to previous lattice-based proof systems. While the concrete sizes are still significantly larger than in code-based constructions for practical sizes of w, we believe that the techniques in this work and the asymptotic improvement paves the way for future work that will lead to more practical lattice-based proof systems.

We discuss several extensions including support for efficient public proof aggregation and inner product argument. We also show how to use linear-map vector commitments over $\mathcal{R}_q$ to embed commitments to polynomials of degree $d = wn$ over $\mathbb{Z}_M$ for $M \leq 2 \cdot \alpha + 1$. Since n is generally very large, we can consider w orders of magnitudes smaller d when determining our proof size, which we expect will produce a huge concrete efficiency improvement—though concrete analysis remains future work. We discuss this along with several other possible techniques for optimizing the concrete complexity of our polynomial commitments.

---

[1] Named for the lattice Orbweaver spider (araneus thaddeus).
[2] Proof size is $O(\log(w \cdot \alpha))$ and verifier time is $O(\log(w \cdot \alpha) \log \log(w \cdot \alpha))$.

1.2 Related Work

Efficient lattice-based proof systems have been constructed in the designated verifier setting [36,42]. In the publicly verifiable setting, there are many results that achieve succinct proof sizes but require linear verifier time [6,8,14,19,20]. There are also works focusing on practical lattice-based ZK proofs, which have proof size linear in the witness size, but are concretely efficient for small statements [30–32,46,47].

Recently, Albrecht et al. [2] constructed extractable lattice-based functional commitments supporting arbitrary degree polynomial maps. For degree d maps their prover time and CRS length are $\tilde{O}(w^{2d})$, while proof size and verifier time are $O(d \log(w))$. Wee and Wu [53] construct non-extractable lattice-based functional commitments for linear functions including polynomial commitments with polylog(w) openings and $\tilde{O}(w^2)$ CRS size and prover time. Castro and Peikert [27] construct non-extractable functional commitments for functions of bounded complexity based on the standard SIS assumption. Their polynomial commitments achieve proof size $O(\log^4 w)$. Balbás, Catalano, Fiore, and Lai construct extractable lattice-based functional commitments supporting arithmetic circuits of width w and depth d that achieve proof size $O(d \log^2 w)$, but have a CRS of size $O(w^5)$ [7]. LaBRADOR [14] designs a SNARK for quadratic relations with quasilinear prover and verifier time, but via a complex recursive argument achieve $O(\log^2 w)$ proofs that concretely surpass the best results from hash-based proof systems.

There is a much longer history of succinct arguments constructed from Merkle hashes that begins with [44] and more recently includes FRI [11], Ligero [4], Aurora [12], Brakedown [38], and Orion [54] among others.

1.3 Technical Overview

At a high level, our construction uses an assumption from the k-R-ISIS assumption family introduced in [2] to translate the knowledge-of-exponent (KEA) based linear functional commitment scheme sketched in [5, section 9] (which is in turn based on [40]) to the lattice setting. The construction should enable a prover to commit to a vector x and later open any linear function $f(x) = \langle [f_i]_{i=1}^w, [x_i]_{i=1}^w \rangle = \sum_{i=1}^w f_i x_i$.

As observed in [5], given a function $x(v) = \sum_{i=1}^w x_i v^i$, and a function $f(v) = \sum_{i=0}^{w-1} f_i v^{-i}$, then $h(v) = x(v)f(v) = \sum_{i=-w+1}^{w-1} a_i v^i$, where $a_0 = \sum_{i=1}^w f_i x_i$. The idea is that the prover sends $c = x(v)$, $y = f(x)$, and $\pi = \sum_{i=-w+1, i \neq 0}^{w-1} a_i v^i$, and then the verifier computes $f(v) = \mathsf{ck}_f$ and checks $c \cdot \mathsf{ck}_f - y = \pi$.

In order to achieve both binding and succinctness, we situate this abstract protocol in lattice setting using the techniques of [2]. A trusted setup generates a universal (i.e., the same setup works for any linear function up to a given size) structured reference string (SRS) $(a, v, u_{-w+1}, \ldots, u_{-1}, u_1, \ldots, u_{w-1}) \in \mathcal{R}_q^\ell \times \mathcal{R}_q^\times \times (\mathcal{R}_q^\ell)^{2w-2}$, where for each u_i it holds that $\langle a, u_i \rangle \equiv v^i \bmod q$ and u_i is "short" relative to q. Note that no preimage u_0 is given out such that $\langle a, u_0 \rangle \equiv 1 \bmod q$. Our k-R-ISIS assumption states that it should be hard to find short $(s, \boldsymbol{u}) \neq (0, \boldsymbol{0}) \in \mathcal{R} \times \mathcal{R}^\ell$ such that $\langle \boldsymbol{a}, \ \boldsymbol{u} \rangle \equiv s \bmod q$ even given these preimages for other powers of v. In general, it should be hard to find the preimage of any target not in the linear span of $[v_i]_{i=-w+1, i \neq 0}^{w-1}$.

Let α be a bound on the ℓ-infinity norm of both the witness and function. The computation of commitment c, commitment key ck_f, and y are exactly as in the abstract protocol, but taken mod q for prime $q \gg \alpha$. The prover now computes

$$\pi_0 := \sum_{i=-w+1, i \neq 0}^{w-1} a_i \boldsymbol{u}_i \bmod q \ ,$$

and the verifier checks

$$\langle \boldsymbol{a}, \ \pi_0 \rangle \equiv c \cdot \mathsf{ck}_f - y \bmod q, \tag{1}$$

and that π_0 and y have small norm. When correctly executing the protocol it follows from the fact that $\alpha \ll q$ and $\beta \ll q$, where β is a norm bound on the $\boldsymbol{u}_i$, that the proof and output will have small norm. Fixing $\mathcal{R}_q$ with respect to the security parameter, one can see that the size of π_0 is of size $O(\log w + \log \alpha)$. We also achieve (almost) the same verifier time[3] in the preprocessing setting: while computing the commitment key $\mathsf{ck}_f = \sum_{i=1}^{w} f_i v^{-i}$ takes linear time, it may be computed once in advance then subsequently used to verify openings wrt any c and y.

Our scheme thus far achieves evaluation binding: an adversary who can open a commitment c to two different outputs for the same function can be used to break k-R-ISIS. To see this, we subtract one verifying Eq. 1 from the other to obtain

$$\langle \boldsymbol{a}, \ \pi_0 - \pi_0' \rangle \equiv y' - y \bmod q$$

Since both proofs and outputs are small, this gives k-R-ISIS solution $s = y' - y, \boldsymbol{u} = \pi_0 - \pi_0'$.

Achieving Extractability. While this construction is evaluation binding, this is insufficient to guarantee that the prover knows some witness consistent with the commitment. For example, the prover can randomly sample a short proof π_0, and compute the commitment $c = \langle \boldsymbol{a}, \ \pi_0 \rangle / (\sum_{i=1}^{w} f_i v^{-i})$. In this case, the prover can pass the verifier checks without knowledge of the input.

To achieve extractability we require an additional knowledge assumption from [2], one from the knowledge k-R-ISIS assumption family. Our knowledge k-R-ISIS assumption states that there is an extractor that extracts short $\boldsymbol{x}^*$ s.t. $c = \sum_{i=1}^{w} x_i^* v^i$ from any prover who, given $[\boldsymbol{u}_i']_{i \in [w]}$ s.t. $\langle \boldsymbol{a}, \ \boldsymbol{u}_i' \rangle \equiv v^i \cdot t \bmod q$ (for some t drawn from a special subset of $\mathcal{R}$), outputs commitment c and a short knowledge proof π_1 s.t. $\langle \boldsymbol{a}, \ \pi_1 \rangle \equiv c \cdot t \bmod q$.

Using this assumption, it suffices to include as part of the commitment an additional value $\pi_1 = \sum_{i=1}^{w} x_i \boldsymbol{u}_i$ in order to achieve extractability. Observe that if for a verifying (c, y, π_0, π_1) it held that $f(\boldsymbol{x}^*) \neq y$, then $\boldsymbol{x}^*$ could be used to

---

[3] Our verifier time is $O(\log(w \cdot \alpha) \log \log(w \cdot \alpha))$ in the preprocessing setting.

create verifying $(c, y' = f(\boldsymbol{x}^*), \pi'_0, \pi'_1)$, which violates binding and could be used to break plain k-R-ISIS as explained above. Therefore, the extracted witness must be consistent with the evaluation.

Lastly, we note our extracted witness has "stretch", i.e., the best norm bound we can hope to enforce on $\boldsymbol{x}^*$ is the norm bound on π_1, which in order to achieve correctness is necessarily bigger than the norm bound we impose on $\boldsymbol{x}$.

2 Preliminaries

Let $\mathbb{Z}(b) := (-b, b) \cap \mathbb{Z}$ and $[a] := [1, a] \cap \mathbb{Z}$. For a ring $\mathcal{R}$ of degree n, let $\mathsf{vec}(r) \in \mathbb{Z}^n$ denote the coefficient vector of $r \in \mathcal{R}$ in the integral basis.

For $m \in \mathbb{N}$, let $\zeta_m \in \mathbb{C}$ be any fixed primitive m-th root of unity. Let $\mathcal{R} = \mathbb{Z}[\zeta_m]$ denote its ring of integers, called a cyclotomic ring. We have $\mathcal{R} \cong \mathbb{Z}[x]/\langle \Phi_m(x)\rangle$, where $\Phi_m(x)$ is the m-th cyclotomic polynomial. If m is a power of 2, we call $\mathcal{R}$ a power-of-2 cyclotomic ring. In this paper, we exclusively use power-of-2 cylotomic rings. Let $q \in \mathbb{N}$ be a prime number, we let $\mathcal{R}_q := \mathcal{R}/q\mathcal{R}$ and let $\mathcal{R}_q^\times$ denote all invertible elements in $\mathcal{R}_q$. For any $f \in \mathcal{R}$, let $\mathsf{ct}(f)$ denote the constant term of f (i.e., $\mathsf{ct}(f) = \mathsf{vec}(f)_0$).

For $x \in \mathcal{R}$, let $\|x\|$ denote the ℓ-infinity norm of its coefficient vector, i.e., $\|x\| = \max_{i \in [n]} \mathsf{vec}(x)$. We use $\|\cdot\|_p$ for the ℓ_p-norm (e.g., $\|\cdot\|_2$ for the ℓ_2 norm).

Definition 1 (Ring expansion factor). *Let $\mathcal{R}$ be a ring. The* expansion factor *of $\mathcal{R}$ is defined as $\gamma_\mathcal{R} := \max_{a,b \in \mathcal{R}} \frac{\|a \cdot b\|}{\|a\| \cdot \|b\|}$.*

Theorem 1 ([3]). *If $\mathcal{R} = \mathbb{Z}[\zeta_m]$ is a power-of-2 cyclotomic ring, then $\gamma_\mathcal{R} \le n$.*

Theorem 2 ([2]). *Let $q = \omega((w \cdot f)^{f/\phi(m)})$ be a rational prime such that $\mathcal{R}_q$ splits into f fields each of size $q^{\phi(m)/f}$. For $v \leftarrow_\$ \mathcal{R}_q^w$, we have $v \in (\mathcal{R}_q^\times)^w$ with non-negligible probability.*

Subsequently in this work, we set q large enough so that uniformly random $v \leftarrow_\$ \mathcal{R}_q$ satisfies $v \in \mathcal{R}_q^\times$ with non-negligible probability.

2.1 Functional Commitments

Definition 2 (Functional commitment). *A (pre-processing non-interactive) functional commitment (FC) scheme is parameterized by a function family*

$$\mathcal{F} := \{\mathcal{F}_w \subseteq \{f : \mathcal{X}^w \to \mathcal{Y}\}\}_{w \in \mathbb{N}}$$

over a ring $\mathcal{R}$ for input alphabet $\mathcal{X} \subseteq \mathcal{R}$ and image space $\mathcal{Y} \subseteq \mathcal{R}$, where w is the dimension of the secret (committed) input. The FC scheme is defined by a 5-tuple of PPT algorithms (Setup, Com, Open, PreVerify, Verify), *working as follows:*

- Setup$(1^\lambda, 1^w) \to$ ck: *Input (in unary) security parameter λ and secret input dimension w, samples commitment key* ck.

- Com(ck, $\boldsymbol{x}$) $\rightarrow$ (c, π_1): *Input commitment key ck and secret input $\boldsymbol{x} \in \mathcal{X}^w$, computes commitment c and a proof of knowledge π_1 of vector $\boldsymbol{x}$ such that $c =$ Com(ck, $\boldsymbol{x}$).*
- Open(ck, $f, \boldsymbol{x}$) $\rightarrow$ π_0: *Input commitment key ck, function $f \in \mathcal{F}_w$, and secret input $\boldsymbol{x} \in \mathcal{R}^w$, computes opening proof π_0 for the evaluation $f(\boldsymbol{x})$.*
- PreVerify(ck, f) $\rightarrow$ ck$_f$: *Input commitment key ck and function $f \in \mathcal{F}_w$, computes preprocessed commitment key ck$_f$. Preprocessing only needs to be performed once per function and allows Verify to run in time sublinear in f.*
- Verify(ck$_f, c, y, \pi_1, \pi_0$) $\rightarrow$ $\{0,1\}$: *Input preprocessed commitment key ck$_f$, commitment c, output $y \in \mathcal{Y}$, and proofs π_1 and π_0, the verifier returns 1 if the proofs convince them the verifier knows some $\boldsymbol{x} \in \mathcal{X}^w$ such that Com(ck, $\boldsymbol{x}$) $= c$ and $f(\boldsymbol{x}) = y$ (else 0).*

We require that functional commitments satisfy correctness, extractability, and succinctness as defined below.

Definition 3 (Correctness). *An FC scheme for $(\mathcal{F}, \mathcal{X}, \mathcal{Y})$ is correct if for any $\lambda, w \in \mathbb{N}$, any ck $\leftarrow$ Setup($1^\lambda, 1^w$), and for any $(f, \boldsymbol{x}, y) \in \mathcal{F} \times \mathcal{X}^w \times \mathcal{Y}$ satisfying $f(\boldsymbol{x}) = y$, any $(c, \pi_1) \leftarrow$ Com(ck, $\boldsymbol{x}$), any $\pi_0 \leftarrow$ Open(ck, $f, \boldsymbol{x}$), and any ck$_f \leftarrow$ PreVerify(ck, f), it holds that $\Pr[\text{Verify}(ck_f, c, y, \pi_1, \pi_0) = 1] = 1$.*

At a high level, extractability of an FC scheme requires that if an adversary can produce a commitment c and a valid opening (π_1, π_0) for some function f and some evaluation y, it must know $\boldsymbol{x} \in \mathcal{X}^w$ satisfying Com(ck, $\boldsymbol{x}$) $= c$ and $f(\boldsymbol{x}) = y$. Note that extractability implies *weak binding* (meaning that it is not possible to open a commitment to two different evaluations for the same function).

Definition 4 (Extractability). *An FC scheme for $(\mathcal{F}, \mathcal{X}, \mathcal{Y})$ is $(\kappa, \mathcal{X}^*)$-extractable if for any PPT adversary $\mathcal{A}$, there exists a PPT extractor $\mathcal{E}_\mathcal{A}$ that, input ck and given black-box access to $\mathcal{A}$ and any randomness it uses, returns $\boldsymbol{x}^* \in (\mathcal{X}^*)^w$ such that*

$$\Pr\left[\begin{array}{c} \text{Verify}(ck_f, c, y, \pi_1, \pi_0) = 1 \\ \wedge \left(\begin{array}{c} \boldsymbol{x} \notin (\mathcal{X}^*)^w \\ \vee\ c \neq \text{Com}(ck, \boldsymbol{x}) \\ \vee\ f(\boldsymbol{x}) \neq y \end{array}\right) \end{array} \middle| \begin{array}{c} ck \leftarrow \text{Setup}(1^\lambda, 1^w) \\ (f, c, y, \pi_1, \pi_0) \leftarrow \mathcal{A}(ck) \\ \boldsymbol{x} \leftarrow \mathcal{E}_\mathcal{A}(ck) \\ ck_f \leftarrow \text{PreVerify}(ck, f) \end{array}\right] \leq \kappa(\lambda, w) \ .$$

We say the scheme is $\mathcal{X}^*$-extractable if its knowledge error $\kappa(\lambda, w)$ is negligible in λ for $w = \text{poly}(\lambda)$.

Definition 5 (Succinctness). *Let Π be a FC scheme for the alphabet $\mathcal{X} = \{r \in \mathcal{R} \mid r \leq \alpha\}$. We say Π is succinct if it satisfies the following properties:*

- *Proof succinctness:* $|c + \pi_1 + \pi_0| = \text{poly}(\log w + \log \alpha)$.
- *Verifier succinctness:* Verify *runs in time* $\text{poly}(\log w + \log \alpha)$.

2.2 Sampling Algorithm

The following relies on the Leftover Hash Lemma over rings to generate some vector a that is indistinguishable from a uniformly randomly sample vector, and some trapdoor that makes it possible to easily generate vectors in the kernel of a. We let $\mathsf{lhl}(\mathcal{R}_q, \beta)$ denote an algorithm that outputs the minimum $\ell \in \mathbb{N}$, which ensures that the resulting distribution of the vector a is indistinguishable from the uniform distribution. It is formally defined as follows, adapted from [2,34,37,50]:

A sampling algorithm has the following three PPT algorithms (taking 1^λ as input implicitly):

- $(a, \mathsf{td}) \leftarrow \mathsf{TrapGen}(1^\ell, q, \mathcal{R}, \beta)$: takes dimension $\ell \in \mathbb{N}$, a modulus $q \in \mathbb{N}$, a ring $\mathcal{R}$, and a norm bound $\beta \in \mathbb{R}$, and outputs a vector $a \in \mathcal{R}_q^\ell$ and a trapdoor td. For any $n \in \mathrm{poly}(\lambda)$, $\ell \geq \mathsf{lhl}(\mathcal{R}_q, b)$ where $b = O(\beta)$, the distribution of a is within $\mathrm{negl}(\lambda)$ statistical distance to $U(\mathcal{R}_q^\ell)$.
- $u \leftarrow \mathsf{SampD}(1^\ell, \mathcal{R}_q, \beta)$: for $\ell \geq \mathsf{lhl}(\mathcal{R}_q, \beta)$, outputs u such that $\|u\| \leq \beta$ and the distribution of $\langle a, u \rangle \bmod q$ is withing $\mathrm{negl}(\lambda)$ statistical distance to $U(\mathcal{R}_q)$.
- $u \leftarrow \mathsf{SampPre}(\mathsf{td}, v, \beta)$: for $\ell \geq \mathsf{lhl}(\mathcal{R}_q, \beta)$ and $v \in \mathcal{R}_q$, outputs $u \in \mathcal{R}_q^\ell$ satisfying $\|u\| \leq \beta$, $\langle a, u \rangle \equiv v \bmod q$, and that distribution of u is within $\mathrm{negl}(\lambda)$ statistical distance the distribution of $v' \leftarrow \mathsf{SampD}(1^\lambda, 1^\ell, \mathcal{R}_q, \beta)$ conditioned on $\langle a, u \rangle \equiv v' \bmod q$.

2.3 Cryptographic Assumptions

The Short Integer Solution (SIS) problem was first introduced in [1], which asks to find a short element (of ℓ_2 norm) in the kernel of a random matrix over the ring $\mathbb{Z}_q$. An inhomogeneous version, ISIS, instead asks for a short solution to some linear equation system [49]. It has been shown that the SIS and ISIS problems are equivalent.

We define the ring version of SIS (R-SIS) from [49] as follows.

Definition 6 (R-SIS [49]). *Let $\mathcal{R}, q, \ell, \beta$ be parameters depending on λ. The R-SIS problem states the following: for $a \leftarrow_\$ \mathcal{R}_q^\ell$ sampled uniformly at random, and $t = 0$, find $u \neq 0 \in \mathcal{R}^\ell$ such that $\|u\| \leq \beta$ and $\langle a, u \rangle \equiv t \bmod q$.*

When $t \leftarrow_\$ \mathcal{R}_q$ this becomes the ring inhomogeneous SIS (R-ISIS) assumption, which is known to be equivalent. For appropriate parameters, there are no known efficient algorithms for solving R-SIS for cyclotomic rings.

k-R-ISIS Assumptions. We define a family of assumptions over rings, k-R-ISIS, introduced in [2]. k-R-ISIS assumptions can be trivially broken if some basic conditions are not satisfied, so we begin by defining those via the notion of k-R-ISIS admissibility:

Definition 7 (k-R-ISIS admissible). *Let $g \in \mathcal{R}(X)$ be a Laurent monomial, i.e., $g(X) := X^e := \prod_{i \in [y]} X_i^{e_i}$ for some exponent vector $e \in \mathbb{Z}^y$. Let $\mathcal{G} \subset \mathcal{R}(X)$ be a set of Laurent monomials with $k := |\mathcal{G}|$. Let $g^* \in \mathcal{R}(X)$ be a target*

Laurent monomial. We say a monomial family $(\mathcal{G}, g^*)$ *is k-R-ISIS* admissible *if the following conditions are satisfied:*

1. *All* $g \in \mathcal{G}$ *and* g^* *have constant degree*
2. *All* $g \in \mathcal{G}$ *are distinct*
3. $0 \notin \mathcal{G}$
4. $g^* \notin \mathcal{G}$

Remark 1. Condition 1 rules out the monomials that depend on $\mathcal{R}$. Condition 2 rules out that trivial linear combinations of preimages give a preimage for the target. Condition 3 rules out a trivially producing multiple preimages of the same target. Condition 4 rules out the trivial solution to get the preimage of the target.

We then define the k-R-ISIS assumption as follows:

Definition 8 (k-R-ISIS assumption). *Let* $\ell \in \mathbb{N}$. *Let* q *be a rational prime,* $\mathcal{R}$ *a cyclotomic ring, and* $\mathcal{R}_q := \mathcal{R}/q\mathcal{R}$. *Let* $\mathcal{G} \subset \mathcal{R}(X)$ *be a set of y-variate Laurent monomials and let* $g^* \in \mathcal{R}(X)$ *be a target Laurent monomial such that* $(\mathcal{G}, g^*)$ *is* k-R-ISIS-*admissible. Let* $\beta, \beta^* \geq 1$ *be reals. For* $g \in \mathcal{G}$, $\ell \geq \mathsf{lhl}(\mathcal{R}_q, \beta)$, $\mathbf{a} \in \mathcal{R}_q^\ell$, *and* $\mathbf{v} \in (\mathcal{R}_q^\times)^y$, *let* $\mathcal{D}_{g,a,v}$ *be a distribution over*

$$\{\mathbf{u}_g \in \mathcal{R}^\ell \mid \langle \mathbf{a}, \mathbf{u}_g \rangle \equiv g(\mathbf{v}) \bmod q \ \wedge \ \|\mathbf{u}_g\| \leq \beta\} \ .$$

Let $\mathcal{D} := \{\mathcal{D}_{g,a,v} : \ell \in \mathbb{N}, \ g \in \mathcal{G}, \ \mathbf{a} \in \mathcal{R}_q^\ell, \ \mathbf{v} \in (\mathcal{R}_q^\times)^y\}$ *be the family of these distributions. Define* $\mathsf{pp} := (\mathcal{R}_q, \ell, y, \mathcal{G}, g^*, \mathcal{D}, \beta, \beta^*)$. *The* k-R-ISIS$_{\mathsf{pp}}$ *assumption states that for any PPT adversary $\mathcal{A}$, we have* $\mathsf{Adv}_{\mathsf{pp},\mathcal{A}}^{k\text{-}R\text{-ISIS}}(\lambda) \leq \mathsf{negl}(\lambda)$, *where* $\mathsf{Adv}_{\mathsf{pp},\mathcal{A}}^{k\text{-}R\text{-ISIS}}(\lambda)$ *is the following probability:*

$$\Pr\left[\begin{array}{c|c} \langle \mathbf{a}, \mathbf{u}_{g^*} \rangle \equiv s^* \cdot g^*(\mathbf{v}) \bmod q & \mathbf{a} \leftarrow\!\!\$ \ \mathcal{R}_q^\ell \\ \wedge \ \|s^*\| \leq \beta^* & \mathbf{v} \leftarrow\!\!\$ \ (\mathcal{R}_q^\times)^y \\ \wedge \ \|\mathbf{u}_{g^*}\| \leq \beta^* & \mathbf{u}_g \leftarrow\!\!\$ \ \mathcal{D}_{g,a,v}, \ \forall g \in \mathcal{G} \\ \wedge \ (s^* \cdot g^*, \mathbf{u}_{g^*}) \neq (0, \mathbf{0}) & (s^*, \mathbf{u}_{g^*}) \leftarrow \mathcal{A}(\mathbf{a}, t, [\mathbf{u}_g]_{g \in \mathcal{G}}, \mathbf{v}) \end{array}\right] .$$

Remark 2. We adapt Definition 8 [2, Def 23]. For simplicity, we set t in [2, Def 23] to be fixed to 1. This is w.o.l.g, as $\langle\{t\}\rangle = \mathcal{R}_q$ and we have $\langle\{1\}\rangle = \mathcal{R}_q$, and thus for any t that can be used, there exists $x, y \in \mathcal{R}_q$ such that $x \cdot y = 1 \bmod q, x \cdot t = 1 \bmod q$ and $y \cdot 1 = t$.

Another thing to note is that this assumption requires v to be $\in \mathcal{R}_q^\times$. Otherwise, the scheme can be insecure. For example, for a power-of-two $\mathcal{R}$, if $q = 2^k$, the ideal $q\mathcal{R}$ splits into $\mathcal{I}^{k \cdot \phi(n)}$ for some ideal $\mathcal{I}$ with norm 2. Then, for $v \leftarrow\!\!\$ \ \mathcal{R}_q$, $\Pr[v = 0 \bmod \mathcal{I}] = 1/2$. Thus, $v^{k \cdot \phi(n)} = 0 \bmod q$. Therefore, we have $p(X) = X^{k \cdot \phi(n)}$ being a solution to any R-V-SIS instance over $\mathcal{R}_q$.

In [2] they also introduce the following meta assumption:

Assumption 1 (k-R-ISIS meta assumption) *For any* k-R-ISIS *admissible* $(\mathcal{G}, g^*)$, k-R-ISIS$_{\mathcal{R}_q, \ell, y, \mathcal{G}, g^*, \mathcal{D}, \beta, \beta^*}$ *is hard if* R-ISIS$_{\mathcal{R}_q, \ell, \beta^*}$ *is hard and if* R-SIS$_{\mathcal{R}_q, k, \beta^*}$ *is hard.*

To achieve extractability we also require an additional knowledge assumption:

Definition 9 (Knowledge k-R-ISIS). *Let the parameters $(\mathcal{R}_q, \ell, y, \mathcal{G}, \beta, \beta^*)$ be defined as in Definition 8. Let $\alpha^* \geq 1$ be a real. Let $\mathcal{T} \subset \mathcal{R}_q$ be such that for all $t \in \mathcal{T}$ it holds that:*

1. $|\langle t \rangle|/|\mathcal{R}_q| = \mathrm{negl}(\lambda)$, and
2. finding $s' \in \mathcal{R}_q$ satisfying $s' \cdot t \equiv 0 \bmod q$ and $0 < \|s'\| \leq \alpha^*$ is hard.

For $g \in \mathcal{G}$, $\ell \geq \mathsf{lhl}(\mathcal{R}_q, \beta)$, $\boldsymbol{a} \in \mathcal{R}_q^\ell$, $t \in \mathcal{T}$, and $\boldsymbol{v} \in (\mathcal{R}_q^\times)^y$, let $\mathcal{D}_{g,a,t,v}$ be a distribution over

$$\{\boldsymbol{u}_g \in \mathcal{R}^\ell \mid \langle \boldsymbol{a}, \boldsymbol{u}_g \rangle \equiv g(\boldsymbol{v}) \cdot t \bmod q \ \wedge \ \|\boldsymbol{u}_g\| \leq \beta\} \ .$$

Let $\mathcal{D} := \{\mathcal{D}_{g,a,t,v} : \ell \in \mathbb{N}, \ g \in \mathcal{G}, \ \boldsymbol{a} \in \mathcal{R}_q^\ell, \ t \in \mathcal{T}, \ \boldsymbol{v} \in (\mathcal{R}_q^\times)^y\}$ be the family of these distributions. Define $\mathsf{pp} := (\mathcal{R}_q, \ell, y, \mathcal{G}, \mathcal{D}, \mathcal{T}, \alpha^*, \beta, \beta^*)$. The knowledge k-R-ISIS_{pp} assumption states that for any PPT adversary $\mathcal{A}$ there exists a PPT extractor $\mathcal{E}_\mathcal{A}$ s.t. $\mathsf{Adv}_{pp,\mathcal{A}}^{k\text{-}R\text{-}\mathsf{ISIS}} \leq \mathrm{negl}(\lambda)$, where $\mathsf{Adv}_{pp,\mathcal{A}}^{k\text{-}R\text{-}\mathsf{ISIS}}$ is the following probability:

$$\Pr \left[\begin{array}{c} \langle \boldsymbol{a}, \boldsymbol{u} \rangle \equiv c \cdot t \bmod q \ \wedge \ \|\boldsymbol{u}\| \leq \beta^* \\ \wedge \ \neg \left(\begin{array}{c} c = \sum_{g \in \mathcal{G}} x_g \cdot g(\boldsymbol{v}) \bmod q \\ \wedge \ \|x_g\| \leq \alpha^*, \ \forall g \in \mathcal{G} \end{array} \right) \end{array} \right| \begin{array}{l} \boldsymbol{a} \leftarrow_\$ \mathcal{R}_q^\ell \bmod q; \ t \leftarrow_\$ \mathcal{T}; \ \boldsymbol{v} \leftarrow_\$ (\mathcal{R}_q^\times)^w \\ \boldsymbol{u}_g \leftarrow_\$ \mathcal{D}_{g,a,v}, \ \forall g \in \mathcal{G} \\ ((c, \boldsymbol{u}), [x_g]_{g \in \mathcal{G}}) \leftarrow (\mathcal{A} \| \mathcal{E}_\mathcal{A})(\boldsymbol{a}, t, [\boldsymbol{u}_g]_{g \in \mathcal{G}}, \boldsymbol{v}) \\ (c, \boldsymbol{u}), [x_g]_{g \in \mathcal{G}}) \leftarrow (\mathcal{A} \| \mathcal{E}_\mathcal{A})(\boldsymbol{a}, t, [\boldsymbol{u}_g]_{g \in \mathcal{G}}, \boldsymbol{v}) \end{array} \right] .$$

To understand the first restriction on $\mathcal{T}$, consider an adversary who samples a random short $\boldsymbol{u}$ and then checks if $\langle \boldsymbol{a}, \boldsymbol{u} \rangle \in \langle t \rangle$, setting the commitment to be c s.t. $\langle \boldsymbol{a}, \boldsymbol{u} \rangle \equiv c \bmod q$ if so. Since $\langle \boldsymbol{a}, \boldsymbol{u} \rangle$ is close to uniformly distributed over $\mathcal{R}_q$, restriction 1 ensures such an adversary succeeds with negligible probability. To understand the second restriction, consider an adversary who finds s' as above and outputs $(c, \boldsymbol{u}) = (s', s' \cdot \boldsymbol{u}_g)$ for an arbitrary $g \in \mathcal{G}$. Observe that $\boldsymbol{u}$ is short since s' and $\boldsymbol{u}_g$ are, and since $\langle \boldsymbol{a}, \boldsymbol{u}_g \rangle \equiv g(\boldsymbol{v}) \cdot t \bmod q$ it follows $\langle \boldsymbol{a}, \boldsymbol{u} \rangle \equiv s' \cdot g(\boldsymbol{v}) \cdot t \equiv 0 \equiv c \cdot t \bmod q$. However, we have that $s' \cdot g(\boldsymbol{v}) \not\equiv c \equiv s' \bmod q$ unless $g(\boldsymbol{v}) \equiv 1 \bmod q$, which should only happen with negligible probability.

In addition to the two constraints on $\mathcal{T}$ in our knowledge k-R-ISIS definition, in [2] they give a third. Namely, that $1/|\langle t \rangle| = \mathrm{negl}(\lambda)$. We have omitted this constraint given it is implied by constraint 2. Let $\phi : \mathcal{R}_q \mapsto \langle t \rangle$. Then $|\ker(\phi)|/|\mathcal{R}_q| = 1/|\langle t \rangle|$. If $1/|\langle t \rangle|$ is not negligible, then $s' \leftarrow_\$ \mathcal{R}_q$ satisfies $s' \cdot t \equiv 0 \bmod q$ with non-negligible probability.

The k-P-R-ISIS Assumption. Our construction relies on a particular assumption in the k-R-ISIS assumption family and its knowledge counterpart, parameterized by the monomial sets $[X^i]_{i \in \mathbb{Z}(w) \setminus \{0\}}$ and $[X^i]_{i \in [w]}$, respectively. This assumption could be seen as a lattice analogue of the k-Strong-Diffie-Hellman (k-SDH) problem, and we refer to it as the k-Powers R-ISIS (k-P-R-ISIS) assumption.

Assumption 2 (k-P-R-ISIS assumption) *Define k-P-R-$\mathsf{ISIS}_{\mathcal{R}_q, \ell, \mathcal{D}, \beta, \beta^*} := k$-$R$-$\mathsf{ISIS}_{\mathcal{R}_q, \ell, y, \mathcal{G}, g^*, \mathcal{D}, \beta, \beta^*}$ with fixed $\mathcal{G} = [X^i]_{i \in \mathbb{Z}(k) \setminus \{0\}}$, $g^*(X) = 1$, and consequently $y = 1$. The k-P-R-ISIS assumption is hard if R-$\mathsf{ISIS}_{\mathcal{R}_q, \ell, \beta^*}$ is.*

In the discrete log setting, this is akin to asking an adversary to compute g given $(g^{x^{w-1}}, \ldots, g^{x^{-1}}, g^x, \ldots, g^{x^w})$. Since $(\mathcal{G}, g^*)$ is k-M-ISISadmissible (Definition 7), our assumption follows from the much broader meta assumption of Lai et al. (Assumption 1). We also require the following knowledge assumption:

Assumption 3 (Knowledge k-P-R-ISIS assumption)   *Define knowledge k-P-R-ISIS$_{\mathcal{R}_q, \ell, \mathcal{D}, \mathcal{T}, \alpha^*, \beta, \beta^*}$ as knowledge k-R-ISIS$_{\mathcal{R}_q, \ell, y, \mathcal{G}, \mathcal{D}, \mathcal{T}, \alpha^*, \beta, \beta^*}$ with $\alpha^* \geq \beta^* \geq 1$, fixed $\mathcal{G} = [X^i]_{i \in [k]}$, and consequently $y = 1$. The knowledge k-P-R-ISIS assumption holds if R-ISIS$_{\mathcal{R}_q, \ell, \beta^*}$ does.*

3   Cryptanalysis of k-P-R-ISIS

In this section, we consider how the k-P-R-ISISassumption may be attacked. We begin by formulating a special case of R-SIS assumption when $\boldsymbol{a}$is generated by the powers of a single ring element, which we call ring Vandermonde SIS (R-V-SIS). Then we show how an attacker who efficiently solves R-V-SIS can break the security of Orbweaver.

Definition 10. *(R-V-SIS) Let $\mathcal{R}, q, \beta_V$ be parameters depending on λ and w. The R-V-SIS problem asks the following: given $\boldsymbol{v} := [v^i]_{i \in \mathbb{Z}(w) \setminus \{0\}} \in \mathcal{R}_q^{2w-3}$ for $v \leftarrow_\$ \mathcal{R}_q^\times$, find $(s, \boldsymbol{z}) \neq (0, \boldsymbol{0}) \in \mathcal{R} \times \mathcal{R}^{2w-3}$ such that $0 < \|s\| \leq \beta_V, \|\boldsymbol{z}\| \leq \beta_V$, and $\langle \boldsymbol{v}, \ \boldsymbol{z} \rangle \equiv s \bmod q$.*

We note that similar assumptions have been proposed by prior works (see [22] for a summary). Thus far, there are no known algorithms which solve these variants faster than their non-Vandermonde counterparts.

We now show how an adversary who breaks R-V-SIS can break k-P-R-ISIS. Since we are given $\boldsymbol{a} \cdot \boldsymbol{u}_i \equiv v^i \bmod q$ for all $i \in \mathbb{Z}(w) \setminus \{0\}$, and our goal is to find short $(s^*, \boldsymbol{u}_{g^*}) \neq (0, \boldsymbol{0})$ such that $\boldsymbol{a} \cdot \boldsymbol{u}_{g^*} \equiv s^* \cdot v^0 \bmod q$. We first solve R-V-SIS, obtaining $s, \boldsymbol{z}$ satisfying the constraints in Definition 10. Then, we let $\boldsymbol{u}_{g^*} = \sum_{i \in \mathbb{Z}(w) \setminus \{0\}} z_i \cdot \boldsymbol{u}_i$ and $s^* = s$. We observe that $\langle \boldsymbol{a}, \ \boldsymbol{u}_{g^*} \rangle \equiv \sum_{i \in \mathbb{Z}(w) \setminus \{0\}} z_i \cdot \langle \boldsymbol{a}, \ \boldsymbol{u}_i \rangle \equiv s^* v^0 \bmod q$.

Notice, however, we do get some blowup in the norm, where now $\|\boldsymbol{u}_{g^*}\| \leq (2w-3) \cdot \beta_V \cdot \beta \cdot \gamma_{\mathcal{R}}$. So we must solve R-V-SIS for a β_V such that $(2w-3) \cdot \beta_V \cdot \beta \cdot \gamma_{\mathcal{R}} \leq \beta^*$.

In [2], they generalize this attack, requiring the attacker find (not necessarily short) $\boldsymbol{z}$ and short s^* satisfying $\langle \boldsymbol{a}, \ \boldsymbol{u}_{g^*} \rangle \equiv s^* v^0 \bmod q$ and $\|\boldsymbol{u}_{g^*}\| \leq \beta^*$ for $\boldsymbol{u}_{g^*} = \sum_{i \in \mathbb{Z}(w) \setminus \{0\}} z_i \cdot \boldsymbol{u}_i$. This attack applies to our scheme as well. See Sect. 4.1 of their paper for details.

Setting Parameters According to the Direct SIS Attack. Given there are no specific algorithms for the above problems, when picking parameters we consider the cost of a direct SIS attack that ignores the preimages and their algebraic dependencies. The following analysis is standard. We first reduce R-ISIS to R-SIS: recall that to break the assumption, the attacker needs to find some

u_g such that $\langle a, u_g \rangle \equiv s^*$ mod q; instead, we ask the attacker to find u'_g such that $\langle a', u'_g \rangle \equiv 0$ mod q, where $a' := a\|-1$. Then, here the last entry of u'_g becomes s^*.

We can then view this as a SIS instance[4]: for $A \in \mathbb{Z}_q^{n \times n(\ell+1)}$ find $u \in \mathbb{Z}_q^{n(\ell+1)}$ such that $A \cdot u \equiv 0$ mod q. Let $L \in \mathbb{Z}_q^{n(\ell+1) \times n\ell}$ be a basis for the right kernel of A. Then solving this SIS instance is equivalent to finding a short vector in $\Lambda(L)$. Observe that

$$L' = \left[L \left| \begin{array}{c} 0 \\ qI_n \end{array} \right. \right]$$

is an equivalent basis for this lattice. If we compute the Gram-Schmidt format of L', we get the form $\left[\begin{array}{c|c} I & 0 \\ \tilde{L} & qI_n \end{array} \right]$ for some $\tilde{L} \in \mathbb{Z}_q^{n(\ell+1) \times n\ell}$.

Thus, it is easy to compute the volume $\mathsf{Vol}(\Lambda) = \prod_{i \in [n(\ell+1)]} \|b_i\|_\infty = q^n$, where $[b_1, \ldots, b_{n(\ell+1)}] = \tilde{L}$. Thus, the goal is to find a vector in $\Lambda(L)^\intercal$ in a $d \leq n \cdot (\ell+1)$ dimensional lattice with volume q^n. We thus consider the adversary wins if it finds a vector with ℓ_2 norm of $\sqrt{d} \cdot \beta^*$, where β^* is the ℓ_∞ norm we allow in our hardness assumption.

Recall that lattice reduction with lattice parameter n (i.e., our ring degree) returns a vector with ℓ_2 norm $\approx \delta^d \cdot \mathsf{Vol}(\Lambda)^{1/d}$, where δ is the root Hermite factor. With the state-of-the-art lattice reduction algorithm [9], to achieve $\delta \approx (\frac{n}{2\pi e})^{1/(2n)}$, it takes roughly $2^{0.292n + o(n)}$ time. When $d \approx \sqrt{n \cdot log(q)/log(\delta)}$, the norm of the vector found (i.e., $\delta^d \cdot \mathsf{Vol}(\Lambda)^{1/d}$) is minimized [51].

Thus, we can simply set $\delta^d \cdot \mathsf{Vol}(\Lambda)^{1/d} \geq \sqrt{d} \cdot \beta^*$ for the d that minimizes the left hand side, and $2^{0.292n + o(n)} \geq 2^\lambda$. Thus, when we set parameters for R-SIS problem with parameter $\mathcal{R}, q, \ell, \beta^*$ (where $\mathcal{R}$ has ring degree n), essentially, we are requiring that the adversary cannot find a vector with ℓ_2 norm $\leq \sqrt{n \cdot log(q)/log(\delta)} \cdot \beta^*$ in $\leq 2^\lambda$ time using the attack above, except with negligible probability.[5]

4   Orbweaver: Linear Map Commitments for $\mathcal{R}_q$

We present Orbweaver, a functional commitment (FC) for linear maps that is non-interactive, publicly verifiable, preprocessing, and structure-preserving. Together, these features enable efficient recursive composition of our construction.

Orbweaver supports opening committed vectors wrt. the function family $\mathcal{F} = \{\mathcal{F}_w\}_{w \in \mathbb{N}}$, where $\mathcal{F}_w = \mathcal{X}^w$ and $f \in \mathcal{F}_w$ is computed as $f(x) \equiv \langle [f_i]_{i=1}^w, x \rangle$ mod q. The input alphabet $\mathcal{X} = \{x \in \mathcal{R} \mid x \leq \alpha\}$ is specified by

---

[4] We are again ignoring the structure of A as to our knowledge there is no attack that works better for R-SIS than SIS.

[5] Note that there are known poly-time attacks against some parameter selection for R-SIS, e.g., [21]. Thus, we also need to avoid those parameter selections. In more detail, we follow what is suggested in [2] and pick q such that $\mathcal{R}_q$ fully splits and pick t as specified in Definition 9.

the ring $\mathcal{R}$ and norm bound α. Let $\delta_M = w \cdot \alpha^2 \cdot \gamma_{\mathcal{R}}$, where $\gamma_{\mathcal{R}}$ is the expansion factor of $\mathcal{R}$ (see Definition 1). The image space $\mathcal{Y}$ is then $\mathcal{Y} = \{y \in \mathcal{R} \mid y \leq \delta_M\}$.

Let $P := \mathbb{Z}(w) \setminus \{0\}$. We use the monomial set $\mathcal{G}_0 := [g_i(X) = X^i]_{i \in P}$ to generate our opening proof $[\boldsymbol{u}_{0,i}]_{i \in P}$, the monomial set $\mathcal{G}_1 := [g_i(X) = X^i]_{i \in [w]}$ to generate our knowledge proof SRS $[\boldsymbol{u}_{1,i}]_{i \in [w]}$, the target monomial $g^*(X) := 1$, and the distribution $\mathcal{T}$ satisfying the requirements of Assumption 3[6] (Table 1).

Table 1. A list of parameters used in Orbweaver.

$w \in \mathbb{N}$		Dimension of secret input $\boldsymbol{x}$
$n \in \mathbb{N}$		Degree of $\mathcal{R}$
$\alpha \in \mathbb{R}$	poly(λ)	Norm bound for $\boldsymbol{x}$ and f
$\beta_0 \in \mathbb{R}$	poly(λ)	Norm bound for public preimages $\boldsymbol{u}_{0,\cdot}$ for π_0
$\beta_1 \in \mathbb{R}$	poly(λ)	Norm bound for public preimages $\boldsymbol{u}_{1,\cdot}$ for π_1
$\delta_0 \in \mathbb{R}$	$w^2 \cdot \alpha^2 \cdot \beta_0 \cdot \gamma_{\mathcal{R}}^2$	Norm bound for opening proof π_0
$\delta_1 \in \mathbb{R}$	$w \cdot \alpha \cdot \beta_1 \cdot \gamma_{\mathcal{R}}$	Norm bound for commitment knowledge proof π_1
$\delta_M \in \mathbb{R}$	$w \cdot \alpha^2 \cdot \gamma_{\mathcal{R}}$	Norm bound for evaluation of a linear map with coefficients of norm bounded by α at a point of norm bounded by α
$q \in \mathbb{R}$		Modulus for $\mathcal{R}_q$
$\ell_i \in \mathbb{N}$	$\geq \mathsf{lhl}(\mathcal{R}_q, \beta_i)$	Number of ring elements in $\boldsymbol{a}$
$\gamma_{\mathcal{R}}$		Ring expansion factor of $\mathcal{R}$
$\mathcal{X}$	$\{x \in \mathcal{R} : \|x\| \leq \alpha\}$	$\mathcal{R}$ elements with norm bound α
$\mathcal{F}$		family of w-variate linear maps over $\mathcal{X}$

$\underline{\mathsf{Setup}(1^\lambda, 1^w) \to \mathsf{ck}}$

$v \leftarrow_\$ \mathcal{R}_q^\times; \quad t \leftarrow_\$ \mathcal{T}$

$(\boldsymbol{a}_0, \mathsf{td}_0) \leftarrow \mathsf{TrapGen}(1, 1^\ell, \mathcal{R}_q, \beta_0); \quad (\boldsymbol{a}_1, \mathsf{td}_1) \leftarrow \mathsf{TrapGen}(1, 1^\ell, \mathcal{R}_q, \beta_1)$

$\boldsymbol{u}_{0,i} \leftarrow \mathsf{SampPre}(\mathsf{td}_0, v^i, \beta_0), \quad \forall i \in P; \quad \boldsymbol{u}_{1,i} \leftarrow \mathsf{SampPre}(\mathsf{td}_1, v^i \cdot t, \beta_1), \quad \forall i \in [w]$

Return $\mathsf{ck} := (\boldsymbol{a}_0, [\boldsymbol{u}_{0,i}]_{i \in P}, \boldsymbol{a}_1, t, [\boldsymbol{u}_{1,i}]_{i \in [w]}, v)$

$\underline{\mathsf{Com}(\mathsf{ck}, \boldsymbol{x}) \to (c, \pi_1)}$

$c := \sum_{i=1}^w x_i v^i \bmod q$

$\pi_1 := \sum_{i=1}^w x_i \cdot \boldsymbol{u}_{1,i} \bmod q$

Return (c, π_1)

$\underline{\mathsf{Open}(\mathsf{ck}, f, \boldsymbol{x}) \to \pi_0}$

Let $a_{-w+1}, ..., a_{w-1}$ denote the $2w - 1$ coefficients of $\boldsymbol{x}(v)f(v) := \left(\sum_{i=1}^w x_i v^i\right)\left(\sum_{i=1}^w f_i v^{-i}\right)$

---

[6] Concretely, we can use the set of all $\mathcal{R}_q$ elements t where half of its components in the Chinese remainder theorem representation are zero and the other half are non-zero, as shown in [2].

Return $\pi_0 := \sum_{i \in P} a_i \cdot \boldsymbol{u}_{0,i} \bmod q$

PreVerify(ck, f) $\rightarrow$ ck$_f$
$\overline{\text{If } \|f\| > \alpha, \text{ abort}}$
Return ck$_f := \sum_{i=1}^{w} f_i \cdot v^{-i} \bmod q$

Verify(ck$_f, c, \pi_1, y, \pi_0$) $\rightarrow \{0, 1\}$
$\overline{\text{Output 1 if the following conditions}}$ all hold (else 0):
$\|y\|_\infty \le \delta_M; \quad \|\pi_1\|_\infty \le \delta_1; \quad \|\pi_0\|_\infty \le \delta_0$
$\langle \boldsymbol{a}_1, \ \pi_1 \rangle \equiv c \cdot t \bmod q$
$\langle \boldsymbol{a}_0, \ \pi_0 \rangle \equiv \text{ck}_f \cdot c - y \bmod q$

We next prove that Orbweaver satisfies correctness, extractability, and succinctness.

Theorem 3. *Orbweaver is correct (Definition 3) for $\delta_1 \ge w \cdot \alpha \cdot \beta_0 \cdot \gamma_\mathcal{R}$ and $\delta_0 \ge w^2 \cdot \alpha^2 \cdot \beta_1 \cdot \gamma_\mathcal{R}^2$.*

Proof. We begin by proving the norm bound checks hold. $y = f(\boldsymbol{x}) = \sum_{i=1}^{w} f_i \cdot x_i \bmod q$, where $\|f_i \cdot x_i\| \le \alpha^2 \cdot \gamma_\mathcal{R}$ for all i. Therefore, $\|y\| \le w \cdot \alpha^2 \cdot \gamma_\mathcal{R} = \delta_M$. Next, $\pi_1 = \sum_{i=1}^{w} x_i \cdot \boldsymbol{u}_{1,i} \bmod q$, where $\|x_i \cdot \boldsymbol{u}_{1,i}\| \le \alpha \cdot \beta_1 \cdot \gamma_\mathcal{R}$ for all i. It follows $\|\pi_1\| \le w \cdot \alpha \cdot \beta_1 \cdot \gamma_\mathcal{R} = \delta_1$. Last, $\pi_0 = \sum_{i \in P} a_i \cdot \boldsymbol{u}_{1,i} \bmod q$, where $a_{-w+1}, ..., a_{w-1}$ denote the $2w - 2$ coefficients of $\boldsymbol{x}(v)f(v) = \left(\sum_{i=1}^{w} x_i v^i\right)\left(\sum_{i=1}^{w} f_i v^{-i}\right)$. Since $\|\boldsymbol{u}_{0,i}\| \le \beta_0$ for all i, $\|\pi_0\| \le \beta_0 \cdot \gamma_\mathcal{R} \cdot \sum_{i \in P} a_i$. Then $\|a_{|i|}\| \le (w - i) \cdot \alpha^2 \cdot \gamma_\mathcal{R}$ for $i \in [w - 1]$. Thus, $\|\pi_0\| \le w^2 \cdot \alpha^2 \cdot \beta_0 \cdot \gamma_\mathcal{R}^2 = \delta_0$.
Next, we show the verification equations hold:

$$\begin{aligned}
\langle \boldsymbol{a}_1, \ \pi_1 \rangle &\equiv \langle \boldsymbol{a}_1, \ \textstyle\sum_{i=1}^{w} x_i \cdot \boldsymbol{u}_{1,i} \rangle \bmod q \\
&\equiv \textstyle\sum_{i=1}^{w} x_i \cdot \langle \boldsymbol{a}_0, \ \boldsymbol{u}_{1,i} \rangle \bmod q \\
&\equiv \textstyle\sum_{i=1}^{w} x_i \cdot v^i \cdot t \bmod q \\
&\equiv c \cdot t \bmod q \\
\langle \boldsymbol{a}_0, \ \pi_0 \rangle &\equiv \langle \boldsymbol{a}_0, \ \textstyle\sum_{i \in P} a_i \cdot \boldsymbol{u}_i \rangle \bmod q \\
&\equiv \textstyle\sum_{i \in P} a_i \cdot v^i \bmod q \\
&\equiv \left(\textstyle\sum_{i=1}^{w} x_i v^i\right)\left(\textstyle\sum_{i=1}^{w} f_i v^{-i}\right) - a_0 \cdot v^0 \bmod q \\
&\equiv \text{ck}_f \cdot c - \textstyle\sum_{i=1}^{w} f_i \cdot x_i \equiv \text{ck}_f \cdot c - y \bmod q \ .
\end{aligned}$$

Theorem 4. *Let $\mathcal{X}^* := \{x \in \mathcal{R} \mid x \le \alpha^*\}$. Orbweaver is $\mathcal{X}^*$-extractable if*

$$\begin{aligned}
&\ell_0 \ge \mathsf{lhl}(\mathcal{R}_q, b_0), \quad \ell_1 \ge \mathsf{lhl}(\mathcal{R}_q, b_1) \\
&\alpha^* \ge \beta_1^* \ge \delta_1 \\
&\beta_0^* \ge 2 \cdot w^2 \cdot \alpha \cdot \alpha^* \cdot \beta_0 \cdot \gamma_\mathcal{R}^2
\end{aligned}$$

where $b_0 = O(\beta_0), b_1 = O(\beta_1)$, and the k-R-$\mathsf{ISIS}_{\mathcal{R}_q, \ell_0, 1, \mathcal{G}_0, g_0^*, \mathcal{D}_0, \beta_0, \beta_0^*}$ (i.e., k-P-R-ISIS) and knowledge k-R-$\mathsf{ISIS}_{\mathcal{R}_q, \ell_1, 1, \mathcal{G}_1, \mathcal{D}_1, \mathcal{T}, \alpha^*, \beta_1, \beta_1^*}$ (i.e., knowledge k-P-R-ISIS) assumptions hold, where $\mathcal{D}_0$ and $\mathcal{D}_1$ are such that

$$\left\{ (a_0, [u_{0,g}]_{g \in \mathcal{G}_0}, v) \middle| \begin{array}{l} a_0 \leftarrow\!\!\$ \, \mathcal{R}_q^{\ell_0}; \quad v \leftarrow\!\!\$ \, \mathcal{R}_q^{\times} \\ u_{0,g} \leftarrow\!\!\$ \, \mathcal{D}_{g,a_0,v}, \;\; \forall i \in P \end{array} \right\}$$
$$\approx \left\{ (a_0, [u_{0,g}]_{g \in \mathcal{G}_0}, v) \middle| \begin{array}{l} a_0 \leftarrow\!\!\$ \, \mathcal{R}_q^{\ell_0}; \quad v \leftarrow\!\!\$ \, \mathcal{R}_q^{\times} \\ u_{0,g} \leftarrow\!\!\$ \, \mathsf{SampD}(1^{\ell_0}, \mathcal{R}_q, \beta_0) : \langle a_0, \, u_{0,g} \rangle \equiv v^i \bmod q, \;\; \forall i \in P \end{array} \right\}$$

and

$$\left\{ (a_1, t_i, [u_{1,g}]_{g \in \mathcal{G}_1}, v) \middle| \begin{array}{l} a_1 \leftarrow\!\!\$ \, \mathcal{R}_q^{\ell_1}; \quad t \leftarrow\!\!\$ \, \mathcal{T}; \;\; v \leftarrow\!\!\$ \, \mathcal{R}_q^{\times} \\ u_{1,g} \leftarrow\!\!\$ \, \mathcal{D}_{g,a_1,t,v}, \;\; \forall i \in [w] \end{array} \right\}$$
$$\approx \left\{ (a_1, t_i, [u_{1,g}]_{g \in \mathcal{G}_1}, v) \middle| \begin{array}{l} a_1 \leftarrow\!\!\$ \, \mathcal{R}_q^{\ell_1}; \quad t \leftarrow\!\!\$ \, \mathcal{T}; \;\; v \leftarrow\!\!\$ \, \mathcal{R}_q^{\times} \\ u_{1,g} \leftarrow\!\!\$ \, \mathsf{SampD}(1^{\ell_1}, \mathcal{R}_q, \beta_1) : \langle a_1, \, u_{1,g} \rangle \equiv v^i \cdot t \bmod q, \;\; \forall i \in [w] \end{array} \right\}.$$

Proof. Suppose there exists a PPT adversary $\mathcal{A}$ that, on input $\mathsf{ck} \leftarrow \mathsf{Setup}(1^\lambda, 1^w)$, outputs (f, c, y, π_1, π_0) such that $\mathsf{PreVerify}(\mathsf{ck}, f)$ does not abort and $\mathsf{Verify}(\mathsf{ck}_f, c, y, \pi_1, \pi_0) = 1$ with non-negligible probability in λ over any randomness it uses and the choice of ck. We construct an extractor $\mathcal{E}_{\mathcal{A}}$ that, input ck and given black-box access to $\mathcal{A}$ and any randomness it uses, returns $x^* \in (\mathcal{X}^*)^w$ such that $c = \mathsf{Com}(\mathsf{ck}, x^*)$ and $f(x^*) = y$ with all but negligible probability in λ when $\mathcal{A}$ succeeds.

For commitment key $\mathsf{ck} = (a_0, [u_{0,i}]_{i \in P}, a_1, t, [u_{1,i}]_{i \in [w]}, v)$, define $\mathsf{ck}_0 := (a_0, [u_{1,i}]_{i \in [w]}, v)$ and $\mathsf{ck}_1 := (a_1, t, [u_{1,i}]_{i \in [w]}, v)$. Let $\mathcal{B}_{\mathcal{A}}$ be an adversary with black-box access to $\mathcal{A}$ that runs on input ck' sampled according to the knowledge $k\text{-}R\text{-}\mathsf{ISIS}_{\mathcal{R}_q, \ell_1, 1, \mathcal{G}_1, \mathcal{D}_1, \mathcal{T}, \alpha^*, \beta_1, \beta_1^*}$ definition (Definition 9). First, $\mathcal{B}_{\mathcal{A}}$ samples ck_0' according to the $k\text{-}R\text{-}\mathsf{ISIS}_{\mathcal{R}_q, \ell_0, 1, \mathcal{G}_0, g_0^*, \mathcal{D}_0, \beta_0, \beta_0^*}$ definition (Definition 8), except fixing $v' = v$. Then $\mathcal{B}_{\mathcal{A}}$ runs $\mathcal{A}$ on $(\mathsf{ck}_0', \mathsf{ck}_1)$ (passing its own random input tape) to obtain (f, c, y, π_1, π_0), which it parses to output (c, π_1).

Let $\mathcal{E}_{\mathcal{B}_{\mathcal{A}}}$ be the extractor promised by our knowledge assumption for $\mathcal{B}_{\mathcal{A}}$. Extractor $\mathcal{E}_{\mathcal{A}}$, on input $\mathsf{ck} = (\mathsf{ck}_0, \mathsf{ck}_1)$, runs $\mathcal{E}_{\mathcal{B}_{\mathcal{A}}}(\mathsf{ck}_1)$ to obtain x^*. Next consider the following hybrid experiments:

1. Hyb_0: the real experiment, where $\mathsf{ck} \leftarrow \mathsf{Setup}(1^\lambda, 1^w)$, $(f, c, y, \pi_1, \pi_0) \leftarrow \mathcal{A}(\mathsf{ck})$, and $x^* \leftarrow \mathcal{E}_{\mathcal{A}}(\mathsf{ck})$.
2. Hyb_1: the same as Hyb_0, but $\mathsf{ck} = (\mathsf{ck}_0, \mathsf{ck}_1')$, where ck_1' is sampled according to the knowledge $k\text{-}R\text{-}\mathsf{ISIS}_{\mathcal{R}_q, \ell_1, 1, \mathcal{G}_1, \mathcal{D}_1, \mathcal{T}, \alpha^*, \beta_1, \beta_1^*}$ definition, conditioned on $v' = v$.
3. Hyb_2: the same as Hyb_1, but $\mathsf{ck} = (\mathsf{ck}_0'', \mathsf{ck}_1')$, where ck_1' is sampled as in Hyb_1, but ck_0'' is sampled according to the $k\text{-}R\text{-}\mathsf{ISIS}_{\mathcal{R}_q, \ell_0, 1, \mathcal{G}_0, g_0^*, \mathcal{D}_0, \beta_0, \beta_0^*}$ definition, again conditioned on $v'' = v'$.

By our assumption on $\mathcal{D}_1$ (resp., $\mathcal{D}_0$) hybrids 0 and 1 (resp., 1 and 2) are statistically close. Therefore, they are all statistically close. This implies if a property holds with respect to the output of one hybrid with a certain probability, it will hold with respect to the output of the others with statistically close probability.

From our knowledge assumption, we know that in Hyb_1 the extractor outputs x^* satisfying $c \equiv \sum_{i=1}^w x_i \cdot v^i \bmod q$ and $\|x_i\| \leq \alpha^*$ for all $i \in [w]$ with probability all but negligible in λ. Now consider the output in Hyb_2 satisfies $c \equiv \sum_{i=1}^w x_i \cdot v^i \bmod q$ for $x^* \in \mathcal{X}^*$, but $f(x^*) \neq y$. When this happens we can break $k\text{-}R\text{-}\mathsf{ISIS}_{\mathcal{R}_q, \ell_0, 1, \mathcal{G}_0, g_0^*, \mathcal{D}_0, \beta_0, \beta_0^*}$ as follows. Let $y^* := f(x^*)$ and

$\pi_0^* \leftarrow \mathsf{Open}(\mathsf{ck}, f, \boldsymbol{x}^*)$. Then we obtain the solution $(y^* - y, \pi_0 - \pi_0^*)$ for k-R-ISIS, where

$$\langle \boldsymbol{a}_0, \ \pi_0 - \pi_0^* \rangle \equiv \mathsf{ck}_f \cdot c - y - (\mathsf{ck}_f \cdot c - y^*) \equiv (y^* - y) \cdot 1 \equiv (y^* - y) \cdot g^*(v) \bmod q \ .$$

To see that the norm bounds hold, we can bound $\delta_M^* := \|y^*\| \le w\alpha^*\alpha\gamma_{\mathcal{R}}$ and $\delta_0^* := \|\pi_0^*\| \le w^2\alpha^*\alpha\beta_0\gamma_{\mathcal{R}}^2 \le \beta_0^*/2$ by modifying the calculations of δ_M and δ_0 in the correctness proof. Therefore, this can only happen with negligible probability in λ. Together, these two properties about the results of Hyb_1 and Hyb_2 show that Orbweaver is $\mathcal{X}^*$-extractable.

Theorem 5. *Orbweaver is succinct (Definition 5).*

Proof. We first show Orbweaver has $O(\log w + \log \alpha)$ size commitments and proofs. From our construction we have that $|c| = n\lceil\log(q)\rceil$, $|\pi_0| = n\ell_0\lceil\log\delta_0\rceil$, and $|\pi_1| = n\ell_1\lceil\log\delta_1\rceil$. We set a base $b_0 = O(\beta_0), b_1 = O(\beta_1)$ for trapdoor generation and let $\ell_0 := \mathsf{lhl}(\mathcal{R}_q, b_0) = O(\log(q)/\log(\beta_0))), \ell_1 := \mathsf{lhl}(\mathcal{R}_q, b_1) = O(\log(q)/\log(\beta_1))$. We consider the ring degree nto be a function of the security parameter and treat it as a constant for the following analysis. As implicated by our extractability theorem (Theorem 4) together with our assumptions relating the hardness of plain and knowledge k-P-R-$\mathsf{ISIS}$to R-SIS (Assumptions 2 and 3), we must have that R-$\mathsf{SIS}_{\mathcal{R}_q,\ell,\beta_0^*}$ and R-$\mathsf{SIS}_{\mathcal{R}_q,\ell,\delta_1}$ are hard. Recall $\beta_0^* = 2w^2\alpha\alpha^*\beta_0\gamma_{\mathcal{R}}^2$. Using $\alpha^* = \delta_1 = w\alpha\beta_1\gamma_{\mathcal{R}}$, we can write $\beta_0^* = 2w^3\alpha^2\beta_0\beta_1\gamma_{\mathcal{R}}^3$. Since $\delta_1 < \beta_0^*$, we can just pick qs.t. R-$\mathsf{SIS}_{\mathcal{R}_q,\ell,\beta_0^*}$ is hard.

In particular, we let $q \approx \beta_0^* n\log(n)$ such that $\log(q) = O(\log\beta_0^*) = O(\log(w) + \log(\alpha) + \log(\beta_0) + \log(\beta_1))$ since for power-of-two cyclotomic rings $\gamma_{\mathcal{R}} \le n$ (Theorem 1). Setting $\beta_0 := \max\{w, \alpha\}$ and $\beta_1 := \max\{w, \alpha\}$, we obtain logarithmic commitment and proof sizes:

$$\begin{aligned}
|c| &= n\lceil\log(q)\rceil & |\pi_0| &= n\ell_0\lceil\log\delta_0\rceil \\
&\approx n\log(n\log(n)\beta_0^*) & &= 2\lceil\log(q)/\log(\beta_0)\rceil n\lceil\log\delta_0\rceil \\
&= O(\log\beta_0^*) & &\approx 2n\log(\beta_0^* n\log n)\log\delta_0/\log\beta_0 \\
&= O(\log w + \log\alpha) & &= O(\log(\beta_0^*)\cdot\log(\delta_0)/\log\beta_0) \\
& & &= O(\log w + \log\alpha)
\end{aligned}$$

$$\begin{aligned}
|\pi_1| &= n\ell_0\lceil\log\delta_1\rceil \\
&= 2\lceil\log(q)/\log(\beta_1)\rceil n\lceil\log\delta_1\rceil \\
&\approx 2n\log(\beta_0^* n\log n)\log\delta_1/\log\beta_1 \\
&= O(\log\beta_0^*\cdot\log\delta_1/\log\beta_1) \\
&= O(\log w + \log\alpha)
\end{aligned}$$

Next, we show that the Orbweaver verifier runs in time $O(\log w + \log \alpha)$ time. Ignoring small constant addends, the verifier first checks the norm of $(\ell_0 + \ell_1) \cdot n$ elements in $\mathbb{Z}_q$. The two inner products similarly require $(\ell_0 + \ell_1)$ multiplications and $(\ell_0 + \ell_1)$ additions in $\mathcal{R}_q$. Using the NTT, $(\ell_0 + \ell_1)$ multiplications in $\mathcal{R}_q$requires $(\ell_0 + \ell_1)n\log n$ multiplications in $\mathbb{Z}_q$. Since we we have fixed n as a constant depending on λ, we observe the verifier is performing $O(\ell_0 + \ell_1) = O(\log q/\log\beta_0 + \log q/\log\beta_1) = O(\log\beta_0^*/\log\beta_0 + \log\beta_0^*/\log\beta_1) = O((\log w + \log\alpha)/\log\beta_0 + (\log w + \log\alpha)/\log\beta_1) = O(1)$ operations over the ring $\mathbb{Z}_q$, where elements have bit length $\log q = O(\log w + \log \alpha)$. As a $\mathbb{Z}_q$ operation takes at most $\log(q) \log \log(q)$ time [...], our verifier time is $O(\log(w \cdot \alpha) \log \log(w \cdot \alpha))$.

4.1   Extensions

This section discuss extensions to Orbweaver including support for public proof aggregation, an inner product argument, recursive proof composition, and polynomial commitments for polynomials over $\mathbb{F}[X] = \mathbb{Z}_M[X]$.

Supporting Smaller Instances. In order to support all instances of length $w \le W$, observe it suffices to run the protocol without modification using only powers in $\mathbb{Z}(w)$. Since parameters are set such that R-SIS is hard for β_0^* based on W, it is not an issue that the extractor outputs an input of length W.

Public Proof Aggregation. Orbweaver can be extended to support public proof aggregation (i.e., the aggregator can be an untrusted third party) by taking advantage of the linearly homomorphic property of the opening proofs. Using short challenges $[[h_{i,j}]_{i=1}^t]_{j=1}^{T[i]}$ we can check that commitments $[c_i]_{i=1}^t$, evaluated at function sets $[f_j]_{j=1}^{T[i]}$, output values $[[y_{i,j}]_{i=1}^t]_{j=1}^{T[i]}$, respectively. The verifier checks the opening proof equation

$$\langle \boldsymbol{a}, \, \pi_0 \rangle \equiv \sum_{i=1}^t \sum_{j=1}^{T[i]} h_{i,j} \cdot \left(c_i \cdot \mathsf{ck}_{f_{i,j}} - y_{i,j} \right) \bmod q \, , \text{ where } \quad \pi_0 = \sum_{i=1}^t \sum_{j=1}^{T[i]} h_{i,j} \pi_{0,i,j} \quad \bmod q$$

Inner Product Argument. We can easily construct an inner product argument (IPA) using Orbweaver, allowing a prover to prove the inner product $y := \langle \boldsymbol{x}, \, \boldsymbol{x}' \rangle \bmod q$ between two committed vectors. The prover runs commit twice to produce c, c', π_1, and π_1', and runs $\mathsf{Open}(\mathsf{ck}, \boldsymbol{x}', \boldsymbol{x})$ to obtain π_0. The verifier checks the norm bounds of all three proofs, verifies both knowledge proofs as in Verify, and then checks the opening proof satisfies $\langle \boldsymbol{a}, \, \pi_0 \rangle \equiv c' \cdot c - y \bmod q$.

It should be noted that this requires a modification of the norm bound β_0^* for which R-SIS must be hard. In the modified proof of Theorem 4 the extractor would generate π_0^* using extracted values $\boldsymbol{x}^*$ and f^*, both of norm α^* (whereas in the linear map case they use f of norm α). Then we must set $\beta_0^* = w^2 (\alpha^*)^2 \beta_0 \gamma_{\mathcal{R}}^2 = w^4 \alpha^2 \beta_1^2 \beta_0 \gamma_{\mathcal{R}}^4$.

Recursive Proof Composition. Observe that $\mathsf{ck}_f \cdot \mathsf{ck} - y \bmod q$ and $c \cdot t \bmod q$ are Ajtai R-SIS commitments to π_0 and π_1 for respective public vectors $\boldsymbol{a}_0$ and $\boldsymbol{a}_1$. Using any proof-succinct argument of knowledge for R-SIS commitment preimages (e.g., [14]), we can achieve better proof sizes by instead sending an AoK of π_0 and π_1. The composed scheme will still have log-time verification even if the outer argument has a linear-time verifier.

5   Linear Map Commitments for $\mathbb{Z}_M$

We construct a functional commitment for linear maps over $\mathbb{Z}_M$, i.e., given $\hat{\boldsymbol{x}}, \hat{f} \in \mathbb{Z}_M^N$ we wish to show $\hat{f}(\hat{\boldsymbol{x}}) \equiv y \bmod M \in \mathbb{Z}_M$. Our starting point is as follows. Using the centered representation, we need $\alpha \geq (M - 1)/2$ in order to represent any element in $\mathbb{Z}_M$. Wlog, let $N = wn$. Our Orbweaver commitment will be to the coefficient embedding of the centered representation of $\hat{x}$, denoted $x \in \mathcal{R}^w$ such that $\mathcal{X} = \{r \in \mathcal{R} \mid r \leq \alpha\}$. (Use of the centered representation will be subsequently implicit.) The commitment key will be to the vector $f = [\sigma_{-1}(f_i)]_{i \in [w]}$, where $[f_i]_{i \in [w]} \in \mathcal{R}^w$ is the coefficient embedding of $\hat{f}$ and $\sigma_{-1} \in \mathsf{aut}(\mathcal{R}_q)$ is the Galois automorphism corresponding to $\sigma_{-1}(X) = X^{-1}$. This gives us $\langle \hat{x}, \hat{f} \rangle = \mathsf{ct}(\langle x, f \rangle) \bmod q$, where ct returns the constant coefficient. The prover sends $y = \langle x, f \rangle \in \mathcal{R}$ (now counted as a part of the proof) together with π_0. The verifier checks the resulting Orbweaver verification equations and that $\mathsf{ct}(y) \bmod M$ is the claimed evaluation.

Just as how in Orbweaver we pair each f_i and x_i with "negated" powers of v whose product is v^0 in order to obtain the inner product $f(x)$ as the constant coefficient of the polynomial product $c \cdot \mathsf{ck}_f \in \mathcal{R}_q$, we apply σ_{-1} above to do the same within each ring element multiplication $f_i x_i$ to obtain the $\mathbb{Z}_M$ inner product in the constant coefficient. While it would be simpler to commit to each $\hat{f}_i \in \mathbb{Z}_M$ as a constant polynomial in $\mathcal{R}$, using all coefficients of the polynomial improves CRS size by a factor of n and the runtime of Com, Open, and PreVerify significantly as we are able to take advantage of the NTT. Unfortunately, this does not affect proof size as the improvement $w = N/n$ vs. $w = N$ is exactly cancelled out in our norm bounds by the fact we can set $\gamma_{\mathcal{R}} = 1$ (rather than n) when multiplying by a constant (rather than arbitrary) polynomial.

Enforcing mod M. It follows from the security of Orbweaver that we obtain an extractable functional commitment for $\mathbb{Z}_q$ above. However, the guarantee that $\hat{f}(\hat{x}^*) - y \equiv 0 \bmod q$ does not tell us this holds mod M. If $\|\hat{f}(\hat{x}^*) - y\| \leq q$ then this equation holds over the integers and thus mod M. In other words, we require $\delta_M + \delta_M^* < q$. Recall from our proof of Theorem 4 that $\beta_0^* \geq 2w\gamma_{\mathcal{R}}\delta_M^* > \delta_M + \delta_M^*$ and we require $q \approx \beta_0^* n \log n$ for R-SIS$_{\mathcal{R}_q, \ell, \beta_0^*}$ to be hard. Then this condition will always hold when setting Orbweaver parameters correctly.

Smaller Proofs with Decomposition and Proof Aggregation. We improve on the protocol above via ternary decomposition and proof aggregation. Ternary decomposition has the advantage that we can work with polynomials of norm bound 1, and the since higher powers of α appear in our proof norm bounds than other variables it is almost always better to trade $\alpha = 1$ for $w' = w \log_3(M)$ and having to create a batch proof for $\log_3(M)$ functions f_i, as we now show is possible. We note some such decomposition can be done in the polynomial setting as well, but it is more straightforward in the integer setting.

Wlog, let $M = 3^t$ and $N = wn$. For $a \in \mathbb{Z}_M^N$, let a_0 denote the vector of the least significant ternary-bit of each element of a, defining a_i for $i \in \{0, \ldots, t - 1\}$ analogously (i.e., $a = \sum_{i=0}^{t-i} a_i 3^i$). We can turn any $\mathbb{Z}_M$ inner product into a $\mathbb{Z}_3$ inner product as follows:

$$\langle \boldsymbol{a},\, \boldsymbol{b} \rangle \equiv \langle \boldsymbol{a}_0 \| \dots \| \boldsymbol{a}_{t-1},\, (3^0 \cdot \boldsymbol{b} \| \dots \| 3^{t-1} \cdot \boldsymbol{b} \bmod M) \rangle := \langle \boldsymbol{a}',\, \boldsymbol{b}' \rangle$$

$$\equiv \sum_{i=0}^{t-1} 3^i \langle \boldsymbol{a}',\, \boldsymbol{b}'_i \rangle \bmod M$$

where $\boldsymbol{a}', \boldsymbol{b}'_i \in \mathbb{Z}_3^{Nt}$.

The prover makes a commitment (c, π_1) to the polynomial vector $\boldsymbol{x} \in \mathcal{R}^{wt}$ corresponding to the coefficient embedding of the ternary-decomposition of their witness in $\boldsymbol{a} \in \mathbb{Z}_M^{Nt}$. For $i \in \{0, \dots, t-1\}$, they then make claimed evaluations and proofs $y_i, \pi_{0,i}$ with respect to each commitment key ck_{f_i} obtained committing to the Galois automorphisms of the elements in the $\mathcal{R}_q$vector $\boldsymbol{f}'_i \in \mathcal{R}^{wt}$ corresponding to the coefficient embedding of the vector $\boldsymbol{b}'_i \in \mathbb{Z}^{Nt}$. The verifier replies with a challenge $h \leftarrow_{\$} \mathcal{H}$, and then the prover sends aggregated opening proof $\pi_0 = \prod_{i=0}^{t-1} h^i \pi_{0,i}$. The verifier checks the equation

$$\langle \boldsymbol{a},\, \pi_0 \rangle \equiv c \cdot \mathsf{ck}_f - y \bmod q$$

where

$$\mathsf{ck}_f = \sum_{i=0}^{t-1} h^i \cdot \mathsf{ck}_{f_i} \qquad \text{and} \qquad y = \sum_{i=0}^{t-1} h^i \cdot y_i$$

In this case the actual evaluation is given by $\langle \boldsymbol{a},\, \boldsymbol{b} \rangle \equiv \sum_{i=0}^{t-1} 3^i \cdot \mathsf{ct}(y_i) \bmod M$.

Below we present a secure instantiation of the challenge set $\mathcal{H}$ of small operator norm c. Then we establish the following parameters:

$$\delta_0 = cw^2 \log_3^3(M) \beta_0 \gamma_{\mathcal{R}}^2$$
$$\delta_1 = w \log_3(M) \beta_1 \gamma_{\mathcal{R}}$$
$$\beta_0^* = 2cw^2 \log_3^3(M) \delta_1 \beta_0 \gamma_{\mathcal{R}}^2 = 2cw^3 \log_3^4(M) \beta_0 \beta_1 \gamma_{\mathcal{R}}^3$$

We must also factor in cost of sending $\log_3 M$ values y_i, each of which has norm bound $\delta_p = w \log_3(M) \gamma_{\mathcal{R}}$. Experimentally, when M is 16 bits or more we find decomposition results in smaller proofs.

5.1   Polynomial Commitments for $\mathbb{Z}_M$

We show how to construct $O(\log N)$ proof size and $O(\log N \log \log N)$ verifier time polynomial commitment (PC) for degree N polynomials over $\mathbb{Z}_M$ using Orbweaver. How to do this while preserving a quasi-log-verifier is not immediate. In a PC protocol based on Orbweaver, the prover commits to the coefficients of the polynomial and the function fbecomes the powers of a challenge evaluation point z. Previously we considered the preprocessing setting, where we assume the same function will be evaluated repeatedly on different commitments. In this amortized setting the cost to run PreVerifyonce is considered a constant. On the other hand, in the PC setting fis defined by z, which is usually a fresh challenge sampled uniformly at random from $\mathbb{Z}_M$—a setting in which preprocessing no longer makes sense.

Again we choose $\alpha \geq (M - 1)/2$ and assume wlog that $\alpha = 3^t$, $wn = N$, and w is a power of 2. We show how to compute, in log-time, a commitment key $\mathsf{ck}'_z \equiv \mathsf{ck}_z \bmod M$, where ck_z is the commitment key corresponding to running PreVerify on the function $f = (f_1, ..., f_w) \in \mathbb{Z}_M^w$, where $\sigma_{-1}(f_i) \in \mathcal{R}_q$ is equal to the coefficient embedding of the vector $z^{n(i-1)} \cdot (z^0, z^{1+n(i-1)}, \ldots, z^{n-1}) :=$ $z^{n(i-1)} \cdot f_\heartsuit \in \mathbb{Z}_M^n$. This choice of f follows the techniques we used in Sect. 5 such that the evaluation of the committed polynomial at z will be equal to the constant coefficient of y. The verifier computes

$$\mathsf{ck}'_z := f_\heartsuit \cdot v^{-w} \cdot \prod_{i=0}^{\log(w)-1} ((z^{n \cdot 2^i} \bmod M) + v^{2^i}) = \sum_{i=1}^{w} f_\heartsuit \cdot \hat{z}_{i-1} \cdot v^{-i} \equiv \mathsf{ck}_z \bmod M$$

In particular this holds because each $\hat{z}_i \equiv z^{in} \bmod M$. The downside of computing the key this way is that it corresponds to a commitment key for the function $\hat{f} := f_\heartsuit \cdot \hat{z} \in \mathcal{R}_q^w$, where $\|\hat{f}\| \leq \alpha^{\log w + 1}$ since the norm of $\hat{z}_i$ is bounded by α to the power of the Hamming weight of i. Roughly speaking, computing the commitment key this way comes at a cost of a $\log \alpha$ times larger opening proof.

6 Evaluation

6.1 Optimizations

Sending Only π_1 and Not c. Observe that it is sufficient to just send π_1 and check the singular verification equation

$$\langle a_0, \pi_0 \rangle \cdot t = \langle a_1, \pi_1 \rangle \cdot \mathsf{ck}_f - z \cdot t$$

improving both communication and complexity. Since c is a deterministic function of π_1, an extractor can still obtain x^* given π_1. To see the evaluation proof check still holds, note that $t \leftarrow_\$ \mathcal{T}$ is sampled such that finding $s' = 0$ and $s't = 0$ is hard. This implies that if $lt = rt$, then $l - r = 0$.

Separate β_0, β_1. We could fix a single public RSIS vector with respect to which preimages for v^i and $v^i t$ are produced. however, using two trapdoor matrices a_0, a_1 let us optimize β_0, β_1 separately to minimize $\|\pi_0\| + \|\pi_1\|$. While setting β_0, β_1 as small as possible minimizes the norm bounds δ_0, δ_1, $\|\pi_0\|, \|\pi_1\|$ also grows with the width of a_0, a_1, which grows inversely with δ_0, δ_1. Our code finds δ_0, δ_1 which minimizes $\|\pi_0\| + \|\pi_1\|$.

Computationally Indistinguishable Trapdoor Matrix. Recall that trapdoor public RSIS vectors in [50] are of the form $a = [\hat{a}|g - r\hat{a}]$, where $\hat{a} \leftarrow_\$ \mathcal{R}_q^\ell$, g is the public gadget vector and r is the trapdoor/ In prior work [2], $\ell = \lceil \log_\beta q \rceil$ was chosen, where it can be shown using the leftover hash lemma the resulting a is indistinguishable from random. We can instead use $\ell = 2$, where one can see the resulting a is an RLWE sample, $[\hat{a}, g - \hat{A}r]$ where $\hat{a} = [1|\hat{a}^\intercal \leftarrow \mathcal{R}_q^{\log_b q}] \in \mathcal{R}_q^{\log_b q \times 2}$, for some $b = O(\beta)$ and $r \leftarrow_\$ \mathcal{D}$ where $\mathcal{D}$

is some distribution for the RLWE secret and error. Experimentally, we find the best distribution, b, β such that the proof size is minimized and the RLWE problem has 128-bit hardness.

Norm Bound on Average Case f, x. Note that, however, the norm bound and proof size estimation is based on the worst case f, x, as we are bounding $\|f\|_\infty$ and $\|x\|_\infty$ to be α. However, if we instead bound $\|f(x)\|$ by α', δ_0 then becomes $\alpha' \cdot \beta_0 \gamma_{\mathcal{R}}$. For average case (i.e., randomly sampled f, x), $\alpha' \approx w^2 \alpha^2 \gamma_{\mathcal{R}}/4$, and size of π_0 is about $1/4$ smaller. For sparse f, x, we can do better. Similarly, we can bound the size of π_1 as well with a tighter norm bound.

6.2   Proof and CRS Sizes

Comparison to [2]. For sake of better comparison with [2], we consider an unoptimized version of Orbweaver (as bit decomposition in Sect. 5, better trapdoor sampling, and many other types of optimizations in Sect. 6.1 can also be applied to [2]). We also note that due to errors in their code, they (1) set a root Hermite factor much smaller than currently achievable (resulting in a security level higher than 128 bits); and (2) overestimate the desired preimage quality, i.e., the shortness/norm bound of the preimages. In the comparison below, we apply the same errors that "oversecure" our scheme for $\lambda = 128$.

Unlike in the asymptotic analysis, we no longer fix n and β_0^*. Concretely, for fixed α and w, we wish to compute optimal values for n, q, β_0^* to minimize $|c + \pi_1 + \pi_0|$ subject to the constraints that $\beta_0^* \geq 2w^3\alpha^2\beta^2 n^3$ and $R\text{-SIS}_{\mathcal{R}_q, \ell, \beta_0^*}$ is hard.[7]

Proof Sizes. In Fig. 1 we compare combined commitment and proof lengths for input lengths w from 2^{15} to 2^{28} and for input alphabets of $\mathcal{R}$ elements bounded by $\alpha = 2$ and $\alpha = 2^{16}$. We compare our commitment and proof sizes to [2] for these parameters, showing a more than $2\times$ reduction. In order to make the comparison as fair as possible, we modified the code of [2] to remove the overhead induced by their schemes support for batching and higher degree polynomial maps.

Prover Time and CRS Size. Even more important, practically speaking, was our reduction of the CRS size and prover time in [2] from quadratic to quasilinear in w and α. The Orbweaver CRS size is calculated as $3w\ell n \log \beta$ bits, as it consists of $3w$ vectors of ring elements, each of which with bit length bounded by $\log(\beta)$. In contrast, [2] requires about $w^2\ell n \log \beta$ bits for the CRS. For our optimized version, CRS size is $\sim$40 GB for functions up to length 2^{30}.

---

[7] β_0 and β_1 do not have to be equal, but for simplicity, we set both to β. In practice, β_1 may be $\ll \beta_0$, and thus by separating the two, we can greatly reduce the size of $|\pi_1|$, but such optimization does not change the asymptotic behavior.

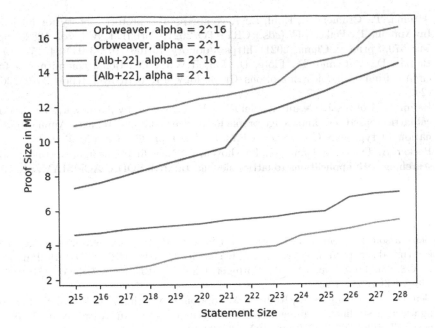

Fig. 1. Comparison of combined commitment and proof size $|c + \pi_0 + \pi_1|$ for Orbweaver and [2].

Acknowledgments. We would like to thank Martin Albrecht and Russell W.F. Lai for answering questions about [2]. We would also like to thank Nicholas Genise for answering our questions about lattice trapdoors.

References

1. Ajtai, M.: Generating hard instances of lattice problems (extended abstract). In: Twenty-Eighth Annual ACM Symposium on Theory of Computing. STOC '96, pp. 99–108 (1996)
2. Albrecht, M.R., Cini, V., Lai, R.W.F., Malavolta, G., Thyagarajan, S.A.K.: Lattice-based SNARKs: publicly verifiable, preprocessing, and recursively composable - (extended abstract). In: Dodis, Y., Shrimpton, T. (eds.) CRYPTO 2022, Part II. LNCS, vol. 13508, pp. 102–132. Springer, Cham (2022). https://doi.org/10.1007/978-3-031-15979-4_4
3. Albrecht, M.R., Lai, R.W.F.: Subtractive sets over cyclotomic rings. In: Malkin, T., Peikert, C. (eds.) CRYPTO 2021, Part II. LNCS, vol. 12826, pp. 519–548. Springer, Cham (2021). https://doi.org/10.1007/978-3-030-84245-1_18
4. Ames, S., Hazay, C., Ishai, Y., Venkitasubramaniam, M.: Ligero: lightweight sublinear arguments without a trusted setup. In: 2017 ACM SIGSAC Conference on Computer and Communications Security, pp. 2087–2104 (2017)
5. Attema, T., Cramer, R.: Compressed Σ-protocol theory and practical application to plug & play secure algorithmics. In: Micciancio, D., Ristenpart, T. (eds.) CRYPTO 2020. LNCS, vol. 12172, pp. 513–543. Springer, Cham (2020). https://doi.org/10.1007/978-3-030-56877-1_18

6. Attema, T., Cramer, R., Kohl, L.: A compressed Σ-protocol theory for lattices. In: Malkin, T., Peikert, C. (eds.) CRYPTO 2021, Part II. LNCS, vol. 12826, pp. 549–579. Springer, Cham (2021). https://doi.org/10.1007/978-3-030-84245-1_19

7. Balbás, D., Catalano, D., Fiore, D., Lai, R.W.F.: Functional commitments for circuits from falsifiable assumptions. Cryptology ePrint Archive, Report 2022/1365 (2022)

8. Baum, C., Bootle, J., Cerulli, A., del Pino, R., Groth, J., Lyubashevsky, V.: Practical lattice-based zero-knowledge proofs for integer relations. In: 38th Annual International Cryptology Conference. CRYPTO 2019, pp. 669–699 (2019)

9. Becker, A., Ducas, L., Gama, N., Laarhoven, T.: New directions in nearest neighbor searching with applications to lattice sieving. In: 27th SODA. ACMSIAM, pp. 10–24, January 2016

10. Ben-Sasson, E., Bentov, I., Horesh, Y., Riabzev, M.: Fast reed-solomon interactive oracle proofs of proximity. In: ICALP 2018, Vol. 107. LIPIcs. Schloss Dagstuhl, pp. 14:1–14:17, July 2018

11. Ben-Sasson, E., Bentov, I., Horesh, Y., Riabzev, M.: Scalable zero knowledge with no trusted setup. In: Boldyreva, A., Micciancio, D. (eds.) CRYPTO 2019, Part III. LNCS, vol. 11694, pp. 701–732. Springer, Cham (2019). https://doi.org/10.1007/978-3-030-26954-8_23

12. Ben-sasson, E., Chiesa, A., Riabzev, M., Spooner, N., Virza, M., Ward, N.: Ligero: lightweight sublinear arguments without a trusted setup. In: Advances in Cryptology - EUROCRYPT 2019, pp. 103–128 (2019)

13. Ben-Sasson, E., et al.: Functional commitments for all functions, with transparent setup. In: 2014 IEEE Symposium on Security and Privacy, pp. 459–474. IEEE Computer Society Press, May 2014

14. Beullens, W., Seiler, G.: LaBRADOR: compact proofs for R1CS from module- SIS. Cryptology ePrint Archive, Paper 2022/1341 (2022)

15. Bitansky, N., Canetti, R., Chiesa, A., Tromer, E.: Functional commitments for all functions, with transparent setup. In: ITCS 2012, pp. 326–349. ACM, January 2012

16. Bitansky, N., Canetti, R., Chiesa, A., Tromer, E.: Progression-free sets and sublinear pairing-based non-interactive zero-knowledge arguments. In: 45th ACM STOC, pp. 111–120. ACM Press, June 2013

17. Bitansky, N., Chiesa, A., Ishai, Y., Paneth, O., Ostrovsky, R.: Succinct non-interactive arguments via linear interactive proofs. In: Sahai, A. (ed.) TCC 2013. LNCS, vol. 7785, pp. 315–333. Springer, Heidelberg (2013). https://doi.org/10.1007/978-3-642-36594-2_18

18. Bootle, J., Cerulli, A., Chaidos, P., Groth, J., Petit, C.: Efficient zero-knowledge arguments for arithmetic circuits in the discrete log setting. In: Fischlin, M., Coron, J.-S. (eds.) EUROCRYPT 2016, Part II. LNCS, vol. 9666, pp. 327–357. Springer, Heidelberg (2016). https://doi.org/10.1007/978-3-662-49896-5_12

19. Bootle, J., Chiesa, A., Sotiraki, K.: Sumcheck arguments and their applications. In: Malkin, T., Peikert, C. (eds.) CRYPTO 2021. LNCS, vol. 12825, pp. 742–773. Springer, Cham (2021). https://doi.org/10.1007/978-3-030-84242-0_26

20. Bootle, J., Lyubashevsky, V., Nguyen, N.K., Seiler, G.: A non-PCP approach to succinct quantum-safe zero-knowledge. In: Micciancio, D., Ristenpart, T. (eds.) CRYPTO 2020, Part II. LNCS, vol. 12171, pp. 441–469. Springer, Cham (2020). https://doi.org/10.1007/978-3-030-56880-1_16

21. Boudgoust, K., Gachon, E., Pellet-Mary, A.: Some easy instances of ideal- SVP and implications on the partial Vandermonde knapsack problem. In: Dodis, Y., Shrimpton, T. (eds.) CRYPTO 2022. LNCS, vol. 13508, pp. 480–509. Springer, Cham (2022). https://doi.org/10.1007/978-3-031-15979-4_17

22. Boudgoust, K., Sakzad, A., Steinfeld, R.: Vandermonde meets Regev: public key encryption schemes based on partial Vandermonde problems. Des. Codes Cryptogr. 1899–1936 (2022)

23. Bowe, S., Grigg, J., Hopwood, D.: Halo: recursive proof composition without a trusted setup. Cryptology ePrint Archive, Report 2019/1021 (2019). https://eprint.iacr.org/2019/1021

24. Bünz, B., Bootle, J., Boneh, D., Poelstra, A., Wuille, P., Maxwell, G.: Efficient zero-knowledge arguments for arithmetic circuits in the discrete log setting. In: 2018 IEEE Symposium on Security and Privacy, pp. 315–334. IEEE Computer Society Press, May 2018

25. Bünz, B., Fisch, B., Szepieniec, A.: Transparent SNARKs from DARK compilers. Cryptology ePrint Archive, Report 2019/1229 (2019). https://eprint.iacr.org/2019/1229

26. Bünz, B., Fisch, B., Szepieniec, A.: Transparent SNARKs from DARK compilers. In: Canteaut, A., Ishai, Y. (eds.) EUROCRYPT 2020. LNCS, vol. 12105, pp. 677–706. Springer, Cham (2020). https://doi.org/10.1007/978-3-030-45721-1_24

27. de Castro, L., Peikert, C.: Functional commitments for all functions, with transparent setup. Cryptology ePrint Archive, Paper 2022/1368 (2022)

28. Chiesa, A., Hu, Y., Maller, M., Mishra, P., Vesely, N., Ward, N.: Marlin: preprocessing zkSNARKs with universal and updatable SRS. In: Canteaut, A., Ishai, Y. (eds.) EUROCRYPT 2020. LNCS, vol. 12105, pp. 738–768. Springer, Cham (2020). https://doi.org/10.1007/978-3-030-45721-1_26

29. Chiesa, A., Ojha, D., Spooner, N.: Transparent SNARKs from DARK compilers. Cryptology ePrint Archive, Report 2019/1076 (2019). https://eprint.iacr.org/2019/1076

30. Esgin, M., Nguyen, N.K., Seiler, G.: Practical lattice-based zero-knowledge proofs for integer relations. In: Advances in Cryptology - ASIACRYPT 2020, pp. 259–288 (2020)

31. Esgin, M.F., Steinfeld, R., Liu, D., Ruj, S.: Functional commitments for all functions, with transparent setup. Cryptology ePrint Archive, Paper 2022/141 (2022)

32. Esgin, M.F., Steinfeld, R., Liu, J.K., Liu, D.: Lattice-based zero-knowledge proofs: new techniques for shorter and faster constructions and applications. In: Boldyreva, A., Micciancio, D. (eds.) CRYPTO 2019. LNCS, vol. 11692, pp. 115–146. Springer, Cham (2019). https://doi.org/10.1007/978-3-030-26948-7_5

33. Gabizon, A., Williamson, Z.J., Ciobotaru, O.: PLONK: permutations over lagrange-bases for oecumenical noninteractive arguments of knowledge. Cryptology ePrint Archive, Report 2019/953 (2019). https://eprint.iacr.org/2019/953

34. Genise, N., Micciancio, D.: Faster Gaussian sampling for trapdoor lattices with arbitrary modulus. In: Nielsen, J.B., Rijmen, V. (eds.) EUROCRYPT 2018. LNCS, vol. 10820, pp. 174–203. Springer, Cham (2018). https://doi.org/10.1007/978-3-319-78381-9_7

35. Gennaro, R., Gentry, C., Parno, B., Raykova, M.: Progression-free sets and sublinear pairing-based non-interactive zero-knowledge arguments. In: Johansson, T., Nguyen, P.Q. (eds.) EUROCRYPT 2013. LNCS, vol. 7881, pp. 626–645. Springer, Heidelberg (2013). https://doi.org/10.1007/978-3-642-38348-9_37

36. Gennaro, R., Minelli, M., Nitulescu, A., Orrù, M.: Lattice-based Zk-SNARKs from square span programs. In: 2018 ACM SIGSAC Conference on Computer and Communications Security. CCS '18, pp. 556–573 (2018)
37. Gentry, C., Peikert, C., Vaikuntanathan, V.: Faster Gaussian sampling for trapdoor lattices with arbitrary modulus. In: Fortieth Annual ACM Symposium on Theory of Computing. STOC '08, pp. 197–206 (2008)
38. Golovnev, A., Lee, J., Setty, S., Thaler, J., Wahby, R.S.: Brakedown: lineartime and post-quantum SNARKs for R1CS. Cryptology ePrint Archive, Paper 2021/1043 (2021)
39. Groth, J.: On the size of pairing-based non-interactive arguments. In: Fischlin, M., Coron, J.-S. (eds.) EUROCRYPT 2016. LNCS, vol. 9666, pp. 305–326. Springer, Heidelberg (2016). https://doi.org/10.1007/978-3-662-49896-5_11
40. Groth, J.: Functional commitments for all functions, with transparent setup. In: Abe, M. (ed.) ASIACRYPT 2010. LNCS, vol. 6477, pp. 321–340. Springer, Heidelberg (2010). https://doi.org/10.1007/978-3-642-17373-8_19
41. Groth, J., Maller, M.: Snarky signatures: minimal signatures of knowledge from simulation-extractable SNARKs. In: Katz, J., Shacham, H. (eds.) CRYPTO 2017. LNCS, vol. 10402, pp. 581–612. Springer, Cham (2017). https://doi.org/10.1007/978-3-319-63715-0_20
42. Ishai, Y., Su, H., Wu, D.J.: Shorter and faster post-quantum designated- verifier ZkSNARKs from lattices. In: 2021 ACM SIGSAC Conference on Computer and Communications Security. CCS '21, pp. 212–234 (2021)
43. Kate, A., Zaverucha, G.M., Goldberg, I.: Constant-size commitments to polynomials and their applications. In: Abe, M. (ed.) ASIACRYPT 2010. LNCS, vol. 6477, pp. 177–194. Springer, Heidelberg (2010). https://doi.org/10.1007/978-3-642-17373-8_11
44. Kilian, J.: A note on efficient zero-knowledge proofs and arguments (extended abstract). In: Symposium on the Theory of Computing (1992)
45. Lipmaa, H.: Progression-free sets and sublinear pairing-based non-interactive zero-knowledge arguments. In: Cramer, R. (ed.) TCC 2012. LNCS, vol. 7194, pp. 169–189. Springer, Heidelberg (2012). https://doi.org/10.1007/978-3-642-28914-9_10
46. Lyubashevsky, V., Nguyen, N.K., Plançon, M.: Lattice-based zero-knowledge proofs and applications: shorter, simpler, and more general. In: Dodis, Y., Shrimpton, T. (eds.) CRYPTO 2022. LNCS, vol. 13508, pp. 71–101. Springer, Cham (2022). https://doi.org/10.1007/978-3-031-15979-4_3
47. Lyubashevsky, V., Nguyen, N.K., Seiler, G.: Practical lattice-based zero- knowledge proofs for integer relations. In: 2020 ACM SIGSAC Conference on Computer and Communications Security. CCS '20, pp. 1051–1070 (2020)
48. Maller, M., Bowe, S., Kohlweiss, M., Meiklejohn, S.: Sonic: zero-knowledge SNARKs from linear-size universal and updatable structured reference strings. In: ACM CCS 2019. ACM Press, pp. 2111–2128, November 2019
49. Micciancio, D.: Generalized compact knapsacks, cyclic lattices, and efficient oneway functions from worst-case complexity assumptions. In: The 43rd Annual IEEE Symposium on Foundations of Computer Science. Proceedings, pp. 356–365 (2002)
50. Micciancio, D., Peikert, C.: Trapdoors for lattices: simpler, tighter, faster, smaller. In: Pointcheval, D., Johansson, T. (eds.) EUROCRYPT 2012. LNCS, vol. 7237, pp. 700–718. Springer, Heidelberg (2012). https://doi.org/10.1007/978-3-642-29011-4_41
51. Micciancio, D., Regev, O.: Functional commitments for all functions, with transparent setup. In: Bernstein, D.J., Buchmann, J., Dahmen, E. (eds.) Post-Quantum Cryptography, pp. 147–191 (2009)

52. Parno, B., Howell, J., Gentry, C., Raykova, M.: Progression-free sets and sublinear pairing-based non-interactive zero-knowledge arguments. In: 2013 IEEE Symposium on Security and Privacy, pp. 238–252. IEEE Computer Society Press, May 2013

53. Wee, H., Wu, D.J.: Succinct Vector, Polynomial, and Functional Commitments from Lattices. Cryptology ePrint Archive, Paper 2022/1515 (2022)

54. Xie, T., Zhang, Y., Song, D.: Orion: zero knowledge proof with linear prover time. In: Dodis, Y., Shrimpton, T. (eds.) CRYPTO 2022. LNCS, vol. 13510, pp. 299–328. Springer, Cham (2022). https://doi.org/10.1007/978-3-031-15985-5_11

Non-interactive Universal Arguments

Nir Bitansky, Omer Paneth$^{(\boxtimes)}$, Dana Shamir, and Tomer Solomon

Tel Aviv University, Tel Aviv, Israel
{nirbitan,omerpa,danashamir1,tomersolomon}@mail.tau.ac.il

Abstract. In 2002, Barak and Goldreich introduced the notion of a *universal argument* and constructed an interactive universal argument for non-deterministic computations based on polynomially hard collision-resistant hash functions. Since then, and especially in recent years, there have been tremendous developments in the construction of *non-interactive* succinct arguments for deterministic computations under standard hardness assumptions. However, the constructed succinct arguments can be proven universal only under *sub-exponential* assumptions.

Assuming *polynomially hard* fully homomorphic encryption and a widely believed worst-case complexity assumption, we prove a general lifting theorem showing that all existing non-interactive succinct arguments can be made universal. The required complexity assumption is that non-uniformity does not allow arbitrary polynomial speedup. In the setting of uniform adversaries, this extra assumption is not needed.

1 Introduction

A succinct argument for a language $\mathcal{L}$ (in **P** or **NP**) allows proving membership in $\mathcal{L}$ so that verification is only polylogarithmic in the time T needed to decide $\mathcal{L}$ (deterministically or non-deterministically). Since the pioneering works of Kilian [Kil92] and Micali [Mic94], succinct arguments have become a central concept in cryptography, with far reaching applications. As such, different notions of succinct arguments have been (and are still being) studied.

One influential notion in this context is that of *universal arguments*, put forth by Barak and Goldreich [BG08]. A universal argument allows proving membership *in any* language in **NP**. More generally, such an argument system enables proving statements $y = (M, x, T)$ in the *universal language* $\mathcal{L}_\mathcal{U}$ attesting that "*M non-deterministically accepts x in time T*". Unlike a succinct argument for a *specific* language $\mathcal{L} \in \mathbf{NP}$, here T is not bounded by any specific polynomial and may be, in fact, as large as 2^λ, where λ is a security parameter. The prover complexity is accordingly polynomial in T. Soundness of universal arguments

Nir Bitansky and Omer Paneth are members of the checkpoint institute of information security. Omer Paneth is supported by an Azrieli Faculty Fellowship, and ISF grant 1789/19. Nir Bitansky, Dana Shamir, and Tomer Solomon are supported by the European Research Council (ERC) under the European Union's Horizon Europe research and innovation programme (grant agreement No. 101042417, acronym SPP).

© International Association for Cryptologic Research 2023
H. Handschuh and A. Lysyanskaya (Eds.): CRYPTO 2023, LNCS 14082, pp. 132–158, 2023.
https://doi.org/10.1007/978-3-031-38545-2_5

is guaranteed against provers that are polynomially bounded in the security parameter λ. Analogously to universal arguments for non-deterministic computations, one may consider a universal argument for deterministic computations, which will be the focus of this work.

The need for universal arguments arises in different scenarios where we are required to verify the correctness of arbitrary computations and do not have a guarantee on the time it will take for them to terminate. In some scenarios, even the honest prover may not know apriori when the computation will terminate. Such is the scenario of *incrementally verifiable computation* [Val08], where the prover gradually computes and updates its proofs as it progresses along the computation. Another salient use case, expressed in the work of Barak and Goldreich, is *diagonalization*. Following the work of Barak [Bar01], universal arguments have been repeatedly used in non-black-box proofs of security in order to prove assertions pertaining to the code of the adversary, whose running time is not known in advance (c.f. [BG08, PR08, DGS09, BKP18]).

Universal Arguments Based on Polynomial Assumptions. The challenge in constructing universal arguments is in basing them on standard *polynomial* assumptions. Indeed, existing non-universal succinct arguments, deterministic and non-deterministic alike, can be made universal by relying on *sub-exponential* assumptions, or assuming super-polynomial security $\ell(\lambda) = \lambda^{-\omega(1)}$, and restricting the universal language to computations of time $T \leq \ell(\lambda)$. Here the complexity of the security reduction does not scale polynomially in that of the adversary as we usually aim for, but rather scales with the complexity of computations that the adversary asserts about, which may be super-polynomially larger. In the regime of polynomial assumptions, this yields a weaker notion that we call *semi-universal arguments* where soundness is only guaranteed when the computation time T is polynomially bounded.

In the interactive setting, Barak and Goldreich overcome this challenge. Assuming *polynomially secure* collision-resistant hash functions, they prove the existence of a four-message argument for non-deterministic computations that is *fully universal* (namely, sound for super-polynomial computation time $T \leq 2^\lambda$).

Non-interactive Universal Arguments. In this work, we aim to base *non-interactive* universal arguments on polynomial assumptions. In the non-interactive setting, the verifier generates a short public key (sometime referred to as a common reference string) once and for all, and this public key can be then used to generate the proofs non-interactively. Faced with known barriers on non-interactive succinct arguments [GW11] and focusing on standard assumptions, we follow the common restriction to *deterministic* computations. Here non-interactive succinct arguments have tremendously developed over recent years and can now be based on standard polynomial assumptions, with strong features like public verification as well and incremental proof updatability (c.f. [KPY19, CJJ21b, PP22, DGKV22]). While these recent constructions can too be made universal under sub-exponential assumptions, or semi universal under polynomial assumptions, non-interactive (fully) universal arguments, based on polynomial assumptions, remain out of reach.

1.1 Results

Our main result is a general lifting theorem from semi universal arguments to universal arguments, based on polynomial security assumptions.

Theorem 1.1 (Informal). *Assuming polynomially-secure fully-homomorphic encryption, any non-interactive semi-universal argument can be lifted to a universal argument. The resulting universal argument is secure against polynomial-time uniform adversaries. Assuming that for any $c \in \mathbb{N}$, $P \not\subset \textbf{ioSIZE}(n^c)$, it is secure against polynomial-size non-uniform adversaries.*

The theorem holds both in the setting of public verification (maintaining public verifiability) and of private verification. It also holds both for deterministic and non-deterministic computations, as well as interactive arguments, without increasing round complexity. We shall keep our focus on the setting of non-interactive publicly-verifiable arguments for deterministic computations, where new results under standard assumptions are obtained. For instance, relying on recent constructions of SNARGs for P from polynomial assumptions [CJJ21b, WW22, KLVW22], we obtain the following corollary.

Corollary 1.2 (of Theorem 1.1). *Assuming fully homomorphic encryption and either LWE or DLIN, there exists a universal argument for deterministic computations. (Non-uniform security additionally requires the same complexity assumption as in the theorem.)*

The assumption that for all $c \in \mathbb{N}$, $P \not\subset \textbf{ioSIZE}(n^c)$, required in the non-uniform setting, essentially says that circuits of a fixed polynomial size n^c, cannot decide all of P in the worst case. (Formally, there is a language $\mathcal{L}_c$ in P, which they fail to decide in the worst-case for all large enough instances.) This can be viewed as a natural generalization of *the time hierarchy theorem*, which holds unconditionally. It further follows from widely believed worst-case assumptions such as *the non-uniform exponential time hypothesis* (**nuETH**). In fact, relying on this assumption has a certain win-win flavour. Morally, if the assumption does not hold, then any language in P can already be verified in fixed polynomial time, making succinct arguments somewhat obsolete. (This connection is not precise because verification is guaranteed infinitely often and requires non-uniform advice, similarly to other constructions in the literature that use the adversary's circuit [KY18, RV22].)

Universal Incrementally Verifiable Computation. We prove an analogous lifting theorem for the case of incrementally verifiable computation. Here we need an extra complexity assumption in both the uniform and non-uniform settings, for simplicity we focus on the latter.

Theorem 1.3 (Informal). *Assuming polynomially-secure fully-homomorphic encryption and that there exists $d \in \mathbb{N}$ such that for any $c \in \mathbb{N}$, $P \cap DSPACE(n^d) \not\subset \textbf{ioSIZE}(n^c)$, any incrementally verifiable semi-universal argument can be lifted to an incrementally verifiable universal argument. (The universal argument is secure against polynomial-size non-uniform adversaries.)*

Relying on recent constructions of incrementally verifiable arguments from polynomial assumptions [PP22, DGKV22], we obtain the following corollary.

Corollary 1.4 (of Theorem 1.3**).** *Assuming fully homomorphic encryption, LWE, and the same complexity assumption as in the theorem, there exists an incrementally verifiable universal argument.*

The complexity assumption required here is stronger (leading to a stronger end result), however, we still view it as rather mild; in particular it is still a worst-case assumption and follows from **nuETH**.

A General Approach Based on Cryptographic Puzzles. Behind our lifting theorems is a general approach based on certain average-case cryptographic puzzles. The statements above reflect standard assumptions from which we manage to construct these puzzles. There are in fact other conceivable ways to construct the corresponding puzzles, as well as potential for future constructions under different assumptions. This is further discussed in the technical overview in the next section. We note that in [BS23], a stronger form of cryptographic puzzles (based on indistinguishability obfuscation) is used to avoid super-polynomial assumptions in the context of fully-homomorphic encryption constructions. We compare the approaches at the end of the technical overview.

1.2   Technical Overview

We start with an overview of our main lifting theorem from semi-universal arguments to universal ones. We shall focus on the case of deterministic computations and public verification.

Recall that our starting point is a semi-universal argument for the language

$$\mathcal{L}_{\mathcal{U}} = \{(M, x, T) : M(x) \text{ deterministically accepts in time } T\} \ .$$

In such an argument, it is possible to generate public verification and proving keys (vk, pk), corresponding to a given security parameter λ. The prover can use pk to generate a proof for statement $y = (M, x, T) \in \mathcal{L}_{\mathcal{U}}$ in time poly(T), which the verifier can verify in time polylog(T).[1] Soundness is guaranteed against efficient provers that only ever cheat on statements $y = (M, x, T) \notin \mathcal{L}_{\mathcal{U}}$ such that T is bounded by some polynomial in the security parameter λ. In contrast, for statements where T is super-polynomial, soundness is no longer guaranteed, even though the prover itself is efficient.

Put Your Money Where Your Mouth Is. At a high level, our approach toward lifting is natural: if the prover wishes to convince the verifier that $(M, x, T) \in \mathcal{L}_{\mathcal{U}}$, then it should:

a. Provide a semi-universal argument for this fact, and

---

[1] Formally, these polynomials also depend on λ, we suppress this dependence to simplify exposition.

b. **Prove that it actually performed a T-long computation.**

The honest prover that anyhow runs in time $\mathrm{poly}(T)$ should have no trouble doing so. In contrast, a malicious prover that runs in time $\mathrm{poly}(\lambda)$, should now only be able to prove that it performed a computation of length $T \leq \mathrm{poly}(\lambda)$, in which case the soundness of the semi-universal argument kicks in.

Cryptographic Puzzles. Realizing the above idea requires an appropriate notion of cryptographic puzzles. For such puzzles, a mildly hard instance can be generated fast, but cannot be solved without the investment of some pre-scribed amount of resources. Starting from the seminal work of Dwork and Naor [DN92], different notions of cryptographic puzzles have been studied in the liter-ature, with different interpretations of the above requirements. For our purpose, we need a rather weak form of puzzles satisfying the following:

- **Fast Sampling:** Given a difficulty parameter T and security parameter λ, it is possible to sample a puzzle Z in time $\mathrm{poly}(\lambda, \log T)$.
- **Completeness:** The puzzle Z can be solved in time $\approx T$.
- **Fast Verification:** A solution to the puzzle Z, can be verified in time $\mathrm{poly}(\lambda, \log T)$.
- **Soundness:** An adversary running in time t, should fail to solve puzzles Z of difficulty $T \gg t^C$ for some constant $C > 1$. In fact, we rely on a relaxed soundness requirement, where the above holds only for polynomially bounded T (analogously to soundness of semi-universal arguments).

Given such puzzles, we realize the previously described strategy as follows. On top of the verification and proving keys (vk, pk) for the semi-universal argument, we add puzzles $Z_1, \ldots, Z_\lambda$, where Z_i is generated with difficulty $T_i = 2^i$. To prove a statement of the form $(M, x, T) \in \mathcal{L}_\mathcal{U}$, with the sole restriction that $T \leq 2^\lambda$, the prover must provide solutions for all puzzles $Z_1, \ldots, Z_{\log T}$ (in addition to the semi-universal argument).

   The completeness of puzzles guarantees that the honest prover can generate a proof in time polynomial in T. As for soundness, a cheating adversary of running time $t = \mathrm{poly}(\lambda)$ that cheats on statements $(M, x, T) \notin \mathcal{L}_\mathcal{U}$ must violate the soundness of either the semi-universal argument or the underlying puzzles:

- If $T = O(t^C)$, the soundness of the semi-universal arguments is violated.
- If $T \gg t^C$, the soundness of the puzzle $Z_{\log t^C}$ is broken. (The adversary also solves allegedly more difficult puzzles like $Z_{\log T}$, but if T is super-polynomial, this does not constitute an attack according to our relaxed definition.)

Puzzles from FHE and Semi-universal Arguments. There are several conceivable ways to construct puzzles satisfying the properties that we need. One simple approach is to require the inversion of a one-way function with domain of size $\approx T$ for the difficulty parameter T. The downside is that this requires assuming exponential hardness of the one-way function. Another app-roach from [BGJ+16] is to combine worst-case mild hardness, for instance based on appropriate hierarchy theorems, together with succinct randomized encodings [BCG+18], which can be obtained assuming indistinguishability obfuscation or (polynomially secure) functional encryption [AL18,GS18,KNTY19]. In our setting, resorting to succinct randomized encodings seems to be an overkill. Indeed the puzzles in [BCG+18] are also required to enable sampling of solved puzzles, which we do not need.

We provide relatively simple constructions of the required puzzles by combining hierarchy theorems, fully homomorphic encryption, and semi-universal arguments. In a nutshell, our approach is the following: Start from puzzles that are only hard in the worst case, based on appropriate hierarchy theorems. Then, lift their hardness to the average case using fully-homomorphic encryption (alla [CKV10]). Finally, make the puzzles verifiable using semi-universal arguments. We next explain these steps in more detail, addressing the different subtleties that arise in the process.

Hierarchy Theorems and Worst-Case Puzzles. Generally speaking, hierarchy theorems are statements of the form *there exist languages that can be decided in the worst case with a certain amount T of resources, but not with significantly smaller amount $t \ll T$*. Basic examples of such theorems are unconditional hierarchy theorems for (uniform) time and space and (non-uniform) circuit size. The specific type of hierarchy theorem needed to carry out our approach depends on whether we consider uniform or non-uniform adversaries. For the first, we can rely on an unconditional hierarchy theorem for probabilistic time by Barak [Bar02], whereas for the latter we need the complexity assumption, mentioned earlier, that for any $c \in \mathbb{N}$, $\mathbf{P} \not\subset \mathbf{ioSIZE}(n^c)$.

In this overview, we will focus on the non-uniform case, which is simpler, yet conveys the main ideas. Here the previously mentioned complexity assumption directly yields worst case puzzles $Z = (M, x, T)$, where T is the difficulty parameter and the solution is $M_T(x)$, the result of running M on x for T steps. The complexity assumption exactly says that for any polynomial $t = \lambda^c$, there exists a language $\mathcal{L}$ and polynomial $T = t^C$, such that $\mathcal{L}$ can be decided in the worst-case by a T-time Turing machine M, but not by circuits of size t (for all large enough inputs).

Average-Case Hardness from FHE. To turn worst-case hardness to average-case hardness, puzzles will now include encrypted pairs (M, x), namely $Z = (\mathsf{Enc}_{\mathsf{pk}}(M, x), T)$, and the solution is $\widehat{\mathsf{Enc}}_{\mathsf{pk}}(M_T(x)) = \mathsf{Eval}(U_T, \mathsf{Enc}_{\mathsf{pk}}(M, x))$, the result of homomorphically computing the universal circuit U_T that emulates T steps of the underlying computation. The actual puzzle sampler will in fact sample encryptions of some arbitrary pair (M, x), say the all-zero string. The basic idea, inspired by [CKV10], is that if an adversary can solve the puzzles on average, namely compute $\mathsf{Eval}(U_T, \cdot)$, on zero-encryptions, then it also does so on encryptions of *any* pair (M, x). This gives a worst case to average case reduction, namely we can use the average-case adversary to obtain a worst-case adversary of roughly the same size.

A subtlety with the above argument is that the adversary might only solve the average case puzzle with some noticeable probability δ, say $1/\lambda$, rather than with probability ≈ 1. The reduction, however, should solve the underlying worst-case *decision* problem with probability noticeably larger than $1/2$. Accordingly, the reduction has to make $\approx \delta^{-1}$ attempts to solve the average case puzzle to make sure it succeeds. The problem is that the reduction cannot test in which of the attempts the adversary actually succeeds, namely computes $\mathsf{Eval}(U_T, \cdot)$, as testing this requires time $\approx T$ rather than $t \ll T$.[2] For exactly the same reason, currently verification of solutions is not fast, but rather requires time $\approx T$.

Adding Semi-Universal Arguments. We remedy both issues raised in the last paragraph in one-shot. We require as part of the solution a semi-universal argument that the claimed result (ciphertext) is actually the result of applying $\mathsf{Eval}(U_T, \cdot)$ to the ciphertext given by the puzzle Z. Relying on the soundness of the universal arguments, we now get fast verification. At the same time, the worst case to average case reduction can now also rely on fast verification to check which of the repeated attempts succeeds. Since we use semi-universal arguments, the puzzles are only sound provided a polynomial bound on T, which as argued before is sufficient for our purpose.

Under the Hood. The reductions should deal with additional details, such as accounting for the overhead of encryption, the repeated solving attempts, and verification of the semi-universal arguments. Overall, the overhead is a fixed polynomial in the adversary size t, the inverse breaking probability δ^{-1}, and the security parameter, so this does not present a problem.

We also note that in the actual paper, we define an intermediate notion of puzzle soundness against non-faulty solvers, which do not err in solving the puzzle, but sometimes identifiably fail. This is meant to capture the minimal notion of puzzles sufficient for universal lifting. We refer the reader to the body for the details.

Incremental Verification. The setting of incrementally verifiable universal arguments generalizes the one of universal arguments. Here we think of the universal relation as

$$\mathcal{L}_\mathcal{U} = \left\{ (M, \mathsf{cf}, \mathsf{cf}', T) : M \text{ transitions from } \mathsf{cf} \text{ to } \mathsf{cf}' \text{ in time } T \right\} \ .$$

Universal (and semi-universal) arguments are defined exactly the same, but now there is an additional *proof update* algorithm that allows to take a proof for $(M, \mathsf{cf}_0, \mathsf{cf}_T, T) \in \mathcal{L}_\mathcal{U}$ and update it to a proof of $(M, \mathsf{cf}_0, \mathsf{cf}_{T+1}, T + 1) \in \mathcal{L}_\mathcal{U}$ in time independent of T. As already mentioned also here there exists semi-universal constructions [PP22, DGKV22]. Our lifting theorem essentially works a similar way to the non-incremental case, only that solutions for the puzzles $Z_1, \ldots, Z_\lambda$ are now computed incrementally. That is the proof for step T also includes the T-th state in the computation of each of the puzzles $Z_1, \ldots, Z_\lambda$.

To keep the incremental nature of the computation it is important though that the puzzles can be computed with a fixed amount of space (independent of

---

[2] This difficulty does not arise in [CKV10], who use this technique to construct delegation with preprocessing, where the reduction could run for as long as the preprocessing time T.

T). For this purpose we need to strengthen our complexity theoretic assumption. We now assume that there exists a constant $d \in \mathbb{N}$ such that for any $c \in \mathbb{N}$, $\mathbf{P} \cap \mathbf{DSPACE}(n^d) \not\subset \mathbf{ioSIZE}(n^c)$. This is arguably still a rather mild worst-case assumption (in particular, it still follows from **nuETH**). Using the fact that homomorphically evaluating a space-efficient computation can be done roughly in the same space, computing the corresponding puzzle solution is space efficient.

Future Direction: Polynomial Hardness of PPAD, Generically. One appealing application of incrementally verifiable proofs has been in the context of proving hardness in the complexity class **CLS = PPAD∩PLS** (which implies the hardness of finding Nash equilibria and more) [JPY88, Pap94, FGHS21]. While by now there are hardness results based on subexponentially hard LWE [JKKZ21], hardness results based on polynomial assumptions have been harder to achieve [GPS16, BCH+22]. In particular, results based on polynomial LWE, or in fact any post-quantum assumption, are not known.

Incrementally-verifiable universal arguments give a generic way of proving hardness in **CLS**, assuming that they also satisfy *uniqueness,* namely that ambiguous proofs (even for true statements) are hard to find (c.f. [KPY20]). In the body, we prove a stronger lifting theorem then the one described above that also preserves *uniqueness.* That is, if the underlying semi-universal incrementally-verifiable argument has uniqueness, so will the lifted one. (In a nutshell, this is done by also adding incremental proofs for the computation of the puzzles themselves.)

At this point, semi-universal incrementally-verifiable arguments from polynomial LWE [PP22, DGKV22] do not satisfy uniqueness, and achieving this remains an open problem. Solving it will imply, combined with our results, PPAD hardness from polynomial LWE and the worst-case complexity assumption discussed above. Our lifting theorem does imply under these assumptions average-case hardness in **PLS** following [BG20].

Comparison to [BS23]. The work of [BS23] also relies on a form of cryptographic puzzles to reduce super-polynomial assumptions to polynomial ones in the context of constructing fully-homomorphic encryption. They rely on a stronger form of puzzles that can be sampled together with solutions (similarly to time-lock puzzles [RSW96], but with no depth considerations). Such puzzles are constructed in [BGJ+16] based on succinct randomized encodings, which can in turn be based on inditinguishability obfuscation (with small input space). Indeed, the use of puzzles in [BS23] is quite different from the one in this work: it is meant to reduce the number of hybrids in a certain reduction.

We view finding additional settings where cryptographic puzzles can be used to avoid super-polynomial loss as an appealing research direction for future work.

2   Preliminaries

Languages: Given a language $\mathcal{L} \subseteq \{0,1\}^*$, we define $\mathcal{L}(\cdot)$ to be its characteristic function.

Efficient Adversaries:

- PPT stands for probabilistic polynomial-time.
- For a PPT algorithm M, we denote by $M(x; r)$ the output of M on input x and random coins r, and by $M(x)$ the random variable, given by sampling the coins r uniformly at random.
- A polynomial-size circuit family $\mathcal{C}$ is a sequence of circuits $\mathcal{C} = \{C_\lambda\}_{\lambda \in \mathbb{N}}$, such that each circuit C_λ is of polynomial size $\lambda^{O(1)}$. We also consider probabilistic circuits that may toss random coins.

2.1 Homomorphic Encryption

In this section we define a fully homomorphic encryption scheme.

Definition 2.1 (Fully Homomorphic Encryption). *A (public key) fully homomorphic encryption scheme* FHE *consists of four PPT algorithms (*Gen, Enc, Dec, Eval*) satisfying:*

Correctness. *For any polynomial ℓ, large enough $\lambda \in \mathbb{N}$, circuit C of size at most $\ell(\lambda)$, and message m,*

$$\Pr\left[\mathsf{Dec}_{\mathsf{sk}}(\mathsf{Eval}(C,\ \mathsf{Enc}_{\mathsf{pk}}(m))) = C(m) \mid (\mathsf{sk},\ \mathsf{pk}) \leftarrow \mathsf{Gen}(1^\lambda)\right] = 1 \ .$$

Semantic Security. *For any pair of equal-length messages $m_0, m_1 \in \{0, 1\}^*$,*

$$\mathsf{pk}, \mathsf{Enc}_{\mathsf{pk}}(m_0) \approx_c \mathsf{pk}, \mathsf{Enc}_{\mathsf{pk}}(m_1) \ ,$$

where $(\mathsf{sk},\ \mathsf{pk}) \leftarrow \mathsf{Gen}(1^\lambda)$.

Compactness. *There exists a polynomial $p(\cdot)$, such that for any $\lambda \in \mathbb{N}$, $(\mathsf{sk}, \mathsf{pk}) \leftarrow \mathsf{Gen}(1^\lambda)$, message $m \in \{0,1\}^*$, and circuit C with input size $|m|$,*

$$|\mathsf{Eval}(C, \mathsf{Enc}_{\mathsf{pk}}(m))| = |C(m)| \cdot p(\lambda) \ .$$

Complexity Preservation. *There exists a polynomial q such that any circuit of size t and width w, can be homomorphically evaluated in time $t \cdot q(\lambda)$ and space $w \cdot (\lambda)$.*

On Complexity Preservation and Homomorphic Evaluation of Turing Machines. The complexity preservation property defined above is typically not required in applications and accordingly not explicitly defined. It is satisfied though by typical FHE schemes, such as any *gate-by-gate* FHE.

We also note that complexity preservation implies, by standard reductions, that we can homomorphically evaluate any time-$t(n)$, space-$s(n)$ Turing machine in time $t \cdot \mathrm{poly}(\log t, n, \lambda)$ and space $s \cdot \mathrm{poly}(\log t, n, \lambda)$ for an appropriate polynomial poly. Accordingly, in our construction of puzzles, it will be convenient to directly address homomorphic evaluation of Turing machines.

2.2   Non-interactive Arguments for Deterministic Computations

In this section we define non-interactive arguments for deterministic computations. Such arguments allow a prover to convince a verifier of the outcome of a long computation. For a T-time computation, the prover should run in time $\text{poly}(T)$ while the verifier runs in time significantly less than T.

The Universal Language. Let $\mathcal{L}_\mathcal{U}$ be the language of all quadruplets $(M, \text{cf}, \text{cf}', T)$ such that M is a deterministic Turing machine that starting from configuration cf transitions to configuration cf' in T steps. A Turing machine configuration includes the machine's state and its entire memory.

A non-interactive argument for $\mathcal{L}_\mathcal{U}$ consists of algorithms (Gen, Prove, Verify) with the following syntax:

Setup: The probabilistic setup algorithm Gen takes as input a security parameter $\lambda \in \mathbb{N}$. It outputs a prover key pk and a verifier key vk.

Prover: The deterministic prover algorithm Prove takes as input a prover key pk and an instance $y \in \mathcal{L}_\mathcal{U}$. It outputs a proof π.

Verifier: The deterministic verifier algorithm Verify takes as input a verifier key vk, an instance y and a proof π. It outputs a bit indicating if it accepts or rejects.

We next define the formal requirements from non-interactive arguments for $\mathcal{L}_\mathcal{U}$. The definition distinguishes between plain soundness and universal soundness. The former only guarantees soundness for computations that are polynomially bounded (this corresponds to the semi-universal arguments discussed in the introduction), while the later guarantees soundness also for super-polynomial computations.

Definition 2.2. *A non-interactive argument for $\mathcal{L}_\mathcal{U}$ satisfies the following requirements:*

Completeness. *For every $\lambda \in \mathbb{N}$ and $y = (M, \text{cf}, \text{cf}', T) \in \mathcal{L}_\mathcal{U}$ such that $|y|, T \leq 2^\lambda$:*

$$\Pr\left[\text{Verify}(\text{vk}, y, \pi) = 1 \, \middle| \, \begin{array}{l} (\text{pk}, \text{vk}) \leftarrow \text{Gen}(\lambda) \\ \pi \leftarrow \text{Prove}(\text{pk}, y) \end{array}\right] = 1 \; .$$

Efficiency. *In the completeness experiment above:*
  - *The setup algorithm runs in time $\text{poly}(\lambda)$.*
  - *The prover algorithm runs in time $\text{poly}(\lambda, |y|, T)$ and outputs a proof π of length $\text{poly}(\lambda)$.*
  - *The verifier algorithm runs in time $\text{poly}(\lambda, |y|)$.*

Soundness. *For every polynomial $\bar{T} = \bar{T}(\lambda)$ and $\text{poly}(\lambda)$-size adversary $\mathcal{A}$ there exists a negligible function μ such that for every $\lambda \in \mathbb{N}$:*

$$\Pr\left[\begin{array}{l} \text{Verify}(\text{vk}, y, \pi) = 1 \\ T \leq \bar{T}(\lambda) \\ y \notin \mathcal{L}_M \end{array} \, \middle| \, \begin{array}{l} (\text{pk}, \text{vk}) \leftarrow \text{Gen}(\lambda) \\ \left(y = \left(M, \text{cf}, \text{cf}', T\right), \pi\right) \leftarrow \mathcal{A}(\text{pk}, \text{vk}) \end{array}\right] \leq \mu(\lambda) \; .$$

We say that:

- *The scheme has* universal soundness *if we set $\bar{T}$ to be 2^λ instead of polynomial in λ. Schemes satisfying universal soundness are called universal arguments. Schemes satisfying (plain) soundness are called semi-universal arguments.*
- *The scheme is* privately verifiable *if it satisfies a weaker notion of soundness where $\mathcal{A}$ is only given* pk *but not* vk.
- *The scheme is* sound against uniform adversaries, *if the adversary in the soundness requirement is restricted to be a uniform PPT algorithm.*

Below we state existing results on non-interactive arguments for $\mathcal{L}_\mathcal{U}$ based on *polynomial* assumptions. These constructions are semi-universal, meaning that they satisfy soundness but are not known to satisfy universal soundness.

Theorem 2.3 ([CJJ21a, WW22, KLVW22]). *Assuming the hardness of either the Learning with Errors (LWE) problem or the Decisional Linear (DLIN) problem in bilinear groups, there exist semi-universal non-interactive arguments for $\mathcal{L}_\mathcal{U}$.*

Theorem 2.4 ([KRR14, BHK17]). *Assuming PIR schemes exist, there exist semi-universal privately-verifiable non-interactive arguments for $\mathcal{L}_\mathcal{U}$.*

2.3 Incrementally Verifiable Computation

In this section we define incrementally verifiable computation. An incrementally verifiable computation scheme is a non-interactive argument for $\mathcal{L}_\mathcal{U}$ that is equipped with an additional update algorithm with the following syntax: The deterministic algorithm Update takes as input the public key pk, a statement $y \in \mathcal{L}_\mathcal{U}$ and a proof π. It outputs a proof π'.

Definition 2.5. *A non-interactive argument* (Gen, Prove, Verify) *for $\mathcal{L}_\mathcal{U}$ together with an update algorithm* Update *is called* incremental *if it satisfies the following requirements:*

Incremental Completeness. *For every $\lambda \in \mathbb{N}$ and machine M:*
- *For every configuration* cf*:*

$$\Pr\left[\text{Verify}\left(\text{vk}, (M, \text{cf}, \text{cf}, 0), \mathcal{E}\right) = 1 \mid (\text{pk}, \text{vk}) \leftarrow \text{Gen}(\lambda)\right] = 1 .$$

   where $\mathcal{E}$ is the empty proof.
- *For every $T < 2^\lambda$, pair of statements $y, y' \in \mathcal{L}_\mathcal{U}$ of the form $y = (M, \text{cf}, \text{cf}', T)$ and $y' = (M, \text{cf}, \text{cf}'', T+1)$ and a proof π:*

$$\Pr\left[\begin{array}{l} \text{Verify}(\text{vk}, y, \pi) = 1 \\ \text{Verify}(\text{vk}, y', \pi') = 0 \end{array} \,\middle|\, \begin{array}{l} (\text{pk}, \text{vk}) \leftarrow \text{Gen}(\lambda) \\ \pi' \leftarrow \text{Update}(\text{pk}, y, \pi) \end{array}\right] = 0 .$$

Update Efficiency. *In the incremental completeness experiments above, the update algorithm runs in time $|y| \cdot \text{poly}(\lambda)$, and outputs a proof π of length $\text{poly}(\lambda)$.*

2.4   Average-Case Puzzles

In this section we define hard on average puzzles.

Syntax. A puzzle is given by a deterministic uniform algorithm F that takes as input a difficulty parameter $t \in \mathbb{N}$ and $x \in \{0,1\}^*$ and outputs $y \in \{0,1\}^{m(|x|)}$, for some polynomial $m(\cdot)$. An average-case puzzle is also given by a probabilistic uniform sampler D that takes as input a difficulty parameter $t \in \mathbb{N}$ and a security parameter $\lambda \in \mathbb{N}$ and outputs $x \in \{0,1\}^{n(\lambda)}$, for some polynomial $n(\cdot)$. For a function $t(\cdot)$, we denote by $\mathsf{F}_{t,\lambda}(x)$ the function $\mathsf{F}(t(\lambda), x)$, and by F_t the function ensemble $\{\mathsf{F}_{t,\lambda}\}_{\lambda \in \mathbb{N}}$. Similarly, we denote by $\mathsf{D}_{t,\lambda}$ the distribution $\mathsf{D}(t(\lambda), \lambda)$, and by D_t the distribution ensemble $\{\mathsf{D}(t(\lambda), \lambda)\}_{\lambda \in \mathbb{N}}$.

Before defining puzzle average-case we define the notion of non-faulty solver:

Definition 2.6 $((\delta,\ \mathcal{D})$-faulty solver). *Let $F = \{F_\lambda\}_{\lambda \in \mathbb{N}}$ be a function ensemble, and let $D = \{D_\lambda\}_{\lambda \in \mathbb{N}}$ be a distribution ensemble, and $\delta : \mathbb{N} \to [0,1]$. An algorithm $\mathcal{A}$ is a (δ, D)-faulty F-solver if for all large enough $\lambda \in \mathbb{N}$, $\Pr[\mathcal{A}(x) \notin \{\bot, F_\lambda(x)\} \mid x \leftarrow D_\lambda] \leq \delta(\lambda)$, where the probability is also over the random coins tosses of $\mathcal{A}$.*

Definition 2.7 (Average-Case Puzzle Against Non-Faulty Solvers). *An average-case puzzle against non-faulty solvers satisfies the following requirements:*

Efficiency.
  – *$\mathsf{F}(t, x)$ runs in time $t \cdot \mathrm{poly}(\log t, |x|)$.*
  – *$\mathsf{D}(t, \lambda)$ runs in time $\mathrm{poly}(\log t, \lambda)$.*
We further say that the puzzle is space efficient *if $\mathsf{F}(t, x)$ runs in space $\mathrm{poly}(\log t, |x|)$.*

Average-case hardness against non-faulty solvers. *For every polynomial p, there exists a constant c, such that for any polynomially bounded $t \geq p^c$, $\delta \leq \frac{0.9}{p}$, any (δ, D_t)-faulty F_t-solver $\mathcal{A}$ with size at most p, and any large enough $\lambda \in \mathbb{N}$,*

$$\Pr[\mathcal{A}(x) = \mathsf{F}_{t,\lambda}(x) \mid x \leftarrow \mathsf{D}_{t,\lambda}] \leq \frac{1}{p(\lambda)} \ .$$

Such a puzzle is called Average-Case Puzzle Against Uniform Non-Faulty Solvers (denoted ACPU) if it is secure against uniform PPT adversaries with running time at most p.

3   Universal Lifting

In this section we show how to lift any semi-universal non-interactive argument to a universal one, based on average case puzzles.

Theorem 3.1. *Assume there exists a (semi-universal) non-interactive argument for $\mathcal{L}_{\mathcal{U}}$. Additionally, assume there exists an average-case puzzle against non-faulty solvers. Then there exists a non-interactive universal argument for $\mathcal{L}_{\mathcal{U}}$, namely one with universal soundness.*

If the original argument is only privately verifiable then so is the resulting universal argument.

If the puzzle is only sound against uniform adversaries then so is the resulting universal argument.

In the rest of this section we prove theorem 3.1.

Construction. Let $(\mathsf{Gen}, \mathsf{Prove}, \mathsf{Verify})$ be the semi-universal argument. Let D be the algorithm sampling puzzle instances and let F be the puzzle solver. We construct a universal argument $(\mathsf{Gen}', \mathsf{Prove}', \mathsf{Verify}')$.

We start with a high level overview of the construction. The setup algorithm generates the keys of the original argument and also generates puzzles $Z_0, Z_1, \ldots, Z_\lambda$ with increasing difficulty levels $1, 2, \ldots, 2^\lambda$ that the prover is challenged to solve. Given a statement $y = (M, \mathsf{cf}, \mathsf{cf}', T)$, the prover creates a proof that $y \in \mathcal{L}_{\mathcal{U}}$ using the semi-universal argument. In addition, it attaches a solution to all puzzles up to difficulty level T together with a proof that it is indeed the solution.

More precisely, let $\bar{i} \leq \lambda$ be the largest such that $2^{\bar{i}} \leq T$. Let $\mathsf{cf}\,[t, Z]$ be the starting configuration of F containing (t, Z) as input and $\mathsf{cf}'\,[\mathsf{S}]$ the ending configuration of F containing S as output. Let T_i be the running time of F on puzzles with security parameter λ and difficulty 2^i. For every $0 \leq i \leq \bar{i}$, the prover attaches the solution S_i of Z_i and the proof that $\left(\mathsf{F}, \mathsf{cf}\,[2^i, Z_i], \mathsf{cf}'\,[\mathsf{S}_i], T_i\right) \in \mathcal{L}_{\mathcal{U}}$.

We now fully describe $(\mathsf{Gen}', \mathsf{Prove}', \mathsf{Verify}')$.

Setup: Given a security parameter λ:
- Sample $(\mathsf{pk}, \mathsf{vk}) \leftarrow \mathsf{Gen}(\lambda)$.
- Sample $Z_i \leftarrow \mathsf{D}(2^i, \lambda)$, for every $0 \leq i \leq \lambda$.
- Output $\mathsf{pk}' = \left(\mathsf{pk}, (Z_i)_{0 \leq i \leq \lambda}\right), \mathsf{vk}' = \left(\mathsf{vk}, (Z_i)_{0 \leq i \leq \lambda}\right)$.

Prover: Given a key $\mathsf{pk}' = \left(\mathsf{pk}, (Z_i)_{0 \leq i \leq \lambda}\right)$ and an instance $y = (M, \mathsf{cf}, \mathsf{cf}', T)$:
- Compute $\pi \leftarrow \mathsf{Prove}(\mathsf{pk}, y)$.
- Solve $\mathsf{S}_i \leftarrow \mathsf{F}(2^i, Z_i)$, for every $0 \leq i \leq \bar{i}$.
- Compute $\pi_i \leftarrow \mathsf{Prove}\left(\mathsf{pk}, (\mathsf{F}, \mathsf{cf}\,[2^i, Z_i], \mathsf{cf}'\,[\mathsf{S}_i], T_i)\right)$, for every $0 \leq i \leq \bar{i}$.
- Output the proof $\pi' = \left(\pi, (\mathsf{S}_i, \pi_i)_{0 \leq i \leq \bar{i}}\right)$.

Verifier: Given a key $\mathsf{vk}' = \left(\mathsf{vk}, (Z_i)_{0 \leq i \leq \lambda}\right)$, an instance $y = (M, \mathsf{cf}, \mathsf{cf}', T)$ and a proof $\pi' = \left(\pi, (\mathsf{S}_i, \pi_i)_{0 \leq i \leq \bar{i}}\right)$:
- Run $\mathsf{Verify}(\mathsf{vk}, y, \pi)$.
- Run $\mathsf{Verify}\left(\mathsf{vk}, (\mathsf{F}, \mathsf{cf}\,[2^i, Z_i], \mathsf{cf}'\,[\mathsf{S}_i], T_i), \pi_i\right)$, for every $0 \leq i \leq \bar{i}$.
- Accept iff all of the verifiers accept.

Completeness and efficiency follow readily from the completeness and efficiency of the underlying argument and the puzzle. We focus on proving universal soundness.

Universal Soundness. We prove soundness against non-uniform adversaries, assuming the puzzle is sound against non-uniform adversaries. The uniform case is analogous.

Assume by contradiction that there exists a poly(λ)-size adversary $\mathcal{A}'$ and a function $\delta(\lambda) = 1/\text{poly}(\lambda)$ such that for infinitely many λ, for

$$(\text{pk}', \text{vk}') \leftarrow \text{Gen}'(\lambda)$$
$$\left(y = \left(M, \text{cf}, \text{cf}', T\right), \pi'\right) \leftarrow \mathcal{A}'(\text{pk}', \text{vk}') ,$$

it holds that:

$$\Pr \begin{bmatrix} \text{Verify}'(\text{vk}', y, \pi') = 1 \\ T \leq 2^\lambda \\ y \notin \mathcal{L}_\mathcal{U} \end{bmatrix} \geq \delta . \tag{1}$$

Denote this experiment by Exp and say that $\mathcal{A}'$ succeeds in Exp if the event in Eq. 1 occurs.

First we describe the general idea of the reduction. We consider different cases, where in some, we show a reduction to the soundness of the underlying semi-universal argument, and in the others, a reduction to the average-case hardness of the puzzle:

- If $\mathcal{A}'$ proves a false statement with a small number of steps T, i.e. number of steps that $\mathcal{A}'$ is capable of computing, we can use it to construct an adversary for the semi-universal argument that proves a false statement corresponding to a polynomial number of steps T, and hence breaks soundness.
- If $\mathcal{A}'$ proves a false statement with a large number of steps T, it has to give a solution and a proof to all puzzles up to difficulty level T. We focus on puzzle number i that is not too difficult but difficult enough. i.e., its difficulty parameter 2^i is bounded by a polynomial, but it is too big for $\mathcal{A}'$ to compute. Now, if $\mathcal{A}'$ solves the puzzle correctly, we can use it to construct a solver breaking the average case puzzle. If $\mathcal{A}'$ doesn't solve the puzzle correctly, it convinces the verifier with a false statement. In this case we use $\mathcal{A}'$ to construct an adversary that breaks the semi-universal argument.

We now describe the reduction in detail. Let $p = \text{poly}(\lambda)$ be a polynomial such that $p \geq \frac{3}{\delta}$. The polynomial p will in fact satisfy more constraints that depend polynomially on the size of the adversary. We will specify how to exactly fix it later on (see dedicated paragraph within Case 2.a below).

By our choice of p,

$$\Pr[\mathcal{A}' \text{ succeeds}] \geq \frac{3}{p} .$$

Let c be the parameter of the puzzle (D, F) such that for any $t \geq p^c$, $\delta' \leq \frac{0.9}{p}$, and (δ', D_t)-faulty F_t-solver $\mathcal{A}^{\text{puz}}$ with size at most p, and any large enough $\lambda \in \mathbb{N}$,

$$\Pr\left[\mathcal{A}^{\text{puz}}(\mathsf{Z}) = \mathsf{F}_{t,\lambda}(\mathsf{Z}) \mid \mathsf{Z} \leftarrow \mathsf{D}_{t,\lambda}\right] \leq \frac{1}{p} .$$

Let T be the number of steps in the statement that $\mathcal{A}'$ outputs. We consider several cases according to the value of $\Pr[\mathcal{A}' \text{ succeeds } \wedge T/2 \leq p^c]$.

Case 1. Reduction to Semi-Universal Arguments. For infinitely many λ,

$$\Pr\left[\mathcal{A}' \text{ succeeds } \wedge T/2 \leq p^c\right] \geq \frac{3}{2p} .$$

Let $\bar{T} = 2p^c$. We define a polynomial adversary $\mathcal{A}$ against the semi-universal argument, proving false statements with number of steps $\leq \bar{T}$.

$\mathcal{A}(\mathsf{pk}, \mathsf{vk})$ simulates the experiment Exp, only the inner keys are replaced with $(\mathsf{pk}, \mathsf{vk})$. It outputs the main statement y and its proof π that $\mathcal{A}'$ outputs. When $(\mathsf{pk}, \mathsf{vk})$ are generated by Gen, we get the same probability space as in Exp and therefore

$$\Pr\begin{bmatrix} \mathsf{Verify}(\mathsf{vk}, y, \pi) = 1 \\ T \leq \bar{T} \\ y \notin \mathcal{L}_{\mathcal{U}} \end{bmatrix} \geq \Pr[\mathcal{A}' \text{ succeeds } \wedge T/2 \leq p^c] \geq \frac{3}{2p} ,$$

in contradiction to plain soundness.

Case 2. Assume that for infinitely many λ,

$$\Pr[\mathcal{A}' \text{ succeeds } \wedge T/2 > p^c] \geq \frac{3}{2p} .$$

Then for such λ, $\exists i \leq \bar{i}$ such that $2^{i-1} \leq p^c \leq 2^i$. Again we split into cases:

Case 2.a. Reduction to Puzzles. Assume that for infinitely many λ,

$$\Pr[\mathcal{A}' \text{ succeeds } \wedge T/2 > p^c \wedge \mathsf{F}(2^i, Z_i) \neq \mathsf{S}_i] < \frac{1}{3} \cdot \frac{3}{2p} .$$

Let $t = 2^i$ and $\delta' = \frac{1}{2p}$. Note that $t \geq p^c$ and $\delta' \leq \frac{0.9}{p}$. We define a (δ', D_t)-faulty F_t-solver $\mathcal{A}^{\mathsf{puz}}$, with size at most p that solves puzzles of difficulty t w.p. $> \frac{1}{p}$.

$\mathcal{A}^{\mathsf{puz}}(Z)$ simulates the experiment Exp, only the i'th puzzle in the key is replaced with Z. It then passes the output of $\mathcal{A}'$ to Verify'. If Verify' doesn't accept or $p^c \geq T/2$, it outputs $\bot$. Otherwise, it outputs $\mathcal{A}''$s solution to the i'th puzzle: S_i.

When Z is generated by D_t, we get the same probability space as in Exp and so

$$\Pr[\mathcal{A}^{\mathsf{puz}}(Z) \notin \{\bot, \mathsf{F}(t, Z)\}] =$$
$$= \Pr\left[\mathcal{A}' \text{ succeeds } \wedge T/2 > p^c \wedge \mathsf{F}(2^i, Z_i) \neq \mathsf{S}_i\right] < \frac{1}{2p} = \delta' ,$$

and

$$\Pr[\mathcal{A}^{\mathsf{puz}}(Z) = \mathsf{F}(t, Z)] =$$
$$= \Pr\left[\mathcal{A}' \text{ succeeds } \wedge T/2 > p^c \wedge \mathsf{F}(2^i, Z_i) = \mathsf{S}_i\right] > \frac{2}{3} \cdot \frac{3}{2p} = \frac{1}{p} .$$

This contradicts the average-case hardness of the puzzle provided that the size of $\mathcal{A}^{\mathsf{puz}}$ is at most p.

$\mathcal{A}^{\mathsf{puz}}$'s **Size, Choice of** p, **and the Uniform Case.** Note that $\mathcal{A}^{\mathsf{puz}}$'s size is a polynomial in the size of $\mathcal{A}'$ and running times of Gen' and Verify', and all together it is a fixed polynomial in λ. We take p to be the maximum of this polynomial and $\frac{3}{8}$, and so the solver runs in time $\leq p$. Also note that this is the only place in the proof where relying on uniform (as opposed to non-uniform) puzzles makes a difference. Here we note that if the adversary $\mathcal{A}'$ is uniform then so is the solver $\mathcal{A}^{\mathsf{puz}}$.

Case 2.b. Reduction to Semi-Universal Arguments. For infinitely λ,

$$\Pr[\mathcal{A}' \text{ succeeds } \wedge\, T/2 > p^c \wedge \mathsf{F}(2^i, \mathsf{Z}_i) \neq \mathsf{S}_i] \geq \frac{1}{3} \cdot \frac{3}{2p} \ .$$

Recall that $\mathcal{A}'$ outputs, amongst others, a proof π_i that $\left(\mathsf{F}, \mathsf{cf}\left[2^i, \mathsf{Z}_i\right], \mathsf{cf}'\left[\mathsf{S}_i\right], T_i\right) \in \mathcal{L}_\mathcal{U}$. In the case that $\mathcal{A}'$ succeeds and $\mathsf{F}(2^i, \mathsf{Z}_i) \neq \mathsf{S}_i$, we get that $\left(\mathsf{F}, \mathsf{cf}\left[2^i, \mathsf{Z}_i\right], \mathsf{cf}'\left[\mathsf{S}_i\right], T_i\right) \notin \mathcal{L}_\mathcal{U}$ and Verify accepts π_i. This means that Verify is convinced by a proof of a wrong statement. In addition, the running time T_i of $\mathsf{F}(2^i, \mathsf{Z}_i)$ satisfies $T_i = 2^i \cdot \mathsf{poly}(\lambda) \leq 2p^c \cdot \mathsf{poly}(\lambda)$ and so there exists a polynomial $\bar{T}(\lambda)$ such that $T_i \leq \bar{T}$. We use this to construct an adversary $\mathcal{A}$ against the semi-universal argument, proving false statements with number of steps $\leq \bar{T}$.

$\mathcal{A}(\mathsf{pk}, \mathsf{vk})$ simulates the experiment Exp, only the inner keys are replaced with $(\mathsf{pk}, \mathsf{vk})$. It outputs the instance $y_i = \left(\mathsf{F}, \mathsf{cf}\left[2^i, \mathsf{Z}_i\right], \mathsf{cf}'\left[\mathsf{S}_i\right], T_i\right)$ and its proof π_i, both generated by $\mathcal{A}'$. When $(\mathsf{pk}, \mathsf{vk})$ are generated by Gen, we get the same probability space as in Exp and therefore:

$$\Pr \begin{bmatrix} \mathsf{Verify}(\mathsf{vk}, y_i, \pi_i) = 1 \\ T_i \leq \bar{T} \\ y_i \notin \mathcal{L}_\mathcal{U} \end{bmatrix} \geq \Pr[\mathcal{A}' \text{ succeeds } \wedge\, p^c < T/2 \wedge \mathsf{F}(2^i, \mathsf{Z}_i) \neq \mathsf{S}_i] \geq \frac{1}{2p} \ ,$$

contradicting soundness.

On the Security Loss of the Reduction. Most cryptographic reductions in the literature have a fixed security loss — there is a universal constant c, such that if the adversary breaks a given scheme in time t and probability $1/t$, then the reduction breaks the underlying assumption in time t^c and probability $1/t^c$. We note that as is, our reduction does not have such a fixed loss, due to the fact that we assume a very weak form of puzzles that do not have a fixed gap (namely for any polynomial p there exists a constant c such that there is no $(p, 1/p)$-solver for puzzles of difficulty p^c). If we assume a stronger form of puzzles that switches the quantifiers and has a universal gap c (independent of p), then our reduction has a fixed loss as well. Puzzles with a universal gap indeed follow in the uniform case (with no additional assumptions) or in the non-uniform case assuming **nuETH** (see Sect. 4 for the corresponding constructions).

3.1 Incrementally Verifiable Computation Lifting

In this section we extend the universal non-interactive argument construction and construct a universal IVC based on a semi-universal IVC.

Theorem 3.2. *Assume that there exists an incrementally verifiable computation for $\mathcal{L}_\mathcal{U}$. Additionally, assume that there exists a space-efficient average-case puzzle against non-faulty solvers. Then there exists an incrementally verifiable computation for $\mathcal{L}_\mathcal{U}$ with universal soundness.*

If the original IVC is only privately verifiable then the resulting universal IVC is also privately verifiable.

If the puzzle is only sound against uniform adversaries then the resulting universal IVC is also sound against uniform adversaries.

In the rest of this section, we prove theorem 3.2. We use the construction from Theorem 3.1, only we add to the proof partial computation data, allowing us to define the Update algorithm.

Construction. Let (Gen, Prove, Update, Verify) be the semi-universal IVC. Let (D, F) be the puzzle. We construct a universal IVC (Gen′, Prove′, Update′, Verify′).

We use the same setup algorithm Gen′ as in Theorem 3.1. i.e., the keys (pk′, vk′) contain the keys of the underlying IVC (pk, vk), and puzzle instances $Z_0, Z_1, \ldots, Z_\lambda$ with increasing difficulty levels $2^0, 2^1, \ldots, 2^\lambda$.

The proof π' includes the proof of the main statement using the underlying IVC, and partial computations of all the puzzles including proofs of these partial computations (again, using the underlying IVC). More precisely, let q be the polynomial such that $F(t, Z)$ runs in time $t \cdot q(\lambda)$ (there is an extra factor of poly $\log t$ in F's running time, but $\log t \leq \lambda$). The proof π' of a statement with number of steps T, contains for every $0 \leq i \leq \lambda$, a configuration cf_i of the machine F, which is the result of computing $T \cdot q(\lambda)$ steps starting from the configuration $\mathsf{cf}\left[2^i, Z_i\right]$. In addition, for every $0 \leq i \leq \lambda$ we attach a proof π_i that cf_i is indeed the result of this partial computation.

Note that for every i such that $2^i \leq T$, cf_i is the final configuration of the computation and so it contains the puzzle solution. It is similar to the non-interactive argument proof in 3.1 where we have a solution (and a proof) to puzzle i for every i such that $2^i \leq T$.

We now describe Update′, Prove′, Verify′ in detail.

Update: Given a key $\mathsf{pk}' = \left(\mathsf{pk}, (Z_i)_{0 \leq i \leq \lambda}\right)$, an instance $y = \left(M, \mathsf{cf}, \mathsf{cf}', T\right)$ and a proof $\pi' = \left(\pi, (\mathsf{cf}_i, \pi_i)_{0 \leq i \leq \lambda}\right)$:

– Update the inner proof $\pi^+ \leftarrow \mathsf{Update}(\mathsf{pk}, y, \pi)$.
– For every $0 \leq i \leq \lambda$, advance the ith puzzle computation and update the proof:
  • Let $\mathsf{cf}_i^0 = \mathsf{cf}_i, \pi_i^0 = \pi_i$. If $T = 1$ (i.e., all the components in π' are empty), take $\mathsf{cf}_i^0 = \mathsf{cf}\left[2^i, Z_i\right]$.

- For every $1 \leq j \leq q(\lambda)$, compute one step of F from cf_i^{j-1} to cf_i^j. Then update the proof:

  $$\pi_i^j \leftarrow \mathsf{Update}\left(\mathsf{pk}, \left(\mathsf{F}, \mathsf{cf}\left[2^i, \mathsf{Z}_i\right], \mathsf{cf}_i^j, (T-1)\, q + j\right), \pi_i^{j-1}\right).$$

- Set $\mathsf{cf}_i^+ \leftarrow \mathsf{cf}_i^q, \pi_i^+ \leftarrow \pi_i^q$.

  - Output the proof $\pi'^+ = \left(\pi^+, \left(\mathsf{cf}_i^+, \pi_i^+\right)_{0 \leq i \leq \lambda}\right)$.

Prover: To prove a statement with number of steps T, we run the update algorithm Update' for T times one after the other, starting from an empty proof.

Verifier: Given a key $\mathsf{vk}' = \left(\mathsf{vk}, (\mathsf{Z}_i)_{0 \leq i \leq \lambda}\right)$, an instance $y = (M, \mathsf{cf}, \mathsf{cf}', T)$ and a proof $\pi' = \left(\pi, (\mathsf{cf}_i, \pi_i)_{0 \leq i \leq \lambda}\right)$, the verifier simply verifies all the inner proofs:

  - Verify: $\mathsf{Verify}\,(\mathsf{vk}, y, \pi)$.
  - For every $0 \leq i \leq \lambda$, verify: $\mathsf{Verify}\left(\mathsf{vk}, \left(\mathsf{F}, \mathsf{cf}\left[2^i, \mathsf{Z}_i\right], \mathsf{cf}_i, T \cdot q\right), \pi_i\right)$.

Incremental Completeness. Since the verifier verifies all the inner proofs $\pi, (\pi_i)_{0 \leq i \leq \lambda}$ using the underlying IVC, and the update algorithm updates these inner proofs with the underlying IVC, incremental completeness follows from incremental completeness of the underlying IVC.

Efficiency. The update algorithm computes $q(\lambda)$ steps of F for all the puzzles and the proof includes the configuration of F after this computation. Since F is space efficient, the configuration is of size $\mathrm{poly}(\lambda)$. This, together with update efficiency of the underlying IVC implies update efficiency of the universal IVC.

Universal Soundness. As mentioned above, for every i such that the non-interactive argument proof contains the solution to the ith puzzle, also the IVC proof contains the solution, since it contains the final configuration of the puzzle computation. Therefore, universal soundness can be proved analogously to the proof in Theorem 3.1.

4 Constructing Average-Case Puzzles

In this section we construct hard-on-average puzzles (Definition 2.7). Our construction is based on FHE combined with appropriate hierarchy theorems/assumptions, where different hierarchy theorems/assumptions yield different efficiency and security guarantees. For security against uniform adversaries, we rely on a probabilistic time hierarchy theorem for slightly non-uniform computations (Theorem 4.9) by Barak [Bar02]. For puzzles against non-uniform adversaries, and for space efficient puzzles we make mild hierarchy assumptions for space bounded computations (4.1 and 4.2). Both assumptions follow from **nuETH** (see Assumption 4.3 and Theorem 4.4).

4.1 Worst-Case Hardness Assumptions

In this section we define complexity worst-case assumptions for instantiating average-case puzzles.

Assumption 4.1. *For any polynomial $q(\cdot)$ there exists a polynomial $Q(\cdot)$ and a language $\mathcal{L} \in \textbf{DTIME}(Q)$ such that any family $\mathcal{C} = \{\mathcal{C}_\lambda\}$ of size-$q(\lambda)$ circuits fails to decide $\mathcal{L}_\lambda = \mathcal{L} \cap \{0,1\}^\lambda$ for all large enough λ.*

Assumption 4.2. *There exists a polynomial $s(\cdot)$ such that for any polynomial $q(\cdot)$ there exists a polynomial Q and a language $\mathcal{L} \in \textbf{DTIME}(Q) \cap \textbf{DSPACE}(s)$ such that any family $\mathcal{C} = \{\mathcal{C}_\lambda\}$ of size-$q(\lambda)$ circuits fails to decide $\mathcal{L}_\lambda = \mathcal{L} \cap \{0,1\}^\lambda$ for all large enough λ.*

Non-Uniform ETH. For $a, b \in \mathbb{N}$, let $3SAT[a, b]$ be the language of satisfiable 3-CNF formulas with a variables and b clauses.

Assumption 4.3 (nuETH [IP01,IPZ01]**).** *There exists constants $c, d > 0$ such that any family $\mathcal{C} = \{\mathcal{C}_\lambda\}$ of size-$2^{\lambda/d}$ circuits fails to decide $3SAT[\lambda, c \cdot \lambda]$ for all large enough λ.*

Theorem 4.4. *Assuming **nuETH** (Assumption 4.3), Assumptions 4.1 and 4.2 hold.*

Proof (Proof Sketch). Let c, d be the constants given by **nuETH**. Let $q(\lambda) = \lambda^k$ be a polynomial. For $\lambda \in \mathbb{N}$, let $n = d \cdot k \cdot \log(\lambda)$ and consider the language $3SAT[n, cn, \lambda]$ that consists of satisfiable 3-CNF formulas with n variables and cn clauses, padded to size λ.

By **nuETH**, for large enough λ any family of circuits of size λ^k fails to decide $3SAT[n, cn, \lambda]$. On the other hand, a SAT solver can enumerate through all $\lambda^{d \cdot k}$ possible assignments. The algorithm runs (deterministically) in time $Q(\lambda) = \lambda^{d \cdot k} \cdot \text{polylog}(\lambda)$, implying Assumption 4.1. Moreover, the algorithm runs in $O(\log(\lambda))$ space, which also implies Assumption 4.2.

4.2 Average-Case Puzzles from FHE

In this section we prove the following three theorems.

Theorem 4.5. *Assuming FHE, there exists an Average-Case Puzzle Against Uniform Non-Faulty Solvers.*

Theorem 4.6. *Assuming FHE and assumption 4.1, there exists an Average-Case Puzzle Against Non-Faulty Solvers.*

Theorem 4.7. *Assuming FHE and assumption 4.2, there exists a space-efficient Average-Case Puzzle Against Non-Faulty Solvers.*

The constructions behind all of the above follow a common blueprint. We next describe this blueprint, and then address the proof for each one of the theorems.

At a high level, the construction is as follows. The sampler samples an encryption of garbage. The associated puzzle algorithm evaluates the universal machine for t steps on the ciphertext. To prove security, the reduction switches the ciphertext to an encryption of an instance of an underlying worst-case language. In this case, a correct answer of the non-faulty solver decrypts to a correct decision about the input. Finally, the success probability is amplified.

Construction. For the formal definition, we fix some encoding such that $x \in \{0,1\}^*$ is viewed as $x = (M, x')$ where M is a Turing machine and x' is an input for M. Let $U_{t,s}$ be the universal Turing machine, which on input $x = (M, x') \in \{0,1\}^n$ outputs $M(x')$ provided that M halts after at most t steps, using at most space s, and outputs a single bit. Let $U_t = U_{t,t}$ (where there is no space restriction). By known constructions $U_{t,s}$ runs in time at most $t \cdot \text{poly}(\log t, n)$ and uses space at most $s \cdot \text{poly}(\log t, n)$.

We next define a puzzle sampler D and puzzle solvers F and F^s. In what follows, let (Gen, Enc, Dec, Eval) be an FHE scheme.

D - **Puzzle Sampler:** Given a difficulty parameter t and a security parameter λ:

  – Samples $pk, sk \leftarrow \text{Gen}(1^\lambda)$
  – Returns $ct \leftarrow \text{Enc}_{pk}(0^{3\lambda})$

F - **Average-Case Puzzle:** Given a difficulty parameter t and input x:
  – Homomorphically evaluates U_t on x

F^s - **Space-Efficient Average-Case Puzzle:** Given a difficulty parameter t and input x:
  – Homomorphically evaluates $U_{t,s}$ on x

We start by proving Theorem 4.6, and then extend the proof to account for Theorem 4.5 and Theorem 4.7.

Proof of Theorem 4.6. We show that (D, F) is an Average-Case Puzzle Against Non-Faulty Solvers under Assumption 4.1.

First note that the efficiency requirements follow from the complexity preservation of homomorphic evaluation. We henceforth focus on proving hardness.

Fix any polynomial $p = p(\lambda)$ and assume toward contradiction that for every constant c, there exists a polynomially bounded function $t \geq p^c$, $\delta \leq \frac{0.9}{p}$, and a (δ, D_t)-faulty F_t-solver $\mathcal{A}$ with size at most p, such that for infinitely many λ,

$$\Pr[\mathcal{A}(x) = F_{t,\lambda}(x) \mid x \leftarrow D_{t,\lambda}] > \frac{1}{p(\lambda)} \ . \tag{2}$$

We prove that there exists a polynomial q such that for any polynomial Q and language $\mathcal{L} \in \mathbf{DTIME}(Q)$, there exists a size-$q$ circuit family $\mathcal{B}$ that decides $\mathcal{L}$ on infinitely many input lengths, thereby contradicting Assumption 4.1.

Let Q be a polynomial and let $\mathcal{L} \in \mathbf{DTIME}(Q)$. Also, let M be a deterministic Turing machine that decides $\mathcal{L}$ in time Q. Consider a sampler $\widehat{D}_M(x)$ that given $x \in \{0,1\}^\lambda$, samples $pk, sk \leftarrow \text{Gen}(1^\lambda)$, and outputs an encryption $\widehat{x} \leftarrow \text{Enc}_{pk}(x')$, where $x' = (M, x)$, padded to size 3λ.

We construct a probabilistic circuit family $\mathcal{B}'$ that decides $\mathcal{L}$ with error $< 2^{-\lambda}$. In particular, we can non-uniformly fix its randomness to get a deterministic decider that decides $\mathcal{L}$ on inputs $x \in \{0,1\}^\lambda$. (The size of $\mathcal{B}'$ will be a polynomial $q(\lambda)$ independent of Q.)

On input $x \in \{0,1\}^\lambda$, $\mathcal{B}'$ repeats the following process $\mathcal{D}$, $k(\lambda)$ times, for some polynomial $k(\cdot)$ to be determined later. $\mathcal{D}(x)$ samples $\widehat{x}_i \leftarrow \widehat{\mathsf{D}}_M(x)$, runs $\mathcal{A}$ on $\widehat{x}_i$, and obtains its output y_i. If $y_i \neq \perp$, $\mathcal{D}$ outputs $b_i = \mathsf{Dec}_{\mathsf{sk}}(y)$, and otherwise outputs $b_i = \perp$. Finally, $\mathcal{B}'$ outputs the majority among the values $\{b_1, \ldots, b_k\} \setminus \{\perp\}$ generated by $\mathcal{D}$.

Claim 4.8. *There exists a polynomial $t \geq Q$ and constants $0 < \alpha < 1 < \beta$, such that for infinitely many λ it holds that for any $x \in \{0,1\}^\lambda$,*

$$\Pr\left[\mathcal{D}(x) = \mathcal{L}(x)\right] \geq \max\left\{\frac{\alpha}{p(\lambda)}, \beta \cdot \Pr\left[\mathcal{D}(x) \notin \{\perp, \mathcal{L}(x)\}\right]\right\} .$$

Proof. Let c be such that $p^c \geq Q$, and let $t \geq p^c$ be such that Eq. 2 holds. For every large enough λ such that 2 holds,

$$
\begin{array}{lll}
\Pr\left[\mathcal{D}(x) = \mathcal{L}(x)\right] & = & (M \text{ decides } \mathcal{L}) \\
\Pr\left[\mathcal{D}(x) = M(x)\right] & = & (\text{FHE correctness}) \\
\Pr\left[\mathcal{A}(\widehat{x}) = \mathsf{F}_{t,\lambda}(\widehat{x}) \mid \widehat{x} \leftarrow \widehat{\mathsf{D}}_M(x)\right] & \geq & (\text{FHE semantic security}) \\
\Pr\left[\mathcal{A}(\widehat{x}) = \mathsf{F}_{t,\lambda}(\widehat{x}) \mid \widehat{x} \leftarrow \mathsf{D}_{t,\lambda}\right] - \dfrac{0.01}{p(\lambda)} & \geq & (\text{Equation 2}) \\
\dfrac{1}{p(\lambda)} - \dfrac{0.01}{p(\lambda)} & = & \\
\dfrac{0.99}{p(\lambda)} & . &
\end{array}
$$

In addition,

$$
\begin{array}{lll}
\Pr\left[\mathcal{D}(x) \notin \{\perp, \mathcal{L}(x)\}\right] & = & (\text{FHE correctness}) \\
\Pr\left[\mathcal{A}(\widehat{x}) \notin \{\perp, \mathsf{F}_{t,\lambda}(\widehat{x})\} \mid \widehat{x} \leftarrow \widehat{\mathsf{D}}_M(x)\right] & \leq & (\text{FHE semantic security}) \\
\Pr\left[\mathcal{A}(\widehat{x}) \notin \{\perp, \mathsf{F}_{t,\lambda}(\widehat{x})\} \mid \widehat{x} \leftarrow \mathsf{D}_{t,\lambda}\right] + \dfrac{0.01}{p(\lambda)} & \leq & (\mathcal{A} \text{ is } \delta \text{ faulty}) \\
\delta(\lambda) + \dfrac{0.01}{p(\lambda)} & \leq & \\
\dfrac{0.91}{p(\lambda)} & . &
\end{array}
$$

In particular, the claim holds with $\alpha = 0.99$ and $\beta = \frac{0.99}{0.91}$.

So, by Claim 4.8, taking $k(\lambda) = C \cdot p(\lambda)$ for a large enough constant C (and assuming w.l.o.g that $p(\lambda) \geq \lambda$), it follows by a Chernoff bound that for any $x \in \{0,1\}^\lambda$,

$$\Pr\left[\mathcal{B}'(x) \neq \mathcal{L}(x)\right] < 2^{-p(\lambda)} \leq 2^{-\lambda} .$$

The Size of $\mathcal{B}$. First, note each invocation of $\mathcal{D}$ can be done in fixed polynomial size $\ell(\lambda)$, which depends only on the size $p(\lambda)$ of $\mathcal{A}$ and fixed polynomial running time of the FHE algorithms. Overall the size of $\mathcal{B}'$, and hence also of the derandomized $\mathcal{B}$, is $q = \ell \cdot k = O(\ell \cdot p)$.

Extending to Space-Efficient Puzzles (Proof of Theorem 4.7). Let s be the space bound given by Assumption 4.2. First, by the complexity preservation of homomorphic evaluation F^s, which evaluates $U_{t,s}$, can be computed in space $s \cdot \mathrm{poly}(\log t, \lambda)$ space. The proof of security is the same, with the exception that we consider $\mathcal{L} \in \mathbf{DTIME}(Q) \cap \mathbf{DSPACE}(s)$.

The Uniform Case (Proof of Theorem 4.5). Recall that here we focus on puzzles against uniform solvers (that are not necessarily space-efficient). We show how to remove ?? 4.1, on which we relied in the non-uniform case. Instead, we rely on the following (unconditional) hierarchy theorem for slightly non-uniform probabilistic time.

Theorem 4.9 ([Bar02]). *For any polynomial q, there exists a polynomial Q such that*

$$\mathbf{BPTIME}(Q)_{/\log n} \not\subseteq \mathbf{ioBPTIME}(q)_{/\log n} \ .$$

The differences from Theorem 4.6 is only in the security proof. The security proof has a similar outline. Below, the parts that are similar to the Proof of Theorem 4.6 are in grey, whereas only the new parts are in black.

Fix any polynomial $p = p(\lambda)$ and assume toward contradiction that for every constant c, there exists a polynomially bounded function $t \geq p^c$, $\delta \leq \frac{0.9}{p}$, and a (δ, D_t)-faulty F_t-solver $\mathcal{A}$ of running time at most p, such that for infinitely many λ,

$$\Pr\left[\mathcal{A}(x) = \mathsf{F}_{t,\lambda}(x) \mid x \leftarrow \mathsf{D}_{t,\lambda}\right] > \frac{1}{p(\lambda)} \ . \tag{3}$$

We prove that there exists a polynomial q such that for any polynomial Q and language $\mathcal{L} \in \mathbf{BPTIME}(Q)_{/\log n}$, there exists a q-time probabilistic algorithm $\mathcal{B}$ that decides $\mathcal{L}$ on infinitely many input lengths, thereby contradicting **Theorem 4.9.**

Let Q be a polynomial and let $\mathcal{L} \in \mathbf{BPTIME}(Q)_{/\log n}$. Also, let M be a Q-time probabilistic Turing machine with non-uniform description of size $O(\log \lambda)$, for inputs of size λ, that decides $\mathcal{L}$ with error $< 1/3$.

Claim 4.10. *Assuming one-way functions (and in particular, assuming FHE), there exists a polynomial Q' and a Q'-time probabilistic M', with non-uniform description of size $O(\log \lambda)$, and randomness of size λ, that decides $\mathcal{L}$ with error $\frac{0.01}{p(\lambda)}$, on all inputs of large enough size λ.*

Proof (Proof Sketch.). First consider an amplified version M'' of M with error $\frac{0.01}{2p(\lambda)}$. M'' also has non-uniform description of size $O(\log \lambda)$ and polynomial running time, but may use randomness of polynomial size $\gg \lambda$. Then to get M', derandomize M'' using a cryptographic pseudorandom generator with seed length λ (which follows from one-way functions [HILL99]). Then by pseudorandomness, for all large enough λ, the error of M' is at most $\frac{0.01}{2p(\lambda)} + \frac{0.01}{2p(\lambda)} = \frac{0.01}{p(\lambda)}$, and it has some polynomial running time $Q'(\lambda)$, as required.

Consider a sampler $\widehat{\mathsf{D}}_{M'}(x)$ that given $x \in \{0,1\}^\lambda$, samples $\mathsf{pk}, \mathsf{sk} \leftarrow \mathsf{Gen}(1^\lambda)$, $r \leftarrow \{0,1\}^\lambda$, and outputs an encryption $\widehat{x} \leftarrow \mathsf{Enc}_{\mathsf{pk}}(x')$, where $x' = (M'_r, x)$, padded to size 3λ, and M'_r is M' with randomness r hardwired (note that M' has description of size $\lambda + O(\log \lambda)$).

We construct a probabilistic Turing machine $\mathcal{B}$ with non-uniform description of size $O(\log \lambda)$ that decides $\mathcal{L}$ (with error $< 1/3$) for infinitely many λ. (The time of $\mathcal{B}$ will be a polynomial $q(\lambda)$ independent of Q.)

On input $x \in \{0,1\}^\lambda$, $\mathcal{B}$ repeats the following process $\mathcal{D}$, $k(\lambda)$ times, for some polynomial $k(\cdot)$ to be determined later. $\mathcal{D}(x)$ samples $\widehat{x}_i \leftarrow \widehat{\mathsf{D}}_{M'}(x)$, runs $\mathcal{A}$ on $\widehat{x}_i$, and obtains its output y_i. If $y_i \neq \perp$, $\mathcal{D}$ outputs $b_i = \mathsf{Dec}_{\mathsf{sk}}(y)$, and otherwise outputs $b_i = \perp$. Finally, $\mathcal{B}$ outputs the majority among the values $\{b_1, \ldots, b_k\} \setminus \{\perp\}$ generated by $\mathcal{D}$.

Claim 4.11. *There exists a polynomial $t \geq Q'$ and constants $0 < \alpha < 1 < \beta$, such that for infinitely many λ it holds that for any $x \in \{0,1\}^\lambda$,*

$$\Pr\left[\mathcal{D}(x) = \mathcal{L}(x)\right] \geq \max\left\{\frac{\alpha}{p(\lambda)}, \beta \cdot \Pr\left[\mathcal{D}(x) \notin \{\perp, \mathcal{L}(x)\}\right]\right\} .$$

Proof. Let c be such that $p^c \geq Q'$, and let $t \geq p^c$ be such that Eq. 2 holds. For every large enough λ such that 3 holds,

$$\Pr\left[\mathcal{D}(x) = \mathcal{L}(x)\right] \qquad\qquad\qquad = \text{(FHE correctness)}$$

$$\Pr\left[\mathcal{A}(\widehat{x}) = \mathsf{F}_{t,\lambda}(\widehat{x}) \,\middle|\, \widehat{x} \leftarrow \widehat{\mathsf{D}}_{M'}(x)\right] - \Pr\left[M'(x) \neq \mathcal{L}(x)\right] \geq (M' \text{ error probability})$$

$$\Pr\left[\mathcal{A}(\widehat{x}) = \mathsf{F}_{t,\lambda}(\widehat{x}) \,\middle|\, \widehat{x} \leftarrow \widehat{\mathsf{D}}_{M'}(x)\right] - \frac{0.01}{p(\lambda)} \qquad \geq \text{(FHE semantic security)}$$

$$\Pr\left[\mathcal{A}(\widehat{x}) = \mathsf{F}_{t,\lambda}(\widehat{x}) \mid \widehat{x} \leftarrow \mathsf{D}_{t,\lambda}\right] - \frac{0.01}{p(\lambda)} - \frac{0.01}{p(\lambda)} \qquad \geq \text{(Equation 3)}$$

$$\frac{0.98}{p(\lambda)} .$$

In addition,

$$\Pr\left[\mathcal{D}(x) \notin \{\perp, \mathcal{L}(x)\}\right] \qquad\qquad\qquad = \text{(FHE correctness)}$$

$$\Pr\left[\mathcal{A}(\widehat{x}) \notin \{\perp, \mathsf{F}_{t,\lambda}(\widehat{x})\} \,\middle|\, \widehat{x} \leftarrow \widehat{\mathsf{D}}_{M'}(x)\right] + \Pr\left[M'(x) \neq \mathcal{L}(x)\right] \leq (M' \text{ error probability})$$

$$\Pr\left[\mathcal{A}(\widehat{x}) \notin \{\perp, \mathsf{F}_{t,\lambda}(\widehat{x})\} \,\middle|\, \widehat{x} \leftarrow \widehat{\mathsf{D}}_{M'}(x)\right] + \frac{0.01}{p(\lambda)} \qquad \leq \text{(FHE semantic security)}$$

$$\Pr\left[\mathcal{A}(\widehat{x}) \notin \{\perp, \mathsf{F}_{t,\lambda}(\widehat{x})\} \mid \widehat{x} \leftarrow \mathsf{D}_{t,\lambda}\right] + \frac{0.01}{p(\lambda)} + \frac{0.01}{p(\lambda)} \qquad \leq (\mathcal{A} \text{ is } \delta \text{ faulty})$$

$$\delta(\lambda) + \frac{0.02}{p(\lambda)} \qquad\qquad\qquad\qquad\qquad \leq$$

$$\frac{0.92}{p(\lambda)} .$$

In particular, the claim holds with $\alpha = 0.99$ and $\beta = \frac{0.98}{0.92}$.

So, by Claim 4.11, taking $k(\lambda) = C \cdot p(\lambda)$ for a large enough constant C (and assuming w.l.o.g that $p(\lambda) \geq \lambda$), it follows by a Chernoff bound that for any $x \in \{0,1\}^\lambda$,

$$\Pr\left[\mathcal{B}(x) \neq \mathcal{L}(x)\right] < 2^{-p(\lambda)} \leq 2/3 \ .$$

The Time and Non-uniformity of $\mathcal{B}$. First, note that each invocation of $\mathcal{D}$ can be done in fixed polynomial time $\ell(\lambda)$, which depends only on the size $p(\lambda)$ of $\mathcal{A}$ and fixed polynomial running time of the FHE algorithms. Overall the running time of $\mathcal{B}$ is $q = \ell \cdot r = O(\ell \cdot p)$. The non-uniform description of $\mathcal{B}$ is dominated by that of M, and hence is of size $O(\log \lambda)$, as required.

References

AL18. Ananth, P., Lombardi, A.: Succinct garbling schemes from functional encryption through a local simulation paradigm. In: Beimel, A., Dziembowski, S. (eds.) TCC 2018. LNCS, vol. 11240, pp. 455–472. Springer, Cham (2018). https://doi.org/10.1007/978-3-030-03810-6_17

Bar01. Barak, B.: How to go beyond the black-box simulation barrier. In: 42nd Annual Symposium on Foundations of Computer Science, FOCS 2001, 14–17 October 2001, Las Vegas, Nevada, USA, pp. 106–115. IEEE Computer Society (2001)

Bar02. Barak, B.: A probabilistic-time hierarchy theorem for "slightly non-uniform" algorithms. In: Randomization and Approximation Techniques, 6th International Workshop, RANDOM 2002, Cambridge, MA, USA, 13–15 September 2002, Proceedings, pp. 194–208 (2002)

BCG+18. Bitansky, N., et al.: Indistinguishability obfuscation for RAM programs and succinct randomized encodings. SIAM J. Comput. **47**(3), 1123–1210 (2018)

BCH+22. Bitansky, N., et al.: PPAD is as hard as LWE and iterated squaring. In: Kiltz, E., Vaikuntanathan, V. (eds.) Theory of Cryptography - 20th International Conference, TCC 2022, Chicago, IL, USA, November 7–10, 2022, Proceedings, Part II, volume 13748 of Lecture Notes in Computer Science, pp. 593–622. Springer, Cham (2022)

BG08. Barak, B., Goldreich, O.: Universal arguments and their applications. SIAM J. Comput. **38**(5), 1661–1694 (2008)

BG20. Bitansky, N., Gerichter, I.: On the cryptographic hardness of local search. In: Vidick, T. (ed.) 11th Innovations in Theoretical Computer Science Conference, ITCS 2020, 12–14 January 2020, Seattle, Washington, USA, volume 151 of LIPIcs, pp. 6:1–6:29. Schloss Dagstuhl - Leibniz-Zentrum für Informatik (2020)

BGJ+16. Bitansky, N., Goldwasser, S., Jain, A., Paneth, O., Vaikuntanathan, V., Waters, B.: Time-lock puzzles from randomized encodings. In: Sudan, M. (ed.) Proceedings of the 2016 ACM Conference on Innovations in Theoretical Computer Science, Cambridge, MA, USA, 14–16 January 2016, pp. 345–356. ACM (2016)

BHK17. Brakerski, Z., Holmgren, J., Kalai, Y.: Non-interactive delegation and batch NP verification from standard computational assumptions. In: Proceedings of the 49th Annual ACM SIGACT Symposium on Theory of Computing, pp. 474–482 (2017)

BKP18. Bitansky, N., Tauman Kalai, Y., Paneth, O.: Multi-collision resistance: a paradigm for keyless hash functions. In: Diakonikolas, I., Kempe, D., Henzinger, M. (eds.) Proceedings of the 50th Annual ACM SIGACT Symposium on Theory of Computing, STOC 2018, Los Angeles, CA, USA, 25–29 June 2018, pp. 671–684. ACM (2018)

BS23. Bitansky, N., Solomon, T.: Bootstrapping homomorphic encryption via functional encryption. In: Kalai, Y.T. (ed.) 14th Innovations in Theoretical Computer Science Conference, ITCS 2023, 10–13 January 2023, MIT, Cambridge, Massachusetts, USA, volume 251 of LIPIcs, pp. 17:1–17:23. Schloss Dagstuhl - Leibniz-Zentrum für Informatik (2023)

CJJ21a. Choudhuri, A.R., Jain, A., Jin, Z.: Non-interactive batch arguments for NP from standard assumptions. In: Malkin, T., Peikert, C. (eds.) CRYPTO 2021. LNCS, vol. 12828, pp. 394–423. Springer, Cham (2021). https://doi.org/10.1007/978-3-030-84259-8_14

CJJ21b. Choudhuri, A.R., Jain, A., Jin, Z.: Snargs for $\mathcal{P}$ from LWE. In: 62nd IEEE Annual Symposium on Foundations of Computer Science, FOCS 2021, Denver, CO, USA, 7–10 February 2022, pp. 68–79. IEEE (2021)

CKV10. Chung, K.-M., Kalai, Y., Vadhan, S.: Improved delegation of computation using fully homomorphic encryption. In: Rabin, T. (ed.) CRYPTO 2010. LNCS, vol. 6223, pp. 483–501. Springer, Heidelberg (2010). https://doi.org/10.1007/978-3-642-14623-7_26

DGKV22. Devadas, L., Goyal, R., Kalai, Y., Vaikuntanathan, V.: Rate-1 non-interactive arguments for batch-NP and applications. In: 63rd IEEE Annual Symposium on Foundations of Computer Science, FOCS 2022, Denver, CO, USA, 31 October–3 November 2022, pp. 1057–1068. IEEE (2022)

DGS09. Deng, Y., Goyal, V., Sahai, A.: Resolving the simultaneous resettability conjecture and a new non-black-box simulation strategy. In: 50th Annual IEEE Symposium on Foundations of Computer Science, FOCS 2009, 25–27 October 2009, Atlanta, Georgia, USA, pp. 251–260. IEEE Computer Society (2009)

DN92. Dwork, C., Naor, M.: Pricing via processing or combatting junk mail. In: Brickell, E.F. (ed.) CRYPTO 1992. LNCS, vol. 740, pp. 139–147. Springer, Heidelberg (1993). https://doi.org/10.1007/3-540-48071-4_10

FGHS21. Fearnley, J., Goldberg, P.W., Hollender, A., Savani, R.: The complexity of gradient descent: CLS = PPAD ∩ PLS. In: STOC, pp. 46–59. ACM (2021)

GPS16. Garg, S., Pandey, O., Srinivasan, A.: Revisiting the cryptographic hardness of finding a Nash equilibrium. In: Robshaw, M., Katz, J. (eds.) CRYPTO 2016. LNCS, vol. 9815, pp. 579–604. Springer, Heidelberg (2016). https://doi.org/10.1007/978-3-662-53008-5_20

GS18. Garg, S., Srinivasan, A.: A simple construction of iO for turing machines. In: Beimel, A., Dziembowski, S. (eds.) TCC 2018. LNCS, vol. 11240, pp. 425–454. Springer, Cham (2018). https://doi.org/10.1007/978-3-030-03810-6_16

GW11. Gentry, C., Wichs, D.: Separating succinct non-interactive arguments from all falsifiable assumptions. In: Fortnow, L., Vadhan, S.P. (eds.) Proceedings of the 43rd ACM Symposium on Theory of Computing, STOC 2011, San Jose, CA, USA, 6–8 June 2011, pp. 99–108. ACM (2011)

HILL99. Håstad, J., Impagliazzo, R., Levin, L.A., Luby, M.: A pseudorandom generator from any one-way function. SIAM J. Comput. 28(4), 1364–1396 (1999)

IP01. Impagliazzo, R., Paturi, R.: On the complexity of k-sat. J. Comput. Syst. Sci. 62(2), 367–375 (2001)

IPZ01. Impagliazzo, R., Paturi, R., Zane, F.: Which problems have strongly exponential complexity? J. Comput. Syst. Sci. **63**(4), 512–530 (2001)

JKKZ21. Jawale, R., Tauman Kalai, Y., Khurana, D., Yun Zhang, R.: SNARGs for bounded depth computations and PPAD hardness from sub-exponential LWE. In: Khuller, S., Williams, V.V. (eds.) STOC 2021: 53rd Annual ACM SIGACT Symposium on Theory of Computing, Virtual Event, Italy, 21–25 June 2021, pp. 708–721. ACM (2021)

JPY88. Johnson, D.S., Papadimitriou, C.H., Yannakakis, M.: How easy is local search? J. Comput. Syst. Sci. **37**(1), 79–100 (1988)

Kil92. Kilian, J.: A note on efficient zero-knowledge proofs and arguments (extended abstract). In: Rao Kosaraju, S., Fellows, M., Wigderson, A., Ellis, J.A. (eds.) Proceedings of the 24th Annual ACM Symposium on Theory of Computing, 4–6 May 1992, Victoria, British Columbia, Canada, pp. 723–732. ACM (1992)

KLVW22. Kalai, Y.T., Lombardi, A., Vaikuntanathan, V., Wichs, D.: Boosting batch arguments and ram delegation, Cryptology ePrint Archive (2022)

KNTY19. Kitagawa, F., Nishimaki, R., Tanaka, K., Yamakawa, T.: Adaptively secure and succinct functional encryption: improving security and efficiency, simultaneously. In: Boldyreva, A., Micciancio, D. (eds.) CRYPTO 2019. LNCS, vol. 11694, pp. 521–551. Springer, Cham (2019). https://doi.org/10.1007/978-3-030-26954-8_17

KPY19. Tauman Kalai, Y., Paneth, O., Yang, L.: How to delegate computations publicly. In: Charikar, M., Cohen, E. (eds.) Proceedings of the 51st Annual ACM SIGACT Symposium on Theory of Computing, STOC 2019, Phoenix, AZ, USA, 23–26 June 2019, pp. 1115–1124. ACM (2019)

KPY20. Kalai, Y.T., Paneth, O., Yang, L.: Delegation with updatable unambiguous proofs and PPAD-hardness. In: Micciancio, D., Ristenpart, T. (eds.) CRYPTO 2020. LNCS, vol. 12172, pp. 652–673. Springer, Cham (2020). https://doi.org/10.1007/978-3-030-56877-1_23

KRR14. Kalai, Y.T., Raz, R., Rothblum, R.D.: How to delegate computations: the power of no-signaling proofs. In: Proceedings of the Forty-Sixth Annual ACM Symposium on Theory of Computing, pp. 485–494 (2014)

KY18. Komargodski, I., Yogev, E.: On distributional collision resistant hashing. In: Shacham, H., Boldyreva, A. (eds.) CRYPTO 2018. LNCS, vol. 10992, pp. 303–327. Springer, Cham (2018). https://doi.org/10.1007/978-3-319-96881-0_11

Mic94. Micali, S.: CS proofs (extended abstracts). In: 35th Annual Symposium on Foundations of Computer Science, Santa Fe, New Mexico, USA, 20–22 November 1994, pp. 436–453. IEEE Computer Society (1994)

Pap94. Papadimitriou, C.H.: On the complexity of the parity argument and other inefficient proofs of existence. J. Comput. Syst. Sci. **48**(3), 498–532 (1994)

PP22. Paneth, O., Pass, R.: Incrementally verifiable computation via rate-1 batch arguments. In: 63rd IEEE Annual Symposium on Foundations of Computer Science, FOCS 2022, Denver, CO, USA, 31 October–3 November 2022, pp. 1045–1056. IEEE (2022)

PR08. Pass, R., Rosen, A.: Concurrent nonmalleable commitments. SIAM J. Comput. **37**(6), 1891–1925 (2008)

RSW96. Rivest, R.L., Shamir, A., Wagner, D.A.: Time-lock puzzles and timed-release crypto. Technical report, MIT (1996)

RV22.   Rothblum, R.D., Vasudevan, P.N.: Collision-resistance from multi-collision-resistance. In: Dodis, Y., Shrimpton, T. (eds.) Advances in Cryptology - CRYPTO 2022–42nd Annual International Cryptology Conference, CRYPTO 2022, Santa Barbara, CA, USA, 15–18 August 2022, Proceedings, Part III, volume 13509 of Lecture Notes in Computer Science, pp. 503–529. Springer, Cham (2022)

Val08.   Valiant, P.: Incrementally verifiable computation or proofs of knowledge imply time/space efficiency. In: Canetti, R. (ed.) TCC 2008. LNCS, vol. 4948, pp. 1–18. Springer, Heidelberg (2008). https://doi.org/10.1007/978-3-540-78524-8_1

WW22.   Waters, B., Wu, D.J.: Batch arguments for SFNP and more from standard bilinear group assumptions. In: Dodis, Y., Shrimpton, T. (eds.) Advances in Cryptology - CRYPTO 2022–42nd Annual International Cryptology Conference, CRYPTO 2022, Santa Barbara, CA, USA, 15–18 August 2022, Proceedings, Part II, volume 13508 of Lecture Notes in Computer Science, pp. 433–463. Springer, Cham (2022)

Succinct Arguments for RAM Programs via Projection Codes

Yuval Ishai[1]([⊠]), Rafail Ostrovsky[2], and Akash Shah[2]

[1] Technion - Israel Institute of Technology, Haifa, Israel
`yuvali@cs.technion.ac.il`
[2] University of California Los Angeles, Los Angeles, USA

Abstract. Motivated by the goal of proving statements that involve small subsets of a big database, we introduce and study the notion of *projection codes*. A standard error-correcting code allows one to encode a message $\mathbf{x}$ into a codeword $\mathbf{X}$, such that even if a constant fraction of $\mathbf{X}$ is corrupted, the message $\mathbf{x}$ can still be recovered. A projection code extends this guarantee to any *subset* of the bits of $\mathbf{x}$. Concretely, for every projection of $\mathbf{x}$ to a subset $\mathbf{s}$ of its coordinates, there is a subset $\mathbf{S}$ of comparable size such that the projected encoding $\mathbf{X}|_\mathbf{S}$ forms a robust encoding of the projected message $\mathbf{x}|_\mathbf{s}$.

Our first main result is a construction of projection codes with a near-optimal increase in the length of $\mathbf{x}$ and size of $\mathbf{s}$. We then apply this to obtain our second main result: succinct arguments for the computation of a RAM program on a (big) committed database, where the communication and the run-time of both the prover and the verifier are close to optimal even when the RAM program run-time is much smaller than the database size. Our solution makes only a black-box use of a collision-resistant hash function, providing the first black-box alternative to previous non-black-box constructions with similar asymptotic efficiency.

1 Introduction

Succinct Arguments [46,49] are computationally sound interactive proof systems that allow a prover $\mathcal{P}$ to convince a verifier $\mathcal{V}$ that a given statement $\mathbf{x}$ is true, using an extremely short proof and very little computation overhead. A bit more formally, consider an NP-language $\mathcal{L}$ defined by a relation $\mathcal{R}(\mathbf{x}, w)$ that can be verified in $\mathsf{DTIME}(T)$. Succinct arguments allow a polynomial-time $\mathcal{P}$, with input $(\mathbf{x}, w) \in \mathcal{R}$, to convince $\mathcal{V}$ that $\mathbf{x} \in \mathcal{L}$, where the communication and runtime of $\mathcal{V}$ are bounded by $\mathsf{poly}(\lambda, \log T)$ and $\mathsf{poly}(\lambda, |\mathbf{x}|, \log T)$ respectively, and where λ is a computational security parameter.

In this work, we consider a natural extension of succinct arguments in which $\mathcal{P}$ first commits to a large database $\mathbf{x} \in \{0,1\}^n$, and later wishes to succinctly prove the correctness of the execution of RAM programs on $\mathbf{x}$ that run in *sublinear time* $T \ll n$. We refer to this notion as "Succinct Argument for RAM programs on committed database" (or SArg-RAM, in short). More formally, SArg-RAM comprises of two phases, the *offline* and the *online* phase. In the offline phase, $\mathcal{P}$ commits to $\mathbf{x}$. In the online phase, $\mathcal{P}$ proves to $\mathcal{V}$ statements of

© International Association for Cryptologic Research 2023
H. Handschuh and A. Lysyanskaya (Eds.): CRYPTO 2023, LNCS 14082, pp. 159–192, 2023.
https://doi.org/10.1007/978-3-031-38545-2_6

the form: $\exists w$ s.t. $\mathcal{R}(\mathbf{x}, w) = \texttt{accept}$, where $\mathcal{R}$ is an NP-relation that can be efficiently verified by a RAM program. The nontrivial efficiency goal is to respect the efficient verification requirements of standard succinct arguments, while ensuring that the online runtime of the prover is comparable to T, which is sublinear in n. The notion of SArg-RAM is very compelling and can be motivated by many application that involve sublinear-time computations over databases. Such applications include proving statements about small subsets of entries, searching data structures, sequence matching (e.g., for genomic data or blockchains), statistical analysis, and more.

Indeed, notions similar to SArg-RAM have been considered in prior works. Examples include zero-knowledge[1] sets [20,50], where $\mathcal{P}$ proves membership or non-membership assertions on the committed set, consistency proofs on committed databases [52], and sublinear zero-knowledge arguments for the execution of RAM programs on committed database [51].

A Generic Non-black-box Approach. Traditional approaches for constructing succinct arguments or their non-interactive variants called SNARKs[2] [15, 17,30,31,37,46,49] typically rely on a circuit representation of the relation $\mathcal{R}$. Even when optimized for RAM programs [9,10], they do not directly yield arguments with sublinear prover runtime. However, as already observed in [52] in the context of zero-knowledge proofs for data structures, there is a simple and general technique for converting any succinct "argument of knowledge" into a SArg-RAM with a low communication and computation overhead. In the offline phase, $\mathcal{P}$ succinctly commits to $\mathbf{x}$ using a *vector commitment* scheme, say based on a Merkle tree [48]. In the online phase, $\mathcal{P}$ then argues that it knows a way to open a subset of the committed entries of $\mathbf{x}$ which is consistent with some (short) accepting transcript. The downside of this approach is that it requires proofs for NP statements that involve the succinct commitment primitive, thus inherently making a *non-black-box* use of this primitive. Such non-black-box constructions are undesirable both in theory and in practice. In particular, they cannot be implemented unconditionally in generic models (such as the random oracle model), and typically involve a big concrete efficiency overhead. As a relevant example, non-black-box constructions of incrementally verifiable computation [16,21,57] (via recursive SNARKs) are much less efficient than black-box constructions of standard SNARKs. Indeed, there has been a large body of work on replacing non-black-box cryptographic constructions by black-box counterparts (see, e.g., [22,24,35,36,39,42,53,54] and references therein).

The above state of affairs gives rise to the following question:

Is there a SArg-RAM on committed databases that respects the runtime of the RAM program and only makes a black-box use of cryptography?

---

[1] Zero-knowledge means no information beyond the validity of the statement is leaked to $\mathcal{V}$.

[2] A SNARK satisfies the additional *knowledge* property, which intuitively requires that if a prover can make the verifier accept, then it must know an NP-witness.

We answer this question in the affirmative, making a black-box use of any collision-resistant hash function. Alternatively, we get an *unconditional* non-interactive variant of this result in the random oracle model. Prior to our work, such black-box protocols were not known even if we only restrict the prover's runtime and the communication, but not the verifier's runtime.

1.1 Black-Box Succincts Argument for RAM Programs

We now give a more detailed overview of our results and techniques, starting with a more precise statement of the main feasibility result described above.

Definition 1 (SArg-RAM, informal). *An* SArg-RAM *allows a computationally bounded prover to succinctly commit to a database in an offline phase, such that in a later online phase it can prove the execution of RAM programs whose runtime is bounded by T.*

- *Completeness: If the statement about the execution of a RAM program on the committed database is true, $\mathcal{P}$ should always be able to convince $\mathcal{V}$.*
- *Soundness: If the statement is false, then any efficient malicious $\mathcal{P}^*$ can only make $\mathcal{V}$ accept with negligible probability.*
- *Efficiency: The online runtime of $\mathcal{P}$ should scale with T and not with the database size. Moreover, the protocol should be* succinct *in the sense that the communication, as well as the runtime of $\mathcal{V}$, are polylogarithmic in n.*

We obtain the following main result.

Theorem 1 (Black-box SArg-RAM, informal). *Assume a black-box access to a collision-resistant hash function. Then, for every $\alpha > 0$, there is $c_\alpha > 1$ for which there is an* SArg-RAM *with the following features:*

- *In the offline phase, $\mathcal{P}$ commits to an n-bit database $\mathbf{x}$ in time $\tilde{O}(n^{c_\alpha})$ and using $\mathrm{polylog}(n)$ bits of communication;*
- *Each invocation of the online phase proves the validity of (a possibly different) NP-relation $R(\mathbf{x}, w)$ that can be verified by a RAM program in (possibly sublinear) time $T(n)$. $\mathcal{P}$ runs in time $\tilde{O}(T^{1+\alpha})$ and $\mathcal{V}$ in time $\mathrm{polylog}(n)$.*

Alternatively, $\mathcal{P}$'s offline runtime can be improved to $\tilde{O}(n^{1+\alpha})$ at the expense of $\tilde{O}(T^2)$ online runtime, for any $\alpha > 0$.

At the heart of our construction for SArg-RAM is a new primitive that we call "projection codes," which we describe in detail next.

1.2 Projection Codes

The main technical challenge in constructing a black-box SArg-RAM involves a conversion of a robust encoding of the database into a compact but robust encoding of a small subset of the database. This task is captured by the notion of projection codes. Consider an encoding scheme Enc that encodes an n-bit message $\mathbf{x}$ into an N-bit codeword $\mathbf{X}$. The guarantee we seek is that given any sequence $\mathbf{s} \in [n]^k$ of k distinct message locations, there is a sequence $\mathbf{S} \in [N]^K$ of K codeword locations, such that $\mathbf{x}|_{\mathbf{s}}$ can be recovered from $\mathbf{X}|_{\mathbf{S}}$ even in the presence of a constant fraction of errors. Here, $\mathbf{x}|_{\mathbf{s}}$ denotes the sequence of bits in $\mathbf{x}$ restricted to indices in $\mathbf{s}$. Naturally, we would like N and K to be not much larger than n and k respectively. More formally:

Definition 2 (Projection code). *Let* $\mathsf{Enc} : \{0,1\}^n \to \{0,1\}^N$ *be an encoding function and* $\mathsf{Proj} : [n]^k \to [N]^K$ *be a projection algorithm. We say that* Enc *is an* (n, N, k, K, δ)-*projection code if for every sequence* $\mathbf{s} \in [n]^k$ *of k distinct message locations,* Proj *outputs a sequence* $\mathbf{S} \in [N]^K$ *of K codeword locations such that there exists a subset decoder* Dec *with the following robustness guarantee. For every* $\mathbf{x} \in \{0,1\}^n$, *and every* $\tilde{\mathbf{X}}|_{\mathbf{S}}$ *which is δ-close to* $\mathbf{X}|_{\mathbf{S}}$ *in relative Hamming distance, where* $\mathbf{X} = \mathsf{Enc}(\mathbf{x})$, *we have* $\mathsf{Dec}(\tilde{\mathbf{X}}|_{\mathbf{S}}) = \mathbf{x}|_{\mathbf{s}}$.

We construct projection codes with the following (near-optimal) parameters.

Theorem 2 (Near-optimal projection codes, informal). *For any $\alpha > 0$ and $k = k(n)$ there is an efficient* $(n, O(n^{1+\alpha}), k, \tilde{O}(k), \Omega(1))$-*projection code.*

In this construction, the runtimes of Enc and Proj are $\tilde{O}(n^{1+\alpha})$ and $\tilde{O}(k^2)$ respectively. The quadratic overhead of Proj can be avoided by an alternative (simpler) construction, at the expense of a bigger encoding size. Concretely, for any $\alpha > 0$, there is $c_\alpha > 1$ for which there is an efficient $(n, O(n^{c_\alpha}), k, O(k^{1+\alpha}), \Omega(1))$ projection code such that the runtimes of Enc and Proj are $\tilde{O}(n^{c_\alpha})$ and $\tilde{O}(k^{1+\alpha})$ respectively. These two families of projection codes correspond to the two possible tradeoffs between the online and offline runtime given by Theorem 1.

1.3 Related Work

Locally Decodable Codes. Our construction of projection codes is inspired by a construction of *multi-point locally decodable codes* from the work of Cramer, Xing, and Yuan [23]. A standard locally decodable code (LDC) [44,59] allows a single bit of the encoded message to be decoded with high probability by only querying a small number of bits of a possibly corrupted codeword. Cramer et al. showed how to optimize the query complexity when decoding k bits simultaneously. Interestingly, while our construction of projection codes is technically very similar, projection codes are a conceptually different object, and we are not aware of a *general* construction of projection codes from multi-point LDCs. In particular, if an extra polylog factor is allowed, multi-point decoding can be trivially realized by invoking the decoder of a polylog-query LDC k times. This approach does not work for our purposes, since we need the projected codeword to be robust. Additionally, while LDCs are inherently randomized, projection codes are fully deterministic: for a set $\mathbf{s}$, the projected set $\mathbf{S}$ is fixed. As will be highlighted in Sect. 2, this requirement is used in the construction of SArg-RAM using projection codes.

SArg-RAM with Superlinear $T(n)$. The question of efficient succinct arguments for the execution of RAM programs was first explicitly studied by Ben-Sasson et al. [9,11]. These works aim to minimize the overhead of arguing about the execution of a RAM program with runtime T on a statement of size n when $T \gg n$. In contrast, we focus on the case of RAM programs that take sublinear time (e.g., $T = O(n^{1/4})$) in the size of a *committed* database. Applying the results of [9,11] in this setting would lead to $\tilde{O}(n)$ online prover runtime.

Zero-Knowledge SArg-RAM. The question of *zero-knowledge* SArg-RAM was considered in [26,51]. Mohassel et al. [51] obtain such black-box protocols in which the online communication is $\tilde{O}(T)$. Franzese et al. [26] improve this by eliminating the polylogarithmic terms. In the above works, the online communication scales (at least) linearly with the RAM runtime T, whereas in our SArg-RAM it is polylogarithmic in n. One should note in this context that black-box SArg-RAM without zero knowledge are trivialized if we allow the online communication to scale linearly with the T. Indeed, the prover can just reveal the values read by the RAM program, including committed database bits and bits of the NP-witness. The verifier can then run the RAM program to check that the database is accepted. The question becomes nontrivial when one additionally requires the SArg-RAM to be zero knowledge.

2 Overview of Techniques

2.1 Projection Codes

We start by recalling the definition of standard Reed-Muller codes, on which our projection code constructions are based.

Reed-Muller encoding. Let $\mathbf{u} = (u_1, \ldots, u_v)$ and let us denote the multivariate polynomial ring $\mathbb{F}_q[u_1, \ldots, u_v]$ by $\mathbb{F}_q[\mathbf{u}]$. The Reed-Muller encoding is defined using a polynomial $p(\cdot) \in \mathbb{F}_q[\mathbf{u}]$ of total degree at most d over message space $\mathcal{M} = \mathbb{F}_q^n$ such that $n = \binom{v+d}{v}$. For $i \in [n]$, let $\mathbf{C}_i = (C_{i,1}, \ldots, C_{i,v}) \in \mathbb{F}_q^v$ denote n distinct but fixed vectors in $\mathbb{F}_q^v$ such that the corresponding linear system has full-rank. Reed-Muller code $\mathcal{E}_{\mathsf{RM}}$ with parameters (n, N, q, d, v) is defined with encoding Enc as below. For message $\mathbf{x} = (x_1, \ldots, x_n)$, $\mathcal{E}_{\mathsf{RM}}.\mathsf{Enc}(\mathbf{x}) = \{(p(\mathbf{u}))_{\mathbf{u} \in \mathbb{F}_q^v} : p(\mathbf{u}) \in \mathbb{F}_q[\mathbf{u}]$, degree of $p(\cdot) \leq d$ and $p(\mathbf{C}_i) = x_i, \forall i \in [n]\}$. The codeword length is $N = q^v$ and the message length satisfies $n = \binom{v+d}{v}$. We say that the codeword is *systematic* if the message symbols appear directly as the part of the codeword at pre-defined locations. Thus, Reed-Muller encoding is systematic.

A Simple Construction. We begin with a simple example for projection codes that uses the standard local decoding procedure for Reed-Muller codes [6,47]. <u>Global codeword</u>. Given a message $\mathbf{x}$ in $\mathbb{F}_q^n$, encode it using the systematic Reed-Muller encoding to obtain a codeword $\mathbf{X} \in \mathbb{F}_q^N$. <u>Projector</u>. Given k message indices $s_1, \ldots, s_k$, let $\mathbf{R}_1, \ldots, \mathbf{R}_k$ be the corresponding codeword locations as defined in the systematic encoding procedure (i.e., $\mathbf{R}_i = \mathbf{C}_{s_i}$, defined above). Define v univariate polynomials $g_1(t), \ldots, g_v(t)$, corresponding to each of the v variables $u_1, \ldots, u_v$ satisfying the following: i) Each polynomial $g_i(t)$ is of degree at most $k - 1$; ii) $\mathbf{g}(t) = (g_1(t), \ldots, g_v(t))$ passes through $\mathbf{R}_1, \ldots, \mathbf{R}_k$, i.e., for each $j \in [k]$, $\mathbf{R_j} = \mathbf{g}(j)$. The projector outputs q locations obtained by evaluating $\mathbf{g}$ over its domain, namely $\mathbf{g}(i)$ for $i \in \mathbb{F}_q$.

<u>Analysis.</u> Restricting any multivariate polynomial of degree at most d to a univariate polynomial of degree at most $k - 1$ yields a univariate polynomial of degree at most $d \cdot (k - 1)$. Thus, when we project the global Reed-Muller code to the output of the projector, we end up with a Reed-Solomon code over $\mathbb{F}_q$ corresponding to a univariate polynomial of degree at most $d \cdot (k - 1)$. This is exactly our projection code with distance $q - d \cdot (k - 1)$.

Using the above approach, we can get projection codes of polynomial length that have a near-optimal projection size. However, the parameters it can achieve are limited in two ways. First, they cannot simultaneously achieve near-optimal encoding size and projection size, as in Theorem 2. Second, they do not yield good projection codes that are also locally testable and correctable with poly-logarithmic queries (see Sect. 3.2). This additional feature, while not essential, simplifies our main SArg-RAM construction. To get around these two limitations, we need to look for a more general approach.

A Generalized Construction. At a very high level, the idea is to encode the given codeword locations using a suitable encoding scheme in the projection.

<u>Projector: Encode the codeword locations.</u> Let the k codeword indices, say $\mathbf{R}_1, \ldots, \mathbf{R}_k \in [N]$, correspond to the given k message indices based on the systematic encoding procedure. For each $i \in [k]$, parse $\mathbf{R}_i = (R_{i,1}, \ldots, R_{i,v})$ as $\mathbb{F}_q^v \equiv [N]$. Then for each $j \in [v]$, encode $(R_{1,j}, \ldots, R_{k,j}) \in \mathbb{F}_q^k$ into K symbols $(S_{1,j}, \ldots, S_{K,j}) \in \mathbb{F}_q^K$ using an encoding scheme that will be appropriately chosen. For each $i \in [K]$, get v symbols $(S_{i,1}, \ldots, S_{i,v}) \in \mathbb{F}_q^v$ and parse them as a codeword location $\mathbf{S}_i \in [N]$. The projector outputs these K locations, $(\mathbf{S}_1, \ldots, \mathbf{S}_K) \in [N]^K$. Figure 1 illustrates the above process pictorially.

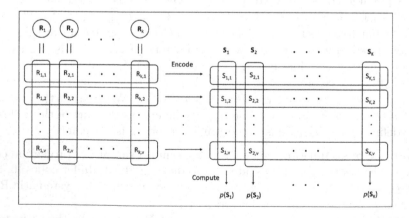

Fig. 1. Our projector in nutshell. Codeword indices $s_1, s_2, \ldots, s_k$ correspond to the given k message indices and p is the v-variate polynomial of our Reed-Muller encoding of total degree d.

We now consider the codeword $\mathbf{Y} = (p(\mathbf{S}_1), \ldots, p(\mathbf{S}_K)) \in \mathbb{F}_q^K$ formed by projecting the Reed-Muller codeword to these K locations, $(\mathbf{S}_1, \ldots, \mathbf{S}_K)$. For $\mathbf{Y}$ to encode $\mathbf{x}|_\mathbf{s}$, we need the encoding scheme used in the projector to be a d-multiplicative linear code. Informally, a d-multiplicative linear code is a linear code that encodes k elements of $\mathbb{F}_q$ into K elements of $\mathbb{F}_q$ such that pointwise product (coordinate-wise multiplication) of up to d codewords in the code results in a new codeword (in a larger linear code); see Sect. 3.2 for a formal definition of d-multiplicative codes and Lemma 2 for a formal version of the above projection procedure using such codes.

In Sect. 4.2, we analyze the achievable parameters when the projector code is instantiated with either Reed-Muller codes or algebraic-geometric (AG) codes, as used in [23,28]. These two options correspond to the two alternative parameters in Theorem 2. In a nutshell, the projector based on AG codes has near-optimal code length and projection size parameters but runs in time $\tilde{O}(k^2)$, whereas the RM-based projector can run in near-linear time $O(k^{1+\alpha})$ at the expense of a polynomial-size encoding.

We leave open the existence of projection codes with a linear-time encoding algorithm. Indeed, our approach heavily relies on multiplication-friendly codes, for which no linear-time instances are known. This should be contrasted with existing constructions of linear-time succinct arguments that can rely on standard linear-time encodable codes [18,19,33,55,58].

2.2 Holographic PCPs for RAM Programs

As an information-theoretic application of projection codes, which serves as a stepping stone for SArg-RAM, we obtain a RAM analogue of classical PCPs [2,3] that we call a *holographic PCP for RAM programs* (HPCP-RAM).[3] For ease of exposition, we first consider a simpler notion of a holographic PCP for *subsets* (HPCP-SS). In HPCP-SS, $\mathcal{P}$ encodes a database $\mathbf{x}$ in the offline phase using an encoding function E_1 to obtain $\mathbf{X} = \mathsf{E}_1(\mathbf{x})$. In the online phase, for $\mathbf{s}$ encoded by another encoding function E_2, $\mathcal{P}$ is interested to prove an NP-statement on the projected message $\mathbf{x}|_\mathbf{s}$. More formally, for an NP relation $\mathcal{R}$, $\mathcal{P}$ wants to generate a PCP proof for $\exists w$ s.t. $\mathcal{R}(\mathbf{x}|_\mathbf{s}, w) = \mathtt{accept}$. Informally, an HPCP-SS construction should satisfy the following properties (cf. Definition 9):

- Completeness: If $\mathbf{x}|_\mathbf{s}$ satisfies the input statement, then $\mathcal{P}$ can generate a PCP proof which is always accepted by $\mathcal{V}$.
- Soundness: If $\mathbf{x}|_\mathbf{s}$ does not satisfy the input statement, then for any proof generated by $\mathcal{P}$, $\mathcal{V}$ should accept the proof only with negligible probability.

We would like the runtime of $\mathcal{P}$ in the online phase to be comparable to the size of the input set $\mathbf{s}$, independently of the size of $\mathbf{x}$, while $\mathcal{V}$ is fully succinct in that its runtime is polylog(n). It is easy to discern that if there exists an

---

[3] The term "holographic PCP" [4] refers to a PCP on an *encoded* input statement. This allows the verifier to only make a small number of queries to *both* the encoded input and the proof. Such PCPs can be constructed from *PCPs of proximity* [13].

encoding of $\mathbf{x}|_\mathbf{s}$, say $\mathbf{Y}$, which is proven to be consistent with global encoding, i.e., $\mathbf{X} = \mathsf{E}_1(\mathbf{x})$, $\mathcal{P}$ could generate a PCP proof with respect to codeword $\mathbf{Y}$. This is exactly the scenario in which projection codes are applicable.

In the offline phase, $\mathcal{P}$ encodes $\mathbf{x}$ using global encoder of projection codes. For the online phase, note that the projected codeword $\mathbf{X}|_\mathbf{s}$ forms an encoding of $\mathbf{x}|_\mathbf{s}$ and is part of the global codeword. Thus, $\mathcal{P}$ can generate a PCP proof with respect to the projected codeword. A deterministic projection procedure from $\mathbf{s}$ to $\mathbf{S}$ allows $\mathcal{P}$ to ascertain the encoded input for PCP without having the need to interact with $\mathcal{V}$ to sample randomness. Using PCPs, $\mathcal{P}$ then proves that projection of $\mathbf{s}$ is indeed $\mathbf{S}$, and the input statement on $\mathbf{x}|_\mathbf{s}$ (encoded with $\mathbf{X}|_\mathbf{s}$) is valid. Through this approach, we obtain a construction of HPCP-SS with the desired asymptotic complexity. HPCP-SS are easily extendable to HPCP-RAM. The idea is to view the bits accessed by the RAM program as the subset of bits on which we would like to prove an input statement. We obtain this extension based on a standard reduction of RAM programs to TM [38] (see Theorem 5).

Why aren't Standard LDCs Enough? For the purpose of the above HPCP-SS construction, it may appear that projection codes are an overkill and one could apply a standard locally decodable code (LDC) instead. However, that is not the case. Let the size of the subset $\mathbf{s}$ be $k \ll n$. The crucial point is that we need to apply a *short* holographic PCP, of length comparable to k, to a *robust* encoding of $\mathbf{x}|_\mathbf{s}$. If we implicitly encode each entry of $\mathbf{x}|_\mathbf{s}$ using the answers to a standard LDC, this encoding is not robust (since each entry is encoded separately). If we try to define an NP statement that involves the entire global encoding of $\mathbf{x}$, it is not clear how to make the PCP short.

2.3   Succinct Arguments for RAM Programs

As our final application, we construct a black-box SArg-RAM as follows. In the offline phase, $\mathcal{P}$ does the offline processing of $\mathbf{x}$ by encoding it using the global encoder of the projection code to obtain $\mathbf{X} \leftarrow \mathsf{Enc}(\mathbf{x})$. $\mathcal{P}$ then uses Merkle hashing [48] to commit to $\mathbf{X}$, and sends short commitment to $\mathcal{V}$. The online phase is executed as in the Kilian's argument system [5, 12, 46].

In the online phase, $\mathcal{P}$ generates a PCP proof using HPCP-RAM construction and commits to the proof using Merkle hashing. $\mathcal{V}$ runs the verifier of HPCP-RAM, $\mathcal{V}'$. For every query of $\mathcal{V}'$, $\mathcal{V}$ forwards the query to $\mathcal{P}$, who opens the Merkle tree hashes corresponding to that query.

3   Preliminaries

We summarize the denotations of frequently used symbols in Table 1. For a vector $\mathbf{x} = (x_1, x_2, \ldots, x_\ell)$, $|\mathbf{x}|$ denotes length of vector $\mathbf{x}$. For a positive integer ℓ, $[\ell] = \{1, \ldots, \ell\}$. For a sequence $\mathbf{s} = (s_1, s_2, \ldots, s_\ell)$ and a $\leq \ell$-sized sequence $A = (j_1, j_2, \ldots, j_a) \in [\ell]^a$, $\mathbf{s}|_A = (s_{j_1}, s_{j_2}, \ldots, s_{j_a})$. Let $\mathbf{x} = (x_1, \ldots, x_\ell)$ and $\mathbf{y} = (y_1, \ldots, y_\ell)$, $\mathbf{x} \circ \mathbf{y}$ denotes concatenation of two sequences. We abuse this notation by using it for some scalar a. Unless stated explicitly, the size of the alphabet space of all the codewords that we use is q, i.e., $\mathbb{F}_q$ is the code alphabets space. For $\mathbf{u}, \mathbf{v} \in \mathbb{F}_q^\ell$, $\mathbf{u} * \mathbf{v}$ denotes the pointwise product of the vectors defined as $(u_1 v_1, \ldots, u_\ell v_\ell) \in \mathbb{F}_q^\ell$ and $w_H(\mathbf{u}, \mathbf{v})$ denotes the hamming distance between $\mathbf{u}$ and $\mathbf{v}$. We denote empty-string by $\varnothing$. We use $\log(\cdot)$ to denote logarithm to the base 2. Unless otherwise stated, we assume that all the algorithms in the computational setting implicitly take the security parameter λ as input.

Table 1. Table of Notations

Symbol	Denotation
$\mathcal{M}$	Message Space
$\mathbf{x}, \mathbf{y}$	Lower-case boldface letters denoting message vectors
n	Length of the global message
$\mathcal{C}$	Codeword Space
$\mathbf{X}, \mathbf{Y}$	Upper-case boldface letters denoting codeword vectors
N	Length of the global codeword
k	Size of the projected message sequence, i.e., $|\mathbf{s}|$
$\mathbf{s}$	Sequence of distinct message locations to be projected ($\mathbf{s} \in [n]^k$)
K	Size of the projected codeword sequence, i.e., $|\mathbf{S}|$
$\mathbf{S}$	Sequence of projected codeword locations ($\mathbf{S} \in [N]^K$)
δ	Fractional distance of projection code
λ	Computational security parameter

3.1 Model of Computation

We consider the Random Access Memory (RAM) model of computation and Turing Machines (TM). We denote a deterministic TM (resp. a non-deterministic TM) that on input of length n runs in time $T(n)$ (where $T : \mathbb{Z}^+ \to \mathbb{Z}^+$) by $\mathsf{DTIME}(T(n))$ (resp. $\mathsf{NTIME}(T(n))$) machines. If not mentioned explicitly, an algorithm is assumed to run in RAM model of computation.

We consider the standard concept of RAM model [1]. We adopt the definition of RAM model of computation from [32] which models it as an interactive TM communicating with Random Access Memory (RAM). We focus on RAM programs M that execute on a large RAM memory, $\mathbf{x}$, of size n.[4]

M accesses certain locations in $\mathbf{x}$ through a series of read/write instructions. Similar to [26,29,34], we consider a RAM program to be defined by a *next-instruction* computation unit. In this work, we define the RAM program by *next-instruction TM* Π. Π takes the current state st and an input bit $b \in \{0, 1\}$, and outputs the updated state st' along with the next instruction to execute. More formally, initialize $\mathsf{st} = \mathsf{start}$ and $b = 0$, and then until termination compute $(\mathsf{op}, \ell, b', \mathsf{st}') \leftarrow \Pi(\mathsf{st}, b)$, and set $\mathsf{st} = \mathsf{st}'$.

---

[4] The RAM memory $\mathbf{x}$ comprises of the database as well as additional working space needed by M. The space reserved for database is instantiated with initial value of the database, i.e., before the first RAM program is executed. If operations are performed by RAM program over a bit in reserved working memory space, the first such operation is always a Write operation. This setting is similar to [29,41,51].

- If op = Stop, terminate with output b'.
- If op = Read, set $b = x_\ell$.
- If op = Write, set $x_\ell = b'$ and $b = b'$.

Thus, execution of RAM program M consists of executions of series of next-instruction TM Π initialized with start state until an instance of next-instruction TM outputs operation Stop. Here, we are interested in next-instruction TM Π whose computation time is polylog$n$.

3.2   Encoding Scheme

Definition 3 (Encoding Scheme). *An encoding scheme over $\mathbb{F}_q$ with message length n, codeword length N, relative distance δ, and relative decoding radius ρ, is defined by a pair of algorithms (Enc, Dec) defined below.*

1. *Enc : $\mathbb{F}_q^n \to \mathbb{F}_q^N$. Enc maps a message $\mathbf{x} \in \mathbb{F}_q^n$ to codeword $\mathbf{X} \in \mathbb{F}_q^N$ such that for any $\mathbf{x} \neq \mathbf{x}'$, $w_H(\mathsf{Enc}(\mathbf{x}), \mathsf{Enc}(\mathbf{x}')) \geq \delta N$.*
2. *Dec : $\mathbb{F}_q^N \to \mathbb{F}_q^n$. Dec takes as input (possibly corrupted) codeword $\mathbf{X}' \in \mathbb{F}_q^N$. For $\mathbf{x} \in \mathbb{F}_q^n$, if $w_H(\mathsf{Enc}(\mathbf{x}), \mathbf{X}') \leq \rho N$, where $\rho < \delta/2$, then Dec outputs $\mathbf{x}$.*

A family of such encoding schemes $(\mathsf{Enc}_n, \mathsf{Dec}_n)$ with $q = \text{polylog}(n)$, $N = N(n)$ for some polynomial $N(.)$, and fixed $\delta > 0$, is efficiently encodable (resp. decodable) if Enc (resp. Dec) runs in probabilistic polynomial time (PPT) in n. We refer to $\mathcal{E} = (\mathsf{Enc}, \mathsf{Dec})$ as an (n, N, δ)-encoding scheme with relative decoding radius ρ. Let $\mathcal{C} = \{\mathcal{E}.\mathsf{Enc}(\mathbf{x}) | \forall \mathbf{x} \in \mathbb{F}_q^n\} \subseteq \mathbb{F}_q^N$ denote the codeword space of $\mathcal{E}$.

Locally Testable Codes. An encoding scheme is locally testable code with parameters: number of queries Q, relative distance δ', and error bound ϵ (or (Q, δ', ϵ)-locally testable, in short) if there is a randomized local testing algorithm $\mathcal{A}$ (probabilistic TM) that takes as input ϵ (in binary) and is given oracle access to $\mathbf{X}$. $\mathcal{A}$ is required to run in polylog(N/ϵ) time and read at most Q locations in a codeword $\mathbf{X}$. At the end of the execution, $\mathcal{A}$ outputs either accept/reject. $\mathcal{A}$ satisfies the following properties:

- Completeness: For every $\mathbf{x} \in \mathbb{F}_q^n$, given oracle access to $\mathsf{Enc}(\mathbf{x})$, $\mathcal{A}$ accepts with probability 1, i.e.,

$$\Pr[\mathcal{A}^{\mathsf{Enc}(\mathbf{x})}(\epsilon) = \mathtt{accept}] = 1.$$

- Soundness: For any $\mathbf{X}'$ which is more than δ' far from a valid codeword, $\mathcal{A}$ accepts $\mathbf{X}'$ with probability at most ϵ. That is, for any $\mathbf{X}'$ s.t. $\forall \mathbf{x} \in \mathbb{F}_q^n$, $w_H(\mathbf{X}', \mathsf{Enc}(\mathbf{x})) \geq \delta' N$,

$$\Pr[\mathcal{A}^{\mathbf{X}'}(\epsilon) = \mathtt{accept}] \leq \epsilon.$$

Locally Decodable Codes. An encoding scheme is locally decodable code with parameters: number of queries Q, relative distance δ', and error bound ϵ (or (Q, δ', ϵ)-locally decodable, in short)if there is a randomized decoder $\mathcal{A}$ (probabilistic TM) that takes as input ϵ (in binary) and index $i \in [n]$, and is given oracle access to $\mathbf{X}$. $\mathcal{A}$ is required to run in $\text{polylog}(N/\epsilon)$ time and make at most Q many non-adaptive queries to codeword $\mathbf{X}$. At the end of the execution, $\mathcal{A}$ outputs $Y \in \mathbb{F}_q$. $\mathcal{A}$ satisfies the following properties:

- For every $\mathbf{x} = (x_1, x_2, \ldots, x_n) \in \mathbb{F}_q^n$ and index $i \in [n]$, given oracle access to $\text{Enc}(\mathbf{x})$, $\mathcal{A}$ outputs x_i with probability 1, i.e.

$$\Pr[\mathcal{A}^{\text{Enc}(\mathbf{x})}(\epsilon, i) = x_i] = 1.$$

- For every message $\mathbf{x} = (x_1, x_2, \ldots, x_n) \in \mathbb{F}_q^n$, index $i \in [n]$ and codeword $\mathbf{X}'$ such that $w_H(\text{Enc}(\mathbf{x}), \mathbf{X}') \leq \delta' N$,

$$\Pr[\mathcal{A}^{\mathbf{X}'}(\epsilon, i) = x_i] \geq 1 - \epsilon.$$

Locally correctable codes are defined similarly [59]. For a (Q, δ', ϵ)-locally correctable code, there exists a randomized algorithm $\mathcal{A}$ that given index i, makes at most Q-many oracle queries to $\mathbf{X}'$ that is at most $\delta' N$ far away from a valid codeword $\mathbf{X}$ and outputs X_i with probability at least $1 - \epsilon$.

There exists RM code with parameters $q = \text{polylog}(n), d = \text{polylog}(n), v = \log(n)/c \log \log n$, and $N = O(n^{1+\alpha})$ for $c, \alpha > 0$ (cf. [40, Theorem 2.2]). Moreover, there exists $\epsilon = \text{negl}(n)$ and $Q = \text{polylog}(n)$ such that for any $0 < \delta < \frac{1}{2}$, the RM code with aforementioned parameters is (Q, δ, ϵ)-locally testable code [27, Theorem 7],[56, Theorem 9], and (Q, δ, ϵ)-locally decodable/(Q, δ, ϵ)-locally correctable code [59, Proposition 2.6].

Multiplicative Linear Codes. Our projection code construction utilizes *multiplicative linear codes*. We recall the definition of multiplicative linear code that are often used for non-interactive computation of low-degree polynomials. This idea can be traced back to Ben-Or, Goldwasser, and Wigderson [7].

Definition 4 ($\mathcal{C}^{*d}$: d^{th}-power of $\mathcal{C}$). *For an $\mathbb{F}_q$-linear code $\mathcal{C} \subseteq \mathbb{F}_q^N$, the $\mathbb{F}_q$-linear code $\mathcal{C}^{*d} \subseteq \mathbb{F}_q^N$, the dth power of $\mathcal{C}$, is defined as the $\mathbb{F}_q$-linear subspace generated by all terms of the form $\mathbf{C}_1 * \ldots * \mathbf{C_d}$ with $\mathbf{C}_1, \ldots, \mathbf{C_d} \in \mathcal{C}$.*

Definition 5. *An efficient (n, N, δ)-encoding scheme $\mathcal{E} = (\text{Enc}, \text{Dec})$ with codeword space $\mathcal{C} \subseteq \mathbb{F}_q^N$ is d-multiplicative linear, if there exist an efficient algorithm[5] Dec^* (called special decoder) and a decoder for $\mathcal{C}^{*d}$, $\text{Dec}^{(d)}$, such that the following conditions are satisfied:*

1. *$\mathcal{C} \subseteq \mathbb{F}_q^N$ is a $\mathbb{F}_q$-linear code and $\text{Dec}^* : \mathcal{C} \to \mathbb{F}_q^n$ is a surjective $\mathbb{F}_q$-vector space morphism.*

---

[5] Polynomial time (possibly probabilistic) in (n, d).

2. *It is unital, i.e., $\mathbf{1} \in \mathcal{C}$ and $\mathsf{Dec}^*(\mathbf{1}) = \mathbf{1}$.*
3. *The map Dec^* extends uniquely to an $\mathbb{F}_q$-linear map $\mathsf{Dec}^* : \mathcal{C}^{*d} \to \mathbb{F}_q^n$ such that the following holds:*
   - Dec^* *satisfies the multiplicative relation*

$$\mathsf{Dec}^*(\mathbf{X}_1 * \ldots * \mathbf{X}_d) = \mathsf{Dec}^*(\mathbf{X}_1) * \ldots * \mathsf{Dec}^*(\mathbf{X}_d) \in \mathbb{F}_q^n$$

   for all $\mathbf{X}_1, \ldots, \mathbf{X}_d \in \mathcal{C}$.
   - $\mathcal{C}^{*d}$ *has minimum distance at least δN.*
4. *Given $\mathbf{X}' \in \mathbb{F}_q^N$ that is at most δ-far from a codeword $\mathbf{X} \in \mathcal{C}^{*d}$, $\mathsf{Dec}^{(d)}(\mathbf{X}')=\mathbf{X}$.*

Succinctly, we refer $\mathcal{E}$ as (n, N, d, δ)-multiplicative linear encoding scheme.

3.3   Probabilistically Checkable Proofs of Proximity (PCPPs)

Informally, for an NP relation $\mathcal{R}$, probabilistic checkable proofs (PCPs) [3] are proofs that can be verified by reading only few bits of the proofs. In this work, we consider the notion of PCPs of Proximity (PCPPs) [14,25] which we recall below. Similar to [14], we consider *pair languages* in which an input is of the form $(\mathbf{v}, \mathbf{x})$. For instance, $\mathbf{v}$ can be a description of a TM and $\mathbf{x}$ an input accepted by this TM. The first part of the input $\mathbf{v} \in \{0,1\}^\ell$ is the *explicit* part, read entirely by the verifier, and the second part $\mathbf{x} \in \{0,1\}^n$ is the *implicit* part to which the verifier has oracle access (we typically have $\ell \ll n$). For the application of PCPPs in our work (see Sect. 5), it will be convenient to associate with a PCPP a specific encoding function E, where the verifier has oracle access not to $\mathbf{x}$ but to $\mathbf{X} = \mathsf{E}(\mathbf{x})$. The case of encoded implicit inputs $\mathbf{X}$ can be handled by simply defining an NP language of encoded instances. Then, a PCPP for NP (as defined in [14]) suffices.

Definition 6. *(PCPs of Proximity (PCPPs).) Let $\mathcal{R}((\mathbf{v}, \mathbf{x}), w) \in \mathsf{DTIME}(T(n))$ be an NP relation where $n = |\mathbf{x}|$ and $T : \mathbb{Z}^+ \to \mathbb{Z}^+$. A probabilistic proof system $(\mathcal{P}, \mathcal{V})$ (where $\mathcal{P}$ is a probabilistic RAM program and $\mathcal{V}$ is a probabilistic TM) with parameters: query complexity of $\mathcal{V}$ (Q), runtime of prover (t_p), runtime of verifier (t_v), proof length (ℓ_p), soundness error (ϵ), and proximity parameter (δ), is a PCPP system for $\mathcal{R}$ with respect to encoding function E if the following holds for every pair $(\mathbf{v}, \mathbf{x})$:*

- *Input: $\mathcal{P}$ receives $\mathbf{v} \in \{0,1\}^\ell, \mathbf{x} \in \{0,1\}^n$ and $w \in \{0,1\}^\mu$ as input, and $\mathcal{V}$ receives $n \in \mathbb{N}, \mathbf{v} \in \{0,1\}^\ell$ as input.*
- *Input encoding: $\mathcal{P}$ computes $\mathbf{X} = \mathsf{E}(\mathbf{x})$.*
- *Prover's proof: $\mathcal{P}$ generates a proof π (corresponding to statement $\mathcal{R}((\mathbf{v}, \mathbf{x}), w) = \mathtt{accept}$) such that $|\pi| \le \ell_p(n)$. We require runtime of $\mathcal{P}$ in proof generation to be bounded by $t_p(n)$.*
- *Verifier's queries: $\mathcal{V}$ makes $Q = Q(n)$ oracle queries $\mathbf{X}$ and π, and based on the responses outputs either $\mathtt{accept}$ or $\mathtt{reject}$. We require the runtime of $\mathcal{V}$ to be within $t_v(n, \ell)$.*
- *Completeness: If $\mathcal{R}((\mathbf{v}, \mathbf{x}), w) = \mathtt{accept}$, then when $\mathcal{V}$ queries the proof π generated by $\mathcal{P}$, it accepts with probability 1.*

– *Soundness:* Suppose $\mathbf{v}$, $\mathbf{X}^*$ are such that for all $\mathbf{x}'$ for which there exists w such that $\mathcal{R}(\mathbf{v}, \mathbf{x}', w) = \mathtt{accept}$, we have that $\mathbf{X}^*$ is δ-far from $\mathsf{E}(\mathbf{x}')$. Then, $\mathcal{V}$ accepts $(\mathbf{v}, \mathbf{X}^*)$ with probability at most $\epsilon = \epsilon(n)$.

Succinctly, we refer to such a system as a $(Q, t_p, t_v, \ell_p, \epsilon, \delta)$-PCPP system.

4   Projection Codes

In this section, we first formalize our new primitive, i.e., *projection codes*. Later in the section, we provide efficient construction of projection codes inspired from techniques used in [23] to build multi-point locally decodable codes.

Definition 7. *(Projection code.) For $k \leq n$, $K \leq N$, and $0 \leq \delta < 1$, a (binary) (n, N, k, K, δ)-Projection code is a triple of algorithms $\Pi = (\mathsf{Enc}, \mathsf{Proj}, \mathsf{Dec})$ with the following syntax:*

– $\mathsf{Enc} : \{0,1\}^n \to \{0,1\}^N$ *is an encoding algorithm mapping a message $\mathbf{x}$ to codeword $\mathbf{X}$.*
– $\mathsf{Proj} : [n]^k \to [N]^K$ *is a projection algorithm mapping a sequence of distinct k message coordinates to a sequence of K codeword coordinates.*
– $\mathsf{Dec} : \{0,1\}^K \to \{0,1\}^k$ *is a decoding algorithm, mapping a sequence of message coordinates and the corresponding codeword projection to a message projection.*

We say that Π is an (n, N, k, K, δ)-projection code if for every sequence $\mathbf{s} \in [n]^k$ of k message locations there is a subset $\mathbf{S} \in [N]^K$ of K codeword locations and a subset decoder Dec with the following robustness guarantee. For every $\mathbf{x} \in \{0,1\}^n$, and every $\tilde{\mathbf{X}}|_{\mathbf{S}}$ which is δ-close to $\mathbf{X}|_{\mathbf{S}}$ in relative Hamming distance, where $\mathbf{X} = \mathsf{Enc}(\mathbf{x})$, we have $\mathsf{Dec}(\tilde{\mathbf{X}}|_{\mathbf{S}}) = \mathbf{x}|_{\mathbf{s}}$.

In our paper, we typically consider a uniform family of projection codes defined by polynomial-time algorithms $(\mathsf{Enc}, \mathsf{Proj}, \mathsf{Dec})$ that apply to any choice of message length n and projection size k. In such a case, we will view N as a function of n and K as a function of k and n.

For ease of exposition, we define the notion of projection codes over $\mathbb{F}_2$ keeping in mind the final application goal, i.e., to obtain succinct argument over a committed database of bits. From a coding theory perspective, we would like to stress that the notion of projection codes holds for any alphabet space. Indeed, our construction (see Fig. 2) is over $\mathbb{F}_q$.

4.1   Constructing Projection Codes

We construct projection codes for the entire parameter regime. Precisely, we first give a construction in which the execution time of Enc is $\mathsf{poly}(n)$ but the execution time of Proj is quasi-linear in k. Second, we give a construction in which the execution time of Enc is quasi-linear in n but the runtime of Proj is quadratic in k. More formally, we prove the below theorem.

Theorem 3 (Projection Codes). *For any $\alpha > 0$, there exists $c_\alpha > 1$ such that there exists an efficient $(n, O(n^{c_\alpha}), k, O(k^{1+\alpha}), \Omega(1))$ projection code. The runtime of* Enc *and* Proj *is $\tilde{O}(n^{c_\alpha})$ and $\tilde{O}(k^{1+\alpha})$ respectively. Alternatively, for any $\alpha > 0$, there exists an efficient $(n, O(n^{1+\alpha}), k, \tilde{O}(k), \Omega(1))$-projection code. The running time of* Enc *and* Proj *algorithms is $\tilde{O}(n^{1+\alpha})$ and $\tilde{O}(k^2)$ respectively.*

In order to obtain our result, we recall the following lemma on multiplicative linear code that is implicit in [23].

Lemma 1. *Suppose $\mathcal{E}_{\mathsf{Mul}}$ with (codeword space, special decoder)=$(\mathcal{C}, \mathsf{Dec}^*)$ is a $(k, K, d, 2\delta)$-multiplicative linear encoding scheme over $\mathbb{F}_q$ and $\mathbf{C}_1, \ldots, \mathbf{C}_v$ are any v codewords in $\mathcal{C}$. Then for any v-variate polynomial $p : \mathbb{F}_q^v \to \mathbb{F}_q$ of total degree at most d, we have*

$$p^{(K)}(\mathbf{C}_1, \ldots, \mathbf{C}_v) \in \mathcal{C}^{*d}$$

$$\mathsf{Dec}^*(p^{(K)}(\mathbf{C}_1, \ldots, \mathbf{C}_v)) = p^{(k)}(\mathsf{Dec}^*(\mathbf{C}_1), \ldots, \mathsf{Dec}^*(\mathbf{C}_v)),$$

where $\mathbf{C_i} = (C_{i,1}, \ldots, C_{i,K})$ for $i \in [v]$. For $\mathbf{u}_1, \ldots, \mathbf{u}_v \in \mathbb{F}_q^\ell$, where $\mathbf{u}_i = (u_{i,1}, \ldots, u_{i,\ell})$ for each $i \in [v]$, we have $p^{(\ell)}((u_{1,1}, \ldots, u_{1,\ell}), \ldots, (u_{v,1}, \ldots, u_{v,\ell}))$ defined as $(p(u_{1,1}, \ldots, u_{v,1}), \ldots, p(u_{1,\ell}, \ldots, u_{v,\ell}))$.

Proof. Let M be the number of terms in v-variate polynomial $p(\mathbf{u}_1, \ldots, \mathbf{u}_v)$, i.e., $p = \sum_{i=1}^M \beta_i \Pi_{j=1}^v \mathbf{u}_j^{d_{i,j}}$, where $\beta_i \in \mathbb{F}_q$ and $d_{i,j} \in \mathbb{N}$ such that $\sum_{j=1}^v d_{i,j} \leq d$, for all $(i, j) \in [M] \times [v]$. Let $(\mathbf{C}_1, \ldots, \mathbf{C}_v)$ be the v codewords in C. For $i \in [v]$, let $\mathsf{Dec}^*(\mathbf{C}_i) = \mathbf{m}_i = (m_{i,1}, \ldots, m_{i,k})$.

$$\mathsf{Dec}^*(p^{(K)}(\mathbf{C}_1, \ldots, \mathbf{C}_v)) = \mathsf{Dec}^* \left(\sum_{i=1}^M \beta_i \Pi_{j=1}^v C_{j,1}^{d_{i,j}}, \ldots, \sum_{i=1}^M \beta_i \Pi_{j=1}^v C_{j,K}^{d_{i,j}} \right)$$

$$= \mathsf{Dec}^* \left(\sum_{i=1}^M \beta_i \Pi_{j=1}^v \mathbf{C}_j^{d_{i,j}} \right) \tag{1}$$

$$= \sum_{i=1}^M \beta_i \mathsf{Dec}^* \left(\Pi_{j=1}^v \mathbf{C}_j^{d_{i,j}} \right) \tag{2}$$

$$= \sum_{i=1}^M \beta_i \Pi_{j=1}^v \mathsf{Dec}^* \left(\mathbf{C}_j^{d_{i,j}} \right) \tag{3}$$

$$= \sum_{i=1}^M \beta_i \Pi_{j=1}^v \mathsf{Dec}^* \left(\mathbf{C}_j \right)^{d_{i,j}} \tag{4}$$

$$= \left(\sum_{i=1}^M \beta_i \Pi_{j=1}^v m_{j,1}^{d_{i,j}}, \ldots, \sum_{i=1}^M \beta_i \Pi_{j=1}^v m_{j,k}^{d_{i,j}} \right)$$

$$= (p(m_{1,1}, \ldots, m_{v,1}), \ldots, p(m_{1,k}, \ldots, m_{v,k}))$$

$$= p^{(k)}(\mathsf{Dec}^*(\mathbf{C}_1), \ldots, \mathsf{Dec}^*(\mathbf{C}_v)). \tag{5}$$

(2) follows from (1) as Dec^* is an $\mathbb{F}_q$-linear map. (3) follows from (2) and (4) follows from (3) from property (3) of multiplicative linear codes.   □

Next, we give a projection code construction using systematic Reed-Muller code and multiplicative linear code. Our projection code construction $\mathcal{E}_{\mathsf{Proj}}$ is formally described in Fig. 2. Notice that we denote the length of the global codeword (output of Enc) and projected codeword in our projection codes construction in bits, i.e., N' and K' denote the length in bits.

Parameters. Let $d > 0$ be some integer. 1) Systematic (n, N, q, d, v)-RM encoding scheme $\mathcal{E}_{\mathsf{RM}}$ over $\mathbb{F}_q$. 2) $(k, K, d, 2\delta)$-multiplicative linear encoding scheme $\mathcal{E}_{\mathsf{Mul}}$ over $\mathbb{F}_q$ with codeword space denoted by $\mathcal{C}_{\mathsf{Mul}} \subseteq \mathbb{F}_q^K$, special decoder Dec^* and decoder $\mathsf{Dec}^{(d)}$ for $\mathcal{C}_{\mathsf{Mul}}^{*d}$.

$\mathsf{Enc}(\mathbf{x} \in \mathbb{F}_q^n)$:

  1. Output $\mathcal{E}_{\mathsf{RM}}.\mathsf{Enc}(\mathbf{x})$.

$\mathsf{Proj}(\mathbf{s} = (s_1, \ldots, s_k) \in [n]^k)$:

  1. Let $(\mathbf{R}_1, \ldots, \mathbf{R}_k) \in [N]^k$ be the corresponding k codeword coordinates corresponding to $(s_1, \ldots, s_k)$ as $\mathcal{E}_{\mathsf{RM}}$ is systematic.
  2. For all $i \in [k]$, parse $\mathbf{R}_i = (R_{i,1}, \ldots, R_{i,v})$ as $\mathbf{R}_i \in [N] \equiv \mathbb{F}_q^v$ and $R_{i,j} \in \mathbb{F}_q$.
  3. For all $i \in [v]$, select $\mathbf{C}_i \in \mathcal{C}_{\mathsf{Mul}}$ such that $\mathsf{Dec}^*(\mathbf{C}_i) = (R_{1,i}, \ldots, R_{k,i})$. Parse each $\mathbf{C}_i \in \mathbb{F}_q^K$ as $(C_{i,1}, \ldots, C_{i,K})$.
  4. Output a sequence of K codeword locations $\mathbf{S} = (\mathbf{S}_1, \ldots, \mathbf{S}_K) \in [N]^K$, where location $\mathbf{S}_j$ is defined as $(C_{1,j}, \ldots, C_{v,j}) \in \mathbb{F}_q^v \equiv [N]$.

$\mathsf{Dec}(\tilde{\mathbf{Y}} \in \mathbb{F}_q^K)$:

  1. Compute $\mathbf{Z} \leftarrow \mathsf{Dec}^{(d)}(\tilde{\mathbf{Y}})$, where $\mathbf{Z} \in \mathcal{C}_{\mathsf{Mul}}^{*d}$.
  2. Output $\mathsf{Dec}^*(\mathbf{Z}) \in \mathbb{F}_q^k$.

Fig. 2. $(n, N' = N \cdot \lceil \log(q) \rceil, k, K' = K \cdot \lceil \log(q) \rceil, \delta)$-projection code construction $\mathcal{E}_{\mathsf{Proj}}$

Lemma 2. *If there exists $(k, K, d, 2\delta)$-multiplicative linear encoding scheme $\mathcal{E}_{\mathsf{Mul}}$ over $\mathbb{F}_q$ then the systematic (n, N, q, d, v)-RM code over $\mathbb{F}_q$ results in $(n, N' = N \cdot \lceil \log(q) \rceil, k, K' = K \cdot \lceil \log(q) \rceil, \delta)$-projection code $\mathcal{E}_{\mathsf{Proj}}$ (Fig. 2) over $\mathbb{F}_q$.*

Proof. Let $\mathbf{x} \in \mathbb{F}_q^n$ be the message that is encoded by $\mathcal{E}_{\mathsf{Proj}}.\mathsf{Enc}$ into a projection code $\mathbf{X} \in \mathbb{F}_q^N$. Let $p(\cdot)$ be the v-variate polynomial of degree at most d that is associated with the underlying Reed-Muller code. Given a sequence $\mathbf{s}$ of k distinct message coordinates, let $\mathbf{S}$ be the sequence of K codeword coordinates produced by $\mathcal{E}_{\mathsf{Proj}}.\mathsf{Proj}$. Let $\mathbf{Y} \leftarrow \mathbf{X}|_{\mathbf{S}}$ be the projected codeword.

Next, if we can show that the projected codeword $\mathbf{Y}$ belongs to $\mathcal{C}_{\mathsf{Mul}}^{*d}$, then we can rely on the guarantees of the decoder $\mathsf{Dec}^{(d)}(\cdot)$ of the multiplicative codes to recover $\mathbf{Y}$ from any corrupted $\tilde{\mathbf{Y}}$ as long as $\tilde{\mathbf{Y}}$ is obtained by changing at most δ-fraction of symbols in $\mathbf{Y}$. We may then finish the proof by proving that $\mathsf{Dec}^*(\mathbf{Y})$ indeed equals to the projected message $\mathbf{x}|_{\mathbf{s}}$. Details follow.

Let $(\mathbf{C}_1, \ldots, \mathbf{C}_v)$ be the v codewords in $\mathcal{C}_{\mathsf{Mul}}$ computed within $\mathcal{E}_{\mathsf{Proj}}.\mathsf{Proj}$ and let $(\mathbf{S}_1, \ldots, \mathbf{S}_K)$ be the output of $\mathcal{E}_{\mathsf{Proj}}.\mathsf{Proj}$.

$$\mathbf{Y} = \mathbf{X}|_{\mathbf{S}} = (p(\mathbf{S}_1), \ldots, p(\mathbf{S}_K))$$
$$= p^K(\mathbf{C}_1, \ldots, \mathbf{C}_v). \tag{6}$$

Thus, $\mathbf{Y} \in \mathcal{C}_{\mathsf{Mul}}^{*d}$. As a result, by Lemma 1, we get

$$\mathsf{Dec}^*(p^K(\mathbf{C}_1, \ldots, \mathbf{C}_v)) = p^k(\mathsf{Dec}^*(\mathbf{C}_1), \ldots, \mathsf{Dec}^*(\mathbf{C}_v))$$
$$= p^k((\mathbf{R}_{1,1}, \ldots, \mathbf{R}_{k,1}), \ldots, (\mathbf{R}_{1,v}, \ldots, \mathbf{R}_{k,v}))$$
$$= (p(\mathbf{R}_1), \ldots, p(\mathbf{R}_k))$$
$$= \mathbf{x}|_{\mathbf{s}}. \tag{7}$$

Thus, $\mathcal{E}_{\mathsf{Proj}}.\mathsf{Dec}$ correctly decodes the desired k message symbols that appear at locations $s_1, \ldots, s_k$. $\qquad\square$

Remark. In our construction, we use Reed-Muller encoding as the global encoder, i.e., $\mathsf{Enc}(\cdot)$ is RM-code. Thus, $\mathsf{Enc}(\cdot)$ is systematic, and there exists $Q = \mathsf{polylog}(n), \epsilon = \mathsf{negl}(n)$ such that for $0 < \delta < \frac{1}{2}$, $\mathsf{Enc}(\cdot)$ is (Q, δ, ϵ)-locally testable, (Q, δ, ϵ)-locally decodable, and (Q, δ, ϵ)-locally correctable code (See Sect. 3.2).

4.2 Instantiations

Case 1. Here, we instantiate Proj algorithm using Reed-Muller code as they satisfy the notion of d-multiplicativity over $\mathbb{F}_q$. Let the degree of the underlying polynomial in Reed-Muller encoding of Enc algorithm be denoted by d_E. Similarly, let d_P be the degree of polynomial in Reed-Muller encoding of Proj algorithm. Thus, the degree of polynomial of projected codeword is at most $d_E \cdot d_P$ which has to be less than $\sigma(q-1)$, for constant $\sigma > 0$ [59, Proposition 2.6]. Let v_E and v_P denote the number of variables in underlying polynomial of Reed-Muller encoding in Enc and Proj algorithm respectively. We require that $\binom{v_E + d_E}{v_E} \geq n$ and $\binom{v_P + d_P}{v_P} \geq k$. Observe that, $\binom{v_E + d_E}{v_E} \geq (d_E / v_E)^{v_E}$. Thus, we can set d_E and v_E such that $(d_E / v_E)^{v_E} \geq n$. Let $(d_E / v_E) = \log^{c_E}(n)$, for some constant $c_E > 1$. Let $a = \log(n)$. Thus, we can set $v_E = \log_a(n)/c_E$ and $d_E = \log^{c_E + 1}(n)$. By a similar analysis, we obtain $v_P = \log_a(k)/c_P$ and $d_P = \log^{c_P + 1}(n)$, for some constant $c_P > 0$. Now, $q \approx \log^{c_E + c_P + 2}(n)$. We have $N = q^{v_E} = n^{1 + (c_P + 2)/c_E}$ and $K = q^{v_P} = k^{1 + (c_E + 2)/c_P}$. Setting $(c_E + 2)/c_P = \alpha$ for some $\alpha > 0$, we obtain $c_\alpha = 1 + (c_P + 2)/(\alpha c_P - 2) \approx 1 + 1/\alpha$ such that $N = n^{c_\alpha}$ and $K = k^{1 + \alpha}$.

To encode a message $\mathbf{x} \in \mathbb{F}_q^n$ to codeword $\mathbf{X} \in \mathbb{F}_q^N$, the encoding time in Reed-Muller codes is $O(N \cdot \mathsf{polylog} N) = \tilde{O}(N)$ [40,45]. Plugging the parameters in Lemma 2, for $\alpha > 0$ there exists $c_\alpha > 1$ such that we have a $(n, O(n^{c_\alpha}), k, O(k^{1+\alpha}), \Omega(1))$ projection code with runtime of Enc and Proj being $\tilde{O}(n^{c_\alpha})$ and $\tilde{O}(k^{1+\alpha})$ respectively. This proves the first part of Theorem 3.

Case 2. For this case, we instantiate Proj algorithm using the multiplicative code construction of Cramer et al. [23, Proposition 2.5].

We require $\binom{v+d}{v} \geq n$ to encode n field elements using v-variate polynomials of degree at most d. Set $d = \log^{\left(1 + \frac{1}{0.9\alpha}\right)} n$, applying Stirling's approximation, we see that $v = \frac{0.9\alpha \log n}{\log \log n}$ suffices. Setting $q = 2d$, we get that $N = q^v = \left(2\log^{\left(1 + \frac{1}{0.9\alpha}\right)} n\right)^{\frac{0.9\alpha \log n}{\log \log n}} = n^{1 + 0.9\alpha + o(1)}$. Thus $N = O(n^{1+\alpha})$ and $q = \mathsf{poly} \log n$ as α is constant > 0. Now, we recall the construction of multiplicative code from Cramer et al. [23].

Lemma 3. *There is a $(k, K, d, \Omega(1))$-multiplicative code $(\mathcal{C}, \mathsf{Dec}^*)$ over $\mathbb{F}_q$ with decoder Dec for $\mathcal{C}^{*d}$ with $K = k \cdot q^2$ and $d = q/5$.*

Plugging the above in Lemma 2 yields a $(n, O(n^{1+\alpha}), k, \tilde{O}(k), \Omega(1))$-projection code with the running time of Enc and Proj algorithms being $\tilde{O}(n^{1+\alpha})$ and $\tilde{O}(k^2)$ respectively. This proves the second part of Theorem 3.

5 Holographic PCPs for RAM Programs

For an NP-language $\mathcal{L}$, a PCP allows a prover $\mathcal{P}$ to convince a verifier $\mathcal{V}$ that $x \in \mathcal{L}$ by having the verifier read just few bits of the proof. However, in certain applications $\mathcal{P}$ may be interested to prove a statement pertaining to only specific bits of the input $\mathbf{x}$ and not the entire input. This is especially the case in execution of RAM programs. For such scenarios, the cost of PCPs is prohibitive as it scales with the input length $|\mathbf{x}|$.

In this section, we are interested to construct *Holographic PCPs for RAM programs* (HPCP-RAM) in which the runtime of the prover scales only with the runtime of the RAM program (i.e., it is independent of the size of the memory $\mathbf{x}$) and the verifier is succinct, i.e., the runtime of verifier is polylog$n$, where $n = |\mathbf{x}|$. As an intermediate step, we introduce the notion of *holographic PCPs for subsets* (HPCP-SS) and provide its first construction using projection codes in Sect. 5.1. The notion of HPCP-SS is intricate and addresses the primary technical challenge that one faces in construction of HPCP-RAM.

In Sect. 5.2, we formalize the notion of HPCP-RAM and extend our HPCP-SS construction to obtain the first HPCP-RAM construction with the aforementioned computation complexity goal.

5.1 Holographic PCPs for Subsets

In obtaining HPCP-RAM, the first step is to prove statements that are consistent on a subset of bits of input $\mathbf{x}$. Looking ahead, these are the set of bits in $\mathbf{x}$ that are accessed by the RAM program of interest. Now, as we would like to prove statements about subsets of the message, we would like to also include the information about the location of the subset apart from the projection of the message, for greater generality. This is exactly achieved by the following notion.

Definition 8. *(Addressable projection* $\mathbf{x}\|_{\mathbf{s}}$*)* *For any* $\mathbf{x} = (x_1, \ldots, x_n) \in \Sigma^n$ *and any sequence* $\mathbf{s} = (s_1, \ldots, s_k) \in [n]^k$ *of k-distinct locations in* $\mathbf{x}$*, we define addressable projection* $\mathbf{x}\|_{\mathbf{s}}$ *as the following sequence of k symbols* $((s_1, x_{s_1}), \ldots, (s_k, x_{s_k}))$ *with each symbol belonging to* $([n] \times \Sigma)$*.*

We consider an NP relation $\mathcal{R}$, where the input is split to two parts $\mathbf{v} \in \{0,1\}^\ell$ and $\mathbf{x} \in \{0,1\}^n$ such that $\ell \ll n$. The NP relation $\mathcal{R}$ takes as input[6] $\mathbf{v}$, addressable projection of $\mathbf{x}$, i.e., $\mathbf{x}\|_{\mathbf{s}}$ and the witness $w \in \{0,1\}^\mu$, where $|\mathbf{s}| = k$. Then, $\mathcal{R}(\mathbf{v}, \mathbf{x}\|_s, w) \in \mathsf{DTIME}(T(k) + T'(\ell))$, where $T, T' : \mathbb{Z}^+ \to \mathbb{Z}^+$. In this work, we are interested in the setting in which $\ell < k$, typically $\ell \leq \mathrm{polylog}n$ and $\exists d_0$, s.t. $\mathsf{DTIME}(T'(d)) \subseteq \mathsf{DTIME}(T(d))$, for every $d > d_0 \in \mathbb{Z}^+$. Hence, $\mathcal{R}(\mathbf{v}, \mathbf{x}\|_s, w) \in \mathsf{DTIME}(T(k))$.

Definition 9. *(Holographic PCP for subsets)* *A holographic PCP for subsets (HPCP-SS) for an NP relation* $\mathcal{R} \in \mathsf{DTIME}(T(k))$ *with respect to* $(Q_1, \delta_1, \epsilon_1)$*-locally-testable code* E_1 *and* $(Q_2, \delta_2, \epsilon_2)$*-locally-testable code* E_2 *is a pair* $(\mathcal{P}, \mathcal{V})$ *(where* $\mathcal{P}$ *is a probabilistic RAM program and* $\mathcal{V}$ *is a probabilistic TM) with parameters: query complexity of the verifier (Q), offline proof computation complexity* (t_{off})*, offline proof size* (p_{off})*, online proof computation complexity* (t_{on})*, online proof size* (p_{on})*, runtime of* $\mathcal{V}$ (t_v)*, proximity parameter* (δ)*, and the soundness error of the HPCP system* (ϵ)*, such that* $(\mathcal{P}, \mathcal{V})$ *satisfies the following requirements:*

- **Offline Phase:**
  - *Inputs:* $\mathcal{P}$ *receives* $\mathbf{x} \in \{0,1\}^n$*.*
  - *Database encoding:* $\mathcal{P}$ *computes* $\mathbf{X} = \mathsf{E}_1(\mathbf{x})$*. We require that* $|\mathbf{X}| \leq p_{\mathsf{off}}(n)$ *and is computed within time* $t_{\mathsf{off}}(n)$ *by prover's RAM program.*
- **Online Phase:**
  - *Inputs:* $\mathcal{P}$ *receives* $\mathbf{v} \in \{0,1\}^\ell, \mathbf{s} \in [n]^k$*, and a witness* $w \in \{0,1\}^\mu$ *as input.* $\mathcal{V}$ *receives* $k, n \in \mathbb{N}$*, and* $\mathbf{v} \in \{0,1\}^\ell$ *as input.*
  - *Subset encoding:* $\mathcal{P}$ *computes* $\mathbf{T} = \mathsf{E}_2(\mathbf{s})$*.*
  - *Proof generation:* $\mathcal{P}$ *computes* π *(for statement* $\mathcal{R}(\mathbf{v}, \mathbf{x}\|_s, w) = \mathsf{accept}$*) by running a RAM program. We require that* $\mathbf{T}$ *and* π *are of total length* $\leq p_{\mathsf{on}}(n, k)$ *and are generated within time* $t_{\mathsf{on}}(n, k)$ *by* $\mathcal{P}$*'s RAM program.*
  - *Verification:* $\mathcal{V}$ *makes* $Q(n)$ *oracle queries to* $(\mathbf{X}, \mathbf{T}, \pi)$*, and based on the responses outputs either* accept *or* reject*. We require the runtime of* $\mathcal{V}$ *to be within* $t_v(n)$*.*
- *Completeness: If* $\mathcal{R}(\mathbf{v}, \mathbf{x}\|_s, w) = \mathsf{accept}$*, then* $\mathcal{V}$ *with oracle access to the correct* $(\mathbf{X}, \mathbf{T}, \pi)$ *always accepts.*
- *Soundness[7]: Suppose* $(\mathbf{v}, \mathbf{X}^*, \mathbf{T}^*)$ *are such that for all* $\mathbf{x}', \mathbf{s}'$ *for which there exists* w *such that* $\mathcal{R}(\mathbf{v}, \mathbf{x}'\|_{s'}, w) = \mathsf{accept}$*, either* $\mathbf{X}^*$ *is* δ_1*-far from* $\mathsf{E}_1(\mathbf{x}')$ *or* $\mathbf{T}^*$ *is* δ_2*-far from* $\mathsf{E}_2(\mathbf{s}')$*. Then,* $\mathcal{V}$ *accepts* $(\mathbf{v}, \mathbf{X}^*, \mathbf{T}^*)$ *with probability at most* $\epsilon = \epsilon(n)$*. Here,* δ *is a function of* δ_1 *and* δ_2*.*

---

[6] Jumping ahead, i) $\mathbf{v}$ denotes the description of the RAM program on input $\mathbf{x}$. ii) $\mathbf{s}$ denotes the sequence of memory locations accessed by the RAM program.

[7] One can aim to achieve the stronger notion of soundness, i.e., *knowledge soundness* (witness extractability) [10, Definition 12.35] by using PCPs with *knowledge soundness*. As it is not the focus of this work, we consider the simpler notion.

Succinctly, we refer to such system as an $(n, k, Q, t_{\text{off}}, p_{\text{off}}, t_{\text{on}}, p_{\text{on}}, t_v, \delta, \epsilon)$-HPCP-SS.

Next, we will prove the following theorem.

Theorem 4 (HPCP-SS). *For any* $\alpha > 0$, *there exists* $c_\alpha > 1$ *such that there exists an* $(n, k, Q = \text{polylog}(n), t_{\text{off}} = \tilde{O}(n^{c_\alpha}), p_{\text{off}} = O(n^{c_\alpha}), t_{\text{on}} = \tilde{O}(k^{1+\alpha}), p_{\text{on}} = O(k^{1+\alpha}), t_v = \text{polylog}(n), \delta = 1/\text{polylog}(n), \epsilon = \text{negl}(n))$-HPCP-SS.

Alternatively, for any $\alpha > 0$, *there exists an* $(n, k, Q = \text{polylog}(n), t_{\text{off}} = \tilde{O}(n^{1+\alpha}), p_{\text{off}} = O(n^{1+\alpha}), t_{\text{on}} = \tilde{O}(k^2), p_{\text{on}} = \tilde{O}(k), t_v = \text{polylog}(n), \delta = 1/\text{polylog}(n), \epsilon = \text{negl}(n))$-HPCP-SS.

To prove Theorem 4, we recall two results from prior works. The first result is on an efficient reduction of RAM programs to TMs [38]. It states that for every non-deterministic computation M in RAM model that runs in time T, there exists a non-deterministic TM M' with runtime $\tilde{O}(T)$ that simulates M. Their result [38, Theorem 2] is stated formally in Theorem 5. Theorem 5 is reworded and uses different terminology than used in the original result [38, Theorem 2] in order to be consistent with the terminology used in our work.

In Theorem 5, the RAM program M is given access to $\mathbf{x}$ and w. It verifies the NP relation $\mathcal{R}(\mathbf{x}, w)$ that runs in time T. Let $\mathbf{v} \in \{0,1\}^\ell$ denote the description of the RAM program, i.e., $\ell = |M|$ and $\mathbf{s}$ denote the sequence of locations accessed by M in $\mathbf{x}$. We define an NP-relation $\mathcal{R}'$ that takes as input $\mathbf{v}$, $\mathbf{x}\|_{\mathbf{s}}$ and witness w' (comprising of w) s.t. for a fixed $\mathbf{v}$, $\mathcal{R}'$ is equivalent to $\mathcal{R}$. That is, for given input memory $\mathbf{x}$, witness w and w', $\mathcal{R}'(\mathbf{v}, \mathbf{x}|_{\mathbf{s}}, w')$ outputs accept iff $\mathcal{R}(\mathbf{x}, w)$ outputs accept. Notice that, $\mathcal{R}$ is a RAM NP-relation, whereas $\mathcal{R}'$ is computed by TM. This allows us to use PCPPs to prove statements for NP relation $\mathcal{R}'$.

Theorem 5 ([38, Theorem 2]). *There exists a RAM program* Conv *and turing machine* M' *such that for every RAM program* M *(with description* $\mathbf{v} \in \{0,1\}^\ell$) *verifying an NP relation* $\mathcal{R}$ *in time* T,

- *The converter RAM program* Conv *with running time* $\tilde{O}(T)$ *takes as input description of RAM program* M, *i.e.,* $\mathbf{v}$, *and witness* w. *It is given random-access to memory* $\mathbf{x}$. Conv *outputs a witness* w' *and a sequence* $\mathbf{s} \in [n]^k$ *that are the sequence of indices of bits in* $\mathbf{x}$ *accessed by RAM program* M, *where* $k \leq T$.
- *The Turing Machine* M' *that runs in time* $\tilde{O}(T)$ *for NP relation* $\mathcal{R}'$. M' *takes as input* $\mathbf{v}$, $\mathbf{x}|_{\mathbf{s}}$ *and witness* w'.

- *Completeness. If* $\exists w$ *s.t.* $M(\mathbf{x}, w) = \texttt{accept}$, *then* $(w', \mathbf{s}) \leftarrow \text{Conv}(\mathbf{v}, \mathbf{x}, w)$ *s.t.* $M'(\mathbf{v}, \mathbf{x}\|_{\mathbf{s}}, w') = \texttt{accept}$, *and*
- *Soundness. If* $\nexists w$ *s.t.* $M(\mathbf{x}, w) = \texttt{accept}$, *then* $\nexists(w', \mathbf{s}')$ *s.t.* $M'(\mathbf{v}, \mathbf{x}\|_{\mathbf{s}'}, w') = \texttt{accept}$.

Next, we recall the follow result on the existence of "quasi-optimal" PCPP proof system for any NP relation $\mathcal{R}$, implicit in [10].[8]

---

[8] Theorem 1 in [10] states this for a PCP, but this can be extended to the PCPP case [8]. A similar PCPP with a slightly higher prover complexity appears in [13].

Theorem 6 (Quasilinear PCPPs). *Let $\mathcal{R}(\mathbf{v}, \mathbf{x}, w) \in$ DTIME$(T(n))$ be an NP relation for a pair language, where $n = |\mathbf{x}|$ and $T : \mathbb{Z}^+ \to \mathbb{Z}^+$. Then there exists a PCPP system (P, V) for $\mathcal{R}$ with respect to an encoding function E, with the following parameters:*

- *Query Complexity: $Q = \text{polylog}(T(n))$.*
- *Prover Complexity: $t_p = \tilde{O}((T(n)))$.*
- *Verifier Complexity: $t_v = \text{polylog}(T(n))$.*
- *Proof Size: $\ell_p = \tilde{O}((T(n)))$.*
- *Proximity parameter: $\delta = 1/\text{polylog}(T(n))$.*
- *Soundness error: $\epsilon = \text{negl}(n)$.*

With the intention to motivate our construction for HPCP-SS, we first discuss simpler black-box approaches and observe why these approaches fail. In the offline phase, $\mathcal{P}$ can compute an encoding of input $\mathbf{x}$ denoted by $\mathbf{X}$. In the online phase, given k-length sequence $\mathbf{s} \in [n]^k$, the task of $\mathcal{P}$ is to prove an NP relation $\mathcal{R}$ on input $\mathbf{x} \| \mathbf{s}$. $\mathcal{P}$ computes an encoding of $\mathbf{s}$ which we denote by $\mathbf{T}$. $\mathcal{P}$ can now generate a PCPP with respect to encoded inputs $\mathbf{X}$ and $\mathbf{T}$. Unfortunately, the online runtime of $\mathcal{P}$ in this approach is proportional to the size of input $\mathbf{x}$, i.e., n. An alternative approach for $\mathcal{P}$ is to compute a fresh encoding $\mathbf{Y}$ of bits in $\mathbf{x}$ at coordinates in sequence $\mathbf{s}$, i.e., $\mathbf{Y}$ is an encoding of $\mathbf{x}|_\mathbf{s}$. $\mathcal{P}$ can now produce a PCPP with respect to encoded inputs $\mathbf{Y}$ and $\mathbf{T}$. This approach does achieve the desired complexity but does not satisfy *soundness* as $\mathcal{P}$ can encode an input inconsistent with $\mathbf{x}$ in the online phase. To remedy this situation, $\mathcal{P}$ is required to generate an additional proof to prove that $\mathbf{Y}$ is an encoding of an input that is consistent with $\mathbf{x}$, again resulting in $\tilde{O}(n)$ online computation load on $\mathcal{P}$.

Parameters.

1. $(n, N' = N \cdot \lceil \log(q) \rceil), k, K' = K \cdot \lceil \log(q) \rceil, \delta_P)$-projection code $\Pi = (\text{Enc}, \text{Proj}, \text{Dec})$ such that the runtime of Enc and Proj algorithm is $O(t_{\text{Enc}}(n))$ and $O(t_{\text{Proj}}(n, k))$ respectively. Moreover, let Enc be $(Q_t^{(1)}, \delta_t^{(1)}, \epsilon_t^{(1)})$-locally testable code and $(Q_c^{(1)}, \delta_c^{(1)}, \epsilon_c^{(1)})$-locally correctable code.

2. $(Q_t^{(2)}, \delta_t^{(2)}, \epsilon_t^{(2)})$-locally testable code $\mathsf{E}_2 : [n]^k \to \{0,1\}^{\Gamma_2}$ with encoding time $O(t_{\mathsf{E}_2}(n, k))$.

3. $(Q_t^{(3)}, \delta_t^{(3)}, \epsilon_t^{(3)})$-locally testable and $(Q_d^{(3)}, \delta_d^{(3)}, \epsilon_d^{(3)})$-locally decodable code $\mathsf{E}_3 : [N]^K \to \{0,1\}^{\Gamma_3}$ with encoding time $O(t_{\mathsf{E}_3}(N, K))$.

4. i) $(Q^{\text{vproj}}, t_p^{\text{vproj}}, t_v^{\text{vproj}}, \ell_p^{\text{vproj}}, \epsilon^{\text{vproj}}, \delta^{\text{vproj}})$-PCPP proof system $(\mathcal{P}_{\text{vproj}}, \mathcal{V}_{\text{vproj}})$ for NP relation $\mathcal{R}'$. ii) Description of RAM program M_{vproj}, i.e., $\mathbf{v}_{\text{vproj}}$.

5. $(Q', t_p', t_v', \ell_p', \epsilon', \delta')$-PCPP proof system $(\mathcal{P}', \mathcal{V}')$ for NP relation $\mathcal{R}$.

Fig. 3. Parameters of our HPCP-SS construction

As it turns out, this is exactly the issue that our projection code can resolve! In the offline phase, $\mathcal{P}$ computes the projection encoding (Enc) of $\mathbf{x}$ denoted by $\mathbf{X}$. In the online phase, $\mathcal{P}$ maps sequence of k message coordinates $\mathbf{s}$ to sequence of K codeword coordinates $\mathbf{S}$ using Proj. Using PCPP, $\mathcal{P}$ proves that the message coordinates were projected correctly. By the robustness guarantee of projection code, we have that given oracle access to $\mathbf{X}$ and $\mathbf{S}$, one can obtain oracle access to the robust encoding of $\mathbf{x}|_{\mathbf{s}}$ with only polylog overhead. $\mathcal{P}$ can then use this encoding to produce a PCPP for NP relation $\mathcal{R}$. This way we obtain a HPCP-SS construction in which the online runtime of $\mathcal{P}$ depends on the size of $\mathbf{s}$, i.e., k, and is independent of the size of $\mathbf{x}$, i.e., n (ignoring polylog factors).

We formally describe the parameters used in our construction in Fig. 3. All the parameters are self-explanatory except PCPP proof system $(\mathcal{P}_{\mathsf{vproj}}, \mathcal{V}_{\mathsf{vproj}})$ for NP relation $\mathcal{R}_{\mathsf{vproj}}$. The NP relation $\mathcal{R}_{\mathsf{vproj}}$ takes as input $\mathbf{s}$ and $\mathbf{S}$ and outputs accept iff all indices in $\mathbf{s}$ are distinct and $\mathbf{S} = \mathsf{Proj}(\mathbf{s})$. The runtime of Proj algorithm is $O(t_{\mathsf{Proj}}(n, k))$. There exists a RAM program M_{vproj} that on input $(\mathbf{s}, \mathbf{S})$ and witness $w = \varnothing$, checks if all indices in $\mathbf{s}$ are distinct and $\mathbf{S} = \mathsf{Proj}(\mathbf{s})$. The former check can be performed using sorting, thus, incurring at most $\tilde{O}(k)$ computation overhead. If the two checks are satisfied, M_{vproj} outputs accept, else it outputs reject. The computation complexity of M_{vproj} is $\tilde{O}(t_{\mathsf{Proj}}(n, k))$. From Theorem 5, we have that there exists a converter RAM program Conv and a turing machine M' s.t. M' computes NP relation $\mathcal{R}'$ such that given description of M_{vproj} denoted by $\mathbf{v}_{\mathsf{vproj}}$, $\mathcal{R}'$ is equivalent to $\mathcal{R}_{\mathsf{vproj}}$. For input $\mathbf{v}_{\mathsf{vproj}}$, the runtime of M'_{vproj} is $\tilde{O}(t_{\mathsf{Proj}}(n, k))$. Thus, $\mathcal{R}'(\mathbf{v}_{\mathsf{vproj}}, \cdot, \cdot) \in \mathsf{DTIME}(\tilde{O}(t_{\mathsf{Proj}}(n, k)))$. We denote $\mathcal{R}'(\mathbf{v}_{\mathsf{vproj}}, \cdot, \cdot)$ by $\mathcal{R}'_{\mathsf{vproj}}(\cdot, \cdot)$.

Offline Phase.
1. Input: $\mathcal{P}$ receives $\mathbf{x} \in \{0, 1\}^n$.
2. Database Encoding: $\mathcal{P}$ computes $\mathbf{X} = \Pi.\mathsf{Enc}(\mathbf{x})$, i.e., $\mathsf{E}_1(\cdot) = \Pi.\mathsf{Enc}(\cdot)$.

Online Phase.
1. Input: $\mathcal{P}$ receives $\mathbf{s} \in [n]^k$, $\mathbf{v} \in \{0, 1\}^\ell$, and a witness $w \in \{0, 1\}^\mu$ as input.
2. Subset Encoding: $\mathcal{P}$ computes $\mathbf{T} = \mathsf{E}_2(\mathbf{s})$.
3. Proof Generation: $\mathcal{P}$ performs the following computation to generate proof π.
   - i) Compute $\mathbf{S} \leftarrow \Pi.\mathsf{Proj}(\mathbf{s})$ and set $\pi_{\mathsf{E}_3} \leftarrow \mathsf{E}_3(\mathbf{S})$.
   - ii) $(w_{\mathsf{vproj}}, \mathbf{s}_{\mathsf{vproj}}) \leftarrow \mathsf{Conv}(\mathbf{v}_{\mathsf{vproj}}, (\mathbf{s}, \mathbf{S}), \varnothing)$.
   - iii) Invoke $\mathcal{P}_{\mathsf{vproj}}$ with input $(\mathbf{v}_{\mathsf{vproj}}, (\mathbf{s}, \mathbf{S}))$, and witness w_{vproj} to obtain proof π_{vproj}.
   - iii) Invoke $\mathcal{P}'$ on input $(\mathbf{v}, \mathbf{x}\|_{\mathbf{s}})$ and witness w to generate proof π'.
   - iv) $\mathcal{P}$ sets proof $\pi \leftarrow \pi_{\mathsf{E}_3} \circ \pi_{\mathsf{vproj}} \circ \pi'$.

Fig. 4. Prover $\mathcal{P}$ of our HPCP-SS construction

Remark. Observe that we use Theorem 5 only for relation $\mathcal{R}_{\mathsf{vproj}}$ and not for our primary relation $\mathcal{R}$ as $\mathcal{R}_{\mathsf{vproj}}$ is a RAM NP-relation whereas $\mathcal{R}$ is computable by a deterministic TM.

We present the computation of $\mathcal{P}$ and $\mathcal{V}$ in our HPCP-SS construction formally in Fig. 4 and 5 respectively. For the PCPP proof system $(\mathcal{P}_{\mathsf{vproj}}, \mathcal{V}_{\mathsf{vproj}})$ in our construction, instead of obtaining a single encoding for inputs $(\mathbf{s}, \mathbf{S})$, $\mathcal{V}_{\mathsf{vproj}}$ receives separate encodings $\mathbf{T}$ (encoding of $\mathbf{s}$), and π_{E_3} (encoding of $\mathbf{S}$). However, observe that $\mathbf{T} \circ \pi_{\mathsf{E}_3}$ is a valid encoding of input $(\mathbf{s}, \mathbf{S})$ but with the proximity parameter of the overall encoding reduced compared to proximity parameter of individual encodings $\mathbf{T}$ and π_3. Similarly, the verifier of $(\mathcal{P}', \mathcal{V}')$ PCPP system receives separate encoding for its individual input components. In our construction, we instantiate these individual encodings using schemes with appropriate parameters in order to obtain HPCP-SS scheme with desired parameters. See proof of Lemma 4 for a formal treatment of the aforementioned subtlety.

In step (2.iii), Fig. 5, we utilize the fact that the global codeword is locally-correctable. However, this is not a necessity, as we can generically compile any protocol that assumes an honest database encoding into one that does not by using an LDC (such as a Reed-Muller code) and PCPP for NP. The idea is that if an honest prover is supposed to commit to $\mathbf{X} = \Pi.\mathsf{Enc}(\mathbf{x})$, the prover will commit to an LDC encoding of $\mathbf{X}$ denoted by $\mathbf{Y}$ and give a PCPP that $\mathbf{Y}$ is indeed close to the LDC-encoding of a valid $\mathbf{X}$. Then whenever we need to access $\mathbf{X}$ in the online phase, we emulate this by applying the local decoding algorithm of the LDC to $\mathbf{Y}$. With this approach, we can even use Reed-Solomon code for projection as described in Sect. 2. However, for simplicity and efficiency reasons we exploit the local correctability property of global codeword in our application.

Using Theorem 5 and Theorem 6, we prove Lemma 4 below. We obtain proof of Theorem 4 by using Theorem 3 in Lemma 4. In Lemma 4, let $t_t^{(1)}$ and $t_c^{(1)}$ respectively denote the time taken to check local-testability and local-correctability of code E_1. Similarly, let $t_t^{(2)}$ denote the local-testability of code E_2. Finally, let $t_t^{(3)}$ and $t_d^{(3)}$ denote the time taken for local-testability and local decoding of code E_3 respectively.

Lemma 4. *Given the primitives listed in Fig. 3, for n-bit inputs, and k-sized sequences, there exist efficient encoding functions $\mathsf{E}_1 : \{0,1\}^n \to \mathbb{F}_q^N$ and $\mathsf{E}_2 : [n]^k \to \{0,1\}^{\Gamma_2}$ for which the following holds. For every NP relation $\mathcal{R} \in \mathsf{DTIME}(T(k))$ there exists HPCP-SS for k-sized projections with respect to E_1 and E_2 satisfying the following parameters:*

1. *Query Complexity:* $Q = Q_t^{(1)} + Q_t^{(2)} + Q_t^{(3)} + Q^{\mathsf{vproj}} + Q'(Q_d^{(3)} + Q_c^{(1)})$.
2. *Offline proof computation complexity:* $t_{\mathsf{off}} = O(t_{\mathsf{Enc}}(n))$.
3. *Offline proof size:* $p_{\mathsf{off}} = N'$.
4. *Online proof computation complexity:* $t_{\mathsf{on}} = \tilde{O}(t_{\mathsf{Proj}}(n,k) + t_{\mathsf{E}_2}(n,k) + t_{\mathsf{E}_3}(N,K) + t_p^{\mathsf{vproj}} + t_p')$.
5. *Runtime of $\mathcal{V}$:* $t_v = \tilde{O}(t_t^{(1)} + t_t^{(2)} + t_t^{(3)} + t_v^{\mathsf{vproj}} + Q' \cdot (t_d^{(3)} + t_c^{(1)}) + t_v')$.
6. *Online proof size:* $\Gamma_2 + \Gamma_3 + \ell^{\mathsf{vproj}} + \ell'$.
7. *Soundness error:* $\epsilon \leq \epsilon_t^{(1)} + \epsilon_t^{(2)} + \epsilon_t^{(3)} + Q'\epsilon_d^{(3)} + \epsilon^{\mathsf{vproj}} + \epsilon'$.
8. *Proximity parameter:* δ *(see proof for details).*

Proof. **Completeness.** We need to show that for given $\mathbf{v}, \mathbf{x}$, and $\mathbf{s}$, if $\exists w$ s.t. $\mathcal{R}(\mathbf{v}, \mathbf{x}\|_\mathbf{s}, w) = \mathsf{accept}$, then $\mathcal{V}$ always outputs accept. By completeness of local-testable codes $\Pi.\mathsf{Enc}$, E_2, and E_3, if $\mathbf{X} = \Pi.\mathsf{Enc}(\mathbf{x})$, $\mathbf{T} = \mathsf{E}_2(\mathbf{s})$ and $\pi_{\mathsf{E}_3} = \mathsf{E}_3(\mathbf{S})$, $\mathcal{V}$ doesn't output reject at step (3.i) of Fig. 5 with probability 1.

Now, let us show that $\mathcal{V}$ doesn't output reject in step (3.ii) of Fig. 5 with probability 1. If M_{vproj} outputs accept on input s and S, then $\mathbf{S} = \Pi.\text{Proj}(\mathbf{s})$ (by definition of M_{vproj}). By the completeness property listed in Theorem 5, we have that $\exists w'_{\text{vproj}}$ such that TM M' on input $\mathbf{v}_{\text{vproj}}$, s and S outputs accept. From the completeness property of PCPP system $(\mathcal{P}^{\text{vproj}}, \mathcal{V}^{\text{vproj}})$ for NP relation $\mathcal{R}'$ (using TM M'), we have that $\mathcal{V}^{\text{vproj}}$ outputs accept with probability 1.

Online Phase.

1. Input: $\mathcal{V}$ receives $n, k \in \mathbb{N}$ and $\mathbf{v} \in \{0,1\}^\ell$ as input.
2. Verification: $\mathcal{V}$ has oracle access to $\mathbf{X}$, $\mathbf{T}$, and $\pi = (\pi_{\mathsf{E}_3} \circ \pi_{\text{vproj}} \circ \pi')$. $\mathcal{V}$ performs the following computation:

    i) $\mathcal{V}$ performs at most $Q_t^{(1)}$, $Q_t^{(2)}$, and $Q_t^{(3)}$-many queries to oracles $\mathbf{X}$, $\mathbf{T}$, and π_{E_3} to check its local-testability. $\mathcal{V}$ outputs reject if any of the test fails.

    ii) $\mathcal{V}$ invokes $\mathcal{V}_{\text{vproj}}$ with input $\mathbf{v}_{\text{vproj}}$. For any oracle query of $\mathcal{V}_{\text{vproj}}$ to encoded inputs $\mathbf{T}/\pi_{\mathsf{E}_3}$ or proof oracle π_{vproj}, $\mathcal{V}$ makes the corresponding query request to oracles $\mathbf{T}/\pi_{\mathsf{E}_3}/\pi_{\text{vproj}}$ and forwards the response it receives to $\mathcal{V}_{\text{vproj}}$. If $\mathcal{V}_{\text{vproj}}$ returns reject then output reject.

    iii) $\mathcal{V}$ invokes $\mathcal{V}'$ with input $\mathbf{v}$. $\mathcal{V}'$ requires oracle access to encoding of input $\mathbf{x}|_{\mathbf{s}}$, and proof π'. For any query of $\mathcal{V}'$ to proof π, $\mathcal{V}$ can simply make the corresponding query to proof π and forward the received response to $\mathcal{V}'$. For queries of $\mathcal{V}'$ to input oracle, if the query is to encoding of s, i.e., $\mathbf{T}$, $\mathcal{V}$ makes the query to oracle $\mathbf{T}$ and sends the received response to $\mathcal{V}'$. Else, if the query is to encoding of input $\mathbf{x}$, i.e., $\mathbf{X}_{\mathbf{S}}$, $\mathcal{V}$ responds to the query as described next. Let $\mathcal{V}'$ request i^{th} bit in $\mathbf{X}_{\mathbf{S}}$. $\mathcal{V}$ determines $j \in [N]$ s.t. $(j-1) \cdot \lceil \log(q) \rceil \leq (i-1) < j \cdot \lceil \log(q) \rceil$. $\mathcal{V}$ makes $Q_d^{(3)}$ queries to locally decode π_{E_3} for index j to obtain j'. $\mathcal{V}$ performs $Q_c^{(1)}$ (locally-correctable) queries on codeword $\mathbf{X}$ to obtain the symbol ψ at index j'. Send bit at index $i' = (i-1) \mod \lceil \log(q) \rceil + 1$ of ψ as response to $\mathcal{V}'$. Finally, if $\mathcal{V}'$ returns reject then output reject.

    iv) $\mathcal{V}$ outputs accept.

Fig. 5. Verifier $\mathcal{V}$ of our HPCP-SS construction

Finally, it is easy to see that all the oracle queries of $\mathcal{V}'$ to π_{E_3} and π' are responded correctly. By the robustness property of projection code, we have that $\mathbf{X}|_{\mathbf{s}}$ is a robust encoding of input $\mathbf{x}|_{\mathbf{s}}$. For queries to encoding $\mathbf{X}|_{\mathbf{s}}$, we first determine the index $j \in [K]$ that contains the ith bit (query of $\mathcal{V}'$) in $\mathbf{X}|_{\mathbf{s}}$. By completeness property of locally decodable code E_3, we have $j' = S_j$. By the completeness property of locally-correctable code $\Pi.\text{Enc}$, we have $\psi = \mathbf{X}_{S_j}$. Thus, the ith bit in $\mathbf{X}|_{\mathbf{s}}$ is indeed the bit i' of $\mathbf{X}_{S_j}$. Completeness of step (3.iii) then follows from completeness property of PCPP system $(\mathcal{P}', \mathcal{V}')$ for NP relation $\mathcal{R}$. Thus, $\mathcal{V}$ outputs accept if $\exists w$ s.t. $\mathcal{R}(\mathbf{v}, \mathbf{x}\|_{\mathbf{s}}, w) = $ accept with probability 1.

Prover Complexity. In the offline phase, $\mathcal{P}$ computes $\Pi.\text{Enc}(\mathbf{x})$. Thus, $\ell_{\text{off}} = N'$ and $t_{\text{off}} = t_{\text{Enc}}(n)$. In the online phase, $\mathcal{P}$ in step (2) of Fig. 4 computes $\mathbf{T} = \mathsf{E}_2(\mathbf{s})$ which takes $O(t_{\mathsf{E}_2}(n,k))$ computation time. In step (3.i), computing projection of sequence $\mathbf{s}$, i.e., $\mathbf{S}$, takes $O(t_{\mathsf{Proj}}(n, k))$ computation time and computing encoding of $\mathbf{S}$ takes additional $O(t_{\mathsf{E}_3}(N, K))$ time. $\mathcal{P}$ then invokes Conv in step (3.ii) that runs in $\tilde{O}(t_{\mathsf{Proj}}(n, k))$ time. The computation cost of Step (3.iii) and (3.iv) is t_p^{vproj} and t'_p respectively. Thus, $t_{\mathsf{on}} = \tilde{O}(t_{\mathsf{Proj}}(n, k) + t_{\mathsf{E}_2}(n, k) + t_{\mathsf{E}_3}(N, K) + t_p^{\mathsf{vproj}} + t'_p)$. Further, in the online phase $\mathcal{P}$ generates oracle access to $\mathbf{T}$, π_{E_3}, π_{vproj}, and π'. Thus, $\ell_{\mathsf{on}} = \Gamma_2 + \Gamma_3 + \ell^{\mathsf{vproj}} + \ell'$.

Verifier Complexity. The computation cost to locally test codewords $\mathbf{X}$, $\mathbf{T}$, and π_{E_3} in step (3.i) of Fig. 5 is $t_t^{(1)} + t_t^{(2)} + t_t^{(3)}$ and the number of queries required to test the same is at most $Q_t^{(1)} + Q_t^{(2)} + Q_t^{(3)}$. In step (3.ii), $\mathcal{V}$ invokes $\mathcal{V}^{\mathsf{vproj}}$ that runs in time t_v^{vproj} and makes at most Q^{vproj} many queries in total to oracles $\mathbf{T}$, π_{E_3}, and π_{vproj}. Finally, $\mathcal{V}$ invokes $\mathcal{V}^{\mathsf{vproj}}$ that runs in t'_v time and makes Q' queries in total to oracles $\mathbf{T}$, $\mathbf{X}|_{\mathbf{S}}$, and π'. However, responding to a single query to encoding of input $\mathbf{x}|_{\mathbf{s}}$ requires $Q_d^{(3)}$ queries to oracle π_3 and $Q_c^{(2)}$ queries to oracle $\mathbf{X}$. Thus, in order to respond to a query of $\mathcal{V}'$, $\mathcal{V}$ makes at most $Q_d^{(3)} + Q_c^{(1)}$ oracle queries in worst-case. Thus, the overall computation and query cost incurred by $\mathcal{V}$ on invoking $\mathcal{V}'$ is $Q' \cdot (t_d^{(3)} + t_c^{(1)}) + t'_v$ and $Q'(Q_d^{(3)} + Q_c^{(1)})$ respectively. Hence, $t_v = \tilde{O}(t_t^{(1)} + t_t^{(2)} + t_t^{(3)} + t_v^{\mathsf{vproj}} + Q' \cdot (t_d^{(3)} + t_c^{(1)}) + t'_v)$ and $Q = Q_t^{(1)} + Q_t^{(2)} + Q_t^{(3)} + Q^{\mathsf{vproj}} + Q'(Q_d^{(3)} + Q_c^{(1)})$.

Soundness. In step (3.i) of Fig. 5, $\mathcal{V}$ accepts ill-formed codeword $\mathbf{X}$ or $\mathbf{T}$ or π_{E_3} with probability at most $\epsilon_t^{(1)} + \epsilon_t^{(2)} + \epsilon_t^{(3)}$. For the rest of the computation of $\mathcal{V}$, with probability $(1-(\epsilon_t^{(1)} + \epsilon_t^{(2)} + \epsilon_t^{(3)}))$, we have $\mathbf{X} = \Pi.\mathsf{Enc}(\mathbf{x}')$, $\mathbf{T} = \mathsf{E}_2(\mathbf{s}')$, and $\pi_{\mathsf{E}_3} = \mathsf{E}_3(\mathbf{S}')$, for some $\mathbf{x}' \in \{0,1\}^n$, $\mathbf{s}' \in [n]^k$, and $\mathbf{S}' \in [N]^K$.

From Theorem 5, if inputs $\mathbf{s}'$ and $\mathbf{S}'$ to M_{vproj} are such that $\mathbf{s}$ is not a sequence of distinct locations or $\mathbf{S}' \neq \Pi.\mathsf{Proj}(\mathbf{s}')$, then $\not\exists w_{\mathsf{vproj}}$ such that TM M' outputs accept. Thus, $\mathcal{R}'$ on inputs v_{vproj}, $\mathbf{s}'$ and $\mathbf{S}'$, outputs reject. Moreover, $\mathcal{V}^{\mathsf{vproj}}$ receives access to input encodings $(\mathbf{T} \circ \pi_{\mathsf{E}_3})$. $\mathbf{T}$ (resp. π_{E_3}) is a codeword of length Γ_2 (resp. Γ_3) with proximity parameter $\delta_t^{(2)}$ (resp. $\delta_t^{(3)}$). Thus, the proximity parameter of the overall codeword is,

$$\rho_1 = \min\left\{ \frac{\delta_t^{(2)} \cdot \Gamma_2}{\Gamma_2 + \Gamma_3}, \frac{\delta_t^{(3)} \cdot \Gamma_3}{\Gamma_2 + \Gamma_3} \right\}.$$

If $\delta^{\mathsf{vproj}} = \rho_1$, then by soundness property of PCPP system $(\mathcal{P}^{\mathsf{vproj}}, \mathcal{V}^{\mathsf{vproj}})$, we have that $\mathcal{V}^{\mathsf{vproj}}$ outputs accept with probability at most $\epsilon^{\mathsf{vproj}}$. Thus, for the rest of the computation, $\mathbf{S}' = \Pi.\mathsf{Proj}(\mathbf{s}')$ with probability $1 - (\epsilon_t^{(1)} + \epsilon_t^{(2)} + \epsilon_t^{(3)} + \epsilon^{\mathsf{vproj}}))$.

Finally, $\mathcal{V}'$ of the $(\mathcal{P}', \mathcal{V}')$ receives oracle access to $\mathbf{T}$ and $\mathbf{X}|_{\mathbf{s}'}$. The queries to $\mathbf{T}$ are always responded correctly. Whereas each query to codeword $\mathbf{X}|_{\mathbf{s}'}$, requires local-decoding of codeword π_{E_3} which is incorrect with probability at most $\epsilon_d^{(3)}$. Thus, queries of $\mathcal{V}'$ are responded incorrectly with probability at most $Q' \epsilon_d^{(3)}$. The query for $\mathbf{X}_{j'}$ is answered on performing locally-correctable queries on codeword $\mathbf{X}$ which is incorrect with probability at most $\epsilon_c^{(1)}$. That is, $\mathcal{V}'$ receives response with respect to a codeword which is $\epsilon_c^{(1)}$-far away from codeword $\mathbf{X}|_{\mathbf{s}'}$. Recall that projection scheme Π has proximity parameter δ_P and the projected codeword has length $\Gamma_p = K\lceil \log_2(q)\rceil$. Therefore, we require that $\epsilon_c^{(1)} \le \delta_P$. Thus, the proximity parameter of the overall codeword $(\mathbf{T} \circ \pi_{\mathsf{E}_3} \circ \mathbf{X}|_{\mathbf{S}'})$ is,

$$\rho_2 = \min\left\{ \frac{\delta_t^{(2)} \cdot \Gamma_2}{\Gamma_2 + \Gamma_3 + \Gamma_p}, \frac{\delta_d^{(3)} \cdot \Gamma_3}{\Gamma_2 + \Gamma_3 + \Gamma_p}, \frac{\delta_p \cdot \Gamma_p}{\Gamma_2 + \Gamma_3 + \Gamma_p} \right\}.$$

Now, if the inputs $\mathbf{x}'$ and $\mathbf{s}'$ are such that $\nexists w$ s.t. $\mathcal{R}(\mathbf{v}, \mathbf{x}'\|_{\mathbf{s}'}, w) = \mathsf{accept}$ and proximity parameter of PCPP system $(\mathcal{P}', \mathcal{V}')$, i.e., $\delta' = \rho_2$, then by soundness property of PCPP system we have that $\mathcal{V}'$ accepts with probability at most ϵ'.

To conclude, our HPCP-SS system $(\mathcal{P}, \mathcal{V})$ has proximity parameter $\delta = \rho_2$ and soundness error (ϵ) is at most $(\epsilon_t^{(1)} + \epsilon_t^{(2)} + \epsilon_t^{(3)} + Q'\epsilon_d^{(3)} + \epsilon^{\mathsf{vproj}} + \epsilon')$. $\square$

Using $(Q_t^{(2)} = \mathrm{polylog}(n), \delta_t^{(2)} = \Omega(1), \epsilon_t^{(2)} = \mathsf{negl}(n))$-locally testable code E_2 with codeword length $\Gamma_2 = cK \log n$ and $(Q_t^{(3)} = \mathrm{polylog}(n), \delta_t^{(3)} = \Omega(1), \epsilon_t^{(3)} = \mathsf{negl}(n))$-locally testable code and $(Q_d^{(3)} = \mathrm{polylog}(n), \delta_d^{(3)} = \Omega(1), \epsilon_d^{(3)} = \mathsf{negl}(n))$-locally decodable code E_3 with codeword length $c'K \log n$, where $c = O(1)$ and $c' = O(1)$, and with result of Theorem 6 and Theorem 3, we obtain proof of Theorem 4.

Remark. We include the length of $\mathbf{s}$, i.e., k as part of the parameters list of HPCP-SS system $(\mathcal{P}, \mathcal{V})$ in order to explicitly state the overall complexity of our protocol in terms of n and k. However, the parameters of the offline phase of our HPCP-SS construction are independent of k. In fact, the offline phase computation can be reused for varying length of $\mathbf{s}$. Thus, our HPCP-SS construction can be used as a building block in scenarios where support for varying sequence length is required such as in execution of RAM programs. Thus, in the rest of our paper we drop parameter k from the parameter list of HPCP-SS system.

5.2 Holographic PCPs for RAM Programs

In this section, we extend the notion of HPCP-SS to obtain Holographic PCPs for RAM programs (HPCP-RAM). We define the notion of HPCP-RAM below. In the online phase, both the parties obtain description of NP relation $\mathcal{R}$ that is given random access to memory $\mathbf{x}$ and takes as input a witness w. $\mathcal{P}$ is interested to prove $\mathcal{V}$ that $\exists w$ s.t. $\mathcal{R}(\mathbf{x}, w) = \mathsf{accept}$. We denote the description of NP relation $\mathcal{R}$ by $P_{\mathcal{R}}$.

Definition 10. *(Holographic PCP for RAM programs) A holographic PCP for RAM programs (HPCP-RAM) with respect to $(Q_1, \delta_1, \epsilon_1)$-locally-testable code E_1 is executed between $\mathcal{P} = (\mathcal{P}_{\mathsf{off}}, \mathcal{P}_{\mathsf{on}})$ and $\mathcal{V}$ (where $\mathcal{P}$ is a probabilistic RAM program and $\mathcal{V}$ is a probabilistic TM) with parameters: query complexity of the verifier (Q), offline proof computation complexity (t_{off}), offline proof size (p_{off}), online proof computation complexity (t_{on}), online proof size (p_{on}), runtime of $\mathcal{V}$ (t_v), proximity parameter (δ), and the soundness error of the HPCP system (ϵ), such that $(\mathcal{P}, \mathcal{V})$ satisfies the following requirements:*

- **Offline Phase:**
  - *Input:* $\mathcal{P}_{\text{off}}$ *receives* $\mathbf{x} \in \{0,1\}^n$.
  - *Database Encoding:* $\mathcal{P}_{\text{off}}$ *computes* $\mathbf{X} = \mathsf{E}_1(\mathbf{x})$ *and outputs state* st. *We require that* $|\mathbf{X}| \leq p_{\text{off}}(n)$ *and is computed within time* $t_{\text{off}}(n)$ *by prover's RAM program.*
- **Online Phase:**
  - *Inputs:* $\mathcal{P}_{\text{on}}$ *receives* st, $P_{\mathcal{R}} \in \{0,1\}^\ell$ *and a witness* $w \in \{0,1\}^\mu$ *as input.* $\mathcal{V}$ *receives* $n \in \mathbb{N}$, *and* $P_{\mathcal{R}} \in \{0,1\}^\ell$ *as input.*
  - *Proof Generation:* $\mathcal{P}_{\text{on}}$ *generates a proof* π *(for statement* $\mathcal{R}(\mathbf{x}, w) = \mathsf{accept})$ *which* $\mathcal{V}$ *gets oracle access to. We require that* $|\pi| \leq p_{\text{on}}(n, T)$ *and is generated within time* $t_{\text{on}}(n, T)$, *where* T *is the bound on the runtime of RAM program* $\mathcal{R}$.
  - *Verification:* $\mathcal{V}$ *makes at most* $Q(n)$ *queries to* $(\mathbf{X}, \pi)$, *and based on the responses outputs either* accept *or* reject. *We require the runtime of* $\mathcal{V}$ *to be within* $t_v(n)$.
- *Perfect Completeness: If* $\mathcal{R}(\mathbf{x}, w) = \mathsf{accept}$, *then* $\mathcal{V}$ *with oracle access to* $(\mathbf{X}, \pi)$ *always accepts.*
- *ϵ-Soundness: Suppose* $\mathbf{X}^*$ *is such that for all* $\mathbf{x}'$ *for which there exists* w *such that* $\mathcal{R}(\mathbf{x}', w) = \mathsf{accept}$, $\mathbf{X}^*$ *is* δ_1-far *from* $\mathsf{E}_1(\mathbf{x}')$. *Then,* $\mathcal{V}$ *accepts* $\mathbf{X}^*$ *with probability at most* $\epsilon = \epsilon(n)$. *In this definition,* δ *denotes the proximity parameter of our* HPCP-RAM *system that depends on proximity parameter of encoding* E_1, *i.e.,* δ_1.

Succinctly, we refer to such system as an $(n, Q, t_{\text{off}}, p_{\text{off}}, t_{\text{on}}, p_{\text{on}}, t_v, \delta, \epsilon)$-HPCP-RAM.

Let M be the RAM program that verifies NP relation $\mathcal{R}$ in time T and let $P_{\mathcal{R}}$ denote the description of M. Our HPCP-RAM construction is a straightforward extension of our HPCP-SS construction. The TM M' verifies NP relation $\mathcal{R}'$ that on first input fixed to $P_{\mathcal{R}}$ is equivalent NP relation $\mathcal{R}$. We describe our HPCP-RAM construction formally in Fig. 6. In Fig. 6, we denote the offline and online computations of $\mathcal{P}'$, the prover of HPCP-SS system, by $\mathcal{P}'_{\text{off}}$ and $\mathcal{P}'_{\text{on}}$ respectively. $\mathcal{P}'_{\text{off}}$ and $\mathcal{P}'_{\text{on}}$ share a state between them. In our construction, Conv and M' denote the converter RAM program and the TM of Theorem 5.

Lemma 5. *If there exists an* $(n, Q', t'_{\text{off}}, p'_{\text{off}}, t'_{\text{on}}, p'_{\text{on}}, t'_v, \delta', \epsilon')$-HPCP-SS *system* $(\mathcal{P}' = (\mathcal{P}'_{\text{off}}, \mathcal{P}'_{\text{on}}), \mathcal{V}')$ *for* NP *relation* $\mathcal{R}'$, *then there exists an* $(n, Q = Q' + \log n, t_{\text{off}} = t'_{\text{off}}, p_{\text{off}} = p'_{\text{off}}, t_{\text{on}} = t'_{\text{on}} + \tilde{O}(T), p_{\text{on}} = p'_{\text{on}} + \lceil \log n \rceil, t'_v = t_v + \lceil \log n \rceil, \delta = \delta', \epsilon = \epsilon')$-HPCP-RAM *for* NP *relation* $\mathcal{R}$ *(RAM program that runs in time at most* T *).*

Proof of Lemma 5 is deferred to the full version. Using Theorem 4 and 5, for a RAM NP relation $\mathcal{R}$ that runs in time at most T we have the following result.

Theorem 7 (HPCP-RAM). *For any* $\alpha > 0$, *there exists* $c_\alpha > 1$ *such that there exists an* $(n, Q = \text{polylog}(n), t_{\text{off}} = \tilde{O}(n^{c_\alpha}), p_{\text{off}} = O(n^{c_\alpha}), t_{\text{on}} = \tilde{O}(T^{1+\alpha}), p_{\text{on}} = O(T^{1+\alpha}), t_v = \text{polylog}(n), \delta = 1/\text{polylog}(n), \epsilon = \text{negl}(n))$-HPCP-RAM.

Alternatively, for any $\alpha > 0$, there exists an $(n, Q = \text{polylog}(n), t_{\text{off}} = \tilde{O}(n^{1+\alpha}), p_{\text{off}} = O(n^{1+\alpha}), t_{\text{on}} = \tilde{O}(T^2), p_{\text{on}} = \tilde{O}(T), t_v = \text{polylog}(n), \delta = 1/\text{polylog}(n), \epsilon = \text{negl}(n))$-HPCP-RAM.

Remark. More precisely, the verifier runtime is $O(\text{polylog}\,n + \ell)$, where $\ell = |P_{\mathcal{R}}|$ denotes the size of the program description. Since a RAM program (similarly to TM) is a uniform computational model that works on all input lengths n, the program length can be viewed as constant in n. Consequently, we omit ℓ relative to n when presenting asymptotic complexities in the rest of the paper.

Parameters.
1. Projection code $\Pi = (\text{Enc}, \text{Proj}, \text{Dec})$, where Enc is $(Q_1, \delta_1, \epsilon_1)$-locally testable.
2. $(Q_2, \delta_2, \epsilon_2)$-locally testable code E_2.
3. $(n, Q', t'_{\text{off}}, p'_{\text{off}}, t'_{\text{on}}, p'_{\text{on}}, t'_v, \delta', \epsilon')$-HPCP-SS system $(\mathcal{P}' = (\mathcal{P}'_{\text{off}}, \mathcal{P}'_{\text{on}}), \mathcal{V}')$ for NP relation $\mathcal{R}'$.

Instantiation.
1. Instantiate HPCP-SS system $(\mathcal{P}', \mathcal{V}')$ with encodings $(E_1(\cdot) = \Pi.\text{Enc}(\cdot), E_2(\cdot))$.

Offline Phase.
Computation of $\mathcal{P}_{\text{off}}$:
1. Input: $\mathcal{P}_{\text{off}}$ receives $\mathbf{x} \in \{0,1\}^n$.
2. Database Encoding: $\mathcal{P}_{\text{off}}$ invokes $\mathcal{P}'_{\text{off}}$ with input $\mathbf{x}$. $\mathcal{P}'_{\text{off}}$ returns $\mathbf{X}$. $\mathcal{P}_{\text{off}}$ sets $\text{st} = \mathbf{x} \circ \mathbf{X}$.

Online Phase.
Computation of $\mathcal{P}_{\text{on}}$:
1. Input: $\mathcal{P}_{\text{on}}$ receives st, $P_{\mathcal{R}} \in \{0,1\}^\ell$, and a witness w as input.
2. Proof Generation:
    i) $\mathcal{P}_{\text{on}}$ computes $(w', \mathbf{s}) \leftarrow \text{Conv}(P_{\mathcal{R}}, \mathbf{x}, w)$ and sets $k \leftarrow |\mathbf{s}|$.
    ii) $\mathcal{P}_{\text{on}}$ invokes $\mathcal{P}'_{\text{on}}$ with inputs $\mathbf{s}, P_{\mathcal{R}}$, and w'. $\mathcal{P}'_{\text{on}}$ returns encoding $\mathbf{T}$ and proof π'.
    iii) $\mathcal{P}_{\text{on}}$ sets $\pi \leftarrow k \circ \mathbf{T} \circ \pi'$.
Computation of $\mathcal{V}$:
1. Input: $\mathcal{V}$ receives $n \in \mathbb{N}$, and $P_{\mathcal{R}} \in \{0,1\}^\ell$ as input.
2. Verification: $\mathcal{V}$ has oracle access to $\mathbf{X}, \pi = k \circ \mathbf{T} \circ \pi'$. $\mathcal{V}$ performs the following computation:
    i) $\mathcal{V}$ makes queries to oracle π to obtain k.
    ii) $\mathcal{V}$ invokes $\mathcal{V}'$ with inputs $n, k, \ell \in \mathbb{N}$, and $P_{\mathcal{R}}$.
    iii) For any query of $\mathcal{V}'$ to encoded inputs $\mathbf{X}/\mathbf{T}$ or proof oracle π', $\mathcal{V}$ makes the corresponding query request to oracles $\mathbf{X}/\mathbf{T}/\pi'$ and forwards the response it receives to $\mathcal{V}'$.
    iv) $\mathcal{V}$ outputs the output received from $\mathcal{V}'$.

Fig. 6. Our HPCP-RAM construction

6 Succinct Arguments for RAM Programs

In this section, we provide the first black-box construction for succinct arguments for RAM programs (SArg-RAM) over a succinctly committed database. Here, we first formalize the notion SArg-RAM. We use the standard definition of commitment scheme (cf. [43, Definition 5.13]).

Definition 11. *(Succinct Argument for RAM programs (SArg-RAM)) A succinct argument for RAM programs (SArg-RAM) with respect to commitment scheme* $\Pi_C = (\mathsf{Gen}, \mathsf{Commit}, \mathsf{Verify})$ *is executed between* $\mathcal{P} = (\mathcal{P}_{\mathsf{off}}, \mathcal{P}_{\mathsf{on}})$ *and* $\mathcal{V}$ *(where* $\mathcal{P}$ *is a probabilistic RAM program and* $\mathcal{V}$ *is a probabilistic TM) with parameters: offline proof computation complexity* (t_{off}), *size of commitment in the offline phase* (c_{off}), *online proof computation complexity* (t_{on}), *online communication complexity* (c_{on}), *runtime of* $\mathcal{V}$ (t_v), *soundness error* (γ), *such that* $(\mathcal{P}, \mathcal{V})$ *satisfies the following requirements:*

- **Trusted Setup** *(*$\mathsf{Setup}(1^\lambda)$*):* $\mathsf{ck} \xleftarrow{\$} \Pi_C.\mathsf{Gen}(1^\lambda)$.
- **Offline Phase:**
  - *Input:* $\mathcal{P}_{\mathsf{off}}$ *receives* λ, ck, *and* $\mathbf{x} \in \{0,1\}^n$.
  - *Offline Commitment: On receiving input,* $\mathcal{P}_{\mathsf{off}}$ *outputs a state* st *and publishes commitment* $\mathsf{com} = \Pi_C.\mathsf{Commit}(\mathsf{ck}, \mathbf{x})$. *We require* $\mathsf{com} \leq c_{\mathsf{off}}(n, \lambda)$ *and the runtime of* $\mathcal{P}_{\mathsf{off}}$ *within* $t_{\mathsf{off}}(n, \lambda)$.
- **Online Phase:**
  - *Input:* $\mathcal{P}_{\mathsf{on}}$ *receives state* st, *RAM program* $P_{\mathcal{R}} \in \{0,1\}^\ell$ *defining an NP-relation* $\mathcal{R}$, *and a witness* $w \in \{0,1\}^\mu$ *as input.* $\mathcal{V}$ *receives* $n, \lambda \in \mathbb{N}$, $P_{\mathcal{R}}$, ck, *and* com *as input.*
  - *Interaction:* $\mathcal{P}_{\mathsf{on}}$ *and* $\mathcal{V}$ *interact and* $\mathcal{V}$ *decides to* accept *or* reject *based on the interaction, and commitment* com. *We require the runtime of* $\mathcal{P}_{\mathsf{on}}$ *and* $\mathcal{V}$ *to be respectively bounded by* $t_{\mathsf{on}}(n, \lambda, T)$ *and* $t_v(n, \lambda)$, *and the communication cost to be within* $c_{\mathsf{on}}(n, \lambda)$, *where* T *denotes the bound on the runtime of RAM program* $\mathcal{R}$.
- *Completeness: If* $\mathcal{R}(\mathbf{x}, w) = \mathsf{accept}$, *then after the honest* $\mathcal{P}$ *and* $\mathcal{V}$ *execute the offline phase and then the online phase on inputs* $(\mathbf{x}, w)$, $\mathcal{V}$ *always accepts.*
- *Soundness: An SArg-RAM system is* $\gamma(n, \lambda)$*-sound, if there exists PPT oracle machine* EXT, *called extractor, such that for every prover* $\mathcal{P}^*$ *and security parameter* λ, *equation (8) holds for the two experiments* $\mathsf{Real\text{-}Exp}_{(\mathcal{P}^*, \mathcal{V})}^{\mathsf{SArg\text{-}RAM}}(\lambda)$ *and* $\mathsf{Ideal}_{(\mathcal{P}^*, \mathsf{EXT})}^{\mathsf{SArg\text{-}RAM}}(\lambda)$ *defined below.*

$\underline{\mathsf{Real\text{-}Exp}_{(\mathcal{P}^*, \mathcal{V})}^{\mathsf{SArg\text{-}RAM}}(\lambda):}$

1. $\mathsf{ck} \xleftarrow{\$} \mathsf{Setup}(1^\lambda)$.
2. $(\mathsf{st}^*, \mathsf{com}^*, P_{\mathcal{R}^*}) \leftarrow \mathcal{P}^*(\mathsf{ck}, \mathbf{x})$.
3. $\mathcal{P}^*(\mathsf{ck}, \mathsf{st}^*, P_{\mathcal{R}^*}, w/\varnothing)$ *and* $\mathcal{V}(\lambda, \mathsf{ck}, P_{\mathcal{R}^*})$ *interact in the online phase.*
4. *Return 1 if* $\mathcal{V}$ *accepts, else return 0.*

$\underline{\mathsf{Ideal}_{(\mathcal{P}^*, \mathsf{EXT})}^{\mathsf{SArg\text{-}RAM}}(\lambda):}$

1. $\mathsf{ck} \xleftarrow{\$} \mathsf{Setup}(1^\lambda)$.

2. $(\mathsf{st}^*, \mathsf{com}^*, P_{\mathcal{R}^*}) \leftarrow \mathcal{P}^*(\mathsf{ck}, \mathbf{x})$.

3. $\mathbf{x}' \leftarrow \mathsf{EXT}^{\mathcal{P}^*(\mathsf{ck}, \mathsf{st}^*, P_{\mathcal{R}^*}, w/\varnothing)}(\mathsf{com}^*, P_{\mathcal{R}^*})$.

4. Return 1 if $(\exists w \text{ s.t. } \mathcal{R}^*(\mathbf{x}', w) = 1 \text{ AND } \mathsf{com}^* = \Pi_C.\mathsf{Commit}(\mathbf{x}'))$, else return 0.

$$\Pr[\mathsf{Ideal}^{\mathsf{SArg\text{-}RAM}}_{(\mathcal{P}^*, \mathsf{EXT})}(\lambda) = 1] \geq \Pr[\mathsf{Real\text{-}Exp}^{\mathsf{SArg\text{-}RAM}}_{(\mathcal{P}^*, \mathcal{V})}(\lambda) = 1] - \gamma(n, \lambda). \quad (8)$$

- *Succinctness:* An SArg-RAM *is succinct if* $t_v(n, \lambda)$ *and* $c_{\mathsf{on}}(n, \lambda)$ *are* $\mathsf{poly}(\lambda, \log n)$.

Succinctly, we refer to such system as an $(n, t_{\mathsf{off}}, c_{\mathsf{off}}, t_{\mathsf{on}}, c_{\mathsf{on}}, t_v, \gamma)$-SArg-RAM.

We present our SArg-RAM construction (see Fig. 7) that uses standard techniques [5,12,46] on top of our construction of HPCP-RAM. Our construction makes use of well-known construct *Merkle Trees* (MT) [48]. MT.Gen($\cdot$) denotes the algorithm to generate commitment key ck for merkle trees, MT.ComputeTree(ck, $\mathbf{x}$) computes merkle tree $\mathsf{D_{Tree}}$ on input $\mathbf{x}$, MT.GetRoot ($\mathsf{D_{Tree}}$) returns root of $\mathsf{D_{Tree}}$, MT.GetPath($\mathsf{D_{Tree}}, i$) returns path in $\mathsf{D_{Tree}}$ corresponding to index i, MT.VerifyPath verifies if path for index i is consistent with the root of $\mathsf{D_{Tree}}$. We direct readers to full-version of the paper for a formal description.

Lemma 6. *Given the following two primitives:*

- *A family of collision-resistant hash functions* $\mathcal{H}$.
- $(n, Q', t'_{\mathsf{off}}, p'_{\mathsf{off}}, t'_{\mathsf{on}}, p'_{\mathsf{on}}, t'_v, \delta', \epsilon')$-HPCP-RAM *system* $(\mathcal{P}' = (\mathcal{P}'_{\mathsf{off}}, \mathcal{P}'_{\mathsf{on}}), \mathcal{V}')$ *with respect to* $(Q_1, \delta_1, \epsilon_1)$-*locally-testable code* E_1.

There exists an $(n, t_{\mathsf{off}}, c_{\mathsf{off}}, t_{\mathsf{on}}, c_{\mathsf{on}}, t_v)$-SArg-RAM *system* $(\mathcal{P} = (\mathcal{P}_{\mathsf{off}}, \mathcal{P}_{\mathsf{on}}), \mathcal{V})$, *satisfying the following parameters:*

1. $t_{\mathsf{off}} = t'_{\mathsf{off}} + \tilde{O}(p'_{\mathsf{off}} \log(p'_{\mathsf{off}}))$.
2. $c_{\mathsf{off}} = \lambda$.
3. $t_{\mathsf{on}} = t'_{\mathsf{on}} + \tilde{O}(p'_{\mathsf{on}} \log(p'_{\mathsf{on}}) + (Q_1 + Q') \log(p'_{\mathsf{off}}))$.
4. $c_{\mathsf{on}} = \tilde{O}((Q_1 + Q') \log(p'_{\mathsf{off}}))$.
5. $t_v = t'_v + \tilde{O}((Q_1 + Q') \log(p'_{\mathsf{off}}))$.
6. $\gamma = \mathsf{negl}(\lambda) + \epsilon'$.

Complete proof of Lemma 6 is deferred to the full-version. Using Theorem 7 with the above lemma, we obtain the following result:

Theorem 8 (SArg-RAM). *If there exists a family of collision-resistant hash functions, then*

- *For* $\alpha > 0$ *there exists a* $c_\alpha > 1$ *such that there exists an* $(\tilde{O}(n^{c_\alpha}), \lambda, \tilde{O}(T^{1+\alpha}), \mathsf{poly}(\lambda, log(n)), \mathsf{poly}(\lambda, log(n), \mathsf{negl}(\lambda))$-SArg-RAM, *Or*
- *For* $\alpha > 0$, *there exists an* $(\tilde{O}(n^{1+\alpha}), \lambda, \tilde{O}(T^2), \mathsf{poly}(\lambda, log(n)), \mathsf{poly}(\lambda, log(n), \mathsf{negl}(\lambda))$-SArg-RAM.

Parameters.

1. A family of compressible functions $\mathcal{H} = \{h_\alpha : \{0,1\}^{2\lambda} \to \{0,1\}^\lambda\}_{\alpha \in \{0,1\}^{\text{poly}(\lambda)}}$ to instantiate merkle tree MT.
2. $(n, Q', t'_{\text{off}}, p'_{\text{off}}, t'_{\text{on}}, p'_{\text{on}}, t'_v, \delta', \epsilon')$-HPCP-RAM system $(\mathcal{P}' = (\mathcal{P}'_{\text{off}}, \mathcal{P}'_{\text{on}}), \mathcal{V}')$ with respect to $(Q_1, \delta_1, \epsilon_1)$-locally-testable code E_1.

Setup(1^λ):

1. ck $\xleftarrow{\$}$ MT.Gen(1^λ).

Offline Phase.

Computation of $\mathcal{P}_{\text{off}}$:

1. Input: $\mathcal{P}_{\text{off}}$ receives λ, ck, and $\mathbf{x} \in \{0,1\}^n$.
2. Offline Commitment: $\mathcal{P}_{\text{off}}$ invokes $\mathcal{P}'_{\text{off}}$ on input $\mathbf{x}$. $\mathcal{P}'_{\text{off}}$ return $\mathbf{X}$. $\mathcal{P}$ computes $D_{\text{Tree}}^{(x)} \leftarrow$ MT.ComputeTree(ck, $\mathbf{X}$) and $,_x \leftarrow$ MT.GetRoot$(D_{\text{Tree}}^{(x)})$. $\mathcal{P}_{\text{off}}$ sets st $= \mathbf{x} \circ \mathbf{X} \circ D_{\text{Tree}}^{(x)}$ and publishes $,_x$.

Online Phase.

Computation of $\mathcal{P}_{\text{on}}$:

1. Input: $\mathcal{P}_{\text{on}}$ receives state st $= \mathbf{x} \circ \mathbf{X} \circ D_{\text{Tree}}^{(x)}$, RAM program $P_\mathcal{R} \in \{0,1\}^\ell$ defining an NP-relation $\mathcal{R}$, and a witness $w \in \{0,1\}^\mu$ as input.
2. Interaction:
   i) $\mathcal{P}_{\text{on}}$ invokes $\mathcal{P}'_{\text{on}}$ with inputs st$' = \mathbf{X}$, $P_\mathcal{R}$, and w. $\mathcal{P}'_{\text{on}}$ returns proof π'.
   ii) $\mathcal{P}_{\text{on}}$ computes $D_{\text{Tree}}^{(\pi)} \leftarrow$ MT.ComputeTree(ck, π) and $,_\pi \leftarrow$ MT.GetRoot$(D_{\text{Tree}}^{(\pi)})$.
   iii) $\mathcal{P}_{\text{on}}$ sends $,_\pi$ to $\mathcal{V}$.
   iv) On receiving request for i^{th} block of $\mathbf{X}$ (resp. π) from $\mathcal{V}$, $\mathcal{P}_{\text{on}}$ computes and sends $(v_x, \text{path}_x) \leftarrow$ MT.GetPath$(D_{\text{Tree}}^{(x)}, i)$ (resp. $(v_\pi, \text{path}_\pi) \leftarrow$ MT.GetPath$(D_{\text{Tree}}^{(\pi)}, i)$) to $\mathcal{V}$.

Computation of $\mathcal{V}$:

1. Input: $\mathcal{V}$ receives $n, \lambda \in \mathbb{N}$, $P_\mathcal{R}$, ck, and $,_x$ as input.
2. Interaction:
   i) $\mathcal{V}$ receives $,_\pi$ from $\mathcal{P}_{\text{on}}$.
   ii) $\mathcal{V}$ generates at most Q_1-many queries $j_1, j_2, \ldots, j_r$ ($r \leq Q_1$) to check local-testability of codeword committed to $,_x$. For each $\ell \in [r]$, $\mathcal{V}$ computes $i_\ell = \lfloor (j_\ell - 1)/\lambda \rfloor + 1$. $\mathcal{V}$ queries $\mathcal{P}_{\text{on}}$ for block i_ℓ of $\mathbf{X}$. $\mathcal{V}$ receives $(v_{x,\ell}, \text{path}_{x,\ell})$ as response from $\mathcal{P}_{\text{on}}$. $\mathcal{V}$ computes MT.VerifyPath(ck, $,_x, i, v_{x,\ell}, \text{path}_{x,\ell}$). If MT.VerifyPath outputs reject, $\mathcal{V}$ outputs reject and aborts. Else, $\mathcal{V}$ sets a_ℓ to bit at index $((j-1) \bmod \lambda + 1)$ of $v_{x,\ell}$. Given responses $a_1, \ldots, a_r$ to queries $j_1, \ldots, j_r$, $\mathcal{V}$ outputs reject and aborts, if local-testability fails.
   iii) $\mathcal{V}$ invokes $\mathcal{V}'$ with inputs n and $P_\mathcal{R}$.
   iv) On receiving query for bit j of $\mathbf{X}$ (resp. π) from $\mathcal{V}'$, $\mathcal{V}$ computes $i = \lfloor (j-1)/\lambda \rfloor + 1$. $\mathcal{V}$ queries $\mathcal{P}_{\text{on}}$ for block i of $\mathbf{X}$ (resp. π). $\mathcal{V}$ receives (v_x, path_x) (resp. (v_π, path_π)) as response from $\mathcal{P}_{\text{on}}$. $\mathcal{V}$ computes MT.VerifyPath(ck, $,_x, i, v_x, \text{path}_x$) (resp. MT.VerifyPath(ck, $,_\pi, i, v_\pi, \text{path}_\pi$)). If MT.VerifyPath outputs reject, $\mathcal{V}$ outputs reject and aborts. Else, $\mathcal{V}$ sends bit at index $((j-1) \bmod \lambda + 1)$ of v_x (resp. v_π) to $\mathcal{V}'$.
   v) $\mathcal{V}$ outputs the output received from $\mathcal{V}'$.

Fig. 7. Our SArg-RAM construction

Acknowledgments. We would like to thank Ashutosh Kumar for his contributions to this research, and the anonymous Crypto reviewers for their helpful comments. Y. Ishai was supported in part by ERC Project NTSC (742754), BSF grant 2018393, ISF grant 2774/20, and a Google Faculty Research Award. R. Ostrovsky was supported in part by DARPA under Cooperative Agreement HR0011-20-2-0025, the Algorand Centers of Excellence programme managed by Algorand Foundation, NSF grants CNS-2001096 and CCF-2220450, US-Israel BSF grant 2015782, Amazon Faculty Award, Cisco Research Award and Sunday Group. Any views, opinions, findings, conclusions or recommendations contained herein are those of the author(s) and should not be interpreted as necessarily representing the official policies, either expressed or implied, of DARPA, the Department of Defense, the Algorand Foundation, or the U.S. Government. The U.S. Government is authorized to reproduce and distribute reprints for governmental purposes not withstanding any copyright annotation therein.

References

1. Aho, A.V., Hopcroft, J.E., Ullman, J.D.: The Design and Analysis of Computer Algorithms. Addison-Wesley (1974)
2. Arora, S., Lund, C., Motwani, R., Sudan, M., Szegedy, M.: Proof verification and the hardness of approximation problems. J. ACM (JACM) **45**(3), 501–555 (1998)
3. Arora, S., Safra, S.: Probabilistic checking of proofs: a new characterization of NP. J. ACM (JACM) **45**(1), 70–122 (1998)
4. Babai, L., Fortnow, L., Levin, L.A., Szegedy, M.: Checking computations in poly-logarithmic time. In: Proceedings of the 23rd Annual ACM Symposium on Theory of Computing, 5–8 May 1991, New Orleans, Louisiana, USA. ACM (1991)
5. Barak, B., Goldreich, O.: Universal arguments and their applications. In: Proceedings 17th IEEE Annual Conference on Computational Complexity, pp. 194–203. IEEE (2002)
6. Beaver, D., Feigenbaum, J.: Hiding instances in multioracle queries. In: Choffrut, C., Lengauer, T. (eds.) STACS 1990. LNCS, vol. 415, pp. 37–48. Springer, Heidelberg (1990). https://doi.org/10.1007/3-540-52282-4_30
7. Ben-Or, M., Goldwasser, S., Wigderson, A.: Completeness theorems for non-cryptographic fault-tolerant distributed computation. In: Proceedings of the Twentieth Annual ACM Symposium on Theory of Computing, STOC '88, pp. 1–10. Association for Computing Machinery, New York, NY, USA (1988)
8. Ben-Sasson, E., Chiesa, A.: Personal communication (2023)
9. Ben-Sasson, E., Chiesa, A., Genkin, D., Tromer, E.: Fast reductions from rams to delegatable succinct constraint satisfaction problems: extended abstract. In: Innovations in Theoretical Computer Science, ITCS '13, Berkeley, CA, USA, 9–12 January 2013, pp. 401–414. ACM (2013)
10. Ben-Sasson, E., Chiesa, A., Genkin, D., Tromer, E.: On the concrete efficiency of probabilistically-checkable proofs. In: STOC. ACM (2013)
11. Ben-Sasson, E., Chiesa, A., Genkin, D., Tromer, E., Virza, M.: SNARKs for C: verifying program executions succinctly and in zero knowledge. In: Canetti, R., Garay, J.A. (eds.) CRYPTO 2013. LNCS, vol. 8043, pp. 90–108. Springer, Heidelberg (2013). https://doi.org/10.1007/978-3-642-40084-1_6
12. Ben-Sasson, E., Chiesa, A., Spooner, N.: Interactive oracle proofs. In: Hirt, M., Smith, A. (eds.) TCC 2016. LNCS, vol. 9986, pp. 31–60. Springer, Heidelberg (2016). https://doi.org/10.1007/978-3-662-53644-5_2

13. Ben-Sasson, E., Goldreich, O., Harsha, P., Sudan, M., Vadhan, S.: Robust PCPs of proximity, shorter PCPs, and applications to coding. SIAM J. Comput. **36**(4), 889–974 (2006)
14. Ben-Sasson, E., Goldreich, O., Harsha, P., Sudan, M., Vadhan, S.P.: Short PCPs verifiable in polylogarithmic time. In: 20th Annual IEEE Conference on Computational Complexity (CCC 2005), 11–15 June 2005, San Jose, CA, USA, pp. 120–134. IEEE Computer Society (2005)
15. Bitansky, N., et al.: The hunting of the SNARK. J. Cryptol. **30**(4), 989–1066 (2017)
16. Bitansky, N., Canetti, R., Chiesa, A., Tromer, E.: Recursive composition and bootstrapping for snarks and proof-carrying data. In: Proceedings of the Forty-Fifth Annual ACM Symposium on Theory of Computing, pp. 111–120 (2013)
17. Bitansky, N., Chiesa, A., Ishai, Y., Paneth, O., Ostrovsky, R.: Succinct non-interactive arguments via linear interactive proofs. In: Sahai, A. (ed.) TCC 2013. LNCS, vol. 7785, pp. 315–333. Springer, Heidelberg (2013). https://doi.org/10.1007/978-3-642-36594-2_18
18. Bootle, J., Cerulli, A., Ghadafi, E., Groth, J., Hajiabadi, M., Jakobsen, S.K.: Linear-time zero-knowledge proofs for arithmetic circuit satisfiability. In: Takagi, T., Peyrin, T. (eds.) ASIACRYPT 2017. LNCS, vol. 10626, pp. 336–365. Springer, Cham (2017). https://doi.org/10.1007/978-3-319-70700-6_12
19. Bootle, J., Chiesa, A., Liu, S.: Zero-knowledge IOPs with linear-time prover and polylogarithmic-time verifier. In: Dunkelman, O., Dziembowski, S. (eds.) EUROCRYPT 2022. LNCS, vol. 13276, pp. 275–304. Springer, Cham (2022). https://doi.org/10.1007/978-3-031-07085-3_10
20. Chase, M., Healy, A., Lysyanskaya, A., Malkin, T., Reyzin, L.: Mercurial commitments with applications to zero-knowledge sets. In: Cramer, R. (ed.) EUROCRYPT 2005. LNCS, vol. 3494, pp. 422–439. Springer, Heidelberg (2005). https://doi.org/10.1007/11426639_25
21. Chen, M., Chiesa, A., Gur, T., O'Connor, J., Spooner, N.: Proof-carrying data from arithmetized random oracles. In: Hazay, C., Stam, M. (eds.) EUROCRYPT 2023. LNCS, vol. 14005, pp. 379–404. Springer, Cham (2023). https://doi.org/10.1007/978-3-031-30617-4_13
22. Choi, S.G., Dachman-Soled, D., Malkin, T., Wee, H.: Simple, black-box constructions of adaptively secure protocols. In: Reingold, O. (ed.) TCC 2009. LNCS, vol. 5444, pp. 387–402. Springer, Heidelberg (2009). https://doi.org/10.1007/978-3-642-00457-5_23
23. Cramer, R., Xing, C., Yuan, C.: Efficient multi-point local decoding of reed-muller codes via interleaved codex. IEEE Trans. Inf. Theory **66**(1), 263–272 (2019)
24. Damgård, I., Ishai, Y.: Constant-round multiparty computation using a black-box pseudorandom generator. In: Shoup, V. (ed.) CRYPTO 2005. LNCS, vol. 3621, pp. 378–394. Springer, Heidelberg (2005). https://doi.org/10.1007/11535218_23
25. Dinur, I.: The PCP theorem by gap amplification. J. ACM (JACM) **54**(3), 12-es (2007)
26. Franzese, N., Katz, J., Lu, S., Ostrovsky, R., Wang, X., Weng, C.: Constant-overhead zero-knowledge for ram programs. In: Proceedings of the 2021 ACM SIGSAC Conference on Computer and Communications Security, pp. 178–191 (2021)
27. Friedl, K., Sudan, M.: Some improvements to total degree tests. In: ISTCS. IEEE Computer Society (1995)
28. Garcia, A., Stichtenoth, H.: A tower of Artin-Schreier extensions of function fields attaining the Drinfeld-Vladut bound. Invent. Math. **121**(1), 211–222 (1995)

29. Garg, S., Steve, L., Ostrovsky, R.: Black-box garbled RAM. In: FOCS. IEEE Computer Society (2015)

30. Gennaro, R., Gentry, C., Parno, B., Raykova, M.: Quadratic span programs and succinct NIZKs without PCPs. In: Johansson, T., Nguyen, P.Q. (eds.) EUROCRYPT 2013. LNCS, vol. 7881, pp. 626–645. Springer, Heidelberg (2013). https://doi.org/10.1007/978-3-642-38348-9_37

31. Gentry, C., Wichs, D.: Separating succinct non-interactive arguments from all falsifiable assumptions. In: Fortnow, L., Vadhan, S.P. (eds.) Proceedings of the 43rd ACM Symposium on Theory of Computing, STOC 2011, San Jose, CA, USA, 6–8 June 2011, pp. 99–108. ACM (2011)

32. Goldreich, O., Ostrovsky, R.: Software protection and simulation on oblivious rams. J. ACM **43**(3), 431–473 (1996)

33. Golovnev, A., Lee, J., Setty, S.T.V., Thaler, J., Wahby, R.S.: Brakedown: linear-time and post-quantum snarks for R1CS. IACR Cryptology ePrint Archive (2021)

34. Gordon, S.D., et al.: Secure two-party computation in sublinear (amortized) time. In: CCS, pp. 513–524. ACM (2012)

35. Goyal, V.: Constant round non-malleable protocols using one way functions. In: Proceedings of the Forty-Third Annual ACM Symposium on Theory of Computing, pp. 695–704 (2011)

36. Goyal, V., Ostrovsky, R., Scafuro, A., Visconti, I.: Black-box non-black-box zero knowledge. In: Proceedings of the Forty-Sixth Annual ACM Symposium on Theory of Computing, pp. 515–524 (2014)

37. Groth, J.: Short pairing-based non-interactive zero-knowledge arguments. In: Abe, M. (ed.) ASIACRYPT 2010. LNCS, vol. 6477, pp. 321–340. Springer, Heidelberg (2010). https://doi.org/10.1007/978-3-642-17373-8_19

38. Gurevich, Y., Shelah, S.: Nearly linear time. In: Meyer, A.R., Taitslin, M.A. (eds.) Logic at Botik 1989. LNCS, vol. 363, pp. 108–118. Springer, Heidelberg (1989). https://doi.org/10.1007/3-540-51237-3_10

39. Haitner, I., Ishai, Y., Kushilevitz, E., Lindell, Y., Petrank, E.: Black-box constructions of protocols for secure computation. SIAM J. Comput. **40**(2), 225–266 (2011)

40. Hamlin, A., Ostrovsky, R., Weiss, M., Wichs, D.: Private anonymous data access. In: Ishai, Y., Rijmen, V. (eds.) EUROCRYPT 2019. LNCS, vol. 11477, pp. 244–273. Springer, Cham (2019). https://doi.org/10.1007/978-3-030-17656-3_9

41. Hu, Z., Mohassel, P., Rosulek, M.: Efficient zero-knowledge proofs of non-algebraic statements with sublinear amortized cost. In: Gennaro, R., Robshaw, M. (eds.) CRYPTO 2015. LNCS, vol. 9216, pp. 150–169. Springer, Heidelberg (2015). https://doi.org/10.1007/978-3-662-48000-7_8

42. Ishai, Y., Khurana, D., Sahai, A., Srinivasan, A.: On the round complexity of black-box secure MPC. In: Malkin, T., Peikert, C. (eds.) CRYPTO 2021. LNCS, vol. 12826, pp. 214–243. Springer, Cham (2021). https://doi.org/10.1007/978-3-030-84245-1_8

43. Katz, J., Lindell, Y.: Introduction to Modern Cryptography, 2nd edn. CRC Press, Boca Raton (2014)

44. Katz, J., Trevisan, L.: On the efficiency of local decoding procedures for error-correcting codes. In: Proceedings of the Thirty-Second Annual ACM Symposium on Theory of Computing, pp. 80–86 (2000)

45. Kedlaya, K.S., Umans, C.: Fast modular composition in any characteristic. In: 49th Annual IEEE Symposium on Foundations of Computer Science, FOCS 2008, 25–28 October 2008, Philadelphia, PA, USA. IEEE Computer Society (2008)

46. Kilian, J.: A note on efficient zero-knowledge proofs and arguments. In: Proceedings of the Twenty-Fourth Annual ACM Symposium on Theory of Computing, pp. 723–732 (1992)
47. Lipton, R.J.: Efficient checking of computations. In: Choffrut, C., Lengauer, T. (eds.) STACS 1990. LNCS, vol. 415, pp. 207–215. Springer, Heidelberg (1990). https://doi.org/10.1007/3-540-52282-4_44
48. Merkle, R.C.: A certified digital signature. In: Brassard, G. (ed.) CRYPTO 1989. LNCS, vol. 435, pp. 218–238. Springer, New York (1990). https://doi.org/10.1007/0-387-34805-0_21
49. Micali, S.: CS proofs (extended abstracts). In: FOCS. IEEE Computer Society (1994)
50. Micali, S., Rabin, M.O., Kilian, J.: Zero-knowledge sets. In: FOCS. IEEE Computer Society (2003)
51. Mohassel, P., Rosulek, M., Scafuro, A.: Sublinear zero-knowledge arguments for RAM programs. In: Coron, J.-S., Nielsen, J.B. (eds.) EUROCRYPT 2017. LNCS, vol. 10210, pp. 501–531. Springer, Cham (2017). https://doi.org/10.1007/978-3-319-56620-7_18
52. Ostrovsky, R., Rackoff, C., Smith, A.: Efficient consistency proofs for generalized queries on a committed database. In: Díaz, J., Karhumäki, J., Lepistö, A., Sannella, D. (eds.) ICALP 2004. LNCS, vol. 3142, pp. 1041–1053. Springer, Heidelberg (2004). https://doi.org/10.1007/978-3-540-27836-8_87
53. Ostrovsky, R., Rao, V., Scafuro, A., Visconti, I.: Revisiting lower and upper bounds for selective decommitments. In: Sahai, A. (ed.) TCC 2013. LNCS, vol. 7785, pp. 559–578. Springer, Heidelberg (2013). https://doi.org/10.1007/978-3-642-36594-2_31
54. Pass, R., Wee, H.: Black-box constructions of two-party protocols from one-way functions. In: Reingold, O. (ed.) TCC 2009. LNCS, vol. 5444, pp. 403–418. Springer, Heidelberg (2009). https://doi.org/10.1007/978-3-642-00457-5_24
55. Ron-Zewi, N., Rothblum, R.D.: Proving as fast as computing: succinct arguments with constant prover overhead. In: Leonardi, S., Gupta, A. (eds.) STOC '22: 54th Annual ACM SIGACT Symposium on Theory of Computing, Rome, Italy, 20–24 June 2022, pp. 1353–1363. ACM (2022)
56. Rubinfeld, R., Sudan, M.: Robust characterizations of polynomials with applications to program testing. SIAM J. Comput. (1996)
57. Valiant, P.: Incrementally verifiable computation or proofs of knowledge imply time/space efficiency. In: Canetti, R. (ed.) TCC 2008. LNCS, vol. 4948, pp. 1–18. Springer, Heidelberg (2008). https://doi.org/10.1007/978-3-540-78524-8_1
58. Xie, T., Zhang, Y., Song, D.: Orion: zero knowledge proof with linear prover time, In: Dodis, Y., Shrimpton, T. (eds.) CRYPTO 2022. LNCS, vol. 13510, pp. 299–328. Springer, Cham (2022). https://doi.org/10.1007/978-3-031-15985-5_11
59. Yekhanin, S.: Locally decodable codes. Found. Trends® Theor. Comput. Sci. 6(3), 139–255 (2012)

Brakedown: Linear-Time and Field-Agnostic SNARKs for R1CS

Alexander Golovnev[1]($\boxtimes$), Jonathan Lee[2], Srinath Setty[3], Justin Thaler[1], and Riad S. Wahby[4]

[1] Georgetown University, Washington, D.C., USA
alexgolovnev@gmail.com
[2] Nanotronics, New York, USA
[3] Microsoft Research, Cambridge, USA
[4] Stanford University, Stanford, USA

Abstract. This paper introduces a SNARK called *Brakedown*. Brakedown targets R1CS, a popular NP-complete problem that generalizes circuit-satisfiability. It is the first built system that provides a *linear-time* prover, meaning the prover incurs $O(N)$ finite field operations to prove the satisfiability of an N-sized R1CS instance. Brakedown's prover is faster, both concretely and asymptotically, than prior SNARK implementations. It does not require a trusted setup and may be post-quantum secure. Furthermore, it is compatible with *arbitrary* finite fields of sufficient size; this property is new among built proof systems with sublinear proof sizes. To design Brakedown, we observe that recent work of Bootle, Chiesa, and Groth (BCG, TCC 2020) provides a polynomial commitment scheme that, when combined with the linear-time interactive proof system of Spartan (CRYPTO 2020), yields linear-time IOPs and SNARKs for R1CS (a similar theoretical result was previously established by BCG, but our approach is conceptually simpler, and crucial for achieving high-speed SNARKs). A core ingredient in the polynomial commitment scheme that we distill from BCG is a linear-time encodable code. Existing constructions of such codes are believed to be impractical. Nonetheless, we design and engineer a new one that is practical in our context.

We also implement a variant of Brakedown that uses Reed-Solomon codes instead of our linear-time encodable codes; we refer to this variant as *Shockwave*. Shockwave is *not* a linear-time SNARK, but it provides shorter proofs and lower verification times than Brakedown, and also provides a faster prover than prior plausibly post-quantum SNARKs.

1 Introduction

A SNARK [18,37,47,55] is a cryptographic primitive that enables a *prover* to prove to a *verifier* the knowledge of a satisfying witness to an NP statement by producing a proof π such that the size of π and the cost to verify it are both sub-linear in the size of the witness. Given their many applications, constructing SNARKs with excellent asymptotics and concrete efficiency is a highly active area of research. Still, one of the key bottlenecks preventing application of existing SNARKs to large NP statements is the prover's asymptotic and concrete

© International Association for Cryptologic Research 2023
H. Handschuh and A. Lysyanskaya (Eds.): CRYPTO 2023, LNCS 14082, pp. 193–226, 2023.
https://doi.org/10.1007/978-3-031-38545-2_7

cost. This has limited the use of SNARKs to practical applications in which NP statements of interest are relatively small (for example, cryptocurrencies).

As with much of the literature on SNARKs, we focus on rank-1 constraint satisfiability (R1CS) over a finite field $\mathbb{F}$, an NP-complete problem that generalizes arithmetic circuit satisfiability. An R1CS instance comprises a set of M constraints, with a vector w over $\mathbb{F}$ said to *satisfy* the instance if it satisfies all M constraints. The term "rank-1" means that the constraints should have a specific form. Specifically, each constraint asserts that the product of two specified linear combinations of the entries of w equals a third linear combination of those entries. See Definition 1 for details. R1CS is amenable to probabilistic checking and is highly expressive. For example, in theory, any nondeterministic random access machine running in time T can be transformed into an R1CS instance of size "close" to T. In practice, there exist efficient transformations and compiler toolchains to transform applications of interest to R1CS [13, 25, 50, 58, 59, 64, 66, 73].

Our focus in this work is designing SNARKs for R1CS with the fastest possible prover. We also wish for the SNARK to be *transparent* (or be without a trusted setup): there should be no need to run a complex multi-party computation to generate a so-called *structured reference string* that is needed for proof generation.

Furthermore, we desire a verifier that runs in time sub-linear in the size of the R1CS instance. Since the verifier must at least read the statement that is being proven, we allow a one-time public preprocessing phase for general (unstructured) R1CS instances. In this phase, the verifier computes a *computation commitment*, a cryptographic commitment to the structure of a circuit or R1CS instance [63]. (For "structured" computations, our SNARKs, like several prior works, can avoid this pre-processing phase.) After the pre-processing phase, the verifier must run in time sub-linear in the size of the R1CS instance. Furthermore, the pre-processing phase should be at least as efficient as the SNARK prover. Subsequent works to Spartan [63] refer to such public preprocessing to achieve fast verification as leveraging *holography* [21, 31, 32].

A second focus of our work is designing SNARKs that can operate over arbitrary (sufficiently large) finite fields. Prior SNARKs apply over fields that are "discrete-log friendly"[1] or "FFT-friendly", or otherwise require one or many multiplicative or additive subgroups of specified sizes. Yet many cryptographic applications naturally work over fields that do not satisfy these properties. Examples include proofs regarding encryption or signature schemes that themselves work over fields that do not satisfy the properties needed by the SNARK. Indeed, most practically relevant elliptic curve groups are defined over fields that are not FFT-friendly. Even in applications where SNARK designers do have flexibility in field choice, field size restrictions can still create engineering challenges or

---

[1] It is possible to construct elliptic curves with specified group order [26], which suffices for many discrete log–based SNARKs. Unfortunately, the most efficient elliptic curve implementations are tailored to specific curves—so using a newly constructed curve may entail a performance or engineering cost.

inconveniences, as well as performance overheads. For example, they may limit the size of R1CS statements that can be handled over the chosen field, or force instance sizes to be padded to a length corresponding to the size of a subgroup.

In this work we design transparent SNARKs that asymptotically have the fastest possible prover, may be post-quantum secure, and work over arbitrary (sufficiently large) finite fields.[2] We refer to this latter property as being *field-agnostic*, and to the best of our knowledge, it is new amongst implemented arguments with sublinear proof size and even *quasi*linear runtime. We optimize and implement our new SNARKs, and demonstrate the fastest prover performance in the SNARK literature (even compared to SNARKs that require FFT-friendly or discrete-log–friendly fields).

Formalizing "fastest possible" Provers. How fast can we hope for the prover in a SNARK to be? Letting N denote the size of the R1CS or arithmetic-circuit-satisfiability instance over an *arbitrary* finite field $\mathbb{F}$, a lower bound on the prover's runtime is N operations in $\mathbb{F}$. Here, the size of an arithmetic-circuit-satisfiability instance is the number of gates in the circuit. The size of an R1CS instance of the form $Az \circ Bz = Cz$ is the number of non-zero entries in A, B, C, where $\circ$ denotes the Hadamard (entry-wise) product. This is because any prover that knows a witness w for the instance has to at least convince *itself* (much less the verifier) that w is valid. We refer to this procedure as *native evaluation* of the instance. So the natural goal, roughly speaking, is to achieve a SNARK prover that is only a constant factor slower than native evaluation. Such a prover is said to run in *linear-time*.

Achieving a linear-time prover may sound like a simple and well-defined goal, but it is in fact subtle to formalize, because one must be precise about what operations can be performed in one "time-step", as well as the soundness error achieved and the choice of the finite field.

In known SNARKs, the bottleneck for the prover (both asymptotically and concretely) is typically one or more of the following operations: (1) Performing an FFT over a vector of length $O(N)$. (2) Building a Merkle-hash tree over a vector consisting of $O(N)$ elements of $\mathbb{F}$. (3) Performing a multiexponentiation of size $O(N)$ in a (multiplicative) cryptographic group $\mathbb{G}$. In this case, the field $\mathbb{F}$ is of prime order p and $\mathbb{G}$ is typically an elliptic curve group (or subgroup) of order p. A multiexponentiation of size N in $\mathbb{G}$ refers to a product of N exponentiations, i.e., $\prod_{i=1}^{N} g_i^{c_i}$, where each $g_i \in \mathbb{G}$ and each $c_i \in \{0, \ldots, p-1\}$.

Should any of these operations count as "linear-time"?

FFTs. An FFT of length $\Theta(N)$ over $\mathbb{F}$ should *not* count as linear-time, because the fastest known algorithms require $\Theta(N \log N)$ operations over $\mathbb{F}$, which is a $\log N$ factor, rather than a constant factor, larger than native evaluation.

However, the remaining operations are trickier to render judgment upon, because they do not refer to field operations.

---

[2] For our SNARKs, a field of size $\exp(\lambda)$ is sufficient to achieve λ bits of security with a linear-time prover. More generally, our SNARK can work over any field $\mathbb{F}$ of size $|\mathbb{F}| \geq \Omega(N)$ with a prover runtime that is superlinear by a factor of $O(\lambda / \log |\mathbb{F}|)$, where N denotes instance size.

Merkle-Hashing. Build a Merkle tree over a vector of $O(N)$ elements of $\mathbb{F}$, computing $O(N)$ cryptographic hashes is necessary and sufficient, assuming the hash function takes as input $O(1)$ elements of $\mathbb{F}$. However, this is only "linear-time" if hashing $O(N)$ elements of $\mathbb{F}$ can be done in time comparable to $O(N)$ operations over $\mathbb{F}$. It is not clear whether or not applying a standard hash function such as SHA-256 to hash a field element should be considered comparable to performing a single field operation.

Theoretical work of Bootle et al. [20] sidesteps this issue by observing that (assuming the intractability of certain lattice problems over $\mathbf{F}_2$, specifically finding a low-Hamming vector in the kernel of a sparse matrix), a collision-resistant hash family of Applebaum et al. [5] is capable of hashing strings consisting of $k \gg \lambda$ bits in $O(k)$ bit operations, with security parameter λ. This means that a vector of $O(N)$ elements of $\mathbb{F}$ can be Merkle-hashed in $O(N \log |\mathbb{F}|)$ bit operations, which Bootle et al. [20] consider comparable to the cost of $O(N)$ operations in $\mathbb{F}$. The aforementioned hash functions appear to be of primarily theoretical interest because they can be orders of magnitude slower than standard hash functions (e.g., SHA-256). Hence, in this paper our implementations make use of standard hash functions, and with this choice, Merkle-hashing is not the concrete bottleneck in our implementations. Accordingly, and to simplify discussion, we consider our implemented Merkle-hashing procedure to be linear-time, even if this may not be strictly justified from a theoretical perspective.

Multiexponentiation. Pippenger's algorithm [60] (see also [16,44]) can perform an $O(N)$-sized multiexponentiation in a group $\mathbb{G}$ of size $\sim 2^\lambda$ by performing $O(N \cdot \lambda / \log(N \cdot \lambda))$ group operations (i.e., group multiplications). Typically, one thinks of the security parameter λ as $\omega(\log N)$ (so that 2^λ is superpolynomial in N, ensuring the intractability of problems such as discrete logarithm in $\mathbb{G}$), and so $O(N \cdot \lambda / \log(N \cdot \lambda))$ group operations is considered $\omega(N)$ group operations. Each group operation is at least as expensive (in fact, several times slower) than a field operation—typically, an operation in the elliptic-curve group $\mathbb{G}$ requires performing a constant number of field operations within a field that is of similar size to, but different than, then prime-order field $\mathbb{F}$ over which the circuit or R1CS instance is defined. Hence, we do *not* consider this to be linear time.

However, note that *for a fixed value of the security parameter λ*, the cost of a multiexponentiation of size N performed using Pippenger's algorithm scales only linearly (in fact, *sub*linearly) with N. That is, Pippenger's algorithm incurs $\Theta(N \cdot (\lambda / \log(N\lambda))) = \Theta_\lambda(N / \log N)$ group operations and in turn this cost is comparable up to a constant factor to the same number of operations over a field of size $\exp(\lambda)$. In practice, protocol designers fix a cryptographic group (and hence fix λ), and then apply the resulting protocol to R1CS instances of varying sizes N. For this reason, systems (e.g., Spartan [63]) whose dominant prover cost is a multiexponentiation of size N will scale (sub-)linearly as a function of N. Specifically, in the experimental results [63], Spartan's prover exhibits the behavior of a linear-time prover (as the cost of native evaluation of the instance also scales linearly as a function of N). Nonetheless, since λ should be thought of as $\omega(\log N)$, we do not consider a multiexponentiation of size N to be a linear-time operation.

In summary, we do *not* consider FFTs and multiexponentiations of size $O(N)$ to be linear-time operations, but *do* consider Merkle-hashing of vectors of size $O(N)$ to be linear-time.

Closely Related Work. We cover additional related work in the full version of this paper [40]. Building on Bootle et al. [20], Bootle, Chiesa, and Groth [21] give an *interactive oracle proof* (IOP) [15] with *constant* soundness error, in which the prover's work is $O(N)$ finite field operations for an N-sized R1CS instance over any finite field of size $\Omega(N)$. Here, an interactive oracle proof (IOP) [15,61] is a generalization of an interactive proof, where in each round, the prover sends a string as an oracle, and the verifier may read one or more entries in the oracle. To achieve soundness error that is exponentially small in the security parameter λ in the IOP of [21], one must restrict to R1CS instances over a "sufficiently large" finite field i.e., where $|\mathbb{F}| = 2^{\Theta(\lambda)}$, or else sacrifice the linear-time prover.

Applying standard transformations to their IOP, one can obtain a SNARG in the random oracle model with similar prover costs, or an interactive argument assuming linear-time computable cryptographic hash functions [5]. Unlike prior SNARGs (even those with a *quasi*-linear time prover), the resulting protocol does not require the field to be FFT-friendly nor discrete-log friendly.

Their IOP construction does not achieve zero-knowledge nor polylogarithmic proofs and verification times (the proof sizes and verification times are $O_\lambda(N^{1/t})$, where t is a constant, and not $O_\lambda(\log N)$ or $O_\lambda(1)$). Bootle, Chiesa, and Liu [23] address these issues by achieving zero-knowledge as well as polylogarithmic proof sizes and verification times (a more detailed discussion of the relationship between our results and those of [23] is in the full version of this paper [40]). Both [21,23] are theoretical in nature; they do not implement their schemes nor report performance results.

There is also very recent work related to our goal of working over arbitrary finite fields. Ben-Sasson et al. [11,12] improve the efficiency of FFT-like algorithms that apply over fields with no smooth order root of unity, by a factor of $\exp(\log^* N)$. An explicit motivation for their work is to improve the efficiency of known SNARKs that perform FFTs (e.g., Fractal [32]) when operating over "non-FFT-friendly" fields. These results do not eliminate the superlinearity of the prover's runtime in their target SNARKs. The algorithms given in [11,12] also perform significant pre-computation that is field-specific and have not to date yielded implemented SNARKs. We seek (and achieve) high-speed SNARKs that require only black-box access to the addition and multiplication operations of the field, with the only additional information required being a lower bound on the field size to ensure soundness.

In summary, prior works leave open the problem of achieving concretely efficient SNARKs that support arbitrary (sufficiently large) finite fields, much less one with a linear-time prover.

1.1 Results and Contributions

We address the above problems with *Brakedown*, a new linear-time field-agnostic SNARK that we design, implement, optimize, and experimentally evaluate.

Concretely, Brakedown achieves the fastest SNARK prover in the literature, even over fields to which prior SNARKs apply. We also implement and evaluate *Shockwave*, a variant of Brakedown that reduces proof sizes and verification times at the cost of sacrificing a linear-time prover, but nonetheless provides a faster prover than prior plausibly post-quantum SNARKs. Brakedown and Shockwave are unconditionally secure in the random oracle model.

SNARK Design Background. Modern SNARKs work by combining a type of interactive protocol called a *polynomial IOP* [28] with a cryptographic primitive called a *polynomial commitment scheme* [45]. The combination yields succinct *interactive* argument, which can then be rendered non-interactive via the Fiat-Shamir transformation [35], yielding a SNARK.

Roughly, a polynomial IOP is an interactive protocol where, in one or more rounds, the prover "sends" to the verifier a very large polynomial q. Because q is so large, one does not wish for the verifier to read a complete description of q. Instead, the verifier only "queries" q at one point (or a handful of points). This means that the only information the verifier needs about q to check that the prover is behaving honestly is one (or a few) evaluations of q.

In turn, a polynomial commitment scheme enables an untrusted prover to succinctly *commit* to a polynomial q, and later provide to the verifier any evaluation $q(r)$ for a point r chosen by the verifier, along with a proof that the returned value is indeed consistent with the committed polynomial.

Essentially, a polynomial commitment scheme is exactly the cryptographic primitive that one needs to obtain a succinct argument from a polynomial IOP. Rather than having the prover send a large polynomial q to the verifier as in the polynomial IOP, the argument system prover cryptographically commits to q and later reveals any evaluations of q required by the verifier to perform its checks.

Design of Our Linear-Time SNARK. We first distill from [21] a polynomial commitment scheme with a linear-time commitment procedure, and show that it satisfies extractability, a key property required in the context of SNARKs (the commitment scheme itself is little more than a rephrasing of the results in [21], though [21] did not analyze extractability). This improves over the prior state-of-the-art polynomial commitment schemes [28,45,49,65,74,78,79] by offering the first in which the time to commit to a polynomial is linear in the size of the polynomial. We focus on multilinear polynomials over the Lagrange basis, but the scheme generalizes to many other types of polynomials such as univariate polynomials over the standard monomial basis (see e.g., [49]).

To obtain linear-time SNARKs for R1CS, we first make explicit a polynomial IOP for R1CS from Spartan [63] and then use our new linear-time polynomial commitment scheme in conjunction with prior compilers [28,63] to transform it into a SNARK for R1CS.

A New and Concretely Fast Linear-Time Encodable Code. A major component in the linear-time polynomial commitment scheme that we distill from [21] is a linear-time encodable linear code. Unfortunately, to the best of our knowledge, existing linear-time encodable codes are highly impractical. We therefore design a new linear-time encodable code that is concretely fast in our context. Our code builds on classic results [34, 36, 67], but designing this code is involved and represents a significant technical contribution. We achieve a fast linear code that works over any (sufficiently large) field by leveraging the following four observations: (1) In our setting, to achieve sublinear sized proofs, it is sufficient for the code to achieve relative Hamming distance only a small constant, rather than very close to 1 (higher minimum distance would improve Brakedown's proof length by a constant factor, but would not meaningfully reduce the prover time); (2) Efficient decoding is not necessary for reasons elaborated upon below; (3) We can (and indeed want to) work over large fields, say, of size at least 2^{127}; and (4) We can use randomized constructions instead of deterministic constructions of pseudorandom objects, so long as the probability that the construction fails to satisfy the necessary distance properties is cryptographically small (e.g., $\leq 2^{-100}$).

Observation (2) holds for the following two reasons: (1) the prover and verifier only execute the code's encoding procedure (this observation also appears in prior work [21]); (2) we describe an efficient extractor for our polynomial commitment scheme that does not invoke the code's decoding procedure. Hence, efficient decoding is not even needed to establish that our SNARK is knowledge-sound.

Observations (1)–(4) together allow us to strip out much of the complexity of prior constructions. For example, Spielman's celebrated work [67] is focused on achieving both linear-time encoding and decoding, while Druk and Ishai [34] focus on improving the minimum distance of Spielman's code. On top of this, we further optimize and simplify the code construction, and provide a detailed, quantitative analysis to show that the probability our code fails to achieve the necessary minimum distance is cryptographically small.

Implementation, Optimization, and Experimental Results. We implement the aforementioned linear-time SNARK, yielding a system we call Brakedown. Because our linear-time code works over any (sufficiently large) field, and the polynomial IOP from Spartan does as well, Brakedown is field-agnostic. This is the first built SNARK to achieve this property. It is also the first built system with a linear-time prover and sub-linear proof sizes and verification times.

We also implement Shockwave, a variant of Brakedown that uses Reed-Solomon codes instead of our fast linear-time code. Since Shockwave uses Reed-Solomon codes, it is not a linear-time SNARK and requires an FFT-friendly finite field, but it provides concretely shorter proofs and lower verification times than Brakedown and is faster than prior plausibly post-quantum secure SNARKs.

Both Shockwave and Brakedown contain simple but crucial concrete optimizations to the polynomial commitment scheme to reduce proof sizes. Neither Shockwave's nor Brakedown's implementations are currently zero-knowledge. However, Shockwave can be rendered zero-knowledge using standard techniques with minimal overhead [4, 30, 76]. Brakedown could be rendered zero-knowledge while maintaining linear prover time by using one layer of recursive composition with zkShockwave (or another zkSNARK). Indeed, subsequent work, called Orion [77], uses Virgo [78] to prove in zero-knowledge the knowledge of valid proofs produced by (a variant of) Brakedown. It is also plausible that Brakedown could be rendered zero-knowledge more directly using techniques from [23].

In terms of experimental results, Brakedown achieves a faster prover than all prior SNARKs for R1CS. Its primary downside is that its proofs are on the larger side, but they are still far smaller than the size of the NP-witness for R1CS instance sizes beyond several million constraints. Shockwave reduces Brakedown's proof sizes and verification times by about a factor of 6×, at the cost of a slower prover (both asymptotically and concretely). Nonetheless, Shockwave already features a concretely faster prover than prior plausibly post-quantum SNARKs. Furthermore, although Shockwave's proof sizes are somewhat larger than most prior schemes with sublinear proof size, they are surprisingly competitive with prior post-quantum schemes such as Fractal [32] and Aurora [14] that have lower *asymptotic* proof size (polylog(N) rather than $\Theta_\lambda(\sqrt{N})$). Its verification times are competitive with discrete-logarithm based schemes, and in fact superior to prior plausibly post-quantum SNARKs.

Public Parameter Generation. The public parameters of Brakedown include a description of the encoding procedure of our error-correcting code. This involves randomly generating certain sparse matrices (we provide details of this in the full version of the paper [40]). Our implementation generates the matrices deterministically using a cryptographic PRG with a public, fixed seed, which could be chosen in a "nothing-up-my-sleeve" way (e.g., as in Bulletproofs [27]). Generating the matrices is concretely fast: our implementation takes under 700 milliseconds to sample parameters suitable for encoding inputs of length 2^{20}, and 22 seconds for encoding inputs of length 2^{25}. The latter setting is suitable for committing to polynomials of degree over 2^{40}, and for giving SNARKs for R1CS instances with roughly 2^{40} constraints. Note that any party acting as the prover or verifier in Brakedown need only generate these matrices once, no matter how many times the SNARK is used.

Subsequent Work on Linear-Time Provers. Xie et al. [77] improve the concrete parameters of the error-correcting code underlying Brakedown. They also compose Brakedown with a different SNARK called Virgo [78] that requires an FFT-friendly field but has smaller proofs. This asymptotically reduces the proof size from $\Theta_\lambda(\sqrt{N})$ to $\Theta_\lambda(\log^2 N)$. The resulting implementation, called Orion, requires an FFT-friendly field, but has substantially smaller proofs than Brakedown, and a slightly faster prover due to the improved code parameters. Orion+ [29] improves Brakedown (this work) and the work of Xie et al. [77] by providing proofs of ≈10 KB at the cost of requiring a (universal) trusted setup and giving up plausible post-quantum security. Vortex [7] builds on Brakedown and uses lattice-based hash functions for improved recursion capabilities.

Recent theoretical works have obtained interactive arguments with constant soundness error and a linear-time prover even over small fields [22,62].

2   Preliminaries

We use $\mathbb{F}$ to denote a finite field, λ to denote the security parameter, and $\mathsf{negl}(()\lambda)$ to denote a negligible function in λ. Unless we specify otherwise, $|\mathbb{F}| = 2^{\Theta(\lambda)}$.

Polynomials. We recall a few basic facts about polynomials. Detailed treatment of these facts can be found elsewhere [69].

- A polynomial over $\mathbb{F}$ is an expression consisting of a sum of *monomials* where each monomial is the product of a constant and powers of one or more variables (which take values from $\mathbb{F}$); all arithmetic is performed over $\mathbb{F}$.
- The degree of a monomial is the sum of the exponents of variables in the monomial; the (total) degree of a polynomial g is the maximum degree of any monomial in g. Also, the degree of a polynomial g in a particular variable x_i is the maximum exponent that x_i takes in any of the monomials in g.
- A *multivariate* polynomial is a polynomial with more than one variable; otherwise it is called a *univariate* polynomial. A multivariate polynomial is called a *multilinear* polynomial if the degree of the polynomial in each variable is at most one.

Rank-1 Constraint Satisfiability (R1CS)

Definition 1. *An R1CS instance is a tuple* $(\mathbb{F}, A, B, C, M, N, \mathsf{io})$, *where* $A, B, C \in \mathbb{F}^{M \times M}$, $M \geq |\mathsf{io}| + 1$, io *denotes the public input and output, and there are at most* $N = \Omega(M)$ *non-zero entries in each matrix.*

We denote the set of R1CS (instance, witness) pairs as $\mathcal{R}_{\mathrm{R1CS}}$, defined as:
$\{\langle(\mathbb{F}, A, B, C, \mathsf{io}, M, N), w\rangle: A \cdot (w, 1, \mathsf{io}) \circ B \cdot (w, 1, \mathsf{io}) = C \cdot (w, 1, \mathsf{io})\}.$

In the rest of the paper, WLOG, we assume that M and N are powers of 2, and that $M = |\mathsf{io}| + 1$. Throughout this paper, all logarithms are to base 2.

SNARKs. We adapt the definition provided in [48].

Definition 2. *Consider a relation $\mathcal{R}$ over public parameters, structure, instance, and witness tuples. A non-interactive argument of knowledge for $\mathcal{R}$ consists of PPT algorithms $(\mathcal{G}, \mathcal{P}, \mathcal{V})$ and deterministic $\mathcal{K}$, denoting the generator, the prover, the verifier and the encoder respectively with the following interface.*

- $\mathcal{G}(1^\lambda) \rightarrow \mathsf{pp}$: *On input security parameter λ, samples public parameters pp.*
- $\mathcal{K}(\mathsf{pp}, \mathsf{s}) \rightarrow (\mathsf{pk}, \mathsf{vk})$: *On input structure s, representing common structure among instances, outputs the prover key pk and verifier key vk.*
- $\mathcal{P}(\mathsf{pk}, u, w) \rightarrow \pi$: *On input instance u and witness w, outputs a proof π proving that $(\mathsf{pp}, \mathsf{s}, u, w) \in \mathcal{R}$.*
- $\mathcal{V}(\mathsf{vk}, u, \pi) \rightarrow \{0, 1\}$: *On input the verifier key vk, instance u, and a proof π, outputs 1 if the instance is accepting and 0 otherwise.*

A non-interactive argument of knowledge satisfies completeness if for any PPT adversary $\mathcal{A}$

$$\Pr\left[\mathcal{V}(\mathsf{vk}, u, \pi) = 1 \,\middle|\, \begin{array}{l} \mathsf{pp} \leftarrow \mathcal{G}(1^\lambda), \\ (\mathsf{s}, (u, w)) \leftarrow \mathcal{A}(\mathsf{pp}), \\ (\mathsf{pp}, \mathsf{s}, u, w) \in \mathcal{R}, \\ (\mathsf{pk}, \mathsf{vk}) \leftarrow \mathcal{K}(\mathsf{pp}, \mathsf{s}), \\ \pi \leftarrow \mathcal{P}(\mathsf{pk}, u, w) \end{array} \right] = 1.$$

pagebreak *A non-interactive argument of knowledge satisfies knowledge sound-ness if for all PPT adversaries $\mathcal{A}$ there exists a PPT extractor $\mathcal{E}$ such that for all randomness ρ*

$$\Pr\left[\begin{array}{c}\mathcal{V}(\mathsf{vk}, u, \pi) = 1, \\ (\mathsf{pp}, \mathsf{s}, u, w) \notin \mathcal{R}\end{array}\middle|\begin{array}{l}\mathsf{pp} \leftarrow \mathcal{G}(1^\lambda), \\ (\mathsf{s}, u, \pi) \leftarrow \mathcal{A}(\mathsf{pp}; \rho), \\ (\mathsf{pk}, \mathsf{vk}) \leftarrow \mathcal{K}(\mathsf{pp}, \mathsf{s}), \\ w \leftarrow \mathcal{E}(\mathsf{pp}, \rho)\end{array}\right] = \mathsf{negl}(\lambda).$$

A non-interactive argument of knowledge is succinct if the size of the proof π and the time to verify it are at most polylogarithmic in the size of the statement proven, where a statement includes both the structure and the instance.

Remark 1. In this paper, we consider an argument system to be succinct as long as the proof sizes and verification times are sublinear in the size of the statement proven. We accept this weakening as proofs produced by such proof systems can be shortened (both asymptotically and concretely) without substantial overheads using depth-1 recursion (e.g., see a subsequent work called Orion [77]).

Polynomial Commitment Scheme. We adapt the definition from [28]. A polynomial commitment scheme for multilinear polynomials is a tuple of four protocols $\mathsf{PC} = (\mathsf{Gen}, \mathsf{Commit}, \mathsf{Open}, \mathsf{Eval})$:

- $pp \leftarrow \mathsf{Gen}(1^\lambda, \mu)$: takes as input μ (the number of variables in a multilinear polynomial); produces public parameters pp.
- $\mathcal{C} \leftarrow \mathsf{Commit}(pp, \mathcal{G})$: takes as input a μ-variate multilinear polynomial over a finite field $\mathcal{G} \in \mathbb{F}[\mu]$; produces a commitment $\mathcal{C}$.
- $b \leftarrow \mathsf{Open}(pp, \mathcal{C}, \mathcal{G})$: verifies the opening of commitment $\mathcal{C}$ to the μ-variate multilinear polynomial $\mathcal{G} \in \mathbb{F}[\mu]$; outputs $b \in \{0, 1\}$.
- $b \leftarrow \mathsf{Eval}(pp, \mathcal{C}, r, v, \mu, \mathcal{G})$ is a protocol between a PPT prover $\mathcal{P}$ and verifier $\mathcal{V}$. Both $\mathcal{V}$ and $\mathcal{P}$ hold a commitment $\mathcal{C}$, the number of variables μ, a scalar $v \in \mathbb{F}$, and $r \in \mathbb{F}^\mu$. $\mathcal{P}$ additionally knows a μ-variate multilinear polynomial $\mathcal{G} \in \mathbb{F}[\mu]$. $\mathcal{P}$ attempts to convince $\mathcal{V}$ that $\mathcal{G}(r) = v$. At the end of the protocol, $\mathcal{V}$ outputs $b \in \{0, 1\}$.

Definition 3. *A tuple of four protocols* $(\mathsf{Gen}, \mathsf{Commit}, \mathsf{Open}, \mathsf{Eval})$ *is an extractable polynomial commitment scheme for multilinear polynomials over a finite field* $\mathbb{F}$ *if the following conditions hold.*

- **Completeness.** *For any μ-variate multilinear polynomial $\mathcal{G} \in \mathbb{F}[\mu]$,*

$$\Pr\left\{\begin{array}{l}pp \leftarrow \mathsf{Gen}(1^\lambda, \mu); \mathcal{C} \leftarrow \mathsf{Commit}(pp, \mathcal{G}): \\ \mathsf{Eval}(pp, \mathcal{C}, r, v, \mu, \mathcal{G}) = 1 \wedge v = \mathcal{G}(r)\end{array}\right\} \geq 1 - \mathsf{negl}(\lambda)$$

- **Binding.** *For any PPT adversary $\mathcal{A}$, size parameter $\mu \geq 1$,*

$$\Pr\left\{\begin{array}{c}pp \leftarrow \mathsf{Gen}(1^\lambda, m); (\mathcal{C}, \mathcal{G}_0, \mathcal{G}_1) = \mathcal{A}(pp); \\ b_0 \leftarrow \mathsf{Open}(pp, \mathcal{C}, \mathcal{G}_0); b_1 \leftarrow \mathsf{Open}(pp, \mathcal{C}, \mathcal{G}_1): \\ b_0 = b_1 \neq 0 \wedge \mathcal{G}_0 \neq \mathcal{G}_1\end{array}\right\} \leq \mathsf{negl}(\lambda)$$

- **Knowledge Soundness.** Eval *is a succinct argument of knowledge for the following NP relation given* $pp \leftarrow \mathsf{Gen}(1^\lambda, \mu)$.

$$\mathcal{R}_{\mathsf{Eval}}(pp) = \{\langle (\mathcal{C}, r, v), (\mathcal{G}) \rangle : \mathcal{G} \in \mathbb{F}[\mu] \wedge \mathcal{G}(r) = v \wedge \mathsf{Open}(pp, \mathcal{C}, \mathcal{G}) = 1\}$$

3 Linear-Time Polynomial Commitments

We distill from Bootle et al. [21] a result establishing the existence of a linear-time commitment scheme for multilinear polynomials over the Lagrange basis with proofs of size $O(N^{1/t})$ for any desired integer constant $t > 0$. Note that this result is implicit in their work.

We then explicitly describe the linear-time polynomial commitment scheme for the case when the parameter $t = 2$. We additionally describe optimizations and prove that the scheme satisfies knowledge soundness.

A General Result Distilled from Bootle et al. [21].

Theorem 1. *For security parameter λ and a positive integer t, given a hash function that can compute a Merkle-hash of N elements of $\mathbb{F}$ with the same time complexity as $O(N)$ $\mathbb{F}$-ops, there exists a linear-time polynomial commitment scheme for multilinear polynomials. Specifically, there exists an algorithm that, given as input the coefficient vector of an ℓ-variate multilinear polynomial over $\mathbb{F}$ over the Lagrange basis, with $N = 2^\ell$, commits to the polynomial, where:*

- *the size of the commitment is $O_\lambda(1)$; and*
- *the running time of the commit algorithm is $O(N)$ operations over $\mathbb{F}$.*

Furthermore, there exists a non-interactive argument of knowledge in the random oracle model to prove the correct evaluation of a committed polynomial with the following parameters:

- *the prover's running time is $O(N)$ operations over $\mathbb{F}$;*
- *the verifier's running time is $O_\lambda(N^{1/t})$ operations over $\mathbb{F}$; and*
- *the proof size is $O_\lambda(N^{1/t})$.*

A proof of this theorem is in the full version of this paper [40].

3.1 Polynomial Commitments for $t = 2$

Notation. g is a multilinear polynomial with n coefficients. We assume for simplicity that $n = m^2$ for some integer m. Let u denote the coefficient vector of g in the Lagrange basis (equivalently, u is the vector of all evaluations of g over inputs in $\{0, 1\}^{\log n}$). Recalling that $[m] = \{1, \ldots, m\}$, we can naturally index entries of u by elements of the set $[m]^2$. It is well known that for any input r to g there exist vectors $q_1, q_2 \in \mathbb{F}^m$ such that $g(r) = \langle (q_1 \otimes q_2), u \rangle$.

For each $i \in [m]$, let us view u as an $m \times m$ matrix, and let u_i denote the ith row of this matrix, i.e., $u_i = \{u_{i,j}\}_{j \in [m]}$.

Let $N = \rho^{-1} \cdot m$, and let $\mathsf{Enc} \colon \mathbb{F}^m \to \mathbb{F}^N$ denote the encoding function of a linear code with constant rate $\rho > 0$ and constant relative distance $\gamma > 0$. We assume that Enc runs in time proportional to that required to perform $O(N)$ operations over $\mathbb{F}$. We assume for simplicity that Enc is systematic, since explicit systematic codes with the properties we require are known [67].

Commitment Phase. Let $\hat{u} = \{\mathsf{Enc}(u_i)\}_{i \in [m]} \in (\mathbb{F}^N)^m$ denote the vector obtained by encoding each row of u. In the IOP setting, the commitment to u is just the vector $\hat{u}$, i.e., the prover sends $\hat{u}$ to the verifier, and the verifier is given point query access to $\hat{u}$. In the derived polynomial commitment scheme in the plain or random oracle model, the commitment to u will be the Merkle-hash of the vector $\hat{u}$. As with u, we may view $\hat{u}$ as a matrix, with $\hat{u}_i \in \mathbb{F}^N$ denoting the ith row of $\hat{u}$ for $i \in [m]$.

Testing Phase. Upon receiving the commitment message, the IOP verifier will interactively test it to confirm that each "row" of u is indeed (close to) a codeword of Enc. We describe this process as occurring in a separate "testing phase" so as to keep the commitment size constant in the plain or random oracle models. In practice, the testing phase can occur during the commit phase, during the evaluation phase, or sometime in between the two.

The verifier sends the prover a random vector $r \in \mathbb{F}^m$, and the prover sends a vector $u' \in \mathbb{F}^m$ claimed to equal the random linear combination of the m rows of u, in which the coefficients of the linear combination are given by r. The verifier reads u' in its entirety.

Next, the verifier tests u' for consistency with $\hat{u}$. That is, the verifier will pick $\ell = \Theta(\lambda)$ random entries of the codeword $\mathsf{Enc}(u') \in \mathbb{F}^N$ and confirm that $\mathsf{Enc}(u')$ is consistent with $v \in \mathbb{F}^N$ at those entries, where v is:

$$\sum_{i=1}^{m} r_i \hat{u}_i \in \mathbb{F}^N. \tag{1}$$

Observe that, by definition of v (Eq. (1)), any individual entry v_j of v can be learned by querying m entries of $\hat{u}$ (we refer to these m entries as the "j'th column" of $\hat{u}$). Meanwhile, since the verifier reads u' in its entirety; $\mathcal{V}$ can compute $\mathsf{Enc}(u')_j$ for all desired $j \in [N]$ in $O(m)$ time.

Evaluation Phase. Let $q_1, q_2 \in \mathbb{F}^m$ be such that $g(r) = \langle (q_1 \otimes q_2), u \rangle$. The evaluation phase is identical to the testing phase, except that r is replaced with q_1 (and the verifier uses fresh randomness to choose the sets of coordinates used for consistency testing). Let $u'' \in \mathbb{F}^m$ denote the vector that the prover sends in this phase, which is claimed to equal $\sum_{i=1}^{m} q_{1,i} \cdot u_i$. If the prover is honest, then u'' satisfies $\langle u'', q_2 \rangle = \langle (q_1 \otimes q_2), u \rangle$. Hence, if the verifier's consistency tests all pass in the testing and evaluation phases, the verifier outputs $\langle u'', q_2 \rangle$ as $g(r)$.

Concrete Optimizations to the Commitment Scheme. We discuss optimizations to reduce proof sizes in the testing and evaluation phases by large constant factors without affecting the correctness guarantees of the commitment scheme.

Description of polynomial commitment in the language of IOPs. Following standard transformations [15,47,55,70], in the actual polynomial commitment scheme, vectors sent by the prover in the IOP may be replaced with a Merkle-commitment to that vector, and each query the verifier makes to a vector is answered by the prover along with Merkle-tree authentication path for the answer. Each phase of the scheme can be rendered non-interactive using the Fiat-Shamir transformation [35].

Commit phase.

- $\mathcal{P} \rightarrow \mathcal{V}$: a vector $\hat{u} = (\hat{u}_1, \ldots, \hat{u}_m) \in \left(\mathbb{F}^N\right)^m$. If $\mathcal{P}$ is honest, each "row" $\hat{u}_i$ of $\hat{u}$ contains a codeword in Enc.

Testing phase.

- $\mathcal{V} \rightarrow \mathcal{P}$: a random vector $r \in \mathbb{F}^m$.
- $\mathcal{P} \rightarrow \mathcal{V}$ sends a vector $u' \in \mathbb{F}^m$ claimed to equal $v = \sum_{i=1}^m r_i \cdot u_i \in \mathbb{F}^m$.
- //Now $\mathcal{V}$ probabilistically checks consistency between $\hat{u}$ and u' ($\mathcal{V}$ reads u' in entirety).
- $\mathcal{V}$: chooses Q to be a random set of size $\ell = \Theta(\lambda)$ with $Q \subseteq [N]$. For each $j \in Q$:
  - $\mathcal{V}$ queries all m entries of the corresponding "column" of $\hat{u}$, namely $\hat{u}_{1,j}, \ldots, \hat{u}_{m,j}$.
  - $\mathcal{V}$ confirms that $\mathsf{Enc}(u')_j = \sum_{i=1}^m r_i \cdot \hat{u}_{i,j}$, halting and rejecting if not.

Evaluation phase.

- Let $q_1, q_2 \in \mathbb{F}^m$ be such that $g(r) = \langle (q_1 \otimes q_2), z \rangle$.
- The evaluation phase is identical to the testing phase, except that r is replaced with q_1 (and fresh randomness is used to choose a set Q' of columns for use in consistency checking).
- If all consistency tests pass, then $\mathcal{V}$ outputs $\langle u', q_2 \rangle$ as $g(r)$.

- In settings where the evaluation phase will only be run once, the testing phase and evaluation phase can be run in parallel and the same query set Q can be used for both testing and evaluation. This saves $\approx 2\times$ in proof sizes.
- For simplicity, we describe the commitment scheme in the setting where u is indexed by $[m]^2$, i.e., u was viewed as a square matrix, this is not a requirement, and the proof size in the testing and evaluation phases can be substantially reduced by exploiting this flexibility. Specifically, if r and c denote the number of rows and columns of u, so that the number of entries in u is $c \cdot r = N$, then the proof length of the commitment scheme is roughly $2c + r \cdot \ell$ field elements where ℓ is the number of columns of the encoded matrix opened by the verifier. Here, the $2c$ term comes from the prover sending two different linear combination of the rows of u, one in the commitment phase and one in the evaluation phase, while the $r \cdot \ell$ term comes from the

verifier querying ℓ different columns of u in the testing and evaluation phases. (This optimization appeared in Ligero [4] in the context of the Reed-Solomon code.) To minimize proof length, one should set $c \approx r\ell/2$, or equivalently, one should set $r \approx \sqrt{2/\ell} \cdot \sqrt{N}$ and $c \approx \sqrt{\ell/2} \cdot \sqrt{N}$. This reduces the proof length from roughly $\ell \cdot \sqrt{N}$ if a square matrix is used, to roughly $\sqrt{2\ell} \cdot \sqrt{N}$, a savings of a factor of $\sqrt{\ell/2}$. Asymptotically, this means the proof length falls from $\Theta(\lambda\sqrt{N})$ if a square matrix is used, down to $\Theta(\sqrt{\lambda N})$, a quadratic improvement in the dependence on λ. To achieve soundness error, say, 2^{-100}, ℓ will be on the order of hundreds or thousands depending on the relative Hamming distance of the code used, and hence this optimization will lead to a reduction in proof length relative to the use of square matrices by one or more orders of magnitude.

– In settings where the commitment is trusted (e.g., applying the polynomial commitment to achieve holography), the testing phase can be omitted. An additional concrete optimization that applies when working over fields of size smaller than $\exp(\lambda)$ is in the full version of the paper [40].

– If $\mathcal{P}$ commits to the vector $\hat{u} \in (\mathbb{F}^N)^m$ with a Merkle tree, then revealing ℓ columns of $\hat{u}$ in the Testing and Evaluation phases would require providing $m \cdot \ell$ Merkle-authentication paths. Naively, this may require $\mathcal{P}$ to send up to $\Theta(m \cdot \ell \cdot \log m)$ hash values. However, by arranging the vector $\hat{u}$ in column-major order before Merkle-hashing it, the communication cost of revealing ℓ columns of $\hat{u}$ can be reduced to just the $m \cdot \ell$ requested field elements plus $O(\log m)$ hash values (a similar optimization appears in prior work [9]).

Soundness Analysis for the Testing Phase. The following claim roughly states that if $\hat{u} = (\hat{u}_1, \ldots, \hat{u}_m) \in (\mathbb{F}^N)^m$, then if even a single $\hat{u}_i$ is far from all codewords in Enc, then a random linear combination of the $\hat{u}_i$'s is also far from all codewords with high probability.

Claim. (Ames, Hazay, Ishai, and Venkitasubramaniam [4], Roth and Zémor) Let $\hat{u} = (\hat{u}_1, \ldots, \hat{u}_m) \in (\mathbb{F}^N)^m$ and for each $i \in [m]$ let c_i be the closest codeword in Enc to $\hat{u}_i$. Let E with $|E| \leq (\gamma/3)N$ be a subset of the columns $j \in [N]$ of $\hat{u}$ on which there is even one row $i \in [m]$ such that $\hat{u}_{i,j} \neq c_{i,j}$. With probability at least $1 - (|E| + 1)/|\mathbb{F}| > 1 - N/|\mathbb{F}|$ over the choice of $r \in \mathbb{F}^m$, $\sum_{i=1}^m r_i \cdot \hat{u}_i$ has distance at least $|E|$ from any codeword in Enc.

Lemma 1. *If the prover passes all of the checks in the testing phase with probability at least $N/|\mathbb{F}| + (1 - \gamma/3)^\ell$, then there is a sequence of m codewords $c_1, \ldots, c_m$ in Enc such that*

$$E := |\{j \in [N]: \exists i \in [m] \text{ such that } c_{i,j} \neq \hat{u}_{i,j}\}| \leq (\gamma/3)N. \tag{2}$$

Proof. Let $d(b, c)$ denote the relative Hamming distance between two vectors $b, c \in \mathbb{F}^N$. Assume by way of contradiction that Eq. (2) does not hold. We explain that the prover passes the consistency tests during the testing phase with probability less than $N/|\mathbb{F}| + (1 - \gamma/3)^\ell$.

Recall that v denotes $\sum_{i=1}^{m} r_i \hat{u}_i$. By Claim 3.1, the probability over the verifier's choice of r that there exists a codeword a satisfying $d(a, v) > \gamma/3$ is less than $N/|\mathbb{F}|$. If no such a exists, then $d(\mathsf{Enc}(u'), v) \geq \gamma/3$. In this event, all of the verifier's consistency tests pass with probability at most $(1 - \gamma/3)^{\ell}$.

Completeness and Binding. Completeness holds by design. To argue binding, recall from the analysis of the testing phase that c_i denotes the codeword in Enc that is closest to row i of $\hat{u}$, and let $w := \sum_{i=1}^{m} q_{1,i} \cdot c_i$. We show that, if the prover passes the verifier's checks in the testing phase with probability more than $N/|\mathbb{F}| + (1 - \gamma/3)^{\ell}$ and passes the verifier's checks in the evaluation phase with probability more than $(1 - (2/3)\gamma)^{\ell}$, then $w = \mathsf{Enc}(u'')$.

If $w \neq \mathsf{Enc}(u'')$, then w and $\mathsf{Enc}(u'')$ are two distinct codewords in Enc and hence they can agree on at most $(1 - \gamma) \cdot N$ coordinates. Denote this agreement set by A. The verifier rejects in the evaluation phase if there is any $j \in Q'$ such that $j \notin A \cup E$, where E is as in Eq. (2). $|A \cup E| \leq |A| + |E| \leq (1 - \gamma) \cdot N + (\gamma/3)N = (1 - (2/3)\gamma)N$, and hence a randomly chosen column $j \in [N]$ is in $A \cup E$ with probability at most $1 - (2/3)\gamma$. It follows that u'' will pass the verifier's consistency checks in the evaluation phase with probability at most $(1 - (2/3)\gamma)^{\ell}$.

In summary, if the prover passes the verifier's checks in the commitment phase with probability at least

$$N/|\mathbb{F}| + (1 - \gamma/3)^{\ell}, \tag{3}$$

then, in the following sense, the prover is *bound* to the polynomial g^* whose coefficients in the Lagrange basis are given by $c_{1,1}, \ldots, c_{m,m}$, where $c_i \in \mathbb{F}^N$ denotes the closest codeword to row i of the vector $\hat{u}$ sent in the commitment phase: on evaluation query r, the verifier either outputs $g^*(r)$, or else rejects in the evaluation phase with probability at least

$$1 - (1 - (2/3)\gamma)^{\ell}. \tag{4}$$

The polynomial commitment scheme provides standard extractability properties. We show this by giving two different extractors.

Extractability via Efficient Decoding. The first is a simple straight-line extractor that is efficient if the error-correcting code Enc has a polynomial-time decoding procedure that can correct up to a $\gamma/4$ fraction of errors. This is because with the IOP-to-succinct-argument transformation of [15,47,55,70], it is known that, given a prover $\mathcal{P}$ that convinces the argument-system verifier to accept with non-negligible probability, there is an efficient straight-line extractor capable of outputting IOP proof string π that "opens" the Merkle commitment sent by the argument system prover in the commitment phase. Moreover, there is an IOP prover strategy $\mathcal{P}'$ for the testing and evaluation phases by which $\mathcal{P}'$ can convince the IOP verifier in those phases to accept with non-negligible probability when the first IOP message is π ($\mathcal{P}'$ merely simulates $\mathcal{P}$ in those phases).

Our analysis of the testing phase of the polynomial commitment scheme (Lemma 1) then guarantees that each row of the extracted string π has relative Hamming distance at most $\gamma/3$ from some codeword. Hence, row-by-row decoding provides the coefficients of the multilinear polynomial that the prover is bound to. If the decoding procedure runs in polynomial time, the extractor is efficient.

Extractability Without Decoding. If the error-correcting code does not support efficient decoding, then even though one can efficiently extract the IOP proof string π underlying the Merkle-commitment sent in the commitment phase of the commitment scheme, one can not necessarily decode (each row of) the string to efficiently extract from π the polynomial that the commiter is bound to.

Instead, the extractor can proceed as follows. We assume throughout the below that Expressions (3) and (4) are negligible (say, exponentially small in the security parameter λ), which holds so long as $|\mathbb{F}| \geq \exp(\lambda)$ and the number of column openings is $\ell = \Theta(\lambda)$.

The testing phase of the commitment scheme can be viewed as a 3-move public-coin argument in which the verifier moves first. First, the verifier sends a challenge vector $r \in \mathbb{F}^m$. Second, the prover responds with a vector claimed to equal $\sum_{i=1}^m r_i u_i$. Third, the verifier chooses a set Q of random columns to use in the consistency test, and performs the consistency test by querying the committed proof string π at all entries of the columns in Q.

Given any efficient prover strategy that passes the verifier's checks in the testing phase with non-negligible probability, we show in the following lemma that there is a polynomial-time extraction procedure capable of outputting m linearly independent challenge vectors $r_1, \ldots, r_m \in \mathbb{F}^m$ from the testing phase of the protocol, and m response vectors $u'_1, \ldots, u'_m \in \mathbb{F}^m$ of the prover, each of which pass the verifier's consistency checks in the testing phase with non-negligible probability.

Lemma 2. *Suppose there is a deterministic prover strategy $\mathcal{P}$ that, following the commitment phase of the polynomial commitment scheme, passes the verifier's checks in the testing phase of the polynomial commitment scheme with probability ϵ. Then there is a randomized extraction procedure $\mathcal{E}$ that runs in expected time $\mathrm{poly}(m, \lambda, 1/\epsilon)$ and such that the following holds. Given the ability to repeatedly rewind $\mathcal{P}$ to the start of the testing phase, with probability at least $1 - 2^{-\Omega(\lambda)}$, $\mathcal{E}$ outputs m linearly independent challenge vectors $r_1, \ldots, r_m \in \mathbb{F}^m$ from the testing phase, and m corresponding response vectors $u'_1, \ldots, u'_m \in \mathbb{F}^m$ of the prover, each of which pass the verifier's checks in the testing phase with probability at least ϵ.*

Before proving Lemma 2, we explain how to extract the desired polynomial given the extracted challenge vectors $r_1, \ldots, r_m \in \mathbb{F}^m$ and m response vectors $u'_1, \ldots, u'_m \in \mathbb{F}^m$. Observe that the testing phase and the evaluation phase of the polynomial commitment scheme are identical up to how the challenge vector is selected. In addition, for each challenge r_i the prover's response u'_i passes the verifier's consistency checks with non-negligible probability. Hence, the binding analysis for the commitment scheme implies that $u'_1, \ldots, u'_m$ are all consistent with the evaluations of a fixed multilinear polynomial g^*, i.e., for $i = 1, \ldots, m$, $u'_i = r_i^T \cdot C$ where C is the coefficient matrix of g^* in the Lagrange basis. Since the r_i vectors are linearly independent, these m linear equations uniquely specify C, and in fact C can be found in polynomial time using Gaussian elimination.

Proof. We begin the proof by assuming that the extractor knows ϵ. We later explain how to remove this assumption. We refer to the extraction procedure that depends on ϵ as the "base extraction procedure".

If $\epsilon < 1/\sqrt{|\mathbb{F}|}$, then the base extractor can simply abort, by assumption that the field size is at least $\exp(\lambda)$. Below, we assume that $\epsilon > 1/\sqrt{|\mathbb{F}|}$.

Fix the extracted proof string $\pi = (\pi_1, \ldots, \pi_m) \in (\mathbb{F}^N)^m$ that "opens" the Merkle-commitment sent by the committer during the commitment phase.

Observe that for any verifier challenge $r' \in \mathbb{F}^m$ and prover response u', one can efficiently compute the probability (over the random choice of column set Q) that u' will pass the verifier's consistency checks. Specifically, if η is the number of columns i such that $\left(\sum_{j=1}^m r'_j \pi_j \right)_i = u'_i$, and ℓ is the number of columns selected by the verifier, then this probability is $(\eta/N)^\ell$ (here, for simplicity let us assume columns are selected with replacement, but an exact expression can also be given when columns are selected without replacement).

Let T denote the set of all challenges r such that $\mathcal{P}$'s response u to r passes the consistency checks with probability at least $\epsilon/2$. By averaging, since $\mathcal{P}$ passes all checks in the testing phase with probability at least ϵ, $|T| \geq (\epsilon/2) \cdot |\mathbb{F}|^m$. The extractor's goal is to efficiently identify a subset $S = \{r_1, \ldots, r_m\}$ of T that spans $\mathbb{F}^m$.

The extractor $\mathcal{E}$ works by repeatedly picking challenge vectors r uniformly at random from $\mathbb{F}^m$, and running $\mathcal{P}$ on challenge r to get a response u; this enables $\mathcal{E}$ to determine whether $r \in T$, and if so, $\mathcal{E}$ adds r to S. The extractor tries $\ell = 18(m + \lambda)/\epsilon$ vectors r, aborting if it fails to identify at least m vectors in T. We claim that the probability the extractor fails to identify m vectors to add to S is at most $1 - 2^{-(m+\lambda)}$. To see this, model each choice of challenge vector r as a Poisson trial with success probability at least $\epsilon/2$. Let μ be the expected number of successes after ℓ Poisson trials each with success probability at least $\epsilon/2$. Then μ is at least $\ell \cdot \epsilon/2 \geq 9(m+\lambda)$. Let $\delta = 1/2$. Since $m \leq \mu/9 \leq (1-\delta) \cdot \mu$, standard Chernoff bounds (e.g., [56, Theorem 4.5]) upper bound the probability that the number of successes is less than m by $e^{-\mu\delta^2/2} \leq e^{-9(m+\lambda)/8} \leq 2^{-(m+\lambda)}$.

We now argue that with probability at least $1 - (m - 1) \cdot (2/\epsilon) \cdot |\mathbb{F}|^{-1}$, the first m vectors that $\mathcal{E}$ adds to S are linearly independent (in the event that this is not the case, the extractor aborts). Denote these m vectors by $r_1, \ldots, r_m \in \mathbb{F}^m$. Observe that each vector r_i is a random element of T. We now explain that for each $i = 2, \ldots, m$, the probability that $r_i \in \text{span}(r_1, \ldots, r_{i-1})$ is at most $(m - 1) \cdot (2/\epsilon) \cdot |\mathbb{F}|^{-1}$. To see this, observe that since the dimension of $\text{span}(r_1, \ldots, r_{i-1})$ is at most $i-1$, the span contains at most $|\mathbb{F}|^{i-1}$ vectors. Since r_i is a uniform random vector from T and $|T| \geq (\epsilon/2) \cdot \mathbb{F}^m$, the probability that $r_i \in \text{span}(r_1, \ldots, r_{i-1})$ is at most $(2/\epsilon) \cdot |\mathbb{F}|^{i-1}/|\mathbb{F}|^m \leq (2/\epsilon) \cdot |\mathbb{F}|^{-1}$. The claim then follows by a union bound over all $m-1$ vectors $r_2, \ldots, r_m$. That is, the probability that $r_1, \ldots, r_m$ are not linearly independent is at most $(m-1) \cdot (2/\epsilon) \cdot |\mathbb{F}|^{-1}$.

Since $\epsilon > 1/\sqrt{|\mathbb{F}|}$, we conclude that the extractor aborts with probability at most $2^{-(m+\lambda)} + (m-1)/\sqrt{|\mathbb{F}|}$. This is a negligible function, by the assumption that $|\mathbb{F}|$ is at least $\exp(\lambda)$.

The above base extraction procedure depends on ϵ, because the extractor tries out $\ell = 18(m+\lambda)/\epsilon$ vectors r (aborting if it fails to identify m vectors in T within that many tries). The following modification eliminates this dependence. Iteratively run the base extraction procedure with ϵ set to the geometrically decreasing sequence of values $\epsilon' = 2^{-1}, 2^{-2}, \ldots, 2^{-\lambda/8}$ halting when the extraction procedure succeeds, and aborting if the extractor reaches $\epsilon' < 2^{-\lambda/8}$ without a witness being identified. The above analysis guarantees that when the extraction procedure is run with ϵ' less than or equal to ϵ, it successfully outputs a witness with probability at least $1 - 2^{-(m+\lambda)} - (m-1)/\sqrt{|\mathbb{F}|} \geq 1 - 2^{-\lambda/3}$. The expected runtime of this modified extraction procedure is at most $36(m+\lambda)/\epsilon + 2^{-\lambda/3} \cdot 18(m+\lambda) \cdot 2^{\lambda/8} \leq \mathrm{poly}(m, \lambda, 1/\epsilon)$. $\square$

The extraction procedure given in Lemma 2 succeeds with overwhelming probability and runs in expected time $\mathrm{poly}(m, \lambda, 1/\epsilon)$ given access to a prover that produces an accepting proof with probability at least ϵ. However, if ϵ is not inverse-polynomial in m and λ, this expected runtime is not polynomial in m and λ. The definition of knowledge soundness (Definition 2) and extractable polynomial commitments (Definition 3) requires that the extractor run in expected polynomial time *regardless of* ϵ, and that whenever the prover succeeds in outputting a convincing proof π, the extractor outputs a witness with all but negligible probability. The lemma below achieves this.

Lemma 3. *There is a randomized extraction procedure $\mathcal{E}$ that runs in expected time $\mathrm{poly}(m, \lambda)$ and such that the following holds. $\mathcal{E}$ first runs $\mathcal{P}$ once during the testing phase of the above polynomial commitment scheme. If $\mathcal{P}$ fails to pass the verifier's checks on the first run, the extractor aborts. Otherwise, with probability at least $1 - 2^{-\Omega(\lambda)}$, $\mathcal{E}$ outputs m linearly independent challenge vectors $r_1, \ldots, r_m \in \mathbb{F}^m$ from the testing phase, and m corresponding response vectors $u'_1, \ldots, u'_m \in \mathbb{F}^m$ of the prover, each of which pass the verifier's checks in the testing phase with probability at least ϵ.*

Proof. We follow the presentation of Hazay and Lindell [43, Theorem 6.5.6] of an extraction strategy originally due to Goldreich [38].

As described in the statement of the lemma, $\mathcal{E}$ first runs $\mathcal{P}$ once during the testing phase, and if $\mathcal{P}$ does not pass the verifier's checks, then $\mathcal{E}$ aborts. If $\mathcal{P}$ does pass the verifier's checks in the testing phase, then $\mathcal{E}$ proceeds to estimate the value ϵ (i.e., the probability that $\mathcal{P}$ indeed passes the verifier's checks in the testing phase). It does this by rewinding $\mathcal{P}$ to the start of the testing phase until $12 \cdot (m+\lambda)$ successful verifications occur. If T runs of $\mathcal{P}$ are required before $12 \cdot (m+\lambda)$ successful verifications occur, then the extractor uses $\epsilon' = 12 \cdot (m+\lambda)/T$ as an estimate of ϵ. The extractor then runs the base extraction procedure from the proof of Lemma 2 with ϵ set to $\epsilon'/2$. Throughout its entire execution, the extractor also keeps a counter of how many times it has run the prover through the testing phase of the polynomial commitment scheme, and if this number ever exceeds 2^m, it aborts. In this event, we say that the extractor has "timed out".

Let us analyze the success probability of the extractor under the assumption that $\epsilon > 2^{-m/2}$ (if $\epsilon \leq 2^{-m/2}$, then ϵ is negligible, and hence it is acceptable for the extractor to succeed with probability 0). [43, Proof of Theorem 6.5.6] shows that with probability at least $1 - 2^{-m+\lambda}$, ϵ' is between $2\epsilon/3$ and 2ϵ. We call this the "good event". Since $\epsilon > 2^{-m/2}$, if the good event occurs, the extractor runs in fewer than 2^m steps and hence does not time out. And the proof of Lemma 2 shows that, conditioned on the good event occurring, the extractor succeeds with probability at least $1 - 2^{-(m+\lambda)} - (m-1)/\sqrt{|\mathbb{F}|}$. Hence, by a union bound, the extractor succeeds with probability at least $1 - 2^{-(m+\lambda)} - (m-1)/\sqrt{|\mathbb{F}|} - 2^{-m+\lambda} \geq 1 - 2^{-\Omega(\lambda)}$.

We now explain that the above extractor runs in expected polynomial time, regardless of the value of ϵ. Let us first consider the case that $\epsilon \leq 2^{-m}$. The probability that the prover passes the verifier's checks in the first prover execution is ϵ, and the extractor never runs for more than 2^m steps. So in this case the expected runtime of the extractor is at most $\epsilon \cdot 2^m \leq 1$, plus the time required to run the verification procedure of the testing phase, which is polynomial in m and λ.

Now consider the case that $\epsilon > 2^{-m}$. The first run of the prover passes the verifier's tests with probability ϵ. If this does not happen, the extractor aborts. Otherwise, the extractor proceeds. If the extractor proceeds and the good event occurs, the extractor runs in time at most $O((m + \lambda)/\epsilon)$. The good event fails to occur with probability only at most $2^{-(m+\lambda)}$, and in this case the extractor still does not run for more than 2^m steps.

Hence, the expected runtime of the extractor is at most

$$O(\epsilon \cdot (m + \lambda)/\epsilon + 2^m \cdot 2^{-(m+\lambda)}) = O(m + \lambda).$$

□

The runtime of our knowledge extractor that does not perform decoding may imply reduced concrete security, but the effect is small. Compared to the extractor that uses efficient decoding, the rewinding extractor requires m "successful" executions of the prover rather than just one, where $m = \sqrt{n}$, for n equal to the degree of the committed polynomial. So, roughly speaking, the runtime of the rewinding extractor is worse by a factor of m, plus an additive term that accounts for the cost of Gaussian elimination.

In the context of Brakedown (our SNARK for R1CS that utilizes this polynomial commitment scheme, see Sect. 5), n is roughly equal to the number of R1CS constraints. As an example, when Brakedown is used to prove a statement about a cryptographic primitive, e.g., knowledge of pre-image of a hash function that is implemented in (say) $1000 \cdot \lambda$ R1CS constraints, then a factor-of-m increase in extractor time corresponds to a loss of roughly $(1/2) \cdot \log(1000\lambda)$ bits of security, which in practice is less than 10 bits.

4 Fast Linear Codes with Linear-Time Encoding

This section describes our construction of practical linear codes with linear-time encoding that we use in Brakedown's implementation of the polynomial commitment scheme from Sect. 3.1. We begin with a sketch of our encoding procedure and of the analysis of its minimum distance.

Overview of Encoding. In this overview we restrict our attention to a construction of a code with distance $\delta = 1/20$ and rate $\rho = 3/5$. The encoding procedure is recursive. For a message $x \in \mathbb{F}^n$ of length n, the codeword consists of three parts $\mathsf{Enc}(x) = (x, z, v)$. The first is the "systematic part" that just copies the message x of length n. The other parts (z, v) are obtained via the following three-step process. First, multiply x by a random sparse $n \times n/5$ matrix to "compress" x to a vector y of length $n/5$. Then obtain z of length $n/3$ by recursively encoding y, and finally obtain v of length $n/3$ by multiplying z by a random sparse $n/3 \times n/3$ matrix B.

Overview of Distance Analysis. The distance analysis proceeds in three cases. Since the code is linear, we merely need to show that the encoding of any non-zero message x has Hamming weight at least $\delta n/\rho = n/12$. We sketch the analysis for a fixed x, but the formal analysis in our full version of the paper [40] holds with overwhelming probability for all x simultaneously.

- If the Hamming weight of x is $> n/12$, then the systematic part x of $\mathsf{Enc}(x)$ already ensures that $\mathsf{Enc}(x)$ has a sufficiently large Hamming weight.
- Otherwise, we show that with overwhelming probability over the random choice of A, y will be non-zero. This, in turn, ensures by induction that $z = \mathsf{Enc}(y)$ has "reasonably large" Hamming weight, at least $n/60$. If the Hamming weight of z is in fact larger than $n/12$ then we are done because z is part of $\mathsf{Enc}(x)$.
- Otherwise, the Hamming weight of z is between $n/60$ and $n/12$. In this case, we show that, with overwhelming probability, B "mixes" the non-zero coordinates of z, and results in a $v = zB$ of Hamming weight at least $n/12$, completing the analysis.

A full version of our paper [40] provides details of our linear-time codes.

5 Linear-Time SNARKs for R1CS

The following theorem captures our main result.

Theorem 2. *Assuming that $|\mathbb{F}| = 2^{\Theta(\lambda)}$ there exists a preprocessing SNARK for $\mathcal{R}_{R1CS}$ in the random oracle model, with the following efficiency characteristics, where M denotes the dimensions of the R1CS matrices, N denotes the number of non-zero entries, and a fixed positive integer t:*

- *the preprocessing cost to the verifier is $O(N)$ $\mathbb{F}$-ops;*
- *the running time of the prover is $O(N)$ $\mathbb{F}$-ops;*

- *the running time of the verifier is $O_\lambda(N^{1/t})$ $\mathbb{F}$-ops; and*
- *the proof size is $O_\lambda(N^{1/t})$.*

A proof of Theorem 2 is in the full version of the paper [40]. In a nutshell, we obtain a SNARK with the claimed performance profile as follows. We first make explicit Spartan's polynomial IOP for R1CS. We then combine our polynomial commitment schemes with Spartan's polynomial IOP to obtain a succinct argument per prior compilers [28]. Finally, to achieve linear-time computation commitments (also called holography) we invoke prior techniques [63] to transform our polynomial commitment scheme from Theorem 1 into one that handles so-called *sparse* multilinear polynomials. This step is necessary because the polynomials used in Spartan's IOP to "capture" the R1CS matrices are sparse.

5.1   A Self-contained Description of Brakedown and Shockwave

For an R1CS instance, $\mathbb{X} = (\mathbb{F}, A, B, C, M, N, \text{io})$ and a purported witness W, let $Z = (W, 1, \text{io})$. For ease of notation, we assume that the vector W and the vector $(1, \text{io})$ have the same length. We interpret the matrices A, B, C as functions mapping domain $\{0,1\}^{\log M} \times \{0,1\}^{\log M}$ to $\mathbb{F}$ in the natural way. That is, an input in $\{0,1\}^{\log M} \times \{0,1\}^{\log M}$ is interpreted as the binary representation of an index $(i, j) \in [M] \times [M]$, where $[M] := \{1, \ldots, M\}$ and the function outputs the (i, j)'th entry of the matrix. Similarly we interpret Z and $(1, \text{io})$ as functions with the following respective signatures in the same manner: $\{0,1\}^s \to \mathbb{F}$ and $\{0,1\}^{s-1} \to \mathbb{F}$.

Note that the *multilinear extension (MLE) polynomial* $\widetilde{Z}$ of Z satisfies

$$\widetilde{Z}(X_1, \ldots, X_{\log M}) = (1 - X_1) \cdot \widetilde{W}(X_2, \ldots, X_{\log M}) + $$
$$X_1 \cdot \widetilde{(1, \text{io})}(X_2, \ldots, X_{\log M}). \tag{5}$$

Here, the MLE refers to the unique multilinear polynomial $\widetilde{Z}$ satisfying $\widetilde{Z}(x_1, \ldots, x_{\log M}) = Z(x_1, \ldots, x_{\log M})$ for all $(x_1, \ldots x_{\log M}) \in \{0,1\}^{\log M}$. Indeed, the RHS of Eq. (5) is a multilinear polynomial, and it is easily checked that $\widetilde{Z}(x_1, \ldots, x_{\log M}) = Z(x_1, \ldots, x_{\log M})$ for all $x_1, \ldots, x_{\log M}$ (since the first half of the evaluations of Z are given by W and the second half are given by the vector $(1, \text{io})$).

From [63, Theorem 4.1], checking if $(\mathbb{X}, W) \in \mathcal{R}_{\text{R1CS}}$ is equivalent, except for a soundness error of $\log M / |\mathbb{F}|$ over the choice of $\tau \in \mathbb{F}^s$, to checking if the following identity holds:

$$0 \stackrel{?}{=} \sum_{x \in \{0,1\}^s} \widetilde{eq}(\tau, x) \cdot$$

$$\left[\left(\sum_{y \in \{0,1\}^s} \widetilde{A}(x,y) \cdot \widetilde{Z}(y) \right) \cdot \left(\sum_{y \in \{0,1\}^s} \widetilde{B}(x,y) \cdot \widetilde{Z}(y) \right) \right.$$

$$\left. - \sum_{y \in \{0,1\}^s} \widetilde{C}(x,y) \cdot \widetilde{Z}(y) \right] \tag{6}$$

where $\widetilde{eq}$ is the MLE of $eq : \{0,1\}^s \times \{0,1\}^s \to \mathbb{F}$:

$$eq(x, e) = \begin{cases} 1 & \text{if } x = e \\ 0 & \text{otherwise.} \end{cases}$$

That is, if $(\mathbb{X}, W) \in \mathcal{R}_{\text{R1CS}}$, then Eq. (6) holds with probability 1 over the choice of τ, and if $(\mathbb{X}, W) \notin \mathcal{R}_{\text{R1CS}}$, then Eq. (6) holds with probability at most $O(\log M/|\mathbb{F}|)$ over the random choice of τ.

Consider computing the right hand side of Eq. (6) by applying the well-known *sum-check protocol* [54] to the polynomial

$$g(x) := \widetilde{eq}(\tau, x) \cdot$$

$$\left[\left(\sum_{y \in \{0,1\}^s} \widetilde{A}(x,y) \cdot \widetilde{Z}(y) \right) \cdot \left(\sum_{y \in \{0,1\}^s} \widetilde{B}(x,y) \cdot \widetilde{Z}(y) \right) \right.$$

$$\left. - \sum_{y \in \{0,1\}^s} \widetilde{C}(x,y) \cdot \widetilde{Z}(y) \right]$$

From the verifier's perspective, this reduces the task of computing the right hand side of Eq. (6) to the task of evaluating g at a random input $r_x \in \mathbb{F}^s$. Note that the verifier can evaluate $\widetilde{eq}(\tau, r_x)$ unassisted in $O(\log M)$ field operations, as it is easily checked that $\widetilde{eq}(\tau, r_x) = \prod_{i=1}^s (\tau_i r_{x,i} + (1 - \tau_i)(1 - r_{x,i}))$. With $\widetilde{eq}(\tau, r_x)$ in hand, $g(r_x)$ can be computed in $O(1)$ time given the three quantities $\sum_{y \in \{0,1\}^s} \widetilde{A}(r_x, y) \cdot \widetilde{Z}(y)$, $\sum_{y \in \{0,1\}^s} \widetilde{B}(r_x, y) \cdot \widetilde{Z}(y)$, and $\sum_{y \in \{0,1\}^s} \widetilde{C}(r_x, y) \cdot \widetilde{Z}(y)$.

These three quantities can be computed by applying the sum-check protocol three more times in parallel, once to each of the following three polynomials (using the same random vector of field elements, $r_y \in \mathbb{F}^s$, in each of the three invocations): $\widetilde{A}(r_x, y) \cdot \widetilde{Z}(y)$, $\widetilde{B}(r_x, y) \cdot \widetilde{Z}(y)$, $\widetilde{C}(r_x, y) \cdot \widetilde{Z}(y)$.

To perform the verifier's final check in each of these three invocations of the sum-check protocol, it suffices for the verifier to evaluate each of the above 3 polynomials at the random vector r_y, which means it suffices for the verifier to evaluate $\widetilde{A}(r_x, r_y)$, $\widetilde{B}(r_x, r_y)$, $\widetilde{C}(r_x, r_y)$, and $\widetilde{Z}(r_y)$. We present the protocol in this section assuming that the verifier can evaluate $\widetilde{A}$, $\widetilde{B}$, and $\widetilde{C}$ at the point (r_x, r_y) in time $O(\sqrt{N})$—if this is not the case, then as discussed in Sect. 5.1 and detailed in the full version of the paper, these polynomials can each be committed in pre-processing and the necessary evaluations revealed by the prover, thereby achieving holography. $\widetilde{Z}(r_y)$ can be obtained from one query to $\widetilde{W}$ and one query to $\widetilde{(1, \text{io})}$ via Eq. (5).

In summary, we have the following succinct interactive argument. It is public coin, and can be rendered non-interactive via the Fiat-Shamir transformation.

---

1. $\mathcal{P} \to \mathcal{V}$: a commitment to the $(\log M - 1)$-variate multilinear polynomial $\widetilde{W}$ using the polynomial commitment scheme of §3.1.

2. $\mathcal{V} \to \mathcal{P}$: $\tau \in_R \mathbb{F}^s$

3. $\mathcal{V} \leftrightarrow \mathcal{P}$: run the sum-check reduction to reduce the check in Equation (6) to checking if the following hold, where r_x, r_y are vectors in $\mathbb{F}^s$ chosen at random by the verifier over the course of the sum-check protocol:
   - $\widetilde{A}(r_x, r_y) \overset{?}{=} v_A$, $\widetilde{B}(r_x, r_y) \overset{?}{=} v_B$, and $\widetilde{C}(r_x, r_y) \overset{?}{=} v_C$; and
   - $\widetilde{Z}(r_y) \overset{?}{=} v_Z$.

4. $\mathcal{V}$:
   - check if $\widetilde{A}(r_x, r_y) \overset{?}{=} v_A$, $\widetilde{B}(r_x, r_y) \overset{?}{=} v_B$, and $\widetilde{C}(r_x, r_y) \overset{?}{=} v_C$, (recall that we have assumed that each of $\widetilde{A}, \widetilde{B}, \widetilde{C}$ can be evaluated in $O(\sqrt{N})$ time).
   - check if $\widetilde{Z}(r_y) \overset{?}{=} v_Z$ by checking if: $v_Z = (1 - r_y[1]) \cdot v_W + r_y[1] \cdot \widetilde{(\text{io}, 1)}(r_y[2..])$, where $r_y[2..]$ refers to a slice of r_y without the first element of r_y (Eq. (5)), and $v_W \leftarrow \widetilde{W}(r_y[2..])$ is obtained via the evaluation procedure of the polynomial commitment scheme (§3.1).

By composing the SNARK of Theorem 2 with known zkSNARKs [41,63,65], we obtain zkSNARKs with shorter proofs (the full version of this paper [40] provides detailed cost profiles of the resulting zkSNARKs). Specifically, the prover in the composed SNARKs proves that it knows a proof π that would convince the SNARK verifier in Theorem 2 to accept. Perfect zero-knowledge of the resulting composed SNARK is immediate from the zero-knowledge property of the SNARKs from these prior works [41,63,65]. Perfect completeness follows from the perfect completeness properties of these prior works and of Theorem 2. Knowledge soundness follows from a standard argument [19,70]: one composes the knowledge extractors of the two constituent SNARKs to get a knowledge extractor for the composed SNARK.

6   Implementation and Evaluation

We evaluate the performance of two polynomial commitment schemes and two SNARKs based on these schemes. Specifically, we evaluate two instantiations of the polynomial commitment scheme of Sect. 3.1: Ligero-PC, which uses the Reed-Solomon code (this scheme is implicit in Ligero [4]), and Brakedown-PC, which uses the new linear-time error-correcting code described in Sect. 4.

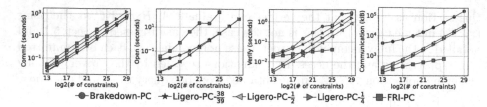

Fig. 1. Microbenchmark results (Sect. 6.1); lower is better. Brakedown-PC uses the parameters in the third line of [40, Figure 7]; Ligero-PC-$38/39$, Ligero-PC-$1/2$, Ligero-PC-$1/4$, and FRI-PC are instantiated with Reed-Solomon rates of $38/39$, $1/2$, $1/4$, and $1/4$, respectively. FRI-PC results are incomplete as the prover ran out of memory for larger instances.

Implementation. We implement Ligero-PC and Brakedown-PC in ≈ 3500 lines of Rust. This includes an implementation of the polynomial commitment of Sect. 3.1 that is generic over fields, error-correcting codes, and hash functions; implementations of the Reed-Solomon code and our new linear-time code; and a fast parallelized FFT. We also integrate our implementation with Spartan [3], yielding a SNARK library; this took less than 100 lines of glue Rust code.

All reported measurements of our implementation use the BLAKE3 hash function [57]. Because Ligero-PC needs to perform FFTs, our measurements use fields of characteristic p such that $p - 1$ is divisible by 2^{40}, which ensures that reasonably large FFTs are possible in the field; we choose p at random.

6.1   Evaluation of Polynomial Commitment Schemes

This section evaluates the concrete costs of our polynomial commitment schemes and a prior baseline, for univariate polynomials, over the standard monomial basis, of degree 2^{13} to 2^{29} (for our schemes, the costs for such univariate polynomials is identical to the costs for multilinear polynomials having 13 to 29 variables).

Baseline. The FRI protocol [8] underlies all prior IOP-based polynomial commitment schemes and all built post-quantum schemes. (Lattice-based Bulletproofs [24] could also be used to construct post-quantum schemes, but to our knowledge these have not been implemented.) Like Ligero-PC, FRI requires an FFT-friendly field for efficiency. Vlasov and Panarin [71] use FRI to construct a univariate polynomial commitment, which we call FRI-PC; Virgo [78] effectively extends FRI-PC to multilinear polynomials by invoking an interactive proof, increasing costs.[3] We evaluate the C++ FRI implementation in libiop [52]. Following the best known soundness analysis [10,71], we set the Reed-Solomon rate to $1/4$ and number of queries to 189.

---

[3] RedShift and ethStark [1,46] use FRI to construct a related primitive called a *list polynomial commitment* with a relaxed notion of soundness, and smaller opening proofs (by up to $\approx 30\%$ using Reed-Solomon rate $1/4$ and existing analyses). That primitive, however, is not a drop-in replacement for polynomial commitments, so we restrict our focus to the latter.

Parameters of the Error-Correcting Codes. We instantiate Brakedown-PC with the parameters given on the third line of [40, Figure 7]. For Ligero-PC, the rate of the Reed-Solomon code trades between proving and verification costs: roughly, a lower rate gives a slower prover but smaller proofs and faster verification. To explore this tradeoff, we test Ligero-PC with three different code rates: 38/39 gives proof sizes roughly matching Brakedown-PC, 1/2 gives smaller proofs than Brakedown-PC at roughly comparable prover cost, and 1/4 gives even smaller proofs at the cost of greater prover computation.[4]

Other Parameters. We evaluate all schemes over 255-bit prime fields. We set parameters of the commitment schemes to obtain 128 bits of security (the exception is that the randomized code generation procedure in Brakedown-PC is designed to have at most a 2^{-100} probability of failing to satisfy the requisite distance properties according to the analysis of Sect. 4; this is acceptable because code generation is done in public). To achieve this, we set the number of columns opened in Brakedown-PC to 6593, in Ligero-PC-38/39 to 7054, in Ligero-PC-1/2 to 309, and in Ligero-PC-1/4 to 189.

Setup and Method. Our testbed for this section is an Azure Standard F64s_v2 virtual machine (64 Intel Xeon Platinum 8272CL vCPUs, 128 GiB memory) with Ubuntu 18.04. We measure single-threaded speed for committing, opening, and verifying; and we report communication cost. For each experiment, we run the operation 10 times and report the average; in all cases, variation is negligible.

Results. Figure 1 reports the results. The FRI-PC prover ran out of memory for polynomials of degree greater than 2^{25}.

For Brakedown-PC and Ligero-PC, the dominant cost for the prover is committing to the polynomial. For large enough polynomials, Brakedown-PC's commitment computation is as fast or faster than Ligero-PC-1/2's, and roughly 2–3× faster than Ligero-PC-1/4's. Computing commitments in Ligero-PC-38/39 is faster than in Brakedown-PC, but Ligero-PC-38/39 does not support multilinear polynomials (see Footnote 4).

For FRI-PC, committing and opening have similar (high) costs: on the sizes where the FRI prover succeeded ($\leq 2^{25}$), committing and opening with FRI-PC is ≈2–9× slower than Brakedown-PC and ≈3–7× slower than the slowest Ligero-PC; for Brakedown-PC, the gap widens with increasing size.

Ligero-PC-1/2 and Ligero-PC-1/4 have lower verification cost than Ligero-PC-38/39 and Brakedown-PC, though this advantage shrinks as instances grow. FRI-PC's verification cost is up to 17× lower than the other schemes.

---

[4] Rate parameter 38/39 *cannot* be used in the Ligero-PC scheme for multilinear polynomials (as required by Shockwave; Sect. 6.2). This is because Ligero-PC's FFT uses power-of-two–length codewords, and multilinear polynomial evaluation can only be decomposed into tensor products with power-of-two-sized tensors (see Sect. 3.1). Since ρ is the ratio of one tensor's size to codeword length, ρ^{-1} must be a power of two. As a result, $\rho = 1/2$ is the highest rate Ligero-PC supports for multilinear polynomials.

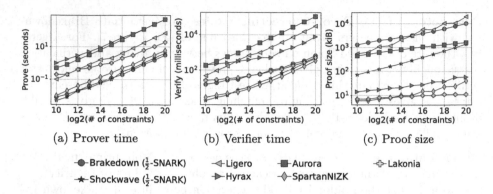

(a) Prover time   (b) Verifier time   (c) Proof size

Fig. 2. $\frac{1}{2}$-SNARK results (Sect. 6.2); lower is better. Brakedown, Shockwave, Ligero, and Aurora are plausibly post-quantum secure.

Brakedown-PC and Ligero-PC-38/39 have nearly the same communication cost, by design. Ligero-PC-1/2 has $\approx$5–15× less communication than Brakedown-PC, and Ligero-PC-1/4 has $\approx$6–21× less than Brakedown-PC; like verification time, their proof size advantage shrinks as instance size grows. FRI-PC's communication is significantly lower: $\approx$22–66× less than Brakedown-PC or Ligero-PC-38/39, $\approx$2–13× less than Ligero-PC-1/2, and $\approx$1.3–10× less than Ligero-PC-1/4.

In sum, Brakedown-PC has a concretely and asymptotically fast prover (especially for multilinear polynomials) but gives large proofs and slower verification than the other schemes. Brakedown-PC's proofs are larger because higher ρ implies more column openings; for large polynomials, the overhead is $\approx \sqrt{\ell'}$, where ℓ' is the ratio of the number of column openings. For these instance sizes, Ligero-PC's prover is competitive with Brakedown-PC's and its proof size and verification cost are lower. FRI-PC gives much smaller proofs and lower verification cost but has a much slower prover. Of course, neither Ligero-PC nor FRI-PC is field-agnostic; Brakedown-PC is.

In our full paper [40] we report on Brakedown-PC and Ligero-PC experiments with 64 threads. For large polynomials, proving times improve by $\approx$16–34×.

6.2   Evaluation of Brakedown and Shockwave SNARKs

Metrics, Method, and Baselines. As is standard in the SNARKs literature, our metrics are: (1) the prover time to produce a proof; (2) the verifier time to verify a proof; (3) proof sizes; and (4) the verifier's preprocessing costs. As baselines, we consider two types of SNARKs: (1) schemes that achieve verification costs sub-linear in the size of the statement (which implies sub-linear proof sizes); and (2) schemes that only achieve proof sizes that are sub-linear in the size of the statement. We refer to the latter type of schemes as $\frac{1}{2}$-*SNARKs*. Additionally, we focus on schemes that do not require a trusted setup (we refer the reader to Spartan [63] for a comparison between our baselines with state-of-the-art SNARKs with trusted setup).

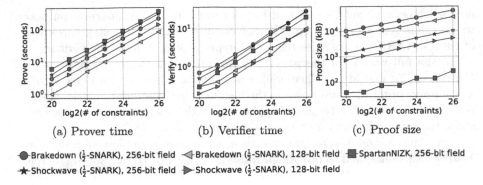

(a) Prover time   (b) Verifier time   (c) Proof size

● Brakedown ($\frac{1}{2}$-SNARK), 256-bit field   ◁ Brakedown ($\frac{1}{2}$-SNARK), 128-bit field   ■ SpartanNIZK, 256-bit field
★ Shockwave ($\frac{1}{2}$-SNARK), 256-bit field   ▷ Shockwave ($\frac{1}{2}$-SNARK), 128-bit field

Fig. 3. $\frac{1}{2}$-SNARK results for varying field sizes (Sect. 6.2); lower is better. Brakedown and Shockwave are plausibly post-quantum secure.

The reader may wonder why we include results for our $\frac{1}{2}$-SNARK given that our implementation is not yet zero-knowledge; after all, the verifier runtime in any non-zero-knowledge $\frac{1}{2}$-SNARK is commensurate with that of the trivial proof system in which the prover explicitly sends the NP-witness to the verifier. The answer is three-fold. First, the proof length in our $\frac{1}{2}$-SNARK is smaller than the witness size for sufficiently large instances ($N \geq 2^{13}$ for Shockwave and $N \geq 2^{18}$ for Brakedown). Second, our $\frac{1}{2}$-SNARK actually *can* save the verifier time relative to the trivial proof system for structured R1CS instances. In particular, if the R1CS is data parallel, then the verifier can run in time proportional to the size of a single sub-computation, independent of the number of times the sub-computation is performed (this is entirely analogous to how prior proof systems save the verifier work for structured computations [9,68]). Third, we expect that the reported performance results are indicative of the performance of future zero-knowledge implementations.

Unless we specify otherwise, we run our experiments in this section on an Azure Standard F16s_v2 virtual machine (16 vCPUs, 32 GB memory) with Ubuntu 20.10. We report results from a single-threaded configuration since not all our baselines leverage multiple cores. As with prior work [14,32,63,65], we vary the size of the R1CS instance by varying the number of constraints and variables m and maintain the ratio n/m to approximately 1.

Performance of Shockwave's and Brakedown's $\frac{1}{2}$-SNARK Scheme.
Prior state-of-the-art $\frac{1}{2}$-SNARK schemes include: Ligero [4], Bulletproofs [27], Aurora [14], SpartanNIZK [63], and Lakonia [65]. Note that for uniform computations (e.g., data-parallel circuits), Hyrax [74] and STARK [9] are SNARKs, but for computations without any structure, they are $\frac{1}{2}$-SNARKs. We do not compare with Ligero++ [17] since its source code is not public. Broadly speaking, Ligero++ has shorter proofs than Ligero at the cost of a slower prover, so its prover will be significantly slower than both Brakedown and Shockwave. We do not report results from Bulletproofs or STARK as they feature a more expensive prover than other baselines considered here [14,27]. Hyrax [74] supports only lay-

ered arithmetic circuits, so as used in prior work [63] for comparison purposes, we translate R1CS to depth-1 arithmetic circuits (without any structure). None of the $\frac{1}{2}$-SNARKs we consider require a preprocessing step for the verifier.

In the full version of the paper [40], we provide a rough comparison with Wolverine [75] and Mac'n'Cheese [6], which unlike schemes considered here do *not* support proof sizes sub-linear in the instance size. Another potential baseline is Virgo [78], which like Hyrax [74] applies only to low-depth circuits as they both share the same information-theoretic component [33,39,72,76].

For Aurora and Ligero, we use their open-source implementations from libiop [52], configured to provide provable security. For Hyrax, we use its reference (i.e., unoptimized) implementation [51]. For SpartanNIZK, we use its open-source implementation [3]. Unless we specify otherwise, we use 256-bit prime fields. Hyrax uses curve25519 and SpartanNIZK uses ristretto255 [2,42] for a group where the discrete-log problem is hard, so R1CS instances are defined over the scalar field of these curves. For Aurora and Ligero, we use the 256-bit prime field option in libiop. Finally, our schemes use the scalar field of BLS12-381, which supports FFTs (Brakedown does not need FFTs but Shockwave does). However, we note that none of these implementations leverages the specifics of the prime field to speed up scalar arithmetic.

We first experiment with Brakedown and Shockwave and their baselines with varying R1CS instance sizes up to 2^{20} constraints defined over a 256-bit prime field. Figures 2a, 2b, and 2c depict respectively the prover time, the verifier time, and the proof size from these experiments. We find the following.

- Brakedown's and Shockwave's provers are faster than prior work at all instance sizes we measure. Compared to basslines that are plausibly post-quantum secure (Ligero and Aurora), Brakedown's and Shockwave's provers are over an order of magnitude faster.
- Brakedown's proof size is larger than other depicted systems except for Ligero. Still, its proofs are substantially smaller than the size of the NP-witness for instance sizes $N \geq 2^{18}$. Shockwave provides shorter proofs than Brakedown as well as prior post-quantum secure baselines (Ligero and Aurora). Note that Aurora has asymptotically shorter proofs than Shockwave, and hence the proof size comparison would "cross over" at larger instance sizes). Shockwave's proof sizes are smaller than that of the NP-witness for instance sizes $N \geq 2^{13}$.
- Despite their larger proofs, Brakedown's and Shockwave's verifiers are competitive with those of SpartanNIZK and Lakonia, and is well over an order of magnitude faster than the plausibly post-quantum secure baselines.

Performance for Larger Instance Sizes. To demonstrate Brakedown's and Shockwave's scalability to larger instance sizes, we experiment with them and SpartanNIZK for instance sizes beyond 2^{20} constraints.

For these larger-scale experiments, we use an Azure Standard F32s_v2 VM which has 32 vCPUs and 64 GB memory. Figures 3a, 3b, and 3c depict results from these larger-scale experiments. Our findings from these experiments are similar to results from the smaller-scale results.

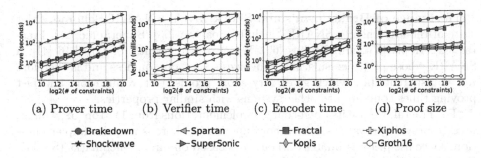

(a) Prover time   (b) Verifier time   (c) Encoder time   (d) Proof size

●—Brakedown   ◀—Spartan   ■—Fractal   ◇—Xiphos
★—Shockwave   ▶—SuperSonic   ◆—Kopis   ○—Groth16

Fig. 4. SNARK results (Sect. 6.2); lower is better. Brakedown, Shockwave, and Fractal are plausibly post-quantum secure. Fractal results are incomplete because the prover and encoder ran out of memory for larger instances.

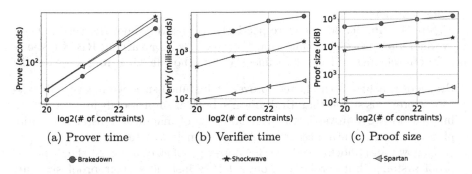

(a) Prover time   (b) Verifier time   (c) Proof size

●—Brakedown   ★—Shockwave   ◀—Spartan

Fig. 5. SNARK results (Sect. 6.2); lower is better. Brakedown and Shockwave are plausibly post-quantum secure.

Performance over Small Fields. To demonstrate flexibility with different field sizes, we also run Brakedown and Shockwave with a prime field where the prime modulus is 128 bits. For the latter case, our choice of parameters achieve at least 100 bits security. We depict these results together with results from our larger-scale experiments (Figs. 3a, 3c, and 3b).

Recall that our asymptotic results require $|\mathbb{F}| > \exp(\Omega(\lambda))$ to achieve a linear-time prover, because if the field is smaller than this, certain parts of the protocol need to be repeated $\omega(1)$ times to drive the soundness error below $\exp(-\lambda)$. However, Brakedown and Shockwave are quite efficient over small fields. The reason is that only some parts of the protocol need to be repeated to drive the soundness error below $\exp(-\lambda)$ and those repetitions produce only low-order effects on the prover's runtime and the proof length. This means that for a fixed security level, our prover is faster over small fields than large fields, because the effect of faster field arithmetic dominates the overhead due to the need to repeat parts of the protocol to drive down soundness error. Similar observations appear in prior work [9].

Performance of Brakedown's and Shockwave's SNARK Scheme. Prior state-of-the-art schemes SNARKs include: Spartan [63], SuperSonic [28], Fractal [32], Kopis [65], and Xiphos [65]. We also give results for Groth16 [41], a SNARK whose preprocessing phase involves secret randomness and is therefore *not* transparent, but which gives very short proofs, fast verification, and fast proving times compared to other systems with similar properties.

For Fractal, we use its open-source implementations from libiop [52], configured to provide provable security. For SuperSonic, there is no prior implementation, so we use prior estimates of their costs based on microbenchmarks (See [65] for a detailed discussion of how they estimate these costs). For Spartan, we use its open-source implementation [3]. For Groth16, we benchmark the libsnark implementation using the BN254 elliptic curve [53]. For preprocessing costs, we ignore the use of "untrusted assistant" technique [65], which applies to all schemes considered here except Groth16.

Figures 4a, 4b, 4c, 4d depict respectively the prover time, the verifier time, the verifier's preprocessing time, and the proof size for varying R1CS instance sizes for our schemes and their baselines. We find the following from these results.

- Brakedown achieves the fastest prover at instance sizes we measure. Shockwave's prover is slower than Brakedown's, both asymptotically and concretely, but Shockwave's prover is still over an order of magnitude faster than prior plausibly post-quantum secure SNARKs (namely Fractal [32]).
- Brakedown and Shockwave have the largest proof sizes amongst the displayed proof systems, but for large enough R1CS instances their proof sizes are sublinear in the size of the NP-witness ($N > 2^{16}$ for Shockwave and $N \geq 2^{22}$ for Brakedown).
- Brakedown's verifier is slower than Shockwave and most other schemes, particularly Xiphos [65] which is specifically designed for achieving a fast verifier. However, Shockwave's verifier is competitive with prior plausibly post-quantum secure SNARKs.
- Brakedown's and Shockwave's preprocessing costs for the verifier are competitive with those of prior high-speed SNARKs such as Spartan [63] and Xiphos [65], and an order of magnitude faster than the prior post-quantum secure SNARK (Fractal).

Performance for Larger Instance Sizes. To demonstrate Brakedown's and Shockwave's scalability to larger instance sizes, we experiment with them and Spartan for instance sizes beyond 2^{20} constraints.

For these larger-scale experiments, we use an Azure Standard F64s_v2 VM which has 64 vCPUs and 128 GB memory. Figures 5a, 5c, and 5b depict results from these larger-scale experiments. Our findings from these experiments are similar to results from the smaller-scale results.

References

1. ethSTARK. https://github.com/starkware-libs/ethSTARK
2. The Ristretto group. https://ristretto.group/
3. Spartan: High-speed zkSNARKs without trusted setup. https://github.com/Microsoft/Spartan
4. Ames, S., Hazay, C., Ishai, Y., Venkitasubramaniam, M.: Ligero: lightweight sublinear arguments without a trusted setup. In: CCS (2017)
5. Applebaum, B., Haramaty, N., Ishai, Y., Kushilevitz, E., Vaikuntanathan, V.: Low-complexity cryptographic hash functions. In: ITCS (2017)
6. Baum, C., Malozemoff, A.J., Rosen, M., Scholl, P.: Mac'n'cheese: zero-knowledge proofs for arithmetic circuits with nested disjunctions. Cryptology ePrint Archive, Report 2020/1410 (2020)
7. Belling, A., Soleimanian, A.: Vortex: building a lattice-based snark scheme with transparent setup. Cryptology ePrint Archive, Paper 2022/1633 (2022)
8. Ben-Sasson, E., Bentov, I., Horesh, Y., Riabzev, M.: Fast reed-solomon interactive oracle proofs of proximity. In: ICALP (2018)
9. Ben-Sasson, E., Bentov, I., Horesh, Y., Riabzev, M.: Scalable zero knowledge with no trusted setup. In: Boldyreva, A., Micciancio, D. (eds.) CRYPTO 2019. LNCS, vol. 11694, pp. 701–732. Springer, Cham (2019). https://doi.org/10.1007/978-3-030-26954-8_23
10. Ben-Sasson, E., Carmon, D., Ishai, Y., Kopparty, S., Saraf, S.: Proximity gaps for Reed-Solomon codes. In: FOCS (2020)
11. Ben-Sasson, E., Carmon, D., Kopparty, S., Levit, D.: Elliptic Curve Fast Fourier Transform (ECFFT) part I: fast polynomial algorithms over all finite fields. Electronic Colloquium on Computational Complexity, Report 2021/103 (2021)
12. Ben-Sasson, E., Carmon, D., Kopparty, S., Levit, D.: Scalable and transparent proofs over all large fields, via elliptic curves. Electronic Colloquium on Computational Complexity, Report 2022/110 (2022)
13. Ben-Sasson, E., Chiesa, A., Genkin, D., Tromer, E.: Fast reductions from RAMs to delegatable succinct constraint satisfaction problems: extended abstract. In: ITCS (2013)
14. Ben-Sasson, E., Chiesa, A., Riabzev, M., Spooner, N., Virza, M., Ward, N.P.: Aurora: transparent succinct arguments for R1CS. In: Ishai, Y., Rijmen, V. (eds.) EUROCRYPT 2019. LNCS, vol. 11476, pp. 103–128. Springer, Cham (2019). https://doi.org/10.1007/978-3-030-17653-2_4
15. Ben-Sasson, E., Chiesa, A., Spooner, N.: Interactive oracle proofs. In: Hirt, M., Smith, A. (eds.) TCC 2016. LNCS, vol. 9986, pp. 31–60. Springer, Heidelberg (2016). https://doi.org/10.1007/978-3-662-53644-5_2
16. Bernstein, D.J., Doumen, J., Lange, T., Oosterwijk, J.-J.: Faster batch forgery identification. Cryptology ePrint Archive, Paper 2012/549 (2012)
17. Bhadauria, R., Fang, Z., Hazay, C., Venkitasubramaniam, M., Xie, T., Zhang, Y.: Ligero++: a new optimized sublinear IOP. In: CCS, pp. 2025–2038 (2020)
18. Bitansky, N., Canetti, R., Chiesa, A., Tromer, E.: From extractable collision resistance to succinct non-interactive arguments of knowledge, and back again. In: ITCS (2012)
19. Bitansky, N., Canetti, R., Chiesa, A., Tromer, E.: Recursive composition and bootstrapping for SNARKs and proof-carrying data. In: STOC (2013)
20. Bootle, J., Cerulli, A., Ghadafi, E., Groth, J., Hajiabadi, M., Jakobsen, S.K.: Linear-time zero-knowledge proofs for arithmetic circuit satisfiability. In: Takagi,

T., Peyrin, T. (eds.) ASIACRYPT 2017. LNCS, vol. 10626, pp. 336–365. Springer, Cham (2017). https://doi.org/10.1007/978-3-319-70700-6_12

21. Bootle, J., Chiesa, A., Groth, J.: Linear-time arguments with sublinear verification from tensor codes. In: Pass, R., Pietrzak, K. (eds.) TCC 2020. LNCS, vol. 12551, pp. 19–46. Springer, Cham (2020). https://doi.org/10.1007/978-3-030-64378-2_2

22. Bootle, J., Chiesa, A., Guan, Z., Liu, S.: Linear-time probabilistic proofs over every field. Cryptology ePrint Archive, Paper 2022/1056 (2022)

23. Bootle, J., Chiesa, A., Liu, S.: Zero-knowledge succinct arguments with a linear-time prover. ePrint Report 2020/1527 (2020)

24. Bootle, J., Lyubashevsky, V., Nguyen, N.K., Seiler, G.: A non-PCP approach to succinct quantum-safe zero-knowledge. In: Micciancio, D., Ristenpart, T. (eds.) CRYPTO 2020. LNCS, vol. 12171, pp. 441–469. Springer, Cham (2020). https://doi.org/10.1007/978-3-030-56880-1_16

25. Braun, B., Feldman, A.J., Ren, Z., Setty, S., Blumberg, A.J., Walfish, M.: Verifying computations with state. In: SOSP (2013)

26. Bröker, R., Stevenhagen, P.: Efficient CM-constructions of elliptic curves over finite fields. Math. Comp. **76**(260), 2161–2179 (2007)

27. Bünz, B., Bootle, J., Boneh, D., Poelstra, A., Wuille, P., Maxwell, G.: Bulletproofs: short proofs for confidential transactions and more. In: S&P (2018)

28. Bünz, B., Fisch, B., Szepieniec, A.: Transparent SNARKs from DARK compilers. In: Canteaut, A., Ishai, Y. (eds.) EUROCRYPT 2020. LNCS, vol. 12105, pp. 677–706. Springer, Cham (2020). https://doi.org/10.1007/978-3-030-45721-1_24

29. Chen, B., Bünz, B., Boneh, D., Zhang, Z.: Hyperplonk: plonk with linear-time prover and high-degree custom gates. In: Hazay, C., Stam, M. (eds.) EUROCRYPT 2023. LNCS, vol. 14005, pp. 499–530. Springer, Cham (2023). https://doi.org/10.1007/978-3-031-30617-4_17

30. Chiesa, A., Forbes, M.A., Spooner, N.: A zero knowledge sumcheck and its applications. CoRR, abs/1704.02086 (2017)

31. Chiesa, A., Hu, Y., Maller, M., Mishra, P., Vesely, N., Ward, N.: Marlin: preprocessing zkSNARKs with universal and updatable SRS. In: Canteaut, A., Ishai, Y. (eds.) EUROCRYPT 2020. LNCS, vol. 12105, pp. 738–768. Springer, Cham (2020). https://doi.org/10.1007/978-3-030-45721-1_26

32. Chiesa, A., Ojha, D., Spooner, N.: FRACTAL: post-quantum and transparent recursive proofs from holography. In: Canteaut, A., Ishai, Y. (eds.) EUROCRYPT 2020. LNCS, vol. 12105, pp. 769–793. Springer, Cham (2020). https://doi.org/10.1007/978-3-030-45721-1_27

33. Cormode, G., Mitzenmacher, M., Thaler, J.: Practical verified computation with streaming interactive proofs. In: ITCS (2012)

34. Druk, E., Ishai, Y.: Linear-time encodable codes meeting the Gilbert-Varshamov bound and their cryptographic applications. In: ITCS, pp. 169–182 (2014)

35. Fiat, A., Shamir, A.: How To prove yourself: practical solutions to identification and signature problems. In: Odlyzko, A.M. (ed.) CRYPTO 1986. LNCS, vol. 263, pp. 186–194. Springer, Heidelberg (1987). https://doi.org/10.1007/3-540-47721-7_12

36. Gelfand, S.I., Dobrushin, R.L., Pinsker, M.S.: On the complexity of coding. pp. 177–184 (1973)

37. Gentry, C., Wichs, D.: Separating succinct non-interactive arguments from all falsifiable assumptions. In: STOC, pp. 99–108 (2011)

38. Goldreich, O., Kahan, A.: How to construct constant-round zero-knowledge proof systems for NP. J. Cryptol. **9**(3), 167–189 (1996)

39. Goldwasser, S., Kalai, Y.T., Rothblum, G.N.: Delegating computation: Interactive proofs for muggles. In: STOC (2008)
40. Golovnev, A., Lee, J., Setty, S., Thaler, J., Wahby, R.S.: Brakedown: linear-time and post-quantum snarks for r1cs. Cryptology ePrint Archive, Paper 2021/1043 (2021)
41. Groth, J.: On the size of pairing-based non-interactive arguments. In: Fischlin, M., Coron, J.-S. (eds.) EUROCRYPT 2016. LNCS, vol. 9666, pp. 305–326. Springer, Heidelberg (2016). https://doi.org/10.1007/978-3-662-49896-5_11
42. Hamburg, M.: Decaf: eliminating cofactors through point compression. In: Gennaro, R., Robshaw, M. (eds.) CRYPTO 2015. LNCS, vol. 9215, pp. 705–723. Springer, Heidelberg (2015). https://doi.org/10.1007/978-3-662-47989-6_34
43. Hazay, C., Lindell, Y.: Efficient Secure Two-Party Protocols: Techniques and Constructions. Springer, Heidelberg (2010). https://doi.org/10.1007/978-3-642-14303-8
44. Housni, Y.E., Botrel, G.: EdMSM: multi-scalar-multiplication for SNARKs and faster montgomery multiplication. Cryptology ePrint Archive, Paper 2022/1400 (2022)
45. Kate, A., Zaverucha, G.M., Goldberg, I.: Constant-size commitments to polynomials and their applications. In: Abe, M. (ed.) ASIACRYPT 2010. LNCS, vol. 6477, pp. 177–194. Springer, Heidelberg (2010). https://doi.org/10.1007/978-3-642-17373-8_11
46. Kattis, A., Panarin, K., Vlasov, A.: RedShift: transparent SNARKs from list polynomial commitment IOPs. Cryptology ePrint Archive, Report 2019/1400 (2019)
47. Kilian, J.: A note on efficient zero-knowledge proofs and arguments (extended abstract). In: STOC (1992)
48. Kothapalli, A., Setty, S., Tzialla, I.: Nova: recursive zero-knowledge arguments from folding schemes. In: Dodis, Y., Shrimpton, T. (eds.) CRYPTO 2022. LNCS, vol. 13510, pp. 359–388. Springer, Cham (2022). https://doi.org/10.1007/978-3-031-15985-5_13
49. Lee, J.: Dory: efficient, transparent arguments for generalised inner products and polynomial commitments. Cryptology ePrint Archive, Report 2020/1274 (2020)
50. Lee, J., Nikitin, K., Setty, S.: Replicated state machines without replicated execution. In: S&P (2020)
51. libfennel. Hyrax reference implementation. https://github.com/hyraxZK/fennel
52. libiop. A C++ library for IOP-based zkSNARK. https://github.com/scipr-lab/libiop
53. libsnark. A C++ library for zkSNARK proofs. https://github.com/scipr-lab/libsnark
54. Lund, C., Fortnow, L., Karloff, H., Nisan, N.: Algebraic methods for interactive proof systems. In: FOCS, October 1990
55. Micali, S.: CS proofs. In: FOCS (1994)
56. Mitzenmacher, M., Upfal, E.: Probability and Computing: Randomization and Probabilistic Techniques in Algorithms and Data Analysis. Cambridge University Press, Cambridge (2017)
57. O'Connor, J., Aumasson, J.-P., Neves, S., Wilcox-O'Hearn, Z.: BLAKE3: one function, fast everywhere, February 2020. https://github.com/BLAKE3-team/BLAKE3-specs/blob/master/blake3.pdf
58. Ozdemir, A., Brown, F., Wahby, R.S.: Unifying compilers for SNARKs, SMT, and more. Cryptology ePrint Archive, Report 2020/1586 (2020)
59. Parno, B., Gentry, C., Howell, J., Raykova, M.: Pinocchio: nearly practical verifiable computation. In: S&P, May 2013

60. Pippenger, N.: On the evaluation of powers and related problems. In: SFCS (1976)
61. Reingold, O., Rothblum, G.N., Rothblum, R.D.: Constant-round interactive proofs for delegating computation. In: STOC, pp. 49–62 (2016)
62. Ron-Zewi, N., Rothblum, R.D.: Proving as fast as computing: succinct arguments with constant prover overhead. In: STOC (2022)
63. Setty, S.: Spartan: efficient and general-purpose zkSNARKs without trusted setup. In: Micciancio, D., Ristenpart, T. (eds.) CRYPTO 2020. LNCS, vol. 12172, pp. 704–737. Springer, Cham (2020). https://doi.org/10.1007/978-3-030-56877-1_25
64. Setty, S., Angel, S., Gupta, T., Lee, J.: Proving the correct execution of concurrent services in zero-knowledge. In: OSDI, October 2018
65. Setty, S., Lee, J.: Quarks: quadruple-efficient transparent zkSNARKs. Cryptology ePrint Archive, Report 2020/1275 (2020)
66. Setty, S., Vu, V., Panpalia, N., Braun, B., Blumberg, A.J., Walfish, M.: Taking proof-based verified computation a few steps closer to practicality. In: USENIX Security, August 2012
67. Spielman, D.A.: Linear-time encodable and decodable error-correcting codes. IEEE Trans. Inf. Theory **42**(6), 1723–1731 (1996)
68. Thaler, J.: Time-optimal interactive proofs for circuit evaluation. In: Canetti, R., Garay, J.A. (eds.) CRYPTO 2013. LNCS, vol. 8043, pp. 71–89. Springer, Heidelberg (2013). https://doi.org/10.1007/978-3-642-40084-1_5
69. Thaler, J.: Proofs, arguments, and zero-knowledge (2020). http://people.cs.georgetown.edu/jthaler/ProofsArgsAndZK.html
70. Valiant, P.: Incrementally verifiable computation or proofs of knowledge imply time/space efficiency. In: Canetti, R. (ed.) TCC 2008. LNCS, vol. 4948, pp. 1–18. Springer, Heidelberg (2008). https://doi.org/10.1007/978-3-540-78524-8_1
71. Vlasov, A., Panarin, K.: Transparent polynomial commitment scheme with polylogarithmic communication complexity. Cryptology ePrint Archive, Report 2019/1020 (2019)
72. Wahby, R.S., et al.: Full accounting for verifiable outsourcing. In: CCS (2017)
73. Wahby, R.S., Setty, S., Ren, Z., Blumberg, A.J., Walfish, M.: Efficient RAM and control flow in verifiable outsourced computation. In: NDSS (2015)
74. Wahby, R.S., Tzialla, I., Shelat, A., Thaler, J., Walfish, M.: Doubly-efficient zkSNARKs without trusted setup. In: S&P (2018)
75. Weng, C., Yang, K., Katz, J., Wang, X.: Wolverine: fast, scalable, and communication-efficient zero-knowledge proofs for Boolean and arithmetic circuits. Cryptology ePrint Archive, Report 2020/925 (2020)
76. Xie, T., Zhang, J., Zhang, Y., Papamanthou, C., Song, D.: Libra: succinct zero-knowledge proofs with optimal prover computation. In: Boldyreva, A., Micciancio, D. (eds.) CRYPTO 2019. LNCS, vol. 11694, pp. 733–764. Springer, Cham (2019). https://doi.org/10.1007/978-3-030-26954-8_24
77. Xie, T., Zhang, Y., Song, D.: Orion: zero knowledge proof with linear prover time. In: Dodis, Y., Shrimpton, T. (eds.) CRYPTO 2022. LNCS, vol. 13510, pp. 299–328. Springer, Cham (2022). https://doi.org/10.1007/978-3-031-15985-5_11
78. Zhang, J., Xie, T., Zhang, Y., Song, D.: Transparent polynomial delegation and its applications to zero knowledge proof. In: S&P (2020)
79. Zhang, Y., Genkin, D., Katz, J., Papadopoulos, D., Papamanthou, C.: vSQL: Verifying arbitrary SQL queries over dynamic outsourced databases. In: S&P (2017)

Lattice-Based Succinct Arguments for NP with Polylogarithmic-Time Verification

Jonathan Bootle[1]($\boxtimes$), Alessandro Chiesa[2], and Katerina Sotiraki[3]

[1] IBM Research Europe, Zurich, Switzerland
jbt@zurich.ibm.com
[2] EPFL, Lausanne, Switzerland
alessandro.chiesa@epfl.ch
[3] UC Berkeley, Berkeley, USA
katesot@berkeley.edu

Abstract. Succinct arguments that rely on the Merkle-tree paradigm introduced by Kilian (STOC 92) suffer from larger proof sizes in practice due to the use of generic cryptographic primitives. In contrast, succinct arguments with the smallest proof sizes in practice exploit homomorphic commitments. However these latter are quantum insecure, unlike succinct arguments based on the Merkle-tree paradigm.

A recent line of works seeks to address this limitation, by constructing quantum-safe succinct arguments that exploit lattice-based commitments. The eventual goal is smaller proof sizes than those achieved via the Merkle-tree paradigm. Alas, known constructions lack succinct verification.

In this paper, we construct the first interactive argument system for NP with succinct verification that, departing from the Merkle-tree paradigm, exploits the homomorphic properties of lattice-based commitments. For an arithmetic circuit with N gates, our construction achieves verification time $\mathsf{polylog}(N)$ based on the hardness of the Ring Short-Integer-Solution (RSIS) problem.

The core technique in our construction is a delegation protocol built from commitment schemes based on leveled bilinear modules, a new notion that we deem of independent interest. We show that leveled bilinear modules can be realized from pre-quantum and from post-quantum cryptographic assumptions.

Keywords: succinct arguments · lattices · short-integer-solution problem

1 Introduction

Succinct arguments enable an untrusted prover to convince a skeptical verifier that a given computation is correctly executed, while incurring communication complexity, and sometimes also verification time, that is much smaller than the computation size. Succinct arguments were first constructed by Kilian in [47],

© International Association for Cryptologic Research 2023
H. Handschuh and A. Lysyanskaya (Eds.): CRYPTO 2023, LNCS 14082, pp. 227–251, 2023.
https://doi.org/10.1007/978-3-031-38545-2_8

and since then much research has been devoted to improving their efficiency and security. Kilian shows how to compile a PCP into a succinct argument by using a Merkle tree, given any collision-resistant hash function. This "Merkle-tree paradigm" can also be used to construct succinct arguments from IOPs [10,62], which are more efficient generalizations of PCPs (and, in particular, are used in practice).

In anticipation of the threat of quantum computers, cryptographers have started investigating quantum-safe constructions of succinct arguments. Kilian's construction is such a construction: recent work [30] establishes that Kilian's interactive argument is quantum-safe if the used hash function is quantum-safe.

Split-and-Fold Techniques in the Pre-quantum Setting: A Success Story. Departing from the Merkle-tree paradigm, an approach based on *split-and-fold techniques* [25–27,48,50] has led to succinct arguments that are remarkably efficient and successful in practice. Even though asymptotically these constructions have similar proof sizes to constructions based on Merkle trees, in practice, they obtain smaller proofs by exploiting the algebraic structure of homomorphic commitment schemes.

This approach has several advantages over Merkle-tree constructions beyond smaller communication complexity. For example, the sumcheck protocol [52] underlies split-and-fold techniques [22], which facilitates space-efficient constructions [16,17]. In contrast, no space-efficient constructions are known for succinct arguments based on Merkle trees.

Unfortunately, the required homomorphic commitment schemes are known *only from pre-quantum cryptography that relies on groups and bilinear groups.*

What Happens in the Post-quantum Setting? The success story of split-and-fold techniques in the pre-quantum setting has motivated a line of work studying similar approaches in the post-quantum setting using lattices [5,7,22,24]. The eventual goal is to achieve succinct arguments from lattice-based split-and-fold techniques that have better efficiency compared to their Merkle-tree-based counterparts (and possibly have other benefits such as space efficiency). In the meantime, the cited works have laid initial foundations for such succinct arguments, but more work is needed to achieve this goal.

The inspiration comes from quantum-safe constructions of signature schemes, where using the algebraic structure of lattices eventually led to shorter signatures compared to using hash functions. For instance, among the standardization candidates in the NIST Post-Quantum Competition [57], lattice-based signature schemes such as Falcon [1] and Dilithium [2] offer shorter signatures compared to hash-based signatures such as SPHINCS+ [3] and Picnic [4].

Succinct Verification. The above lattice-based succinct arguments lack succinct verification (the time complexity of the verifier is at least the time of the proved computation). This is in contrast to constructions based on Merkle trees (and some pre-quantum constructions based on split-and-fold techniques [26,50]), which offer succinct verification. This leads to the main question motivating our work:

How to construct interactive arguments with succinct verification from split-and-fold techniques based on lattices?

1.1 Our Results

We answer this question in the affirmative, achieving succinct verification for R1CS, a popular circuit-like NP problem, in the *preprocessing setting*.

Definition 1 (informal). *The R1CS problem over a ring $R_\bullet$ asks: given coefficient matrices $A, B, C \in R_\bullet^{N \times N}$ each containing at most $M = \Omega(N)$ non-zero entries, and an instance vector $\underline{x}$ over $R_\bullet$, is there a witness vector $\underline{w}$ over $R_\bullet$ such that $\underline{z} := (\underline{x}, \underline{w}) \in R_\bullet^N$ and $A\underline{z} \circ B\underline{z} = C\underline{z}$? (Here "$\circ$" is the entry-wise product.)*

In the preprocessing setting, an *indexer* algorithm performs a public computation that depends on the coefficient matrices A, B and C (the "circuit description"), leading to a long proving key and a short verification key. Thereafter, anyone can use the proving/verification key to prove/verify statements for the preprocessed coefficient matrices. The argument verifier may achieve succinct verification because it only needs the verification key and the instance vector $\underline{x}$, with no need to read the (much larger) coefficient matrices. (Non-uniform computations require some form of preprocessing to enable succinct verification.)

We construct a succinct interactive argument with preprocessing for the R1CS problem over rings.

Theorem 1 (informal). *Let $R := \mathbb{Z}[X]/\langle \Phi_d(X) \rangle$ where Φ_d is the d-th cyclotomic polynomial and d is a prime power. Let p, q be primes such that $p \ll q$. If the SIS problem is hard over R/qR then there is a preprocessing interactive argument of knowledge (with a transparent setup algorithm) for R1CS over $R_\bullet := R/pR$ with the following efficiency:*

- *round complexity $O(\log^2(M + N))$;*
- *communication complexity $O(\log^2(M + N))$ elements of R/qR;*
- *indexer complexity $O(M + N)$ operations in R/qR;*
- *prover complexity $O(M + N)$ operations in R/qR;*
- *verifier complexity $O(\log^2(M + N))$ operations in R/qR.*

In fact, we construct a preprocessing succinct interactive argument for R1CS based on *leveled bilinear modules*, a new abstraction with multiple instantiations that we deem of independent interest. Theorem 1 follows by instantiating this abstraction using lattices, as we now outline.

An (unleveled) bilinear module [22] consists of modules M_L, M_R, M_T over a ring R with an R-bilinear map $e: M_L \times M_R \to M_T$. Example instantiations include the following.

- **Bilinear groups:** $(R, M_L, M_R, M_T, e) = (\mathbb{F}_p, \mathbb{G}_0, \mathbb{G}_1, \mathbb{G}_T, e)$, where $|\mathbb{G}_0| = |\mathbb{G}_1| = |\mathbb{G}_T| = p$ and $e: \mathbb{G}_0 \times \mathbb{G}_1 \to \mathbb{G}_T$ is a bilinear (pairing) map.

- **Lattices:** $(R, M_{\mathrm{L}}, M_{\mathrm{R}}, M_{\mathrm{T}}, e) = (R, R, R/q, R/q, e)$, where $R = \mathbb{Z}[X]/\langle \Phi_d(X) \rangle$, q is a large prime, and $e \colon R \times R/q \to R/q$ computes multiplication of ring elements modulo q.

Prior work [22] constructs commitment schemes based on bilinear modules, with messages defined over M_{L}, keys defined over M_{R}, and commitments defined over M_{T}, and gives interactive arguments of knowledge of commitment openings based on the sumcheck protocol. These arguments have linear verification costs in the length of the commitment key, which is the best one can hope for because they are not preprocessing arguments (and so the verifier must receive the long commitment key as input).

In a *leveled* bilinear module, which we introduce, the key space is associated with the message space of another bilinear module.

Definition 2 (informal). *A K-level bilinear-module system is a collection of K bilinear modules*

$$\{(R, M_{\mathrm{L},i}, M_{\mathrm{R},i}, M_{\mathrm{T},i}, e_i)\}_{i \in [K]}$$

with the same ring R such that $M_{\mathrm{R},i}$ can be "embedded" inside $M_{\mathrm{L},i+1}$ while preserving arithmetic operations (possibly up to some correction factors).

Example instantiations of leveled bilinear modules include the following.

- **Bilinear groups:** $(R, M_{\mathrm{L},i}, M_{\mathrm{R},i}, M_{\mathrm{T},i}, e_i) = (\mathbb{F}_p, \mathbb{G}_{i \bmod 2}, \mathbb{G}_{i+1 \bmod 2}, \mathbb{G}_{\mathrm{T}}, e)$, where $|\mathbb{G}_0| = |\mathbb{G}_1| = |\mathbb{G}_{\mathrm{T}}| = p$ and $e \colon \mathbb{G}_0 \times \mathbb{G}_1 \to \mathbb{G}_{\mathrm{T}}$ is a bilinear (pairing) map.
- **Lattices:** $(R, M_{\mathrm{L},i}, M_{\mathrm{R},i}, M_{\mathrm{T},i}, e_i) = (R, R, R/q, R/q, e)$, where $R := \mathbb{Z}[X]/\langle \Phi_d(X) \rangle$ and $e \colon R \times R/q \to R/q$ computes multiplication of ring elements modulo q. The "embedding map" computes the bit decomposition of ring elements viewed as vectors modulo q: it maps an element of $M_{\mathrm{R},i} := R/q$ viewed as a vector of polynomial coefficients modulo q to $\log q$ elements in $M_{\mathrm{L},i+1} := R$ with coefficients in $\{0, 1\}$.

We use leveled bilinear modules to construct delegation protocols for evaluating polynomials over $M_{\mathrm{L},1}$, which enables achieving succinct verification for commitment openings. In turn, we obtain succinct verification for R1CS from leveled bilinear modules, from which Theorem 1 follows as a special case.

Theorem 2 (informal). *Let $\mathcal{M}$ be a leveled bilinear module with $\ell = O(\log(M + N))$ levels, for which the leveled bilinear relation assumption holds. Suppose that $M_{\mathrm{L},1}$ is a ring and I a suitable ideal of $M_{\mathrm{L},1}$. There is a preprocessing interactive argument of knowledge for R1CS over $R_\bullet := M_{\mathrm{L},1}/I \simeq \mathbb{F}^k$ with the following efficiency:*

- *communication complexity $O(\log^2(M + N))$ elements of $M_{\mathrm{T},\ell}$;*
- *round complexity $O(\log^2(M + N))$;*
- *indexer complexity $O(M + N)$ operations in $M_{\mathrm{T},\ell}$ and applications of e_ℓ;*
- *prover complexity $O(M + N)$ operations in $M_{\mathrm{T},\ell}$ and applications of e_ℓ;*

- *verifier complexity* $O(\log^2(M + N))$ *operations in* $M_{T,\ell}$ *and applications of* e_ℓ.

The interactive argument in Theorem 2 relies on the *leveled bilinear relation assumption*. This is a falsifiable assumption on leveled bilinear modules implied by the SXDH assumption in the bilinear group instantiation, and by the SIS assumption in the lattice instantiation. For these instantiations, the interactive argument has a transparent (public-coin) setup algorithm.

1.2   Related Work

We summarize work on split-and-fold techniques, lattice-based arguments, and Merkle-tree-based arguments.

Split-and-Fold Techniques over Groups. [25, 27] construct succinct arguments in the discrete logarithm setting, but lack succinct verification. [50] constructs succinct arguments in the bilinear group setting, achieving succinct verification with preprocessing. [17, 26] construct succinct arguments in the unknown-order group setting, achieving succinct verification without preprocessing (they target uniform computations). Drawing inspiration from [17, 26, 50], we achieve succinct verification with preprocessing from an abstract algebraic structure (leveled bilinear modules), which in particular specializes to lattices.

Lattice-Based Interactive Arguments. [9] construct a lattice-based zero-knowledge argument for NP with sublinear (specifically, square-root) communication complexity. [24] use split-and-fold techniques to construct an interactive argument of knowledge for commitment openings with polylogarithmic communication complexity; subsequently [5] reduced the slackness of the openings. [7, 22] extend the approach to work for NP statements. [5, 7] also provide complete security proofs for protocols in [24], while [22] shows that split-and-fold techniques are related to the sumcheck protocol [52]. Our starting point is the protocol of [22]: we construct a delegation protocol (itself also related to the sumcheck protocol) for the expensive computation of the verifier in [22]. Finally, [14] uses a more complex recursive approach to achieve logarithmic proof sizes with concrete estimates of communication complexity in the tens of kilobytes for R1CS instances of size 2^{20}. All the aforementioned lattice-based argument systems lack succinct verification.

Many other works aim to provide concretely efficient arguments for NP statements [58] and specialized applications including group/ring signatures and proofs of knowledge for lattice-based commitments [8, 23, 37–39, 53–55, 60, 61, 66].

Lattice-Based Non-interactive Arguments. Several works construct succinct non-interactive arguments (SNARGs) based on non-falsifiable assumptions (believed to be necessary [43]) about lattices. [18, 19] construct designated-verifier SNARGs by following a paradigm based on linear PCPs [15]. These works were subsequently optimized [41, 46, 59], and a similar approach was used to obtain public-verifier SNARGs [6]. All of these works rely on a private-coin setup algorithm that samples a structured reference string with a trapdoor. This line of work is not directly comparable to our results (we construct interactive arguments from falsifiable assumptions, and moreover the bilinear group and lattice instantiations of our construction have a public-coin setup algorithm).

Merkle-Tree-Based Interactive Arguments. A long line of works [11–13, 21, 29, 44, 51, 63, 65] constructs preprocessing succinct arguments for general NP statements using the Merkle-tree paradigm. These works offer transparent setup and succinct verification with preprocessing. While some of these proof systems offer benefits such as reduced prover complexity in theory [21, 63] and practice [44, 51, 65], the communication complexity of these arguments is at present larger than split-and-fold-based proof systems built from classical assumptions (e.g., [27]), which offers communication complexity on the order of a few kilobytes.

2 Techniques

We summarize the main ideas behind our results.

2.1 Our Approach

A common approach for constructing succinct arguments is to combine two ingredients: (a) a polynomial interactive oracle proof (PIOP); and (b) a suitable polynomial commitment scheme. PIOPs are information-theoretic proof systems, in which the prover sends polynomials in the form of oracle messages to the verifier, who then performs polynomial evaluation queries to these oracles. The polynomial commitment scheme enables the argument prover to commit to these polynomials and subsequently authenticate answers to queries received from the argument verifier.

The succinct argument that we construct follows this common approach, and our contribution is to achieve a suitable realization of each ingredient. To obtain Theorem 2 it suffices to construct, in the preprocessing model, a PIOP for R1CS with succinct verification (an information-theoretic object) and a polynomial commitment scheme with succinct verification from leveled bilinear modules (a cryptographic object). Below we briefly discuss each ingredient, and we elaborate further on them in later sections; note that, for PIOPs, preprocessing is known as *holography*.

(a) Holographic PIOP for R1CS over Product Rings. We construct a holographic PIOP for R1CS over product rings $R_\bullet \simeq \mathbb{F}^k$, by extending prior constructions over finite fields $\mathbb{F}$. This is useful because cyclotomic rings commonly employed in lattice cryptography can be expressed as product rings using facts from algebraic number theory. See Sect. 2.6 for more details.

(b) Polynomial Commitment Scheme from Bilinear Modules. Prior constructions of polynomial commitment schemes with succinct verifier based on split-and-fold techniques [17, 26, 50] use delegation protocols and/or preprocessing. We similarly construct a delegation protocol with preprocessing, leveraging an algebraic module-theoretic abstraction called "leveled bilinear modules"; these can be obtained from lattices, for example. Drawing inspiration from [50], this abstraction captures the ability to commit to commitment keys. We explain our construction across several subsections.

- In Sect. 2.2, we review a polynomial commitment scheme whose proofs of polynomial evaluation, which are based on the sumcheck protocol, have linear-time verification.
- In Sect. 2.3, we describe a delegation protocol over bilinear groups that reduces verification time to polylogarithmic.
- In Sect. 2.4, we introduce leveled bilinear modules, and instantiate them using bilinear groups or lattice rings.
- In Sect. 2.5, we extend the delegation protocol to work over leveled bilinear modules.

Combining. In Sect. 2.7, we obtain our main result by combining the polynomial commitment scheme with succinct verification and the PIOP over rings.

2.2   Polynomial Commitments from Sumcheck Arguments

Sumcheck arguments [22] are a generalization of the sumcheck protocol and of split-and-fold techniques for proving the correct opening of "sumcheck-friendly" commitments. They are used to construct succinct interactive arguments for NP over an abstract algebraic structure, which can be instantiated with lattices. This gives a succinct interactive argument for NP that exploits the structure of lattice-based commitment schemes.

Sumcheck arguments reduce the task of proving knowledge of a commitment opening to the task of evaluating a polynomial whose coefficients are derived from the commitment key. The verifier has access to the commitment key and can perform this evaluation on its own. The commitment key, however, has linear size, leading to linear verification time.

We now describe how to obtain *polynomial commitment schemes* from sumcheck arguments. We restrict our attention to deterministic commitment schemes (without a hiding property) because these suffice for (non-zero-knowledge) interactive arguments. First, we present the necessary background related to the sumcheck protocol. Then, we focus on sumcheck arguments defined over finite fields $\mathbb{F}$ and discrete logarithm groups $\mathbb{G}$ of prime order. Finally, we discuss sumcheck arguments defined over bilinear modules, an abstract mathematical structure that we will use to express pairing and lattice-based commitments.

Sumcheck Protocol. The prover wants to convince the verifier that a given ℓ-variate polynomial P sums to τ over the hypercube $\mathcal{H}^\ell$. While the sumcheck protocol [52] was introduced for polynomials over fields, it directly extends to work with polynomials over *modules* as we describe below. The following construction is a reduction from the claim $\sum_{\underline{\omega} \in \mathcal{H}^\ell} P(\underline{\omega}) = \tau$ to a claim of the form $P(\underline{r}) = v$.

Protocol 1: sumcheck protocol

The prover P_{SC} and the verifier V_{SC} receive an instance $\mathrm{x}_{\mathrm{SC}} = (R, M, \mathcal{H}, \ell, \tau, \mathcal{C})$, where
- R is a ring,
- M is a module over R,
- $\mathcal{H}$ is a subset of R,
- ℓ is a number of variables,
- $\tau \in M$ is a claimed sum, and
- $\mathcal{C} \subseteq R$ is a sampling set (more about this below).

The prover P_{SC} additionally receives a polynomial $P \in M[X_1, \ldots, X_\ell]$ such that $\sum_{\underline{\omega} \in \mathcal{H}^\ell} P(\underline{\omega}) = \tau$. The protocol has ℓ rounds; in each round the prover sends a univariate polynomial $Q_i(X_i)$ and the verifier responds with a challenge r_i.

1. For $i = 1, \ldots, \ell$:
   (a) P_{SC} sends to V_{SC} the polynomial

   $$Q_i(X_i) := \sum_{\omega_{i+1}, \ldots, \omega_\ell \in \mathcal{H}} P(r_1, \ldots, r_{i-1}, X_i, \omega_{i+1}, \ldots, \omega_\ell) \in M[X_i];$$

   (b) V_{SC} sends to P_{SC} a random challenge $r_i \leftarrow \mathcal{C}$.
2. V_{SC} checks that $\sum_{\omega_1 \in \mathcal{H}} Q_1(\omega_1) = \tau$ and, for $i \in \{2, \ldots, \ell\}$, that $\sum_{\omega_i \in \mathcal{H}} Q_i(\omega_i) = Q_{i-1}(r_{i-1})$.
3. If the checks pass, then V_{SC} sets $v := Q_\ell(r_\ell) \in M$ and outputs the tuple $((r_1, \ldots, r_\ell), v)$.

If $\sum_{\underline{\omega} \in \mathcal{H}^\ell} P(\underline{\omega}) = \tau$, then at the end of Protocol 1, the verifier V_{SC} will always output $((r_1, \ldots, r_\ell), v)$ satisfying $P(r_1, \ldots, r_\ell) = v$. On the other hand, if $\sum_{\underline{\omega} \in \mathcal{H}^\ell} P(\underline{\omega}) \neq \tau$, then for any malicious prover $\tilde{P}_{\mathrm{SC}}$, the verifier's output will only satisfy $P(r_1, \ldots, r_\ell) = v$ with probability at most $\frac{\ell \deg(P)}{|\mathcal{C}|}$. This follows from a strengthening of the analysis of the sumcheck protocol over finite fields, relying on the additional requirement that $\mathcal{C}$ is a "sampling set", which guarantees that non-zero polynomials of a given degree d have at most d roots. The sumcheck protocol over modules is discussed further in [22].

Polynomial Commitment Scheme. A polynomial commitment scheme enables a prover to commit to a polynomial and later prove that a claimed polynomial evaluation at a given point is correct. For concreteness, we consider multilinear polynomials whose coefficients are defined by a vector of elements as follows.

Definition 1. *We index the entries of a vector $\underline{v}$ of length $n = 2^\ell$ via binary strings $(i_1, \ldots, i_\ell) \in \{0, 1\}^\ell$, and define the corresponding multilinear polynomial*

$$p_{\underline{v}}(X_1, \ldots, X_\ell) := \sum_{i_1, \ldots, i_\ell \in \{0,1\}} X_1^{i_1} \cdots X_\ell^{i_\ell} \cdot v_{i_1, \ldots, i_\ell}.$$

We describe a polynomial commitment scheme based on Pedersen commitments for committing to the polynomial $p_{\underline{m}}(X_1, \ldots, X_{\log n})$, where $\underline{m} \in \mathbb{F}^n$ and $\mathbb{F}$ is a finite field of prime order p. The commitment is an element of a group $\mathbb{G}$ of order p. In the proof of polynomial evaluation, the prover wishes to convince the verifier of the following $\mathcal{NP}$ statement:

Task 1. *Given a commitment* $\mathsf{C} \in \mathbb{G}$, *a commitment key* $\underline{\mathsf{G}} \in \mathbb{G}^n$, *an evaluation point* $\underline{z} \in \mathbb{F}^{\log n}$, *and a claimed evaluation* $u \in \mathbb{F}$, *prove knowledge of the polynomial* $p_{\underline{m}}$ *(i.e., of the coefficients* $\underline{m} \in \mathbb{F}^n$*) such that* $p_{\underline{m}}(\underline{z}) = u$ *and* $\mathsf{C} = \langle \underline{m}, \underline{\mathsf{G}} \rangle$.

Using Definition 1 we define the polynomial $p_{\underline{\mathsf{G}}}(X_1, \ldots, X_{\log n})$. Here, $p_{\underline{\mathsf{G}}}(\underline{X})$ defines a polynomial function $p_{\underline{\mathsf{G}}} \colon \mathbb{F}^{\log n} \to \mathbb{G}$ over $\mathbb{G}$, where addition corresponds to the group operation and multiplication with an element in $\mathbb{F}$ corresponds to scalar multiplication with the same element. Observe that $\sum_{\underline{\omega} \in \{-1,1\}^\ell} p_{\underline{m}}(\underline{\omega}) p_{\underline{\mathsf{G}}}(\underline{\omega}) = 2^\ell \cdot \mathsf{C}$.

Protocol 2 is a succinct interactive argument for Task 1 based on a sumcheck argument. The only non-succinct verifier operation is colored blue.

Protocol 2: sumcheck argument for polynomial evaluation

For $n = 2^\ell$, the prover and verifier receive as input a commitment key $\underline{\mathsf{G}} \in \mathbb{G}^n$, a commitment $\mathsf{C} \in \mathbb{G}$, an evaluation point $\underline{z} := (z_1, z_2, \ldots, z_\ell) \in \mathbb{F}^\ell$, and a claimed evaluation $u \in \mathbb{F}$. The prover also receives as input an opening $\underline{m} \in \mathbb{F}^n$ such that $\mathsf{C} = \langle \underline{m}, \underline{\mathsf{G}} \rangle$.

The prover and verifier engage in a sumcheck protocol for the claim

$$\sum_{\underline{\omega} \in \{-1,1\}^\ell} P'(\underline{\omega}) = 2^\ell \cdot (\mathsf{C}, u) \ ,$$

where $P'(\underline{X}) := (p_{\underline{m}}(\underline{X}) \cdot p_{\underline{\mathsf{G}}}(\underline{X}), p_{\underline{m}}(\underline{X}) \cdot p_{\underline{\tilde{z}}}(\underline{X}))$ and $\underline{\tilde{z}} := \bigotimes_{i=1}^\ell (1, z_i) = (1, z_1, z_2, z_1 z_2, \ldots, z_1 \cdots z_\ell)$. As defined in Protocol 1, the sumcheck protocol uses the instance

$$\mathbb{x}_{\mathsf{SC}} := (R = \mathbb{F}, \ M = \mathbb{G} \times \mathbb{F}, \ \mathcal{H} = \{-1, 1\}, \ \ell = \log n, \ \tau = 2^\ell \cdot (\mathsf{C}, u), \ \mathcal{C} = \mathbb{F}) \ ,$$

and the prover additionally knows the polynomial $P'(\underline{X}) \in (\mathbb{G} \times \mathbb{F})[\underline{X}]$.

After the end of the sumcheck protocol, if the verifier's checks pass, the prover learns the randomness $\underline{r} \in \mathbb{F}^\ell$ used in the protocol, and the verifier learns $(\underline{r}, v) \in \mathbb{F}^\ell \times \mathbb{F}$. Then, the prover computes and sends $w := p_{\underline{m}}(\underline{r}) \in \mathbb{F}$; the verifier computes $p_{\underline{\mathsf{G}}}(\underline{r}) \in \mathbb{G}$ and $p_{\underline{\tilde{z}}}(\underline{r}) \in \mathbb{F}$ and checks that $(w \cdot p_{\underline{\mathsf{G}}}(\underline{r}), w \cdot p_{\underline{\tilde{z}}}(\underline{r})) = v$.

The Task to Delegate. The only expensive operation that the verifier has to compute is the final multilinear polynomial evaluation $p_{\underline{\mathsf{G}}}(\underline{r})$; because $\underline{\tilde{z}} :=$

$\bigotimes_{i=1}^{\ell}(1, z_i)$, it holds that $p_{\underline{z}}(\underline{r}) = \prod_{i=1}^{\ell}(1 + r_i z_i)$ which can be evaluated in $O(\ell) = O(\log n)$ operations. Our goal is to reduce the verifier complexity by delegating the polynomial evaluation $p_{\underline{G}}(\underline{r})$ to the prover. This means that the prover sends $V \in \mathbb{G}$ and has to prove the following $\mathcal{P}$ statement to the verifier.

Task 2. *Given a commitment key $\underline{G} \in \mathbb{G}^n$, an evaluation point $\underline{r} \in \mathbb{F}^{\log n}$, and a claimed evaluation $V \in \mathbb{G}$, prove that $p_{\underline{G}}(\underline{r}) = V$.*

It is not known how to delegate this task over finite fields $\mathbb{F}$ and discrete logarithm groups $\mathbb{G}$ of prime order. However, we will show a delegation protocol for bilinear groups and lattices. First, we define bilinear modules, an algebraic abstraction that allows us to instantiate Protocol 2 in these settings.

Generalization to Bilinear Modules. We need the commitment scheme and sumcheck argument above to work over more general algebraic structures, specifically over bilinear modules. A bilinear module $\mathsf{BM} = (R, M_\mathrm{L}, M_\mathrm{R}, M_\mathrm{T}, e)$ consists of a ring R, three R-modules $M_\mathrm{L}, M_\mathrm{R}, M_\mathrm{T}$, and an R-bilinear map $e \colon M_\mathrm{L} \times M_\mathrm{R} \to M_\mathrm{T}$.

In a *generalized Pedersen commitment* over a bilinear module BM, the commitment key is a random vector $\underline{G} \in M_\mathrm{R}^n$ and the commitment to the message $\underline{m} \in M_\mathrm{L}^n$ is $C := \langle \underline{m}, \underline{G} \rangle := \sum_{i=1}^{n} e(\mathsf{m}_i, \mathsf{G}_i) \in M_\mathrm{T}$. The commitment scheme is binding for messages of *bounded norm* if given a random vector $\underline{G} \in M_\mathrm{R}^n$, it is hard to find $\underline{m} \in M_\mathrm{L}^n$ with $\underline{m} \neq 0$ and $\|\underline{m}\| \leq B_\mathrm{c}$ such that $\langle \underline{m}, \underline{G} \rangle = 0$. We call this assumption *bilinear relation assumption*.

The generalized Protocol 2 works exactly as before, except for a new check on the norm of w to guarantee that the commitment opening is binding.

In the case of discrete logarithm groups, which is used in Protocol 2, we have $(R, M_\mathrm{L}, M_\mathrm{R}, M_\mathrm{T}, e) := (\mathbb{F}, \mathbb{F}, \mathbb{G}, \mathbb{G}, e)$, using group exponentiation for e. Other instantiations of bilinear modules include bilinear groups and ideal lattices. In the bilinear group setting, $(R, M_\mathrm{L}, M_\mathrm{R}, M_\mathrm{T}, e) := (\mathbb{F}, \mathbb{G}_0, \mathbb{G}_1, \mathbb{G}_\mathrm{T}, e)$ using the bilinear (pairing) operation for e. In the lattice setting, $(R, M_\mathrm{L}, M_\mathrm{R}, M_\mathrm{T}, e) := (R, R, R/qR, R/qR, \times)$, where $R := \mathbb{Z}[X]/\langle \Phi_d(X) \rangle$, Φ_d is the d-th cyclotomic polynomial and $\times$ is polynomial multiplication modulo q. The bilinear relation assumption for the three instantiations corresponds to discrete logarithm, double pairing, and SIS assumptions respectively. In the discrete logarithm and the bilinear group setting, the underlying norm is such that all non-zero elements have norm 1, whereas in the ideal lattice setting we consider the ℓ_∞-norm.

2.3   Warmup: Delegation over Bilinear Groups

Consider the setting of bilinear groups: there are three groups $\mathbb{G}_0, \mathbb{G}_1, \mathbb{G}_\mathrm{T}$ of prime size p and a bilinear map $e \colon \mathbb{G}_0 \times \mathbb{G}_1 \to \mathbb{G}_\mathrm{T}$. When the polynomial commitment scheme and sumcheck argument from Sect. 2.2 are realized over this instantiation of bilinear modules, Task 2 becomes the following.

Task 3. *Given a commitment key $\underline{G} \in \mathbb{G}_1^n$, an evaluation point $\underline{r} \in \mathbb{F}^{\log n}$, and a claimed evaluation $V \in \mathbb{G}_1$, prove that $p_{\underline{G}}(\underline{r}) = V$.*

We describe an interactive proof with succinct verification for this task that is based on techniques from [50] (and variants [64]). Below we review the main ideas behind these techniques, and then discuss the challenges that arise in extending them to work for more general algebraic structures.

Review: Delegation Ideas from [50]. Consider an additional polynomial commitment scheme whose message space is $\mathbb{G}_1^n$ and whose key space is $\mathbb{G}_0^n$:

- a commitment key is a random $\underline{H} \in \mathbb{G}_0^n$;
- a message is $\underline{G} \in \mathbb{G}_1^n$ (which can be the commitment key from Task 3);
- $C' := \langle \underline{H}, \underline{G} \rangle = \sum_{i=1}^n e(H_i, G_i)$ is a commitment to $\underline{G}$ using key $\underline{H}$.

Since $\underline{G}$ and $\underline{H}$ are sampled during the setup phase, C' can be computed during a preprocessing phase. Then, Task 3 can be replaced by the following task.

Task 4. *Given a commitment $C' = \langle \underline{H}, \underline{G} \rangle \in \mathbb{G}_T$ computed in a preprocessing phase by the (honest) indexer, an evaluation point $\underline{r} \in \mathbb{F}^{\log n}$, and a claimed evaluation $V \in \mathbb{G}_1$, prove that $p_{\underline{G}}(\underline{r}) = V$.*

This opens up the possibility of succinct verification because the verifier receives as input $C' \in \mathbb{G}_T$ rather than $\underline{G} \in \mathbb{G}_1^n$. In fact, Task 4 is similar to the original task (Task 1) defined in the setting of bilinear groups. A difference is that in Task 1 the verifier is also given the commitment key. However, to achieve succinct verification the verifier here cannot receive $\underline{H} \in \mathbb{G}_0^n$ as input.

Reducing the Key Size. With further ideas from [50], one can reduce to a *smaller* commitment key over $\mathbb{G}_0^{n/2}$, and then apply the same technique with the roles of $\mathbb{G}_0$ and $\mathbb{G}_1$ reversed. One can repeat this until the verifier need only perform a computation on a constant-size commitment key.

Instead of committing to $\underline{G}$ using a commitment key of length n, split $\underline{G}$ into two halves: $\underline{G} := (\underline{G}[L], \underline{G}[R]) \in \mathbb{G}_1^{n/2} \times \mathbb{G}_1^{n/2}$. During the preprocessing phase, the indexer computes the commitments $C_L := \langle \underline{H}, \underline{G}[L] \rangle \in \mathbb{G}_T$ and $C_R := \langle \underline{H}, \underline{G}[R] \rangle \in \mathbb{G}_T$ using the commitment key $\underline{H} \in \mathbb{G}_0^{n/2}$.

Instead of C', which is a commitment to $\underline{G}$, the verifier now has C_L and C_R, so we can no longer apply the sumcheck argument for polynomial evaluation (Protocol 2) to Task 4. To remedy this, we use the fact that the verifier can compute a commitment to any linear combination of $\underline{G}[L]$ and $\underline{G}[R]$. Then, it suffices to find a linear combination $\underline{G}' \in \mathbb{G}_1^{n/2}$ and an evaluation point $\underline{r}' \in \mathbb{F}^{\log n - 1}$ such that $p_{\underline{G}}(\underline{r}) = p_{\underline{G}'}(\underline{r}')$.

From Definition 1, $p_{\underline{G}}(\underline{X}) := \sum_{i_1,\ldots,i_{\log n} \in \{0,1\}} X_1^{i_1} \cdots X_\ell^{i_{\log n}} \cdot G_{i_1,\ldots,i_{\log n}}$ where $\underline{G} := (G_1,\ldots,G_n)$. Hence, $p_{\underline{G}}(\underline{X}) = p_{\underline{G}[L]+X_1\underline{G}[R]}(X_2,\ldots,X_{\log n})$ and Task 4 reduces to the following task.

Task 5. *Given a commitment $C' := C_L + r_1 C_R$, where $C_L := \langle \underline{H}, \underline{G}[L] \rangle \in \mathbb{G}_T$ and $C_R = \langle \underline{H}, \underline{G}[R] \rangle \in \mathbb{G}_T$ are computed in a preprocessing phase, an evaluation point $\underline{r}' \in \mathbb{F}^{\log n - 1}$, and a claimed evaluation $V \in \mathbb{G}_1$, prove that $p_{\underline{G}'}(\underline{r}') = V$, where $\underline{G}' := \underline{G}[L] + r_1 \underline{G}[R] \in \mathbb{G}_1^{n/2}$.*

Challenge: What Happens over Bilinear Modules? The ideas described above work over bilinear groups due to two fortunate coincidences.

– There are two bilinear modules $(\mathbb{F}, \mathbb{G}_0, \mathbb{G}_1, \mathbb{G}_T, e)$ and $(\mathbb{F}, \mathbb{G}_1, \mathbb{G}_0, \mathbb{G}_T, e)$ that lead to two commitment schemes *with opposite message space and key space.*
– The output claim produced by a sumcheck argument over the first bilinear module is a claim that can be proved using a sumcheck argument over the second bilinear module, and vice versa.

Unfortunately, the situation with general bilinear modules is not so straight-forward. Even if the first property is satisfied (namely, both $\mathsf{BM}_1 = (R, M_\mathrm{L}, M_\mathrm{R}, M_\mathrm{T}, e)$ and $\mathsf{BM}_2 = (R, M_\mathrm{R}, M_\mathrm{L}, M_\mathrm{T}, e)$ are bilinear modules), the second property is not. Since $\underline{\mathsf{G}} \in M_\mathrm{R}^n$ is *random* (so to act as a commitment key over BM_1), $\underline{\mathsf{G}}$ may not have *bounded norm*. The norm bound is required in order to make a binding commitment to $\underline{\mathsf{G}}$, when it acts as a message for BM_2! *This precludes using the same repeated reduction idea over BM_1 and BM_2.*

2.4 Leveled Bilinear Modules

In order to build a delegation protocol for general bilinear modules and prove Theorem 2 (and thus Theorem 1), we want the ability to commit to commitment keys from successive reductions using new bilinear modules. To this end, we consider *multiple levels* of compatible bilinear modules, capable of mapping statements about commitment keys for "lower-level" commitment schemes to statements about messages in "higher-level" commitment schemes. We formalize this new abstract algebraic structure and call it a *leveled bilinear module system*. We also give post-quantum instantiations based on ideal lattices.

Defining Leveled Bilinear Modules. A K-level bilinear module system is a list of K bilinear module systems over the *same* ring R, each satisfying the bilinear relation assumption:

$$\{\mathsf{BM}_i\}_{i \in [K]} = \{(R, M_{\mathrm{L},i}, M_{\mathrm{R},i}, M_{\mathrm{T},i}, ei)\}_{i \in [K]} .$$

Further, to allow commitments to Pedersen commitment keys, successive levels are connected by two maps:

– an *upward map* $\mathsf{up}_i \colon M_{\mathrm{R},i} \to M_{\mathrm{L},i+1}^{\delta_{i+1}}$ that lifts keys at level i to δ_{i+1} small-norm messages at level $i+1$; and
– a *downward map* $\mathsf{dn}_i \colon M_{\mathrm{L},i+1}^{\delta_{i+1}} \to M_{\mathrm{R},i}$ that projects messages at level $i+1$ to keys at level i.

The two maps up_i and dn_i cancel each other out: $\mathsf{dn}_i \circ \mathsf{up}_i$ is the identity map on $M_{\mathrm{R},i}$. Messages produced by up_i are within the binding space of the commitment scheme at level $i+1$. For each level $i \in [K-1]$, the upward map up_i (and hence also dn_i) must satisfy some homomorphic properties:

– for every $m_1, m_2 \in M_{\mathrm{R},i}$, $\mathsf{up}_i(m_1 + m_2) = \mathsf{up}_i(m_1) + \mathsf{up}_i(m_2) \bmod \ker \mathsf{dn}_i$;

– for every $r \in R$ and $m \in M_{\mathrm{R},i}$, $\mathsf{up}_i(r \cdot m) = r \cdot \mathsf{up}_i(m) \bmod \ker \mathsf{dn}_i$.

In fact, these conditions imply that $M_{\mathrm{R},i}$ and $M_{\mathrm{L},i+1}^{\delta_{i+1}} / \ker \mathsf{dn}_i$ are isomorphic as R-modules via up_i and dn_i. Note that if "$\bmod \ker \mathsf{dn}_i$" was removed from the two conditions above, then $M_{\mathrm{R},i}$ and $M_{\mathrm{L},i+1}^{\delta_{i+1}}$ would be isomorphic as R-modules. This would be too rigid for lattice instantiations, in which for every $i \in [K-1]$ the upward map up_i takes statements about commitment keys modulo a prime q to multiple statements about integers of bounded norm, which can be messages for higher-level commitment schemes. Also, equations modulo q may not hold exactly over the integers, and working $\bmod \ker \mathsf{dn}_i$ allows for correction factors.

Using up_i, claims about polynomial evaluations over commitment key elements can be lifted from $M_{\mathrm{R},i}$ to $M_{\mathrm{L},i+1}$ to act as inputs for proof systems over BM_{i+1}. Conversely, using dn_i, statements proved about lifted polynomial evaluations reduce to similar statements about polynomial evaluations over the commitment keys. Leveled bilinear module systems neatly encapsulate the algebraic requirements for interactive arguments like [50], and facilitate extending those ideas to other cryptographic settings.

Instantiations. We describe three instantiations of leveled bilinear-module systems.

– A "2-cycle" based on bilinear groups. Given a bilinear group $(\mathbb{F}, \mathbb{G}_0, \mathbb{G}_1, \mathbb{G}_T, e)$, we set $M_{\mathrm{L},i} := \mathbb{G}_{i \bmod 2}$, $M_{\mathrm{R},i} := \mathbb{G}_{i+1 \bmod 2}$, $M_{\mathrm{T},i} := \mathbb{G}_T$, $\delta_i = 1$, and $e_i := e$. Hence $M_{\mathrm{R},i}$ and $M_{\mathrm{L},i+1}$ are equal. For each level $i \in [K-1]$, the upward map $\mathsf{up}_i \colon \mathbb{G}_{i \bmod 2} \to \mathbb{G}_{i+1 \bmod 2}$ and downward map $\mathsf{dn}_i \colon \mathbb{G}_{i+1 \bmod 2} \to \mathbb{G}_{i \bmod 2}$ are the identity map. At each level, the bilinear relation assumption is implied by the SXDH assumption. This instantiation works for any number of levels.

– A first instantiation based on ideal lattices. Let d be a prime power, $\Phi_d(X)$ the d-th cyclotomic polynomial, $R = \mathbb{Z}[X]/\langle \Phi_d(X) \rangle$ the corresponding cyclotomic ring, and $q_1, \ldots, q_K \in \mathbb{N}$. Let $M_{\mathrm{L},i} := R$, $M_{\mathrm{R},i} := R/q_i R$, $M_{\mathrm{T},i} := R/q_i R$, and e_i be the multiplication of ring elements modulo q_i.

We "lift" an element m of $M_{\mathrm{R},i} = R/q_i R$ to an element of $M_{\mathrm{L},i+1} = \mathbb{Z}[X]/\langle X^d + 1 \rangle$ with norm at most q_i by viewing it as a polynomial over the integers rather than modulo q_i. For each level $i \in [K-1]$, the upward map $\mathsf{up}_i \colon R/qR \to R$ lifts polynomials modulo q to integer polynomials, and the downward map $\mathsf{dn}_i \colon R \to R/q_i R$ performs the reverse operation, i.e., reduction modulo q_i. At each level, the bilinear relation assumption follows from the ring SIS assumption modulo q_i.

Unfortunately, this first instantiation is somewhat inefficient, and insecure when K is super-constant. This is because in order for the ring SIS assumption modulo q_i to be hard with respect to messages of norm up to q_{i-1}, we require $q_i \gg q_{i-1}$, so that $q_K \gg \cdots \gg q_1$. Moreover, based on the parameters required by the proof system that we use, the gap between each modulus can force q_K to be exponentially large when $K = \omega(1)$, which poses problems for the hardness of ring SIS.

This motives the following improved instantiation.

– A "1-cycle" based on ideal lattices. Let d be a prime power, $\Phi_d(X)$ the d-th cyclotomic polynomial, $R = \mathbb{Z}[X]/\langle\Phi_d(X)\rangle$ the corresponding cyclotomic ring, and $q \in \mathbb{N}$. Let $M_{L,i} := R$, $M_{R,i} := R/qR$, $M_{T,i} := R/qR$, and e_i be the multiplication of ring elements modulo q.

An element in R can be viewed as a polynomial with d coefficients. We "lift" an element m of $M_{R,i} = R/qR$ to $\log q$ elements of $M_{L,i+1} = \mathbb{Z}[X]/\langle X^d + 1\rangle$ with norm at most 1 by computing the bit decomposition of the coefficients of m. For each level $i \in [K - 1]$, the upward map $\mathsf{up}_i \colon R/qR \to R$ lifts polynomials modulo q to integer polynomials using bit decomposition, and the downward map $\mathsf{dn}_i \colon R \to R/qR$ performs the reverse operation, i.e., bit composition modulo q. At each level, the bilinear relation assumption follows from the ring SIS assumption modulo q. This instantiation works for any number of levels.

2.4.1 Comparison with Prior Algebraic Structures Tiered Commitment Schemes.

Some prior works also use leveled algebraic structures to construct argument systems. [45] constructs two-tiered commitment schemes, in which commitments in $\mathbb{G}_0$ (to messages in $\mathbb{F}$) are themselves treated as messages and used to produce "commitments to commitments" in $\mathbb{G}_T$. [24] uses a lattice construction to "commit to commitments" over multiple levels. In contrast to our work, the focus in these works is committing to commitments, which would lead to an abstraction that is different from ours ($M_{T,i}$, rather than $M_{R,i}$, is identified with $M_{L,i+1}$).[1]

Graded Encodings (a.k.a. Multilinear Maps). Leveled modules may be reminiscent of graded encoding schemes, in which elements of groups can be multiplied together up to a certain number of multiplications. We explain the main differences between graded encoding schemes and leveled bilinear-module systems.

Graded encodings of different levels usually consist of elements of the same ring, with homomorphic properties when combining encodings at different levels. By contrast, leveled bilinear modules feature different modules at each level, and the embedding maps between levels do not fully preserve homomorphism. This means that only objects at the same level can be multiplied together, and since homomorphism is limited, leveled bilinear modules cannot be used to construct a multilinear map.

Constructions of graded encoding schemes typically rely on lattice assumptions [40,42,49] or integer assumptions (e.g., the approximate GCD problem) [32,33,56] that have been subject to many attacks [28,34–36]. By contrast, we give comparatively simple instantiations of leveled bilinear modules based on bilinear groups and ideal lattices, providing the relevant security properties under standard cryptographic assumptions (SXDH and SIS respectively).

---

[1] Of course, in our lattice instantiation, $M_{R,i}$ and $M_{T,i}$ happen to be the same.

2.5   Delegation over Leveled Bilinear-Module Systems

The polynomial commitment scheme and the sumcheck argument from Sect. 2.2 can be defined over a bilinear module, and in particular over the first level of a leveled bilinear-module system. In this case, the prover's goal is to convince the verifier of the following $\mathcal{NP}$ statement.

Task 6. *Given a commitment* $C \in M_{T,1}$, *a commitment key* $\underline{G} \in M_{R,1}^n$, *an evaluation point* $\underline{z} \in R^{\log n}$, *and a claimed evaluation* $u \in M_{L,1}$, *prove knowledge of* $\underline{m} \in M_{L,1}^n$ *such that* $p_{\underline{m}}(\underline{z}) = u$ *and* $C = \langle \underline{m}, \underline{G} \rangle$.

The succinct interactive protocol for the above task is a generalization of Protocol 2 over bilinear modules. Even though for certain settings (e.g., lattices) norm manipulations and selecting appropriate challenge spaces $\mathcal{C} \subseteq R$ are important, for simplicity in this overview we ignore these issues.

Protocol 3: sumcheck argument for polynomial evaluation over $\mathcal{M}$

For $n = 2^\ell$, the prover and verifier receive as input a commitment key $\underline{G} \in M_{R,1}^n$, a commitment $C \in M_{T,1}$, an evaluation point $\underline{z} := (z_1, z_2, \ldots, z_\ell) \in R^\ell$, and a claimed evaluation $u \in M_{L,1}$. The prover also receives as input an opening $\underline{m} \in M_{L,1}^n$ such that $C = \langle \underline{m}, \underline{G} \rangle$.

The prover and verifier engage in a sumcheck protocol for the claim

$$\sum_{\underline{\omega} \in \{-1,1\}^\ell} P'(\underline{\omega}) = 2^\ell \cdot (C, u),$$

where $P'(\underline{X}) := (p_{\underline{m}}(\underline{X}) \cdot p_{\underline{G}}(\underline{X}), p_{\underline{m}}(\underline{X}) \cdot p_{\underline{z}}(\underline{X}))$ and $\tilde{z} := \bigotimes_{i=1}^\ell (1, z_i) = (1, z_1, z_2, z_1 z_2, \ldots, z_1 \cdots z_\ell)$. As defined in Protocol 1, the sumcheck protocol uses the instance

$$\mathbb{x}_{SC} := (R, \ M = M_{T,1} \times M_{L,1}, \ \mathcal{H} = \{-1,1\}, \ \ell = \log n, \ \tau = 2^\ell \cdot (C, u), \ \mathcal{C} \subseteq R) \ ,$$

and the prover additionally knows the polynomial $P'(\underline{X}) \in (M_{T,1} \times M_{L,1})[\underline{X}]$.

After the end of the sumcheck protocol, if the verifier's checks pass, the prover learns the randomness $\underline{r} \in \mathcal{C}^\ell$ used in the protocol, and the verifier learns $(\underline{r}, v) \in \mathcal{C}^\ell \times (M_{T,1} \times M_{L,1})$. Then, the prover computes and sends $w := p_{\underline{m}}(\underline{r}) \in M_{L,1}$; the verifier computes $p_{\underline{G}}(\underline{r}) \in M_{R,1}$ and $p_{\tilde{z}}(\underline{r}) \in R$ and checks that $(w \cdot p_{\underline{G}}(\underline{r}), w \cdot p_{\tilde{z}}(\underline{r})) = v$.

Delegation Using the Leveled Bilinear-Module System. The above protocol reduces proving that $p_{\underline{m}}(\underline{z}) = u \in M_{L,1}$ to checking the polynomial evaluation $p_{\underline{G}}(\underline{r}) = V \in M_{R,1}$. Using the maps of the leveled bilinear-module system, we compute $\mathsf{up}_1(\underline{G}) \in (M_{L,2}^{\delta_2})^n$, where up_1 is applied to each coordinate of

$\underline{\mathsf{G}}$, and $\mathsf{V}' \equiv \mathsf{up}_1(\mathsf{V}) \bmod \ker(\mathsf{dn}_1) \in M_{\mathrm{L},2}^{\delta_2}$. Then, we transform the evaluation $p_{\underline{\mathsf{G}}}(\underline{r}) = \mathsf{V} \in M_{\mathrm{R},1}$ to δ_2 evaluations over $M_{\mathrm{L},2}$:

$$p_{\mathsf{up}_1(\underline{\mathsf{G}})}(\underline{r}) = \mathsf{V}' \ .$$

The function up_1 maps an element in $M_{\mathrm{R},1}$ to multiple elements in $M_{\mathrm{L},2}$. We reduce to a single element of $M_{\mathrm{L},2}$ by computing a random linear combination using challenges sent by the verifier. For the rest of this section, we ignore this issue and focus on the case where up_i maps an element of an $M_{\mathrm{R},i}$ to a *single* element of $M_{\mathrm{L},i+1}$ (i.e., $\delta_{i+1} = 1$).

We can apply the key reduction idea presented in Sect. 2.3 to reduce to a statement of smaller size. During the preprocessing phase, the indexer computes the commitments $C_L = \langle \mathsf{up}_1(\underline{\mathsf{G}}[L]), \underline{\mathsf{H}} \rangle \in M_{\mathrm{T},2}$ and $C_R = \langle \mathsf{up}_1(\underline{\mathsf{G}}[R]), \underline{\mathsf{H}} \rangle \in M_{\mathrm{T},2}$, where $\underline{\mathsf{G}} := (\underline{\mathsf{G}}[L], \underline{\mathsf{G}}[R]) \in M_{\mathrm{R},1}^{n/2} \times M_{\mathrm{R},1}^{n/2}$. Task 6 reduces to the following.

Task 7. *Given a commitment $C' := C_L + r_1 C_R$, where $C_L := \langle \mathsf{up}_1(\underline{\mathsf{G}}[L]), \underline{\mathsf{H}} \rangle \in M_{\mathrm{T},2}$ and $C_R = \langle \mathsf{up}_1(\underline{\mathsf{G}}[R]), \underline{\mathsf{H}} \rangle \in M_{\mathrm{T},2}$ are computed in a preprocessing phase, an evaluation point $\underline{r}' \in R^{\log n - 1}$, and a claimed evaluation $\mathsf{V}' \in M_{\mathrm{L},2}$, prove that $p_{\underline{\mathsf{G}}'}(\underline{r}') = \mathsf{V}'$, where $\underline{\mathsf{G}}' := \mathsf{up}_1(\underline{\mathsf{G}}[L]) + r_1 \cdot \mathsf{up}_1(\underline{\mathsf{G}}[R]) \in M_{\mathrm{L},2}^{n/2}$.*

Final Protocol: Delegation of Polynomial Evaluations with Succinct Verifier. Below we sketch the final protocol. There are $\ell := \log n$ iterations of Protocol 3. In the i-th iteration the instance has size $n/2^i$ and is defined over the i-th level of the leveled bilinear module. After ℓ iterations of Protocol 3, the verifier checks the evaluation of a constant polynomial, which can be done without help from the prover.

Protocol 4: delegation of polynomial evaluations over $\underline{M}$

Setup Given an upper bound n on the size of $\underline{m}$ (the number of polynomial coefficients), the setup algorithm samples a leveled bilinear-module system with $\log n$ levels and commitment keys $\underline{\mathsf{G}}_i \in M_{\mathrm{R},i}^{n/2^{i-1}}$ for $i \in \{1, \ldots, \log n + 1\}$.

Indexer In a preprocessing phase (i.e., before receiving $\underline{m}$), the indexer computes

$$\mathsf{C}_{L,i} := \langle \mathsf{up}_i(\underline{\mathsf{G}}_i[L]), \underline{\mathsf{G}}_{i+1} \rangle \in M_{\mathrm{T},i+1} \ , \ \text{and} \mathsf{C}_{R,i} = \langle \mathsf{up}_i(\underline{\mathsf{G}}_i[R]), \underline{\mathsf{G}}_{i+1} \rangle \in M_{\mathrm{T},i+1}$$

for $i \in \{1, \ldots, \log n\}$. Finally, the indexer sets outputs the proving key $\mathsf{ipk} := (\underline{\mathsf{G}}_i)_{i=1}^{\log n + 1}$ and verification key $\mathsf{ivk} := ((\mathsf{C}_{L,i}, \mathsf{C}_{R,i})_{i=1}^{\log n}, \underline{\mathsf{G}}_{\log n})$.

Interactive phase For $n = 2^\ell$, the prover and verifier receive as input a commitment $C \in M_{\mathrm{T},1}$, an evaluation point $\underline{z} := (z_1, z_2, \ldots, z_\ell) \in R^\ell$, and a claimed evaluation $u \in M_{\mathrm{L},1}$. The prover also receives as input the proving key ipk and an opening $\underline{m} \in M_{\mathrm{L},1}^n$ such that $C = \langle \underline{m}, \underline{\mathsf{G}} \rangle$. The verifier also receives as input the verification key ivk.

The prover and verifier engage in $\log n$ iterations of Protocol 3. The first iteration reduces the claim $p_{\underline{m}}(\underline{z}) = u$ to proving that $p_{\underline{G}_1}(\underline{r}_1) = V_1$, which can be reduced to the claim $p_{\underline{G}'_1}(\underline{r}'_1) = V'_1 \in M_{L,2}$ as in Task 7. Similarly, the i-th iteration reduces the claim $p_{\underline{G}'_{i-1}}(\underline{r}'_{i-1}) = V'_{i-1} \in M_{L,i}$ to proving that $p_{\underline{G}'_i}(\underline{r}'_i) = V'_i \in M_{L,i+1}$. Finally, the last claim is $p_{\underline{G}_{\log n}}(\underline{r}_{\log n}) = V_{\log n}$, which the verifier can check directly using the key $\underline{G}_{\log n}$.

The indexer performs $O(n)$ operations. Subsequently, the prover and verifier interact over $O(\log^2 n)$ rounds. The communication complexity is $O(\log^2 n)$ elements of the ring and modules of the leveled bilinear-module system: each iteration of the $O(\log n)$ iterations of Protocol 3 has communication complexity $O(\log n)$ elements of a bilinear module. The prover performs $O(n)$ operations over the ring and modules of the leveled bilinear-module system; and the verifier performs $O(\log^2 n)$ such operations. (Indeed, in the i-th sumcheck argument the prover performs $O(n/2^i)$ operations and the verifier performs $O(\log n - i)$ operations.)

Completeness of the protocol is straightforward, since the i-th iteration reduces a true statement about a polynomial evaluation over the i-th level into a true statement about a polynomial evaluation over the $(i+1)$-th level, using the embedding map up_i. The verifier accepts because each iteration is a sumcheck argument for a valid polynomial evaluation. In contrast, establishing soundness requires more care, as we now explain.

Soundness. The protocol consists of $\log n$ sumcheck arguments, so a starting point for arguing soundness is to follow the approach in [22]. There, a valid witness is extracted from an extraction tree (a collection of accepting transcripts with a special tree-like structure). For instance, in the case of polynomial commitments as in Protocol 2, the extraction tree is a ternary tree of depth $\log n$. An extraction tree can be obtained, from a suitable malicious prover, in time exponential in its depth (e.g. see the forking lemma in [7, Lemma 5]). While this technique works in a single iteration of Protocol 3 to prove knowledge soundness, it fails when applied in the final delegation protocol which consists of $\log n$ iterations. This is because now we would need an extraction tree of depth $\log^2 n$, and producing such a tree takes quasi-polynomial time.

An alternative approach is to start from the knowledge soundness of each iteration of Protocol 3, which is based on an extraction tree of depth only $\log n$. Informally, the soundness of the final delegation protocol then follows by a union bound on the $\log n$ iterations. This approach is used, e.g., to establish the soundness of the $O(\log^2 n)$-round version of [50] presented in [64]. However, in our case, which also captures the lattice setting, this has a negative impact in the parameters.

For example, in the lattice setting, it is only known how to prove knowledge soundness of Protocol 3 for a relaxed statement [22]. More precisely, if the verifier accepts in Protocol 3, then we can extract a *relaxed opening* $\underline{m} \in M_{L,1}^n$ to C such that $c \cdot C = \langle \underline{m}, \underline{G} \rangle$ and $p_{\underline{m}}(\underline{z}) = u$, where c is called the *slackness*. Then, establishing soundness by simply applying the knowledge soundness property of

Task 6 recursively ℓ times causes the slackness to accumulate at each extraction step. This approach can only prove that the final delegation protocol has slackness exponential in $\log n$.

We avoid the accumulation of slackness by leveraging the fact that the statement to be proved is a deterministic computation: if the prover does not send a correct evaluation of the key polynomial at the end of each iteration, then the verifier rejects (with some good probability). There is no witness to extract, since the commitment keys are part of the public parameters. In the security proof we can check whether the prover sends an incorrect evaluation in each iteration of Protocol 3. If any of the evaluations is incorrect, then we extract a message that breaks the binding property of the commitment of this iteration. The i-th iteration of Protocol 3 has soundness error $O(\frac{\log n - i}{|C|})$; hence, the soundness error of the entire protocol is $O(\frac{\log n^2}{|C|})$. The final slackness remains c.

From Relaxed to Exact Openings. Relaxed openings prove approximate statements about polynomial evaluations. This is a problem when we wish to reason about exact satisfiability of algebraic relations, such as R1CS. We modify the polynomial commitment scheme to allow us to divide out the slackness, and hence to extract exact openings. Specifically, we consider $M_{\mathrm{L},1}$ to be a ring and I an ideal of $M_{\mathrm{L},1}$ in which multiplication by slackness c is invertible. Then, intuitively, an opening of a commitment $c \cdot \mathsf{C}$ to message $\underline{\mathsf{m}} \in M_{\mathrm{L},1}^n$ can be viewed as an opening of C to $c^{-1}\underline{\mathsf{m}} \in (M_{\mathrm{L},1}/I)^n$. The message space for the modified commitment scheme is $M_{\mathrm{L},1}/I$. To commit to a polynomial with coefficients in $M_{\mathrm{L},1}/I$, we first lift them to elements in $M_{\mathrm{L},1}$ and then apply the original, unmodified commitment scheme. Specifically, our lattice-based instantiation of the leveled modules and rings leads to a polynomial commitment scheme over a ring R/pR.

2.6   Polynomial IOP for Product Rings

As described in Sect. 2.1, our succinct argument is obtained by combining the polynomial commitment scheme described in Sect. 2.5 and a polynomial IOP (PIOP). In a PIOP, the prover can send polynomials to the verifier as oracle messages, and the verifier's queries request evaluations of these polynomials.

While there are PIOPs that work over finite fields $\mathbb{F}$, to prove Theorem 2 we need a PIOP that works over rings satisfying $R_\bullet \simeq \mathbb{F}^k$. This suffices to prove Theorem 1 as a special case of Theorem 2 because the cyclotomic rings that arise from the lattice instantiation can be expressed as product rings using facts from algebraic number theory.[2]

---

[2] In more detail, consider a cyclotomic ring of the form $R := \mathbb{Z}[X]/\langle \Phi_d(X) \rangle$ where $\Phi_d(X)$ is the d-th cyclotomic polynomial. The polynomial $\Phi_d(X)$ modulo a prime p with $\gcd(p, d) = 1$ factors into irreducible polynomials of the same degree t for some $t \in \mathbb{N}$ (e.g., from [31, Theorem 5.3]). This means that R/pR is isomorphic to $k := \phi(d)/t$ copies of $\mathbb{F}_{p^t}$.

PIOPs over Product Rings. We obtain a holographic PIOP for R1CS over product rings $R_\bullet \simeq \mathbb{F}^k$ by using k times "in parallel" an existing PIOP construction over $\mathbb{F}$, as we now explain. First, we apply the isomorphism between $R_\bullet$ and $\mathbb{F}^k$ to an R1CS instance defined over $R_\bullet$, producing k R1CS instances defined over $\mathbb{F}$. Observe that the non-zero entries in each of the k R1CS instances over $\mathbb{F}$ are a subset of the non-zero entries in the instance over $R_\bullet$. Second, we use the holographic PIOP with succinct verification for R1CS instances over $\mathbb{F}$ from prior work [20]. More precisely, we run this PIOP for the k R1CS instances over $\mathbb{F}$ using the same random verifier challenges (which are sampled from $\mathbb{F}$). This gives a PIOP with similar complexity parameters defined over $R_\bullet$ by mapping all of the prover and verifier messages back into $R_\bullet$.

This approach works because the PIOP in [20] has the following special property: the indexer, prover, and verifier can be modeled as arithmetic circuits which have hard-coded the positions of non-zero entries in the R1CS instance[3]. Since the set of non-zero entries in the R1CS instance over $R_\bullet$ is a superset of the non-zero entries in the k R1CS instances over $\mathbb{F}$, the arithmetic circuits for the indexer, prover, and verifier are the same for the k instances over $\mathbb{F}$. Thus, a PIOP for R1CS over $\mathbb{F}$ can be converted into a PIOP over $R_\bullet$ with the same proof size and computational complexity as the original PIOP, but measured as elements and operations over $R_\bullet$.

In sum, we obtain a ring-based PIOP with linear prover time and logarithmic verifier time.

Lemma 1. (informal). *For every ring $R_\bullet$ such that $R_\bullet \simeq \mathbb{F}^k$, there is a holographic polynomial IOP for R1CS over the ring $R_\bullet$ with instances of size N with M non-zero entries, with the following properties:*

- *the round complexity is $O(\log(M + N))$;*
- *the proof length is $O(M + N)$ elements in $R_\bullet$;*
- *the query complexity is $O(1)$;*
- *the communication complexity is $O(\log(M + N))$ messages in $R_\bullet$;*
- *the indexer uses $O(M)$ operations in $R_\bullet$;*
- *the prover uses $O(N + M)$ operations in $R_\bullet$;*
- *the verifier uses $O(\log M)$ operations in $R_\bullet$.*

Here, "proof length" refers to the total number of elements of $R_\bullet$ in oracle messages, while "communication complexity" refers to the total number of (non-oracle) message elements received by the verifier.

2.7   Final Protocol: Combining Polynomial Commitments and PIOP

To obtain Theorem 2, we combine the polynomial commitment scheme described in Sect. 2.5 and the PIOP over product rings of Sect. 2.6. Then, Theorem 1 follows as a special case by using the lattice-based instantiation of a leveled bilinear module.

---

[3] This is despite the fact that the PIOP construction in full generality sometimes uses non-algebraic operations such as linear scans.

Protocol 5: succinct interactive argument for R1CS over $\underline{\mathcal{M}}$

Setup On input $N \in \mathbb{N}$, the setup algorithm runs the setup algorithm for the polynomial commitment scheme to generate public parameters for committing to messages of length N. As part of this algorithm, the setup algorithm samples a levelled bilinear module with $\underline{\mathcal{M}}$, containing the description of a ring $M_{\mathrm{L},1}$, an ideal I_1, and a module $M_{\mathrm{T},\ell}$, where $\ell = \log(N)$.

Indexer On input an R1CS instance of size N with M non-zero entries defined over the ring $R_\bullet = M_{\mathrm{L},1}/I_1 \simeq \mathbb{F}^k$, the indexer algorithm runs the indexer algorithm for the PIOP for $R_\bullet$ of Section 2.6, producing polynomial oracle messages defined over $R_\bullet$. Then the indexer runs the indexer of the polynomial commitment scheme of Section 2.5, and computes commitments to each of the polynomials. The indexer computes a proving key ipk consisting of the polynomials, their commitments, and the proving key for the polynomial commitment scheme. The indexer computes a verification key ivk consisting of the commitments and the verification key for the polynomial commitment scheme. Finally, the indexer outputs ipk and ivk.

Prover and verifier The prover receives ipk, while the verifier receives ivk. The prover and verifier run the prover and verifier algorithms for the PIOP of Section 2.6, forwarding messages between the PIOP prover and verifier. Whenever the PIOP prover produces a polynomial oracle message over $R_\bullet$, the prover commits to it using the polynomial commitment scheme and sends the result to the verifier. Whenever the PIOP verifier makes a polynomial evaluation query, the verifier forwards it to the prover, who evaluates the polynomial, and sends the evaluation back to the verifier. The prover and verifier then use the polynomial commitment scheme to prove that the evaluation is consistent with the correct committed polynomial. The verifier accepts if all evaluations are consistent, and the PIOP verifier acccepts.

The verifier must perform $O(\log M)$ operations over $R_\bullet$ as part of the PIOP, and $O(\log^2(M + N))$ operations over $M_{\mathrm{T},\ell}$ to use the polynomial commitment scheme to verify each of the $O(1)$ PIOP query responses. The communication complexity of the argument is dominated by the $O(\log^2(M + N))$ elements of $M_{\mathrm{T},\ell}$ sent when using the polynomial commitment scheme. This yields a succinct argument with efficient verification for NP over a leveled bilinear-module system.

References

1. URL: https://falcon-sign.info/
2. URL: https://pq-crystals.org/dilithium/index.shtml
3. URL: https://sphincs.org/
4. URL: https://microsoft.github.io/Picnic/

5. Albrecht, M.R., Lai, R.W.F.: Subtractive sets over cyclotomic rings: limits of Schnorr-like arguments over lattices. In: Malkin, T., Peikert, C. (eds.) CRYPTO 2021. LNCS, vol. 12826, pp. 519–548. Springer, Cham (2021). https://doi.org/10.1007/978-3-030-84245-1_18

6. Albrecht, M.R., Cini, V., Lai, R.W.F., Malavolta, G., Thyagarajan, S.A.: Lattice-based SNARKs: publicly verifiable, preprocessing, and recursively composable. In: Dodis, Y., Shrimpton, T. (eds.) CRYPTO 2022. LNCS, vol. 13508, pp. 102–132. Springer, Cham (2022). https://doi.org/10.1007/978-3-031-15979-4_4

7. Attema, T., Cramer, R., Kohl, L.: A compressed Σ-protocol theory for lattices. In: Malkin, T., Peikert, C. (eds.) CRYPTO 2021. LNCS, vol. 12826, pp. 549–579. Springer, Cham (2021). https://doi.org/10.1007/978-3-030-84245-1_19

8. Attema, T., Lyubashevsky, V., Seiler, G.: Practical product proofs for lattice commitments. In: Micciancio, D., Ristenpart, T. (eds.) CRYPTO 2020. LNCS, vol. 12171, pp. 470–499. Springer, Cham (2020). https://doi.org/10.1007/978-3-030-56880-1_17

9. Baum, C., Bootle, J., Cerulli, A., del Pino, R., Groth, J., Lyubashevsky, V.: Sublinear lattice-based zero-knowledge arguments for arithmetic circuits. In: Shacham, H., Boldyreva, A. (eds.) CRYPTO 2018. LNCS, vol. 10992, pp. 669–699. Springer, Cham (2018). https://doi.org/10.1007/978-3-319-96881-0_23

10. Ben-Sasson, E., Chiesa, A., Spooner, N.: Interactive oracle proofs. In: Hirt, M., Smith, A. (eds.) TCC 2016. LNCS, vol. 9986, pp. 31–60. Springer, Heidelberg (2016). https://doi.org/10.1007/978-3-662-53644-5_2

11. Ben-Sasson, E., et al.: Aurora: transparent succinct arguments for R1CS. In: Proceedings of the 38th Annual International Conference on the Theory and Applications of Cryptographic Techniques. EUROCRYPT'19, pp. 103–128 (2019). Full version available at https://eprint.iacr.org/2018/828

12. Ben-Sasson, E., et al.: Fast Reed-Solomon interactive oracle proofs of proximity. In: Proceedings of the 45th International Colloquium on Automata, Languages and Programming. ICALP'18, pp. 14:1–14:17 (2018)

13. Ben-Sasson, E., Chiesa, A., Goldberg, L., Gur, T., Riabzev, M., Spooner, N.: Linear-size constant-query IOPs for delegating computation. In: Hofheinz, D., Rosen, A. (eds.) TCC 2019. LNCS, vol. 11892, pp. 494–521. Springer, Cham (2019). https://doi.org/10.1007/978-3-030-36033-7_19

14. Beullens, W., Seiler, G.: LaBRADOR: compact proofs for R1CS from module - SIS (2022)

15. Bitansky, N., Chiesa, A., Ishai, Y., Paneth, O., Ostrovsky, R.: Succinct non-interactive arguments via linear interactive proofs. In: Sahai, A. (ed.) TCC 2013. LNCS, vol. 7785, pp. 315–333. Springer, Heidelberg (2013). https://doi.org/10.1007/978-3-642-36594-2_18

16. Block, A.R., Holmgren, J., Rosen, A., Rothblum, R.D., Soni, P.: Public-coin zero-knowledge arguments with (almost) minimal time and space overheads. In: Pass, R., Pietrzak, K. (eds.) TCC 2020. LNCS, vol. 12551, pp. 168–197. Springer, Cham (2020). https://doi.org/10.1007/978-3-030-64378-2_7

17. Block, A.R., Holmgren, J., Rosen, A., Rothblum, R.D., Soni, P.: Time- and space-efficient arguments from groups of unknown order. In: Malkin, T., Peikert, C. (eds.) CRYPTO 2021. LNCS, vol. 12828, pp. 123–152. Springer, Cham (2021). https://doi.org/10.1007/978-3-030-84259-8_5

18. Boneh, D., Ishai, Y., Sahai, A., Wu, D.J.: Lattice-based SNARGs and their application to more efficient obfuscation. In: Coron, J.-S., Nielsen, J.B. (eds.) EUROCRYPT 2017. LNCS, vol. 10212, pp. 247–277. Springer, Cham (2017). https://doi.org/10.1007/978-3-319-56617-7_9

19. Boneh, D., Ishai, Y., Sahai, A., Wu, D.J.: Quasi-optimal SNARGs via linear multi-prover interactive proofs. In: Nielsen, J.B., Rijmen, V. (eds.) EUROCRYPT 2018. LNCS, vol. 10822, pp. 222–255. Springer, Cham (2018). https://doi.org/10.1007/978-3-319-78372-7_8

20. Bootle, J., Chiesa, A., Groth, J.: Linear-time arguments with sublinear verification from tensor codes. In: Pass, R., Pietrzak, K. (eds.) TCC 2020. LNCS, vol. 12551, pp. 19–46. Springer, Cham (2020). https://doi.org/10.1007/978-3-030-64378-2_2

21. Bootle, J., Chiesa, A., Liu, S.: Zero-knowledge succinct arguments with a linear-time prover. In: Dunkelman, O., Dziembowski, S. (eds.) EUROCRYPT 2022. LNCS, vol. 13276, pp. 275–304. Springer, Cham (2022). https://doi.org/10.1007/978-3-031-07085-3_10

22. Bootle, J., Chiesa, A., Sotiraki, K.: Sumcheck arguments and their applications. In: Malkin, T., Peikert, C. (eds.) CRYPTO 2021. LNCS, vol. 12825, pp. 742–773. Springer, Cham (2021). https://doi.org/10.1007/978-3-030-84242-0_26

23. Bootle, J., Lyubashevsky, V., Seiler, G.: Algebraic techniques for short(er) exact lattice-based zero-knowledge proofs. In: Boldyreva, A., Micciancio, D. (eds.) CRYPTO 2019. LNCS, vol. 11692, pp. 176–202. Springer, Cham (2019). https://doi.org/10.1007/978-3-030-26948-7_7

24. Bootle, J., Lyubashevsky, V., Nguyen, N.K., Seiler, G.: A non-PCP approach to succinct quantum-safe zero-knowledge. In: Micciancio, D., Ristenpart, T. (eds.) CRYPTO 2020. LNCS, vol. 12171, pp. 441–469. Springer, Cham (2020). https://doi.org/10.1007/978-3-030-56880-1_16

25. Bootle, J., Cerulli, A., Chaidos, P., Groth, J., Petit, C.: Efficient zero-knowledge arguments for arithmetic circuits in the discrete log setting. In: Fischlin, M., Coron, J.-S. (eds.) EUROCRYPT 2016. LNCS, vol. 9666, pp. 327–357. Springer, Heidelberg (2016). https://doi.org/10.1007/978-3-662-49896-5_12

26. Bünz, B., Fisch, B., Szepieniec, A.: Transparent SNARKs from DARK compilers. In: Canteaut, A., Ishai, Y. (eds.) EUROCRYPT 2020. LNCS, vol. 12105, pp. 677–706. Springer, Cham (2020). https://doi.org/10.1007/978-3-030-45721-1_24

27. Bünz, B., et al.: Bulletproofs: short proofs for confidential transactions and more. In: Proceedings of the 39th IEEE Symposium on Security and Privacy. S&P'18, pp. 315–334 (2018)

28. Cheon, J.H., Fouque, P.-A., Lee, C., Minaud, B., Ryu, H.: Cryptanalysis of the new CLT multilinear map over the integers. In: Fischlin, M., Coron, J.-S. (eds.) EUROCRYPT 2016. LNCS, vol. 9665, pp. 509–536. Springer, Heidelberg (2016). https://doi.org/10.1007/978-3-662-49890-3_20

29. Chiesa, A., Ojha, D., Spooner, N.: FRACTAL: post-quantum and transparent recursive proofs from holography. In: Canteaut, A., Ishai, Y. (eds.) EUROCRYPT 2020. LNCS, vol. 12105, pp. 769–793. Springer, Cham (2020). https://doi.org/10.1007/978-3-030-45721-1_27

30. Chiesa, A., et al.: Post-quantum succinct arguments: breaking the quantum rewinding barriers. In: Proceedings of the 62nd Annual IEEE Symposium on Foundations of Computer Science. FOCS'21 (2021)

31. Conrad, K.: Cyclotomic Extensions (2013). https://kconrad.math.uconn.edu/math5211s13/handouts/cyclotomic.pdf

32. Coron, J.-S., Lepoint, T., Tibouchi, M.: New multilinear maps over the integers. In: Gennaro, R., Robshaw, M. (eds.) CRYPTO 2015. LNCS, vol. 9215, pp. 267–286. Springer, Heidelberg (2015). https://doi.org/10.1007/978-3-662-47989-6_13

33. Coron, J.-S., Lepoint, T., Tibouchi, M.: Practical multilinear maps over the integers. In: Canetti, R., Garay, J.A. (eds.) CRYPTO 2013. LNCS, vol. 8042, pp. 476–493. Springer, Heidelberg (2013). https://doi.org/10.1007/978-3-642-40041-4_26

34. Coron, J.-S., Lee, M.S., Lepoint, T., Tibouchi, M.: Cryptanalysis of GGH15 multilinear maps. In: Robshaw, M., Katz, J. (eds.) CRYPTO 2016. LNCS, vol. 9815, pp. 607–628. Springer, Heidelberg (2016). https://doi.org/10.1007/978-3-662-53008-5_21

35. Coron, J.-S., Lee, M.S., Lepoint, T., Tibouchi, M.: Zeroizing attacks on indistinguishability obfuscation over CLT13. In: Fehr, S. (ed.) PKC 2017. LNCS, vol. 10174, pp. 41–58. Springer, Heidelberg (2017). https://doi.org/10.1007/978-3-662-54365-8_3

36. Coron, J.-S., et al.: Zeroizing without low-level zeroes: new MMAP attacks and their limitations. In: Gennaro, R., Robshaw, M. (eds.) CRYPTO 2015. LNCS, vol. 9215, pp. 247–266. Springer, Heidelberg (2015). https://doi.org/10.1007/978-3-662-47989-6_12

37. Esgin, M.F., Nguyen, N.K., Seiler, G.: Practical exact proofs from lattices: new techniques to exploit fully-splitting rings. In: Moriai, S., Wang, H. (eds.) ASIACRYPT 2020. LNCS, vol. 12492, pp. 259–288. Springer, Cham (2020). https://doi.org/10.1007/978-3-030-64834-3_9

38. Esgin, M.F., Steinfeld, R., Zhao, R.K.: MatRiCT+: More efficient post-quantum private blockchain payments. In: Proceedings of the 43rd IEEE Symposium on Security and Privacy, SP'22, pp. 1281–1298 (2022)

39. Esgin, M.F., Steinfeld, R., Sakzad, A., Liu, J.K., Liu, D.: Short lattice-based one-out-of-many proofs and applications to ring signatures. In: Deng, R.H., Gauthier-Umaña, V., Ochoa, M., Yung, M. (eds.) ACNS 2019. LNCS, vol. 11464, pp. 67–88. Springer, Cham (2019). https://doi.org/10.1007/978-3-030-21568-2_4

40. Garg, S., Gentry, C., Halevi, S.: Candidate multilinear maps from ideal lattices. In: Johansson, T., Nguyen, P.Q. (eds.) EUROCRYPT 2013. LNCS, vol. 7881, pp. 1–17. Springer, Heidelberg (2013). https://doi.org/10.1007/978-3-642-38348-9_1

41. Gennaro, R., et al.: Lattice-based zk-SNARKs from square span programs. In: Proceedings of the 25th ACM Conference on Computer and Communications Security. CCS'18, pp. 556–573 (2018)

42. Gentry, C., Gorbunov, S., Halevi, S.: Graph-induced multilinear maps from lattices. In: Dodis, Y., Nielsen, J.B. (eds.) TCC 2015. LNCS, vol. 9015, pp. 498–527. Springer, Heidelberg (2015). https://doi.org/10.1007/978-3-662-46497-7_20

43. Gentry, C., Wichs, D.: Separating succinct non-interactive arguments from all falsifiable assumptions. In: Proceedings of the 43rd Annual ACM Symposium on Theory of Computing. STOC'11, pp. 99–108 (2011)

44. Golovnev, A., et al.: Brakedown: linear-time and post-quantum SNARKs for R1CS. Cryptology ePrint Archive, Report 2021/1043, p. 21 (2021)

45. Groth, J.: Efficient zero-knowledge arguments from two-tiered homomorphic commitments. In: Lee, D.H., Wang, X. (eds.) ASIACRYPT 2011. LNCS, vol. 7073, pp. 431–448. Springer, Heidelberg (2011). https://doi.org/10.1007/978-3-642-25385-0_23

46. Ishai, Y., Su, H., Wu, D.J.: Shorter and faster post-quantum designated-verifier zkSNARKs from lattices. In: Proceedings of the 28th ACM Conference on Computer and Communications Security. CCS'21, pp. 212–234 (2021)

47. Kilian., J.: A note on efficient zero-knowledge proofs and arguments. In: Proceedings of the 24th Annual ACM Symposium on Theory of Computing. STOC'92, pp. 723–732 (1992)

48. Lai, R.W.F., Malavolta, G., Ronge, V.: Succinct arguments for bilinear group arithmetic: practical structure-preserving cryptography. In: Proceedings of the 26th ACM Conference on Computer and Communications Security. CCS'19, pp. 2057–2074 (2019)
49. Langlois, A., Stehlé, D., Steinfeld, R.: GGHLite: more efficient multilinear maps from ideal lattices. In: Nguyen, P.Q., Oswald, E. (eds.) EUROCRYPT 2014. LNCS, vol. 8441, pp. 239–256. Springer, Heidelberg (2014). https://doi.org/10.1007/978-3-642-55220-5_14
50. Lee, J.: Dory: efficient, transparent arguments for generalised inner products and polynomial commitments. In: Nissim, K., Waters, B. (eds.) TCC 2021. LNCS, vol. 13043, pp. 1–34. Springer, Cham (2021). https://doi.org/10.1007/978-3-030-90453-1_1
51. Lee, J., et al.: Linear-time zero-knowledge SNARKs for R1CS. Cryptology ePrint Archive, Report 2021/030 (2021)
52. Lund, C., et al.: Algebraic methods for interactive proof systems. J. ACM **39**(4), 859–868 (1992)
53. Lyubashevsky, V., Nguyen, N.K., Seiler, G.: Lattice-based zero-knowledge proofs and applications: shorter, simpler, and more general. In: Dodis, Y., Shrimpton, T. (eds.) CRYPTO 2022. LNCS, vol. 13508, pp. 71–101. Springer, Cham (2022). https://doi.org/10.1007/978-3-031-15979-4_3
54. Lyubashevsky, V., Nguyen, N.K., Seiler, G.: Practical lattice-based zero-knowledge proofs for integer relations. In: Proceedings of the 2020 ACM SIGSAC Conference on Computer and Communications Security. CCS'20, pp. 1051–1070 (2020)
55. Lyubashevsky, V., Nguyen, N.K., Seiler, G.: SMILE: set membership from ideal lattices with applications to ring signatures and confidential transactions. In: Malkin, T., Peikert, C. (eds.) CRYPTO 2021. LNCS, vol. 12826, pp. 611–640. Springer, Cham (2021). https://doi.org/10.1007/978-3-030-84245-1_21
56. Ma, F., Zhandry, M.: The MMap strikes back: obfuscation and new multilinear maps immune to CLT13 zeroizing attacks. In: Beimel, A., Dziembowski, S. (eds.) TCC 2018. LNCS, vol. 11240, pp. 513–543. Springer, Cham (2018). https://doi.org/10.1007/978-3-030-03810-6_19
57. NIST. Post-Quantum Cryptography (2016). https://csrc.nist.gov/Projects/Post-Quantum-Cryptography
58. Nguyen, N.K., Seiler, G.: Practical sublinear proofs for R1CS from lattices. In: Dodis, Y., Shrimpton, T. (eds.) CRYPTO 2022. LNCS, vol. 13508, pp. 133–162. Springer, Cham (2022). https://doi.org/10.1007/978-3-031-15979-4_5
59. Nitulescu, A.: Lattice-based zero-knowledge SNARGs for arithmetic circuits. In: Schwabe, P., Thériault, N. (eds.) LATINCRYPT 2019. LNCS, vol. 11774, pp. 217–236. Springer, Cham (2019). https://doi.org/10.1007/978-3-030-30530-7_11
60. del Pino, R., Lyubashevsky, V., Seiler, G.: Lattice-based group signatures and zero-knowledge proofs of automorphism stability. In: Proceedings of the 25th Conference on Computer and Communications Security. CCS'18, pp. 574–591 (2018)
61. del Pino, R., Lyubashevsky, V., Seiler, G.: Short discrete log proofs for FHE and ring-LWE ciphertexts. In: Lin, D., Sako, K. (eds.) PKC 2019. LNCS, vol. 11442, pp. 344–373. Springer, Cham (2019). https://doi.org/10.1007/978-3-030-17253-4_12
62. Reingold, O., Rothblum, G., Rothblum, R.: Constant-round interactive proofs for delegating computation. SIAM J. Comput. **50**(3) (2021). Preliminary version appeared in STOC'16
63. Ron-Zewi, N., Rothblum, R.D.: Proving as fast as computing: succinct arguments with constant prover overhead. In: Proceedings of the 54th Annual ACM Symposium on Theory of Computing. STOC'22, pp. 1353–1363 (2022)

64. Thaler, J.: Proofs, arguments, and zero-knowledge. Unpublished manuscript (2022). https://people.cs.georgetown.edu/jthaler/ProofsArgsAndZK.pdf
65. Xie, T., Zhang, Y., Song, D.: Orion: zero knowledge proof with linear prover time. In: Dodis, Y., Shrimpton, T. (eds.) CRYPTO 2022. LNCS, vol. 13510, pp. 299–328. Springer, Cham (2022). https://doi.org/10.1007/978-3-031-15985-5_11
66. Yang, R., Au, M.H., Zhang, Z., Xu, Q., Yu, Z., Whyte, W.: Efficient lattice-based zero-knowledge arguments with standard soundness: construction and applications. In: Boldyreva, A., Micciancio, D. (eds.) CRYPTO 2019. LNCS, vol. 11692, pp. 147–175. Springer, Cham (2019). https://doi.org/10.1007/978-3-030-26948-7_6

SNARGs for Monotone Policy Batch NP

Zvika Brakerski[1]([✉]), Maya Farber Brodsky[2], Yael Tauman Kalai[3],
Alex Lombardi[4], and Omer Paneth[2]

[1] Weizmann Institute of Science,Rehovot, Israel
zvika.brakerski@weizmann.ac.il
[2] Tel Aviv University,Tel Aviv, Israel
[3] Microsoft Research and MIT,Cambridge, USA
[4] Simons Institute and UC Berkeley,Berkeley, USA

Abstract. We construct a succinct non-interactive argument (SNARG) for the class of monotone policy batch NP languages, under the Learning with Errors (LWE) assumption. This class is a subclass of NP that is associated with a monotone function $f : \{0,1\}^k \to \{0,1\}$ and an NP language $\mathcal{L}$, and contains instances $(x_1, \ldots, x_k)$ such that $f(b_1, \ldots, b_k) = 1$ where $b_j = 1$ if and only if $x_j \in \mathcal{L}$. Our SNARGs are arguments of knowledge in the non-adaptive setting, and satisfy a new notion of somewhere extractability against adaptive adversaries.

This is the first SNARG under standard hardness assumptions for a sub-class of NP that is not known to have a (computational) non-signaling PCP with parameters compatible with the standard framework for constructing SNARGs dating back to [Kalai-Raz-Rothblum, STOC '13]. Indeed, our approach necessarily departs from this framework.

Our construction combines existing quasi-arguments for NP (based on batch arguments for NP) with a new type of cryptographic encoding of the instance and a new analysis going from local to global soundness. The main novel ingredient used in our encoding is a *predicate-extractable hash* (PEHash) family, which is a primitive that generalizes the notion of a somewhere extractable hash. Whereas a somewhere extractable hash allows to extract a single input coordinate, our PEHash extracts a *global* property of the input. We view this primitive to be of independent interest, and believe that it will find other applications.

1 Introduction

Succinct non-interactive arguments (SNARGs) are a powerful cryptographic primitive whose feasibility is still poorly understood. Informally, a SNARG for an NP language $\mathcal{L}$ is a computationally sound non-interactive argument system for $\mathcal{L}$ whose proofs are short (much shorter than the length of an NP witness) and easy to verify.

© International Association for Cryptologic Research 2023
H. Handschuh and A. Lysyanskaya (Eds.): CRYPTO 2023, LNCS 14082, pp. 252–283, 2023.
https://doi.org/10.1007/978-3-031-38545-2_9

In the random oracle model, it is known that there are SNARGs for *every* NP language [24, 26]. However, constructing SNARGs for NP in the "plain model" under falsifiable and preferably standard cryptographic assumptions remains a grand challenge, and will require overcoming some serious barriers [13]. As such, the main focus of this work is making progress on the following question.

Which NP *languages have* SNARGs *in the standard model?*

Prior Positive Results. Constructing SNARGs in the standard model has received extensive attention over the last 15 years, both in the privately verifiable [1, 3, 18, 20, 22] and publicly verifiable [5, 7, 8, 16, 19, 29–31] settings. At this point in time, the achieved results in the privately and publicly verifiable settings are similar,[1] so we focus on the latter. There are two main results to summarize:

1. [7, 23] construct SNARGs for a *restricted* class of NP languages: those that have a "(computational) non-signaling PCP" with good enough parameters (including low locality) [3, 21]. This is a class of NP languages that have a certain kind of information-theoretic proof system, and is known to include all languages in P [3, 22] and all languages with low (read-once) non-deterministic space complexity [1].
2. [30] constructs a variant of SNARG for any NP language, with the following caveats:
   - The scheme requires a (non-succinct) common reference string that is as large as the NP verification circuit, and in particular as long as the instance and witness.
   - The scheme is only non-adaptively sound; this means that an adversarial prover is only unable to prove false statements that are fixed in advance (before the crs is sampled).
   - The scheme is secure assuming (in addition to one-way functions) the existence of indistinguishability obfuscation (iO) [2, 11], which is not a falsifiable assumption [12]. This issue was partially circumvented by [15] for some specific languages in NP ∩ coNP.
   - The scheme does not provide any knowledge extraction (or *argument of knowledge*) guarantee. That is, it is not possible to argue that a convincing prover in their argument system *knows* an NP witness for the statement x.

The Non-Signaling Barrier. Given result (1), it is natural to ask if we are already done – does this give us SNARGs for NP? Probably not. It is unlikely that all languages in NP have (computational) non-signaling PCPs with small locality.Indeed, it is known that if a language $\mathcal{L}$ has a non-signaling PCP with locality

---

[1] There are some differences in the computational assumptions required for SNARGs in the two settings.

ℓ then $\mathcal{L}$ is contained in DTIME(2^ℓ) [10,22].[2] Thus, under widely believed complexity assumptions, there is no non-signaling PCP for all of NP with non-trivial locality.

To explain why all previous SNARG constructions that are not based on iO are limited to languages with (computational) non-signaling PCPs, we recognize that all these constructions follow the same blueprint:

- Use cryptography to build a "quasi-argument system" for NP, which is an argument system for 3-SAT with a weak soundness guarantee: roughly speaking, any successful cheating prover P^* can be used to produce a "locally satisfiable assignment distribution[3]" to the underlying SAT formula.
- Use an information-theoretic encoding of an NP instance x into a SAT formula $\phi_x = \mathsf{Encode}(x)$ such that any locally satisfiable assignment distribution to ϕ_x gives an NP witness for x.

The power of this approach is inherently limited since deciding if there exists an encoding of x as a SAT formula ϕ_x such that local satisfiability implies global satisfiability is equivalent to the question of whether it has a (computational) non-signaling PCP [3,21], which limits the scope of results in this framework to a strict subclass of NP.

In this work, we show how to modify the above approach and circumvent the known complexity-theoretic barrier by **making additional use of cryptography in the encoding of the NP instance into a SAT formula**. In slightly more detail, the idea is to use a cryptographic encoding of an NP instance x into a SAT formula ϕ_x, such that if x is not in the language, there may still exist a locally satisfiable assignment distribution to ϕ_x, but producing such a distribution is intractable.

We remark that a few works have successfully used cryptography in the encoding of the instance, but these were only to achieve better *efficiency guarantees* in SNARGs for certain languages:

- Delegation for RAM programs [3,7,18] combines quasi-arguments with a *hash tree*, which results with an encoding that contains local openings of the hash. This is done in order to enable sublinear-time proof generation and verification for languages in P.
- More refined variants of hash trees and RAM delegation have also been used to improve the efficiency of "batch argument systems" (BARGs) [9,17,28], which led to constructions of new cryptographic primitives (incrementally verifiable computation, stronger RAM delegation) and constructions of SNARGs from different computational assumptions.

---

[2] Loosely speaking, a computational non-signaling PCP with locality ℓ consists of a distribution of answers for every set of ℓ PCP queries $q_1, \ldots, q_\ell$, with the guarantee that for any two sets of queries Q and Q', each of size ℓ, the distributions of answers, denoted by A and A' respectively, satisfy that A restricted to $Q \cap Q'$ is computationally indistinguishable from A' restricted to $Q \cap Q'$.

[3] It is required that this local assignment is non-signaling in the sense that for any (local) set of variables I and J, the corresponding assignments x_I and x_J are computationally indistinguishable on the variables $I \cap J$.

However, we have yet to employ additional cryptography to obtain SNARGs for any *new languages*; in this respect, there has been no progress since [21] constructed (privately verifiable) SNARGs from non-signaling PCPs.

1.1   Our Results

In this work, we go beyond the information-theoretic non-signaling approach and construct SNARGs for new languages.

More specifically, we construct a SNARG for the class of "monotone policy BatchNP" languages, which is a subclass of NP defined as follows. Fix any NP language $\mathcal{L}$ with witness relation $\mathcal{R}$ and any monotone function f. Let

$$\mathcal{L}_f^{(k)} = \left\{ (x_1, \ldots, x_k) : \exists (w_1, \ldots, w_k) \text{ s.t. } f(b_1, \ldots, b_k) = 1, \text{ where } b_i = \mathcal{R}(x_i, w_i) \right\}.$$

That is, a statement $(x_1, \ldots, x_k)$ is in $\mathcal{L}_f^{(k)}$ if *enough* of the statements $x_1, \ldots, x_k$ are true to provide a satisfying input assignment to f. Our main result is a construction of SNARGs for $\mathcal{L}_f^{(k)}$ for every f that has a polynomial-size monotone circuit. This generalizes the notion of batch arguments (BARGs) captured by the special case where f is the conjunction $b_1 \wedge b_2 \wedge \ldots \wedge b_k$.

Theorem 1.1 (informal). *Assuming the polynomial hardness of learning with errors (LWE), there exist SNARGs for monotone policy BatchNP for all polynomial-size monotone circuit policies. Our SNARG has the following quantitative succinctness:*

- *The length of the SNARG proof is $m \cdot \mathsf{poly}(\lambda)$ – growing with the length of a single NP witness $|w_i| = m$ rather than k of them.*
- *The common reference string has length $(m + k)\mathsf{poly}(\lambda)$.*

In particular, the communication complexity of our SNARG matches the efficiency of BARGs, and achieving sublinear dependence on m would imply SNARGs for NP.

Our SNARG additionally has the following properties:

1. **Short CRS for low-width C.** The crs length in Theorem 1.1 can actually be reduced to $(m + \min\{k, \mathrm{width}(C)\}) \cdot \mathsf{poly}(\lambda)$, where $\mathrm{width}(C)$ is the width of the monotone circuit C. In our circuit model (see Sect. 4), we allow wires in the $(i+1)$th layer to be computed from wires in the ith layer along with the input layer. This allows for sublinear circuit width which corresponds roughly to the space complexity of the evaluation of C.

   As a result, for circuits of width $\mathsf{poly}(\lambda, \log k)$, we obtain a fully succinct crs.

2. **Argument of Knowledge.** Our SNARG is an argument of knowledge. Namely, for any prover that convinces the verifier to accept some fixed statement $(x_1, \ldots, x_k)$ there exists a PPT extractor that extracts valid witnesses for a subset $J \subseteq [k]$ of the instances, such that $f(b_1, \ldots, b_k) = 1$, where $b_j = 1$ if and only if $j \in J$.

3. **Efficient Verification.** In our protocol, the verifier runs in time polynomial in the proof length plus time linear in the length of the input $(C, x_1, \ldots, x_k)$. When the input has a succinct representation (or if the verifier has a hash of $(C, x_1, \ldots, x_k)$), verification is even faster.

Importantly, we remark that Theorem 1.1 appears to be beyond the reach of the framework used by previous SNARG constructions, dating back to [21].[4] Instead, we introduce a new technique for building SNARGs that we believe is of independent interest and likely to be used to obtain SNARGs for other NP languages.

Somewhere Argument of Knowledge. Theorem 1.1 above achieves non-adaptive soundness (and argument of knowledge). We strengthen our result to achieve a variant of soundness against provers that can choose the statements $x_1, \ldots, x_k$ *adaptively* based on the common reference string.

Theorem 1.2 (informal). *Assuming the polynomial hardness of learning with errors, there exist* somewhere extractable SNARGs *for monotone policy* BatchNP *where the common reference string is of size* $(m + k) \cdot \mathsf{poly}(\lambda)$.

We define somewhere extractable SNARGs for $\mathcal{L}_f^{(k)}$ with respect to "necessary subsets" for the policy f. We say that a subset $J \subset [k]$ is necessary for f if every input $b_1, \ldots, b_k$ satisfying $f(b_1, \ldots, b_k) = 1$ has the property that $b_j = 1$ for some $j \in J$. For example, if f is the conjunction $b_1 \wedge b_2 \wedge \ldots \wedge b_k$, then every non-empty subset of $[k]$ is necessary.

Our extractability (somewhere argument of knowledge) property says that for every necessary subset $J \subset [k]$, it is possible to sample a computationally indistinguishable common reference string crs_J that is extractable on J in the following sense: if the prover adaptively chooses statements $x_1, \ldots, x_k$ and provides a proof π for $(x_1, \ldots, x_k)$, then it is possible to extract a valid NP witness w_j for *some* $j \in J$. In general, even an honest prover may not have a witness for multiple indices in J, so this is in some sense the best possible argument of knowledge property for $\mathcal{L}_f^{(k)}$.

We remark that the common reference string in Theorem 1.2 *must*, in general, grow with k. This is because the common reference string crs_J must encode the set J, and the number of necessary subsets for a language $\mathcal{L}_f^{(k)}$ may be exponential in k.

---

[4] For those familiar with [22], the framework builds SNARGs using PCPs that are sound against *statistically* (or even *computationally*) non-signaling strategies. If the PCP is sound against δ-non-signaling strategies, the resulting SNARG has proof length that grows with $\log(1/\delta)$. All prior SNARG constructions implicitly construct non-signaling PCPs with good enough parameters to be plugged into this transformation, while monotone policy BatchNP languages do not appear to have such PCPs.

Our somewhere extractability property immediately implies that if the crs is sampled to be extractable on J, an adversarial prover P^* cannot produce statements $x_1, \ldots, x_k$ and an accepting proof π such that $x_j \notin \mathcal{L}$ for all $j \in J$. Since this property is testable in time 2^m, under a subexponential security assumption the same must hold when the crs is sampled honestly. *However*, this is still weaker than a full adaptive soundness property: an adaptive adversary may still be able to prove a false statement $(x_1, \ldots, x_k) \notin \mathcal{L}_f^{(k)}$ while "avoiding" a J-contradiction when given crs$_J$.

Comparison With [30]. Compared to the general NP SNARG result of [30], our results above (1) achieve significantly shorter common reference string for all languages ([30] requires a crs of size $k \cdot m \gg k + m$) and sometimes achieve a fully compact crs (for width$(C) \leq \text{poly}(\lambda, \log k)$), (2) achieve forms of somewhere extractability and semi-adaptive soundness (with a crs of size $k+m$), and (3) rely on the (polynomial) hardness of LWE instead of indistinguishability obfuscation.

Low-depth Monotone Policies. Theorems 1.1 and 1.2 give SNARGs for BatchNP with policy implemented by any monotone circuit. Next we give a complementary result constructing SNARGs for policies given by a monotone circuit with low-depth with different efficiency and under different assumptions.[5]

Theorem 1.3 (informal).   *Assuming 2^d-secure   (somewhere extractable) BARGs and collision-resistant hash functions, there exist SNARGs for monotone policy BatchNP for all depth-d polynomial-size monotone circuit policies. The common reference string and the proof in this SNARG scheme have size $m \cdot \text{poly}(d, \lambda)$.*

In particular, based on existing constructions of BARGs [6–8,17,31], we get SNARGs for policies given by a *monotone formula* with CRS and proof of size $m \cdot \text{poly}(\lambda)$ under polynomial LWE, DLIN or sub-exponential DDH.

A New Tool: Predicate Extractable Hash Functions. In order to prove Theorems 1.1 and 1.2, we introduce (and use) a new primitive called a *predicate extractable hash* (PEHash) family. This primitive generalizes the notion of a somewhere extractable hash family [14,27]. While the latter enforces binding to (and extractability of) a single input coordinate, our notion enforces binding to (and extractability of) a potentially *global* property of the input string x.

Specifically, a PEHash family is a hash family with local opening, such that a hash key hk encodes a secret predicate P. Given a trapdoor td$_P$ for hk one can extract the predicate evaluation $P(x)$ from the hash value $\mathsf{v} = h(x)$. Somewhere extractable hash families have exactly this syntax when P is restricted to be an *index function* $x \mapsto x_i$.

---

[5] This is based on an unpublished work of Brakerski and Kalai [4] which is merged with this work.

In this work, we construct and use PEHash families for *bit-fixing predicates*, where each such predicate $P_{J,y}$ is associated with a subset $J \subseteq [|x|]$ and a string $y \in \{0,1\}^{|J|}$. The predicate is defined as

$$P_{J,y}(x) = \bigwedge_{j \in J} \mathbb{1}(x_j = y_j).$$

In other words, the predicate $P_{J,y}$ checks that the input string x matches y on all indices in J simultaneously.

Theorem 1.4 (informal). *Assuming the polynomial hardness of* LWE, *there exist* PEHash *families for bit-fixing predicates. The size of the hash key is $\ell \cdot$ poly(λ), where ℓ is a bound on the maximum size of a set J supported by the family.*

Defining security of PEH families is quite subtle; we defer a detailed discussion of this to the technical overview, but we roughly require that it is computationally infeasible for an adversary to produce a hash value v along with a local opening at an index j that contradicts the value of the predicate P. We discuss this in more detail in the technical overview in the technical overview. A formal definition of this primitive can be found in Sect. 5.

We believe that the notion of PEH is of independent interest and will be useful in future SNARG constructions and elsewhere in cryptography.

2   Our Techniques

We first give an overview of our proof of Theorem 1.1, focusing on our new technique involving *predicate-extractable hash functions*. We mainly discuss the problem of obtaining short proof length; at the end, we briefly list additional ideas for minimizing the crs length and verification time, and for obtaining somewhere extractable soundness.

Monotone Policy BatchNP. Fix any NP language $\mathcal{L}$ with witness relation $\mathcal{R}$ and fix any function f computable by a monotone circuit family C. Recall that we wish to construct a SNARG for the NP language $\mathcal{L}_f^{(k)}$ defined as follows:

$$\mathcal{L}_f^{(k)} = \left\{ (x_1, \ldots, x_k) : \exists (w_1, \ldots, w_k) \text{ s.t. } f(b_1, \ldots, b_k) = 1, \text{ where } b_i = \mathcal{R}(x_i, w_i) \right\}.$$

Our goal is to construct a SNARG for $\mathcal{L}_f^{(k)}$ with proof length $m \cdot$ poly(λ), where m denotes the length of a single witness w_i.

Why Don't BARGs Just Work? Before discussing our techniques, we briefly mention a naive idea that is fundamentally flawed but highlights a key difficulty of the problem. For any instance $(x_1, \ldots, x_k) \in \mathcal{L}_f^{(k)}$, there is a set of witnesses $\{w_i\}_{i \in S}$ for a subset $S \subset [k]$ such that $f(\chi_S) = 1$, where χ_S denotes the indicator vector for S. Therefore, one can prove that $(x_1, \ldots, x_k) \in \mathcal{L}_f^{(k)}$ using a BARG to prove the claim that "$x_i \in L$ for all $i \in S$."

This idea results in a sound argument system; however, *the verifier does not know the set S.* As a result, the prover would at least have to communicate S, which may require sending an additional $O(k)$ bits, ruining succinctness.

As a result, one key technical challenge in this work is finding a way to argue about these implicitly defined sets S of size $O(k)$ even though the SNARG proof cannot contain this much information. For a concrete example, one can think about the case where f is the *majority* function, where the sets S in question have size $\lceil \frac{k}{2} \rceil$.

2.1   The Canonical Protocol

We first describe a simple candidate SNARG for monotone policy BatchNP. While we cannot show its soundness, our results are based on variants of this canonical protocol. Roughly following [7,23], a candidate argument system for an *arbitrary* NP language can be built from a (somewhere extractable) *batch argument system* (BARG), which enables proving that a large number of NP statements are *all true*, at the communication cost of roughly one NP witness. Somewhere extractable BARGs are now known from a wide variety of assumptions, including LWE [7].

Tailored to our setting, the candidate argument system for $\mathcal{L}_f^{(k)}$ is constructed as follows:

- Given an instance $(x_1, \ldots, x_k) \in \mathcal{L}_f^{(k)}$ together with a witness $(w_1, \ldots, w_k)$ compute the bits $b_j = \mathcal{R}_{\mathcal{L}}(x_j, w_j)$ for $1 \le j \le k$ and evaluate the circuit $C(b_1, \ldots, b_k)$.
- Compute a succinct commitment (i.e., tree hash) v of the values of all the wires in the evaluation of C.
- Use the batch argument system to prove the conjunction of the following $|C|+1$ statements:
  - *Input wires:* For every $j \in [k]$ there exists a witness w_j and a local opening of v in location j to a value b_j such that $b_j = \mathcal{R}_{\mathcal{L}}(x_j, w_j)$.
  - *Internal wires:* For every gate of C connecting the wires $j, j_1, j_2 \in [|C|]$ there exist local openings of v in locations j, j_1, j_2 to values b_j, b_{j_1}, b_{j_2} that are consistent with the gate.
  - *Output wire:* There exists a local opening of v in location $|C|$ (corresponding to the output wire) to the value 1 (indicating that C accepts).

Since the witness to each claim proven in the BARG is of length at most $m + \mathsf{poly}(\lambda)$, the overall proof length is $m \cdot \mathsf{poly}(\lambda)$. This style of argument system enforces the *local consistency* of a claimed execution of the NP verifier for $\mathcal{L}_f^{(k)}$. Unfortunately, **we do not know whether, in general, this argument system is sound!**

Prior works can be thought of as using a variant of the canonical protocol with ℓ independent BARG executions, where ℓ is a locality parameter. In this case, the canonical protocol turns out to be a "quasi-argument" with locality ℓ.

Low-depth Circuits. We next describe how to obtain Theorem 1.3 using the canonical protocol (with locality $\ell = 2$). We focus on the case where C is a logarithmic depth monotone circuit. More generally, we can prove soundness for depth d circuits with proof length $m \cdot \text{poly}(\lambda, d)$, under a 2^d-time security assumption.

To prove soundness we rely on the fact that the BARG is *somewhere extractable*. This means that for every $j \in [|C|+1]$, we can sample a computationally indistinguishable CRS_j together with a corresponding trapdoor td_j, so that given any accepting proof under CRS_j we can efficiently extract a witness for the jth claim from the proof using td_j. We use the protocol variant that includes two independent BARG executions (with respect to the same commitment v). This allows us to extract witnesses for two of the claims at once. Moreover, we can extract from one of the BARG proofs while the index where the other BARG is extractable remains hidden.

To argue non-adaptive soundness, fix a false statement $(x_1, \ldots, x_k) \notin \mathcal{L}_f^{(k)}$. For $j \in [k]$, let $b_j^* = 1$ if $x_j \in \mathcal{L}$ and $b_j^* = 0$ otherwise. Let $(b_j^*)_{1 \leq j \leq |C|}$ denote the values of all the wires in the evaluation of $C(b_1^*, \ldots, b_k^*) = 0$. The idea is to argue inductively that if an efficient adversary P^* breaks the argument system, then for every layer, there exists a wire j in the layer such that if the BARGs are extractable on the statement involving the jth wire value, then the committed value b_j in the extracted witness is *greater than* b_j^* (i.e., $b_j = 1$ but $b_j^* = 0$) with non-negligible probability.

For the output layer of the circuit, this is clear since $b_{|C|}^* = 0$ but $b_{|C|} = 1$ or the BARG proofs are rejected. Then, inductively, assume that $b_j > b_j^*$ with probability p when the BARGs are extractable on the jth claim and let j_1, j_2 be the two *child* wires of the jth wire. Then for some $\alpha \in [2]$, we must have that $b_{j_\alpha} > b_{j_\alpha}^*$ with probability at least $p/2$ because the (j, j_1, j_2) gate is monotone (AND or OR). Furthermore, the same holds when the BARGs are extractable on the j_αth claim by the following non-signaling argument: consider a hybrid experiment where one of our BARG proofs is extractable on the jth claim and the other BARG proof is extractable on the j_αth claim. We use the binding of the commitment v to argue that the value b_{j_α} extracted from both BARGs is identical and we use the fact that the CRSs are indistinguishable to argue that $b_{j_\alpha} > b_{j_\alpha}^*$ with almost the same probability in the hybrid experiment and in the two original experiments (where the two BARGs are are extractable on the jth claim and on the j_αth claim). Since the circuit is of logarithmic depth, we can apply this argument inductively and show that for one of the input wires $j \in [k]$ the extracted value b_j is greater than b_j^* with noticeable probability in the appropriate hybrid experiment. However, this is a contradiction since if $b_j \neq \mathcal{R}_\mathcal{L}(x_j, w_j) = b_j^*$ then the BARG proofs are rejected.

We can extend this analysis to consider circuits of any depth d where the loss in the reduction grows exponentially with d. We can still obtain soundness by relying on subexponential hardness assumptions, however, in this case the security parameter and thus also the length of the SNARG proof must grow with d. We prove this formally in the full version of this work.

Avoiding the Exponential Decay. Constructing SNARGs for monotone policy BatchNP where the circuit C has arbitrary depth under polynomial hardness assumptions requires a new type of analysis where the success probability does not decay exponentially with the depth. Previous work [21,22] introduce two techniques for avoiding this exponential decay in the context of SNARGs for P. Next, we describe these techniques and explain why they are insufficient in our context.

The solution of [21] was restricted to circuits of small width, allowing the proof to grow with the width. In particular, in this setting it is possible to extract from the proof an entire layer of the circuit instead of just a single gate. Accordingly, in their inductive argument, the success probability only decreases by a negligible amount in each layer, instead of by a factor of 2.

To deal with circuits with unbounded width, [22] proposed the following modification: instead of extracting an entire layer of the circuit (which would require the proof to grow), the prover augments each layer with a short hash of the layer.[6] Now, by extracting only the hash of the layer and comparing it against the hash of the layer values in the correct evaluation of the deterministic circuit we can certify that each value in the layer was computed correctly.

In our context, however, the circuit in question is non-deterministic and may have many possible evaluations. Instead, we want to make sure that the value extracted for each wire b_j is not *greater than* the value b_j^* of the wire in the evaluation of $C(b_1^*, \ldots, b_k^*) = 0$ described above. Indeed, it is not at all clear that such global information can be discerned from a short hash of the layer.

2.2 Enforcing Global Properties with Predicate Extractable Hashing

Our solution for general circuits extends the paradigm from [22] to the regime of non-deterministic languages. We modify the "canonical protocol" by defining and using a more powerful cryptographic hash family to commit to the wire values $b_1, \ldots, b_{|C|}$. At a high level of generality, imagine that we want a hash function h that maps a long input x to a short output v, such that the evaluation $v = h(x)$ is binding to a (potentially arbitrary) predicate $P(x)$. We formalize this with a following syntax for a "predicate-extractable hash family" PEHash:

- Given the description of a predicate P, it should be possible to sample a hash key hk along with a trapdoor td_P. The hash key hk should computationally hide the choice of predicate P.
- Given hk and an input x, we can compute a short hash $v = H(hk, x)$.
- As in a standard hash tree, we require that it is possible to locally open a hash value v on an index j to the bit x_j. The opening should be short and $\mathsf{poly}(\lambda)$-efficient to verify.

---

[6] In fact, [22] proposed an information theoretic analog of this idea where the short hash is replaced by a few random locations in the low-degree extension of the layer.

- Finally, given a hash value v and trapdoor td_P, it should be possible to *extract* a bit $\mathsf{Extract}(td_P, v)$ which is supposed to correspond to the evaluation $P(x)$ (at least on an honestly generated $v = H(\mathsf{hk}, x)$).

We view this object as a syntactic generalization of somewhere statistically binding (and somewhere extractable) hash families [14], which have proved to be extremely useful in the construction of cryptographic protocols. In our formalization, SEHash families correspond to the case where the predicate P is an *index* function $x \mapsto x_i$. In this special case, security is defined as follows: if the hash key hk is sampled to be binding on index i, then it is infeasible for an adversary to produce a hash value v and an opening of v to a bit b on location i such that $\mathsf{Extract}(td_i, v) = 1 - b$. In other words, the ith location opening must be consistent with the extracted bit value.

PEHash *Families for Bit-Fixing Predicates.* In this work, we define, construct, and make use of predicate-extractable hash families for "bit-fixing" predicates. That is, for inputs of length N, a predicate P is specified by a subset $J \subseteq [N]$ and a string $y \in \{0,1\}^J$. The predicate $P_{J,y}(x)$ is defined to be 1 if $y_j = x_j$ for all $j \in J$.

Defining security for bit-fixing PEH requires significant care. Specifically, security is asymmetric with respect to whether $P(x) = 1$ or $P(x) = 0$.

- Security in the $P(x) = 1$ case is relatively easy to describe. We require that if the hash key hk is extractable on bit-fixing predicate (J, y), an adversary cannot produce a hash value v such that $\mathsf{Extract}(td, v) = 1$ together with an opening of v to a bit b on index $j \in J$ such that $b \neq y_j$. We note that the adversary here can choose j adaptively. This corresponds to the intuition that an evaluation $\mathsf{Extract}(td, v) = 1$ should *simultaneously* bind every value x_j to y_j.
- Security in the $P(x) = 0$ case is more subtle. Intuitively, we want to say that if $\mathsf{Extract}(td, v) = 0$ then the adversary *cannot* simultaneously open on every index $j \in J$ to y_j. However, this security property is insufficiently "succinct" to be useful in our construction. Instead, we require that, in addition to the predicate value, we can extract a specific index $j^* = \mathsf{ExtractIndex}(td, v)$ such that the adversary cannot open v to y_{j^*} on the j^*th location.

Constructing PEHash *for Bit-Fixing Predicates.* The high-level idea for constructing a bit-fixing PEHash family is simple and takes inspiration from [14]: we can hash a string x in a way that is binding to $P_{J,y}$, via a tree of homomorphic evaluations on pairs of ciphertexts. In more detail, the hash key will contain an encryption of the predicate (J, y). We hash x as follows:

- First, for every j we homomorphically evaluate $\mathsf{Enc}(\mathbb{1}((x_j = y_j) \vee (j \notin J)))$.
- At each layer given sibling ciphertexts $\mathsf{ct}_{j||0}, \mathsf{ct}_{j||1}$ containing bits $z_{j||0}, z_{j||1}$, we compute the parent ct_j by homomorphically evaluating $z_{j||0} \wedge z_{j||1}$.
- To enforce correctness with respect to a malicious committer, we implement the evaluation tree with an FHE bootstrapping mechanism (each layer has

its own FHE secret key, and homomorphic operations are always computed on ciphertexts encrypting sk_{i+1} under pk_i, which are included as part of the hash key).

- The construction above is sufficient to satisfy "one-sided" $(P(x) = 1)$ security. To obtain two-sided security, we have the FHE evaluation tree also keep track of the lexicographically first index j^* on which $x_j \neq y_j$. This invariant can be maintained throughout the evaluation.

As a result, an honestly evaluated hash of x will be an encryption of $(P_{J,y}(x), j^*)$, where $j^* = \bot$ if $P_{J,y}(x) = 1$ and j^* equals to the lexicographically first index such that $x_j \neq y_j$ if $P_{J,y}(x) = 0$. We prove in the full version of this work that this construction satisfies both sides of our security definition.

Unfortunately, the construction above is too simplistic: specifically, verifying an opening requires recomputing a path along the tree (as is typical for Merkle-style commitments), but each step of our tree evaluation requires doing a computation involving $\mathsf{Enc}(J)$, which is not succinct if J is a large set. However, this opening verification can be delegated to the opening *generation* using a RAM delegation scheme, enabling the verifier to check correctness efficiently given a short hash of hk (generated at setup time).

2.3 New SNARG Construction

Having defined and constructed a predicate extractable hash family for bit-fixing predicates, we now show how to use it to build a SNARG for monotone policy BatchNP. Our SNARG construction is similar in structure to the canonical construction, but (for reasons that will become clear later) in place of a the hash tree we make use of *two* instantiations of a PEHash family. Roughly speaking, the SNARG proof is computed as follows.

- Using two independent hash keys $\mathsf{hk}^{(1)}, \mathsf{hk}^{(2)}$, succinctly commit to $b_1, \ldots, b_{|C|}$, which are all the wire values of the circuit C. Let $\mathsf{v}^{(1)}, \mathsf{v}^{(2)}$ denote the two resulting hash values.
- Use the batch argument system to prove the conjunction of the following $|C|$ statements:
  - b_j is indeed equal to $\mathcal{R}_\mathcal{L}(x_j, w_j)$ for all $j \in [k]$,
  - For every gate (j, j_1, j_2) of C, we have local openings of $\mathsf{v}^{(1)}, \mathsf{v}^{(2)}$ to a correct gate evaluation on a fixed triple of bits (b_j, b_{j_1}, b_{j_2}).
  - The final wire value of C is 1 (according to both commitments $\mathsf{v}^{(1)}, \mathsf{v}^{(2)}$).

How are we better equipped to prove soundness of this argument system? The idea is that predicate extractability gives us a means to argue about the consistency of an entire layer of C based on a single bit.

More specifically, to argue non-adaptive soundness, we again fix a false statement $(x_1, \ldots, x_k)$ and define "correct wire values" $b_1^*, \ldots, b_{|C|}^*$ as before. Next, for a fixed layer i, we switch to a computationally indistinguishable world in which the predicate $P^{(1)}$ on which $\mathsf{hk}^{(1)}$ is extractable is the predicate $P_{J_i,0}$ that checks for the "forced zeroes" of the circuit evaluation. That is, $P(b_1, \ldots, b_{|C|})$ is defined to be 1 if and only if $b_j = 0$ for all j in the ith layer of C such that $b_j^* = 0$. We know that in any honest evaluation of the circuit, this predicate $P^{(1)}$ would evaluate to 1.

We first argue that if an adversary cheats and produces an accepting proof for a false statement with $i = d$ then it must be the case that $P^{(1)} = 0$ (except with negligible probability). This follows from the fact that if the proof is accepting then by the soundness of the BARG it must be that $b_{|C|} = 1$ and hence $P^{(1)} = 0$. We then get a contradiction by arguing (by induction on i) that if the adversary cheats with $i = 1$ then it must be the case that $P^{(1)} = 0$ (except with negligible probability), which contradicts the security of the underlying BARG. This is where we utilize the two hash keys. Specifically, we argue that given two hash keys $\mathsf{hk}^{(1)}$ and $\mathsf{hk}^{(2)}$, encoding predicates $P^{(i)}$ and $P^{(i-1)}$ respectively, for any adversary that generates a valid proof $(\mathsf{v}^{(1)}, \mathsf{v}^{(2)}, \pi)$, it must be the case that $\mathsf{Extract}(\mathsf{td}^{(1)}, \mathsf{v}^{(1)}), \mathsf{Extract}(\mathsf{td}^{(2)}, \mathsf{v}^{(2)})$ *agree* (except with negligible probability). This follows from the binding properties of the PEHash along with the (extractable) soundness of the batch argument system, because:

- If $\mathsf{Extract}(\mathsf{td}^{(1)}, \mathsf{v}^{(1)}) = 0$, there must be some specific index j^* on which $b_j > b_j^*$ (where b_j is defined if the seBARG is extractable on the jth gate).
- Thus, if the jth gate is correct, there exists a child j_α such that $b_{j_\alpha} > b_{j_\alpha}^*$.
- However, this implies that we should have $\mathsf{Extract}(\mathsf{td}^{(2)}, \mathsf{v}^{(2)}) = 0$ except with a negligible error probability.

Finally, we can argue that $\mathsf{Extract}(\mathsf{td}^{(1)}, \mathsf{v}^{(1)}) = 0$ with roughly the same probability when $(\mathsf{hk}^{(1)}, \mathsf{td}^{(1)})$ is sampled w.r.t. layer $i - 1$ by a non-signaling argument, and continue via a similar argument, relating $\mathsf{Extract}(\mathsf{td}^{(1)}, \mathsf{v}^{(1)})$ to $\mathsf{Extract}(\mathsf{td}^{(2)}, \mathsf{v}^{(2)})$ which is extractable on $P^{(i-2)}$. Importantly, the "exponential decay" in success probability from layer to layer has disappeared – the local gate-by-gate analysis has been replaced by a global layer-by-layer analysis that suffers from a linear loss in the depth, as opposed to an exponential loss.

2.4   Achieving Somewhere Extractability

Having sketched our proof of Theorem 1.1, we now turn our attention to Theorem 1.2. Namely, can we modify our SNARG to obtain a guarantee that an accepting proof π can be used to obtain a valid witness w_j for an instance in the necessary subset?

In this setting, we no longer have a fixed false statement $\vec{x} = (x_1, \ldots, x_k)$. Instead, we have a necessary subset $J \subseteq [k]$ of instances, and given a prover $\mathcal{P}^*$ that produces instances $(x_1, \ldots, x_k)$ and a proof π that makes the verifier accept, we would like to extract a witness w_j for some $j \in J$.

We begin by following the analysis of the non-adaptive case. Rather than programming the PEHash on predicates $P_{J_i,0}$ that check for "forced zeroes" in layer i of the circuit evaluation on $\vec{x}$, we set J_i to be the set of wires that are 0 when evaluating the circuit on any set of inputs that is 0 on the necessary subset J. Then, we can show that since $\mathcal{P}^*$ produces an accepting proof, we must have $\mathsf{Extract}(\mathsf{td}^{(1)}, \mathsf{v}^{(1)}) = 0$ for the predicate $P_{J_d,0}$, and using a global layer-by-layer analysis, we get that $\mathsf{Extract}(\mathsf{td}^{(1)}, \mathsf{v}^{(1)}) = 0$ for the predicate $P_{J_0,0}$, where $J_0 = J$.

Thus, if we program the crs such that the PEHash is extractable on $P_{J,0}$, we can use the trapdoor $\mathsf{td}^{(1)}$ to extract from the proof an index $j^* = \mathsf{ExtractIndex}(\mathsf{td}^{(1)}, \mathsf{v}^{(1)}) \in J$ where, intuitively, the predicate must be violated, so we should have that $x_{j^*} \in \mathcal{L}$. However, we do not yet have a mechanism for extracting the witness w_{j^*}.

One may hope that we would be able to extract this witness from the seBARG. Unfortunately, this would require us to know the index j^* during crs generation (or set the seBARG to be extractable on all of J, which would ruin succinctness). Instead, we extend our notion of PEHash, to one which would enable us to extract the witness from the hash value itself.

Predicate Extractable Hash Families With Tags. We define and construct an extended notion of PEHash families for bit-fixing predicates, which we call PEHash families with tags. This object supports hashing the input $x \in \{0,1\}^N$ together with tags $t_1, \ldots, t_N$, attaching a tag to each bit of the input. Similarly, the opening and verification algorithms also receive tags.

We define an additional security requirement for this object, which we call consistency of tag extraction. Extending the requirement that if $\mathsf{Extract}(\mathsf{td}, \mathsf{v}) = 0$ then we can extract $j^* = \mathsf{ExtractIndex}(\mathsf{td}, \mathsf{v})$ such that the adversary cannot open the j^*th location to the bit y_{j^*}, we require that the adversary can only open the j^*th location together with a specific tag $t = \mathsf{ExtractTag}(\mathsf{td}, \mathsf{v})$.

We construct this object via a simple modification to our original construction of PEHash for bit-fixing predicates: in the FHE evaluation tree, in addition to (b, j), we also keep track of the tag t attached to the index j. An honestly evaluated hash is an encryption of $(P_{J,y}(x), j^*, t)$ where t is the tag attached to index j^*, which guarantees that the adversary is bound to t when opening j^*.

Achieving Somewhere Extractability. We now describe how we can augment our non-adaptive SNARG construction with a PEHash family with tags to achieve a SNARG with a stronger somewhere extractability property. Recall that the non-adaptive SNARG proof π consists of PEHash values $\mathsf{v}^{(1)}, \mathsf{v}^{(2)}$ of the circuit wires, and a seBARG proof.

We modify the SNARG proof π as follows:

- We append to the proof an additional hash value $\mathsf{v}_{\mathsf{PEHT}}$ of the input wires $b_1, \ldots, b_k$, with the witnesses $w_1, \ldots, w_k$ as attached tags. This hash value is computed using a PEHash family with tags, with a hash key $\mathsf{hk}_{\mathsf{PEHT}}$ extractable on the predicate $P_{J,0}$ which checks that $b_j = 0$ for each $j \in J$.
- We modify the seBARG proof, so that on each input wire $j \in [k]$ we not only validate openings of $\mathsf{v}^{(1)}, \mathsf{v}^{(2)}$ to b_j on location j and that $b_j = \mathcal{R}(x_j, w_j)$, but additionally validate an opening of $\mathsf{v}_{\mathsf{PEHT}}$ to b_j with the witness w_j as its tag.

Now, to extract a witness from the SNARG proof π, we extract it from our new hash value v_{PEHT}, using $\mathsf{ExtractTag}(\mathsf{td}_{\mathsf{PEHT}}, v_{\mathsf{PEHT}})$.

Analysis. We show that if a malicious prover $\mathcal{P}^*$ produces instances $(x_1, \ldots, x_k)$ and a proof π that causes the verifier to accept, then the extracted witness $w_{j^*} = \mathsf{ExtractTag}(\mathsf{td}_{\mathsf{PEHT}}, v_{\mathsf{PEHT}})$ is a valid witness for the instance x_{j^*}, for $j^* = \mathsf{ExtractIndex}(\mathsf{td}_{\mathsf{PEHT}}, v_{\mathsf{PEHT}})$.

First, as in our non-adaptive soundness analysis, we use a global layer-by-layer argument to show that since we have $\mathsf{Extract}(\mathsf{td}^{(1)}, v^{(1)}) = 0$ where $v^{(1)}$ is programmed on the predicate $P_{J_d,0}$, except with negligible probability we must also have $\mathsf{Extract}(\mathsf{td}^{(1)}, v^{(1)}) = 0$ for the predicate $P_{J,0}$.

Next, we claim that except with negligible probability we must also have $\mathsf{Extract}(\mathsf{td}_{\mathsf{PEHT}}, v_{\mathsf{PEHT}}) = 0$. Indeed, otherwise, we can program the seBARG to be extractable on a random index, which with non-negligible probability will be equal to $j = \mathsf{ExtractIndex}(\mathsf{td}^{(1)}, v^{(1)})$, and extract openings of both $v^{(1)}, v_{\mathsf{PEHT}}$ to the input bit b_j, which from the PEHash consistency must be 1 in $v^{(1)}$ but 0 in v_{PEHT}, which is a contradiction.

Finally, we argue that if $\mathsf{Extract}(\mathsf{td}_{\mathsf{PEHT}}, v_{\mathsf{PEHT}}) = 0$, then except with negligible probability the extracted witness w_{j^*} must be valid. Indeed, otherwise, we again program the seBARG on a random index, and when it is equal to j^* we can extract an opening of v_{PEHT} to b_{j^*} together with some witness w'_{j^*}, which also satisfies $b_{j^*} = \mathcal{R}(x_{j^*}, w'_{j^*})$. Since j^* is the extracted index we get from PEHash consistency that b_{j^*} must violate the predicate $P_{J,0}$, so $b_{j^*} = 1$. Thus w'_{j^*} is a valid witness, but we assumed that w_{j^*} is invalid - so the adversary has opened v_{PEHT} in the j^*th location together with a tag w'_{j^*} that differs from the extracted tag w_{j^*}, which contradicts the consistency of tag extraction property.

2.5   Shortening the CRS

We describe an optimization that allows us to shorten the prover common reference string $\mathsf{crs}_{\mathcal{P}}$ in our SNARG from length $(m + \mathrm{width}(C)) \cdot \mathrm{poly}(\lambda)$ to $(m + \min\{k, \mathrm{width}(C)\}) \cdot \mathrm{poly}(\lambda)$. This is especially useful in our somewhere extractable SNARG, where the size of $\mathsf{crs}_{\mathcal{P}}$ must be at least k since it is binding on a subset $J \subseteq [k]$ of input wires, so the optimization allows us to achieve a length $(m + k) \cdot \mathrm{poly}(\lambda)$ which is fully succinct.

The main bottleneck in $\mathsf{crs}_{\mathcal{P}}$ which requires length $\mathrm{width}(C) \cdot \mathrm{poly}(\lambda)$ is the hash key for the PEHash family, which is as long as the predicate $P_{J,y}$. In our SNARG, we use the predicates $P_{J,0}$ where J is a set of wires in a single layer of the circuit C, so its size is at most the size of the largest layer of C, i.e. its width.

However, we observe that the sets J that we actually use have structure; specifically, they are not arbitrary sets of wires in a layer, but can be described as the set of wires in a layer that are 0 in a computation of C on some input $(b_1, \ldots, b_k)$. Therefore, to encode the predicate $P_{J,0}$, it is enough to give an encryption under FHE of an input of length k, and an index of a layer. Then, the prover can compute the full hash key by homomorphically evaluating the circuit on that description.

3 Preliminaries

Notations. We use PPT to denote probabilistic polynomial-time, and denote the set of all positive integers up to n as $[n] := \{1, \ldots, n\}$. For any $x \in \{0,1\}^n$ and any subset $J \subset [n]$ we denote by $x_J = (x_j)_{j \in J}$. For any finite set S, $x \leftarrow S$ denotes a uniformly random element x from the set S. Similarly, for any distribution $\mathcal{D}$, $x \leftarrow \mathcal{D}$ denotes an element x drawn from the distribution $\mathcal{D}$.

3.1 Hash Family with Local Opening

In this section we recall the definition of a hash family with local opening [25].[7]

Syntax. A hash family (HT) with succinct local opening consists of the following algorithms:

$\mathsf{Gen}(1^\lambda) \to \mathsf{hk}$. This is a PPT algorithm that takes as input the security parameter 1^λ in unary and outputs a hash key hk.

$\mathsf{Hash}(\mathsf{hk}, x) \to \mathsf{rt}$. This is a deterministic poly-time algorithm that takes as input a hash key hk and an input $x \in \{0,1\}^N$ for $N \leq 2^\lambda$, and outputs a hash value rt.

$\mathsf{Open}(\mathsf{hk}, x, j) \to \rho$. This is a deterministic poly-time algorithm that takes as input a hash key hk, an input $x \in \{0,1\}^N$ for $N \leq 2^\lambda$, and an index $j \in [N]$, and outputs an opening ρ.

$\mathsf{Verify}(\mathsf{hk}, \mathsf{rt}, j, b, \rho) \to 0/1$. This is a deterministic poly-time algorithm that takes as input a hash key hk, a hash value rt, an index $j \in [N]$, a bit $b \in \{0,1\}$ and an opening ρ. It outputs 1 (accept) or 0 (reject).

Definition 3.1. *(Properties of HT) A HT family* $(\mathsf{Gen}, \mathsf{Hash}, \mathsf{Open}, \mathsf{Verify})$ *is required to satisfy the following properties.*

Opening completeness. *For any* $\lambda \in \mathbb{N}$, *any* $N \leq 2^\lambda$, *any* $x \in \{0,1\}^N$, *and any index* $j \in [N]$,

$$\Pr\left[\mathsf{Verify}(\mathsf{hk}, \mathsf{rt}, j, x_j, \rho) = 1 \; : \; \begin{array}{l} \mathsf{hk} \leftarrow \mathsf{Gen}(1^\lambda), \\ \mathsf{rt} = \mathsf{Hash}(\mathsf{hk}, x), \\ \rho = \mathsf{Open}(\mathsf{hk}, x, j) \end{array}\right] = 1 - \mathsf{negl}(\lambda).$$

Succinctness. *In the completeness experiment above, we have that* $|\mathsf{hk}| + |\mathsf{rt}| + |\rho| = \mathsf{poly}(\lambda)$.

---

[7] In what follows we use the notation HT to denote a hash family with local opening, where HT symbolizes a Hash Tree construction. We emphasize that we are not restricted to such a construction, and use this notation only to give the reader an example to have in mind.

Collision resistance w.r.t. opening. *For any poly-size adversary $\mathcal{A}$ there exists a negligible function* $\mathsf{negl}(\cdot)$ *such that for every* $\lambda \in \mathbb{N}$,

$$\Pr\left[\begin{matrix} \mathsf{Verify}(\mathsf{hk}, \mathsf{rt}, j, 0, \rho_0) = 1 \\ \wedge\ \mathsf{Verify}(\mathsf{hk}, \mathsf{rt}, j, 1, \rho_1) = 1 \end{matrix} : \begin{matrix} \mathsf{hk} \leftarrow \mathsf{Gen}(1^\lambda), \\ (\mathsf{rt}, j, \rho_0, \rho_1) \leftarrow \mathcal{A}(\mathsf{hk}) \end{matrix}\right] = \mathsf{negl}(\lambda).$$

Remark 3.1. We say that a hash family with local opening is T-secure, for $T = T(\lambda)$, if the collision resistance w.r.t. opening property holds against any $\mathsf{poly}(T)$-size adversary (as opposed to $\mathsf{poly}(\lambda)$-size) and the probability that the adversary finds a collision is $\mathsf{negl}(T)$ (as opposed to $\mathsf{negl}(\lambda)$). We refer to this property as T-collision-resistance w.r.t. opening.

Remark 3.2. One can naturally extend the definition of a hash family with local opening to allow the Open algorithm to take as input (hk, x, J) where $J \subseteq [N]$ consists of a set of indices, as opposed to a single index. $\mathsf{Open}(\mathsf{hk}, x, J)$ will simply run $\mathsf{Open}(\mathsf{hk}, x, j)$ for every $j \in J$. Verify can be extended in a similar way to take as input $(\mathsf{hk}, \mathsf{rt}, J, b_J, \rho_J)$, and accept if and only if $\mathsf{Verify}(\mathsf{hk}, \mathsf{rt}, j, b_j, \rho_j) = 1$ for every $j \in J$.

Theorem 3.1 ([25]). *Assuming the existence of a collision resistant hash family there exists a hash family with local opening (according to Definition 3.1).*

3.2 Fully Homomorphic Encryption

In this section we define fully homomorphic encryption.

Syntax. A fully homomorphic encryption scheme consists of a fixed ciphertext size $\ell_{ctxt} = \ell_{ctxt}(\lambda)$ and the following polynomial time algorithms:

$\mathsf{FHE.Setup}(1^\lambda) \to (\mathsf{pk}, \mathsf{sk})$. This is a probabilistic algorithm that takes as input a security parameter 1^λ. It outputs a public key pk and a secret key sk.

$\mathsf{FHE.Enc}_{\mathsf{pk}}(b) \to c$. This is a probabilistic algorithm that takes as input a public key pk and a bit $b \in \{0, 1\}$. It outputs a ciphertext $c \in \{0, 1\}^{\ell_{ctxt}}$.

$\mathsf{FHE.Dec}_{\mathsf{sk}}(c) \to b$. This is a deterministic algorithm that takes as input a secret key sk and a ciphertext $c \in \{0, 1\}^{\ell_{ctxt}}$. It outputs a bit $b \in \{0, 1\}$.

$\mathsf{FHE.Eval}_{\mathsf{pk}}(f, c_1, \ldots, c_n) \to c^*$. This is a deterministic algorithm that takes as input a public key pk, a circuit representing a function $f : \{0, 1\}^n \to \{0, 1\}$ and n ciphertexts $c_1, \ldots, c_n \in \{0, 1\}^{\ell_{ctxt}}$. It outputs a ciphertext $c^* \in \{0, 1\}^{\ell_{ctxt}}$.

Definition 3.2 (FHE). *A fully homomorphic encryption scheme* $\mathsf{FHE} = (\mathsf{FHE.Setup}, \mathsf{FHE.Enc}, \mathsf{FHE.Eval}, \mathsf{FHE.Dec})$ *is required to satisfy the following properties:*

Encryption Correctness. *For any choice of* $(\mathsf{pk}, \mathsf{sk}) \leftarrow \mathsf{FHE.Setup}(1^\lambda)$, *any* $b \in \{0, 1\}$ *and any* $c \leftarrow \mathsf{FHE.Enc}_{\mathsf{pk}}(b)$ *we have* $\mathsf{FHE.Dec}_{\mathsf{sk}}(c) = b$.

Evaluation Correctness. *For any choice of* $(\mathsf{pk}, \mathsf{sk}) \leftarrow \mathsf{FHE.Setup}(1^\lambda)$, *any ciphertexts* $c_1, \ldots, c_n \in \{0, 1\}^{\ell_{ctxt}}$ *such that* $\mathsf{FHE.Dec}_{\mathsf{sk}}(c_i) = b_i \in \{0, 1\}$ *and any circuit* $f : \{0, 1\}^n \to \{0, 1\}$, *if we set* $c = \mathsf{FHE.Eval}(f, c_1, \ldots, c_n)$ *then* $\mathsf{FHE.Dec}_{\mathsf{sk}}(c) = f(b_1, \ldots, b_n)$.

Security. *The encryption scheme is semantically secure.*

Remark 3.3. Given a FHE scheme, one can extend the definition of the encryption algorithm FHE.Enc to take as input a longer message $m \in \{0,1\}^n$, as opposed to a single bit. FHE.Enc$_{pk}(m)$ will simply run $c_i =$ FHE.Enc$_{pk}(m_i)$ for every $i \in [n]$, and set $c = (c_1, \ldots, c_n) \in \{0,1\}^{n \cdot \ell_{ctxt}}$. Similarly, we extend FHE.Eval to take as input a function $f : \{0,1\}^n \to \{0,1\}^u$ with multi-bit output.

3.3   Somewhere Extractable Batch Arguments (seBARGs)

A batch argument system BARG for an NP language $\mathcal{L}$ enables proving that k NP statements are true with communication cost that is polylogarithmic in k. There are many BARG variants which are known to be existentially equivalent under mild computational assumptions (see, e.g., [7,17,23]). In this work, for simplicity in our constructions, we make use of an argument system for what we call "batch index Turing machine SAT" (BatchTMSAT), defined below.

Definition 3.3. *The language* BatchIndexTMSAT *consists of instances of the form $x = (M, z, k, T)$, where:*

- *M is the description of a Turing machine.*
- *z is an input string (to M)*
- *k is a batch size, and*
- *T is a running time.*

An instance $x = (M, z, k, T)$ is in BatchIndexTMSAT *if for all $i \leq i \leq k$, there exists a string w_i such that $M(z, i, w_i)$ accepts within T steps.*

We sometimes use the notation $\mathcal{R}(x, i, w_i)$ to denote the relation with instance (x, i) and corresponding witness w_i.

Syntax. A (publicly verifiable and non-interactive) somewhere extractable batch argument system seBARG for BatchIndexTMSAT consists of the following polynomial time algorithms:

Gen$(1^\lambda, 1^n, 1^m, i^*) \to$ (crs, td). This is a probabilistic polynomial-time algorithm that takes as input a security parameter 1^λ, input length 1^n, witness length 1^m, and an index $i^* \in [2^\lambda]$. It outputs a common reference string crs along with a trapdoor td.

$\mathcal{P}$(crs, $M, z, 1^T, w_1, \ldots, w_k) \to \pi$. This deterministic polynomial-time algorithm takes as input a crs, Turing machine M, input z, runtime 1^T, and k witnesses $w_1, \ldots, w_k$. It outputs a proof π.

$\mathcal{V}$(crs, $x, \pi) \to 0/1$. This deterministic polynomial-time algorithm takes as input a crs, instance $x = (M, z, k, T)$, and a proof π. It outputs a bit (1 to accept, 0 to reject).

Extract(td, $\pi) \to w^*$. This deterministic polynomial-time algorithm takes as input a trapdoor td and a proof π. It outputs a single witness w^*.

Definition 3.4 (seBARG). *A somewhere-extractable batch argument scheme* seBARG $= (\text{Gen}, \mathcal{P}, \mathcal{V}, \text{Extract})$ *for* BatchIndexTMSAT *is required to satisfy the following properties:*

Completeness. *For any* $\lambda \in \mathbb{N}$, *any* $k(\lambda), n(\lambda), m(\lambda), T(\lambda) \leq 2^\lambda$, *any instance* $x = (M, z, k, T) \in$ BatchIndexTMSAT *with* $|M| + |z| = n$, *any corresponding witnesses* $w_1, \ldots, w_k \in \{0,1\}^m$ *and any index* $i^* \in [k]$,

$$\Pr\left[\mathcal{V}(\text{crs}, x, \pi) = 1 \ : \ \begin{array}{l} (\text{crs}, \text{td}) \leftarrow \text{Gen}(1^\lambda, 1^n, 1^m, i^*), \\ \pi \leftarrow \mathcal{P}(\text{crs}, M, z, 1^T, w_1, \ldots, w_k) \end{array} \right] = 1.$$

Efficiency. *In the completeness experiment above,* $|\text{crs}| + |\pi| \leq m \cdot$ $\text{poly}(\lambda, \log(knT))$. *The running time of the verifier is at most* $\text{poly}(|\text{crs}| + |\pi|) +$ $\text{poly}(\lambda) \cdot |x|$.

Index Hiding. *For any poly-size adversary* $\mathcal{A}$ *and any polynomials* $k(\lambda)$, $n(\lambda), m(\lambda)$, *there exists a negligible function* $\text{negl}(\cdot)$ *such that for every* $\lambda \in \mathbb{N}$ *and every pair of indices* $i_0, i_i \in [k]$,

$$\Pr\left[\mathcal{A}(\text{crs}) = b \ : \ \begin{array}{l} b \leftarrow \{0,1\}, \\ (\text{crs}, \text{td}) \leftarrow \text{Gen}(1^\lambda, 1^n, 1^m, i_b) \end{array} \right] \leq \frac{1}{2} + \text{negl}(\lambda).$$

Somewhere Argument of Knowledge. *For any poly-size adversary* $\mathcal{A}$ *and any polynomials* $k(\lambda), n(\lambda), m(\lambda), T(\lambda)$ *there exists a negligible function* $\text{negl}(\cdot)$ *such that for any index* $i^* \in [k]$ *and for every* $\lambda \in \mathbb{N}$,

$$\Pr\left[\begin{array}{l} \mathcal{V}(\text{crs}, x, \pi) = 1 \\ \wedge \ (x, i^*, w^*) \notin \mathcal{R} \end{array} \ : \ \begin{array}{l} (\text{crs}, \text{td}) \leftarrow \text{Gen}(1^\lambda, 1^n, 1^m, i^*) \\ (M, z, \pi) = \mathcal{A}(\text{crs}) \\ w^* \leftarrow \text{Extract}(\text{td}, \pi) \end{array} \right] \leq \text{negl}(\lambda).$$

Remark 3.4. We say that a seBARG scheme is T-secure, for $T = T(\lambda)$, if the index hiding property and the somewhere argument of knowledge property hold w.r.t. a $\text{poly}(T)$-size adversary (as opposed to a $\text{poly}(\lambda)$-size), and the advantage probability is $\text{negl}(T)$ (as opposed to $\text{negl}(\lambda)$). We refer to these properties as T-index-hiding and T-somewhere-argument-of-knowledge, respectively.

Throughout this paper, when we refer to a BARG or seBARG, we will implicitly mean a seBARG for BatchIndexTMSAT.

Remark 3.5. Given an seBARG, one can naturally extend the definition of the key generation algorithm Gen to take as input an index set $I \subset [k]$, as opposed to a single index. $\text{Gen}(1^\lambda, 1^n, 1^m, I)$ will simply run $\text{Gen}(1^\lambda, 1^n, 1^m, i)$ for every $i \in I$. The prover algorithm $\mathcal{P}$, given a crs that encodes the $|I|$ indices, will simply generate $|I|$ proofs (one for each crs), and the verifier will check these $|I|$ proofs independently.

Theorem 3.2 ([6,7,17,31]). *There exists an* seBARG *for* BatchIndexTMSAT *assuming* LWE *or* DLIN *or subexponential* DDH.

Remark 3.6. While seBARGs for BatchIndexTMSAT were not discussed explicitly in the above works, they can be constructed generically from all previous "flavors" of BARG along with a somewhere extractable hash family with local opening. This follows from a similar proof to that of Theorem 12 in [7]; an index seBARG for batch circuit SAT can be run to batch verify the executions of a RAM delegation scheme (or memory delegation scheme), which checks the computation of $M(z, i, w_i)$ in time $\mathsf{poly}(\lambda, \log k, \log T)$ given a tree hash of (M, z).

3.4 RAM SNARGs

In this section we define RAM SNARGs.

A RAM machine $\mathcal{R}$ is modeled as a deterministic machine with random access to memory of size 2^{ℓ} bits and a local state of size S. At every step, the machine reads or writes a single memory bit and updates its state.

For convenience, we think of the input to the RAM machine as a pair $x = (x_{\mathsf{imp}}, x_{\mathsf{exp}})$, where x_{imp} is large and is stored in the random access memory, and x_{exp} is a short explicit input.

Syntax. A RAM SNARG for machine $\mathcal{R}$ consists of the following polynomial time algorithms:

$\mathsf{Gen}(1^{\lambda}, T) \to \mathsf{crs}$. This is a probabilistic algorithm that takes as input a security parameter 1^{λ} and a time bound T. It outputs a common reference string crs.

$\mathsf{Digest}(\mathsf{crs}, x_{\mathsf{imp}}) \to \mathsf{d}$. This is a deterministic algorithm that takes as input a crs and a string x_{imp}. It outputs a digest d of size $\mathsf{poly}(\lambda)$.

$\mathcal{P}(\mathsf{crs}, (x_{\mathsf{imp}}, x_{\mathsf{exp}})) \to (b, \pi)$. This is a deterministic algorithm that takes as input a crs and a pair $(x_{\mathsf{imp}}, x_{\mathsf{exp}})$ which consists of a (long) input x_{imp} and a (short) input x_{exp}. It outputs a bit $b = \mathcal{R}(x_{\mathsf{imp}}, x_{\mathsf{exp}}) \in \{0, 1\}$ and a proof π.

$\mathcal{V}(\mathsf{crs}, \mathsf{d}, x_{\mathsf{exp}}, b, \pi) \to \{0, 1\}$. This is a deterministic algorithm that takes as input a crs, a digest d of the long input, a short input x_{exp}, a bit $b \in \{0, 1\}$ and a proof π. It outputs a bit (1 to accept, 0 to reject).

Definition 3.5 (RAM SNARG). *A RAM SNARG for machine $\mathcal{R}$ with local state of size $S \geq |x_{\mathsf{exp}}| + \log|x_{\mathsf{imp}}|$ is required to satisfy the following properties:*

Completeness. *For any $\lambda, n \in \mathbb{N}$ such that $n \leq T(n) \leq 2^{\lambda}$ and any $x = (x_{\mathsf{imp}}, x_{\mathsf{exp}}) \in \{0, 1\}^n$ such that $\mathcal{R}(x)$ halts within T time steps, we have that*

$$\Pr\left[\begin{array}{l} \mathcal{V}(\mathsf{crs}, \mathsf{d}_{x_{\mathsf{imp}}}, x_{\mathsf{exp}}, b, \pi) = 1 \wedge \\ b = \mathcal{R}(x) \end{array} : \begin{array}{l} \mathsf{crs} \leftarrow \mathsf{Gen}(1^{\lambda}, T) \\ (b, \pi) = \mathcal{P}(\mathsf{crs}, x) \\ \mathsf{d}_{x_{\mathsf{imp}}} = \mathsf{Digest}(\mathsf{crs}, x_{\mathsf{imp}}) \end{array}\right] = 1.$$

Efficiency. *In the completeness experiment above, the length of crs and the proof π is at most $\mathsf{poly}(\lambda, S, \log T)$.*

Collision resistance of RAM digest. *For any poly-size adversary $\mathcal{A}$ and any polynomial $T = T(\lambda)$ there exists a negligible function* negl$(\cdot)$ *such that for every $\lambda \in \mathbb{N}$,*

$$\Pr\left[\begin{array}{l} \mathsf{Digest}(\mathsf{crs}, x_{\mathsf{imp}}) = \mathsf{Digest}(\mathsf{crs}, x'_{\mathsf{imp}}) \wedge \\ x_{\mathsf{imp}} \neq x'_{\mathsf{imp}} \end{array} : \begin{array}{l} \mathsf{crs} \leftarrow \mathsf{Gen}(1^\lambda, T) \\ (x_{\mathsf{imp}}, x'_{\mathsf{imp}}) \leftarrow \mathcal{A}(\mathsf{crs}) \end{array}\right] \leq \mathsf{negl}(\lambda).$$

Soundness. *For any poly-size adversary $\mathcal{A}$ and any polynomial $T = T(\lambda)$ there exists a negligible function* negl$(\cdot)$ *such that for every $\lambda \in \mathbb{N}$,*

$$\Pr\left[\begin{array}{l} \mathcal{V}(\mathsf{crs}, \mathsf{d}, x_{\mathsf{exp}}, b, \pi) = 1 \wedge \\ \mathsf{Digest}(\mathsf{crs}, x_{\mathsf{imp}}) = \mathsf{d} \wedge \\ \mathcal{R}(x_{\mathsf{imp}}, x_{\mathsf{exp}}) \neq b \end{array} : \begin{array}{l} \mathsf{crs} \leftarrow \mathsf{Gen}(1^\lambda, T) \\ (\mathsf{d}, x_{\mathsf{imp}}, x_{\mathsf{exp}}, b, \pi) \leftarrow \mathcal{A}(\mathsf{crs}) \end{array}\right] \leq \mathsf{negl}(\lambda).$$

Theorem 3.3 ([6,7,17,31]). *There exists a RAM SNARG assuming LWE or DLIN or subexponential DDH.*

4   SNARGs for Monotone Policy BatchNP

Monotone Policy BatchNP Model. Fix any NP language $\mathcal{L}$ with witness relation $\mathcal{R}$ and fix any function f computable by a monotone circuit family C.
   The complexity of C (and its topology) is described in the following way:

- C has some input length $k = k(n)$ and size $|C| = s = s(n)$. These parameters are functions of n, the length of an instance of $\mathcal{L}$.
- C may have a more efficient uniform description, i.e., polynomial-time Turing machine M that generates C on input aux of length less than s.
- The circuit C is *layered* if the wires of C can be partitioned into "layers" $J_0, J_1, \ldots, J_d \subset [s]$ such that for every gate $(j, j_0, j_1, c \in \{\mathsf{AND}, \mathsf{OR}\}) \in$ Gates(C), if $j \in J_i$ then $j_0, j_1 \in J_{i-1} \cup J_0$. In other words, wire values in layer i are computed from wires in layer $i - 1$ along with input wires.
- We say that a layered circuit C has *depth* d if it has d layers (not including the input layer), and has *width* w if each layer (besides the input layer) has size at most w. We note that this notion allows for C to have width less than k.

In what follows, we construct a SNARG for the NP language $\mathcal{L}_f^{(k)}$ defined as follows:

$$\mathcal{L}_f^{(k)} = \left\{(x_1, \ldots, x_k) : \exists (w_1, \ldots, w_k) \text{ s.t. } f(b_1, \ldots, b_k) = 1, \text{ where } b_i = \mathcal{R}(x_i, w_i)\right\}.$$

We first define the notion of a SNARG for $\mathcal{L}_f^{(k)}$.

4.1   Definition

We now define succinct non-interactive arguments (SNARGs) for languages of the form $\mathcal{L}_f^{(k)}$ above. The syntax follows that of SNARGs for general (NP) languages; however, similarly to the case of batch arguments (Definition 3.4), we allow the proof size (and other parameters) to grow with the size of a single NP witness w_i.

Syntax. A SNARG for $\mathcal{L}_f^{(k)}$ consists of the following PPT algorithms:

$\mathsf{Gen}(1^\lambda, k, n) \to (\mathsf{crs}_\mathcal{P}, \mathsf{crs}_\mathcal{V})$. This is a probabilistic algorithm that takes as input the security parameter 1^λ as well as a batch size k and instance size n. It outputs a common reference string $(\mathsf{crs}_\mathcal{P}, \mathsf{crs}_\mathcal{V})$, separated into two parts for efficiency reasons.

$\mathcal{P}(\mathsf{crs}_\mathcal{P}, C, x_1, \ldots, x_k, w_1, \ldots, w_k) \to \pi$. This is a deterministic polynomial-time algorithm that takes as input the crs $\mathsf{crs}_\mathcal{P}$, a description of the monotone circuit C, the k NP instances $x_1, \ldots, x_k$, and corresponding witnesses $w_1, \ldots, w_k$. It outputs a proof string π.

$\mathcal{V}(\mathsf{crs}_\mathcal{V}, C, x_1, \ldots, x_k, \pi) \to 0/1$. This is a deterministic polynomial-time algorithm that takes as input the verification key $\mathsf{crs}_\mathcal{V}$, a description of C, the k NP instances $x_1, \ldots, x_k$, and a proof string π. It outputs a bit (1 to accept, 0 to reject).

We will sometimes drop C from our algorithm notation, as it is fixed once and for all based on the language $\mathcal{L}_f^{(k)}$ and choice of implementation C of f.

We next define the properties of a SNARG scheme. We consider two soundness guarantees: non-adaptive soundness and semi-adaptive soundness (somewhere extractability).

Definition 4.1 (SNARG for Monotone Policy BatchNP). *A SNARG scheme* $(\mathsf{Gen}, \mathcal{P}, \mathcal{V})$ *for* $\mathcal{L}_f^{(k)}$ *is required to satisfy the following properties.*

Completeness. *For any* $\lambda \in \mathbb{N}$, *any* $k = k(\lambda)$, $n = n(\lambda)$, *and* $x = (x_1, \ldots, x_k) \in \mathcal{L}_f^{(k)}$, *such that* $|x| \leq 2^\lambda$ *and* $|x_i| = n$ *for every* $i \in [k]$, *and any corresponding witness* $w = (w_1, \ldots, w_k) \in \{0,1\}^{k \cdot m}$,

$$\Pr\left[\mathcal{V}(\mathsf{crs}_\mathcal{V}, C, x, \pi) = 1 \;:\; \begin{array}{l} (\mathsf{crs}_\mathcal{P}, \mathsf{crs}_\mathcal{V}) \leftarrow \mathsf{Gen}(1^\lambda, k, n), \\ \pi \leftarrow \mathcal{P}(\mathsf{crs}_\mathcal{P}, C, x, w) \end{array} \right] = 1.$$

Succinctness. *In the completeness experiment above, the size of* $\mathsf{crs}_\mathcal{V}$ *and* π *are at most* $\mathsf{poly}(\lambda, \log k, m)$.

Non-Adaptive Soundness. *For any polynomials* $k = k(\lambda)$ *and* $n = n(\lambda)$ *and any polynomial-size* $\mathcal{P}^*$ *there exists a negligible function* $\mathsf{negl}(\cdot)$ *such for any instance* $x = (x_1, \ldots, x_k) \notin \mathcal{L}_f^{(k)}$ *such that* $|x_i| = n$ *for every* $i \in [k]$, *it holds that for every* $\lambda \in \mathbb{N}$,

$$\Pr\left[\mathcal{V}(\mathsf{crs}_\mathcal{V}, C, x, \pi) = 1 \;:\; \begin{array}{l} (\mathsf{crs}_\mathcal{P}, \mathsf{crs}_\mathcal{V}) \leftarrow \mathsf{Gen}(1^\lambda, k, n), \\ \pi \leftarrow \mathcal{P}^*(\mathsf{crs}_\mathcal{P}, \mathsf{crs}_\mathcal{V}) \end{array} \right] \leq \mathsf{negl}(\lambda).$$

In addition to the standard soundness definition, we introduce a variant of "somewhere extractability" for SNARGs for monotone policy BatchNP. Roughly speaking, our definition says that for any "necessary subset" $J \subset [k]$ for C (meaning that if $C(b_1, \ldots, b_k) = 1$ then $b_j = 1$ for some $j \in J$), the common reference string can be programmed to be "extractable on J," meaning that it is possible to extract (from an efficiently generated proof π on an adaptively chosen statement) a witness w_j for some $j \in J$.

Definition 4.2 (Somewhere Extractable SNARGs for Monotone Policy BatchNP). *A SNARG for* $\mathcal{L}_f^{(k)}$ *is somewhere extractable if it additionally supports the following syntax:*

$\mathsf{Gen}(1^\lambda, k, n, J) \rightarrow (\mathsf{crs}_\mathcal{P}, \mathsf{crs}_\mathcal{V}, \mathsf{td})$. *This is a probabilistic algorithm that takes as input the security parameter* 1^λ, *batch size* k, *input length* n, *and the description of a set* $J \subset [k]$. *It outputs a common reference string* $(\mathsf{crs}_\mathcal{P}, \mathsf{crs}_\mathcal{V})$ *along with a trapdoor* td.

$\mathsf{Extract}(\mathsf{td}, \pi) \rightarrow (i, w_i)$. *This is a polynomial-time algorithm that takes as input a trapdoor* td *and proof string* π. *It outputs an index* i *and witness* w_i.

We additionally require the following two properties (which together imply soundness):

Key Indistinguishability. *For any poly-size adversary* $\mathcal{A}$, *any polynomials* $k = k(\lambda)$ *and* $n = n(\lambda)$, *and any sets* $J_0, J_1 \subseteq [k]$ *there exists a negligible function* $\mathsf{negl}(\cdot)$ *such that for every* $\lambda \in \mathbb{N}$,

$$\Pr\left[\mathcal{A}(\mathsf{crs}_\mathcal{P}, \mathsf{crs}_\mathcal{V}) = b \;:\; \begin{array}{l} b \leftarrow \{0,1\}, \\ (\mathsf{crs}_\mathcal{P}, \mathsf{crs}_\mathcal{V}, \mathsf{td}) \leftarrow \mathsf{Gen}(1^\lambda, k, n, J_b) \end{array}\right] \leq \frac{1}{2} + \mathsf{negl}(\lambda).$$

Somewhere Argument of Knowledge. *For any polynomials* $k = k(\lambda)$ *and* $n = n(\lambda)$ *and any polynomial-size* $\mathcal{P}^*$, *there exists a negligible function* $\mathsf{negl}(\cdot)$ *such that for any set* $J \subseteq [k]$ *where the assignment* $b_i = 1_{i \notin J}$ *satisfies* $f(b_1, \ldots, b_k) = 0$, *and every* $\lambda \in \mathbb{N}$,

$$\Pr\left[\begin{array}{l} \mathcal{V}(\mathsf{crs}_\mathcal{V}, C, x_1, \ldots, x_k, \pi) = 1 \wedge \\ i \notin J \vee \mathcal{R}(x_i, w_i) = 0 \end{array} \;:\; \begin{array}{l} (\mathsf{crs}_\mathcal{P}, \mathsf{crs}_\mathcal{V}, \mathsf{td}) \leftarrow \mathsf{Gen}(1^\lambda, k, n, J) \\ (x_1, \ldots, x_k, \pi) \leftarrow \mathcal{P}^*(\mathsf{crs}_\mathcal{P}, \mathsf{crs}_\mathcal{V}) \\ (i, w_i) \leftarrow \mathsf{Extract}\,(\mathsf{td}, \pi) \end{array}\right] \leq \mathsf{negl}(\lambda).$$

5   Predicate Extractable Hash Families

In order to construct a SNARG scheme for monotone policy BatchNP languages, we first introduce a new tool: a *predicate extractable hash family* (PEHash). PEHash extends the commonly used notion of a *somewhere extractable hash* (SEHash) in the following way:

- A PEHash is associated with a class of predicates $\mathcal{F}$. A SEHash can be viewed as an instance of PEHash where $\mathcal{F}$ consists of all *index* functions $f_i(x) = x_i$.
- A hash key hk is sampled to be *binding* on a specific predicate f; however, hk itself computationally hides f.
- When hk is binding on f, it should be possible to *extract* $f(x)$ from a hash of x.

Defining security of PEHash for general predicates is somewhat challenging. In the case of SEHash, the key security property (aside from index hiding) is that if the bit b is extracted from a hash value v, and the hash function is binding on index i, then it should be hard (or impossible) to locally open v to $1 - b$ on the ith input location.

In this work, we define and construct PEHash for the class of *bit-fixing* predicates $f_{y,J}$ where $f_{y,J}(x) = 1$ if and only if $y_i = x_i$ for all $i \in J$. However, we view PEHash as a more general object and expect extensions to be useful in the future. Therefore, in what follows we define the syntax and basic properties of PEHash for general predicates. Our security definitions, however, are tailored to bit-fixing predicates.

5.1 Syntax and Basic Properties

A predicate extractable hash family PEHash with respect to a family $\mathcal{F}$ consists of the following PPT algorithms:

Gen$(1^\lambda, N, f) \to (\mathsf{hk}, \boldsymbol{k}, \mathsf{td})$. This is a PPT setup algorithm that takes as input a security parameter 1^λ, a message length N, and a predicate $f : \{0,1\}^N \to \{0,1\}$ in $\mathcal{F}$. It outputs a hash key hk, a verification key $\boldsymbol{k}$, and a trapdoor td.

Hash$(\mathsf{hk}, x) \to \mathsf{v}$. This is a poly-time deterministic algorithm that takes as input a hash key hk and an input $x \in \{0,1\}^N$, and outputs a hash value $\mathsf{v} \in \{0,1\}^{\mathsf{poly}(\lambda)}$.

Open$(\mathsf{hk}, x, j) \to \rho$. This is a poly-time deterministic algorithm that takes as input a hash key hk, an input $x \in \{0,1\}^N$ and an index $j \in [N]$, and outputs an opening $\rho \in \{0,1\}^{\mathsf{poly}(\lambda)}$.

Verify$(\boldsymbol{k}, \mathsf{v}, j, b, \rho) \to 0/1$. This is a poly-time deterministic algorithm that takes as input a verification key $\boldsymbol{k}$, a hash value $\mathsf{v} \in \{0,1\}^{\mathsf{poly}(\lambda)}$, an index $j \in [N]$, a bit $b \in \{0,1\}$ and an opening $\rho \in \{0,1\}^{\mathsf{poly}(\lambda)}$, and outputs 1 (accept) or 0 (reject).

Extract$(\mathsf{td}, \mathsf{v}) \to u$. This is a deterministic extraction algorithm that takes as input a trapdoor td and a hash value v, and outputs a bit u.

Most properties of a PEHash can be stated independently of the predicate class $\mathcal{F}$: we require that a PEHash hash key should hide the predicate, the extraction algorithm should output the predicate $f(x)$ on Hash(x), and that PEHash should be a secure hash family with local opening.

Definition 5.1 (PEHash Basic Properties). *A predicate extractable hash family*

$$\mathsf{PEHash} = (\mathsf{Gen}, \mathsf{Hash}, \mathsf{Open}, \mathsf{Verify}, \mathsf{Extract})$$

satisfies the following properties:

Opening completeness. *For any $\lambda \in \mathbb{N}$, any $N \leq 2^\lambda$, any predicate $f \in \mathcal{F}$, any index $j \in [N]$, and any $x \in \{0,1\}^N$,*

$$\Pr\left[\mathsf{Verify}(\boldsymbol{k}, \mathsf{v}, j, x_j, \rho) = 1 \; : \; \begin{array}{l} (\mathsf{hk}, \boldsymbol{k}, \mathsf{td}) \leftarrow \mathsf{Gen}(1^\lambda, N, f), \\ \mathsf{v} = \mathsf{Hash}(\mathsf{hk}, x), \\ \rho = \mathsf{Open}(\mathsf{hk}, x, j), \end{array}\right] = 1.$$

Succinctness. *In the completeness experiment above, the size of the verification key $\boldsymbol{k}$ and the hash value v is $\mathsf{poly}(\lambda)$. The size of the hash key hk is at most $|f| \cdot \mathsf{poly}(\lambda, \log N)$.*

Computational Binding. *For any poly-size adversary $\mathcal{A}$ it holds that for any polynomial $N = N(\lambda)$ and any predicate $f \in \mathcal{F}$ there exists a negligible function μ such that for any $\lambda \in \mathbb{N}$,*

$$\Pr \left[\begin{array}{l} \mathsf{Verify}(\boldsymbol{k}, \mathsf{v}, j, 0, \rho_0) = 1 \wedge \\ \mathsf{Verify}(\boldsymbol{k}, \mathsf{v}, j, 1, \rho_1) = 1 \end{array} : \begin{array}{l} (\mathsf{hk}, \boldsymbol{k}, \mathsf{td}) \leftarrow \mathsf{Gen}(1^\lambda, N, f), \\ (\mathsf{v}, j, \rho_0, \rho_1) \leftarrow \mathcal{A}(\mathsf{hk}, \boldsymbol{k}) \end{array} \right] \leq \mathsf{negl}(\lambda).$$

Predicate Hiding. *For any poly-size adversary $\mathcal{A}$, any polynomial $N = N(\lambda)$, and any two predicates $f_0, f_1 \in \mathcal{F}$ such that $|f_0| = |f_1|$, there exists a negligible function $\mathsf{negl}(\cdot)$ such that for every $\lambda \in \mathbb{N}$,*

$$\Pr \left[\mathcal{A}(\mathsf{hk}, \boldsymbol{k}) = b : \begin{array}{l} b \leftarrow \{0, 1\} \\ (\mathsf{hk}, \boldsymbol{k}, \mathsf{td}) \leftarrow \mathsf{Gen}(1^\lambda, N, f_b) \end{array} \right] \leq \frac{1}{2} + \mathsf{negl}(\lambda),$$

Extraction Correctness. *For any $\lambda \in \mathbb{N}$, any $N \leq 2^\lambda$, any predicate $f \in \mathcal{F}$, and any $x \in \{0, 1\}^N$, there exists a negligible function $\mathsf{negl}(\cdot)$ such that for every $\lambda \in \mathbb{N}$,*

$$\Pr \left[f(x) \neq \mathsf{Extract}(\mathsf{td}, \mathsf{v}) : \begin{array}{l} (\mathsf{hk}, \boldsymbol{k}, \mathsf{td}) \leftarrow \mathsf{Gen}(1^\lambda, N, f) \\ \mathsf{v} = \mathsf{Hash}(\mathsf{hk}, x) \end{array} \right] \leq \mathsf{negl}(\lambda).$$

5.2 Extractable Hash for Bit-Fixing Predicates

Next, we describe what it means for a PEHash to be secure for *bit-fixing predicates*. Recall that for $x \in \{0, 1\}^n$, we define $f_{y,J}(x) = 1$ if and only if $y_i = x_i$ for all $i \in J$. We want a security notion that restricts the behavior of an adversarial sender, which given $(\mathsf{hk}, \boldsymbol{k})$ produces a hash value v. It turns out that security is *asymmetric* depending on whether $\mathsf{Extract}(\mathsf{td}, \mathsf{v})$ is equal to 0 or 1:

- If $\mathsf{Extract}(\mathsf{td}, \mathsf{v}) = 1$, we want it to be hard for the adversary to open the ith bit of x to $1 - y_i$ for any $i \in J$.
- If $\mathsf{Extract}(\mathsf{td}, \mathsf{v}) = 0$, we want to say that there is *some* index $j \in J$ such that the adversary cannot open the jth bit of x to y_j. To formalize this, we introduce an auxiliary algorithm $\mathsf{ExtractIndex}(\mathsf{td}, \mathsf{v}) \rightarrow j$ that "points" to which index the adversary is constrained on.

We give a formal definition below.

Definition 5.2 (Bit-fixing PEHash). *A predicate extractable hash family PEHash with respect to the bit-fixing predicate family is a PEHash satisfying the basic properties above (Definition 5.1), augmented with the following algorithm:*

$\mathsf{ExtractIndex}(\mathsf{td}, \mathsf{v}) \rightarrow j$. *This is a deterministic extraction algorithm that takes as input a trapdoor td and a hash value $\mathsf{v} \in \{0, 1\}^{\mathsf{poly}(\lambda)}$, and outputs an index $j \in [N]$.*

The hash family is furthermore required to satisfy the following consistency *properties:*

Index Extraction Correctness. *For any* $\lambda \in \mathbb{N}$, *any* $N \leq 2^\lambda$, *any predicate* $f = (J, y) \in \mathcal{F}$ *such that* $J \neq \emptyset$, *and any hash value* v,

$$\Pr\left[\mathsf{ExtractIndex}(\mathsf{td}, \mathsf{v}) \in J \; : \; (\mathsf{hk}, \boldsymbol{k}, \mathsf{td}) \leftarrow \mathsf{Gen}(1^\lambda, N, J, y)\right] = 1 .$$

Consistency of Extraction. *For any poly-size adversary* $\mathcal{A}$ *it holds that for any polynomial* $N = N(\lambda)$ *and any bit-fixing predicate described by a set* $J \subset [N]$ *and string* $y \in \{0,1\}^J$, *there exists a negligible function* $\mathsf{negl}(\cdot)$ *such that for any* $\lambda \in \mathbb{N}$,

$$\Pr\left[\begin{matrix} j \in J \wedge \; \mathsf{Extract}(\mathsf{td}, \mathsf{v}) = 1 \wedge \\ \mathsf{Verify}(\boldsymbol{k}, \mathsf{v}, j, 1 - y_j, t, \rho) = 1 \end{matrix} \; : \; \begin{matrix} (\mathsf{hk}, \boldsymbol{k}, \mathsf{td}) \leftarrow \mathsf{Gen}(1^\lambda, N, J, y), \\ (\mathsf{v}, j, t, \rho) \leftarrow \mathcal{A}(\mathsf{hk}, \boldsymbol{k}) \end{matrix}\right] \leq \mathsf{negl}(\lambda),$$

and

$$\Pr\left[\begin{matrix} \mathsf{Extract}(\mathsf{td}, \mathsf{v}) = 0 \wedge \\ \mathsf{ExtractIndex}(\mathsf{td}, \mathsf{v}) = j \wedge \\ \mathsf{Verify}(\boldsymbol{k}, \mathsf{v}, j, y_j, t, \rho) = 1 \end{matrix} \; : \; \begin{matrix} (\mathsf{hk}, \boldsymbol{k}, \mathsf{td}) \leftarrow \mathsf{Gen}(1^\lambda, N, J, y), \\ (\mathsf{v}, j, t, \rho) \leftarrow \mathcal{A}(\mathsf{hk}, \boldsymbol{k}) \end{matrix}\right] \leq \mathsf{negl}(\lambda).$$

Theorem 5.1. *Assuming the hardness of* LWE, *there exists a* PEHash *family for bit-fixing predicates.*

The proof of this theorem appears in the full version of this work.

5.3 Extractable Hash with Tags for Bit-Fixing Predicates

In this section we define an extension of PEHash for bit-fixing predicates, which we call a PEHash family with tags. This object supports hashing the input together with a vector of tags, such that each bit of the input has an attached tag.

We use this extended definition in to achieve a somewhere extractable SNARG. We modify the syntax of the basic PEHash algorithms to support tags, as follows:

- Gen, Extract and ExtractIndex are identical.
- Hash and Open receive a vector of tags $\vec{t} = (t_1, \ldots, t_N)$ as an additional input.
- Verify receives a tag t as an additional input, which should correspond to the tag attached to the jth bit of x.

We additionally introduce an auxiliary algorithm ExtractTag that is defined similarly to ExtractIndex except that it extracts the tag associated with input that the adversary is constrained on instead of its index. We give the full syntax below.

Syntax. A predicate extractable hash family PEHash with tags with respect to the bit-fixing predicate family consists of the following PPT algorithms:

$\mathsf{Gen}(1^\lambda, N, J, y) \to (\mathsf{hk}, \boldsymbol{k}, \mathsf{td})$. This is a probabilistic setup algorithm that takes as input a security parameter 1^λ in unary, a message length N, a set of indices $J \subseteq [N]$, and a string $y \in \{0,1\}^J$. It outputs a hash key hk, verification key $\boldsymbol{k}$ and trapdoor td.

$\mathsf{Hash}(\mathsf{hk}, x, \vec{t}) \to \mathsf{v}$. This is a deterministic algorithm that takes as input a hash key hk, an input $x \in \{0,1\}^N$, and tags $\vec{t} = (t_1, \ldots, t_N) \in (\{0,1\}^T)^N$. It outputs a hash value $\mathsf{v} \in \{0,1\}^{T \cdot \mathsf{poly}(\lambda)}$.

$\mathsf{Open}(\mathsf{hk}, x, \vec{t}, j) \to \rho$. This is a deterministic algorithm that takes as input a hash key hk, an input $x \in \{0,1\}^N$, tags $\vec{t} = (t_1, \ldots, t_N) \in (\{0,1\}^T)^N$ and an index $j \in [N]$. It outputs an opening $\rho \in \{0,1\}^{T \cdot \mathsf{poly}(\lambda)}$.

$\mathsf{Verify}(\boldsymbol{k}, \mathsf{v}, j, b, t, \rho) \to 0/1$. This is a deterministic algorithm that takes as input a verification key $\boldsymbol{k}$, a hash value $\mathsf{v} \in \{0,1\}^{T \cdot \mathsf{poly}(\lambda)}$, an index $j \in [N]$, a bit $b \in \{0,1\}$, a tag $t \in \{0,1\}^T$ and an opening $\rho \in \{0,1\}^{T \cdot \mathsf{poly}(\lambda)}$, and outputs 1 (accept) or 0 (reject).

$\mathsf{Extract}(\mathsf{td}, \mathsf{v}) \to u$. This is a deterministic extraction algorithm that takes as input a trapdoor td and a hash value $\mathsf{v} \in \{0,1\}^{T \cdot \mathsf{poly}(\lambda)}$, and outputs a bit $u \in \{0,1\}$.

$\mathsf{ExtractIndex}(\mathsf{td}, \mathsf{v}) \to j$. This is a deterministic extraction algorithm that takes as input a trapdoor td and a hash value $\mathsf{v} \in \{0,1\}^{T \cdot \mathsf{poly}(\lambda)}$, and outputs an index $j \in [N]$.

$\mathsf{ExtractTag}(\mathsf{td}, \mathsf{v}) \to t$. This is a deterministic extraction algorithm that takes as input a trapdoor td and a hash value $\mathsf{v} \in \{0,1\}^{T \cdot \mathsf{poly}(\lambda)}$, and outputs a tag $t \in \{0,1\}^T$.

The basic properties of PEHash with tags are as in Definition 5.1, with minor adjustments to account for the modified syntax. For security, we extend the consistency of extraction property to hold also for tags.

Definition 5.3 (Bit-fixing PEHash with Tags). *A predicate extractable hash family PEHash with tags with respect to the bit-fixing predicate family is a PEHash satisfying the basic properties defined in Definition 5.1 modified to account for tags, and the following consistency properties:*

Index Extraction Correctness. *For any $\lambda \in \mathbb{N}$, any $N \leq 2^\lambda$, any predicate $f = (J, y) \in \mathcal{F}$ such that $J \neq \emptyset$, and any hash value v,*

$$\Pr\left[\mathsf{ExtractIndex}(\mathsf{td}, \mathsf{v}) \in J \ : \ (\mathsf{hk}, \boldsymbol{k}, \mathsf{td}) \leftarrow \mathsf{Gen}(1^\lambda, N, J, y)\right] = 1 .$$

Consistency of Extraction. *For any poly-size adversary $\mathcal{A}$ it holds that for any polynomial $N = N(\lambda)$ and any bit-fixing predicate described by a set $J \subseteq [N]$ and string $y \in \{0,1\}^J$, there exists a negligible function $\mathsf{negl}(\cdot)$ such that for any $\lambda \in \mathbb{N}$,*

$$\Pr\left[\begin{array}{l} j \in J \wedge \mathsf{Extract}(\mathsf{td}, \mathsf{v}) = 1 \wedge \\ \mathsf{Verify}(\boldsymbol{k}, \mathsf{v}, j, \bar{y}_j, t, \rho) = 1 \end{array} : \begin{array}{l} (\mathsf{hk}, \boldsymbol{k}, \mathsf{td}) \leftarrow \mathsf{Gen}(1^\lambda, N, J, y), \\ (\mathsf{v}, j, t, \rho) \leftarrow \mathcal{A}(\mathsf{hk}, \boldsymbol{k}) \end{array}\right] \leq \mathsf{negl}(\lambda),$$

and

$$\Pr\left[\begin{array}{l}\mathsf{Extract}(\mathsf{td},\mathsf{v}) = 0 \;\wedge \\ \mathsf{ExtractIndex}(\mathsf{td},\mathsf{v}) = j \;\wedge \\ \mathsf{Verify}(\boldsymbol{k},\mathsf{v},j,y_j,t,\rho) = 1 \end{array} \; : \; \begin{array}{l}(\mathsf{hk},\boldsymbol{k},\mathsf{td}) \leftarrow \mathsf{Gen}(1^\lambda, N, J, y),\\ (\mathsf{v},j,t,\rho) \leftarrow \mathcal{A}(\mathsf{hk},\boldsymbol{k})\end{array}\right] \leq \mathsf{negl}(\lambda).$$

Consistency of Tag Extraction. *For any poly-size adversary $\mathcal{A}$ it holds that for any polynomial $N = N(\lambda)$ and any bit-fixing predicate described by a set $J \subseteq [N]$ and string $y \in \{0,1\}^J$, there exists a negligible function $\mathsf{negl}(\cdot)$ such that for any $\lambda \in \mathbb{N}$,*

$$\Pr\left[\begin{array}{l}\mathsf{Extract}(\mathsf{td},\mathsf{v}) = 0 \;\wedge \\ \mathsf{ExtractIndex}(\mathsf{td},\mathsf{v}) = j \;\wedge \\ \mathsf{ExtractTag}(\mathsf{td},\mathsf{v}) \neq t \;\wedge \\ \mathsf{Verify}(\boldsymbol{k},\mathsf{v},j,\bar{y}_j,t,\rho) = 1 \end{array} \; : \; \begin{array}{l}(\mathsf{hk},\boldsymbol{k},\mathsf{td}) \leftarrow \mathsf{Gen}(1^\lambda, N, J, y),\\ (\mathsf{v},j,t,\rho) \leftarrow \mathcal{A}(\mathsf{hk},\boldsymbol{k})\end{array}\right] \leq \mathsf{negl}(\lambda).$$

The construction and proof appears in the full version of this work.

6 Non-Adaptive SNARG Construction

In what follows we construct a SNARG scheme $(\mathsf{Gen}, \mathcal{P}, \mathcal{V})$ for the language $\mathcal{L}_f^{(k)}$ defined in Sect. 4 with respect to an underlying NP language $\mathcal{L}$ and a monotone circuit C computing function f.

Our construction uses the following building blocks:

– A PEHash family (Definition 5.2)

$$\mathsf{PEHash} = (\mathsf{Gen}_{\mathsf{PEH}}, \mathsf{Hash}_{\mathsf{PEH}}, \mathsf{Open}_{\mathsf{PEH}}, \mathsf{Verify}_{\mathsf{PEH}}, \mathsf{Extract}_{\mathsf{PEH}}, \mathsf{ExtractIndex}_{\mathsf{PEH}})$$

with respect to the bit-fixing predicate family $\mathcal{F}$ where each $f \in \mathcal{F}$ is a Boolean function with domain $\{0,1\}^N$, where $N = s := |C|$. Each function $f \in \mathcal{F}$ is associated with a subset $J \subseteq [N]$ of size $\ell \leq \mathrm{width}(C)$ and a string $y \in \{0,1\}^\ell$.

– A seBARG scheme (Definition 3.4)

$$(\mathsf{Gen}_{\mathsf{seBARG}}, \mathcal{P}_{\mathsf{seBARG}}, \mathcal{V}_{\mathsf{seBARG}}, \mathsf{Extract}_{\mathsf{seBARG}}).$$

We are now ready to define our SNARG for $\mathcal{L}_f^{(k)}$.

$\mathsf{Gen}(1^\lambda, k, n)$ does the following:

1. Fix two arbitrary predicates $f_1, f_2 \in \mathcal{F}$. Recall that $|f_\beta| = \ell \cdot (\log s + 1)$ for every $\beta \in \{1,2\}$.
2. Generate $(\mathsf{hk}_{\mathsf{PEH}}^{(\beta)}, \boldsymbol{k}_{\mathsf{PEH}}^{(\beta)}, \mathsf{td}_{\mathsf{PEH}}^{(\beta)}) \leftarrow \mathsf{Gen}_{\mathsf{PEH}}(1^\lambda, N, f_\beta)$ for each $\beta \in \{1,2\}$.
3. Generate $(\mathsf{crs}_{\mathsf{seBARG}}, \mathsf{td}_{\mathsf{seBARG}}) \leftarrow \mathsf{Gen}_{\mathsf{seBARG}}(1^\lambda, 1^{n'}, 1^{m'}, I)$, where

$$n' = O(1) + \log N + 2|\boldsymbol{k}_{\mathsf{PEH}}| + 2|\mathsf{v}|,$$

$$m' = m + 3 + 6|\rho|,$$

$|\mathsf{v}|$ is the length of the output of $\mathsf{Hash}_{\mathsf{PEH}}(\mathsf{hk}_{\mathsf{PEH}}, \cdot)$, $|\rho|$ is the length of the output of $\mathsf{Open}_{\mathsf{PEH}}(\mathsf{hk}_{\mathsf{PEH}}, \cdot)$, and where $I \subset [N]$ is a set of size three initialized to $\{1, 2, N\}$.

4. Let $\text{crs}_\mathcal{P} = (\text{hk}_{\text{PEH}}^{(1)}, k_{\text{PEH}}^{(1)}, \text{hk}_{\text{PEH}}^{(2)}, k_{\text{PEH}}^{(2)}, \text{crs}_{\text{seBARG}})$ and let $\text{crs}_\mathcal{V} = (k_{\text{PEH}}^{(1)}, k_{\text{PEH}}^{(2)}, \text{crs}_{\text{seBARG}})$.

5. Output $(\text{crs}_\mathcal{P}, \text{crs}_\mathcal{V})$.

$\mathcal{P}(\text{crs}_\mathcal{P}, C, x_1, \ldots, x_k, w_1, \ldots, w_k)$ does the following:

1. For every $1 \leq j \leq k$, compute $b_j = \mathcal{R}_\mathcal{L}(x_j, w_j)$. Then, compute the values of all the wires in the circuit evaluation $C(b_1, \ldots, b_k)$. Denote these values by $b_1, \ldots, b_N$ (the first k bits are the input wire values).

2. Parse $\text{crs}_\mathcal{P} = (\text{hk}_{\text{PEH}}^{(1)}, k_{\text{PEH}}^{(1)}, \text{hk}_{\text{PEH}}^{(2)}, k_{\text{PEH}}^{(2)}, \text{crs}_{\text{seBARG}})$.

3. Compute $\mathsf{v}^{(\beta)} = \text{Hash}_{\text{PEH}}(\text{hk}_{\text{PEH}}^{(\beta)}, (b_1, \ldots, b_N))$ for $\beta \in \{1, 2\}$.

4. Define an instance $X = (M, z, N, T)$ of BatchIndexTMSAT. The input z is defined as $z = (C, x_1, \ldots, x_k, (k_{\text{PEH}}^{(\beta)}, \mathsf{v}^{(\beta)})_{\beta \in \{1, 2\}})$. The batch size is set to N. The Turing machine $M(z, j, \omega_j)$ is defined to operate as follows:

   (a) Parse $z = (C, x_1, \ldots, x_k, (k_{\text{PEH}}^{(\beta)}, \mathsf{v}^{(\beta)})_{\beta \in \{1, 2\}})$.

   (b) If $1 \leq j \leq k$:

      i Parse $\omega_j = (w_j, b_j, \rho^{(1)}, \rho^{(2)})$.

      ii Check that $\text{Verify}(k_{\text{PEH}}^{(\beta)}, \mathsf{v}^{(\beta)}, j, b_j, \rho^{(\beta)}) = 1$ for $\beta \in \{1, 2\}$.

      iii Check that $\mathcal{R}_\mathcal{L}(x_j, w_j) = b_j$.

   (c) If $j > k$:

      i Compute the jth gate of C, $g_j = (j, j_1, j_2, c \in \{\text{AND}, \text{OR}\})$.

      ii Parse $\omega_j = \left(b_j, b_{j_1}, b_{j_2}, \left(\rho_j^{(\beta)}, \rho_{j_1}^{(\beta)}, \rho_{j_2}^{(\beta)}\right)_{\beta \in \{1, 2\}}\right)$.

      iii Check that $\text{Verify}_{\text{PEH}}(k_{\text{PEH}}^{(\beta)}, \mathsf{v}^{(\beta)}, j, b_j, \rho_j^{(\beta)}) = 1$ for $\beta \in \{1, 2\}$.

      iv Check that $\text{Verify}_{\text{PEH}}(k_{\text{PEH}}^{(\beta)}, \mathsf{v}^{(\beta)}, j_\alpha, b_{j_\alpha}, \rho_{j_\alpha}^{(\beta)}) = 1$ for $\alpha, \beta \in \{1, 2\}$.

      v Check that $b_j = c(b_{j_1}, b_{j_2})$. (That is, check that the gate is satisfied.)

      vi If $j = N$ is the output wire then check that $b_j = 1$.

   The description length of M is a constant. Finally, the time bound $T = \text{poly}(N, n, m, k)$ is set so that the pseudocode above terminates.

5. For every $j \in [N]$, construct a witness (j, ω_j) for X, using the Open_{PEH} algorithm to produce openings for $(b_1, \ldots, b_N)$ as appropriate.

6. Compute $\pi_{\text{seBARG}} = \mathcal{P}_{\text{seBARG}}(\text{crs}_{\text{seBARG}}, M, z, 1^T, \omega_1, \ldots, \omega_N)$.

7. Output $(\mathsf{v}^{(1)}, \mathsf{v}^{(2)}, \pi_{\text{seBARG}})$.

$\mathcal{V}(\text{crs}_\mathcal{V}, C, x_1, \ldots, x_k, \pi)$ does the following:

1. Parse $\text{crs}_\mathcal{V} = (k_{\text{PEH}}^{(1)}, k_{\text{PEH}}^{(2)}, \text{crs}_{\text{seBARG}})$.

2. Parse $\pi = (\mathsf{v}^{(1)}, \mathsf{v}^{(2)}, \pi_{\text{seBARG}})$.

3. Define $X = (M, z, N, T)$ as above.

4. Output $\mathcal{V}_{\text{seBARG}}(\text{crs}_{\text{seBARG}}, X, \pi_{\text{seBARG}})$.

6.1   Analysis

Theorem 6.1. *The construction given in Sect. 6 is a SNARG for $\mathcal{L}_f^{(k)}$ (Definition 4.1) with the following additional efficiency properties:*

– *The runtime of the verifier is $\text{poly}(|\text{crs}_\mathcal{V}| + |\pi|) + (kn + |C|)\text{poly}(\lambda, \log k)$.*

– *The (prover) common reference string* $\mathsf{crs}_\mathcal{P}$ *has size* $\mathsf{poly}(\lambda, \log k)(m + \mathsf{width}(C))$.

The proof of this theorem appears in the full version of this work.

The constructions and security proofs of somewhere extractable SNARGs for monotone policy BatchNP, and of SNARGs for low-depth monotone policies, appear in the full version of this work.

Acknowledgements. Zvika Brakerski is supported by the Israel Science Foundation (Grant No. 3426/21), and by the European Union Horizon 2020 Research and Innovation Program via ERC Project REACT (Grant 756482).

Maya Farber Brodsky is supported by an ISF grant 1789/19.

Yael Tauman Kalai is supported by DARPA under Agreement No. HR00112020023. Any opinions, findings and conclusions or recommendations expressed in this material are those of the author(s) and do not necessarily reflect the views of the United States Government or DARPA.

Alex Lombardi was supported in part by a Simons-Berkeley postdoctoral fellowship, and in part by DARPA under Agreement No. HR00112020023.

Omer Paneth is a member of the Checkpoint Institute of Information Security and is supported by an Azrieli Faculty Fellowship, and ISF grant 1789/19.

References

1. Badrinarayanan, S., Kalai, Y.T., Khurana, D., Sahai, A., Wichs, D.: Succinct delegation for low-space non-deterministic computation. In: Diakonikolas, I., Kempe, D., Henzinger, M. (eds.) 50th ACM STOC, pp. 709–721. ACM Press (2018). https://doi.org/10.1145/3188745.3188924
2. Barak, B., et al.: On the (im)possibility of obfuscating programs. In: Kilian, J. (ed.) CRYPTO 2001. LNCS, vol. 2139, pp. 1–18. Springer, Heidelberg (2001). https://doi.org/10.1007/3-540-44647-8_1
3. Brakerski, Z., Holmgren, J., Kalai, Y.T.: Non-interactive delegation and batch NP verification from standard computational assumptions. In: Hatami, H., McKenzie, P., King, V. (eds.) 49th ACM STOC, pp. 474–482. ACM Press (2017). https://doi.org/10.1145/3055399.3055497
4. Brakerski, Z., Kalai, Y.T.: Monotone batch np-delegation with applications to access control. IACR Cryptol. ePrint Arch. **2018**, 375 (2018). https://eprint.iacr.org/archive/2018/375/20180513:062615
5. Canetti, R., et al.: Fiat-Shamir: from practice to theory. In: Charikar, M., Cohen, E. (eds.) 51st ACM STOC, pp. 1082–1090. ACM Press (2019). https://doi.org/10.1145/3313276.3316380
6. Choudhuri, A.R., Garg, S., Jain, A., Jin, Z., Zhang, J.: Correlation intractability and SNARGs from sub-exponential DDH. Cryptology ePrint Archive (2022)
7. Choudhuri, A.R., Jain, A., Jin, Z.: SNARGs for $\mathcal{P}$ from LWE. In: 62nd IEEE Annual Symposium on Foundations of Computer Science, FOCS 2021, Denver, CO, USA, 7–10 February 2022, pp. 68–79. IEEE (2021). https://doi.org/10.1109/FOCS52979.2021.00016
8. Choudhuri, A.R., Jain, A., Jin, Z.: Non-interactive batch arguments for np from standard assumptions. In: Malkin, T., Peikert, C. (eds.) CRYPTO 2021. LNCS, vol. 12828, pp. 394–423. Springer, Cham (2021). https://doi.org/10.1007/978-3-030-84259-8_14

9. Devadas, L., Goyal, R., Kalai, Y., Vaikuntanathan, V.: Rate-1 non-interactive arguments for batch-NP and applications. In: Proceedings of FOCS 2022 (2022)
10. Dwork, C., Langberg, M., Naor, M., Nissim, K., Reingold, O.: Succinct proofs for np and spooky interactions. Unpublished manuscript. http://www.cs.bgu.ac.il/~kobbi/papers/spooky_sub_crypto.pdf (2004)
11. Garg, S., Gentry, C., Halevi, S., Raykova, M., Sahai, A., Waters, B.: Candidate indistinguishability obfuscation and functional encryption for all circuits. In: 54th FOCS, pp. 40–49. IEEE Computer Society Press (2013). https://doi.org/10.1109/FOCS.2013.13
12. Garg, S., Gentry, C., Sahai, A., Waters, B.: Witness encryption and its applications. In: Boneh, D., Roughgarden, T., Feigenbaum, J. (eds.) 45th ACM STOC, pp. 467–476. ACM Press (2013). https://doi.org/10.1145/2488608.2488667
13. Gentry, C., Wichs, D.: Separating succinct non-interactive arguments from all falsifiable assumptions. In: Fortnow, L., Vadhan, S.P. (eds.) 43rd ACM STOC, pp. 99–108. ACM Press (2011). https://doi.org/10.1145/1993636.1993651
14. Hubacek, P., Wichs, D.: On the communication complexity of secure function evaluation with long output. In: Roughgarden, T. (ed.) ITCS 2015, pp. 163–172. ACM (2015). https://doi.org/10.1145/2688073.2688105
15. Jain, A., Jin, Z.: Indistinguishability obfuscation via mathematical proofs of equivalence. In: 63rd IEEE Annual Symposium on Foundations of Computer Science, FOCS 2022, Denver, CO, USA, October 31 - November 3 2022, pp. 1023–1034 (2022)
16. Jawale, R., Kalai, Y.T., Khurana, D., Zhang, R.Y.: SNARGs for bounded depth computations and PPAD hardness from sub-exponential LWE. In: Khuller, S., Williams, V.V. (eds.) STOC 2021: 53rd Annual ACM SIGACT Symposium on Theory of Computing, Virtual Event, Italy, 21–25 June 2021, pp. 708–721. ACM (2021). https://doi.org/10.1145/3406325.3451055
17. Kalai, Y.T., Lombardi, A., Vaikuntanathan, V., Wichs, D.: Boosting batch arguments and RAM delegation. Cryptology ePrint Archive, Report 2022/1320 (2022). https://eprint.iacr.org/2022/1320
18. Kalai, Y., Paneth, O.: Delegating RAM computations. In: Hirt, M., Smith, A. (eds.) TCC 2016. LNCS, vol. 9986, pp. 91–118. Springer, Heidelberg (2016). https://doi.org/10.1007/978-3-662-53644-5_4
19. Kalai, Y.T., Paneth, O., Yang, L.: How to delegate computations publicly. In: Charikar, M., Cohen, E. (eds.) 51st ACM STOC, pp. 1115–1124. ACM Press (2019). https://doi.org/10.1145/3313276.3316411
20. Kalai, Y.T., Raz, R.: Probabilistically checkable arguments. In: Halevi, S. (ed.) CRYPTO 2009. LNCS, vol. 5677, pp. 143–159. Springer, Heidelberg (2009). https://doi.org/10.1007/978-3-642-03356-8_9
21. Kalai, Y.T., Raz, R., Rothblum, R.D.: Delegation for bounded space. In: Boneh, D., Roughgarden, T., Feigenbaum, J. (eds.) 45th ACM STOC, pp. 565–574. ACM Press (2013). https://doi.org/10.1145/2488608.2488679
22. Kalai, Y.T., Raz, R., Rothblum, R.D.: How to delegate computations: the power of no-signaling proofs. In: Shmoys, D.B. (ed.) 46th ACM STOC, pp. 485–494. ACM Press (2014). https://doi.org/10.1145/2591796.2591809
23. Kalai, Y.T., Vaikuntanathan, V., Zhang, R.Y.: Somewhere statistical soundness, post-quantum security, and SNARGs. In: Nissim, K., Waters, B. (eds.) TCC 2021. LNCS, vol. 13042, pp. 330–368. Springer, Cham (2021). https://doi.org/10.1007/978-3-030-90459-3_12

24. Kilian, J.: A note on efficient zero-knowledge proofs and arguments (extended abstract). In: 24th ACM STOC, pp. 723–732. ACM Press (1992). https://doi.org/10.1145/129712.129782

25. Merkle, R.C.: A digital signature based on a conventional encryption function. In: Pomerance, C. (ed.) CRYPTO 1987. LNCS, vol. 293, pp. 369–378. Springer, Heidelberg (1988). https://doi.org/10.1007/3-540-48184-2_32

26. Micali, S.: CS proofs (extended abstracts). In: 35th FOCS, pp. 436–453. IEEE Computer Society Press (1994). https://doi.org/10.1109/SFCS.1994.365746

27. Okamoto, T., Pietrzak, K., Waters, B., Wichs, D.: New realizations of somewhere statistically binding hashing and positional accumulators. In: Iwata, T., Cheon, J.H. (eds.) ASIACRYPT 2015. LNCS, vol. 9452, pp. 121–145. Springer, Heidelberg (2015). https://doi.org/10.1007/978-3-662-48797-6_6

28. Paneth, O., Pass, R.: Incrementally verifiable computation via rate-1 batch arguments. In: Proceedings of FOCS 2022 (2022)

29. Paneth, O., Rothblum, G.N.: On zero-testable homomorphic encryption and publicly verifiable non-interactive arguments. In: Kalai, Y., Reyzin, L. (eds.) TCC 2017. LNCS, vol. 10678, pp. 283–315. Springer, Cham (2017). https://doi.org/10.1007/978-3-319-70503-3_9

30. Sahai, A., Waters, B.: How to use indistinguishability obfuscation: deniable encryption, and more. In: Shmoys, D.B. (ed.) 46th ACM STOC, pp. 475–484. ACM Press (2014). https://doi.org/10.1145/2591796.2591825

31. Waters, B., Wu, D.J.: Batch arguments for NP and more from standard bilinear group assumptions. In: Dodis, Y., Shrimpton, T. (eds.) Advances in Cryptology – CRYPTO 2022. CRYPTO 2022. Lecture Notes in Computer Science, vol. 13508, pp. 433–463. Springer, Cham (2022). https://doi.org/10.1007/978-3-031-15979-4_15

TreePIR: Sublinear-Time and Polylog-Bandwidth Private Information Retrieval from DDH

Arthur Lazzaretti$^{(\boxtimes)}$ and Charalampos Papamanthou

Yale University, New Haven, USA
{arthur.lazzaretti,charalampos.papamanthou}@yale.edu

Abstract. In Private Information Retrieval (PIR), a client wishes to retrieve the value of an index i from a public database of N values without leaking any information about i. In their recent seminal work, Corrigan-Gibbs and Kogan (EUROCRYPT 2020) introduced the first two-server PIR protocol with sublinear amortized server time and sublinear $O(\sqrt{N}\log N)$ bandwidth. In a followup work, Shi et al. (CRYPTO 2021) reduced the bandwidth to polylogarithmic by proposing a construction based on privately puncturable pseudorandom functions, a primitive whose only construction known to date is based on heavy cryptographic primitives such as LWE. Partly because of this, their PIR protocol does not achieve concrete efficiency. In this paper we propose TreePIR, a two-server PIR protocol with sublinear amortized server time and polylogarithmic bandwidth whose security can be based on just the DDH assumption. TreePIR can be partitioned in two phases that are both sublinear: The first phase is remarkably simple and only requires pseudorandom generators. The second phase is a single-server PIR protocol on *only* $\sqrt{N}$ indices, for which we can use the protocol by Döttling et al. (CRYPTO 2019) based on DDH, or, for practical purposes, the most concretely efficient single-server PIR protocol. Not only does TreePIR achieve better asymptotics than previous approaches while resting on weaker cryptographic assumptions, it also outperforms existing two-server PIR protocols in practice. The crux of our protocol is a new cryptographic primitive that we call weak privately puncturable pseudorandom functions, which we believe can have further applications.

Keywords: Private Information Retrieval · Puncturable Pseudorandom Functions · Privacy-Preserving Primitives

1 Introduction

Private Information Retrieval (PIR) is classically a two-player protocol where the client holds an index $i \in \{0, \ldots, N-1\}$ and the server holds a public string DB of N bits. The goal of the protocol is for the client to learn DB$[i]$, and for the server *not to learn any information related to i*. Since the problem was introduced [14], PIR has become a building block for a myriad of privacy-preserving applications [3, 4, 24, 32, 44].

© International Association for Cryptologic Research 2023
H. Handschuh and A. Lysyanskaya (Eds.): CRYPTO 2023, LNCS 14082, pp. 284–314, 2023.
https://doi.org/10.1007/978-3-031-38545-2_10

PIR has been studied extensively over the years [2,6,9,10,14,25,33,37,38][1] and unfortunately, all space-efficient PIR protocols are bound to a well-known linear server time lower bound by Beimel et al. [6]. Intuitively, linear server time is required since otherwise some index-specific portion of the database will remain untouched, and therefore information about the queried index will be leaked. To address this problem, Corrigan-Gibbs and Kogan [15] propose a model with *client preprocessing* and *two* non-colluding servers that store copies of the database: After one expensive *query-independent* offline phase where the client interacts with the first server and stores a small amount of information, subsequent queries run privately in time sublinear in the database size, resulting in *amortized* sublinear time per query. The online phase involves the second server and may or may not involve the first server. This model has shown to have many useful applications in practice, and brings PIR query times substantially closer to the non-private query baseline.

1.1 Client-Preprocessing PIR

The core idea of client-preprocessing PIR, as proposed by Corrigan-Gibbs and Kogan [15], is the following: In the offline phase, the client samples a certain number (in particular $\sqrt{N}$) of random index sets and asks the first server to compute parities of those sets, storing these parities, along with the respective sets, locally. In the online phase (query to index i), the client finds a preprocessed set S that contains i, and sends $S \setminus \{i\}$ to the second server. The server then returns the parity of the set $S \setminus \{i\}$, and the client can compute the value of index i through the difference of its preprocessed parity and the new parity. (The actual protocol is a little more complicated but we want to keep the exposition at a high level for now.) Note that since the online server time is a computation over a set of $\sqrt{N}$ indices, the server computation is sublinear.

Reducing communication complexity in client-preprocessing PIR. Several optimizations of the above idea have been proposed. For example, Corrigan-Gibbs and Kogan [15] observe that instead of sending the actual sets to the first server, one can send small PRP keys representing those sets, allowing the server to compute the sets itself—this ensures sublinear offline communication and sublinear client storage. Still, the online query cannot be further compressed and the client must send $S \setminus \{i\}$, as before. To reduce online communication, Kogan and Corrigan-Gibbs [32] propose representing their sets with keys derived from *puncturable* PRFs [22,31]—such keys can be updated to represent a set with a removed element i while still (i) hiding which element i was removed; (ii) maintaining the small key size. Unfortunately, this approach does not directly support fast membership testing (which is crucial in order to find the preprocessed set that contains i during the online phase), due to the non-invertibility of PRFs. Therefore finding a set containing i during the online phase requires $O(N)$ expected time. (In their work, they propose a faster membership test by

---

[1] A non-exhaustive list, we provide more background on related work in Sect. 1.3.

using a linear-space data structure. For some use cases of PIR however, using linear client storage can be prohibitive.)

Client-preprocessing PIR via privately puncturable PRFs. In CRYPTO 2021, Shi et al. [43] addressed the above shortcomings by proposing *puncturable pseudorandom sets*. Their seminal construction achieves the following three properties: First, a set can be represented with a small key k; Second, this small key k can be updated to k_i to represent a set with a removed element i, while (i) hiding what i is and (ii) maintaining the small key size; Third, one can check membership of any element in key k efficiently, i.e., in polylogarithmic time. Their construction is based on *privately puncturable* PRFs, whose only instantiation is based on LWE [7,13]). As such, although the Shi et al. scheme has excellent asymptotic complexities, it does not seem to have concrete efficiency. Our back-of-the-envelope calculations show communication overhead of hundreds of megabytes, which make it unusable in practice for now. (We discuss this further in Sect. 5.)

Therefore, we still do not have a suitable sublinear-time PIR scheme with concrete efficiencies and low communication. Our scheme, TreePIR, was developed to bridge the gap. We paint a full picture of the asymptotics mentioned above, including our new scheme TreePIR, in Fig. 1.

1.2   Our Contribution

In this work, we present a new two-server PIR scheme that achieves polylogarithmic bandwidth and sublinear server time and client storage, from DDH. *To the best of our knowledge, ours is the first scheme achieving such complexities from such a well-established cryptographic assumption.* (For comparison with existing work, see Fig. 1.) Our construction is simple and reuses ideas from the celebrated GGM PRF construction [22] in a novel way, introducing a new primitive that we call *weak privately puncturable pseudorandom functions* (wpPRFs). Due to its conceptual simplicity, our scheme lends itself to an efficient implementation, showing strong performance improvements over past schemes for many use cases of PIR. We now summarize our core technical ideas.

Weak privately puncturable PRFs. A wpPRF satisfies the strong notion of privacy of privately puncturable PRFs, where the punctured key hides both the point that was punctured and its evaluation, but with relaxed correctness. The relaxed correctness property states that one is only able to compute the PRF values from the punctured key if they know the point that was punctured. The punctured point is an additional input to the evaluation algorithm for the punctured key. A second property that a wpPRF must satisfy is to allow the enumeration the whole domain for all "potentially punctured points" in quasilinear time. We note here that previously, the only known way to construct puncturable PRFs that hide both the evaluation at the punctured point and the punctured index was using LWE with superpolynomial modulus, in conjunction with other inefficient cryptographic primitives [8,13]. Instead, we show that we are able to construct a weaker version of puncturable PRFs (that fits our application) relying solely on the existence of one-way functions. This is shown in Sect. 3.

Protocol	Server* Time	Client Storage	Bandwidth*	Assump.
TreePIR, Theorem 4.1	$O(\sqrt{N}\log N)$	$O(\sqrt{N}\log N)$	$O(\sqrt{N})$	OWF
TreePIR, Lemma 4.1	$O(\sqrt{N}\log N)$	$O(\sqrt{N})$	$O(\text{poly}\log N)$	DDH
Shi et al. [43][β]	$O(\sqrt{N}\log^2 N)$	$O(\sqrt{N}\log^2 N)$	$O(\text{poly}\log N)$	LWE
Checklist [32]	$O(\sqrt{N})$	$O(N\log N)$	$O(\log N)$	OWF
PRP-PIR [15]	$O(\sqrt{N})$	$O(\sqrt{N})$	$O(\sqrt{N}\log N)$	OWF

[β] The big O notation hides factors very large in the security parameter for this scheme.

Fig. 1. Complexities for different PIR schemes over a database of size N. Server time and bandwidth are amortized over $\sqrt{N}$ queries (denoted amortized with a *). Client time is omitted because it is the same for all schemes, $O(\sqrt{N}\log N)$.

Applying weak privately puncturable PRFs to PIR. We use our new primitive, the weak privately puncturable PRF, with domain and range $\sqrt{N}$ to construct sets that are concise, remain concise after removing one element, and support fast membership testing. This is the first construction to achieve all three properties in unison from only one-way functions. The tricky part is that given the relaxed notion of correctness of our new primitive, it is not straightforward exactly how we can use these sets in PIR. We expand on this in Sect. 4 and show to use our primitive to reduce the problem of PIR on N elements to PIR on $\sqrt{N}$ elements during the online query, using sublinear time and logarithmic communication.

To reduce communication further, one can recursively apply a second PIR scheme to retrieve the element of interest from the resulting database, incurring the cost of the PIR scheme used on the database of size $\sqrt{N}$, because we know exactly which index is of interest within the smaller database. This means that TreePIR benefits from previous (and future) work on non-preprocessing PIR, since it is compatible with the state-of-the-art single-server PIR schemes. Our techniques paired with previous results enable us to achieve PIR with polylogarithmic amortized bandwidth and sublinear amortized server time.

Notably, paired with the result from Döttling et al. [18], our technique implies the first sublinear time PIR scheme with non-trivial client storage and polylogarithmic communication complexity from only the Decisional Diffie-Hellman (DDH) assumption.

A TreePIR implementation. As a second contribution, we provide an implementation of TreePIR. We benchmark our implementation in Sect. 5, and show strong evidence of its practical value. For many usecases, somewhat surprisingly, downloading the $\sqrt{N}$ bits without recursing presents itself as a better alternative to employing a second PIR scheme over $\sqrt{N}$ databases. This is because, in general, current single-server PIR schemes incur somewhat large baseline communication costs and cannot handle small elements well.

Our implementation of TreePIR shows an amortized query time of over three times faster than Checklist [32] over different tests, using up to 8,000× less client storage. We also outperform the other known implementation of client-preprocessing PIR by Corrigan-Gibbs and Kogan and Ma et al. [15,42]. The price we pay for the improvements in client storage and query time is increased communication, which we believe is still reasonable for many applications, given the other improvements. We provide a full picture of performance comparisons against previous schemes in Sect. 5.

1.3   Related Work

The first PIR protocol to achieve non-trivial communication was introduced, along with the problem of PIR itself, by Chor et al. [14]. This scheme relies on a two-server assumption, where the database is replicated in two non-colluding servers. This has proven to be a reasonable assumption in practice [24,29,32]. Later, it was shown that non-trivial communication can also be achieved without the two-server assumption [33], albeit paying a hefty computational price on the server. Subsequent to the seminal works on two-server PIR and single-server PIR, many works have inched towards bringing PIR closer to being practical [5,17,19–21,30,35,36,47].

In 2000, Beimel et al. [6] showed that a PIR scheme must incur at least linear work per query when the server stores no extra bits. In the same work, it was shown that we can decrease server work by storing additional bits at the server (the server-preprocessing model), since the client is not involved. To date, many efforts have been directed towards improving PIR in this model, which is also sometimes called Doubly Efficient PIR [10,28]. These works can achieve very good server time and bandwidth (polylogarithmic). One drawback of these works is that many of them rely on non-standard assumptions, and we have yet to evaluate how well these perform in practice. However, it is an interesting direction to be able to store some small amount of preprocessed bits on the server that allow client queries to run in amortized sublinear time, since this would imply the possibility to amortize queries across different clients (as opposed to the client-preprocessing model, where each offline phase is client specific).

1.4   Notation

We define $\nu(\cdot)$ to be a negligible function, such that for every polynomial $p(\cdot)$, $\nu(\cdot) < 1/p(\cdot)$. We define overwhelming probability to be the probability $1 - \nu(\cdot)$. Unless otherwise noted, let $\lambda \in \mathbb{N}$ be the security parameter and $m, n \in \mathbb{N}$ be arbitrary natural numbers and $N = 2^n$. We index a bitstring x at index i using notation x_i and an array a at index i with notation $a[i]$, both are 0-indexed. For any bitstring x, we define x^ℓ, x^r such that $x = x^\ell || x^r$, where $|x^\ell| = |x^r| = |x|/2$. For any $q \in \mathbb{N}$, let $[q]$ denote the set $\{0, \ldots, q-1\}$. We use the notation $i \xleftarrow{R} S$ to denote that i is an element sampled uniformly at random from the set of elements of S. Unless explicitly stated, our big-O notation $O(\cdot)$ hides factors in the security parameter.

1.5   Paper Outline

On Sect. 2, we recall definitions and constructions from previous work that will be useful in constructing our scheme. On Sect. 3, we introduce our new primitive, the weak privately puncturable PRF, and show how to construct it from one way functions. Next, we provide our PIR scheme, TreePIR on Sect. 4, and prove its correctness, privacy and efficiency. Finally, we benchmark an implementation of our scheme against previous PIR schemes in Sect. 5.

2   Preliminaries

Here we outline definitions and primitives that we will need throughout the paper.

2.1   Security Definitions for PIR

We first formally define correctness and privacy for PIR.

Definition 2.1 (PIR correctness). *A PIR scheme ($server_0$, $server_1$, client) is correct if, for any polynomial-sized sequence of queries $x_1, \ldots, x_Q$, the honest interaction of **client** with $server_0$ and $server_1$ that store a polynomial-sized database $DB \in \{0,1\}^N$, returns $DB[x_1], \ldots, DB[x_Q]$ with probability $1 - \nu(\lambda)$.*

Definition 2.2 (PIR privacy). *A PIR scheme ($server_0$, $server_1$, client) is private with respect to $server_1$ if there exists a PPT simulator Sim, such that for any algorithm $serv_0$, no PPT adversary $\mathcal{A}$ can distinguish the following experiments with non-negligible probability:*

- ***$Expt_0$**: **client** interacts with $\mathcal{A}$ who acts as $server_1$ and $serv_0$ who acts as the $server_0$. At every step t, $\mathcal{A}$ chooses the query index x_t, and **client** is invoked with input x_t as its query.*
- ***$Expt_1$**: Sim interacts with $\mathcal{A}$ who acts as $server_1$ and $serv_0$ who acts as the $server_0$. At every step t, $\mathcal{A}$ chooses the query index x_t, and Sim is invoked with no knowledge of x_t.*

In the above definition our adversary $\mathcal{A}$ can deviate arbitrarily from the protocol. Intuitively the privacy definition implies that queries made to $server_1$ will appear random to $server_1$, assuming servers do not collude (as is the case in our model). Privacy for $server_0$ is defined symmetrically.

We will need these when constructing our scheme in Sect. 4. Until then, we shift our focus slightly to other primitives we will require to build TreePIR.

2.2   Pseudorandom Generators (PRGs) and Pseudorandom Functions (PRFs)

Our core technique builds upon the celebrated construction of a PRF from a length-doubling PRG by Goldreich, Goldwasser and Micali [22], henceforth denoted the GGM construction. We introduce both the definitions of a PRG, a PRF, and give the GGM construction in the remainder of this section.

Definition 2.3 (PRG). *A PRG $G : \{0,1\}^\lambda \to \{0,1\}^{2\lambda}$ satisfies security if, for any $k \in \{0,1\}^\lambda$ and $r \in \{0,1\}^{2\lambda}$ sampled uniformly at random, for any PPT adversary $\mathcal{A}$, there is a negligible function $\nu(\lambda)$ such that*

$$|\Pr[\mathcal{A}(G(k)) \to 1] - \Pr[\mathcal{A}(r) \to 1]| \leq \nu(\lambda).$$

We also define below the pseudorandomness property for a PRF.

Definition 2.4 (PRF). *A PRF $F : \{0,1\}^\lambda \times \{0,1\}^n \to \{0,1\}^m$ satisfies security if, for any $k \in \{0,1\}^\lambda$ sampled uniformly at random, for any function $\mathcal{F}$ sampled uniformly at random from the set of functions mapping $\{0,1\}^n \to \{0,1\}^m$, for any PPT adversary $\mathcal{A}$, there is exists a negligible function $\nu(\lambda)$ such that*

$$|\Pr[\mathcal{A}^{\mathcal{O}_{\mathcal{F}(\cdot)}} \to 1] - \Pr[\mathcal{A}^{\mathcal{O}_{F(k,\cdot)}} \to 1]| \leq \nu(\lambda).$$

2.3   The GGM PRF Construction and Puncturing

Given a PRG G as above, the GGM construction of a PRF F works as follows. Let us define for any output of G on input k, $G(k) = G_0(k)\|G_1(k)$, where $|G_b(\cdot)| = \lambda$ for $b \in \{0,1\}$. To simplify sequential applications of G, we also define $G_{10}(\cdot) = G_1(G_0(\cdot))$. From G, we construct a PRF $F : \{0,1\}^\lambda \times \{0,1\}^n \to \{0,1\}^\lambda$ as follows. For key $k \in \{0,1\}^\lambda$ and input $x \in \{0,1\}^n$, let $F_k(x) = G_x(k)$. As shown in [22], this outputs a secure PRF with evaluation time n, assuming the PRG is secure. The construction can be visualized as a tree with k as the root with recursive applications of G split in half as its children.

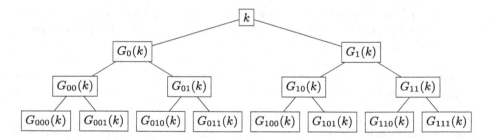

Fig. 2. The GGM PRF tree.

Figure 2 represents the tree for a GGM PRF with input length $n = 3$, key length λ and output length $m = \lambda$.[2] Now, this PRF construction is not ideal in terms of practical evaluation time, since it requires sequential applications of G linear in the size of the input. However, it is also very powerful since it allows us to constrain the PRF key so as to *disallow evaluation at one point*. In the literature

---

[2] We note that this construction is only secure for a fixed input length. Also, we can support any output length either truncating an output to be less than λ or reapplying G sequentially on the final leaf node to increase the output size.

this is commonly referred to as a puncturing constraint. The constraint can be picked selectively after the key generation. We denote a PRF that selectively allows for a puncturing constraint as a puncturable PRF (pPRF)[3]. We define a pPRF below and give additional security properties it must satisfy.

Definition 2.5 (Punctforable PRFs). *Let n and m be public parameters. A pPRF P maps n-bit inputs to m-bit outputs and is defined as a tuple of four algorithms.*

- *Gen$(1^\lambda) \to k$: Generates key $k \in \{0, 1\}^\lambda$ given security parameter λ.*
- *Eval$(k, x) \to y$: Takes in a key k and a point $x \in \{0, 1\}^n$ and outputs $y \in \{0, 1\}^m$, the evaluation of P on key k at point x.*
- *Puncture$(k, x) \to k_x$: Outputs k_x, the key k punctured at point x.*
- *PEval$(k_x, x') \to y$: Takes in a punctured key k_x and a point $x' \in \{0, 1\}^n$ and outputs y, the evaluation of P's key k_x at point x'.*

Along with standard pseudorandomness (Definition 2.4), the pPRF P must satisfy the following additional (informal) properties.

1. The punctured key k_x reveals nothing about $P.\mathsf{Eval}(k, x)$, the evaluation of the point x on the unpunctured key.
2. For any point x' not equal to x, $P.\mathsf{Eval}(k, x')$ equals $P.\mathsf{PEval}(k_x, x')$.

We formalize these below.

Definition 2.6 (Security in puncturing). *A puncturable pseudorandom function (Gen, Eval, Puncture, PEval) satisfies security in puncturing if for $r \in \{0, 1\}^m$ sampled uniformly, $k \leftarrow$ Gen(1^λ), there exists a negligible function $\nu(\lambda)$ such for any PPT adversary $\mathcal{A}$, $\mathcal{A}$ cannot distinguish between the following experiments below with probability more than $\nu(\lambda)$.*

- ***Expt$_0$:** $x \leftarrow \mathcal{A}(1^\lambda)$, Puncture$(k, x) \to k_x$, $b' \leftarrow \mathcal{A}(k_x, \mathsf{Eval}(k, x))$.*
- ***Expt$_1$:** $x \leftarrow \mathcal{A}(1^\lambda)$, Puncture$(k, x) \to k_x$, $b' \leftarrow \mathcal{A}(k_x, r)$.*

Definition 2.7 (Correctness in puncturing). *A puncturable pseudorandom function (Gen, Eval, Puncture, PEval) satisfies correctness in puncturing if for $k \leftarrow$ Gen(1^λ), for any point $x \in \{0, 1\}^n$, for $k_x \leftarrow$ Puncture(k, x), it holds that $\forall x' \in \{0, 1\}^n$ x' not equal to x, Eval$(k, x') =$ PEval(k_x, x').*

A pPRF construction based on a GGM style PRF was widely referenced in the literature for many years before it was finally formalized by Kiayias et al. [31]. The construction goes as follows: When puncturing a point x, we remove the "path to x" from the evaluation tree created using k and output the keys so that the adversary can reconstruct all the other values except for x. We will be handing the adversary a key of size $n \cdot \lambda$ (instead of just λ), that allows evaluation of the pPRF in every point of the domain *except for x*. We also note that the

---

[3] Other works have studied adaptively picked constraints for pPRFs [27,41].

punctured point x is part of the punctured key, so that the adversary is able to reconstruct the pPRF's structure. We expand on this in the next section. Kiayias et al. [31] conduct a formal analysis of this initial pPRF scheme and show that it satisfies the security and correctness properties above.

Then, we show how one can modify this well-know GGM construction to achieve our new desired primitive with stronger privacy guarantees.

3 Weak Privately Puncturable PRFs

In this section we introduce a new primitive called *weak privately puncturable pseudorandom functions* that is going to be useful for our final construction. Weak privately puncturable PRFs are privately puncturable PRFs [7,11,13,40] that satisfy a weaker notion of *correctness*.

But first, let us see what a privately puncturable PRF is: privately puncturable PRFs satisfy a stricter security definition than the pPRF introduced in Sect. 2. Note that although the punctured key k_x of a pPRF P reveals nothing about $P.\mathsf{Eval}(k, x)$, it still reveals the punctured point, x. In fact, without revealing x, there is no way to evaluate the pPRF punctured key at the other points. This is not necessarily inherent to all pPRFs but it is certainly inherent to the GGM scheme. In contrast, privately puncturable PRFs also hide the punctured point! This very powerful primitive was built using techniques that depart significantly from the GGM construction, and current schemes employ heavy machinery, such as lattices with super-polynomial moduli and fully-homomorphic encryption to achieve private puncturing. Because of this, these are unfortunately very far from being practical, especially for smaller domains.

So, can we have Privately Puncturable PRFs from simpler assumptions, ones that would allow more efficient implementation? Let us take a step back and look at one specific goal, i.e., that of hiding the index that was punctured.

We examine how this could be achieved on a standard GGM pPRF. This requires a closer look into exactly what comprises a pPRF punctured key given our current GGM pPRF construction. Suppose that we take the pPRF P defined by the tree in Fig. 2 and would like to puncture the point 010. In order to satisfy our Definition 2.6 we need to remove all the nodes on the path to 010, so that it cannot be computed given a punctured key. We are left with the tree in Fig. 3.

After removing the nodes in red, note that the strings on the nodes highlighted in yellow, and the punctured point, 010 are necessary (and sufficient) [31] to reconstruct the remaining outputs of P. Put together, we require our punctured key for the pPRF to be the tuple $(010, [G_{00}(k), G_{011}(k), G_1(k)])$, where the array is *ordered* (in a left-to-right fashion with respect to the tree)[4]. This punctured key satisfies our privacy and correctness definitions for the pPRF [31].

Our first attempt to hide the punctured point is to simply remove it from the key. In our example, instead of outputting the tuple $(010, [G_{00}(k), G_{011}(k), G_1(k)])$ as our punctured key, we output only the ordered

---

[4] This is equivalent to a depth-first ordering up to some deterministic shifting, however this ordering will be more intuitive for our approach moving forward.

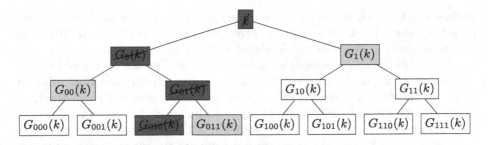

Fig. 3. Puncturing a GGM PRF.

array $[G_{00}(k), G_{011}(k), G_1(k)]$. By security of the PRG (Definition 2.3), this should not leak any information about the punctured point (intuitively, the array is just a sequence of random strings). We now have a construction that satisfies privacy in the point punctured! However, it is not clear as of now how this will be useful. How do we evaluate anything with this when not given the punctured point? After all, as was noted in [31], the point is necessary to reconstruct the original function evaluations at the other indices.

One approach is to guess the punctured point, meaning that evaluating a point in the punctured key now takes two inputs other than the key: both the point to be evaluated (as before) and the point at which the original key was punctured (new). A correct guess will enable us be able to evaluate the function correctly, since a correct guess means that we have exactly the same key as before. An incorrect guess will likely yield some other random string. For example, if we guess 000 as the punctured point, we can arrange our array $[G_{00}(k), G_{011}(k), G_1(k)]$ in a tree *as if* the punctured index was 000 (it is important that to note the ordering of the array). We construct this tree in Fig. 4.

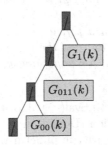

Fig. 4. Reconstructing attempted GGM tree from index and strings.

In Fig. 4, although the first half of the tree is not consistent with our initial evaluation, $G_1(k)$ is placed correctly and therefore the evaluations of the last four indices will be consistent with our unpunctured key. This is not good enough to satisfy any current definition of correctness, but it points us in the right direction. *Some evaluations will be shared across different guesses.*

The key observation required for our work is that if we are interested in *every evaluation in the domain* except the punctured point, the fact that different "puncture guesses" are related can be used to our advantage. By construction, we can evaluate the whole domain of input-output pairs for our initial guess of the punctured point 000 in N time (the tree has $2N$ nodes total). Let us denote this set S_{000}. Now, using this S_{000}, we can compute the entire domain of input-output pairs for the PRF on a "puncture guess" of 001, S_{001}, by only performing one removal and one addition to S_{000}.

Applying this observation across all possible punctured guesses, we iteratively obtain the set of all input-output pairs for every "potential punctured point" in just $N \log N$ time! Out of these N sets, one is correct (using correctness as defined in Definition 2.7[5]). In our example, this would be S_{010}. Crucially, the "correct evaluation set" still does not reveal the evaluation at the punctured point, by security of the pPRF construction we saw in Sect. 2.

In the remainder of this section, we will define our new primitive, the weak privately puncturable PRF (wpPRF), give its security definitions, and provide our construction. It follows a generalized version of the example above.

Definition 3.1 (Weak Privately Puncturable PRF). *We define a weak privately puncturable pseudorandom function (wpPRF) F as a tuple of four algorithms.*

- *$Gen(1^\lambda) \rightarrow k$: Takes in a security parameter λ and returns the wpPRF key $k \in \{0,1\}^\lambda$.*
- *$Eval(k, x) \rightarrow y$: Takes $x \in \{0,1\}^n$ as input and outputs the evaluation on key k at x, $y \in \{0,1\}^m$.*
- *$Puncture(k, i) \rightarrow k_i$: Takes in the wpPRF key k and an input from the domain i and outputs the privately punctured key k_i punctured at point i.*
- *$PEval(k_i, j, x) \rightarrow y$: Takes in a privately punctured key k_i, a guess j of the point that k_i was punctured on, and the point to be evaluated x, and outputs the evaluation of the point x for punctured key k_i with potential puncturing index j.*

First, note that our $Gen(\cdot)$ and $Eval(\cdot, \cdot)$ algorithms must satisfy the standard PRF pseudorandomness definition (Definition 2.4). We also require our wpPRF to satisfy the same notion of security in puncturing as the pPRF (Definition 2.6. Since the adversary *picks* and therefore *knows* x, it can evaluate $PEval(k_x, x, \cdot)$ on every input except x, which is equivalent to the experiment on the original pPRF (Definition 2.5).

Our $Puncture$ algorithm must satisfy an additional notion of privacy with respect to the puncture operation, aside from Definition 2.6. The puncture must

---

[5] These sets are related, and there are only $N \log N$ unique elements across all sets. We can exploit this, defining the first set in full and the following ones as set differences.

hide both the evaluation at the point punctured *and* the point punctured. We capture the second property below:

Definition 3.2 (Privacy in puncturing). *A weak privately puncturable PRF (Gen, Eval, Puncture, PEval) satisfies privacy in puncturing if given a uniformly random* $b \in \{0, 1\}$*,* $k \in \{0, 1\}^\lambda$ *there exists a negligible function* $\nu(\lambda)$ *such that for any probabilistic polynomial time adversary* $\mathcal{A}$*,* $\mathcal{A}$ *cannot correctly guess* b *with probability more than* $\frac{1}{2} + \nu(\lambda)$ *in the experiment below.*

- $k \leftarrow \text{Gen}(1^\lambda)$.
- $(x_0, x_1) \leftarrow \mathcal{A}(1^\lambda)$.
- $k_{x_b} \leftarrow \text{Puncture}(k, x_b)$.
- $b' \leftarrow \mathcal{A}(k_{x_b})$.

Finally, we also redefine correctness with respect to private puncturing, where, intuitively, we only require $\text{PEval}(k_i, j, x)$ to be equal to $\text{Eval}(k, x)$ on the unpunctured key k if i equals j. Note that by Definition 3.2 k_i gives no information about i. For i not equal to j, the output will look random, but will not necessarily map to the original PRF output.

Definition 3.3 (Weak correctness in puncturing). *A weak privately puncturable PRF (Gen, Eval, Puncture, PEval) satisfies weak correctness in private puncturing if given* $k \leftarrow \text{Gen}(1^\lambda)$*, for any point* $x \in \{0, 1\}^n$*,* $k_x \leftarrow \text{Puncture}(k, x)$*, it holds that* $\forall x' \in \{0, 1\}^n$*,* $x' \neq x$*,* $\text{Eval}(k, x') = \text{PEval}(k_x, x, x')$*.*

Lastly, for our scheme to be useful, we require one final property, which we will denote *efficient full evaluation*. This will ensure that given some punctured key, we can evaluate our wpPRF on its full domain, for every possible punctured index, in $O(N \log N)$. The definition below captures this property.

Definition 3.4 (Efficient full evaluation). *Let F be a weak privately puncturable PRF (Gen, Eval, Puncture, PEval) and let* $N = 2^n$*. Also let* $k \leftarrow \text{Gen}(1^\lambda)$ *and* $k_i \leftarrow \text{Puncture}(k, i)$ *for some* $i \in \{0, 1\}^n$*. Define*

$$S_j = \{(x, \text{PEval}(k_i, j, x)) \mid x \in \{0, 1\}^n \wedge x \neq j\}.$$

We say that F satisfies efficient full evaluation *if all sets* $\{S_j\}_{j \in \{0,1\}^n}$ *can be enumerated in* $O(N \log N)$ *time.*

It is clear that to satisfy efficient full evaluation there needs to be overlap between the sets S_j, as will be the case with our construction. Otherwise, $\Omega(N^2)$ computation and space is needed. For our case, we will show that due to the tree construction, there are at most $N \log N$ unique elements that can be enumerated, and so if we define each set iteratively from the first, we can evaluate the whole domain of the PRF for every punctured guess in $O(N \log N)$ time.

Our wpPRF construction.

Let G be a length-doubling PRG (satisfying Definition 2.3).
- Gen(1^λ) $\to k$:

  – Output a uniform random string of length λ.

- Eval(k, x) $\to y$:

  – Let $y \leftarrow G_x(k)$, output y.

- Puncture(k, i) $\to k_i$:

  – Output list of seeds *not* in path to i, ordered left to right, as shown in Figure 3.

- PEval(k_i, j, x) $\to y$:

  – Let $y \leftarrow G_x((j, k_i))$. We denote with $G_x((j, k_i))$ the leaf node at position x of the tree reconstructed from (j, k_i) as shown in Figure 4. Output y.

Fig. 5. Our wpPRF construction.

3.1 A wpPRF Construction

Our construction follows exactly our earlier description in this section, slightly modified from the GGM pPRF to fit the new definitions. We give the full construction in Fig. 5.

Theorem 3.1 (wpPRFs). *Assuming the security of the pseudorandom generator G (Definition 2.3), our wpPRF scheme (Definition 3.1) satisfies pseudorandomness (Definition 2.4), security in puncturing (Definition 2.6), privacy in puncturing Definition 2.6, weak correctness in puncturing (Definition 3.3) and efficient full evaluation (Definition 3.4).*

Proof. Note that pseudorandomness follows from the standard GGM construction and proof from [22]. Weak correctness in puncturing follows directly by construction. Security in puncturing follows from the pPRF security proof in [31], since our privately punctured key is a strict subset of the punctured key in the GGM construction.

Privacy in puncturing follows from directly from the security of G. Our punctured key is an ordered array of random strings, and therefore cannot leak any information about the index that was punctured. The key can be simulated by generating $\log N$ random strings of size λ, and by security of G that will be indistinguishable from our key for any probabilistic polynomial time adversary.

Finally, we show that our scheme also satisfies efficient full evaluation. Given a punctured key k_i, we enumerate all sets S_j using the following algorithm.

– Step 1: Compute S_{0^n}, as defined in Definition 3.4. This takes $O(N \log N)$ time.

- Step 2: For $j = 1, \ldots, N - 1$:
  1. Let h be the height of the node between index $j - 1$ and index j on the tree. We denote leaf nodes to have $h = 0$.
  2. $S_j = \{(v, F.\mathsf{PEval}(k_i, j, v)\}_{v \in \{j - 2^{h-1}, \ldots, j + 2^{h-1}\}}$.

Given that we run into a transition of height h with exactly $2^n/2^h$ times, we have that going through this loop we will take

$$\sum_{h=1}^{n} \frac{2^n}{2^h} \times 2^h = n2^n = N \log N$$

steps. Then, this whole process of evaluating every S_j takes time $2N \log N = O(N \log N)$. Note that each S_j as defined above has 2^h elements and so by a similar argument we have that this conjunction of all sets will have $O(N \log N)$ elements. (Intuitively, the first set will be constructed normally and the remaining sets will be constructed iteratively from the first, reusing evaluations.)

Finally, we have to show that each of this set of $\{S_i\}_{i \in [N]}$ does indeed represent the appropriate full evaluation for all potential puncture at points $j \in [N]$. We define the real set of mappings for a puncture guess of j to be $S_j' = S_{j-1}' + S_j$, where we define the $+$ operation to be the union of both sets, except when there are two mappings of the same index, we overwrite to the value to the latter value. As an example, if we have S contain the entry (x, y) and S' contain (x, y'), the set $S + S'$ contains only (x, y'). It is straightforward to verify that for any j, $S_j' = S_0 + S_1 + \ldots + S_j$ corresponds to the set of all evaluations of the domain of F given a puncture guess of j. $\qquad \square$

4 Applying wpPRFs to PIR

In this section we focus on showing how to utilize our new primitive, the wpPRF, to achieve a PIR scheme with the complexities outlined in Fig. 1. We first show how our wpPRFs can be used to construct pseudorandom sets, and then use these sets to build TreePIR.

4.1 Constructing Pseudorandom Sets from wpPRFs

As we glanced over in the introduction, all current PIR schemes in the client-preprocessing model use some notion of pseudorandom sets. Here, we explore how we can construct these sets from our new wpPRF primitive. In a general sense, we want sets that satisfy the following properties:

- Have a short description.
- Maintain a short description after removing one element.
- Support fast (non-trivial) membership testing.

Our Approach. Here we show how to use wpPRFs to address the shortcomings of prior work. Suppose we have a wpPRF $F := (\mathsf{Gen}, \mathsf{Eval}, \mathsf{Puncture}, \mathsf{PEval})$ whose domain and range is $\sqrt{N}$. We can then define a set S of $\sqrt{N}$ elements in $[N]$ using F. For exposition, let N be an even power of two. Given a uniform random key $k \in \{0,1\}^\lambda$, we define our set S as:

$$S = \left\{ i \| F.\mathsf{Eval}(k,i) : i \in \left[\sqrt{N}\right] \right\}.$$

The $\|$ notation concatenates the binary representation of both numbers. The set S will contain each element in $[N]$ with probability $1/\sqrt{N}$. Also the set will be "partitioned" within $[N]$, and will contain exactly one element for each interval of size $\sqrt{N}$ within $[N]$. We look at a small example below to aid in our exposition.

Let us take an example where $N = 16$. We represent the database with a box for each index below. The darker boxes represent chunks of size $\sqrt{N} = 4$ indices:

We pick some uniform k, and evaluate it at $\sqrt{16} = 4$ points, such that

$$F.\mathsf{Eval}(k,00) = 01, F.\mathsf{Eval}(k,01) = 00, F.\mathsf{Eval}(k,10) = 01, F.\mathsf{Eval}(k,11) = 11.$$

Then, our set would be $S = \{0001, 0100, 1001, 1111\}$. The coverage with respect to the database would look as follows:

As aforementioned, we have exactly one element within each of the darker boxes. This is intrinsic to our set definition. Now, assuming we were using a regular GGM style pPRF, a puncture to a point would reveal its'box'. Let us say we want to puncture the element 0001 from the set. To do this, we run $F.\mathsf{Puncture}(k,00) = k_{00}$. Using a regular pPRF, k_{00} does not reveal the evaluation 01, but it does reveal the punctured index. What this means is that given the punctured pPRF key, one can infer that the element removed from the set is within the green elements below:

In the context of PIR, this would enable the adversary to narrow down the query index to $\sqrt{N}$ indices.

Intuitively, because our wpPRF enables us to also hide the point that was punctured, we hide both the index within the partition *and* which partition we are puncturing. If we define the set using a wpPRF key, a punctured key would reveal no information about what element was removed from the set.

To summarize, our set, as defined above, initialized with a wpPRF key, satisfies the following properties:

1. It can be represented in λ bits by its key k.
2. We can check membership with one wpPRF evaluation. For any $x = x^\ell || x^r \in [N]$, x will be part of S if and only if $F.\mathsf{Eval}(k, x^\ell)$ evaluates to x^r.
3. If we puncture at a point x (by puncturing position x^ℓ as defined above), the punctured key remains concise, and reveals nothing about the punctured point or the punctured index (Definition 2.6, 3.2).

Applying Our New Sets to PIR. We now explore how to use a punctured key to retrieve a desired database index value. Recall that our set is defined as:

$$S = \left\{ i || F.\mathsf{Eval}(k, i) : i \in \left[\sqrt{N} \right] \right\} .$$

We want to find the value $\mathsf{DB}[x]$ for some $x \in S$, note that for $x = x^\ell || x^r$, it follows from the set definition above that:

$$x \in S \iff F.\mathsf{Eval}(k, x^\ell) = x^r .$$

Suppose we happen to have the respective set parity:

$$p = \bigoplus_{i \in S} \mathsf{DB}[i] .$$

Let us now define :

$$p_t = \bigoplus_{i \in S \setminus \{t\}} \mathsf{DB}[i] .$$

To retrieve $\mathsf{DB}[x]$, where $x = x^\ell || x^r = x^\ell || F.\mathsf{Eval}(k, x^\ell)$, we first send $k_{x_\ell} \leftarrow F.\mathsf{Puncture}(k, x^\ell)$ to the server. Then, without revealing x to the server, we must have the server compute p_x. This would allow us to locally compute $\mathsf{DB}[x] = p \oplus p_x$. Since we are using a wpPRF, k_{x^ℓ} does not allow the server to compute p_x. However, because the wpPRF that we are using satisfies efficient full evaluation, per Definition 3.4, the server uses k_{x_ℓ} and computes all $\sqrt{N}$ values S_j (and thus all p_j) in $O(\sqrt{N} \log N)$ time.

We have successfully reduced the problem of fetching a record privately from a database of N records to fetching a record privately from a database of $\sqrt{N}$ records. There are two different ways we can proceed from here.

1. Download all the $\sqrt{N}$ parities.
2. Use a single-server PIR scheme to fetch the record p_x from the smaller database. The record we want from this smaller database p_x is exactly the x^ℓ-th index.

Using approach number two, our bandwidth then becomes the size of the wpPRF key (which is $\lambda \log N$) plus whatever bandwidth is incurred from the single-server PIR scheme used. Since the single-server PIR is run over a smaller database of size $\sqrt{N}$, the server cost of each query is still sublinear in N.

4.2 Our TreePIR Scheme

In Fig. 6, we give the full scheme, based on the intuition above. For the scheme. We assume that N is an even power of two, so that $\sqrt{N}$ is a natural number and that x's bit representation can be split in half. We discuss how to generalize to any size of database in Appendix A. We note that wpPRFs makes our scheme considerably simpler than previous schemes based on the same paradigm [15,32, 43], since we do not require "failing" with certain probability and executing a secondary protocol or executing λ instances in parallel.

We argue our scheme's privacy and correctness in Theorem 4.1.

Theorem 4.1 (TreePIR). *Assuming Theorem 3.1, TreePIR, for any $N \in \mathbb{N}$ which is an even power of two, and security parameter λ, our scheme given in Fig. 6 satisfies correctness and privacy for multi-query PIR schemes as defined in Definition 2.1, 2.2 and its complexities are:*

- *$O(\lambda N \log N)$ offline server time and $O(\lambda \sqrt{N})$ offline client time.*
- *$O(\sqrt{N} \log N)$ online server time and $O(\sqrt{N} \log N)$ probabilistic online client time.*
- *No additional server space and $O(\sqrt{N})$ client space.*
- *$O(\lambda \sqrt{N})$ offline bandwidth.*
- *$O(\lambda \log N)$ upload bandwidth and $\sqrt{N}$ download bandwidth.*

Proof Our efficiencies follow directly from construction and from Theorem 3.1. We specifically highlight that Step 2 of the Answer algorithm runs in $O(\sqrt{N} \log N)$ time by the efficient full evaluation property. In Step 1 of our online query phase, we run the $F.\mathsf{Gen}(\cdot)$ *until* we find the mapping from x^ℓ to x^r. As is, this runs in *probabilistic $O(\sqrt{N})$* time.[6]

Privacy with respect to **server**$_1$. Offline, **server**$_1$ sees nothing, so we do only consider online privacy. We first show that for the first query, we satisfy the indistinguishability experiment. Then, since we show how to induct on this argument and extend it for any polynomial number of queries. Assume the adversary picked query index x_1 for query Q_1. Now consider the hybrid experiment below:

- **Hyb: client** interacts with $\mathcal{A}$ who acts as **server**$_1$ and $serv_0$ who acts as **server**$_0$. **client** is invoked with query x_1, and instead of finding a key that contains x to puncture and send to **server**$_1$, it instead samples a fresh key $k^* \leftarrow F.\mathsf{Gen}(1^\lambda)$, punctures it at x_1, and sends $q_1^* \leftarrow F.\mathsf{Puncture}(k^*, x_1)$ to **server**$_1$.

---

[6] Client time is probabilistic because sampling a set that contains x takes $O(\sqrt{N})$ time probabilistically by naively sampling keys and testing until we find one that contains x. We discuss an optimization to this naive approach in Appendix A.

Our TreePIR construction.

Let $F := (\mathsf{Gen}, \mathsf{Eval}, \mathsf{Puncture}, \mathsf{PEval})$ be a wpPRF as defined in Definition 3.1 that maps $\sqrt{N}$ bits to $\sqrt{N}$ bits. Let $M = \lambda\sqrt{N}$ and DB be a vector of N indices.

- Offline: Preprocessing(**client**, **server**$_0$).

  1. **client** sets $k_i \leftarrow F.\mathsf{Gen}(1^\lambda)$, $i = 1, \ldots, M-1$, and sends $k_0, \ldots, k_{M-1}$ to **server**$_0$.
  2. For all $i = 0, \ldots, M-1$ **server**$_0$ computes parities

  $$p_i = \bigoplus_{j \in S_i} \mathsf{DB}[j],$$

  where

  $$S_i = \left\{ v \| F.\mathsf{Eval}(k_i, v) : v \in \left[\sqrt{N}\right] \right\},$$

  and sends $p_0, \ldots, p_{M-1}$ to **client**.
  3. **client** stores pairs of keys and parities in a table

  $$\mathsf{T} = \{T_j = (k_j, p_j) : j \in [M]\} .$$

- Online: Query(**client**, x) $\to (q_0, q_1)$, $x \in [N]$.

  1. Sample $k' \leftarrow F.\mathsf{Gen}(1^\lambda)$ until $F.\mathsf{Eval}(k', x^\ell) = x^r$.
  2. Find T_j such that $F.\mathsf{Eval}(k_j, x^\ell) = x^r$.
  3. Let $q_0 \leftarrow F.\mathsf{Puncture}(k', x^\ell)$.
  4. Let $q_1 \leftarrow F.\mathsf{Puncture}(k_j, x^\ell)$.
  5. Send (q_0, q_1) to **server**$_0$ and **server**$_1$ respectively.

- Online Answer(**server**$_b$, q_b) $\to \mathcal{P}_b$ for $b \in \{0, 1\}$.

  1. Parse $q_b = (k_{punc})$.
  2. Compute an array of parities $\mathcal{P}_b = [\phi_0, \ldots, \phi_{\sqrt{N}}]$, where $\phi_i = \bigoplus_{j \in S_i} \mathsf{DB}[j]$,

  $$S_i = \left\{ v \| F.\mathsf{PEval}(k_{punc}, i, v) : \text{ for } v \in \left[\sqrt{N}\right] \right\}_{i \in \left[\sqrt{N}\right]} .$$

  3. Return $\mathcal{P}_b$.

- Online Reconstruct(**client**, $\mathcal{P}_0, \mathcal{P}_1$) $\to \mathsf{DB}[x]$.

  1. $\mathsf{DB}[x] \leftarrow p_j \oplus \mathcal{P}_1[x^\ell]$.
  2. $T_j \leftarrow (k', \mathcal{P}_0[x^\ell] \oplus \mathsf{DB}[x])$.

Fig. 6. Our novel PIR scheme, TreePIR.

By security in puncturing (Definition 2.6), our wpPRF key punctured key reveals nothing about the evaluation at the punctured point. A distinguisher $\mathcal{D}$ that distinguishes **Expt**$_0$ and **Hyb** can be used to break the security in puncturing experiment through the following steps:

1. Send point x_1^ℓ to the security in puncturing experiment, get back $(k_{x_1^\ell}, u)$.
2. Send $k_{x_i^\ell}$ and $x_1^\ell \| u$ to $\mathcal{D}$; if $\mathcal{D}$ outputs $\mathbf{Expt}_0$, output 0. Else, output 1.

Note that the probability that we output correctly is exactly the probability that $\mathcal{D}$ can distinguish whether u is uniform or the original evaluation of $k_{x_1^\ell}$ at x_1^ℓ. Then, since a PPT algorithm $\mathcal{D}$ that can distinguish between $\mathbf{Expt}_0$ and $\mathbf{Hyb}$ allows us to break the security in puncturing experiment, it follows that assuming security in puncturing, $\mathbf{Expt}_0$ and $\mathbf{Hyb}$ are computationally indistinguishable.

Next, we define our algorithm Sim as follows.

- Sim: Run $k \leftarrow F.\mathsf{Gen}(1^\lambda)$. Let α be an element sampled uniformly from $\left[\sqrt{N}\right]$. Output $q_{sim} \leftarrow F.\mathsf{Puncture}(k, \alpha)$.

Now, if we show that there Sim is computationally indistinguishable from $\mathbf{Hyb}$, we have shown privacy with respect to $\mathbf{server}_1$. Note that both k and k^* are sampled from Gen. Now, suppose there exists a distinguisher $\mathcal{D}$ that can distinguish between Sim and $\mathbf{Hyb}$. Then, we can use $\mathcal{D}$ to break our privacy in puncturing experiment Definition 3.2 as follows:

1. Send to the privacy in puncturing experiment the points $(\sigma_0 := \alpha^\ell, \sigma_1 := x_1^\ell)$ and get back a key k_{σ_b}.
2. Send k_{σ_b} to $\mathcal{D}$. If $\mathcal{D}$ outputs Sim, output 0, else output 1.

Again, we see that advantage in the experiment corresponds exactly to the privacy in puncturing experiment, and thus a PPT algorithm $\mathcal{D}$ that distinguishes between Sim and $\mathbf{Hyb}$ allows one to break the privacy in puncturing property of the underlying wpPRF. Then, by contrapositive, assuming privacy in puncturing of the wpPRF, Sim and $\mathbf{Hyb}$ are computationally indistinguishable from the point of view of $\mathbf{server}_1$. Finally, we have shown privacy with respect to $\mathbf{server}_1$ for the first query, since our protocol is computationally indistinguishable from an algorithm Sim that runs without knowledge of x_1.

For subsequent queries, we replace our used key k with a new key $k' \leftarrow F.\mathsf{Gen}(1^\lambda)$ *until* $F.\mathsf{Eval}(k', x^\ell) = x^r$. But since our key, k, that was used in the first query can also *be seen as* the output of $F.\mathsf{Gen}(1^\lambda)$ *until* $F.\mathsf{Eval}(k, x_1^\ell) = x^r$, because it was the *first* key generated that contained x_1, we note that k and k' are computationally indistinguishable and therefore swapping k for k' maintains the distribution of T. Then, by induction, since each query maintains the distribution of T, by the same argument as above we conclude that for any sequence of queries $\{1, \ldots, t\}$, our scheme satisfies privacy with respect to $\mathbf{server}_1$.

Privacy with respect to $\mathbf{server}_0$. Offline privacy follows directly from the fact that the keys are picked before any query, and therefore cannot leak any information. Online privacy with respect to $\mathbf{server}_0$ can be argued symmetrically from the same arguments as privacy with respect to $\mathbf{server}_1$. The only difference is that we have to be careful to pick fresh keys from a *different* randomness so they are independent from the keys sent to $\mathbf{server}_0$ offline.

Correctness. We argue correctness by construction and Theorem 3.1, using an induction argument on the client's state.

Let us first consider the first query Q_1 to index x_1. For any query index x_1, the probability that we *do not* find a set that contains x_1, for some negligible function $\nu(\cdot)$, is:

$$\Pr\left[x_1 \notin \{S_i\}_{i \in [\lambda\sqrt{N}]}\right] = \Pr\left[\forall i \in [\lambda\sqrt{N}], F.\mathsf{Eval}(k_i, x_1^\ell) \neq x_1^r\right] \quad (1)$$

$$= \left(1 - \frac{1}{\sqrt{N}}\right)^{\lambda\sqrt{N}} \quad (2)$$

$$\leq \left(\frac{1}{e}\right)^\lambda \leq \nu(\lambda). \quad (3)$$

This means that Step 2 in our Query algorithm will always succeed for the first query except with negligible probability. Then, by construction of our scheme and weak correctness of our wpPRF (Definition 3.3), it follows that, if $x_1 \in S_j = \left\{i \| F.\mathsf{Eval}(k_j, i) : i \in \left[\sqrt{N}\right]\right\}$, then:

$$\mathsf{DB}[x_1] = \left(\bigoplus_{i \in S_j} \mathsf{DB}[i]\right) \oplus \left(\bigoplus_{i \in S_j \setminus \{x_1\}} \mathsf{DB}[i]\right) \quad (4)$$

$$= p_j \oplus \left(\bigoplus_{k \in S_{j,x_1^\ell}} \mathsf{DB}[k]\right) \quad (5)$$

$$= p_j \oplus \mathcal{P}_1[x_1^\ell], \quad (6)$$

where:

$$S_{j,x_1^\ell} = \left\{i \| F.\mathsf{PEval}(k_{j,x_1^\ell}, x_1^\ell, i) : i \in \left[\sqrt{N}\right]\right\}, k_{j,x_1^\ell} = F.\mathsf{Puncture}(k_j, x_1^\ell).$$

We have shown that the first query Q_1 to index x_1 is correct except with negligible probability. At the end of the query, we update T by setting $T_j = (k', \mathcal{P}[x^\ell] \oplus \mathsf{DB}[x])$. Correctness of the parity follows in a similar argument as above. Also, our updated table T maintains its distribution, and holds only sets never seen by **server₁**, as we have shown in the privacy proof. Then, it follows that the next query Q_2 to index x_2 will also be correct by the same argument as above. By induction, this will hold for query Q_t to index x_t for any $t < \frac{1}{\nu(\lambda)}$, for any negligible function $\nu(\cdot)$. □

4.3 Sublinear Time, Polylog Bandwidth PIR from the DDH Assumption

Prior works [18,37] have studied single-server PIR and have achieved schemes with polylogarithmic bandwidth. The bottleneck of these schemes is that the server time grows linearly with the database size. Applying TreePIR with one of these schemes, we can achieve a practical PIR scheme with sublinear time and polylogarithmic bandwidth. Applying the scheme by Döttling et al. [18] we achieve our claimed result, a two-server PIR scheme with sublinear online time and polylog bandwidth, reliant only on the DDH assumption [16]. This is reflected on the following lemma:

Lemma 4.1 (Sublinear time, polylog bandwidth PIR from DDH).
Assuming the Decisional Diffie-Hellman problem is hard, Theorem 4.1 implies a two-server PIR with the same complexities except with polylogarithmic online bandwidth.

Proof. We can replace the last step of the server answer in our protocol with a single-server PIR that has linear work and polylogarithmic bandwidth. This is because we know what index we want from the string of $\sqrt{N}$ words ahead of time, it corresponds to exactly x^ℓ. The protocol then replaces the last step of downloading $\sqrt{N}$ words with fetch the x^ℓ-th word using a single-server scheme. The privacy, efficiency, and correctness follow from Theorem 4.1 and previous work on single-server PIR [12,18,21,35,37]. This means that we also have to introduce any assumptions used by the scheme selected. By recursing with the single-server PIR scheme by Döttling et al., which has polylog bandwidth and relies only on DDH, we achieve the claimed complexities.   □

On Sect. 5 we benchmark the performance of our TreePIR paired with SPI-RAL [37]. Note that we *cannot* recurse with a PIR scheme that uses preprocessing based on the database elements (and this includes our TreePIR), since the $\sqrt{N}$ words from the last step of the Answer phase are dynamically generated and entirely dependent on the index we decide to query.

4.4 Tuning Efficiencies in TreePIR

We have picked wpPRFs of domain and range $\sqrt{N}$ so that we achieve $O(\sqrt{N}\log N)$ server time and $O(\sqrt{N})$ client space. This is not the only tradeoff supported by TreePIR. We can trade off client storage and online client time for online server time and bandwidth. If we change our set size to N^D, then this makes our online time and bandwidth N^D. In exchange, we get client storage and online client time proportional to N^{1-D}. This will work for any D in the range $(0, 1)$. Intuitively, this says that if we have smaller sets in the client, we get faster server time, but we need more sets at the client to ensure coverage of all indices. Conversely, to have less sets at the client, they need to represent more indices and we would have to pay for it in server time. For this work we fixed the $D = 1/2$ tradeoff. Ideal tradeoffs between the parameters depend largely on application and therefore for the rest of this work we fix this tradeoff.

5 Performance

In this section, we benchmark both TreePIR as introduced in Sect. 4 and TreePIR paired with SPIRAL to reduce the communication of the last step, on databases of different sizes and with different size elements (not only bits as defined previously). As we will see, there are use cases where plain TreePIR performs well, specifically for databases with small elements.

Our Tests. We implement TreePIR in 530 lines of C++ code and 470 lines of Go code. The source code is available on GitHub [1]. Our starting point was the previous optimized implementations of PIR by Kogan and Corrigan Gibbs [32] and Kales et al. [29]. Given that the only client-preprocessing scheme with comparable asymptotics does not have any known implementation, we benchmark PIR with two other client-preprocessing PIR schemes: PRP-PIR [15] implemented by Ma et al. [42], which has online bandwidth of $O(\sqrt{N} \log N)$ and requires parallel instantiations, and Checklist by Kogan and Corrigan-Gibbs [32], which requires persistent client storage proportional to the number of elements in the database ($O(N \log N)$ client storage). Across all tests, it will be clear that in many use cases of PIR, TreePIR provides the best alternative out of the three. The tests results reflect microbenchmarks run on a single thread in an Amazon Web Services EC2 instance of size m5d.8xlarge.

Comparison with Shi et al. [43]. The only known client-preprocessing PIR scheme with comparable asymptotics to TreePIR is the scheme by Shi et al. [43]. However, we do not benchmark the Shi et al. scheme [43] because there is no known implementation of the Privately Puncturable PRF primitive. Given the sample parameter instantiation of privately puncturable PRFs by [7], a conservative estimate on the online bandwidth is of at least $2\lambda^4 \log(\lambda) \cdot \log N$. This means an online per query communication cost of over 400 megabytes, given a security parameter of size 128 bits, for any database size. This means that by our estimates the communication using TreePIR presents a communication of 8,000x or more over the scheme by Shi et al. in all databases benchmarked (as will be clear later in the section). This large communication is largely due to the underlying primitive, the *privately puncturable PRF*, which means that improvements in the privately puncturable PRF construction imply improvements to their scheme. However, for now, the best known constructions yield the complexities discussed above.

5.1 TreePIR with No Recursion

First, we consider TreePIR as outlined in Fig. 6, without recursion. Without using a second PIR scheme to recurse in the online phase, TreePIR incurs $O(\sqrt{N})$ online bandwidth, since we are required to download the parity for each "potential set". Although asymptotically suboptimal, in applications where the database elements are very small, it actually outperforms not only other schemes, but also the recursive solution, in both time and bandwidth.

One such application was recently introduced by Henzinger et al. [26]. Henzinger et al. study the use of PIR for secure certificate transparency (SCT) auditing. Their protocol for SCT requires the use of PIR over a database of

2^{33} elements of size only 1 bit. Another application that might involve large databases of 1 bit entries would be compromised credential checking services, among other usecases where we are basically 'checking membership' using PIR, but the query is sensitive.

The work by Henzinger et al. [26] considers the problem given only one server. Here we consider a similar-sized database in the client-preprocessing, two-server scenario. We provide evaluations for such scenario on how plain TreePIR (no recursion) compares to another two state-of-the-art two-server client preprocessing schemes, Checklist [32] and PRP-PIR [15], implemented by Ma et al. [42] in Fig. 7. We benchmark using a similar sized database of 2^{32} 1-bit elements. We note that PRP-PIR query time is marked with a '−' because we were not able to benchmark PRP-PIR time in this experiment, the implementation did not support the large database size .

Results for database of 2^{32} 1-bit elements.

Protocol	Amortized Query Time	Client Storage	Online Bandwidth
Checklist	12574ms	8.6GB	0.51KB
PRP-PIR	-	1.05MB	33.5MB
TreePIR	3508ms	1.05MB	16.6KB

Fig. 7. Amortized query time for a large database of small elements. Query time is amortized per client, over 2000 queries.

After an initial offline phase, queries are run in $\sqrt{N}\log N$ server time.[7] Although not asymptotically optimal, for this usecase, and other usecases with very small elements, incurring $\sqrt{N}$ is better than recursing with a single-server scheme in practice. When comparing with previous approaches to client-preprocessing PIR, such as Checklist, TreePIR incurs additional communication, but makes up for it in both query speed and client space used. Note that using Checklist for this usecase would allow for queries with half a kilobyte of bandwidth, but since Checklist incurs client storage proportional to $N\log N$, this would mean persistent client storage larger than the size of the database (upwards of 8 giga-bytes, as seen in Fig. 7) to perform the queries. In contrast, TreePIR incurs persistent client storage of only around one megabyte to perform its queries. Therefore, in this case, compared to Checklist TreePIR reduces persistent client storage by over 8,000x. Additionally, TreePIR improves total query time by more than 3.5x. We pay for this in communication, but a price small enough to still be practical. When compared to PRP-PIR, we see a very large gain in online bandwidth, largely due to the fact that while TreePIR has bandwidth proportional to $\sqrt{N}$, PRP-PIR requires $\lambda\sqrt{N}\log N$ bandwidth in order to perform the same query. With respect to client storage, both store PRP-PIR and TreePIR store the same information, $\lambda\sqrt{N}$ parities and a random seed of size λ to generate the sets.

---

[7] This is amortized per client.

5.2   Recursing to Improve Bandwidth

Next, we run benchmarks for larger database sizes, where we use TreePIR paired with a single-server PIR scheme to reduce the bandwidth. We found SPIRAL [37] to be the most suitable scheme to recurse with in practice. We run the analysis of amortized query time across two thousand queries for a database of four million elements of 256 bytes (Fig. 8) and a database of 268 million elements of 32 bytes (Fig. 9). Running benchmarks on both databases with a large collection of small elements and a smaller selection of large elements is common practice to test the flexibility of the PIR scheme.

Results for database of 2^{22} 256-byte elements.

Protocol	Amortized Query Time	Client Storage	Online Bandwidth
Checklist [32]	140ms	78MB	0.7KB
PRP-PIR [15, 42]	315ms	67MB	721KB
TreePIR + SPIRAL	(89+61)ms	67MB	50KB

Fig. 8. Amortized query time for moderate database size. Query time is amortized over 200 queries.

Results for database of 2^{28} 32-byte elements.

Protocol	Amortized Query Time	Client Storage	Online Bandwidth
Checklist [32]	711ms	570MB	0.3KB
PRP-PIR [15, 42]	-	67MB	7.3MB
TreePIR + SPIRAL	(251+61)ms	67MB	50KB

Fig. 9. Amortized query time for large database of small elements. Query time is amortized over 2000 queries.

The times seen in Fig. 8 and Fig. 9 for TreePIR + SPIRAL represent the time that each takes, respectively. As shown in the figures, to recurse with SPIRAL, we pay 61ms on a database of 2^{11} elements of size 256 bytes, and the same 61ms to recurse on a database of 2^{14} elements of size 32 bytes. This means that, in reducing bandwidth, our amortized query time would be slower than Checklist's for the databases of 2^{22} elements of 256 bytes, but still considerably faster for a database with 2^{28} elements of size 32 bytes each. In total then, Checklist outperforms TreePIR for small databases of large elements. However, once the database is scaled, the client storage incurred by Checklist is upwards of half a gigabyte. For many client use-cases, such as mobile phones and even laptop computers, half a gigabyte of storage is extremely undesirable. In such cases,

TreePIR provides an alternative with faster query times and small client storage, at the cost of higher bandwidth per query. Furthermore, the overhead seen in the experiment is largely due to the security parameters, meaning that TreePIR with recursion can support larger database elements with much less overhead than these small ones.

In cases where the database size is small but its elements are large, Checklist still presents itself as a very good candidate. Whenever the size of the database is large or the elements are small, TreePIR provides the best trade-offs in practice, either through recursion or just using it plainly. Below we provide additional remarks with respect to the schemes that we compared against.

On the Performance of PRP-PIR [15]. To benchmark PRP-PIR [15], we use a separate library provided by Ma et al. [42]. This library does not use optimized instructions to perform the xor operation and that could partially explain its poor performance. The other factor is that small-domain PRPs [39,46] put overhead in the membership testing and evaluation, both of which are performed numerous times throughout the scheme. We were not able to successfully benchmark the times for PRP-PIR against databases with more than 2^{22} elements.

On the Performance of Checklist [32]. Checklist will always have a shorter faster online server time than TreePIR by construction. However, when running many queries on large databases, such as was the case to benchmark, the Checklist query time is inconsistent. The hashmap used to find the set with the desired query index does not contain a full mapping of every set, it only contains one entry per index. If x and y are in the same set i with the map pointing both x and y to set i, a query to x will make the mapping of y invalid on the map with very high probability. This means that a query to y after a query to x requires enumerating $\sqrt{N}$ sets in expectation and therefore requires around linear client work. This explains why over many queries, TreePIR outperforms Checklist. This problem could be fixed by keeping a full mapping of all sets in the hashmap, although this would require an additional λ factor of client storage, bringing Checklist's storage up to $\lambda N \log N$. We do not benchmark this scenario since the client storage would be too large, but we note that the asymptotics reported in Fig. 1 reflect this latter case, since without this extra λ factor, Checklist's client time is $O(N)$ in the worst case.

5.3   Supporting Changing Databases

Techniques to support preprocessing in databases that change over time have been studied in previous work [32,42]. These techniques can also be applied to TreePIR and are able to maintain most of the benefits of preprocessing with small overhead.

In specific, the technique introduced by Kogan and Corrigan-Gibbs [32] is a waterfall-based approach to updates also used in other related primitives such as oblivious RAM [23] and searchable encryption [45]. We re-iterate the main ideas of the technique here, and refer to previous works for a complete analysis.

Update Types. A changing database can be given three different kinds of operations: $\mathsf{Add}(i, v)$, $\mathsf{Remove}(i)$ or $\mathsf{Edit}(i, v)$.

PIR by Keywords. The first step in supporting updates via a waterfall approach is converting our classical PIR algorithm TreePIR algorithm. Chor et al. [14] showed that this can be done in a blackbox fashion with $O(\log N)$ overhead for almost all modern PIR schemes.

Initializing Subdatabases. We initialize i 'subdatabases'. The i-th subdatabase is of size 2^i, for $i \in \{1, \ldots, \log N\}$ (for simplicity, again, we assume that N is a power of two). We will refer to the i-th subdatabase as the i-th layer. Initially, every layer is empty except for the $\log N$-th layer, which stores the whole database. For each query, the client must send its query to each layer. Here we incur another constant factor of overhead in client space, client time, server time and bandwidth, to query each layer.

Updating the Database. For each update to the database, the update is directed to the 0-th layer. If the 0-th layer is empty, then the client runs the preprocessing over the 0-th layer and is done. Else, the update is directed to the next non-full layer j, along with the updates from all other layers from 0 to j, and the preprocessing is redone for the j-th layer, and zeroed out for layers 0 through i. The updates to the database defined by a tuple consisting of a key (the index to the updated) and value (the value of this index). If there are conflicts, they are resolved upon merging (with priority given to the newest values, the same is true when clients receive conflicting values from different layers for the same index). We can reserve a special value for deletion to support deletes as well. Note that in this manner, updates are amortized, and we go through N updates before having to re-run the preprocessing for the whole database again. In Checklist [32], they show that the update costs are manageable. Furthermore, [23] show how to de-amortize these more expensive preprocessing steps over multiple updates.

Another approach suitable for some applications, outlined by Henzinger et al. [26] is to have a pre-determined update schedule. In the SCT application discussed before, for example, it is acceptable to update the certificates monthly, meaning that we would perform the expensive preprocessing phase only once a month for each client.

Acknowledgements. This research was supported by the National Science Foundation, the Algorand Foundation and Protocol Labs. We thank Samir Menon for a helpful exchange regarding SPIRAL and the reviewers for helping improve our work.

A   Further Optimizations

We discuss here some further optimizations to TreePIR.

A.1   Deterministic Client Time

Our protocol in Fig. 6 has probabilistic client time due to Step 1 of the Online Query algorithm, which is:

1. Sample $k' \leftarrow F.\mathsf{Gen}(1^\lambda)$ until $F.\mathsf{Eval}(k', x^\ell) = x^r$.

In practice, sampling several keys until finding one can be time consuming, and as N increases, the worst case run-time can be very expensive. To achieve both faster and more consistent run-times, it is desirable to have a fully deterministic PIR algorithm. This is achievable by introducing an additional parameter to each of our 'sets', a *shift*. The shift will permute every element in the set by a fixed offset (this technique was used before in [15]). We modify the TreePIR by include a shift $s \in \left[\sqrt{N}\right]$ to be a part of every pseudorandom set (which is now defined as a tuple of a wpPRF key and a shift).

Offline, the client now generates tuples (k_i, s_i) for $i = 1, \ldots, M - 1$; where $k_i \leftarrow F.\mathsf{Gen}(1^\lambda)$ as before, and s_i is sampled uniformly from $\left[\sqrt{N}\right]$. Then, for all $i = 0, \ldots, M - 1$, **server$_0$** computes the appropriate parities p_i as before, except we now define our set S_i as:

$$S_i = \left\{ v || (F.\mathsf{Eval}(k_i, v) \oplus s_i) : v \in \left[\sqrt{N}\right] \right\}.$$

The membership check also is changed accordingly. Finally, the reason for this change is that we can now run Step 1 of the online query as:

1. Sample $k' \leftarrow F.\mathsf{Gen}(1^\lambda)$. Let $s' = x^r \oplus F.\mathsf{Eval}(k', x^\ell)$.

Note that this guarantees that we generate a set with x sampling only a single k' instead of an expected $\sqrt{N}$ (and potentially many more) different keys. We sketch the privacy proof here and include refer to the full version of the paper [34] for a complete proof. For sets generated offline, the shifts are sampled uniformly at random, and therefore do not affect privacy or correctness for the initially generated sets, they only shift all elements of the initial sets by a fixed offset. However, in Step 1 of the Online Query, s' is dependent on x, our query index.

Then, we must now show that upon sending such tuple to **server$_0$** does not reveal any additional information. We must show that the tuple (q_0, s') can be simulated without knowledge of x. This follows from the fact that we can replace our q_0 by some freshly sampled key punctured at a uniformly sampled point in the functions domain. We denote u to be a point sampled uniformly from the range of the PRF. Then, since $F.\mathsf{Eval}(k', x^\ell)$ for a freshly sampled key is computationally indistinguishable from u given only q_0 (follows from Definition 2.6), and completely independent from x (since we are using a fresh sample key), from the server's view, $s' = x^r \oplus u$. Since the xor operation is randomness preserving, we can replace the whole s' by a uniformly sampled point in $\left[\sqrt{N}\right]$. Then, if we do this for the Sim algorithm, we have shown that our query is computationally indistinguishable from a query generated without knowledge of x. The rest of the proof follows as in Sect. 4.

A.2   Generalizing TreePIR to More Flexible Database Sizes

In Sect. 4 we assume that N is a perfect square *and* a power of two for simplicity and exposition. This allows us to use concatenations and splitting to go between our index x and the building blocks x^ℓ and x^r. With some extra steps, TreePIR can be generalized to work with any N that is a perfect square by replacing the concatenation operation by a multiplication by $\sqrt{N}$ and addition by the function evaluation value. Our sets S_i are therefore now defined as:

$$S_i = \left\{ v * \sqrt{N} + F.\mathsf{Eval}(k_i, v) : v \in \left[\sqrt{N} \right] \right\}.$$

Here, $*$ and $+$ are plain addition and multiplication over the natural numbers. Checking membership is done in the corresponding fashion. For an index $x \in [N]$, let $x^\ell = \left\lfloor x/\sqrt{N} \right\rfloor$ (where $\lfloor \cdot \rfloor$ denotes the floor function, rounding *down* to the nearest integer). We can check if x is in S_i by checking whether $x - x^\ell * \sqrt{N} = F.\mathsf{Eval}(k_i, x^\ell)$

If a database size N is *not* a perfect square, one can simply use the domain and range of F to be $\left\lceil \sqrt{N} \right\rceil$ with little to no overhead at the client or server and treat elements larger than N as 0-strings (when necessary for calculating parities). We use $\lceil \cdot \rceil$ to denote the ceil function, rounding *up* to the nearest integer.

References

1. Source code for TreePIR. https://github.com/alazzaretti/treePIR
2. Aguilar-Melchor, C., Barrier, J., Fousse, L., Killijian, M.O.: XPIR: private information retrieval for everyone. Proc. Privacy Enhancing Technol. **2016**(2), 155–174 (2016). https://doi.org/10.1515/popets-2016-0010. https://petsymposium.org/popets/2016/popets-2016-0010.php
3. Angel, S., Setty, S.: Unobservable communication over fully untrusted infrastructure. In: Proceedings of the 12th USENIX Conference on Operating Systems Design and Implementation, OSDI 2016, pp. 551–569. USENIX Association, USA, November 2016
4. Backes, M., Kate, A., Maffei, M., Pecina, K.: ObliviAd: provably secure and practical online behavioral advertising. In: 2012 IEEE Symposium on Security and Privacy, pp. 257–271, May 2012. https://doi.org/10.1109/SP.2012.25. iSSN: 2375-1207
5. Beimel, A., Ishai, Y.: Information-theoretic private information retrieval: a unified construction. In: Orejas, F., Spirakis, P.G., van Leeuwen, J. (eds.) ICALP 2001. LNCS, vol. 2076, pp. 912–926. Springer, Heidelberg (2001). https://doi.org/10.1007/3-540-48224-5_74
6. Beimel, A., Ishai, Y., Malkin, T.: Reducing the servers computation in private information retrieval: PIR with preprocessing. In: Bellare, M. (ed.) CRYPTO 2000. LNCS, vol. 1880, pp. 55–73. Springer, Heidelberg (2000). https://doi.org/10.1007/3-540-44598-6_4

7. Boneh, D., Kim, S., Montgomery, H.: Private puncturable PRFs from standard lattice assumptions. In: Coron, J.-S., Nielsen, J.B. (eds.) EUROCRYPT 2017. LNCS, vol. 10210, pp. 415–445. Springer, Cham (2017). https://doi.org/10.1007/978-3-319-56620-7_15

8. Boneh, D., Lewi, K., Wu, D.J.: Constraining pseudorandom functions privately. In: Fehr, S. (ed.) PKC 2017. LNCS, vol. 10175, pp. 494–524. Springer, Heidelberg (2017). https://doi.org/10.1007/978-3-662-54388-7_17

9. Boyle, E., Gilboa, N., Ishai, Y.: Function secret sharing. In: Oswald, E., Fischlin, M. (eds.) EUROCRYPT 2015. LNCS, vol. 9057, pp. 337–367. Springer, Heidelberg (2015). https://doi.org/10.1007/978-3-662-46803-6_12

10. Boyle, E., Ishai, Y., Pass, R., Wootters, M.: Can We Access a Database Both Locally and Privately? pp. 662–693, November 2017. https://doi.org/10.1007/978-3-319-70503-3_22

11. Brakerski, Z., Tsabary, R., Vaikuntanathan, V., Wee, H.: Private constrained PRFs (and More) from LWE. In: Kalai, Y., Reyzin, L. (eds.) TCC 2017. LNCS, vol. 10677, pp. 264–302. Springer, Cham (2017). https://doi.org/10.1007/978-3-319-70500-2_10

12. Cachin, C., Micali, S., Stadler, M.: Computationally private information retrieval with polylogarithmic communication. In: Stern, J. (ed.) EUROCRYPT 1999. LNCS, vol. 1592, pp. 402–414. Springer, Heidelberg (1999). https://doi.org/10.1007/3-540-48910-X_28

13. Canetti, R., Chen, Y.: Constraint-hiding constrained PRFs for NC^1 from LWE. In: Coron, J.-S., Nielsen, J.B. (eds.) EUROCRYPT 2017. LNCS, vol. 10210, pp. 446–476. Springer, Cham (2017). https://doi.org/10.1007/978-3-319-56620-7_16

14. Chor, B., Gilboa, N., Naor, M.: Private Information Retrieval by Keywords (1998). https://eprint.iacr.org/1998/003, report Number: 003

15. Corrigan-Gibbs, H., Kogan, D.: Private information retrieval with sublinear online time. In: Canteaut, A., Ishai, Y. (eds.) EUROCRYPT 2020. LNCS, vol. 12105, pp. 44–75. Springer, Cham (2020). https://doi.org/10.1007/978-3-030-45721-1_3

16. Diffie, W., Hellman, M.: New directions in cryptography. IEEE Trans. Inf. Theory **22**(6), 644–654 (1976). https://doi.org/10.1109/TIT.1976.1055638. conference Name: IEEE Transactions on Information Theory

17. Dong, C., Chen, L.: A fast single server private information retrieval protocol with low communication cost. In: Kutyłowski, M., Vaidya, J. (eds.) ESORICS 2014. LNCS, vol. 8712, pp. 380–399. Springer, Cham (2014). https://doi.org/10.1007/978-3-319-11203-9_22

18. Döttling, N., Garg, S., Ishai, Y., Malavolta, G., Mour, T., Ostrovsky, R.: Trapdoor hash functions and their applications. In: Boldyreva, A., Micciancio, D. (eds.) CRYPTO 2019. LNCS, vol. 11694, pp. 3–32. Springer, Cham (2019). https://doi.org/10.1007/978-3-030-26954-8_1

19. Dvir, Z., Gopi, S.: 2-Server PIR with Subpolynomial Communication. J. ACM **63**(4), 1–15 (2016). https://doi.org/10.1145/2968443

20. Efremenko, K.: 3-query locally decodable codes of subexponential length. SIAM J. Comput. **41**(6), 1694–1703 (2012). https://doi.org/10.1137/090772721. http://epubs.siam.org/doi/10.1137/090772721

21. Gentry, C., Ramzan, Z.: Single-database private information retrieval with constant communication rate. In: Caires, L., Italiano, G.F., Monteiro, L., Palamidessi, C., Yung, M. (eds.) ICALP 2005. LNCS, vol. 3580, pp. 803–815. Springer, Heidelberg (2005). https://doi.org/10.1007/11523468_65

22. Goldreich, O., Goldwasser, S., Micali, S.: How to construct random functions (extended abstract). In: FOCS (1984). https://doi.org/10.1109/SFCS.1984.715949

23. Goldreich, O., Ostrovsky, R.: Software protection and simulation on oblivious RAMs. J. ACM **43**(3), 431–473 (1996). https://doi.org/10.1145/233551.233553

24. Gupta, T., Crooks, N., Mulhern, W., Setty, S., Alvisi, L., Walfish, M.: Scalable and private media consumption with Popcorn. In: Proceedings of the 13th Usenix Conference on Networked Systems Design and Implementation, NSDI 2016, pp. 91–107. USENIX Association, USA, March 2016

25. Hafiz, S.M., Henry, R.: A Bit More Than a Bit Is More Than a Bit Better: Faster (essentially) optimal-rate many-server PIR. Proceedings on Privacy Enhancing Technologies **2019**(4), 112–131 (2019). https://doi.org/10.2478/popets-2019-0061. https://petsymposium.org/popets/2019/popets-2019-0061.php

26. Henzinger, A., Hong, M.M., Corrigan-Gibbs, H., Meiklejohn, S., Vaikuntanathan, V.: One Server for the Price of Two: Simple and Fast Single-Server Private Information Retrieval, p. 27 (2022)

27. Hohenberger, S., Koppula, V., Waters, B.: Adaptively secure puncturable pseudorandom functions in the standard model. In: Iwata, T., Cheon, J.H. (eds.) ASIACRYPT 2015. LNCS, vol. 9452, pp. 79–102. Springer, Heidelberg (2015). https://doi.org/10.1007/978-3-662-48797-6_4

28. Holmgren, J., Canetti, R., Richelson, S.: Towards Doubly Efficient Private Information Retrieval. Technical report 568 (2017). https://eprint.iacr.org/2017/568

29. Kales, D., Omolola, O., Ramacher, S.: Revisiting User Privacy for Certificate Transparency. In: 2019 IEEE European Symposium on Security and Privacy (EuroS&P), pp. 432–447. IEEE, Stockholm, Sweden, June 2019. https://doi.org/10.1109/EuroSP.2019.00039. https://ieeexplore.ieee.org/document/8806754/

30. Kiayias, A., Leonardos, N., Lipmaa, H., Pavlyk, K., Tang, Q.: Optimal Rate Private Information Retrieval from Homomorphic Encryption. Proceedings on Privacy Enhancing Technologies **2015**(2), 222–243 (2015). https://doi.org/10.1515/popets-2015-0016. https://www.sciendo.com/article/10.1515/popets-2015-0016

31. Kiayias, A., Papadopoulos, S., Triandopoulos, N., Zacharias, T.: Delegatable pseudorandom functions and applications. In: Proceedings of the 2013 ACM SIGSAC conference on Computer & communications security, CCS 2013, pp. 669–684. Association for Computing Machinery, New York, NY, USA, November 2013. https://doi.org/10.1145/2508859.2516668

32. Kogan, D., Corrigan-Gibbs, H.: Private blocklist lookups with checklist. In: 30th USENIX Security Symposium (USENIX Security 21), pp. 875–892. USENIX Association (2021). https://www.usenix.org/conference/usenixsecurity21/presentation/kogan

33. Kushilevitz, E., Ostrovsky, R.: Replication is not needed: single database, computationally-private information retrieval. In: Proceedings 38th Annual Symposium on Foundations of Computer Science. pp. 364–373. IEEE Comput. Soc, Miami Beach, FL, USA (1997). https://doi.org/10.1109/SFCS.1997.646125. http://ieeexplore.ieee.org/document/646125/

34. Lazzaretti, A., Papamanthou, C.: TreePIR: Sublinear-Time and Polylog-Bandwidth Private Information Retrieval from DDH (2023). https://eprint.iacr.org/2023/204, report Number: 204

35. Lipmaa, H.: An oblivious transfer protocol with log-squared communication. In: Proceedings of the 8th international conference on Information Security, ISC 2005, pp. 314–328. Springer, Heidelberg (Sep 2005). https://doi.org/10.1007/11556992_23

36. Lipmaa, H., Pavlyk, K.: A Simpler Rate-Optimal CPIR Protocol. In: Financial Cryptography and Data Security, 2017 (2017). http://eprint.iacr.org/2017/722

37. Menon, S.J., Wu, D.J.: Spiral: fast, high-rate single-server PIR via FHE composition. In: IEEE Symposium on Security and Privacy, 2022 (2022). http://eprint.iacr.org/2022/368
38. Mughees, M.H., Chen, H., Ren, L.: OnionPIR: response efficient single-server PIR. In: Proceedings of the 2021 ACM SIGSAC Conference on Computer and Communications Security, CCS 2021, pp. 2292–2306. Association for Computing Machinery, New York, November 2021. https://doi.org/10.1145/3460120.3485381
39. Patarin, J.: Security of random feistel schemes with 5 or more rounds. In: Franklin, M. (ed.) CRYPTO 2004. LNCS, vol. 3152, pp. 106–122. Springer, Heidelberg (2004). https://doi.org/10.1007/978-3-540-28628-8_7
40. Peikert, C., Shiehian, S.: Constraining and watermarking PRFs from milder assumptions. In: Kiayias, A., Kohlweiss, M., Wallden, P., Zikas, V. (eds.) PKC 2020. LNCS, vol. 12110, pp. 431–461. Springer, Cham (2020). https://doi.org/10.1007/978-3-030-45374-9_15
41. Pietrzak, Momchil Konstantinov, K.G.F., Rao, V.: Adaptive Security of Constrained PRFs (2014). http://eprint.iacr.org/undefined/undefined
42. Rabin, Ke Zhong, T.Y.M., Angel, S.: Incremental Offline/Online PIR (extended version). In: USENIX Security 2022 (2022). http://eprint.iacr.org/2021/1438
43. Shi, E., Aqeel, W., Chandrasekaran, B., Maggs, B.: Puncturable pseudorandom sets and private information retrieval with near-optimal online bandwidth and time. In: Malkin, T., Peikert, C. (eds.) CRYPTO 2021. LNCS, vol. 12828, pp. 641–669. Springer, Cham (2021). https://doi.org/10.1007/978-3-030-84259-8_22
44. Singanamalla, S., et al.: Oblivious DNS over HTTPS (ODoH): a practical privacy enhancement to DNS. Proc. Privacy Enhancing Technol. 2021(4), 575–592 (2021). https://doi.org/10.2478/popets-2021-0085. https://www.sciendo.com/article/10.2478/popets-2021-0085
45. Stefanov, E., Papamanthou, C., Shi, E.: Practical Dynamic Searchable Encryption with Small Leakage, January 2014. https://doi.org/10.14722/ndss.2014.23298
46. Stefanov, E., Shi, E.: FastPRP: Fast pseudo-random permutations for small domains. Cryptology ePrint Report 2012/254. Technical report (2012)
47. Yekhanin, S.: Towards 3-query locally decodable codes of subexponential length. J. ACM 55(1), 1–16 (2008). https://doi.org/10.1145/1326554.1326555

Multi-party Homomorphic Secret Sharing and Sublinear MPC from Sparse LPN

Quang Dao[1]([✉]), Yuval Ishai[2], Aayush Jain[1], and Huijia Lin[3]

[1] Carnegie Mellon University, Pittsburgh, USA
{qvd,aayushja}@andrew.cmu.edu
[2] Technion, Haifa, Israel
yuvali@cs.technion.ac.il
[3] University of Washington, Seattle, USA
rachel@cs.washington.edu

Abstract. Over the past few years, homomorphic secret sharing (HSS) emerged as a compelling alternative to fully homomorphic encryption (FHE), due to its feasibility from an array of standard assumptions and its potential efficiency benefits. However, all known HSS schemes, with the exception of schemes built from FHE or indistinguishability obfuscation (iO), can only support two parties.

In this work, we give the first construction of a *multi-party* HSS scheme for a non-trivial function class, from an assumption not known to imply FHE. In particular, we construct an HSS scheme for an *arbitrary* number of parties with an *arbitrary* corruption threshold, supporting evaluations of multivariate polynomials of degree $\log / \log \log$ over arbitrary finite fields. As a consequence, we obtain a secure multiparty computation (MPC) protocol for any number of parties, with (slightly) *sub-linear* per-party communication of roughly $O(S/\log \log S)$ bits when evaluating a layered Boolean circuit of size S.

Our HSS scheme relies on the *sparse* Learning Parity with Noise (LPN) assumption, a standard variant of LPN with a sparse public matrix that has been studied and used in prior works. Thanks to this assumption, our construction enjoys several unique benefits. In particular, it can be built on top of *any* linear secret sharing scheme, producing noisy output shares that can be error-corrected by the decoder. This yields HSS for low-degree polynomials with optimal download rate. Unlike prior works, our scheme also has a low computation overhead in that the per-party computation of a constant degree polynomial takes $O(M)$ work, where M is the number of monomials.

1 Introduction

Homomorphic secret sharing (HSS) [19] is the secret sharing analogue of homomorphic encryption [37,51], which supports local evaluation of functions on shares of secret inputs. A standard N-party t-private secret sharing scheme randomly splits an input x into N shares, $(x_1, \ldots, x_N)$, such that any subset of t shares reveals nothing about the input. An HSS scheme additionally supports computations on shared inputs by means of local computations on their

© International Association for Cryptologic Research 2023
H. Handschuh and A. Lysyanskaya (Eds.): CRYPTO 2023, LNCS 14082, pp. 315–348, 2023.
https://doi.org/10.1007/978-3-031-38545-2_11

shares. More concretely, there is a local evaluation algorithm Eval and reconstruction algorithm Rec satisfying the following homomorphism requirement. Given a description of a function f, the algorithm $\mathsf{Eval}(f, x_j)$ maps an input share x_j to a corresponding output share y_j such that $\mathsf{Rec}(y_1, \ldots, y_m) = f(x)$. To avoid trivial solutions,[1] the HSS output shares should be *compact* in the sense that their length depends only on the output length of f and the security parameter, and hence the reconstruction time does not grow in the function size. HSS enables private outsourcing of computation to multiple non-colluding servers. It also has applications to secure multiparty computation (MPC) with sublinear communication [19,27,29], multi-server private information retrieval (PIR) and secure keywords search [18,39,53], generating correlated pseudorandomness [15,16], and much more.

The work of Boyle, Gilboa and Ishai [19] gave the first nontrivial example of a 2-party HSS scheme without FHE. Their scheme supports the class of polynomial-size branching programs (which contains NC^1) and is based on the Decisional Diffie-Hellman (DDH) assumption. A series of followup works have extended their result, improving efficiency [17,20,22], and diversifying the underlying assumptions to Decision Composite Residuosity (DCR) [33,50,52] or assumptions based on class groups of imaginary quadratic fields [1]. For more limited function classes, which include constant-degree polynomials, 2-party HSS can be based on different flavors of the Learning Parity with Noise (LPN) assumption [16,29]. However, when it comes to the general setting of HSS with $N \geq 3$ parties, constructions have been lacking, with the only known solutions relying on either FHE [11,12,21,26,32,48] or Indistinguishability Obfuscation (iO) [18].[2]

The same "multi-party barrier" exists when it comes to the construction of sublinear-communication MPC protocols, the goal is to achieve (per-party) communication cost that is sublinear in the size of the circuit being computed. Until the DDH-based construction of HSS [19], this could only be achieved using FHE. It is easy to see that an N-party $(N-1)$-private HSS for a function class $\mathcal{F}$ directly implies an MPC protocol for functions in $\mathcal{F}$ with communication depending only on the input and output lengths. Thus, all 2-party HSS schemes in previous works immediately yield 2-party low-communication MPC for low-depth computations (log- or log log-depth). Furthermore, these protocols can be extended to handle general layered circuits with a communication cost sublinear in the circuit size (by a log or log log factor). Unfortunately, when it comes to general multiparty settings, with up to $N-1$ corruption, the only known solutions again rely on FHE or $i\mathcal{O}$.

Motivated by the state-of-the-art, we ask:

---

[1] A trivial solution is letting the output shares be (f, x_j) and Rec reconstruct x from the shares and then compute f. However, this solution is uninteresting since it is not useful.

[2] The work of [18] builds 2-party HSS for general polynomial-sized computation from subexponentially secure iO and one-way functions. Their construction can be extended to the multiparty setting.

Can we have general N-party t-private HSS for useful classes of functions, and sublinear communication MPC for general number of parties, without FHE or iO?

1.1   Our Results

In this work, based on the sparse LPN assumption (described shortly), we construct general N-party t-private HSS for log log-depth arithmetic circuits, and more generally, for the class of multivariate polynomials with log / log log degree and a polynomial number of monomials. Our HSS natively supports arithmetic computation over arbitrary field $\mathbb{F}_q$ (assuming sparse LPN over $\mathbb{F}_q$). It also enjoys concrete efficiency. In particular, the server computation overhead can be made constant (independent of the security parameter) when evaluating constant degree polynomials, and shares of multiple outputs can be packed together to achieve optimal download rate [35]. As an application of our HSS, we obtain the first sublinear-communication MPC for general layered circuits and arbitrary number of parties without relying on FHE or $i\mathcal{O}$. We now describe our results in more detail.

Sparse LPN. Given two sparsity parameters $k = \omega(1) \in \mathbb{N}$ and $\delta \in (0,1)$, the (k, δ)-sparse LPN assumption over a finite field $\mathbb{F}_q$ states that the following distributions are computationally indistinguishable:

$$(\mathbf{A}, \mathbf{s}^T \mathbf{A} + \mathbf{e}^T \mod q) \approx_c (\mathbf{A}, \mathbf{r}) , \text{ where } \mathbf{A} \in \mathbb{F}_q^{n \times m}, \mathbf{s} \leftarrow \mathbb{F}_q^n, \mathbf{e} \in \mathbb{F}_q^m, \mathbf{r} \leftarrow \mathbb{F}_q^m .$$

The public matrix $\mathbf{A} \in \mathbb{F}_q^{n \times m}$ is k-sparse, meaning that each column is sampled randomly subject to having Hamming weight exactly k, while the error vector $\mathbf{e}$ is $n^{-\delta}$-sparse in the sense that each coordinate e_i is random non-zero with probability $1/n^\delta$ and 0 otherwise. This work relies on the *sparse LPN assumption* that the above indistinguishability holds for every super-constant k, every constant $\delta \in (0,1)$, every prime modulus q (potentially exponentially large in λ), and any polynomial number m of samples. See Assumption 4.1 for the precise formulation. In fact, in this work it suffices to require the above indistinguishability to hold for *some* $\delta > 0$ (though we believe that the assumption should hold for any constant $\delta \in (0,1)$).

Variants of this assumption in the binary field $\mathbb{F}_2$ have been proposed and studied for at least a couple of decades in average-case complexity (see works such as [2,3,10,30,34,40,45,47]). The work of [6] generalized the assumption to large fields $\mathbb{F}_q$. Both of these variants have been used in a number of works (see for example [2,4,7,42]). The related assumption of local PRGs [40] has also been used in a number of works including the recent construction of program obfuscation scheme [44]. Comparing with previous variants, our assumption is relatively conservative in two aspects. First, we consider public matrices that are $(k = \omega(1))$-sparse, instead of constant sparse $k = O(1)$. In fact, for our constructions of HSS and sublinear communication MPC, it suffices to set $k = \mathrm{poly}(\log \lambda)$. Second, the error-rate $1/n^\delta$ can be an arbitrary inverse polynomial, whereas for some application such as PKE [4] we require δ to be greater than some fixed constant.

The work of [4] showed how to construct PKE from sparse LPN over $\mathbb{F}_2$ with constant sparsity $k = 3$, sample complexity $n^{1.4}$ and error probability $o(n^{-0.2})$. Their scheme could be naturally extended to work with the variant of the assumption for a fairly general choice of parameters. In particular, they could work with any choice of constant $k \geq 3$, assuming a sample complexity of $m = n^{1+(k/2-1)(1-\delta)}$ for $\delta > 0$, where the noise probability should be $o(n^{-\delta})$. In our case, k is set to be $\omega(1)$ (so n^k is super-polynomial), and our sample complexity is only polynomial in n. For these parameters the noise probability implying PKE through [4] is smaller than any inverse polynomial, while for us, the noise probability could be $n^{-\delta}$ for any $\delta > 0$. Therefore, to the best of our knowledge, our parameters are not known to imply PKE. We survey cryptanalysis of the sparse LPN problem, and give more details on the PKE scheme, in the full version.

General N-party t-private HSS Scheme. Assuming sparse LPN, we present a construction of HSS schemes for general number of parties N and privacy threshold t. Our schemes support computing functions represented by multivariate polynomials with degree $O(\log \lambda / \log \log \lambda)$ and polynomial number of monomials; in particular, this class of functions contains $O(\log \log)$-depth arithmetic circuits. However, similar to the DDH-based HSS construction of [19], our schemes have a noticeable correctness error, which can be made as small as any inverse polynomial, at the cost of worse efficiency.

Theorem 1.1 (Multi-party HSS, informal). *Assume sparse LPN. For any number of parties $N \geq 2$, privacy threshold $t < N$, modulus q, error probability $\epsilon = 1/\operatorname{poly}(\lambda)$, there is a N-party, t-private HSS with correctness error ϵ for the following class of functions:*

- *Function Class $\mathcal{P}(\mathbb{F}_q, D, M)$: multivariate polynomials over the finite field $\mathbb{F}_q$ with degree $D = O(\log \lambda / \log \log \lambda)$ and number of monomials $M = \operatorname{poly}(\lambda)$.*

The reconstruction of the above HSS scheme is linear. Furthermore, the scheme can be modified to have compact (but non-linear) reconstruction and negligible error rate.

Previously, sparse LPN with specific parameters was used to build public-key encryption (PKE) through the classic work of [4]. However, as remarked above, our parameters implying HSS are not known to imply PKE. Therefore, we obtain the first multi-party HSS scheme for useful classes of functions from a plausibly mini-crypt assumption. In contrast, previous (2-party) HSS schemes were either based on LWE, on various number theoretic assumptions (DDH/DCR/QR), or on standard LPN (with dense public matrix) that required the error rate to be below $n^{-0.5}$; all of these assumptions are known to imply PKE. See Fig. 1 for details.

Besides accommodating general N and t, our construction enjoys several other desirable features. First, thanks to the fact that the sparse LPN assumption

Assumptions	(N, t)	Function Class	Error
DDH [17,19,20], DCR [33]	$(2, 1)$	Branching programs (NC^1)	1/poly
LWE [22]	$(2, 1)$	Branching programs (NC^1)	negl
DCR [50,52]	$(2, 1)$	Branching programs (NC^1)	negl
Class Groups [1]	$(2, 1)$	Branching programs (NC^1)	negl
LPN [16]	$(2, 1)$	Constant-degree polynomials	none
Quasi-poly LPN [29]	$(2, 1)$	Loglog-depth circuits	none
Degree-k Homomorphic Encryption [43,46]	$\left(\lfloor \frac{dt}{k+2} \rfloor, t\right)$	Degree-d polynomials	none [a]
Unconditional (Shamir-based) [35]	$(dt + 1, t)$	Degree-d polynomials	none
iO and OWF [18]	$(\star, \star)$	Circuits (P/poly)	none
FHE [21,32] [b]	$(\star, \star)$	Circuits (P/poly)	negl
Sparse LPN (Ours)	$(\star, \star)$	Loglog-depth circuits	1/poly

[a] reconstruction is non-linear
[b] relies on multi-key FHE schemes that can be based on "circular-secure" LWE

Fig. 1. Comparison between existing N-party, t-private HSS schemes and ours. The reconstruction process is linear unless stated otherwise.

"arithmetize" to arbitrary field $\mathbb{F}_q$, our HSS schemes natively support evaluating these polynomials (and arithmetic circuits) over arbitrary field $\mathbb{F}_q$. Second, our construction can also accommodate general reconstruction threshold $t < t' \leq N$, namely, how many output shares are needed in order to reconstruct the output. Having a smaller reconstruction threshold are useful in certain applications, for instance, it implies fault tolerance to server failures in the scenario of outsourcing computation to multiple servers via HSS. Furthermore, our schemes have constant server-computation overhead when computing low degree polynomials and optimal download rate, which we expand in detail later.

Sublinear Communication MPC for Any Number of Parties. Using our HSS construction, we circumvent the "circuit-size barrier" for general MPC, for the first time, without restricting the number of parties N or the function classes, nor using FHE or $i\mathcal{O}$. We construct such protocols where the communication cost of each party is sublinear in the size S of the Boolean layered circuit being computed, roughly by a factor of $\log \log S$ (plus other lower order terms).

Theorem 1.2 (Sublinear MPC, informal). *Assume sparse LPN and the existence of an oblivious transfer protocol. Then, for any $\kappa(\lambda) \in \omega(1)$ and any number of parties N, there exist N-party MPC protocols tolerating up to $(N-1)$ semi-honest corruptions that can evaluate Boolean layered circuits of size S, depth D, and width W, with per-party communication*

$$O(\kappa \cdot S/\log \log S) + D \cdot S^{o(1)} \cdot \mathsf{poly}(\lambda, N) + W \cdot \mathsf{poly}(\log N, \log \lambda)/N.$$

Besides sparse LPN, our sublinear-communication MPC also (inevitably) needs to rely on an Oblivious Transfer (OT) protocol. The latter can be based on standard LPN with noise rate below $n^{-0.5}$ [2,31] or a specific sparse LPN-type assumption [4].[3] In summary, sublinear-communication MPC can be obtained using only assumptions in the LPN family.

Finally, we note that by an existing compiler due to Naor and Nissim [49], we can upgrade our MPC protocols to be maliciously secure while preserving per-party sublinear communication cost, assuming the existence of Collision-Resistant Hash (CRH) functions. Again, CRH can be constructed from standard LPN with low-noise rate $\log^2(n)/n$ [24].

Low Server Computation Overhead. If assuming stronger variants of sparse LPN assumption where the public matrix is constant-sparse,[4] i.e., $k = O(1)$, we can slightly adapt the evaluation procedure of our HSS construction, so that, the computation overhead of each party/server for computing *constant-degree* polynomials represented as a sum of monomials is only a constant. More precisely, to compute a single degree d monomial over $\mathbb{F}_q$, the local homomorphic evaluation procedure can be represented by a degree d arithmetic circuit over $\mathbb{F}_q$ of size $O((k+1)^d)$. Next, homomorphic addition of the outputs of t monomials involves only t addition over $\mathbb{F}_q$. Therefore, when both k and d are constants, the overhead is at most $O((k+1)^d/d)$ (i.e., the ratio between the server cost and the cost of computing a single monomial) a constant. In comparison, almost all previous HSS schemes (tolerating $N - 1$ corruption) have a server computation overhead proportional to the security parameter $\mathsf{poly}(\lambda)$ [1,22,29,33,50,52]; the only exception is using FHE [38] with polylogarithmic overhead, which implies HSS with $\mathsf{poly}(\log \lambda)$ overhead.

We remark that HSS for low-degree polynomials is well-motivated by a variety of applications, for instance, multi-server private information retrieval, for computing inner product between two integer-valued vectors (a degree-2 function) which is a measure of correlation, and for computing intersection of d sets where each set is represented by a characteristic vector in $\mathbb{F}_2^\ell$, and intersection can be computed by ℓ instances of a degree-d monomial over $\mathbb{F}_2$. See [35,43,46] for more examples.

Simple Reconstruction and Optimal Download Rate. In fact, our HSS is also "compatible" with an arbitrary *multi-secret sharing scheme* LMSS. This allows us to achieve much better download rate[5] by packing many function evaluations into a single set of output shares. In particular, by plugging in the multi-secret Shamir sharing [36], we achieve a rate of $1-t/N$, which matches the best possible rate for information-theoretic HSS. In fact, this also applies to computational

---

[3] Namely, the PKE constructed in [4] can be directly transformed into a semi-honest OT.

[4] In such a setting, we shall use public matrices from specific distributions instead of being uniform. See Remark 4.2 for a discussion.

[5] The download rate is the ratio of the output size over the sum of all output share sizes (for details, see [35]).

HSS with linear reconstruction, or where the output share size is independent of the computational security parameter.[6]

Theorem 1.3 (General Linear Output Shares, informal). *For any field* $\mathbb{F}_q$, *assume sparse LPN over* $\mathbb{F}_q$. *For any* $N \geq 2$, $t < N$, $\epsilon = 1/\text{poly}(\lambda)$, *and any* N-*party,* t-*private linear secret sharing scheme* LSS, *there is an* N-*party,* t-*private HSS with correctness error* ϵ *for the same function class as in Theorem 1.1 satisfying the following properties:*

- *the output shares are* LSS *secret shares of the output* y *with probability* $1 - \epsilon$ *(and* LSS *secret shares of some wrong value with probability* ϵ).
- *using an appropriate* LMSS, *the output shares can be packed together to achieve download rate* $1 - t/N$.

The above should be compared with the $1 - Dt/N$ rate of the (perfectly correct) *information-theoretic* construction from [35], which is in fact optimal for HSS in which *both* the sharing and the reconstruction are linear. To the best of our knowledge, the only other computationally secure HSS scheme with $(1-t/N)$ download rate uses FHE with certain properties. This scheme is sketched in the full version.

1.2 Related Work

2-party sublinear MPC. The work of Boyle, Gilboa, and Ishai [19] showed how to build sublinear 2PC for layered circuits of size S with communication complexity roughly $O(S/\log S)$, under the DDH assumption. Following this template, later works showed that we can replace DDH with various other assumptions such as DCR [33,50,52], poly-modulus LWE [22], or class group assumptions [1]. More recently, Couteau and Meyer [29] showed that assuming the quasi-polynomial hardness of (dense) LPN, we can have 2PC with sublinear communication complexity roughly $O(S/\log \log S)$. Finally, in the correlated randomness model with polynomial storage, Couteau constructed information theoretically secure MPC protocols with communication complexity O(S/log log S) [27].

Beyond 2 parties. In a very recent and independent work, Boyle, Couteau and Meyer [14] constructed the first sublinear MPC protocols for $N \geq 3$ parties from assumptions that are not known to imply FHE. This includes a 3-party protocol from a combination of a variant of the (dense) LPN assumption and *either* DDH or QRA, as well as a 5-party protocol additionally assuming DCR and a local PRG. In contrast, we obtain a sublinear MPC protocol for *any* number of parties N, based entirely on variants of the LPN assumption (sparse LPN and OT, which is implied from low-noise dense LPN).

Our technical approach is very different from that of [14]. The results of [14] are based on a novel compiler that obtains a sublinear N-party MPC protocol

---

[6] The latter conditions rule out HSS schemes in which the output shares contain a homomorphic encryption of the output. Such schemes can only achieve good rate when the output size is much bigger than the (computational) security parameter.

from an $(N-1)$-party HSS scheme satisfying an extra "Las-Vegas"[7] correctness property, along with a PIR scheme with special properties. (See [14] for details, and Proposition 1 in [14] for a more general framework.) We cannot use the compiler from [14] to obtain our MPC result (Theorem 1.2), for two reasons: our HSS scheme does not satisfy the extra Las-Vegas property, and (even standard) PIR is not known to follow from any variant of LPN.

Instead, our sublinear MPC protocol follows the blueprint of a similar (2-party) HSS-based construction from [19], adapting it to the lower complexity class supported by our HSS scheme and extending it to cope with a big number of parties. This approach is more direct and simpler than the compiler from [14], thanks to the fact that we can use an N-party (rather than an $(N-1)$-party) HSS scheme to construct N-party sublinear MPC protocols.

Finally, we note that while our MPC protocol inherently has a negligible correctness error, the construction in [14] can leverage HSS schemes with Las-Vegas correctness to yield perfectly correct (3-party or 5-party) MPC protocols [28]. We leave open the possibility of obtaining a Las-Vegas variant of our HSS scheme or a perfectly correct sublinear MPC from sparse LPN and OT.

2   Technical Overview

Our results are facilitated mainly due to structural properties underlying our assumption of *sparse LPN*.

Sparse LPN. We start by recalling the *sparse LPN* assumption. Our assumption states that the following two distributions are computationally indistinguishable:

$$\{\boldsymbol{a}_i, \langle \boldsymbol{a}_i, \boldsymbol{s}\rangle + e_i\}_{i\in[m]} \approx_c \{\boldsymbol{a}_i, u_i\}_{i\in[m]},$$

where $\boldsymbol{a}_i$ are randomly chosen k-sparse vectors over $\mathbb{F}_q^n$ for a prime power q, and m is an arbitrarily chosen polynomial in n. The error e_i is chosen sparsely from a Bernoulli random variable over $\mathbb{F}_q$ with probability of error being $n^{-\delta}$ for a constant $\delta > 0$. On the other hand, $\{u_i\}$ are chosen at random from $\mathbb{F}_q$. In this work, we can work with any $\delta > 0$ and typically consider $k = \omega(1)$ as an appropriately chosen super constant, however the assumption is plausible even when k is chosen to be a constant integer greater than equal to 3 as long as $m = o(n^{k/2})$. Such an assumption will allow our homomorphic secret sharing scheme to support a slightly bigger function class. We discuss the history and cryptanalysis of this assumption in the full version. Our function class consists of multivariate polynomials over $\mathbb{F}_q$, and the sparse LPN assumption we will use to build such an HSS will also be over the same $\mathbb{F}_q$. We now illustrate how this assumption gives rise to a conceptually clean construction of a homomorphic secret sharing scheme.

---

[7] An HSS scheme has Las-Vegas correctness with error ϵ if each output share can be set to $\bot$ with at most ϵ probability, and if no output share is set to $\bot$ then the shares must always add up to the correct output.

2.1 HSS Construction

We now describe the ideas behind our HSS construction. In this work, we consider the function class $\mathcal{P}(\mathbb{F}_q, D, M)$ which consists of polynomials evaluated on inputs that are vectors of arbitrary polynomial length over $\mathbb{F}_q$. These polynomials are of degree D, and are subject to an upper bound of M on the number of monomials. Looking ahead, we will handle $D = \frac{\log \lambda}{\log \log \lambda}$ and $M = \mathsf{poly}(\lambda)$ where λ is the security parameter. This already lets us evaluate Boolean circuits that are local where the locality[8] is bounded by $D = \frac{\log \lambda}{\log \log \lambda}$ - any circuit that has a locality bounded by D, can be represented by such a polynomial. We refer to the definitions for a homomorphic-secret sharing scheme $\mathsf{HSS} = (\mathsf{Share}, \mathsf{Eval}, \mathsf{Rec})$ in Sect. 3.2.

Template from Boyle et al. Our scheme follows the same high-level template that was first suggested by [19] and has been later adopted in a number of follow-ups such as [1,22,50,52], but introduces a number of important twists. Suppose we want to secret share a vector $\boldsymbol{x} \in \mathbb{F}_q^m = (x_1, \ldots, x_m)$ amongst N parties. We work with a suitable linear secret sharing scheme over $\mathbb{F}_q$. In this overview, we will work with the additive secret sharing for N parties, but it could be any linear secret sharing scheme over $\mathbb{F}_q$ (or its field extensions).

Each party can be handed over the shares of $\boldsymbol{x}$: a party P_ℓ for $\ell \in [N]$ is given shares that are denoted by $[\![x_i]\!]_\ell$ for $i \in [m]$, respectively. This is already enough to build a homomorphic secret sharing scheme supporting linear functions. Namely, parties can locally compute shares of linear functions of $\boldsymbol{x}$ by applying appropriate linear functions over their shares $[\![x_i]\!]_\ell$.

The main ingredient in prior HSS schemes is a method that lets one noninteractively compute share of multiplication of an intermediate computation y with an input symbol x_i. The idea is that one publishes an encryption of the input $\{\mathsf{ct}_s(x_i)\}$ and encryptions of the products $\{\mathsf{ct}_s(x_i \cdot s_j)\}$, where $\boldsymbol{s} = (s_1, \ldots, s_n)$ is the secret key, using a suitably chosen linearly homomorphic encryption scheme (such schemes can typically be instantiated from any of the LWE/DDH/DCR/QR assumptions). Since we are encrypting functions of the secret key inside the ciphertext, the encryption scheme must also be KDM secure (or we must assume it is KDM secure).

These encryptions are given to all parties. Along with these encryptions and the shares of the input $[\![x_i]\!]_\ell$, each party P_ℓ receives a share $[\![x_i \cdot s_j]\!]_\ell$ of the product $x_i s_j$. The key step is a procedure that allows one to start with a share $[\![y]\!]_\ell$ for an intermediate computation y and shares $[\![y \cdot s_j]\!]_\ell$ of products $y \cdot s_j$ and compute not only a share of $[\![y \cdot x_i]\!]_\ell$ for any input x_i but also shares of the form $[\![y \cdot x_i \cdot s_j]\!]_\ell$. This step leverages structural properties of the linearly homomorphic encryption scheme. Typically in such settings, one homomorphically computes on the ciphertext by "multiplying" $\mathsf{ct}_s(x_i)$ with $[\![y]\!]_\ell$. The resulting ciphertext is then "decrypted" in a distributed fashion using the secret-shares of the form $[\![y \cdot s_j]\!]_\ell$, assuming that the decryption is almost linear. This produces

---

[8] The locality of any Boolean circuit is the number of input bits it depends on.

shares of $[\![y \cdot x_i]\!]_\ell$. The shares of $[\![y \cdot x_i \cdot s_j]\!]_\ell$ can be computed by starting with $\mathsf{ct}_s(x_i s_j)$ instead.

Which linearly homomorphic encryption one chooses can present different sets of challenges for realizing the above step. [19,50] relied on DDH/Pallier based encryption. Since the ambient space of shares is over some field, whereas the encryption consists of group elements, this step include some operations done over the groups followed by a "distributed discrete-log" step that works specifically for two parties. In LWE based schemes such as [22], the ciphertexts live in the same space as that of the shares. The issue is that while the ciphertexts are almost linear in the secret, they have a low-norm error. The authors suggest a rounding based idea that was inspired by earlier works on homomorphic encryption [23,25] that for some (not so) coincidental reason works specifically for two parties. Our main approach consists of devising a suitable linearly homomorphic encryption that sits naturally over the field $\mathbb{F}_q$, and does not suffer from the issues that prevented scaling of previous ideas beyond two parties.

Suitable Linearly Homomorphic Encryption. The main issue with prior linear homomorphic encryption schemes that restricts constructions to two parties is that they don't work naturally with the linear secret sharing scheme. As a result, special share conversion methods have to be devised (which seem to be stuck at two parties). It is instructive to ask what properties a linear homomorphic encryption could satisfy so that it works more naturally with the linear secret sharing scheme.

To this end, consider the following (broken) encryption scheme that encrypts input x_i as $\mathsf{ct}_s(x_i) = (\boldsymbol{a}_i, b_i = \langle \boldsymbol{a}_i, \boldsymbol{s} \rangle + x_i)$ where $\boldsymbol{s}$ is a vector of $\mathbb{F}_q^n$ and $\boldsymbol{a}_i \leftarrow \mathbb{F}_q^n$ is randomly chosen. Similarly, we have $\mathsf{ct}_s(x_i s_j) = (\boldsymbol{a}_{i,j}, b_{i,j} = \langle \boldsymbol{a}_{i,j}, \boldsymbol{s} \rangle + x_i s_j)$. Such an encryption scheme is both linearly homomorphic and has a linear decryption function over $\mathbb{F}_q$. On the other hand, it is obviously not secure: one could find the secret $\boldsymbol{s}$ by solving a properly constructed linear equation system.

But, for the time being assume that the scheme was secure. If this were true, then this will give rise to a homomorphic secret sharing scheme supporting corruption patterns governed by any linear secret sharing scheme over $\mathbb{F}_q$, thanks to it being linearly homomorphic over $\mathbb{F}_q$ and having linear decryption over $\mathbb{F}_q$. Indeed, observe that

$$b_i [\![y]\!]_\ell - \langle \boldsymbol{a}_i, ([\![ys_1]\!]_\ell, \ldots, [\![ys_n]\!]_\ell) \rangle = [\![x_i \cdot y]\!]_\ell \tag{1}$$

$$b_{i,j} [\![y]\!]_\ell - \langle \boldsymbol{a}_{i,j}, ([\![ys_1]\!]_\ell, \ldots, [\![ys_n]\!]_\ell) \rangle = [\![x_i \cdot y \cdot s_j]\!]_\ell \tag{2}$$

LPN-Based Linearly Homomorphic Encryption. While the above proposal would work, as described before, it is obviously not secure. To fix the security issue, one could leverage an encryption scheme based on the *standard LPN assumption*. We could instead have $\mathsf{ct}_s(x_i) = (\boldsymbol{a}_i, b_i = \langle \boldsymbol{a}_i, \boldsymbol{s} \rangle + x_i + e_i)$ and $\mathsf{ct}_s(x_i s_j) = (\boldsymbol{a}_{i,j}, b_{i,j} = \langle \boldsymbol{a}_{i,j}, \boldsymbol{s} \rangle + x_i s_j + e_{i,j})$ where e_i and $e_{i,j}$ are chosen from the generalized Bernoulli random variables $\mathsf{Ber}(\mathbb{F}_q, \eta)$ where $\eta(n)$ is chosen to be a small inverse polynomial $n^{-\delta}$. The resulting scheme is now secure by the LPN assumption, it is also linearly homomorphic and has a linear decryption over $\mathbb{F}_q$. Although, the decryption has a small probability correctness error due to noise. The problem we now face is correctness of the output.

We can observe that if one is initially given $[\![x_i]\!]_\ell$ and $[\![x_i \cdot s_j]\!]_\ell$, as one computes shares for degree two computations $x_{i_1} \cdot x_{i_2}$, Eq. 1 instead yields noisy shares $\langle\!\langle x_{i_1} \cdot x_{i_2} \rangle\!\rangle_\ell$ and $\langle\!\langle x_{i_1} \cdot x_{i_2} \cdot s_j \rangle\!\rangle_\ell$. Here by "noisy" we don't mean that the shares of individual parties are corrupted, but rather that, with some small probability the shares reconstruct to something else other than the desired computation (but they are still consistent secret sharing of some "noisy" output). Each computed share can be corrupted with probability η due to the LPN noise. Moreover, as one evaluates further to compute degree three terms, the noise increases further. To compute degree three shares of the form $\langle\!\langle x_{i_1} \cdot x_{i_2} \cdot x_{i_3} \rangle\!\rangle_\ell$, the noise probability could already be overwhelming. This is because due to Eq. 1,

$$b_{i_3} \langle\!\langle x_{i_1} x_{i_2} \rangle\!\rangle_\ell - \langle \boldsymbol{a}_i, (\langle\!\langle x_{i_1} x_{i_2} s_1 \rangle\!\rangle_\ell , \dots, \langle\!\langle x_{i_1} x_{i_2} s_n \rangle\!\rangle_\ell) \rangle = \langle\!\langle x_{i_1} x_{i_2} x_{i_3} \rangle\!\rangle_\ell .$$

Thus, each conversion is a function of one LPN sample and n shares derived in the previous layer. The probability of having no noise in the reconstructed output is roughly the probability that all the shares derived in the previous layer are non-noisy and the LPN sample used in that layer has no noise. This probability is roughly $(1 - \eta)^{O(n)}$ assuming that the errors are independent. As $\eta \gg \frac{1}{n}$, this probability is already negligible.

Sparse LPN for Error Control. We can observe that in Eq. 1 above (now with noisy shares),

$$b_{i_3} \langle\!\langle x_{i_1} x_{i_2} \rangle\!\rangle_\ell - \langle \boldsymbol{a}_i, (\langle\!\langle x_{i_1} x_{i_2} s_1 \rangle\!\rangle_\ell , \dots, \langle\!\langle x_{i_1} x_{i_2} s_n \rangle\!\rangle_\ell) \rangle = \langle\!\langle x_{i_1} x_{i_2} x_{i_3} \rangle\!\rangle_\ell ,$$

if $\boldsymbol{a}_i$ was only k-sparse, where k is a parameter that could be a constant or slightly super-constant, the error build up will be manageable. The probability that the share is non-noisy is can now be lower-bounded by $1 - (k + 1)\eta$. This is because this equation now depends only on $k + 1$ noisy shares derived in the previous layer and one LPN sample, both with noise rate η.

Going inductively, the shares at level D for computing a degree D monomial are non-noisy with probability at least $1 - O((k + 1)^D \eta)$. If one further adds M such degree D monomials to compute the polynomial of desired form the resulting shares are non-noisy with probability is at least $1 - O(M(k + 1)^D \eta)$. We can make sure that this probability is $1 - O(\frac{1}{\lambda})$ if $M(k+1)^D \eta$ is kept smaller than $\frac{1}{\lambda}$. If M is some polynomial in λ, $D = \frac{\log \lambda}{\log \log \lambda}$, and $\eta = n^{-\delta}$ for some constant $\delta > 0$, we can set $k = \log^{O(1)} \lambda$ and n as some other polynomial in λ. More details of our HSS scheme can be found in Sect. 5.1.

Summing up. To sum up, one would compute

$$\mathsf{ct}_s(x_i) = (\boldsymbol{a}_i, \langle \boldsymbol{a}_i, \boldsymbol{s} \rangle + e_i + x_i), \tag{3}$$

where $\boldsymbol{a}_i$ is chosen to be a random sparse vector as in the distribution specified by the sparse LPN assumption, and e_i is generated as a sparse noise. $\{\mathsf{ct}_s(x_i s_j)\}_{i,j}$

are generated analogously. Since our assumption works naturally over the field $\mathbb{F}_q$ one could use any linear secret sharing scheme over $\mathbb{F}_q$. One can then evaluate any function in $\mathcal{P}(\mathbb{F}_q, D, M)$. For any function f in the function class, at the end of the evaluation each party gets a noisy share $\langle\!\langle f(x_1, \ldots, x_m) \rangle\!\rangle_\ell$. With all but a small inverse polynomial probability, these shares reconstruct to $f(\boldsymbol{x})$ using the same linear reconstruction that is used for the base secret sharing scheme.

2.2 Arguing KDM Security

One issue that we have not discussed thus far is that in our HSS scheme, one gives out encryptions that are dependent on the key $\boldsymbol{s}$. Namely, all parties not only get encryptions of the input $\mathsf{ct}_{\boldsymbol{s}}(x_i)$, but also encryptions $\mathsf{ct}_{\boldsymbol{s}}(x_i s_j)$ of the products $x_i s_j$. Therefore, we need to argue that KDM security follows from sparse LPN. Note that indeed if $\mathsf{ct}_{\boldsymbol{s}}(x_i s_j)$ were encrypted using the standard LPN assumption, namely by setting $\mathsf{ct}_{\boldsymbol{s}}(x_i s_j) = (\boldsymbol{a}_{i,j}, \langle \boldsymbol{a}_{i,j}, \boldsymbol{s} \rangle + e_{i,j} + x_i s_j)$, where $\boldsymbol{a}_{i,j}$ is chosen randomly over $\mathbb{F}_q^n$, then such KDM security holds directly from LPN. The idea is that one can "simulate" such an encryption from an LPN sample $(\boldsymbol{a}', b' = \langle \boldsymbol{a}', \boldsymbol{s} \rangle + e)$ as follows. We can simply set $\boldsymbol{a}_{i,j} = \boldsymbol{a}' - \underbrace{(0, \ldots, 0, x_i, 0, \ldots 0)}_{x_i \text{ at } j^{th} \text{ coordinate}} = \boldsymbol{a}' - x_i \cdot \boldsymbol{v}_j$ for the jth unit vector $\boldsymbol{v}_j$, and $b_{i,j} = b'$.

Observe that $b' = \langle \boldsymbol{a}', \boldsymbol{s} \rangle + e = \langle \boldsymbol{a}_{i,j}, \boldsymbol{s} \rangle + x_i s_j + e$. Since $\boldsymbol{a}'$ is chosen at random, the distribution of $\boldsymbol{a}_{i,j}$ is also identically random even given x_i.

The above simulation strategy fails to work when $\boldsymbol{a}_{i,j}$ are exactly k-sparse for some k. This is because the vector $\boldsymbol{a}_{i,j}$ that is used to construct $\mathsf{ct}_{\boldsymbol{s}}(x_i \cdot s_j)$ might actually be distinguishable from the distribution of $\boldsymbol{a}' - x_j \boldsymbol{v}_j$. Not only there could be a difference in the number of non-zero coordinates, this could also leak out x_i (by observing the value at of $\boldsymbol{a}_{i,j}$ formed this way at the jth coordinate).

We modify slightly the distribution of the coefficient vectors $\boldsymbol{a}_{i,j}$ used to generate $\mathsf{ct}_{\boldsymbol{s}}(x_i \cdot s_j)$ so that one could prove KDM security under sparse LPN assumption. Below we sketch the main ideas assuming q is a prime power greater than 2.

Modified Distribution. In the actual scheme in Sect. 5, we encrypt the vector $\boldsymbol{x}$ as $\mathsf{ct}_{\boldsymbol{s}}(x_i) = (\boldsymbol{a}_i, \langle \boldsymbol{a}_i, \boldsymbol{s} \rangle + e_i + x_i)$ where $\boldsymbol{a}_i$ are exactly k-sparse. However, to encrypt the products $x_i s_j$, we compute $\mathsf{ct}_{\boldsymbol{s}}(x_i s_j) = (\boldsymbol{a}_{i,j}, \langle \boldsymbol{a}_{i,j}, \boldsymbol{s} \rangle + e_{i,j} + x_{i,j})$ where $\boldsymbol{a}_{i,j}$ are chosen differently. They are chosen to be $2k - 1$ sparse with the constraint that the jth coordinate of $\boldsymbol{a}_{i,j}$ is non-zero. This constraint enables us to prove security from sparse LPN as long as $q > 2$.

Our main idea is that such a sample $\boldsymbol{a}_{i,j}, b_{i,j}$ can be simulated from sufficiently (polynomially) many samples of sparse LPN with sparsity k. Say we have two samples of the form $\boldsymbol{c}_1, d_1$ and $\boldsymbol{c}_2, d_2$ such that $d_i = \langle \boldsymbol{c}_i, \boldsymbol{s} \rangle + e_i$ for $i \in \{1, 2\}$. Additionally, $\boldsymbol{c}_1$ and $\boldsymbol{c}_2$ are non-zero at the jth coordinate and that is the only coordinate at which both $\boldsymbol{c}_1$ and $\boldsymbol{c}_2$ are non-zero. Any pair of samples will satisfy this property with an inverse polynomial probability provided

k is reasonably small. We sample a random non-zero field element r, and two non-zero elements $\mu_1, \mu_2 \in \mathbb{F}_q$ so that $\mu_1 c_{1,j} + \mu_2 c_{2,j} = r + x_i$. Computing such non-zero μ_1 and μ_2 requires that $q > 2$. Indeed if $q = 2$, there is only one choice for μ_1 and μ_2 and then our condition $\mu_1 c_{1,j} + \mu_2 c_{2,j} = r + x_i$ may not hold. Now let $\alpha = \mu_1 c_1 + \mu_2 c_2$, and set $a_{i,j} = \alpha - x_i v_j$. Our desired sample then becomes $\mathsf{ct}_s(x_i s_j) = (a_{i,j}, b_{i,j} = \mu_1 d_1 + \mu_2 d_2)$. Observe that $b_{i,j} = \mu_1 \langle c_1, s \rangle + \mu_2 \langle c_2, s \rangle + \mu_1 e_1 + \mu_2 e_2$. As $a_{i,j} = \mu_1 c_1 + \mu_2 c_2 - x_i v_j$, we have that $b_{i,j} = \langle a_{i,j}, s \rangle + (\mu_1 e_1 + \mu_2 e_2) + x_i s_j$.

Note that the error $\mu_1 e_1 + \mu_2 e_2$ is still sparse (with noise rate close to 2η); our remaining task is to show that $a_{i,j}$ has the right distribution. This follows from the following argument. Since c_1 and c_2 have disjoint support aside from the jth coordinate, the distribution of $a_{i,j}$ on coordinates not equal to j is identical to a random $(2k - 2)$-sparse vector. On the other hand, at the jth coordinate $a_{i,j}$ is set to be equal to r, which is random non-zero.

When $q = 2$, we are not able to prove KDM security of our distribution under (exactly) k-sparse LPN. On the other hand, relying on a related assumption we can indeed show KDM security. In this assumption, the samples will consist of two kinds of coefficient vectors a_i: with half probability, a_i will be k-sparse, otherwise it will be $(k - 1)$-sparse. We refer to Sect. 4.1 for more details.

2.3 Sublinear MPC Construction

We can leverage our homomorphic secret sharing scheme to build a sublinear MPC protocol for (Boolean) layered circuits. Here too, our result follows the main conceptual outline suggested by [19], with a number of low-level, yet important, differences in the implementation. The differences in implementation come from three sources: handling arbitrary number of parties, dealing with restricted function classes supported by the HSS, and dealing with correctness error. In the following, recall that Boolean layered circuits of width W, depth D and size S are designed so that every layer is computed by applying some gates on inputs only on the previous layer. Our sublinear MPC will can compute such a circuit supporting N with a communication of $O(\omega(1) \cdot S/\log \log S + (D + W) \cdot S^{o(1)} \cdot \mathsf{poly}(N, \lambda))$ for an arbitrarily small tunable $\omega(1)$.

Recipe for Sublinear MPC from HSS from Boyle et al. The intuition why an HSS scheme could be helpful for this task was first brought out by [19] and can be described as follows. Suppose that our HSS scheme supported arbitrary circuits and had no correctness error. Then parties can then run any MPC protocol that distributes shares $\mathsf{sh}_1, \ldots, \mathsf{sh}_N$ that correspond to a homomorphic secret sharing of x of their combined input. The amount of communication per-party for this would be polynomial in the security parameter λ, $|x|$ and the number of parties N. Each party P_ℓ can then locally evaluate on their share sh_ℓ to compute the desired layered circuit C to form evaluation st_ℓ and output this value. For our purposes, let the length of the output be M, which is the width of the last layer. Let $\mathsf{st}_\ell = (\mathsf{st}_{\ell,1}, \ldots, \mathsf{st}_{\ell,M})$. The jth output bit can be reconstructed by adding $\{\mathsf{st}_{\ell,j}\}_{\ell \in [N]}$. This yields an additional communication of $|\mathsf{st}_\ell| = O(M)$

bits per-party. Thus, the total communication is $\mathsf{poly}(\lambda, N, |x|) + O(M)$ which is sublinear in the circuit size.

There are two typical challenges that arise in materializing the intuition above. First, the HSS scheme typically could have an error in output reconstruction. For all currently known schemes with erroneous outputs, leaking out which outputs don't reconstruct correctly can jeopardize security (much as how leaking which LPN samples have error can break the assumption). The second challenge is that typically HSS schemes don't support circuits of arbitrary size; instead, they may only handle circuits of depth $\log S$ or even $\log \log S$. Indeed, our HSS can only handle circuits of depth $c \cdot \log \log S$, for any constant $c < 1$.

To address the challenges of circuit depth, Boyle et al. suggested the following. They suggested dividing the circuit C into $L = S/\log S$ special layers (or $S/\log \log S$ in our case depending on the depth supported by the HSS scheme), such that HSS can be performed from one layer to the next. Unfortunately, this won't work as is because one cannot afford to run a general-purpose MPC for every chunk to generate HSS sharings of the state of the circuit at that layer. This is because the communication for this step could grow as $O(W \, \mathsf{poly}(\lambda, N))$ where W is the width of the circuit. Any savings by running HSS evaluation of circuits with depth $\log S$ (or $\log \log S$ in our case) could be drowned out by multiplicative $\mathsf{poly}(\lambda, N)$ term. To address this, Boyle et al. suggested that for every chunk $i \in [L]$, the MPC is run to generate an HSS sharing of N secret keys $\{\mathsf{sk}_{i,\ell}\}_{i \in [L], \ell \in [N]}$ for a rate-one encryption scheme. Since keys are smaller in size compared to the state of the circuit, this could be done with significantly less communication. The keys $\mathsf{sk}_{i,\ell}$ for every chunk $i \in [L]$ and party P_ℓ is known only to party P_ℓ. The evaluation will follow in encrypt-then-evaluate cycles. Namely, (rate-one) encrypted HSS evaluated shares will be decrypted by HSS, computed upon according the circuit chunk description, and then the resulting HSS evaluations are encrypted by each party using their key for that chunk. This process could go on, but at the end we must reconstruct the output. If our HSS is perfectly/statistically correct each party could simply release the HSS share evaluations unencrypted corresponding to the output layer.

If the HSS evaluations do not satisfy correctness as described above, there could be multiple additional issues. First, the output of computation for each chunk might not be correct. More importantly, for the output layer, when parties reveal the HSS evaluations it could jeopardize security. The fix for the first issue that was proposed was to evaluate the circuit in a fault tolerant fashion using appropriate error correction. Each HSS evaluation will now not only correspond to a decryption followed by evaluation, it will also have an error correction step. To address the second issue, Boyle et al. suggested using MPC at the final layer to reconstruct the final output as opposed to clearly releasing the evaluations. This will introduce additional communication but only about $M \cdot \mathsf{poly}(N, \lambda)$.

Specific Issues in Our Context. We now discuss specific issues that we need to address in our context.

- We can handle circuits of depth $\log \log S$, so we have to implement both error correction and decryption within that depth.

– Each party P_ℓ encrypt their HSS evaluation under their secret key $\mathsf{sk}_{i,\ell}$. Even if the decryption circuit of the encryption is very simple, decrypting $O(N)$ encryptions, followed by HSS reconstruction and evaluation corresponding to the chunk all under the hood of HSS could be too complex for us as such a function has a locality of $\Omega(N)$.

To address error correction issue, we will do naive majority-based error correction. We will have $\kappa = \omega(1)$ copies of HSS shares for the same set of encryption keys, where κ could be any super-constant. Each party will then release κ rate-one encryptions, one for each of the κ HSS evaluations. For the error correction, each HSS evaluation function will simply use majority decoding and compute the majority of κ HSS reconstructions and then apply the circuit corresponding to the chunk. If HSS reconstruction and the decryption are very local, then the whole circuit is very local. This introduces a κ factor larger communication that the previous approach, but we can choose $\kappa = o(\log \log S)$ so that our communication is sublinear.

To implement the encryption with a very local decryption, we rely on sparse LPN yet again. In particular, we revisit the encryption scheme described in Eq. 3, whose decryption circuit has locality equal to the sparsity parameter k. We can handle decryption errors via the same majority-based fault tolerance approach, as described above.

To solve the third issue, we leverage the fact that our encryption scheme is key-homomorphic. Instead of setting up HSS shares for keys $\{\mathsf{sk}_{i,\ell}\}_{\ell \in [N]}$, we set up HSS shares for the sum $\Sigma_{\ell \in [N]} \mathsf{sk}_{i,\ell} = \mathsf{sk}_i$. The ciphertexts encrypting HSS shares under key $\mathsf{sk}_{i,\ell}$ could be homomorphically added to form a ciphertext under sk_i of the HSS reconstruction of the circuit state for the chunk, thanks to the additive reconstruction of our HSS scheme and the additive homomorphism of the encryption scheme. Now, the HSS evaluation could decrypt just the resulting ciphertext encrypted under sk_i as opposed to decrypting N ciphertexts.

While these are the main ideas, there are a number of low-level details that we could not dive into in this overview. The details of our sublinear MPC can be found in Sect. 6.

3   Preliminaries

Notation. Let $\mathbb{N} = \{1, 2, \dots\}$ be the natural numbers, and define $[a, b] := \{a, a + 1, \dots, b\}$, $[n] := [1, n]$. Our logarithms are in base 2. For a finite set S, we write $x \leftarrow S$ to denote uniformly sampling x from S. We denote the security parameter by λ; our parameters depend on λ, e.g. $n = n(\lambda)$, and we often drop the explicit dependence. We abbreviate PPT for probabilistic polynomial-time. Our adversaries are non-uniform PPT ensembles $\mathcal{A} = \{\mathcal{A}_\lambda\}_{\lambda \in \mathbb{N}}$. We write $\mathsf{negl}(\lambda)$ to denote negligible functions in λ. Two ensembles of distributions $\{\mathcal{D}_\lambda\}_{\lambda \in \mathbb{N}}$ and $\{\mathcal{D}'_\lambda\}_{\lambda \in \mathbb{N}}$ are computationally indistinguishable if for any non-uniform PPT adversary $\mathcal{A}$ there exists a negligible function negl such that $\mathcal{A}$ can distinguish between the two distributions with probability at most $\mathsf{negl}(\lambda)$.

For $q \in \mathbb{N}$ that is a prime power, we write $\mathbb{F}_q$ to denote the finite field with q elements, and $\mathbb{F}_q^\times$ to denote its non-zero elements. We write vector and matrices in boldcase, e.g. $v \in \mathbb{F}^m$ and $A \in \mathbb{F}^{n \times m}$. We recall the model of arithmetic circuits, and properties of the Bernoulli distribution $\mathsf{Ber}(\mathbb{F}_q, \epsilon)$, in the full version

3.1   Linear Secret Sharing Schemes

We describe linear (multi-)secret sharing schemes, denoted L(M)SS. Looking ahead, our HSS construction will work with an arbitrary LMSS/LSS scheme. The reader can think of the Shamir LMSS as a running example, described in Definition 3.3 below.

Definition 3.1 (Linear Multi-Secret Sharing Scheme). *A N-party, t-private, s-secret linear multi-secret sharing scheme (LMSS) over a finite field $\mathbb{F}$ is a tuple of PPT algorithms* $\mathsf{LMSS} = (\mathsf{Share}, \mathsf{Rec})$ *with the following syntax:*

- $\mathsf{Share}(x_1, \ldots, x_s; \rho) \to (\mathsf{sh}_1, \ldots, \mathsf{sh}_N)$. *Given secrets $x_1, \ldots, x_s \in \mathbb{F}$, this algorithm samples randomness $\rho \in \mathbb{F}^r$ and return shares $\mathsf{sh}_i \in \mathbb{F}^{b_i}$ for all $i \in [N]$. Note that $r, b_1, \ldots, b_N \in \mathbb{N}$ are also part of the description of LMSS. We require $\mathsf{Share} : \mathbb{F}^s \times \mathbb{F}^r \to \mathbb{F}^{b_1} \times \cdots \times \mathbb{F}^{b_N}$ to be a $\mathbb{F}$-linear map.*
- $\mathsf{Rec}(\mathsf{sh}_1, \ldots, \mathsf{sh}_N) \to (x_1, \ldots, x_s)$. *Given shares $(\mathsf{sh}_1, \ldots, \mathsf{sh}_N)$, return the secrets $(x_1, \ldots, x_s)$ or $\perp$. We require $\mathsf{Rec} : \mathbb{F}^{b_1} \times \cdots \times \mathbb{F}^{b_N} \to \mathbb{F}^s$ to be a $\mathbb{F}$-linear map.*

We require the following properties:

- **Correctness.** *For any $x_1, \ldots, x_s \in \mathbb{F}$, we have*

$$\Pr_{\rho \in \mathbb{F}^r} [\mathsf{Rec}(\mathsf{sh}_1, \ldots, \mathsf{sh}_N) = (x_1, \ldots, x_s) \mid (\mathsf{sh}_1, \ldots, \mathsf{sh}_N) \leftarrow \mathsf{Share}(x_1, \ldots, x_s; \rho)] = 1.$$

- **Privacy.** *For any tuples $(x_1, \ldots, x_s), (x'_1, \ldots, x'_s) \in \mathbb{F}^s$ and any subset $T \subset [N]$ of size at most t, the following distributions are the same:*

$$\{(\mathsf{sh}_i)_{i \in T} \mid (\mathsf{sh}_i)_{i \in [N]} \leftarrow \mathsf{Share}(x_1, \ldots, x_s)\} \equiv \{(\mathsf{sh}'_i)_{i \in T} \mid (\mathsf{sh}'_i)_{i \in [N]} \leftarrow \mathsf{Share}(x'_1, \ldots, x'_s)\}.$$

We define the rate *of LMSS to be $r := s/(b_1 + \cdots + b_N)$. When $s = 1$, we denote the (single-)secret sharing scheme by LSS.*

Notation. We will denote by $[\![x_1 \| \ldots \| x_s]\!]$ a LMSS of s secrets $x_1, \ldots, x_s$, and $[\![x_1 \| \ldots \| x_s]\!]_\ell$ the ℓ'th share for $\ell \in [N]$. When we have a LSS that encodes a single secret, i.e., $s = 1$, its shares are denoted as $[\![x]\!]$ and $[\![x]\!]_\ell$, respectively. When sharing a vector x element-wise using a LSS, we denote the ℓ'th share of x by $[\![x]\!]_\ell$.

Remark 3.2 (LMSS to LSS). A LMSS instance for s secrets can be "split" into s LSS instances $\mathsf{LSS}^{(1)}, \ldots, \mathsf{LSS}^{(s)}$, where for all $\sigma \in [s]$, $\mathsf{LSS}^{(\sigma)}$ shares input x in the σth slot of LMSS as $(0, \ldots, x, \ldots, 0) = x \cdot u_\sigma$, where $u_\sigma = (0, \cdots, 0, 1, 0, \cdots, 0)$ is the σ'th unit vector of dimension s and with a single 1 at coordinate σ.

These LSS instances can be "merged" back into a LMSS instance in the following sense: there exists an operation Pack, such that for any $\ell \in [N]$, given party P_ℓ's shares of the LSS instances $[\![x_1 \cdot \boldsymbol{u}_1]\!]_\ell^{(1)}, \ldots, [\![x_s \cdot \boldsymbol{u}_s]\!]_\ell^{(s)}$, returns party P_ℓ's share of the LMSS instance:

$$\mathsf{Pack}\left([\![x_1 \cdot \boldsymbol{u}_1]\!]_\ell^{(1)}, \ldots, [\![x_s \cdot \boldsymbol{u}_s]\!]_\ell^{(s)}\right) := \sum_{\sigma \in [s]} [\![x_\sigma \cdot \boldsymbol{u}_\sigma]\!]_\ell^{(\sigma)} = [\![x_1\| \ldots \|x_s]\!]_\ell .$$

We recall the construction of the Shamir LMSS in e.g. [36]. Note that this LMSS achieves the *optimal* tradeoff (see [35]) between the rate and the privacy threshold t, meaning that $r = 1 - t/N$.

Definition 3.3 (Multi-secret Shamir sharing). *Let $\mathbb{F}$ be a finite field, N be the number of parties, and t the privacy threshold. Let $d = \lceil \log_{|\mathbb{F}|}(2N - t) \rceil$, and define $\mathbb{E}$ to be the unique extension field of $\mathbb{F}$ of degree d. Let γ be a primitive element of $\mathbb{E}$ over $\mathbb{F}$. For any $s \leq N - t$, the N-party, t-private, (ds)-secret Shamir LMSS is defined as follows. Pick arbitrary distinct field elements $\alpha_1, \ldots, \alpha_N, \beta_1, \ldots, \beta_s \in \mathbb{E}$.*

- $\mathsf{Share}(x_1, \ldots, x_{ds}) \rightarrow (\mathsf{sh}_1, \ldots, \mathsf{sh}_N)$. *On input $(x_1, \ldots, x_{ds}) \in \mathbb{F}^{ds}$, we pack every d elements $(x_{dj}, \ldots, x_{dj+d-1})$ into a field element y_j of $\mathbb{E}$ by setting $y_j = \sum_{i=0}^{d-1} x_{dj+i} \gamma^i$. We then choose a random polynomial $p(X) \in \mathbb{E}[X]$ of degree at most $s+t-1$ such that $p(\beta_j) = y_j$ for all $j \in [s]$. Return $\mathsf{sh}_i = p(\alpha_i)$ for all $i \in [N]$.*
- $\mathsf{Rec}(\mathsf{sh}_1, \ldots, \mathsf{sh}_N) \rightarrow (x_1, \ldots, x_{ds})$. *On input the shares $(\mathsf{sh}_1, \ldots, \mathsf{sh}_N)$, we interpolate the unique polynomial $p(X) \in \mathbb{E}[X]$ of degree at most $s + t - 1$ such that $p(\alpha_i) = \mathsf{sh}_i$ for all $i \in I$. We then compute $y_j = p(\beta_j)$ for all $j \in [s]$, and break y_j down into d elements $(x_{dj}, \ldots, x_{dj+d-1})$ of $\mathbb{F}$ (which is a $\mathbb{F}$-linear operation). Return $(x_1, \ldots, x_{ds})$.*

3.2 Homomorphic Secret Sharing

We recall the definition of homomorphic secret sharing schemes from [18, 21], in the setting with a single client, an arbitrary number N of servers, and security against t colluding servers. The functions we consider are arithmetic circuits over a finite field.

Definition 3.4. *Let $N(\lambda), t(\lambda), q(\lambda), \epsilon_{\mathsf{corr}}(\lambda)$ be polynomials in λ. A N-party, t-private homomorphic secret sharing (HSS) scheme with correctness error ϵ_{corr}, for a class of arithmetic circuits $\mathcal{F} = \{\mathcal{F}_\lambda\}_{\lambda \in \mathbb{N}}$ over the finite field $\mathbb{F}_q$, is a tuple of PPT algorithms $\mathsf{HSS} = (\mathsf{Share}, \mathsf{Eval}, \mathsf{Rec})$ with the following syntax:*

- $\mathsf{Share}(\boldsymbol{x}) \rightarrow (\mathsf{sh}_1, \ldots, \mathsf{sh}_N)$: *given a vector $\boldsymbol{x} \in \mathbb{F}_q^m$ of field elements, this algorithm returns a secret sharing $(\mathsf{sh}_1, \ldots, \mathsf{sh}_N)$ of $\boldsymbol{x}$.*
- $\mathsf{Eval}(i, f, \mathsf{sh}_i) \rightarrow \mathsf{osh}_{f,i}$: *given party index $i \in [N]$, a function $f \in \mathcal{F}_\lambda$ and the share sh_i, this algorithm returns an output share $\mathsf{osh}_{f,i}$.*

- Rec($\{\mathsf{osh}_{f,i}\}_{i\in[N]}$) $\to y_f$: given the output shares $\{\mathsf{osh}_{f,i}\}_{i\in[N]}$, this algorithm returns the final output y_f or $\bot$.

We require HSS to satisfy the following properties:

- **Correctness.** We say that the HSS scheme is ϵ_{corr}-correct, if in an honest execution of HSS algorithms with error bound ϵ_{corr}, one can reconstruct the correct output given the output shares with probability at least $1 - \epsilon_{\mathsf{corr}}$. Formally, for all $\lambda \in \mathbb{N}$, all functions $f \in \mathcal{F}_\lambda$, and inputs x to f, we have

$$\Pr\left[\mathsf{Rec}(\{\mathsf{osh}_{f,i}\}_{i\in[N]}) = f(x) \;\middle|\; \begin{array}{l}(\mathsf{sh}_i)_{i\in[N]} \leftarrow \mathsf{HSS.Share}(x) \\ \mathsf{osh}_{f,i} \leftarrow \mathsf{HSS.Eval}(i,f,\mathsf{sh}_i) \; \forall\, i \in [N]\end{array}\right] \geq 1 - \epsilon_{\mathsf{corr}}(\lambda).$$

- **Security.** We say that the HSS scheme is secure if any subset of no more than t shares of the input x reveals no information about x. Formally, for any sequence of subsets $\{T_\lambda\}_\lambda$, where $T = T_\lambda \subset [N]$ has size t, and any PPT adversary $\mathcal{A} = (\mathcal{A}_1, \mathcal{A}_2)$, the advantage of $\mathcal{A}$ in the following experiment is bounded by $1/2 + \mathsf{negl}(\lambda)$ for a negligible function negl.
  1. $\mathcal{A}$ picks challenge inputs $((x_0, x_1), \mathsf{st}) \leftarrow \mathcal{A}_1(1^\lambda, T)$.
  2. $\mathcal{C}(x_0, x_1)$ samples a random bit $b \leftarrow \{0,1\}$ and computes $(\mathsf{sh}_{b,1}, \ldots, \mathsf{sh}_{b,N}) \leftarrow \mathsf{HSS.Share}(x_b)$.
  3. $\mathcal{A}$ outputs a guess $b' \leftarrow \mathcal{A}_2(\mathsf{st}, (\mathsf{sh}_{b,i})_{i\in T})$.
  The advantage of $\mathcal{A}$ in the above experiment is the probability that b equals b'.
- **Compactness.** There exists a polynomial p such that for any $\lambda \in \mathbb{N}$, any $i \in [N]$, any $f \in \mathcal{F}_\lambda$, any input x to f, given $(\mathsf{sh}_j)_{j\in[N]} \leftarrow \mathsf{Share}(x)$, the output share $\mathsf{osh}_{f,i} \leftarrow \mathsf{Eval}(i,f,\mathsf{sh}_i)$ satisfies $|\mathsf{osh}_{f,i}| \leq p(\lambda)$. In particular, the output share sizes do not depend on the size of the function f.

Remark 3.5 (Linear Reconstruction). We say that an HSS scheme for a class of arithmetic circuits $\mathcal{F}$ over a field $\mathbb{F}_q$ has *linear reconstruction* if for every $f \in \mathcal{F}$, input x to f, shares $(\mathsf{sh}_j)_{j\in[N]}$, and party $i \in [N]$, the operation $\mathsf{Eval}(i,f,\mathsf{sh}_i) \to \mathsf{osh}_{f,i}$ produces output shares that are vectors of field elements in $\mathbb{F}_q$. Furthermore, the reconstruction $\mathsf{Rec}(\{\mathsf{osh}_{f,i}\}_{i\in[N]}) \to y_f$ consists of applying a $\mathbb{F}_q$-linear map over the output shares $\mathsf{osh}_{f,i}$.

4   Sparse LPN

In this section, we define our *sparse learning parity with noise (sLPN)* assumption. sLPN is a natural variant of the LPN assumption, where each column of the public matrix is now k-sparse for a parameter k. First introduced by Alekhnovich [2], who used it for obtaining hardness of approximation results, variants of the sLPN assumption were subsequently used for constructing local pseudorandom generators [8], cryptography with constant computational overhead [42], public-key encryption schemes [4], pseudorandom correlation generators [15] and more. In the full version, we give an overview of known attacks against sLPN that may help establish a plausible concrete tradeoff between the parameters.

Definition 4.1 (Sparse LPN distribution). *Let $\lambda \in \mathbb{N}$ be the security parameter, $n = n(\lambda)$ be the dimension, $m = m(\lambda) \in \mathbb{N}$ the number of samples, $k = k(\lambda) \leq n$ the sparsity parameter, $q = q(\lambda) \in \mathbb{N}$ the field size, and $\epsilon = \epsilon(\lambda) \in (0,1)$ the noise rate. We define the sparse LPN distribution $\mathcal{D}_{\mathsf{sLPN},n,m,k,\epsilon,q}$ to be output distribution of the following process:*

- *Sample $s \leftarrow \mathbb{F}_q^{1 \times n}$ uniformly at random.*
- *Sample A randomly from $\mathbb{F}_q^{n \times m}$ such that every column of A has exactly k non-zero elements.*
- *Sample $e \leftarrow (\mathsf{Ber}(\mathbb{F}_q, \epsilon))^{1 \times m}$, where $\mathsf{Ber}(\mathbb{F}_q, \epsilon)$ returns 0 with probability $1 - \epsilon$, and a uniformly random non-zero element of $\mathbb{F}_q$ otherwise.*
- *Compute $b = s \cdot A + e$. Output (A, b).*

Similarly, we define $\mathcal{D}_{\mathsf{rand},n,m,k,\epsilon,q}$ to be identical to the distribution $\mathcal{D}_{\mathsf{sLPN},n,m,k,\epsilon,q}$ except that b is chosen uniformly at random from $\mathbb{F}_q^{1 \times m}$.

We now state our Sparse LPN assumption. Note the following two parameter choices: $k = \omega(1)$ is a super-constant, and the noise rate $\epsilon = O(n^{-\delta})$ for some $\delta \in (0,1)$.

Assumption 4.1 (The (δ, q)-sLPN Assumption). *Let $\lambda \in \mathbb{N}$ be the security parameter, $\delta \in (0,1)$ be a constant, and $q = q(\lambda)$ is a sequence of prime powers computable in $\mathsf{poly}(\lambda)$ time. We say that the (δ, q)-sLPN holds if for all functions $n = n(\lambda), m = m(\lambda), k = k(\lambda), \epsilon = \epsilon(\lambda)$ efficiently computable in $\mathsf{poly}(\lambda)$ time, with $k = \omega(1) \leq n$ and $\epsilon = O(n^{-\delta})$, the following two distributions are computationally indistinguishable:*

$$\{\mathcal{D}_{\mathsf{sLPN},n,m,k,\epsilon,q}\}_{\lambda \in \mathbb{N}} \approx_c \{\mathcal{D}_{\mathsf{rand},n,m,k,\epsilon,q}\}_{\lambda \in \mathbb{N}}.$$

We will also use $\mathsf{sLPN}_{n,m,k,\epsilon,q}$ to refer to the (decisional) sparse LPN problem with fixed parameters, where an adversary needs to distinguish between the two distributions above.

Remark 4.2. In our sparse LPN assumption, we choose $k = \omega(1)$ to be a super-constant (in particular, polylogarithmic) to avoid dealing with syntactical issues arising when k is a constant. Formulations of sparse LPN are well-studied and believed to be hard over $\mathbb{F}_2$ when $k \geq 3$ is a constant (See for example [2,4,34]). Such formulations can support even up to $m = n^{k/2-\epsilon}$ samples for arbitrary constant $\epsilon > 0$. In such cases, however, we require the m columns of A to not admit a sparse combination of columns say $(i_1, \ldots, i_\ell)$ such that $A_{i_i} + \ldots A_{i_\ell} = 0$ for some constant ℓ. This is achieved by requiring the k-regular bipartite graph formed with the columns of A satisfies certain expansion conditions. Unfortunately, this criterion fails to hold for a random graph/random A with inverse polynomial probability $\frac{1}{n^{O(1)}}$.

We could have worked with a stronger assumption, where k is a constant and the matrix A comes from a special distribution of sparse matrices,[9] to achieve a slightly more expressive function class supported by our HSS scheme. Namely, in such a case we could handle $D = O(\log \lambda)$. But for simplicity, we choose to work with super-constant k and uniform k-sparse matrix A.

---

[9] For example, the distribution in the work of Applebaum and Kachlon [9].

4.1 KDM Security

For the security proof of our HSS construction, we will also require the pseudo-randomness of a specific secret-dependent sLPN distribution. In this distribution, we essentially encrypt each input x_i and $x_i \cdot s_j$ for all i, j under sLPN. We note that the result proved in this section corresponds to the notion of KDM security with function $f_{x,j}(\boldsymbol{s}) = x \cdot s_j$ for a given index $j \in [n]$ and for all $x \in \mathbb{F}_q$, defined in prior works [5,13,22].

Definition 4.3 (Sparse LPN KDM distribution). *Let $\delta \in (0,1)$ be a constant and $q = q(\lambda)$ a sequence of prime powers efficiently computable in $\mathsf{poly}(\lambda)$ time. Let $\lambda \in \mathbb{N}$ be the security parameter, and $n(\lambda), m(\lambda), k(\lambda), \epsilon(\lambda) \in \mathbb{N}$ be efficiently computable functions of 1^n such that q is a prime power, $k = \omega(1) < n/2$, and $\epsilon = O(n^{-\delta})$. For any sequence of vectors $\{\boldsymbol{x} = \boldsymbol{x}_\lambda\}_\lambda$ where $\boldsymbol{x}_\lambda \in \mathbb{F}_q^m$, we define the distribution $\mathcal{D}^{\mathsf{kdm}}_{\mathsf{sLPN},n,m,k,\epsilon,q}(\boldsymbol{x})$ to be the output of the following process:*

- *Sample $\boldsymbol{s} \leftarrow \mathbb{F}_q^n$.*
- *For all $i \in [m]$, sample a random k-sparse vector $\boldsymbol{a}_i \in \mathbb{F}_q^n$.*
- *For all $i \in [m], j \in [n]$, sample a random $(2k-1)$-sparse vector $\boldsymbol{a}_{i,j} \in \mathbb{F}_q^n$ conditioned on the jth coordinate of $\boldsymbol{a}_{i,j}$ being nonzero.*
- *For every $i \in [m]$, compute $b_i = \langle \boldsymbol{a}_i, \boldsymbol{s} \rangle + x_i + e_i$, where $e_i \leftarrow \mathsf{Ber}(\mathbb{F}_q, \epsilon)$.*
- *For every $i \in [m], j \in [n]$, compute $b_{i,j} = \langle \boldsymbol{a}_{i,j}, \boldsymbol{s} \rangle + x_i \cdot s_j + e_{i,j}$, where $e_{i,j} \leftarrow \mathsf{Ber}(\mathbb{F}_q, \epsilon)$.*
- *Output $\{(\mathbf{a}_i, b_i)\}_{i \in [m]}$ and $\{(\mathbf{a}_{i,j}, b_{i,j})\}_{i \in [m], j \in [n]}$.*

Similarly, we define $\mathcal{D}^{\mathsf{kdm}}_{\mathsf{rand},n,m,k,\epsilon,q}$ to be exactly the distribution above except that $b_i, b_{i,j}$ are chosen uniformly at random from $\mathbb{F}_q$ for all $i \in [m]$, $j \in [n]$.

We now show that the above KDM distribution is also computationally indistinguishable from random, assuming the sparse LPN assumption for the same parameters n, k, q, slightly lower noise rate $\epsilon/2$, and a polynomially larger m'. Note that the lemma requires $q > 2$ due to a technical detail, sketched in the technical overview. We give a full proof in the full version, and discuss a few workarounds for the case $q = 2$.

Lemma 4.4 (KDM security of Sparse LPN). *Let $\delta, q, n, m, k, \epsilon$ and $\boldsymbol{x}$ be as specified in Definition 4.3. For $q > 2$ and $k \in \omega(1) \cap o(\sqrt{n})$, assuming the (δ, q)-sLPN assumption holds (c.f. Assumption 4.1), the following distributions are computationally indistinguishable:*

$$\left\{ \mathcal{D}^{\mathsf{kdm}}_{\mathsf{sLPN},n,m,k,\epsilon,q}(\boldsymbol{x}) \right\}_{n \in \mathbb{N}} \approx_c \left\{ \mathcal{D}^{\mathsf{kdm}}_{\mathsf{rand},n,m,k,\epsilon,q} \right\}_{n \in \mathbb{N}}.$$

5 HSS Construction

In this section, we describe our main HSS construction from Sparse LPN (c.f. Assumption 4.1). Our scheme can handle $\log / \log\log$-degree polynomials containing a polynomial number of monomials, and achieve ϵ-correctness for an arbitrary inverse polynomial ϵ.

Function Class. Our HSS supports the function class $\mathcal{P}(\mathbb{F}_q, D, M)$ consists of multivariate polynomials over field $\mathbb{F}_q$ with degree D and number of monomials M. We do not put any constraint on the number of variables m of the polynomial, as long as it is $\mathsf{poly}(\lambda)$. In particular, every function $f \in \mathcal{P}(D, M)$ can be represented as a sum of monomials:

$$f(x_1, \cdots, x_m) = \sum_{\gamma \in [M]} c_\gamma \cdot M_\gamma(x_1, \cdots, x_m) \,,$$

where $c_\gamma \in \mathbb{F}_q$ is a coefficient and M_γ is a monomial of degree at most D over $\boldsymbol{x}$. Our HSS construction will require polynomials to be represented this way, which is without loss of generality since one can efficiently pre-process any polynomial to be of this form. Looking ahead, our scheme will achieve $D = O\left(\frac{\log \lambda}{\log \log \lambda}\right)$ and $M = \mathsf{poly}(\lambda)$.

In particular, this function class allows us to evaluate arbitrary arithmetic circuits (with fan-in 2) of depth $d = c \cdot \log \log \lambda$, for any $c < 1$. This is because every output of such a circuit can be computed by a degree-2^d polynomial in 2^d number of variables. Since the degree is $D = 2^d = \log^c \lambda = O\left(\frac{\log \lambda}{\log \log \lambda}\right)$, and the number of monomials is $M \le (2^d)^{2^d} < (\log^c \lambda)^{\log \lambda / \log \log \lambda} = \lambda^c$, we can see that this circuit can be supported by our HSS.

5.1 Scheme Description

Parameters for Sparse LPN. We will use below the Sparse LPN assumption over $\mathbb{F}_q$ with noise rate $n^{-\delta}$ for an arbitrary constant $\delta \in (0, 1)$, chosen such that the assumption holds, and dimension n which is a polynomial in the security parameter λ depending on D and M.

Ingredient: A Linear Secret Sharing Scheme. In our scheme, we require an arbitrary N-party, t-private LSSS scheme $\mathsf{LSS} = (\mathsf{Share}, \mathsf{Rec})$ supported over the field $\mathbb{F}_q$ of computation. For convenience, the reader may think of the Shamir secret sharing scheme (c.f. Definition 3.3). When $N > q$, note that the shares in the Shamir LSSS live in a suitable extension field $\mathbb{E}$ of $\mathbb{F}_q$ such that $|\mathbb{E}| > N$.

Scheme Overview. We now give a high-level overview of our multi-party HSS scheme, expanding on some points made in the technical overview. The full construction is presented in Fig. 2. In our scheme, HSS.Setup will choose a suitable LSS scheme with reconstruction over $\mathbb{F}_q$ and suitably set sLPN parameters n and k. To share an input $\boldsymbol{x} \in \mathbb{F}_q^m$, HSS.Share will generate encryptions $\mathsf{ct}_s(\boldsymbol{x})$, $\mathsf{ct}_s(\boldsymbol{x} \otimes \boldsymbol{s})$ drawn from the distribution $\mathcal{D}_{\mathsf{sLPN}, n, m, k, \epsilon, q}^{\mathsf{kdm}}(\boldsymbol{x})$ in Definition 4.3, along with secret sharings of $\boldsymbol{x}$ and $\boldsymbol{x} \otimes \boldsymbol{s}$. Namely:

– We sample a random k sparse coefficient vector $\boldsymbol{a}_i \in \mathbb{F}_q^n$ for every $i \in [m]$. Similarly, for every $i \in [m], j \in [n]$, we sample a random $2k - 1$ sparse vector $\boldsymbol{a}_{i,j} \in \mathbb{F}_q^n$ so that it is non-zero at the jth coordinate.

- To encrypt x_i for $i \in [m]$, we sample a random secret vector $\boldsymbol{s} \leftarrow \mathbb{F}_q^n$ and compute $b_i = \langle \boldsymbol{a}_i, \boldsymbol{s} \rangle + x_i + e_i$ for all $i \in [m]$, where $e_i \leftarrow \mathsf{Ber}(\mathbb{F}_q, \epsilon)$ is Bernoulli with noise rate $\epsilon = n^{-\delta}$.
- We also encrypt $x_i \cdot s_j$ for every $i \in [m], j \in [n]$ as follows. We compute $b_{i,j} = \langle \boldsymbol{a}_{i,j}, \boldsymbol{s} \rangle + x_i \cdot s_j + e_{i,j}$, where $e_{i,j} \leftarrow \mathsf{Ber}(\mathbb{F}_q, \epsilon)$ is Bernoulli with noise rate $\epsilon = n^{-\delta}$. Notice that together $\mathsf{ct_s}(\boldsymbol{x}) := \{(\boldsymbol{a}_i, b_i), \{(\boldsymbol{a}_{i,j}, b_{i,j})\}_{j \in [n]}\}_{i \in [m]}$ is exactly from the $\mathcal{D}_{\mathsf{sLPN}, n, m, k, \epsilon, q}^{\mathsf{kdm}}$ distribution.
- We secret share each x_i, for $i \in [m]$, and products $x_i \cdot s_j$, for $i \in [m], j \in [n]$, using our LSSS scheme. Let us denote the shares of each party P_ℓ with $\ell \in [N]$ by $[\![x_i]\!]_\ell$ and $[\![x_i \cdot s_j]\!]_\ell$, respectively.
- Each party P_ℓ's share $\mathsf{sh}_\ell(\boldsymbol{x})$ consists of $\left(\mathsf{ct_s}(\boldsymbol{x}), \{[\![x_i]\!]_\ell, \{[\![x_i \cdot s_j]\!]_\ell\}_{j \in [n]}\}_{i \in [m]} \right)$.

Homomorphic Evaluation. To execute HSS.Eval, each party P_ℓ (for $\ell \in [N]$) will perform homomorphic operations on its local shares. Intitially, the parties start with sharings of the form $[\![x_i]\!]_\ell, \{[\![x_i \cdot s_j]\!]_\ell\}_{j \in [n]}$. Relying additionally on the sparse LPN encodings, we will maintain the invariant that for every intermediate value of computation y, each party P_ℓ stores shares of y and $y \cdot s_j$ for $j \in [n]$. However, as a result of the computation each share can be corrupted by a low-probablity noise over $\mathbb{F}_q$. We will denote these shares using a special notation $\langle\!\langle \alpha \rangle\!\rangle_\ell$ for the intermediate variable α. To be precise $\langle\!\langle \alpha \rangle\!\rangle_\ell = [\![\alpha + e_\alpha]\!]_\ell$ where e_α is a low-probability noise.

The Eval operations will involve both the linear shares and the noisy ciphertext $\mathsf{ct}_x(\boldsymbol{s})$, leading to a build-up of noise as each party continue its local computation. The homomorphic operations are performed as follows:

- To add together two intermediate values y and z, each party P_ℓ can just add its local noisy shares:

$$\langle\!\langle y + z \rangle\!\rangle_\ell := \langle\!\langle y \rangle\!\rangle_\ell + \langle\!\langle z \rangle\!\rangle_\ell, \quad \langle\!\langle (y + z) \cdot s_j \rangle\!\rangle_\ell := \langle\!\langle y \cdot s_j \rangle\!\rangle_\ell + \langle\!\langle z \cdot s_j \rangle\!\rangle_\ell \ \forall j \in [n].$$

This operation increases the noise rate only by a factor of 2. Therefore, this extends straightforwardly to handle arbitrary linear combinations of a polynomial number of intermediate values assuming that the initial noise rate is small enough.

- To multiply an intermediate value y with an input x_i, each party P_ℓ will utilize its encryptions $(\boldsymbol{a}_i, b_i), \{(\boldsymbol{a}_{i,j}, b_{i,j})\}_{j \in [n]}$ along with its noisy shares of y to compute:

$$\langle\!\langle x_i \cdot y \rangle\!\rangle_\ell := b_i \cdot \langle\!\langle y \rangle\!\rangle_\ell - \sum_{\sigma \in \mathsf{Supp}(\boldsymbol{a}_i)} a_{i,\sigma} \cdot \langle\!\langle y \cdot s_\sigma \rangle\!\rangle_\ell,$$

$$\langle\!\langle (x_i \cdot y) \cdot s_j \rangle\!\rangle_\ell := b_{i,j} \cdot \langle\!\langle y \cdot s_j \rangle\!\rangle_\ell - \sum_{\sigma \in \mathsf{Supp}(\boldsymbol{a}_{i,j})} a_{i,j,\sigma} \cdot \langle\!\langle y \cdot s_\sigma \rangle\!\rangle_\ell \ \ \forall j \in [n].$$

$$(4)$$

The reason why the above holds is the following. Recall that $\mathsf{Supp}(\boldsymbol{a})$ denotes the non-zero coordinates of $\boldsymbol{a}$. Without any noise, the above computation gives the right result, since the equation

$$b_i \approx \langle \boldsymbol{a}_i, \boldsymbol{s} \rangle + x_i = \sum_{\sigma \in \mathsf{Supp}(\boldsymbol{a}_i)} a_{i,\sigma} \cdot s_\sigma + x_i,$$

together with the linearity of the shares, imply that

$$b_i \cdot \langle\!\langle y \rangle\!\rangle_\ell - \sum_\sigma a_{i,\sigma} \cdot \langle\!\langle y \cdot s_\sigma \rangle\!\rangle_\ell \approx \langle\!\langle x_i \cdot y \rangle\!\rangle_\ell .$$

In other words, as long as the potentially noisy shares $\langle\!\langle y \rangle\!\rangle_\ell, \{\langle\!\langle y \cdot s_j \rangle\!\rangle_\ell\}_{j \in \mathsf{Supp}(\boldsymbol{a}_i)}$ were noise-free and the sample b_i was also noise free, then the share produced by $\langle\!\langle\!\langle (x_i \cdot y) \rangle\!\rangle\!\rangle_\ell$ in Eq. 4 will be noise free. A similar argument applies for correctness of computing $\langle\!\langle\!\langle (x_i \cdot y) \cdot s_j \rangle\!\rangle\!\rangle_\ell$.

The presence of noise affects the correctness as follows. Because both $\boldsymbol{a}_i$ and $\boldsymbol{a}_{i,j}$ have sparsity at most $2k - 1$, at every multiplication step the error probability grows by a factor at most $O(k)$. On careful analysis, this growth at each level is just right to set parameters so that we can handle the desired function class.

Using the homomorphic operations described above, we can evaluate any multivariate polynomial $f \in \mathcal{P}(D, M)$, written as $f(x_1, \ldots, x_m) = \sum_{S \in \Lambda} c_S \cdot x_S$, by first locally evaluating each monomial x_S, then locally taking a linear combination of the results. Finally, we describe the reconstruction algorithm HSS.Rec. At the end of the local computations, each party P_ℓ will hold a noisy share $\langle\!\langle y \rangle\!\rangle_\ell$ of the output $y = f(\boldsymbol{x})$. Since these are LSS shares, we may reconstruct a noisy version of y by applying the reconstruction algorithm of LSS.

5.2 Security Analysis

Noise growth analysis. We now analyze the noise growth of our homomorphic operations. Here, we will write explicit noise terms (colored in red) for our noisy shares:

$$\langle\!\langle y \rangle\!\rangle_\ell = [\![y + e_y]\!]_\ell, \quad \langle\!\langle y \cdot s_j \rangle\!\rangle_\ell = [\![y \cdot s_j + e_{y,j}]\!]_\ell \quad \forall j \in [n],$$

We start by considering party ℓ's homomorphic multiplication of an input x_i, shared as $\mathsf{sh}_\ell(x_i)$, with an intermediate value y, shared as $\langle\!\langle y \rangle\!\rangle_\ell, \{\langle\!\langle y \cdot s_j \rangle\!\rangle_\ell\}_{\ell \in [N]}$. Recalling that

$$b_i = \langle \boldsymbol{a}_i, \boldsymbol{s} \rangle + x_i + e_i = \sum_{\sigma \in \mathsf{Supp}(\boldsymbol{a}_i)} a_{i,\sigma} \cdot s_\sigma + x_i + e_i,$$

HSS from Sparse LPN

Parameters. Number of parties N, threshold t, field $\mathbb{F}_q$, a N-party, (t, t')-private LSSS scheme LSS over $\mathbb{F}_q$, the function class $\mathcal{P}(D, M)$, sLPN parameters (k, n, δ) chosen according to Remark 5.1.

- Share$(\boldsymbol{x}) \to \{\mathsf{sh}_\ell(\boldsymbol{x})\}_{\ell \in [N]}$. On input $\boldsymbol{x} \in \mathbb{F}_q^m$, sample from the KDM sparse LPN distribution (with secret vector $\boldsymbol{s} \in \mathbb{F}_q^n$)

$$\{\mathsf{ct}_s(\boldsymbol{x}), \mathsf{ct}_s(\boldsymbol{x} \otimes \boldsymbol{s})\} := \Big\{(\boldsymbol{a}_i, b_i), \{(\boldsymbol{a}_{i,j}, b_{i,j})\}_{j \in [n]}\Big\}_{i \in [m]} \leftarrow \mathcal{D}_{\mathsf{sLPN}, n, m, k, \delta, q}^{\mathsf{kdm}}(\boldsymbol{x}).$$

Next, compute secret sharings (for all $i \in [m], j \in [n]$):

$$\mathsf{LSS.Share}(x_i) \to \Big\{[\![x_i]\!]_\ell\Big\}_{\ell \in [N]}, \quad \mathsf{LSS.Share}(x_i \cdot s_j) \to \Big\{[\![x_i \cdot s_j]\!]_\ell\Big\}_{\ell \in [N]}.$$

Return $\mathsf{sh}_\ell(\boldsymbol{x}) := \left(\mathsf{ct}_s(\boldsymbol{x}), \mathsf{ct}_s(\boldsymbol{x} \otimes \boldsymbol{s}), \Big\{[\![x_i]\!]_\ell, \{[\![x_i \cdot s_j]\!]_\ell\}_{j \in [n]}\Big\}_{i \in [m]} \right)$.

- Eval$(\ell, P, \mathsf{sh}_\ell(\boldsymbol{x})) \to \mathsf{osh}_{P,\ell}$. Given a party index $\ell \in [N]$, a m-variate polynomial $P \in \mathcal{P}(D, M)$, and the corresponding share $\mathsf{sh}_\ell(\boldsymbol{x})$, we first evaluate each monomial of P, then add these monomials together. The party P_ℓ stores, for each intermediate value z during the computation, a noisy share $\{\!\{z\}\!\}_\ell := \left(\langle\!\langle z \rangle\!\rangle_\ell, \{\langle\!\langle z \cdot s_j \rangle\!\rangle_\ell\}_{j \in [n]} \right)$ defined as follows:
  - If $z = x_i$ for some $i \in [m]$, set $\langle\!\langle z \rangle\!\rangle_\ell := [\![x_i]\!]_\ell$, $\langle\!\langle z \cdot s_j \rangle\!\rangle_\ell = [\![x_i \cdot s_j]\!]_\ell$ for all $j \in [n]$.
  - If $z = y \cdot x_i$, where y is an intermediate value and x_i is an input, parse $\{\!\{y\}\!\}_\ell$ as above, then compute

$$\langle\!\langle z \rangle\!\rangle_\ell := b_i \cdot \langle\!\langle y \rangle\!\rangle_\ell - \sum_{\sigma \in \mathsf{Supp}(\boldsymbol{a}_i)} a_{i,\sigma} \cdot \langle\!\langle y \cdot s_\sigma \rangle\!\rangle_\ell,$$

$$\langle\!\langle z \cdot s_j \rangle\!\rangle_\ell := b_{i,j} \cdot \langle\!\langle y \rangle\!\rangle_\ell - \sum_{\sigma \in \mathsf{Supp}(\boldsymbol{a}_{i,j})} a_{i,j,\sigma} \cdot \langle\!\langle y \cdot s_\sigma \rangle\!\rangle_\ell \quad \text{for all } j \in [n].$$

  - If $z = \sum_\gamma c_\gamma \cdot y_\gamma$ where c_γ are coefficients and y_γ are intermediate values, parse $\{\!\{y_\gamma\}\!\}_\ell$ as above, then compute

$$\langle\!\langle z \rangle\!\rangle_\ell := \sum_\gamma c_\gamma \cdot \langle\!\langle y_\gamma \rangle\!\rangle_\ell, \quad \langle\!\langle z \cdot s_j \rangle\!\rangle_\ell := \sum_\gamma c_\gamma \cdot \langle\!\langle y_\gamma \cdot s_j \rangle\!\rangle_\ell \quad \text{for all } j \in [n].$$

Once party P_ℓ has computed the noisy share $\{\!\{z\}\!\}_\ell$ for the final output $P(\boldsymbol{x})$, return $\mathsf{osh}_{P,\ell} := \langle\!\langle z \rangle\!\rangle_\ell$.

- Rec$(I, \{\mathsf{osh}_\ell\}_{\ell \in I}) \to z$. Given a subset of parties $I \subset [N]$ and corresponding output shares $\{\mathsf{osh}_\ell\}_{\ell \in I}$, return $z \leftarrow \mathsf{LSS.Rec}(I, \{\mathsf{osh}_\ell\}_{\ell \in I})$.

Fig. 2. HSS from Sparse LPN

where we denote the noise term in blue (which has a fixed noise rate $O(n^{-\delta})$), we can compute the following:

$$b_i \cdot [\![y + e_y]\!]_\ell - \sum_{\sigma \in \mathsf{Supp}(a_i)} a_{i,\sigma} \cdot [\![y \cdot s_\sigma + e_{y,\sigma}]\!]_\ell$$

$$= \left[\!\!\left[\left(\sum_{a_{i,\sigma} \neq 0} a_{i,\sigma} \cdot s_\sigma + x_i + e_i \right) \cdot y + b_i \cdot e_y - \left(\sum_{a_{i,\sigma} \neq 0} a_{i,\sigma} \cdot s_\sigma \right) \cdot y - \sum_{a_{i,\sigma} \neq 0} a_{i,\sigma} \cdot e_{y,\sigma} \right]\!\!\right]_\ell$$

$$= [\![x_i \cdot y + e_{x_i \cdot y}]\!]_\ell, \quad \text{where} \quad e_{x_i \cdot y} = y \cdot e_i + b_i \cdot e_y - \sum_{a_{i,\sigma} \neq 0} a_{i,\sigma} \cdot e_{y,\sigma}.$$

Similarly, we can compute the noise growth for the noisy shares $\langle\!\langle x_i \cdot y \cdot s_j \rangle\!\rangle_\ell$ for all $j \in [n]$, keeping in mind that $b_{i,j} = \sum_{\sigma \in \mathsf{Supp}(a_{i,j})} a_{i,j,\sigma} \cdot s_\sigma + x_i \cdot s_j + e_{i,j}$:

$$b_{i,j} \cdot [\![y + e_y]\!]_\ell - \sum_{\sigma \in \mathsf{Supp}(a_{i,j})} a_{i,j,\sigma} \cdot [\![y \cdot s_j + e_{y,\sigma}]\!]_\ell$$

$$= \left[\!\!\left[\left(\sum_{a_{i,j,\sigma} \neq 0} a_{i,j,\sigma} \cdot s_\sigma + x_i \cdot s_j + e_{i,j} \right) \cdot y + b_{i,j} \cdot e_y - \left(\sum_{a_{i,j,\sigma} \neq 0} a_{i,j,\sigma} \cdot s_\sigma \right) \cdot y - \sum_{a_{i,j,\sigma} \neq 0} a_{i,j,\sigma} \cdot e_{y,\sigma} \right]\!\!\right]_\ell$$

$$= \left[\!\!\left[x_i \cdot y \cdot s_j + e_{x_i \cdot y \cdot j} \right]\!\!\right]_\ell, \quad \text{where} \quad e_{x_i \cdot y \cdot j} = y \cdot e_{i,j} + b_{i,j} \cdot e_y - \sum_{a_{i,j,\sigma} \neq 0} a_{i,j,\sigma} \cdot e_{y,\sigma}.$$

We observe that after multiplication, the noisy shares $\langle\!\langle x_i \cdot y \rangle\!\rangle$ and $\langle\!\langle x_i \cdot y \cdot s_j \rangle\!\rangle$ both contain one new noise term, and due to the k-sparsity of $\boldsymbol{a}_i$ and $(2k - 1)$-sparsity of $\boldsymbol{a}_{i,j}$, aggregate at most $2k$ prior noises. Therefore, the rate of noise increase by a factor of at most $2k + 1$. As we started out with noise level $n^{-\delta}$ for some arbitrary $\delta \in (0, 1)$, after D steps the noise level is at most $(2k + 1)^D n^{-\delta}$.

Next, we consider the noise growth for homomorphic linear combination. Here, the error growth is much less, allowing us to aggregate M error terms for arbitrary $M = \mathsf{poly}(\lambda)$. Namely, for any coefficients $c_\gamma \in \mathbb{F}_q$ and any intermediate noisy shares $\{y_\gamma\}_\ell$ with $\gamma \in [M]$, we have:

$$\sum_{\gamma=1}^{M} c_\gamma \cdot [\![y_\gamma + e_{y_\gamma}]\!]_\ell = \left[\!\!\left[\sum_{\gamma=1}^{M} c_\gamma \cdot y_\gamma + \sum_{\gamma=1}^{M} c_\gamma \cdot e_{y_\gamma} \right]\!\!\right]_\ell$$

$$\sum_{\gamma=1}^{M} c_\gamma \cdot [\![y_\gamma \cdot s_j + e_{y_\gamma,j}]\!]_\ell = \left[\!\!\left[\sum_{\gamma=1}^{M} c_\gamma \cdot y_\gamma \cdot s_j + \sum_{\gamma=1}^{M} c_\gamma \cdot e_{y_\gamma,j} \right]\!\!\right]_\ell \quad \forall j \in [n].$$

The noise level for the final share grows by a factor of M.

Remark 5.1 (Parameter Selection for HSS). For a given program class $\mathcal{P}(\mathbb{F}_q, D, M)$, given any constant $\delta \in (0, 1)$ for which the Sparse LPN assumption holds, and given desired correctness error $\epsilon \in (0, 1)$, we need to choose k and n so that

$$k = \omega(1) \quad \text{and} \quad (2k + 1)^D \cdot M \cdot n^{-\delta} < \epsilon. \tag{5}$$

When $D = O(\log \lambda / \log \log \lambda)$, $M = \mathsf{poly}(\lambda)$, and $\epsilon = 1/\mathsf{poly}(\lambda)$, we may choose $k = \log^c \lambda$ for a sufficiently small constant $c > 0$, and $n = \lambda^{c'}$ for a sufficiently large constant $c' > 0$ for the above conditions to hold.

Remark 5.2 (Efficiency). Our HSS input share size $|\mathsf{sh}_\ell(\boldsymbol{x})|$, for $\boldsymbol{x} \in \mathbb{F}_q^m$, is equal to $m(n+1)+mn(n+1)+(m+mn)|\mathsf{LSS}| = m(n+1)((n+1)+|\mathsf{LSS}|)$, where $|\mathsf{LSS}|$ is the share size of the linear secret sharing scheme. In particular, by Remark 5.1 this share size depends on program class $\mathcal{P}(D, M)$ supported (since n depends on D and M). In contrast, our HSS output share is just an LSS share. We also note that when LSS is the Shamir secret sharing scheme, the share size $|\mathsf{LSS}|$ is e field elements, where $e \in \mathbb{N}$ is the smallest integer such that $t < q^e$.

For computation, our HSS evaluation only has an overhead of $O(nk|\mathsf{LSS}|)$, since we need to compute on $n+1$ shares $\langle\!\langle y \rangle\!\rangle$, $\{\langle\!\langle y \cdot s_j \rangle\!\rangle\}_{j \in [n]}$, and during multiplication we suffer another $O(k)$ overhead in computing a linear combination of $(k+1)$ terms.

Remark 5.3 (On concrete parameter settings). While Sparse LPN has been extensively studied in the asymptotic setting (see our discussion in Sect. 1.1), there have been little work on determining concrete parameters for the assumption. Prior works such as [6,54] proposed parameters for Sparse LPN in the constant noise regime, while our noise rate is smaller, namely $1/n^\delta$ for an arbitrary $0 < \delta < 1$. Thus, we leave as interesting open questions the task of figuring out concrete parameters for Sparse LPN in our noise regime, and optimizing our HSS to be more efficient.

Remark 5.4 (Constant overhead for constant-degree polynomials). In fact, our HSS construction can be made even more efficient than Remark 5.2 for polynomials of *constant* degree D, where we may achieve $O(k^D \cdot M)$ computation overhead for polynomials with M monomials. If we were to set $k = O(1)$, then the overhead is constant in M. This follows from a more conservative computation of only the necessary values required to evaluate the polynomial. Namely, each homomorphic multiplication of an intermediate value y with an input x_i requires only $(k+1)$ secret shares $\{[\![ys_\sigma]\!]\}_{\sigma \in \mathsf{Supp}(a)}$. As a consequence, each degree D monomial computation will touch at most $O(k^D)$ sparse LPN samples and secret shares and involve roughly these many binary additions and multiplications.

From our noise growth analysis above and the subsequent Remark 5.1 on parameter selection, we can conclude the correctness of our HSS construction.

Lemma 5.5 (Correctness of HSS). *Assume the Sparse LPN assumption holds with constant $\delta \in (0,1)$. For any $\epsilon = 1/\mathsf{poly}(\lambda)$, any $D = O(\log\lambda/\log\log\lambda)$, and any $M = \mathsf{poly}(\lambda)$, for parameters n and k chosen according to Remark 5.1, the resulting HSS construction in Fig. 2 is correct except with probability ϵ.*

Remark 5.6 (Decreasing the correctness error). We note that our correctness error can be decreased to $\mathsf{negl}(\lambda)$, at the cost of larger share sizes, more computation, and making reconstruction non-additive. This is done by giving out some $\kappa = \omega(1)$ copies of the same HSS sharings, each with fresh randomness, doing HSS evaluations of the same function for each of these sharings, then taking majority.

We will now show that our HSS scheme is secure. Again, most of the heavy lifting is done in Lemma 4.4, from which our proof follows almost immediately.

Lemma 5.7 (Security of HSS). *Assume the Sparse LPN assumption holds with constant $\delta \in (0,1)$. For any finite field $\mathbb{F}_q$, any number of parties $N \geq 2$, any threshold $t < N$, any $D = O(\log \lambda / \log \log \lambda)$, and any $M = \text{poly}(\lambda)$, with parameters chosen as in Remark 5.1, the N-party HSS construction in Fig. 2 for the class $\mathcal{P}(\mathbb{F}_q, D, M)$ satisfies HSS security with threshold t.*

Proof. Recall that for security of HSS, we need to show that for any subset $I \subset [N]$ of size $|I| \leq t$ and any vectors $\boldsymbol{x}, \boldsymbol{x}' \in \mathbb{F}_q^m$, the shares $\{\text{sh}_\ell(\boldsymbol{x})\}_{\ell \in I}$ and $\{\text{sh}_\ell(\boldsymbol{x}')\}_{\ell \in I}$ are computationally indistinguishable. By construction of HSS.Share, these shares consist of two parts, the KDM ciphertexts $\{\text{ct}_s(\boldsymbol{x}), \text{ct}_s(\boldsymbol{x} \otimes \boldsymbol{s})\}$ versus $\{\text{ct}_s(\boldsymbol{x}'), \text{ct}_s(\boldsymbol{x}' \otimes \boldsymbol{s})\}$, along with the LSS shares $\{[\![\boldsymbol{x}]\!]_\ell, [\![\boldsymbol{x} \otimes \boldsymbol{s}]\!]\}_{\ell \in I}$ versus $\{[\![\boldsymbol{x}']\!]_\ell, [\![\boldsymbol{x}' \otimes \boldsymbol{s}]\!]\}_{\ell \in I}$. The former is indistinguishable due to Lemma 4.4 (for $q = 2$, we may take any of the approaches, detailed in the full version, to conclude Lemma 4.4), and the latter is indistinguishable due to t-privacy of LSS. $\qquad\square$

Putting everything together, we get our HSS with desired functionality.

Theorem 5.8 (Multi-party HSS). *Assume the Sparse LPN assumption (c.f. Assumption 4.1) holds. For any number of parties $N \geq 2$, privacy threshold $t < N$, finite field $\mathbb{F}_q$, and error probability $\epsilon = 1/\text{poly}(\lambda)$, there is a N-party, t-private HSS with correctness error ϵ for the function class $\mathcal{P}(\mathbb{F}_q, D, M)$ with degree $D = O(\log \lambda / \log \log \lambda)$ and number of monomials $M = \text{poly}(\lambda)$.*

In the full version, we will present the packed HSS variant that allows us to conclude Theorem 1.3.

6 Sublinear MPC

In this section, we leverage our HSS in Sect. 5 to build a sublinear MPC, with per-party communication dominated by the term $O(S/\log \log S)$, for layered Boolean circuits of size S.[10] Our MPC construction can support an arbitrary $N = \text{poly}(\lambda)$ parties with up to $(N-1)$-out-of-N corruptions.

6.1 Protocol Description

Layered Boolean Circuits. Our MPC construction achieves sublinear communication for the class of *layered Boolean circuits*. A Boolean circuit $C : \{0,1\}^n \to \{0,1\}^m$ is *layered* if its nodes can be partitioned into $D = \text{depth}(C)$ layers $(L_1, \ldots, L_D)$ such that any edge (u, v) of C satisfies $u \in L_i$ and $v \in L_{i+1}$ for some $i \leq D - 1$. The width $\text{width}(C)$ of a layered circuit C is defined to be

---

[10] More generally, our construction can generalize to any constant-size field. For simplicity, we only cover the Boolean case.

the maximum number of non-output gates contained in any single layer. In our MPC, we assume that the parties input are $x_1, \ldots, x_N$, concatenated into $x := x_1 \| x_2 \| \ldots \| x_N$. Then x is the overall input to the circuit C, and at the end of the MPC, each party should get $C(x)$.

Remark 6.1 (Circuit Decomposition). From an existing result in [19], for any $d \in \mathbb{N}$, we have a decomposition of C into $L = \lceil D/d \rceil$ *special layers* $(L_1^\star, \ldots, L_L^\star)$ such that: (1) two consecutive layers are of distance at most $2d$ from each other, and (2) letting w_i be the width of layer L_i for all $i \in [L]$, we have $\sum_{i=1}^{L} w_i \leq S/d$. We denote by $C_{i,j}$ the circuit computing the jth output of layer L_{i+1} from the inputs of layer L_i, for all $i \in [L-1], j \in [w_{i+1}]$.

For simplicity, in our MPC construction we will assume that all the inputs to C are in the first layer, and all outputs are in the last layer. This is without loss of generality, as all intermediate values in our construction are represented in the same form; thus, we can "delay" an input until it is needed in an intermediate layer, and similarly delay an output till the end.

Protocol Description. Following the main ideas discussed in Sect. 2.3, we now give our MPC construction in Figs. 3 and 4. In our construction, we assume that each party has access to a broadcast channel. This is simply for ease of presentation, since in the semi-honest model we can simulate such a broadcast channel by letting parties pass messages in a cyclic or star-like fashion. In the full version, we will prove that our MPC is secure, with desired sublinear per-party communication as in Theorem 1.2.

Remark 6.2 (Removing dependence on width). We note that our MPC incurs a communication cost proportional to the circuit width W, due to the use of the public vectors $\{a_{i_2,i_3}\}_{i_2 \in [W], i_3 \in [\kappa]}$. We suggest two main approaches to reduce/eliminate the additive term proportional to the width.

- If the number of parties are large, since this is a semi-honest protocol, each party can be required to output $\frac{W \cdot \kappa}{N}$ such vectors, as opposed to running the MPC for computing $W \cdot \kappa$ such vectors. In this case this additive term can be replaced by a term that grows like $W \cdot \text{poly}(\log N, \log \lambda)/N$. This per party communication becomes sublinear for big enough N.
- Since these vectors are chosen randomly (among all k_{Enc}-sparse vectors), this term can be removed altogether if we are willing to assume any of the following: 1) a uniform random string, 2) a random oracle, or 3) an *explicit* family of k_{Enc}-sparse matrices for which the sparse LPN assumption holds. Any of these assumptions allow the parties to have the description of a_{i_2,i_3} without any further communication.

Sublinear MPC construction, part 1

Local Inputs. Each party P_ℓ, for $\ell \in [N]$, has input $\boldsymbol{x}_\ell$, concatenated into $\boldsymbol{x} = \boldsymbol{x}_1 \| \ldots \| \boldsymbol{x}_\ell$.

Circuit. A layered Boolean circuit $\mathsf{C} : \{0,1\}^n \to \{0,1\}^m$ of size S, depth D and width W, decomposed as in Remark 6.1. In particular, we choose depth parameter $d = 0.1 \cdot \log \log S$. This gives special layers $(\mathsf{L}_1^\star, \ldots, \mathsf{L}_L^\star)$, where $L = D/d$, of widths $w_1, \ldots, w_L$ respectively.

Output. The evaluation $\boldsymbol{y} = \mathsf{C}(\boldsymbol{x})$, delivered to each party.

Ingredients.
- Number of repetitions κ, set to be an arbitrary super-constant $\omega(1)$.
- Our encryption scheme $(\mathsf{Enc}, \mathsf{Dec})$ from Sparse LPN, described in Equation 3, with noise rate $\epsilon_{\mathsf{Enc}} = 1/(2N\lambda)$. We denote the encryption parameters as follows: the dimension is n_{Enc} and the sparsity is k_{Enc}.
- Our N-party, $(N-1)$-secure HSS in Figure 2, with correctness error $\epsilon_{\mathsf{HSS}} = 1/(2\lambda)$, for the class of Boolean circuits of depth $d' = (0.9 \cdot \log \log S)$ and using the additive secret sharing scheme AdSS. We denote the HSS parameters as follows: the dimension is n_{HSS} and the sparsity is k_{HSS}.
- A general semi-honest MPC protocol, secure against $(N-1)$-out-of-N corruptions, that can evaluate a Boolean circuit C of size S with communication $O(N \cdot S)$ per party. Such a protocol can be based on the existence of oblivious transfer [41].

Protocol Execution:

1. Perform a MPC for the circuit $\mathsf{GenVec} \to \{\boldsymbol{a}_{i_2,i_3}\}_{i_2 \in [W], i_3 \in [\kappa]}$, described as follows:

   For all $i_2 \in [W]$, $i_3 \in [\kappa]$, sample a random k_{Enc}-sparse vector $\boldsymbol{a}_{i_2,i_3} \leftarrow \mathbb{F}_2^{n_{\mathsf{Enc}}}$. Return $\{\boldsymbol{a}_{i_2,i_3}\}_{i_2 \in [W], i_3 \in [\kappa]}$ to all parties.

Fig. 3. Semi-honest sublinear MPC from OTs and Sparse LPN

Sublinear MPC construction, part 2

2. Perform a MPC for the circuit GenKeyShares $\rightarrow$ $\left\{ [\![k_{i_1}]\!]_{\ell,i_3}, \mathsf{sh}_{i_1,i_3,\ell} \right\}_{i_1 \in [L], i_3 \in [\kappa], \ell \in [N]}$, described as follows:

For all $i_1 \in [0, L-1]$:
   - Sample a random key $k_{i_1} \leftarrow \mathbb{F}_2^{n_{\mathsf{Enc}}}$.
   - For each $i_3 \in [\kappa]$, compute $\{[\![k_{i_1}]\!]_{\ell,i_3}\}_{\ell \in [N]} \leftarrow \mathsf{AdSS.Share}(k_{i_1})$, each time with fresh randomness.
   - For each $i_3 \in [\kappa]$, compute $\{\mathsf{sh}_{i_1,i_3,\ell}\}_{\ell \in [N]} \leftarrow \mathsf{HSS.Share}(k_{i_1})$ for all $i_3 \in [\kappa]$, each time with fresh randomness.

For each $\ell \in [N]$, return $\{[\![k_{i_1}]\!]_{\ell,i_3}, \mathsf{sh}_{i_1,i_3,\ell}\}_{i_1 \in [L], i_3 \in [\kappa]}$ to party P_ℓ.

3. For each $\ell \in [N]$, party P_ℓ secret-shares its input x_ℓ for κ times $\{[\![\mathsf{st}_{1,i_2,\ell}]\!]_{\ell',i_3}\}_{\ell' \in [N], i_2 \in [n], i_3 \in [\kappa]} \leftarrow \mathsf{AdSS.Share}(x_\ell)$, and sends $\{[\![\mathsf{st}_{1,i_2,\ell}]\!]_{\ell',i_3}\}_{i_2 \in [n], i_3 \in [\kappa]}$ to each party $P_{\ell'}$. Then P_ℓ concatenate input shares coming from all other parties to get $\{[\![\mathsf{st}_{1,i_2}]\!]_{\ell,i_3}\}_{i_2 \in [n], i_3 \in [\kappa]}$.

4. For each layer $i_1 \in [L-1]$ and party index $\ell \in [N]$:
   (a) For each $i_2 \in [w_{i_1}]$, $i_3 \in [\kappa]$, party P_ℓ samples $e_{i_1,i_2,i_3,\ell} \leftarrow \mathsf{Ber}(\mathbb{F}_2, \epsilon_{\mathsf{Enc}})$ and broadcasts its partial ciphertext $\mathsf{ct}_{i_1,i_2,i_3,\ell} = \langle a_{i_2,i_3}, [\![k_{i_1}]\!]_{\ell,i_3} \rangle + [\![\mathsf{st}_{i_1,i_2}]\!]_{\ell,i_3} + e_{i_1,i_2,i_3,\ell}$.
   (b) Party P_ℓ receives partial ciphertexts $\mathsf{ct}_{i_1,i_2,i_3,\ell'}$ from all other parties $P_{\ell'}$ and reconstructs $\mathsf{ct}_{i_1,i_2,i_3} \leftarrow \mathsf{AdSS.Rec}(\{\mathsf{ct}_{i_1,i_2,i_3,\ell}\}_{\ell \in [N]})$.
   (c) For each $i_2' \in [w_{i_1+1}]$, $i_3 \in [\kappa]$, P_ℓ computes $\mathsf{HSS.Eval}(\ell, \mathsf{ComputeLayer}_{i_1,i_2'}, \mathsf{sh}_{i_1,i_3,\ell})$ where $\mathsf{ComputeLayer}_{i_1,i_2'}$ is the following function:
      - Use input k_{i_1} to decrypt $\mathsf{st}_{i_1,i_2,i_3'} \leftarrow \mathsf{Dec}(k_{i_1}, \mathsf{ct}_{i_1,i_2,i_3'})$ for all $i_3' \in [\kappa]$.
      - Compute majority $\mathsf{st}_{i_1,i_2} \leftarrow \mathsf{Majority}(\{\mathsf{st}_{i_1,i_2,i_3'}\}_{i_3' \in [\kappa]})$.
      - Then compute $\mathsf{st}_{i_1+1,i_2'} \leftarrow C_{i_1,i_2'}(\{\mathsf{st}_{i_1,i_2}\}_{i_2 \in [w_{i_1}]})$, where $C_{i_1,i_2'}$ is the circuit computing the $(i_2')^{th}$ output of the $(i_1+1)^{th}$ layer.
   (d) At this point, each party P_ℓ has shares for the next layer $\{[\![\mathsf{st}_{i_1+1,i_2}]\!]_{\ell,i_3}\}_{i_2 \in [w_{i_1+1}], i_3 \in [\kappa]}$.

5. Perform a final MPC for the following circuit $\mathsf{FinalRec} \rightarrow y$:
   - For each $i_2 \in [m]$, $i_3 \in [\kappa]$, compute $y_{i_2,i_3} \leftarrow \mathsf{AdSS.Rec}(\{[\![\mathsf{st}_{L,i_2}]\!]_{\ell,i_3}\}_{\ell \in [N]})$.
   - For each $i_2 \in [m]$, compute majority $y_{i_2} \leftarrow \mathsf{Majority}(\{\mathsf{osh}_{i_2,i_3}\}_{i_3 \in [\kappa]})$.
   - Return $\{y_{i_2}\}_{i_2 \in [m]}$ to each party.

Fig. 4. Sublinear MPC construction, continued

Acknowledgments. We thank the anonymous Crypto reviewers for helpful comments and suggestions and the authors of [14] for sharing an early version of their manuscript and answering our questions. Y. Ishai was supported in part by ERC Project NTSC (742754), BSF grant 2018393, and ISF grant 2774/20. A. Jain is supported in part by the Google Research Scholar Award and through various gifts from CYLAB, CMU. H. Lin was supported by NSF grants CNS-1936825 (CAREER), CNS-2026774, a JP Morgan AI Research Award, a Cisco Research Award, and a Simons Collaboration on the Theory of Algorithmic Fairness.

References

1. Abram, D., Damgård, I., Orlandi, C., Scholl, P.: An algebraic framework for silent preprocessing with trustless setup and active security. In: Dodis, Y., Shrimpton, T. (eds.) CRYPTO. Lecture Notes in Computer Science, vol. 13510, pp. 421–452. Springer (2022). https://doi.org/10.1007/978-3-031-15985-5_15
2. Alekhnovich, M.: More on average case vs approximation complexity. In: 44th FOCS, pp. 298–307. IEEE Computer Society Press (Oct 2003)
3. Allen, S.R., O'Donnell, R., Witmer, D.: How to refute a random CSP. In: Guruswami, V. (ed.) 56th FOCS, pp. 689–708. IEEE Computer Society Press (Oct 2015)
4. Applebaum, B., Barak, B., Wigderson, A.: Public-key cryptography from different assumptions. In: Schulman, L.J. (ed.) 42nd ACM STOC, pp. 171–180. ACM Press (Jun 2010)
5. Applebaum, B., Cash, D., Peikert, C., Sahai, A.: Fast cryptographic primitives and circular-secure encryption based on hard learning problems. In: Halevi, S. (ed.) CRYPTO 2009. LNCS, vol. 5677, pp. 595–618. Springer, Heidelberg (2009). https://doi.org/10.1007/978-3-642-03356-8_35
6. Applebaum, B., Damgård, I., Ishai, Y., Nielsen, M., Zichron, L.: Secure arithmetic computation with constant computational overhead. In: Katz, J., Shacham, H. (eds.) CRYPTO 2017. LNCS, vol. 10401, pp. 223–254. Springer, Cham (2017). https://doi.org/10.1007/978-3-319-63688-7_8
7. Applebaum, B., Ishai, Y., Kushilevitz, E.: On Pseudorandom Generators with Linear Stretch in NC^0. In: Díaz, J., Jansen, K., Rolim, J.D.P., Zwick, U. (eds.) APPROX/RANDOM -2006. LNCS, vol. 4110, pp. 260–271. Springer, Heidelberg (2006). https://doi.org/10.1007/11830924_25
8. Applebaum, B., Ishai, Y., Kushilevitz, E.: On pseudorandom generators with linear stretch in nc^0. Comput. Complex. **17**(1), 38–69 (2008). https://doi.org/10.1007/s00037-007-0237-6
9. Applebaum, B., Kachlon, E.: Sampling graphs without forbidden subgraphs and unbalanced expanders with negligible error. In: Zuckerman, D. (ed.) 60th FOCS, pp. 171–179. IEEE Computer Society Press (Nov 2019)
10. Applebaum, B., Lovett, S.: Algebraic attacks against random local functions and their countermeasures. In: Wichs, D., Mansour, Y. (eds.) 48th ACM STOC, pp. 1087–1100. ACM Press (Jun 2016)
11. Asharov, G., Jain, A., López-Alt, A., Tromer, E., Vaikuntanathan, V., Wichs, D.: Multiparty computation with low communication, computation and interaction via threshold FHE. In: Pointcheval, D., Johansson, T. (eds.) EUROCRYPT 2012. LNCS, vol. 7237, pp. 483–501. Springer, Heidelberg (2012). https://doi.org/10.1007/978-3-642-29011-4_29
12. Boneh, D., et al.: Threshold cryptosystems from threshold fully homomorphic encryption. In: Shacham, H., Boldyreva, A. (eds.) CRYPTO 2018. LNCS, vol. 10991, pp. 565–596. Springer, Cham (2018). https://doi.org/10.1007/978-3-319-96884-1_19
13. Boneh, D., Halevi, S., Hamburg, M., Ostrovsky, R.: Circular-Secure encryption from decision Diffie-Hellman. In: Wagner, D. (ed.) CRYPTO 2008. LNCS, vol. 5157, pp. 108–125. Springer, Heidelberg (2008). https://doi.org/10.1007/978-3-540-85174-5_7
14. Boyle, E., Coateau, G., Meyer, P.: Sublinear-communication secure multiparty computation does not require FHE. In: Eurocrypt (2023)

15. Boyle, E., Couteau, G., Gilboa, N., Ishai, Y.: Compressing vector OLE. In: Lie, D., Mannan, M., Backes, M., Wang, X. (eds.) ACM CCS 2018, pp. 896–912. ACM Press (Oct 2018)

16. Boyle, E., Couteau, G., Gilboa, N., Ishai, Y., Kohl, L., Scholl, P.: Efficient pseudo-random correlation generators: silent OT extension and more. In: Boldyreva, A., Micciancio, D. (eds.) CRYPTO 2019. LNCS, vol. 11694, pp. 489–518. Springer, Cham (2019). https://doi.org/10.1007/978-3-030-26954-8_16

17. Boyle, E., Couteau, G., Gilboa, N., Ishai, Y., Orrù, M.: Homomorphic secret sharing: Optimizations and applications. In: Thuraisingham, B.M., Evans, D., Malkin, T., Xu, D. (eds.) ACM CCS 2017, pp. 2105–2122. ACM Press (Oct / Nov 2017)

18. Boyle, E., Gilboa, N., Ishai, Y.: Function secret sharing. In: Oswald, E., Fischlin, M. (eds.) EUROCRYPT 2015. LNCS, vol. 9057, pp. 337–367. Springer, Heidelberg (2015). https://doi.org/10.1007/978-3-662-46803-6_12

19. Boyle, E., Gilboa, N., Ishai, Y.: Breaking the circuit size barrier for secure computation under DDH. In: Robshaw, M., Katz, J. (eds.) CRYPTO 2016. LNCS, vol. 9814, pp. 509–539. Springer, Heidelberg (2016). https://doi.org/10.1007/978-3-662-53018-4_19

20. Boyle, E., Gilboa, N., Ishai, Y.: Group-Based Secure computation: optimizing rounds, communication, and computation. In: Coron, J.-S., Nielsen, J.B. (eds.) EUROCRYPT 2017. LNCS, vol. 10211, pp. 163–193. Springer, Cham (2017). https://doi.org/10.1007/978-3-319-56614-6_6

21. Boyle, E., Gilboa, N., Ishai, Y., Lin, H., Tessaro, S.: Foundations of homomorphic secret sharing. In: Karlin, A.R. (ed.) ITCS 2018, vol. 94, pp. 21:1–21:21. LIPIcs (Jan 2018)

22. Boyle, E., Kohl, L., Scholl, P.: Homomorphic secret sharing from lattices without FHE. In: Ishai, Y., Rijmen, V. (eds.) EUROCRYPT 2019. LNCS, vol. 11477, pp. 3–33. Springer, Cham (2019). https://doi.org/10.1007/978-3-030-17656-3_1

23. Brakerski, Z., Gentry, C., Vaikuntanathan, V.: (Leveled) fully homomorphic encryption without bootstrapping. In: Goldwasser, S. (ed.) ITCS 2012, pp. 309–325. ACM (Jan 2012)

24. Brakerski, Z., Lyubashevsky, V., Vaikuntanathan, V., Wichs, D.: Worst-Case hardness for LPN and cryptographic hashing via code smoothing. In: Ishai, Y., Rijmen, V. (eds.) EUROCRYPT 2019. LNCS, vol. 11478, pp. 619–635. Springer, Cham (2019). https://doi.org/10.1007/978-3-030-17659-4_21

25. Brakerski, Z., Vaikuntanathan, V.: Efficient fully homomorphic encryption from (standard) LWE. In: Ostrovsky, R. (ed.) 52nd FOCS, pp. 97–106. IEEE Computer Society Press (Oct 2011)

26. Clear, M., McGoldrick, C.: Multi-identity and multi-key leveled FHE from learning with errors. In: Gennaro, R., Robshaw, M. (eds.) CRYPTO 2015. LNCS, vol. 9216, pp. 630–656. Springer, Heidelberg (2015). https://doi.org/10.1007/978-3-662-48000-7_31

27. Couteau, G.: A note on the communication complexity of multiparty computation in the correlated randomness model. In: Ishai, Y., Rijmen, V. (eds.) EUROCRYPT 2019. LNCS, vol. 11477, pp. 473–503. Springer, Cham (2019). https://doi.org/10.1007/978-3-030-17656-3_17

28. Couteau, G.: Personal communication (2023)

29. Couteau, G., Meyer, P.: Breaking the circuit size barrier for secure computation under quasi-polynomial LPN. In: Canteaut, A., Standaert, F.-X. (eds.) EUROCRYPT 2021. LNCS, vol. 12697, pp. 842–870. Springer, Cham (2021). https://doi.org/10.1007/978-3-030-77886-6_29

30. Cryan, M., Miltersen, P.B.: On pseudorandom generators in NC^0. In: Sgall, J., Pultr, A., Kolman, P. (eds.) MFCS 2001. LNCS, vol. 2136, pp. 272–284. Springer, Heidelberg (2001). https://doi.org/10.1007/3-540-44683-4_24

31. David, B., Dowsley, R., Nascimento, A.C.A.: Universally composable oblivious transfer based on a variant of LPN. In: Gritzalis, D., Kiayias, A., Askoxylakis, I. (eds.) Cryptology and Network Security, pp. 143–158. Springer International Publishing, Cham (2014). https://doi.org/10.1007/978-3-319-12280-9_10

32. Dodis, Y., Halevi, S., Rothblum, R.D., Wichs, D.: Spooky encryption and its applications. In: Robshaw, M., Katz, J. (eds.) CRYPTO 2016. LNCS, vol. 9816, pp. 93–122. Springer, Heidelberg (2016). https://doi.org/10.1007/978-3-662-53015-3_4

33. Fazio, N., Gennaro, R., Jafarikhah, T., Skeith, W.E.: Homomorphic secret sharing from Paillier encryption. In: Okamoto, T., Yu, Y., Au, M.H., Li, Y. (eds.) ProvSec 2017. LNCS, vol. 10592, pp. 381–399. Springer, Cham (2017). https://doi.org/10.1007/978-3-319-68637-0_23

34. Feige, U.: Relations between average case complexity and approximation complexity. In: 34th ACM STOC, pp. 534–543. ACM Press (May 2002)

35. Fosli, I., Ishai, Y., Kolobov, V.I., Wootters, M.: On the download rate of homomorphic secret sharing. In: Braverman, M. (ed.) 13th Innovations in Theoretical Computer Science Conference (ITCS 2022). Leibniz International Proceedings in Informatics (LIPIcs), vol. 215, pp. 71:1–71:22. Schloss Dagstuhl - Leibniz-Zentrum für Informatik, Dagstuhl, Germany (2022). https://drops.dagstuhl.de/opus/volltexte/2022/15667

36. Franklin, M.K., Yung, M.: Communication complexity of secure computation (extended abstract). In: 24th ACM STOC, pp. 699–710. ACM Press (May 1992)

37. Gentry, C.: Fully homomorphic encryption using ideal lattices. In: Mitzenmacher, M. (ed.) 41st ACM STOC, pp. 169–178. ACM Press (May/Jun 2009)

38. Gentry, C., Halevi, S., Smart, N.P.: Fully homomorphic encryption with polylog overhead. In: Pointcheval, D., Johansson, T. (eds.) EUROCRYPT 2012. LNCS, vol. 7237, pp. 465–482. Springer, Heidelberg (2012). https://doi.org/10.1007/978-3-642-29011-4_28

39. Gilboa, N., Ishai, Y.: Distributed point functions and their applications. In: Nguyen, P.Q., Oswald, E. (eds.) EUROCRYPT 2014. LNCS, vol. 8441, pp. 640–658. Springer, Heidelberg (2014). https://doi.org/10.1007/978-3-642-55220-5_35

40. Goldreich, O.: Candidate one-way functions based on expander graphs. Electronic Colloquium on Computational Complexity (ECCC) **7**(90) (2000)

41. Goldreich, O., Micali, S., Wigderson, A.: How to play any mental game or A completeness theorem for protocols with honest majority. In: Aho, A. (ed.) 19th ACM STOC, pp. 218–229. ACM Press (May 1987)

42. Ishai, Y., Kushilevitz, E., Ostrovsky, R., Sahai, A.: Cryptography with constant computational overhead. In: Ladner, R.E., Dwork, C. (eds.) 40th ACM STOC, pp. 433–442. ACM Press (May 2008)

43. Ishai, Y., Lai, R.W.F., Malavolta, G.: A geometric approach to homomorphic secret sharing. In: Garay, J.A. (ed.) PKC 2021. LNCS, vol. 12711, pp. 92–119. Springer, Cham (2021). https://doi.org/10.1007/978-3-030-75248-4_4

44. Jain, A., Lin, H., Sahai, A.: Indistinguishability obfuscation from well-founded assumptions. In: Khuller, S., Williams, V.V. (eds.) STOC '21: 53rd Annual ACM SIGACT Symposium on Theory of Computing, Virtual Event, Italy, June 21–25, 2021, pp. 60–73. ACM (2021)

45. Kothari, P.K., Mori, R., O'Donnell, R., Witmer, D.: Sum of squares lower bounds for refuting any CSP. In: Hatami, H., McKenzie, P., King, V. (eds.) 49th ACM STOC, pp. 132–145. ACM Press (Jun 2017)

46. Lai, R.W.F., Malavolta, G., Schröder, D.: Homomorphic secret sharing for low degree polynomials. In: Peyrin, T., Galbraith, S. (eds.) ASIACRYPT 2018. LNCS, vol. 11274, pp. 279–309. Springer, Cham (2018). https://doi.org/10.1007/978-3-030-03332-3_11
47. Mossel, E., Shpilka, A., Trevisan, L.: On e-biased generators in NC0. In: FOCS, pp. 136–145 (2003)
48. Mukherjee, P., Wichs, D.: Two round multiparty computation via multi-key FHE. In: Fischlin, M., Coron, J.-S. (eds.) EUROCRYPT 2016. LNCS, vol. 9666, pp. 735–763. Springer, Heidelberg (2016). https://doi.org/10.1007/978-3-662-49896-5_26
49. Naor, M., Nissim, K.: Communication preserving protocols for secure function evaluation. In: 33rd ACM STOC, pp. 590–599. ACM Press (Jul 2001)
50. Orlandi, C., Scholl, P., Yakoubov, S.: The Rise of Paillier: homomorphic secret sharing and public-key silent OT. In: Canteaut, A., Standaert, F.-X. (eds.) EUROCRYPT 2021. LNCS, vol. 12696, pp. 678–708. Springer, Cham (2021). https://doi.org/10.1007/978-3-030-77870-5_24
51. Rivest, R.L., Dertouzos, M.L.: On data banks and privacy homomorphisms (1978)
52. Roy, L., Singh, J.: Large message homomorphic secret sharing from DCR and applications. In: Malkin, T., Peikert, C. (eds.) CRYPTO 2021. LNCS, vol. 12827, pp. 687–717. Springer, Cham (2021). https://doi.org/10.1007/978-3-030-84252-9_23
53. Wang, F., Yun, C., Goldwasser, S., Vaikuntanathan, V., Zaharia, M.: Splinter: Practical private queries on public data. In: Akella, A., Howell, J. (eds.) 14th USENIX Symposium on Networked Systems Design and Implementation, NSDI 2017, Boston, MA, USA, March 27–29, 2017, pp. 299–313. USENIX Association (2017). https://www.usenix.org/conference/nsdi17/technical-sessions/presentation/wang-frank
54. Zichron, L.: Locally computable arithmetic pseudorandom generators. Ph.D. thesis, Master's thesis, School of Electrical Engineering, Tel Aviv University (2017)

Anonymous Credentials

Lattice Signature with Efficient Protocols, Application to Anonymous Credentials

Corentin Jeudy[1,2(✉)], Adeline Roux-Langlois[3], and Olivier Sanders[1]

[1] Orange Labs, Applied Crypto Group, Cesson-Sévigné, France
{corentin.jeudy,olivier.sanders}@orange.com
[2] Univ Rennes, CNRS, IRISA, Rennes, France
[3] Normandie Univ, UNICAEN, ENSICAEN, CNRS, GREYC, 14000 Caen, France
adeline.roux-langlois@cnrs.fr

Abstract. Digital signature is an essential primitive in cryptography, which can be used as the digital analogue of handwritten signatures but also as a building block for more complex systems. In the latter case, signatures with specific features are needed, so as to smoothly interact with the other components of the systems, such as zero-knowledge proofs. This has given rise to so-called *signatures with efficient protocols*, a versatile tool that has been used in countless applications. Designing such signatures is however quite difficult, in particular if one wishes to withstand quantum computing. We are indeed aware of only one post-quantum construction, proposed by Libert et al. at Asiacrypt'16, yielding very large signatures and proofs.

In this paper, we propose a new construction that can be instantiated in both standard lattices and structured ones, resulting in each case in dramatic performance improvements. In particular, the size of a proof of message-signature possession, which is one of the main metrics for such schemes, can be brought down to less than 650 KB. As our construction retains all the features expected from signatures with efficient protocols, it can be used as a drop-in replacement in all systems using them, which mechanically improves their own performance, and has thus a direct impact on many applications. It can also be used to easily design new privacy-preserving mechanisms. As an example, we provide the first lattice-based anonymous credentials system.

Keywords: Lattice-Based Cryptography · Signature · Efficient Protocols · Privacy · Anonymous Credentials

1 Introduction

Electronic authentication massively relies on digital signatures, a cryptographic primitive that can be traced back to the Diffie-Hellman seminal paper [22]. The strong point of digital signatures is that they act in the digital world in the same way as handwritten signatures do in the real world: they add a short element S to some data m attesting that m has been validated by the signer and that it

© International Association for Cryptologic Research 2023
H. Handschuh and A. Lysyanskaya (Eds.): CRYPTO 2023, LNCS 14082, pp. 351–383, 2023.
https://doi.org/10.1007/978-3-031-38545-2_12

has not been modified afterwards. By emulating handwritten signatures, they represent the perfect electronic counterpart and are indeed ubiquitous today.

However, for several decades, cryptographers have questioned this hegemony in some situations as these signatures may give rise to many privacy issues. Typically, presentation of the same certificate[1] S each time m needs to be authenticated allows tracing S and hence its owner. Moreover, if m is a set of elements m_i, then verification of S requires knowledge of all these elements even if they are irrelevant for the current authentication.

For example, let us consider the classical use-case of age control (e.g., to check that a customer is an adult) where some customer owns a digital certificate (embedded in some ID document) authenticating his attributes (name, birthdate, address, etc). With standard digital signature, this customer has no other choice than providing the full set of attributes to the controller as they are required to run the verification algorithm. This is clearly a significant privacy issue but here one could argue that the situation already occurs in the real world: it is indeed quite common to present an ID document displaying many personal information to a cashier that needs to control your age.

This apparent paradox epitomizes the differences between the real world and the digital one. In the former, it is natural to assume that the cashier will not memorize all the information contained in the document for further commercial exploitation or identity theft. This does not hold true in the digital world where the users definitely lose control of their data as soon as they reveal them and it is very likely that the same customer will be much more reluctant to provide the same information to a website that needs to verify that he is an adult.

1.1 Related Works

Since the problems of the two worlds are different it is actually logical that standard digital signatures are not best suited for all use-cases. In particular, the fact that electronic data can no longer be controlled once they are revealed calls for solutions disclosing as few information as possible during authentication. This has given rise to countless advanced cryptographic primitives, tailored to very specific use-cases, such as anonymous credentials [14,17,26], group signatures [3, 18], Direct Anonymous Attestations (DAA) [13], EPID [12], etc. Far from simply being theoretical constructions, some of them have been included in standards (e.g., [29,30]) and even embedded in billions of devices (e.g., [28,45]).

Surprisingly, the diversity of use-cases addressed by these privacy-preserving authentication mechanisms contrasts with the very few mathematical settings allowing efficient designs. A closer look at these standards indeed shows that all of them make use of RSA moduli or cyclic groups and thus cannot withstand the power of quantum computing. The emerging success of such systems is thus based on foundations that will crumble as soon as a sufficiently powerful quantum computer appears.

---

[1] All along this paper, the words *signature* and *certificate* will be used interchangeably.

This unsatisfying state of affairs clearly calls for the design of post-quantum alternatives to such systems. However, when we look at the cryptographic literature on this topic, it is striking to see that the existing post-quantum solutions are not only much less efficient than their classical[2] counterparts but also extremely rare. Typically, we are not aware of any explicit post-quantum anonymous credentials system. Even when we consider popular primitives such as group signatures, we note that the most efficient solutions [21,36] depart from the traditional model [3] as they do not achieve non-frameability, a property implying that the certificate issuer does not know users' secret keys and that is thus incompatible with their construction. Although this might seem to be a minor restriction for group signatures, this has very important consequences on their industrial variants such as DAA [19] and EPID [7]. Indeed, for the latter, the knowledge of the users' secret keys allows one to break anonymity, which makes the whole construction totally pointless.

To understand the contrasting situations of classical constructions and post-quantum ones in the area of privacy-preserving authentication mechanisms, it is important to recall that all of them require, at some point, to prove knowledge of a signature on some (potentially secret) attributes. For example, in an anonymous credential system, the user generally receives a signature on their attributes and some secret key at the time of issuance. To show their credentials they then reveal the requested attributes and prove knowledge of the signature, the hidden attributes and the secret key so as to remain anonymous. In non-frameable group signatures, DAA or EPID schemes, the user first receives a certificate C on a secret key s and then generates their own signatures by including a zero-knowledge proof that C is valid on s. Of course, the resulting signatures also contains additional elements that define the specificity of each primitive but the point is that the common core is this proof of knowledge which essentially needs two kinds of building blocks: a "signature scheme with efficient protocols" as coined by Camenisch and Lysyanskaya [15] and an associated zero-knowledge (ZK) proof system.

The latter notion is well-known and has seen several advances over the past few years, in particular in the lattice setting, e.g., [8,35,47]. The former notion is rather informal but it usually refers to a digital signature scheme with some specific features such as the ability to sign committed (hidden) messages and to prove knowledge of a signature on such messages. This places some restrictions on the design of the signature scheme as it for example proscribes hash functions and hence most popular paradigms such as Hash-and-Sign and Fiat-Shamir. Yet, several extremely efficient constructions from number theoretic assumptions exist, in particular in bilinear (pairing) environments [6,16,43]. They constitute a very powerful and simple-to-use building block which explains the countless applications using them.

This situation stands in sharp contrast with the one of post-quantum cryptography where we are aware of only one lattice-based construction [33] with such

---

[2] In this paper, we use "classical" to denote cryptographic constructions that rely on computational assumptions broken by quantum algorithms.

features. Moreover the latter was designed with Stern's proof of knowledge in mind and thus does not leverage the recent advances in the area of lattice-based zero-knowledge proofs. The original paper only provides asymptotic estimation but our thorough analysis (deferred in the full version [31, Sec. H]) shows that, even with the recent ZK protocol from [47], a proof of knowledge of a signature is still, at best, 670 MB large, which is far too high for practical applications. This leaves designers of privacy-preserving systems with no other solution than constructing the whole system from scratch, as was done for example in the case of EPID [7] and DAA [19], which requires skills in many different areas and thus limits the number of contributions.

1.2   Our Contributions

The goal of our paper is to propose the lattice counterpart of [6, 16, 43], that is, a signature scheme with efficient protocols that is specifically designed to smoothly and efficiently interact with the most recent lattice-based zero-knowledge proof systems. More precisely, we provide a lattice-based signature scheme for which we can (1) obtain signatures on potentially hidden (in a commitment) messages, and (2) prove in zero-knowledge the possession of a message-signature pair. Compared to the only such construction [33], our scheme is not only much more efficient but also transposes well to an algebraically structured setting which leads to further performance improvements, as summarized in Table 1.

Our natural starting point is [33] which consists in a Boyen signature [11] on a randomly chosen tag $\tau \in \{0,1\}^\ell$ and for a syndrome shifted by the binary decomposition of the commitment $c = D_0 r + D_1 m$ to a binary message m, the commitment scheme being implicit in [1]. At first sight, this scheme perfectly fits the recent zero-knowledge proof system proposed by Yang et al. [47] but yet leads to an extremely large proof of knowledge as explained above (a thorough complexity analysis is provided in the full version [31, Sec. F.3, Tab. H.1]). We then undertake a complete overhaul of this scheme, pointing out at the same time the reasons of such a high complexity.

The main novelty is that we adopt a much more global approach as we look simultaneously at the three components of such systems, namely the commitment scheme (necessary to obtain signature on hidden messages), the signature scheme and the zero-knowledge proof systems, and the possible synergies. We, in particular, emphasize that the design choices we made for each component were not driven by the will to improve the latter individually but rather by their impact on the whole system. Typically, some of the modifications we introduce in the signature scheme itself has almost no impact on its complexity but yet results in very significant gains when it comes to proving knowledge of a signature. More generally, our approach leads to a series of contributions that we regroup in three main parts.

The Signature Scheme. One of the first consequences of having to sign committed messages is that the signature must now include the randomness added to the commitment by the signer. In [33], this randomness has the same dimension as the one of the Boyen signature but a much larger width (see full version [31, Tab. H.1]) and thus represents the largest part of the signature. This is amplified by the proof of knowledge, which explains in part the high complexity of the latter. One of the reasons of such a large width is that the security proof requires to embed a hidden relation in the matrix $\mathbf{D}$ that is applied to the binary decomposition of the Ajtai commitment $\mathbf{c}$. More precisely, it defines $\mathbf{D} = \mathbf{AU}$ for the matrix $\mathbf{A}$ from the Boyen public key and some short matrix $\mathbf{U}$. This (along with other design choices discussed below) deteriorates the quality of the SIS solution extracted during the security proof and thus leads to large parameters.

To address this issue, we depart from [33] by generating conjointly the parameters of the signature scheme and the ones of the commitment scheme and in particular by re-using parts of the former in the latter. More specifically, in our construction, a commitment to $\mathbf{m}$ is $\mathbf{c} = \mathbf{Ar} + \mathbf{Dm}$, for a Gaussian randomness $\mathbf{r}$, where $\mathbf{A}$ is a matrix from the signer's public key and $\mathbf{D}$ is a public random matrix. From the efficiency standpoint, this has two important effects. First, this allows merging the randomness $\mathbf{r}$ with the other parts of the signatures, as we explain below, and thus to reduce the number of elements that we have to prove knowledge of. Second, as $\mathbf{A}$ is no longer hidden by a matrix $\mathbf{U}$, this significantly reduces the discrepancy between the adversary output and the extracted SIS solution in the security proof, leading to much better parameters.

Obviously, this has important consequences on the construction as the commitment matrix $\mathbf{A}$ is now selected by the signer, which is usually embodied by the adversary in privacy security games. To ensure that $\mathbf{A}$ is random to make the Ajtai commitment hiding, we need to generate it as a hash output. This solution is then totally incompatible with the [33] approach where the signer needs to generate $\mathbf{A}$ together with an associated trapdoor.

Instead of Boyen's signature, we then choose to use the trapdoors of [39], which interface well with the Ajtai commitment. More precisely, our public key is composed of a random matrix $\mathbf{A}$, a matrix $\mathbf{B} = \mathbf{AR}$ and a random syndrome $\mathbf{u}$, and the secret key is a random ternary matrix $\mathbf{R}$. In order to sign a binary message $\mathbf{m}$ hidden in a commitment $\mathbf{c} = \mathbf{Ar} + \mathbf{Dm}$, we use pre-image sampling to sample a Gaussian vector $\mathbf{v}'$ such that $[\mathbf{A}|\tau\mathbf{G} - \mathbf{B}]\mathbf{v}' = \mathbf{u} + \mathbf{c}$, where τ is a tag from a tag space $\mathcal{T} \subseteq \mathbb{Z}_q^\times$ and $\mathbf{G}$ is the gadget matrix from [39]. As $\mathbf{A}$ is involved in both the left hand side of the equation and in $\mathbf{c}$, we can set the signature as $(\tau, \mathbf{v} = \mathbf{v}' - [\mathbf{r}^T|\mathbf{0}]^T)$. Verification consists in checking

$$[\mathbf{A}|\tau\mathbf{G} - \mathbf{B}]\mathbf{v} = \mathbf{u} + \mathbf{Dm} \bmod q \text{ and } \|\mathbf{v}\|_\infty \text{ small.} \tag{1}$$

One can note that we have removed in the process the binary decomposition of $\mathbf{c}$. We indeed choose a very different approach in the security proof which shows that this step is actually not necessary. Removing this decomposition is also crucial in order to compact the commitment randomness $\mathbf{r}$ with the pre-image $\mathbf{v}'$. It avoids further intermediate steps that deteriorate the SIS solution extracted from the forgery, as explained above, which leads to better parameters overall. Moreover, when it comes to proving knowledge of the signature, each intermediate step makes the whole statement harder to prove and requires to create additional witnesses, i.e., each bit of $\mathbf{c}$, that must be committed, whose membership in $\{0, 1\}$ must be proven, etc. Our point here is that each seemingly innocent modification is considerably amplified when considering the full protocol and therefore results in major gains.

At this stage, a reader familiar with the construction in [21] might wonder why we do not try to embed the committed message in the tag τ, instead of having this $\mathbf{Dm}$ component in our verification equation. Here, we need to recall that the situation of [21] is very specific as the signer (the group manager in their application) knows the signed message $\mathbf{m}$, which belongs to some bounded set in their application. In our case, we want to hide this message that may have a very large entropy (this is for example the case in anonymous credentials systems). In all cases, the security reduction must guess, at the setup stage, the value of the tag τ^* involved in the forgery. Therefore, if τ is generated from $\mathbf{m}$ itself, then the reduction would have to guess this message, which would result in an exponential security loss in most scenarios. A workaround could be to construct τ from $H(\mathbf{m})$ for some appropriate function H (most likely a hash function because of the properties it would have to satisfy) whose image has lower entropy so as to guess $H(\mathbf{m})$ instead of $\mathbf{m}$. Alternatively, H could be modelled as a random oracle. The problem with this solution is that verification would now require to prove that $H(\mathbf{m})$ has been correctly evaluated. For very specific scenarios (*e.g., blind signature* [5,20]) where $\mathbf{m}$ can be revealed at the verification time, this would work with a security loss depending on the entropy of $H(\mathbf{m})$. For all others (*e.g.*, group signature, anonymous credentials, e-cash, etc), where the message must remain secret, this would not be possible with the zero-knowledge frameworks we target because of the nature of H. As we aim to design a versatile tool, suitable for all applications, we choose to have a tag uncorrelated to the message, hence the $\mathbf{Dm}$ component mentioned above. As per the security proof, there are two constraints in the way to choose tags: generate tags without encountering collisions to only emit one signature per tag, and without enduring an exponential loss in the security proof due to guesses. Given that we essentially target privacy-preserving applications such as group signatures or anonymous credentials, we focus, in the body of our paper, on a stateful construction that inherently solves these two problems. For all these applications, it is indeed natural for the signer to keep track of the signatures it has issued. For group signature, this is even a requirement of the security model [3]: a registration table must be updated after each addition of a group member. However, for completeness, we show in the full version [31, Sec. G] that our construction can easily be tweaked to be stateless, at the cost of a very mild increase of the signature size, while complying with the two constraints above.

So far, we have essentially discussed improvements of both the commitment and the signature schemes. Table 1 shows that our resulting signature is between 30 and 40 times smaller than that of [33] when considering the same setting (standard lattices). However, this gain is still not sufficient to lead to practical proofs as ZK lattice proofs are still complex, even with the recent framework of [47]. We now focus on the proofs of knowledge necessary for our protocol and explain how we can modify the previous framework for a better efficiency.

Table 1. Comparison of efficiency estimates of the signature schemes of [33], of Sect. 3 and of Sect. 3.3 for $\lambda = 128$ bits of quantum security, with the size of zero-knowledge proof of possession of a message-signature pair. In the setting column, *stand.* stands for standard lattices, as opposed to the ring setting of our last construction. The proofs for [33] and Sect. 3 are either exact proofs or approximate ones using the *fast mode* of Sect. 4.2 and described in the technical overview. The complete analysis and parameter sets used for these estimates can be found in the full version [31, Sec. H].

	setting	λ	|pk| (MB)	|sk| (MB)	|sig| (kb)	|π| (kb)
[33] (exact proof)	stand.	128	$296 \cdot 10^4$	$156 \cdot 10^2$	$862 \cdot 10$	$102 \cdot 10^5$
[33] (fast mode)	stand.	128	$707 \cdot 10^4$	$372 \cdot 10^2$	$139 \cdot 10^2$	$671 \cdot 10^3$
Sect. 3 (exact proof)	stand.	128	$115 \cdot 10$	892	261	$306 \cdot 10^3$
Sect. 3 (fast mode)	stand.	128	$296 \cdot 10$	$229 \cdot 10$	418	$177 \cdot 10^2$
Sect. 3.3 (exact proof)	module	128	7.8	8.9	273	639

Efficient Protocols and Zero-Knowledge Arguments. A "signature scheme with efficient protocols" requires two kinds of protocols, one to get a signature on a committed message and one for proving possession of a message-signature pair. Regarding the former, the problem is rather simple as the message $\mathbf{m}$ to sign is already embedded in a commitment $\mathbf{c} = \mathbf{Ar} + \mathbf{Dm}$. However, we have to slightly modify this construction because both the user requesting the signature and the signer must contribute to the randomness of the commitment. This leads to a commitment $\mathbf{c} = \mathbf{A}(\mathbf{r}' + \mathbf{r}'') + \mathbf{Dm}$ where $\mathbf{r}'$ is added by the user to enforce the hiding property of $\mathbf{c}$ and $\mathbf{r}''$ is added by the signer to be able to handle any query in the security proof. Only the former needs to prove knowledge of $\mathbf{r}'$ and $\mathbf{m}$ so as to rely on the EUF-CMA property of the signature scheme we introduced. In all cases, the user ends up with a signature $(\tau, \mathbf{v})$ on a binary $\mathbf{m}$ verifying (1) and needs to prove it in a zero-knowledge way.

For that, we employ the recent zero-knowledge framework proposed by Yang et al. [47] which can be used to prove linear relations with quadratic constraints. The latter feature is very useful in our case as our verification equation (1) is quadratic in $(\mathbf{m}; (\tau, \mathbf{v}))$ because of the term $\tau \mathbf{Gv}_2$ (where $\mathbf{v}_2$ is the bottom part of $\mathbf{v}$). Moreover, this allows one to prove that an element is short by first writing its binary decomposition and then proving that each resulting component x is indeed binary through the quadratic equation $x(x - 1) = 0$.

Unfortunately, this nice feature comes at a price as this decomposition procedure entails a $(\log_2 B)$-fold increase of the size of the witness $\mathbf{v}$, where B is a bound on $\|\mathbf{v}\|_\infty$. For a high dimensional vector $\mathbf{v}$ in $\mathbb{Z}^m$, this results in a very large proof which has led the authors of [47] to propose a so-called *fast mode* for their protocol. In a nutshell, this variant relies on the observation that the norm of $\mathbf{Hv}$, for a random short matrix $\mathbf{H}$ of dimension $k \times m$, implies some bound on the norm of $\mathbf{v}$, even when the latter is chosen by the adversary. As $\mathbf{Hv}$ must be hidden, one must still use the quadratic relation above to prove shortness but on a witness with a much smaller dimension as k is in practice much smaller than m. The efficiency gains are very significant but we point out several short-comings with the solution proposed in [47]. First, contrarily to the claim in [47], this fast mode *cannot* be used to prove that $\mathbf{v}$ is positive and we provide a concrete counter-example in Sect. 4. This is not a problem in our case as we only want to prove results on the ℓ_∞ norm of $\mathbf{v}$ but this can be a problem for specific applications such as the e-cash system considered in [47]. Second, the authors in [47] make use of a binary matrix $\mathbf{H}$ which significantly deteriorates the overall statement as one must set a bound $m\beta$ on the norm of $\mathbf{Hv}$, when $\|\mathbf{v}\|_\infty$ is bounded by β. Although this soundness gap seems unavoidable with this mode, we show that we can do better with a matrix $\mathbf{H} \in \{-1, 0, 1\}^{k \times m}$, which allows selecting better parameters and thus leads to more efficient protocols.

Finally, we also propose in the full version only [31, Sec. E] a series of optimizations for the protocol of [47] that range from better parameter selection to compression of the commitments, resulting in further efficiency improvements. For a fair comparison, the figures in Table 1 take into account these improvements for both our scheme and the one from [33]. This table shows that our contributions reduce the size of a proof of knowledge (using the fast mode) to roughly 18 MB, which can be interpreted in two ways. On the one hand, this is an important improvement over [33]. On the other hand, this is still large and probably impractical for many applications. The next part of our contributions thus investigates how to instantiate our construction in another setting to further reduce this size.

Extending to Structured Lattices. Our construction extends to the module setting where we replace the integers by polynomials with integer coefficients. More concretely, we consider a power-of-two cyclotomic ring, i.e., $R = \mathbb{Z}[X]/\langle X^n + 1\rangle$ with n a power-of-two. The additional structure yields more efficient computations, as well as more compact keys. The trapdoors of [39] have already been used over such algebraic rings, e.g., [4,21,24], which makes our module construction very similar to the one based on standard lattice assumptions. All the tools required to prove the security of our scheme also have a ring counterpart, which therefore leads to almost no differences in the security proofs either. The main difference comes when considering exact zero-knowledge proofs over algebraic rings. Our verification equation in the module setting is

$$[\mathbf{A}|\tau\mathbf{G} - \mathbf{B}]\mathbf{v} = \mathbf{u} + \mathbf{Dm} \bmod qR \text{ and } \mathbf{v} \text{ short.} \tag{2}$$

Proving knowledge of (2) requires to prove that (1) τ is in the specified tag space, (2) $\mathbf{v}$ is short, (3) $\mathbf{m}$ is a vector of binary polynomials, and (4) that the quadratic equation is verified. Based on state-of-the-art proof systems, (1) constrains which tag space to choose so that we can efficiently prove membership, while ensuring that a difference of tags is in $(R/qR)^\times$ as needed per the security proofs. Statement (2) requires to define a notion of shortness over the ring, which is usually defined based on the size of the polynomials' coefficients. Up until recently, exact proofs performing the latter task [8,25] (also used for (3)) used NTT packing, i.e., interpreting the coefficients of $\mathbf{v}$ as the NTT (Number

Theoretic Transform) of another vector $\mathbf{v}'$, which is most efficient when $X^n + 1$ splits into low-degree irreducible factors modulo q. This splitting makes it harder to choose a proper tag space for which differences are always invertible. Finally, (4) requires a proof system able to deal with quadratic equations. Similar relations [21, 36] were handled by transforming the relation quadratic in the witnesses into a linear relation in the commitment of the witnesses. Since efficient proofs of commitment opening rely on relaxed openings, this solution introduces a soundness gap in the proven statement, which we would like to avoid.

Instead, we use the very recent framework of Lyubashevsky et al. [35] which provides a unified method to prove all our statements. It extends the previous works of [8, 25] and enables proving quadratic relations exactly, as well as quadratic evaluations. The latter can be used to prove exact bounds directly in the ℓ_2 norm, which leads to more efficient proofs than proving ℓ_∞ bounds.

In the module setting, we therefore end up with a signature scheme that is efficient on all metrics, as highlighted in Table 1. In particular, we manage to keep our proofs of knowledge of a message-signature pair below 650 KB[3]. As these proofs are one of the main building blocks of privacy-preserving protocols, these efficiency gains readily translate to the latter and thus should have a significant impact on the area. More generally, our construction is designed to be used as a black box, which should foster many applications, as was the case with the pairing-based signatures with efficient protocols [6, 16, 43].

Application: Anonymous Credentials. Signature with efficient protocols like the one we propose gives a single signature construction that can be turned into several privacy-preserving primitives such as group signatures, anonymous credentials, e-cash etc. We give an example of one such construction based on our signature to show how it interfaces with the "efficient protocols". More precisely, we propose an anonymous credentials system following the syntax and security model from [26]. At a high-level, the security relies on the zero-knowledge and soundness properties of the proof system and on the EUF-CMA security of our signature. To the best of our knowledge, this provides the first explicit lattice-based anonymous credentials system.

2   Preliminaries

Throughout this paper, for two integers $a \leq b$, we define $[a, b] = \{k \in \mathbb{Z} : a \leq k \leq b\}$. When $a = 1$ and $b \geq 1$, we simply use $[b]$ to denote $[1, b]$. For a positive integer q, we define $\mathbb{Z}_q = \mathbb{Z}/q\mathbb{Z}$. In this work, we consider q to be an odd prime (or product of odd primes), and we sometimes identify $\mathbb{Z}_q$ with the set of representatives $[-(q-1)/2, (q-1)/2]$. The vectors are written in bold lowercase letters $\mathbf{a}$, while the matrices are in bold uppercase letters $\mathbf{A}$. The transpose operator is denoted with the superscript T. The identity matrix of

---

[3] To remain as broad as possible, we use statistical trapdoors and related tools. One could however get further efficiency gains by using a computational instantiation.

size $n \times n$ is denoted by $\mathbf{I}_n$. For any $\mathbf{a} \in \mathbb{R}^n$, we define its Euclidean (ℓ_2) norm as $\|\mathbf{a}\|_2 = (\sum_{i \in [n]} |a_i|^2)^{1/2}$ and its infinity (ℓ_∞) norm as $\|\mathbf{a}\|_\infty = \max_{i \in [n]} |a_i|$. For a matrix $\mathbf{A} = [\mathbf{a}_i]_{i \in [m]} \in \mathbb{R}^{n \times m}$, we define $\|\mathbf{A}\|_{\max} = \max_{i \in [m]} \|\mathbf{a}_i\|_\infty$, and $\|\mathbf{A}\|_2 = \max_{\mathbf{x} \neq 0} \|\mathbf{A}\mathbf{x}\|_2 / \|\mathbf{x}\|_2$. We denote by λ the security parameter.

2.1 Lattices

A (full-rank) *lattice* $\mathcal{L}$ of rank n is a discrete additive subgroup of $\mathbb{R}^n$. The *dual lattice* of a lattice $\mathcal{L}$ is defined by $\mathcal{L}^* = \{\mathbf{x} \in \mathrm{Span}_{\mathbb{R}}(\mathcal{L}) : \forall \mathbf{y} \in \mathcal{L}, \langle \mathbf{x}, \mathbf{y} \rangle \in \mathbb{Z}\}$. In this work, we consider the family of q-ary lattices defined by $\mathcal{L}_q^\perp(\mathbf{A}) = \{\mathbf{e} \in \mathbb{Z}^m : \mathbf{A}\mathbf{e} = \mathbf{0} \bmod q\}$ for $\mathbf{A} \in \mathbb{Z}_q^{n \times m}$.

2.2 Probabilities

For a finite set S, we define $|S|$ to be its cardinality, and $U(S)$ to be the uniform probability distribution over S. The action of sampling $x \in S$ from a probability distribution P is denoted by $x \hookleftarrow P$. We use $x \sim P$ to say that the random variable x follows the distribution P. The *statistical distance* between two discrete probability distributions P and Q over a countable set S is defined as $\Delta(P, Q) = \frac{1}{2} \sum_{x \in S} |P(x) - Q(x)|$. We start by recalling the leftover hash lemma from [27] which we write to match our context and notations.

Lemma 2.1 (Adapted from [23,27]). Let n, m, q be positive integers such that q is an odd prime. For $\mathbf{A} \sim U(\mathbb{Z}_q^{n \times m})$, $\mathbf{x} \sim U(\{-1, 0, 1\}^m)$, and $\mathbf{u} \sim U(\mathbb{Z}_q^n)$, it holds that $\Delta((\mathbf{A}, \mathbf{A}\mathbf{x} \bmod q), (\mathbf{A}, \mathbf{u})) \leq \frac{1}{2}\sqrt{q^n/3^m}$. In particular, whenever $m \log_2 3 \geq n \log_2 q + \omega(\log_2 \lambda)$, the statistical distance is negligible.

For any *center* vector $\mathbf{c} \in \mathbb{R}^n$, and *Gaussian width* $\sigma > 0$, we define the Gaussian function $\rho_{\sigma,\mathbf{c}} : \mathbf{x} \in \mathbb{R}^n \mapsto \exp(-\pi \|\mathbf{x} - \mathbf{c}\|_2^2 / \sigma^2)$. For a lattice $\mathcal{L}$ of rank n, we define the *discrete Gaussian distribution* $\mathcal{D}_{\mathcal{L},\sigma,\mathbf{c}}$ of support $\mathcal{L}$, width σ and center $\mathbf{c}$ by $\mathcal{D}_{\mathcal{L},\sigma,\mathbf{c}} : \mathbf{x} \in \mathcal{L} \mapsto \rho_{\sigma,\mathbf{c}}(\mathbf{x})/\rho_{\sigma,\mathbf{c}}(\mathcal{L})$, where $\rho_{\sigma,\mathbf{c}}(\mathcal{L}) = \sum_{\mathbf{x} \in \mathcal{L}} \rho_{\sigma,\mathbf{c}}(\mathbf{x})$. When $\mathbf{c} = \mathbf{0}$, we omit it in the notations. We then use it to define the *smoothing parameter* of a lattice $\mathcal{L}$ [41], parameterized by a real $\varepsilon > 0$, by $\eta_\varepsilon(\mathcal{L}) = \inf\{s > 0 : \rho_{1/s}(\mathcal{L}^*) \leq 1 + \varepsilon\}$. If the standard deviation is wider than the smoothing parameter, the discrete Gaussian distribution benefits from properties that are similar to the ones of the continuous Gaussian distribution. In particular, the sum of two independent discrete Gaussians is a discrete Gaussian.

Lemma 2.2 (Adapted from [44, Claim 3.9][40, Thm. 3.3]). Let $\mathcal{L}$ be lattice of rank n. Let $r, s > 0$ and $t = \sqrt{r^2 + s^2}$ be such that $rs/t \geq \eta_\varepsilon(\mathcal{L})$ for some $\varepsilon \in (0, 1/2]$. Then, we have $\Delta(\mathcal{D}_{\mathcal{L},r} + \mathcal{D}_{\mathcal{L},s}, \mathcal{D}_{\mathcal{L},t}) \leq 7\varepsilon/4$. The condition on r, s is satisfied for example when $r, s \geq \sqrt{2}\eta_\varepsilon(\mathcal{L})$.

When centered around $\mathbf{0}$, the discrete Gaussian distribution benefits from tail bounds similar to the standard Gaussian distribution. In this work, we use tail bounds on the ℓ_2 and ℓ_∞ norms. We also recall the result of [34] bounding the magnitude of $\langle \mathbf{x}, \mathbf{v} \rangle$ for a discrete Gaussian $\mathbf{x}$ and an arbitrary vector $\mathbf{v}$. Although the tail bound on the ℓ_∞ norm follows directly from the latter, it was first proven in [42, Cor. 5.3].

Lemma 2.3 ([2, Lem. 1.5][42, Cor. 5.3][34, Lem 4.3]). *Let $\mathcal{L}$ be a lattice of rank n. Let $\sigma > 0$ and $\mathbf{v} \in \mathbb{R}^n$. Then, for all $t > 0$, it holds that*

1. $\mathbb{P}_{\mathbf{x} \sim \mathcal{D}_{\mathcal{L},\sigma}} [\|\mathbf{x}\|_2 > \sigma \sqrt{n}] < 2^{-2n}$,
2. $\mathbb{P}_{\mathbf{x} \sim \mathcal{D}_{\mathcal{L},\sigma}} [\|\mathbf{x}\|_\infty > \sigma \log_2 n] \leq 2ne^{-\pi \log_2^2 n}$,
3. $\mathbb{P}_{\mathbf{x} \sim \mathcal{D}_{\mathcal{L},\sigma}} [|\langle \mathbf{x}, \mathbf{v} \rangle| > \sigma t \|\mathbf{v}\|_2] \leq 2e^{-\pi t^2}$.

We also use the following bound on the spectral norm of a matrix with independent sub-Gaussian entries. We recall the definition of a sub-Gaussian random vector.

Definition 2.1 (Sub-Gaussian Distribution). *Let n be a positive integer, and $\mathbf{x}$ a (discrete or continuous) random vector over $\mathbb{R}^n$. We say that $\mathbf{x}$ is sub-Gaussian with sub-Gaussian moment s if for all unit vector $\mathbf{u} \in \mathbb{R}^n$ and all $t \in \mathbb{R}$, we have $\mathbb{E}[\exp(t \langle \mathbf{x}, \mathbf{u} \rangle)] \leq e^{s^2 t^2 / 2}$.*

Lemma 2.4 ([46]). *Let ℓ, m be two positive integers, and $\mathcal{P}$ a sub-Gaussian distribution of moment s. There exists a universal constant $C > 0$ such that for all $t > 0$, $\mathbb{P}_{\mathbf{U} \hookrightarrow \mathcal{P}^{\ell \times m}} [\|\mathbf{U}\|_2 \geq Cs(\sqrt{\ell} + \sqrt{m} + t)] \leq 2e^{-\pi t^2}$.*

By noticing that $\mathcal{P} = U([-1,1])$ is sub-Gaussian with moment $\sqrt{2/3}$, we can bound the spectral norm of ternary uniform matrix by $C\sqrt{2/3}(\sqrt{\ell} + \sqrt{m} + t)$ except with probability $2e^{-\pi t^2}$, for some constant $C > 0$ that does not depend on the dimensions. We can verify experimentally that in this case $C\sqrt{2/3} \leq 1$, and we thus omit it in the rest of the paper for clarity. The security proof of our signature requires a bound on $\|\mathbf{U}\mathbf{m}\|_2$ for an arbitrary message $\mathbf{m} \in \{0,1\}^m$ and uniform ternary $\mathbf{U}$. When m is small, Lemma 2.4 gives a close to optimal bound by $\|\mathbf{U}\mathbf{m}\|_2 \leq \|\mathbf{U}\|_2 \sqrt{m}$. However, when m is large, we expect a tighter bound. By using the fact that square sub-Gaussian random variables are sub-exponential and tail bounds on sub-exponential distributions, we get the following lemma. The proof and associated definitions are provided in the full version [31, Sec. A].

Lemma 2.5. *Let ℓ, m be two positive integers and $x > 0$. We assume that $\ell > x \cdot 10/\log_2 e$. Let $\mathbf{m} \in \{0,1\}^m$. We have $\mathbb{P}_{\mathbf{U} \hookrightarrow U([-1,1])^{\ell \times m}} [\|\mathbf{U}\mathbf{m}\|_2 \geq 2\sqrt{\ell m}] \leq 2^{-x}$.*

In our situation, $x = \Theta(\lambda)$ with λ the security parameter, and $\ell = O(n \log_2 q + \omega(\log_2 \lambda))$. The condition $\ell > 10x/\log_2 e$ is then verified. Note that this condition is necessary only to obtain the simple bound $2\sqrt{\ell m}$ with probability 2^{-x}, but one could use a different bound or different probability to avoid this condition. Combining both lemmas gives the following

$$\mathbb{P}_{\mathbf{U} \hookrightarrow U([-1,1]^{\ell \times m})} [\|\mathbf{U}\mathbf{m}\|_2 \geq \min(2\sqrt{\ell}, \sqrt{\ell} + \sqrt{m} + t)\sqrt{m}] \leq 2^{-2\lambda} + 2e^{-\pi t^2}, \quad (3)$$

whenever $\ell \geq 20\lambda/\log_2 e$ which is the case in our context. The spectral bound of Lemma 2.4 is also necessary to set the correct parameters to sample Gaussian vectors $\mathbf{v}$ verifying $[\mathbf{A}|\tau\mathbf{G} - \mathbf{AR}]\mathbf{v} = \mathbf{u}$, where $\mathbf{A}$ is a uniform matrix, $\mathbf{R}$ a short random matrix and $\mathbf{G}$ the gadget matrix of [39] used for efficient pre-image sampling. Our signature uses the following pre-image sampling algorithm.

Lemma 2.6 ([39]). *There exists an algorithm* SampleD *that takes as input a trapdoor matrix* $\mathbf{R} \in \mathbb{Z}^{m_1 \times n\lceil \log_2 q \rceil}$, *a partial parity-check matrix* $\mathbf{A} \in \mathbb{Z}_q^{n \times m_1}$, *an invertible tag matrix* $\mathbf{H} \in \mathbb{Z}_q^{n \times n}$, *a syndrome* $\mathbf{u} \in \mathbb{Z}_q^n$ *and a standard deviation* $\sigma \geq \eta_\varepsilon(\mathbb{Z})\sqrt{7}\sqrt{1 + \|\mathbf{R}\|_2^2}$, *and that outputs* $\mathbf{v}$ *that is statistically close to* $\mathcal{D}_{\mathbb{Z}^{m_1 + n\lceil \log_2 q \rceil}, \sigma}$ *conditioned on* $[\mathbf{A}|\mathbf{HG} - \mathbf{AR}]\mathbf{v} = \mathbf{u} \bmod q$, *with* $\mathbf{G} = \mathbf{I}_n \otimes \mathbf{g}$ *and* $\mathbf{g} = [1 \ldots 2^{\lceil \log_2 q \rceil - 1}]$.

2.3 Hardness Assumption

The security of our signature scheme relies on the *Short Integer Solution* (SIS) problem [1], which we recall here.

Definition 2.2 (Short Integer Solution). *Let* n, m, q *be positive integers, and* $\beta_2 \geq \beta_\infty \geq 1$. *The* Short Integer Solution *problem* $\text{SIS}_{n,m,q,\beta_\infty,\beta_2}^{\infty,2}$ *asks to find* $\mathbf{x} \in \mathcal{L}_q^\perp(\mathbf{A})\backslash\{\mathbf{0}\}$ *given* $\mathbf{A} \hookleftarrow U(\mathbb{Z}_q^{n \times m})$ *such that* $\|\mathbf{x}\|_\infty \leq \beta_\infty$ *and* $\|\mathbf{x}\|_2 \leq \beta_2$.

Note that the original formulation of SIS considers a single bound β on the ℓ_2 norm. There is a trivial reduction from the latter to $\text{SIS}_{n,m,q,\beta_\infty,\beta_2}^{\infty,2}$ by setting $\beta = \min(\beta_\infty\sqrt{m}, \beta_2)$. As discussed by Micciancio and Peikert [40, Thm. 1.1], using both norm bounds leads to more precise hardness results, and sometimes smaller approximation factors when relating the problem to worst-case problems on lattices. Moreover, it seems to be relevant for the concrete hardness of the problem as well. Indeed, most lattice reduction algorithms aim at finding vectors in the ball of radius β_2 but without constraining the magnitude of the coefficients. Finding a lattice vector in the intersection of the ball of radius β_2 and the hypercube of half side β_∞ is at least as hard as the same task without the β_∞ bound. When $\beta_\infty \ll \beta_2$, it may even be substantially harder.

2.4 Signature Scheme

A signature scheme is defined by four algorithms. The Setup algorithm is a probabilistic algorithm that, on input a security parameter λ, outputs the public parameters pp that will be common to all users. The key generation algorithm KeyGen is a probabilistic algorithm that, on input pp, outputs a secret signing key sk and a public verification key pk. The signing algorithm Sign is a probabilistic algorithm which, on inputs sk and a message $\mathbf{m}$ (and pk, pp), outputs a signature sig. Finally, the verification algorithm Verify is a deterministic algorithm that, on inputs pk, $\mathbf{m}$, sig (and pp), outputs 1 if sig is a valid signature on $\mathbf{m}$ under pk, and 0 otherwise. We use the *Existential Unforgeability against Chosen Message Attacks* (EUF-CMA) security model, which we formally recall in the full version [31, Sec. B] along with the security proofs of our signature scheme.

3   A Lattice-Based Signature Scheme

We present here our signature scheme which interfaces smoothly with privacy-enhancing protocols. It provides an alternative to the only such scheme based on lattices due to Libert et al. [33].

One of the main differences between their construction and ours is that we aim at optimizing the interactions between the commitment scheme implicitly used by such kind of protocols and the signature scheme itself. In [33], the public parameters of these two components were generated independently. We depart completely from this approach by generating these parameters conjointly and even by using a common matrix $\mathbf{A}$ for these two parts. Besides the natural gain in the public key size, this strategy allows one to merge different components of the signature itself. In particular, compared to [33], our signature no longer has to include the commitment opening, which significantly reduces its size.

Obviously, this has important consequences on the design of the scheme itself. One of them is that it forbids to re-use the approach of [33], inherited from Boyen signature [11], where $\mathbf{A}$ was generated together with a trapdoor, because it would clearly break the hiding property of the commitment scheme. We instead rely on a $\mathbf{G}$-trapdoor $\mathbf{R}$ of size $m_1 \times m_2$ in the sense of [39] and then use a matrix $[\mathbf{A}|\tau\mathbf{G} - \mathbf{AR}]$ where τ is a tag from $\mathbb{Z}_q^\times$. We can therefore generate $\mathbf{A}$ as a random matrix[4] of size $n \times m_1$, where m_1 is the dimension of the commitment randomness. We then use it to construct the commitment $\mathbf{c}$ to a message $\mathbf{m} \in \{0, 1\}^{m_3}$ as $\mathbf{c} = \mathbf{Ar} + \mathbf{Dm} \bmod q$, where $\mathbf{D}$ is a random matrix of size $n \times m_3$ and m_3 is the dimension of the message. The randomness $\mathbf{r}$ can then be merged with the short vector $\mathbf{v}$ generated thanks to the trapdoor, as mentioned above.

In [33], the authors had to first compute a binary decomposition $\mathbf{c}'$ of the commitment $\mathbf{c}$ to the message before generating a short pre-image of $\mathbf{u} + \mathbf{Dc}'$ where $\mathbf{u}$ (resp. $\mathbf{D}$) was some public vector (resp. matrix). This might look harmless when we only consider the signature because it does not increase its size. However, when plugged in the Yang et al. ZK framework [47] this replaces one secret vector $\mathbf{c}$ by $\log_2 q$ ones and makes the overall statement to prove more complex[5]. To remove this binary decomposition we revisit the security proof and show how to avoid it by using an argument based on the Rényi Divergence. Additionally, this change seems necessary to extend our construction to polynomial rings, as described in Sect. 3.3.

More generally, all the modifications we introduce have a second positive effect on complexity. In both our security proof and the one of [33], it is necessary to generate the public matrices with hidden relations, usually by multiplying one by some low-norm matrix $\mathbf{U}$ to generate the other. This impacts the norm of the extracted solutions, which grows with the number of such matrices and computational steps, and therefore impacts the system parameters. By reusing $\mathbf{A}$ for different purposes and by removing some computational steps (e.g.,

---

[4] In our protocol for signing hidden messages, we will have to enforce this requirement but this can be done easily by setting $\mathbf{A}$ as some hash output.

[5] Considering a binary tag also leads to similar inefficiencies.

multiplication by $\mathbf{D}$), we significantly reduce the discrepancy between the adversary output and the resulting SIS solution, leading to much better parameters.

3.1   Description of the Signature

We now describe the four algorithms that define our signature scheme. The signature is designed to sign a binary message $\mathbf{m}$. We present our scheme for the more general case of a message with variable length m_3 rather than a variable number of blocks of fixed length which may require unnecessary padding. Except for m_3 which is chosen depending on the use case, the other parameters are determined by the correctness and security analysis of the scheme, which are the object of Lemmas 3.1, 3.2, and 3.3.

Algorithm 3.1: Setup

Input: Security parameter λ.

1. Select a positive integer n.   ▷ SIS dimension driving security
2. Select a prime integer q.   ▷ modulus driving security
3. Select a positive integer $Q \leq q' \leq q$.   ▷ Bound on tags
4. $\mathcal{T} \leftarrow \mathbb{Z}_{q'} \setminus \{0\}$.   ▷ Tag space
5. Select $f(\lambda) \leftarrow \omega(\log_2 \lambda)$.   ▷ Leftover Hash Lemma slack
6. $m_1 \leftarrow \lceil (n \log_2 q + f(\lambda)) / \log_2 3 \rceil$. ▷ Commitment randomness dimension
7. $m_2 \leftarrow n \lceil \log_2 q \rceil$.
8. $m \leftarrow m_1 + m_2$.   ▷ Signature dimension
9. Choose a positive integer m_3.   ▷ Maximum bit-size of $\mathbf{m}$
10. $\mathbf{g} \leftarrow [2^0 | \ldots | 2^{\lceil \log_2 q \rceil - 1}] \in \mathbb{Z}_q^{1 \times \lceil \log_2 q \rceil}$. ▷ Gadget vector
11. $r \leftarrow \eta_\varepsilon(\mathbb{Z})$.   ▷ $r = 5.4$ leads to $\varepsilon \approx 2^{-131}$
12. Select $t > 0$.   ▷ Spectral norm slack (Equation (3))
13. $\sigma \leftarrow r\sqrt{7}\sqrt{(\sqrt{m_1} + \sqrt{m_2} + t)^2 + 1}$. ▷ Preimage sampling width
14. $\sigma_2 \leftarrow \max\left(\sqrt{m_3} \min(2\sqrt{m_1}, \sqrt{m_1} + \sqrt{m_2} + t)^2 - \sigma^2, \omega(\sqrt{\log_2 m_1}) \right)$.
15. $\sigma_1 \leftarrow \sqrt{\sigma^2 + \sigma_2^2}$.
16. $\mathbf{D} \hookleftarrow U(\mathbb{Z}_q^{n \times m_3})$.   ▷ Message commitment key

Output: $\mathsf{pp} = (\mathbf{D}; \mathbf{g}; \lambda, n, m_1, m_2, m_3, q, \sigma, \sigma_2, \sigma_1)$.

Algorithm 3.2: KeyGen

Input: Public parameters pp as in Algorithm 3.1.

1. $\mathbf{A} \hookleftarrow U(\mathbb{Z}_q^{n \times m_1})$.
2. $\mathbf{R} \hookleftarrow U([-1, 1]^{m_1 \times m_2})$.
3. $\mathbf{B} \leftarrow \mathbf{A}\mathbf{R} \bmod q \in \mathbb{Z}_q^{n \times m_2}$.
4. $\mathbf{u} \hookleftarrow U(\mathbb{Z}_q^n)$.

Output: $\mathsf{pk} = (\mathbf{A}, \mathbf{B}, \mathbf{u})$, and $\mathsf{sk} = \mathbf{R}$.

Algorithm 3.3: Sign

Input: Signing key sk, Message $\mathbf{m} \in \{0,1\}^{m_3}$, Public key pk, Public Param. pp, State st.

1. $\mathbf{r} \hookleftarrow \mathcal{D}_{\mathbb{Z}^{m_1}, \sigma_2}$.

2. $\mathbf{c} \leftarrow \mathbf{Ar} + \mathbf{Dm} \bmod q$.   ▷ Commitment to $\mathbf{m}$
3. $\tau \leftarrow F(\mathsf{st})$.   ▷ $\tau \in \mathcal{T}$
4. $\mathbf{v} \leftarrow \mathsf{SampleD}(\mathbf{R}, \mathbf{A}, \tau \mathbf{I}_n, \mathbf{u} + \mathbf{c}, \sigma) - [\mathbf{r}^T | \mathbf{0}_{m_2}]^T$.   ▷ $\mathbf{A}_\tau = [\mathbf{A}|\tau(\mathbf{I}_n \otimes \mathbf{g}) - \mathbf{B}]$
5. $\mathsf{st} \leftarrow \mathsf{st} + 1$.

Output: sig $= (\tau, \mathbf{v})$.

───────────────── **Algorithm 3.4: Verify** ─────────────────

Input: Public key pk, Message $\mathbf{m} \in \{0,1\}^{m_3}$, Signature sig, Public Param. pp.

1. $\mathbf{A}_\tau \leftarrow [\mathbf{A}|\tau(\mathbf{I}_n \otimes \mathbf{g}) - \mathbf{B}] \in \mathbb{Z}_q^{n \times m}$.
2. Split $\mathbf{v}$ into $[\mathbf{v}_1^T | \mathbf{v}_2^T]^T$, with $\mathbf{v}_1 \in \mathbb{Z}^{m_1}$, $\mathbf{v}_2 \in \mathbb{Z}^{m_2}$.
3. $b \leftarrow (\mathbf{A}_\tau \mathbf{v} = \mathbf{u} + \mathbf{Dm} \bmod q) \wedge (\|\mathbf{v}_1\|_\infty \leq \sigma_1 \log_2 m_1) \wedge (\|\mathbf{v}_2\|_\infty \leq \sigma \log_2 m_2) \wedge (\tau \in \mathcal{T})$

Output: b.   ▷ $b = 1$ if valid, 0 otherwise

The correctness of the signature scheme simply relies on the sum of discrete Gaussians (Lemma 2.2) and the Gaussian tail bound (Lemma 2.3). The former guarantees that $\mathbf{v}_1$ is statistically close to $\mathcal{D}_{\mathbb{Z}^{m_1}, \sigma_1}$, and the latter ensures that for an honest signature it holds that $\|\mathbf{v}_1\|_\infty \leq \sigma_1 \log_2 m_1$, and $\|\mathbf{v}_2\|_\infty \leq \sigma \log_2 m_2$ with overwhelming probability.

Lemma 3.1 (Correctness). *The signature scheme of Algorithms 3.1, 3.2, 3.3, and 3.4 is correct with negligible correctness error.*

Proof Let pp $\leftarrow$ Setup(1^λ), (pk, sk) $= ((\mathbf{A}, \mathbf{B}, \mathbf{u}), \mathbf{R}) \leftarrow$ KeyGen(pp). Let $\mathbf{m} \in \{0,1\}^{m_3}$ and $(\tau, \mathbf{v}) \leftarrow$ Sign(sk, $\mathbf{m}$, pk, pp, st). Then, there exists a vector $\mathbf{r} \in \mathbb{Z}^{m_1}$ drawn from $\mathcal{D}_{\mathbb{Z}^{m_1}, \sigma_2}$ such that $\mathbf{v} = \mathbf{v}' - [\mathbf{r}^T | \mathbf{0}]^T$, where $\mathbf{v}'$ was obtained from SampleD($\mathbf{R}, \mathbf{A}, \tau \mathbf{I}_n, \mathbf{u} + \mathbf{Ar} + \mathbf{Dm} \bmod q, \sigma$). By Lemma 2.6, it holds that $[\mathbf{A}|\tau(\mathbf{I}_n \otimes \mathbf{g}) - \mathbf{B}]\mathbf{v} = [\mathbf{A}|\tau(\mathbf{I}_n \otimes \mathbf{g}) - \mathbf{B}]\mathbf{v}' - \mathbf{Ar} = \mathbf{u} + \mathbf{Ar} + \mathbf{Dm} - \mathbf{Ar} \bmod q = \mathbf{u} + \mathbf{Dm} \bmod q$.

Then, also by Lemma 2.6, it holds that $\mathbf{v}'$ is statistically close to $\mathcal{D}_{\mathbb{Z}^{m_1+m_2}, \sigma}$ conditioned on $\mathbf{A}_\tau \mathbf{v}' = \mathbf{u} + \mathbf{Ar} + \mathbf{Dm} \bmod q$. Hence, by Lemma 2.2, $\mathbf{v}$ is statistically close to $\mathcal{D}_{\mathbb{Z}^{m_1+m_2}, \mathbf{S}}$ conditioned on $\mathbf{A}_\tau \mathbf{v} = \mathbf{u} + \mathbf{Dm} \bmod q$ and where $\mathbf{S} = \mathrm{diag}(\sqrt{\sigma^2 + \sigma_2^2}\mathbf{I}_{m_1}, \sigma \mathbf{I}_{m_2}) = \mathrm{diag}(\sigma_1 \mathbf{I}_{m_1}, \sigma \mathbf{I}_{m_2})$. Finally, applying Lemma 2.3 yields the bounds on $\|\mathbf{v}_1\|_\infty$ and $\|\mathbf{v}_2\|_\infty$. It gives that $b = 1$ except with negligible probability as claimed.   □

Note that the randomness $\mathbf{r}$ used to commit to the message can be drawn from a Gaussian with any width $\sigma_2 > 0$. However, the security proofs require σ_1 to be at least $\min(2\sqrt{m_1}, \sqrt{m_1} + \sqrt{m_3} + t)\sqrt{m_3}$ in order to hide the shifted center of the Gaussian vector, which in turns restricts the value of σ_2. Additionally, the goal of this signature scheme being to allow signing on committed messages, σ_2 must be chosen so that the commitment scheme is statistically hiding, which is why we take it at least $\omega(\sqrt{\log_2 m_1})$. We present our signature scheme in the most general way, thus explaining the multitude of dimensions m_i and Gaussian widths σ_i. This also allows fine-tuning of the parameters depending on the specific application. Typically, an application requiring to sign only small messages of constant bit-size m_3 would be able to select a much smaller σ_1 and would then yield smaller signatures.

We also point out the fact that we express the shortness condition on $\mathbf{v}$ in the ℓ_∞ norm. This is due to the fact that the zero-knowledge argument framework from [47] that we consider to prove possession of a message-signature pair allows one to prove bounds on the coefficients more naturally. As a result, we can base the security of our signature scheme on $\mathrm{SIS}^{\infty,2}$ which is at least as hard as SIS^2 as explained in Sect. 2.3.

Remark 3.1. As discussed in Sect. 1, we choose to describe a stateful version of our construction that better suits our applications, hence the fact that our tags τ are generated as $F(\mathsf{st})$. The only requirements placed on F are that it must be injective, with outputs in the tag space, which should easily be met in practice. For example, in the case of group signatures, one can proceed as in [21] and set the tags as the group members' identities. Nevertheless, if selecting such a function F proved to be difficult for some use case, we recall that a stateless version of our construction is provided in the full version [31, Sec. G].

3.2   Security of the Signature

We distinguish two types of forgeries that an attacker can produce, which we treat separately for the sake of clarity. More precisely we distinguish between the cases depending on whether or not the tag τ^* of the forgery has been re-used from the signature queries. Combining the corresponding lemmas proves the EUF-CMA security of the signature under the SIS assumption. It consists in the SIS challenger tossing a coin and proceeding as in either Lemma 3.2 or 3.3 and aborting if the forgery does not match the coin toss. The proofs are provided in the full version [31, Sec. B.2 & B.3] for completeness.

Lemma 3.2. *An adversary produces a Type I forgery* $(\tau^*, \mathbf{v}^*)$ *if the tag* τ^* *does not collide with the tags of the signing queries. If an adversary can produce a Type I forgery with advantage* δ, *then we can construct an adversary* $\mathcal{B}$ *that solves the* $\mathrm{SIS}^{\infty,2}_{n,m_1+1,q,\beta_\infty,\beta_2}$ *problem with advantage* $\mathrm{Adv}[\mathcal{B}] \gtrsim \delta/(|\mathcal{T}| - Q)$, *for* $\beta_\infty = \sigma_1 \log_2 m_1 + m_2 \sigma \log_2 m_2 + m_3$ *and* $\beta_2 = \sqrt{1 + (\sqrt{m_1} + \sqrt{m_2} + t)^2} \cdot \sqrt{m_1(\sigma_1 \log_2 m_1)^2 + m_2(\sigma \log_2 m_2)^2 + \min(2\sqrt{m_1}, \sqrt{m_1} + \sqrt{m_3} + t)\sqrt{m_3} + 1}$.

Lemma 3.3. *An adversary produces a Type II forgery* $(\tau^*, \mathbf{v}^*)$ *if the tag* τ^* *is re-used from some* i^*-*th signing query* $(\tau^{(i^*)}, \mathbf{v}^{(i^*)})$, *i.e.,* $\tau^* = \tau^{(i^*)}$. *If an adversary can produce a Type II forgery with advantage* δ, *we can construct* $\mathcal{B}$ *solving* $\mathrm{SIS}^{\infty,2}_{n,m_1,q,\beta'_\infty,\beta'_2}$ *with advantage* $\mathrm{Adv}[\mathcal{B}] \gtrsim \delta^{\alpha^*}/(\alpha^*-1)e^{-\alpha^*\pi}/Q$, *with* $\alpha^* = 1 + \sqrt{\log_2(1/\delta)/(\pi \log_2 e)}$, *and for* $\beta'_\infty = 2\sigma_1 \log_2 m_1 + m_2 \cdot 2\sigma \log_2 m_2 + m_3$, $\beta'_2 = \sqrt{1 + (\sqrt{m_1} + \sqrt{m_2} + t)^2} \cdot \sqrt{\sigma_1^2 m_1(1 + \log_2^2 m_1) + \sigma^2 m_2(1 + \log_2^2 m_2) + \min(2\sqrt{m_1}, \sqrt{m_1} + \sqrt{m_3} + t)\sqrt{m_3}}$.

3.3   Our Signature on Modules

The results of Table 1 show that the performances of the signature scheme from Sect. 3.1 and associated protocols are greatly improved over [33]. However, the complexity is still rather high and we therefore investigate in this section a way to decrease it. Concretely, we show that the signature scheme from Sect. 3.1 can be extended over the ring of integers of a number field. For the zero-knowledge arguments required by the efficient protocols, we employ the recent framework from [35], which we detail in Sect. 4.3. We use a tag space that corresponds to the identity space of their group signature construction. We also use a message space that is similar to the latter but with no restriction on the number of non-zero coefficients. We present our construction with a single power-of-two cyclotomic ring, but we note that it can be adapted to use subrings for efficiency gains. For more details on the use of subrings, we refer to [35,36]. In what follows, we take n a power of two and R the $2n$-th cyclotomic ring, i.e., $R = \mathbb{Z}[X]/\langle X^n + 1 \rangle$. We also define $R_q = \mathbb{Z}_q[X]/\langle X^n + 1 \rangle$ for any modulus $q \geq 2$. We call θ the coefficient embedding of R, i.e., for all $r = \sum_{i \in [0,n-1]} r_i X^i \in R$, $\theta(r) = [r_0 \ldots r_{n-1}]^T$. We then define $S_{bin} = \theta^{-1}(\{0,1\}^n)$ and $S_1 = \theta^{-1}(\{-1,0,1\}^n)$. We also define the usual norms $\|\cdot\|_p$ over R by $\|r\|_p := \|\theta(r)\|_p$. Finally, we define the discrete Gaussian distribution over R by $\theta^{-1}(\mathcal{D}_{\theta(R),\sigma})$, which we denote by $\mathcal{D}_{R,\sigma}$.

Remark 3.2. The Gaussian distributions are defined with respect to the coefficient embedding θ. Theoretical works usually define Gaussian distributions with respect to the Minkowski embedding (or canonical embedding) σ_H. We refer to [37] for more details. In our specific case of power-of-two cyclotomic rings, it holds that $\sigma_H = \sqrt{n}\mathbf{P}\theta$ where $\mathbf{P}$ is a unitary matrix. Hence, by denoting $\mathcal{D}_{R,\sigma}^{\theta}$ (resp. $\mathcal{D}_{R,\sigma}^{\sigma_H}$) the Gaussian distribution with respect to θ (resp. σ_H), we can show that $\mathcal{D}_{R,\sigma\sqrt{n}}^{\sigma_H}$ is exactly the same distribution as $\mathcal{D}_{R,\sigma}^{\theta}$.

3.3.1   Description

Our module signature scheme is described by Algorithms 3.5, 3.6, 3.7 and 3.8.

Algorithm 3.5: Setup

Input: Security parameter λ.

1. Select a positive integer d.   ▷ M-SIS rank driving security
2. Select $k \leq n$ to be a power of two.   ▷ Number of splitting factors
3. Select a prime integer q such that $q = 2k + 1 \bmod 4k$ and $q \geq (2\sqrt{k})^k$.
4. Select positive integers w, κ.   ▷ w such that $\binom{n}{w} \geq Q$
5. $\mathcal{T}_w \leftarrow \{\tau \in S_{bin} : \|\tau\|_2 = \sqrt{w}\}$.   ▷ Tag space
6. $g \leftarrow \lceil q^{1/\kappa} \rfloor$.
7. $m_1 \leftarrow \lceil (d \log_2 q + f(\lambda))/\log_2 3 \rceil$ ▷ $f(\lambda) = \omega(\log_2 \lambda)$
8. $m_2 \leftarrow d\kappa$
9. $m \leftarrow m_1 + m_2$.   ▷ Signature dimension
10. Choose a positive integer m_3.   ▷ Maximum bit-size of $\mathbf{m}$ is $n \cdot m_3$
11. $\mathbf{g} = [1 \cdots g^{\kappa-1}] \in R_q^{1 \times \kappa}$.   ▷ Gadget vector
12. $r \leftarrow \eta_\varepsilon(\mathbb{Z})$.   ▷ $r = 5.4$ leads to $\varepsilon \approx 2^{-131}$

13. Select $t > 0$.   ▷ Spectral norm slack
14. $\sigma \leftarrow r\sqrt{g^2 + 1}\sqrt{(\sqrt{nm_1} + \sqrt{nm_2} + t)^2 + 1}$.   ▷ Pre-image sampling width
15. $\sigma_2 \leftarrow \sqrt{(\sqrt{nm_1} + \sqrt{nm_3} + t)^2 \cdot nm_3 - \sigma^2}$.   ▷ Commitment randomness width
16. $\sigma_1 \leftarrow \sqrt{\sigma^2 + \sigma_2{}^2}$.
17. $\mathbf{D} \hookleftarrow U(R_q^{d \times m_3})$.   ▷ Message Commitment Key

Output: $\mathsf{pp} = (\mathbf{D}; \mathbf{g}; \lambda, n, d, m_1, m_2, m_3, q, w, \kappa, \sigma, \sigma_2, \sigma_1)$.

Algorithm 3.6: KeyGen

Input: Public parameters pp as in Algorithm 3.5.

1. $\mathbf{A} \hookleftarrow U(R_q^{d \times m_1})$.
2. $\mathbf{R} \hookleftarrow U(S_1^{m_1 \times m_2})$.
3. $\mathbf{B} \leftarrow \mathbf{A}\mathbf{R} \bmod qR \in R_q^{d \times m_2}$.
4. $\mathbf{u} \hookleftarrow U(R_q^d)$.

Output: $\mathsf{pk} = (\mathbf{A}, \mathbf{B}, \mathbf{u})$, and $\mathsf{sk} = \mathbf{R}$.

Algorithm 3.7: Sign

Input: Signing key sk, Message $\mathbf{m} \in S_{bin}^{m_3}$, Public key pk, Public Parameters pp, State st

1. $\mathbf{r} \hookleftarrow \mathcal{D}_{R^{m_1}, \sigma_2}$.
2. $\mathbf{c} \leftarrow \mathbf{A}\mathbf{r} + \mathbf{D}\mathbf{m} \bmod qR$.   ▷ Commitment to $\mathbf{m}$
3. $\tau \leftarrow F(\mathsf{st})$.   ▷ $\tau \in \mathcal{T}_w$
4. $\mathbf{v} \leftarrow \mathsf{SampleD}(\mathbf{R}, \mathbf{A}, \tau\mathbf{I}_d, \mathbf{u} + \mathbf{c}, \sigma) - [\mathbf{r}^T | \mathbf{0}_{m_2}]^T$.   ▷ $\mathbf{A}_\tau = [\mathbf{A} | \tau(\mathbf{I}_d \otimes \mathbf{g}) - \mathbf{B}]$
5. $\mathsf{st} \leftarrow \mathsf{st} + 1$.

Output: $\mathsf{sig} = (\tau, \mathbf{v})$.

Algorithm 3.8: Verify

Input: Public key pk, Message $\mathbf{m} \in S_{bin}^{m_3}$, Signature sig, Public Parameters pp.

1. $\mathbf{A}_\tau \leftarrow [\mathbf{A} | \tau(\mathbf{I}_d \otimes \mathbf{g}) - \mathbf{B}] \in R_q^{d \times m}$.
2. $b \leftarrow (\mathbf{A}_\tau \mathbf{v} = \mathbf{u} + \mathbf{D}\mathbf{m} \bmod qR) \wedge (\|\mathbf{v}\|_2 \leq \sqrt{\sigma_1^2 nm_1 + \sigma^2 nm_2}) \wedge (\tau \in \mathcal{T}_w)$

Output: b.   ▷ $b = 1$ if valid, 0 otherwise

3.3.2 Security Analysis

The security of the scheme is now based on the problem M-SIS$_{d, m_1, q, \beta}$ [32]. It asks to find $\mathbf{w} \in R^{m_1}$ such that $\mathbf{A}\mathbf{w} = \mathbf{0} \bmod qR$ and $0 < \|\mathbf{w}\|_2 \leq \beta$ given $\mathbf{A} \hookleftarrow U(R_q^{d \times m_1})$. The security proofs rigorously follow that of Lemma 3.2 and 3.3. This is due to the fact that all the tools that we use have a ring counterpart. We briefly explain what tools are needed to carry out the proofs in the module case. We stress that the construction can also be used over rings $(d = 1)$.

First, we need to ensure that a difference of distinct tags is invertible in R_q. By [38, Cor. 1.2], when $q = 2k + 1 \bmod 4k$, a ring element r is invertible in R_q if $0 < \|r\|_\infty \leq q^{1/k}/\sqrt{k}$. We chose q so that a difference of tags $\tau_1 - \tau_2$ has ℓ_∞ norm at most $2 \leq q^{1/k}/\sqrt{k}$. Hence, a difference of distinct tags is in $R_q^\times$. Then, the leftover hash lemma of Lemma 2.1 has been adapted to general rings of integer by Boudgoust et al. and further generalized in [9]. In our case, it ensures that $\mathbf{A}\mathbf{s}$ is within statistical distance ε of $U(R_q^d)$, where $\mathbf{A}\sim U(R_q^{d\times m})$, $\mathbf{s}\sim U(S_1^m)$ and $\varepsilon=\frac{1}{2}\sqrt{(1+q^d/3^m)^n-1}$.

The use of the Rényi divergence in the proof of Lemma 3.3 applies on the discrete Gaussian distributions, which are defined by their embedding to $\mathbb{R}^n$. As such, the argument remains unchanged. We also need to argue that for $\mathbf{A}\hookleftarrow U(R_q^{d\times m_1+m_2})$ and $\mathbf{v}\hookleftarrow \mathcal{D}_{R^{m_1+m_2},\boldsymbol{\Sigma}}$ with $\boldsymbol{\Sigma}=\mathrm{diag}(\sigma_1\mathbf{I}_{nm_1},\sigma\mathbf{I}_{nm_2})$, then $\mathbf{u}=\mathbf{A}\mathbf{v}\bmod q$ is close to uniform. For that, we use [37, Thm. 7.4] which states that if $\sigma,\sigma_1\geq 2nq^{(d+2/n)/(m_1+m_2)}$, then the public syndrome $\mathbf{u}$ is close to uniform in R_q^d. We note that this results holds when the Gaussian over R is defined with respect to the Minkowski embedding. As explained in Remark 3.2, in the case of our Gaussian distributions, we only need $\sigma,\sigma_1\geq 2\sqrt{n}q^{\frac{d+2/n}{m_1+m_2}}$. Since $m_1+m_2\geq d(\log_2(q)/\log_2(3)+\kappa)+f(\lambda)/\log_2(3)$, the result holds whenever $\sigma,\sigma_1\geq 3^{1+2/n}\cdot 2\sqrt{n}$, which is the case in our context.

Finally, we need to bound the spectral norm of structured matrices that are of size $nm_1\times nm_2$ (or $nm_1\times nm_3$). In power-of-two cyclotomic rings, the structured matrix considered is a block matrix whose blocks are nega-circulant matrices of size $n\times n$. The entries are thus all distributed according to $U([-1,1])$ but they are not all independent within a block. This means we cannot apply Lemma 2.4 directly. The spectral norm of such a structured matrix of size $nm_1\times nm_2$ is proven to be the maximal spectral norm of the n complex-embedded matrices of size $m_1\times m_2$ [9, Lem. 2.3], which all have i.i.d. entries that are sub-Gaussian of moment $\sqrt{2n/3}$. Applying Lemma 2.4 to these embedded matrices with the union bound (on half the complex embeddings) gives $\|\mathbf{R}\|_2\leq C\sqrt{2n/3}(\sqrt{m_1}+\sqrt{m_2}+t)$ with high probability for an absolute constant $C>0$. Although this bound is proven, we can verify experimentally that it is not tight, and rather that the original bound (when there is no structure) of $\sqrt{nm_1}+\sqrt{nm_2}+t$ for a small t (typically $6-7$) is satisfied with overwhelming probability. Further, we use the latter bound for setting parameters in the description of the signature.

Lemma 3.4. *If an adversary can produce a Type I forgery with advantage δ, then we can construct $\mathcal{B}$ that solves* M-SIS$_{d,m_1+1,q,\beta}^2$ *with advantage $Adv[\mathcal{B}]\gtrsim$ $\delta/(|\mathcal{T}_w|-Q)$, for $\beta=\sqrt{1+(\sqrt{nm_1}+\sqrt{nm_2}+t)^2}\sqrt{\sigma_1^2 nm_1+\sigma^2 nm_2}+(\sqrt{nm_1}+\sqrt{nm_3}+t)\sqrt{nm_3}+1$.*

Lemma 3.5. *If an adversary can produce a Type II forgery with advantage δ, we can construct $\mathcal{B}$ that solves the* M-SIS$_{d,m_1,q,\beta'}^2$ *problem with advantage $Adv[\mathcal{B}]\gtrsim$ $\delta^{\alpha^*/(\alpha^*-1)}e^{-\alpha^*\pi}/Q$, with $\alpha^*=1+\sqrt{\log_2(1/\delta)/(\pi\log_2 e)}$, and for for $\beta'=\sqrt{1+(\sqrt{nm_1}+\sqrt{nm_2}+t)^2}\cdot\sqrt{2\sigma_1^2 nm_1+2\sigma^2 nm_2}+(\sqrt{nm_1}+\sqrt{nm_3}+t)\sqrt{nm_3}$.*

4   Zero-Knowledge Arguments of Knowledge

We now detail out the zero-knowledge arguments of knowledge (ZKAoK) that we use to instantiate the protocols from Sect. 5. Since we propose a construction over $\mathbb{Z}_q$ and another over structured lattices, we employ the frameworks from [47] and [35] respectively to tackle the relations to be proven. We first discuss some aspects of the former, and later explain in Sect. 4.3 how to use both frameworks to instantiate the necessary relations.

4.1   A Framework for Quadratic Relations over $\mathbb{Z}_q$

Our construction requires a proof system that handles exact quadratic relations, over $\mathbb{Z}_q$ for our first construction and another framework over R_q for our structured variant. Let us first focus on the former. To handle such relations, we could have used Stern-like protocols but this would only reach constant soundness error, thus implying a large number of repetitions and hence bad performance. Additionally, the decomposition-extension methods used in the original scheme [33] make the relation to be proven much larger. To circumvent these two shortcomings, we instead use the more recent framework by Yang et al. [47]. It combines the perks of Stern-like ZKAoK and Fiat-Shamir with Aborts ZKAoK to reach a framework with standard soundness and inverse polynomial soundness error. This requires fewer iterations as a result. More precisely, the framework of [47] provides a ZKAoK for the relation

$$\mathcal{R}^* = \{((\overline{\mathbf{A}}, \mathbf{y}, \mathcal{M}); \mathbf{x}) \in (\mathbb{Z}_q^{k \times L_{\mathbf{x}}} \times \mathbb{Z}_q^k \times ([L_{\mathbf{x}}]^3)^{L_{\mathcal{M}}}) \times \mathbb{Z}_q^{L_{\mathbf{x}}} : \overline{\mathbf{A}}\mathbf{x} = \mathbf{y} \bmod q$$
$$\wedge \forall (h, i, j) \in \mathcal{M}, \mathbf{x}[h] = \mathbf{x}[i] \cdot \mathbf{x}[j] \bmod q\}.$$

This relation can be used to prove that the witness vector is short, which we need for our verification equation for example. Concretely, any witness $x \in \mathbb{Z}_q$ that we need to prove smaller than some bound B is decomposed as $x_1, \ldots, x_\ell$, where $\ell = \lceil \log_2 B \rceil$, which are proved binary using the quadratic relation $x_i^2 = x_i \bmod q$. The downside of this approach is that it adds ℓ witnesses for each short element, which quickly becomes cumbersome. To address this issue, the authors of [47] introduced a so-called *fast mode* that significantly reduces the size of the witness. We describe such a mode in Sect. 4.2 but also show that its analysis in [47] is not entirely correct and thus provide a more thorough one. We also propose additional optimizations in the full version [31, Sec. E].

4.2   Zero-Knowledge Fast Mode Revisited

As explained above, the decomposition technique entails a $(\ell + 1)$-fold increase of the witness, which is prohibitive for high-dimensional vectors. This has led the authors of [47] to sketch a so-called *fast mode* to obtain drastic efficiency gains in this case. The idea is to relax the zero-knowledge argument, thus introducing a soundness gap, and prove knowledge of a solution $\mathbf{w}'$ of $\mathbf{P}\mathbf{w}' = \mathbf{v} \bmod q$ such that $\mathbf{w}'$ is nB-bounded instead of B-bounded, where n is the dimension of $\mathbf{w}$. More precisely, they consider the following relation

$$\mathcal{R}' = \{((\mathbf{P}, \mathbf{v}, \mathbf{H}, \mathbf{c}), (\mathbf{w}, \mathbf{u}, \mathbf{r})) \in (\mathbb{Z}_q^{m \times n} \times \mathbb{Z}_q^m \times [0, 1]^{\lambda \times n} \times C) \times (\mathbb{Z}_q^n \times [0, nB]^\lambda \times R) :$$
$$\mathbf{P}\mathbf{w} = \mathbf{v} \bmod q \wedge \mathbf{H}\mathbf{w} - \mathbf{u} = 0 \bmod q \wedge \mathbf{c} = \texttt{Commit}(\mathbf{w}; \mathbf{r})\}$$

The point is that the prover now only has to prove a bound on the λ elements of $\mathbf{u}$ instead of the n elements from $\mathbf{w}$, which is very interesting when $\lambda \ll n$, a condition easily met in practice. The authors argue that, if one knows a witness $(\mathbf{w}, \mathbf{u}, \mathbf{r})$ satisfying $\mathcal{R}'$, it ensures that $\mathbf{w}$ is in $[0, nB]^n$, except with negligible probability over the randomness of $\mathbf{H}$. We provide a simple counter-example to the above. For example, assume a prover knows $\mathbf{w} = [-1, 1, \ldots, 1]^T$ such that $\mathbf{Pw} = \mathbf{v} \bmod q$. We now consider $\mathbf{H}$ to be a random matrix whose entries are independently distributed according to $U(\{0,1\})$. We denote by $\mathbf{h}_i$ the i-th row of $\mathbf{H}$ for $i \in [\lambda]$. For all $i \in [\lambda]$, we have $\mathbb{P}_{\mathbf{h}_i}[\mathbf{h}_i^T \mathbf{w} \in [0, nB]] = 1 - 2^{-n}$ by simply conditioning on the first coefficient of $\mathbf{h}_i$. It yields $\mathbb{P}_{\mathbf{H}}[\mathbf{Hw} \in [0, nB]^\lambda] = (1 - 2^{-n})^\lambda \geq 1 - \lambda 2^{-n}$. Since the *fast mode* is only relevant when $n \geq \lambda$, it holds that $\mathbf{Hw} \in [0, nB]^\lambda$ with overwhelming probability. This shows that $\mathcal{R}'$ cannot be used to prove that $\mathbf{w}$ has non-negative coefficients and thus for example invalidates the use of the fast mode in the e-cash use-case in [47].

Fortunately, a more thorough analysis shows that $\mathbf{Hw} \bmod q$ is in $[0, B]^\lambda$ implies that $\mathbf{w} \bmod q \in [-2B, 2B]^n$ with high probability, which would be sufficient in our case as we only need to prove bounds on the ℓ_∞ norm. However, we have so far only discussed of soundness. When it comes to correctness, we note that the choices made in [47] results in an unwieldy situation.

First, because one has to set an upper bound on $\mathbf{Hw}$ that will be satisfied with high probability for any $\mathbf{w}$ in $[-B, B]^n$. For a binary matrix $\mathbf{H}$, it seems hard to do much better than $[-nB, nB]^\lambda$ since we will be close to this bound for $\mathbf{w} = [B, \ldots, B]^T$, hence the factor n in the soudness gap mentioned above.

Second, because one cannot start the argument with $\mathbf{w} \in [-B, B]^n$ as it can lead to having $\mathbf{Hw}$ with negative coefficients. One must shift all the coefficients of $\mathbf{w}$ before running the protocol, but it results in a skewed statement on $\mathbf{w}$. Indeed, it would prove that $\mathbf{w} + B\mathbf{1}_n$ is in $[-2nB, 2nB]^n$ and therefore that $\mathbf{w} \in [-(2n+1)B, (2n-1)B]^n$, where $\mathbf{1}_n = [1 \ldots 1]^T \in \mathbb{Z}^n$.

For these reasons, we believe it is much more natural to sample the coefficients of $\mathbf{H}$ uniformly from $\{-1, 0, 1\}$. We prove below that $\mathbf{Hw} \bmod q$ is in $[-B, B]^\lambda$ still implies that $\mathbf{w} \bmod q \in [-2B, 2B]^n$, which avoids to shift the witness and thus the problem mentioned above. Moreover, such distribution of $\mathbf{H}$ allows us to derive much better upper bounds on $\mathbf{Hw}$ using for example an argument similar to the one of Lemma 2.5. However, we do not study more thoroughly this general problem as we are able to derive sharp bounds for our specific use case (see Remark 4.1 below).

More formally, let $\mathbf{H} \in [-1, 1]^{k \times n}$, with $k = \lambda / \log_2(9/5)$. The following lemma, proven in the full version [31, Sec. D], argues that $\mathbf{Hw} \bmod q \in [-B, B]^k$ implies $\mathbf{w} \bmod q \in [-2B, 2B]^n$ with overwhelming probability over the choice of $\mathbf{H}$.

Lemma 4.1. *Let $B \in \mathbb{Z}$ be such that $6B < q/2$. Let k be a positive integer. Let $\mathbf{w} \in \mathbb{Z}^n$ be a vector. Assuming that $\|\mathbf{w} \bmod q\|_\infty > 2B$, it then holds that $\mathbb{P}_{\mathbf{H} \hookleftarrow U(\{-1,1\}^{k \times n})} [\|\mathbf{Hw} \bmod q\|_\infty \leq B] \leq (5/9)^k$.*

The fast mode that we consider now corresponds to the following relation, where B is chosen so that $\|\mathbf{Hw} \bmod q\|_\infty \leq B$ with overwhelming probability for an honest witness $\mathbf{w}$.

$$\mathcal{R}'' = \{((\mathbf{P}, \mathbf{v}, \mathbf{H}, \mathbf{c}), (\mathbf{w}, \mathbf{u}, \mathbf{r})) \in (\mathbb{Z}_q^{m \times n} \times \mathbb{Z}_q^m \times [-1, 1]^{k \times n} \times \mathbf{C}) \times$$

$$(\mathbb{Z}_q^n \times [-B, B]^k \times \mathbf{R}) : \mathbf{P}\mathbf{w} = \mathbf{v} \bmod q \wedge \mathbf{H}\mathbf{w} - \mathbf{u} = \mathbf{0} \bmod q \wedge \mathbf{c} = \mathtt{Commit}(\mathbf{w}; \mathbf{r})\}$$

Remark 4.1. For our relations, the vectors that we need to prove short are sampled from discrete Gaussian distributions. For example the vector $\mathbf{v}_1$ follows $\mathcal{D}_{\mathbb{Z}^{m_1}, \sigma_1}$. For a fixed $\mathbf{H} \in \{-1, 0, 1\}^{k \times m_1}$, the third statement of Lemma 2.3 yields that $\mathbb{P}_{\mathbf{v}_1}[|\langle \mathbf{v}_1, \mathbf{h}_i \rangle| \geq \sigma_1 t \sqrt{m_1}] \leq \mathbb{P}_{\mathbf{v}_1}[|\langle \mathbf{v}_1, \mathbf{h}_i \rangle| \geq \sigma_1 t \|\mathbf{h}_i\|_2] \leq 2e^{-\pi t^2}$, where $\mathbf{h}_i$ is the i-th row of $\mathbf{H}$ and the first inequality follows by event inclusion as $\|\mathbf{h}_i\|_2 \leq \sqrt{m_1}$. The union bound yields $\mathbb{P}_{\mathbf{v}_1}[\|\mathbf{H}\mathbf{v}\|_\infty \geq \sigma_1 t \sqrt{m_1}] \leq 2ke^{-\pi t^2}$, where $k = \lambda / \log_2(9/5)$ as per Lemma 4.1. Hence, taking $t = \log_2 \lambda$ gives that $\|\mathbf{H}\mathbf{v}\|_\infty \leq \sigma_1 \sqrt{m_1} \log_2 \lambda$ with overwhelming probability. This improves on the trivial bound $\sigma_1 m_1 \log_2 m_1$. By making sure that $2\sigma_1 \sqrt{m_1} \log_2 \lambda < (q-1)/2$, which is generally the case, we have no wrap-around modulo q in $\mathbf{H}\mathbf{v}_1$ and therefore $\|\mathbf{H}\mathbf{v}_1 \bmod q\|_\infty \leq \sigma_1 \sqrt{m_1} \log_2 \lambda$. The conditions of Lemma 4.1 allow one to choose $B = \sigma_1 \sqrt{m_1} \log_2 \lambda \ll q/12$. Then, proving that $\|\mathbf{H}\mathbf{v}_1 \bmod q\|_\infty \leq \sigma_1 \sqrt{m_1} \log_2 \lambda$ implies that $\|\mathbf{v}_1 \bmod q\|_\infty \leq 2\sigma_1 \sqrt{m_1} \log_2 \lambda$.

4.3   Zero-Knowledge Arguments and Relations

The zero-knowledge framework from [47] allows to prove quadratic relations over $\mathbb{Z}_q$. The protocols accompanying our signature that we present in Sect. 5 require a proof system to prove knowledge of a commitment opening, and to prove knowledge of a message-signature pair, which are both quadratic relations. At a high level, the commitment opening proof requires to prove a linear relation and that the witness is short. As explained when describing $\mathcal{R}^*$, the latter can be dealt with by decomposing each entry in a binary vector, and proving that the latter indeed has binary coefficients. Similarly, proving knowledge of $(\mathbf{m}, \tau, \mathbf{v})$ such that $\mathsf{Verify}(\mathsf{pk}, \mathbf{m}, (\tau, \mathbf{v}), \mathsf{pp}) = 1$, requires proving that some elements have small magnitude, and that $\mathbf{A}\mathbf{v}_1 - \mathbf{B}\mathbf{v}_2 + \tau \mathbf{G}\mathbf{v}_2 = \mathbf{u} + \mathbf{D}\mathbf{m} \bmod q$ which is quadratic because of the term $\tau \mathbf{v}_2$. Due to lack of space, we defer to the full version [31, Sec. F] the details on how to use the framework of [47] to instantiate them.

We however give more details for our construction over structured lattices. Although the framework of [47] straightforwardly adapts to the ring or module setting, it results in relations of the form $\mathbf{A}\mathbf{x} = \mathbf{y} \bmod qR$ and $\mathbf{x}[h] = \mathbf{x}[i]\mathbf{x}[j] \bmod qR$. In our case, we aim to prove that the witness is short (or binary for the message part) with respect to the coefficient embedding of R. Taking the example of the message, $\mathbf{m}[i] = \mathbf{m}[i]^2 \bmod qR$ does not imply that the coefficients of the polynomial $\mathbf{m}[i]$ are binary, but only that the number theoretic transform (NTT) of $\mathbf{m}[i]$ is a binary vector. A naive alternative would be to embed the entire relation into $\mathbb{Z}$ via the coefficient embedding and applying [47] in a non-structured way. This would indeed prove the desired relation but it would also ignore the underlying structure and all the optimizations that come with it. Instead, we use the very recent framework by Lyubashevsky, Nguyen and Plançon [35], which generalizes the previous work of [8] and [25] used to obtain exact proofs. The advantage of this framework is that it provides a way to prove bounds on the ℓ_2 norm of the witness without resorting to bounds on the ℓ_∞ norm. As explained in [35], this leads to proving tighter bounds on the ℓ_2 norm, and in a more efficient way as a result. We denote by σ_{-1} to be the automorphism of R_q that can be defined as $\sigma_{-1}(\sum_{i=0}^{n-1} r_i X^i) = r_0 - \sum_{i=1}^{n-1} r_i X^{n-i}$. Their proof system allows one to prove relations of the form

$$\begin{cases} \forall i \in [\rho], f_i(\mathbf{s}) = 0 \bmod qR & \forall i \in [v_e], \left\| \mathbf{E}_i^{(e)} \mathbf{s} - \mathbf{u}_i^{(e)} \right\|_2 \leq \beta_i^{(e)} \\ \forall i \in [\rho_{eval}], \widetilde{F}_i(\mathbf{s}) = 0 & \forall i \in [v_a], \left\| \mathbf{E}_i^{(a)} \mathbf{s} - \mathbf{u}_i^{(a)} \right\|_\infty \leq \beta_i^{(a)}, \end{cases}$$

where the f_i, F_i are quadratic functions in $\mathbf{s} = [\mathbf{s}_1^T, \sigma_{-1}(\mathbf{s}_1)^T]^T$ ($\mathbf{s}_1$ being the committed vector), and $\widetilde{F}_i(\mathbf{s})$ denotes the constant coefficient of the polynomial $F_i(\mathbf{s})$. The norm conditions with superscript (e) are proven exactly, while those with superscript (a) are proven approximately. We note for completeness that the considered automorphism is not necessarily σ_{-1}. We present here how our relations can be instantiated in their framework, which consists in describing the functions f_i, F_i and matrices and vectors for the norm conditions.

Let $q_1 < q$ be a prime integer such that $q_1 = 2k + 1 \bmod 4k$, and define $q_\pi = q_1 q$ as the modulus of the proof system, which is different from the modulus of our signature. We take q_1 having the same splitting as q in R to ensure the invertibility of challenge differences in R_{q_π} as discussed in [35, Sec. 2.3].

4.3.1   Proof of Commitment Opening
Consider the relation

$$q_1(\mathbf{Ar'} + \mathbf{Dm}) = q_1 \mathbf{c} \bmod q_\pi R \wedge \|\mathbf{r'}\|_2 \leq \sigma_3 \sqrt{nm_1} =: \alpha_3 \wedge \mathbf{m} \in S_{bin}^{m_3},$$

where the private input is $\mathbf{r'}, \mathbf{m}$ and the public input is $\mathbf{A}, \mathbf{D}, \mathbf{c}$. We multiply the linear equation by q_1 to work with the proof system modulus. We now instantiate this relation in the framework of [35]. Using the notations of [35], we define $\mathbf{s}_1 = [\mathbf{r'}|\mathbf{m}] \in R^{m_1+m_3}$ and $\mathbf{s} = [\mathbf{s}_1 | \sigma_{-1}(\mathbf{s}_1)] \in R^{2(m_1+m_3)}$.

Quadratic Equations: Define $f_i(\mathbf{s}) = (\mathbf{e}_i^T [q_1\mathbf{A}|q_1\mathbf{D}|\mathbf{0}_{d\times m_1+m_3}]) \cdot \mathbf{s} + (-\mathbf{e}_i^T q_1 \mathbf{c})$ for all $i \in [d]$, where $\mathbf{e}_i$ is the zero vector with a 1 at position i. Then, proving $f_i(\mathbf{s}) = 0 \bmod q_\pi R$ for all $i \in [d]$ yields $q_1(\mathbf{Ar'} + \mathbf{Dm}) = q_1 \mathbf{c} \bmod q_\pi R$.

Quadratic Evaluations: We define $r = \sum_{j\in[0,n-1]} X^j$. For all $i \in [m_3]$, define $F_i(\mathbf{s}) = \mathbf{s}^T \mathbf{E}_{2m_1+m_3+i,m_1+i}\mathbf{s} + (-r\mathbf{e}_{2m_1+m_3+i})^T \mathbf{s} = \sigma_{-1}(\mathbf{m}[i])(\mathbf{m}[i] - r)$, where $\mathbf{E}_{k,\ell}$ denotes the zero matrix with a 1 at position (k,ℓ). Then, proving $\widetilde{F}_i(\mathbf{s}) = 0$ for all $i \in [m_3]$ implies $\mathbf{m} \in S_{bin}^{m_3}$. This relies on the fact that for $m \in R$, the constant coefficient of $\sigma_{-1}(m)(m - r)$ is $\langle \theta(m), \theta(m) - \mathbf{1}_n \rangle$. Then, proving that this inner product is 0 over $\mathbb{Z}$ is equivalent to proving that $\theta(m) \in \{0,1\}^n$, i.e., $m \in S_{bin}$.

Norm Conditions: We define $\mathbf{E}^{(e)} = [\mathbf{I}_{m_1}|\mathbf{0}_{m_1\times m_1+2m_3}]$, $\mathbf{u}^{(e)} = \mathbf{0}_{m_1}$, and $\beta^{(e)} = \alpha_3$. Then $\left\| \mathbf{E}^{(e)}\mathbf{s} - \mathbf{u}^{(e)} \right\|_2 \leq \beta^{(e)}$ is equivalent to $\|\mathbf{r'}\|_2 \leq \alpha_3$.

Remark 4.2. The above aims at proving the relation exactly. However, we note that the commitment scheme employed in [35] already contains a part $\mathbf{A}_1\mathbf{s}_1 + \mathbf{A}_2\mathbf{s}_2$. By setting the public matrices $\mathbf{A}_1, \mathbf{A}_2$ as $\mathbf{A}, \mathbf{D}$ respectively, $\mathbf{s}_2 = \mathbf{r}'$ which is chosen from a Gaussian distribution, and $\mathbf{s}_1 = \mathbf{m}$, we can directly use the protocol of [35, Fig. 8]. We simply have to set $\|\mathbf{s}_1\|_2 \leq \sqrt{nm_3} =: \alpha$, and the quadratic evaluations as above to prove (exactly) that $\mathbf{s}_1 = \mathbf{m}$ is indeed in $S_{bin}^{m_3}$. It then proves the correct statement but with a soundness gap on the norm of $\mathbf{r}'$.

4.3.2   Proof of Message-Signature Pair Possession.

Consider the relation

$$q_1(\mathbf{Av}_1 - \mathbf{Bv}_2 + \tau\mathbf{Gv}_2 - \mathbf{Dm}) = q_1\mathbf{u} \bmod q_\pi R$$
$$\text{with } \|\mathbf{v}\|_2 \leq \sqrt{\sigma_1^2 nm_1 + \sigma^2 nm_2} =: \alpha \wedge \mathbf{m} \in S_{bin}^{m_3} \wedge \tau \in \mathcal{T}_w,$$

where the private input is $\tau, \mathbf{v} = [\mathbf{v}_1^T|\mathbf{v}_2^T]^T, \mathbf{m}$ and the public input is composed of $\mathbf{A}, \mathbf{B}, \mathbf{D}, \mathbf{G}, \mathbf{u}$. We define $\mathbf{s}_1 = [\mathbf{v}_1|\mathbf{v}_2|\mathbf{m}|\tau] \in R^{m_1+m_2+m_3+1}$ and $\mathbf{s} = [\mathbf{s}_1|\sigma_{-1}(\mathbf{s}_1)] \in R^{2(m_1+m_2+m_3+1)}$.

Quadratic Equations: We define $\mathbf{A}' = q_1[\mathbf{A}|-\mathbf{B}|-\mathbf{D}|\mathbf{0}_{d\times m_1+m_2+m_3+2}]$, and for all $i \in [d]$, we define

$$\mathbf{G}_i = q_1 \begin{bmatrix} \mathbf{0}_{(m_1+m_2+m_3)\times 2(m_1+m_2+m_3+1)} \\ \mathbf{0}_{1\times m_1} \; \mathbf{e}_i^T\mathbf{G} \; \mathbf{0}_{1\times m_1+m_2+2(m_3+1)} \\ \mathbf{0}_{(m_1+m_2+m_3+1)\times 2(m_1+m_2+m_3+1)} \end{bmatrix}.$$

Then, for all $i \in [d]$, define $f_i(\mathbf{s}) = \mathbf{s}^T\mathbf{G}_i\mathbf{s} + (\mathbf{e}_i^T\mathbf{A}')\mathbf{s} + (-q_1\mathbf{e}_i^T\mathbf{u})$. Proving $f_i(\mathbf{s}) = 0 \bmod q_\pi R$ for all $i \in [d]$ yields $q_1(\mathbf{Av}_1 - \mathbf{Bv}_2 + \tau\mathbf{Gv}_2 - \mathbf{Dm}) = q_1\mathbf{u} \bmod q_\pi R$.

Quadratic Evaluations: We define $r = \sum_{j\in[0,n-1]} X^j$. For all $i \in [m_3 + 1]$, define $F_i(\mathbf{s}) = \mathbf{s}^T\mathbf{E}_{2(m_1+m_2)+m_3+1+i,m_1+m_2+i}\mathbf{s} + (-r\mathbf{e}_{2(m_1+m_2)+m_3+1+i})^T\mathbf{s}$. We also define $F_{m_3+2}(\mathbf{s}) = \mathbf{s}^T\mathbf{E}_{2(m_1+m_2+m_3+1),m_1+m_2+m_3+1}\mathbf{s} - w = \sigma_{-1}(\tau)\tau - w$. Proving $\widetilde{F}_i(\mathbf{s}) = 0$ for $i \in [m_3]$ is equivalent to $\mathbf{m} \in S_{bin}^{m_3}$ as before. Then, showing $\widetilde{F}_{m_3+1}(\mathbf{s}) = 0$ proves $\tau \in S_{bin}$, while $\widetilde{F}_{m_3+2}(\mathbf{s}) = 0$ proves that $\|\tau\|_2^2 = \langle\theta(\tau), \theta(\tau)\rangle = w$, thus giving $\tau \in \mathcal{T}_w$.

Norm Conditions: We define $\mathbf{E}^{(e)} = [\mathbf{I}_{m_1+m_2}|\mathbf{0}_{m_1+m_2\times m_1+m_2+2(m_3+1)}]$, $\mathbf{u}^{(e)} = \mathbf{0}_{m_1+m_2}$, and $\beta^{(e)} = \alpha$. Then $\|\mathbf{E}^{(e)}\mathbf{s} - \mathbf{u}^{(e)}\|_2 \leq \beta^{(e)}$ proves $\|\mathbf{v}\|_2 \leq \alpha$.

5   Privacy-Preserving Protocols and Anonymous Credentials

The very purpose of a signature scheme with efficient protocols (SEP) is to be used as a building block for privacy-preserving primitives such as group signature, anonymous credentials or e-cash. For such applications, one usually needs (1) to get a signature on committed (hidden) messages and (2) to prove knowledge of a signature, without revealing it. This has led previous papers, e.g., [16, 33, 43], providing such types of signatures to describe specific protocols addressing those needs. We here follow the same approach. More specifically, we give a first protocol in Sect. 5.1 which allows a signer to obliviously sign a message, by only knowing a commitment to the message. The second protocol, presented in Sect. 5.2, enables a user to prove the possession of a message-signature pair, where the signature has been obtained by the oblivious signing protocol. As in previous works, we do not identify any properties expected from such protocols nor prove any results regarding their security. As this might look unconventional, we need to recall a few facts about SEPs and their use in privacy-preserving applications.

The use of signature schemes in the latter applications can be done based on formal generic frameworks, e.g., [3] for group signature or [10] for e-cash, or on some rather common heuristics, e.g., for anonymous credentials [16]. In all cases, the point is that, in theory, no specific property is expected from the signatures beyond EUF-CMA security. Typically, [3, 10] consider standard digital signature schemes for their framework.

However, in practice, the use of any digital signature is likely to lead to a totally impractical construction because of the difficult interactions between general-purpose signatures and the other building blocks such as zero-knowledge proofs. This is where SEPs prove handy. They are specifically designed to smoothly interact with the other building blocks so as to optimize the efficiency of the resulting construction.

In this context, defining security notions that such protocols should achieve would be meaningless as no such formal properties are expected by the constructions using them. Worse, this is likely to lead to unnecessary complications as it is difficult to define a relevant security model for SEPs. Typically, an SEP allows one to get a signature on hidden messages and then to prove knowledge of the message-signature pair. How to define a relevant security model in this context? Unforgeability indeed means the inability to produce a signature on new messages but here we do not know the messages requested by the adversary to the signing oracle and we do not know which message-signature pairs it is proving knowledge of. In other words, we cannot decide if the adversary won.

Libert et al. [33] circumvents this issue by forcing the user to provide an encryption of the messages in the blind issuance process. This does not address the problem of formalizing the properties expected from the protocols (1) and (2) of SEPs (and indeed [33] does not define such properties) but this enables to provide some results regarding security as a reduction can recover all the messages it has signed (by decrypting the ciphertexts) and thus decide when a forgery occurs. Besides being unconventional (this led [33] to prove "security" of the protocols without defining what "security" means), this approach complicates the protocols by adding this encryption step that is not necessary in most applications using such signatures. Indeed, in concrete applications, this problem is usually solved by other means. For example, in e-cash systems, "forgeries" can be detected by comparing the amount of withdrawn coins with the one of spent coins. In group signatures, there is an opening procedure that allows to trace back a group signature to a group member. This enables to detect forgeries as the latter will be involved in group signatures that cannot be opened to anyone.

To sum up, SEPs constitute an informal subclass of digital signatures designed for privacy-preserving applications. Defining specific security properties for the protocols associated with SEPs is not necessary for such applications and artificially increases complexity. In accordance with previous works, we therefore do not consider such security properties.

However, to demonstrate how an SEP can easily be plugged in a privacy-preserving construction and how security is concretely managed in this case, we provide in Sect. 5.3 the description of an anonymous credentials system based on our SEP scheme.

In this section, we present the protocols for the construction over structured lattices, but they can be naturally adapted for the construction over $\mathbb{Z}_q$. We thus use the zero-knowledge arguments presented in Sect. 4.3 using the framework from [35]. One would instead use the framework of [47] for the relations over $\mathbb{Z}_q$, which are detailed in the full version [31, Sec. F].

5.1 Oblivious Signing Protocol

We present here our first protocol between a signer S and a user U. The user U is interacting with S in order to obtain a signature $(\tau, \mathbf{v})$ on a message $\mathbf{m}$, by only providing S with a commitment $\mathbf{c}$ to the message $\mathbf{m}$. We assume that Algorithms 3.5 and 3.6 have been run prior to entering the protocol but with some slight modifications that we detail below. First, instead of choosing σ_2 as in Algorithm 3.5, it chooses $\sigma_3 \geq \sqrt{2}\eta_\varepsilon(R^{m_1})$ and then

$$\sigma_4 \geq \max\left(\sqrt{((\sqrt{nm_1} + \sqrt{nm_3} + t)\sqrt{nm_3} + \sigma_3\sqrt{nm_1})^2 - \sigma^2}, \sqrt{2}\eta_\varepsilon(R^{m_1})\right).$$

It then re-defines $\sigma_2 = \sqrt{\sigma_3^2 + \sigma_4^2}$ and $\sigma_1 = \sqrt{\sigma^2 + \sigma_2^2}$. The new widths σ_3, σ_4 are also included in pp in addition to $\sigma, \sigma_1, \sigma_2$. We explain this change in Remark 5.1. Second, as we use the public key matrix $\mathbf{A}$ as part of the commitment matrices, we must ensure that it cannot be tempered with by the attacker. As such, we generate $\mathbf{A}$ as the hash of a public string. In the random oracle model, the matrix can be assumed to follow the prescribed uniform distribution over $R_q^{d \times m_1}$.

Algorithm 5.1: OblSign (Oblivious Signing Interactive Protocol)

Input: Signer S with $\mathsf{sk}, \mathsf{pk}, \mathsf{pp}, \mathsf{st}$, and a user U with $\mathbf{m} \in S_{bin}^{m_3}$ and pk, pp.

  <u>User U.</u>
1. $\mathbf{r}' \hookleftarrow \mathcal{D}_{R^{m_1}, \sigma_3}$.   ▷ $\sigma_3 \geq \sqrt{2}\eta_\varepsilon(R^{m_1})$
2. $\mathbf{c} \leftarrow \mathbf{A}\mathbf{r}' + \mathbf{D}\mathbf{m} \bmod qR$.
3. Send $\mathbf{c}$ to S.
  <u>User $U \longleftrightarrow$ Signer S.</u>
4. Interactive zero-knowledge argument between U and S, where U proves that $\mathbf{c}$ is commitment to $\mathbf{m}$ with randomness $\mathbf{r}'$. If S is not convinced, the protocol aborts.
  <u>Signer S.</u>
5. $\mathbf{r}'' \hookleftarrow \mathcal{D}_{R^{m_1}, \sigma_4}$.

6. $\mathbf{c}' \leftarrow \mathbf{c} + \mathbf{Ar}'' \bmod qR$.
7. $\tau \leftarrow F(\mathsf{st})$.   ▷ $\tau \in \mathcal{T}_w$
8. $\mathbf{v}' \leftarrow \mathsf{SampleD}(\mathbf{R}, \mathbf{A}, \tau\mathbf{I}_d, \mathbf{u} + \mathbf{c}', \sigma) - [\mathbf{r}''^T|\mathbf{0}]^T$.
9. Send $(\tau, \mathbf{v}')$ to U.
10. $\mathsf{st} \leftarrow \mathsf{st} + 1$
    User U.
11. $\mathbf{v} \leftarrow \mathbf{v}' - [\mathbf{r}'^T|\mathbf{0}]^T$.
12. **if** $\mathsf{Verify}(\mathsf{pk}; \mathbf{m}; (\tau, \mathbf{v}); \mathsf{pp}) = 1$, **then return** $(\tau, \mathbf{v})$.   ▷ Algorithm 3.8
13. **else return** $\perp$

Remark 5.1. Notice that Algorithm 5.1 does not exactly rely on the signature scheme of Sect. 3. This is because the signer S also contributes to the randomness of the commitment to the message $\mathbf{m}$ via $\mathbf{r}''$. If the randomness came only from the user U, the signer, who is embodied by the SIS adversary in the security proofs, would have no control over the randomness part of the signing query. In the proof of Lemma 3.4 (and Lemma 3.5 for the i-th query with $i \neq i^+$), the randomness $\mathbf{r}$ is legitimately sampled from $\mathcal{D}_{R^{m_1},\sigma_2}$. As such, it could instead be sampled as $\mathbf{r}' + \mathbf{r}''$ with $\mathbf{r}' \hookleftarrow \mathcal{D}_{R^{m_1},\sigma_3}$ sampled by the forger $\mathcal{A}$, and $\mathbf{r}'' \hookleftarrow \mathcal{D}_{R^{m_1},\sigma_4}$ sampled by the SIS adversary, thus matching with Algorithm 5.1. This would restrict $\sigma_2 = \sqrt{\sigma_3^2 + \sigma_4^2}$. If $\sigma_3, \sigma_4 \geq \sqrt{2}\eta_\varepsilon(R^{m_1})$, Lemma 2.2 guarantees that $\mathbf{r}'+\mathbf{r}''$ is $7\varepsilon/4$-close to $\mathcal{D}_{R^{m_1},\sigma_2}$ as required. However, when dealing with the i^+-th query in Lemma 3.5, the SIS adversary needs to control part of the randomness. At this step of the proof, $\mathbf{r}_0$ would be distributed according to $\mathcal{D}_{R^{m_1},\sigma_4}$, and it would construct $\mathbf{v}_1'^{(i^+)} = \mathbf{v}_1 - (\mathbf{r}_0 - \mathbf{Um}^{(i^+)} - \mathbf{r}'^{(i^+)})$ with $\mathbf{r}'^{(i^+)}$ sampled from $\mathcal{D}_{R^{m_1},\sigma_3}$ by the forger $\mathcal{A}$. The rest remains the same, but this modification introduces the condition $\sqrt{\sigma^2 + \sigma_4^2} \geq \alpha + \sigma_3\sqrt{m_1}$, where $\alpha = (\sqrt{nm_1} + \sqrt{nm_3} + t)\sqrt{nm_3}$. It yields $\sigma_2 \geq \sqrt{(\alpha + \sigma_3\sqrt{nm_1})^2 + \sigma_3^2 - \sigma^2}$, leading to $\sigma_1 = \sqrt{\sigma^2 + \sigma_2^2} \geq \sqrt{(\alpha + \sigma_3\sqrt{nm_1})^2 + \sigma_3^2}$ instead of just α. In most applications, m_3 is much larger than σ_3 and it thus only entails a mild increase of σ_1.

5.2 Message-Signature Pair Possession Protocol

The second protocol provides a user, who obtained a certificate $\mathsf{sig} = (\tau, \mathbf{v})$ on a message $\mathbf{m}$, with the ability to prove possession of this valid message-signature pair. For that, they only have to prove that $\mathsf{Verify}(\mathsf{pk}, \mathbf{m}, (\tau, \mathbf{v}), \mathsf{pp}) = 1$ without revealing neither $\mathbf{m}$ nor $(\tau, \mathbf{v})$. The protocol of Algorithm 5.2 thus simply consists in using the ZKAoK presented in Sect. 4.3 to prove this relation. The proof can be made non-interactive in the random oracle model using the Fiat-Shamir transform.

Algorithm 5.2: Prove (Message-Signature Pair Possession)

Input: User U with $\mathsf{pk}, \mathsf{pp}, \mathbf{m}, (\tau, \mathbf{v})$, and a verifier V with pk, pp.

User $U \longleftrightarrow$ Verifier V.

1. Interactive zero-knowledge argument between U and V, where U proves knowledge of $(\mathbf{m}; (\tau, \mathbf{v}))$ such that $\mathsf{Verify}(\mathsf{pk}, \mathbf{m}, (\tau, \mathbf{v}), \mathsf{pp}) = 1$.

5.3   Application to Anonymous Credentials

Anonymous credentials (AC), a.k.a. attribute-based credentials, is a generic term covering a wide spectrum of privacy-preserving systems considering essentially two main use-cases. One where a user interacts with an organization to get a signature on potentially concealed attributes, and one where this user will prove possession of this signature on his attributes while limiting leakage to some threshold depending on the concrete applications. For example, one may agree to reveal some attributes but wants to retain unlinkability of showings, which implies to hide the signature. We refer to [26] for a discussion on the different features of such systems. In all cases, one can note that our two protocols above readily address those needs. To demonstrate that, we formally describe the anonymous credentials system resulting from our SEP construction and prove that it satisfies the security model introduced in [26]. This model is recalled in full version [31, Sec. C.1] for completeness but, in a few words, anonymous credentials is defined by two Keygen algorithms, one (OKeyGen) for the organization issuing credentials and one (UKeyGen) for the user, along with two interactive protocols, one (Issue) run by the organization and the user who wants to obtain a certificate and one (Show) run by some user and some verifier to check the validity of the claimed attributes. From the security standpoint, two properties are expected: anonymity and unforgeability. The former informally requires that Show does not leak more information than necessary, i.e., the set of disclosed attributes. The latter requires that no user can claim a credential on some attributes unless it has personally received a certificate from the organization. This in particular implies that nobody can present a credential that they do not own.

The OKeyGen and UKeyGen algorithms and the (Issue) and (Show) protocols based on our SEP construction are presented below. It gives, to our knowledge, the first lattice-based anonymous credential system. The algorithm Setup (Alg. 3.5) is modified so that $m_3 = m_s + m_3'$ where $m_s = 2d$ and $m_3' \cdot n$ is the maximal total bitsize of the attributes. We consider a system with ℓ attributes, where $h_i \cdot n$ is the bitsize of the i-th attribute $\mathbf{m}_i$ which means $m_3' = \sum_{i \in [\ell]} h_i$. The commitment matrix $\mathbf{D}$ is decomposed into $\mathbf{D} = [\mathbf{D}_s | \mathbf{D}_1 | \dots | \mathbf{D}_k]$ where $\mathbf{D}_s \in R_q^{n \times m_s}$ and $\mathbf{D}_i \in R_q^{n \times h_i}$.

Algorithm 5.3: OKeyGen

Input: Public parameters pp as in Algorithm 3.5.
Output: $(\mathsf{opk}, \mathsf{osk}) \leftarrow \mathsf{KeyGen}(\mathsf{pp})$.   ▷ Algorithm 3.6

Algorithm 5.4: UKeyGen

Input: Public parameters pp as in Algorithm 3.5.

1. $\mathbf{s} \hookleftarrow U(S_{bin}^{m_s})$.
2. $\mathbf{t} \leftarrow \mathbf{D}_s \mathbf{s} \bmod qR$.

Output: $(\mathsf{upk}, \mathsf{usk}) = (\mathbf{t}, \mathbf{s})$.

————— Algorithm 5.5: Issue (Credential Issuance Protocol) —————

Input: Organization O with $\mathsf{osk}, \mathsf{opk}, \mathsf{upk}, \mathsf{pp}, \mathsf{st}$, and a user U with $\mathbf{m} \in S_{bin}^{m_3'}$ and $\mathsf{usk}, \mathsf{upk}, \mathsf{opk}, \mathsf{pp}, \mathbf{m}$.

User $U \longleftrightarrow$ Organization O.
1. Run the interactive protocol OblSign from Algorithm 5.1, where O plays the signer and with message $\widetilde{\mathbf{m}} = [\mathsf{usk}^T | \mathbf{m}^T]^T$. In this syntax, i.e., [26], the signer knows $\mathbf{m}$ but not usk. Hence the ZKAoK is adapted to prove knowledge of short $(\mathbf{r}', \mathbf{s})$ such that $\mathbf{c} - \sum_i \mathbf{D}_i \mathbf{m}_i = \mathbf{A}\mathbf{r}' + \mathbf{D}_s \mathbf{s} \bmod qR$, and additionally that $\mathbf{D}_s \mathbf{s} = \mathsf{upk} \bmod qR$.

————— Algorithm 5.6: Show (Credential Showing Protocol) —————

Input: User U with $\mathsf{usk}, \mathsf{opk}, \mathsf{pp}, \mathbf{m}, (\tau, \mathbf{v}), \mathcal{I}$, and verifier V with $\mathsf{opk}, \mathsf{pp}, (\mathbf{m}_i)_{i \in \mathcal{I}}$.

User $U \longleftrightarrow$ Verifier V.
1. Interactive zero-knowledge argument between U and V, where U proves knowledge of $(\mathbf{s}, (\mathbf{m}_i)_{i \notin \mathcal{I}}; (\tau, \mathbf{v}))$ such that $\mathsf{Verify}(\mathsf{pk}, \widetilde{\mathbf{m}}, (\tau, \mathbf{v}), \mathsf{pp}) = 1$.

Theorem 5.1. *The AC described in Algorithms 5.3, 5.4, 5.5 and 5.6 is correct, anonymous under the zero-knowledge property of the underlying ZKAoKs, and unforgeable under the hardness of Inhomogeneous M-SIS, M-LWE, the soundness of the ZKAoKs and the EUF-CMA security of our SEP.*

The proof of Theorem 5.1 is given in the full version [31, Sec. C.2] for lack of space. We also defer the detailed performance analysis in the full version [31, Sec. H]. As an example, for 10 128-bit attributes with 4 disclosed ones, the proof size in the Show protocol is less than 730 KB.

Conclusion

In this paper, we have proposed a new signature scheme with efficient protocols which is several orders of magnitude more efficient than the current state-of-the-art [33]. This improvement was obtained by revisiting the latter construction in a systematic way, considering not only the signature scheme itself but also its interactions with the other components such as the commitment scheme and the zero-knowledge proofs. In the process, we have also rectified a problem with the fast mode of the zero-knowledge framework of [47] and introduced some optimizations, which are of independent interest.

Our construction was designed to remain as generic as possible in order to be compatible with the broadest possible spectrum of applications. In particular, it can be instantiated in both standard lattices and structured ones so as to suit any lattice-based system. Despite this versatility, the size of a proof of knowledge of a message-signature pair, one of the core component of privacy-preserving systems, can be much lower than 1 MB, which should foster the development of practical post-quantum constructions in this area. We made a step in this direction by giving the first lattice-based anonymous credentials system.

Acknowledgments. This work has received a French government support managed by the National Research Agency in the France 2030 program, with reference ANR-22-PETQ-0008 PQ-TLS, as well as in the ASTRID program, under the national project AMIRAL with reference ANR-21-ASTR-0016, and finally in the MobiS5 project, with reference ANR-18-CE-39-0019-02 MobiS5. We also thank our anonymous reviewers from Crypto'23.

References

1. Ajtai, M.: Generating hard instances of lattice problems (extended abstract). In: Proceedings of the Twenty-Eighth Annual ACM Symposium on Theory of Computing (STOC) (1996)
2. Banaszczyk, W.: New bounds in some transference theorems in the geometry of numbers. Math. Ann. **296**, 625–635 (1993)
3. Bellare, M., Shi, H., Zhang, C.: Foundations of group signatures: the case of dynamic groups. In: Menezes, A. (ed.) CT-RSA 2005. LNCS, vol. 3376, pp. 136–153. Springer, Heidelberg (2005). https://doi.org/10.1007/978-3-540-30574-3_11
4. Bert, P., Eberhart, G., Prabel, L., Roux-Langlois, A., Sabt, M.: Implementation of lattice trapdoors on modules and applications. In: International Conference on Post-Quantum Cryptography (PQCrypto) (2021)
5. Beullens, W., Lyubashevsky, V., Nguyen, N.K., Seiler, G.: Lattice-based blind signatures: Short, efficient, and round-optimal. IACR Cryptol. ePrint Arch. p. 77 (2023)
6. Boneh, D., Boyen, X.: Short signatures without random oracles and the SDH assumption in bilinear groups. J. Cryptol. **21**(2), 149–177 (2007). https://doi.org/10.1007/s00145-007-9005-7
7. Boneh, D., Eskandarian, S., Fisch, B.: Post-quantum EPID signatures from symmetric primitives. In: Matsui, M. (ed.) CT-RSA 2019. LNCS, vol. 11405, pp. 251–271. Springer, Cham (2019). https://doi.org/10.1007/978-3-030-12612-4_13
8. Bootle, J., Lyubashevsky, V., Seiler, G.: Algebraic techniques for Short(er) exact lattice-based zero-knowledge proofs. In: Boldyreva, A., Micciancio, D. (eds.) CRYPTO 2019. LNCS, vol. 11692, pp. 176–202. Springer, Cham (2019). https://doi.org/10.1007/978-3-030-26948-7_7
9. Boudgoust, K., Jeudy, C., Roux-Langlois, A., Wen, W.: On the hardness of module learning with errors with short distributions. J. Cryptol. **36**(1), 1 (2023)
10. Bourse, F., Pointcheval, D., Sanders, O.: Divisible E-cash from constrained pseudorandom functions. In: 25th International Conference on the Theory and Application of Cryptology and Information Security (ASIACRYPT) (2019)
11. Boyen, X.: Lattice mixing and vanishing trapdoors: a framework for fully secure short signatures and more. In: Nguyen, P.Q., Pointcheval, D. (eds.) PKC 2010. LNCS, vol. 6056, pp. 499–517. Springer, Heidelberg (2010). https://doi.org/10.1007/978-3-642-13013-7_29
12. Brickell, E., Li, J.: Enhanced privacy ID: a direct anonymous attestation scheme with enhanced revocation capabilities. In: Proceedings of the 2007 ACM Workshop on Privacy in Electronic Society (WPES) (2007)

13. Brickell, E.F., Camenisch, J., Chen, L.: Direct anonymous attestation. In: Proceedings of ACM Conference on Computer and Communications Security (CCS) (2004)
14. Camenisch, J., Lysyanskaya, A.: An efficient system for non-transferable anonymous credentials with optional anonymity revocation. In: Pfitzmann, B. (ed.) EUROCRYPT 2001. LNCS, vol. 2045, pp. 93–118. Springer, Heidelberg (2001). https://doi.org/10.1007/3-540-44987-6_7
15. Camenisch, J., Lysyanskaya, A.: A signature scheme with efficient protocols. In: Cimato, S., Persiano, G., Galdi, C. (eds.) SCN 2002. LNCS, vol. 2576, pp. 268–289. Springer, Heidelberg (2003). https://doi.org/10.1007/3-540-36413-7_20
16. Camenisch, J., Lysyanskaya, A.: Signature schemes and anonymous credentials from bilinear maps. In: Franklin, M. (ed.) CRYPTO 2004. LNCS, vol. 3152, pp. 56–72. Springer, Heidelberg (2004). https://doi.org/10.1007/978-3-540-28628-8_4
17. Chaum, D.: Showing credentials without identification. In: Pichler, F. (ed.) EUROCRYPT 1985. LNCS, vol. 219, pp. 241–244. Springer, Heidelberg (1986). https://doi.org/10.1007/3-540-39805-8_28
18. Chaum, D., van Heyst, E.: Group signatures. In: Davies, D.W. (ed.) EUROCRYPT 1991. LNCS, vol. 547, pp. 257–265. Springer, Heidelberg (1991). https://doi.org/10.1007/3-540-46416-6_22
19. Chen, L., El Kassem, N., Lehmann, A., Lyubashevsky, V.: A framework for efficient lattice-based DAA. In: Proceedings of the 1st ACM Workshop on Workshop on Cyber-Security Arms Race (CYSARM@CCS) (2019)
20. del Pino, R., Katsumata, S.: A new framework for more efficient round-optimal lattice-based (partially) blind signature via trapdoor sampling. In: Dodis, Y., Shrimpton, T. (eds) Advances in Cryptology - CRYPTO 2022. CRYPTO 2022. Lecture Notes in Computer Science, vol 13508. Springer, Cham (2022). https://doi.org/10.1007/978-3-031-15979-4_11
21. del Pino, R., Lyubashevsky, V.: and G. Seiler. Lattice-based group signatures and zero-knowledge proofs of automorphism stability. In: Proceedings of the 2018 ACM SIGSAC Conference on Computer and Communications Security (CCS) (2018)
22. Diffie, W., Hellman, M.E.: New directions in cryptography. IEEE Trans. Inf. Theor. **22**(6), 644–654 (1976)
23. Dodis, Y., Ostrovsky, R., Reyzin, L., Smith, A.D.: Fuzzy extractors: how to generate strong keys from biometrics and other noisy data. SIAM J. Comput. **38**(1), 97–139 (2008)
24. L. Ducas and D. Micciancio. Improved short lattice signatures in the standard model. In: International Cryptology Conference (CRYPTO) (2014)
25. Esgin, M.F., Nguyen, N.K., Seiler, G.: Practical exact proofs from lattices: new techniques to exploit fully-splitting rings. In: 26th International Conference on the Theory and Application of Cryptology and Information Security (ASIACRYPT) (2020)
26. Fuchsbauer, G., Hanser, C., Slamanig, D.: Structure-preserving signatures on equivalence classes and constant-size anonymous credentials. J. Cryptol. **32**(2), 498–546 (2019)
27. Håstad, J., Impagliazzo, R., Levin, L.A., Luby, M.: A pseudorandom generator from any one-way function. SIAM J. Comput. **28**(4), 1364–1396 (1999)
28. Intel. A cost-effective foundation for end-to-end IoT security, white paper (2016). https://www.intel.com/content/dam/www/public/us/en/documents/white-papers/intel-epid-iot-security-white-paper.pdf

29. ISO/IEC. ISO/IEC 18370–2:2016 information technology - security techniques - blind digital signatures - part 2: Discrete logarithm based mechanisms (2013). https://www.iso.org/standard/62544.html

30. ISO/IEC. ISO/IEC 20008–2:2013 information technology - security techniques - anonymous digital signatures - part 2: Mechanisms using a group public key (2013). https://www.iso.org/standard/56916.html

31. Jeudy, C., Roux-Langlois, A., Sanders, O.: Lattice signature with efficient protocols, application to anonymous credentials. IACR Cryptol. ePrint Arch. p. 509 (2022)

32. Langlois, A., Stehlé, D.: Worst-case to average-case reductions for module lattices. DCC (2015)

33. Libert, B., Ling, S., Mouhartem, F., Nguyen, K., Wang, H.: Signature schemes with efficient protocols and dynamic group signatures from lattice assumptions. In: Cheon, J.H., Takagi, T. (eds.) ASIACRYPT 2016. LNCS, vol. 10032, pp. 373–403. Springer, Heidelberg (2016). https://doi.org/10.1007/978-3-662-53890-6_13

34. Lyubashevsky, V.: Lattice signatures without trapdoors. In: Pointcheval, D., Johansson, T. (eds.) EUROCRYPT 2012. LNCS, vol. 7237, pp. 738–755. Springer, Heidelberg (2012). https://doi.org/10.1007/978-3-642-29011-4_43

35. Lyubashevsky, V., Nguyen, N.K., Plançon, M.: Lattice-based zero-knowledge proofs and applications: Shorter, simpler, and more general. IACR Cryptol. ePrint Arch. p. 284 (2022). Version dated from March 07th 2022

36. Lyubashevsky, V., Nguyen, N.K., Plançon, M., Seiler, G.: Shorter lattice-based group signatures via "almost free" encryption and other optimizations. In: International Conference on the Theory and Application of Cryptology and Information Security (ASIACRYPT) (2021)

37. Lyubashevsky, V., Peikert, C., Regev, O.: A toolkit for ring-LWE cryptography. In: Johansson, T., Nguyen, P.Q. (eds.) EUROCRYPT 2013. LNCS, vol. 7881, pp. 35–54. Springer, Heidelberg (2013). https://doi.org/10.1007/978-3-642-38348-9_3

38. Lyubashevsky, V., Seiler, G.: Short, invertible elements in partially splitting cyclotomic rings and applications to lattice-based zero-knowledge proofs. In: Nielsen, J.B., Rijmen, V. (eds.) EUROCRYPT 2018. LNCS, vol. 10820, pp. 204–224. Springer, Cham (2018). https://doi.org/10.1007/978-3-319-78381-9_8

39. Micciancio, D., Peikert, C.: Trapdoors for lattices: simpler, tighter, faster, smaller. In: Pointcheval, D., Johansson, T. (eds.) EUROCRYPT 2012. LNCS, vol. 7237, pp. 700–718. Springer, Heidelberg (2012). https://doi.org/10.1007/978-3-642-29011-4_41

40. Micciancio, D., Peikert, C.: Hardness of SIS and LWE with small parameters. In: Canetti, R., Garay, J.A. (eds.) CRYPTO 2013. LNCS, vol. 8042, pp. 21–39. Springer, Heidelberg (2013). https://doi.org/10.1007/978-3-642-40041-4_2

41. Micciancio, D., Regev, O.: Worst-case to average-case reductions based on gaussian measures. SIAM J. Comput. **37**(1), 267–302 (2007)

42. Peikert, C.: Limits on the hardness of lattice problems in l_p norms. Comput. Complex. **17**, 300–351 (2008). https://doi.org/10.1007/s00037-008-0251-3

43. Pointcheval, D., Sanders, O.: Short randomizable signatures. In: Sako, K. (ed.) CT-RSA 2016. LNCS, vol. 9610, pp. 111–126. Springer, Cham (2016). https://doi.org/10.1007/978-3-319-29485-8_7

44. Regev, O.: On lattices, learning with errors, random linear codes, and cryptography. In: Proceedings of the 37th Annual ACM Symposium on Theory of Computing (STOC) (2005)

45. TCG (2015). https://trustedcomputinggroup.org/authentication/

46. Vershynin, R.: Introduction to the non-asymptotic analysis of random matrices. In: Compressed Sensing (2012)
47. Yang, R., Au, M.H., Zhang, Z., Xu, Q., Yu, Z., Whyte, W.: Efficient lattice-based zero-knowledge arguments with standard soundness: construction and applications. In: Boldyreva, A., Micciancio, D. (eds.) CRYPTO 2019. LNCS, vol. 11692, pp. 147–175. Springer, Cham (2019). https://doi.org/10.1007/978-3-030-26948-7_6

A Framework for Practical Anonymous Credentials from Lattices

Jonathan Bootle[1](✉), Vadim Lyubashevsky[1], Ngoc Khanh Nguyen[2], and Alessandro Sorniotti[1]

[1] IBM Research Europe, Zurich, Switzerland
{jbt,vad,aso}@zurich.ibm.com
[2] EPFL, Lausanne, Switzerland
khanh.nguyen@epfl.ch

Abstract. We present a framework for building practical anonymous credential schemes based on the hardness of lattice problems. The running time of the prover and verifier is independent of the number of users and linear in the number of attributes. The scheme is also compact in practice, with the proofs being as small as a few dozen kilobytes for arbitrarily large (say up to 2^{128}) numbers of users with each user having several attributes. The security of our scheme is based on a new family of lattice assumptions which roughly states that given short pre-images of random elements in some set S, it is hard to create a pre-image for a fresh element in such a set. We show that if the set admits efficient zero-knowledge proofs of knowledge of a commitment to a set element and its pre-image, then this yields practically-efficient privacy-preserving primitives such as blind signatures, anonymous credentials, and group signatures. We propose a candidate instantiation of a function from this family which allows for such proofs and thus yields practical lattice-based primitives.

1 Introduction

With the recent announcement that the American National Institute of Standards and Technology (NIST) will be standardizing three lattice-based encryption and digital signature schemes, together with the NSA releasing their new CNSA 2.0 crypto suite which mandates that lattice-based constructions be the main cryptographic tools for communication security beginning from 2030, it is looking increasingly likely that lattices will form the future foundation of public key cryptography. While we already have several very efficient almost-standardized schemes for encryption and digital signatures [13,23,52], the state of more advanced quantum-safe cryptography is more murky with a lot of constructions being noticeably less efficient than their classical counterparts. The last several years, however, have seen tremendous progress in constructing efficient zero-knowledge proofs for lattice relations [6,11,24,25,42,57] and this led to rather compact and practical constructions of schemes like ring signatures, group signatures and confidential payment protocols [26,42,44,45]. A set of important

© International Association for Cryptologic Research 2023
H. Handschuh and A. Lysyanskaya (Eds.): CRYPTO 2023, LNCS 14082, pp. 384–417, 2023.
https://doi.org/10.1007/978-3-031-38545-2_13

primitives that are currently lacking in truly efficient instantiations fall under the global umbrella of *anonymous credentials*.

At a very high level, in an anonymous credential scheme [18–20,36] an issuer signs a set of credentials for a user. The user can then present a subset of this credential set and give a zero-knowledge proof that they were indeed signed by the issuer. For the scheme to be secure, it should be impossible for a user to present a credential that the issuer never signed. For anonymity, when a user presents his credential, all his other credentials should remain hidden – even from the issuer. Furthermore, multiple credential presentations by the same user should remain unlinkable. Manifestations of such schemes have been adopted by the *self-sovereign identity* community, which has developed open-source projects [30,31,46,55] and standard drafts [35,54] catering for a market whose size is estimated in the billions of US dollars [49]. While there are some very efficient instantiations of these schemes based on non-quantum-safe assumptions, to the best of our knowledge there are no truly practical quantum-safe instantiations that are available.[1]

Some recent lattice-based constructions of related primitives that previously didn't have any efficient quantum-safe instantiation based the security of the scheme on novel, but very plausible, lattice assumptions. For example, the recent blind signature in [3] was based on the new "one-more-ISIS" assumption and publicly-verifiable SNARKs were recently instantiated using a new k-R-ISIS assumption in [5]. The blind signature in [3] is one of the most concretely-efficient quantum-safe constructions to date, while the work in [5] is the first construction of its kind that gets within the vicinity of practicality. It is not too surprising that the range of assumptions needed to be expanded in order to construct more efficient lattice-based primitives. Analogously to the non-post-quantum setting, simple primitives like digital signatures can be efficiently based on the hardness of the basic discrete logarithm problem, while the most efficient constructions of other more advanced schemes crucially rely on much more esoteric assumptions. And so, analogously to the classical setting, it makes sense to explore other assumptions for constructing advanced lattice-based primitives as well.

In this paper we propose a new family of lattice problems some of whose members admit a practically-efficient zero-knowledge proof for proving knowledge of a solution. We then show how to apply this zero-knowledge proof to create fairly simple constructions of various efficient privacy-preserving lattice-based primitives, such as blind signatures and anonymous credentials, based on the presumed hardness of the new problem. The specific assumption we use in our paper is a particular instantiation from this family of assumptions that yields efficient zero-knowledge proofs. The family of problems is very natural and can be seen as a generalization of the underlying problem upon which the classic GPV signature scheme [28] is based.

---

[1] It is of course possible to construct these schemes using succinct zero-knowledge proofs such as STARKs, but the cost of these constructions appears to be in the hundreds of kilobytes range.

Lattice-Based Hash-and-Sign Signatures and Extensions. Privacy-based primitives are often constructed as some combination of a hash-and-sign digital signature scheme and a zero-knowledge proof system. Hash-and-sign lattice-based digital signatures based on the hardness of the standard SIS problem, first constructed in [28], are abstractly based on the hardness of the following problem over some distribution of input matrices A, which is parametrized by a global function f (there are also specific parameters n, m, β, β' which are determined based on the security parameter):

Definition 1.1 (The ISIS_f Problem (informal)). *We are given a matrix $A \in \mathbb{Z}_p^{n \times m}$ (chosen from some distribution), a function $f : [N] \to \mathbb{Z}_p^n$, and access to an oracle who chooses a random input $x \in [N]$ and outputs it together with a vector $\|\vec{s}\| \leq \beta$ satisfying $A\vec{s} = f(x)$. The game is won by coming up with a fresh tuple $(x', \vec{s}') \in [N] \times \mathbb{Z}^m$ where $\|\vec{s}'\| \leq \beta'$ and $A\vec{s}' = f(x').$*[2]

The hardness of the above problem depends on the choice of f, the distribution of A and how the oracle chooses the vector $\vec{s}$.[3] When the function f is instantiated as a cryptographic hash function (e.g. SHA) which is modelled as a random oracle, A is chosen uniformly-random, and $\vec{s}$ is chosen from a distribution with enough entropy, then the ISIS_f problem is equivalent to the well-known SIS and ISIS problems. If f is modelled as a random oracle, then $f(x)$ is uniformly-random in $\mathbb{Z}_p^n$, and so there is no advantage gained by seeing a pre-image $\vec{s}$ of a random element in $\mathbb{Z}_p^n$ because one could, in principle, do the pre-image sampling in reverse. That is, one could instead generate a random $\vec{s}$ and if the distribution of $\vec{s}$ has enough entropy, then it is the pre-image of a uniformly-random $\vec{t} = A\vec{s}$ (since $(A, \vec{t} = A\vec{s})$ is uniformly-random by the leftover hash lemma).

Modelling f as a random oracle and furthermore being able to create a matrix A together with a trapdoor which allows for pre-image sampling, gives rise to lattice-based hash-and-sign signatures based on the hardness of ISIS_f [28]. The idea is simply to sign a message (digest) x with the pre-image $\vec{s}$. This allows us to sign random messages x, but when f is modelled as a random oracle, it doesn't matter whether x is chosen at random or adaptively because $f(x)$ is uniformly-random regardless – thus allowing the signing of arbitrary messages is as secure as only being able to sign random ones.

When f is not a cryptographic hash function, then we don't immediately obtain a signature scheme based on ISIS_f by treating x as the message to be signed precisely because the ISIS_f problem requires x to be random, whereas in an attack on a signature scheme the x is chosen by the adversary. One could, of course, propose a stronger version of ISIS_f in which the x is chosen by the attacking algorithm, but we feel that this may require the function f to be needlessly "complicated" (e.g. something that's close to a cryptographic hash function like

---

[2] Note that x' can be equal to one of the x, as long as $\vec{s}' \neq \vec{s}$.

[3] We will also want the set $[N]$ to be exponentially large so that there is a negligible chance of obtaining pre-images on the same $f(x)$.

SHA) in order for the problem to remain hard.[4] And we do not want the function circuit to be too complex because building anonymous credentials from a signature scheme will additionally require proving knowledge of the signature. Even though recent techniques for proving arbitrarily large circuits have proof sizes of around 60 KB [9], this is still larger than proofs of simple linear or quadratic relations which can be as small as a dozen KB for common lattice relations [42]. Furthermore, the more complex proofs of arbitrary circuits will be less efficient, in terms of computation time, than proofs of simpler relations.

The main result of this work is to show how one can build an anonymous credential scheme based upon the above-sketched construction of a signature scheme for random messages. We also propose a simple function f which admits a very efficient zero-knowledge proof of the relation $A\vec{s} = f(x')$, and for which we believe that the ISIS_f problem is hard. We now discuss our choice of f and will sketch the anonymous credential scheme construction and proof in Sect. 1.1.

Arguably the simplest way to instantiate $f(x)$ is to let it be a linear function. For example, if we use the natural correspondence between binary vectors of length $\log N$ with the set $[N]$, then if $f(\vec{v}) = B\vec{v}$, where $\vec{v} \in \{0,1\}^{\log N}$, one can use the practically-efficient zero-knowledge proofs from [42] to commit to $\vec{s}$ and $\vec{v}$ and show that they have small norms and satisfy $A\vec{s} = B\vec{v}$. At first glance, it might seem that the linearity of the function interacts dangerously with the inherent linearity of lattices. For example, if $\vec{v}_1 + \vec{v}_2 = \vec{v}_3$ and we have $A\vec{s}_i = f(\vec{v}_i)$ for $i = 1,2$, then $A(\vec{s}_1 + \vec{s}_2) = f(\vec{v}_3)$. In our definition of the problem, however, the $\vec{v}_i$ are chosen at random and it is very unlikely that the sum of two randomly-chosen binary vectors will sum to another binary one (i.e. the probability is $(3/4)^{\log N}$). And if we sum more than 2 binary vectors, then the probability that the resulting pre-image $\vec{s}$ which is a sum of the pre-images, will still be as small becomes negligible.[5] So the hardness of ISIS_f for the above-defined function relies in large part on the fact that the domain of f is not closed under addition, even though f is a linear function over a larger domain. And so we conjecture that instantiating f in this way (i.e. choosing f as a random linear function over some ring and its domain as binary vectors) leads to a hard instance of ISIS_f. Furthermore, proving $A\vec{s} = B\vec{v}$ for some short $\vec{s}$ and binary $\vec{v}$ can be done very efficiently using the proofs from [42]. In particular, we do not see any better algorithm for solving the ISIS_f problem when f is defined as above vs. when f is a cryptographic hash function as in [28].

---

[4] Still, investigating this stronger assumption with appropriate functions f could be an interesting research direction. The one-more-ISIS assumption in [3] does allow the adversary access to an oracle to obtain pre-images of arbitrary vectors, but requires him to find pre-images for a random set of vectors to win the game.

[5] For example, the expected squared norm of a 512-dimensional Gaussian of standard deviation σ is $512\sigma^2$. The probability that the sum of three such Gaussians have squared norm less than this is less than 2^{-160}.

1.1   Blind Signatures and Anonymous Credentials from ISIS_f

We will now give a high level sketch of our main construction – an efficient anonymous credential scheme based on the hardness of the ISIS_f problem when one is able to give an efficient zero-knowledge proof of a solution to ISIS_f. We will first sketch the construction and proof of a blind signature scheme and then explain how essentially the same protocol can be turned into an anonymous credential scheme.

The Blind Signature Scheme. Recall that in a blind signature scheme, the user asks a signer to sign a message $\vec{m}$ and can then prove to everyone that he has a signature for $\vec{m}$. The blindness property of the scheme states that the signer cannot know during which interaction he signed $\vec{m}$, and the soundness property states that a user who interacted with the signer k times can only produce k valid signed messages.

The signer creates a matrix A and a trapdoor which allows him to sample short $\vec{s} \sim D_\sigma$, for some standard deviation σ, satisfying $A\vec{s} = \vec{t}$ for any $\vec{t} \in \mathbb{Z}_p^n$. In the concrete instantiation, the matrix A, along with the trapdoor and sampling algorithm, is as in the NTRU-based signature scheme [21,52].[6] The signer also creates random matrices B_1 and B_2 (their dimensions will be clear from their usage). The public key is A, B_1, B_2 and the function f, while the secret key is the trapdoor for A.

If the user wants to sign a (digest of a) message $\vec{m}$, he sends to the signer an Ajtai commitment of his message committed under randomness $\vec{r}$ as $\vec{c} = B_1\vec{m} + B_2\vec{r}$, along with a zero-knowledge proof (using [42]) that $\vec{m}$ and $\vec{r}$ have small norms and the linear relation $\vec{c} = B_1\vec{m} + B_2\vec{r}$ is satisfied. The signer checks the proof, creates a uniformly-random "tag" $x \in [N]$ and then uses the trapdoor for A to create a short pre-image $\vec{s}$ satisfying

$$A\vec{s} = f(x) + B_1\vec{m} + B_2\vec{r}. \tag{1}$$

The pre-image $\vec{s}$ and the tag x are sent to the user. In order to prove that he has a signature of a message $\vec{m}$, the user reveals $\vec{m}$ and creates a zero-knowledge proof of knowledge of $\vec{s}, x$ satisfying (1). In the case that f is a linear function, the exact same proof from [42] for proving $\vec{c} = B_1\vec{m} + B_2\vec{r}$ can be used here as well.

The anonymity of the blind signature (i.e. that the signer cannot figure out during which interaction $\vec{m}$ was signed) is ensured by the fact that $\vec{m}$ is transferred to the signer in a computationally-hiding commitment scheme and all the proofs are zero-knowledge. The more interesting part of the proof is showing that a user cannot produce more signed messages than the number of queries

---

[6] This implies that the scheme would be instantiated over some polynomial ring rather than $\mathbb{Z}_p$, as in the description in this section. But since $\mathbb{Z}_p$ is a sub-ring of the polynomial ring, all operations in the polynomial ring can also be described as operations over vectors over $\mathbb{Z}_p$, and so the description in this section is actually more general than we will need to be.

that he makes to the signer. We will show that if there is an adversary who can forge in the blind signature scheme, then there is an algorithm who can solve the ISIS_f problem.

Given the matrix A and a function f in the ISIS_f problem, the reduction chooses matrices with small coefficients R_1 and R_2, and then creates $B_1 = AR_1$ and $B_2 = AR_2$. By the LWE assumption, these look indistinguishable from uniform. The public key for the blind signature is thus A, B_1, B_2, along with the function f. In his first move, the adversary sends an Ajtai commitment to a message $\vec{m}$ using randomness $\vec{r}$ along with a zero-knowledge proof that the commitment is valid. In particular, the zero-knowledge proof ensures that the commitment is of the form $B_1\vec{m} + B_2\vec{r}$, and the reduction can extract the $\vec{m}$ and $\vec{r}$. By the construction of B_1 and B_2, we have $B_1\vec{m} + B_2\vec{r} = A(R_1\vec{m} + R_2\vec{r})$. The reduction then calls the oracle in the ISIS_f definition and receives some $\vec{s}, x$ satisfying $A\vec{s} = f(x)$. Notice that the reduction can now create $\vec{s}' = \vec{s} + R_1\vec{m} + R_2\vec{r}$ that satisfies

$$A\vec{s}' = f(x) + B_1\vec{m} + B_2\vec{r}. \tag{2}$$

The tuple $(\vec{s}', x)$ could be a valid signature except for the fact that the distribution of $\vec{s}'$ is not a discrete Gaussian (as in the real scheme), but is a Gaussian perturbed by $R_1\vec{m} + R_2\vec{r}$. To get $\vec{s}'$ to be a discrete Gaussian, the reduction can use rejection sampling as in [38, Theorem 4.6] which converts shifted Gaussians into zero-centered ones. If we accept, then we can send $\vec{s}'$ and x to the adversary as the signature of $\vec{m}$. If there is a rejection, then we can again query the oracle to obtain another $\vec{s}$ and x and create another potential vector $\vec{s}'$, and so on until the rejection sampling procedure accepts.

The above shows that the view of the adversary is identical in both the simulation and the real signature scheme, and thus the adversary should be successful in creating a signature for a new message $\vec{m}$. In other words, he is able to prove knowledge of an $x \in [N]$ and vectors $\vec{m}, \vec{r}$ satisfying (1), and these can be extracted by the extractor. Since $B_1 = AR_1$ and $B_2 = AR_2$, we have the potential solution to the ISIS_f problem being

$$A(\vec{s} - R_1\vec{m} - R_2\vec{r}) = f(x). \tag{3}$$

There are three possibilities for the x that is used in the forgery

1. x has not been queried to the oracle
2. x has been queried to the oracle, but was not seen by the adversary (i.e. it was discarded by the reduction during rejection sampling)
3. x has been queried to the oracle and seen by the adversary

In case 1, Eq. (3) directly gives a solution to the ISIS_f problem. In case 2, the fact that x was already queried means that the reduction has a vector $\vec{s}'$ satisfying $A\vec{s}' = f(x)$. If $\vec{s}' \neq \vec{s} - R_1\vec{m} - R_2\vec{r}$, then we again have a solution to ISIS_f. Because the adversary never saw $\vec{s}'$ and the entropy of pre-image sampling is (exponentially) large, there is only a negligible chance that $\vec{s}' = \vec{s} - R_1\vec{m} - R_2\vec{r}$.

In case 3, the adversary knows the value $\tilde{s} = \vec{s}' + R_1\vec{m}' + R_2\vec{r}'$ where $\vec{s}'$ was such that $A\vec{s}' = f(x)$, and it produces a forgery $\vec{s}, \vec{m} \neq \vec{m}', \vec{r}$ satisfying

$A(\vec{s} - R_1\vec{m} - R_2\vec{r}) = f(x)$. If $\vec{s}' = \tilde{s} - R_1\vec{m}' - R_2\vec{r} \neq \vec{s} - R_1\vec{m} - R_2\vec{r}$, then we have a solution to the ISIS_f problem. In order for this to not be a solution, the adversary would need to create $\vec{s}, \vec{m} \neq \vec{m}', \vec{r}$ such that

$$(\tilde{s} - \vec{s}) + R_1(\vec{m} - \vec{m}') + R_2(\vec{r} - \vec{r}') = 0. \tag{4}$$

To prove that even an all-powerful adversary will fail to create such an equality, we need to rely on the entropy of the matrix R_1. In particular, we can set the distribution of R_1 such that for every column of R_1, there exists another R_1' which differs from R_1 in only that column, satisfying $AR_1 = AR_1'$ (c.f. [40, Lemma 4.4]). If for every R_1, there is such a set of R_1', then for the R_1' which differs in the column corresponding to the coordinate where $\vec{m}$ and $\vec{m}'$ differ, we will have $R_1(\vec{m} - \vec{m}') \neq R_1'(\vec{m} - \vec{m}')$. An important point is also that when receiving the vector $\tilde{s}$, which is a result of rejection sampling that involves $R_1\vec{m}$, the value of R_1 is hidden since the output of the rejection sampling hides the specific $R_1\vec{m}$. In short, the success probability of the reduction breaking the ISIS_f problem is at least half the probability that an adversary can forge the blind signature.

Adapting the Above to Anonymous Credentials and Other Privacy Primitives. The framework for creating an anonymous credential scheme is virtually identical to the one above for a blind signature scheme. The first part of the scheme is the issuance of a credential for a set of attributes $\vec{m}$. This is done in the exact same manner as signing in the blind signature scheme. The user submits a commitment to a vector of credentials $\vec{m}$ along with a zero-knowledge proof that the commitment is validly formed, and the issuer creates a random tag x along with a pre-image vector $\vec{s}$ satisfying (1). The one difference in an anonymous credential scheme over a blind signature is that the user may not wish to reveal the entire attribute vector $\vec{m}$, whereas in the blind signature scheme, the whole message is revealed. In this case, he can simply reveal the sub-vector $\vec{m}'$ of $\vec{m}$ that he wishes and then prove knowledge of the remaining part of $\vec{m}$ in the zero-knowledge proof. The security proof for the anonymous credential scheme is virtually identical to the one for the blind signature.

One can also easily adapt the framework to create a group signature scheme. The only change versus an anonymous credential scheme would be that the user would additionally create a lattice-based encryption of x along with the zero-knowledge proof, and additionally prove (again using the zero-knowledge proof from [42]) that the ciphertext is a valid encryption of x. The size of the signature will be larger than that in [41], but the advantage is that signing and verification time does not scale linearly in the group size.

1.2 Related Work

Prior works building privacy-preserving primitives such as group signatures, blind signatures, and anonymous credentials [45,50,51], circumvented the need to prove knowledge of a random oracle pre-image by using the standard-model digital signature framework of [1] instead of the hash-and-sign based approach. But these standard-model signatures are a factor 5X - 10X longer because instantiating standard-model signatures requires larger parameters and does not allow instantiating the trapdoored matrix A via the NTRU assumption as we do.

Other constructions of efficient blind signatures [3,10] which do not start from the signature in [1], and do in fact use the NTRU trapdoor, unfortunately cannot be extended to anonymous credential schemes while utilizing the the the compact proofs from [42] for simple lattice relations. The technical reason is that in these blind signature schemes, the user gets the signer to blindly sign $H(\mu)$ for some message μ and cryptographic hash function H. In the proof, he reveals the whole μ, and proves knowledge of a simple relation that includes $H(\mu)$. Because the user will only ever give one proof that includes μ, revealing μ is perfectly fine. In an anonymous credential scheme, however, one may want to get a set of credentials (i.e. $\mu = \mu'||\mu''$) blindly signed, and then reveal only the μ' part of it. This will require proving knowledge of a μ'' that satisfies some relation involving $H(\mu'||\mu'')$, which results in longer and slower proofs.[7]

1.3 Concurrent Work

We discuss concurrent works [32,33], of which [32] was recently updated with applications to anonymous credentials, and will appear at CRYPTO'23.

In common with prior work [45,50,51], both [32,33] avoid proving knowledge of random oracle preimages. Both works follow the paradigm of 'signatures with efficient protocols' and design lattice-based digital signature schemes tailored towards efficient zero-knowledge proofs of a message and signature. The second work, [33] defines a new cryptographic primitive called commit-transferable signatures (CTS) in order to instantiate this paradigm more efficiently. Similarly to our work, they rely on existing frameworks such as [43] (with [32] additionally relying on [57])) to produce efficient zero-knowledge proofs to use inside their constructions.

The biggest difference between our work and [32,33] lies in the use of cryptographic assumptions. The anonymous credential constructions of [32,33] rely solely on the SIS and LWE assumptions and their ring variants. In contrast, our work relies on the new ISIS_f assumption which we introduce. The main benefit of this new assumption over the approaches in [32,33] is that it allows us to use zero-knowledge proofs of [43] to prove significantly fewer and simpler relations. This leads to a large efficiency improvement in our anonymous credential constructions, with [32,33] offering credential sizes of roughly 640KB and 500KB respectively, and our work offering sizes of roughly 120KB (under ISIS_f). Further, while [32,33] rely on trapdoor sampling techniques for standard lattices from [47], we rely on NTRU lattices and NTRU-based trapdoors [21,52]. Finally, as noted in [33], we use minimalistic definitions of anonymous credentials which

---

[7] The blind signature protocol of [10] does require a zero-knowledge proof involving $H(\cdot)$, but this proof is only done in the intermediate interaction between the user and the signer, and so its relative inefficiency does not affect the signature size.

do not incorporate pseudonyms or user secret keys. Including these aspects would require additional commitments and zero-knowledge proofs which would increase the complexity of our anonymous credentials, although we do not believe they would add too much extra overhead.

1.4   Discussion and Open Problems

The most pertinent open problem is to analyze the hardness of the ISIS_f problem when instantiated with a random linear f, or perhaps other classes of slightly higher-degree functions f which still yield efficient zero-knowledge proofs.

Another open problem is to come up with a possibly stronger assumption that would result in tighter reductions for our schemes. In particular, we feel that breaking our blind signature and anonymous credential scheme is more difficult than what the security reductions imply. For example, we need to set parameters so as to allow rejection sampling to work and for the matrix R_1 to be chosen such that with high probability there is another R_1' satisfying $AR_1 = AR_1'$.

If one looks closely at the proof sketch in Sect. 1.1, what we have essentially done is give a reduction from ISIS_f to an "interactive" version of ISIS_f in which the adversary has more control over the pre-images that he receives. In the ISIS_f problem, the adversary is given an oracle that outputs $\vec{s}, x$ satisfying $A\vec{s} = f(x)$, whereas in the "interactive" version, the adversary can choose $\vec{m}$ and $\vec{r}$ as in (1) and then receives a random x and $\vec{s}$ satisfying (1). His goal is then to satisfy (1) for a fresh $\vec{m}$. We have shown that if the random matrices B_1 and B_2 are constructed as AR_1 and AR_2, and other parameters are set appropriately, then using rejection sampling we are able to transform $\vec{s}, x$ that satisfy $A\vec{s} = f(x)$ into $\vec{s}', x$ that satisfy (1). Furthermore, picking an R_1 from a wide-enough distribution to guarantee the existence of another R_1' satisfying $AR_1 = AR_1'$ was required to assure that the adversary could not create a forgery that satisfied (4). It is very much possible, however, that setting the scheme parameters to allow for these particularities of the proof to go through is not really necessary for security. Since asymptotically, the interactive ISIS_f problem is as hard as ISIS_f, it makes sense to examine the interactive version on its own with a more favorable parameter setting. That is, one could make the assumption that the interactive version of the ISIS_f problem is hard in the parameter range that does not yield a reduction from ISIS_f.[8] In Table 1, we give example parameters of instantiations of an anonymous credential scheme based on the ISIS_f assumption and parameters required if one assumes hardness of the interactive version. The scheme based on ISIS_f is noticeably more compact than the previously most efficient anonymous credential scheme [32], which has output sizes of around 650KB. But as we also see, there is a noticeable advantage in setting the scheme parameters smaller

---

[8] This is similar to how the SIS and LWE problems were first introduced – solving their random instances was shown to be as hard as solving lattice problems in the worst case [4,48,53], but now the SIS and LWE problems are used with parameters which do not satisfy these original reductions because these problems have since been very well-studied on their own.

Table 1. Output sizes for the anonymous credential schemes with 8 and 16 attributes.

Attributes	Assumption			
	ISIS_f	interactive ISIS_f	Strong-RSA [17]	qSDH [16]
8	122KB	26KB	1319B	608B
16	133KB	29KB	1910B	865B

and assuming that the problem (interactive ISIS_f) is still hard. We believe that analyzing the security of this version of the problem, and possibly building other more efficient schemes based on it, is a promising research direction when it comes to building practical lattice-based schemes.

One of the main appeals of lattice cryptography, in addition to its versatility, is that its underlying operations are very fast when instantiated over polynomial rings. It is therefore quite conceivable that lattice-based constructions will be the fastest option out of all the post-quantum alternatives. Since most anonymous credential schemes involve real-time interaction (e.g. credit card usage), speed is a very important consideration in their real world deployment. Unlike the many efforts to construct efficient software for discrete log, pairing-based, and PCP/IOP-based proof systems, there has not been much concentrated effort to develop software for efficient lattice-based primitives. Part of the problem has been that there were not many lattice-based protocols which were compact enough to be considered for practical deployment. We hope that this paper provides some motivation for creating implementations of lattice-based privacy primitives that are real-world ready.

2   Preliminaries

Let λ be a security parameter which is provided in unary to all involved algorithms. For $n \in \mathbb{N}$, let $[n] := \{1, \ldots, n\}$. Let $\mathbb{Z}_p$ denote the ring of integers modulo p. We write $\vec{v} \in \mathbb{Z}_p^m$ to denote vectors over a ring $\mathbb{Z}_p$. Matrices over $\mathbb{Z}_p$ will be written as regular capital letters. By default, all vectors are column vectors.

We define $\mathcal{U}(S)$ to be the uniform distribution on the finite set S. We write $x \leftarrow D$ when x is sampled according to the distribution D. Sometimes, we abuse the notation and write $x \leftarrow S$ to denote $x \leftarrow \mathcal{U}(S)$.

Lattices. Let $B = \{\vec{b}_1, \ldots, \vec{b}_n\} \subseteq \mathbb{R}^n$ be a set of linearly independent vectors. The n-dimensional full-rank lattice generated by B is defined as follows:

$$\Lambda = \Lambda(B) := \left\{ \sum_{i=1}^{n} c_i \vec{b}_i : c_1, \ldots, c_n \in \mathbb{Z} \right\}.$$

We denote $\tilde{B} = (\vec{b}_i')_{i \in [n]}$ to be the Gram-Schmidt orthogonalization of B. Further, define the Gram-Schmidt norm of B as $\|\tilde{B}\| := \max_{i \in [n]} \|\vec{b}_i'\|$.

Cyclotomic Rings. For a power of two $d \geq 4$ and a positive integer p, let $\mathcal{K} = \mathbb{Q}[X]/(X^d + 1)$ denote the $2d$-th cyclotomic field and $\mathcal{R} = \mathbb{Z}[X]/(X^d + 1)$ be the corresponding ring of integers. Lower-case letters denote elements in $\mathcal{R}$ and bold lower-case (resp. upper-case) letters represent column vectors (resp. matrices) with coefficients in $\mathcal{R}$. For a modulus $q \in \mathbb{N}$, we define $\mathcal{R}_q := \mathcal{R}/(q) = \mathbb{Z}_q[X]/(X^d + 1)$. Further, we define $\mathcal{R}_q^{\times}$ to be the set of polynomials in $\mathcal{R}_q$ which are invertible over $\mathcal{R}_q$. For $\eta \in \mathbb{N}$, define $S_\eta := \{x \in \mathcal{R} : \|x\|_\infty \leq \eta\}$. Recall that, for any $\mathbf{A} \in \mathcal{R}_q^{n \times m}$, the q-ary lattice $\Lambda_q^{\perp}(\mathbf{A})$ is defined as $\Lambda_q^{\perp}(\mathbf{A}) := \{\mathbf{x} \in \mathcal{R}^m : \mathbf{Ax} = \mathbf{0} \bmod q\}$.

Coefficient Representation and Multiplication Matrices. For a polynomial vector $\mathbf{x} \in \mathcal{R}^l$, define $\mathsf{Coeffs}(\mathbf{x}) \in \mathbb{Z}^{ld}$ to be coefficient vector of $\mathbf{x}$. Similarly, $\mathsf{Coeffs}^{-1}(\vec{x}) \in \mathcal{R}^l$ is the polynomial vector with coefficients $\vec{x}$.

For a polynomial $f = f_0 + f_1 X + \ldots + f_{d-1} X^{d-1} \in \mathcal{R}$, we define the *multiplication* matrix $\mathsf{rot}(f) \in \mathbb{Z}^{d \times d}$ as:

$$\mathsf{rot}(f) = \begin{bmatrix} f_0 & -f_{d-1} & \cdots & -f_1 \\ f_1 & f_0 & \cdots & -f_2 \\ \vdots & \vdots & \vdots & \vdots \\ f_{d-1} & \cdots & f_1 & f_0 \end{bmatrix}.$$

In particular, we will use the property that for $f, g \in \mathcal{R}$, $\mathsf{rot}(fg) = \mathsf{rot}(f)\mathsf{rot}(g)$. We extend this definition to matrices over $\mathcal{R}$. Namely, for a matrix $\mathbf{F} = (f_{i,j}) \in \mathcal{R}_q^{n \times m}$, we define

$$\mathsf{rot}(\mathbf{F}) = \begin{bmatrix} \mathsf{rot}(f_{1,1}) & \mathsf{rot}(f_{1,2}) & \cdots & \mathsf{rot}(f_{1,m}) \\ \vdots & \vdots & \vdots & \vdots \\ \mathsf{rot}(f_{n,1}) & \mathsf{rot}(f_{n,2}) & \cdots & \mathsf{rot}(f_{n,m}) \end{bmatrix} \in \mathbb{Z}^{nd \times md}.$$

Then, for any polynomial vector $\mathbf{x} \in \mathcal{R}_q^m$ we have the following property over $\mathbb{Z}_q$:

$$\mathsf{Coeffs}(\mathbf{Fx}) = \mathsf{rot}(\mathbf{F})\mathsf{Coeffs}(\mathbf{x}).$$

Discrete Gaussian Distribution. We recall the discrete Gaussian distribution used for the rejection sampling and trapdoor sampling.

Definition 2.1 *The n-dimensional Gaussian function $\rho_{\mathsf{s},\vec{c}} : \mathbb{R} \to (0, 1]$ is defined by*

$$\rho_{\mathsf{s},\vec{c}}(\vec{x}) := \exp\left(-\frac{\|\vec{x} - \vec{c}\|^2}{2\mathsf{s}^2}\right).$$

For any coset $\Lambda + \vec{t}$ of a full-rank lattice $\Lambda \subset \mathbb{R}^n$, $\rho_{\mathsf{s},\vec{c}}(\Lambda + \vec{t}) := \sum_{\vec{x} \in \Lambda + \vec{t}} \rho_{\mathsf{s},\vec{c}}(\vec{x})$. Then, the discrete Gaussian distribution over a coset of a lattice $\Lambda + \vec{t}$ centred around $\vec{c} \in \mathbb{R}^n$ with standard deviation $\mathsf{s} > 0$ is given by

$$\forall \vec{x} \in \Lambda + \vec{t}, D_{\Lambda + \vec{t}, \mathsf{s}, \vec{c}}(\vec{x}) := \frac{\rho_{\mathsf{s},\vec{c}}(\vec{x})}{\rho_{\mathsf{s},\vec{c}}(\Lambda + \vec{t})}.$$

We write $D^n_{s,\vec{c}}$ when $\Lambda = \mathbb{Z}^n$. Similarly, we ignore the subscript $\vec{c}$ when the distribution is centred around $\vec{0} \in \mathbb{Z}^n$.

Smoothing Parameter. We recall the definition of a smoothing parameter [48]. Namely, for any n-dimensional lattice Λ and a real number $\epsilon > 0$, the smoothing parameter $\eta_\epsilon(\Lambda)$ is the smallest $s > 0$ such that $\rho_{\frac{1}{s\sqrt{2\pi}}}(\Lambda^* \backslash \{0\}) \leq \epsilon$. We also consider the scaled version $\eta'_\epsilon(\Lambda) = \frac{1}{\sqrt{2\pi}}\eta_\epsilon(\Lambda)$. Further, for any $\epsilon > 0$ we define $\eta_{\min}(\epsilon) \in \mathbb{R}$ to be such that $\Pr_{\mathbf{A} \leftarrow \mathcal{R}_q^{n \times m}}[\eta'_\epsilon(\Lambda_q^\perp(\mathbf{A})) > \eta_{\min}(\epsilon)] \leq 2^{-d}$. Note that $\eta_{\min}$ can be computed as in [14, Lemma 2.5].

Tail Bounds. We recall the following tail bounds which are widely used in the literature. The first one focuses on discrete Gaussians over integers and follows from [7, Lemma 1.5(i)] and was adapted in [38, Lemma 4.4]. The next one by Micciancio and Regev [48, Lemma 4.4] is a tail bound on discrete Gaussians over any full-rank lattices.

Lemma 2.2 ([38]). *Let $\vec{x} \leftarrow D^n_s$ and $t > 1$. Then*

$$\Pr\left[\|\vec{x}\| > t \cdot s\sqrt{n}\right] < \left(te^{\frac{1-t^2}{2}}\right)^n.$$

Lemma 2.3 ([48]). *Let Λ be an n-dimensional full-rank lattice, $\vec{c} \in \mathbb{R}^n$, $0 < \epsilon < 1$ and $s \geq \eta'_\epsilon(\Lambda)$. Let $\vec{x} \leftarrow D_{\Lambda,s,\vec{c}}$. Then $\Pr\left[\|\vec{x} - \vec{c}\| \geq s\sqrt{n}\right] < \frac{1+\epsilon}{1-\epsilon} \cdot 2^{-n}$.*

Preimage Sampling. Let $\mathbf{A} \in \mathcal{R}_q^{n \times m}$. Then, we denote $\mathbf{A}_s^{-1}(\mathbf{u})$ to be the random variable $\mathbf{x} \leftarrow D_s^{md}$ conditioned on $\mathbf{Ax} = \mathbf{u}$ over $\mathcal{R}_q$.

Rejection Sampling. Rejection sampling [37,38] is a widely used technique to ensure the zero-knowledge property of many lattice-based (non-)interactive proofs.

Lemma 2.4 (Rejection Sampling [38]). *Let $V \subseteq \mathcal{R}^\ell$ be a set of polynomials with norm at most T and $\rho: V \to [0,1]$ be a probability distribution. Fix the standard deviation $s = \alpha T$ for $\alpha = O(\sqrt{\lambda})$. Let*

$$M = \exp\left(\sqrt{\frac{2(\lambda+1)}{\log e}} \cdot \frac{1}{\alpha} + \frac{1}{2\alpha^2}\right) = O(1).$$

Now, sample $\mathbf{v} \leftarrow \rho$ and $\mathbf{y} \leftarrow D_s^\ell$, set $\mathbf{z} = \mathbf{y} + \mathbf{v}$, and run $b \leftarrow \mathsf{Rej}_1(\mathbf{z}, \mathbf{v}, s, M)$ as defined in Fig. 1. Then, the probability that $b = 1$ is at least $(1 - 2^{-\lambda})/M$ and the distribution of $(\mathbf{v}, \mathbf{z})$, conditioned on $b = 1$, is within statistical distance of $2^{-\lambda}$ of the product distribution $\rho \times D_s^\ell$.

$$\begin{array}{|l|}
\hline
\text{Rej}\,(\vec{z}, \vec{v}, \mathfrak{s}, M) \\
\hline
1:\ u \leftarrow [0, 1) \\
2:\ \textbf{if } u > \frac{1}{M} \cdot \exp\left(\frac{-2\langle \vec{z}, \vec{v}\rangle + \|\vec{v}\|^2}{2\mathfrak{s}^2}\right) \textbf{ then} \\
3:\quad \textbf{return } 0 \text{ (i.e. } reject) \\
4:\ \textbf{else} \\
5:\quad \textbf{return } 1 \text{ (i.e. } accept) \\
\hline
\end{array}$$

Fig. 1. Standard rejection sampling algorithm [38].

RejSamp$(\mathbf{A}, \mathbf{v}, \mathbf{t}, \mathbf{w})$	SimRS$(\mathbf{A}, \mathbf{t}, \mathbf{w})$
1: **if** $\mathbf{Av} \neq \mathbf{t}$ **then return** $\perp$	1: **if** $\mathbf{Av} \qquad\qquad \neq$
2: $\mathbf{y} \leftarrow \mathbf{A}_\mathfrak{s}^{-1}(\mathbf{w})$	$\quad\mathbf{t}$ **then return** $\perp$
3: $\mathbf{z} = \mathbf{y} + \mathbf{v}$	2: $\mathbf{z} \leftarrow \mathbf{A}_\mathfrak{s}^{-1}(\mathbf{t} + \mathbf{w})$
4: **return** $(\mathbf{A}, \mathbf{t}, \mathbf{w}, \mathbf{z})$ with prob.	3: **return** $(\mathbf{A}, \mathbf{t}, \mathbf{w}, \mathbf{z})$ with
$\quad \min\left(\frac{D_\mathfrak{s}^{md}(\mathbf{z})}{M \cdot D_{\mathfrak{s}, \mathbf{v}}^{md}(\mathbf{z})}, 1\right)$	prob. $\frac{1}{M}$

Fig. 2. Rejection sampling on q-ary lattices.

Recently, Boschini et al. [14] proposed a generalized rejection sampling method for ellipsoidal Gaussians over any lattice, which was later used in the context of multi-signatures. Here, we use the (simplified) result from [14, Theorem B.1] to apply rejection sampling on q-ary lattices[9].

Lemma 2.5 (Generalized Rejection Sampling [14]). *Take any $\alpha, T > 0$ and $\epsilon \leq 1/2$. Let $\mathbf{v} \in \mathcal{R}_q^m$ be such that $\|\mathbf{v}\| \leq T$, $\mathbf{A} \in \mathcal{R}_q^{n \times m}$, $\mathbf{w} \in \mathcal{R}_q^n$ and $\mathbf{t} := \mathbf{Av} \in \mathcal{R}_q^n$. Also, pick $\mathfrak{s} \geq \max(\alpha T, \eta_\epsilon'(\Lambda_q^\perp(\mathbf{A})))$. Then, for any*

$$t > 0, \quad M := \exp\left(\frac{1}{2\alpha^2} + \frac{t}{\alpha}\right), \quad \varepsilon := 2\left(\frac{1+\epsilon}{1-\epsilon}\right)\exp\left(-2t^2 \cdot \frac{\pi - 1}{\pi}\right),$$

the statistical distance between distributions RejSamp *and* SimRS *defined in Fig. 2 is at most $\frac{\varepsilon}{2M} + \frac{2\epsilon}{M}$. Moreover, the probability that* RejSamp *outputs something is at least $\frac{1-\varepsilon}{M}\left(1 - \frac{4\epsilon}{(1+\epsilon)^2}\right)$.*

2.1 NTRU Lattices

Using terminology from above, let d be a power of two, q a positive integer and $f, g \in \mathcal{R}$ such that f is invertible over $\mathcal{R}_q$. Let $h = g/f \in \mathcal{R}_q$. The NTRU lattice associated to h and q is defined as

$$\Lambda_{h,q} := \{(u, v) \in \mathcal{R}^2 : u + vh = 0 \bmod q\}\ .$$

---

[9] An almost identical application was described in [14, Section B.4] in the context of proving statistical honest-verifier zero-knowledge of the Fiat-Shamir with aborts protocol [38].

Then, $\Lambda_{h,q}$ is a $2d$-dimensional full-rank lattice generated by the rows of

$$A_{h,q} := \begin{bmatrix} -\mathsf{rot}(h) & I_d \\ q \cdot I_d & 0 \end{bmatrix} \in \mathbb{Z}^{2d \times 2d}.$$

We recall that there is an efficient algorithm $\mathtt{NTRU.TrapGen}$, which given modulus q and the ring dimension d, outputs $h \in \mathcal{R}_q$ and a short basis of $\Lambda_{h,q}$. This is the core part of the key generation of the Falcon signature scheme [52].

Lemma 2.6 ([21,52]).   *There is a PPT algorithm* $\mathtt{NTRU.TrapGen}(q,d)$ *which outputs* $h \in \mathcal{R}_q$ *and a basis* $\mathbf{B}$ *of* $\Lambda_{h,q}$ *such that* $\|\tilde{\mathbf{B}}\| \le 1.17\sqrt{q}$.

The short basis can now be used for preimage sampling using the well-known GPV framework [28] and its concrete instantiation in [21]. Namely, for any $c \in \mathcal{R}$, one can efficiently sample $(u,v) \in \mathcal{R}^2$ from a discrete Gaussian distribution conditioned on $u + vh = c \bmod q$. We use the extended result following [56, Lemma 2.7], i.e. given additionally $\mathbf{a} \in \mathcal{R}^m$, we can efficiently sample $(u,v,\mathbf{w}) \in \mathcal{R}^{m+2}$ from a discrete Gaussian distribution conditioned on $u + vh + \mathbf{a}^T\mathbf{m} = c \bmod q$.

Lemma 2.7 ([21,22,28]).   *Let* $n \in \mathbb{N}$ *and* $\epsilon = 2^{-\lambda}/(4d)$. *There is a PPT algorithm* $\mathtt{GSampler}$, *which takes* $(h,\mathbf{B}) \leftarrow \mathtt{NTRU.TrapGen}(q,d)$, $\mathbf{a} \in \mathcal{R}_q^m$, *standard deviation* $\mathfrak{s} > 0$ *and a target vector* $c \in \mathcal{R}_q$ *as input, and outputs a triple* $(u,v,\mathbf{w}) \in \mathcal{R}_q^{m+2}$ *such that*

$$\Delta\left(\left[h\ \mathbf{a}^T\ 1 \right]_{\mathfrak{s}}^{-1}(c), \mathtt{GSampler}(h,\mathbf{a},\mathbf{B},\mathfrak{s},c) \right) \le 2^{-\lambda}$$

as long as

$$\mathfrak{s} \ge 1.17\sqrt{q} \cdot \eta'_\epsilon(\mathbb{Z}) \quad where \quad \eta'_\epsilon(\mathbb{Z}) \approx \frac{1}{\pi} \cdot \sqrt{\frac{1}{2}\ln\left(2 + \frac{2}{\epsilon}\right)}.$$

2.2   Module-SIS and Module-LWE Problems

The security of our schemes relies on the well-known computational lattice problems Module-LWE (MLWE) and Module-SIS (MSIS) [34]. Both problems are defined over $\mathcal{R}_q$.

Definition 2.8 ($\mathsf{MSIS}_{n,m,\mathcal{B}}$)**.** *Given* $A \leftarrow \mathcal{R}_q^{n \times m}$, *the Module-SIS problem with parameters* $n, m > 0$ *and* $0 < \mathcal{B} < q$ *asks to find* $\mathbf{z} \in \mathcal{R}_q^m$ *such that* $A\mathbf{z} = \mathbf{0}$ *over* $\mathcal{R}_q$ *and* $0 < \|\mathbf{z}\| \le \mathcal{B}$. *An algorithm* $\mathcal{A}$ *is said to have advantage* ϵ *in solving* $\mathsf{MSIS}_{n,m,\mathcal{B},q}$ *if*

$$\mathsf{Adv}_{n,m,\mathcal{B},q}^{\mathsf{MSIS}}(\mathcal{A}) := \Pr\left[0 < \|\mathbf{z}\|_\infty \le \mathcal{B} \wedge A\mathbf{z} = \mathbf{0} \,\middle|\, A \leftarrow \mathcal{R}_q^{n \times m}; \mathbf{z} \leftarrow \mathcal{A}(A) \right] \ge \epsilon.$$

If the modulus is clear from the context, then we drop q *from the subscript.*

As for Module-LWE, we consider its "knapsack version" which is equivalent to its standard definition up to an additive negligible factor for typically chosen parameters [26, Appendix C]. In the paper we will use both versions and assume they are equivalent.

Definition 2.9 (MLWE$_{n,m,\chi,q}$). *The* Module-LWE *problem with parameters* $m \geq n > 0$ *and an error distribution* χ *over* $\mathcal{R}$ *asks the adversary* $\mathcal{A}$ *to distinguish between the following two cases: 1)* (A, As) *for* $A \leftarrow \mathcal{R}_q^{n \times m}$, *a secret vector* $s \leftarrow \chi^m$, *and 2)* $(A, b) \leftarrow \mathcal{R}_q^{n \times m} \times \mathcal{R}_q^n$. *Then,* $\mathcal{A}$ *is said to have advantage* ϵ *in solving* MLWE$_{n,m,\chi,q}$ *if*

$$\mathsf{Adv}_{n,m,\chi,q}^{\mathsf{MLWE}}(\mathcal{A}) := \Big| \Pr \Big[b = 1 \Big| A \leftarrow \mathcal{R}_q^{n \times m}; \, s \leftarrow \chi^m; \, b \leftarrow \mathcal{A}(A, As) \Big]$$

$$- \Pr \Big[b = 1 \Big| A \leftarrow \mathcal{R}_q^{n \times m}; \, b \leftarrow \mathcal{R}_q^n; \, b \leftarrow \mathcal{A}(A, b) \Big] \Big| \geq \epsilon. \quad (5)$$

For simplicity, if χ *is a uniform distribution over* S_η *then we simply write* MLWE$_{n,m,\eta,q}$. *Also, we drop the subscript* q *if the modulus is clear from the context.*

2.3   Non-interactive Zero-Knowledge Proofs in the ROM

In this paper, we consider binary relations $R \subseteq \{0,1\}^* \times \{0,1\}^*$. Then define $L_R := \{x \in \{0,1\}^* : \exists w, (x, w) \in R\}$ to be the language corresponding to R. We refer to x as a statement and w as a witness.

We recall the (slightly adapted) definitions of non-interactive zero-knowledge proofs (NIZK) in the random oracle model from [50].

Definition 2.10 (NIZK). *A non-interactive zero-knowledge proof system* Π_{NIZK} *for the relation* R *consists of three PPT algorithms* (Setup, Prove, Verify) *which are defined as follows:*

- Setup$(1^\lambda) \rightarrow$ crs : *the setup algorithm which outputs the common reference string* crs $\in \{0,1\}^{\ell(\lambda)}$,
- Prove^{H}(crs, x, w) $\rightarrow \pi/\bot$: *the prover algorithm takes as input the common reference string* crs $\in \{0,1\}^\ell$, *statement* x *and witness* w, *either outputs a proof* π *or an abort symbol* $\bot$,
- Verify^{H}(crs, x, π) $\rightarrow 0/1$: *the verifier algorithm takes as input the common reference string* crs $\in \{0,1\}^\ell$, *statement* x *and a proof* π *and outputs a bit* b *where* b = 1 *means accept and* b = 0 *means reject.*

Unless stated otherwise, we assume that crs can be generated as the output of another random oracle. In other words, crs is a common random string. Hence, our protocols do not require a trusted setup.

We recall the key properties of NIZK used in this paper: (i) correctness, (ii) zero-knowledge, and (iii) multi-proof extractability (i.e. straight-line extractability).

Definition 2.11 (Correctness). *We say that a NIZK proof system Π_{NIZK} is correct if for all* $\mathsf{crs} \in \{0,1\}^\ell$ *and* $(\mathsf{crs}, x, w) \in R$, *the probability that* $\mathsf{Prove}^{\mathsf{H}}(\mathsf{crs}, x, w)$ *outputs* $\perp$ *is* $\mathsf{negl}(\lambda)$, *and:*

$$\Pr\left[\pi \leftarrow \mathsf{Prove}^{\mathsf{H}}(\mathsf{crs}, x, w) : \mathsf{Verify}(\mathsf{crs}, x, w) = 1 \,\middle|\, \pi \neq \perp\right] = 1 - \mathsf{negl}(\lambda).$$

Definition 2.12 (Zero-Knowledge). *We say that a NIZK proof system Π_{NIZK} is zero-knowledge if there exists a simulator* $\mathcal{S} = (\mathcal{S}_0, \mathcal{S}_1)$ *which consists of two PPT algorithms with a shared state such that for any PPT adversary $\mathcal{A}$ we have*

$$\mathsf{Adv}^{\mathsf{ZK}}_{\Pi_{\mathsf{NIZK}}}(\mathcal{A}) := \left|\Pr[1 \leftarrow \mathcal{A}^{\mathsf{H},\mathsf{Prove}}(\mathsf{crs})] - \Pr[1 \leftarrow \mathcal{A}^{\mathcal{S}_0,\mathcal{S}_1}(\mathsf{crs})]\right| = \mathsf{negl}(\lambda)$$

where Prove *and $\mathcal{S}$ are prover and simulator oracles which, given* (x, w), *output* $\perp$ *if* $(\mathsf{crs}, x, w) \notin R$ *and otherwise return* $\mathsf{Prove}^{\mathsf{H}}(\mathsf{crs}, x, w)$ *and* $\mathcal{S}_1(\mathsf{crs}, x)$ *respectively. The probability is also taken over the randomness of generating the common reference string* $\mathsf{crs} \leftarrow \mathsf{Setup}(1^\lambda)$.

Finally, we consider multi-proof extractability which corresponds to straight-line extractability. Here, the adversary can pick the statements adaptively. In order to perform extraction in this stronger setting, the common reference string is simulated and the corresponding trapdoor is provided to the extractor.

Definition 2.13 (Multi-Proof Extractability). *The following hold:*

CRS Simulatability. For any PPT adversary $\mathcal{A}$, we have:

$$\mathsf{Adv}^{\mathsf{crs}}_{\Pi_{\mathsf{NIZK}}}(\mathcal{A}) := \left|\Pr[\mathsf{crs} \leftarrow \mathsf{Setup}(1^\lambda) : 1 \leftarrow \mathcal{A}^{\mathsf{H}}(\mathsf{crs})] - \Pr[(\tilde{\mathsf{crs}}, \tau) \leftarrow \mathcal{S}_{\mathsf{crs}}(1^\lambda) : 1 \leftarrow \mathcal{A}^{\mathsf{H}}(\tilde{\mathsf{crs}})]\right|$$

is negligible.

Straight-Line Extractability. There exist constants e_1, e_2, c such that for any $Q_{\mathsf{H}}, Q_s \in \mathsf{poly}(\lambda)$ and any PPT adversary $\mathcal{A}$ that makes at most Q_{H} random oracle queries with

$$\Pr\left[\begin{array}{l}(\tilde{\mathsf{crs}}, \tau) \leftarrow \mathcal{S}_{\mathsf{crs}}(1^\lambda), \\ \{(x_i, \pi_i)\}_{i \in [Q_s]} \leftarrow \mathcal{A}^{\mathsf{H}}(\tilde{\mathsf{crs}})\end{array} : \forall i \in [Q_s], \mathsf{Verify}^{\mathsf{H}}(\tilde{\mathsf{crs}}, x_i, \pi_i) = 1\right] \geq \varepsilon(\lambda),$$

where $\varepsilon(\lambda)$ is non-negligible, we have

$$\Pr\left[\begin{array}{l}(\tilde{\mathsf{crs}}, \tau) \leftarrow \mathcal{S}_{\mathsf{crs}}(1^\lambda), \{(x_i, \pi_i)\}_{i \in [Q_s]} \leftarrow \mathcal{A}^{\mathsf{H}}(\tilde{\mathsf{crs}}), \\ \{w_i \leftarrow \textit{Multi-Extract}(Q_{\mathsf{H}}, Q_s, 1/\varepsilon, \tilde{\mathsf{crs}}, \tau, x_i, \pi_i)\}_{i \in [Q_s]} : \\ \forall i \in [Q_s], (\tilde{\mathsf{crs}}, x_i, w_i) \in R \wedge \mathsf{Verify}^{\mathsf{H}}(\tilde{\mathsf{crs}}, x_i, \pi_i)\end{array}\right] \geq \frac{1}{2} \cdot \varepsilon(\lambda) - \mathsf{negl}(\lambda)$$

where the runtime of the extractor is upper-bounded by $Q_{\mathsf{H}}^{e_1} \cdot Q_s^{e_2} \cdot \frac{1}{\varepsilon(\lambda)^c} \cdot \mathsf{poly}(\lambda)$.

For proving various soundness properties, we will deal with *expected* PPT knowledge extractors. Since security of our protocols rely on computation assumptions, it is essential for us to transform these extractors into *strict* PPT algorithms. Below, we show a standard way to achieve this goal.

Lemma 2.14 (Expected-Time to Strict-Time Transformation). *Take any efficient binary relation R and any statement x. Let $\mathcal{A}$ be a probabilistic algorithm which runs in expected time at most T and*

$$\Pr_{\mathsf{crs} \leftarrow \{0,1\}^\ell}[\mathcal{A}(\mathsf{crs}, x) \to w : (x, w) \in R] = \varepsilon.$$

Then, there is an algorithm $\mathcal{B}$ with an oracle access to $\mathcal{A}$, which runs in time at most $\frac{2T}{\varepsilon}$ and

$$\Pr_{\mathsf{crs} \leftarrow \{0,1\}^\ell}[\mathcal{B}^{\mathcal{A}}(\mathsf{crs}, x) \to 1] \geq \varepsilon/2.$$

Proof The algorithm $\mathcal{B}$ is pretty intuitive: given input (crs, x), it runs $\mathcal{A}(\mathsf{crs}, x)$ and checks whether $\mathcal{A}$ did output a valid witness w. However, if the total runtime is more than $T_{\max} := 2T/\varepsilon$, then $\mathcal{B}$ aborts.

Denote X to be the binary random variable, which determines whether the output w from $\mathcal{A}$ is valid. Similarly, let Y be the runtime of $\mathcal{A}(\mathsf{crs}, x)$. Then, we are interested in

$$\Pr[X = 1 \wedge Y \leq T_{\max}] \geq \Pr[X = 1] - \Pr[Y > T_{\max}].$$

Note that $\Pr[X = 1] = \varepsilon$, and also by Markov inequality we have $\Pr[Y > T_{\max}] \leq \varepsilon/2$. Hence, this concludes the proof.   □

3   The ISIS$_f$ Assumption

This section introduces a new family of lattice-based assumptions called ISIS$_f$ (where ISIS stands for Inhomogenous Shortest Integer Solution). With a similar flavour to the recently proposed lattice assumptions [2,5], the adversary is given short preimages of random (but not necessarily uniformly random) images and its task is to come up with either a short preimage of a new image, or a new preimage (i.e. not the one received earlier) to one of the images which was sent. More formally, let $n, m, k \in \mathbb{N}$ where the first two variables correspond to the matrix dimensions and the last one represents the number of samples. We consider a uniformly random $n \times m$ matrix $\mathbf{A}$ over $\mathcal{R}_q$, and an efficiently computable function $f : [N] \to \mathbb{Z}_q^n$. The adversary is given $x_1, \ldots, x_k \leftarrow [N]$ as well as vectors $\mathbf{s}_1, \ldots, \mathbf{s}_k \in \mathbb{Z}_q^m$, where each $\mathbf{s}_i \leftarrow \mathbf{A}_{\mathfrak{s}}^{-1}(f(x_i))$. Then, it needs to come up with a new pair $(x^*, \mathbf{s}^*)$ (in particular, different from the previous ones) such that $\mathbf{A}\mathbf{s}^* = f(x^*)$ and $\mathbf{s}^*$ is short.

Definition 3.1 (The ISIS$_f$ Problem). *Let* $\mathsf{pp} := (q, d, n, m, N, k, \mathfrak{s}, \mathcal{B})$ *be a tuple of functions of the security parameter λ. Consider any efficiently com-*

$$\frac{\mathsf{Exp}_{\mathsf{pp}}^{\mathsf{ISIS}_f}(\mathcal{A})}{}$$

1: $\mathbf{A} \leftarrow \mathcal{R}_q^{n \times m}$
2: **for** $i \in [k]$:
3:     $x_i \leftarrow [N]$
4:     $\mathbf{s}_i \leftarrow \mathbf{A}_{\mathsf{s}}^{-1}(f(x_i))$
5: $(x^*, \mathbf{s}^*) \leftarrow \mathcal{A}(\mathbf{A}, (x_i, \mathbf{s}_i)_{i \in [k]})$
6: **if** $\big(\mathbf{As}^* = f(x^*)\big) \wedge \big(0 < \|\mathbf{s}^*\| \leq \mathcal{B}\big) \wedge \big((x^*, \mathbf{s}^*) \notin \{(x_i, \mathbf{s}_i) : i \in [k]\}\big)$
7:     **then return** 1
8: **else return** 0

Fig. 3. The ISIS_f experiment.

putable function $f : [N] \to \mathcal{R}_q^n$. The ISIS_f assumption is defined by the experiment in Fig. 3. For an adversary $\mathcal{A}$, we define

$$\mathsf{Adv}_{\mathsf{pp}}^{\mathsf{ISIS}_f}(\mathcal{A}) = \Pr[\mathsf{Exp}_{\mathsf{pp}}^{\mathsf{ISIS}_f}(\mathcal{A}) \to 1].$$

The $\mathsf{ISIS}_f^{\mathsf{pp}}$ assumption states that for every PPT adversary $\mathcal{A}$, $\mathsf{Adv}_{\mathsf{pp}}^{\mathsf{ISIS}_f}(\mathcal{A})$ is negligible.

3.1 Concrete Instantiations of f

3.1.1 Random Function

An intuitive choice for $f = \mathsf{RF}$ is a random function, modelled in the security analysis as a random oracle. In this case, if $N = \omega(\mathsf{poly}(\lambda))$ then following the GPV signature proof [28, Proposition 6.1], ISIS_f can be tightly reduced to the plain Module-SIS assumption. Unfortunately, the issue with picking f to be random is that in our constructions we need to prove knowledge of a preimage of f. This becomes slightly awkward since then we would require proof systems that can actually prove statements related to the random oracle f.

3.1.2 Binary Encoding

In our constructions we will use the following family of functions f. Let $t \in \mathbb{N}$ and take any matrix $B \in \mathbb{Z}_q^{nd \times t}$. Then, the function is defined as:

$$f(x) := \mathsf{Coeffs}^{-1}(B \cdot \mathsf{enc}(x)) \in \mathcal{R}_q^n$$

where $\mathsf{enc}(x) \in \{0,1\}^t$ is a binary decomposition of $x - 1$. Hence, naturally $N = 2^t$. Clearly, proving knowledge of a preimage x of f, i.e. $f(x) = \mathbf{y}$, is equivalent to proving knowledge of a binary vector $\vec{u} \in \{0,1\}^t$ such that $B\vec{u} = \mathsf{Coeffs}(\mathbf{y})$. This, in turn, can be proven using the [42] framework. The main purpose of the matrix B is to provide flexibility when setting N and has no significant impact on the security (apart from a few naive special cases). We denote the corresponding ISIS_f problem as $\mathsf{ISIS}_{\mathsf{bin}}$. In the following, we propose a few standard attacks on $\mathsf{ISIS}_{\mathsf{bin}}$.

Relations to Finding a Short Vector in the Lattice. Regardless of the choice of f, one of the most naive attacks would be to simply try any x and then use the lattice attacks to find a short vector $\mathbf{s}^*$ such that

$$\mathbf{As}^* = f(x)$$

which has a flavour of the Inhomogenous-MSIS problem. Now, if B is a zero (resp. identity) matrix then this corresponds to the plain (resp. Hermite Normal Form) Module-SIS [23].

We propose another attack, which this time actually makes use of the k pairs $(x_i, \mathbf{s}_i)_{i \in [k]}$. Denote $\vec{u}_i = \mathsf{enc}(x_i)$ and $\vec{s}_i = \mathsf{Coeffs}(\mathbf{s}_i)$ for $i \in [k]$. Then, by definition of $\mathsf{ISIS}_{\mathsf{bin}}$ we have[10]:

$$\left[\mathsf{rot}(\mathbf{A}) - B\right] S = 0 \quad \text{where} \quad S := \begin{bmatrix} \vec{s}_1 \cdots \vec{s}_k \\ \vec{u}_1 \cdots \vec{u}_k \end{bmatrix} \in \mathbb{Z}_q^{(md+t) \times k}. \tag{6}$$

Here, the attack is to consider the lattice Λ generated by columns of S and find a short vector $(\vec{s}^*, \vec{u}^*) \in \Lambda$, such that $\|\vec{s}^*\| \le B, \vec{u}^* \in \{0,1\}^t$ and $(\vec{s}^*, \vec{u}^*) \notin S$. We briefly explain why this allows us to solve $\mathsf{ISIS}_{\mathsf{bin}}$. Suppose we found a vector $(v_1, \dots, v_k) \in \mathbb{Z}_q^k$ such that $\vec{s}^* = \sum_{i=1}^k v_i \vec{s}_i$ and $\vec{u}^* = \sum_{i=1}^k v_i \vec{u}_i$, where $\vec{s}^*$ and $\vec{u}^*$ satisfy all the conditions above. Then, for $\mathbf{s}^* = \mathsf{Coeffs}^{-1}(\vec{s}^*)$ we have

$$\mathbf{As}^* = \sum_{i=1}^k v_i \mathbf{s}^* = \sum_{i=1}^k v_i \mathsf{Coeffs}^{-1}(B\vec{u}_i) = \mathsf{Coeffs}^{-1}\left(\sum_{i=1}^k v_i \cdot B\vec{u}_i\right) = \mathsf{Coeffs}^{-1}(B\vec{u}^*).$$

Finally, by the conditions above, this gives us a valid $\mathsf{ISIS}_{\mathsf{bin}}$ solution.

A naive solution to obtain $(\vec{s}^*, \vec{u}^*)$ would be to hope that S has full-rank $md + t$ for large enough instances k. Then, the adversary could pick any valid $(\vec{s}^*, \vec{u}^*)$ and compute the linear combination $v_1, \dots, v_k \in \mathbb{Z}_q$ using linear algebra. The hardness of this problem lies in the fact that by (6) and the rank-nullity theorem, we have that the rank of S is at most nd. Since in all our applications $n \le m$, this implies that S will never have rank at least $md + t$.

Relations to Integer Linear Programming. Let us denote $\vec{u}_i = \mathsf{enc}(x_i)$ for $i \in [k]$. The attack involves finding a short non-zero vector $\vec{v} \in \mathbb{Z}_q^k$ such that $\sum_{i=1}^k v_i \vec{u}_i = \vec{0} \pmod q$. Note that if $\vec{u}_1, \dots, \vec{u}_k$ as well as $\vec{v}$ are sufficiently short w.r.t. q then the equation above holds over integers. Now, we can use techniques from integer linear programming (ILP) [12,29] to find such a vector $\vec{v}$. In particular, Herold and May [29, Theorem 1] showed that under some mild assumptions, one can efficiently find such a binary vector $\vec{v} \in \{0,1\}^k$, as long as $k \ge 2t$. Let $i \in [k]$ such that $v_i \ne 0$. Then, if we denote $\mathbf{s}^* := -(\sum_{j \ne i} v_j \mathbf{s}_j)$, then

$$\mathbf{As}^* = -\sum_{j \ne i} v_j \mathbf{As}_j = -\sum_{j \ne i} v_j \mathsf{Coeffs}^{-1}(B\vec{u}_j) = v_i \mathsf{Coeffs}^{-1}(B\vec{u}_i) = \mathsf{Coeffs}^{-1}(B\vec{u}_i).$$

---

[10] We recall the skew-circulant matrices and the function rot in Sect. 2.

$$
\begin{array}{ll}
\underline{\mathsf{Exp}_{\mathsf{pp}}^{\mathsf{Int\text{-}ISIS}_f}(\mathcal{A})} & \underline{\mathcal{O}_{\mathsf{pre}}(\mathbf{m},\mathbf{r})} \\[4pt]
1:\ \mathbf{A} \leftarrow \mathcal{R}_q^{\mathsf{n}\times\mathsf{m}} & 1:\ \textbf{if } \|(\mathbf{m},\mathbf{r})\| < \mathcal{B}_m \\
2:\ \mathbf{C} \leftarrow \mathcal{R}_q^{\mathsf{n}\times(\ell_m+\ell_r)} & 2:\quad \textbf{then return } \bot \\
3:\ \mathcal{M} = \emptyset & 3:\ x \leftarrow [N] \\
4:\ (x^*,\mathbf{s}^*,\mathbf{m}^*,\mathbf{r}^*) \leftarrow \mathcal{A}^{\mathcal{O}_{\mathsf{pre}}}(\mathbf{A},\mathbf{C}) & 4:\ \mathbf{s} \leftarrow \mathbf{A}_\mathfrak{s}^{-1}\left(f(x) + \mathbf{C}\begin{bmatrix}\mathbf{m}\\\mathbf{r}\end{bmatrix}\right) \\
5:\ \textbf{if } (\mathbf{m}^* \notin \mathcal{M}) \quad\wedge\quad \left(\mathbf{A}\mathbf{s}^* = f(x^*) + \mathbf{C}\begin{bmatrix}\mathbf{m}^*\\\mathbf{r}^*\end{bmatrix}\right) & 5:\ \mathcal{M} \leftarrow \mathcal{M} \cup \{\mathbf{m}\} \\
\quad (0 < \|\mathbf{s}^*\| \le \mathcal{B}_s) \wedge (\|(\mathbf{m}^*,\mathbf{r}^*)\| \le \mathcal{B}_m) & 6:\ \textbf{return } (x,\mathbf{s}) \\
6:\quad \textbf{then return } 1 & \\
7:\ \textbf{else return } 0 &
\end{array}
$$

Fig. 4. Interactive version of the ISIS_f problem.

If $\mathfrak{s}$ is larger than the norm of the shortest norm of $\Lambda_q^\perp(\mathbf{A})$, then by the unpredictability argument (c.f. Lemma 3.8), with non-negligible probability we have $\mathbf{s}^* \neq \mathbf{s}_i$. Now, using the standard tail bounds (c.f. Sect. 2), we can upper-bound the norm of $\mathbf{s}^*$ by $(k-1) \cdot \mathfrak{s}\sqrt{\mathsf{md}}$. Hence, if $\mathcal{B}$ is larger than that value then $(\mathbf{s}^*, f^{-1}(\mathbf{b}_i))$ is a valid $\mathsf{ISIS}_{\mathsf{bin}}$ solution[11]. Therefore, in order to prevent such attacks, we need to set $\mathcal{B} \approx \mathfrak{s}\sqrt{\mathsf{md}}$ to be close to the tail bound of the discrete Gaussian distribution with standard deviation $\mathfrak{s}$.

3.2 Interactive Version

We are ready to introduce the interactive version of the ISIS_f problem which will be used as an underlying cryptographic assumption for our anonymous credentials. The main difference is that we allow the adversary to make *preimage queries* with respect to adaptively chosen messages, i.e. it has access to the preimage oracle $\mathcal{O}_{\mathsf{pre}}$. Here, $\mathcal{O}_{\mathsf{pre}}$ on input $(\mathbf{m}_i, \mathbf{r}_i)$ first samples $x_i \leftarrow [N]$ and then returns x_i along with

$$
\mathbf{s}_i \leftarrow \mathbf{A}_\mathfrak{s}^{-1}\left(f(x_i) + \mathbf{C}\begin{bmatrix}\mathbf{m}_i\\\mathbf{r}_i\end{bmatrix}\right)
$$

where $\mathbf{C}$ is a uniformly random public matrix. The adversary's goal is to come up with a new tuple $(x^*, \mathbf{s}^*, \mathbf{m}^*, \mathbf{r}^*)$ such that $\mathbf{s}^*, \mathbf{m}^*, \mathbf{r}^*$ are short vectors,

$$
\mathbf{A}\mathbf{s}^* = f(x^*) + \mathbf{C}\begin{bmatrix}\mathbf{m}^*\\\mathbf{r}^*\end{bmatrix} \tag{7}
$$

and $\mathbf{m}^* \notin \{\mathbf{m}_1, \ldots, \mathbf{m}_k\}$ where k is the number of oracle queries. In order to avoid trivial attacks, we require the inputs $(\mathbf{m}_i, \mathbf{r}_i)$ to the preimage oracle $\mathcal{O}_{\mathsf{pre}}$ to be short vectors as well.

Definition 3.2 (The Interactive ISIS_f Problem). *Define public parameters* $\mathsf{pp} := (q, d, \mathsf{n}, \mathsf{m}, \ell_m, \ell_r, N, \mathfrak{s}, \mathcal{B}_s, \mathcal{B}_m)$ *as a tuple of functions of the security parameter* λ. *Consider any efficiently computable function* $f : [N] \to \mathcal{R}_q^\mathsf{n}$. *The* $\mathsf{Int\text{-}ISIS}_f$ *assumption is defined by the experiment in Fig. 4. For an adversary* $\mathcal{A}$, *we define*

$$
\mathsf{Adv}_{\mathsf{pp}}^{\mathsf{Int\text{-}ISIS}_f}(\mathcal{A}) = \Pr[\mathsf{Exp}_{\mathsf{pp}}^{\mathsf{Int\text{-}ISIS}_f}(\mathcal{A}) \to 1].
$$

---

[11] Obviously, one could try to use ILP for smaller k to decrease the bound on $\mathbf{s}^*$.

$\mathcal{O}_1(\mathbf{m,r})$	$\mathcal{O}_2(\mathbf{m,r})$	$\mathcal{O}_3(\mathbf{m,r})$
1: **if** $\|(\mathbf{m,r})\| > \mathcal{B}_m$	1: **if** $\|(\mathbf{m,r})\| > \mathcal{B}_m$	1: **if** $\|(\mathbf{m,r})\| > \mathcal{B}_m$
2: **then return** $\bot$	2: **then return** $\bot$	2: **then return** $\bot$
3: ctr $= 0$	3: ctr $= 0$	3: $\mathbf{v} = \mathbf{D}\begin{bmatrix}\mathbf{m}\\\mathbf{r}\end{bmatrix}$
4: **while**ctr ≥ 0 **do**	4: $\rho = \bot$	4: ctr $= 0$
5: $x \leftarrow [N]$	5: **while**ctr $< T_{\max}$ **do**	5: $\rho = \bot$
6: $\mathbf{s} \leftarrow \mathbf{A}_\mathfrak{s}^{-1}\left(f(x) + \mathbf{C}\begin{bmatrix}\mathbf{m}\\\mathbf{r}\end{bmatrix}\right)$	6: $x \leftarrow [N]$	6: **while**ctr $< T_{\max}$ **do**
7: $u \leftarrow [0,1)$	7: $\mathbf{s} \leftarrow \mathbf{A}_\mathfrak{s}^{-1}\left(f(x) + \mathbf{C}\begin{bmatrix}\mathbf{m}\\\mathbf{r}\end{bmatrix}\right)$	7: $x \leftarrow [N]$
8: **if** $u \leq \frac{1}{M}$:	8: $u \leftarrow [0,1)$	8: $\bar{\mathbf{s}} \leftarrow \mathbf{A}_\mathfrak{s}^{-1}(f(x))$
9: $\mathcal{M} \leftarrow \mathcal{M} \cup \{\mathbf{m}\}$	9: **if** $u \leq \frac{1}{M} \wedge \rho = \bot$:	9: $\mathbf{s} = \bar{\mathbf{s}} + \mathbf{v}$
10: **return** $(x,\mathbf{s})$	10: $\mathcal{M} \leftarrow \mathcal{M} \cup \{\mathbf{m}\}$	10: $u \leftarrow [0,1)$
11: ctr $= $ ctr $+ 1$	11: $\rho = (x,\mathbf{s})$	11: **if** $u \leq \min\left(\frac{D_\mathfrak{s}^{md}(\mathbf{s})}{M \cdot D_{\mathfrak{s},\mathbf{v}}^{md}(\mathbf{s})},1\right) \wedge$
12: **return** $\bot$	12: ctr $= $ ctr $+ 1$	$\rho = \bot$:
	13: **return** ρ	12: $\mathcal{M} \leftarrow \mathcal{M} \cup \{\mathbf{m}\}$
		13: $\rho = (x,\mathbf{s})$
		14: ctr $= $ ctr $+ 1$
		15: **return** ρ

Fig. 5. Preimage oracles $\mathcal{O}_{\text{pre}}$ used in the hybrid argument.

The $\mathsf{Int\text{-}ISIS}_f^{\mathsf{pp}}$ assumption states that for every PPT adversary $\mathcal{A}$, $\mathsf{Adv}_{\mathsf{pp}}^{\mathsf{Int\text{-}ISIS}_f}(\mathcal{A})$ is negligible.

The main result of this section is an efficient reduction from the interactive ISIS_f to the one in Definition 3.2.

Theorem 3.3 ($\mathsf{Int\text{-}ISIS}_f \implies \mathsf{ISIS}_f$). *Let* $\mathsf{pp} := (q,d,\mathsf{n},\mathsf{m},\ell_m,\ell_r,N,\mathfrak{s},\mathcal{B}_s,\mathcal{B}_m)$ *be public parameters such that* $q/2 > \mathcal{B}_m \geq 1, \mathsf{m} = \mathsf{n}\log q + r$, *and*

$$M := \exp\left(1 + \frac{1}{2\alpha^2}\right) \quad \text{and} \quad \varepsilon := 2\left(\frac{1+\epsilon}{1-\epsilon}\right)\exp\left(-2\alpha^2 \cdot \frac{\pi-1}{\pi}\right)$$

where $\epsilon \leq 1/2, \alpha \geq 1$ *and* $r > 0$. *Suppose* $\mathfrak{s} \geq \max\left(\eta_{\min}(\epsilon), \alpha\mathcal{B}_m d\sqrt{(\ell_m + \ell_r)\mathsf{m}}\right)$. *Then, for every adversary* $\mathcal{A}$ *which makes at most* Q *queries to* $\mathcal{O}_{\text{pre}}$, *there is an adversary* $\mathcal{A}'$ *which runs in time essentially identical to* $\mathcal{A}$ *and*

$$\mathsf{Adv}_{\mathsf{pp}'}^{\mathsf{ISIS}_f}(\mathcal{A}') \geq \frac{1}{6Q}\mathsf{Adv}_{\mathsf{pp}}^{\mathsf{Int\text{-}ISIS}_f}(\mathcal{A}) - \frac{\ell_m + \ell_r}{12Q}\sqrt{\left(1+2^{-r}\right)^d - 1} - \frac{2^{-\lambda}}{6} - \frac{T_{\max}^2 Q}{12N}$$

$$- \frac{\ell_m}{3} \cdot 2^{-rd} - \left(Q - \frac{2}{3}\right)T_{\max}\left(\frac{\varepsilon}{2M} - \frac{2\epsilon}{M}\right) - \frac{2^{-d+2}}{3}$$

where $\mathsf{pp}' := (q,d,\mathsf{n},\mathsf{m},N,T_{\max}Q,\mathfrak{s},\mathcal{B} = \mathcal{B}_s + \mathcal{B}_m d\sqrt{(\ell_m + \ell_r)\mathsf{m}})$ *and* $T_{\max}$ *satisfies* $\left(1 - \frac{1}{M}\right)^{T_{\max}} \leq 2^{-\lambda}$.

Proof. Assume without loss of generality that $\mathcal{A}$ makes exactly Q queries. We will prove the statement using a hybrid argument. Namely, in each game we will either modify the execution of the $\mathcal{O}_{\mathsf{pre}}$ oracle, or change the execution of the challenger. In the following, define E_i to be the event that $\mathcal{A}$ wins the Int-ISIS$_f$ experiment.

Game$_1$: This is the standard Interactive ISIS$_f$ game. Hence, $\Pr[\mathsf{E}_1] = \varepsilon$. Let us denote the preimage oracle $\mathcal{O}_0 := \mathcal{O}_{\mathsf{pre}}$.

Game$_2$: Here, instead of sampling $\mathbf{C}$ uniformly random, the challenger first picks a uniformly random matrix of binary polynomials $\mathbf{D} \in \mathcal{R}_q^{m \times (\ell_m + \ell_r)}$ and sets $\mathbf{C} = \mathbf{AD}$.

Lemma 3.4. $\Pr[\mathsf{E}_2] \geq \Pr[\mathsf{E}_1] - \frac{\ell_m + \ell_r}{2} \sqrt{\left(1 + 2^{-r}\right)^d - 1}.$

Proof. The result follows directly from the ring version of the leftover hash lemma [15, Lemma 7]. □

Game$_3$: In this game, we run $\mathcal{O}_{\mathsf{pre}}$ as $\mathcal{O}_1$ defined in Fig. 5.

Lemma 3.5. $\Pr[\mathsf{E}_3] = \Pr[\mathsf{E}_2].$

Proof. Define CTR to be the random variable which is the value of ctr when $\mathcal{O}_1$ actually outputs $(x, \mathbf{s})$. Then, for any $(\mathbf{m}, \mathbf{r})$ such that $\|(\mathbf{m}, \mathbf{r})\| \leq \mathcal{B}_m$, and any possible output $(x, \mathbf{s})$ we have:

$$
\begin{aligned}
\Pr[(x, \mathbf{s}) \leftarrow \mathcal{O}_1(\mathbf{m}, \mathbf{r})] &= \sum_{i=0}^{\infty} \Pr[(x, \mathbf{s}) \leftarrow \mathcal{O}_1(\mathbf{m}, \mathbf{r}) \wedge \mathsf{CTR} = i] \\
&= \sum_{i=0}^{\infty} \frac{1}{M} \left(1 - \frac{1}{M}\right)^i \Pr[(x, \mathbf{s}) \leftarrow \mathcal{O}_0(\mathbf{m}, \mathbf{r})] \\
&= \Pr[(x, \mathbf{s}) \leftarrow \mathcal{O}_0(\mathbf{m}, \mathbf{r})].
\end{aligned}
$$

When $\|(\mathbf{m}, \mathbf{r})\| > \mathcal{B}_m$, then both $\mathcal{O}_1$ and $\mathcal{O}_0$ output $\perp$ in the first step. Hence, the two oracles behave identically and thus $\Pr[\mathsf{E}_3] = \Pr[\mathsf{E}_2]$. □

Game$_4$: In this game, we run $\mathcal{O}_{\mathsf{pre}}$ as $\mathcal{O}_2$ defined in Fig. 5.

Lemma 3.6. $\Pr[\mathsf{E}_4] \geq \Pr[\mathsf{E}_3] - Q2^{-\lambda}.$

Proof. The only change is that we abort when ctr reaches $T_{\max}$. Hence, the statistical distance between $\mathcal{O}_2(\mathbf{m}, \mathbf{r})$ and $\mathcal{O}_1(\mathbf{m}, \mathbf{r})$ is at most $\left(1 - \frac{1}{M}\right)^{T_{\max}} \leq 2^{-\lambda}$. Hence, $\Pr[\mathsf{E}_4] \geq \Pr[\mathsf{E}_3] - Q\left(1 - \frac{1}{M}\right)^{T_{\max}} \geq \Pr[\mathsf{E}_3] - Q2^{-\lambda}$. □

Game$_5$: It differs from the previous game in a sense that we abort whenever $\mathcal{O}_2$ picks an index x, which was already sampled, even if it was not sent to the adversary. Recall that we still use the preimage oracle $\mathcal{O}_2$.

Lemma 3.7. $\Pr[\mathsf{E}_5] \geq \Pr[\mathsf{E}_4] - \frac{T_{\max}^2 Q^2}{2N}.$

Proof. The inequality follows directly from the birthday bound.   □

Game_6: We still use the preimage oracle $\mathcal{O}_2$. The only change is in the challenger execution. First, the challenger additionally keeps track of all generated variables. Namely, define

$$\mathcal{X} := \left\{ \left(x, \mathbf{s} - \mathbf{D} \begin{bmatrix} \mathbf{m} \\ \mathbf{r} \end{bmatrix} \right) : x \text{ and } \mathbf{s} \text{ were generated while querying } \mathcal{O}_2(\mathbf{m}, \mathbf{r}) \right\}. \tag{8}$$

In particular, $\mathcal{X}$ contains pairs which were not sent to adversary. Further,

$$\mathcal{Y} := \left\{ \left(x, \mathbf{s} - \mathbf{D} \begin{bmatrix} \mathbf{m} \\ \mathbf{r} \end{bmatrix} \right) : x \text{ and } \mathbf{s} \text{ were sent to } \mathcal{A} \text{ by } \mathcal{O}_2(\mathbf{m}, \mathbf{r}) \right\}. \tag{9}$$

Then, we have the following simple relations: $|\mathcal{X}| = T_{\max}Q, |\mathcal{Y}| = |\mathcal{M}| \leq Q$ and $\mathcal{Y} \subseteq \mathcal{X}$. In this game, the challenger aborts when the output vectors from $\mathcal{A}$ satisfy the following:

$$\left(x^*, \mathbf{s}^* - \mathbf{D} \begin{bmatrix} \mathbf{m}^* \\ \mathbf{r}^* \end{bmatrix} \right) \in \mathcal{X} \backslash \mathcal{Y}.$$

Lemma 3.8. $\Pr[\mathsf{E}_6] \geq \frac{1}{2} \cdot \Pr[\mathsf{E}_5]$.

Proof. Denote $\mathcal{X}_0 := \{ x \in [N] : \exists \mathbf{s}, (x, \mathbf{s}) \in \mathcal{X} \}$ and similarly for $\mathcal{Y}_0$. It is easy to see that

$$\Pr[\mathsf{E}_6 \wedge x^* \in \mathcal{Y}_0] = \Pr[\mathsf{E}_5 \wedge x^* \in \mathcal{Y}_0] \quad \text{and} \quad \Pr[\mathsf{E}_6 \wedge x^* \notin \mathcal{X}_0] = \Pr[\mathsf{E}_5 \wedge x^* \notin \mathcal{X}_0].$$

In the following, we show $\Pr[\mathsf{E}_6 \wedge x^* \in \mathcal{X}_0 \backslash \mathcal{Y}_0] \geq \frac{1}{2} \Pr[\mathsf{E}_5 \wedge x^* \in \mathcal{X}_0 \backslash \mathcal{Y}_0]$ which concludes the proof. Suppose that $\mathcal{A}$ wins Game_5 and the output index is in $\mathcal{X}_0 \backslash \mathcal{Y}_0$, i.e. there exists a unique $\mathbf{z}$ such that $(x^*, \mathbf{z}) \in \mathcal{X} \backslash \mathcal{Y}$ (by conditions of Game_5). Because this pair does not belong to $\mathcal{Y}$, it was rejected during the execution of $\mathcal{O}_2$ on some input $(\mathbf{m}', \mathbf{r}')$. Define

$$\mathbf{z}^* := \mathbf{s}^* - \mathbf{D} \begin{bmatrix} \mathbf{m}^* - \mathbf{m}' \\ \mathbf{r}^* - \mathbf{r}' \end{bmatrix}.$$

By definition of $\mathcal{X} \backslash \mathcal{Y}$, $\mathbf{s}' := \mathbf{z} + \mathbf{D} \begin{bmatrix} \mathbf{m}' \\ \mathbf{r}' \end{bmatrix}$ is perfectly hidden among the preimages of $f(x^*) + \mathbf{C} \begin{bmatrix} \mathbf{m}' \\ \mathbf{r}' \end{bmatrix}$ under $\mathbf{A}$ since the adversary did not actually see $\mathbf{s}'$. Let $\mathbf{u}$ be a polynomial vector with ternary coefficients in $\Lambda_q^{\perp}(\mathbf{A})$, which exists since $m > n \log q$. Note that $\|\mathbf{u}\| \leq \sqrt{md}$ and $\mathfrak{s} \geq \alpha \mathcal{B}_m d \sqrt{(\ell_m + \ell_r)m} \geq \sqrt{md} \geq \|\mathbf{u}\|$.

Therefore, $\mathbf{s}^* - \mathbf{D} \begin{bmatrix} \mathbf{m}^* \\ \mathbf{r}^* \end{bmatrix} = \mathbf{z} \iff \mathbf{s}' = \mathbf{z}^*$, and also

$$\Pr\left[\mathbf{s}' = \mathbf{z}^* \middle| \mathsf{E}_5 \wedge x^* \in \mathcal{X}_0 \backslash \mathcal{Y}_0\right] \leq \frac{\exp\left(\frac{-\|\mathbf{z}^*\|^2}{-2s^2}\right)}{\exp\left(\frac{-\|\mathbf{z}^*\|^2}{2s^2}\right) + \exp\left(\frac{-\|\mathbf{z}^* + \mathbf{u}\|^2}{2s^2}\right) + \exp\left(-\frac{\|\mathbf{z}^* + \mathbf{u}\|^2}{2s^2}\right)}$$

$$\leq \frac{1}{1 + \left(\exp\left(-\frac{\langle \mathbf{z}^*, \mathbf{u}\rangle}{s^2}\right) + \exp\left(\frac{\langle \mathbf{z}^*, \mathbf{u}\rangle}{s^2}\right)\right)\exp\left(-\frac{\|\mathbf{u}\|^2}{2s^2}\right)}$$

$$\leq \frac{1}{1 + 2\exp\left(-\frac{\|\mathbf{u}\|^2}{2s^2}\right)}$$

$$\leq \frac{1}{1 + 2\exp\left(-\frac{1}{2}\right)} \leq \frac{1}{2}.$$

By taking the complement, we deduce that

$$\Pr\left[\mathbf{s}^* - \mathbf{D} \begin{bmatrix} \mathbf{m}^* \\ \mathbf{r}^* \end{bmatrix} \neq \mathbf{z} \middle| \mathsf{E}_5 \wedge x^* \in \mathcal{X}_0 \backslash \mathcal{Y}_0\right] \geq \frac{1}{2}.$$

Finally, note that if $\mathsf{E}_5 \wedge x^* \in \mathcal{X}_0 \backslash \mathcal{Y}_0$ hold and additionally $\mathbf{s}^* - \mathbf{D} \begin{bmatrix} \mathbf{m}^* \\ \mathbf{r}^* \end{bmatrix} \neq \mathbf{z}$, then we must have

$$\left(x^*, \mathbf{s}^* - \mathbf{D} \begin{bmatrix} \mathbf{m}^* \\ \mathbf{r}^* \end{bmatrix}\right) \notin \mathcal{X} \backslash \mathcal{Y}$$

since $(x^*, \mathbf{z}) \in \mathcal{X} \backslash \mathcal{Y}$ and there is at most one pair in $\mathcal{X}$ of the form $(x^*, \cdot)$ by the condition introduced in Game_5. This implies that

$$\Pr[\mathsf{E}_6 \wedge x^* \in \mathcal{X}_0 \backslash \mathcal{Y}_0] \geq \frac{1}{2} \Pr[\mathsf{E}_5 \wedge x^* \in \mathcal{X}_0 \backslash \mathcal{Y}_0]$$

which concludes the proof. $\qquad \square$

Game_7: At the beginning, the challenger samples an index $j^* \leftarrow [Q]$. Then at the end, if $x^* \in \mathcal{Y}_0$ and x^* was *not* sampled in the j^*-th query then the challenger aborts. We still use the preimage oracle $\mathcal{O}_2$.

Lemma 3.9. $\Pr[\mathsf{E}_7] \geq \frac{1}{Q} \Pr[\mathsf{E}_6]$.

Proof. Clearly, if $x^* \notin \mathcal{Y}_0$ then the game behaves identically as before. However, if $x^* \in \mathcal{Y}$ then with probability at least $1/Q$ we have that x^* was sampled during the j^*-th oracle query. $\qquad \square$

Game_8: In this game, only for the j^*-th oracle query, instead of executing $\mathcal{O}_2$ we run $\mathcal{O}_3$ as in Fig. 5.

Lemma 3.10. $\Pr[\mathsf{E}_8] \geq \Pr[\mathsf{E}_7] - T_{\max}\left(\frac{\varepsilon}{2M} + \frac{2\epsilon}{M}\right) - 2^d$.

Proof. First, we exclude the case that $\eta_\epsilon'(\Lambda_q^\perp(\mathbf{A})) > \eta_{\min}$ which occurs with probability 2^{-d}. Then, by our parameter selection and Lemma 2.5, the statistical distance between $\mathcal{O}_3(\mathbf{m}, \mathbf{r})$ and $\mathcal{O}_2(\mathbf{m}, \mathbf{r})$ is at most $\frac{\varepsilon}{2M} + \frac{2\epsilon}{M}$. Hence, the statement follows by the hybrid argument. $\qquad \square$

Game$_9$

1. Generate $\mathbf{A} \leftarrow \mathcal{R}_q^{n \times m}$.
2. Sample $\mathbf{D} \leftarrow \{0,1\}^{md \times (\ell_m + \ell_r)d}$ and set $\mathbf{C} = \mathbf{AD}$.
3. Set $\mathcal{M} = \emptyset$.
4. Sample $j^* \leftarrow [Q]$.
5. Run $(x^*, \mathbf{s}^*, \mathbf{m}^*, \mathbf{r}^*) \leftarrow \mathcal{A}^{\mathcal{O}'}(\mathbf{A}, \mathbf{C})$, where $\mathcal{O}'$ is defined below.
6. Define $\tilde{\mathbf{s}} = \mathbf{s}^* - \mathbf{D}\begin{bmatrix} \mathbf{m}^* \\ \mathbf{r}^* \end{bmatrix}$
7. If all the conditions below hold, then return 1 and 0 otherwise:
   - $\mathbf{m}^* \notin \mathcal{M}$ and $\|(\mathbf{m}^*, \mathbf{r}^*)\| \le \mathcal{B}_m$ and $\|\mathbf{s}^*\| \le \mathcal{B}_s$ (from the Int-ISIS$_f$ game),
   - $\mathbf{A}\tilde{\mathbf{s}} = f(x^*)$ (from the Int-ISIS$_f$ game),
   - $\forall (x, \mathbf{s}) \neq (x', \mathbf{s}') \in \mathcal{X}$, $x \neq x'$ (from Game$_5$),
   - $(x^*, \tilde{\mathbf{s}}) \notin \mathcal{X} \backslash \mathcal{Y}$ (from Game$_6$),
   - if $x^* \in \mathcal{Y}_0$, then x^* must have been generated in the j^*-th oracle query (from Game$_7$),
   - $(x^*, \tilde{\mathbf{s}}) \notin \mathcal{Y}$ (from Game$_9$).

Fig. 6. Description of Game$_9$. Here, $\mathcal{O}'$ behaves as $\mathcal{O}_2$, apart from the j^*-th query where it behaves like $\mathcal{O}_3$ (defined in Fig. 5.)

Game$_9$: For presentation purposes, we summarise the security game in Fig. 6. The difference from the previous game is that the adversary loses whenever

$$\left(x^*, \mathbf{s}^* - \mathbf{D}\begin{bmatrix} \mathbf{m}^* \\ \mathbf{r}^* \end{bmatrix} \right) \in \mathcal{Y}.$$

Lemma 3.11. $\Pr[\mathsf{E}_9] \ge \frac{1}{3}\Pr[\mathsf{E}_8] - \frac{\ell_m \cdot 2^{-rd}}{3}$.

Proof. We follow the proof strategy from [39, Theorem 3.2]. Note that conditioned on $x^* \notin \mathcal{Y}_0$ the two security games are identical. Hence, in the following we show

$$\Pr[\mathsf{E}_9 \wedge x^* \in \mathcal{Y}_0] \ge \frac{1}{3}\Pr[\mathsf{E}_8 \wedge x^* \in \mathcal{Y}_0] - \frac{\ell_m \cdot 2^{-rd}}{3}.$$

Let us consider the following alternative game Game$_9'$ defined in Fig. 7 and denote E_9' to be the event that the adversary wins Game$_9'$. We claim that $\Pr[\mathsf{E}_9'] = \Pr[\mathsf{E}_9 \wedge x^* \in \mathcal{Y}_0]$. Indeed, the only change is that the challenger *resamples* the vectors $\tilde{\mathbf{s}}_{j^*}$ (which is the preimage generated in the j^*-th query) and $\mathbf{D}$ according to their original distributions conditioned on what the adversary $\mathcal{A}$ already knows (e.g. it knows the value $\mathbf{s}_j$). Hence, from now on we focus on Game$_9'$.

Let us denote $\tilde{\mathbf{s}}_{j^*} := \mathbf{s}^* - \mathbf{D}\begin{bmatrix} \mathbf{m}^* \\ \mathbf{r}^* \end{bmatrix}$. In the following, we will use the fact that when $b = 0$, we have $\tilde{\mathbf{s}}_{j^*} = \tilde{\mathbf{s}}$. Next, we partition the success probability into two

---

Game_9'

1. Generate $\mathbf{A} \leftarrow \mathcal{R}_q^{n \times m}$.
2. Sample $\mathbf{D} = (\mathbf{d}_i)_{i \in [\ell_m + \ell_r]} \leftarrow \{0,1\}^{md \times (\ell_m + \ell_r)d}$ and set $\mathbf{C} = \mathbf{A}\mathbf{D}$.
3. Set $\mathcal{M} = \emptyset$.
4. Sample $j^* \leftarrow [Q]$.
5. Run $(x^*, \mathbf{s}^*, \mathbf{m}^*, \mathbf{r}^*) \leftarrow \mathcal{A}^{\mathcal{O}'}(\mathbf{A}, \mathbf{C})$, where $\mathcal{O}'$ as in Fig. 6.
6. If one of the conditions below does not hold, then return 0:
   - $\mathbf{m}^* \notin \mathcal{M}$ and $\|(\mathbf{m}^*, \mathbf{r}^*)\| \leq \mathcal{B}_m$ and $\|\mathbf{s}^*\| \leq \mathcal{B}_s$ (from the Int-ISIS$_f$ game),
   - $\forall(x, \mathbf{s}) \neq (x', \mathbf{s}') \in \mathcal{X}$, $x \neq x'$ (from Game_5),
   - x^* must have been generated in the j^*-th oracle query (from Game_7 and the condition $x^* \in \mathcal{Y}_0$).
7. Let $(\mathbf{m}_{j^*}, \mathbf{r}_{j^*})$ be the input for the j^*-th query, $\bar{\mathbf{s}}_{j^*}$ be the generated preimage, and denote the query output as $(x^*, \mathbf{s}_{j^*}) \in \mathcal{Y}$.
8. Let $i^* \in [\ell_m]$ be the index for which $m_{i^*}^* \neq m_{j^*, i^*}$.
9. Flip a bit $b \leftarrow D$, where D is defined as $D(0) = 1/3$ and $D(1) = 2/3$.
10. If $b = 0$, then set $\bar{\mathbf{s}} = \bar{\mathbf{s}}_{j^*}$ and $\bar{\mathbf{D}} = \mathbf{D}$.
11. If $b = 1$, sample $\bar{\mathbf{s}} \leftarrow D_s^{md}$ and $\bar{\mathbf{d}} \leftarrow \{0,1\}^{md}$ conditioned on

$$\mathbf{A}\bar{\mathbf{s}} = f(x^*), \quad \mathbf{A}\bar{\mathbf{d}} = \mathbf{A}\mathbf{d}_{i^*}, \quad \mathbf{s}_{j^*} = \bar{\mathbf{s}} + \bar{\mathbf{D}}\begin{bmatrix} \mathbf{m}_{j^*} \\ \mathbf{r}_{j^*} \end{bmatrix}$$

where $\bar{\mathbf{D}} := \begin{bmatrix} \mathbf{d}_1 \cdots \mathbf{d}_{i^*-1} \ \bar{\mathbf{d}} \ \mathbf{d}_{i^*+1} \cdots \mathbf{d}_{\ell_m + \ell_r} \end{bmatrix}$.
12. Define $\tilde{\mathbf{s}} = \mathbf{s}^* - \bar{\mathbf{D}}\begin{bmatrix} \mathbf{m}^* \\ \mathbf{r}^* \end{bmatrix}$
13. If all the conditions below hold, then return 1 and 0 otherwise:
   - $\mathbf{A}\tilde{\mathbf{s}} = f(x^*)$ (from the Int-ISIS$_f$ game),
   - $\tilde{\mathbf{s}} \neq \bar{\mathbf{s}}$ (from Game_9 and the condition that $x^* \in \mathcal{Y}_0$).

Fig. 7. Description of the alternative game Game_9'.

parts: $\Pr[E_9'] = \Pr[E_9' \wedge \tilde{\mathbf{s}}_{j^*} \neq \mathbf{s}_j] + \Pr[E_9' \wedge \tilde{\mathbf{s}}_{j^*} = \mathbf{s}_j]$. Now, one observes that

$$\Pr[E_9' \wedge \tilde{\mathbf{s}}_{j^*} \neq \mathbf{s}_j] \geq \Pr[E_9' \wedge \tilde{\mathbf{s}}_{j^*} \neq \bar{\mathbf{s}}_{j^*} \wedge b = 0]$$

$$\geq \frac{1}{3} \cdot \Pr[E_9' \wedge \tilde{\mathbf{s}}_{j^*} \neq \bar{\mathbf{s}}_{j^*} | b = 0]$$

$$\geq \frac{1}{3} \Pr\left[E_8 \wedge x^* \in \mathcal{Y}_0 \wedge \tilde{\mathbf{s}} \neq \bar{\mathbf{s}} \wedge \tilde{\mathbf{s}}_{j^*} \neq \bar{\mathbf{s}}_{j^*} | b = 0\right]$$

$$\geq \frac{1}{3} \Pr\left[E_8 \wedge x^* \in \mathcal{Y}_0 \wedge \tilde{\mathbf{s}}_{j^*} \neq \bar{\mathbf{s}}_{j^*}\right].$$

For the second part, let us denote

$$S(\mathbf{D}, i^*) := \left\{ \begin{bmatrix} \mathbf{d}_1 \cdots \mathbf{d}_{i^*-1} \ \mathbf{e} \ \mathbf{d}_{i^*+1} \cdots \mathbf{d}_{\ell_m + \ell_r} \end{bmatrix} : \mathbf{A}\mathbf{e} = \mathbf{A}\mathbf{d}_{i^*} \wedge \mathbf{e} \in \{0,1\}^{(\ell_m + \ell_r)d} \right\}.$$

Clearly, $\mathbf{D} \in S(\mathbf{D}, i^*)$. Further,

$$\Pr[E_9' \wedge \tilde{\mathbf{s}}_{j^*} = \mathbf{s}_j] \geq \Pr[E_9' \wedge \tilde{\mathbf{s}}_{j^*} = \bar{\mathbf{s}}_{j^*} \wedge |S(\mathbf{D}, i^*)| \geq 2]$$

$$\geq \Pr[E_9' \wedge \tilde{\mathbf{s}}_{j^*} = \bar{\mathbf{s}}_{j^*} \wedge |S(\mathbf{D}, i^*)| \geq 2 \wedge b = 1].$$

For presentation purposes, define the event

$$E := (\mathsf{E}_8) \wedge (x^* \in \mathcal{Y}_0) \wedge (\tilde{\mathbf{s}}_{j^*} = \bar{\mathbf{s}}_{j^*}) \wedge (|S(\mathbf{D}, i^*)| \geq 2) \wedge (b = 1).$$

Then,

$$
\begin{aligned}
\Pr[E] &\geq \frac{2}{3} \Pr[\mathsf{E}_8 \wedge x^* \in \mathcal{Y}_0 \wedge \tilde{\mathbf{s}}_{j^*} = \bar{\mathbf{s}}_{j^*} \wedge |S(\mathbf{D}, i^*)| \geq 2] \\
&\geq \frac{2}{3} \left(\Pr[\mathsf{E}_8 \wedge x^* \in \mathcal{Y}_0 \wedge \tilde{\mathbf{s}}_{j^*} = \bar{\mathbf{s}}_{j^*}] - \Pr[\mathsf{E}_8 \wedge x^* \in \mathcal{Y}_0 \wedge \tilde{\mathbf{s}}_{j^*} = \bar{\mathbf{s}}_{j^*} \wedge |S(\mathbf{D}, i^*)| = 1] \right) \\
&\geq \frac{2}{3} \left(\Pr[\mathsf{E}_8 \wedge x^* \in \mathcal{Y}_0 \wedge \tilde{\mathbf{s}}_{j^*} = \bar{\mathbf{s}}_{j^*}] - \ell_m \left(\frac{q^n}{2^m} \right)^d \right)
\end{aligned}
$$

where for the last inequality we used the fact from [38, Lemma 5.2] to deduce that

$$
\begin{aligned}
\Pr[\mathsf{E}_8 \wedge x^* \in \mathcal{Y}_0 \wedge \tilde{\mathbf{s}}_{j^*} = \bar{\mathbf{s}}_{j^*} \wedge |S(\mathbf{D}, i^*)| = 1] & \\
&\leq \Pr[\mathsf{E}_8 \wedge x^* \in \mathcal{Y}_0 \wedge \tilde{\mathbf{s}}_{j^*} = \bar{\mathbf{s}}_{j^*} \wedge \exists i, |S(\mathbf{D}, i)| = 1] \\
&\leq \Pr[\exists i, |S(\mathbf{D}, i)| = 1] \\
&\leq \sum_{i=1}^{\ell_m} \Pr[|S(\mathbf{D}, i)| = 1] \\
&\leq \ell_m \left(\frac{q^n}{2^m} \right)^d = \ell_m \cdot 2^{-rd}.
\end{aligned}
$$

Thus,

$$
\begin{aligned}
\Pr[\mathsf{E}_9' \wedge \tilde{\mathbf{s}}_{j^*} = \bar{\mathbf{s}}_{j^*}] &\geq \Pr[\mathsf{E}_9' \wedge \tilde{\mathbf{s}}_{j^*} = \bar{\mathbf{s}}_{j^*} \wedge |S(\mathbf{D}, i^*)| \geq 2 \wedge b = 1] \\
&\geq \Pr[\tilde{\mathbf{s}} \neq \bar{\mathbf{s}} | E] \cdot \Pr[E].
\end{aligned}
$$

We claim that
$$\Pr[\tilde{\mathbf{s}} = \bar{\mathbf{s}} | E] \leq \Pr[\tilde{\mathbf{s}} = \bar{\mathbf{s}}_{j^*} \wedge \bar{\mathbf{D}} = \mathbf{D} | E].$$

Indeed, suppose $\tilde{\mathbf{s}} = \bar{\mathbf{s}}$ which by definition implies

$$\mathbf{s}^* = \bar{\mathbf{s}} + \bar{\mathbf{D}} \begin{bmatrix} \mathbf{m}^* \\ \mathbf{r}^* \end{bmatrix}.$$

We know from E that $\tilde{\mathbf{s}}_{j^*} = \bar{\mathbf{s}}_{j^*}$, i.e.

$$\bar{\mathbf{s}}_{j^*} + \mathbf{D} \begin{bmatrix} \mathbf{m}^* \\ \mathbf{r}^* \end{bmatrix} = \mathbf{s}^* = \bar{\mathbf{s}} + \bar{\mathbf{D}} \begin{bmatrix} \mathbf{m}^* \\ \mathbf{r}^* \end{bmatrix}.$$

Also, we know from Step 11 of Fig. 7 that:

$$\bar{\mathbf{s}}_{j^*} + \mathbf{D} \begin{bmatrix} \mathbf{m}_{j^*} \\ \mathbf{r}_{j^*} \end{bmatrix} = \mathbf{s}_{j^*} = \bar{\mathbf{s}} + \bar{\mathbf{D}} \begin{bmatrix} \mathbf{m}_{j^*} \\ \mathbf{r}_{j^*} \end{bmatrix}.$$

By subtracting the two equations, we end up with

$$(\mathbf{D} - \bar{\mathbf{D}}) \begin{bmatrix} \mathbf{m}^* - \mathbf{m}_{j^*} \\ \mathbf{r}^* - \mathbf{r}_{j^*} \end{bmatrix} = \mathbf{0}.$$

Since both matrices $\mathbf{D}, \bar{\mathbf{D}}$ belong to $S(\mathbf{D}, i^*)$, we have $(m_{i^*}^* - m_{j^*, i^*})(d_{j, i^*} - \bar{d}_{i^*}) = \mathbf{0}$ where $\mathbf{d}_{i^*}, \bar{\mathbf{d}}_{i^*}$ are the i^*-th columns of $\mathbf{D}, \bar{\mathbf{D}}$ respectively. Since $2\mathcal{B}_m < q$, we deduce that this equation holds over integers. Further, we know that $m_{i^*}^* \neq m_{j^*, i^*}$ which implies that $\mathbf{d}_{i^*} = \bar{\mathbf{d}}_{i^*}$ and thus $\mathbf{D} = \bar{\mathbf{D}}$. Consequently, $\bar{\mathbf{s}} = \bar{\mathbf{s}}_{j^*}$ and the claim follows. Hence, we have

$$\Pr[\tilde{\mathbf{s}} = \bar{\mathbf{s}}|E] \leq \Pr[\tilde{\mathbf{s}} = \bar{\mathbf{s}}_{j^*} \wedge \bar{\mathbf{D}} = \mathbf{D}|E] \leq \Pr[\bar{\mathbf{D}} = \mathbf{D}|E] \leq \frac{1}{2}.$$

This is because E includes the event that $S(\mathbf{D}, i^*)$ contains at least two elements. Therefore, we conclude that

$$\Pr[E_9' \wedge \tilde{\mathbf{s}}_{j^*} = \bar{\mathbf{s}}_{j^*}] \geq \frac{1}{2} \cdot \frac{2}{3} \left(\Pr[E_8 \wedge x^* \in \mathcal{Y}_0 \wedge \tilde{\mathbf{s}}_{j^*} = \bar{\mathbf{s}}_{j^*}] - 2^{-rd} \right)$$

$$\geq \frac{1}{3} \Pr[E_8 \wedge x^* \in \mathcal{Y}_0 \wedge \tilde{\mathbf{s}}_{j^*} = \bar{\mathbf{s}}_{j^*}] - \frac{\ell_m \cdot 2^{-rd}}{3}.$$

and thus

$$\Pr[E_9 \wedge x^* \in \mathcal{Y}_0] \geq \Pr[E_9'] \geq \frac{1}{3} \Pr[E_8 \wedge x^* \in \mathcal{Y}_0] - \frac{\ell_m \cdot 2^{-rd}}{3}$$

which finishes the proof.   □

Game$_{10}$: In this game, throughout the experiment $\mathcal{A}$ queries $\mathcal{O}_{\mathsf{pre}}$ defined as $\mathcal{O}_3$ in Fig. 5 (not only for the j^*-th query).

Lemma 3.12. $\Pr[E_{10}] \geq \Pr[E_9] - (Q-1)T_{\max} \left(\frac{\varepsilon}{2M} + \frac{2\epsilon}{M} \right) - 2^{-d}.$

Proof. It follows identically as in Lemma 3.10.   □

Finally, our reduction runs as a challenger in Game$_{10}$. Namely, it first gets $T_{\max}Q$ pairs $(x_i, \mathbf{s}_i)_{i \in [T_{\max}Q]}$ from the ISIS_f challenger, i.e. $\mathbf{As} = f(x_i)$, and then uses them to simulate the query outputs from $\mathcal{O}_3$. Note that if $\mathcal{A}$ wins Game$_{10}$ then the set $\mathcal{X}$ contains exactly these pairs, and further the output $(x^*, \tilde{\mathbf{s}})$ does not belong to $\mathcal{X}$ (from Game$_6$ and Game$_9$). Also,

$$\|\tilde{\mathbf{s}}\| \leq \|\mathbf{s}^*\| + \left\| \mathbf{D} \begin{bmatrix} \mathbf{m}^* \\ \mathbf{r}^* \end{bmatrix} \right\| \leq \mathcal{B}_s + \mathcal{B}_m d \sqrt{(\ell_m + \ell_r)\mathsf{m}} = \mathcal{B}.$$

Therefore, the reduction outputs a valid ISIS_f solution. Now, using all the previous lemmas, the probability that the reduction wins the ISIS_f game can be lower-bounded as

$$\Pr[E_{10}] \geq \Pr[E_9] - (Q-1)T_{\max}\left(\frac{\varepsilon}{2M} + \frac{2\epsilon}{M}\right) - 2^{-d}$$

$$\geq \frac{1}{3}\Pr[E_8] - \frac{\ell_m \cdot 2^{-rd}}{3} - (Q-1)T_{\max}\left(\frac{\varepsilon}{2M} + \frac{2\epsilon}{M}\right) - 2^{-d}$$

$$\geq \frac{1}{3}\Pr[E_7] - \frac{\ell_m \cdot 2^{-rd}}{3} - \left(Q-\frac{2}{3}\right)T_{\max}\left(\frac{\varepsilon}{2M} + \frac{2\epsilon}{M}\right) - \frac{2^{-d+2}}{3}$$

$$\geq \frac{1}{3Q}\Pr[E_6] - \frac{\ell_m \cdot 2^{-rd}}{3} - \left(Q-\frac{2}{3}\right)T_{\max}\left(\frac{\varepsilon}{2M} + \frac{2\epsilon}{M}\right) - \frac{2^{-d+2}}{3}$$

$$\geq \frac{1}{6Q}\Pr[E_5] - \frac{\ell_m \cdot 2^{-rd}}{3} - \left(Q-\frac{2}{3}\right)T_{\max}\left(\frac{\varepsilon}{2M} + \frac{2\epsilon}{M}\right) - \frac{2^{-d+2}}{3}$$

$$\geq \frac{1}{6Q}\Pr[E_4] - \frac{T_{\max}^2 Q}{12N} - \frac{\ell_m \cdot 2^{-rd}}{3} - \left(Q-\frac{2}{3}\right)T_{\max}\left(\frac{\varepsilon}{2M} + \frac{2\epsilon}{M}\right) - \frac{2^{-d+2}}{3}$$

$$\geq \frac{1}{6Q}\Pr[E_3] - \frac{2^{-\lambda}}{6} - \frac{T_{\max}^2 Q}{12N} - \frac{\ell_m \cdot 2^{-rd}}{3} - \left(Q-\frac{2}{3}\right)T_{\max}\left(\frac{\varepsilon}{2M} + \frac{2\epsilon}{M}\right) - \frac{2^{-d+2}}{3}$$

$$\geq \frac{1}{6Q}\Pr[E_2] - \frac{2^{-\lambda}}{6} - \frac{T_{\max}^2 Q}{12N} - \frac{\ell_m \cdot 2^{-rd}}{3} - \left(Q-\frac{2}{3}\right)T_{\max}\left(\frac{\varepsilon}{2M} + \frac{2\epsilon}{M}\right) - \frac{2^{-d+2}}{3}$$

$$\geq \frac{1}{6Q}\Pr[E_1] - \mathsf{AddLoss}$$

where

$$\mathsf{AddLoss} := \frac{\ell_m + \ell_r}{12Q}\sqrt{\left(1+2^{-r}\right)^d - 1} + \frac{2^{-\lambda}}{6} + \frac{T_{\max}^2 Q}{12N} + \frac{\ell_m \cdot 2^{-rd}}{3}$$

$$+ \left(Q-\frac{2}{3}\right)T_{\max}\left(\frac{\varepsilon}{2M} + \frac{2\epsilon}{M}\right) + \frac{2^{-d+2}}{3}$$

which concludes the proof. $\qquad\square$

Asymptotic Parameter Selection. Let $d = O(\lambda)$, $\alpha = O(\sqrt{\lambda})$ and $\epsilon = \mathsf{negl}(\lambda)$. Then, $M = O(1)$, $\varepsilon = \mathsf{negl}(\lambda)$ and $T_{\max} = O(\lambda)$.

Suppose we want $\mathsf{Int\text{-}ISIS}_f$ to be hard against efficient adversaries, and thus $Q = \mathsf{poly}(\lambda)$. This implies that we need N to be exponential in λ. Next, to use the leftover hash lemma, we set $r \geq \omega(\log d)$. With these parameters, if a PPT adversary $\mathcal{A}$ solves $\mathsf{Int\text{-}ISIS}_f$ with probability δ, then there is a PPT adversary which solves ISIS_f with probability $\delta/(12Q) - \mathsf{negl}(\lambda)$.

3.3 Applications to Exotic Signatures

We briefly explain how to build digital signatures [28,52], group signatures [8,51] and blind signatures [3,27,50] from the (interactive) ISIS_f assumption.

Signature Schemes. We can directly build standard model signatures using the hash-and-sign GPV framework. Namely, the secret key is a trapdoor for the public matrix $\mathbf{A}$. Let $\mathbf{C}$ be another uniformly random matrix (which corresponds to the $\mathbf{C}$ in the interactive ISIS_f problem). Then, to sign a (short) message $\mathbf{m}$, we sample a uniformly random $x \leftarrow [N]$ and compute a short preimage $\mathbf{s}$ which satisfies $\mathbf{As} = f(x) + \mathbf{Cm}$. Thus, the signature is a pair $(x, \mathbf{s})$. Unforgeability follows directly from the $\mathsf{Int\text{-}ISIS}_f$ assumption.

Group Signatures. Let L be the size of the group and for $i \in [L]$, let $\mathbf{m}_i$ to be the polynomial vector whose coefficient vector is the binary representation of i. We follow the standard sign-and-encrypt approach. Namely, the setup authority generates matrices $(\mathbf{A}, \mathbf{C})$, along with the trapdoor for preimage sampling. Then, for each user $i \in [L]$, it generates a uniformly random $x_i \leftarrow [N]$ and computes a short preimage $\mathbf{s}_i$ that satisfies $\mathbf{As}_i = f(x_i) + \mathbf{Cm}_i$. Hence, the signature for user i consists of a zero-knowledge proof of knowledge π that $i \in [L], x_i \in [N]$, and short $\mathbf{s}_i$ such that $\mathbf{As}_i = f(x_i) + \mathbf{Cm}_i$[12]. Since we obtain π by applying the Fiat-Shamir transformation to an interactive proof, the message to sign is included as an input to the hash function.

Blind Signatures. We follow the Fischlin framework for constructing round-optimal blind signatures. The public key are the matrices $(\mathbf{A}, \mathbf{C})$, while the secret key is a trapdoor for $\mathbf{A}$. Suppose the user wants to obtain a signature on a short message vector $\mathbf{m}$. It first computes the Ajtai commitment [4] on $\mathbf{m}$, i.e. $\mathbf{u} := \mathbf{C} \begin{bmatrix} \mathbf{m} \\ \mathbf{r} \end{bmatrix}$, where $\mathbf{r}$ is a fresh, short randomness vector, and sends $\mathbf{u}$ to the signer along with a proof π_u of well-formedness of $\mathbf{u}$. The signer, who possess the trapdoor for matrix $\mathbf{A}$, samples $x \leftarrow [N]$ and returns to the user a short vector $\mathbf{s}$ which satisfies $\mathbf{As} = f(x) + \mathbf{u}$. Finally, the user outputs as a signature a zero-knowledge proof of knowledge π_s of $x \in [N]$, short randomness $\mathbf{r}$ and a short vector $\mathbf{s}$ such that

$$\mathbf{As} = f(x) + \mathbf{C} \begin{bmatrix} \mathbf{m} \\ \mathbf{r} \end{bmatrix},$$

where $\mathbf{m}$ is a part of the statement. This is also the approach we take for constructing anonymous credentials in the full version of this paper.

References

1. Agrawal, S., Boneh, D., Boyen, X.: Lattice basis delegation in fixed dimension and shorter-ciphertext hierarchical IBE. In: Rabin, T. (ed.) CRYPTO 2010. LNCS, vol. 6223, pp. 98–115. Springer, Heidelberg (2010). https://doi.org/10.1007/978-3-642-14623-7_6
2. Agrawal, S., Stehlé, D., Yadav, A.: Towards practical and round-optimal lattice-based threshold and blind signatures. IACR Cryptol. ePrint Arch., p. 381 (2021)
3. Agrawal, S., Kirshanova, E., Stehlé, D., Yadav, A.: Practical, round-optimal lattice-based blind signatures (2022)
4. Ajtai, M.: Generating hard instances of lattice problems (extended abstract). In: STOC, pp. 99–108 (1996)

---

[12] The signature should also contain a verifiable encryption of i using the opener's public key.

5. Albrecht, M.R., Cini, V., Lai, R.W.F., Malavolta, G., Thyagarajan, S.A.: Lattice-based SNARKs: publicly verifiable, preprocessing, and recursively composable. In: Dodis, Y., Shrimpton, T. (eds) CRYPTO 2022. LNCS, vol. 13508. Springer, Cham (2022). https://doi.org/10.1007/978-3-031-15979-4_4

6. Attema, T., Lyubashevsky, V., Seiler, G.: Practical product proofs for lattice commitments. In: Micciancio, D., Ristenpart, T. (eds.) CRYPTO 2020. LNCS, vol. 12171, pp. 470–499. Springer, Cham (2020). https://doi.org/10.1007/978-3-030-56880-1_17

7. Banaszczyk, W.: New bounds in some transference theorems in the geometry of numbers. Mathematische Annalen **296**(1): 625–635 (1993). ISSN 1432–1807. https://doi.org/10.1007/BF01445125. https://doi.org/10.1007/BF01445125

8. Bellare, M., Micciancio, D., Warinschi, B.: Foundations of group signatures: formal definitions, simplified requirements, and a construction based on general assumptions. In: Biham, E. (ed.) EUROCRYPT 2003. LNCS, vol. 2656, pp. 614–629. Springer, Heidelberg (2003). https://doi.org/10.1007/3-540-39200-9_38

9. Beullens, W., Seiler, G.: Labrador: compact proofs for R1CS from module-sis. IACR Cryptol. ePrint Arch., p. 1341 (2022)

10. Beullens, W., Lyubashevsky, V., Nguyen, N.K., Seiler, G.: Lattice-based blind signatures: Short, efficient, and round-optimal. Cryptology ePrint Archive, Paper 2023/077 (2023). https://eprint.iacr.org/2023/077. https://eprint.iacr.org/2023/077

11. Bootle, J., Lyubashevsky, V., Seiler, G.: Algebraic techniques for short(er) exact lattice-based zero-knowledge proofs. In: Boldyreva, A., Micciancio, D. (eds.) CRYPTO 2019. LNCS, vol. 11692, pp. 176–202. Springer, Cham (2019). https://doi.org/10.1007/978-3-030-26948-7_7

12. Bootle, J., Delaplace, C., Espitau, T., Fouque, P.-A., Tibouchi, M.: LWE without modular reduction and improved side-channel attacks against BLISS. In: Peyrin, T., Galbraith, S. (eds.) ASIACRYPT 2018. LNCS, vol. 11272, pp. 494–524. Springer, Cham (2018). https://doi.org/10.1007/978-3-030-03326-2_17

13. Bos, J.W., et al.: CRYSTALS - kyber: a cca-secure module-lattice-based KEM. In: 2018 IEEE European Symposium on Security and Privacy, EuroS&P, pp. 353–367 (2018)

14. Boschini, C., Takahashi, A., Tibouchi, M.: Musig-l: Lattice-based multi-signature with single-round online phase. Cryptology ePrint Archive, Paper 2022/1036 (2022). https://eprint.iacr.org/2022/1036. https://eprint.iacr.org/2022/1036

15. Boudgoust, K., Jeudy, C., Roux-Langlois, A., Wen, W.: Towards classical hardness of module-LWE: the linear rank case. In: Moriai, S., Wang, H. (eds.) ASIACRYPT 2020. LNCS, vol. 12492, pp. 289–317. Springer, Cham (2020). https://doi.org/10.1007/978-3-030-64834-3_10

16. Camenisch, J., Drijvers, M., Lehmann, A.: Anonymous attestation using the strong Diffie Hellman assumption revisited. In: Franz, M., Papadimitratos, P. (eds.) Trust 2016. LNCS, vol. 9824, pp. 1–20. Springer, Cham (2016). https://doi.org/10.1007/978-3-319-45572-3_1

17. Camenisch, J., Lysyanskaya, A.: A signature scheme with efficient protocols. In: Cimato, S., Persiano, G., Galdi, C. (eds.) SCN 2002. LNCS, vol. 2576, pp. 268–289. Springer, Heidelberg (2003). https://doi.org/10.1007/3-540-36413-7_20

18. Chaum, D.: Security without identification: transaction systems to make big brother obsolete. Commun. ACM **28**(10), 1030–1044 (1985). https://doi.org/10.1145/4372.4373. https://doi.org/10.1145/4372.4373

19. Chen, L.: Access with pseudonyms. In: Dawson, E., Golić, J. (eds.) CPA 1995. LNCS, vol. 1029, pp. 232–243. Springer, Heidelberg (1996). https://doi.org/10.1007/BFb0032362

20. Damgård, I.B.: Payment systems and credential mechanisms with provable security against abuse by individuals. In: Goldwasser, S. (ed.) CRYPTO 1988. LNCS, vol. 403, pp. 328–335. Springer, New York (1990). https://doi.org/10.1007/0-387-34799-2_26

21. Ducas, L., Lyubashevsky, V., Prest, T.: Efficient identity-based encryption over NTRU lattices. In: Sarkar, P., Iwata, T. (eds.) ASIACRYPT 2014. LNCS, vol. 8874, pp. 22–41. Springer, Heidelberg (2014). https://doi.org/10.1007/978-3-662-45608-8_2

22. Ducas, L., Nguyen, P.Q.: Learning a zonotope and more: cryptanalysis of NTRUSign countermeasures. In: Wang, X., Sako, K. (eds.) ASIACRYPT 2012. LNCS, vol. 7658, pp. 433–450. Springer, Heidelberg (2012). https://doi.org/10.1007/978-3-642-34961-4_27

23. Ducas, L., Kiltz, E., Lepoint, T., Lyubashevsky, V., Schwabe, P., Seiler, G., Stehlé, D.: Crystals-dilithium: a lattice-based digital signature scheme. IACR Trans. Cryptogr. Hardw. Embed. Syst. **2018**(1), 238–268 (2018)

24. Esgin, M.F., Nguyen, N.K., Seiler, G.: Practical Exact Proofs from Lattices: New Techniques to Exploit Fully-Splitting Rings. In: Moriai, S., Wang, H. (eds.) ASIACRYPT 2020. LNCS, vol. 12492, pp. 259–288. Springer, Cham (2020). https://doi.org/10.1007/978-3-030-64834-3_9

25. Esgin, M.F., Steinfeld, R., Liu, J.K., Liu, D.: Lattice-Based Zero-Knowledge Proofs: New Techniques for Shorter and Faster Constructions and Applications. In: Boldyreva, A., Micciancio, D. (eds.) CRYPTO 2019. LNCS, vol. 11692, pp. 115–146. Springer, Cham (2019). https://doi.org/10.1007/978-3-030-26948-7_5

26. Esgin, M.F., Zhao, R.K., Steinfeld, R., Liu, J.K., Liu, D.: Matrict: Efficient, scalable and post-quantum blockchain confidential transactions protocol. In: CCS, pp. 567–584. ACM (2019)

27. Fischlin, M.: Round-Optimal Composable Blind Signatures in the Common Reference String Model. In: Dwork, C. (ed.) CRYPTO 2006. LNCS, vol. 4117, pp. 60–77. Springer, Heidelberg (2006). https://doi.org/10.1007/11818175_4

28. Gentry, C., Peikert, C., Vaikuntanathan, V.: Trapdoors for hard lattices and new cryptographic constructions. In: STOC, pp. 197–206 (2008)

29. Herold, G., May, A.: LP solutions of vectorial integer subset sums – cryptanalysis of galbraith's binary matrix LWE. In: Fehr, S. (ed.) PKC 2017. LNCS, vol. 10174, pp. 3–15. Springer, Heidelberg (2017). https://doi.org/10.1007/978-3-662-54365-8_1

30. Hyperledger Foundation. Hyperledger Aries. https://www.hyperledger.org/use/aries. Accessed 06 Oct 2022

31. Hyperledger Foundation. Hyperledger Indy. https://www.hyperledger.org/use/hyperledger-indy. Accessed 06 Oct 2022

32. Jeudy, C., Roux-Langlois, A., Sanders, O.: Lattice signature with efficient protocols, application to anonymous credentials. Cryptology ePrint Archive, Paper 2022/509 (2022). https://eprint.iacr.org/2022/509

33. Lai, Q., Liu, F.-H., Lysyanskaya, A., Wang, Z.: Lattice-based commit-transferrable signatures and applications to anonymous credentials. Cryptology ePrint Archive, Paper 2023/766, (2023). https://eprint.iacr.org/2023/766

34. Langlois, A., Stehlé, D.: Worst-case to average-case reductions for module lattices. Des. Codes Crypt. **75**(3), 565–599 (2015)

35. Looker, T., Kalos, V., Whitehead, A., Lodder, M.: The BBS Signature Scheme (2022). https://www.ietf.org/id/draft-looker-cfrg-bbs-signatures-01.html. Accessed 06 Oct 2022
36. Lysyanskaya, A., Rivest, R.L., Sahai, A., Wolf, S.: Pseudonym Systems. In: Heys, H., Adams, C. (eds.) SAC 1999. LNCS, vol. 1758, pp. 184–199. Springer, Heidelberg (2000). https://doi.org/10.1007/3-540-46513-8_14
37. Lyubashevsky, V.: Fiat-Shamir with aborts: applications to lattice and factoring-based signatures. In: Matsui, M. (ed.) ASIACRYPT 2009. LNCS, vol. 5912, pp. 598–616. Springer, Heidelberg (2009). https://doi.org/10.1007/978-3-642-10366-7_35
38. Lyubashevsky, V.: Lattice signatures without trapdoors. In: Pointcheval, D., Johansson, T. (eds.) EUROCRYPT 2012. LNCS, vol. 7237, pp. 738–755. Springer, Heidelberg (2012). https://doi.org/10.1007/978-3-642-29011-4_43
39. Lyubashevsky, V., Micciancio, D.: Asymptotically efficient lattice-based digital signatures. Cryptology ePrint Archive, Paper 2013/746 (2013). https://eprint.iacr.org/2013/746
40. Lyubashevsky, V., Micciancio, D.: Asymptotically efficient lattice-based digital signatures. J. Cryptol., **31**(3), 774–797 (2018). https://eprint.iacr.org/2013/746. Preliminary version appeared in TCC 2008
41. Lyubashevsky, V., Nguyen, N.K.: Bloom: bimodal lattice one-out-of-many proofs and applications. Cryptology ePrint Archive, Paper 2022/1307 (2022). https://eprint.iacr.org/2022/1307
42. Lyubashevsky, V., Nguyen, N.K., Plançon, M.: Lattice-based zero-knowledge proofs and applications: shorter, simpler, and more general. IACR Cryptol. ePrint Arch., p. 284 (2022). Appears in Crypto 2022
43. Lyubashevsky, V., Nguyen, N.K., PlanM.: Lattice-based zero-knowledge proofs and applications: shorter, simpler, and more general. In: Dodis, Y., Shrimpton, T. (eds) CRYPTO 2022. LNCS, vol. 13508, pp. 71–101. Springer, Cham (2022). https://doi.org/10.1007/978-3-031-15979-4_3
44. Lyubashevsky, V., Nguyen, N.K., Seiler, G.: SMILE: set membership from ideal lattices with applications to ring signatures and confidential transactions. In: Malkin, T., Peikert, C. (eds.) CRYPTO 2021. LNCS, vol. 12826, pp. 611–640. Springer, Cham (2021). https://doi.org/10.1007/978-3-030-84245-1_21
45. Lyubashevsky, V., Nguyen, N.K., Plancon, M., Seiler, G.: Shorter lattice-based group signatures via "Almost Free" encryption and other optimizations. In: Tibouchi, M., Wang, H. (eds.) ASIACRYPT 2021. LNCS, vol. 13093, pp. 218–248. Springer, Cham (2021). https://doi.org/10.1007/978-3-030-92068-5_8
46. MATTR. MATTR. https://github.com/mattrglobal. Accessed 06 Oct 2022
47. Micciancio, D., Peikert, C.: Trapdoors for lattices: simpler, tighter, faster, smaller. In: Pointcheval, D., Johansson, T. (eds.) EUROCRYPT 2012. LNCS, vol. 7237, pp. 700–718. Springer, Heidelberg (2012). https://doi.org/10.1007/978-3-642-29011-4_41
48. Micciancio, D., Regev, O.: Worst-case to average-case reductions based on gaussian measures. SIAM J. Comput. **37**(1), 267–302 (2007)
49. NFCW. Digital identity market revenues to reach US$53bn in 2026 (2022). https://www.nfcw.com/2022/01/31/375825/digital-identity-market-revenues-to-reach-us53bn-in-2026/. Accessed 06 Oct 2022
50. del Pino, R., Katsumata, S.: A new framework for more efficient round-optimal lattice-based (partially) blind signature via trapdoor sampling. Cryptology ePrint Archive, Paper 2022/834 (2022). https://eprint.iacr.org/2022/834. https://eprint.iacr.org/2022/834

51. del Pino, R., Lyubashevsky, V., Seiler, G.: Lattice-based group signatures and zero-knowledge proofs of automorphism stability. In: ACM Conference on Computer and Communications Security, pp. 574–591. ACM (2018)

52. Prest, T., et al.: FALCON. Technical report, National Institute of Standards and Technology (2017). https://csrc.nist.gov/projects/post-quantum-cryptography/round-1-submissions

53. Regev, O.: On lattices, learning with errors, random linear codes, and cryptography. J. ACM **56**(6) (2009)

54. The AnonCreds Specification Working Group. The AnonCreds Specification. https://github.com/AnonCreds-WG/anoncreds-spec (2022). Accessed 06 Oct 2022

55. Veramo. Veramo core development. https://github.com/uport-project. Accessed 06 Oct 2022

56. Wee, H., Wu, D.J.: Succinct vector, polynomial, and functional commitments from lattices. Cryptology ePrint Archive, Paper 2022/1515 (2022). https://eprint.iacr.org/2022/1515. https://eprint.iacr.org/2022/1515

57. Yang, R., Au, M.H., Zhang, Z., Xu, Q., Yu, Z., Whyte, W.: Efficient lattice-based zero-knowledge arguments with standard soundness: construction and applications. In: Boldyreva, A., Micciancio, D. (eds.) CRYPTO 2019. LNCS, vol. 11692, pp. 147–175. Springer, Cham (2019). https://doi.org/10.1007/978-3-030-26948-7_6

Anonymous Tokens with Stronger Metadata Bit Hiding from Algebraic MACs

Melissa Chase[1], F. Betül Durak[1(✉)], and Serge Vaudenay[2]

[1] Microsoft Research, Redmond, WA, USA
melissac@microsoft.com
[2] EPFL, Lausanne, Switzerland
betul.durak@microsoft.com

Abstract. On the one hand, the web needs to be secured from malicious activities such as bots or DoS attacks; on the other hand, such needs ideally should not justify services tracking people's activities on the web. Anonymous tokens provide a nice tradeoff between allowing an issuer to ensure that a user has been vetted and protecting the users' privacy. However, in some cases, whether or not a token is issued reveals a lot of information to an adversary about the strategies used to distinguish honest users from bots or attackers.

In this work, we focus on designing an anonymous token protocol between a client and an issuer (also a verifier) that enables the issuer to support its fraud detection mechanisms while preserving users' privacy. This is done by allowing the issuer to embed a hidden (from the client) metadata bit into the tokens. We first study an existing protocol from CRYPTO 2020 which is an extension of Privacy Pass from PoPETs 2018; that protocol aimed to provide support for a hidden metadata bit, but provided a somewhat restricted security notion. We demonstrate a new attack, showing that this is a weakness of the protocol, not just the definition. In particular, the metadata bit hiding is weak in the setting where the attacker can redeem some tokens and get feedback on whether the bit extraction succeeded.

We then revisit the formalism of anonymous tokens with private metadata bit, consider the more natural notion, and design a scheme which achieves it. In order to design this new secure protocol, we base our construction on algebraic MACs instead of PRFs. Our security definitions capture a realistic threat model where adversaries could, through direct feedback or side channels, learn the embedded bit when the token is redeemed. Finally, we compare our protocol with one of the CRYPTO 2020 protocols. We obtain 20% more efficient performance.

1 Introduction

There has been significant industry interest recently in anonymous tokens, including Google's Trust Tokens (TT) [23] and Cloudflare's Privacy Pass (PP)

© International Association for Cryptologic Research 2023
H. Handschuh and A. Lysyanskaya (Eds.): CRYPTO 2023, LNCS 14082, pp. 418–449, 2023.
https://doi.org/10.1007/978-3-031-38545-2_14

[11]. These protocols are used to transfer trust signals without compromising users' privacy. Anonymous tokens define a protocol between three types of parties: a client, an issuer, and a redeemer. The client wishes to obtain tokens from an issuer and then present them to a redeemer. The issuer determines the trustworthiness of clients and issues tokens; and the redeemer (a.k.a. the verifier) verifies the tokens. These systems are anonymous in that the token issuance and redemption are unlinkable, in the sense that the issuer and redeemer cannot tell which of the issued tokens was used in any given redemption. In the above systems, we consider an issuer and a redeemer which are controlled by the same entity, so these two parties are assumed to share a secret key.

PP was specifically designed in the context of CDNs to assess the trustworthiness of a client at the edge before the client is granted (or denied) access to a web server. In the typical use case, the client is required to solve a CAPTCHA before it accesses a web server for the first time. If the CAPTCHA is successfully solved, the client is given a set of tokens to redeem the next time it visits the web server. At subsequent visits the server checks that the user's token is valid and has not previously been used, and if so allows the client to bypass the CAPTCHA and directly access the content. This allows for a better experience for the user since they only have to complete the CAPTCHA once, even if they are accessing the webserver over Tor or a VPN. Because of the unlinkability, it does so without helping the web server to track the user across different visits.

Even though CAPTCHA is one way to detect bad actors, there are more advanced techniques to assess how trustworthy the client is, for example based on machine learning algorithms for fraud detection. Typically, such fraud detection algorithms are run on the issuer side; when these algorithms determine that a client is likely to be malicious, the issuer should refuse to issue it any tokens. However, such feedback allows a fraudulent client to improve their methods to bypass the fraud detection. Ideally the issuer would instead embed a bit (to indicate if the client is malicious or trusted) inside the token which would be hidden from the client and only recovered by the redeemer during the redemption. That way, the malicious client would not find out that its fraudulent activity has been detected until it tries to redeem the token. This would make this type of attack on the fraud detection algorithms significantly more cumbersome.

Behind anonymous tokens with private metadata bit, there are three desired security and privacy requirements: unforgeability (to prevent malicious clients from forging valid tokens), unlinkability (to prevent a malicious server and redeemer from linking the tokens they issued with those that are redeemed), and privacy of embedded metadata bit (to prevent the clients from learning immediately if they were identified as malicious actors). More specifically, the metadata bit is a covert channel between issuer and redeemer, who as described above will share a key. If this channel were allowed to convey unlimited information, unlinkability would be meaningless, so the protocols must ensure that the embedded signal is only a single bit and no more. Such covert channel with one bit is used to communicate whether or not the issued token should be accepted without revealing the decision to the client until it attempts a redemption.

The initial proposal for including a private metadata bit built directly on the PP protocol where the client picks an arbitrary message t and masks it to hide it from the issuer (i.e., the issuer blindly "signs" the t), and then the client unmasks the signature on t. This idea naturally extends to support private metadata bits with PP: the issuer would choose two PP issuing keys and generate a token under one key or the other depending on the bit it wished to encode.

Because PP is based on an oblivious pseudo random function, a token generated under either key was indistinguishable from random so the client was unable to determine the bit from looking at a correctly generated token. However, this protocol had significant weaknesses; a malicious client can easily make malformed token requests (e.g. keep using the same message t), and then tell from the responses whether the tokens issued encode the same metadata bit. This means that the attacker has to make one request for which he can predict the resulting bit (e.g. by using a genuine user device or by behaving badly enough that it will be guaranteed to be detected as fraudulent), and then it can make an incorrectly formed token request and directly tell from the (invalid) token it receives whether the attacker was attempting to issue a token with metadata bit 0 or 1. This problem essentially comes from the fact that the PP allows the client to pick the messages to be signed arbitrarily. In our design, messages are jointly generated by the client and the issuer so we can ensure they are random.

Two recent papers [14,15,21] aim to address this problem and to formally define and construct anonymous tokens with private metadata bit. The latter is a more generic version of the former where the protocols can accept public metadata as well as the private metadata bit. The authors in these works identify the problem as being that the tokens are deterministic; they propose new randomized protocols. These proposals address the issues above and guarantee that an adversary who can maliciously interact with the token issuing server cannot learn anything about the private metadata bits encoded in the tokens.

However, these schemes still have some counter intuitive properties. In particular, in their protocol, there are two notions for a *token validity*: "validity from verification", where the adversary gets feedback on whether the token verifies correctly, and "validity from extraction", where the adversary gets feedback on whether there is an embedded bit or not without revealing the bit (if it exists). Their definition of privacy for the metadata bit allows the adversary to learn at redemption whether a token is "valid from verification", but not following the other notion. Contrarily, the unforgeability notion is based on the existence of an embedded bit. And this is not just a property of the definition: we will show that the proposed schemes have the property that if the redemption service reveals whether a bit is embedded during the token redemption, the adversary can use only a few malicious interactions with the issuing and redemption service to learn information about the hidden bits embedded in a large batch of tokens.

This separation may make sense in some contexts, where we can guarantee that the adversary gets no feedback at all from the redemption server on whether its token was accepted and what the included bit was. In other cases however, this seems to be a nontrivial weakness. For example, in the CDN application above, the adversary will clearly get feedback on the bit if it is used to determine whether it will be allowed to access the web content. A private metadata bit protocol with this type of weakness would allow the adversary to make many attempts to bypass the fraud detection and thus acquire many tokens, then make a few redemption requests and identify exactly which of the remaining unredeemed tokens successfully avoided the fraud detection. Those tokens could then be collected and, for example, used to mount a DDOS attack.

Thus, it is clear that in at least some settings, we would like a token system which provides stronger guarantees. Moreover, identifying all sources of feedback is challenging. It seems likely that if a new primitive for anonymous tokens is released, it will at some point be used in settings where the adversary can get feedback on the encoded bit, whether or not the security definition allows for that. Thus, the best solution would be the one that provides the most natural security guarantees - an adversary interacting with an issuer and a redeemer may learn the bits encoded *in the tokens it redeems*, but nothing else.

That leaves us with the following questions: *Is such a definition efficiently realizable? What is the overhead as compared to the solutions described above?*

Our Contributions. In the rest of the paper, we begin by summarizing the private metadata bit proposals PMBT of [14,15], describing the known weakness in detail, and explaining an additional attack. Then we present our more natural security definitions. Finally, we present ATHM, a *new construction for anonymous tokens* with private metadata bit which we show satisfies our definitions. We analyze the efficiency of ATHM in Sect. 5 and show that, surprisingly, ATHM is faster than PMBT (1.3 ms vs 1.6 ms). Finally, we show the *flexibility of our approach* by demonstrating that it extends easily to allow for tokens including *public metadata* visible to both issuer/redeemer and client.

Our Techniques. As mentioned above, the initial privacy pass protocol was based around oblivious pseudorandom functions (OPRFs). The proposals of [14,15, 21], as described above, identify the problem as that OPRFs are deterministic, and attempt to address it by making the protocol randomized. However, once we recognize that we do not in fact need a deterministic function, we can ask whether it makes sense to base this primitive around OPRFs, whose defining characteristic is that they are deterministic. Moreover, the obliviousness property of OPRFs turns out to be *not* a very good fit for hiding the metadata bit.

This begs the question: *Is there a better primitive to start from if we want to encode hidden data in anonymous tokens?*

For this, we turn to authentication primitives like MACs. Since we need privacy, we look at anonymous credentials, which allow issuers to certify attributes which can later be presented unlinkably [3,9]. Specifically, we borrow from keyed verification anonymous credentials (KVAC) [5,6], where the credential issuer and verifier share a secret key, and from constructions based on algebraic MACs.

KVAC directly gives us a protocol for blindly issuing credentials, in which an issuer issues a MAC on a set of attributes, some of which are only known to the client. At a high level we can apply this as follows: in token issuance, the client chooses a random nonce, and the issuer uses blind issuance to give a MAC on a pair of messages consisting of the nonce and the hidden bit. If we use the first construction from [5], MACGGM, that gives a construction in elliptic curve groups where tokens consist of the nonce and two additional group elements, which is roughly comparable with PMBT, and only twice as long as PP. But, if we consider the blind issuance protocol from [5], it would be roughly twice as expensive as the issuance for PMBT, and 4 times the cost of PP.[1] It also does not directly provide metadata privacy as that is not a property generally considered in the credentials setting. Technically then, we are left with two questions: 1) *Can we optimize the MACGGM based issuance protocol to the point where it is competitive with PP or PMBT?* and 2) *If the client does not know one of the attributes in the credential, do the protocols still work? Can we prove that this attribute will not be leaked to the client?*

We address the first of these questions with a very careful optimization of the blind issuance protocol to get a result with comparable cost to PMBT. If we wanted to directly reduce to MAC security, we would need the request to include something from which we could extract the nonce in $\mathbb{Z}_p$ which will be the message for the MAC. Extracting messages in $\mathbb{Z}_p$ is extremely expensive.[2] Moreover, the blind issuance protocol in [5] has the client form an ElGamal encryption of the message to be signed, which would result in a client-to-server message twice as long as in PP or PMBT, even before the proofs are added. Instead, we design an optimized blind issuance protocol and prove in the generic group model that the resulting token scheme is unforgeable.

Unlinkability follows in a straightforward way from the privacy of the KVAC scheme. Privacy of the metadata bit is more challenging, as there is no analog in the KVAC context. First, we note that the blind issuance protocol works even if the client does not know one of the messages, and the verifier (the issuance server) can simply verify with both possible bit messages, and output the bit for which the MAC verifies. Intuitively, we also might hope to get privacy for the metadata bit because MACGGM has some pseudorandomness properties: the basic MAC on a message pair (m_0, m_1) is $(U, (x + ym_0 + zm_1)U)$, where U is a random group element, and (x, y, z) are the secret key. DDH then guarantees that this will look like a random pair of messages. However, proving that this satisfies the metadata bit privacy property, where the adversary can interact maliciously with issuance and redemption oracles is significantly more challenging. Here, we again prove security in the generic group model.

Related Work. Beyond the works on anonymous tokens mentioned above, the most closely related work is in anonymous credentials. While there are also works based on RSA groups (beginning with [3,4]) and based on pairings, we focus here on works that can be implemented in prime order elliptic curve groups, since those provide the best efficiency. In that setting, besides MACGGM, there

---

[1] We provide a more precise analysis in the full version of this paper [12].

[2] [5] addresses this by making non-standard assumptions about the extraction properties of Fiat-Shamir.

is one other proposal for a MAC based anonymous credential scheme [7] which is more expensive than MACGGM.

In addition, there are several anonymous credential constructions in elliptic curve groups that take a blind-signature based approach [1,17,22]. It is not clear how to add private issuer values (like the metadata bit) in these schemes, but even if we consider the simpler setting where the bit is known to the user, these schemes have several downsides: First, token redemption is significantly more expensive (4x for [17] or [22], and 8x for [1]). In a setting like the CDN application where we will be using tokens to decrease spam/prevent DDOS attacks, we want the cost to verify tokens to be as low as possible. Secondly, they all require a multi-round issuance protocol, with two round trips between the user and issuer. This requires that the token issuance server to be stateful, and in fact if the issuer can be tricked into completing a protocol in two different ways, then his secret key will be leaked. This means that implementing a token issuer requires careful state management, including storage per client session. In a setting where there are many clients, many of which may be untrusted or on flaky connections, this can be quite expensive.

2   PMBT: A Case Study

We begin with [15] (and its full version [14]) and investigate the shortcomings as well as a new attack. There are two main constructions in these works called Private Metadata Bit Tokens (PMBT) and CMBT. For PMBT, the authors acknowledge that Verify returning always true is not meaningful and then announced their new protocol named CMBT in the full version of their paper [14]. Before the description of protocols, we borrow the interface of anonymous tokens (AT) with private metadata bit and its security and privacy requirements.

2.1   AT Interface and Security

- $(\mathsf{crs}, \mathsf{td}) \leftarrow \mathsf{AT}.\mathsf{Setup}(1^\lambda)$ sets up a common reference string crs and a trapdoor td with security parameter λ.
- $(\mathsf{pp}, \mathsf{sk}) \leftarrow \mathsf{AT}.\mathsf{KeyGen}(\mathsf{crs})$ generates the public parameters pp and a secret key sk from crs.
- $\{\sigma, \bot\} \leftarrow \langle \mathsf{AT}.\mathsf{Client}(\mathsf{pp}, t), \mathsf{AT}.\mathsf{IssueToken}(\mathsf{sk}, b) \rangle$ is an interactive token generation protocol between a *client* (also called a *user*) and the issuer. The client inputs are a string t along with the public parameters, and the issuer inputs are the secret key sk and a *metadata bit b*. The protocol outputs a token (also referred to as signature) σ for the client or $\bot$.
- $\mathsf{bool} \leftarrow \mathsf{AT}.\mathsf{Verify}(\mathsf{sk}, t, \sigma)$ (run by the *redeemer*) verifies a token σ with tag t and returns a boolean value to indicate if the token was valid.
- $\mathsf{ind} \leftarrow \mathsf{AT}.\mathsf{ReadBit}(\mathsf{sk}, t, \sigma)$ (run by the *redeemer*) extracts the metadata bit b from a token (t, σ) and returns b if it succeeds or $\bot$ if it fails.

The issuance protocol is interactive between the user and the issuer. In [15], it is assumed to be a user-to-issuer-to-user protocol (2-move, user-initiated). The security properties of an AT scheme are unforgeability, unlinkability, and privacy of the metadata bit. They are formally (re)defined in Sect. 3. Unforgeability ensures that no adversary can forge "valid" (in the sense that AT.ReadBit does not give an error) tokens. Privacy ensures that no adversary can read a hidden bit, even with access to a "validity" (in the sense of AT.Verify) oracle.

PMBT.Client(X_0, X_1, t)

input: (X_0, X_1, t)

output: σ

$r \leftarrow\!\!\$ \; \mathbb{Z}_p^*$

$T := H_t(t)$

$T' := r^{-1}T$

$$\xrightarrow{\qquad T' \qquad}$$

PMBT.IssueToken$((x_0, y_0), (x_1, y_1), b)$

input: $(x_0, y_0), (x_1, y_1), b$

output: $\{\}$

$s \leftarrow\!\!\$ \; \{0, 1\}^\lambda$

$S' := H_s(T', s)$

$W' := x_b T' + y_b S'$

$\pi \leftarrow \Pi.\mathsf{Prove}((X_0, X_1, T', S', W'), (x_b, y_b))$

$$\xleftarrow{\qquad (s, W', \pi) \qquad}$$

$S' := H_s(T', s)$

if not $\Pi.\mathsf{Verify}((X_0, X_1, T', S', W'), \pi)$ **then return** $\perp$

$S := rS'$

$W := rW'$

output: $\sigma := (S, W)$

Fig. 1. PMBT token issuance protocol as given in [15, Fig 8, p 325]

We recall the PMBT issuance protocol in Fig. 1. As specified in [15], Verify always returns true and ReadBit returns $b \in \{0, 1\}$ such that $W = x_b H_t(t) + y_b S$ when it exists or $\perp$ otherwise.

2.2 Potential Attack for PMBT

In this section, we describe new attacks on PMBT. The authors of PMBT [15] already acknowledge that, given (S_i, W_i) tokens (at least two) which are generated with the same tag $t_i = t$ and the same bit $b_i = b$, the client can generate many other tokens (S, W) with the same tag t by making a weighed average: for scalars α_i such that $\sum_i \alpha_i = 1$, compute $W = \sum_i \alpha_i W_i$ and $S = \sum_i \alpha_i S_i$ to get $W = x_b H_t(t) + y_b S$. This is not considered to be a forgery because tokens with the same tag are considered as the same one. When the b_i's are not necessarily the same, the obtained token is valid (in the sense that ReadBit would read a bit) if and only if all b_i's are the same. So, a validity oracle could be used to check hidden bits equality. This is not considered to be a metadata bit privacy attack as the adversary has no access to this type of validity oracle. However, it can be considered as a side-channel attack.

New attack. In a new attack, we consider an adversary who gets one token (t_1, S_1, W_1) with a known bit b_1. Then, the adversary selects a fresh t^* and makes a challenge query by using $H_t(t^*) - H_t(t_1)$ in the place of T in the protocol with an unknown challenge bit b^*. The adversary would get (S^*, W^*) satisfying

$$W^* = x_{b^*}(H_t(t^*) - H_t(t_1)) + y_{b^*}S^*$$

Then, setting $W_2 = W^* + W_1$ and $S_2 = S^* + S_1$ gives

$$W_2 = x_{b^*}H_t(t^*) + y_{b^*}S_2 + (x_{b_1} - x_{b^*})H_t(t_1) + (y_{b_1} - y_{b^*})S_1$$

(S_2, W_2) with tag t^* would encode a bit (which would be b^*) if and only if $b_1 = b^*$ (except with the negligible probability that $(x_{b_1} - x_{b^*})H_t(t_1) + (y_{b_1} - y_{b^*})S_1 = 0$). Hence, the ability to learn whether ReadBit runs successfully on a chosen token breaks privacy of the hidden bit. Note that the two tokens use different tags.

This attacks generalizes, applies to the CMBT fix, and to other schemes as discussed in the full version of this paper [12].

3 Anonymous Tokens Revisited

3.1 AT Interface

We revisit the interface of AT and update the security notions as follows. We deviate from the previous definitions in three ways: first of all, there is a unique AT.ReadBit algorithm (and no extra AT.Verify) which returns the hidden bit or $\perp$ if invalid. Second, the client no longer chooses the t input in the issuing protocol. Instead, a unique nonce t is returned to the client. Finally, we added, for completeness, the optional *public metadata* m attribute. For protocols not allowing it, input m is ignored in algorithms and games.[3]

- cpp $\leftarrow$ AT.Setup(1^λ) sets up the common public parameters cpp from the security parameter λ. cpp typically contains a group description, its order, and a generator. [4] cpp is input to all other algorithms and omitted for more readability.
- (pk, sk) $\leftarrow$ AT.KeyGen(cpp) generates the public key pk and the secret key sk of the token *issuer*, with cpp as input.
- $\langle t, \sigma, \perp \rangle \leftarrow \langle$AT.Client(pk, m), AT.IssueToken(sk, b, m)$\rangle$ is the interactive token issuance protocol between a *client* and an *issuer*. The client inputs the issuer's public key pk and the *public metadata* m. The issuer inputs their secret key sk, a *metadata bit* $b \in \{0, 1\}$, and m. (Both participants are assumed to agree on m.) The protocol outputs a token (t, σ) composed of a tag t and a token σ for the client and nothing ($\perp$) for the issuer.
  The elements m, b, and t are called *attributes* and can be optionally offered by the protocol. The attribute t is a *nonce*; b is the issuer's private metadata bit; m is a public metadata (on which both participants must agree).
  As we focus on a round-trip protocol which is initiated by the client (2-move, client-initiated), we can specify it by three algorithms:

---

[3] A protocol with this m option is available in the full version of this paper [12].
[4] In the common reference string model, the CRS cpp comes with a trapdoor td.

- AT.ClientQuery(pk, m) → (query, st)   //Client sends query to issuer
- AT.IssueToken(sk, b, m, query) → resp   //Issuer replies with resp
- AT.ClientFinal(st, resp) → (t, σ) //Client locally computes token
- ind ← AT.ReadBit(sk, m, t, σ) extracts a bit b from a token σ with attributes (m, t). It outputs b if it succeeds and an error $\perp$ if it fails, in which case we say the token is *invalid*.

When we run these algorithms in the order they have been introduced and we obtain ind $= b$, we say that the protocol is *correct*.

The security properties of an AT scheme are unforgeability, unlinkability, and privacy of metadata bit. **Unforgeability** implies that an adversary cannot create valid tokens with modified attributes on an existing token. More precisely, if the issuer is invoked $n_{b,m}$ times for each attribute (b, m), then, for no (b, m) the adversary can exhibit $n_{b,m}+1$ valid tokens with pairwise different tags t. The adversary has access to a ReadBit(sk, ·, ·) oracle and can choose the bit b to be hidden in the token by the issuer. **Unlinkability** implies that a malicious issuer cannot link a redeemed token with one of the issuing sessions. The malicious issuer can maliciously set up the public parameters. **Privacy** of metadata means that a malicious client cannot guess the metadata bit hidden during a issuing session, even with access to an oracle for checking if a token is valid (but without access to an oracle which extracts the bit).

3.2   Unforgeability

The one-more unforgeability game (OMUF) is defined in Fig. 2. This is the same as in Kreuter et al. [15] except for a modification in the quantifiers[5] and for the modification in the interface: having the token verification and the bit extraction in the same algorithm and oracle. Notably, (t, σ) making AT.Verify return true and AT.ReadBit return $\perp$ would not exist any more as there is no AT.Verify. Those differences do not change the security notion.

Definition 1. *In the* OMUF *game[6] in Fig. 2, we define the advantage of an adversary $\mathcal{A}$ by*

$$\mathsf{Adv}_{\mathcal{A}}^{\mathsf{OMUF}}(\lambda) = \Pr[\mathsf{win}]$$

We say that AT *is* OMUF-*secure if for any PPT adversary $\mathcal{A}$, the advantage is a negligible function.*

---

[5] In their OMUF security definition, the first condition says that both $q_0 \le \ell$ AND $q_1 \le \ell$ where q_b is the number of oracle queries with bit b. Suppose the adversary made 10 queries with $b = 0$ ($q_0 = 10$) and 1000 queries with $b = 1$ ($q_1 = 1000$). If the adversary forges 11 tokens with $b = 0$, for this to succeed as a forgery, ℓ must be at least 1000. If it is not, this does not succeed.

[6] For protocols with no public metadata m, the variables $n_{b,m}$ in the game shall be changed to n_b and input m shall be removed from AT algorithms.

Game OMUF(1^λ):
1: AT.Setup(1^λ) → cpp
2: AT.KeyGen(cpp) → (pk, sk)
3: initialize $n_{b,m} \leftarrow 0$ for all (b, m)
4: $\mathcal{A}^{\mathcal{O}_{\text{sign}}, \mathcal{O}_{\text{read}}}$(cpp, pk) → $b, m, (t_i, \sigma_i)$
5: **if** $\#\{t_i\} \leq n_{b,m}$ **then** abort   ▷ this
  counts the number of pairwise differ-
  ent t_i values
6: **for** each i **do**
7:    **if** AT.ReadBit(sk, t_i, m, σ_i) $\neq b$
  then abort
8: **end for**
9: adversary wins

Oracle $\mathcal{O}_{\text{sign}}(b, m, \text{query})$:
10: increment $n_{b,m}$
11: AT.IssueToken(sk, b, m, query) → resp
12: **return** resp

Oracle $\mathcal{O}_{\text{read}}(m, t, \sigma)$:
13: **return** AT.ReadBit(sk, m, t, σ)

Fig. 2. One-More UnForgeability Game with Public Metadata m

3.3 Unlinkability

The unlinkability game (UNLINK) is defined in Fig. 3. This is the same as in Kreuter et al. [15] except for the modification in the interface: the tag t is output instead of being an arbitrarily selected input by the client and the public metadata m must be the same for all challenge tokens.

Definition 2. *In the UNLINK game in Fig. 3, we define the advantage of an adversary $\mathcal{A} = (\mathcal{A}_1, \mathcal{A}_2, \mathcal{A}_3)$ for parameter n by*

$$\mathsf{Adv}_{\mathcal{A},n}^{\mathsf{UNLINK}}(\lambda) = \Pr[\mathsf{win}]$$

We say that AT is κ-UNLINK-secure if for any PPT adversary $\mathcal{A}$ and any integer n, the advantage bounded by $\frac{\kappa}{n}$ plus a negligible function.

The issuer knows which bit is hidden during an issuing session and can extract the hidden bit during redeem. Hence, we should only consider unlinkability when the bits are the same.

If an adversary (1) puts n_b tokens with bit b for each b in $\mathcal{Q}$ with total of $n = \sum_b n_b$ tokens; (2) it draws and reads the bit b in out_{i^*}; (3) it outputs i at random among indices where it put the token with $b = b^*$, then the adversary wins with probability $\sum_b \frac{n_b}{n} \times \frac{1}{n_b} = \frac{2}{n}$. So, we focus on 2-UNLINK security.

3.4 Privacy of the Metadata Bit

The privacy of the metadata bit game (PMB) is defined in Fig. 4 with a challenge bit b^*. This is the same as in Kreuter et al. [15] except for the modification in the interface: the verify oracle is implemented by checking if AT.ReadBit does not return $\bot$. We also modified to have a single access to $\mathcal{O}_{\text{chal}}$ and to give access to $\mathcal{O}_{\text{read}}$ until the challenge is released. In the case of [15], the separation between

Game UNLINK$_n(1^\lambda)$:
1: AT.Setup$(1^\lambda) \to$ cpp
2: initialize $\mathcal{Q}_\text{query}, \mathcal{Q}_\text{final} \leftarrow \emptyset$
3: $\mathcal{A}_1(\text{cpp}) \to (\text{pk}, \text{state}_1)$
4: $\mathcal{A}_2^{\mathcal{O}_\text{query}, \mathcal{O}_\text{final}}(\text{state}_1) \to$
   $(\mathcal{Q}, (\text{resp}_i)_{i \in \mathcal{Q}}), \text{state}_2)$
5: if $\mathcal{Q} \not\subseteq \mathcal{Q}_\text{query} - \mathcal{Q}_\text{final}$ then abort
6: if $\#\mathcal{Q} < n$ then abort
7: for all $i \in \mathcal{Q}$ do
8:   $\text{out}_i \leftarrow$ AT.ClientFinal$(\text{st}_i, \text{resp}_i)$
9:   if $\text{out}_i = \perp$ then abort
10: end for
11: if $\#\{m_i; i \in \mathcal{Q}\} > 1$ then abort   ▷
   the m_i must all be the same
12: $i^* \leftarrow\!\!\!_\$ \; \mathcal{Q}$
13: pick a random permutation φ of $\mathcal{Q}$
14: $\mathcal{A}_3(\text{state}_2, \text{out}_{i^*}, (\text{out}_{\varphi(i)})_{i \in \mathcal{Q}}) \to i$
15: win iff $i = i^*$

Oracle $\mathcal{O}_\text{query}(i, m)$:
16: if $i \in \mathcal{Q}_\text{query}$ then return
17: insert i in $\mathcal{Q}_\text{query}$
18: $m_i \leftarrow m$
19: AT.ClientQuery$(\text{pk}, m_i) \to \text{query}_i, \text{st}_i$
20: return query_i

Oracle $\mathcal{O}_\text{final}(i, \text{resp})$:
21: if $i \in \mathcal{Q}_\text{final}$ or $i \notin \mathcal{Q}_\text{query}$ then return
22: insert i in $\mathcal{Q}_\text{final}$
23: return AT.ClientFinal$(\text{st}_i, \text{resp})$

Fig. 3. Unlinkability Game

AT.Verify and AT.ReadBit allowed $\mathcal{O}_\text{verify}$ to return true although AT.ReadBit would return $\perp$. Our interface does not allow it any more so the adversary has more information.

Definition 3. *In the PMB game in Fig. 4, we define the advantage of an adversary $\mathcal{A}$ by*

$$\text{Adv}_{\mathcal{A}}^\text{PMB}(\lambda) = \Pr[\text{PMB}_1 \to 1] - \Pr[\text{PMB}_0 \to 1]$$

We say that AT is PMB-secure if for any PPT adversary $\mathcal{A}$, the advantage is a negligible function.

4   ATHM: Anonymous Tokens with Hidden Metadata

Instead of relying on a deterministic PRF, we construct a protocol which is based on a randomized algebraic MAC, like in keyed-verification anonymous credentials [5,6] and Signal's private group management in group chats [7,8]. A valid MAC for an input b with a nonce t and a secret key (x, y, z) is a pair $\sigma = (P, Q)$ such that $Q = (x + by + tz)P$. In our scheme, a token with a hidden bit b will be a pair (t, σ) such that σ is a valid MAC for the attributes (b, t) with a secret key (x, y, z). In the full version of this paper [12], we present variants and extensions of ATHM to introduce public metadata m or other MAC algorithms.

4.1   The ATHM Components

Our scheme uses as a building block a simulatable non-interactive proof Π_2.

Game $\mathsf{PMB}_{b^*}(1^\lambda)$:
1: $\mathsf{AT.Setup}(1^\lambda) \to \mathsf{cpp}$
2: $\mathsf{AT.KeyGen}(\mathsf{cpp}) \to (\mathsf{pk}, \mathsf{sk})$
3: $\mathsf{flag} \leftarrow \mathsf{false}$
4: $\mathbf{return}\ \mathcal{A}^{\mathcal{O}_{\mathsf{sign}}, \mathcal{O}_{\mathsf{chal}}, \mathcal{O}_{\mathsf{read}}, \mathcal{O}_{\mathsf{valid}}}(\mathsf{cpp}, \mathsf{pk})$

Oracle $\mathcal{O}_{\mathsf{read}}(m, t, \sigma)$:
5: $\mathbf{if}\ \mathsf{flag}\ \text{and}\ m = m^*\ \mathbf{then\ return}\ \bot$
6: $\mathbf{return}\ \mathsf{AT.ReadBit}(\mathsf{sk}, m, t, \sigma)$

Oracle $\mathcal{O}_{\mathsf{valid}}(m, t, \sigma)$
7: $\mathsf{bool} \leftarrow \mathsf{AT.ReadBit}(\mathsf{sk}, m, t, \sigma) \neq \bot$
8: $\mathbf{return}\ \mathsf{bool}$

Oracle $\mathcal{O}_{\mathsf{sign}}(b, m, \mathsf{query})$:
9: $\mathsf{AT.IssueToken}(\mathsf{sk}, b, m, \mathsf{query}) \to \mathsf{resp}$
10: $\mathbf{return}\ \mathsf{resp}$

Oracle $\mathcal{O}_{\mathsf{chal}}(m, \mathsf{query})$:
11: $\mathbf{if}\ \mathsf{flag}\ \mathbf{then\ return}\ \bot$
12: $\mathsf{flag} \leftarrow \mathsf{true}$
13: $m^* \leftarrow m$
14: $\mathsf{AT.IssueToken}(\mathsf{sk}, b^*, m^*, \mathsf{query}) \quad \to$
    resp
15: $\mathbf{return}\ \mathsf{resp}$

Fig. 4. Privacy of the Metadata Bit Game

Setup algorithm. Setup is composed of two phases. The Setup_0 algorithm generates an (additive) group, of prime order p, and a generator G. The Setup_2 algorithm selects common parameters cpp_2 for Π_2.

$\mathsf{Setup}(1^\lambda)$:
1: $\mathsf{Setup}_0(1^\lambda) \to (\mathsf{gp}, p, G)$ ▷ group setup
2: $\mathsf{Setup}_2(\mathsf{gp}, p, G) \to \mathsf{cpp}_2$ ▷ Π_2 setup
3: $\mathsf{cpp} \leftarrow (\mathsf{gp}, p, G, \mathsf{cpp}_2)$

Our proposed Π_2 scheme requires Setup_2 to select uniformly a random non-zero group element $\mathsf{cpp}_2 = H$. (See Subsect. 4.3.)

The KeyGen algorithm. Key generation is composed of several phases.

$\mathsf{KeyGen}(\mathsf{cpp})$:
1: $\mathsf{KeyGen}_0(\mathsf{cpp}) \to (\mathsf{pk}_0, \mathsf{sk}_0)$
2: $\mathsf{KeyGen}_2(\mathsf{cpp}, \mathsf{pk}_0, \mathsf{sk}_0) \to (\mathsf{pk}_2, \mathsf{sk}_2)$ ▷ Π_2 key generation
3: $\mathsf{pk} \leftarrow (\mathsf{pk}_0, \mathsf{pk}_2)$
4: $\mathsf{sk} \leftarrow (\mathsf{sk}_0, \mathsf{sk}_2)$

In KeyGen_0, the issuer selects three secrets $\mathsf{sk}_0 = (x, y, z) \in \mathbb{Z}_p \times (\mathbb{Z}_p^*)^2$ uniformly $(y, z \neq 0)$ and sets $\mathsf{pk}_0 = Z = zG$.

Our proposed Π_2 scheme requires KeyGen_2 to add in pk_2 Pedersen commitments [18] $C_x = xG + r_xH$, $C_y = yG + r_yH$, together with a Schnorr proof of knowledge [19] of z such that $Z = zG$. Clients must verify this proof before starting the issuance protocol, but this is done once for all. (See Subsect. 4.3.)

The token issuance protocol. The user has public parameters. The server's input is the secret (x, y, z) and a bit b to hide inside the token. The protocol works as depicted in Fig. 5: the client selects a random tag share t_C and a random mask $r \in \mathbb{Z}_p$ and sends $T = t_C Z + rG$ to the issuer. The issuer selects a random tag share t_S and generates a pair (U, V) such that $(U, V - rU)$ is a valid MAC for tag $t = t_C + t_S$ and metadata b with key (x, y, z). For this, the issuer selects $U = dG$ for a random $d \in \mathbb{Z}_p^*$ and $V = d(xG + byG + t_S zG + T)$. Π_2 proves that the

(U, V, t_S) triplet was correctly generated and that $b \in \{0, 1\}$. Then, (U, V, t_S, π) is returned. The client computes $(U, V - rU)$. To make it unlinkable, the pair is multiplied by a random mask c to obtain another pair $\sigma = (P, Q)$.

ATHM.Client(G, Z)
input: (G, Z)
$t_C, r \leftarrow\!\!\$\ \mathbb{Z}_p$
$T := t_C Z + rG$

$$\xrightarrow{\quad T \quad}$$

ATHM.IssueToken$((x, y, z), b)$
input: $(x, y, z), b$

$t_S \leftarrow\!\!\$\ \mathbb{Z}_p$
$d \leftarrow\!\!\$\ \mathbb{Z}_p^*$
$U := dG$
$V := d(xG + byG + t_S zG + T)$
$\pi \leftarrow \Pi_2.\mathsf{Prove}(b, d, \mathsf{sk}_0, \mathsf{sk}_2; U, V, t_S, T, \mathsf{cpp}, \mathsf{pk})$

$$\xleftarrow{\quad U, V, t_S, \pi \quad}$$

if not $\Pi_2.\mathsf{Verify}(\pi, U, V, t_S, T, \mathsf{cpp}, \mathsf{pk})$ then return $\perp$
if $U = 0$ then return $\perp$
$c \leftarrow\!\!\$\ \mathbb{Z}_p^*$
$P := cU$
$Q := c(V - rU)$
$t := t_C + t_S$
$\sigma := (P, Q)$
output: (t, σ)

Fig. 5. ATHM token issuance protocol.

The proof Π_2 is a Fiat-Shamir transform of an OR proof of two Schnorr proofs for $b = 0$ and $b = 1$. It is specified in Subsect. 4.3.

The ReadBit *algorithm.* The redemption of (t, P, Q) with (x, y, z) checks $P \neq 0$ and looks for which $b \in \{0, 1\}$, the equality $Q = (x + by + tz)P$ is satisfied. It returns that bit (it must be unique) or an error if there is none.

Rationales. MACGGM (see Subsect. 4.2) ensures OMUF security. It uses two attributes to carry the tag t and hidden bit b. We observe that it is necessary that the issuer contributes to t. If the client could decide $t = t_C$, then PMB security could be broken by getting a challenge with tag t^* then issuing a token with same tag $t = t^*$ and taking the weighted average of both. The obtained token is valid if and only if b^* is equal to the bit b put in the second token. We can also observe that it is necessary to have t_C, r, and c. Without any of them, the malicious issuer can easily break UNLINK security by linking an issued token with a redeemed token.

The same goes with the proof Π_2 which plays two roles. First, it proves that the used sk corresponds to pk. Without Π_2, the issuer could use a set of different sk's and make a selection of sk in this set which would play the role of a marker in the token. Second, Π_2 proves that either $b = 0$ or $b = 1$, thus b only contains one bit. Without Π_2, the issuer could use more than one bit inside b and use this as a marker to link tokens to redeem to clients requesting a token. So, Π_2 is necessary for UNLINK security. The client must also verify $U \neq 0$, because $U = 0$ could be used by the issuer to mark a token.

Beware of double spending. Note that for this protocol, tag t needs to be a nonce as in other protocols [14,15] i.e. the redeemer should check against double-spending of a token with the same t. Otherwise, it is easy to transform a valid token with tag t into another valid token with the same tag t: let $\sigma = (P,Q)$ be a signature on t. Then the client can forge another signature $\sigma' = (c'P, c'Q)$ on t for a random c'.

4.2   The MAC Building Block

Our security results will be based on the security of an algebraic MAC. The simplest one is the MACGGM algorithm [5] defined as follows: given a secret $(x, y, z) \in \mathbb{Z}_p^3$, a valid authentication for $(b, t) \in \mathbb{Z}_p^2$ is a pair $\sigma = (P, Q)$ such that $Q = (x + by + tz)P$. For this MAC to be secure, it is important that no adversary can find any linear relation between the random values of P. Hence, P is selected at random by the issuer.

The security of MACGGM was proven in the generic group model (GGM) [5]. So, we use the same model to prove the security of ATHM. However, our construction generalizes to other MAC algorithms which can be proven in the standard model, and we use non-GGM security for this generalization, as shown in the full version of this paper [12].

4.3   The Simulatable Proof Building Block

As already mentioned, setup and key generation for the π proof is specified in Fig. 6. The setup essentially sets up an additional generator H to make a Pedersen commitment [18]. Key generation computes Pedersen commitments C_x on x and C_y on y together with a Schnorr proof [19] with Fiat-Shamir transform [13] for the knowledge of z such that $Z = zG$. Clients are assumed to verify that pk is correct by running once the Verify$_2$ algorithm.

On a high level, the proof π first commits to b by releasing a Pedersen commitment [18] $C = bC_y + \mu H$, then performs an OR proof [10]: a proof of knowledge for μ such that either $C = \mu H$ or $C = C_y + \mu H$. Finally, it performs a proof of knowledge for (d', ρ, w) such that $-G = d'U$, $-(C_x + C + t_s Z + T) = d'V + \rho H$, and $-T = d'V + wG$. The link with d is that $d' = -\frac{1}{d}$. Hence

$$\exists (d', \rho, w) \quad d' \begin{pmatrix} U \\ V \\ V \end{pmatrix} + \rho \begin{pmatrix} 0 \\ H \\ 0 \end{pmatrix} + w \begin{pmatrix} 0 \\ 0 \\ G \end{pmatrix} = - \begin{pmatrix} G \\ C_x + C + t_s Z + T \\ T \end{pmatrix} \quad (1)$$

$\mathsf{Setup}_2(\mathsf{gp}, p, G)$:
1: $\mathsf{td}_2 \leftarrow\!\!\$ \; \mathbb{Z}_p^*$
2: $H \leftarrow \mathsf{td}_2.G$
3: $\mathsf{cpp}_2 \leftarrow H$
4: **return** cpp_2

$\mathsf{KeyGen}_2(\mathsf{cpp}, \mathsf{pk}_0, \mathsf{sk}_0)$:
5: $(\mathsf{gp}, p, G, H) \leftarrow \mathsf{cpp}$
6: $Z \leftarrow \mathsf{pk}_0$
7: $(x, y, z) \leftarrow \mathsf{sk}_0$
8: $r_x, r_y \leftarrow\!\!\$ \; \mathbb{Z}_p$
9: $C_x \leftarrow xG + r_x H$
10: $C_y \leftarrow yG + r_y H$

11: $\rho_z \leftarrow\!\!\$ \; \mathbb{Z}_p$
12: $\Gamma_z \leftarrow \rho_z G$
13: $\varepsilon \leftarrow \mathsf{Hash}(G, H, Z, \Gamma_z)$
14: $a_z \leftarrow \rho_z + \varepsilon z g$
15: $\mathsf{sk}_2 \leftarrow (r_x, r_y)$
16: $\mathsf{pk}_2 \leftarrow (C_x, C_y, \varepsilon, a_z)$
17: **return** $(\mathsf{pk}_2, \mathsf{sk}_2)$

$\mathsf{Verify}_2(\mathsf{cpp}, \mathsf{pk})$:
18: $(\mathsf{gp}, p, G, H) \leftarrow \mathsf{cpp}$
19: $(Z, C_x, C_y, \varepsilon, a_z) \leftarrow \mathsf{pk}$
20: $\Gamma_z \leftarrow a_z G - \varepsilon Z$
21: **return** $1_{\varepsilon = \mathsf{Hash}(G,H,Z,\Gamma_z)}$

Fig. 6. Initialization of Π_2.

where $\rho = -(r_x + b r_y + \mu)$ and $w = x + by + t_S z$. The proof follows standard NIZK techniques, with (generalized) Schnorr proof [19], OR proof [10], and Fiat-Shamir transform [13].

We will use two properties of Π_2: that we can simulate the proof on any entry by programming the random oracle, and that we have a straightline extractor for (x, y, z, b, d) in the generic group model. We will prove these properties in the security analysis.

To construct Prove, we merge this OR proof with the AND proofs with statement given in Eq. 1 and we transform into a non-interactive proof. We formally define the algorithms in Π_2 below.

Prove. The algorithm $\mathsf{Prove}(b, d, \mathsf{sk}_0, \mathsf{sk}_2; U, V, t_S, T, \mathsf{cpp}, \mathsf{pk})$ parses different elements, picks μ, sets $C = b C_y + \mu H$, $d' = -\frac{1}{d}$, $\rho = -(r_x + b r_y + \mu)$, and $w = x + by + t_S z$.

The issuer (prover) picks $e_{1-b}, a_{1-b}, r_\mu, r_d, r_\rho, r_w$ at random and computes $C_b = r_\mu H$, $C_{1-b} = a_{1-b} H - e_{1-b}(C - (1 - b)C_y)$,

$$\begin{pmatrix} C_d \\ C_\rho \\ C_w \end{pmatrix} = r_d \begin{pmatrix} U \\ V \\ V \end{pmatrix} + r_\rho \begin{pmatrix} 0 \\ H \\ 0 \end{pmatrix} + r_w \begin{pmatrix} 0 \\ 0 \\ G \end{pmatrix}$$

$e = \mathsf{Hash}(G, H, C_x, C_y, Z, U, V, t_S, T, C, C_0, C_1, C_d, C_\rho, C_w)$, $e_b = e - e_{1-b}$, $a_b = r_\mu + e_b \mu$, and $(a_d, a_\rho, a_w) = (r_d, r_\rho, r_w) + e(d', \rho, w)$. Finally, the output is

$$\pi = (C, e_0, e_1, a_0, a_1, a_d, a_\rho, a_w)$$

Verify. The algorithm $\mathsf{Verify}(\pi, U, V, t_S, T, \mathsf{cpp}, \mathsf{pk})$ parses π, cpp, and pk, computes $C_0 = a_0 H - e_0 C$, $C_1 = a_1 H - e_1(C - C_y)$, $e = e_0 + e_1$,

$$\begin{pmatrix} C_d \\ C_\rho \\ C_w \end{pmatrix} = a_d \begin{pmatrix} U \\ V \\ V \end{pmatrix} + a_\rho \begin{pmatrix} 0 \\ H \\ 0 \end{pmatrix} + a_w \begin{pmatrix} 0 \\ 0 \\ G \end{pmatrix} + e \begin{pmatrix} G \\ C_x + C + t_S Z + T \\ T \end{pmatrix}$$

then verifies $e = \mathsf{Hash}(G, H, C_x, C_y, Z, U, V, t_S, T, C, C_0, C_1, C_d, C_\rho, C_w)$.

5   Performance

Implementation. We implemented our construction as given in Fig. 5 in Rust (version 1.66.0). We use the Ristretto group using curve25519-dalek library. We use RistrettoBasePointTable struct (which is a precomputed table for multiplications with the group generator G) to accelerate the scalar multiplications (PMBT implementation does *not* use these tables). We use two of these tables: one for G and one for H which requires 60 KB of memory for constant time cryptography and up to 4 times speed up. For OR proofs and verification, we did *not* rely on any external library, meaning we implemented it in pure Rust. We did *not* use multi-scalar multiplication. It is available at https://github.com/Microsoft/MacTok.

We benchmarked the implementation on a machine with Intel(R) i7-1185G7 3.00GHz CPU. Our benchmarks excludes the key generation (because it is generated only once for all). They include client blinded message generation, server's computation of MACs (blindly, along with the proof Π_2.Prove), client's unblinding (along with the Π_2.Verify$_2$), and server's redemption. It takes 1.3 ms whereas PMBT takes 1.6 ms for the same operations[7]. We note that we disabled SIMD optimizations (which allows curve25519-dalek to run faster curve operations) in both ATHM and PMBT due to the unstable version (1.66.0-nightly) of the Rust compiler that does not allow building PMBT. When we run our ATHM protocol with SIMD optimization, we get 0.9 ms of running time.

Theoretical Complexity. We also computed the number of scalar multiplications to compare ATHM with PMBT and observed that ATHM computes 29 scalar multiplication whereas PMBT computes 31 multiplications in total, for benchmarked operations (client and server side computations including redemption along with the proof and verification).

In ATHM, the issuer computes 11 scalar multiplications during issuance (one for C, 7 for the proof, and 3 for the ATHM protocol). The client computes 17 scalar multiplications (one for $t_S Z$, 11 for the proof, and 5 for ATHM). The total is 28 multiplications.[8] Furthermore, the number of transmission is of 4 group elements (C in the proof and (T, U, V) in the proof) and 8 integers (t_S in ATHM and the 7 elements of π). The total is 12.[9] For redeem, the number of multiplications is 1 and token length is 3 (t, P, and Q). For key generation, the issuer computes 2 multiplications (1 for Z and 1 for pk$_2$) and the client computes 2 multiplications for the Π_2 verification. The public key contains 5 elements (1 for Z and 4 for pk$_2$).

As a comparison, in PMBT, for issuance, the issuer computes 12 multiplications in total and the client computes 15 multiplications. In total, the number

---

[7] PMBT code is available at https://github.com/mmaker/anonymous-tokens.

[8] In this count, we took the computation of $(1 - b)C_y$ as free. Furthermore, the computation of $r_d V$ and $a_d V$ are done twice but count for a single operation.

[9] By setting $t_S = $ Hash(U), the issuer would not have to send t_S any longer and save the transmission of one $\mathbb{Z}_p$ element.

of multiplications is 27 for issuance. The number of transmissions is 2 group elements and 7 scalars. The total is 9. The redemption needs 4 multiplication with a token length 2 group elements. For key generation, the issuer computes 4 multiplication. The public key contains 4 elements.

We provide a complexity comparison in Table 1. We compute the number of scalar multiplications for both participants during issuance, and the amount of communication between them ($\mathbb{G}$ stands for group elements, $\mathbb{Z}_p$ stands for integers, and h stands for hashes), and the same for redeem. We added KVAC reduced to two attributes t and b, as presented in the full version of this paper [12]. Note that PP does not have hidden bit metadata, PMBT uses a weaker PMB security notion, and KVAC does not ensure PMB security.

Table 1. Complexity comparison

	Issuance			Redemption		Total	
	Client	Server	Comm.	Server	Comm.	Comp.	Comm.
ATHM	17×	11×	$4\mathbb{G} + 7\mathbb{Z}_p$	1×	$2\mathbb{G} + 1\mathbb{Z}_p$	29×	$6\mathbb{G} + 8\mathbb{Z}_p$
PP	2×	7×	$2\mathbb{G} + 1\mathbb{Z}_p + 1h$	1×	$1\mathbb{G} + 1h$	10×	$3\mathbb{G} + 1\mathbb{Z}_p + 2h$
PMBT	15×	12×	$2\mathbb{G} + 7\mathbb{Z}_p$	4×	$2\mathbb{G} + 1\mathbb{Z}_p$	31×	$4\mathbb{G} + 8\mathbb{Z}_p$
KVAC	35×	30×	$7\mathbb{G} + 12\mathbb{Z}_p$	1×	$2\mathbb{G} + 1\mathbb{Z}_p$	66×	$9\mathbb{G} + 13\mathbb{Z}_p$
BLOR	11×	7×	$5\mathbb{G} + 6\mathbb{Z}_p$	6×	$3\mathbb{G} + 4\mathbb{Z}_p$	24×	$8\mathbb{G} + 10\mathbb{Z}_p$

We also include BLOR [2] (that we named from the initials of the authors). This protocol has a different model: public verifiability but hidden metadata. This means that anyone can check whether a token hides a hidden bit but only the issuer can determine which bit is hidden. Besides, the issuance protocol has an additional move. So the protocol implies that the issuer is a stateful server.

6   Security Proof for **ATHM** in the Generic Group Model

We consider ATHM as specified in Sect. 4, i.e. with MACGGM, no T_{ext}, and with the nonce t and private metadata bit b attributes. (See the full version of this paper [12] for T_{ext} and other options.) Considering more attributes would work the same. We prove OMUF, 2-UNLINK, and PMB security in the generic group and random oracle models. The security of MACGGM without generic groups is an open problem, so the GGM seems to be unavoidable here. It also helps to build a straightline extractor for Π_2 (in UNLINK). The random oracle is used in the simulation of Π_2 (in OMUF and PMB) and in the soundness of Π_2 (in UNLINK).

We first discuss about the Generic Group Model (GGM). We adopt the model by Maurer [16] which models a lower-level interface to the generic group. In this model, all group operations are outsourced to an external oracle which also keeps the group element values in registers which cannot be read by the adversary. Initially, the setup GGMSetup sets a register Mem[1] set to a "base" group element from the setup: the generator G. Other registers $\mathsf{Mem}[\cdot]$ are initialized to 0. These registers are given an address that the adversary or the game can use. The adversary uses addresses as references when a group operation is requested but never sees the element value itself. Actually, the oracle only computes subtractions GGMSub (from which we can do additions, scalar multiplications, inversion, and get the neutral element) and comparisons GGMCmp (whether or not the group elements referred to by two addresses are equal):

Oracle $\mathsf{GGMSetup}(\lambda)$:
1: $\mathsf{Setup}_0(1^\lambda) \to (\mathsf{gp}, p, G)$
2: initialize $\mathsf{Mem}[\cdot] = 0$
3: $\mathsf{Mem}[1] \leftarrow G$
4: **return** p

Oracle $\mathsf{GGMSub}(i, j, k)$:
5: $\mathsf{Mem}[k] \leftarrow \mathsf{Mem}[i] - \mathsf{Mem}[j]$
6: **return**

Oracle $\mathsf{GGMCmp}(i, j)$:
7: **return** $1_{\mathsf{Mem}[i]=\mathsf{Mem}[j]}$

Clearly, the only oracle leaking information about group element values is the comparison oracle GGMCmp. The main task of the proof is to simulate this oracle to reduce it to a trivial game.

The Maurer generic group model [16] does not allow to efficiently hash group elements or to build dictionaries with group elements as a key, which is essential in generic algorithms such as Pollard Rho or Baby-Step Giant-Step. Managing to do so essentially reduces to simulating the original Shoup generic group model [20]. In the Shoup model, the adversary has access to the *encryption* of the group element values and can interact with an oracle to subtract encrypted elements. An ideal deterministic encryption is set up at the beginning of the game. To simulate the Shoup model with q_{sub} calls to the subtraction oracle, we need $q_{\mathsf{GGMCmp}} = \frac{q_{\mathsf{sub}}(q_{\mathsf{sub}}-1)}{2}$ calls to GGMCmp.

Overview of our proofs in GGM. In our security proofs, we need to distinguish registers which are visible by the adversary from others which are used by the game or other oracles. For that, we imagine an interface between the GGM oracles and a querier who is either the game/oracles or the adversary. The interface controls access privileges, depending on whether the query comes from the adversary or not. For convenience, we partition the memory Mem into three arrays of registers: base elements $\mathsf{Base}[\cdot]$, working registers $R[\cdot]$ for the adversary, and private registers $\mathsf{Rpriv}[\cdot]$ for the game/oracles. $\mathsf{GGMSub}(i, j, k)$ queries which are from the game or oracles should use a k address pointing to the Rpriv array. The interface would make the i address of $\mathsf{Mem}[i]$ correspond to a register address i' in one of the three arrays, depending on i, and likewise for $\mathsf{Mem}[j]$. For instance, the partition could be defined by address i corresponding to the register at address $\lfloor \frac{i}{3} \rfloor$ in one of the three arrays, depending on $i \bmod 3$.

Elements which are new for the adversary (in the sense that they are provided by the game or oracles) are stored in the Base array. Namely, setup stores $\mathsf{Base}[1] = G$ at the beginning of the game. A variable $\dim$ keeps the number of assigned base elements (i.e. $\dim = 1$ after setup). The Rpriv array is not accessible by the adversary (i.e., the interface does not allow a $\mathsf{GGMSub}(i, j, k)$

or GGMCmp(i, j) query from the adversary with any input address i, j, k corresponding to Rpriv). The Base array is a write-once array which is readable but not writable except by a new Reveal(i) system call (i.e. the inputs i and j in any GGMSub(i, j, k) or GGMCmp(i, j) query can point to the Base array, but not k). The new system call Reveal(i), which is *not* accessible by the adversary, increments the value of dim and assigns Base[dim] to Mem[i]. The idea is that Mem[i] corresponds to a Rpriv[i'] result from a computation by the game/oracles which should be returned to the adversary. Hence, Reveal is the only access which is writing inside Base. It is write-once: we make sure that elements are not overwritten. So we have dim "base" elements in the Base array. Actually, "base" should be understood in the sense of linear algebra: it is intended that every element in Base are "linearly free". Any vanishing linear combination would imply solving a discrete logarithm problem.

The adversary can work in the $R[\cdot]$ array and can read in the Base[$\cdot$] array. Given an adversary $\mathcal{A}$ in this model, we can define another adversary $\mathcal{B}$ who does the same as $\mathcal{A}$ but follows step by step the oracles queries made by $\mathcal{A}$ to GGMSub in order to express every $R[i']$ as a known linear combination of the base elements. Initially, $\mathcal{B}$ defines vectors Vec[$\cdot$] from $\mathbb{Z}^\infty$ (i.e., sequences of eventually null integers, but only the first dim coordinates can be nonzero) which are initialized to the zero vector. Upon a query GGMSub(i, j, k) by $\mathcal{A}$, $\mathcal{B}$ forwards the query and does an additional task: first, it defines vectors v_i and v_j corresponding to input i and j. If address i is pointing to $R[i']$, we define $v_i = \text{Vec}[i']$. If address i is pointing to Base[i'], we define $v_i = (0, \ldots, 0, 1, 0, \ldots)$ with 1 at coordinate i'. The same is done with v_j. Note that k must point to some $R[k']$. Hence, $\mathcal{B}$ affects Vec[k'] $\leftarrow (v_i - v_j) \bmod p$. With these operations, we easily prove by induction that at every step of the game, we have

$$R[i'] = \sum_{\ell=1}^{\text{dim}} \text{Vec}[i']_\ell \cdot \text{Base}[\ell]$$

So, from now on, we assume without loss of generality that all adversaries follow this approach to express group elements as a linear combination of "base" elements. We call *linearization* the transform of $\mathcal{A}$ to $\mathcal{B}$.

When the server is modelled by the game, the base elements consist of G and H from setup, Z, C_x, and C_y from key generation, and every (U, V) pair returned by the issuer, as well as a C value from π.

In the next transform, which we call *algebraic transform*, each secret scalar value such as td_2, x, y, z, r_x, r_y, d_i, etc. are associated to a formal variable $\bar{\text{td}}_2$, $\bar{x}$ and so on. Let Var be the tuple of variables and Val be the corresponding tuple of scalar values. Each base element Base[ℓ] will be associated to a multivariate scalar function $P_\ell^{\text{Base}}(\text{Var})$ satisfying the fundamental property that Base[ℓ] $= P_\ell^{\text{Base}}(\text{Val}).G$. The function will be known by $\mathcal{B}$ (only Val remains unknown). Then, $\mathcal{B}$ will define a formal multivariate function

$$P_{i'}^R(\text{Var}) = \sum_{\ell=1}^{\text{dim}} \text{Vec}[i']_\ell \cdot P_\ell^{\text{Base}}(\text{Var})$$

and extend the fundamental property to $R[i'] = P_{i'}^R(\mathsf{Val}).G$ thanks to the linear expression. Those functions will appear to be low-degree polynomials. The goal of this transformation is to be able to simulate OCmp by simply comparing the polynomials. The simulation is not perfect because some polynomials may be different and still evaluate to the same scalar, but this will occur with negligible probability thanks to the Schwartz-Zippel lemma.

6.1 OMUF Security in GGM and ROM

Theorem 1. *For every $\mathcal{A}$ playing OMUF in the generic group and random oracle models and making n oracle calls to $\mathcal{O}_{\mathsf{sign}}$, if Π_2 is perfectly simulatable, we have*

$$\mathsf{Adv}^{\mathsf{OMUF}} \leq (2(n+1+q_{\mathcal{O}_{\mathsf{read}}}) + q_{\mathsf{GGMCmp}} + 1) \times \frac{n+2}{p} + \frac{n}{p} + \frac{q_{\mathsf{Hash}}}{p^6}$$

where n, $q_{\mathcal{O}_{\mathsf{read}}}$, q_{GGMCmp}, and q_{Hash} are the number of queries to $\mathcal{O}_{\mathsf{sign}}$, $\mathcal{O}_{\mathsf{read}}$, GGMCmp, and to the random oracle.

By doing q_{GGMCmp} queries, the adversary can compute the discrete logarithm z of Z with success probability q_{GGMCmp}/p. Then, with $n = 1$ query, the adversary gets one valid token (b, t, P, Q). For any δ, the token $(b, t + \delta, P, Q + \delta z P)$ is valid too. Thus, the OMUF game succeeds with advantage q_{GGMCmp}/p. Hence, our bound is tight.

Proof. We consider an adversary $\mathcal{A}$ playing the OMUF game. Without loss of generality, we assume that $\mathcal{A}$ either aborts, or returns (b_j, t_j, P_j, Q_j) tuples which are all valid, with pairwise different t_j, same $b_j = b$, and the total number equals to $n_b + 1$.

Eliminating π. Before applying the GGM transforms, we first reduce to a game Γ_1 where $\mathcal{O}_{\mathsf{sign}}$ no longer computes a proof π. Instead, a proof

$$\pi = (C, e_0, e_1, a_0, a_1, a_d, a_\rho, a_w)$$

is simulated by the adversary. As only the adversary needs to query the random oracle, this oracle can be simulated by the adversary by lazy sampling. This gives the opportunity to program the oracle too.

To simulate the proof, the adversary picks $\mathcal{V} = (C, e_0, e_1, a_0, a_d, a_1, a_\rho, a_w)$ in $\mathbb{G} \times \mathbb{Z}_p^7$ uniformly at random. After selecting π, the adversary can follow the $\Pi_2.\mathsf{Verify}$ algorithm to compute $C_0, C_1, e, C_d, C_\rho, C_w$. Then, the adversary forms the input to the random oracle

$$q = (G, H, C_x, C_y, Z, U, V, t_S, T, C, C_0, C_1, C_d, C_\rho, C_w)$$

If q is already queried to Hash, the simulation fails and the game aborts. However, since π was randomly picked, this should happen with probability limited to $\frac{q_{\mathsf{Hash}}}{p^6}$.

In the way the normal proof is generated (see Subsect. 4.3), what is randomly selected is $\mathcal{W} = (\mu, e_{1-b}, a_{1-b}, r_\mu, r_d, r_\rho, r_w, e)$ where $e = \mathsf{Hash}(q)$, but there is a one-to-one mapping between $\mathcal{V}$ and $\mathcal{W}$. So, π is well distributed but the link with the random oracle is missing. Since $\mathsf{Hash}(q)$ was not queried before, the adversary can program the random oracle with $\mathsf{Hash}(q) = e$. Hence, the proof becomes valid. Except in the failure case, the proof is perfect.

$$\mathsf{Adv}^{\mathsf{OMUF}} \leq \mathsf{Adv}^{\Gamma_1} + \frac{q_{\mathsf{Hash}}}{p^6}$$

Finally, oracles no longer use H, C_x, C_y. We can reduce to a game where Setup_2 and KeyGen_2 are skipped. The adversary can run them and select H, C_x, and C_y randomly. This simulation is perfect. Hence we can now assume that the remaining Γ^1 game applies to a variant of ATHM with no H, C_x, C_y, and π.

In the ith query to $\mathcal{O}_{\mathsf{sign}}$, we let $(b, \mathsf{query}) = (b_i, T_i)$ denote the input and $(U_i, V_i, t_{S,i})$ denote the output.

Uniform secret values. Our next transform consists of modifying the game Γ_1 into a game Γ_2 in which y and z in KeyGen and every d in $\mathcal{O}_{\mathsf{sign}}$ queries are uniformly selected in $\mathbb{Z}_p$ instead of $\mathbb{Z}_p^*$. The failure case is when one random selection draws zero. By using the difference lemma, we obtain

$$\mathsf{Adv}^{\Gamma_1} \leq \mathsf{Adv}^{\Gamma_2} + \frac{n+2}{p}$$

GGM transforms. We apply the linearization transform in the GGM with base elements $(G, Z, (U_i, V_i)_i)$. For each group element $A = R[i']$, the adversary gets a vector $\mathsf{Vec}[i'] = (a_G, a_Z, (a_{U_i}, a_{V_i})_i, 0, 0, \ldots)$ such that

$$A = a_G.G + a_Z.Z + \sum_i (a_{U_i}.U_i + a_{V_i}.V_i)$$

The adversary has access to group elements in $R[\cdot]$ and $\mathsf{Base}[\cdot]$. For each of those element, the adversary knows a corresponding vector which we denote by Vec_A.

We then apply the algebraic transform in the GGM with the secret scalar values $\mathsf{Val} = (x, y, z, (d_i)_i)$ corresponding to the formal variables $\mathsf{Var} = (\bar{x}, \bar{y}, \bar{z}, (\bar{d}_i)_i)$. We recursively define the polynomials $P_\ell^{\mathsf{Base}}(\mathsf{Var})$ and $P_{i'}^R(\mathsf{Var})$. For convenience, we denote $\mathsf{Pol}_A(\mathsf{Var})$ the polynomial associated to each group element A for which the adversary has access. Clearly, we can set $\mathsf{Pol}_G(\mathsf{Var}) = 1$, $\mathsf{Pol}_Z(\mathsf{Var}) = \bar{z}$, $\mathsf{Pol}_{U_i}(\mathsf{Var}) = \bar{d}_i$ to ensure the fundamental property for these base elements. To define $\mathsf{Pol}_{V_i}(\mathsf{Var})$, we assume that $\mathsf{Pol}_{T_i}(\mathsf{Var})$ is defined (it is by linear combination of previous base elements) and we define

$$\mathsf{Pol}_{V_i}(\mathsf{Var}) = \bar{d}_i(\bar{x} + b_i\bar{y} + t_{S,i}\bar{z}) + \bar{d}_i.\mathsf{Pol}_{T_i}(\mathsf{Var})$$

By induction, for every group element A which is accessible by the adversary, we have $A = \mathsf{Pol}_A(\mathsf{Val}).G$. The formal polynomial Pol_A is known by the adversary but Val remains secret.

We prove by induction the following fact.

Fact 1. *For each A accessible by the adversary after q queries to $\mathcal{O}_{\text{sign}}$, the Pol_A polynomial has total degree bounded by $q + 1$. Furthermore, every partial degree is bounded by 1. Monomials are square-free.*

Indeed, after $q = 0$ queries, the largest degree is for $\text{Pol}_Z(\text{Var}) = \bar{z}$. Making a new query to $\mathcal{O}_{\text{sign}}$ multiplies $\text{Pol}_{T_i}(\text{Var})$ by a fresh $\bar{d}_i$ and adds a degree-2 polynomial $\bar{d}_i.(\bar{x} + b_i\bar{y} + t_{S,i}\bar{z})$.

We can now use out GGM transforms to start the simulation of the GGMCmp oracle. First observe that queries to this oracle are only made by the adversary, and by the game calling $< AT.\text{ReadBit}$ either in the $\mathcal{O}_{\text{read}}$ or in the final verification of the forged tokens. By abuse of notation we define the polynomials associated to A and B in the query (A, B) to the oracle by the game. For a token (P, Q), which is provided by the adversary, we have $\text{Pol}_A(\text{Var}) = \text{Pol}_Q(\text{Var})$ and $\text{Pol}_B(\text{Var}) = (\bar{x} + b\bar{y} + t\bar{z})\text{Pol}_P(\text{Var})$, with b and t provided by the adversary.

If the call to the comparison oracle is made by the adversary, the polynomials have degree bounded by $q + 1$ so we obtain the result. Otherwise, the call must come from the usage of AT.ReadBit in either the game of the $\mathcal{O}_{\text{read}}$ oracle, which multiply a degree-$(q+1)$-bounded polynomial by a degree-1 polynomial $\bar{x} + b\bar{y} + t\bar{z}$. So, the degree is bounded by $q + 2$. The values in Val are uniform in $\mathbb{Z}_p$. By using the Schwartz-Zippel lemma and the bound on the degree of polynomials, we have the following fact.

Fact 2. *Let q be the number of $\mathcal{O}_{\text{sign}}$ queries before an input (A, B) is presented for the first time to a comparison oracle. Except with a probability bounded by $\frac{q+2}{p}$, we have $A = B$ if and only if $\text{Pol}_A = \text{Pol}_B$.*

The adversary, game, or $\mathcal{O}_{\text{read}}$ oracle can simulate that comparison oracle by checking equality between $\text{Pol}_A = \text{Pol}_B$. Hence, by induction, using hybrids, we reduce to a game Γ_3 where no access to the comparison oracle is made, and for every final (b, t, P, Q) output, we have $\text{Pol}_Q(\text{Var}) = (\bar{x} + b\bar{y} + t\bar{z})\text{Pol}_P(\text{Var})$ (in winning cases). The total number of comparisons is bounded by $2(n + 1 + q_{\mathcal{O}_{\text{read}}}) + q_{\text{GGMCmp}}$, where $q_{\mathcal{O}_{\text{read}}}$ is the number of calls to $\mathcal{O}_{\text{read}}$ by the adversary and q_{GGMCmp} is the number of calls to the comparison by the adversary. We obtain

$$|\text{Adv}^{\Gamma_2} - \text{Adv}^{\Gamma_3}| \leq (2(n + 1 + q_{\mathcal{O}_{\text{read}}}) + q_{\text{GGMCmp}}) \times \frac{n+2}{p}$$

In Γ_3, no query to GGMCmp is made. So no information about Mem leaks. Hence, secret values become useless and the game becomes linear.

Analyzing the linear game. We now focus on one of the $n_b + 1$ final (b, t, P, Q) produced by $\mathcal{A}$ in winning cases. Since the tokens are assumed to be valid and thanks to our previous transforms, we know that $\text{Pol}_Q(\text{Var}) = (\bar{x} + b\bar{y} + t\bar{z})\text{Pol}_P(\text{Var})$. $\mathcal{A}$ is only making scalar linear combinations of G, Z, and the U_i and V_i. We write

$$P = a_G.G + a_Z.Z + \sum_i (a_{U_i}.U_i + a_{V_i}.V_i)$$

$$Q = b_G.G + b_Z.Z + \sum_i (b_{U_i}.U_i + b_{V_i}.V_i)$$

$$= (x + by + tz)P$$

Thanks to Fact 1, the partial degree of Pol_Q in $\bar{z}$ is bounded by 1. We can see from the last equation $\mathsf{Pol}_Q = \mathsf{Pol}_P \times (\bar{x} + b\bar{y} + t\bar{z})$ that $a_Z = 0$.

Pol_P has constant term a_G. From the last equation, Pol_Q has a_G as a coefficient of monomial $\bar{x}$. However, no monomial $\bar{x}$ can appear in the linear expression of Pol_Q. (For instance, Pol_{V_i} is always a multiple of $\bar{d}_i$.) Hence, $a_G = 0$.

Similarly, $\bar{x} + b\bar{y} + t\bar{z}$ has no constant term so we must have $b_G = 0$.

By inspecting the monomial $\bar{z}$ we now obtain that $b_Z = 0$.

Hence,

$$P = \sum_i (a_{U_i}.U_i + a_{V_i}.V_i)$$

$$Q = \sum_i (b_{U_i}.U_i + b_{V_i}.V_i)$$

$$= (x + by + tz)P$$

Given a polynomial and a variable $\bar{u}$, we say that $\bar{u}$ appears if the partial degree in $\bar{u}$ is at least 1. We have the following fact.

Fact 3. $\bar{d}_i$ appears in Pol_P if and only if it appears in Pol_Q.

Since the partial degree of Pol_Q in $\bar{x}$ is at most 1 due to Fact 1, the partial degree of Pol_P in $\bar{x}$ must be zero. Hence, a monomial μ is in Pol_P if and only if the monomial $\bar{x}\mu$ is in Pol_Q.

In the ith oracle call to $\mathcal{O}_{\mathsf{sign}}$, we have

$$\mathsf{Pol}_{V_i} = \bar{d}_i(\bar{x} + b_i\bar{y}) + t_{S,i}\bar{d}_i\bar{z} + \bar{d}_i \times \mathsf{Pol}_{T_i}$$

with $t_{S,i}$ sampled as a fresh uniform scalar. Note that $\bar{d}_i$ cannot appear in Pol_{T_i} because it is formed before sampling d_i. Pol_{T_i} may have the monomial $\bar{z}$ (it is actually supposed to) but Pol_{T_i} is set before sampling $t_{S,i}$. Hence, except with probability $\frac{1}{p}$, the $\bar{d}_i\bar{z}$ monomial is present in Pol_{V_i}. We deduce what follows.

Fact 4. For any i, the monomial $\bar{d}_i\bar{z}$ has a nonzero coefficient in Pol_{V_i}, except with probability $\frac{1}{p}$.

We reduce to a game Γ_4 where $\bar{d}_i\bar{z}$ never has a zero coefficient in Pol_{V_i} for every i. We have

$$\mathsf{Adv}^{\Gamma_3} \leq \mathsf{Adv}^{\Gamma_4} + \frac{n}{p}$$

Fact 5. In Γ_4, among all group elements given to $\mathcal{A}$, the monomial $\bar{d}_i\bar{z}$ has a nonzero coefficient in Pol_{V_i} and only in Pol_{V_i}.

Indeed, even though it could be put in a Pol_{T_j} for $j > i$, the monomial would be multiplied by $\bar{d}_j$ and thus $\bar{d}_i\bar{z}$ would not appear as a standalone monomial in Pol_{V_j}. Coming back to the representation of a final P and Q, we deduce that $a_{V_i} = 0$ for every i (as we cannot have $\bar{d}_i\bar{z}^2$ in Pol_Q). By writing $\mathsf{Pol}_{U_i} = \bar{d}_i$, Pol_P is linear in every $\bar{d}_i$. This implies that no monomial in a final Pol_Q can be divisible by any $\bar{d}_i\bar{d}_{i'}$.

We have $\mathsf{Pol}_{V_i} = (\bar{x} + b_i\bar{y} + t_{S,i}\bar{z})\bar{d}_i + \bar{d}_i\mathsf{Pol}_{T_i}$. For every i such that $b_{V_i} \neq 0$, we deduce that no $\bar{d}_{i'}$ appear in Pol_{T_i}. Hence, for every i such that $b_{V_i} \neq 0$, we have that T_i must be a known linear combination of G and Z. We write $T_i = t_{C,i}Z + r_iG$. Hence, $\mathsf{Pol}_{V_i} = \bar{d}_i(\bar{x} + b_i\bar{y} + (t_{C,i} + t_{S,i})\bar{z})$. By writing $t_i = t_{C,i} + t_{S,i}$, we have

$$\mathsf{Pol}_P = \sum_i a_{U_i}.\bar{d}_i$$

$$\mathsf{Pol}_Q = \sum_i (b_{U_i} + b_{V_i}(\bar{x} + b_i\bar{y} + t_i\bar{z} + r_i))\bar{d}_i$$

$$= \mathsf{Pol}_P \times (\bar{x} + b\bar{y} + t\bar{z}))$$

By inspecting $\bar{d}_i$ we can further see that we must have $b_{U_i} = -b_{V_i}r_i$ and $a_{U_i} = b_{V_i}$. Hence, $P = \sum_i a_{U_i}U_i$ and $Q = \sum_i a_{U_i}(V_i - r_iU_i)$.

We say that the ith query is well formed if Pol_{T_i} is a linear combination of Pol_G and Pol_Z (i.e. that Pol_{T_i} is a polynomial in $\bar{z}$ with degree bounded by 1: $\mathsf{Pol}_{T_i} = t_{C,i}\bar{z} + r_i$). For each well formed query we can define $t_i = t_{C,i} + t_{S,i}$. It follows that for every i such that $a_{U_i} \neq 0$, we have that the ith query is well formed and that $b_i = b$ and $t_i = t$. This proves that for any valid (b, t, P, Q), (P, Q) is a known linear combination of all $(U_i, V_i - r_iU_i)$ for well-formed queries satisfying $(b, t) = (b_i, t_i)$. Since P is nonzero, there exists i such that the ith query is well formed and $(b, t) = (b_i, t_i)$. Hence, the number of pairwise different t cannot exceed n_b. We deduce there is no winning case in Γ_4.

We can wrap up by collecting all Adv overheads to get an upper bound for $\mathsf{Adv}^{\mathsf{OMUF}}$.   □

6.2   UNLINK Security in GGM and ROM

Theorem 2. ATHM *is 2-UNLINK-secure in the generic group and random oracle models. More precisely, for any n, given an UNLINK$_n$-adversary $\mathcal{A}$, we have*

$$\mathsf{Adv}_{\mathcal{A}}^{\mathsf{UNLINK}} \leq \frac{2}{n} + \frac{3 + n + q_{\mathsf{GGMCmp}} + 3q_{\mathsf{Hash}}}{p}$$

where q_{GGMCmp} and q_{Hash} are the number of queries to the GGMCmp oracle and the random oracle.

Perfect 2-UNLINK security is when the advantage is bounded by $\frac{2}{n}$. By doing q_{GGMCmp} queries, the adversary can compute the discrete logarithm td_2 of H with success probability q_{GGMCmp}/p. If it succeeds, the adversary can select n pairwise different secrets x_i and use the secret (x_i, y, z) in the ith query. Thanks to td_2, the Pedersen commitment C_x can equivocate to a commitment to x_i for each i. So, the proof Π_2 can be made and verified. Then, each token can be uniquely recognized and the game succeeds with advantage 1. If the discrete logarithm fails, hiding the bit $b = i \bmod 2$ and a random guess works with advantage $\frac{2}{n}$. So, the UNLINK$_n$ game succeeds with advantage roughly $\frac{2}{n} + q_{\mathsf{GGMCmp}}/p$. Hence, our bound is tight.

Incidentally, if the setup is maliciously done and the server gets td_2, it is enough to run the above UNLINK attack. So unlinkability relies on a trusted setup. On the other hand, a malicious setup is only useful for a malicious server: it only harms unlinkability.

Proof. We start with an adversary $\mathcal{A} = (\mathcal{A}_1, \mathcal{A}_2, \mathcal{A}_3)$ playing the UNLINK$_n$ game. To win the game, there must exist $\mathcal{O}_{\text{sign}}$ queries. We assume that AT.ClientQuery verifies pk during at least one query and aborts if not valid. Hence, we could add after the selection of pk by $\mathcal{A}_1$ an explicit verification of pk with abort if not valid. So, we can assume without loss of generality that pk is valid.

ROM. We first reduce to a game Γ_1 in which for every verification of pk (right after $\mathcal{A}_1$ produces pk) and every final verification of π (in every AT.ClientFinal instance at the end of the game, i.e. excluding those in $\mathcal{O}_{\text{final}}$), the Hash query which is made to compute the challenge ε or e was done by the adversary before the verification. Clearly, if this is not the case, the probability that the corresponding verification succeeds is exactly $\frac{1}{p}$. Hence,

$$\text{Adv}_{\mathcal{A}}^{\text{UNLINK}} \leq \text{Adv}_{\mathcal{A}}^{\Gamma_1} + \frac{1+n}{p}$$

Hence, we will be able to discuss on *when* the query was done by the first time by the adversary, when the challenge was unknown and the input to the hash were committed.

GGM. We modify the $\mathcal{O}_{\text{final}}$ oracle so that it would return t_C, r, and c for the issuance session which is finalized and the token revealed. As it gives more information, the winning probability does not decrease. It further helps in the GGM transform by removing from the base elements the group elements provided by the client in the revealed sessions. Hence, we only take as base elements the values of G, H, and T_i from the $\mathcal{O}_{\text{query}}$ responses which have not been finalized. Note that the basis contains independent and uniform elements (with nonzero G and H). We apply the linearization with the remaining basis.

Next, we reduce to a game Γ_2 in which every group equation check in every verification of pk (right after $\mathcal{A}_1$ produces pk) and every group equation check in the final verifications of π (in every AT.ClientFinal instance at the end of the game) are replaced by their corresponding vectorial check. A failure case would give a non-trivial linear relation between base elements, which would solve the discrete logarithm problem. Such success happens with probability bounded by $\frac{q_{\text{GGMCmp}}+1}{p}$ in GGM [16].

$$\text{Adv}_{\mathcal{A}}^{\Gamma_1} \leq \text{Adv}_{\mathcal{A}}^{\Gamma_2} + \frac{1}{p} + \frac{q_{\text{GGMCmp}}+1}{p}$$

Extraction of the secret. We first extract x, r_x, y, r_y, z from $\mathcal{A}_1$ as follows. We use the generic group model and the linearization transform. In GGM, the base elements for $\mathcal{A}_1$ are G and H. So, the elements made by $\mathcal{A}_2$ such as C_x, C_y, and

Z have a linear expression in G and H. Such linearization step clearly extracts x, r_x, y, r_y, z, r_z such that $C_x = xG + r_xH$, $C_y = yG + r_yH$, and $Z = zG + r_zH$. We only have to prove that $r_z = 0$ except with negligible probability. When $r_z = 0$ we say that Z is *proportional* to G by abuse of language.

Thanks to the verification condition, we have $\varepsilon = \mathsf{Hash}(\mathsf{query})$ with $\mathsf{query} = (G, H, Z, \Gamma_z)$ and $\Gamma_z + \varepsilon Z = a_z G$. Due to the Γ_2 reduction, we deduce that $\Gamma_z + \varepsilon Z$ is proportional to G in the vectorial sense.

We reduce to a game Γ_3 in which for every hash query of form (G, H, A, B) by $\mathcal{A}_1$ with $B + \mathsf{Hash}(G, H, A, B)A$ proportional to G, then A and B are also proportional to G. We analyze the probability of the failure case. The first time (G, H, A, B) is queried to the random oracle, A and B are committed and the hash $\mathsf{Hash}(G, H, A, B)$ is random and uniform. Hence, the probability of the failure case is bounded by $\frac{1}{p}$. Hence

$$\mathsf{Adv}_{\mathcal{A}}^{\Gamma_2} \leq \mathsf{Adv}_{\mathcal{A}}^{\Gamma_3} + \frac{q_{\mathsf{Hash}}}{p}$$

In our case, $\Gamma_z + \mathsf{Hash}(G, H, Z, \Gamma_z)Z$ is proportional to G. Hence, both Z and Γ_z are proportional to G in Γ_3. In Γ_3, we can now assume that sk is extracted and that $(\mathsf{pk}, \mathsf{sk})$ is valid.

Extraction of b. For every $\mathsf{AT.ClientFinal}$ instance, the input resp from $\mathcal{A}_2$ parses as $\mathsf{resp} = (U, V, t_S, \pi)$ and $\pi_i = (C, e_0, e_1, a_0, a_1, a_d, a_\rho, a_w)$. Following the verification procedure of π defines $C_0, C_1, e, C_d, C_\rho, C_w$ and the query

$$q = (G, H, C_x, C_y, Z, U, V, t_S, T, C, C_0, C_1, C_d, C_\rho, C_w)$$

to Hash. We want to extract b and d from it.

Thanks to the verification condition, we have $e = \mathsf{Hash}(q)$ with $C_0 = a_0H - e_0C$ and $C_1 = a_1H - e_1(C - C_y)$. Due to the Γ_2 reduction, these last two relations hold in a vectorial sense.

We reduce to a game Γ_4 in which for every hash query of the form of q by $\mathcal{A}_2$ with neither C nor $C - C_y$ being proportional to H, with C_0 being a linear combination of H and C, and with C_1 being a linear combination of H and $C - C_y$, we have $\mathsf{Hash}(q) \neq e_0' + e_1'$ where $C_0 = a_0'H - e_0'C$ and $C_1 = a_1'H - e_1'(C - C_y)$ are the unique linear relations. Clearly, the failure case has probability bounded by $\frac{1}{p}$ for each Hash query. Hence

$$\mathsf{Adv}_{\mathcal{A}}^{\Gamma_3} \leq \mathsf{Adv}_{\mathcal{A}}^{\Gamma_4} + \frac{q_{\mathsf{Hash}}}{p}$$

In our case, we have $e = \mathsf{Hash}(q)$ with $C_0 = a_0H - e_0C$ and $C_1 = a_1H - e_1(C - C_y)$ and the query $\mathsf{Hash}(q)$ was made. So, either C or $C - C_y$ is proportional to H, which gives b. (If both C and $C - C_y$ are proportional to H, we select b arbitrarily.) In Γ_4, we can now assume that b and μ such that $C = bC_y + \mu H$ are extracted for each final $\mathsf{AT.ClientFinal}$ instance.

Extraction of (d', ρ, w). We continue the analysis of the AT.ClientFinal instance by observing that we must have

$$\begin{pmatrix} C_d \\ C_\rho \\ C_w \end{pmatrix} - e \begin{pmatrix} & G & \\ C_x + C & + t_S Z + T \\ & T & \end{pmatrix} \in \left\langle \begin{pmatrix} U \\ V \\ V \end{pmatrix}, \begin{pmatrix} 0 \\ H \\ 0 \end{pmatrix}, \begin{pmatrix} 0 \\ 0 \\ G \end{pmatrix} \right\rangle$$

in a vectorial sense, which we write $V_1 - eV_2 \in \langle V_3, V_4, V_5 \rangle$ for short, where $\langle V_3, V_4, V_5 \rangle$ denotes the linear span of V_3, V_4, V_5. We reduce to a game Γ_5 in which for every hash query of the form of q by $\mathcal{A}_2$ with $V_1 - \mathsf{Hash}(q)V_2 \in \langle V_3, V_4, V_5 \rangle$, then $V_2 \in \langle V_3, V_4, V_5 \rangle$. We analyze the probability of the failure case. Again, the probability of the failure case is bounded by $\frac{1}{p}$. Hence

$$\mathsf{Adv}_{\mathcal{A}}^{\Gamma_4} \leq \mathsf{Adv}_{\mathcal{A}}^{\Gamma_5} + \frac{q_{\mathsf{Hash}}}{p}$$

Since $V_1 - \mathsf{Hash}(q)V_2 \in \langle V_3, V_4, V_5 \rangle$ and $\mathsf{Hash}(q)$ was queried before verification, we deduce that $V_2 \in \langle V_3, V_4, V_5 \rangle$. Hence we can write $-V_2 = d'V_3 + \rho V_4 + wV_5$, which is Eq. 1. We easily deduce d such that $U = dG$ and $V = d((x + by + t_S z)G + T)$.

Information theoretic argument. The rest of the proof is an information theoretic argument for which complexities do not matter. Given $(x, y, z, T_i, U_i, V_i, t_{i,S}, \pi_i)$ we can uniquely determine b_i. The variables $t_{i,C}$ and r_i are uniform but linked by $T_i = t_{i,C} Z + r_i G$ and c_i is still independent and uniform. Since $t_i = t_{i,C} + t_{i,S}$ and $P_i = c_i U_i$, we have that $(t_i, P_i)|(x, y, z, T_i, U_i, V_i, t_{i,S}, \pi_i)$ is uniformly distributed as a pair composed of a scalar and a nonzero group element. Hence, whenever $\mathcal{A}_2$ returns $\mathcal{Q}$ and the list of resp_i, it determines the values of the b_i but the (t_i, P_i) to be released are still uniform. After permutation, $(t_{\sigma(i)}, P_{\sigma(i)}, Q_{\sigma(i)})$ has a value of $Q_{\sigma(i)}$ which is imposed by $Q_{\sigma(i)} = (x + b_{\sigma(i)} y + t_{\sigma(i)} z) P_{\sigma(i)}$ so brings $b_{\sigma(i)}$ as only information.

This reduces to the following game: the adversary chooses a list of bits $(b_i)_{i \in \mathcal{Q}}$ with $\#\mathcal{Q} \geq n$, the game selects a random i^* and a random permutation σ then provides b_{i^*} and $(b_{\sigma(i)})_{i \in \mathcal{Q}}$ to the adversary, and the adversary finally makes a guess i and win if and only if $i = i^*$. If the adversary puts n_0 zeros and n_1 ones, the adversary can only win with probability $\frac{1}{n_0}$ when it is a zero (which happens with probability $\frac{n_0}{n_0+n_1}$), and with probability $\frac{1}{n_1}$ when it is a one (which happens with probability $\frac{n_1}{n_0+n_1}$). Overall, the adversary wins with probability $\frac{2}{n_0+n_1}$ which is at most $\frac{2}{n}$ since $n_0 + n_1 = \#\mathcal{Q} \geq n$. $\qquad\square$

6.3   PMB Security in GGM and ROM

Theorem 3. *For every $\mathcal{A}$ playing* PMB *in the generic group model and making n oracle calls to $\mathcal{O}_{\mathsf{sign}}$, if Π_2 is perfectly simulatable, we have*

$$\mathsf{Adv}^{\mathsf{PMB}} \leq 2(2(n + 1 + q_{\mathcal{O}_{\mathsf{read}}}) + q_{\mathsf{GGMCmp}} + 1) \times \frac{n+2}{p} + \frac{q_{\mathsf{Hash}}}{p^6}$$

where $q_{\mathcal{O}_{\text{read}}}$, q_{GGMCmp}, *and* q_{Hash} *are the number of queries to* $\mathcal{O}_{\text{read}}$, GGMCmp, *and to the random oracle.*

Again, the bound is tight. By computing the logarithm of Z, an adversary can modify an existing valid token to make it a valid token with a chosen t. Two tokens with same t can be combined into a single token which is valid if and only if the hidden bits are equal. Then we have a similar attack as the one we presented on PMBT.

Proof. We now consider an adversary $\mathcal{A}$ playing the $\text{PMB}_{\bar{b}^*}$ game.

The only new element in the generic group model treatment is that there is a new variable $\bar{b}^*$ appearing in polynomials. This variable appears as soon as $\mathcal{A}$ queries $\mathcal{O}_{\text{chal}}$. It appears as a term of form $\text{Pol}_{V_{i^*}} = (\bar{x} + \bar{b}^*\bar{y} + t_{S,i^*}\bar{z} + \text{Pol}_{T_{i^*}})\bar{d}_{i^*}$, where i^* is the index number of the $\mathcal{O}$ query for the $\mathcal{O}_{\text{chal}}$ query.

We treat the variable $\bar{b}^*$ differently than others from Var (as $\bar{b}^*$ takes random values in $\{0,1\}$ instead of random values in $\mathbb{Z}_p$ like other variables.) For each polynomial $\text{Pol}_A(\bar{b}^*, \text{Var})$ in which $\bar{b}^*$ appears, we can make two partial evaluations $\text{Pol}_A(0, \text{Var})$ and $\text{Pol}_A(1, \text{Var})$ corresponding to $\bar{b}^* = 0$ and $\bar{b}^* = 1$. We obtain two polynomials with no $\bar{b}^*$ variable. Hence, this increase the number of polynomials by a factor at most 2.

We first proceed like for OMUF security with games Γ_1 to have no π in the return from the issuer and Γ_2 to sample secrets in $\mathbb{Z}_p$. The transition to Γ_3 to get rid of the GGMCmp oracle (and thus of the $\mathcal{O}_{\text{read}}$ and $\mathcal{O}_{\text{valid}}$ oracles) is also using hybrid arguments but is more complicated. Oracles are simulated in the order they are called. For the simulation of GGMCmp and $\mathcal{O}_{\text{read}}$ until the challenge is made, it works like for OMUF security. After the challenge is made, the $\text{GGMCmp}(A, B)$ made by the adversary are simulated by answering 1 if and only if there exists $\beta \in \{0,1\}$ such that $\text{Pol}_A - \text{Pol}_B$ vanishes in the partial evaluation $\bar{b}^* = \beta$. To simulate $\mathcal{O}_{\text{valid}}(t, P, Q)$ (which is the last one to use GGMCmp), the answer is 1 if and only if there exists $b, \beta \in \{0,1\}$ such that $\text{Pol}_Q - (\bar{x} + b\bar{y} + t\bar{z}) \times \text{Pol}_P$ vanishes in the partial evaluation $\bar{b}^* = \beta$. In the first case, we prove the following variant of Fact 2.

Fact 6. *Let q is the number of $\mathcal{O}_{\text{sign}}$ queries (including $\mathcal{O}_{\text{chal}}$) before an input (A, B) is presented for the first time to the GGMCmp oracle. We assume that the call is made by the adversary. Except with a probability bounded by $\frac{q+2}{p}$, we have $A = B$ if and only if $\text{Pol}_A(0, \text{Var}) = \text{Pol}_B(0, \text{Var})$ or $\text{Pol}_A(1, \text{Var}) = \text{Pol}_B(1, \text{Var})$.*

The direct implication works like in Fact 2 as the match happens for $\bar{b}^* = b^*$. We now want to show the converse implication: if $\text{Pol}_A - \text{Pol}_B$ vanishes for $\bar{b}^* = \beta$ with $\beta \in \{0,1\}$, then we want to prove $A = B$.

Thanks to the generic group model, the adversary knows a linear combination of provided group elements to obtain $A - B$. Let λ_i and μ_i be the coefficients of U_i and V_i respectively. We let i be the largest index such that $(\lambda_i, \mu_i) \neq (0,0)$. The partial derivative of Pol_{A-B} with respect to $\bar{d}_i$ is $\lambda_i + \mu_i(\bar{x} + b_i\bar{y} + t_{S,i}\bar{z} + \text{Pol}_{T_i})$ (with b_i replaced by $\bar{b}^*$ in the $i = i^*$ case). Since $\text{Pol}_{A-B}(\beta, \text{Var}) = 0$, the partial derivative vanishes for $\bar{b}^* = \beta$ too:

$$\lambda_i + \mu_i(\bar{x} + b_i\bar{y} + t_{S,i}\bar{z} + \mathsf{Pol}_{T_i}(\beta, \mathsf{Var})) = 0$$

The adversary knows how to express T_i as a linear combination of provided group elements. We notice that the monomials $\bar{x}$ and $\bar{b}^*\bar{x}$ are in no polynomial of any group element. So, there is no way to make a T_i such that $\mathsf{Pol}_{T_i}(\beta, \mathsf{Var})$ has a monomial $\bar{x}$. Hence, it cannot cancel $\bar{x}$. This implies $\mu_i = 0$ then $\lambda_i = 0$ which contradicts $(\lambda_i, \mu_i) \neq (0,0)$. We deduce that $A - B$ has no U_i and V_i as a component in the linear combination. Hence, it does not depend on b^* and the result is trivial: if $\mathsf{Pol}_A - \mathsf{Pol}_B$ vanishes for $\bar{b}^* = \beta$, it vanishes with the partial evaluation $\bar{b}^* = b^*$ too. Hence, we can apply Fact 2 and conclude. We can simulate the first GGMCmp oracle call, if it is made by the adversary. We now look at what happens it is made by $\mathcal{O}_{\mathsf{valid}}$.

To simulate $\mathcal{O}_{\mathsf{valid}}$, we use the following fact.

Fact 7. *Let q is the number of $\mathcal{O}_{\mathsf{sign}}$ queries (including $\mathcal{O}_{\mathsf{chal}}$) before a $\mathcal{O}_{\mathsf{valid}}(t, P, Q)$ call is made for the first time. We assume there is no GGMCmp call before. Except with a probability bounded by $\frac{q+2}{p}$, the oracle returns 1 if and only if there exists $b, \beta \in \{0,1\}$ such that $\mathsf{Pol}_Q(\beta, \mathsf{Var}) = (\bar{x}+b\bar{y}+t\bar{z})\mathsf{Pol}_P(\beta, \mathsf{Var})$.*

The direct implication uses Fact 2 with $\beta = b^*$ and the right b which makes (b, t, P, Q) valid. For the converse implication, we assume that the polynomial equality is verified for a given (b, β) pair of bits.

We let $a_{U_i}, a_{V_i}, b_{U_i}, b_{V_i}$ be the coefficients of U_i and V_i for P and of U_i and V_i for Q. Let $\lambda_i = b_{U_i} - (\bar{x}+b\bar{y}+t\bar{z})a_{U_i}$ and $\mu_i = b_{V_i} - (\bar{x}+b\bar{y}+t\bar{z})a_{V_i}$. Like in the previous case, let i be the largest index such that (λ_i, μ_i) is nonzero. The partial derivative of $\mathsf{Pol}_Q - (\bar{x} + b\bar{y} + t\bar{z})\mathsf{Pol}_P$ in terms of $\bar{d}_i$ is again $\lambda_i + \mu_i(\bar{x} + b_i\bar{y} + t_{S,i}\bar{z} + \mathsf{Pol}_{T_i})$ (with b_i replaced by $\bar{b}^*$ in the $i = i^*$ case). We know it vanishes when evaluated on $\bar{b}^* = \beta$. Clearly, a_{V_i} must be zero (otherwise, $\bar{x}^2$ appears and cannot vanish). The same argument about the monomial $\bar{x}$ and also about the monomial $\bar{y}$ implies that $(\bar{x} + b\bar{y})a_{U_i} = (\bar{x} + b_i\bar{y})b_{V_i}$. Hence,

$$\frac{\partial \mathsf{Pol}_\Delta}{\partial \bar{d}_i}(\bar{b}^*, \mathsf{Var}) = b_{U_i} + b_{V_i}\left((b_i - b)\bar{y} + (t_{S,i} - t)\bar{z} + \mathsf{Pol}_{T_i}(\bar{b}^*, \mathsf{Var})\right)$$

for $\Delta = Q - (x + by + tz)P$. The adversary also knows a linear combination of T_i in terms of the provided group elements. Let λ'_j and μ'_j be the coefficients of U_j and V_j and let j be the largest index for which they are nonzero. The second partial derivative gives

$$\frac{\partial^2 \mathsf{Pol}_{A-B}}{\partial \bar{d}_j\, \partial \bar{d}_i}(\bar{b}^*, \mathsf{Var}) = b_{U_i}\left(\lambda_j + \mu_j(\bar{x} + b_j\bar{y} + t_j\bar{z} + \mathsf{Pol}_{T_j}(\bar{b}^*, \mathsf{Var}))\right)$$

which should vanish for $\bar{b}^* = \beta$. The same argument than before shows that $\bar{x}$ cannot disappear. Hence, T_i cannot have components in U_j or V_j and does not depend on b^*.

Knowing that T_i has no component is any previous U_i of V_i, we can go to the second largest i such that (λ_i, μ_i) is nonzero and look at the partial derivative with respect to $\bar{d}_i$ (which we know does not appear in a subsequent $V_{i'}$). We obtain the same result that T_i does not have any component in U_j or V_j. We analyze like this all components in every (U_i, V_i) of $\mathsf{Pol}_Q - (\bar{x} + b\bar{y} + t\bar{z})\mathsf{Pol}_P$. Since it vanished on $\bar{b}^* = \beta$, we cannot have any other component. Hence

$$\mathsf{Pol}_Q - (\bar{x} + b\bar{y} + t\bar{z})\mathsf{Pol}_P = \sum_i \left(b_{U_i} + b_{V_i}\left((b_i - b)\bar{y} + (t_{S,i} - t)\bar{z} + \mathsf{Pol}_{T_i}(\bar{b}^*, \mathsf{Var})\right)\right)\bar{d}_i$$

with b_{i^*} to be replaced by $\bar{b}^*$. For all indices i of nonzero terms, we deduce that $b = b_i$ and T_i is or form $T_i = t_{C,i}Z + r_iG$. This boils down to

$$\mathsf{Pol}_Q - (\bar{x} + b\bar{y} + t\bar{z})\mathsf{Pol}_P = b_{V_{i^*}}(\bar{b}^* - b)\bar{y}\bar{d}_{i^*} + \sum_{i \neq i^*} b_{V_i}(b_i - b)\bar{y}\bar{d}_i$$

If $b_{V_{i^*}} = 0$, this vanishing for $\bar{b}^* = \beta$ implies vanishing for $\bar{b}^* = b^*$ too, so we can apply Fact 2 to deduce that $Q = (x + by + tz)P$ most of the cases. If $b_{V_{i^*}} \neq 0$, this vanishing for $\bar{b}^* = \beta$ implies $b = \beta$. We can then see that it vanishes for $\bar{b}^* = b^*$ and $b = b^*$ too. We apply Fact 2 to deduce that $Q = (x + \beta y + tz)P$ most of the cases.

Using hybrids, we obtain

$$|\Pr[\mathsf{PMB}_{b^*} \to 1] - \Pr[\Gamma_{3,b^*} \to 1]| \leq (2(n+1+q_{\mathcal{O}_{\text{read}}}) + q_{\mathsf{GGMCmp}} + 1) \times \frac{n+2}{p} + \frac{q_{\mathsf{Hash}}}{p^6}$$

In the game Γ_3, the oracles $\mathcal{O}_{\text{verify}}$, $\mathcal{O}_{\text{read}}$, and GGMCmp are not used any more.

After getting rid of $\mathcal{O}_{\text{verify}}$ and $\mathcal{O}_{\text{read}}$, we obtain a game in which no information about b^* is given to the adversary. Thus,

$$\Pr[\Gamma_{3,0} \to 1] = \Pr[\Gamma_{3,1} \to 1]$$

$$\square$$

7   Conclusion

In our work, we studied the anonymous tokens with hidden metadata bit from issuer to the verifier. We started our studies with a security weakness in a protocol from CRYPTO 2020 which is an extension of Privacy Pass from PoPETs 2018. The protocol is based on oblivious PRFs. We discussed the real-world implications of the security notions defined in their protocol and showed that such problems can be overcome with a new token protocol from algebraic MACs. We defined the security with more natural and strong notions.

We believe algebraic MACs suit better in anonymous tokens with hidden bit as a primitive. However, it is an open question to understand if there are other OPRFs or another new primitive that would help designing anonymous tokens with strong security and privacy guarantees.

Acknowledgements. We heartily thank Greg Zaverucha, Michele Orrù, and Nirvan Tyagi for the insightful discussions and fruitful comments on the early version of the paper. We are also very thankful to Kim Laine, Radames Cruz Moreno, and Wei Dai for their valuable time and help with the implementation of the protocols and benchmarks in Rust.

References

1. Baldimtsi, F., Lysyanskaya, A.: Anonymous credentials light. In: Sadeghi, A.-R., Gligor, V.D., Yung, M., editors, 2013 ACM SIGSAC Conference on Computer and Communications Security, CCS'13, pp. 1087–1098. ACM (2013)
2. Benhamouda, F., Lepoint, T., Orrù, M., Raykova, M.: Publicly verifiable anonymous tokens with private metadata bit. Cryptology ePrint Archive, Paper 2022/004 (2022). https://eprint.iacr.org/2022/004
3. Camenisch, J., Lysyanskaya, A.: An efficient system for non-transferable anonymous credentials with optional anonymity revocation. In: Pfitzmann, B. (ed.) EUROCRYPT 2001. LNCS, vol. 2045, pp. 93–118. Springer, Heidelberg (2001). https://doi.org/10.1007/3-540-44987-6_7
4. Camenisch, J., Lysyanskaya, A.: A signature scheme with efficient protocols. In: Cimato, S., Persiano, G., Galdi, C. (eds.) SCN 2002. LNCS, vol. 2576, pp. 268–289. Springer, Heidelberg (2003). https://doi.org/10.1007/3-540-36413-7_20
5. Chase, M., Meiklejohn, S., Zaverucha, G.: Algebraic MACs and keyed-verification anonymous credentials. In: Proceedings of the 2014 ACM SIGSAC Conference on Computer and Communications Security, CCS '14, pp. 1205–1216. Association for Computing Machinery (2014)
6. Chase, M., Meiklejohn, S., Zaverucha, G.: Algebraic MACs and keyed-verification anonymous credentials (2014). https://eprint.iacr.org/2013/516
7. Chase, M., Perrin, T., Zaverucha, G.: The signal private group system and anonymous credentials supporting efficient verifiable encryption, pp. 1445–1459. Association for Computing Machinery (2020)
8. Chase, M., Perrin, T., Zaverucha, G.: The signal private group system and anonymous credentials supporting efficient verifiable encryption (2020). https://eprint.iacr.org/2019/1416
9. Chaum, D.: Blind signatures for untraceable payments. In: Advances in Cryptology - CRYPTO. Springer International Publishing (1982)
10. Damgård, I.: On Σ-protocol (2010)
11. Davidson, A., Goldberg, I., Sullivan, N., Tankersley, G., Valsorda, F.: Privacy pass: bypassing internet challenges anonymously. In: PoPETs, pp. 164–180 (2018)
12. Betül Durak, F., Vaudenay, S., Chase, M.: Anonymous tokens with stronger metadata bit hiding from algebraic macs. Cryptology ePrint Archive, Paper 2022/1622 (2022). https://eprint.iacr.org/2022/1622
13. Fiat, A., Shamir, A.: How to prove yourself: practical solutions to identification and signature problems. In: Odlyzko, A.M. (ed.) CRYPTO 1986. LNCS, vol. 263, pp. 186–194. Springer, Heidelberg (1987). https://doi.org/10.1007/3-540-47721-7_12
14. Kreuter, B., Lepoint, T., Orrù, M., Raykova, M.: Anonymous tokens with private metadata bit (2020). https://eprint.iacr.org/2020/072
15. Kreuter, B., Lepoint, T., Orrù, M., Raykova, M.: Anonymous tokens with private metadata bit. In: Micciancio, D., Ristenpart, T. (eds.) CRYPTO 2020. LNCS, vol. 12170, pp. 308–336. Springer, Cham (2020). https://doi.org/10.1007/978-3-030-56784-2_11
16. Maurer, U.: Abstract models of computation in cryptography. In: Smart, N.P. (ed.) Cryptography and Coding 2005. LNCS, vol. 3796, pp. 1–12. Springer, Heidelberg (2005). https://doi.org/10.1007/11586821_1
17. Paquin, C., Zaverucha, G.: U-prove cryptographic specification v1.1 (Revision 3), December (2013). Released under the Open Specification Promise (http://www.microsoft.com/openspecifications/en/us/programs/osp/default.aspx)

18. Pedersen, T.P.: Non-interactive and information-theoretic secure verifiable secret sharing. In: Feigenbaum, J. (ed.) CRYPTO 1991. LNCS, vol. 576, pp. 129–140. Springer, Heidelberg (1992). https://doi.org/10.1007/3-540-46766-1_9
19. Schnorr, C.P.: Efficient identification and signatures for smart cards. In: Brassard, G. (ed.) CRYPTO 1989. LNCS, vol. 435, pp. 239–252. Springer, New York (1990). https://doi.org/10.1007/0-387-34805-0_22
20. Shoup, V.: Lower bounds for discrete logarithms and related problems. In: Fumy, W. (ed.) EUROCRYPT 1997. LNCS, vol. 1233, pp. 256–266. Springer, Heidelberg (1997). https://doi.org/10.1007/3-540-69053-0_18
21. Silde, T., Strand, M.: Anonymous tokens with public metadata and applications to private contact tracing. https://fc22.ifca.ai/preproceedings/40.pdf
22. Tessaro, S., Zhu, C.: Short pairing-free blind signatures with exponential security. In: Dunkelman, O., Dziembowski, S., editors, Advances in Cryptology - EUROCRYPT 2022, volume 13276 of Lecture Notes in Computer Science, pp. 782–811. Springer, Cham (2022). https://doi.org/10.1007/978-3-031-07085-3_27
23. Trust Tokens API. https://developer.chrome.com/docs/privacy-sandbox/trust-tokens/

New Paradigms and Foundations

Revisiting Time-Space Tradeoffs
for Function Inversion

Alexander Golovnev[1], Siyao Guo[2], Spencer Peters[3(✉)],
and Noah Stephens-Davidowitz[3]

[1] Georgetown University, Georgetown, USA
alexgolovnev@gmail.com
[2] NYU Shanghai, Shanghai, China
sg191@nyu.edu
[3] Cornell University, Ithaca, USA
sp2473@cornell.edu, noahsd@gmail.com

Abstract. We study the black-box function inversion problem, which is the problem of finding $x \in [N]$ such that $f(x) = y$, given as input some challenge point y in the image of a function $f : [N] \to [N]$, using T oracle queries to f *and* preprocessed advice $\sigma \in \{0,1\}^S$ depending on f. We prove a number of new results about this problem, as follows.

1. We show an algorithm that works for any T and S satisfying

$$TS^2 \cdot \max\{S, T\} = \widetilde{\Theta}(N^3) \,.$$

   In the important setting when $S < T$, this improves on the celebrated algorithm of Fiat and Naor [STOC, 1991], which requires $TS^3 \gtrsim N^3$. E.g., Fiat and Naor's algorithm is only non-trivial for $S \gg N^{2/3}$, while our algorithm gives a non-trivial tradeoff for any $S \gg N^{1/2}$. (Our algorithm and analysis are quite simple. As a consequence of this, we also give a self-contained and simple proof of Fiat and Naor's original result, with certain optimizations left out for simplicity.)

2. We observe that there is a very simple *non-adaptive* algorithm (i.e., an algorithm whose ith query x_i is chosen based entirely on σ and y, and not on the $f(x_1), \ldots, f(x_{i-1})$) that improves slightly on the trivial algorithm. It works for any T and S satisfying $S = \Theta(N \log(N/T))$, for example, $T = N/\text{poly} \log(N)$, $S = \Theta(N/\log\log N)$. This answers a question due to Corrigan-Gibbs and Kogan [TCC, 2019], who asked whether non-trivial non-adaptive algorithms exist; namely, algorithms that work with parameters T and S satisfying $T + S/\log N < o(N)$. We also observe that our non-adaptive algorithm is what we call a *guess-and-check* algorithm, that is, it is non-adaptive *and* its final output is always one of the oracle queries $x_1, \ldots, x_T$.

   For guess-and-check algorithms, we prove a matching lower bound, therefore completely characterizing the achievable parameters (S, T) for this natural class of algorithms. (Corrigan-Gibbs and Kogan showed that any such lower bound for *arbitrary* non-adaptive algorithms would imply new circuit lower bounds.)

© International Association for Cryptologic Research 2023
H. Handschuh and A. Lysyanskaya (Eds.): CRYPTO 2023, LNCS 14082, pp. 453–481, 2023.
https://doi.org/10.1007/978-3-031-38545-2_15

3. We show equivalence between function inversion and a natural decision version of the problem in both the worst case and the average
   case, and similarly for functions $f : [N] \to [M]$ with different ranges.
   Some of these equivalence results are deferred to the full version
   [ECCC, 2022].

All of the above results are most naturally described in a model with
shared randomness (i.e., random coins shared between the preprocessing
algorithm and the online algorithm). However, as an additional contribution, we show (using a technique from communication complexity due
to Newman [IPL, 1991]) how to generically convert any algorithm that
uses shared randomness into one that does not.

1   Introduction

We revisit the fundamental problem of black-box *function inversion*. That is, we
study the problem of finding $x \in [N]$ such that $f(x) = y$, given as input some
challenge point y in the image of $f : [N] \to [N]$ and oracle access to f.

Of course, given *only* oracle access to f, inverting general functions f will
clearly require roughly N queries, which is not very interesting. However, if we
allow our inversion algorithm access to some additional information about f,
then inversion might be possible with *much* fewer queries. So, we consider the
following model. First, using unlimited computational power, a *preprocessing*
algorithm $\mathcal{P}$ analyzes f and outputs S bits of *advice* $\sigma \in \{0,1\}^S$. Then, an
online algorithm $\mathcal{A}$ is given a point y in the image of f, the advice σ, and oracle
access to f and, using at most T oracle queries, must output some x such that
$f(x) = y$. We wish to design such algorithms that minimize the complexity
measures S and T, which are often referred to informally as "space" and "time."
For example, notice that it is trivial to invert f if $S/\log N + T \geq N$, by simply
including the first $S/\log N$ values of f as advice and querying the remaining
$N - S/\log N \leq T$ values.

This model is very well studied, since it arises naturally in a number of
contexts, from cryptography [6–10,12,13,17,27,29,30] (where an appropriate
version of this problem corresponds to the problem of breaking a black-box
one-way function in the non-uniform model) to data structures and complexity
theory [8,11,14,30]. Indeed, many variants of the problem have been studied. For
example, we might ask for algorithms that invert arbitrary functions f [12], random functions f [17] (in which case the algorithm should work with reasonable
probability over the function f), or special classes of functions f, like permutations [30]; or one might place restrictions on the algorithm by, e.g., requiring the
oracle queries to be non-adaptive [3,8] or requiring that the algorithm otherwise
has some special structure [2]. Other work has considered stronger models of
computation, such as quantum algorithms [4,5,22].

In his celebrated 1980 work, Hellman [17] published the first non-trivial function inversion algorithm. Hellman's algorithm inverts random functions for any
S and T satisfying $TS^2 \gtrsim N^2$, under certain heuristic assumptions. (Here and
elsewhere in the introduction, we use $\gtrsim$ to represent an inequality that holds up

to factors polylogarithmic in N.) In their seminal 1991 paper, Fiat and Naor [12] presented an algorithm that (1) provably achieves Hellman's tradeoff for random functions f; and (2) achieves a different non-trivial tradeoff for *any* function f. Specifically, their algorithm can invert any function f provided that S and T satisfy

$$TS^3 \gtrsim N^3 \,. \tag{1}$$

For example, when $T = S$, this works for any $S = T \gtrsim N^{3/4}$, while the result becomes trivial for $S \lesssim N^{2/3}$ (since in that case they require $T \geq N$, which can be matched by the trivial algorithm).

Despite thirty years of effort, no improvements have been made to Eq. (1). This has naturally led to a search for matching *lower bounds*. Indeed, Barkan, Biham, and Shamir showed that Hellman's algorithm (or Fiat and Naor's variant with proven correctness) gives essentially the optimal tradeoff between S and T for inverting random functions if we restrict our attention to a certain rather specific class of algorithms [2]. However, the best known lower bound [9,13, 30] against arbitrary algorithms (which applies for random functions and even random permutations) only says that S and T must satisfy

$$ST \gtrsim N \,, \tag{2}$$

which is much weaker than Eq. (1). (While the lower bound in Eq. (2) is quite far from the best upper bounds known for arbitrary functions or even for random functions, Hellman proved it is tight in the special case when the function f is a permutation [17].)

Corrigan-Gibbs and Kogan explained the lack of progress on lower bounds by showing that any significant improvement to the lower bound in Eq. (2) would yield a breakthrough in circuit lower bounds [8]. (See also [11], which showed that lower bounds on function inversion are closely related to many other major open problems, such as the hardness of sorting and the Network Coding Conjecture.) In fact, Corrigan-Gibbs and Kogan [8] showed that even a lower bound against *non-adaptive* algorithms that improves upon Eq. (2) would imply new circuit lower bounds. An online algorithm $\mathcal{A}$ is *non-adaptive* if the queries $x_1, \ldots, x_T$ that it makes to its oracle are functions only of its input y, the preprocessed advice σ, and shared randomness r—i.e., if x_{i+1} is chosen independently of the answers $f(x_1), \ldots, f(x_i)$ to the previous queries. This result is quite tantalizing because (1) all of the non-trivial algorithms described above rely crucially on adaptive queries; (2) very strong lower bounds are in fact known for slightly weaker models [3]; and (3) it seems intuitively clear that non-adaptive algorithms should not be able to do much better than the trivial algorithm, which requires $S/\log N + T \geq N$. (Notice that in the context of non-adaptive algorithms, we do not leave out logarithmic factors, as even small improvements are interesting here.) Indeed, Corrigan-Gibbs and Kogan naturally speculated that no non-adaptive algorithm can do significantly better than the trivial algorithm—specifically, that no non-adaptive algorithm can solve function inversion with $S < o(N \log N)$ and $T < o(N)$.

1.1   Our Results

Improving on the Fiat-Naor algorithm for $T > S$. Our first main result is an algorithm that inverts any function $f : [N] \to [N]$ on any challenge y in its image for any T and S satisfying

$$T^2 S^2 \gtrsim N^3 . \tag{3}$$

Recall that the original Fiat-Naor algorithm requires $TS^3 \gtrsim N^3$ (as in Eq. (1)). So, our algorithm is better than Fiat and Naor's algorithm if (and only if) $T > S$. This is arguably the most interesting setting, since non-uniform advice is arguably a more expensive resource than queries (as Hellman pointed out in [17]).[1] In particular, our algorithm remains non-trivial (i.e., outperforms the trivial algorithm that requires $S + T \gtrsim N$) as long as $S \gtrsim N^{1/2}$, whereas the original Fiat-Naor algorithm is trivial for $S \lesssim N^{2/3}$.

In fact, our algorithm is a surprisingly simple variant of Fiat and Naor's original. Our presentation of the algorithm and its analysis is also notably simpler. So, as an additional benefit, we also give a significantly simpler presentation of the original result in [12].[2] Indeed, we present the two algorithms together, as a single algorithm (that behaves differently in one step depending on whether $S > T$) that solves function inversion for any S and T satisfying

$$TS^2 \cdot \max\{S, T\} \gtrsim N^3 . \tag{4}$$

In other words, we give a unified presentation that achieves the best of both worlds, matching the original tradeoff achieved by Fiat and Naor in Eq. (1) and our new tradeoff in Eq. (3).

A Lower Bound Against Guess-and-Check (Non-adaptive) Algorithms. We next address Corrigan-Gibbs and Kogan's question about whether non-trivial non-adaptive algorithms are possible. Corrigan-Gibbs and Kogan naturally guessed the answer was negative. But, surprisingly, we observe that there is a very simple algorithm that (slightly) outperforms the trivial algorithm.[3] Recall that the trivial algorithm simply stores inverses for as many range elements as it can, and achieves parameters $S/\log N + T = N$.

---

[1] However, a big part of the reason that advice is considered to be expensive is because memory is often considered to be more expensive than computing time. Unfortunately, though our algorithm can use much less than T bits of advice, our online algorithm still must use roughly T bits of space. So, though we do show an algorithm that uses less advice, we do not show an algorithm that uses less space.

[2] Admittedly, this simplicity is partially (though not entirely) due to the fact that we chose not to optimize for parameters other than S and T, while Fiat and Naor were quite careful to optimize, e.g., the actual running time and space of both the query algorithm and the preprocessing algorithm. See Sect. 1.4 for more discussion.

[3] In fact, we also missed this algorithm. An earlier version of this paper described a much more complicated algorithm that achieves the same parameters. We are very grateful to the anonymous CRYPTO reviewer who reviewed that version and discovered the simple algorithm.

The simple algorithm, by contrast, stores only *part of* an inverse for each range element. Specifically, for each $y \in [N]$ having at least one inverse, the preprocessing algorithm stores the first $\log(N) - \log(T) = \log(N/T)$ bits of an inverse x_y. On challenge y, the online algorithm queries all $T = 2^{\log T}$ elements whose first $\log(N/T)$ bits match the stored prefix of x_y. One of these queries will discover that $f(x_y) = y$. This simple algorithm evidently achieves the tradeoff

$$S = N \log(N/T) . \tag{5}$$

For example, setting $T = N/\log^C(N)$ for any constant $C > 0$, the simple algorithm uses $S = O(N \log \log N)$ bits of advice, beating the trivial algorithm by a polylogarithmic factor in both time and space.

The simple algorithm is very straightforward by any standard, and in particular, it always outputs one of the points x_i that it queries. We call non-adaptive algorithms with this property *guess-and-check* algorithms, since such an algorithm can be viewed as making T guesses $x_1, \ldots, x_T$ up front, and then using its queries to check whether any of its guesses is in fact a inverse of y.

To our knowledge, we are the first to consider this class of algorithms, though we find them to be quite natural. For example, we note in passing that guess-and-check algorithms can be thought of as "highly parallel algorithms" in the sense that they capture the model in which T processors independently compute and check one potential preimage x_i of y (i.e., one "guess"), and the algorithm succeeds if and only if any of these processors discovers that x_i is in fact a preimage of y. Indeed, Corrigan-Gibbs and Kogan [8] introduced non-adaptive algorithms in part because of their relationship with parallelism. (Other special classes of non-adaptive algorithms were studied in [8] and [3], but none of the previously defined classes captures guess-and-check algorithms, as we explain in Sect. 1.3.)

Our second contribution is a lower bound showing that no *guess-and-check* algorithm can do significantly better than Eq. (5) (even for inverting permutations). Specifically, we show that Eq. (5) is tight up to a constant factor in S and T. We therefore characterize the query-preprocessing tradeoff for guess-and-check non-adaptive function inversion up to a constant factor. If our lower bound could be extended to general non-adaptive algorithms, it would imply new strong circuit lower bounds, using the result of Corrigan-Gibbs and Kogan [8].

Search-to-Decision Reductions. Next, we consider a natural variant of function inversion, which we call *decision function inversion* (DFI). In DFI, the goal is simply to determine whether the input point $y \in [M]$ is in the image of a function $f : [N] \to [M]$, given oracle access to f, shared randomness r, and S bits of preprocessed advice σ that may depend on r and f. (Notice that in the context of DFI, it is natural to consider functions with a range $[M]$ for $M \gg N$. In the full version [15], we show that many versions of function inversion are equivalent to their respective variants when the range is changed.) Given the very slow progress on the *search* function inversion (SFI) problem that we discussed above, it is natural to ask whether the decision variant is any easier.

Unfortunately, we show that this cannot be the case—for either random functions or worst-case functions. Specifically, we show a reduction from average-case SFI to average-case DFI (in which both the function and the target are uniformly random, as in definitions Definitions 4 and 5), and a reduction from worst-case SFI to worst-case DFI. These reductions incur very little overhead—only increasing S and T by a factor that is polylogarithmic in N—and both reductions are non-adaptive, in the sense that they convert non-adaptive DFI algorithms into non-adaptive SFI algorithms. (See Remarks 1 and 2.)

These reductions can be viewed as variants of a reduction presented by Corrigan-Gibbs and Kogan in [8] (as we discuss in Sects. 1.2 and 1.3). In the full version [15], we show another search-to-decision reduction for injective functions, which is a more direct adaptation of the reduction in [8].

Removing Shared Randomness. Our final contribution is a generic way to convert a function inversion algorithm with shared randomness into an algorithm without shared randomness, at the expense of a small (additive) increase in S. Indeed, prior work used slightly different models for function inversion—depending on whether the preprocessing and query algorithms are allowed access to a shared random string, which does not count as part of the preprocessed advice. Often, this shared random string is represented by shared access to a random oracle.

E.g., Corrigan-Gibbs and Kogan [8] allowed their query and preprocessing algorithms access to the same random oracle. In contrast, Fiat and Naor [12] did not allow for this. Even in this more conservative setting, however, it is often far more convenient to first describe algorithms that *do* have access to shared randomness, typically in the form of a random oracle, and then to describe how to remove this shared randomness by, e.g., replacing the random oracle with a suitable carefully chosen hash function (with a suitably short key that can be included as part of the preprocessed advice) and arguing that this has little to no effect on the correctness of the algorithm.

We show a generic way to convert *any* function inversion algorithm with shared randomness into a function inversion algorithm without shared randomness. Our conversion is quite simple (and actually applies to a more general class of problems; see Sect. 6), as it simply replaces the shared randomness r with a string r_i chosen by the preprocessing algorithm from a relatively small number of fixed strings $r_1, \ldots, r_k$. (In fact, a random list of strings will work with high probability.[4]) Because the number of such strings is relatively low (e.g., $k \leq N \cdot \mathrm{poly} \log(N)$ in all of our settings), the index i can be appended to the preprocessed advice essentially for free (costing only an additional $\log k \approx \log N$ bits of advice).

---

[4] At first, this statement might sound trivial, since we started with an algorithm that works with shared randomness r, and we seem to have converted into an algorithm with *more* shared randomness. The difference, however, is in the order of quantifiers. In the shared randomness model, we ask that for any function f with high probability over the randomness r, the algorithm inverts f. Here, we show that with high probability over the random strings $r_1, \ldots, r_k$, for every function f there exists i such that the algorithm inverts f with randomness r_i.

In particular, nearly all of the results listed are most naturally presented using shared randomness, but this procedure shows that this shared randomness can be removed without changing any of our stated results (up to a lower-order additive term in S)! And, this shows that the carefully chosen hash functions in much prior work were *in some sense* not necessary. (In particular, our result implies that it is not necessary to use these hash functions to remove shared randomness. However, these hash functions are still useful for optimizing additional complexity measures that we ignore in this work, like the size of the description of the (nonuniform) preprocessing algorithm. See Sect. 1.4.)

Our proof of this result is an adaptation to our setting of a celebrated result in communication complexity. Specifically, we adapt Newman's beautiful technique for converting public-coin protocols to private-coin protocols [23].

This does not come completely for free, however. Our proof shows that a random list of strings $r_1, \ldots, r_k$ will work with high probability. But, these strings still need to be stored somehow. So, while our conversion process does not increase the number of queries T and only (additively) increases the size S of the advice by a very small amount, it *does* require both the preprocessing algorithm $\mathcal{P}$ and the online algorithm $\mathcal{A}$ to be *non-uniform*.

Since non-uniformity is often assumed in this setting, this does not bother us much. But, there do exist practical applications of function inversion algorithms, e.g., in cryptanalysis, for which truly non-uniform algorithms are an unreasonable model. We note, however, that in practical applications it is typically sufficient to simply use a cryptographic hash function as a replacement for a random oracle. If this is done, our algorithm becomes uniform, while retaining the desirable property from Fiat and Naor's algorithm that preprocessing only requires $\tilde{O}(N)$ time. Thus our improvement over Fiat and Naor's algorithm in the low-space regime $S < T$ also applies in this setting.

1.2   Our Techniques

Improving Fiat-Naor. Our improvement to Fiat and Naor's algorithm starts by recalling the following. In the original Fiat-Naor procedure, the preprocessing algorithm first generates a list of nearly S "heavy hitters"—that is, elements in the image of f having many inverses—and it includes this list together with a preimage for each heavy hitter in its advice to the online algorithm.

The online algorithm then operates in two phases. It first checks this list to see if its input y is a heavy hitter, in which case it immediately outputs the corresponding preimage contained in the advice. Otherwise, (ignoring important technical details for simplicity) the algorithm effectively runs a function inversion algorithm on the function f *restricted to elements whose images are not heavy hitters*. With the heavy hitters removed, the new restricted function is much better behaved than the original, allowing for the final tradeoff. (In particular, the restricted function will have relatively low collision probability, which Fiat and Naor show is sufficient for a Hellman-like algorithm to invert it with the desired tradeoff. See Sect. 3 for the details.)

In fact, as Fiat and Naor observe, it is sufficient to simply include a list of nearly S pairs $(x_i, f(x_i))_{1 \leq i \leq S}$ for uniformly random $x_i \sim [N]$ as part of the advice, rather than explicitly looking for heavy hitters. (Notice that any elements $y \in [N]$ with very many preimages will still be contained in such a list with high probability, which is why this works.)

At this high (and slightly misleading) level of detail, our modification to Fiat and Naor's algorithm is straightforward: rather than having the preprocessing algorithm include many random queries $(x_i, f(x_i))_i$ as part of the preprocessing, we have the online algorithm generate this list itself. This allows us to replace a list of length S with a list of length T, which gives us our advantage over the original algorithm when $T > S$.

Of course, many details must be worked out to make this actually work. Most significantly, it is crucial that the same list $(x_i, f(x_i))_i$ is known to both the preprocessing algorithm and the online algorithm, so that they both work with the same restricted function f'. For this, we rely on shared randomness (which can then be removed quite painlessly using the result from Sect. 6), allowing the online algorithm and the preprocessing algorithm to share the same list $(x_i)_i$ of random query points.

Our reliance on shared randomness also greatly simplifies the description and analysis of both our algorithm *and* Fiat and Naor's original. Indeed, as we mentioned above, we give a simple presentation of a single unified algorithm that works whenever

$$S^2 T \cdot \max\{S, T\} \gtrsim N^3 .$$

This simplified presentation might itself be of independent interest.

A Tight Bound Against Guess-and-Check Algorithms. The proof of our lower bound against guess-and-check algorithms follows the high-level framework used by [9] and [10]. The idea here is to show that a function inversion algorithm with certain properties would imply an unreasonably succinct way to *encode* a function $f : [N] \to [N]$—i.e., a succinct bit string that can be used to recover f. (In this high-level description, we ignore for simplicity the fact that our algorithms $(\mathcal{P}, \mathcal{A})$ may be randomized and the related fact that they might fail some fraction of the time. To fix this, we must work with randomized encodings that themselves have some chance of failure.) In fact, we restrict our attention to permutations f, so that in order to encode f, it suffices to encode the unique inverse of each element $y \in [N]$. (This only makes our lower bound stronger.)

Our encoding will consist of the S bits of preprocessed advice $\sigma \in \{0, 1\}^S$ together with some additional information. Recall that a non-adaptive algorithm has the property that the queries $x_1^{(y)}, \ldots, x_T^{(y)}$ made by $\mathcal{A}$ on input y are fixed for fixed σ (where here we are ignoring any randomness for simplicity). Furthermore, if a guess-and-check (non-adaptive) algorithm succeeds, then one of the x_i must be a preimage of y. Our encoding will therefore simply record for each $y \in [N]$ the index $i_y \in [T]$ such that $x_{i_y}^{(y)}$ is the unique preimage of y. Notice that this information, together with σ, is actually enough to completely reconstruct the function f. (Notice also that this argument relies quite heavily on *guess-and-check* non-adaptivity. For a general non-adaptive algorithm, it might be necessary to include the responses to all queries $x_1^{(y)}, \ldots, x_T^{(y)}$.)

This gives an encoding of f that uses only $N \log T + S$ bits. Since there are $N!$ permutations over $[N]$, this is a contradiction unless $N \log T + S \geq \log(N!) \geq \Omega(N \log N)$. Rearranging gives our lower bound of $S \geq \Omega(N \log(N/T))$.

Search-to-Decision Reductions. Corrigan-Gibbs and Kogan [8] observed that there is a reduction from SFI on *injective* functions $f : [N] \to [M]$ to (a different version of) DFI on worst-case functions, where the reduction works by essentially "asking the DFI oracle for the ith bit of the unique preimage." Specifically, at a high level their reduction works by essentially running the DFI algorithm separately on the functions $f_i : [N/2] \to [M]$ corresponding to f restricted to inputs whose ith bit is, say, zero. By solving DFI on the functions f_i and target point y_i, they can recover the unique preimage to y "one bit at a time."[5] Notice in particular that this reduction is careful to only work with a small number of functions f_i that are defined independently of the target point, which allows the SFI algorithm to work with preprocessed advice from the DFI algorithm for a small number of functions.

Both of our search-to-decision reductions start with the simple (and, on its own, not particularly interesting) observation that the above idea can be generalized to invert *any* function $f : [N] \to [M]$, *provided that the target point y that we are inverting has a unique preimage*.

At a high level, our reduction from worst-case SFI to worst-case DFI then works by directly reducing from worst-case SFI with a general target point y to the variant in which y is promised to have a unique preimage. For this, we use an idea inspired by Valiant and Vazirani's celebrated Isolation Lemma [28]. Specifically, we find a small number of subsets $U_j \subseteq [N]$ of the domain of f (which are chosen independently of y!) such that with high probability y has exactly one preimage when f is *restricted to U_j*. Then, (ignoring many technical details) we can use the ideas described above to solve this search problem using only a DFI algorithm.

For our reduction from average-case SFI to average-case DFI, we can more-or-less assume that the target point y has a unique preimage, since a large fraction of the elements in the image of a random function f have a unique preimage. However, here we run into a different problem: an average-case DFI oracle is only guaranteed to work with some reasonable probability when the function $f : [N] \to [M]$ is uniformly random (see Sect. 5.2 for the details). While the restrictions f_i (as described above) of a uniformly random function f are themselves uniformly random, they are certainly not independent. This means that a DFI oracle could potentially have very high success probability

---

[5] We are oversimplifying quite a bit here and leaving out many important details. Perhaps most importantly, we are assuming here for simplicity that the DFI oracle always outputs the correct answer, while Corrigan-Gibbs and Kogan worked with a much weaker DFI oracle. They were also careful to keep the domain of the functions f_i the same as the domain of the function f, while we are not concerned with this.

but still could, e.g., *always* fail on one (or even many) of the functions f_i (out of $\log N$ total functions $f_1, \ldots, f_{\log N}$), which would cause our search-to-decision reduction to always fail to find the ith bit of the preimage (and therefore to fail).

We solve the above problem by using good error-correcting codes. That is, instead of working with the functions f_i corresponding to the bits of elements in $[N]$ written in binary, we work with a larger number of functions f_i' corresponding to the bits of *encodings* of elements in $[N]$ using a good error-correcting code. That is, f_i' is the function f restricted to the set of elements in $[N]$ whose corresponding codeword has ith bit equal to zero. By using a good enough code, we can recover a preimage of the target by solving just $O(\log N)$ decision problems, even if a $1/4 - \varepsilon$ fraction of the answers are wrong. (Indeed, we can even decode efficiently, though we mostly do not worry about this.)

1.3 Related Work

Here, we describe some of the related work that has not already been discussed, as it relates to the present work.

De, Trevisan, and Tulsiani [9] showed improvements to Fiat and Naor's algorithm along a different axis. Specifically, they showed how to achieve surprisingly small values of S and T in the setting in which the algorithm is only required to invert $y := f(x)$ for uniformly random $x \sim [N]$ with some very small probability ε. (In contrast, all of our algorithms invert such a y with high probability.) They show a slight variant of Fiat and Naor's algorithm that works for any S, T, and ε satisfying $ST \gtrsim \varepsilon N$ for $\varepsilon < N^{-1/3}$ (which they show is optimal) and $TS^3 \gtrsim \varepsilon^5 N^3$ otherwise.

Like us, Chawin, Haitner, and Mazor [3] showed lower bounds on special cases of non-adaptive algorithms. In particular, they considered the function $g_{\sigma,y} : [N]^T \to [N]$ that maps the responses $f(x_1), \ldots, f(x_T)$ to the queries made by $\mathcal{A}$ to the final output of $\mathcal{A}$ (i.e., the guess that $\mathcal{A}$ makes for the preimage of y). For example, they showed that $S \geq \Omega(N)$ (regardless of T) if $g_{\sigma,y}$ is an affine function. They also showed that $dS \log N + T \geq \Omega(N)$ if $g_{\sigma,y}$ can be implemented by a depth-d affine decision tree. We note that neither of these models captures guess-and-check algorithms, for which $g_{\sigma,y}(y_1, \ldots, y_T) = x_i$, where i is such that $y_i = y$. (Such a $g_{\sigma,y}$ is certainly not affine, and it seems that it requires depth $d \approx T$ to implement such a function as an affine decision tree, as one must sequentially check whether $y_i = y$ for all i.)

Corrigan-Gibbs and Kogan also defined a special case of non-adaptive algorithms, which they call *strongly* non-adaptive [8]. For a strongly non-adaptive algorithm, the function $g_{\sigma,y}$ may be arbitrary, but the queries $x_1, \ldots, x_T$ must be computed independently of the preprocessing (and non-adaptively), so that they are effectively completely independent of the function f. [8] showed that lower bounds against even such weak models would imply new circuit lower bounds. However, strongly non-adaptive algorithms are incomparable to our model of guess-and-check algorithms, so that our lower bound on guess-and-check algorithms unfortunately does not directly apply.

For general non-adaptive algorithms, Dvořák, Koucký, Král, and Slívová [11] showed a conditional lower bound of $T \geq \Omega(\log N / \log \log N)$ for any $S \leq \varepsilon N \log N$ for some small constant $\varepsilon > 0$, assuming the Network Coding Conjecture. Notice that this lower bound holds in a more general setting than our lower bound or those of [3] but it requires an unproven conjecture and is quantitatively weaker than ours and those in of [3]. (E.g., for guess-and-check algorithms with $S \leq \varepsilon N \log N$, our lower bound implies that $T \geq N^{1-O(\varepsilon)}$.)

There is also a long line of work [6–10,16] studying a different version of DFI than the one that we study, which is sometimes simply called the PRG problem. Here, the goal is to distinguish (perhaps with relatively small distinguishing advantage) a uniformly random element $y \sim [M]$ from $f(x)$ for uniformly random $x \sim [N]$, where $f : [N] \to [M]$. In particular, Corrigan-Gibbs and Kogan show a search-to-to-decision reduction from SFI over injective functions to the worst-case PRG problem. Our search-to-decision reductions are essentially generalizations of their reduction from [8] to the setting of non-injective functions. We pay for this non-injectivity by requiring our DFI algorithm to solve problems that are harder than the PRG problem, and by requiring significantly more complicated reductions.

1.4   A Note on the Many Facets of Function Inversion

There are *many* variants of the function inversion problem and *many* different complexity measures that one can use to assess algorithms in this context. The landscape is therefore quite complicated. Indeed, our search-to-decision reductions and our proof that shared randomness can be removed (as well as the reductions between versions of SFI with different range sizes in the full version [15]) can be viewed as small steps towards simplifying the picture a bit.

But, there are still certainly many variants and complexity measures that we simply do not address in this work. E.g., while we mostly focus on the number of queries T and the length S of the preprocessed advice, much prior work was also interested in the time and space complexity of the algorithms $\mathcal{P}$ and $\mathcal{A}$, which we largely ignore. E.g., prior work of Fiat and Naor, and of De, Trevisan, and Tulsiani [9,12] used specialized hash functions to replace shared randomness because removing shared randomness is itself a worthy goal, but *also* to optimize the running time of their algorithms (which is not the same as the query complexity T). For the sake of simplicity, we have chosen to largely ignore these additional complexity measures in our algorithms, and we have therefore not optimized our algorithms for these complexity measures at all. (We do note that our algorithms run in essentially optimal time when they are implemented with shared randomness in the form of shared access to a random oracle. In particular, the preprocessing algorithms can be implemented in time $\widetilde{O}(N)$, and the online algorithms can be implemented in time $T \cdot \operatorname{poly} \log(N)$.)

As another example, as we discussed above, De, Trevisan, and Tulsiani [9] studied the dependence of S and T in terms of the fraction ε of inputs $x \in [N]$ for which the algorithm successfully inverts $f(x)$. They showed that for small ε one can do *much* better than Eq. (1), using essentially the same algorithm. It is natural to ask whether their techniques can be applied to our new version of the Fiat-Naor algorithm; we believe that they can be, but we leave this to future work.

2   Preliminaries

We define $\mathbb{1}_\mu$ as $\mathbb{1}_\mu = 1$ if μ is true, and 0 otherwise. All logarithms are base 2, i.e., $\log 2^n = n$.

2.1   Definitions of Function Inversion Problems

In the following definitions, M and N are positive integers, and $(\mathcal{P}, \mathcal{A})$ is a pair of randomized algorithms. For a set $X \subseteq [N]$, $f(X)$ denotes the image of X under f, and for $y \in [N]$, $f^{-1}(y)$ denotes the preimage of y under f. The first few definitions are core to our study of function inversion.

Definition 1. *We say that*

1. *$(\mathcal{P}, \mathcal{A})$ uses S bits of preprocessing if for all inputs, the output of $\mathcal{P}$ has bitlength at most S.*
2. *$(\mathcal{P}, \mathcal{A})$ uses T queries if for all inputs, $\mathcal{A}^f$ makes at most T queries to f.*

Definition 2. *We say that $(\mathcal{P}, \mathcal{A})$ solves (N, M)-search function-inversion $((N, M)$-SFI) with success probability $\delta \in (0, 1]$ if for all $f : [N] \to [M]$ and $y \in f([N])$,*

$$\Pr_{r \sim \{0,1\}^l} [\mathcal{A}^f(\mathcal{P}(f, r), y, r) \in f^{-1}(y)] \geq \delta.$$

Here r is the shared randomness between the algorithms $\mathcal{A}$ and $\mathcal{P}$. It has some (typically unspecified) finite bitlength l.

Definition 3. *We say that $(\mathcal{P}, \mathcal{A})$ solves (N, M)-decision function-inversion $((N, M)$-DFI) with advantage $\varepsilon \in (0, 1/2]$ if for all $f : [N] \to [M]$ and $y \in [M]$,*

$$\Pr_{r \sim \{0,1\}^l} [\mathcal{A}^f(\mathcal{P}(f, r), y, r) = \mathbb{1}_{y \in f([N])}] \geq 1/2 + \varepsilon.$$

In words, $\mathcal{A}$ is likely to output 1 when y is in the image of f, but is unlikely to output 1 when y is in $[M] \setminus f([N])$.

We will abuse terminology slightly and simply refer to $(\mathcal{P}, \mathcal{A})$ as an algorithm when the meaning is clear from context. When $N = M$, we will drop the parameters and just write SFI or DFI. We will also sometimes write "worst-case SFI" or "worst-case DFI" to distinguish from the average-case variants that we define next.

Definition 4. *We say that $(\mathcal{P}, \mathcal{A})$ solves average-case (N, M)-SFI with success probability δ if*

$$\Pr_{\substack{r \sim \{0,1\}^l \\ f \sim \{g:[N] \to [M]\} \\ x \sim [N]; y \leftarrow f(x)}} [\mathcal{A}^f(\mathcal{P}(f, r), y, r) \in f^{-1}(y)] \geq \delta.$$

Definition 5. *We say that* $(\mathcal{P}, \mathcal{A})$ *solves average-case* (N, M)-*DFI with advantage* ε *if*

$$\Pr_{\substack{r \sim \{0,1\}^l \\ f \sim \{g:[N] \to [M]\} \\ x \sim [N]; y \leftarrow f(x)}} [\mathcal{A}^f(\mathcal{P}(f,r), y, r) = 1] \geq 1/2 + \varepsilon,$$

and

$$\Pr_{\substack{r \sim \{0,1\}^l \\ f \sim \{g:[N] \to [M]\} \\ y \sim [M] \setminus f([N])}} [\mathcal{A}^f(\mathcal{P}(f,r), y, r) = 0] \geq 1/2 + \varepsilon.$$

In order to state our results removing shared randomness, we need the following definition of function-inversion algorithms without shared randomness.

Definition 6. *We say that* $(\mathcal{P}, \mathcal{A})$ *solves* (N, M)-*SFI with success probability* δ *without shared randomness if for all* $f : [N] \to [M]$ *and all* $y \in f([N])$,

$$\Pr_{r_1, r_2 \sim \{0,1\}^l} [\mathcal{A}^f(\mathcal{P}(f, r_1), y, r_2) \in f^{-1}(y)] \geq \delta.$$

We make analogous definitions for the 3 other problems ((N, M)-DFI, average-case (N, M)-SFI, average-case (N, M)-DFI).

Note that we will say, for example, "(N, M)-SFI for injective functions", when we mean Definition 2, but with the function f ranging over all injective functions from $[N] \to [M]$. Finally, we define some special classes of algorithms that will be studied in Sect. 4.

Definition 7. *An algorithm* $\mathcal{A}$ *is* non-adaptive *if* $\mathcal{A}^f(\sigma, y, r)$ *only queries* f *on points* $x_1(\sigma, y, r), \ldots, x_T(\sigma, y, r)$ *depending only on the inputs* $\sigma, y,$ *and* r *(i.e., not depending on the results of previous queries).*

Definition 8. *An algorithm* $\mathcal{A}$ *is a* guess-and-check *algorithm if it is non-adaptive and whenever* $x \leftarrow \mathcal{A}^f(\sigma, y, r)$, *then* x *is one of the points queried by* $\mathcal{A}^f$.

We will say that $(\mathcal{P}, \mathcal{A})$ is non-adaptive (resp. a guess-and-check algorithm) if $\mathcal{A}$ is non-adaptive (resp. a guess-and-check algorithm).

2.2 Some Basic Probability Results

We will use the following version of Chernoff's bound (see, e.g., [20]).

Lemma 1. *Suppose* $X_1, \ldots, X_n$ *are independent random variables taking values in {0, 1}. Let* X *denote their sum, and* $\mu := \mathbb{E}[X]$. *Then for any* $\delta \geq 0$,

$$\Pr[X \geq (1 + \delta)\mu] \leq \exp\left(\frac{-\delta^2 \mu}{2 + \delta}\right).$$

Moreover, for $0 \leq \varepsilon \leq 1$,

$$\Pr[X \leq (1 - \varepsilon)\mu] \leq \exp\left(\frac{-\varepsilon^2 \mu}{2}\right).$$

We will also need the following simple bound.

Lemma 2. *For any integers $N \geq 1$ and $M \geq 2$,*

$$\Pr_{f \sim \{g:[N] \to [M]\}, x \sim [N]} [|\{x' \in [N] \; : \; f(x) = f(x')\}| = 1] \geq e^{-N/M - N/M^2} .$$

Proof. This is exactly equal to

$$\Pr_{y_1, \ldots, y_{N-1} \sim [M]} [\forall i, \; y_i \neq 0] = (1 - 1/M)^{N-1} \geq e^{-N/M - N/M^2} .$$

For the last inequality, it suffices to show that $1 - x \geq e^{-x - x^2}$ for $0 \leq x \leq 1/2$. Indeed, plugging in $x = 1/M$ gives $1 - 1/M \geq e^{-1/M - 1/M^2}$, which implies $(1 - 1/M)^{N-1} > (1 - 1/M)^N \geq e^{-N/M - N/M^2}$. To prove this, let $f(x) = 1 - x$, $g(x) = e^{-x - x^2}$, and $h(x) = f(x)/g(x)$. Computing $\frac{d}{dx} \log(h(x)) = \frac{d}{dx}(\log(1 - x) - (-x - x^2)) = -1/(1 - x) + 1 + 2x = x(1 - 2x)/(1 - x)$, we see that it is nonnegative on $[0, 1/2]$. Since the logarithm is increasing, it follows that $\frac{d}{dx} h(x)$ is also nonnegative on $[0, 1/2]$, and so $h(x) \geq h(0) = 1$ on $[0, 1/2]$. But this implies $f(x) \geq g(x)$ for all $0 \leq x \leq 1/2$, which is what we wanted to prove. $\quad\square$

2.3   Binary Linear Codes

Recall that a binary linear code $\mathcal{C}$ with rank n is an n-dimensional subspace $\mathcal{C} \subseteq \mathbb{F}_2^m$, and $\mathbf{C} \in \mathbb{F}_2^{m \times n}$ is a generator matrix for $\mathcal{C}$ if $\mathcal{C} = \mathbf{C}\mathbb{F}_2^n$. For $\mathbf{x} \in \mathbb{F}_2^m$, we write $\|\mathbf{x}\|_H$ for the Hamming weight of $\mathbf{x}$ (i.e., the number of non-zero coordinates). . The notation $m_{n,\varepsilon} \leq O_\varepsilon(n)$ means that there exists a function $f(\varepsilon)$ such that $m_{n,\varepsilon} \leq f(\varepsilon)O(n)$.

Theorem 1 ([1,18,19,25]). *For every constant $\varepsilon > 0$, there exists a family $\mathcal{C}_{n,\varepsilon} \subseteq \mathbb{F}_2^m$ with rank n and $m = m_{n,\varepsilon} \leq O_\varepsilon(n)$, an efficiently computable generator matrices $\mathbf{C}_{n,\varepsilon} \in \mathbb{F}_2^{m \times n}$, and an efficient decoding algorithm Dec such that for every $\mathbf{x} \in \mathbb{F}_2^n$ and every $\mathbf{e} \in \mathbb{F}_2^m$ with $\|\mathbf{e}\|_H \leq (1/4 - \varepsilon) \cdot m$, $\mathsf{Dec}(\mathbf{C}_{n,\varepsilon}\mathbf{x} \oplus \mathbf{e}) = \mathbf{x}$.*

For any $\mathcal{C} \subseteq \mathbb{F}_2^m$ and $1 \leq i \leq m$, we can easily define the subcode $\mathcal{C}_i := \{\mathbf{c} = (c_1, \ldots, c_m) \in \mathcal{C} \; : \; c_i = 0\}$. Notice that we have either $|\mathcal{C}_i| = |\mathcal{C}|$ or $|\mathcal{C}_i| = |\mathcal{C}|/2$ (where the first case only occurs if all $\mathbf{c} \in \mathcal{C}$ have zero ith coordinate), and that given a generator matrix $\mathbf{C} \in \mathbb{F}_2^{m \times n}$ for a code $\mathcal{C}$, it is trivial to compute a generator matrix for $\mathcal{C}_i$. Notice also that we may assume without loss of generality that the codes $\mathcal{C} := \mathcal{C}_{n,\varepsilon}$ in Theorem 1 satisfy $|\mathcal{C}_i| = |\mathcal{C}|/2$ for all i (since we may simply remove any coordinates that are always zero).

3   An Improvement to Fiat and Naor's Algorithm

From our perspective, there are two core techniques used in Fiat and Naor's algorithm [12]. First, Fiat and Naor's algorithm generates a list L of pairs $(x, f(x))$

for random domain elements $x \in [N]$, which effectively serves as a list of preimages of "heavy hitters"—i.e., elements x such that $f(x)$ has many preimages. In the original algorithm, L is included as part of the preprocessed advice. Second, (following Hellman [17]) Fiat and Naor describe a randomized subroutine $(\mathcal{P}', \mathcal{A}')$ that takes L as auxiliary input and for all $y \in f([N])$, inverts y with some small probability. This subroutine is then run many times to boost its success probability (with a fixed list L but independent randomness for $\mathcal{P}'$ and $\mathcal{A}'$). Our improvement differs from the original only in the first part, and the difference can be described in one sentence: if $T > S$, instead of including the list L in the preprocessed advice, we reconstruct it using queries to f. This can be done because the random domain elements x can be derived from *shared* randomness (which we also show in Corollary 1 is available in the non-uniform model for essentially no cost). This allows us to construct a larger list L in the case when $T > S$, with $|L| \approx T$ instead of $|L| \approx S$.

Our formal theorem is the following.

Theorem 2. *For all S, T satisfying $S^2 T \max\{S, T\} \geq N^3$, there exists an algorithm that solves SFI with success probability 1 using $O(S \log^2 N)$ bits of preprocessing and $O(T \log^2 N)$ queries.*

As mentioned above, this improves on Fiat and Naor's tradeoff in the important setting where $S < T$. On the other hand, when $S \geq T$ our algorithm is essentially just Fiat and Naor's algorithm. However, even in this case, we believe that our presentation and analysis is significantly simpler, which we view as an additional contribution. Some (though certainly not all) of this simplicity is because of our choice to optimize only for T and S and not for additional complexity measures like the running time of the online algorithm (see Sect. 1.4) or the use of shared randomness (which we show is essentially without loss of generality in Sect. 6). Fiat and Naor made careful use of k-wise independent hash functions in order to optimize these parameters.

Below, we present an algorithm which succeeds with probability $1 - O(1/N)$. By Corollary 1, this implies the result.

3.1   The Algorithm

Let $K := \max\{S, T\}$, and let $\alpha := 2K \lceil \log N \rceil$. Let $z_1, \ldots, z_\alpha \sim [N]$ be uniformly random and independent elements generated using the shared randomness. Let $L := \{(z_i, f(z_i)) : i \in [\alpha]\}$. Intuitively, we think of L as a list of inverses for "heavy hitters," that is, elements y in the image of f that have many preimages. Let $\widehat{L} := \{y : (x, y) \in L\}$, and let $D := \{x \in [N] : f(x) \notin \widehat{L}\}$ be the domain elements whose images are not trivially inverted by lookup in L. Finally, let $N' := |D|$.

We will show a subroutine $(\mathcal{P}', \mathcal{A}')$ that takes L as input and, provided that $\widehat{L}$ contains all points with at least N/K preimages, inverts any challenge $y \in f(D)$ with small but decent probability. It uses parameters $m := \lfloor N/3T \rfloor$ and $t := \lfloor N'/3S \rfloor$. The subroutine works by constructing m chains of length t as in Fig. 1.

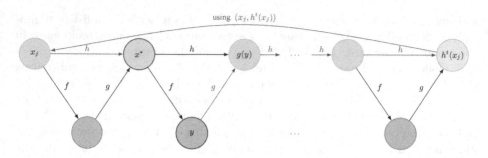

Fig. 1. The picture captures the basic workings of chain-based algorithms, including Hellman's algorithm, Fiat and Naor's algorithm, and our improvement. Here $h = g \circ f$, where g is randomly sampled from some appropriate distribution. Preprocessing constructs the green chain $C(x_j)$ by sampling a random point x_j and iterating h. It stores the pair $(x_j, h^t(x_j))$. On challenge y, online assumes y is a blue point, and follows the red arrows. That is, it proceeds by computing $g(y)$, then iterating h until it reaches the stored endpoint $h^t(x_j)$. Once there, it jumps back to x_j and iterates h until $x^* \in f^{-1}(y)$ is found. (Color figure online)

At a high level, the full algorithm $(\mathcal{P}, \mathcal{A})$ then works by constructing L, and running $(\mathcal{P}', \mathcal{A}')$ many times to boost the success probability. More precisely, let $\ell := \lceil 100ST \log(N)/N \rceil$, and let $r_1, \dots, r_\ell$ be independent random strings derived from shared randomness. On input a function f, the preprocessing algorithm $\mathcal{P}$ first constructs L as described above, then for $i \in [\ell]$, it runs $\mathrm{st}_i \leftarrow \mathcal{P}'(L, f, r_i)$. If $S \geq T$, $\mathcal{P}$ outputs $\sigma := (L, \mathrm{st}_1, \dots, \mathrm{st}_\ell)$. Otherwise, it just outputs $\sigma := (\mathrm{st}_1, \dots, \mathrm{st}_\ell)$.

On input a challenge y and preprocessed advice σ, the online algorithm $\mathcal{A}$ first recovers L as follows. If $S \geq T$, $\mathcal{A}$ just reads L from σ. Otherwise, it queries f on the points $z_1, \dots, z_\alpha$ to recover L. Then $\mathcal{A}$ checks if $y \in \widehat{L}$; if so, it returns the corresponding inverse. If not, for $i \in [\ell]$, it runs $o_i \leftarrow \mathcal{A}'^f(L, \mathrm{st}_i, y, r_i)$. If any run i returns $o_i \neq \bot$, $\mathcal{A}$ outputs o_i. Otherwise, it outputs $\bot$.

The Subroutine. It remains to describe the subroutine $(\mathcal{A}', \mathcal{P}')$. The subroutine receives L as input, but we will view it as receiving g as input instead, where $g : [N] \to [D]$ is a uniformly random function, constructed using L as follows. Let $J := \lceil N/N' \cdot 2 \log N \rceil$, and let $g' : [N] \times [J] \to [N]$ be a random function sampled independently using the shared randomness of $\mathcal{P}'$ and $\mathcal{A}'$. We say that g' is *bad* if there exists an $i \in [N]$ such that $g'(i, j) \notin D$ for all $j \in [J]$. If g' is bad, our subroutine will simply fail. But, it is easy to see that for our choice of J this happens with probability at most $2/N$. We will therefore assume below that g' is not bad, which will cost us at most an additive factor of $2/N$ in the success probability of our subroutine. Now, define $g(y) := g'(y, k)$, where $k \in [J]$ is minimal such that $g'(y, k) \in D$. Notice that g is a uniformly random function

$g : [N] \to D$, and that, given L, $g(y)$ can be computed using at most J queries to f by finding the minimal i such that $f(g'(y,i)) \notin \widehat{L}$.[6]

Finally, let $h := g \circ f$, and for each $x \in [N]$ and $s \geq 1$, define the *chain* $C^s(x) := \{x, h(x), \ldots, h^s(x)\}$. (Here and below, we use the notation h^q to represent h composed with itself q times.) See Fig. 1.

Preprocessing: Stores $(x_i, h^t(x_i))$ for independent $x_1, \ldots, x_m \sim D$. The $h^t(x_i)$ will be called *endpoints*.

Online: On challenge $y \in f(D)$ (recall that $f(D) = f([N]) - \widehat{L}$), online computes $C_y := C^{t-1}(g(y))$ and checks if there is a unique $i \in [m]$ such that $h^t(x_i) \in C_y$.[7] If not, it gives up. Then it computes $C^{t-1}(x_i)$ and checks whether any $x^* \in C^{t-1}(x_i)$ satisfies $f(x^*) = y$. If so, it returns x^*; else it returns $\perp$.

3.2   Analysis

First we analyze the resource costs. It is clear that the sub-algorithm stores at most $2m\lceil \log N \rceil$ bits of advice, and makes at most $2t \cdot J$ queries to f. Hence the data structures $\mathrm{st}_1, \ldots, \mathrm{st}_\ell$ have total bitlength at most

$$\ell \cdot 2m\lceil \log N \rceil = \left\lceil \frac{100ST \log N}{N} \right\rceil \cdot (2\,m\lceil \log N \rceil) \leq \frac{300ST \log^2 N}{N} \frac{N}{3T} = 100\,S \log^2 N.$$

If $S > T$, storing the list L, which consists of $\alpha = 2S\lceil \log N \rceil$ pairs of elements of $[N]$, requires at most an additional $10S \log^2 N$ bits. So $(\mathcal{P}, \mathcal{A})$ uses at most $110S\lceil \log N \rceil^2$ bits of preprocessing. And the total number of queries to f made by $\mathcal{A}$ is at most

$$\ell \cdot (2tJ) \leq \ell \cdot 5t(N/N') \log N = \left\lceil \frac{100ST \log N}{N} \right\rceil \cdot 5 \left\lfloor \frac{N'}{3S} \right\rfloor \cdot \frac{N \log N}{N'} \leq 200\,T \log^2 N.$$

To analyze the success probability, we first observe that

Lemma 3. *Except with probability $2/N$, all $x \in D$ satisfy $|f^{-1}(f(x))| \leq N/K$.*

Proof. The condition above is equivalent to the list $\widehat{L}$ containing all $u \in [N]$ with $|f^{-1}(u)| \geq N/K$. But since $\alpha := 2K\lceil \log N \rceil$, we have $N/K \geq 2 \log N \cdot N/\alpha$, and so for any u with $|f^{-1}(u)| \geq N/K$, there exists $i \in [\alpha]$ with $f(z_i) = u$ (which implies $u \in \widehat{L}$) except with probability $2/N^2$. The lemma then follows by union bound. □

We claim that the subalgorithm satisfies the following guarantee:

---

[6] Indeed, this is the whole purpose of this rather subtle construction of g (which is only a slight variant of the construction in Fiat and Naor [12])—to provide $\mathcal{P}'$ and $\mathcal{A}'$ with access to a shared random function from $[N]$ to D without requiring $\mathcal{A}'$ to make too many queries. Notice that this is non-trivial because the set D is not known to $\mathcal{A}'$ and might not have a succinct description. ($\mathcal{A}'$ instead only knows the image $\widehat{L}$ of $[N] - D$ under f.).

[7] The requirement of uniqueness substantially simplifies the analysis. However, it is possible to use a weaker condition.

Theorem 3. *Let $f : [N] \to [N]$ for some $N \geq 1$. Let $U \geq 1$, and suppose that for all $x \in D$, $|f^{-1}(f(x))| \leq U$. Let $y \in f(D)$. Then the sub-algorithm with parameters $0 \leq m, t \leq N$ finds an inverse of y with probability at least*

$$(1 - 6mt^2U/N') \cdot (1 - t^2U/N') \cdot |f^{-1}(y)| \cdot mt/N' - 2/N .$$

In particular, if N is sufficiently large, the bound $U = N/K$ from Lemma 3 holds, and the parameter settings are $m = \lfloor N/3T \rfloor$, $t = \lfloor N'/3S \rfloor$ as above, the probability is at least

$$mt/(2N') \geq N/(100\,ST).$$

Using Theorem 3, it is straightforward to show Theorem 2. Proof of Theorem 2 *assuming Theorem 3.*

Lemma 3 states that all $x \in D$ satisfy $|f^{-1}(f(x))| \leq U$ except with probability $2/N$ over the random choices of $z_1, \ldots, z_\alpha$. Assuming this holds, Theorem 3 says that for all $y \in f(D)$ (i.e., all $y \notin \widehat{L}$), the subalgorithm $(\mathcal{P}', \mathcal{A}')$ inverts y with probability at least $N/(100ST)$. Thus, for all $y \notin \widehat{L}$, except with probability $O(1/N)$, at least one of the $\ell = \lceil 100 \log N \cdot (ST/N) \rceil$ iterations of $(\mathcal{P}', \mathcal{A}')$ inverts y. Of course, the points $y \in \widehat{L}$ are trivially inverted by lookup in L. Hence for all $y \in f([N])$, $(\mathcal{P}, \mathcal{A})$ inverts y except with probability $O(1/N)$. By Corollary 1, this implies the result.   □

It remains to prove Theorem 3.

Proof of Theorem 3. The particular statement easily follows from the general statement. Indeed,

$$mt^2U/N' \leq (N/3T) \cdot (N'/3S)^2 \cdot (N/K)/N'$$
$$\leq N^2\,N'/(27\,S^2\,TK) \leq N^3/(27\,S^2\,TK) \leq 1/27.$$

And for sufficiently large N, it follows that

$$(1 - 6mt^2U/N') \cdot (1 - t^2U/N') \cdot |f^{-1}(y)| \cdot mt/N' - 2/N$$
$$\geq (1 - 7mt^2U/N') \cdot mt/N' - 2/N$$
$$\geq (1 - 7/27) \cdot mt/N' - 2/N$$
$$\geq 1/2 \cdot (mt/N')$$
$$\geq (N/3T) \cdot (N'/3S)/(2N')$$
$$\geq N/(18ST).$$

We now prove the general statement of Theorem 3. Fix $f, U,$ and y as in the theorem statement. In what follows, we will assume that g' is not bad (so that g is a random function from $[N]$ to $[D]$), at the cost of an additive $2/N$ in the success probability. By inspection, the subalgorithm inverts y if and only if the following event E_i occurs for some $i \in [m]$: (1) y is contained in $f(C^{t-1}(x_i))$ (which implies $h^t(x_i) \in C_y$), and (2), for all $j \neq i$, $h^t(x_j) \notin C_y$. Moreover, these events E_i are disjoint and symmetric. So the probability that the subalgorithm inverts y is exactly $m \Pr[E_1]$.

Let E_1^1 be the event that $h^t(x_j) \notin C_y$ for all $j \neq 1$, and let E_1^2 be the event that $y \in f(C^{t-1}(x_1))$; then $E_1 = E_1^1 \cap E_1^2$. To lower bound $\Pr[E_1]$, we will first lower bound $\Pr[E_1^2]$, then lower bound $\Pr[E_1^1 \mid E_1^2]$.

We claim that

Lemma 4

$$\Pr[E_1^2] := \Pr[y \in f(C^{t-1}(x_1))] \geq (1 - t^2 U/N') \cdot |f^{-1}(y)| \cdot t/N'.$$

For convenience, define

$$(Z_1, \ldots, Z_t) := (x_1, h(x_1), \ldots, h^{t-1}(x_1)) = C^{t-1}(x_1).$$

Let A_0 be the universal event (i.e., $\Pr[A_0] = 1$) and for $1 \leq i \leq t - 1$, let A_i be the event that (1) A_{i-1} holds, (2) $Z_i \notin f^{-1}(y)$, and (3) $f(Z_i) \notin f(\{Z_1, \ldots, Z_{i-1}\})$. More explicitly, for $1 \leq i \leq t - 1$, A_i is the event that (1) $Z_1, Z_2 \ldots, Z_i \notin f^{-1}(y)$, and (2) the values $f(Z_1), f(Z_2), \ldots, f(Z_i)$ are all distinct.

It is not hard to see that for all $1 \leq i \leq t$, conditioned on A_{i-1}, Z_i is uniformly random and independent of $(Z_1, \ldots, Z_{i-1})$. (Here the probability is over $x_1, \ldots, x_m$ and the random function g.) Indeed, the claim is trivial for $i = 1$. For $i > 1$, observe that conditioned on A_{i-1}, it holds that $f(Z_{i-1}) \notin f(\{Z_1, \ldots, Z_{i-2}\})$, so $Z_i = g(f(Z_{i-1}))$ is a fresh uniform sample from D, independent of $(Z_1, \ldots, Z_{i-1})$.

For $1 \leq i \leq t$, let B_i be the event that (1) A_{i-1} holds, and (2) $Z_i \in f^{-1}(y)$. That is, B_i is the event that (1) $Z_i \in f^{-1}(y)$, (2) $Z_j \notin f^{-1}(y)$ for all $j < i$, and (3), the values $f(Z_1), f(Z_2), \ldots, f(Z_{i-1})$ are all distinct. By construction, the events B_i are mutually exclusive. So,

$$\Pr[y \in f(C^{t-1}(x_1))] \geq \Pr\left[\bigcup_{i=1}^t B_i\right] = \sum_{i=1}^t \Pr[B_i] \geq \sum_{i=0}^{t-1} \Pr[A_i] \Pr[B_{i+1} \mid A_i].$$

First we obtain a lower bound on $\Pr[A_i]$.

$$
\begin{aligned}
\Pr[A_{i+1} \mid A_i] &= \Pr[Z_{i+1} \notin f^{-1}(y) \text{ and } f(Z_{i+1}) \notin f(\{Z_1, \ldots, Z_i\}) \mid A_i] \\
&= \Pr[Z_{i+1} \notin (f^{-1}(y) \cup f^{-1}(f(Z_1)) \cup \cdots \cup f^{-1}(f(Z_i))) \mid A_i] \\
&= 1 - |f^{-1}(y) \cup f^{-1}(f(Z_1)) \cup \cdots \cup f^{-1}(f(Z_i))|/N' \\
&\geq 1 - ((i+1)U)/N' \\
&\geq 1 - tU/N'.
\end{aligned}
$$

It follows that for all $0 \leq i \leq t - 1$,

$$\Pr[A_i] \geq (1 - tU/N')^t \geq 1 - t^2 U/N'.$$

By a similar calculation, for all $0 \leq i \leq t - 1$,

$$\Pr[B_{i+1} \mid A_i] = \Pr[Z_{i+1} \in f^{-1}(y) \mid A_i] = |f^{-1}(y)|/N'.$$

Putting everything together, we have the desired lower bound:

$$\Pr[E_1^2] := \Pr[y \in f(C^{t-1}(x_1))] \geq (1 - t^2 U/N') \cdot |f^{-1}(y)| \cdot t/N' .$$

Next we turn to lower bounding $\Pr[E_1^1 \mid E_1^2]$. We claim that

Lemma 5
$$\Pr[E_1^1 \mid E_1^2] \geq 1 - 6mt^2 U/N' .$$

It suffices to prove this claim. Indeed, combining it with Lemma 4 gives

$$\Pr[I] \geq m \Pr[E_1] \geq m \Pr[E_1^2] \cdot \Pr[E_1^1 \mid E_1^2]$$
$$\geq m(1 - 6mt^2 U/N') \cdot (1 - t^2 U/N') \cdot |f^{-1}(y)| \cdot t/N' .$$

Next we prove Lemma 5. By union bound and symmetry,

$$\Pr[E_1^1 \mid E_1^2] := \Pr[\forall j \neq 1, h^t(x_j) \notin C_y \mid E_1^2]$$
$$\geq 1 - m \cdot \Pr[h^t(x_2) \in C_y \mid y \in f(C^{t-1}(x_1))] . \tag{6}$$

Thus, our goal is to upper bound $\Pr[h^t(x_2) \in C_y \mid y \in f(C^{t-1}(x_1))]$. We reason similarly to the proof of Lemma 4.

Notice that, if $y \in f(C^{t-1}(x_1))$, then $g(y) \in C^t(x_1)$, and so $C_y := C^{t-1}(g(y)) \subseteq C^{2t}(x_1)$. It follows that

$$\Pr[h^t(x_2) \in C_y \mid y \in f(C^{t-1}(x_1))] \leq \Pr[h^t(x_2) \in C^{2t}(x_1) \mid y \in f(C^{t-1}(x_1))] .$$

This is convenient, since we have combined two events that would otherwise need to be considered separately; namely, the event that the chain $C^t(x_2)$ starting at x_2 intersects C_y, and the event that $C^t(x_2)$ intersects $C^{t-1}(x_1)$. Next, we reason as follows.

$$\Pr[h^t(x_2) \in C^{2t}(x_1) \mid y \in f(C^{t-1}(x_1))]$$
$$\leq \Pr[f(h^t(x_2)) \in f(C^{2t}(x_1)) \mid y \in f(C^{t-1}(x_1))]$$
$$\leq \Pr[\bigvee_{j=0}^{t} f(h^j(x_2)) \in f(C^{2t}(x_1)) \mid y \in f(C^{t-1}(x_1))]$$
$$\leq \sum_{j=0}^{t} \Pr[f(h^j(x_2)) \in f(C^{2t}(x_1)) \mid$$
$$\forall k < j, f(h^k(x_2)) \notin f(C^{2t}(x_1)), y \in f(C^{t-1}(x_1))] .$$

Intuitively, the j-th term in the sum corresponds to the chain starting at x_2 intersecting the chain starting at x_1 after j steps, but not before. We write

$$\mathsf{COND}_{1,j} := \forall k < j, f(h^k(x_2)) \notin f(C^{2t}(x_1)) \text{ and } \mathsf{COND}_2 := y \in f(C^{t-1}(x_1))$$

We claim that for all $0 \leq j \leq t$, the j-th term satisfies the following bound:

$$\Pr[f(h^j(x_2)) \in f(C^{2t}(x_1)) \mid \mathsf{COND}_{1,j}, \mathsf{COND}_2] \leq |f^{-1}(f(C^{2t}(x_1)))|/N' .$$

Notice that if $j = 0$, then $\text{COND}_{1,j}$ is vacuous, $h^j(x_2) = x_2$ is a fresh independent uniform sample from D, and the claimed bound holds with equality.

For $j \geq 1$, consider the event $\text{COND}_{3,j}$ that, for some $k < j-1$, $f(h^{j-1}(x_2)) = f(h^k(x_2))$. It is not hard to see that

$$\Pr[f(h^j(x_2)) \in f(C^{2t}(x_1)) \mid \text{COND}_{1,j}, \text{COND}_2, \text{COND}_{3,j}] = 0 \,.$$

Indeed, applying $f \circ g$ to both sides of $\text{COND}_{3,j}$ gives $f(h^j(x_2)) = f(h^{k+1}(x_2))$, but $\text{COND}_{1,j}$ implies $f(h^{k+1}(x_2)) \notin f(C^{2t}(x_1))$.

On the other hand, if we condition on $\neg\text{COND}_{3,j}$ (and $\text{COND}_{1,j}$ and COND_2), we know that $v_j := f(h^{j-1}(x_2))$ is distinct from the values $f(h^k(x_2))$ for $0 \leq k < j - 1$. By $\text{COND}_{1,j}$ and COND_2, v_j is also distinct from the values $f(h^i(x_1))$ for $0 \leq i \leq 2t$. In other words, v_j is not in the set V_j defined by

$$V_j := \{f(h^k(x_2)) \mid 0 \leq k < j - 1\} \cup \{f(h^i(x_1)) \mid 0 \leq i \leq 2t\}.$$

But it is not difficult to verify that the events $\text{COND}_{1,j}, \text{COND}_2$, and $\text{COND}_{3,j}$ can be expressed solely in terms of x_1, x_2, and the random variables $g(x)$ for $x \in V_j$. (As a sanity check, it is helpful to note that $h^{j-1}(x_2) = g(f(h^{j-2}(x_2)))$ only depends on the random variables $g(f(h^k(x_2)))$ for $k < j - 1$.) In particular, these events are independent of $g(v_j)$. It follows that, even conditional on $\text{COND}_{1,j}, \text{COND}_2$, and $\neg\text{COND}_{3,j}$, $h^j(x_2) = g(v_j)$ is a fresh uniform sample from D, independent of the random variables in the conditional. So we have

$$\Pr[f(h^j(x_2)) \in f(C^{2t}(x_1)) \mid \text{COND}_{1,j}, \text{COND}_2, \neg\text{COND}_{3,j}]$$
$$= |f^{-1}(f(C^{2t}(x_1)))|/N' \,,$$

and we have established the claimed bound on the terms of the sum. Plugging the bound in, we see

$$\Pr[h^t(x_2) \in C^{2t}(x_1) \mid y \in f(C^{t-1}(x_1))]$$
$$\leq \sum_{j=0}^{t} |f^{-1}(f(C^{2t}(x_1)))|/N'$$
$$\leq \sum_{i=0}^{t} U \cdot (2t+1)/N'$$
$$\leq U \cdot (t+1) \cdot (2t+1)/N' \leq 6t^2 U/N' \,.$$

(The last line only holds if $t > 0$, but otherwise Lemma 5 is trivial.) Combining this with Eq. (6) concludes the proof of Lemma 5 and hence the proof of Theorem 3. □

4   A Lower Bound Against Guess-and-check Non-adaptive Algorithms

In this section, we prove our lower bound against guess-and-check non-adaptive algorithms. The precise statement is as follows.

Theorem 4. *Any guess-and-check algorithm that solves SFI for permutations with success probability at least 3/4 using S bits of preprocessing and T queries must have $S \geq (N/2)\log(N/6T) - 4$.*

Following De et al. [9] and Dodis et al. [10], we will consider randomized encoding and decoding procedures for a set of functions, and rely on the following lemma which lower bounds the encoding length.

Lemma 6. *([9,10]) Suppose there exist randomized encoding and decoding procedures* (Enc, Dec) *for a set $\mathcal{F}$. We say such an encoding has recovery probability δ if for all $f \in \mathcal{F}$,*

$$\Pr_{r \sim \{0,1\}^\ell}[\text{Dec}(\text{Enc}(f,r),r) = f] \geq \delta .$$

The encoding length of (Enc, Dec), *defined to be $\max_{f,r}\{|\text{Enc}(f,r)|\}$, is at least $\log|\mathcal{F}| - \log 1/\delta$.*

Our main lemma gives a randomized encoding for the family of permutations given a guess-and-check inversion algorithm.

Lemma 7. *Suppose that there exists a guess-and-check algorithm $(\mathcal{P}, \mathcal{A})$ that solves SFI for permutations with success probability 3/4 using S bits of preprocessing and T queries. Then there exists a randomized encoding for the set of all permutations from $[N]$ to $[N]$, with recovery probability at least 1/2 and encoding length at most*

$$S + \lceil N/2 \rceil \cdot \log T + \log\frac{N!}{\lceil N/2 \rceil!} + 3 .$$

We first observe that Theorem 4 follows immediately from the above lemmas. Indeed, combining the two lemmas and recalling that there are $N!$ permutations from $[N]$ to $[N]$, we have

$$S + \lceil N/2 \rceil \cdot \log T + \log\frac{N!}{\lceil N/2 \rceil!} + 3 \geq \log N! - \log 2 .$$

Hence,

$$S \geq \log\lceil N/2 \rceil! - \lceil N/2 \rceil \cdot \log T - 4 \geq \frac{N}{2}\log\frac{N}{6T} - 4 ,$$

where the second inequality is due to the fact $m! \geq (m/e)^m \geq (m/3)^m$ (by Stirling's approximation) and $\lceil N/2 \rceil \geq N/2$.

Proof. Fix an arbitrary permutation $f: [N] \to [N]$. We encode f as follows. Given f and randomness r, the encoder simulates $(\mathcal{P}, \mathcal{A})$ on every $y \in [N]$. Let st be the output of $\mathcal{P}(f,r)$ and G be the set of y such that $\mathcal{A}^f(\text{st}, y, r) = f^{-1}(y)$. By an averaging argument,

$$\Pr_{r \sim \{0,1\}^\ell}[\Pr_{y \sim [N]}[\mathcal{A}^f(\text{st}, y, r) = f^{-1}(y)] \geq \frac{1}{2}] \geq \frac{1}{2} .$$

In other words, with probability at least 1/2 the size of G is at least $N' := \lceil N/2 \rceil$. Assuming $|G| \geq N'$, we pick a set $G' \subseteq G$ with size exactly N' and encode f as follows,

1. Include st, and a description of G'. This requires $S + \lceil \log \binom{N}{N'} \rceil$ bits.
2. For each $y \in G'$ (in lexicographic order), run $\mathcal{A}^f(\text{st}, y, r)$ and include the index i such that the answer to the ith oracle query is y. This requires $\lceil N' \cdot \log T \rceil$ bits in total.
3. Store the mapping from $[N] \setminus f^{-1}(G')$ to $[N] \setminus G'$ corresponding to f restricted to $[N] \setminus f^{-1}(G')$ using $\lceil \log(N - N')! \rceil$ bits.

Given the shared randomness r, the decoder does the following:

1. Recover st and G'.
2. For each $y \in G'$, run $\mathcal{A}(\text{st}, y, r)$ to generate T non-adaptive queries $x_1, \ldots, x_T$, recover the index i and set $f(x_i) = y$. We remark that this step heavily relies on the guess-and-check property of $\mathcal{A}$.
3. After the above two steps, the decoder reconstructs $f^{-1}(G')$ and G' (hence $[N] \setminus f^{-1}(G')$ and $[N] \setminus G'$). Then the decoder recovers the values of $[N] \setminus f^{-1}(G')$ using the remainder of the encoding.

Assuming $|G| \geq N/2$, the decoding procedure recovers f. The encoding length is

$$S + \left\lceil \log \binom{N}{N'} \right\rceil + \lceil N' \cdot \log T \rceil + \lceil \log(N - N')! \rceil \leq S + N' \cdot \log T + \log \frac{N!}{N'!} + 3 \,,$$

as claimed.   □

5   Comparing Variants of Function Inversion

In this section, we prove that different formulations of the function inversion problem are equivalent (up to polylogarithmic factors in S and T). First, we prove that the decision version of the Function Inversion problem, that merely asks to check whether a query y is in the image of the preprocessed function f, is as hard as the search version of the problem where the goal is to find a preimage of y. We prove this equivalence for three different settings: for arbitrary (i.e., worst-case) functions in Sect. 5.1, for random functions in Sect. 5.2, and for injective functions in the full version [15].[8] Also, [8, Lemma 21] proves that for worst-case functions and $M > N$, inverting $f: [N] \rightarrow [M]$ is as hard as inverting $f': [N] \rightarrow [N]$. (Of course, for $M < N$, inverting worst-case functions $f: [N] \rightarrow [M]$ trivially reduces to inverting worst-case functions $f': [N] \rightarrow [N]$.) In the full version [15], we show that this result can be extended to the setting of random functions.

These equivalences suggest that the hardness of function inversion is specified by the domain size and the class of functions (worst-case/injective/random), but not by the search/decision type of the problem or the range size.

---

[8] We remark that the result for injective functions is very similar to [8, Theorem 8]. We simply include it for completeness.

5.1   Search-to-decision Reduction for Arbitrary Functions

In this section, we prove an essentially tight search-to-decision reduction for worst-case function inversion. Namely, given an algorithm that solves DFI (for all functions; see Definition 3) in query time T and preprocessing S, we design an algorithm that solves SFI (for all functions) in query time $T \cdot \mathrm{poly}(\log N)$ and preprocessing $S \cdot \mathrm{poly}(\log N)$ (or even query time $O(T \cdot \log N)$ and preprocessing $O(S \cdot \log N)$, see Remark 1).

First, in Lemma 8 we observe that, given an algorithm for DFI, one can solve SFI on all inputs y that have unique preimages. Then, in Theorem 5 we use the Isolation Lemma [21,26,28] to reduce the general case of SFI to the case where y has a unique preimage.[9]

Lemma 8. *Let $N = 2^n$ and $\varepsilon := \varepsilon(N) \in (0,1/2]$. Suppose there exists an algorithm $(\mathcal{P}, \mathcal{A})$ that solves (N,M)-DFI with advantage ε using S bits of pre-processing and T queries. Then there exists an algorithm $(\mathcal{P}', \mathcal{A}')$ that uses $S' \leq O(Sn(\log n)/\varepsilon^2)$ bits of preprocessing and $T' \leq O(Tn(\log n)/\varepsilon^2)$ queries with the following guarantees. For every $f\colon [N] \to [M]$ and every $y \in [M]$ satisfying $|\{f^{-1}(y)\}| = 1$,*

$$\Pr_{r \sim \{0,1\}^{\ell'}}[x' \leftarrow (\mathcal{A}')^f(\mathcal{P}'(f,r),y,r) \ :\ f(x') = y] \geq 1 - 1/(10n^2).$$

Furthermore, for every $f\colon [N] \to [M]$ and every $y \in [M]$,

$$\Pr_{r \sim \{0,1\}^{\ell'}}[x' \leftarrow (\mathcal{A}')^f(\mathcal{P}'(f,r),y,r) \ :\ x' \neq \bot \text{ and } f(x') \neq y] \leq 1/(10n^2).$$

For space reasons, we defer the proofs of Lemma 8 and the other results in this section to the full version [15]. We can now state the main result of this section. The main difference in the statements of Lemma 8 and Theorem 5 is that the SFI algorithm in Lemma 8 is only guaranteed to succeed on queries that have a unique preimage, while the SFI algorithm in Theorem 5 works for all queries.

Theorem 5. *Let $N = 2^n$, and let $\varepsilon := \varepsilon(N) \in (0,1/2]$. Suppose there exists an algorithm $(\mathcal{P}, \mathcal{A})$ that solves (N,M)-DFI with advantage ε using S bits of preprocessing and T queries. Then there exists an algorithm $(\mathcal{P}'', \mathcal{A}'')$ that solves (N,M)-SFI with success probability 0.9, $S'' \leq O(Sn^2(\log n)/\varepsilon^2)$ bits of preprocessing, and $T'' \leq O(Tn^2(\log n)/\varepsilon^2)$ queries.*

Remark 1. A few extensions of Theorem 5 are in order.

1. This search-to-decision reduction is non-adaptive, so a non-adaptive algorithm for DFI implies a non-adaptive algorithm for SFI (and an adaptive algorithm for DFI implies an adaptive algorithm for SFI). See the full version [15].

---

[9] One could reduce the latter probability of failure to 0 with an adaptive reduction, but we prefer to keep the reduction non-adaptive with a small probability of error.

2. In the proof of Lemma 8 in the full version [15], the $\log n$ factor in the advice length and the number of queries comes from the amplification of the success probability of the assumed DFI algorithm from $1/2 + \varepsilon$ to $1 - O(1/n^3)$. We remark that one can get rid of this $\log n$ factor by recovering the bits of $C(x)$ rather than the bits of x for a good linear code C (similarly to how it is done in the proof of Theorem 6). This modification will also improve the parameters S'' and T'' in Theorem 5 by a $\log n$ factor (though unfortunately it does *not* preserve non-adaptivity).

5.2   Search-to-decision Reduction for Average-Case Functions

In this section, we show a different search-to-decision reduction for average-case function inversion. (See Definition 4 for the formal definition of average-case SFI and Definition 5 for the formal definition of average-case DFI.) The proof of Theorem 5 does not work for the case of average-case functions as Lemma 8 heavily relies on the fact that the assumed DFI algorithm works for all functions. Nevertheless, we can extend the techniques of the previous section to recover bits of a certain encoding of x rather than the individual bits of x and prove an essentially tight search-to-decision reduction for average-case function inversion in Theorem 6.

Theorem 6. *Let $N = 2^n$. Suppose there exists an algorithm $(\mathcal{P}, \mathcal{A})$ that solves average-case $(2N, M)$-DFI with advantage $\varepsilon \geq 1/2 - \exp\left(-2N/M - 2N/M^2\right)/4$, using S bits of preprocessing and T queries. Then for any constant $\delta \in (0, 1/4)$, there exists an algorithm $(\mathcal{P}', \mathcal{A}')$ that solves average-case (N, M)-SFI with success probability $\exp\left(-2N/M - 2N/M^2\right) - (1/2 - \varepsilon)/(1/4 - \delta)$ using $S' \leq O_\delta(nS)$ bits of preprocessing and $T' \leq O_\delta(nT)$ queries.*

Remark 2.

1. Similarly to the reduction in Theorem 5, the search-to-decision reduction of Theorem 6 is non-adaptive.
2. A drawback of Theorem 6 is that it requires the DFI algorithm to have very large advantage ε. This is because we actually need the DFI algorithm to have non-negligible advantage in distinguishing between (1) uniformly random y that is not in the image of f; and (2) uniformly random y with $|f^{-1}(y)| = 1$ (i.e., a random image that has a unique preimage). We could have worked directly with this assumption on the DFI algorithm, but we prefer the simpler (but strictly stronger) assumption in Theorem 6.

6   Removing Shared Randomness

In this section, we adapt to our setting Newman's technique for converting public-coin protocols to private-coin protocols [23] in the context of communication complexity. We first define a general notion of a computational problem with preprocessing to which our technique will apply.

Definition 9. *Let $\mathcal{F}$ be a set of functions $f : D \to R$, and let $\mathcal{Y}$, $\mathcal{X}$ be sets. A preprocessing-queries tradeoff problem is a function $g : \mathcal{F} \times \mathcal{Y} \to 2^{\mathcal{X}}$, where $2^{\mathcal{X}}$ denotes the powerset of $\mathcal{X}$. Let $(\mathcal{P}, \mathcal{A})$ be a pair of randomized algorithms. We say that*

1. *$(\mathcal{P}, \mathcal{A})$ solves g with success probability $\delta \in (0, 1]$ if for all $f \in \mathcal{F}$ and $y \in \mathcal{Y}$,*

$$\Pr_{r \sim \{0,1\}^l}[\mathcal{A}^f(\mathcal{P}(f, r), y, r) \in g(f, y)] \geq \delta.$$

2. *$(\mathcal{P}, \mathcal{A})$ solves g without shared randomness with success probability $\delta \in (0, 1]$ if for all $f \in \mathcal{F}$ and $y \in \mathcal{Y}$,*

$$\Pr_{r_1, r_2 \sim \{0,1\}^{l'}}[\mathcal{A}^f(\mathcal{P}(f, r_1), y, r_2) \in g(f, y)] \geq \delta.$$

Our generic lemma for removing shared randomness is as follows.

Lemma 9. *Suppose there exists an algorithm that solves a preprocessing-queries tradeoff problem $g : \mathcal{F} \times \mathcal{Y} \to 2^{\mathcal{X}}$ with success probability $1 - \varepsilon$ using preprocessing S and T. Then there exists another algorithm that solves g without shared randomness, with success probability $1 - 2\varepsilon$, preprocessing $S + \log(K/\varepsilon^2) + O(1)$, and T queries, where $K = \log|\mathcal{F} \times \mathcal{Y}|$. If the first algorithm is non-adaptive (resp. guess-and-check) then so is the second. Moreover, the success probability can be increased to 1 at the cost of an additional $4\varepsilon|\mathcal{Y}|\lceil \log|\mathcal{Y}| \rceil$ bits of preprocessing.*

Proof. The proof is adapted from the proof of Newman's technique given in [24]. Sample $k = O(2K/\varepsilon^2)$ independent random strings $r_1, \ldots, r_k \in \{0,1\}^l$.

We claim that with probability at least $1 - 2^{-K}$, these random strings satisfy the following property: For all functions $f \in \mathcal{F}$ and inputs $y \in \mathcal{Y}$, we have

$$\Pr_{i \sim [k]}[\mathcal{A}^f(\mathcal{P}(f, r_i), y, r_i) \in g(f, y)] \geq 1 - 2\varepsilon. \tag{7}$$

From the claim, it follows that k fixed strings $r_1^*, \ldots, r_k^*$ with this property must exist. Then the algorithms $(\mathcal{A}', \mathcal{P}')$ are simple. On input f, $\mathcal{P}'$ first samples $i \sim [k]$, then simulates $\mathcal{P}$ to compute $st := \mathcal{P}(f, r_i^*)$. It outputs advice (st, i). On input y, $\mathcal{A}'^f$ simply returns $\mathcal{A}^f(st, y, r_i^*)$. Clearly $\mathcal{A}'$ is non-adaptive (resp. guess-and-check) if $\mathcal{A}$ is.

It remains to prove the claim. Fix a function f and an input y. For each independent random string r_i we have

$$\Pr_{r_i}[\mathcal{A}^f(\mathcal{P}(f, r_i), y, r_i) \in g(f, y)] \geq 1 - \varepsilon.$$

Hence by the Chernoff bound (Lemma 1), the probability that $2\varepsilon k$ strings r_i satisfy $\mathcal{A}^f(\mathcal{P}(f, r_i), y, r_i) \notin g(f, y)$ is at most $2^{\Omega(\varepsilon^2 k)} \leq 2^{-2K}$. Since there are at most 2^K possible pairs (f, y), by union bound, the probability that this occurs for any f, y is at most 2^{-K}, as claimed.

For the "Moreover", fix a function $f \in \mathcal{F}$. Notice that by an averaging argument, Eq. (7) implies that for some $i^* \in [k]$, $r_{i^*}^*$ satisfies

$$\Pr_{y \in \mathcal{Y}}[\mathcal{A}^f(\mathcal{P}(f, r_i^*), y, r_i^*) \in g(f, y)] \geq 1 - 2\varepsilon .$$

Thus there are only $b = 2\varepsilon|\mathcal{Y}|$ inputs $y_1, \ldots, y_b$ for which $\mathcal{A}^f(\mathcal{P}(f, r_{i^*}^*), y_j, r_{i^*}^*) \notin g(f, y)$. $\mathcal{P}'$ outputs (st, i^*, E), where $E := \{(y_j, x_j)\}_{j \in [b]}$, and for each $j \in [b]$, $x_j \in g(f, y)$. (Such an x_j is guaranteed to exist because the original algorithm $(\mathcal{A}, \mathcal{P})$ is assumed to have positive success probability on all input-challenge pairs (f, y).) Given challenge y, $\mathcal{A}'^f$ first checks if $(y, x) \in E$ for some $x \in \mathcal{X}$. If so, it returns x. Otherwise, it returns $\mathcal{A}^f(st, y, r_{i^*}^*)$ as before. It is easy to see that $(\mathcal{P}', \mathcal{A}')$ always succeeds, uses at most $S + \log(K/\varepsilon^2) + 4\varepsilon|\mathcal{Y}|\lceil \log|\mathcal{Y}|\rceil + O(1)$ bits of preprocessing, and uses at most T queries. And again, $\mathcal{A}'$ is clearly non adaptive (resp. guess-and-check) if $\mathcal{A}$ is. $\qquad \square$

It's worth noting that while the proof uses the probabilistic method (and so is nonconstructive), it is essentially constructive in the sense that choosing the required strings at random works with very high probability. (Of course, choosing the strings at random will not allow us to obtain success probability 1.) The following is an immediate corollary in our setting.

Corollary 1. *Suppose that for some class $\mathcal{F}$ of functions $f : [N] \to [M]$ there exists a function-inversion algorithm that solves (N, M)-SFI (resp. solves (N, M)-DFI) for $\mathcal{F}$ with success probability $1 - \varepsilon$, using preprocessing S, and queries T. Then there exists a function-inversion algorithm that solves (N, M)-SFI (resp. solves (N, M)-DFI) for $\mathcal{F}$ with success probability $1 - 2\varepsilon$ without shared randomness, using $S + \log(N/\varepsilon^2) + \log \log M + O(1)$ bits of preprocessing and T queries. If the first algorithm is non-adaptive (resp. guess-and-check) then so is the second. Moreover, the success probability can be made 1 at the cost of an additional $4\varepsilon N \log N$ bits of preprocessing.*

Proof. It is easy to check that each of these function-inversion problems is a preprocessing-queries tradeoff problem, with $\mathcal{Y} = [M]$. Thus Lemma 9 applies. So it suffices to observe that

$$
\begin{aligned}
\log(K/\varepsilon^2) &= \log K - \log \varepsilon^2 \\
&= \log \log |\mathcal{F} \times \mathcal{Y}| - \log \varepsilon^2 \\
&= \log \log M^{N+1} - \log \varepsilon^2 \\
&= \log((N+1) \log M) - \log \varepsilon^2 \\
&= \log(N+1) + \log \log M - \log \varepsilon^2 \\
&= O(1) + \log N - \log \varepsilon^2 + \log \log M \\
&= O(1) + \log(N/\varepsilon^2) + \log \log M.
\end{aligned}
$$

$\qquad \square$

Acknowledgements. Siyao Guo was supported by National Natural Science Foundation of China Grant No. 62102260, Shanghai Municipal Education Commission (SMEC) Grant No. 0920000169, NYTP Grant No. 20121201 and NYU Shanghai Boost Fund. Spencer Peters and Noah Stephens-Davidowitz were supported in part by the NSF under Grant No. CCF-2122230. We are indebted to all reviewers of this paper, but we would like to acknowledge specifically the anonymous CRYPTO reviewer who pointed out the existence of the very simple non-adaptive algorithm.

References

1. Alon, N., Bruck, J., Naor, J., Naor, M., Roth, R.M.: Construction of asymptotically good low-rate error-correcting codes through pseudo-random graphs. IEEE Trans. Inf. Theory **38**(2), 509–516 (1992)
2. Barkan, E., Biham, E., Shamir, A.: Rigorous bounds on cryptanalytic time/memory tradeoffs. In: CRYPTO (2006)
3. Chawin, D., Haitner, I., Mazor, N.: Lower bounds on the time/memory tradeoff of function inversion. In: TCC (2020)
4. Chung, K.M., Guo, S., Liu, Q., Qian, L.: Tight quantum time-space tradeoffs for function inversion. In: FOCS (2020)
5. Chung, K.M., Liao, T.N., Qian, L.: Lower bounds for function inversion with quantum advice. In: ITC (2020)
6. Coretti, S., Dodis, Y., Guo, S.: Non-uniform bounds in the random-permutation, ideal-cipher, and generic-group models. In: CRYPTO (2018)
7. Coretti, S., Dodis, Y., Guo, S., Steinberger, J.: Random oracles and non-uniformity. In: Eurocrypt (2018)
8. Corrigan-Gibbs, H., Kogan, D.: The function-inversion problem: barriers and opportunities. In: TCC (2019)
9. De, A., Trevisan, L., Tulsiani, M.: Time space tradeoffs for attacks against one-way functions and PRGs. In: CRYPTO (2010)
10. Dodis, Y., Guo, S., Katz, J.: Fixing cracks in the concrete: random oracles with auxiliary input, revisited. In: EUROCRYPT (2017)
11. Dvořák, P., Koucký, M., Král, K., Slívová, V.: Data structures lower bounds and popular conjectures. In: ESA (2021)
12. Fiat, A., Naor, M.: Rigorous time/space tradeoffs for inverting functions. In: STOC (1991)
13. Gennaro, R., Trevisan, L.: Lower bounds on the efficiency of generic cryptographic constructions. In: FOCS (2000)
14. Golovnev, A., Guo, S., Horel, T., Park, S., Vaikuntanathan, V.: Data structures meet cryptography: 3SUM with preprocessing. In: STOC (2020)
15. Golovnev, A., Guo, S., Peters, S., Stephens-Davidowitz, N.: Revisiting time-space tradeoffs for function inversion (2022). https://eccc.weizmann.ac.il/report/2022/145/
16. Gravin, N., Guo, S., Kwok, T.C., Lu, P.: Concentration bounds for almost k-wise independence with applications to non-uniform security. In: SODA (2021)
17. Hellman, M.: A cryptanalytic time-memory trade-off. IEEE Trans. Inf. Theory **26**(4), 401–406 (1980)
18. Justesen, J.: Class of constructive asymptotically good algebraic codes. IEEE Trans. Inf. Theory **18**(5), 652–656 (1972)
19. MacWilliams, F.J., Sloane, N.J.A.: The theory of error-correcting codes. Elsevier (1977)

20. Mitzenmacher, M., Upfal, E.: Probability and computing: Randomization and probabilistic techniques in algorithms and data analysis. Cambridge University Press (2017)
21. Mulmuley, K., Vazirani, U.V., Vazirani, V.V.: Matching is as easy as matrix inversion. In: STOC (1987)
22. Nayebi, A., Aaronson, S., Belovs, A., Trevisan, L.: Quantum lower bound for inverting a permutation with advice. Quantum Inf. Comput. **15**(11–12), 901–913 (2015)
23. Newman, I.: Private vs. common random bits in communication complexity. Inf. Process. Lett. **39**(2), 67–71 (1991)
24. Rao, A., Yehudayoff, A.: Communication Complexity and Applications. Cambridge University Press (2020)
25. Spielman, D.A.: Linear-time encodable and decodable error-correcting codes. In: STOC (1995)
26. Ta-Shma, N.: A simple proof of the isolation lemma (2015). https://eccc.weizmann.ac.il//report/2015/080/
27. Unruh, D.: Random oracles and auxiliary input. In: CRYPTO (2007)
28. Valiant, L.G., Vazirani, V.V.: NP is as easy as detecting unique solutions. In: STOC (1985)
29. Wee, H.: On obfuscating point functions. In: STOC (2005)
30. Yao, A.C.C.: Coherent functions and program checkers. In: STOC (1990)

The Query-Complexity of Preprocessing Attacks

Ashrujit Ghoshal$^{(\boxtimes)}$ (ID) and Stefano Tessaro (ID)

Paul G. Allen School of Computer Science & Engineering, University of Washington, Seattle, WA, USA
{ashrujit,tessaro}@cs.washington.edu

Abstract. A large number of works prove lower bounds on space-time trade-offs in preprocessing attacks, i.e., trade-offs between the size of the advice and the time needed to break a scheme given such advice. We contend that the question of how much *time* is needed to produce this advice is equally important, and often highly non-trivial. However, this question has received significantly less attention. In this paper, we present lower bounds on the complexity of preprocessing attacks that depend on both offline and online time. As in the case of space-time trade-offs, we focus in particular on settings with ideal primitives, where both the offline and online time-complexities are approximated by the number of queries to the given primitive. We give generic results that highlight the benefits of salting to generically increase the offline costs of preprocessing attacks. The majority of our paper presents several results focusing on *salted* hash functions. In particular, we provide a fairly involved analysis of the pre-image- and collision-resistance security of the (two-block) Merkle-Damgård construction in our model.

1 Introduction

Preprocessing attacks leverage a suitably pre-computed *advice* string that only depends on some underlying primitive (e.g., a hash function, a block cipher, or an elliptic curve) to break a scheme using fewer resources than the best attack without such advice. For example, Hellman's [14] seminal work shows that, for a given permutation $\pi : [N] \to [N]$, one can compute a suitable S-bit advice that allows inverting the permutation on any point in time $T \approx N/S$.

A number of works, starting from [5,6,9,10,21], prove lower bounds that establish inherent trade-offs between the *size* of the advice and the *online* time needed to break the scheme (often referred to as "space-time trade-offs"). A question that has received less attention, however, concerns the study of trade-offs between the *offline* time needed to compute the advice and the online time. To the best of our knowledge, the only such result, due to Corrigan-Gibbs and Kogan [7], focuses on the discrete logarithm problem in the generic-group model.

Initiating a more comprehensive and grounded study of such *offline-online time trade-offs* is the main goal of this paper. As in prior works on space-time trade-offs, we focus on proving lower bounds relying on ideal primitives, thus

© International Association for Cryptologic Research 2023
H. Handschuh and A. Lysyanskaya (Eds.): CRYPTO 2023, LNCS 14082, pp. 482–513, 2023.
https://doi.org/10.1007/978-3-031-38545-2_16

approximating time with query-complexity. In addition to providing a generic overview of how salting makes preprocessing attacks expensive, we revisit under a new lens the recent works [2,3,6,12] on preprocessing attacks against *salted* hash functions and the Merkle-Damgård construction.

WHY DOES TIME-COMPLEXITY MATTER? One main reason to study preprocessing attacks is to model non-uniform security. In this case, it is indeed irrelevant *how long* it takes to compute a good advice string since its mere *existence* suffices for an attack, although such an attack may well never be explicitly found. This perspective has emerged from the debate around the use of non-uniformity in security [4,16], although often the issue can be bypassed entirely via cleverer uniform reductions, as in e.g. [11]. The importance of non-uniform attacks in practice has also been a source of debate [19].

Here, we are concerned with a more practical and less formal perspective where preprocessing is used in practical, explicit attacks for one of two reasons:

1. An attack needs to run very quickly in the online stage (e.g., must succeed before a time-out occurs in an Internet protocol) but can afford to run much slower in an offline stage. For instance, Adrian et al. [1] use offline computation to break 512-bit finite-field discrete logs in less than a minute of online time, hence compromising legacy versions of the Diffie-Hellman handshake.
2. The advice is computed once and for all and is re-used to attack multiple instances. This is the scenario of *Rainbow Tables* [18], which leverage Hellman-type trade-offs to speed up attacks against unsalted password hashes.

In both cases, it is imperative that the offline time remains within a feasible range.

WHEN IS PREPROCESSING WORTH IT? Different preprocessing attacks exhibit very different offline-online time trade-offs. The main goal is to ensure that, thanks to preprocessing, the online complexity of an attack is better than the best preprocessing-free attack. For example, in Rainbow Tables, for a password dictionary of size N, the preprocessing takes time $T_1 \approx N$ to produce advice of size S, for which the online complexity is then $T_2 \approx N/S$. The online complexity bests the optimal online-only attacks, which is $\Omega(N)$; moreover, the preprocessing time is optimal since the *sum* of the offline and online time cannot beat the complexity of the best online only attack.

A more interesting example is finding collisions in the *salted* Merkle-Damgård (MD) construction, as studied in a line of recent works [2,3,12]. Given a (random) compression function $h : [N] \times [M] \to [N]$, the offline phase of the optimal attack for two-block collisions finds S collisions of the form $h(a_i, m_i) = h(a_i, m_i')$ for $m \neq m'$ and salts $a_1, \ldots, a_S$, for which offline time $T_1 \approx S \cdot \sqrt{N}$ is necessary. Then, the online phase, given the salt a, uses time $T_2 = N/S$ to find m such that $h(a, m) = a_i$ for some i, which yields a collision $m\|m_i, m\|m_i'$. This attack achieves the trade-off $T_1 \times T_2 = N^{3/2}$, and the online time beats the naïve Birthday attack whenever $T_1 = \Omega(N)$. It is not clear, however, whether the trade-off is optimal, and this is indeed one of the questions we are addressing below.

OUR CONTRIBUTIONS. This paper initiates an in-depth investigation of the time-complexity of preprocessing attacks, and we focus primarily on salted constructions using hash functions, which is where the most interesting technical questions emerge. In particular:

- **Generic salting.** We propose a generic technique to analyze the common practice of salting to mitigate the effects of preprocessing attacks. We consider a model where every call to the underlying primitive is salted. Qualitatively, our result implies that in most settings, to beat the best online-only attack, one needs to invest an offline effort proportional to compromising the primitive on *every salt*.
- **Concrete bounds for random oracles.** Our generic technique can be combined with a recent work by Jaeger and Tessaro [15] to provide concrete quantitative upper bounds on the advantage of an offline-online adversary. These bounds are not always optimal, and we prove more refined bounds. We exemplify this situation by studying the pre-image-resistance and collision-resistance of a salted random oracle.
- **Merkle Damgård construction.** The technical bulk of this paper studies the salted Merkle-Damgård (MD) construction with a random ideal compression function. Here, salting achieves a more limited effect and still allows for non-trivial trade-offs between the offline and online complexity of an attack. We deliver quantitative upper bounds on the advantage of breaking pre-image-resistance and collision-resistance of the two-block salted MD for offline-online adversaries.

SALTING DEFEATS PREPROCESSING. We start with a result that generically justifies the practice of salting cryptographic primitives to defeat preprocessing attacks. Such results were proved for space-time-complexity in [6], but we give an analogue result for offline-online query-complexity.

Concretely, we assume that we have a scheme Π^g that relies on a random function $g : [M] \to [N]$, and that the advantage in breaking Π^g, as a function of the number of queries to g, is a well understood quantity. (In particular, here we assume that the security depends only on the number of queries to g.) Now, we replace $g(\cdot)$ with a *salted* hash function $h(a, \cdot)$, where $h : [S] \times [M] \to [N]$. We aim to quantify security for an attacker $\mathcal{A}$ which, during an offline phase, is allowed to issue T_1 queries to $h(\cdot, \cdot)$. Then, after learning the random salt $a \leftarrow_\$ [S]$, $\mathcal{A}$ attacks $\Pi^{h(a, \cdot)}$. In this online stage, $\mathcal{A}$ can issue T_2 queries to $h(\cdot, \cdot)$.

We show that if (roughly) T^* queries to g are needed to break Π^g in the *worst case* with very high probability, then for the attacker $\mathcal{A}$ to succeed with high probability as well, $T_1 \geqslant S \cdot T^*/2$ or $T_2 \geqslant T^*/2$ must hold. In other words, the *only* way to beat the best online-only attack is to invest an amount of preprocessing equivalent to that of breaking the scheme *for every choice of the salt*. At the core of this proof is a simple argument that shows how to build an adversary $\mathcal{B}$ against Π^g, achieving the same advantage as $\mathcal{A}$, with *expected* query-complexity $T_1/S + T_2$.

QUANTITATIVE BOUNDS FOR SALTED RANDOM ORACLES. The above generic result holds for adversaries achieving high advantage. Overall, we would like to go one step further to obtain quantitative precise upper bounds on the advantage of $\mathcal{A}$ as a function of T_1 and T_2 and to characterize the whole advantage curve. As our first result, we combine the above reduction to an adversary with expected query-complexity with the work by Jaeger and Tessaro [15]. This allows us to show that any adversary attempting to break pre-image-resistance of a random oracle with a s-bit salt and n-bit outputs succeeds with probability at most

$$\frac{T_1}{S \cdot N} + \frac{T_2}{N} ,$$

where $N = 2^n$, $S = 2^s$ and, once again, T_1 and T_2 are the offline- and online-query-complexity. This bound ends up being nearly *exact* in that there are offline- and online-only attacks achieving each of the two terms.

Unfortunately, the same approach via [15] yields only suboptimal bounds for other properties, such as the collision resistance of a salted random oracle. Here, we give a direct proof that shows a bound of order

$$\frac{T_1}{S \cdot \sqrt{N}} + \frac{T_2^2}{N} .$$

This proof is of independent interest, and uses a compression argument to bound the number of salts for which a collision is found in the preprocessing stage. And indeed, the first term is matched by an attack that finds collisions for $\Omega(\lceil T_1/\sqrt{N} \rceil)$ salts, issuing $\sqrt{N}$ queries for each of these salts.

TRADE-OFFS FOR MERKLE-DAMGÅRD. Our first set of results aims to show that salting prevents offline-online trade-offs–the best attack is either fully offline or fully online. However, we show that this is not true if we cannot afford to salt *each* call to a primitive. We focus in particular on the salted Merkle-Damgård (MD) construction [8,17], which has also been central to a recent wave of works in the context of space-time trade-offs [2,3,12]. Here, we are given a compression function $h : \{0,1\}^n \times \{0,1\}^\ell \to \{0,1\}^n$ and a message M that consists of B blocks $M_1, \ldots, M_B \in \{0,1\}^\ell$. To hash M, one sets the initial value y_0 to equal the salt a and computes the final hash y_B by iterating

$$y_i \leftarrow h(y_{i-1}, M_i) .$$

Here, we focus on the case of messages of length at most two, which, as in the case of space-time trade-offs [2], already captures many of the challenges. (In fact, we believe that going beyond requires significantly new techniques than those we explore in this paper.) For *pre-image-resistance*, we prove a bound (which we show to be tight) of the form (when ignoring constant factors and lower-order terms)

$$\frac{T_2}{N} + \frac{T_1 T_2}{N^2} + \frac{T_1^2}{N^3} .$$

The most interesting term is the middle one: it is leading, e.g., for $T_1 = N^{6/5}$ and $T_2 = N^{4/5}$, and suggests an inherent trade-off between offline and online query-complexities. Indeed, this advantage is (roughly) matched by an actual attack that first evaluates $h(a_i, M)$ on N distinct M's for T_1/N different salts $a_1, \ldots, a_{T_1/N}$. Then, upon learning the value y to invert on, as well as the salt a, the online adversary spends its T_2 queries looking for $M \in \{0,1\}^n$ such that $h(a, M) = a_i$ for some $i \in [T_1/N]$, succeeding with probability $\Omega(T_1 T_2/N)$. Then, given it succeeds, the attacker knows N evaluations of $h(a_i, \cdot)$ and is thus likely able to find $M' \in \{0,1\}^n$ such that $h(a_i, M') = y$. Hence, (M, M') is a pre-image of y.

COLLISION-RESISTANCE OF MD. Our most involved result is the analysis of the *collision-resistance* of the two-block MD construction, which in particular relies on a number of sophisticated compression arguments and results in a bound that we know to be only partially tight. Ignoring lower order terms and constant factors, we show a bound of order

$$\frac{T_2^2}{N} + \frac{T_1 T_2}{N^{3/2}} + \frac{T_1}{N^{5/4}} + \frac{T_1^2}{N^{7/3}} .$$

Here, we show matching attacks for all terms except the last one. This (potential) lack of tightness of the last term is due to our combinatorial analysis of a special type of offline-only attack. Namely, an offline attacker could repeatedly attempt to find a special type of collision called a *diamond* for a (potential) salt a, namely, four (distinct) queries $h(a, x_1) = y_1$, $h(a, x_2) = y_2$, $h(y_1, x_1') = z_1$, $h(y_2, x_2') = z_2$ such that $z_1 = z_2$. If the attacker finds a diamond for k salts, then in the online phase it wins with probability k/N (with no further query). Therefore, this boils down to proving a tail inequality on the number of salts for which a diamond is found with T_1 queries. This is challenging since in the regime $T_1 \gg N$ the combinatorics of random functions are not very well understood. The challenge stems from the fact that the "outer" queries $h(y_1, x_1') = z_1$ and $h(y_2, x_2') = z_2$ in one diamond could, individually, be part of diamonds for different salts. Our proof uses compression arguments to provide a suitable tail bound, but we leave it as an open problem to improve our analysis (or show it is tight).

COMBINING SPACE AND TIME. In conclusion, we observe that our approach is entirely dual to that of space-time trade-offs. The latter completely ignores the issue of *time* to produce advice, whereas we completely ignore the issue of advice size. The obvious question is whether both can be combined, and we currently lack good techniques to combine space and query-complexity.

RELATIONSHIP WITH MULTI-INSTANCE SECURITY. We note that a remark in [7] observed that a lower bound against multiple-discrete-log algorithms also yields lower bounds on the preprocessing time for discrete-log algorithms with prepro-cessing (observation attributed to Dan Bernstein). We can extend this approach to relate the advantage of an offline-online adversary with the advantage of an adversary playing a multi-instance game. However, we find that this does not give tight bounds for the advantage of offline-online adversaries that succeed with small (sub-constant) probability. In the full version [13], we illustrate this via an example.

2   Preliminaries

Let $\mathbb{N} = \{0, 1, 2, \ldots\}$ denote the set of all natural numbers and $\mathbb{N}_{>0} = \mathbb{N} \setminus \{0\}$. For $N \in \mathbb{N}_{>0}$, let $[N] = \{1, 2, \ldots, N\}$. For a set X, let $|X|$ be its size and X^+ denote one or more elements of X. For a set S and $r \in \mathbb{N}_{>0}$ such that $r \leqslant |\mathsf{S}|$, we denote using $\binom{\mathsf{S}}{r}$ the set of subsets of S with r elements. We denote $\mathsf{Fcs}(\mathsf{D}, \mathsf{R})$ the set of all functions mapping elements in D to the elements of R. Security notions are defined via games; for an example see Fig. 2. The probability that a game G outputs true is denoted using $\Pr[\mathsf{G}]$.

We let $x \leftarrow_\$ \mathcal{D}$ denote sampling x according to the distribution $\mathcal{D}$. If D is a set, we overload notation and let $x \leftarrow_\$ \mathsf{D}$ denote uniformly sampling from the elements of D. For a bit-string s we use $|s|$ to denote the number of bits in s. For a random variable X, we use $\mathsf{E}[X]$ to denote its expectation.

MERKLE-DAMGÅRD. We recall the Merkle-Damgård hashing mechanism. For $n, \ell \in \mathbb{N}_{>0}$, let $h : \{0, 1\}^n \times (\{0, 1\}^\ell)^+ \to \{0, 1\}^n$ be a compression function. We recursively define Merkle-Damgård (MD) hashing $\mathsf{MD}^h : \{0, 1\}^n \times (\{0, 1\}^\ell)^+ \to \{0, 1\}^n$ as

$$\mathsf{MD}^h(a, M) = h(a, M)$$

for $a \in \{0, 1\}^n, M \in \{0, 1\}^\ell$ and

$$\mathsf{MD}^h(a, (M_1, M_2, \ldots, M_B)) = h(\mathsf{MD}^h(a, (M_1, M_2, \ldots, M_{B-1})), M_B)$$

for $a \in \{0, 1\}^n$ and $M_1, \ldots, M_B \in \{0, 1\}^\ell$. We refer to a as the *salt*.

THE COMPRESSION LEMMA. The compression lemma states that it is impossible to compress a random element in set $\mathcal{X}$ to a string shorter than $\log |\mathcal{X}|$ bits long, even relative to a random string.

Proposition 1 (E.g., [9]). *Let* Encode *be a randomized map from* $\mathcal{X}$ *to* $\mathcal{Y}$ *and let* Decode *be a randomized map from* $\mathcal{Y}$ *to* $\mathcal{X}$ *such that*

$$\Pr_{x \leftarrow_\$ \mathcal{X}} [\mathsf{Decode}(\mathsf{Encode}(x)) = x] \geqslant \epsilon.$$

Then, $\log |\mathcal{Y}| \geqslant \log |\mathcal{X}| - \log(1/\epsilon)$.

MARKOV'S INEQUALITY. We use Markov's inequality multiple times in this paper. We state it here for the sake of completeness.

Proposition 2. *Let* X *be a non-negative random variable and* $a > 0$. *Then*

$$\Pr[X \geqslant a] \leqslant \frac{\mathsf{E}[X]}{a}.$$

3   Offline-Online Trade-offs and the Role of Salting

We present some basic facts about offline-online trade-offs and discuss the role of salting. To do this, we define a notational framework that captures the generality of our statements.

3.1   A General Framework for Offline-Online Attacks

GAMES. We formalize security guarantees in cryptography using *games*, which we also use for security proofs. A game G describes an environment an adversary $\mathcal{A}$ can interact with, and the combination of G and $\mathcal{A}$ results in a random experiment $G(\mathcal{A})$ (we refer to this as $\mathcal{A}$ "playing" the game G) which produces a Boolean output. We also denote this output as $G(\mathcal{A})$.

GAMES WITH IDEAL PRIMITIVES. We are interested in a special class of games that depend on an *ideal primitive*, such as a random oracle, random permutation, ideal cipher, etc. We model this via a distribution $\mathcal{I}$ on a set of functions. For example, a *random oracle* with (finite) domain D and range R would be modeled by the uniform distribution on $\mathsf{Fcs}(\mathsf{D}, \mathsf{R})$.[1] Similarly, an ideal cipher with key space K and domain X can be modeled as a uniformly chosen function e from the set $\mathsf{Fcs}(\mathsf{K} \times \mathsf{X} \times \{-1, 1\}, \mathsf{X})$ such that $e(k, \cdot, 1)$ is a permutation on X for all $k \in \mathsf{K}$, and $e(k, \cdot, -1)$ is its inverse. We can also model a variant of the generic-group model (GGM) [20] by looking at the uniform distribution of functions $f \in \mathsf{Fcs}(\mathbb{Z}_p \times \mathsf{X} \times \mathsf{X}, \mathsf{X} \times \mathsf{X})$, where $|\mathsf{X}| = p$, and

$$\pi(x, l_1, l_2) = (\phi(x), \phi(\phi^{-1}(l_1) + \phi^{-1}(l_2))) ,$$

where $\phi : \mathbb{Z}_p \to \mathsf{X}$ is a bijective function.

GAMES WITH PRIMITIVES. An *oracle* game G^π is one where both the adversary $\mathcal{A}$ and the game procedures are given access to an oracle π, from an understood set of possible functions π, which we refer to as *compatible* with the game G. We denote by $G^\pi(\mathcal{A}^\pi)$ both the experiment where $\mathcal{A}$ plays the game, and is given access to the same π as the game as well as the random variable denoting the output. We say that an (oracle) game G is *compatible* with an ideal primitive $\mathcal{I}$, if the range of $\mathcal{I}$ is a subset of the compatible oracles for G. We write specifically

$$\mathsf{Adv}^{\mathsf{G}}_{\mathcal{I}}(\mathcal{A}) = \Pr\left[G^\pi(\mathcal{A}^\pi)\right] \tag{1}$$

where $\pi \leftarrow_\$ \mathcal{I}$. One could define a more general notion that permits other advantage formats (e.g., to model distinguishing notions). This is straightforward, and outside the scope of this paper.

DEFINING OFFLINE-ONLINE ATTACKS. With the above formalism, given an oracle game G, we introduce a new oracle game pre-G, which enhances the original game to model offline-online attacks. Both games preserve compatibility with any oracle. In particular, an adversary $\mathcal{A}$ is split into two parts, the offline adversary $\mathcal{A}_1$ and the online adversary $\mathcal{A}_2$. Initially, in the *offline stage*, $\mathcal{A}_1$ is given access *solely* to the game oracle π. At the end of this stage, $\mathcal{A}_1$ outputs a state st. Then, in the *online stage*, adversary $\mathcal{A}_2$ is initialized with state st and run in the game G. Both $\mathcal{A}_2$ and G are given access to the oracle π. Crucially,

---

[1] As usual, one must be more precise when formally defining a random oracle with $\mathsf{D} = \{0, 1\}^*$, but we remain intentionally informal on this front; all of our examples can be assumed to work on a finite domain.

Game pre-$G^\pi(\mathcal{A} = (\mathcal{A}_1, \mathcal{A}_2))$	Game s-pre-$G^\pi(\mathcal{A} = (\mathcal{A}_1, \mathcal{A}_2))$
$\mathsf{st} \leftarrow \mathcal{A}_1^\pi$	$\mathsf{st} \leftarrow \mathcal{A}_1^\pi$
Return $G^\pi(\mathcal{A}_2^\pi(\mathsf{st}))$	$a \leftarrow_\$ \{0,1\}^s$
	Return $G^{\pi_a}(\mathcal{A}_2^\pi(\mathsf{st}, a))$

Fig. 1. Offline-Online security games for an original game G. Left: the unsalted case. Right: the salted case. Here, π is meant to be sampled from a salted ideal primitive $\mathcal{I}_s$, and $\pi_a(\cdot) = \pi(a, \cdot)$, i.e., the primitive with salt fixed to a.

the game G might give $\mathcal{A}_2$ additional oracles plus additional initialization values, etc., which are available in the offline stage. (This is formalized in Fig. 1 on the left). We colloquially refer to $\mathcal{A} = (\mathcal{A}_1, \mathcal{A}_2)$ as an offline-online adversary. Further, we say that $\mathcal{A}$ is a (T_1, T_2)-adversary if $\mathcal{A}_1$ makes at most T_1 queries and $\mathcal{A}_2$ makes at most T_2 queries. (Note that $\mathcal{A}_2$ could make additional game-dependent queries, which we would specify separately if necessary.) We overload notation and define advantage in terms of (T_1, T_2) as follows.

$$\mathsf{Adv}_\mathcal{I}^G(T_1, T_2) = \max_{(T_1, T_2)\text{-adversaries } \mathcal{A}} \mathsf{Adv}_\mathcal{I}^G(\mathcal{A}) . \tag{2}$$

SOME BASIC FACTS. The following elementary fact, while straightforward, establishes some important baselines for when offline-online attacks are interesting. It relies on the basic observation that one can consider $\mathcal{A}_1$ and $\mathcal{A}_2$ to be a single online adversary.

Lemma 1. *Let* G *be a game compatible with the ideal primitive* $\mathcal{I}$*. For any* (T_1, T_2)*-adversary* $\mathcal{A}$*, there exists an adversary* $\mathcal{B}$ *such that*

$$\mathsf{Adv}_\mathcal{I}^{\text{pre-}G}(\mathcal{A}) = \mathsf{Adv}_\mathcal{I}^G(\mathcal{B}) .$$

Here, $\mathcal{B}$ *makes* $T_1 + T_2$ *queries to the primitive, and its time-complexity is the sum of the time-complexities of* $\mathcal{A}_1$ *and* $\mathcal{A}_2$*. Further, for any game-dependent type of query,* $\mathcal{B}$ *makes the same number of queries as* $\mathcal{A}_2$*.*

For an ideal primitive $\mathcal{I}$, we let $Q(\mathcal{I})$ be an upper bound on the number of queries needed by an adversary, given oracle access to $\pi \leftarrow_\$ \mathcal{I}$, to reconstruct π with probability 1. Then, the following also holds true and formalizes the fact that one can simulate an offline-online adversary by having the offline adversary first reconstruct π and then store it in st.

Lemma 2. *Let* $\mathcal{I}$ *be a primitive that is compatible with game* G*. For all offline-online adversaries* $\mathcal{A}$*, there exists a* $(Q(\mathcal{I}), 0)$*-adversary* $\mathcal{B}$ *such that*

$$\mathsf{Adv}_\mathcal{I}^{\text{pre-}G}(\mathcal{A}) = \mathsf{Adv}_\mathcal{I}^{\text{pre-}G}(\mathcal{B})$$

Note that the adversary $\mathcal{B}$ could be much less efficient than $\mathcal{A}$; however, in many cases, we will study games that only target information-theoretic security, and time-complexity will not matter. It also naïvely follows that there always exists an *optimal* adversary that is a $(Q(\mathcal{I}), 0)$-adversary.

WHICH GAMES ARE INTERESTING? Some games are more interesting than others in the context of offline-online trade-offs, and the above two lemmas already provide some guidance.

Consider the problem of inverting a random permutation $\pi : \{0,1\}^n \to \{0,1\}^n$. It is well known that the best adversary takes time $\Omega(N)$ queries, where $N = 2^n$, to invert with constant probability. Then, Lemma 1 implies that any (T_1, T_2)-offline adversary needs $T_1 + T_2 = \Omega(N)$ to invert with constant probability. Thus, to get $T_2 = o(N)$ and beat the naïve inversion attack in the online phase, we need $T_1 = \Omega(N)$. Further, we already have an $(N, 0)$-adversary by Lemma 2, so we cannot really expect interesting trade-offs. The question becomes interesting only if we limit the state size between $\mathcal{A}_1$ and $\mathcal{A}_2$, which is exactly what is considered by prior works on space-time trade-offs.

This is in contrast to the setting of the discrete logarithm problem with preprocessing [7]. There, for a group of order p, by combining Lemma 1 with the well-known result by Shoup [20], we get that $T_1 + T_2 = \Omega(\sqrt{p})$. Lemma 2 guarantees only a $(p, 0)$ attacker, so we can expect that $T_2 = o(\sqrt{p})$ while still having $T_1 = o(p)$. And indeed, one can achieve the trade-off $T_1 \cdot T_2 \geqslant p$, as indicated in [7].

3.2   The Power of Salting

A special case of interest is that of *salting*, where the cryptographic primitive $\mathcal{I}$ permits an additional input–called a *salt*–that is chosen in the online phase of an attack.

GENERIC SALTING. Let $\mathcal{I}$ be an ideal primitive, whose range is a subset of $\mathsf{Fcs}(\mathsf{D}, \mathsf{R})$. We define its s-bit *salted* version, denoted $\mathcal{I}_s$, as the ideal primitive with range $\mathsf{Fcs}(\{0,1\}^s \times \mathsf{D}, \mathsf{R})$; sampling a function $\pi : \{0,1\}^s \times \mathsf{D} \to \mathsf{R}$ occurs by first sampling 2^s independent copies $\pi_a \leftarrow_\$ \mathcal{I}$ for each $a \in \{0,1\}^s$ and then letting

$$\pi(a, x) = \pi_a(x) \,,$$

for all $a \in \{0,1\}^s$ and $x \in \mathsf{D}$.

For any game G compatible with an ideal primitive $\mathcal{I}$, we can now define an s-bit salted version of the game, s-pre-G, that is compatible with $\mathcal{I}_s$. This is given on the right of Fig. 1. Essentially, we now sample a primitive $\pi \leftarrow_\$ \mathcal{I}_s$ to which the adversary $\mathcal{A}$ is given access. However, in the online phase, the games themselves have access only to π_a for a randomly sampled salt a, which is revealed to only the adversary $\mathcal{A}_2$.

FROM SALTED TO UNSALTED GAMES. The following theorem relates the advantage of an offline-online adversary for the salted game with that of an adversary for the original game. We provide an interpretation below (and use this lemma quantitatively in Sect. 4).

Theorem 1. *Let* G *be a game compatible with an ideal primitive* $\mathcal{I}$. *Let* $\mathcal{A} = (\mathcal{A}_1, \mathcal{A}_2)$ *be a* (T_1, T_2) *offline-online adversary. Then, there exists an adversary* $\mathcal{B}$ *playing* G *such that*

$$\mathsf{Adv}^{s\text{-pre-G}}_{\mathcal{I}_s}(\mathcal{A}) = \mathsf{Adv}^{\mathsf{G}}_{\mathcal{I}}(\mathcal{B}) \,.$$

The adversary $\mathcal{B}$ *makes a number of queries, expressed as a random variable* T *with expectation* $\mathsf{E}\,[T] \leqslant T_1/2^s + T_2$.

Proof. Given access to π in the range of $\mathcal{I}$, the adversary $\mathcal{B}$ samples a random salt a from $\{0,1\}^s$ and then samples $\pi_{a'} \leftarrow_\$ \mathcal{I}$ for $a' \neq a$. It then simulates an execution of $\mathcal{A} = (\mathcal{A}_1, \mathcal{A}_2)$ in s-pre-G as follows: it answers the ideal-primitive query of $\mathcal{A}$ for salt a using oracle queries to π, and those for salt $a' \neq a$ using the local evaluation of $\pi_{a'}$. It is immediate that $\mathcal{B}$ perfectly simulates the execution of s-pre-G to $\mathcal{A}$. Therefore, $\mathcal{A}$ wins if and only if $\mathcal{B}$ does and the claim about advantages follows.

Observe that $\mathcal{B}$ queries its ideal primitive, sampled from $\mathcal{I}$ only when it receives an ideal object query from $\mathcal{A}$ that is prefixed by the actual salt a. Since it is not given access to a when simulating $\mathcal{A}_1$, its queries are independent of a, and each of them is indeed on salt a with probability $1/2^s$. In contrast, $\mathcal{A}_2$ makes queries after learning a, and therefore, those queries are on salt a with probability upper bounded by one. By linearity of expectation, the total number of queries T to $\pi = \pi_a$ made by $\mathcal{B}$ satisfies $\mathsf{E}\,[T] \leqslant T_1/|\mathsf{S}| + T_2$, as we intended to show. $\qquad\square$

SALTING GENERICALLY DEFEATS PREPROCESSING ATTACKS. We illustrate one first main application of Theorem 1, i.e., the fact that salting generically defeats preprocessing in a *qualitative* sense. Here, "qualitative" means that we only look at the power of attacks that achieve large advantage. Subsequent sections (Sects. 4 and 5) take a more quantitative angle on this, studying the whole advantage curve.

We now say that a game G compatible with $\mathcal{I}$ is (T^*, ϵ)-hard if $\mathsf{Adv}^{\mathsf{G}}_{\mathcal{I}}(\mathcal{A}) \leqslant \epsilon$ for all T^*-query $\mathcal{A}^*$. We say that game G is (T^*, ϵ)-expected-hard if the same holds for all adversaries running in *expected* time at most T^*. The following fact is helpful.

Lemma 3. *If* G *is* $(T^*, 0.4)$-*hard, then it is* $(T^*/2, 0.9)$-*expected-hard*.

Proof. By contradiction, let $\mathcal{A}$ run in expected time at most $T^*/2$, and $\mathsf{Adv}^{\mathsf{G}}_{\mathcal{I}}(\mathcal{A}) > 0.9$. Then, build $\mathcal{B}$ that runs $\mathcal{A}$ for T^* queries and then aborts with some default answer if $\mathcal{A}$ did not finish running. Let T be the running time of $\mathcal{A}$. Then, for $\pi \leftarrow_\$ \mathcal{I}$,

$$\begin{aligned}
\Pr\,[\mathsf{G}^\pi(\mathcal{B}^\pi)] &= \Pr\,[\mathsf{G}^\pi(\mathcal{A}^\pi) \wedge T \leqslant T^*] \\
&\geqslant \Pr\,[\mathsf{G}^\pi(\mathcal{A}^\pi)] - \Pr\,[T > T^*] > 0.9 - 0.5 = 0.4 \,,
\end{aligned}$$

where we used Markov's inequality and the fact that $\mathsf{E}\,[T] \leqslant T^*/2$. $\qquad\square$

Now, say that s-pre-G is (T_1, T_2, ϵ)-hard if for all (T_1, T_2)-adversaries $\mathcal{A}$, we have that $\mathsf{Adv}_{\mathcal{I}}^{s\text{-pre-G}}(\mathcal{A}) \leqslant \epsilon$. Then, Lemma 3 and Theorem 1 yield the following corollary.

Corollary 1. *If* G *is* $(T^*, 0.4)$-*hard, then* s-pre-G *is* $(T_1, T_2, 0.9)$-*hard for any* T_1, T_2 *such that* $T_1/2^s + T_2 \leqslant T^*/2$.

This means that if a (T_1, T_2)-adversary is to achieve advantage larger than 0.9 in s-pre-G, then $T_1 \geqslant 2^s T^*/4$ or $T_2 \geqslant T^*/4$. In other words, in order to win s-pre-G with an advantage larger than 0.9, an attacker needs to either use online time which is (almost) as large as that of the best online attack achieving advantage 0.4 or run 2^s times that amount of time in the offline stage.

MOVING ON. We can easily revisit the remainder of this paper using what we saw in this section. First of all, our conclusion about salting applies only to large advantage adversaries since otherwise we cannot prove an analogue of Lemma 3. Section 4 examines *tight* exact bounds on the advantage of (T_1, T_2)-adversaries that hold for each choice of T_1 and T_2. Second, this conclusion applies only to the case where G salts *every call* to the primitive. In Sect. 5, we characterize the pre-image- and the collision-resistance of the salted MD construction against offline-online attacks and show that salting, while still useful, has a more limited effect.

4 Offline-Online Security of Salted Random Oracles

In this section, we study the security of salted monolithic random oracles against offline-online adversaries. Specifically, we consider the security properties of pre-image-resistance and collision-resistance. Our analysis begins by applying Theorem 1 in conjunction with [15, Theorem 1] to derive advantage upper bounds for offline-online adversaries against these properties. This approach already yields a tight bound for pre-image-resistance, but not for collision-resistance. We then use a non-generic technique to prove a tight bound for the latter.

4.1 Pre-image-resistance of a Salted Random Oracle

Oracle game PR^h in Fig. 2 formalizes the preimage-resistance of oracle h, which has co-domain $\{0,1\}^n$. In the game the adversary is given as input y, which is randomly sampled from $\{0,1\}^n$. It has oracle access to h and wins if it manages to output x such that $h(x) = y$.

We aim to upper bound the advantage of offline-online adversaries $\mathcal{A}$ against pre-image-resistance of salted random oracles. Let $H_{s,\ell,n}$ be the uniform distribution over $\mathsf{Fcs}(\{0,1\}^s \times \{0,1\}^\ell, \{0,1\}^n)$. The quantity of interest is $\mathsf{Adv}_{H_{s,\ell,n}}^{s\text{-pre-PR}}(T_1, T_2)$. Using Theorem 1 and [15, Theorem 1], we get the following corollary.

Corollary 2. *Let $T_1, T_2, n, s, \ell \in \mathbb{N}_{>0}$. Then*

$$\mathsf{Adv}_{H_{s,\ell,n}}^{s\text{-pre-PR}}(T_1, T_2) \leqslant 5 \left(\frac{T_1}{2^{s+n}} + \frac{T_2}{2^n} \right).$$

Proof. We fix the adversary (T_1, T_2)-adversary $\mathcal{A}$ that maximizes $\mathsf{Adv}_{H_{s,\ell,n}}^{s\text{-pre-PR}}$ (T_1, T_2). From Theorem 1 we have that there exists an adversary $\mathcal{B}$ that makes at most T queries to its h oracle, where $\mathsf{E}[T] \leqslant T_1/2^s + T_2$ and

$$\mathsf{Adv}_{H_{s,\ell,n}}^{s\text{-pre-PR}}(\mathcal{A}) = \mathsf{Adv}_{H_{s,\ell,n}}^{\mathsf{PR}}(\mathcal{B}).$$

Game $\mathsf{PR}^h(\mathcal{B})$	Game $\mathsf{CR}^h(\mathcal{A})$
$x \leftarrow_\$ \{0,1\}^*$	$(M, M') \leftarrow \mathcal{A}^h$
$y \leftarrow h(x)$	If $M \neq M'$ and $h(M) = h(M')$
$x' \leftarrow \mathcal{B}^h(y)$	$\quad$ Return true
If $h(x') = y$:	Return false
$\quad$ Return true	
Return false	

Fig. 2. Left: Oracle Game PR^h for preimage-resistance of oracle h. Right: Oracle Game CR^h for collision-resistance of oracle h.

Using Theorem 1 in [15], we can show that $\mathsf{Adv}_{H_{s,\ell,n}}^{\mathsf{PR}}(\mathcal{B}) \leqslant \frac{5\mathsf{E}[T]}{2^n}$, which completes the proof.

TIGHTNESS. We remark that this bound is tight up to constant factors. To see the tightness of the term $T_2/2^n$, consider the online-only adversary that simply makes k distinct queries with the salt a. It fails only if all the queries have answer different from y, which happens with probability $(1 - 1/2^n)^{T_2} \leqslant e^{-T_2/2^n}$. Since $e^{-x} \leqslant 1 - x/2$ for $x \leqslant 1.5$, for $T_2 \leqslant 2^n$, $e^{-T_2/2^n} \leqslant 1 - T_2/2^{n+1}$. This means the adversary succeeds with probability at least $T_2/2^{n+1}$, meaning the second term in the bound is tight up to constant factors.

To see why the first term is tight, consider the adversary $\mathcal{A}_1$ which makes 2^n queries on different inputs for $k = T_1/2^n$ different salts (where T_1 is a multiple of 2^n). In the online phase, it simply checks whether it had made a query with salt a, that had output y; if so it returns the query input.

Let the set of k salts $\mathcal{A}_1$ had made queries on be S. For each salt in S, the probability that $\mathcal{A}_1$ had not made query with that salt that had answer y is at most $(1 - 1/2^n)^{2^n} \leqslant 1/e$. So, for each salt in S with probability at least $(1 - 1/e)$, $\mathcal{A}_1$ had made a query that had answer y. Now $\mathcal{A}$ wins if the a sampled is in S, and $\mathcal{A}_1$ has made a query with salt a that had answer y; this probability is at least $(1 - 1/e)k/2^s$ since a is sampled at random. Since $k = T_1/2^n$, it follows that the second term in the bound is tight as well.

4.2   Collision-Resistance of a Salted Random Oracle

Oracle game CR^h in Fig. 2 formalizes the collision-resistance of oracle h. In the game the adversary has oracle access to h and wins if it manages to output M, M' such that $M \neq M'$ and $h(M) = h(M')$.

We aim to upper bound the advantage of offline-online adversaries $\mathcal{A}$ against collision-resistance of salted random oracles. Let $H_{s,\ell,n}$ be the uniform distribution over $\mathsf{Fcs}(\{0,1\}^s \times \{0,1\}^\ell, \{0,1\}^n)$. We seek to tightly upper bound $\mathsf{Adv}_{H_{s,\ell,n}}^{s\text{-pre-CR}}(T_1, T_2)$. Using Theorem 1 and [15, Theorem 1] we get the following corollary.

Corollary 3. *Let* $T_1, T_2, n, s, \ell \in \mathbb{N}_{>0}$. *Then*

$$\mathsf{Adv}_{H_{s,\ell,n}}^{s\text{-pre-CR}}(T_1, T_2) \leqslant 5\sqrt{2}\left(\frac{T_1}{2^{s+n/2}} + \frac{T_2}{2^{n/2}}\right).$$

Proof. We fix the adversary (T_1, T_2)-adversary $\mathcal{A}$ that maximizes $\mathsf{Adv}_{H_{s,\ell,n}}^{s\text{-pre-CR}}$ (T_1, T_2). From Theorem 1 we have that there exists an adversary $\mathcal{B}$ such that it makes at most T queries to its h oracle, where $\mathsf{E}\,[T] \leqslant T_1/2^s + T_2$, and

$$\mathsf{Adv}_{H_{s,\ell,n}}^{s\text{-pre-PR}}(\mathcal{A}) \leqslant \mathsf{Adv}_{H_{s,\ell,n}}^{\mathsf{PR}}(\mathcal{B}).$$

Using [15, Theorem 1], we can show that $\mathsf{Adv}_{H_{s,\ell,n}}^{\mathsf{CR}}(\mathcal{B}) \leqslant 5\sqrt{\frac{2\mathsf{E}[T]^2}{2^n}}$, which concludes the proof.

TIGHT BOUND. The bound in Corollary 3 is suboptimal. In Theorem 2, we obtain a better bound for $\mathsf{Adv}_{H_{s,\ell,n}}^{s\text{-pre-CR}}(T_1, T_2)$.

Theorem 2. *Let* $n, s, \ell, T_1, T_2 \in \mathbb{N}_{>0}$. *Let* $H_{s,\ell,n}$ *be the uniform distribution on* $\mathsf{Fcs}(\{0,1\}^s \times \{0,1\}^\ell, \{0,1\}^n)$. *Then, we have that*

$$\mathsf{Adv}_{H_{s,\ell,n}}^{s\text{-pre-CR}}(T_1, T_2) \leqslant \frac{\binom{T_2}{2}}{2^n} + \frac{T_2 T_1}{2^{s+n}} + \frac{eT_1}{2^{s+n/2}} + \frac{n}{2^{s+1}} + \frac{1}{2^n}.$$

TIGHTNESS. We argue that this bound is tight up to constant factors. Initially, observe that for $T_2 \geqslant 2^{n/2}$, the right side becomes greater than one, and the bound always holds. For $T_2 \leqslant 2^{n/2}$, we have that $\frac{T_1 T_2}{2^{n+s}} \leqslant \frac{eT_1}{2^{s+n/2}}$. Therefore, the term $\frac{T_1 T_2}{2^{n+s}}$ is never the dominant term in the bound, and it suffices to show attacks that achieve advantage of the order $\frac{\binom{T_2}{2}}{2^n}$ and $\frac{eT_1}{2^{s+n/2}}$ to show that this bound is tight. A birthday style attack with T_2 queries achieves advantage of the order $\frac{\binom{T_2}{2}}{2^n}$. Finally, we prove the following theorem to show that term $\frac{eT_1}{2^{s+n/2}}$ is tight up to constant factors.

Theorem 3. *Let* $T_1, s, n, \ell \in \mathbb{N}_{>0}$ *such that* n *is a multiple of 2 and* T_1 *is a multiple of* $2^{n/2+1}$. *Let* $H_{s,\ell,n}$ *be the uniform distribution over* $\mathsf{Fcs}(\{0,1\}^s \times \{0,1\}^\ell, \{0,1\}^n)$. *Then there exists a* $(T_1, 0)$-*adversary* $\mathcal{A}$ *such that*

$$\mathsf{Adv}_{H_{s,\ell,n}}^{s\text{-pre-CR}}(\mathcal{A}) \geqslant \frac{(1 - 1/e)T_1}{2^{s+n/2+1}}.$$

We defer the formal proof of this theorem to the full version [13]. We next prove Theorem 2.

Proof. Let $\mathcal{A} = (\mathcal{A}_1, \mathcal{A}_2)$ be the (T_1, T_2)-offline-online adversary that maximizes $\mathsf{Adv}_{H_{s,\ell,n}}^{\text{s-pre-CR}}(T_1, T_2)$. We can treat $\mathcal{A}$ as deterministic by fixing its randomness that maximizes its advantage.

We seek to upper bound the probability that the adversary $\mathcal{A}$ finds a one-block collision for the randomly chosen salt a that it gets as input in its online phase. We can assume without loss of generality that if $\mathcal{A}$ outputs a collision, it must have made the relevant queries either in the offline or the online phase. This is without loss of generality because if $\mathcal{A}$ does not make one of these queries, we can construct a $(T_1, T_2 + 2)$-offline-online adversary $\mathcal{A}'$ that does whatever $\mathcal{A}$ does, and at the end of its online phase, makes the two relevant queries if not made earlier after $\mathcal{A}$ outputs M, M'. The term T_2 would then be replaced by $T_2 + 2$ in our bounds; for ease of readability, we omit this.

Also, without loss of generality we can assume that no query across the offline and online phases is repeated because the adversary can simply remember the query answer since we do not restrict its memory or the amount of advice it can pass on from offline to the online phase.

We define the following three events.

1. $\mathsf{onecoll}_{\mathsf{on}}$: $\mathcal{A}_2$ makes two queries $h(a, M) = z$, $h(a, M') = z$ for some $M \neq M'$
2. $\mathsf{onecoll}_{\mathsf{offon}}$: $\mathcal{A}_1$ makes a query $h(a, M) = z$, and $\mathcal{A}_2$ makes a query whose answer is z
3. $\mathsf{onecoll}_{\mathsf{off}}$: $\mathcal{A}_1$ makes two queries $h(a, M) = z$, $h(a, M') = z$ for some $M \neq M'$

Observe that if none of $\mathsf{onecoll}_{\mathsf{on}}, \mathsf{onecoll}_{\mathsf{offon}}, \mathsf{onecoll}_{\mathsf{off}}$ happen, $\mathcal{A}$ cannot find a collision. We have that

$$\Pr\left[\text{s-pre-CR}_{H_{s,\ell,n}}^{h}(\mathcal{A})\right] \leqslant \Pr\left[\mathsf{onecoll}_{\mathsf{on}}\right] + \Pr\left[\mathsf{onecoll}_{\mathsf{offon}}\right] + \Pr\left[\mathsf{onecoll}_{\mathsf{on}}\right] . \quad (3)$$

We upper bound the probability of these three events one by one.

UPPER BOUNDING $\Pr\left[\mathsf{onecoll}_{\mathsf{on}}\right]$. This event happens only if $\mathcal{A}_2$ makes two queries that collide. The probability of any two queries of $\mathcal{A}_2$ colliding is $1/2^n$. Using a union bound over all pairs of queries of $\mathcal{A}_2$, we have

$$\Pr\left[\mathsf{onecoll}_{\mathsf{on}}\right] \leqslant \frac{\binom{T_2}{2}}{2^n} . \quad (4)$$

UPPER BOUNDING $\Pr\left[\mathsf{onecoll}_{\mathsf{offon}}\right]$. Observe that $\mathsf{onecoll}_{\mathsf{offon}}$ happens only if there is an online query that has the same answer as one of the offline queries that had input salt a. There are a total of T_1 offline queries, and a is random. Therefore, the expected number of offline queries with salt a is $T_1/2^s$. We have that

$$\Pr\left[\mathsf{onecoll}_{\mathsf{offon}}\right] \leqslant \sum_{k=0}^{T_1} \Pr\left[\text{There are } k \text{ offline queries with salt } a\right] \frac{kT_2}{2^n}$$

$$= \mathsf{E}\left[\text{Number of offline queries with salt } a\right] \frac{T_2}{2^n}$$

$$= \frac{T_1 T_2}{2^{s+n}} . \tag{5}$$

UPPER BOUNDING $\Pr\left[\mathsf{onecoll}_{\mathsf{off}}\right]$. The main challenge of this proof is proving an upper bound on $\Pr\left[\mathsf{onecoll}_{\mathsf{off}}\right]$. We do it as follows: we define an event off-oneblk-k since there are k different salts for which a one-block collision has been found in the offline phase. We have that for any k,

$$\Pr\left[\mathsf{onecoll}_{\mathsf{off}}\right] \leqslant \Pr\left[\mathsf{onecoll}_{\mathsf{off}} \mid \neg\text{off-oneblk-}k\right] + \Pr\left[\text{off-oneblk-}k\right] . \tag{6}$$

Since $\mathsf{onecoll}_{\mathsf{off}}$ happens if for the salt a that is chosen uniformly at random from $\{0,1\}^s$, $\mathcal{A}_1$ had queried $h(a, M), h(a, M')$ that have the same answer, we have that $\Pr\left[\mathsf{onecoll}_{\mathsf{off}} \mid \neg\text{off-oneblk-}k\right] \leqslant k/2^s$. We upper bound $\Pr\left[\text{off-oneblk-}k\right]$ using a compression argument.

The encoding procedure encodes the random oracle h as follows.

1. It runs $\mathcal{A}_1^h$ and initializes a list L to the empty list and a set S to the empty set.
2. For every query $h(a, M)$ made by $\mathcal{A}_1$, it does the following:
   (a) Let $z = h(a, M)$. If there was *exactly one* earlier query by $\mathcal{A}_1$ of the form (a, M') for some $M' \neq M$ that had answer z, and $|\mathsf{S}| < 2k$, it adds the index of the query $h(a, M')$ and the current query to S.
   (b) Otherwise, it adds $h(a, M)$ to L.
3. It appends the evaluation of h on the points not queried by $\mathcal{A}_1$ to L in the lexicographical order of the inputs.
4. If $|\mathsf{S}| < 2k$ it outputs $\varnothing$; otherwise, it outputs L, S.

The decoding procedure works as follows.

1. If the encoding is $\varnothing$, it aborts.
2. It runs $\mathcal{A}_1^h$.
3. For every query $h(a, M)$ made by $\mathcal{A}_1$, it does the following:
   (a) If the index of the query is in S, and there is an earlier query $h(a, M')$ for some M' by $\mathcal{A}_1$ such that its index is in S, answer this query with $h(a, M')$.
   (b) Otherwise, it removes the element in front of L and answers with that.
4. It populates h on the points not queried by $\mathcal{A}_1$ in the lexicographical order by the remaining entries of L

Correctness of decoding: For adversary $\mathcal{A}_1$ that causes the event off-oneblk-k to happen, the encoding algorithm will never return $\varnothing$ because by the definition of off-oneblk-k there will be at least k different salts a_i for which $\mathcal{A}_1$ queries $h(a_i, M_i) = z_i$, $h(a_i, M_i') = z_i$; meaning the size of S will be $2k$. For such an adversary $\mathcal{A}$ it is easy to verify the decoding algorithm will always produce the correct output because for the answers of h that were not added to L, the decoding algorithm recovers them using the set of indices S. Therefore, we have that

$$\Pr[\text{ Decoding is correct }] \geqslant \Pr[\text{off-oneblk-}k] .$$

The size of the output space of the encoding algorithm is upper bounded by $\binom{T_1}{2k} \cdot (2^n)^{2^{o\mid\ell}-k}$. The size of the input space is $(2^n)^{2^{s+\ell}}$. From the compression lemma (Proposition 1), we have that

$$\Pr[\text{off-oneblk-}k] \leqslant \Pr[\text{ Decoding is correct }] \leqslant \frac{\binom{T_1}{2k}}{2^{kn}} .$$

We $k = \max\left(\frac{eT_1}{2^{n/2}}, n/2\right)$. If $\max\left(\frac{eT_1}{2^{n/2}}, n/2\right) = \frac{eT_1}{2^{n/2}}$, then $k \geqslant n/2$. Therefore,

$$\frac{\binom{T_1}{2k}}{2^{nk}} \leqslant \left(\frac{eT_1}{2^{n/2}(2k)}\right)^{2k} \leqslant \left(\frac{1}{2}\right)^n .$$

If $\max\left(\frac{eT_1}{2^{n/2}}, n/2\right) = n/2$, then $k \geqslant \frac{eT_1}{2^{n/2}}$. Therefore,

$$\frac{\binom{T_1}{2k}}{2^{nk}} \leqslant \left(\frac{eT_1}{2^{n/2}(2k)}\right)^{2k} \leqslant \left(\frac{1}{2}\right)^n .$$

Therefore, for $k = \max\left(\frac{eT_1}{2^{n/2}}, n/2\right)$, $\Pr[\text{off-oneblk-}k] \leqslant 1/2^n$. Therefore, from (6) we have

$$\Pr[\text{onecoll}_{\text{off}}] \leqslant \frac{eT_1}{2^{s+n/2}} + \frac{n}{2^{s+1}} + \frac{1}{2^n} . \tag{7}$$

Plugging (4), (5) and (7) into (3) gives us that

$$\mathsf{Adv}_{H_{s,\ell,n}}^{\text{s-pre-CR}}(\mathcal{A}) \leqslant \frac{\binom{T_2}{2}}{2^n} + \frac{T_1 T_2}{2^{n+s}} + \frac{eT_1}{2^{s+n/2}} + \frac{n}{2^{s+1}} + \frac{1}{2^n} .$$

$\square$

5   Offline-Online Security of Two-Block Merkle-Damgård

In previous sections, we focused on proving security guarantees against offline-online attacks on constructions where every query to the ideal primitive is salted. Here, we will see an example of a construction (Merkle Damgård) where only the first query to the underlying primitive (random oracle) is salted. Specifically, we will study the pre-image-resistance and collision-resistance for two-block Merkle-Damgård.

The main takeaway from this section is that for primitives that are not salted for every call, we can have parameter regimes where a term of the form $T_1 T_2$

dominates the bound, meaning that in these regimes there are trade-offs between the number of offline and online queries for the advantage to be close to one. This contrasts with what we saw earlier in Sect. 3.2. There we demonstrated that for constructions that salt every query to the ideal primitive, an adversary must have either online time close to the online time of the best online-only attack that attains an advantage close to one, or offline time close to the best offline-only attack that attains an advantage close to one to achieve an advantage close to one.

5.1   Pre-image-resistance of Two-Block Merkle-Damgård

In this section we study the offline-online attacks against the pre-image-resistance of the two-block Merkle-Damgaard (MD) construction. Pre-image-resistance of two-block Merkle-Damgård is formalized in the game 2-PR-MD$_n^h$ in Fig. 3. A salt a and a value y are sampled uniformly at random from $\{0,1\}^n$ and given as input to $\mathcal{A}$. $\mathcal{A}$ can make queries to h and wins if it outputs a message M that is one or two blocks long whose MD evaluation with a is y.

$$
\begin{array}{|l|}
\hline
\text{Game 2-PR-MD}_n^h(\mathcal{A}) \\
\hline
a \leftarrow\!\!\$ \; \{0,1\}^n \\
y \leftarrow\!\!\$ \; \{0,1\}^n \\
M \leftarrow \mathcal{A}^h(a,y) \\
\text{If } |M| \in \{\ell, 2\ell\} \text{ and MD}^h(a,M) = y \\
\quad \text{Return true} \\
\text{Return false} \\
\hline
\end{array}
$$

Fig. 3. Oracle game 2-PR-MD$_n^h$ formalizing the pre-image-resistance of the two-block MD construction.

Let $H_{n,\ell,n}$ be the uniform distribution over $\mathsf{Fcs}(\{0,1\}^n \times \{0,1\}^\ell, \{0,1\}^n)$. We are interested in proving an upper bound on $\mathsf{Adv}_{H_{n,\ell,n}}^{\text{pre-2-PR-MD}}(T_1, T_2)$. We prove the following theorem.

Theorem 4. *Let* $T_1, T_2, n, \ell \in \mathbb{N}_{>0}$. *Let* $H_{n,\ell,n}$ *be the uniform distribution over* $\mathsf{Fcs}(\{0,1\}^n \times \{0,1\}^\ell, \{0,1\}^n)$. *Then*

$$
\mathsf{Adv}_{H_{n,\ell,n}}^{\text{pre-2-PR-MD}}(T_1, T_2) \leqslant \frac{2T_2 + 1}{2^n} + \frac{T_1 T_2 + n T_1 + T_1}{2^{2n}} + \frac{4e T_1^2}{2^{3n}}.
$$

OFFLINE-ONLINE TRADE-OFFS. Note that in the regime $T_1 = 2^{n(1+\epsilon)}, T_2 = 2^{n(1-\epsilon)}$ for $0 < \epsilon < 1/2$, the term $T_1 T_2 / 2^{2n}$ dominates the bound, meaning there is an offline-online query trade-off in that regime.

TIGHTNESS. We show that this bound is tight up to factors of n. Observe that the dominant terms are of the order $T_2/2^n$, $T_1 T_2/2^{2n}$, and $T_1^2/2^{3n}$. We briefly describe how we show this.

The tightness of $T_2/2^n$ follows easily – the online only attack simply makes T_2 queries with the given salt. The advantage of this attack is at least $(1-1/e)T_2/2^n$ for $T_2 \leqslant 2^n$, as argued in the tightness discussion for pre-image-resistance of the salted random oracle.

The following theorem proves that the term $T_1T_2/2^{2n}$ is tight.

Theorem 5. *Let $T_1, T_2, n, \ell \in \mathbb{N}_{>0}$ such that T_1 is a multiple of 2^n, $T_1T_2 \leqslant 2^{2n}$. Let $H_{n,\ell,n}$ be the uniform distribution over $\mathsf{Fcs}(\{0,1\}^n \times \{0,1\}^\ell, \{0,1\}^n)$. Then there exists a (T_1, T_2)-adversary such that*

$$\mathsf{Adv}^{\text{2-PR-MD}}_{H_{n,\ell,n}}(\mathcal{A}) \geqslant \frac{T_1T_2(1 - 2/e)}{2^{2n+1}} .$$

We defer the proof of this theorem to the full version [13].

The following theorem proves that the term $T_1^2/2^{3n}$ is tight.

Theorem 6. *Let $T_1, n, \ell \in \mathbb{N}_{>0}$ such that T_1 is a multiple of 2^{n+1}, $T_1 \leqslant 2^{3n/2}$. Let $H_{n,\ell,n}$ be the uniform distribution over $\mathsf{Fcs}(\{0,1\}^n \times \{0,1\}^\ell, \{0,1\}^n)$. Then there exists a $(T_1, 0)$-adversary such that*

$$\mathsf{Adv}^{\text{2-PR-MD}}_{H_{n,\ell,n}}(\mathcal{A}) \geqslant \frac{T_1^2(1 - 2/e)}{2^{3n+4}} .$$

We defer the proof of this theorem to the full version [13].

Game $H(\mathcal{A} = (\mathcal{A}_1, \mathcal{A}_2))$	Oracle $H(a', M')$
$h \leftarrow\!\!\text{\$}\ \mathsf{Fcs}(\{0,1\}^n \times \{0,1\}^\ell, \{0,1\}^n)$	$\tau \leftarrow \tau \cup \{((a', M'), h(a', M'))\}$
win $\leftarrow$ false	If $\exists M' : ((a, M'), y) \in \tau$:
oneblkinv, twoblkinv $\leftarrow$ false	win $\leftarrow$ true
$\tau \leftarrow [\,], a, y \leftarrow \perp$	oneblkinv $\leftarrow$ true
st $\leftarrow \mathcal{A}_1^H$	If $\exists M', M'', z :$
$a \leftarrow\!\!\text{\$}\ \{0,1\}^n$	$((a, M'), z), ((z, M''), y) \in \tau$:
$y \leftarrow\!\!\text{\$}\ \{0,1\}^n$	win $\leftarrow$ true
If $\exists M : ((a, M), y) \in \tau$:	twoblkinv $\leftarrow$ true
win $\leftarrow$ true	Return $h(a', M')$
oneblkinv $\leftarrow$ true	
If $\exists M, M', z :$	
$((a, M), z), ((z, M'), y) \in \tau$:	
win $\leftarrow$ true	
twoblkinv $\leftarrow$ true	
$\mathcal{A}_2^H(\text{st}, a, y)$	
Return win	

Fig. 4. H using in the analysis of pre-image-resistance of two-block MD. The events introduced in this game are marked in red. (Color figure online)

Proof (Theorem 4). Let $\mathcal{A}$ be the (T_1, T_2)-adversary that maximizes $\mathsf{Adv}^{\text{2-PR-MD}}_{H_{n,\ell,n}}(T_1, T_2)$. Without loss of generality $\mathcal{A}$ is deterministic and does not repeat any queries. We also assume without loss of generality that $\mathcal{A}$ makes all the queries needed to compute the MD evaluation of the messages it outputs.

We can formulate an alternate version of the game for pre-image-resistance of MD in game H in Fig. 4. Note that whenever $\mathcal{A}$ wins 2-PR-MD^h_n, it has to win H because from our assumption that $\mathcal{A}$ makes all the queries needed to compute the MD evaluation of the messages it outputs, it follows that at least one of the following happens.

- $\mathcal{A}$ makes a query $h(a, M') = y$ – meaning it has found a one-block message M' whose MD evaluation with salt a is y.
- $\mathcal{A}$ queries $h(a, M') = z$ and $h(z, M'') = y$ – meaning it has found a two-block message (M', M'') whose MD evaluation with salt a is y.

In either of these cases the flag win is set in H, meaning $\mathcal{A}$ wins the game. Therefore,

$$\mathsf{Adv}^{\text{2-PR-MD}}_{H_{n,\ell,n}}(\mathcal{A}) \leqslant \Pr\left[\mathsf{H}(\mathcal{A})\right] .$$

Note that win is set to true H only if one of oneblkinv, twoblkinv is set to true. It follows that

$$\Pr\left[\mathsf{H}(\mathcal{A})\right] = \Pr\left[\mathcal{A} \text{ sets win}\right] \leqslant \Pr\left[\mathsf{oneblkinv}\right] + \Pr\left[\mathsf{twoblkinv}\right] .$$

We show that

$$\Pr\left[\mathsf{oneblkinv}\right] \leqslant \frac{T_2}{2^n} + \frac{T_1}{2^{2n}} ,$$

and

$$\Pr\left[\mathsf{twoblkinv}\right] \leqslant \frac{T_2 + 1}{2^n} + \frac{T_1 T_2 + n T_1}{2^{2n}} + \frac{4 e T_1^2}{2^{3n}} .$$

Putting it all together would give us the theorem.

We next upper bound $\Pr\left[\mathsf{oneblkinv}\right], \Pr\left[\mathsf{twoblkinv}\right]$.

Towards upper bounding $\Pr\left[\mathsf{oneblkinv}\right]$, we define the two following events:

1. $\mathsf{oneblkinv}_{\mathsf{off}}$: $\mathcal{A}_1$ makes a query with input salt a and output y
2. $\mathsf{oneblkinv}_{\mathsf{on}}$: $\mathcal{A}_2$ makes a query which has output y

It is easy to see that if oneblkinv happens, then at least one of $\mathsf{oneblkinv}_{\mathsf{off}}$, $\mathsf{oneblkinv}_{\mathsf{on}}$ has to happen. Therefore

$$\Pr\left[\mathsf{oneblkinv}\right] \leqslant \Pr\left[\mathsf{oneblkinv}_{\mathsf{off}}\right] + \Pr\left[\mathsf{oneblkinv}_{\mathsf{on}}\right] .$$

We first upper bound $\Pr\left[\mathsf{oneblkinv}_{\mathsf{on}}\right]$. Each query by $\mathcal{A}_2$ has answer y with probability $1/2^n$. Using a union bound over all queries of $\mathcal{A}_2$, we have that

$$\Pr\left[\mathsf{oneblkinv}_{\mathsf{on}}\right] \leqslant T_2/2^n .$$

We next upper bound $\Pr[\mathsf{oneblkinv}_{\mathsf{off}}]$. Consider the set of (s, y) pairs such that there is a query by $\mathcal{A}_1$ with input salt s and answer y. There are at most T_1 such pairs. Note that, $\mathsf{oneblkinv}_{\mathsf{off}}$ happens only if (a, y) which is sampled uniformly at random, is among those at most T_1 pairs. Hence,

$$\Pr[\mathsf{oneblkinv}_{\mathsf{off}}] \leqslant T_1/2^{2n} .$$

Putting this together, we have the required bound on $\Pr[\mathsf{oneblkinv}]$.

We next upper bound $\Pr[\mathsf{twoblkinv}]$. We define the three following events.

1. $\mathsf{twoblkinv}_{\mathsf{off}}$: $\mathcal{A}_1$ makes queries $h(a, M) = z$ and $h(z, M') = y$ for some M, M', z
2. $\mathsf{twoblkinv}_{\mathsf{offon}}$: $\mathcal{A}_1$ makes a query $h(z, M) = y$ and $\mathcal{A}_2$ makes a query $h(a, M') = z$ for some M, M', z
3. $\mathsf{twoblkinv}_{\mathsf{on}}$: $\mathcal{A}_2$ makes a query with answer y

It is easy to see that if $\mathsf{twoblkinv}$ happens then at least one of $\mathsf{twoblkinv}_{\mathsf{off}}$, $\mathsf{twoblkinv}_{\mathsf{offon}}$, $\mathsf{twoblkinv}_{\mathsf{on}}$ has to happen. Therefore,

$$\Pr[\mathsf{twoblkinv}] \leqslant \Pr[\mathsf{twoblkinv}_{\mathsf{off}}] + \Pr[\mathsf{twoblkinv}_{\mathsf{offon}}] + \Pr[\mathsf{twoblkinv}_{\mathsf{on}}] . \quad (8)$$

We upper bound these probabilities one by one starting with $\Pr[\mathsf{twoblkinv}_{\mathsf{on}}]$. Observe that every query by $\mathcal{A}_2$ has probability $1/2^n$ of having answer y. Using a union bound over all queries of $\mathcal{A}_2$, it follows that

$$\Pr[\mathsf{twoblkinv}_{\mathsf{on}}] \leqslant \frac{T_2}{2^n} . \quad (9)$$

We next upper bound $\Pr[\mathsf{twoblkinv}_{\mathsf{offon}}]$. Observe that this event happens only if $\mathcal{A}_2$ makes a query that has answer z such that $\mathcal{A}_1$ made a query with salt z that had answer y. Therefore, using total probability

$$\Pr[\mathsf{twoblkinv}_{\mathsf{offon}}] \leqslant \sum_{k=1}^{T_1} \Pr[\mathcal{A}_1 \text{ made } k \text{ queries with answer } y] \frac{kT_2}{2^n}$$

$$= \frac{T_2}{2^n} \sum_{k=1}^{T_1} \mathsf{E}[\text{Number of queries of } \mathcal{A}_1 \text{ with answer } y]$$

$$= \frac{T_2 T_1}{2^{2n}} . \quad (10)$$

The last equality follows since each query of $\mathcal{A}_1$ has answer y with probability $1/2^n$.

Finally, we upper bound $\Pr[\mathsf{twoblkinv}_{\mathsf{off}}]$. For this we initially take a short detour and define the event $(m+1)$-col as the event that $\mathcal{A}_1$ has made $m+1$ distinct random oracle queries, all of which have the same answer. We claim that

$$\Pr[\mathsf{twoblkinv}_{\mathsf{off}} \mid \neg(m+1)\text{-col}] \leqslant \frac{mT_1}{2^{2n}} .$$

This is because if $(m + 1)$-col does not happen, there can be at most mT_1 pairs of queries such that the answer of the one query of the pair is the input of the other query (as otherwise there would be a $m + 1$-multi-collision since there are T_1 queries made by $\mathcal{A}_1$). Now, twoblkinv$_{\mathsf{off}}$ happens only if (a, y) that is sampled uniformly at random is such that one of these at most mT_1 pairs have a as the salt for one query and y as the answer of the other query. This happens with probability at most $\frac{mT_1}{2^{2n}}$.

Finally, we upper bound $\Pr[(m + 1)\text{-col}]$. For any subset of $m + 1$ queries made by $\mathcal{A}_1$, the probability that they have the same answer is $1/2^{nm}$. Using a union bound over all possible $m + 1$ sized subsets of the queries of $\mathcal{A}_1$, we have that

$$\Pr[(m + 1)\text{-col}] \leqslant \frac{\binom{T_1}{m+1}}{2^{nm}}.$$

We let $m = \max\left(n, \frac{4eT_1}{2^n}\right)$. If $n \leqslant \frac{4eT_1}{2^n}$, we have that $m = \frac{4eT_1}{2^n} \geqslant n$. Therefore,

$$\Pr[(m + 1)\text{-col}] \leqslant \frac{\binom{T_1}{m+1}}{2^{mn}} \leqslant \left(\frac{eT_1}{(m+1)2^n}\right)^{m+1} 2^n \leqslant \left(\frac{1}{4}\right)^m 2^n \leqslant \left(\frac{1}{2}\right)^n.$$

Otherwise, if $n > \frac{4eT_1}{2^n}$, we have that $m = n > \frac{4eT_1}{2^n}$. Therefore,

$$\Pr[(m + 1)\text{-col}] \leqslant \frac{\binom{T_1}{m+1}}{2^{nm}} \leqslant \left(\frac{eT_1}{(m+1)2^n}\right)^{m+1} 2^n \leqslant \left(\frac{1}{4}\right)^{m+1} 2^n \leqslant \left(\frac{1}{2}\right)^n.$$

Therefore, we have that for $m = \max\left(n, \frac{4eT_1}{2^n}\right)$, $\Pr[(m + 1)\text{-col}] \leqslant 1/2^n$. Hence

$$\Pr[\mathsf{twoblkinv_{off}}] \leqslant \frac{nT_1}{2^{2n}} + \frac{4eT_1^2}{2^{3n}} + \frac{1}{2^n}. \tag{11}$$

Plugging (9) to (11) into (8) gives us the required bound for $\Pr[\mathsf{twoblkinv}]$ and concludes the proof. $\qquad\square$

5.2   Collision-Resistance of Two-Block Merkle-Damgård

In this section, we study the collision-resistance of two-block Merkle-Damgård (MD) against offline-online adversaries. Collision-resistance of two-block MD is formalized by the oracle game 2-CR-MD$_n^h$ in Fig. 5. In this game a salt a is picked at random from $\{0, 1\}^n$ that is given to the adversary $\mathcal{A}$. The adversary $\mathcal{A}$ has oracle access to h, and wins if it can output two messages M, M' that are distinct; both at most 2 blocks long, and satisfy $\mathsf{MD}^h(a, M) = \mathsf{MD}^h(a, M')$.

The game pre-2-CR-MD$_n^h$ captures the collision-resistance of 2-block MD against offline-online adversaries. We prove the following upper bound on $\mathsf{Adv}_{H_{n,\ell,n}}^{\mathsf{pre-2-CR-MD},n}$.

Theorem 7. *Let* $T_1, T_2, s, \ell, n \in \mathbb{N}_{>0}$. *Let* $H_{n,\ell,n}$ *be the uniform distribution on* $\mathsf{Fcs}(\{0,1\}^n \times \{0,1\}^\ell, \{0,1\}^n)$.

$$
\mathsf{Adv}^{\mathsf{pre\text{-}2\text{-}CR\text{-}MD}}_{H_{s,\ell,n}}(\mathcal{A}) \leqslant \frac{2T_2^2 + nT_2/2 + 3n^2/2 + 99n/2 + 33}{2^n}
$$
$$
+ \left(\frac{T_1 T_2}{2^{3n/2}}\right)(n^2 + 5n + 83)
$$
$$
+ \left(\frac{T_1}{2^{5n/4}}\right)(53n + 14n^{1/2} + 56n^{1/3} + 342) + 468\left(\frac{T_1^2}{2^{7n/3}}\right).
$$

OFFLINE-ONLINE TRADE-OFFS. Note that, in the regime of parameters $T_1 = 2^{n(1+\epsilon)}, T_2 = 2^{n(1/2-\epsilon)}$ for $0 < \epsilon < 1/6$, the term $T_1 T_2/2^{3n/2}$ dominates the bound, i.e., there is a trade-off between the number of offline and online queries in that regime.

Game 2-CR-MD$_n^h(\mathcal{A})$
$a \leftarrow_\$ \{0,1\}^n$
$(M, M') \leftarrow \mathcal{A}^h(a)$
If $\lvert M \rvert, \lvert M' \rvert \in \{\ell, 2\ell\}$ and $M \neq M'$ and $\mathsf{MD}^h(a, M) = \mathsf{MD}^h(a, M')$
$\quad$ Return true
Return false

Fig. 5. Oracle game 2-CR-MD$_n^h$ formalizing collision-resistance of two-block MD.

TIGHTNESS OF THE BOUND. We show that the first three terms in the above bound are tight by giving matching attacks. We could not find an attack matching the last term in the bound and leave improving it or showing it tight to be future research.

We briefly describe how we show the other terms to be tight. The first term is dominated by $T_2^2/2^n$ – we can show that this is tight up to constant factors using the birthday attack, which achieves advantage of the order $T_2^2/2^n$.

In the second term, ignoring constants and powers of n, the dominant factor is $\frac{T_1 T_2}{2^{3n/2}}$. We prove this theorem to show that it is tight.

Theorem 8. *Let* $T_1, T_2, n, \ell \in \mathbb{N}_{>0}$ *such that* n *is a multiple of 2,* T_1 *is a multiple of* $2^{n/2+1}$, *and* $T_1 T_2 \leqslant 2^{3n/2}$. *Let* $H_{n,\ell,n}$ *be the uniform distribution over* $\mathsf{Fcs}(\{0,1\}^n \times \{0,1\}^\ell, \{0,1\}^n)$. *There exists a* (T_1, T_2) *adversary* $\mathcal{A}$ *such that*

$$
\mathsf{Adv}^{\mathsf{pre\text{-}2\text{-}CR\text{-}MD}}_{H_{n,\ell,n}}(\mathcal{A}) \geqslant \frac{(1 - 2/e)T_1 T_2}{2^{3n/2+3}}.
$$

The proof of this theorem is in the full version [13].

In the third term, ignoring constants and powers of n, the dominant factor is $\frac{T_1}{2^{5n/4}}$. We give an attack that achieves advantage of the order $\frac{T_1^2}{2^{5n/2}}$. While $\frac{T_1^2}{2^{5n/2}} \leqslant \frac{T_1}{2^{5n/4}}$ for $T_1 \leqslant 2^{5n/4}$, observe that both of them become one at $T_1 = 2^{5n/4}$. Formally, we prove the following theorem.

Theorem 9. *Let* $T_1, T_2, n, \ell \in \mathbb{N}_{>0}$ *such that* n *is a multiple of* 2, *and* T_1 *is a multiple of* $2^{n/2+1}$. *Let* $H_{n,\ell,n}$ *be the uniform distribution over* $\mathsf{Fcs}(\{0,1\}^n \times \{0,1\}^\ell, \{0,1\}^n)$. *There exists a* (T_1, T_2) *adversary* $\mathcal{A}$ *such that*

$$\mathsf{Adv}_{H_{n,\ell,n}}^{\mathsf{pre\text{-}2\text{-}CR\text{-}MD}}(\mathcal{A}) \geq \frac{(1 - 2/e)T_1^2}{2^{5n/2+6}} .$$

The proof of this theorem is in the full version.

We now proceed to prove Theorem 7.

Proof. The proof of this theorem fixes the (T_1, T_2)-offline-online adversary $\mathcal{A} = (\mathcal{A}_1, \mathcal{A}_2)$ that maximizes $\mathsf{Adv}_{H_{n,\ell,n}}^{\mathsf{pre\text{-}2\text{-}CR\text{-}MD}}(T_1, T_2)$. We can treat $\mathcal{A}$ as deterministic by fixing its randomness that maximizes its advantage. Without loss of generality we can assume that $\mathcal{A}$ does not repeat any query across the offline and online phases because we have no restrictions on the memory of the adversary.

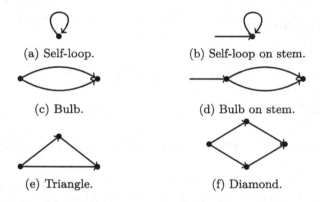

(a) Self-loop.   (b) Self-loop on stem.

(c) Bulb.   (d) Bulb on stem.

(e) Triangle.   (f) Diamond.

Fig. 6. The structure of the six different types of two-block MD collisions in the query graph. The nodes in the query graph are labelled with values in $\{0,1\}^n$, and there is an edge (a, a') labelled with M if the adversary made a query $h(a, M) = a'$. We omit the node and edge labels for simplicity.

We rewrite the collision-resistance game for two-block MD in game H in Fig. 7. Note that whenever $\mathcal{A}$ wins $\mathsf{G}_{n,\ell}^{\mathsf{2\text{-}PR\text{-}MD}}$, from our assumption that $\mathcal{A}$ makes all the queries needed to compute the MD evaluation of the messages it outputs, at least one of the following happens.

- $\mathcal{A}$ makes a query $h(a, M') = a$, meaning it has found a one-block message M' whose MD evaluation with salt a is a. This is sufficient for a two-block collision because for any $M'' \in \{0,1\}^\ell$, (M', M'') and M'' have the same MD evaluation with salt a.
- $\mathcal{A}$ makes queries $h(a, M') = z$ and $h(z, M'') = z$; this is a two-block collision because (M', M'') and M' have the same MD evaluation with salt a.
- $\mathcal{A}$ makes queries $h(a, M') = z$ and $h(a, M'') = z$ for $M' \neq M''$; this is a two-block collision because M', and M'' have the same MD evaluation with salt a.

- $\mathcal{A}$ makes queries $h(a, M') = z$, $h(y, M'') = z$ and $h(y, M''') = z$ for $M'' \neq M'''$; this is a two-block collision because (M', M'') and (M', M'') have the same MD evaluation with salt a.
- $\mathcal{A}$ makes queries $h(a, M') = y$, $h(y, M'') = z$ and $h(a, M''') = z$; this is a two-block collision because (M', M'') and M''' have the same MD evaluation with salt a.
- $\mathcal{A}$ makes queries $h(a, M') = y$, $h(y, M'') = z$, $h(a, M''') = y'$, and $h(y', M''') = z$ for $M' \neq M'''$ and $M'' \neq M''''$; this is a two-block collision because (M', M'') and (M''', M'''') have the same MD evaluation with salt a.

If any of these occur, win is set in H, meaning $\mathcal{A}$ wins the game. Therefore,

$$\mathsf{Adv}_{H_{n,\ell,n}}^{\mathsf{pre\text{-}2\text{-}CR\text{-}MD}}(\mathcal{A}) \leqslant \Pr\left[\mathsf{H}(\mathcal{A})\right] .$$

Game $\mathsf{H}(\mathcal{A} = (\mathcal{A}_1, \mathcal{A}_2))$	Oracle $\mathsf{H}(a, M)$
$h \leftarrow_\$ \mathsf{Fcs}(\{0,1\}^n \times \{0,1\}^m, \{0,1\}^n)$	$\tau \leftarrow \tau \cup \{((a, M), h(a, M))\}$
win $\leftarrow$ false, $\tau \leftarrow []$, $a \leftarrow \perp$	If $\exists M' : ((a, M'), a) \in \tau$:
sl, sos, bulb, bos, tri, dia $\leftarrow$ false	$\quad$ win $\leftarrow$ true, sl $\leftarrow$ true
st $\leftarrow \mathcal{A}_1^{\mathrm{H}}$	If $\exists M', M'', z$:
$a \leftarrow_\$ \{0,1\}^n$	$\quad ((a, M'), z), ((z, M''), z) \in \tau$:
If $\exists M' : ((a, M'), a) \in \tau$:	$\quad$ win $\leftarrow$ true, sos $\leftarrow$ true
$\quad$ win $\leftarrow$ true, sl $\leftarrow$ true	If $\exists M' \neq M'', z$:
If $\exists M', M'', z$:	$\quad ((a, M'), z), ((a, M''), z) \in \tau$:
$\quad ((a, M'), z), ((z, M''), z) \in \tau$:	$\quad$ win $\leftarrow$ true, bulb $\leftarrow$ true
$\quad$ win $\leftarrow$ true, sos $\leftarrow$ true	If $\exists M', M'' \neq M''', y, z$:
If $\exists M' \neq M'', z$:	$\quad ((a, M'), y), ((y, M''), z) \in \tau$,
$\quad ((a, M'), z), ((a, M''), z) \in \tau$:	$\quad ((y, M'''), z) \in \tau$:
$\quad$ win $\leftarrow$ true, bulb $\leftarrow$ true	$\quad$ win $\leftarrow$ true, bos $\leftarrow$ true
If $\exists M', M'' \neq M''', y, z$:	If $\exists M', M'', M''', y, z$:
$\quad ((a, M'), y), ((y, M''), z) \in \tau$,	$\quad ((a, M'), y), ((y, M''), z) \in \tau$,
$\quad ((y, M'''), z) \in \tau$:	$\quad ((a, M'''), z) \in \tau$:
$\quad$ win $\leftarrow$ true, bos $\leftarrow$ true	$\quad$ win $\leftarrow$ true, tri $\leftarrow$ true
If $\exists M', M'', M''', y, z$:	If $\exists M' \neq M''', M'' \neq M'''', x, y, z$:
$\quad ((a, M'), y), ((y, M''), z) \in \tau$,	$\quad ((a, M'), x), ((a, M''), y) \in \tau$,
$\quad ((a, M'''), z) \in \tau$:	$\quad ((x, M'''), z), ((y, M''''), z) \in \tau$:
$\quad$ win $\leftarrow$ true, tri $\leftarrow$ true	$\quad$ win $\leftarrow$ true, dia $\leftarrow$ true
If $\exists M' \neq M''', M'' \neq M'''', x, y, z$:	$\mathcal{A}_2^{\mathrm{H}}(\mathsf{st}, a)$
$\quad ((a, M'), x), ((a, M''), y) \in \tau$,	Return $h(a, M)$
$\quad ((x, M'''), z), ((y, M''''), z) \in \tau$:	
$\quad$ win $\leftarrow$ true, dia $\leftarrow$ true	
$\mathcal{A}_2^{\mathrm{H}}(\mathsf{st}, a)$	
Return win	

Fig. 7. H using in the analysis of collision-resistance of two-block MD against offline-online adversaries. The events introduced in this game are marked in red. (Color figure online)

The game H defines events sl, sos, bulb, bos, tri, dia. We name the events this way because of the following alternative view of MD collisions via the query graph of $\mathcal{A}$: the nodes of the query graph are labelled with strings from $\{0,1\}^n$, and whenever $\mathcal{A}$ makes a query $h(a, M) = a'$, an edge (a, a') labelled M is added to the graph. Finding a two block collision can be viewed as finding one of the following structures in the query graph: self-loop, self-loop on stem, bulb, bulb-on-stem, triangle, and diamond; Fig. 6 shows these structures.

It follows from inspection that in game H, win is set only if one of these event among $\{$sl, sos, bulb, bos, tri, dia$\}$ happen. Therefore, using the union bound we have that

$$\Pr[H(\mathcal{A})] = \Pr[\mathcal{A} \text{ sets win}]$$

$$\leqslant \sum_{\text{event} \in \{\text{sl,sos,bulb,bos,tri,dia}\}} \Pr[\text{event}] \tag{12}$$

Our proof is divided into these following lemmas each of which upper bound the probability of these events.

Lemma 4

$$\Pr[\text{sl}] \leqslant \frac{1}{2^n} + \frac{n}{2^n} + \frac{2eT_1}{2^{2n}} + \frac{T_2}{2^n} .$$

Lemma 5

$$\Pr[\text{sos}] \leqslant \frac{T_2 + 3 + nT_2 + n^2}{2^n} + \frac{2eT_1T_2 + 6enT_1}{2^{2n}} + \frac{8e^2T_1^2}{2^{3n}} .$$

Lemma 6

$$\Pr[\text{bulb}] \leqslant \frac{\binom{T_2}{2}}{2^n} + \frac{T_2T_1}{2^{2n}} + \frac{eT_1}{2^{3n/2}} + \frac{n}{2^{n+1}} + \frac{1}{2^n} .$$

Lemma 7

$$\Pr[\text{bos}] \leqslant \frac{\binom{T_2}{2} + nT_2/2 + n^2/2 + 4}{2^n} + \frac{eT_1T_2 + enT_1}{2^{3n/2}} + \frac{nT_1T_2 + T_1T_2^2 + 2enT_1}{2^{2n}}$$
$$+ \frac{4e^2T_1^2}{2^{5n/2}} + \frac{4eT_1^2T_2}{2^{3n}} .$$

Lemma 8

$$\Pr[\text{tri}] \leqslant \frac{\binom{T_2}{2} + 18n + 8}{2^n} + \frac{3(24e)^{1/2}T_1 + 3(8en)^{1/2}T_1}{2^{3n/2}} + \frac{9(2)^{1/3}eT_1^{4/3}}{2^{5n/3}}$$
$$+ \frac{2nT_1T_2 + T_1T_2 + T_2^2T_1 + 12e(2)^{1/2}T_1^{3/2}}{2^{2n}} + \frac{8eT_1^2T_2 + 2T_1T_2}{2^{3n}} .$$

Lemma 9

$$\Pr[\text{dia}] \leqslant \frac{\binom{T_2}{2} + 30n + 16}{2^n} + \frac{4eT_1^2T_2 + 2T_1T_2 + 4eT_1^2T_2^2}{2^{3n}}$$
$$+ \frac{nT_1T_2 + T_2^2T_1 + n^2T_1T_2 + nT_1T_2^2}{2^{2n}} + \frac{4eT_1^3T_2}{2^{4n}}$$
$$+ \frac{40(en)^{1/3}T_1}{2^{4n/3}} + \frac{(8e)^{1/2}nT_1 + 10(2e)^{1/2}nT_1}{2^{3n/2}}$$
$$+ \frac{240e^{2/3}T_1^2}{2^{7n/3}} + \frac{8(2)^{1/2}e^{3/2}T_1^2 + 40(2e)^{1/2}T_1^2}{2^{5n/2}} .$$

Plugging all probability upper bounds into (12), rearranging terms and simplifying, we get the required bound. We show these calculations in the full version [13].

We prove Lemmas 4 to 6 in Sects. 5.3 to 5.5 respectively. Due to lack of space we defer the proofs of Lemmas 7 to 9 to the full version [13].   □

5.3 Proof of Lemma 4

Proof (Lemma 4). We define the two following events.

1. sl_{off}: $\mathcal{A}_1$ made a query $h(a, M) = a$
2. sl_{on}: $\mathcal{A}_2$ made a query $h(a, M) = a$

Notice that sl happens only if at least one of sl_{off} or sl_{on} happens. Therefore, we have that

$$\Pr[\text{sl}] \leqslant \Pr[\text{sl}_{\text{off}}] + \Pr[\text{sl}_{\text{on}}] . \tag{13}$$

We first prove an upper bound on $\Pr[\text{sl}_{\text{on}}]$. Note that, for every query $h(a, M)$ made by $\mathcal{A}_2$, the probability that its answer is a is $1/2^n$. Therefore, using a union bound over all the queries of $\mathcal{A}_2$, we have that

$$\Pr[\text{sl}_{\text{on}}] \leqslant T_2/2^n .$$

To prove an upper bound on $\Pr[\text{sl}_{\text{off}}]$, we define the following event off-sl-k: $\mathcal{A}_1$ makes at least k different queries such that the input salt of the query is the answer of the query. Using total probability, we have that for any k

$$\Pr[\text{sl}_{\text{off}}] \leqslant \Pr[\text{sl}_{\text{off}} \mid \neg\text{off-sl-}k] + \Pr[\text{off-sl-}k] + \frac{k}{2^n} . \tag{14}$$

Note that, if the adversary $\mathcal{A}_1$ makes at most k different queries, such that the input salt of the query is the answer, sl_{off} happens only if the salt a that is sampled uniformly at random is same as the salt for one of those at most k queries. Therefore, $\Pr[\text{sl}_{\text{off}} \mid \neg\text{off-sl-}k] \leqslant k/2^n$.

We upper bound $\Pr[\text{off-sl-}k]$ as follows. Let B_j be the indicator random variable that indicates whether the j-th query of $\mathcal{A}_1$ is such that its answer is same as its input salt. Since $\mathcal{A}_1$ does not repeat queries, all the B_j's are independent, and $\Pr[B_j] = 1/2^n$. From the definition of B_j's, it follows that

$$\Pr[\text{off-sl-}k] = \Pr\left[\sum_{j=1}^{T_1} B_j \geq k\right].$$

We rewrite the term on the right as

$$\Pr\left[\sum_{j=1}^{T_1} B_j \geq k\right] = \Pr[\exists S \subseteq [T_1], |S| = k : \forall j \in S, B_j = 1].$$

Using a union bound over all subsets of T_1 of size k, we have

$$\Pr[\exists S \subseteq [T_1], |S| = k : \forall j \in S, B_j = 1] \leq \sum_{S \subseteq [T_1], |S| = k} \Pr[\forall j \in S, B_j = 1].$$

Since there are $\binom{T_1}{k}$ subsets of $[T_1]$ of size k, and all the B_j's are independent and $\Pr[B_j = 1] = 1/2^n$, we have that

$$\Pr[\exists S \subseteq [T_1], |S| = k : \forall j \in S, B_j = 1] \leq \frac{\binom{T_1}{k}}{2^{nk}}.$$

Therefore

$$\Pr[\text{off-sl-}k] \leq \frac{\binom{T_1}{k}}{2^{nk}} \leq \left(\frac{eT_1}{k2^n}\right)^k.$$

Plugging this in (14), we have that for any k,

$$\Pr[\text{sl}_{\text{off}}] \leq \left(\frac{eT_1}{k2^n}\right)^k + \frac{k}{2^n}.$$

We let $k = \max\left(n, \frac{2eT_1}{2^n}\right)$. If $n \leq \frac{2eT_1}{2^n}$, we have that $k = \frac{2eT_1}{2^n} \geq n$. Therefore,

$$\frac{\binom{T_1}{k}}{2^{nk}} \leq \left(\frac{eT_1}{k2^n}\right)^k \leq \left(\frac{1}{2}\right)^k \leq \frac{1}{2^n}.$$

Otherwise if $n > \frac{2eT_1}{2^n}$, we have that $k = n > \frac{2eT_1}{2^n}$. Therefore,

$$\frac{\binom{T_1}{k}}{2^{nk}} \leq \left(\frac{eT_1}{k2^n}\right)^k \leq \left(\frac{1}{2}\right)^k = \frac{1}{2^n}.$$

Hence,

$$\Pr[\text{sl}_{\text{off}}] \leq \frac{1}{2^n} + \frac{n}{2^n} + \frac{2eT_1}{2^{2n}}.$$

Plugging this back into (13) gives us

$$\Pr[\text{sl}] \leq \frac{1}{2^n} + \frac{n}{2^n} + \frac{2eT_1}{2^{2n}} + \frac{T_2}{2^n}.$$

$\square$

5.4   Proof of Lemma 5

Proof (Lemma 5). We first define the three following events.

1. $\mathsf{sos_{off}}$: $\mathcal{A}_1$ made queries $h(a, M') = z$ and $h(z, M'') = z$
2. $\mathsf{sos_{offon}}$: $\mathcal{A}_1$ made a query $h(y, M'') = y$ and $\mathcal{A}_2$ made a query $h(a, M') = y$
3. $\mathsf{sos_{on}}$: $\mathcal{A}_2$ made a query $h(z, M') = z$, i.e., a query whose answer is the same as its input salt

From inspection one can verify that sos happens only if at least one of $\mathsf{sos_{off}}$, $\mathsf{sos_{on}}$, $\mathsf{sos_{offon}}$ happen. It follows that

$$\Pr\left[\mathsf{sos}\right] \leqslant \Pr\left[\mathsf{sos_{off}}\right] + \Pr\left[\mathsf{sos_{on}}\right] + \Pr\left[\mathsf{sos_{offon}}\right] . \tag{15}$$

We first upper bound $\Pr\left[\mathsf{sos_{on}}\right]$. Note that for every query $h(a, M)$ made by $\mathcal{A}_2$, the probability that its answer is a is $1/2^n$. Therefore, using a union bound over all the queries of $\mathcal{A}_2$, we have that

$$\Pr\left[\mathsf{sos_{on}}\right] \leqslant T_2/2^n . \tag{16}$$

We next upper bound $\Pr\left[\mathsf{sos_{offon}}\right]$. Recall that the event off-sl-k defined in the proof of Lemma 4: $\mathcal{A}_1$ makes at least k different queries such that the input salt of the query is the answer. We have that

$$\Pr\left[\mathsf{sos_{offon}}\right] \leqslant \Pr\left[\mathsf{sos_{offon}} \mid \neg\text{off-sl-}k\right] + \Pr\left[\text{off-sl-}k\right] .$$

In this case, $\mathsf{sos_{offon}}$ happens only if $\mathcal{A}_2$ makes a query whose answer is the input salt of one of at most k such queries. Therefore, we have that for any k,

$$\Pr\left[\mathsf{sos_{offon}}\right] \leqslant \Pr\left[\text{off-sl-}k\right] + \frac{kT_2}{2^n} .$$

As seen in the proof of Lemma 4, setting $k = \max\left(n, \frac{2eT_1}{2^n}\right)$ makes $\Pr\left[\text{off-sl-}k\right] \leqslant 1/2^n$. Therefore, by setting this value of k, we have that

$$\Pr\left[\mathsf{sos_{offon}}\right] \leqslant \frac{nT_2}{2^n} + \frac{2eT_1T_2}{2^{2n}} + \frac{1}{2^n} . \tag{17}$$

We finally upper bound $\Pr\left[\mathsf{sos_{off}}\right]$. For this we recall $(m + 1)$-col as the event that we defined in the proof of Theorem 4. We say that $(m + 1)$-col happens if the $\mathcal{A}_1$ has made $m + 1$ distinct random oracle queries that all have the same answer. Using total probability, we have that for any k, m

$$\Pr\left[\mathsf{sos_{off}}\right] \leqslant \Pr\left[\mathsf{sos_{off}} \mid \neg\text{off-sl-}k \wedge \neg(m + 1)\text{-col}\right] + \Pr\left[\text{off-sl-}k \vee (m + 1)\text{-col}\right]$$
$$\leqslant \Pr\left[\mathsf{sos_{off}} \mid \neg\text{off-sl-}k \wedge \neg(m + 1)\text{-col}\right] + \Pr\left[\text{off-sl-}k\right] + \Pr\left[(m + 1)\text{-col}\right] . \tag{18}$$

We claim that

$$\Pr\left[\mathsf{sos_{off}} \mid \neg\text{off-sl-}k \wedge \neg(m + 1)\text{-col}\right] \leqslant \frac{mk}{2^n} .$$

This is because if off-sl-k and $(m+1)$-col do not happen, there can be at most $k \cdot m$ salts a that satisfy that $\mathcal{A}_1$ makes a query $h(a, M') = z$ and $h(z, M'') = z$. The probability that the salt a that is sampled uniformly at random is among one of those at most $k \cdot m$ salts is at most $\frac{mk}{2^n}$.

From our calculations in the proof of Theorem 4, we have that for $m = \max\left(n, \frac{4eT_1}{2^n}\right)$, $\Pr\left[(m+1)\text{-col}\right] \leqslant 1/2^n$. We also know that for $k = \max\left(n, \frac{2eT_1}{2^n}\right)$, $\Pr\left[\text{off-sl-}k\right] \leqslant 1/2^n$. We set m, k to these values and obtain from (18) that

$$\Pr\left[\mathsf{sos_{off}}\right] \leqslant \frac{2}{2^n} + \frac{n^2}{2^n} + \frac{6enT_1}{2^{2n}} + \frac{8e^2T_1^2}{2^{3n}} . \tag{19}$$

This is because for $m = \max\left(n, \frac{4eT_1}{2^n}\right)$, $k = \max\left(n, \frac{2eT_1}{2^n}\right)$,

$$k \cdot m \leqslant n^2 + 6enT_1/2^n + 8e^2T_1^2/2^{2n} .$$

Plugging (16), (17) and (19) into (15), we get that

$$\Pr\left[\mathsf{sos}\right] \leqslant \frac{T_2 + 3 + nT_2 + n^2}{2^n} + \frac{2eT_1T_2 + 6enT_1}{2^{2n}} + \frac{8e^2T_1^2}{2^{3n}} .$$

$\square$

5.5   Proof of Lemma 6

Proof. We define the three following events.

1. $\mathsf{bulb_{off}}$: $\mathcal{A}_1$ made queries $h(a, M) = y$, $h(a, M') = y$ for some $M \neq M'$ and y
2. $\mathsf{bulb_{offon}}$: $\mathcal{A}_1$ made queries $h(a, M) = y$, and $\mathcal{A}_2$ made a query with answer y for some M, y
3. $\mathsf{bulb_{on}}$: $\mathcal{A}_2$ made queries $h(a, M) = y$, $h(a, M') = y$ for some $M \neq M'$ and y

Observe that bulb happens only if at least one of $\mathsf{bulb_{off}}$, $\mathsf{bulb_{offon}}$, $\mathsf{bulb_{on}}$ happen. Therefore

$$\Pr\left[\mathsf{bulb}\right] \leqslant \Pr\left[\mathsf{bulb_{off}}\right] + \Pr\left[\mathsf{bulb_{offon}}\right] + \Pr\left[\mathsf{bulb_{on}}\right] . \tag{20}$$

The rest of the proof consists of upper bounding these probabilities one by one. We begin with $\Pr\left[\mathsf{bulb_{on}}\right]$. Observe that $\mathsf{bulb_{on}}$ happens only if $\mathcal{A}_2$ makes two queries that have the same answer. The probability of any two queries of $\mathcal{A}$ having the same answer is $1/2^n$. Using a union bound over all pairs of queries of $\mathcal{A}_2$, we have that

$$\Pr\left[\mathsf{bulb_{on}}\right] \leqslant \frac{\binom{T_2}{2}}{2^n} . \tag{21}$$

We next upper bound $\Pr\left[\mathsf{bulb_{offon}}\right]$. Let Q_a be the random variable denoting the number of queries $\mathcal{A}_1$ makes with salt a. Using total probability

$$\Pr\left[\mathsf{bulb_{offon}}\right] = \sum_{i=1}^{T_1} \Pr\left[Q_a = k\right] \Pr\left[\mathsf{bulb_{offon}} \mid Q_a = k\right]$$

$$= \sum_{i=1}^{T_1} \Pr\left[Q_a = k\right] \cdot \frac{kT_2}{2^n}$$

$$= \frac{T_2}{2^n} \cdot \mathsf{E}\left[Q_a\right] = \frac{T_1 T_2}{2^{2n}} . \tag{22}$$

The second equality above follows because if $\mathcal{A}_1$ makes k queries with salt a, the probability that $\mathsf{bulb_{offon}}$ happens is at most $kT_2/2^n$ using a union bound over all queries of $\mathcal{A}_2$. The final equality uses the fact that $\mathsf{E}\left[Q_a\right] = T_1/2^n$, because $\mathcal{A}_1$ makes T_1 queries and a is sampled uniformly at random.

Finally, we upper bound $\Pr\left[\mathsf{bulb_{off}}\right]$. We define an event off-bulbs-k as follows: there is a set of at least k distinct salts $a_1, \ldots, a_k$ such that for each a_i, $\mathcal{A}_1$ has made a pair of queries $h(a_i, M_i) = z$ and $h(a_i, M_i') = z$ for $M_i \neq M_i'$.

We have that for any k,

$$\Pr\left[\mathsf{bulb_{off}}\right] \leqslant \Pr\left[\mathsf{bulb_{off}} \mid \neg\mathsf{off\text{-}bulbs\text{-}}k\right] + \Pr\left[\mathsf{off\text{-}bulbs\text{-}}k\right] . \tag{23}$$

Since $\mathsf{bulb_{off}}$ happens if for the salt a that is chosen uniformly at random from $\{0, 1\}^n$, $\mathcal{A}_1$ had queried $h(a, M), h(a, M')$ that have the same answer, we have that $\Pr\left[\mathsf{bulb_{off}} \mid \neg\mathsf{off\text{-}bulbs\text{-}}k\right] \leqslant k/2^n$. We upper bound $\Pr\left[\mathsf{off\text{-}bulbs\text{-}}k\right]$ using a compression argument.

Note that the event off-bulbs-k is similar to the event off-oneblk-k we defined in the proof of Theorem 4, the only difference being the salt length was s there and is n here. However, $\Pr\left[\mathsf{off\text{-}oneblk\text{-}}k\right]$ did not depend on s, hence we can prove the same bound for $\Pr\left[\mathsf{off\text{-}bulbs\text{-}}k\right]$. We showed in that proof that for $k = \max\left(\frac{eT_1}{2^{n/2}}, n/2\right)$, $\Pr\left[\mathsf{off\text{-}oneblk\text{-}}k\right] \leqslant 1/2^n$.

Hence from (23) we have

$$\Pr\left[\mathsf{bulb_{off}}\right] \leqslant \frac{eT_1}{2^{3n/2}} + \frac{n}{2^{n+1}} + \frac{1}{2^n} . \tag{24}$$

Plugging (21), (22) and (24) into (20) gives us that

$$\Pr\left[\mathsf{bulb}\right] \leqslant \frac{\binom{T_2}{2}}{2^n} + \frac{T_2 T_1}{2^{2n}} + \frac{eT_1}{2^{3n/2}} + \frac{n}{2^{n+1}} + \frac{1}{2^n} .$$

$\square$

Acknowledgements. This research was partially supported by NSF grants CNS-2026774, CNS-2154174, a JP Morgan Faculty Award, a CISCO Faculty Award, and a gift from Microsoft.

References

1. Adrian, D., et al.: Imperfect forward secrecy: how Diffie-Hellman fails in practice. In: Ray, I., Li, N., Kruegel, C. (eds.) ACM CCS 2015, pp. 5–17. ACM Press, October 2015
2. Akshima, Cash, D., Drucker, A., Wee, H.: Time-space tradeoffs and short collisions in Merkle-Damgård hash functions. In: Micciancio, D., Ristenpart, T. (eds.) CRYPTO 2020, Part I. LNCS, vol. 12170, pp. 157–186. Springer, Heidelberg (2020). https://doi.org/10.1007/978-3-030-56784-2_6
3. Akshima, Guo, S., Liu, Q.: Time-space lower bounds for finding collisions in Merkle-Damgård hash functions. In: Dodis, Y., Shrimpton, T. (eds.) CRYPTO 2022, Part III. LNCS, vol. 13509, pp. 192–221. Springer, Heidelberg (2022). https://doi.org/10.1007/978-3-031-15982-4_7
4. Bernstein, D.J., Lange, T.: Non-uniform cracks in the concrete: the power of free precomputation. In: Sako, K., Sarkar, P. (eds.) ASIACRYPT 2013, Part II. LNCS, vol. 8270, pp. 321–340. Springer, Heidelberg (2013). https://doi.org/10.1007/978-3-642-42045-0_17
5. Coretti, S., Dodis, Y., Guo, S.: Non-uniform bounds in the random-permutation, ideal-cipher, and generic-group models. In: Shacham, H., Boldyreva, A. (eds.) CRYPTO 2018, Part I. LNCS, vol. 10991, pp. 693–721. Springer, Cham (2018). https://doi.org/10.1007/978-3-319-96884-1_23
6. Coretti, S., Dodis, Y., Guo, S., Steinberger, J.: Random oracles and non-uniformity. In: Nielsen, J.B., Rijmen, V. (eds.) EUROCRYPT 2018, Part I. LNCS, vol. 10820, pp. 227–258. Springer, Cham (2018). https://doi.org/10.1007/978-3-319-78381-9_9
7. Corrigan-Gibbs, H., Kogan, D.: The discrete-logarithm problem with preprocessing. In: Nielsen, J.B., Rijmen, V. (eds.) EUROCRYPT 2018, Part II. LNCS, vol. 10821, pp. 415–447. Springer, Cham (2018). https://doi.org/10.1007/978-3-319-78375-8_14
8. Damgård, I.B.: A design principle for hash functions. In: Brassard, G. (ed.) CRYPTO 1989. LNCS, vol. 435, pp. 416–427. Springer, New York (1990). https://doi.org/10.1007/0-387-34805-0_39
9. De, A., Trevisan, L., Tulsiani, M.: Time space tradeoffs for attacks against one-way functions and PRGs. In: Rabin, T. (ed.) CRYPTO 2010. LNCS, vol. 6223, pp. 649–665. Springer, Heidelberg (2010). https://doi.org/10.1007/978-3-642-14623-7_35
10. Dodis, Y., Guo, S., Katz, J.: Fixing cracks in the concrete: random oracles with auxiliary input, revisited. In: Coron, J.-S., Nielsen, J.B. (eds.) EUROCRYPT 2017, Part II. LNCS, vol. 10211, pp. 473–495. Springer, Cham (2017). https://doi.org/10.1007/978-3-319-56614-6_16
11. Gaži, P., Pietrzak, K., Rybár, M.: The exact PRF-security of NMAC and HMAC. In: Garay, J.A., Gennaro, R. (eds.) CRYPTO 2014, Part I. LNCS, vol. 8616, pp. 113–130. Springer, Heidelberg (2014). https://doi.org/10.1007/978-3-662-44371-2_7
12. Ghoshal, A., Komargodski, I.: On time-space tradeoffs for bounded-length collisions in Merkle-Damgård hashing. In: Dodis, Y., Shrimpton, T. (eds.) CRYPTO 2022, Part III. LNCS, vol. 13509, pp. 161–191. Springer, Heidelberg (2022). https://doi.org/10.1007/978-3-662-44371-2_7
13. Ghoshal, A., Tessaro, S.: The query-complexity of preprocessing attacks. Cryptology ePrint Archive, Paper 2023/856 (2023). https://eprint.iacr.org/2023/856

14. Hellman, M.E.: A cryptanalytic time-memory trade-off. IEEE Trans. Inf. Theory **26**(4), 401–406 (1980)
15. Jaeger, J., Tessaro, S.: Expected-time cryptography: generic techniques and applications to concrete soundness. In: Pass, R., Pietrzak, K. (eds.) TCC 2020, Part III. LNCS, vol. 12552, pp. 414–443. Springer, Cham (2020). https://doi.org/10.1007/978-3-030-64381-2_15
16. Koblitz, N., Menezes, A.: Another look at HMAC. Cryptology ePrint Archive, Report 2012/074 (2012). https://eprint.iacr.org/2012/074
17. Merkle, R.C.: A fast software one-way hash function. J. Cryptol. **3**(1), 43–58 (1990)
18. Oechslin, P.: Making a faster cryptanalytic time-memory trade-off. In: Boneh, D. (ed.) CRYPTO 2003. LNCS, vol. 2729, pp. 617–630. Springer, Heidelberg (2003). https://doi.org/10.1007/978-3-540-45146-4_36
19. Rogaway, P.: Formalizing human ignorance. In: Nguyen, P.Q. (ed.) VIETCRYPT 2006. LNCS, vol. 4341, pp. 211–228. Springer, Heidelberg (2006). https://doi.org/10.1007/11958239_14
20. Shoup, V.: Lower bounds for discrete logarithms and related problems. In: Fumy, W. (ed.) EUROCRYPT 1997. LNCS, vol. 1233, pp. 256–266. Springer, Heidelberg (1997). https://doi.org/10.1007/3-540-69053-0_18
21. Unruh, D.: Random oracles and auxiliary input. In: Menezes, A. (ed.) CRYPTO 2007. LNCS, vol. 4622, pp. 205–223. Springer, Heidelberg (2007). https://doi.org/10.1007/978-3-540-74143-5_12

Random Oracle Combiners: Breaking the Concatenation Barrier for Collision-Resistance

Yevgeniy Dodis[1]($\boxtimes$), Niels Ferguson[2], Eli Goldin[1], Peter Hall[1], and Krzysztof Pietrzak[3]

[1] New York University, New York, USA
dodis@cs.nyu.edu, {eg3293,pf2184}@nyu.edu
[2] Microsoft, Redmond, USA
niels@microsoft.com
[3] IST, Klosterneuburg, Austria
krzysztof.pietrzak@ist.ac.at

Abstract. Suppose we have two hash functions h_1 and h_2, but we trust the security of only one of them. To mitigate this worry, we wish to build a *hash combiner* C^{h_1,h_2} which is secure so long as one of the underlying hash functions is. This question has been well-studied in the regime of *collision resistance*. In this case, concatenating the two hash function outputs clearly works. Unfortunately, a long series of works (Boneh and Boyen, CRYPTO'06; Pietrzak, Eurocrypt'07; Pietrzak, CRYPTO'08) showed no (noticeably) shorter combiner for collision resistance is possible.

In this work, we revisit this pessimistic state of affairs, motivated by the observation that collision-resistance is insufficient for many interesting applications of cryptographic hash functions anyway. We argue the right formulation of the "hash combiner" is to build what we call *random oracle (RO) combiners*, utilizing stronger assumptions for stronger constructions.

Indeed, we circumvent the previous lower bounds for collision resistance by constructing a simple length-preserving RO combiner

$$\widetilde{C}^{h_1,h_2}_{\mathcal{Z}_1,\mathcal{Z}_2}(M) = h_1(M, \mathcal{Z}_1) \oplus h_2(M, \mathcal{Z}_2),$$

where $\mathcal{Z}_1, \mathcal{Z}_2$ are random salts of appropriate length. We show that this extra randomness is necessary for RO combiners, and indeed our construction is somewhat tight with this lower bound.

On the negative side, we show that one cannot generically apply the composition theorem to further replace "monolithic" hash functions h_1 and h_2 by some simpler indifferentiable construction (such as the *Merkle-Damgård transformation*) from smaller components, such as fixed-length compression functions. Finally, despite this issue, we directly prove collision resistance of the Merkle-Damgård variant of our combiner, where h_1 and h_2 are replaced by iterative Merkle-Damgård hashes applied to a fixed-length compression function. Thus, we can still subvert the concatenation barrier for collision-resistance combiners while utilizing practically small fixed-length components underneath.

© International Association for Cryptologic Research 2023
H. Handschuh and A. Lysyanskaya (Eds.): CRYPTO 2023, LNCS 14082, pp. 514–546, 2023.
https://doi.org/10.1007/978-3-031-38545-2_17

1 Introduction

Imagine you are a major software company and wrote some important crypto-graphic code utilizing a "cryptographic hash function". You believe that your favorite function h_1 is the best such function to use. One of your customers would like to buy your software. However, the regulations of their country mandates they use a different cryptographic hash function h_2, and they are not allowed to use a different hash function. Your company does not believe h_2 is as secure as h_1, and you do not wish to substitute h_1 by h_2. For example, in the case where h_2 gets broken, you do not want any bad publicity that your software application could suddenly become insecure, even though you wanted to use the "secure" hash function h_1. But you also want to make a sale, as the customer is a big client.

Hash combiners provide a practical solution to this dilemma. Imagine your software will utilize some combined hash function $C = C^{h_1,h_2}$, which depends in a black-box way on both h_1 and h_2, and which is secure as long as either h_1 or h_2 is secure. In this case you can convince the customer to still buy your software, as the security of the hash function C is at least as good as that of h_2. But you are not worried of a future attack, since C is also as secure as your trusted hash function h_1.

How can we build such a combiner $C = C^{h_1,h_2}$? That depends on the notion of security that we want. So far, most of the literature of hash combiners focused on the notion of *collision-resistance* as the most common target security notion. In this case, the following simple *concatenation combiner* works:

$$C^{h_1,h_2}(M) = h_1(M)\|h_2(M)$$

Indeed, a collision for C clearly implies a collision for both h_1 and h_2. Unfortunately, this construction also doubles the output size of the hash function (assuming, for simplicity, that both h_1 and h_2 are n-bit long). As such, this restriction severely limits the applicability of combiner in practice. For example, in hash-then-sign signatures (such as FDH [3] or BLS [5]), this forces one to use much heavier public-key cryptography, and similar considerations apply for virtually any real-world application we can think off.

Perhaps we can do better? Unfortunately, a series of works [4,21,22] showed that this is not the case, even if the combiner is allowed to be randomized (i.e., keyed, with the key chosen independently of h_1 and h_2).

Is There a Way Out? At first, it seems like we are stuck, since collision-resistance is one of the most basic security properties of hash function that we will need to preserve. Fortunately, as was first observed by Mittelbach [19] (see also [18]) and continued in this work, this conclusion is perhaps overly pessimistic. Namely, most applications of "cryptographic hash functions" already require more than collision-resistance. For example, hash-then-sign signatures [3,5] are typically proven in the random oracle model (ROM), and it is in fact unlikely that a standard-model property of hash functions will be enough to instantiate these widely-used schemes (see, e.g., [8,9,20]).

One potential solution, then, is to design a *multi-property preserving* combiner [11], which simultaneously preserves multiple (or possibly all?) required security properties of hash functions. In this setting, the concatenation combiner would fail even more miserably - for example, if one of the input hash functions is not pseudorandom, the concatenation combiner will not be pseudorandom regardless of whether the other is. Hence, it does not solve our original problem.

A better approach, studied by [18,19], is to try to prove collision-resistance (and other individual properties) of the combiner in the random oracle model, where one of the hash functions is modeled as a *random oracle*, and the other may adversarially query the random oracle. While very useful (see Sect. 1.2 for more discussion), this still does not address the issue that most applications of hash functions might need stronger properties than collision resistance. It is also a bit underwhelming to start with a random oracle but only achieve weaker security properties. Thus, in this work, we take this approach one step beyond, and introduce the following, even better solution to the problem:

Random Oracle Combiners!

Ignoring for a second that this notion was never defined prior to this work,—something we will fix shortly—this solution seems to be a much better fit for our application. Indeed, it addresses the fact that most application of cryptographic hash function anyway require something stronger than collision-resistance; in particular, random oracle usually suffices. Even more, perhaps when one of the hash functions h_1 or h_2 is a true random oracle, the lower bound for collision-resistance combiners mentioned above would no longer hold? Intuitively, a stronger assumption (RO rather than collision-resistance) on the hash function might yield a similarly stronger conclusion on the combiner, while being much more efficient. Indeed, this is precisely what we will show in this work: *There does exist simple length-preserving random oracle combiners.*

1.1 Our Results

We now describe our results in more detail.

Defining RO-Combiners. Our first contribution is a formal definition of an RO-combiner. We follow the *indifferentiability framework* of Maurer, Renner, and Holenstein [16] similarly to Coron et al. [7] to say that the combiner C should be indifferentiable from a random oracle provided h_1 or h_2 is an RO.

In our case, we must be careful as to how h_1 and h_2 may depend on each other so as to accurately model real use-cases. For concreteness, suppose h_1 is a random oracle. We would like our combiner C^{h_1,h_2} to be indifferentiable from a random oracle even if h_2 *arbitrarily depends on* h_1. If h_2 was limited to not depend on h_1 at all, trivial constructions such as $C^{h_1,h_2}(M) = h_1(M) \oplus h_2(M)$ would suffice. No reasonable practitioner would be happy with such a combiner, though, as even the reasonable choice of $h_2 = h_1$ results in $C^{h_1,h_2} = 0$ on all inputs. On the other hand, if h_2 can depend on h_1 in some "exponentially-complex" way, this seems to give the adversarial hash function too much power in a way that does not model the real world.

Thus, we settle on the following compromise, which we feel adequately balances real-world threats of the attacker. We allow h_2 to implement an arbitrary (even unbounded-size) circuit g, but on every input, g is allowed to make up some (large, but bounded) number of black-box calls to h_1. This rules out, for example, h_2 being able to access the entire truth table of the random oracle on a single function call. We refer to Definition 3 (and further discussion of our notion in Sect. 2.2) to formally model this *adversarial implementation*.

To see that this notion is non-trivial, we show that no deterministic RO-combiners exist. The formal proof of this result is rather involved (see Theorem 5), but the intuition is as follows: For any deterministic combiner C (which outputs just one bit) we will bias one of the hash functions in a way that $C(0)$ will be biased. This is either accomplished if $C(0)$ does not "meaningfully depend" on (say) h_2, in which case our task is easily accomplished by controlling h_1. Here "meaningfully depend" roughly corresponds to choosing h_1 at random, and seeing if further choosing h_2 at random affect the value of $C(0)$. Otherwise, we will do "rejection sampling" inside the adversarial function h_2 that we design. The adversarial hash h_2 will attempt to evaluate $C(0)$ using its oracle gates to h_1, and will keep randomly changing its answers to h_2 until the result of the $C(0)$ evaluation is 0.

Length-Preserving RO-combiner. Having developed some intuition why building RO-combiners is non-trivial, and requires some randomness, we proceed with our main positive result. Namely, we show that the following *length-preserving* (and, necessarily, randomized) RO-combiner is secure:

$$\widetilde{C}^{h_1,h_2}_{\mathcal{Z}_1,\mathcal{Z}_2}(M) = h_1(M, \mathcal{Z}_1) \oplus h_2(M, \mathcal{Z}_2),$$

where $\mathcal{Z}_1, \mathcal{Z}_2$ are sufficiently long random salts. We refer to Theorem 3.

Specifically, the lengths of salts $\mathcal{Z}_1, \mathcal{Z}_2$ are slightly longer (roughly, by security parameter) than the length of the hash message M. As a high-level intuition, the key to the security of this RO-combiner comes from the fact that no evaluation of $\widetilde{C}(M)$ can completely call $h_1(*, \mathcal{Z}_1)$ inside $h_2(M, \mathcal{Z}_2)$, and vice versa. This is because the message M (which can be chosen by the attacker *after* it learns $\mathcal{Z}_1, \mathcal{Z}_2$) is not long enough to encode the entirety of $\mathcal{Z}_1$ or $\mathcal{Z}_2$. Thus, our indifferentiability simulator (run in the ideal world, where C is now a true random oracle) does not get stuck when adapting one of the hash functions h_1 or h_2 to be consistent with RO C.

We also show that the lower bound on $|\mathcal{Z}_1|, |\mathcal{Z}_2|$ required by our security analysis is tight, by presenting a simple attack on any $\widetilde{C}^{h_1,h_2}_{\mathcal{Z}_1,\mathcal{Z}_2}$ when using significantly shorter salts. For more details, see Theorem 4.

Using Shorter Compression Functions? While our main positive result is length-preserving and already illustrates the usefulness of our approach of modeling "hash function combiners" as RO-combiners, our particular construction

$\widetilde{C}^{h_1,h_2}_{\mathcal{Z}_1,\mathcal{Z}_2}$ is not yet applicable to practical cases in the following sense: Even for reasonably-sized inputs M, it calls the underlying hash functions $h_1(M,\mathcal{Z}_1)$ and $h_2(M,\mathcal{Z}_2)$ on inputs which do not fit into a typical block of existing cryptographic hash functions, such as SHA-2 or SHA-3 (in part, because the salts $\mathcal{Z}_1$ and $\mathcal{Z}_2$ are relatively long).

Instead, practical hash functions typically iterate a given compression function using some mode of operation, such as the Merkle-Damgård transformation. At first, it is tempting to attempt simply apply the composition theorem in the indifferentiability framework [16] - Instead of assuming h_1 and h_2 are monolithic hash functions on "long inputs" $(M,\mathcal{Z})$, imagine they are modeled as fixed-length compression functions on "short-inputs", and we appropriately redefine our RO-combiner to be

$$\mathrm{SufC}^{h_1,h_2}_{\mathcal{Z}_1,\mathcal{Z}_2}(M) = h_1^*(M,\mathcal{Z}_1) \oplus h_2^*(M,\mathcal{Z}_2),$$

where the notation $f^*(m_1,\ldots m_t) = f(m_t, f(m_{t-1},\ldots,f(m_1,0)\ldots))$ corresponds to the Merkle-Damgård (MD) evaluation of the compression function f.

Now, we could use the earlier indifferentiability result of [7] that applying the MD evaluation a fixed number of times on a compression function modeled as a fixed-length random oracle is by itself indifferentiable from a (longer-input) monolithic random oracle. Combined with our previous result, this would imply that SufC is still a good RO-combiner, but now with much more practical parameters for h_1 and h_2.

Unfortunately, this reasoning turns out to be false for a rather subtle reason. Our indifferentiability notion for RO-combiners is technically a two stage game [23], as explained in detail in Sect. 3.1. As such, standard composition theorem cannot be applied to argue security of such game. Indeed, to see this explicitly, we show that a similar-looking combiner

$$\mathrm{PreC}^{h_1,h_2}_{\mathcal{Z}_1,\mathcal{Z}_2}(M) = h_1^*(\mathcal{Z}_1,M) \oplus h_2^*(\mathcal{Z}_2,M).$$

is completely insecure as an RO-combiner on fixed-length compression functions. Namely, the difference between SufC and PreC is whether the salts $\mathcal{Z}_1,\mathcal{Z}_2$ are appended or prepended to the actual message M. For the "monolithic" combiner $\widetilde{C}^{h_1,h_2}_{\mathcal{Z}_1,\mathcal{Z}_2}(M) = h_1(M,\mathcal{Z}_1) \oplus h_2(M,\mathcal{Z}_2)$, this clearly does not matter. Yet, the prepended construction is insecure when instantiated with the Merkle-Damgård based variant. Intuitively, all the useful information about the salts $\mathcal{Z}_1,\mathcal{Z}_2$ is hashed into compact descriptions $h_1^*(\mathcal{Z}_1)$ and $h_2^*(\mathcal{Z}_2)$, respectively, which may then be, e.g., included within M. See Theorem 8 for more details.

Direct Collision-Resistance. While the composition theorem does not immediately imply security of $\mathrm{SufC}(M) = h_1^*(M,\mathcal{Z}_1) \oplus h_2^*(M,\mathcal{Z}_2)$, one could still attempt a direct security proof that this is a secure RO-combiner. We leave this as a great open question. However, as an initial step in this direction, we show that $\mathrm{SufC}(M)$ is at least collision-resistant in our model (Theorem 9). This gives another meaningful (and provably secure) way to circumvent the concatenation barrier for collision-resistant combiners [4,21,22], albeit leveraging stronger assumptions.

We note that our construction is basically a "cryptophia short combiner" as considered in [18,19]. However, we achieve better efficiency and our result is more general in several senses. We discuss this comparison further below.

1.2   Related Work

Combiners for cryptographic primitives were first considered by [15] and [14], followed by numerous works including [2,13–15,17]. Combiners for collision-resistance have been of particular interest. In this space, the concatenation combiner belongs to folklore, and proving its optimality (in terms of output length) was established by a series of works [4,6,21,22]. So-called multi-property preserving combiners have been defined and constructed by [11,12]. These combiners preserve indifferentiability from a random oracle, but as they are also combiners for specific properties, including collision resistance, they necessarily have long output length, in line with the lower bounds above.

Mittelbach [19] considered a similar notion to RO-combiners called "cryptophia short combiners" (additionally, a follow up work [18] identifies and fixes a flaw in the original paper). Mittelbach [19] was the first to show that the lower bounds on the output length of collision-resistance combiners (that is, nearly double the length of the outputs of the input hash functions [4,21,22]) can be overcome by assuming one of the two functions is ideal, even under the strong assumption that the other hash function can arbitrarily depend on the ideal one. Our work follows in this direction, making the following improvements:

Security: While [19] shows that the combined function achieves particular security properties (collision-resistance, pseudorandomness, one-wayness), we show indifferentiability from a random oracle, which is strictly stronger.

Efficiency: Our combiner is conceptually simpler and more efficient: To hash a message of length $\ell = k \cdot n$, we need to hash $2\ell + n = (2k+1)n$ bits with each of the hash functions. In [18] it's $5k \cdot n$ bits.

Completeness of Assumptions: The Cryptophia combiner is defined for arbitrarily compressing hash functions. This is justified (in the Remark of Sect. 3.3 of [19]) by stating their definition is one-stage, allowing them to replace the large-input hash by something indifferentiable from a random oracle, such as the Merkle-Damgard composition of a compression function. However, their model (similarly to ours) allows the adversarial hash function to make oracle queries to the honest one, and so their security game is two stage. Thus, just as with our results from Sect. 3, their security proof does not hold when their combiner is instantiated with "real-world" hash functions. We get around this issue by providing a direct proof of collision-resistance when our combiner is instantiated with Merkle-Damgard hash functions (Theorem 9).

2   Preliminaries

Definition 1. *A random oracle* $\mathcal{H} : \{0,1\}^m \to \{0,1\}^n$ *is an oracle giving access to a function* $\{0,1\}^m \to \{0,1\}^n$ *chosen uniformly at random during initialization.*

We will make frequent use of the following theorem, which we will call a "compression argument." The proof of this theorem is folklore, but is easy to show using the pigeonhole principle.

Theorem 1. *Let* $\mathsf{Enc} : \mathcal{S} \to \mathcal{T}$ *and* $\mathsf{Dec} : \mathcal{T} \to \mathcal{S}$ *be two algorithms such that*

$$\Pr_{s \xleftarrow{\$} \mathcal{S}} [\mathsf{Dec}(\mathsf{Enc}(s)) = s] \geq \epsilon.$$

Then

$$\epsilon \cdot |\mathcal{S}| \leq |\mathcal{T}|.$$

2.1   Hash Combiners

We will use the term hash combiner to refer to the following syntax:

Definition 2. *A hash combiner* $C_{\mathcal{Z}}^{h_1, h_2} : \{0,1\}^\ell \to \{0,1\}^s$ *is an algorithm, keyed by randomness* $\mathcal{Z}$ *with* $|\mathcal{Z}| = k$, *with oracle access to two functions* $h_1, h_2 : \{0,1\}^m \to \{0,1\}^n$.

We also will refer to adversarial implementations of hash functions. When defining security of combiners, we will want security to hold against all adversarial implementations.

Definition 3. *An adversarial implementation of a hash function is an oracle circuit* $g^{\mathcal{O}} : \{0,1\}^m \to \{0,1\}^n$. *We typically bound the number of queries made by* g *to its oracle by* T_g.

In particular, for a hash combiner $C_{\mathcal{Z}}^{h_1, h_2} : \{0,1\}^\ell \to \{0,1\}^s$ to be secure, we will want $C_{\mathcal{Z}}^{h, g^h}$ and $C_{\mathcal{Z}}^{g^h, h}$ to be secure for any adversarial implementation g when h is implemented as an honest hash function. In this work, we will consider the honest hash function to always be implemented as a random oracle.

2.2   Alternative Models

We could consider the model where the adversarial hash function $g^{\mathcal{O}} : \{0,1\}^m \to \{0,1\}^n$ is given access to a common reference string of length r. However, if we bound the number of queries made to $\mathcal{O}$ to q, these models are equivalent up to a $\frac{r}{n} \frac{q}{2^m}$ additive factor. This is because a deterministic g^h can simulate the common reference string by non-uniformly fixing some prefix c of length $m - \log(r/n)$ and using $h(c, 0), \ldots, h(c, r/n)$ as its internal randomness.

We may wish to consider the model where the circuit g is chosen efficiently by the distinguisher instead of being fixed as a separate nonuniform adversary. Note, however, that this model is strictly weaker than the one described in the previous paragraph. Thus, as our positive results hold in a stronger model, they will hold in this model as well. For our negative results, our constructions will indeed be able to be efficiently generated.

Finally, we may wish to consider a one-stage model, where the adversarial hash function is not given oracle access to the honest random oracle. This model is described in more detail in Sect. 7.2, but we do not analyze this model in detail in this work.

2.3 Notation

Throughout this work, we will use certain conventions to make comparisons between constructions and attacks simpler. In general, for a (randomized) hash function h, m will refer to the input length, n will refer to the output length, and k will refer to the length of the randomness. For combiners, we will use ℓ to refer to the input length. Any other notation will be detailed in the section in which it is relevant.

3 Indifferentiability and Hash Combiners

We first introduce the notion of indifferentiability. Indifferentiability was first defined by Maurer, Renner, and Holenstein [16] as a way of arguing (among other things) a notion that some idealized object could be "replaced" by some system or protocol without sacrificing any of the properties of the idealized object. More specifically, in this work, we desire indifferentiability of a hash function combiner with the random oracle. Note that this notion is strictly stronger than collision-resistance. We present the definitions necessary for this notion below, starting with that of indifferentiability itself.

Definition 4 (Maurer, Renner, Holenstein 2003). *Let $\mathcal{F}, \mathcal{G}$ be two ideal primitives, and let $\mathcal{S}_{\mathcal{Z}}^{\mathcal{F}}$ be a family of constructions of $\mathcal{G}$ from $\mathcal{F}$. We say that $\mathcal{S}$ is (statistically) $(T_{\mathsf{Sim}}, \epsilon)$-indifferentiable from $\mathcal{G}$ if there exists a simulator $\mathsf{Sim}^{\mathcal{O}}$ making at most T_{Sim} queries to its oracle such that the following holds: For all (unbounded) oracle algorithms $\mathcal{D}$,*

$$\left| \Pr_{z \xleftarrow{\$} \mathcal{U}} [\mathcal{D}(\mathcal{Z}, \mathcal{F}, \mathcal{S}_{\mathcal{Z}}^{\mathcal{F}}) \to 1] - \Pr_{z \xleftarrow{\$} \mathcal{U}} [\mathcal{D}(\mathcal{Z}, \mathsf{Sim}^{\mathcal{G}}(\mathcal{Z}), \mathcal{G}) \to 1] \right| \leq \epsilon$$

where $\mathcal{U}$ is the uniform distribution.

Theorem 2. *(Informal) If $\mathcal{S}^{\mathcal{F}}$ is ϵ-indifferentiable from $\mathcal{G}$, then for any single-stage cryptographic application using $\mathcal{G}$, replacing $\mathcal{G}$ with $\mathcal{S}^{\mathcal{F}}$ will have at most ϵ security loss.*

That is, if something is indifferentiable from a random oracle, than it can be used as a random oracle in almost all applications. Note that there are some restrictions on the applications of indifferentiability. In particular, for cryptographic systems designed against multiple adversaries who cannot communicate, replacing an ideal model with something indifferentiable may not preserve security [23].

As a random oracle is in some sense the best possible hash function, an ideal hash combiner would be indifferentiable from a random oracle if one of the underlying hash functions is a random oracle. More formally, we give the following definition.

Definition 5. *Let $C_{\mathcal{Z}}^{h_1,h_2}$ be a combiner. Let $\mathcal{H}, \mathcal{G}$ be two random oracles. We say that C is $(T_g, T_{\mathsf{Sim}}, \epsilon)$-random-oracle-secure if, for all oracle circuits $g^{\mathcal{O}}$ making at most T_g oracle queries, both $C_{\mathcal{Z}}^{\mathcal{H},g^{\mathcal{H}}}$ and $C_{\mathcal{Z}}^{g^{\mathcal{H}},\mathcal{H}}$ are $(T_{\mathsf{Sim}}, \epsilon)$-indifferentiable from $\mathcal{G}$. An equivalent formulation is illustrated in Fig. 1.*

Note in particular that we allow our combiner to be keyed. That is, the combiner has access to some public randomness chosen after the adversarial hash function is determined. In the next section, we will show that this is indeed necessary in order for our definition to be achievable.

3.1   On Composability of Random-Oracle-Security

One weakness of our definition of random-oracle-security is that this definition is itself a two-stage game. That is, an adversary against random-oracle-security is composed of both the adversarial implementation $g^{\mathcal{O}}$ as well as the distinguisher $\mathcal{D}$, and neither party is allowed to communicate. Therefore, if one were to instantiate the honest oracle for a random-oracle-combiner with a hash function which is indifferentiable to a random oracle but is not a random oracle itself, the combiner may not preserve security. That is, a random-oracle-secure combiner should be instantiated with candidate hash functions and not transformations of candidate hash functions. We go into more detail on this issue in Sect. 5.

One could consider a stronger definition of hash combiner, which requires indifferentiability from a random oracle when instantiated with a function indifferentiable from a random oracle. We leave it an open question as to whether such a combiner can be achieved, but we suspect that the parameters required for such a transformation are likely to be worse for practitioners.

However, note that this is only an issue when precomposing our definition with indifferentiability. Postcomposing will present no issues aside from those standard for indifferentiability. That is, since our definition requires that the combiner (when instaniated properly) be indifferentiable from a random oracle, Theorem 2 still applies. Any one-stage security property secure when instantiated with a random oracle will also be secure when instantiated with a random-oracle-secure combiner as long as one of the underlying hash functions used by the combiner is itself a random oracle.

As most reasonable security properties one would expect from a hash function are indeed designed for one-stage adversaries, a random-oracle-secure combiner can be used as a random oracle for the vast majority of applications. In particular, when instantiated properly, a random-oracle-secure combiner will be collision resistant, one-way, pseudorandom, and second preimage resistant.

4   Random-Oracle-Secure Hash Combiner Construction

With this definition in mind, we present a construction of a hash function combiner which is indifferentiable from a random oracle. Let $h_1, h_2 : \{0,1\}^m \to \{0,1\}^n$ be two hash functions, and let $\mathcal{Z}_1, \mathcal{Z}_2 \xleftarrow{\$} \{0,1\}^k$ for some $k < m$. Then, our construction is simply the xor of the two hashes evaluated on the input concatenated with $\mathcal{Z}_1, \mathcal{Z}_2$ respectively. That is, we define our combiner $C^{h_1,h_2}_{\mathcal{Z}_1,\mathcal{Z}_2} : \{0,1\}^\ell \to \{0,1\}^n$ as

---

$\underline{REAL - b}$:

Sample $\mathcal{Z} \xleftarrow{\$} \{0,1\}^k$
Sample $h : \{0,1\}^m \to \{0,1\}^n$ u.a.r.
Run $\mathcal{D}^{\mathcal{O}_1,\mathcal{O}_2}(\mathcal{Z}) \to b'$
Output b'.

$\mathcal{O}_1(x)$:
Output $h(x)$

$\mathcal{O}_2(M)$:
If $b = 0$, output $C_{\mathcal{Z}}^{\mathcal{O}_1,g^{\mathcal{O}_1}}(M)$.
If $b = 1$, output $C_{\mathcal{Z}}^{g^{\mathcal{O}_1},\mathcal{O}_1}(M)$.

$\underline{IDEAL}$:

Sample $\mathcal{Z} \xleftarrow{\$} \{0,1\}^k$
Sample $H : \{0,1\}^\ell \to \{0,1\}^s$ u.a.r.
Run $\mathcal{D}^{\mathcal{O}_1,\mathcal{O}_2}(\mathcal{Z}) \to b'$
Output b'.

$\mathcal{O}_1(x)$:
Output $\mathsf{Sim}^{\mathcal{O}_2}(x, \mathcal{Z})$

$\mathcal{O}_2(M)$:
Output $H(M)$.

Fig. 1. We say that the combiner is secure if for all b, $\mathcal{D}^{\mathcal{O}_1,\mathcal{O}_2}$ not necessarily efficient, $g^{\mathcal{O}}$ a query-bounded circuit, there exists a simulator Sim such that $|\Pr[\mathcal{D}(REAL - b) \to 1] - \Pr[\mathcal{D}(IDEAL) \to 1]| \le \epsilon$.

$$C^{h_1,h_2}_{\mathcal{Z}_1,\mathcal{Z}_2}(M) = h_1(M, \mathcal{Z}_1) \oplus h_2(M, \mathcal{Z}_2). \tag{1}$$

This construction relies on k being at least $\frac{m+\log T+\lambda}{2}$, where m is the input length of the hash functions and T is the number of honest hash function h_1 queries the adversarial hash function h_2 may make.

Note that, as m is the length of our hash function input space, this only supports message length at most $\ell = m - k$. In Sect. 5, we will discuss the difficulties of extending this fixed length to arbitrary length.

Theorem 3. *Let* $|\mathcal{Z}_1| = |\mathcal{Z}_2| = k$, $h_1, h_2 : \{0,1\}^m \to \{0,1\}^n$. *We define a hash combiner* $\widetilde{C}^{h_1,h_2}_{\mathcal{Z}_1,\mathcal{Z}_2} : \{0,1\}^\ell \to \{0,1\}^n$ *by*

$$\widetilde{C}^{h_1,h_2}_{\mathcal{Z}_1,\mathcal{Z}_2}(M) = h_1(M, \mathcal{Z}_1) \oplus h_2(M, \mathcal{Z}_2).$$

Then, for all T, $\widetilde{C}^{h_1,h_2}_{\mathcal{Z}_1,\mathcal{Z}_2}$ *is* $\left(T, 1, \frac{T}{2^{k-\ell}} + \frac{1}{2^k}\right)$*-random-oracle-secure.*

To prove Theorem 3, We will rely on the following key lemma.

Lemma 1. *Let* $g^{\mathcal{O}} : \{0,1\}^m \to \{0,1\}^n$ *a circuit making at most* T *oracle calls. Let* $\mathcal{Z}_1, \mathcal{Z}_2 \xleftarrow{\$} \{0,1\}^k$ *and* $h \xleftarrow{\$} \{f : \{0,1\}^m \to \{0,1\}^n\}$ *be random variables. Define* BAD *to be the event that there exists* $x, x' \in \{0,1\}^{\ell:=m-k}$ *such that* $g^h(x, \mathcal{Z}_2)$ *queries* $h(x', \mathcal{Z}_1)$. *Let* $\epsilon = \Pr_{\mathcal{Z}_1,\mathcal{Z}_2,h}[BAD]$. *Then,*

$$\epsilon \leq \frac{T}{2^{k-\ell}}$$

Proof. We write

$$\epsilon_{\mathcal{Z}_2',h'} := \Pr_{\mathcal{Z}_1,\mathcal{Z}_2,h}[BAD | \mathcal{Z}_2 = \mathcal{Z}_2', h = h'] = \Pr_{\mathcal{Z}_1}[\exists\, x, x' : g^h(x, \mathcal{Z}_2') \text{ queries } h'(x', \mathcal{Z}_1)].$$

By an averaging argument, there must exist some $\mathcal{Z}_2^*, h^*$ such that $\epsilon_{\mathcal{Z}_2^*,h^*} \geq \epsilon$. We will build a compressor (Enc, Dec) for $\mathcal{Z}_1$ as follows:

We define $\mathsf{Enc}(\mathcal{Z}_1)$:

1. Find the first lexicographic x such that $g^{h^*}(x, \mathcal{Z}_2^*)$ queries $h^*(x', \mathcal{Z}_1)$ for some x'. If no such x exists, output $\perp$. Otherwise, let t be the index that this query occurs at.
2. Output (x, t).

We also define $\mathsf{Dec}(x, t)$:

1. Let $(x', \mathcal{Z})$ be the t-th query made by $g^{h^*}(x', \mathcal{Z}_1)$.
2. Output $\mathcal{Z}$.

Note that as long as Enc doesn't output $\perp$, it is clear that $\mathsf{Dec}(\mathsf{Enc}(\mathcal{Z}_1)) = \mathcal{Z}_1$. But the probability that Enc fails is $\epsilon_{\mathcal{Z}_2^*,h^*} \geq \epsilon$. Thus, Enc compresses a set of size $\epsilon_{\mathcal{Z}_2^*,h^*} 2^k$ into a set of size $2^\ell \cdot T$. Theorem 1 then gives us

$$\epsilon \leq \epsilon_{\mathcal{Z}_2^*,h^*} \leq \frac{T}{2^{k-\ell}},$$

which completes the proof. $\square$

We now move to the proof of Theorem 3. Note that, since our scheme is symmetric, it suffices to prove $\widetilde{C}^{g^{\mathcal{H}},\mathcal{H}}_{\mathcal{Z}}$ is ϵ-indifferentiable from $\mathcal{G}$ for $\epsilon = \frac{T}{2^{k-\ell}}$.

$Sim^{\mathcal{G}}_{\mathcal{Z}_1, \mathcal{Z}_2}(x)$:

If $x = (M, \mathcal{Z}_1)$ for some M:
-Run $y \leftarrow g^{lazy}(M, \mathcal{Z}_2)$.
-Output $\mathcal{G}(M) \oplus y$.
Else:
-Output $lazy(x)$.

Subroutine $lazy(x)$:
-If $D[x] = \bot$, set $D[x] \xleftarrow{\$} \{0,1\}^n$.
-Output $D[x]$.

Fig. 2. The simulator.

Proof. We first define our simulator Sim as in Fig. 2. Let $REAL$ and $IDEAL$ be the games in Fig. 3. We simply need to show that for any (unbounded) $\mathcal{D}$, $|\Pr[REAL \to 1] - \Pr[IDEAL \to 1]| \leq \epsilon$.

To achieve this, we rely on a series of hybrid games, $REAL, G1, G2, G3, G4, IDEAL$ defined in Figs. 3, 4, and 5.

Claim 1: $\Pr[REAL \to 1] = \Pr[G1 \to 1]$.
In G1, since f and h are sampled uniformly at random, $\tilde{h}$ is a uniformly random function. Thus, since the only difference between these two games is that h (a uniformly random function) is replaced with $\tilde{h}$, $REAL$ and $G1$ are identically distributed.

Claim 2: $|\Pr[G1 \to 1] - \Pr[G2 \to 1]| \leq \epsilon$.
Conditioned on the event that there does not exist any x such that $g^h(x, \mathcal{Z}_2)$ queries h on $(M, \mathcal{Z}_2)$, G2 is identically distributed to G1. But by Lemma 1, this occurs with probability at most ϵ, and so the claim follows.

Claim 3: $\Pr[G2 \to 1] = \Pr[G3 \to 1]$.
Note that the function $g^h(x, \mathcal{Z}_2)$ is independent of f, and so as f is uniformly random, $F(x) = f(x) \oplus g^h(x, \mathcal{Z}_2)$ is also uniformly random. Thus, since the only difference between $G3$ and $G2$ is that f is replaced by F, the two games are identically distributed.

Claim 4: $\Pr[G3 \to 1] = \Pr[G4 \to 1]$.
Note that $G4$ is just $G3$ with algebraic terms reorganized. All values returned by all oracles are identically distributed in both games. The claim trivially follows.

Claim 5: $\Pr[IDEAL \to 1] = \Pr[G4 \to 1]$.
The only difference between $IDEAL$ and $G4$ is that h is replaced by lazy sampling. The claim trivially follows.

Putting the above claims together, we get that $\Pr[REAL \to 1] = \Pr[G1 \to 1]$ and $\Pr[G2 \to 1] = \Pr[IDEAL \to 1]$, and so

$$|\Pr[REAL \to 1] - \Pr[IDEAL \to 1]| \leq \epsilon$$

4.1   Remarks on Parameters

□

Given two $\{0,1\}^m \to \{0,1\}^n$ hash functions, our construction gives a $\{0,1\}^\ell \to \{0,1\}^n$ hash function with security loss $\frac{T}{2^{k-\ell}}$. Note that here, $\ell + k = m$, and so this security loss can be rewritten as $\frac{T}{2^{2k-m}}$. In practice, hash functions are expected to have so called "birthday bound" security for various security properties (such as collision resistance). That is, any attack making q queries to the hash function should have probability of success $\frac{q}{2^\lambda}$, where λ is the security parameter.

REAL:

Sample $Z_1, Z_2 \overset{\$}{\leftarrow} \{0,1\}^k$
Sample $h : \{0,1\}^m \to \{0,1\}^n$ u.a.r.
Run $\mathcal{D}^{\mathcal{O}_1, \mathcal{O}_2}(Z_1, Z_2) \to b'$
Output b'.

$\mathcal{O}_1(x)$:
Output $h(x)$

$\mathcal{O}_2(M)$:
Output $\mathcal{O}_1(M, Z_1) \oplus g^{\mathcal{O}_1}(M, Z_2)$.

(a) Real Game, where $\mathcal{O}_1$ refers to the random oracle and $\mathcal{O}_2$ refers to our combiner construction.

IDEAL:

Sample $Z_1, Z_2 \overset{\$}{\leftarrow} \{0,1\}^k$
Sample $H : \{0,1\}^\ell \to \{0,1\}^n$ u.a.r.
Run $\mathcal{D}^{\mathcal{O}_1, \mathcal{O}_2}(Z_1, Z_2) \to b'$
Output b'.

$\mathcal{O}_1(x)$:
If $x = (M, Z_1)$:
- Compute $y = g^{lazy}(M, Z_2)$. If g ever queries (M', Z_1) for any M', fail.
- Output $\mathcal{O}_2(M) + y$
Else: output $lazy(x)$

$\mathcal{O}_2(M)$:
Output $F(M)$.

Subroutine $lazy(M)$:
If $D[x] = \perp$: $D[x] \overset{\$}{\leftarrow} \{0,1\}^n$.
Output $D[x]$.

(b) Ideal Game, where $\mathcal{O}_1$ refers to our h_1 simulator and $\mathcal{O}_2$ refers to our idealized combiner.

Fig. 3. The real and ideal games for Theorem 3.

G1:
Sample $Z_1, Z_2 \xleftarrow{\$} \{0,1\}^k$
Sample $h : \{0,1\}^m \to \{0,1\}^n$ u.a.r.
Sample $f : \{0,1\}^\ell \to \{0,1\}^n$ u.a.r.
Define $\qquad \widetilde{h}(x) \qquad\qquad =$
$\begin{cases} f(M) & x = (M, Z_1) \text{ for some } M \\ h(x) & o.w. \end{cases}$
Run $\mathcal{D}^{\mathcal{O}_1, \mathcal{O}_2}(Z_1, Z_2) \to b'$
Output b'.

$\mathcal{O}_1(x)$:
Output $\widetilde{h}(x)$

$\mathcal{O}_2(M)$:
Output $\widetilde{h}(M, Z_1) \oplus g^{\widetilde{h}}(M, Z_2)$.

The same as the real game, but with the honest hash function divided into two parts.

G2:
Sample $Z_1, Z_2 \xleftarrow{\$} \{0,1\}^k$
Sample $h : \{0,1\}^m \to \{0,1\}^n$ u.a.r.
Sample $f : \{0,1\}^\ell \to \{0,1\}^n$ u.a.r.
Define $\qquad \widetilde{h}(x) \qquad\qquad =$
$\begin{cases} f(M) & x = (M, Z_1) \text{ for some } M \\ h(x) & o.w. \end{cases}$
Run $\mathcal{D}^{\mathcal{O}_1, \mathcal{O}_2}(Z_1, Z_2) \to b'$
Output b'.

$\mathcal{O}_1(x)$:
Output $\widetilde{h}(x)$

$\mathcal{O}_2(M)$:
Output $f(M) \oplus g^h(M, Z_2)$.

The same as G1, but with $g^{\widetilde{h}}$ replaced with g^h. That is, the compromised hash function's queries to (M, Z_1) are replaced with random values.

Fig. 4. The first two hybrids used for Theorem 3.

G3:
Sample $Z_1, Z_2 \xleftarrow{\$} \{0,1\}^k$
Sample $h : \{0,1\}^m \to \{0,1\}^n$ u.a.r.
Sample $f : \{0,1\}^\ell \to \{0,1\}^n$ u.a.r.
Define $F(x) := f(x) \oplus g^h(x, Z_2)$.
Define $\qquad \widetilde{h}(x) \qquad\qquad =$
$\begin{cases} F(M) & x = (M, Z_1) \text{ for some } M \\ h(x) & o.w. \end{cases}$
Run $\mathcal{D}^{\mathcal{O}_1, \mathcal{O}_2}(Z_1, Z_2) \to b'$
Output b'.

$\mathcal{O}_1(x)$:
Output $\widetilde{h}(x)$

$\mathcal{O}_2(M)$:
Output $F(M) \oplus g^h(M, Z_2)$.

The same as G2, but with $f(x)$ replaced by $f(x) \oplus g^h(x, Z_2)$. That is, the honest hash functions outputs are shifted by $g^h(x, Z_2)$.

G4:
Sample $Z_1, Z_2 \xleftarrow{\$} \{0,1\}^k$
Sample $h : \{0,1\}^m \to \{0,1\}^n$ u.a.r.
Sample $f : \{0,1\}^\ell \to \{0,1\}^n$ u.a.r.
Run $\mathcal{D}^{\mathcal{O}_1, \mathcal{O}_2}(Z_1, Z_2) \to b'$
Output b'.

$\mathcal{O}_1(x)$:
If $x = (M, Z_1)$, output $\mathcal{O}_2(M) \oplus g^h(M, Z_2)$.
Else: output $h(x)$.

$\mathcal{O}_2(M)$:
Output $f(M)$.

The same as G3, but with values reorganized so as to be similar to the simulator.

Fig. 5. The last two hybrids used for Theorem 3.

As our notion of indifferentiability applies to unbounded attackers, the security loss from our construction does not at all depend on the number of queries made by the distinguisher. Thus, to achieve birthday security using our construction, it is sufficient to set

$$k = \frac{m + \log T + \lambda}{2}.$$

Of course, this means our input space is limited to length $\ell = (m - \log T - \lambda)/2$.

4.2   Our Security Proof is Tight

Note that although our proof achieves birthday security for $k = \frac{m+\log T+\lambda}{2}$, one may wonder whether Theorem 3 holds even for smaller values of k. That is, are the parameters required by our security proof optimal for our construction? In this section, we show that the parameters are optimal up to a constant factor.

Theorem 4. *Let $k = \ell$ and let $\widetilde{C}_{\mathcal{Z}_1,\mathcal{Z}_2}^{h_1,h_2} : \{0,1\}^\ell \to \{0,1\}^n$ be as in Eq. (1). Then $\widetilde{C}$ is not $\left(1, 1 - \frac{1}{2^n}\right)$-random oracle secure.*

Proof. Define $g^{\mathcal{H}}(x,y) := h(x,x)$. Then observe that

$$\widetilde{C}_{\mathcal{Z}_1,\mathcal{Z}_2}^{h,g^h}(\mathcal{Z}_1) = h(\mathcal{Z}_1,\mathcal{Z}_1) + g^h(\mathcal{Z}_1,\mathcal{Z}_2) = 0.$$

Thus, we can distinguish $\widetilde{C}$ from a random oracle simply by evaluating on $\mathcal{Z}_1$. This will succeed with probability

$$\left|\Pr[\widetilde{C}(\mathcal{Z}_1) = 0] - \Pr[\mathcal{H}(\mathcal{Z}_1) = 0]\right| = 1 - \frac{1}{2^n}$$

$\square$

In particular, this means that our proof of security for our construction is close to tight. That is, our construction admits an attack when $k \leq \ell$. Since our proof requires that $k \geq \ell + \log T + \lambda$, this means that our randomness requirement is tight up to a $\log T + \lambda$ additive factor. If $\ell = c\lambda$ and $T \leq 2^\lambda$, our proof of security will be tight for our construction up to a $(c+2)$ multiplicative factor.

4.3   Random-Oracle-Secure Combiners Need Randomness

Our construction requires randomness linear in m and the security parameter λ. We now show the dependence on λ is necessary.

In particular, we first prove that no deterministic random-oracle-secure hash combiners can exist - randomness is always needed. This contrasts with the notion of combiners for collision resistance, in which setting concatenation functions as an effective deterministic combiner. We further demonstrate a lower bound on the amount of randomness required for any hash combiner to be

random-oracle-secure, and we argue that in order to achieve "brute-force security", λ bits of randomness are required.

First, we present our main theorem, showing that random-oracle-secure combiners require some randomness.

Theorem 5. *Let C^{h_1,h_2} be a <u>deterministic</u> hash combiner making at most T_C
queries to its underlying hash function. Then, for any value of T_{Sim}, C is not
$(7T_C, T_{\mathsf{Sim}}, 0.25)$-random oracle secure.*

Theorem 6. *Let $C_{\mathcal{Z}}^{h_1,h_2}$ be a hash combiner making T_C oracle queries and uti-
lizing k bits of randomness (i.e. $|\mathcal{Z}| = k$). Then, for any value of T_{Sim}, C is
not $\left(7T_C, T_{\mathsf{Sim}}, \frac{0.25}{2^k}\right)$-secure, even when only considering attacks which can be
generated in time $O(2^k)$.*

Theorem 6 means that any combiner must use superlogarithmic randomness
in order to achieve negligible security loss. In practice, this means that if one
hopes to achieve "brute-force" security, (i.e. no attacker should be able to succeed
with probability $\geq \frac{1}{2^\lambda}$), then it is necessary that $k \geq \lambda - 2$. That is, there should
be at least as much randomness used by the combiner as desired bits of security.

In particular, we note that the adversarial hash functions used in the proofs
of these theorems can be produced in time $O(1)$ and $O((2^k)^2)$ respectively. The
distinguisher in both theorems runs in time $O(1)$.

The proofs of both theorems are a direct result of the following lemma:

Lemma 2. *Let $C_{\mathcal{Z}}^{h_1,h_2} : \{0,1\}^\ell \rightarrow \{0,1\}^s$ be a hash combiner with $|\mathcal{Z}| = k$
making at most T_C queries to its oracles. Let $\epsilon > 0$, $\rho \in (0,1)$, $d \in \mathbb{N}$ such that*

$$\rho\left(1 - \left(\frac{1}{2} + \epsilon\right)^d\right) - \left(\frac{1}{2} + \epsilon\right) > 0$$

Then, C is not $(dT_C, \infty, \frac{\epsilon}{2^k})$-random oracle secure.

In particular, Theorem 6 results from setting $\rho = 0.9$, $\epsilon = 0.25$, and $d = 7$.
Theorem 5 results from setting $k = 1$ in Theorem 6.

4.4   Proof of Lemma 2

Claim. let $C^{h_1,h_2} : \{0,1\}^\ell \rightarrow \{0,1\}^s$ be any deterministic oracle function making
at most T_C queries to its oracles. Let $\mathcal{F} = \{f : \{0,1\}^m \rightarrow \{0,1\}^n\}$. Suppose
that

$$\Pr_{h_1 \xleftarrow{\$} \mathcal{F}}\left[\Pr_{h_2 \xleftarrow{\$} \mathcal{F}} [C^{h_1,h_2}(0) = 0] \geq \frac{1}{2} - \epsilon\right] \geq \rho.$$

Then, for all d, there exists an $\tilde{h}_r^{h_1}$ making at most $d \cdot T_C$ queries to h_1 such that

$$\Pr_{r}[\Pr_{h_1}[C^{h_1, \tilde{h}_r^{h_1}}(0) = 0] \geq \frac{1}{2} + \epsilon] \geq \rho\left(1 - \left(\frac{1}{2} + \epsilon\right)^d\right) - \left(\frac{1}{2} + \epsilon\right)$$

Proof. We will first define a stateful algorithm $lazy_r(x)$:
On initialization, $lazy_r$ sets $D = \{\}$, $ctr = 1$, and parses $r = w_1, \ldots, w_{T_C}$.
On input x, $lazy_r(x)$ does the following:

- If $x \notin D$, set $D[x] = w_{ctr}$ and increase ctr by 1.
- Output $D[x]$.

We will define $\tilde{h}_r^{h_1}(x)$ as follows:

- Parse $r = r_1, \ldots, r_d$.
- For each $i = 1, \ldots, d$: run $C^{h_1, lazy_{r_i}}(0) \to c_i$, keeping track of D_i the database computed by $lazy_{r_i}$.
- If $c_i = 0$ for any i, set i^* to be the smallest such i.
- Output $D_{i^*}[x]$ if $x \in D_{i^*}$. Otherwise output 0.

We make two key observations. First note that if $\tilde{h}_r$ finds i^* for any (and thus all) of its inputs, then $C^{h_1, lazy_{r_{i^*}}}(0) = C^{\tilde{h}_r, h_2}(0) = 0$. Second, note that for uniform w, $C^{h_1, lazy_w}(0)$ is identically distributed to $C^{h_1, h_2}(0)$.

Let h_1 be such that $\Pr_{h_2}[C^{h_1, h_2}(0) = 0] \geq (\frac{1}{2} - \epsilon)$. Then

$$\Pr_w[C^{h_1, lazy_w}(0) = 0] \geq \left(\frac{1}{2} - \epsilon\right)$$

$$\Pr_{w_1, \ldots, w_d}[C^{h_1, lazy_w}(0) = 0 \text{ for some } i] \geq 1 - \left(\frac{1}{2} + \epsilon\right)^d$$

$$\Pr_r[C^{h_1, \tilde{h}_r^{h_1}}(0) = 0] \geq 1 - \left(\frac{1}{2} + \epsilon\right)^d$$

Putting this together with the assumption in the lemma, we get

$$\Pr_{h_1}[\Pr_r[C^{h_1, \tilde{h}_r}(0) = 0] \geq 1 - \left(\frac{1}{2} + \epsilon\right)^d] \geq \rho$$

and so

$$\Pr_{r, h_1}[C^{h_1, \tilde{h}_r}(0) = 0] \geq \rho\left(1 - \left(\frac{1}{2} + \epsilon\right)^d\right)$$

Using basic probability, we get our lemma.   □

Claim. Let C^{h_1, h_2} be such that

$$\Pr_{h_1 \xleftarrow{\$} \mathcal{F}}[\Pr_{h_2 \xleftarrow{\$} \mathcal{F}}[C^{h_1, h_2}(0) = 0] \geq \frac{1}{2} - \epsilon] < \rho$$

Then there exists an efficient $\tilde{h}_r^{h_2}$ making at most T_C queries to h_2 such that

$$\Pr_r[\Pr_{h_2}[C^{\tilde{h}_r, h_2}(0) = 1] \geq \frac{1}{2} + \epsilon] \geq 1 - \rho$$

Proof. We simply define $\bar{h}_r$ to lazily sample the random oracle. In particular, $\bar{h}_r(x)$ is defined by:

- Run $C^{lazy_r, h_2}(0)$ to get database D.
- If $x \in D$, output $D[x]$, otherwise output 0.

It is clear that $C^{lazy_r, h_2}(0)$ is identically distributed to $C^{h_1, h_2}(0)$, so we conclude

$$\Pr_r[\Pr_{h_2}[C^{\bar{h}_r, h_2}(0) = 0] > \frac{1}{2} - \epsilon] < \rho.$$

$\square$

The proof of Lemma 2 comes from the two claims as follows:

Proof. Let ϵ, ρ, and d be as in the theorem statement. We will first consider the case where $\mathcal{Z} = 0$. By the claims, when ρ and d are set appropriately, either

$$\Pr_r[\Pr_{h_1}[C_0^{h_1, \tilde{h}_r}(0) = 0] \geq \frac{1}{2} + \epsilon] > 0$$

or

$$\Pr_r[\Pr_{h_2}[C_0^{\overline{h_1}_r, h_2}(0) = 1] \geq \frac{1}{2} + \epsilon] > 0$$

We will define an attack for the first case, and the attack in the second case will be symmetric.

Observe that in the first case, there must exist some r^* such that $\Pr_{h_1}[C_0^{h_1, \tilde{h}_{r^*}}(0) = 0] \geq \frac{1}{2} + \epsilon$. Thus, we define $g = \tilde{h}_{r^*}$. For $\mathcal{H}, \mathcal{G}$ random oracles, We will develop an attacker $\mathcal{D}$ for the indifferentiability game between $C_{\mathcal{Z}}^{\mathcal{H}, g^{\mathcal{H}}}$ from $\mathcal{G}$.

$\mathcal{D}(\mathcal{Z}, \mathcal{O}_1, \mathcal{O}_2)$:

- If $\mathcal{Z} \neq 0$: flip a coin $b \xleftarrow{\$} \{0, 1\}$ and output b.
- If $\mathcal{Z} = 0$: output 1 if and only if $\mathcal{O}_2(0)$.

We can then compute the advantage of $\mathcal{D}$ as follows:

$\Pr[\mathcal{D}(\mathcal{H}, C_{\mathcal{Z}}^{\mathcal{H}, g^{\mathcal{H}}}) = 1]$

$= \Pr[\mathcal{Z} = 0] \Pr[\mathcal{D}(C_{\mathcal{Z}}^{\mathcal{H}, g^{\mathcal{H}}} = 0 | \mathcal{Z} = 0] + \Pr[\mathcal{Z} \neq 0] \Pr[\mathcal{D}(C_{\mathcal{Z}}^{\mathcal{H}, g^{\mathcal{H}}} = 0 | \mathcal{Z} \neq 0]$

$= \frac{1}{2^k} \Pr_{h_1}[C_0^{h_1, \tilde{h}_{r^*}^{h_1}}(0) = 0] + \left(1 - \frac{1}{2^k}\right) \frac{1}{2}$

$\geq \frac{1}{2} + \frac{1}{2^k} \left(\left(\frac{1}{2} + \epsilon\right) - \frac{1}{2}\right) = \frac{1}{2} + \frac{\epsilon}{2^k}$

But for any simulator Sim,

$$\Pr[\mathcal{D}(\text{Sim}^{\mathcal{G}}, \mathcal{G}) = 1] = \frac{1}{2}$$

and so $C_{\mathcal{Z}}^{\mathcal{H}, g^{\mathcal{H}}}$ is not $\frac{1}{2^k}(1 - (\frac{1}{2} - \epsilon))$-indifferentiable from $\mathcal{G}$. Thus, since in either case g will make at most dT_C queries to its oracle, we get that C^{h_1, h_2} is not $(dT_C, \frac{\epsilon}{2^k})$-random oracle secure. $\square$

A Few Remarks on Efficiency: We remark that the probability of a random r being sufficient for our purposes is

$$\alpha := \min\left(1 - \rho, \rho\left(1 - \left(\frac{1}{2} + \epsilon\right)^d\right) - \left(\frac{1}{2} + \epsilon\right)\right)$$

and we can test whether some r is sufficient by estimating

$$\Pr_{h_1}[C_0^{h_1, \tilde{h}_r}(0) = 0] = \Pr_{r'}[C_0^{lazy_{r'}, \tilde{h}_r}(0) = 0]$$

or

$$\Pr_{h_2}[C_0^{\overline{h}_r, h_2}(0) = 0] = \Pr_{r'}[C_0^{\overline{h}_r, lazy_{r'}}(0) = 0]$$

and seeing if it is larger than $\frac{1}{2} - \frac{1}{2}\frac{\epsilon}{2^k}$. This test can be performed in time $O\left(\left(\frac{2^k}{\epsilon}\right)^2\right)$, and a good r can be found in $O\left(\frac{1}{\alpha}\right)$ trials. Thus, we can produce a g which biases C in time $O\left(\frac{1}{\alpha}\left(\frac{2^k}{\epsilon}\right)^2\right)$.

5   Extensions to Arbitrary Length

In Sects. 3 and 4, we considered a regime where the two input hash functions go from m-bit long strings to n-bit long strings.

Note that there are a number of constructions [7], mostly designed around the Merkle-Damgård transform (Sect. 5.1), which when instantiated on a compressing random oracle, are indifferentiable from a random oracle. In Sect. 5.2, we show how to compose such a construction with a combiner to produce a combiner for arbitrary length input. However, in Sect. 5.3, we see that the parameters of our construction imply that it is not advisable to employ this approach for hash functions used in practice.

One would hope to instead perform a transformation from [7] on the original compression function, and then applying our combiner to the results. However, as we remarked in Sect. 3.1, this construction may not be secure. In fact, in Sect. 5.4, we demonstrate an attack against this approach.

To remedy this issue, in Sect. 6, we explicitly consider the security of precomposing with a Merkle-Damgård transformation instead of relying on the modular approach. In particular, we show that this approach produces a combiner satisfying collision-resistance. We conjecture that indifferentiability will hold for this construction as well.

5.1   The Merkle-Damgård Transformation

First, we define some of the terms necessary to understand the Merkle-Damgård transformation on hash functions. For the remainder of this work, for any hash function h, we will denote by h^* the Merkle-Damgård transformation applied to that hash function.

Definition 6. *(Merkle-Damgård transformation): Let $f : \{0,1\}^{n+\Delta} \to \{0,1\}^n$ be a function. We define $f^* : \{0,1\}^* \to \{0,1\}^n$ as follows: On input x, write $x = (x_1, \ldots, x_\ell)$ where $|x_i| = \Delta$ (if $|x|$ is not a multiple of Δ, pad with 0s). Then,*

$$f^*(x) = f(x_\ell, \ldots, f(x_2, f(x_1, 0)) \ldots)$$

Intuitively, the Merkle-Damgård transform separates the message into Δ-bit blocks and then iteratively evaluates a fixed-length hash function $h : \{0,1\}^{n+\Delta} \to \{0,1\}^n$ on each block in order to extend the length of input arbitrarily.

At times, we will want to consider partial evaluations of the Merkle-Damgård evaluation. In these events, for any hash function $h : \{0,1\}^{n+\Delta} \to \{0,1\}^n$, any message $x = (x_1, \ldots, x_\ell) \in \{0,1\}^{\ell\Delta}$, and any $1 \le i \le \ell$, we denote

$$h^{(i)}(x) := h^*(x_1, \ldots, x_i).$$

5.2 Arbitrary Length Construction

For any hash function transformation from fixed length to arbitrary length which preserves indifferentiability, we can apply this to our fixed-length random-oracle-secure combiner (Eq. (1)) to produce an arbitrary length random-oracle-secure combiner. In fact, this holds for any random-oracle-secure combiner, as seen in the following theorem. Note that the parameters for indifferentiability will depend heavily on the particular construction used, and so we will only provide an informal theorem. The proof is a straightforward application of Theorem 2.

Theorem 7. *(Informal) Let $\mathcal{F} : \{0,1\}^m \to \{0,1\}^n$ and $\mathcal{G} : \{0,1\}^* \to \{0,1\}^{n'}$ be random oracles, and let $T^{\mathcal{F}}$ be indifferentiable from $\mathcal{G}$. Let $C_{\mathcal{Z}}^{h_1,h_2}$ be a random-oracle-secure combiner. Then $\overline{C}_{\mathcal{Z}}^{h_1,h_2}$ defined by*

$$\overline{C}_{\mathcal{Z}}^{h_1,h_2}(M) = T^{C_{\mathcal{Z}}^{h_1,h_2}}(M)$$

is a random-oracle-secure combiner.

Plugging in the NMAC transformation construction from [7] gives us the following corollary.

Corollary 1. *Let $\widetilde{C}$ be as in Theorem 3. Then*

$$ArbC_{\mathcal{Z}}^{h_1,h_2}(M) := \widetilde{C}(1, \widetilde{C}(0, M_\ell, \widetilde{C}(0, M_{\ell-1}, \widetilde{C}(\ldots, \widetilde{C}(0, M_1, 0) \ldots)))))$$

is a random-oracle-secure combiner.

5.3   A Note on Parameters

Note that in order for our random-oracle-secure combiner construction to be a compression function for use in Theorem 7, it is necessary that $\ell > n$. But as $\ell \leq m/2$, this means that the underlying hash functions must satisfy $n \leq m/2$.

In practice, the compression function used for SHA2 maps 768 bits (representing the internal state and the input block) to 256 bits (representing just the internal state) [1]. Thus, for SHA2, $m/2 = \frac{768-256}{2} = 256 = n$, and so the resulting combiner is not compressing. The compression function used for SHA3 maps 2688 bits to 1600 bits [10]. Thus, our combiner cannot be instantiated with either of these hash functions without first truncating the output. However, truncation will reduce security guarantees significantly, and so is not recommended.

5.4   A Prefix Attack on Merkle-Damgård Hash Functions

In order to produce a random oracle with sufficient compression, we could imagine applying Merkle-Damgård to a concrete hash function. Thus, the resulting hash function would be indifferentiable from a random oracle, and will be sufficiently compressing. Unfortunately, we show that if we use the random-oracle-combiner as a black-box, the resulting construction may not be secure.

In particular, applying a combiner on a hash function indifferentiable from a random oracle will not necessarily preserve security.

Define
$$PreC_{\mathcal{Z}_1,\mathcal{Z}_2}^{h_1,h_2}(M) := h_1(\mathcal{Z}_1, M) \oplus h_2(\mathcal{Z}_2, M)$$

Note that the same proof as Theorem 3 shows that $PreC$ is $\left(T, 1, \frac{T}{2^{k-\ell}} + \frac{1}{2^k}\right)$-random-oracle-secure.

Furthermore, [7] shows that if $\mathcal{H} : \{0,1\}^m \to \{0,1\}^n$ is a random oracle, then for any fixed m', $\mathcal{H}^* : \{0,1\}^{m'} \to \{0,1\}^n$ is a random oracle.

However, we will show that composing these two constructions does not lead to a random-oracle-secure combiner. In particular, the resulting hash combiner will not even be a one-way function.

Theorem 8. *Let $h_1, h_2 : \{0,1\}^{2n} \to \{0,1\}^n$.*
Define
$$PreCMD_{\mathcal{Z}_1,\mathcal{Z}_2}^{h_1,h_2}(M) := h_1^*(\mathcal{Z}_1, M) \oplus h_2^*(\mathcal{Z}_2, M).$$

There exists an adversarial implementation $g^{\mathcal{O}}$ such that, if $y = PreCMD_{\mathcal{Z}_1,\mathcal{Z}_2}^{h,g^h}(x)$, there exists an efficient A such that

$$\Pr_{\substack{h \xleftarrow{\$} \{f:\{0,1\}^m \to \{0,1\}^n\} \\ \mathcal{Z}_1,\mathcal{Z}_2 \xleftarrow{\$} \{0,1\}^k, x \xleftarrow{\$} \{0,1\}^\ell}} [PreCMD_{\mathcal{Z}_1,\mathcal{Z}_2}^{h,g^h}(A(y)) = y] \geq 1 - \frac{3}{2^n}.$$

We immediately get the following corollary.

Corollary 2. *$PreCMD$ is not $\left(1, T_{\mathsf{Sim}}, 1 - \frac{4}{2^n}\right)$-random-oracle-secure for any value of T_{Sim}.*

Proof. (of Theorem 8) Define the compromised hash function g^h as follows

$$g^h(x, IV) := \begin{cases} 1 & x = 0 \\ h(x, x) & IV = 1 \\ h(x, IV) \oplus x & \text{else} \end{cases}$$

Let $y \neq 0$. Define $M_y = 0|h^*(\mathcal{Z}_1, 0)|y$. We will show that with high probability over h, that if $g^*(\mathcal{Z}_2, M_y) = h^*(\mathcal{Z}_1, y)$.

We call h good if $h^*(\mathcal{Z}_1, 0) \neq 0$ and $h^*(\mathcal{Z}_1, 0, h^*(\mathcal{Z}_1, 0)) \neq 1$. In this case,

$$\begin{aligned} g^*(\mathcal{Z}_2, M_y) &= g(y, g(h^*(\mathcal{Z}_1, 0), g(0, g^*(\mathcal{Z}_2)))) \\ &= g(y, g(h^*(\mathcal{Z}_1, 0), 1)) \\ &= g(y, h(h^*(\mathcal{Z}_1, 0), h^*(\mathcal{Z}_1, 0))) \\ &= g(y, h^*(\mathcal{Z}_1, 0, h^*(\mathcal{Z}_1, 0))) \\ &= h(y, h^*(\mathcal{Z}_1, 0, h^*(\mathcal{Z}_1, 0))) \oplus y \\ &= h^*(\mathcal{Z}_1, 0, h^*(\mathcal{Z}_1, 0), y) \oplus y \\ &= h^*(\mathcal{Z}_1, M_y) \oplus y \end{aligned}$$

and so

$$PreCMD^{h,g^h}_{\mathcal{Z}_1, \mathcal{Z}_2}(M_y) = h^*(\mathcal{Z}_1, M_y) \oplus h^*(\mathcal{Z}_1, M_y) \oplus y = y$$

Define $A(y) = M_y$. For simplicity, we will write $y = PreCMD^{h,g^h}_{\mathcal{Z}_1, \mathcal{Z}_2}(x)$. Then,

$$\Pr_{h, \mathcal{Z}_1, \mathcal{Z}_2, x}[PreCMD^{h,g^h}_{\mathcal{Z}_1, \mathcal{Z}_2}(A(y)) = y]$$

$$= \Pr[y \neq 0, h^*(\mathcal{Z}_1, 0) \neq 0, h^*(\mathcal{Z}_1, 0, h^*(\mathcal{Z}_1, 0)) \neq 1] \geq 1 - \frac{3}{2^n}$$

$\square$

6 A Short Collision Resistant Hash Function Combiner

Despite the fact that indifferentiability does not precompose with random-oracle-security, we may hope that our construction is secure when instantiated specifically with Merkle-Damgård style hash functions. In particular, define

$$CMD^{h_1, h_2}_{\mathcal{Z}_1, \mathcal{Z}_2}(M) = h_1^*(M, \mathcal{Z}_1) \oplus h_2^*(M, \mathcal{Z}_2).$$

We would like to claim that $CMD^{h_1, h_2}_{\mathcal{Z}_1, \mathcal{Z}_2}$ is random-oracle-secure.

As evidence towards this result, we show that $CMD^{h_1, h_2}_{\mathcal{Z}_1, \mathcal{Z}_2}$ is collision-resistant. We leave the claim that $CMD^{h_1, h_2}_{\mathcal{Z}_1, \mathcal{Z}_2}$ is random-oracle-secure as an open question.

6.1   Collision Resistance Definitions

We present the definitions of collision resistance as well as a collision-resistant hash function combiner in the random oracle model.

Definition 7. *We say that a family of hash functions $\{H_{\mathcal{Z}}^{\mathcal{O}}\}_{\mathcal{Z}}$ is (T_A, ϵ)- collision-resistant in the random oracle model if for all $A^{\mathcal{O}}$ making at most T_A queries to $\mathcal{O}$*

$$\Pr_{\mathcal{Z}}[A^{\mathcal{O}}(\mathcal{Z}) \to M_0, M_1 : H_{\mathcal{Z}}^{\mathcal{O}}(M_0) = H_{\mathcal{Z}}^{\mathcal{O}}(M_1)] \leq \epsilon$$

Definition 8. *Let $C_{\mathcal{Z}}^{h_1,h_2}$ be a combiner. Let $\mathcal{H}, \mathcal{G}$ be two random oracles. We say that C is (T_g, T_A, ϵ)-collision-resistant secure if, for all oracle circuits $g^{\mathcal{O}}$ making at most T_g oracle queries, both $C_{\mathcal{Z}}^{\mathcal{H}, g^{\mathcal{H}}}$ and $C_{\mathcal{Z}}^{g^{\mathcal{H}}, \mathcal{H}}$ are (T_A, ϵ)-collision-resistant in the random oracle model.*

6.2   Merkle-Damgård Yields Collision Resistance

We present the main theorem for the section, and the rest will be dedicated to proving this result.

Theorem 9. *Let $h_1 : \{0,1\}^{n+\Delta} \to \{0,1\}^n$ be a random oracle, and let $h_2 : \{0,1\}^{n+\Delta} \to \{0,1\}^n$ be an oracle circuit with at most T_{h_2} gates to h_1. Let $\mathcal{Z}_1, \mathcal{Z}_2 \xleftarrow{\$} \{0,1\}^{k\Delta}$. Define $CMD_{\mathcal{Z}_1,\mathcal{Z}_2}^{h_1,h_2} : \{0,1\}^{\ell\Delta} \to \{0,1\}^n$ as*

$$CMD_{\mathcal{Z}_1,\mathcal{Z}_2}^{h_1,h_2}(M) = h_1^*(M, \mathcal{Z}_1) \oplus h_2^*(M, \mathcal{Z}_2).$$

Then, $CMD_{\mathcal{Z}_1,\mathcal{Z}_2}^{h_1,h_2}$ is (T_{h_2}, T_A, ϵ)-collision-resistant secure for

$$\epsilon \leq \frac{T_g^{k/\Delta}}{2^{k-\ell-1}} + \frac{2T_A + 4(\ell + k) + 5}{2^n} + \frac{3}{(T_A + 2(\ell + k)) \cdot 2^n}$$

Note that, in particular, the output length of CMD significantly bypasses the impossibility results of [4,21,22].

6.3   Proof of Theorem 9

We now prove Theorem 9. The proof is rather technical, but the high-level intuition is as follows: If the combiner were not collision-resistant, then with noticeable probability we can find $M_0 \neq M_1$ such that $h_2^*(M_0, \mathcal{Z}_2) \oplus h_2^*(M_1, \mathcal{Z}_2) = h_1^*(M_0, \mathcal{Z}_1) \oplus h_1^*(M_1, \mathcal{Z}_1)$. Then, we see that either one or both of the h_2^* evaluations must query the final round of an h_1^* evaluation, or neither will.

1. If one does, then with high probability it must query every intermediate value for computing h_1^* (Lemma 3), and we may use these intermediate values with these queries to compress the random oracle.

2. If neither does, then a similar process may be used to create an algorithm which outputs a random oracle output without querying it, which obviously succeeds only with negligible probability.

So, in either case, we see that a noticeable probability of success at breaking collision resistance corresponds to a noticeable probability of either (1) compressing the random oracle, or (2) learning the random oracle without querying it. Since both of these things cannot succeed with noticeable probability, we are done.

As a note, all notions of h_2 in the theorem statement and proof are h_1 oracle circuits. We denote $h_2 = h_2^{h_1}$ for simplicity.

Proof. Suppose toward contradiction that there exists some $h_2, \mathcal{A}$ which break collision resistance. In particular, $\mathcal{A}(\mathcal{Z}_1, \mathcal{Z}_2)$ outputs some $M_0 \neq M_1$ such that $CMD_{\mathcal{Z}_1,\mathcal{Z}_2}^{h_1,h_2}(M_0) = CMD_{\mathcal{Z}_1,\mathcal{Z}_2}^{h_1,h_2}(M_1)$ with probability $\epsilon \geq 1/p(\lambda)$ for some polynomial p.

We define $\mathcal{A}_{complete}$ as a PPT algorithm which on input $(\mathcal{Z}_1, \mathcal{Z}_2)$ computes $(M_0, M_1) \leftarrow \mathcal{A}(\mathcal{Z}_1, \mathcal{Z}_2)$, queries $h_1^*(M_0)$ and $h_1^*(M_1)$, and outputs (M_0, M_1). In particular, $\mathcal{A}_{complete}$ also breaks collision resistance of $CMD_{\mathcal{Z}_1,\mathcal{Z}_2}^{h_1,h_2}$ with probability ϵ, but $\mathcal{A}_{complete}$ is guaranteed to make every h_1 query needed to compute $h_1^*(M_0)$ and $h_1^*(M_1)$. Let $T_{complete} \leq T_\mathcal{A} + 2(\ell + k)$.

Without loss of generality, we denote by M_0 the message which $\mathcal{A}_{complete}$ queries the final round of first.

With probability ϵ, $(M_0, M_1) \leftarrow \mathcal{A}_{complete}(\mathcal{Z}_1, \mathcal{Z}_2)$ satisfies $CMD_{\mathcal{Z}_1,\mathcal{Z}_2}^{h_1,h_2}(M_0) = CMD_{\mathcal{Z}_1,\mathcal{Z}_2}^{h_1,h_2}(M_1)$. If this is true, then one of the following clearly must hold:

1. $h_2^*(M_0, \mathcal{Z}_2)$ queries h_1 on $(\mathcal{Z}_{1,k}, h^*(M_1, \mathcal{Z}_{1,1}, \ldots, \mathcal{Z}_{1,k-1}))$.
2. $h_2^*(M_1, \mathcal{Z}_2)$ queries h_1 on $(\mathcal{Z}_{1,k}, h^*(M_1, \mathcal{Z}_{1,1}, \ldots, \mathcal{Z}_{1,k-1}))$.
3. Neither $h_2^*(M_0, \mathcal{Z}_2)$ nor $h_2^*(M_1, \mathcal{Z}_2)$ query h_1 on $(\mathcal{Z}_{1,k}, h^*(M_1, \mathcal{Z}_{1,1}, \ldots, \mathcal{Z}_{1,k-1}))$.

We denote by ϵ_1 the probability of Case 1 ocurring, and likewise for ϵ_2 for Case 2 and ϵ_3 for Case 3. By a union bound, $\epsilon \leq \epsilon_1 + \epsilon_2 + \epsilon_3$. We will analyze each of these cases individually.

Before we start the case analysis, we will make heavy use of the following process and technical lemma (Fig. 6).

---

reconstruct($h_{target}, \boldsymbol{q}$):

Let $i_1, \ldots, i_\ell$ be an increasing sequence of indices of $\boldsymbol{q}$ corresponding to queries $q_{i_1} = (s_1, IV_1), \ldots, q_{i_\ell} = (s_\ell, IV_\ell)$ satisfying:
- $IV_1 = 0^n$,
- $\forall i < \ell, IV_{i+1} = h_1(s_i, IV_i)$.
- $h_{target} = h_1(s_\ell, IV_\ell)$. If this sequence is unique in $\boldsymbol{q}$, output $c_1 \circ c_2 \circ \ldots \circ c_\ell$. Else, output $\perp$.

Fig. 6. The algorithm reconstruct.

In essence, reconstruct takes a set of queries as well as a target final output, and reconstructs an ℓ-block input $c = c_1 \circ \ldots \circ c_\ell$ satisfying $h_1^*(c) = h_{target}$, if one exists. This allows us to implicitly reconstruct messages which the query pattern of an algorithm indicates it evaluated.

We also present the technical Lemma 3, whose proof is deferred to Sect. 6.4.

Lemma 3. *Let $h : \{0,1\}^{n+\Delta} \to \{0,1\}^n$ be a random oracle, and let skip^h be a PPT algorithm which makes at most T_{skip} queries to h. Let (x,y) be the output of skip, and let ℓ be such that $|x| = \ell\Delta$. Denote by x_i the i-th block of Δ bits in x. Then, the probability that $(x,y) \leftarrow \mathsf{skip}^h$, $y = h^*(x)$, and there is some $i \le \ell$ such that skip^h queries h on $(x_i, h^{(i)}(x))$ is at most $(q+1)/2^n$.*

As a peek ahead, the proof of Lemma 3 involves using skip as a compressor for the random oracle. As each case reduces to this lemma, then, we are intrinsically hiding a compression argument inside of each case.

Case 1: We define skip' as follows:

1. Sample $\mathcal{Z}_1, \mathcal{Z}_2 \xleftarrow{\$} \{0,1\}^{k\Delta}$.
2. Sample a random index $t_0 \in [T_{complete}]$.
3. Run $\mathcal{A}_{complete}(\mathcal{Z}_1, \mathcal{Z}_2)$ up until before query t_0.
4. Let $\boldsymbol{q} = (q_1, \ldots, q_{T_{complete}}$ denote the $T_{complete}$ h_1-queries made by $\mathcal{A}_{complete}$, where queries made after t_0 are denoted implicitly according to the randomness which $\mathcal{A}_{complete}$ is using.
5. Set $\widetilde{M_0} = \mathsf{reconstruct}(q_{t_0}, \boldsymbol{q})$. If $\mathsf{reconstruct}(q_{t_0}, \boldsymbol{q}) = \perp$, output $\perp$ instead.
6. Compute $y = h_2(\widetilde{M_0}, \mathcal{Z}_2)$.
7. Output $(\widetilde{M_0} \circ \mathcal{Z}_2, y)$.

Because we are running $\mathcal{A}_{complete}$, must some index t_0 such that in the above procedure, $q_{t_0} = (M_{0,\ell}, h_1^{(\ell-1)}(M_0))$. By Lemma 3, then, in this event, with probability at least $1 - (T_{complete} + 1/2^n)$, $\mathcal{A}_{complete}$ will query all of $h_1^*(M_0)$ in order. Furthermore, if there are no queries among these queries, then these queries will be unique. In this case, it is clear that the conditions for $\mathsf{reconstruct}(q_{t_0}, \boldsymbol{q})$ will be fulfilled, and in fact $\mathsf{reconstruct}(q_{t_0}, \boldsymbol{q}) = \widetilde{M_0} = M_0$. By a union bound, then, the probability that this is the case is at least $\rho = (T_{complete} + 1)/2^n + T_{complete}^2/2^n$ (If t_0 is guessed correctly).

So, with probability at least $\epsilon_1 - \rho/T_{complete}$, skip' chooses the correct t_0 runs $h_2^*(M_0, \mathcal{Z}_2)$ as desired, which queries $h_1(\mathcal{Z}_{1,i}, h_1^*(M_0, \mathcal{Z}_{1,1}, \ldots, \mathcal{Z}_{1,i-1})$ for all i by assumption. Note that here, the probability is over any internal randomness of $\mathcal{A}_{complete}$, the choice of h_1, and the sampling of $\mathcal{Z}_1, \mathcal{Z}_2$.

In particular, there must be some choice of $\mathcal{A}_{complete}, h_1, \mathcal{Z}_2$ such that skip' generates $\widetilde{M_0}$ such that $h_2^*(\widetilde{M_0}, \mathcal{Z}_2)$ queries all $h_1(\mathcal{Z}_{1,i}, h_1^*(M_0, \mathcal{Z}_{1,1}, \ldots, \mathcal{Z}_{1,i-1}))$ with probability at least $\epsilon_1 - \rho/T_{complete}$ (where now the probability is only over the random sampling of $\mathcal{Z}_1$). Call these $\mathcal{A}_{complete}^{opt}, h_1^{opt}, \mathcal{Z}_2^{opt}$, respectively. We will at last use these to compress any $\mathcal{Z}_1$.

We define $(\mathsf{Enc}, \mathsf{Dec})$ as so: First, $\mathsf{Enc}(\mathcal{Z}_1)$ is defined as so:

1. Compute $(M_0, M_1) \leftarrow A^{opt}_{complete}(\mathcal{Z}_1, \mathcal{Z}_2^{opt})$.
2. If $h_2^*(M_0, \mathcal{Z}_2^{opt})$ does not query $h_1^{opt}(\mathcal{Z}_{1,i}, (h_1^{opt})^*(M_0, \mathcal{Z}_{1,1}, \ldots, \mathcal{Z}_{1,i-1})$ for all i, output $\perp$.
3. Else, if $h_2^*(M_0, \mathcal{Z}_2^{opt})$ does query every $h_1^{opt}(\mathcal{Z}_{1,i}, (h_1^{opt})^*(M_0, \mathcal{Z}_{1,1}, \ldots, \mathcal{Z}_{1,i-1})$ during its computation, let $\widetilde{q}_1, \ldots, \widetilde{q}_k$ be these indices of these queries.
4. Output $M_0, \widetilde{q}_1, \ldots, \widetilde{q}_k$.

We define $\mathsf{Dec}(M_0, \widetilde{q}_1, \ldots, \widetilde{q}_k)$ as so:

1. Initialize s as the empty string.
2. Run $h_2^*(M_0, \mathcal{Z}_2^{opt})$. Whenever this process makes query $\widetilde{q}_i$, let (s_{q_i}, IV_{q_i}) be the query itself and set $s = s \circ s_i$.
3. Output s.

Intuitively, if every h_1 query is made in step (2) of Enc, then Enc outputs the indices of those exact queries. Then, because $\mathcal{Z}_{1,i}$ is the state of each of those queries, Dec can use those queries to recover $\mathcal{Z}_1$. Correctness of the encoding in fact follows directly from the fact that $s_{q_i} = \mathcal{Z}_{1,i}$ for all $i \in [k]$, giving us $\mathsf{Dec}(\mathsf{Enc}(\mathcal{Z}_1)) = \mathcal{Z}_1$.

Because we chose our other inputs optimally, we see that this encoding is correct on at least an $(\epsilon_1 - \rho/T_{complete})$-fraction of the space of all $\mathcal{Z}_1$. The output space of Enc, meanwhile, is $2^\ell \cdot T_{h_2}^{k/\Delta}$, as each M_0 is ℓ bits long and we must choose the queries from among the k/Δ h_1^{opt}-calls of h_2, each of which makes up to T_{h_2} queries.

Theorem 1 then gives us $(\epsilon_1 - \rho/T_{complete})2^k \leq 2^\ell \cdot T_{h_2}^{k/\Delta}$. Substituting $\rho = (T_{complete} + 1)/2^n + T_{complete}^2/2^n$ and solving for ϵ_1, we see this is satisfied by

$$\epsilon_1 \leq \frac{T_g^{k/\Delta}}{2^{k-\ell}} + \frac{T_{complete}^2 + T_{complete} + 1}{2^n T_{complete}} = \frac{T_g^{k/\Delta}}{2^{k-\ell}} + \frac{T_{complete} + 1}{2^n} + \frac{1}{T_{complete} 2^n}. \tag{2}$$

Case 2: We observe that Case 2 follows the exact same reasoning as in Case 1 when replacing $(M_0, \widetilde{M}_0, t_0)$ with $(M_1, \widetilde{M}_1, t_1)$ respectively. Therefore, we get a similar bound

$$\epsilon_2 \leq \frac{T_g^{k/\Delta}}{2^{k-\ell}} + \frac{T_{complete} + 1}{2^n} + \frac{1}{T_{complete} 2^n}. \tag{3}$$

Case 3: We define skip' as similarly as in the first case with some important adjustments:

1. Sample $\mathcal{Z}_1, \mathcal{Z}_2 \xleftarrow{\$} \{0,1\}^{k\Delta}$.
2. Sample two random indices $t_0 < t_1 \in [T_{complete}]$.
3. Run $\mathcal{A}_{complete}(\mathcal{Z}_1, \mathcal{Z}_2)$ up until before query t_1.
4. Let $\boldsymbol{q} = (q_1, \ldots, q_{T_{complete}})$ denote the $T_{complete}$ h_1-queries made by $\mathcal{A}_{complete}$, where queries made after t_0 are denoted implicitly according to the randomness which $\mathcal{A}_{complete}$ is using.
5. Set $\widetilde{M}_0 = \mathsf{reconstruct}(q_{t_0}, \boldsymbol{q})$ *and* $\widetilde{M}_1 = \mathsf{reconstruct}(q_{t_1}, \boldsymbol{q})$. If either call to reconstruct returns with $\perp$, instead immediately output $\perp$.

6. Compute $y = h_1^*(\widetilde{M_0}, \mathcal{Z}_1) \oplus h_2^*(\widetilde{M_1}, \mathcal{Z}_2) \oplus h_2^*(\widetilde{M_0}, \mathcal{Z}_2)$.
7. Output $(\widetilde{M_1} \circ \mathcal{Z}_2, y)$.

Similar to Cases 1 and 2, we see that with probability that, if both t_0 and t_1 are chosen correctly - i.e., such that $q_{t_0} = (M_{0,\ell}, h_1^{(\ell-1)}(M_0))$ and $q_{t_1} = (M_{1,\ell}, h_1^{(\ell-1)}(M_1))$ - then the probability that $\mathsf{reconstruct}(q_{t_0}, \boldsymbol{q}) = \widetilde{M_0} = M_0$ and $\mathsf{reconstruct}(q_{t_1}, \boldsymbol{q}) = \widetilde{M_1} = M_1$ is at least $\rho = (T_{comlete} + 1)/2^n + T_{complete}^2/2^n$. Note that this is the exact same as in the previous cases as, assuming both t_0 and t_1 are chosen correctly, either both $\mathsf{reconstruct}$ will output a value or both will output $\perp$. So, we only have to account for collisions or errors in $\mathsf{reconstruct}$ once.

Because we must choose two indices correctly this time in order to reconstruct M_0 and M_1, we see that with probability at least $1 - \rho/T_{complete}^2$, we have chosen both t_0, t_1 such that $\widetilde{M_0} = M_0$ and $\widetilde{M_1} = M_1$. In particular, then, with probability at least $\epsilon_3 - \rho/T_{complete}^2$, we see $y = h_1^*(\widetilde{M_0}, \mathcal{Z}_1) \oplus h_2^*(\widetilde{M_1}, \mathcal{Z}_2) \oplus h_2^*(\widetilde{M_0}, \mathcal{Z}_2) = h_1^*(M_0, \mathcal{Z}_1) \oplus h_2^*(M_1, \mathcal{Z}_2) \oplus h_2^*(M_0, \mathcal{Z}_2) = h_1^*(M_1, \mathcal{Z}_1)$. By the assumption of this case, neither $h_2^*(M_1, \mathcal{Z}_2)$ nor $h_2^*(M_0, \mathcal{Z}_2)$ will query h_1 on input $(\mathcal{Z}_{1,k}, h^*(M_1, \mathcal{Z}_{1,1}, \ldots, \mathcal{Z}_{1,k-1}))$. Because $M_0 \neq M_1$, $h_1^*(\widetilde{M_0}, \mathcal{Z}_1)$ also does not make this query. However, we see $y = h_1^*(M_1, \mathcal{Z}_1) = h_1^*(\widetilde{M_1} \circ \mathcal{Z}_2)$. So, we see that skip' has output a pair $(x, h_1^*(x))$ without querying the final h_1 query of $h_1^*(x)$. Because h_1 is chosen uniformly at random, the probability that any algorithm can achieve this is at most $1/2^n$. In particular, this yields

$$\epsilon_3 - \rho/T_{complete}^2 \leq \frac{1}{2^n}.$$

Substituting in $\rho = (T_{comlete} + 1)/2^n + T_{complete}^2/2^n$ and solving for ϵ_3, we have

$$\epsilon_3 \leq \frac{T_{complete}^2 + T_{complete} + 1}{T_{complete}^2 \cdot 2^n} + \frac{1}{2^n} = \frac{1}{2^n} + \frac{1}{2^{n-1}} + \frac{1}{T_{complete}^2 \cdot 2^n}. \qquad (4)$$

Putting it All Together: As stated, we know $\epsilon \leq \epsilon_1 + \epsilon_2 + \epsilon_3$. Substituting in the upper bounds from Eqs. 2, 3, and 4, we get

$$\epsilon \leq \frac{T_g^{k/\Delta}}{2^{k-\ell-1}} + \frac{2T_{complete} + 5}{2^n} + \frac{3}{T_{complete} \cdot 2^n} \qquad (5)$$

Substituting back in $T_{complete} \leq T_{\mathcal{A}} + 2(\ell + k)$, this gives us the bound

$$\epsilon \leq \frac{T_g^{k/\Delta}}{2^{k-\ell-1}} + \frac{2T_{\mathcal{A}} + 4(\ell + k) + 5}{2^n} + \frac{3}{(T_{\mathcal{A}} + 2(\ell + k)) \cdot 2^n} \qquad (6)$$

$\square$

6.4   Proof of Lemma 3

Proof. Let ϵ be the probability over all h, skip that $(x, y) \leftarrow \mathsf{skip}^h$, $y = h^*(x)$, and there is some $i \leq \ell$ such that skip^h queries h on $(x_i, h^{(i)}(x))$. (That is, ϵ is the value we must bound above by $(q + 1)/2^n$.)

In addition, let ϵ_{skip} be the probability that $(x, y) \leftarrow \mathsf{skip}^h$, $y = h^*(x)$, and there is some $i \leq \ell$ such that skip^h queries h on $(x_i, h^{(i)}(x))$, where the probability is over the internal randomness over h. We see by an averaging argument that there must be some skip^{opt} such that $\epsilon_{\mathsf{skip}^{opt}} \geq \epsilon$. We will use this optimal skip to compress the random oracle h.

We define $(\mathsf{Enc}, \mathsf{Dec})$ as so: First, $\mathsf{Enc}(h)$ is defined as so:

1. Find $(x, y) \leftarrow \mathsf{skip}^{opt}$ with $|x| = \ell\Delta$.
2. Let t be the last index such that $h(x_{t+1}, h^{(t)}(x))$ is queried before $h(x_t, h^{(t-1)}(x))$. If no such index exists, output $\perp$.
3. Let $q_t = (x_t, h^{(t-1)}(x))$.
4. Define i as the query index of skip^{opt} where $h(x_{t+1}, h^{(t)}(x))$ is queried. In the case where $t = \ell$ (and therefore the final round of $h^*(x)$ is simply not queried), set $i = -1$.
5. Let $h \setminus q_t$ be the truth table of h except the entry $h(q_t)$ removed. Output $(i, h \setminus q_t)$.

We define $\mathsf{Dec}(i, h \setminus q_t)$ as so:

1. If $i = -1$, run skip^{opt} by referring to $h \setminus q_t$ to receive (x, y). Define $h(q_t) = y$ and output $h \setminus q_t$ with this entry added.
2. Else, run skip^{opt} b referring to $h \setminus q_t$, stopping just before query i would be made. Let (s, IV) be the intended input at this query, and define $h(q_t) = IV$. Output $h \setminus q_t$ with this entry added.

We show that, if Enc does not output $\perp$, then $\mathsf{Dec}(\mathsf{Enc}(h)) = h$. First, if $i = -1$ in Enc, then in particular skip^{opt} never queries $h(x_\ell, h^{(\ell-1)}(x))$. So, we may safely run skip^{opt}. By assumption with probability at least ϵ, skip^{opt} still outputs $y = h^*(x) = h(x_\ell, h^{(\ell-1)}(x))$, and so Dec correctly inputs this value for $h(q_t)$. If $i \geq 0$, on the other hand skip^{opt} behaves equivalently with access to h and $h \setminus q_t$ up to query i. So, $(s, IV) = (x_t, h^{(t-1)}(x))$ with probability at least ϵ, and so we set $h(q_t) = h(x_t, h^{(t-1)}(x)) = h^{(t)}(x) = IV$, as desired. Note that with probability at least ϵ, we are guaranteed that skip^{opt} does query out of order by assumption, and so in these cases we will also not receive $\perp$ from Enc. This satisfies correctness of our encoding.

So, we compress an ϵ-fraction of all possible functions (from m bits to n bits) to a set of query indices with all functions with one entry removed. This means we compress a set of size at least $\epsilon \cdot 2^{n2^m}$ to a set of size $(q+1)2^{n2^m}/2^n$, as q is the maximum number of queries which skip^{opt} may make, but i may also be set to -1. So, we must have

$$\epsilon \leq \frac{q+1}{2^n}.$$

$\square$

7 Conclusion

7.1 Recommendations for Practice

We give two recommendations for practice.

Situation 1: You have two compression functions $h_1, h_2 : \{0,1\}^m \to \{0,1\}^n$, at least one of which is believed to be a random oracle. $n \leq m/4$.

We recommend using the construction from Corollary 1. Note that in this Corollary, T represents the number of times the compromised hash function can evaluate the uncompromised one. That is, if h_b runs in time T_b, then (if $t_1 > t_0$) $T \leq \frac{t_1}{t_0}$. Since it is unlikely that one would wish to combine two hash functions where one of the hash functions takes a million times as long to run, we will assume that $T \leq 2^{30}$.

Recall from Sect. 4.1 that to achieve birthday bound security one should set

$$k \geq \frac{m + \log T + \lambda}{2} = \frac{m + 30 + \lambda}{2}.$$

Note that in order to apply this construction to an input of length s, we require $\frac{s}{m-k-n-1}$ calls to the underlying hash functions. That is, applying this construction requires

$$2 \cdot \frac{m - n}{m - k - n - 1}$$

times as many queries to the underlying hash functions than applying Merkle-Damgård directly to a trusted hash function would.

Suggestion Takeaway: For any hash function property, if $n = \lambda = 256$, $m = 1024$, this construction has birthday bound security loss compared to a random oracle and requires

$$\leq 2 \cdot \frac{768}{227} \leq 7$$

times as many hash evaluations. Furthermore, the hash size is identical to the hash size of the underlying compression functions.

Downside: Our security proof does not hold when the honest hash functions is instantiated as Merkle-Damgård applied to some random oracle. That is, this suggestion should be applied only to the underlying hash functions for SHA2/SHA3/... directly.

Situation 2: You have two hash functions $h_1, h_2 : \{0,1\}^* \to \{0,1\}^n$ both instantiated as Merkle-Damgård applied to some underlying compression functions.

We recommend sampling some $\mathcal{Z}_1, \mathcal{Z}_2 \xleftarrow{\$} \{0,1\}^k$, and using the hash function

$$C_{\mathcal{Z}_1, \mathcal{Z}_2}(M) = h_1(M, \mathcal{Z}_1) \oplus h_2(M, \mathcal{Z}_2)$$

By Theorem 9, this hash function will be collision resistant for k sufficiently large.

In order to achieve near birthday bound security, k should be set such that $\frac{T_g^{k/\Delta}}{2^{k-\ell-1}} + \frac{2T_A+4(\ell+k)+5}{2^n} + \frac{3}{(T_A+2(\ell+k))\cdot 2^n} = 1/2^\lambda$, where $\Delta = m - n$ is the compression of the hash functions underlying h_1 and h_2. As in the previous situation, we can assume $T_g \leq 2^{30}$.

That is, for an appropriately set value of n, we will want

$$\frac{T_g^{k/\Delta}}{2^{k-\ell-1}} \approx \frac{1}{2^\lambda}$$

Note that this construction requires $\frac{k}{\Delta}$ additional compression function evaluations compared to simply concatenating the underlying hash functions. In particular, to achieve near birthday bound security, we require

$$\frac{k}{\Delta} = \frac{\lambda+\ell}{\Delta-30}$$

additional hash evaluations.

Suggestion Takeaway: To achieve a collision resistant hash function from 1024 bits to 256 bits, if $\Delta = \lambda = 256$, then this construction will require

$$\frac{k}{\Delta} \leq \frac{256+\ell}{226} \leq 6$$

additional hash evaluations. Furthermore, the hash size is identical to the hash size of the underlying hash functions.

Downside: The security proof for this construction only holds for collision-resistance. Furthermore, the amount of extra blocks required depends linearly on the length of the input, although the linear factor of $\frac{1}{\Delta-30}$ is quite small.

7.2 Alternative One-stage Model

As observed in Sect. 3.1, our random oracle combiner security definition is two-stage. One may wonder if there is a reasonable one-stage security definition, so that composability properties may be used more easily. Observe that the reason the game is two-stage is because both the distinguisher $\mathcal{D}$ and the hash function g have oracle access to the idealized model, and can thus communicate through their shared state.

We could instead consider a model where g is not allowed oracle access to the idealized model. For example, g may be a fixed (non-oracle) circuit chosen by an adversary which makes polynomial queries to h. This can then be considered a one-stage game, and so this weakened combiner security property composes with indifferentiability.

Note that this model is strictly weaker than the other, since an arbitrary circuit could run the adversary inside of itself. Thus, our positive results also hold in this model. Upon inspection of the proof, we observe that our lower bounds from Sect. 4.3 also apply.

This model represents the scenario where the adversarial hash function g does not "run" h. In the real world, if g were to run h, we may hope that this would be detected by comparing the two hash functions' code and running times. Nevertheless, this leaves the combiner open to some attacks, and so we consider this model to be of lesser practical consideration. For the sake of brevity, we do not analyze it in detail in this work.

7.3   Open Questions

We include a number of open questions on this topic.

Is there a random-oracle-combiner construction which provably composes with indifferentiability?

Our random-oracle-secure construction does not perfectly match the randomness requirement in our lower bound. Is it possible to improve the randomness requirement for the random-oracle-secure construction.

The random-oracle-secure combiner construction presented takes hash functions from m bits to n bits and produces a hash function mapping ℓ bits to n bits, where $\ell = m - |\mathcal{Z}|/2$. Is it possible to construct a random-oracle-secure combiner with longer input length using the same amount of randomness?

As a particular approach to both of the previous two questions, is the CMD construction from Sect. 6 random-oracle-secure?

Is it possible to construct more efficient combiners for weaker security notions than indifferentiability or collision-resistance? For example, is there a more efficient pseudorandom combiner? Is there a more efficient combiner in the one-stage model from Sect. 7.2?

References

1. Specifications for the secure hash standard. Federal Inf. Process. Stds. (NIST FIPS) (2002)
2. Asmuth, C.A., Blakley, G.R.: An efficient algorithm for constructing a cryptosystem which is harder to break than two other cryptosystems. Comput. Math. Appl. **7**(6), 447–450 (1981)
3. Bellare, M., Rogaway, P.: Entity authentication and key distribution. In: Stinson, D.R. (ed.) CRYPTO 1993. LNCS, vol. 773, pp. 232–249. Springer, Heidelberg (1994). https://doi.org/10.1007/3-540-48329-2_21
4. Boneh, D., Boyen, X.: On the impossibility of efficiently combining collision resistant hash functions. In: Dwork, C. (ed.) CRYPTO 2006. LNCS, vol. 4117, pp. 570–583. Springer, Heidelberg (2006). https://doi.org/10.1007/11818175_34
5. Boneh, D., Lynn, B., Shacham, H.: Short signatures from the weil pairing **17**, 297–319 (2004)
6. Canetti, R., Rivest, R., Sudan, M., Trevisan, L., Vadhan, S., Wee, H.: Amplifying collision resistance: a complexity-theoretic treatment. In: Menezes, A. (ed.) CRYPTO 2007. LNCS, vol. 4622, pp. 264–283. Springer, Heidelberg (2007). https://doi.org/10.1007/978-3-540-74143-5_15

7. Coron, J.-S., Dodis, Y., Malinaud, C., Puniya, P.: Merkle-Damgård revisited: how to construct a hash function. In: Shoup, V. (ed.) CRYPTO 2005. LNCS, vol. 3621, pp. 430–448. Springer, Heidelberg (2005). https://doi.org/10.1007/11535218_26

8. Dodis, Y., Haitner, I., Tentes, A.: On the instantiability of hash-and-sign RSA signatures. In: Cramer, R. (ed.) TCC 2012. LNCS, vol. 7194, pp. 112–132. Springer, Heidelberg (2012). https://doi.org/10.1007/978-3-642-28914-9_7

9. Dodis, Y., Oliveira, R., Pietrzak, K.: On the generic insecurity of the full domain hash. In: Shoup, V. (ed.) CRYPTO 2005. LNCS, vol. 3621, pp. 449–466. Springer, Heidelberg (2005). https://doi.org/10.1007/11535218_27

10. Morris Dworkin. Sha-3 standard: Permutation-based hash and extendable output functions. Federal Inf. Process. Stds. (NIST FIPS)

11. Fischlin, M., Lehmann, A.: Multi-property preserving combiners for hash functions. In: Canetti, R. (ed.) TCC 2008. LNCS, vol. 4948, pp. 375–392. Springer, Heidelberg (2008). https://doi.org/10.1007/978-3-540-78524-8_21

12. Fischlin, M., Lehmann, A., Pietrzak, K.: Robust multi-property combiners for hash functions. J. Cryptol. **27**(3), 397–428 (2014)

13. Goldreich, O., Lustig, Y., Naor, M.: On chosen ciphertext security of multiple encryptions. Cryptology ePrint Archive, Report 2002/089 (2002). https://eprint.iacr.org/2002/089

14. Harnik, D., Kilian, J., Naor, M., Reingold, O., Rosen, A.: On robust combiners for oblivious transfer and other primitives. In: Cramer, R. (ed.) EUROCRYPT 2005. LNCS, vol. 3494, pp. 96–113. Springer, Heidelberg (2005). https://doi.org/10.1007/11426639_6

15. Herzberg, A.: On tolerant cryptographic constructions. In: Menezes, A. (ed.) CT-RSA 2005. LNCS, vol. 3376, pp. 172–190. Springer, Heidelberg (2005). https://doi.org/10.1007/978-3-540-30574-3_13

16. Maurer, U., Renner, R., Holenstein, C.: Indifferentiability, impossibility results on reductions, and applications to the random oracle methodology. In: Naor, M. (ed.) TCC 2004. LNCS, vol. 2951, pp. 21–39. Springer, Heidelberg (2004). https://doi.org/10.1007/978-3-540-24638-1_2

17. Meier, R., Przydatek, B.: On robust combiners for private information retrieval and other primitives. In: Dwork, C. (ed.) CRYPTO 2006. LNCS, vol. 4117, pp. 555–569. Springer, Heidelberg (2006). https://doi.org/10.1007/11818175_33

18. Mennink, B., Preneel, B.: Breaking and fixing cryptophia's short combiner. In: Gritzalis, D., Kiayias, A., Askoxylakis, I. (eds.) CANS 2014. LNCS, vol. 8813, pp. 50–63. Springer, Cham (2014). https://doi.org/10.1007/978-3-319-12280-9_4

19. Mittelbach, A.: Cryptophia's short combiner for collision-resistant hash functions. In: Jacobson, M., Locasto, M., Mohassel, P., Safavi-Naini, R. (eds.) ACNS 2013. LNCS, vol. 7954, pp. 136–153. Springer, Heidelberg (2013). https://doi.org/10.1007/978-3-642-38980-1_9

20. Paillier, P.: Impossibility proofs for RSA signatures in the standard model. In: Abe, M. (ed.) CT-RSA 2007. LNCS, vol. 4377, pp. 31–48. Springer, Heidelberg (2006). https://doi.org/10.1007/11967668_3

21. Pietrzak, K.: Non-trivial black-box combiners for collision-resistant hash-functions don't exist. In: Naor, M. (ed.) EUROCRYPT 2007. LNCS, vol. 4515, pp. 23–33. Springer, Heidelberg (2007). https://doi.org/10.1007/978-3-540-72540-4_2

22. Pietrzak, K.: Compression from collisions, or why CRHF combiners have a long output. In: Wagner, D. (ed.) CRYPTO 2008. LNCS, vol. 5157, pp. 413–432. Springer, Heidelberg (2008). https://doi.org/10.1007/978-3-540-85174-5_23
23. Ristenpart, T., Shacham, H., Shrimpton, T.: Careful with composition: limitations of the indifferentiability framework. In: Paterson, K.G. (ed.) EUROCRYPT 2011. LNCS, vol. 6632, pp. 487–506. Springer, Heidelberg (2011). https://doi.org/10.1007/978-3-642-20465-4_27

Individual Cryptography

Stefan Dziembowski[1,2](✉)[iD], Sebastian Faust[3][iD], and Tomasz Lizurej[1,2][iD]

[1] University of Warsaw, Warsaw, Poland
{stefan.dziembowski,tomasz.lizurej}@crypto.edu.pl
[2] IDEAS NCBR, Warsaw, Poland
[3] TU Darmstadt, Darmstadt, Germany
sebastian.faust@tu-darmstadt.de

Abstract. We initiate a formal study of *individual cryptography*. Informally speaking, an algorithm Alg is *individual* if, in every implementation of Alg, there always exists an individual user with full knowledge of the cryptographic data S used by Alg. In particular, it should be infeasible to design implementations of this algorithm that would hide S by distributing it between a group of parties using an MPC protocol or outsourcing it to a trusted execution environment.

We define and construct two primitives in this model. The first one, called *proofs of individual knowledge*, is a tool for proving that a given message is fully known to a single ("individual") machine on the Internet, i.e., it cannot be shared between a group of parties. The second one, dubbed *individual secret sharing*, is a scheme for sharing a secret S between a group of parties so that the parties have no knowledge of S as long as they do not reconstruct it. The reconstruction ensures that if the shareholders attempt to collude, one of them will learn the secret entirely. Individual secret sharing has applications for preventing collusion in secret sharing. A central technique for constructing individual cryptographic primitives is the concept of MPC hardness. MPC hardness precludes an adversary from completing a cryptographic task in a distributed fashion within a specific time frame.

This result is part of a project that received funding from the European Research Council (ERC) under the European Union's *Horizon 2020* and *Horizon Europe* research and innovation programs (grants PROCONTRA-885666 and CRYPTOLAYER-101044770). This work was also partly supported by the National Science Centre, Poland, under research project No. 463393, by the German Research Foundation (DFG) via the DFG CRC 1119 CROSSING (project S7), by the German Federal Ministry of Education and Research and the Hessen State Ministry for Higher Education, Research and the Arts within their joint support of the National Research Center for Applied Cybersecurity ATHENE.

H. Handschuh and A. Lysyanskaya (Eds.): CRYPTO 2023, LNCS 14082, pp. 547–579, 2023.
https://doi.org/10.1007/978-3-031-38545-2_18

1   Introduction

Multiparty computation (MPC) [6,12,20] is a powerful cryptographic technique that enables parties to evaluate any function securely in the presence of an adversary. It guarantees that nothing is revealed about the honest parties' inputs except what can be learned from the function's output. MPC protocols have found countless applications in cryptography and are one of the main tools for achieving privacy. In addition, MPC technology is becoming widely available in practice, e.g., for machine learning and blockchain applications. While MPCs are traditionally used for the "good" with their increasing availability in practice, there is a danger that an adversary misuses this technology to carry out malicious tasks. Let us illustrate this with two examples.

Identity Sharing Over the Internet. Imagine a service provider S that maintains a system in which individual users U can open accounts by paying a subscription fee. To lower this fee, the malicious users decide to open a *single* account and to share the credentials S to it between each other. In this paper, we are interested in situations when these users are individuals $A_1, \ldots, A_a$ connected via the Internet that do not trust each other, i.e., we are *not* concerned about scenarios in which the credentials are shared between different devices that belong to a single person, between members of one family, or between devices that are located physically very close to each other (so the network connection speed does not matter).

Suppose that to discourage such users from simply sharing S in plaintext, the service provider integrates ad-hoc countermeasures such that knowledge of S suffices to damage the account significantly. For example, if the "account" is a cryptocurrency address, then the knowledge of S should suffice to drain the account from all the coins. Alternatively, if it is an online storage system, then knowledge of S should permit deleting all the files. While these countermeasures should suffice to discourage the users from sharing S in plaintext, they are not sufficient to protect against a more sophisticated *identity sharing attack*, where the malicious users share S using secret sharing and jointly emulate a single "virtual" user U using an MPC protocol to authenticate with S.

The identity-sharing attack is similar to the "identity-lease attack" recently introduced by Puddu et al. [29]. In an identity-lease attack, the attacker's primary goal is to temporarily outsource ("lease") its identity to a third party, who can control it for a specific time or purpose. As discussed in [29], this may, for instance, be problematic in electronic voting, where identity leasing can be used to sell votes. While Puddu et al. rely on a trusted execution environment for their attack, it is possible to carry out the same attack using an MPC committee. Here, the committee holds secret shares of the user's identity and is queried by the third party to carry out the desired task (e.g., vote for a certain party in an electronic election).

Collusion in Secret Sharing. Threshold secret sharing is a fundamental primitive in cryptography. It allows an honest dealer to share a secret S among a set of parties $\mathcal{P}_1, \ldots, \mathcal{P}_a$ such that any subset of $t-1$ parties learns nothing about S, while a subset of t parties suffices to recover S. To this end, we typically require that at most $t-1$ parties are malicious, while the remaining parties are honest and do not collude. However, the latter may be unrealistic, particularly when collusion can go undetected and thus cannot easily be financially punished. For example, in standard secret sharing schemes, nothing prevents a set of t parties from simply exchanging their shares to recover the secret S. As discussed in the next paragraph, a trivial attempt to de-incentivize such an attack can be broken by an MPC protocol.

Consider a setting where the dealer wishes that the shareholders only release the secret after a certain time T. This setting is often referred to as "encryption to the future" and has gained some interest due to applications for blockchains [10, 22]. To prevent the simple collusion attack from above, the honest dealer shares $S' := (S, X)$, where if some party $\mathcal{P}_i$ gets to know X before time T, she is able to punish all other shareholders (e.g., this may be done via a smart contract on a blockchain).[1] While this approach de-incentivizes our naive collusion attack from above, it can easily be attacked using an MPC protocol. More concretely, instead of just recovering the entire S' by exchanging their secret shares, the parties run an MPC, which allows them to stripe off X before learning S.

MPC Hardness. By closely examining the two previous examples, we make the following crucial observation. Both attacks rely on the assumption that a distributed adversary can efficiently evaluate the cryptographic task via the MPCs. Hence, to thwart these attacks, our key idea is to make these cryptographic tasks *MPC-hard*. Informally, we say that a task/function is MPC-hard if executing it securely in a distributed way takes a significant amount of time. This implies that if a cryptographic task is MPC-hard, then in order to run it efficiently, the parties need to execute it *individually*. We formalize this new notion through a concept that we call *individual cryptography*.

Let us take a look at how MPC hardness may help us to prevent the previous two attacks. In the case of the identity sharing example, the *distributed adversary*, i.e., a tuple $\mathcal{A}_1, \ldots, \mathcal{A}_a$ of interactive machines (also called the *sub-adversaries*), uses an MPC protocol to ensure that no party individually knows the credentials to authenticate with a service provider S. Suppose the service provider will only accept an authentication attempt if it is completed within a certain time frame. The distributed adversary now has two options. Either it runs the authentication process via the MPC. This, however, will fail due to MPC hardness. Alternatively, the adversary may ask one of the sub-adversaries, say $\mathcal{A}_j$, to execute the task *individually*, in which case $\mathcal{A}_j$ has to know the credential S entirely.[2] We formalize this concept via a new primitive that we call *Proof of Individual Knowledge (PIK)*. Informally, a PIK guarantees that the

---

[1] We note that a similar (but more involved) idea has been used in a recent work of Mangipudi et al. to construct a collusion-deterrent threshold information escrow [27].

[2] Recall that in this case, the sub-adversary $\mathcal{A}_j$ can take full control over the account of the user, which was something that a malicious user tries to avoid.

prover must know the entire secret if it wants to get accepted by a verifier. We will provide further details on PIKs in Sect. 1.2. In the secret sharing example, the distributed adversary uses the MPC to compute some non-trivial function of the shared secret S before time T. Here, we require that the reconstruction algorithm of the secret sharing scheme is MPC hard. Informally, this guarantees that the distributed adversary cannot complete the reconstruction before some time T unless one of the sub-adversaries say $\mathcal{A}_j$, runs the reconstruction individually. We call such a secret sharing scheme an *individual secret sharing (ISS)* and present more details on it in Sect. 5.

Attacks via the Trusted Execution Environment (TEE). An alternative way to perform the aforementioned attacks is to use trusted execution environments (such as Intel's SGX) to accelerate the MPC (see, e.g., [2]) or to outsource secret storage in a way similar to the one described in [29]. To make our schemes secure against such attacks, we need to make some additional assumptions about what kind of fast computation is infeasible in TEEs. One option is to assume that the honest users are equipped with hardware similar to Bitcoin mining rigs that can compute a massive amount of hashes in parallel (note that our PIK protocol is based on massive parallel computation, while the ISS uses sequential computation). Another option is to come up with new hash functions that are infeasible to compute quickly on TEEs (e.g., due to large memory requirements). We leave it as future work to design such hash functions.

1.1 Informal Description of Our Model

As standard in cryptographic modeling, we have to describe the adversarial model (i.e., the adversaries' abilities) and specify what it means for a cryptographic task to be secure. Let us start with the adversarial model.

The Adversarial Model. As our MPC-hard functions will be based on massively evaluating a hash function, we give the distributed adversary $\mathcal{A}_1, \ldots, \mathcal{A}_a$ access to a special oracle Ω_H that allows evaluating a fixed input-length hash function $H : \{0,1\}^\lambda \to \{0,1\}^\kappa$. The oracle accepts queries of the form $(x, mode)$, where $x \in \{0,1\}^\lambda$ and $mode \in \{\text{fast}, \text{slow}\}$. If $mode = \text{fast}$, then a query is called *fast*. It is called *slow* otherwise. Let us give some intuition behind these two modes.

The fast queries are hash function evaluations that a sub-adversary $\mathcal{A}_b$ runs locally. We assume that these evaluations can be done very fast (orders of magnitude faster than slow queries). For example, a party may execute them using a specially designed ASIC, such as used in the context of Bitcoin mining. We assume that the number of fast queries is only bounded by the running time of the adversary, which is polynomial time. On the other hand, the slow queries model an evaluation of the hash function using an MPC protocol. In particular, this means that the sub-adversaries $\mathcal{A}_1, \ldots, \mathcal{A}_a$ can learn $H(x)$ without knowing x. Since the evaluation of a hash function using MPC technology is conceivable much slower than using an ASIC, we assume that the budget of the adversary for such queries is comparably small, i.e., bounded by some parameter σ.

In addition to bounding the number of slow queries that the sub-adversaries may ask for, in our PIK application, we put an additional restriction on the sub-adversaries. We require that they run in at most ρ communication rounds. Notice that we do not require any bounds on the communication complexity as at the end of each round, we allow the sub-adversaries to share any information that they currently possess.

Attacks Exploiting the Hash Function Structure. We need to stress that in the model above, the hash function $H : \{0,1\}^\lambda \to \{0,1\}^\kappa$ needs to be chosen carefully, and it is unrealistic to assume that λ is large. It is also important that H does not have a structure that the adversary could exploit. A natural choice for H is a compression function of a popular hash function (for example, in SHA-256, the compression function is of a type $H : \{0,1\}^{728} \to \{0,1\}^{256}$).

We illustrate this by the following example. Suppose H is a Merkle-Damgard-type hash function, and let $G : \{0,1\}^{2\kappa} \to \{0,1\}^\kappa$ be the compression function that H is built from, i.e., for messages of a form $(S_1 \| S_2 \| W)$ (with $|S_1| = |S_2| = |W| = \kappa$) we have $H(S_1 \| S_2 \| W) = G(G(G(IV \| S_1) \| S_2) \| W)$ (where $IV \in \{0,1\}^\kappa$ is some fixed initial value, and for simplicity, we omit the last block encoding message length). Now, suppose that we want to verify if a message S consisting of two blocks (S_1, S_2) (both of length κ) is stored on one machine by forcing the prover to compute a large number of hashes of a form $H(S, W)$ (for multiple W's), which is the case for our PIK construction (see below). Taking into account the structure of H, two sub-adversaries: $\mathcal{A}_1$ and $\mathcal{A}_2$ can now "split" the computation as follows: the $\mathcal{A}_1$ first computes $h = G(IV, S_1)$, and then sends h to $\mathcal{A}_2$ who can compute $H(S_1 \| S_2 \| W)$ for an arbitrary number of different W's *without* knowing S_1, just by using that fact that $H(S_1 \| S_2 \| W) = G(G(h \| S_2) \| W)$. Hence, if H is a Merkle-Damgard type of hash function, the assumption that the input of every fast query is known to the adversary would be unrealistic. The same applies to sponge-based hash functions and to any other hash functions that read their input blocks in an online way and compress them to a shorter state.

Security Against Distributed Adversaries. By using MPC-hardness, we want to enforce that the distributed adversary must run the cryptographic task individually. More concretely, if the adversaries manage to complete the cryptographic task within some specified time bound (seconds in the case of PIK and hours in the case of ISS), then one of the adversaries, say $\mathcal{A}_j$, must know some secret information S completely. Hence, we need some formal method to model "knowledge".

The question of formalizing knowledge has a long history in cryptography, and in particular, it has been studied in the context of "proofs of knowledge" [3], "knowledge of exponent" [14], or "plaintext-awareness" [5]. None of these approaches considers attacks by a distributed adversary. The most relevant to ours is the model of [5], which considers an adversary with access to a hash function (modeled as a random oracle). It is assumed that if an adversary $\mathcal{A}$ evaluated H on some input x, then $\mathcal{A}$ knows the input x and the corresponding output $H(x)$. Technically: the (input, output) pairs are later given to an algorithm $\mathcal{E}$ called "knowledge extractor". If, based on these tuples, the knowledge extractor outputs some message S, then we assume that "$\mathcal{A}$ knows S" (since $\mathcal{A}$ could have computed S herself just by observing the oracle queries and the replies to them).

In our case, we use the concept of a knowledge extractor but slightly adjust it in the following way. First, we will consider knowledge extractors $\mathcal{E}_b$ for each of the different adversaries $\mathcal{A}_b$. Second, each such knowledge extractor takes as input the transcript of queries T_b^{fast} that $\mathcal{A}_b$ has made to the oracle Ω_H only in $mode = \text{fast}$. Put differently: queries made by $\mathcal{A}_b$ in $mode = \text{slow}$ (recall that these queries model MPC evaluations of H with a potentially unknown input) are not given to the knowledge extractor $\mathcal{E}_b$. Finally, we say that an adversary $\mathcal{A}_j$ individually knows a secret S if there exists an efficient knowledge extractor $\mathcal{E}_j$ such that $S \in \mathcal{E}_j(T_b^{\text{fast}})$.

Allowing Pre-computation of the Hash Function. To model realistic attacks, we do not make any assumptions about how much time the distributed adversary has before the protocol starts. In particular, we allow the sub-adversaries to perform any distributed computation that involves the hash function H before the beginning of the protocol. This will be reflected by assuming that the attack works in two phases: in the first one, called *pre-processing* phase, the adversary will not be restricted in the number of slow hash queries that she can evaluate. Such a restriction will only apply in the second, *online*, phase. We protect our protocols against such pre-computation attacks by making all hashes depend on random values that are unknown before the online phase.

1.2   Informal Description of PIK

As outlined in the introduction, a PIK protocol should allow the prover $\mathcal{P}$ to convince the verifier $\mathcal{V}$ that a secret S (that they both know) is stored on one machine and known to the machine owner. This is done by forcing $\mathcal{P}$ to quickly reply to challenges Z from $\mathcal{V}$ in a way that proves that $\mathcal{P}$ performed intensive computation on the entire value of S. Since $\mathcal{P}$ measures the response time, it will notice any response delays that are due to the fact that S is, in fact, distributed between different "sub-adversaries", and it is not stored on one machine. This distinction is made by performing a large amount of "hash computations" on S, which in practice, for example, can be carried out via a highly optimized ASIC.

As outlined in the previous subsection, two main parameters that characterize the adversary are σ – the number of hashes that can be computed in such a way that no sub-adversary learns their inputs since they are computed using MPC (in our model, this corresponds to the "slow" queries to the oracle), and ρ – the number of communication rounds between the $\mathcal{A}_b$'s. In Sect. 1.1, we already explained the idea behind the slow queries. The bound on the number of communication rounds is relatively mild in practice. Recall that $\mathcal{A}_b$'s are connected over the Internet, and hence assuming that no more than 1000 rounds of communications per second (say) are executed between them is reasonable.

Our scheme is described formally in Sect. 4. The reader may, in particular, look at the diagram in Fig. 2 – we will refer to it while presenting our solution informally below. Let us start with describing a simple scheme for proving knowledge of a message consisting of one block (i.e., messages of a form $S = (S_1)$, where $S_1 \in \{0,1\}^\lambda$), and assuming that (a) the sub-adversaries cannot execute any slow queries, and (b) the sub-adversaries cannot communicate during protocol execution. In this case, the following idea works: the verifier sends a challenge Z to the prover, and the prover has to respond with $h = H(Z \| S_1)$. Since no slow queries are allowed, and the sub-adversaries cannot communicate. Thus one sub-adversary, say $\mathcal{A}_b$, needs to know (Z, S_1). Let us now show how to remove our artificial assumptions in the above example.

Allowing Slow Queries. Recall that above, we assumed that the sub-adversaries could not perform any slow queries (i.e., no H can be computed using MPCs). We eliminate this restriction in the following way: namely, we force the prover to perform multiple computations of hashes on different nonces to find a nonce that leads to a hash starting with ζ zeros. This ensures that to convince the verifier, there must be an individual adversary $\mathcal{A}_b$ that makes a large number of fast queries that contain as input S_1. Notice that our approach is very similar to Bitcoin's puzzles, except that we do it κ times to reduce the variance in finding a solution. The nonce that is used in the ith puzzle is denoted with W^i.

Longer Messages S. Let us now discuss how to eliminate the assumption that S just consists of one block. Let $S = (S_1, \ldots, S_n)$ where $n \geq 1$. Our idea is straightforward (see also the first column on Fig. 2, ignoring the values at the beginning of the hashed blocks): we apply the construction for a single block iteratively, i.e., for the ith nonce W we let $Q_1 := H(Z \| W)$, and then for each $j = 2, \ldots, n + 1$ we let $Q_j := H(S_j \| Q_{j-1})$.

Allowing Communication Between the Sub-adversaries. Note that the above construction is insecure if there are no restrictions on the communication between the $\mathcal{A}_b$'s. Indeed, imagine two sub-adversaries $\mathcal{A}_1$ and $\mathcal{A}_2$ and suppose S has two blocks $S = (S_1, S_2)$, with $\mathcal{A}_1$ holding S_1 and $\mathcal{A}_2$ holding S_2. Then these adversaries can break the above PIK as follows: $\mathcal{A}_1$ computes a massive number of hashes $Q_2 := H(S_1 \| H(Z, W))$ (for different values of W) using fast queries to Ω^{fast} and sends the Q_2's to $\mathcal{A}_2$. Sub-adversary $\mathcal{A}_2$ processes every Q_2 by computing $Q_3 := H(S_2 \| Q_2)$ in order to find Q_2 such that Q_3 starts with ζ zeros. Once such Q_2 is found, she communicates it to $\mathcal{A}_2$, who checks which W this Q_2 corresponds to and sends this Q to the verifier.

The above example shows that we need to restrict communication between the sub-adversaries. As discussed in Sect. 1.1 we choose to do it by putting a bound ρ on the number of rounds (an alternative approach would be to bound the communication size, but it seems more challenging to work with in practice). In our construction, we use this assumption by requiring that the prover needs to compute $d = \rho + 1$ iterations of the procedure outlined above (cf. Fig. 2).

Dealing with Artificial Fast Queries. While from the above, it is clear that one of the sub-adversaries $\mathcal{A}_b$ has to know the entire S, it is not immediately clear how to build an efficient knowledge extractor. One challenge here is that the adversary may try to "confuse" us by making "useless" fast queries to Ω_H. We address this challenge by adding 2-bit flags to the inputs on which the hash function is evaluated. This enables the knowledge extractor to identify starting points for efficiently extracting the most likely values for S.

1.3   Informal Description of ISS

Our individual secret sharing scheme is based on the following simple idea. Let $P_1, \ldots, P_a$ be the parties among which the secret S is shared, and let t be the threshold denoting the minimal number of parties needed to reconstruct the secret. In order to share S in an "individual" way, we first share a random value $X \leftarrow_\$ \{0,1\}^\kappa$ using a standard t-out-of-a secret sharing. We then compute a long chain of hashes H on X. Let K be the output of this computation, and let η be the length of the chain. We then use K to encrypt our secret S using a standard symmetric encryption scheme. The shares of S are the shares of X plus the resulting ciphertext C. Reconstruction works in a natural way: t parties first reconstruct X (using the standard reconstruction procedure), and then one of them computes K. Afterwards, S is computed by decrypting C using key K.

The parameter η is chosen in such a way that it is feasible to compute K from X in plain (e.g. it takes 10 min in hardware), but computing it using MPC is infeasible within the time in which we want S to remain secret. In the security proof we use the fact that if a long chain of hashes was computed by the adversary, then a noticeable fraction of intermediate results of this computation had to be computed using the fast queries. For the details see Sect. 5.

1.4   Related Work

Using cryptography for malicious purposes has been studied before, most notably in the context of "Cryptovirology" proposed by Young and Yung [31]. The approach of [31] focuses on the malicious use of public-key encryption and not the MPCs. Hence, our paper can be viewed as a natural continuation of the approach of [31] (with MPCs being more "advanced" primitives than the public-key encryption schemes). The idea of preventing leaking secrets has been studied extensively in a context such as traitor-tracing, e.g., it [13,26]. To our knowledge, none of these works considers a distributed adversary.

On a higher level, our paper is also related to papers that look at defining the notion of "identity" in cryptography. In particular, it has some similarities to Position-Based Cryptography [11], where an identity of a user is defined by its geographic location. This approach is also based on measuring the prover's response time. Still, it is assumed that the communication is not done over the Internet but via physical signals (the whole approach is based on the fact that the speed of electromagnetic signals is fixed). Another difference is that the users in [11] do not have secret credentials but are identified by their geographic location. As already mentioned, our proof techniques are similar to those used in the context of space-bounded cryptography, in particular in the construction of schemes that are secure based on assumptions about the restricted memory of the adversary and whose security relies on hash functions, see, e.g., [1,15,16,19]. For the differences between our model and the ones used in this area, see Sect. 1.1.

Concurrent Work. In a very recent concurrent work, Kelkar et al. [25] introduce the concept of *complete knowledge*. A proof of complete knowledge (PoCK) guarantees that a single party has complete control/knowledge of its secret. This is very similar to our notion of PIK. We emphasize that while both works aim at similar goals, there are significant differences. Their construction of a PoCK directly achieves a zero-knowledge property. In contrast, our basic PIK construction does not have this property (we outline a generic transformation of any PIK into a zkPIK in Sect. 4.4). In addition, they also present an implementation. On the other hand, their work is very much application-oriented. It lacks a formal model that takes into account the many subtleties that we attempt to model with the concept of individual cryptography (e.g., possible communication, fast/slow queries, and taking into account how hash functions are constructed in practice). In addition, they do not have a construction of individual secret sharing, which shows that our modeling has applications beyond proof of knowledge.

2 Preliminaries

A function $f : \mathbb{N} \to \mathbb{R}$ is *negligible* if for every positive integer c there exists an integer N such that for every $n > N$ we have $|f(n)| \leq n^{-c}$. A sequence of events has an *overwhelming probability* if the probability of their negations is negligible. We will use the following standard fact.

Lemma 1. *For every $p < 1$ we have that $(1 - p)^{1/p} \leq e^{-1}$.*

A pair of algorithms $(\mathsf{Enc} : \{0,1\}^* \times \{0,1\}^* \to \{0,1\}^*, \mathsf{Dec} : \{0,1\}^* \times \{0,1\}^* \to \{0,1\}^*)$ is a *CPA-secure symmetric encryption scheme* (see, e.g., [24]) if for every $K, M \in \{0,1\}^*$ we have that $\mathsf{Dec}(K, \mathsf{Enc}(K, M)) = M$. Moreover, we require that for every poly-time machine $\mathcal{D}_1^{\mathsf{cpa}}$, that takes as input 1^κ, and outputs $S^0, S^1, Y \in \{0,1\}^*$ (such that $|S^0| = |S^1|$) an every every poly-time machine $\mathcal{D}_2^{\mathsf{cpa}}$ it holds that $\Pr\left[\mathcal{D}_2(Y, \mathsf{Enc}(K, S^0)) = 1\right] - \Pr\left[\mathcal{D}_2(Y, \mathsf{Enc}(K, S^1)) = 1\right] \leq \mathsf{negl}(\kappa)$, where $K \leftarrow_\$ \{0,1\}^\kappa$. We will also use the following lemma, whose proof appears in the extended version of this paper [18].

Lemma 2. *Let $\kappa, \zeta \in \mathbb{N}$ be arbitrary parameters (where ζ can be a function of κ). Let $U_1, \ldots, U_C$ be independent random variables distributed over $\{0,1\}$ and such that for each i we have that $\Pr[U_i = 1] = 2^{-\zeta}$. Let $U := U_1 + \cdots + U_C$. We have that (a) if $C = \kappa \cdot 2^{\zeta+1}$ then $\Pr[U \leq \kappa] \leq \mathsf{negl}(\kappa)$ and (b) if $C \leq \kappa \cdot 2^{\zeta-1}$ then $\Pr[U \geq \kappa] \leq \mathsf{negl}(\kappa)$.*

3   The Model

This section provides more details on the model already informally introduced in Sect. 1.1. All protocols are executed in an asynchronous model. Every protocol is parameterized by a security parameter 1^κ and a hash function H that is modeled differently in the honest and adversarial executions. In the honest execution, the parties access H in a black-box way (via a standard random oracle [4]), except for Sect. 4.4, where a "circuit access" to H is needed (in the construction of zkPIK).

In the adversarial model, the malicious parties access H via an interactive machine Ω_H, which chooses a random function $H : \{0,1\}^\lambda \to \{0,1\}^\kappa$ (where λ and κ are parameters of the model) and interacts with parties $\mathcal{A}_1, \ldots, \mathcal{A}_a$ by accepting queries of a form $(x, mode)$, where $x \in \{0,1\}^*$ and $mode \in \{\mathsf{fast}, \mathsf{slow}\}$. If $mode = \mathsf{fast}$, then a query is called *fast*. It is called *slow* otherwise. Each query coming from a party $\mathcal{A}_b$ is answered to $\mathcal{A}_b$ with $H(x)$ (we also say that $\mathcal{A}_b$ *evaluated* H on input x). The execution of a protocol is divided into the *pre-computation* phase and the *online* phase, happening one after another. We say that Ω_H *is σ-bounded* if the total number of slow queries answered in the online phase is at most σ. The queries that exceed this quota are answered with $\bot$. The total number of fast queries is only bounded by the time complexity of the adversaries (i.e., it is polynomial in κ).

The main idea is that the fast queries are "cheap" and the participants will be allowed to send much more of them than the "expensive" slow queries (which correspond to queries computed using MPC/TEE techniques). On the other hand, when analyzing what the adversarial parties learned from the execution (i.e. when defining the "knowledge extractors", see below), only the fast queries will count. Namely, only the inputs to such queries will be considered known to the querying party. The distinction between the pre-computation phase and the online phase serves to model the fact that before the protocol starts, the sub-adversaries have an unbounded (but polynomial) time and can execute any distributed protocol. Note that the *mode* flag is only used for "accounting" purposes: the actions Ω_H do not depend on the value of this flag, except when defining the available budget of queries.

At the end of the execution of a protocol, we look at the information each party received as a result of the fast oracle queries. We define the *local hash transcript of a party* $\mathcal{A}_b$ to be the sequence $\mathcal{T}_b$ of hash inputs that Ω_H received from $\mathcal{A}_b$ (in the same order in which they were received). Let $\mathcal{T}_b^{\mathsf{fast}}$ be the sub-sequence of $\mathcal{T}_b$ containing only the inputs corresponding to fast queries (call it *local fast-hash transcript of a party* $\mathcal{A}_b$). A *(knowledge) extractor* $\mathcal{E}$ is a deterministic poly-time machine that takes $\mathcal{T}_b^{\mathsf{fast}}$ as input and produces as output a finite set $\mathcal{E}(\mathcal{T}_b^{\mathsf{fast}}) \subset \{0,1\}^*$. The extractors have block-box access to H (via the same oracle Ω_H, only using the fast queries).

For future reference, also define the *global hash transcript* to be the sequence $\mathcal{T}$ of hash inputs that Ω_H received (in the same order in which they were received). Let the *global fast-hash transcript* be the sub-sequence $\mathcal{T}^{\mathsf{fast}}$ of $\mathcal{T}$ containing only the inputs corresponding to fast queries.

4   Proofs of Individual Knowledge

We now provide formal details of the definition and the construction that were informally presented in Sect. 1.

4.1   Definition

A *proof of individual knowledge (PIK)* is a protocol $\pi_{\mathsf{PIK}}^{\rho,\sigma}$ between a prover $\mathcal{P}$ and a verifier $\mathcal{V}$ (also denoted $(\mathcal{P} \leftrightarrows \mathcal{V})$), which are probabilistic poly-time machines with access to a hash function $H : \{0,1\}^\lambda \to \{0,1\}^\kappa$. The prover and the verifier take as input a pair $(1^\kappa, S)$, where 1^κ is a security parameter and $S \in \{0,1\}^*$. For $\eta_{\mathcal{P}}, \eta_{\mathcal{V}} \in \mathbb{N}$, we say that the prover and the Verfier are $\eta_{\mathcal{P}}$- and $\eta_{\mathcal{V}}$-*bounded* (respectively) if the prover and the Verfier make at most $\eta_{\mathcal{P}}$ and $\eta_{\mathcal{V}}$ evaluations of H (respectively). We require that the protocol is *complete*, i.e., if both parties are honest (and their inputs are as above), then with overwhelming probability, the verifier outputs yes (in which case we also say that $\mathcal{V}$ *accepts*).

The second required property is *soundness*. Define a (ρ, σ)-*distributed adversary* to be a tuple $(\mathcal{A}_1, \ldots, \mathcal{A}_a)$ of poly-time interactive *sub-adversaries*. The honest verifier $\mathcal{V}$ receives $(1^\kappa, S)$ as input and interacts with $\mathcal{A}_1$ that also receives $(1^\kappa, S)$ as input. Intuitively, $\mathcal{A}_1$ plays the role of the (malicious) prover from the point of view of the verifier $\mathcal{V}$. Initially, the sub-adversaries can run a per-computation phase, where they can send an arbitrary number of slow queries to the oracle Ω_H. Then, the protocol starts, and the sub-adversaries enter the online phase in which they can make at most σ queries to the oracle Ω_H. The adversaries run in at most ρ rounds, where each of them has the following form: (1) each sub-adversary $\mathcal{A}_b$ performs some local computation, at the end of which $\mathcal{A}_b$ outputs a string Str_b, and (2) each Str_b is delivered to every other sub-adversary $\mathcal{A}_{\hat{b}}$. We emphasize that we do not restrict the size of the communicated messages.

Consider an execution of a distributed adversary $(\mathcal{A}_1, \ldots, \mathcal{A}_a)$ against an honest verifier (on input $(1^\kappa, S)$). Define $\mathsf{exec}((\mathcal{A}_1, \ldots, \mathcal{A}_a) \leftrightarrows \mathcal{V}); 1^\kappa; S)$ to be equal to $(\mathcal{T}_1^{\mathsf{fast}}, \ldots, \mathcal{T}_a^{\mathsf{fast}}, Out_{\mathcal{V}})$, where each $\mathcal{T}_b^{\mathsf{fast}}$ is the local fast-hash transcript of $\mathcal{A}_b$ and $Out_{\mathcal{V}} \in \{\mathsf{yes}, \mathsf{no}\}$ is the output of $\mathcal{V}$. We now have the following.

Definition 1. *We say that $\pi_{\mathsf{PIK}}^{\rho,\sigma}$ is a PIK protocol sound against (ρ, σ)-distributed adversary if there exists knowledge extractors $\mathcal{E}_1, \ldots, \mathcal{E}_a$ such that for every (ρ, σ)-distributed adversary $(\mathcal{A}_1, \ldots, \mathcal{A}_a)$ and every $S \in \{0,1\}^*$ we have that*

$$\Pr[Out_{\mathcal{V}} = \mathsf{yes} \text{ and } S \notin \mathcal{E}_1(\mathcal{T}_1^{\mathsf{fast}}) \cup \cdots \cup \mathcal{E}_a(\mathcal{T}_a^{\mathsf{fast}})] \le \mathsf{negl}(\kappa), \qquad (1)$$

where $(\mathcal{T}_1^{\mathsf{fast}}, \ldots, \mathcal{T}_a^{\mathsf{fast}}, Out_{\mathcal{V}}) \leftarrow_{\$} \mathsf{exec}((\mathcal{A}_1, \ldots, \mathcal{A}_a) \leftrightarrows \mathcal{V}); 1^\kappa; S)$. We say that $\pi_{\mathsf{PIK}}^{\rho,\sigma}$ has extraction efficiency $(\alpha_{\mathsf{O}}, \alpha_{\mathsf{T}}, \alpha_{\mathsf{S}})$ if $|\mathcal{E}_1(\mathcal{T}_1^{\mathsf{fast}}) \cup \cdots \cup \mathcal{E}_a(\mathcal{T}_a^{\mathsf{fast}})| \le \alpha_{\mathsf{O}}$, and $\mathcal{E}$ operates in time at most α_{T} and uses space at most α_{S}. The parameters $\alpha_{\mathsf{O}}, \alpha_{\mathsf{T}}$ and α_{S} can be functions of some other parameters in the system.

The idea behind α_{O} is that $\alpha_{\mathsf{O}} - 1$ is the number of "false positives", i.e., values in $\mathcal{E}_1(\mathcal{T}_1^{\mathsf{fast}}) \cup \cdots \cup \mathcal{E}_a(\mathcal{T}_a^{\mathsf{fast}})$ that are not equal to S. Obviously, the smaller α_{O} is, the better. In Sect. 4.4, we describe a method that, with high probability, allows to reduce the number of such false positives to 0 in many applications.

4.2   Construction

In this section, we present our construction of a PIK protocol $\pi_{\mathsf{PIK}}^{\rho;\sigma}$, which was already informally described in Sect. 1.2. The protocol is parameterized by a "moderate hardness parameter" $\zeta \in \mathbb{N}$ and a security parameter 1^κ. It uses a hash function $H : \{0,1\}^\lambda \to \{0,1\}^\kappa$ with $\lambda \geq 2\kappa$. In practice, H could be a compression function of a popular hash function. The protocol participant takes as input $S \in \{0,1\}^*$ and 1^κ. We assume that $|S|$ is a multiple of $\lambda - \kappa - 2$ (if it is not the case, then one can pad S with zeros). Let $S_1, \ldots, S_n$ be such that $S = (S_1 \,||\, \cdots \,||\, S_n)$ where $|S_1| = \cdots = |S_n| = \lambda - \kappa - 2$.

Our PIK protocol is depicted in Fig. 1. It uses a sub-routine scratch (see also Fig. 2 for a graphical representation of the computation of scratch). The protocol starts with the verifier sending a random challenge $Z \in \{0,1\}^\kappa$. Then, the goal of the prover is to find κ nonces $W^1, \ldots, W^\kappa \in \{0,1\}^{\lambda-\kappa-2}$ that convince the verifier that the prover did a substantial amount of work for the challenge Z. This is done by requiring that the output of every scratch(S, Z, W^i) starts with ζ zeros. We have the following definition.

Definition 2. *We call a given* scratch(S, Z, W) *successful if its output starts with ζ zeros (cf. Step 2b on Fig. 1 (b)).*

This is similar to the Bitcoin mining procedure, except that we require κ nonces to be found (in Bitcoin $\kappa = 1$) in order to reduce the variance of the success probability. The main idea behind scratch is that it forces the prover to sequentially compute d times H on every block S_j of S. We also force the prover to compute scratch(S, Z, W) on a large number of W's. The search for the W^i's can be fully parallelized. The only non-parallelizable part is the scratch procedure, which takes as input (S, Z, W), where S is the message, Z is the challenge, and W is the nonce.

The inputs of H in scratch start with two bits: 00 indicates that the hash is computed on (Z, W) (where Z is a challenge and W is a nonce), 01 indicates that the first block (S_1) is hashed (together with some Q), and 10 indicates that the hashed value S_j is one of the subsequent blocks (i.e., $j > 1$). Labels 00, 01, and 10 are used to help the extractor find S (e.g. if the extractor sees that some $(01 \,||\, \widehat{S}_1 \,||\, \widehat{Q}_1)$ was hashed then the extractor guesses that $\widehat{S}_1$ is the first block of S and starts searching for a hash of a form $(10 \,||\, \widehat{S}_2 \,||\, \widehat{Q}_2)$ with $\widehat{Q}_2 = H(01 \,||\, \widehat{S}_1 \,||\, \widehat{Q}_1)$ (see Proof of Theorem 1 for the details). Note that in total scratch computes $nd + 1$ hashes H. Security of $\pi_{\mathsf{PIK}}^{\rho;\sigma}$ is stated in the following theorem.

Theorem 1. *Let κ, n, d be as above and let $\eta_P := (nd + 1) \cdot 2^{\zeta+1} \cdot \kappa$ and $\eta_V := (nd + 1) \cdot \kappa$. Assume $\sigma \leq \kappa \cdot 2^{\zeta-3}$ and $\rho \leq d - 1$. Then $\pi_{\mathsf{PIK}}^{\rho;\sigma}$ from Fig. 1 is a PIK protocol with η_P-bounded prover and η_V-bounded verifier that is sound against a (ρ, σ)-distributed adversary with extraction efficiency $(\alpha_O, \alpha_T, \alpha_S)$, where*

$$\mathbb{E}[\alpha_O] = 2^{-\zeta} \cdot \ell, \mathbb{E}[\alpha_T] = O(\ell_b), and \mathbb{E}[\alpha_S] = O(2^{-\zeta} \cdot \ell_b \cdot |S|).$$

Above, ℓ_b is the number of hashes computed by a sub-adversary $\mathcal{A}_b$, and $\ell := \ell_1 + \cdots + \ell_a$. The unit of time is a computation of H.

Procedure scratch(S, Z, W)

1. Assume $S = (S_1 \mathbin{\|} \cdots \mathbin{\|} S_n)$, where each $|S_j| = \lambda - \kappa - 2$.
2. For $k = 1$ to d do:
    For $j = 1$ to n do:

$$Q_j^k := \begin{cases} H(00 \mathbin{\|} Z \mathbin{\|} W) & \text{if } k = 1 \text{ and } j = 1 \\ H(10 \mathbin{\|} S_n \mathbin{\|} Q_n^{k-1}) & \text{if } k \neq 1 \text{ and } j = 1 \\ H(01 \mathbin{\|} S_1 \mathbin{\|} Q_1^k) & \text{if } j = 2 \\ H(10 \mathbin{\|} S_{j-1} \mathbin{\|} Q_{j-1}^k) & \text{if } j > 2 \end{cases}$$

3. Output $H(10 \mathbin{\|} S_n \mathbin{\|} Q_n^d)$.

(a)

Protocol $\pi_{\mathsf{PIK}}^{\rho,\sigma}$

The protocol is parameterized with a "moderate hardness" parameter $\zeta \leq \kappa$. It is executed between the η_P-bounded prover $\mathcal{P}$ and the η_V-bounded verifier $\mathcal{V}$. Both parties take as input $(1^\kappa, S)$, where $S = (S_1, \ldots, S_n)$.

1. The verifier $\mathcal{V}$ chooses a random *challenge* $Z \in \{0,1\}^\kappa$ and sends it to the prover $\mathcal{P}$.
2. The prover $\mathcal{P}$ does the following **parallel search** across different values of $i = \{1, \ldots, \kappa\}$ and *nonces* $W^i \in \{0,1\}^{\lambda-\kappa-2}$:
    (a) Let $Q^i := \mathsf{scratch}(S, Z, W^i)$.
    (b) If Q^i starts with ζ zeros then record W^i and **stop the parallel search**. The above search is done as long as the prover did not exhaust her budget for computing hashes (recall that she can make at most η_P of them). If this happens before the search is over, then $\mathcal{P}$ outputs $\bot$ to $\mathcal{V}$, who also outputs $\bot$, and then both halt. Otherwise, we proceed to the next step.
3. The prover sends $(W^1, \ldots, W^\kappa)$ to the verifier.
4. Upon receiving $(W^1, \ldots, W^\kappa)$ the verifier outputs yes if for *all* $i \in \{1, \ldots, \kappa\}$ it holds that the output of $\mathsf{scratch}(S, Z, W^i)$ starts with ζ zeros. Otherwise, the verifier outputs no.

(b)

Fig. 1. Proof of individual knowledge (PIK) $\pi_{\mathsf{PIK}}^{\rho,\sigma}$ that satisfies Def. 1 (see Thm. 1). The main procedure is depicted in point (b). It uses a sub-routine scratch depicted in point (a).

The proof of Theorem 1 is presented in Sect. 4.3. Before proceeding to it, let us comment on the parameters in the lemma statement. When it comes to the parameters of the honest prover and verifier, the most important ones are those

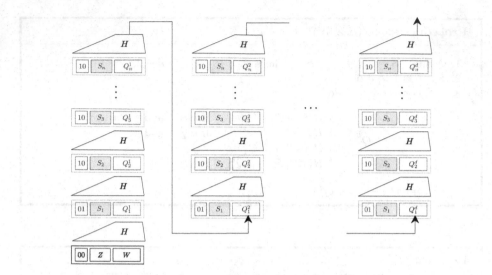

Fig. 2. A diagram representing an execution of $\mathsf{scratch}((S_1, \ldots, S_n), Z, W)$ procedure from Fig. 1.

denoting the "budget" for the hash computations, i.e., $\eta_{\mathcal{P}} = (nd + 1) \cdot 2^{\zeta+1} \cdot \kappa$ and $\eta_{\mathcal{V}} = (nd + 1) \cdot \kappa$ respectively. Note that each computation of the $\mathsf{scratch}$ procedure requires $(nd + 1)$ hash computations. The verifier needs to do such a computation κ times; hence, she needs to perform only $(nd + 1) \cdot \kappa$ hashes. For the prover, observe that each scratch attempt succeeds with probability $2^{-\zeta}$ (by "succeeding" we mean finding a value that starts with ζ zeros). Since the prover needs to be successful κ times, she needs, on average, $(nd + 1) \cdot 2^{\zeta} \cdot \kappa$ scratch attempts. We set $\eta_{\mathcal{P}}$ to be the double of this parameter in order to make the probability that he is successful (see Definition 2) less than κ times exponentially small.

Observe also that if we substitute $2^{-\zeta}$ with $2 \cdot \kappa \cdot (nd+1)/\eta_{\mathcal{P}}$ then the formula $2^{-\zeta} \cdot \ell$ (appearing both in the bounds on $\mathbb{E}[\alpha_O]$ and $\mathbb{E}[\alpha_S]$) can be rewritten as: $2 \cdot \kappa \cdot (nd+1) \cdot \ell / \eta_{\mathcal{P}}$. It is interesting to look at the last factor, i.e., $\ell/\eta_{\mathcal{P}}$. Recall that ℓ is the number of hashes computed by the adversary $\mathcal{A}$. On the other hand, $\eta_{\mathcal{P}}$ is the maximal number of hashes computed by the honest prover. Hence, $\ell/\eta_{\mathcal{P}}$ corresponds to the multiplicative advantage of the adversary with respect to the honest prover, or, in other words, it answers the question "How much more computing power does the adversary have compared to the honest prover?". In our theorem, the bounds on α_O and α_S grow linearly with $\ell/\eta_{\mathcal{P}}$. Intuitively, this comes from the fact that a powerful adversary can always "mislead" the extractor by executing a large number of $\mathsf{scratch}$ procedures on $\widehat{S} \neq S$.

4.3   Proof of Theorem 1

Completeness. Let us start with proving completeness. We first upper-bound the probability that the protocol halts in Step 2 due to the fact that the budget for H computations was exhausted. Note that this budget allows the prover to evaluate scratch $\lfloor \eta_P/(nd+1) \rfloor = 2^{\varsigma+1} \cdot \kappa$ times (since each scratch execution takes $nd+1$ hash evaluations). For $i = 1, \ldots, 2^{\varsigma+1} \cdot \kappa$, let $U_i \in \{0,1\}$ be equal to 1 if and only if the ith scratch execution was successful, i.e., it produced an output that starts with κ zeros. Set $U = U_1 + \cdots + U_{2^{\varsigma+1} \cdot \kappa}$. For simplicity of the analysis assume that $\pi_{\mathsf{PIK}}^{\rho,\sigma}$ does not stop once all the W^j's are found. Clearly, the U_i's are independent. Moreover, we have that each $\Pr[U_i = 1] = 2^{-\varsigma}$ (the probability that a random string starts with ς zeros) and hence each $\mathbb{E}[U_i] = 2^{-\varsigma}$. Therefore by Lemma 2 (Point (a)), we get that $\Pr[U < \kappa] \leq \mathsf{negl}(\kappa)$. Therefore with overwhelming probability the prover finds κ values W such that $\mathsf{scratch}(S, Z, W)$ starts with ς zeros without exhausting her hash budget, and hence she does not output $\bot$. It is also easy to see that the Verifier always accepts in such a case (since she just repeats the same scratch computation as the prover for the W^i values that she received in Step 4, and η_V hash evaluations are needed for this computation).

Soundness. To show soundness, let $\mathcal{A} = (\mathcal{A}_1, \ldots, \mathcal{A}_a)$ be a (ρ, σ)-distributed adversary. Consider an execution of $\mathcal{A}$ against an honest verifier on input $(1^\kappa, S)$ and let Z be the challenge that the verifier sends in Step 1. Recall that the adversary has access to a σ-bounded oracle Ω_H that she can use to evaluate hash function H. For an arbitrary $\widehat{S}$ (necessarily equal to S), such that $\widehat{S} = (\widehat{S}_1 \parallel \cdots \parallel \widehat{S}_n)$ (with each $\widehat{S}_j \in \{0,1\}^{\lambda-\kappa-2}$) and an arbitrary $\widehat{Q}_1 \in \{0,1\}^\kappa$ a *trace on $\mathcal{T}$ for $\widehat{S}$ (starting with $\widehat{Q}_1$)* is a sequence $(i_1, \ldots, i_n)$ such that

- $\mathcal{T}[i_1] = (01 \parallel \widehat{S}_1 \parallel \widehat{Q}_1)$ and
- for every $m = 2, \ldots t$ we have: $\mathcal{T}[i_1] = (10 \parallel \widehat{S}_m \parallel H(\mathcal{T}[i_{m-1}]))$.

Intuitively a trace is a sequence of indices on $\mathcal{T}$ that "look like" an attempt to evaluate a column on Fig. 2 for *some* $\widehat{S}$. For any nonce W, an *S-scratch on $\mathcal{T}$ for W* is a sequence

$$i_0 \parallel (i_1^1, \ldots, i_n^1) \parallel \cdots \parallel (i_1^d, \ldots, i_n^d), \tag{2}$$

where $\mathcal{T}[i_0] = (00 \parallel Z \parallel W)$ and each $(i_1^k, \ldots, i_n^k)$ is a trace for S staring either with $H(\mathcal{T}[i_0])$ (if $k = 1$) or with $H(10 \parallel S_n \parallel H(\mathcal{T}[i_n^{k-1}]))$ (otherwise). In other words: S-scratch is a sequence of indices on $\mathcal{T}$ that correspond to an attempt to evaluate the entire diagram on Fig. 2 for $\widehat{S} = S$.

Claim 1. For a hash transcript $\mathcal{T}$ consider two distinct nonces W and $\widehat{W}$. Let I and $\widehat{I}$ be S-scratches on $\mathcal{T}$ for W and $\widehat{W}$, respectively. Then with overwhelming probability, we have that I and $\widehat{I}$ are disjoint, i.e., there does not exist an index i that appears in both I and $\widehat{I}$.

Proof (sketch). Let Q_i^k's and $\widehat{Q}_i^k$'s be the values of the variables in the scratch procedure when run on input (S, Z, W) and $(S, Z, \widehat{W})$, respectively (see Fig. 1 or the diagram on Fig. 2). Suppose there exists an index i that appears in both I and $\widehat{I}$. Obviously $T[i]$ cannot be of a form $(00 \,\|\, Z \,\|\, W)$, since $W \neq \widehat{W}$. Hence $T[i]$ must have a form $(b_0 \,\|\, b_1 \,\|\, S_j \,\|\, Q)$. This means that $T[i]$ is an output of a sequence of hashes starting with $H(00 \,\|\, Z \,\|\, W)$ *and* simultaneously, it is an output of a sequence of hashes starting with $H(00 \,\|\, Z \,\|\, \widehat{W})$. Using this information, one can efficiently find a collision in H. Since the probability of finding collisions in H is negligible, the probability that such W and $\widehat{W}$ can be found has to be negligible. □

We will need the following definition.

Definition 3. *Let W be a nonce such that there exists an S-scratch on T for W. We call W fast if for every S-scratch $(i_1, \ldots, i_m)$ on T for W each $T[i_j]$ is a fast query. Otherwise, we call it slow.*

We will also use the following simple fact that states that with overwhelming probability, the adversary has to compute the Q_j^k variables in the same order as the honest party executing the scratch procedure.

Claim 2. Fix some $Z \in \{0,1\}^\kappa$ and $W \in \{0,1\}^{\lambda-\kappa-2}$ and let S be as above. Let Q_j^k's be the variables computed in the scratch(S, Z, Q) procedure (see Fig. 1 (a)). For a global hash transcript T

- let i_0^1 be the first position in T on which $(00 \,\|\, Z \,\|\, W)$ appears, and
- for $k \in \{1, \ldots, d\}$ and $j \in \{1, \ldots, n\}$ let i_j^k be the first position in T such that $T[i_j^k]$ ends with Q_j^k.

Then with overwhelming probability the i_j^k's when sorted lexicographically by (k, j) are monotonically increasing, i.e.,

$$\underset{\substack{(k_0, j_0) \\ (k_1, j_1)}}{\forall} \quad k_0 < k_1 \vee ((k_0 = k_1) \wedge (j_0 < j_1)) \text{ implies that } i_{j_0}^{k_0} < i_{j_1}^{k_1}. \tag{3}$$

Proof (sketch). Let $\prec$ be the strict lexicographic order on (k, j)'s used in Eq. (3). Suppose that there exists $(k_0, j_0) \prec (k_1, j_1)$ such that $i_{j_0}^{k_0} \geq i_{j_1}^{k_1}$. Clearly, unless a collision in H is found (which happens with negligible probability), all the Q_j^k's are distinct, and hence we can assume that $i_{j_0}^{k_0} > i_{j_1}^{k_1}$. Without loss of generality assume that (k_0, j_0) immediately precedes (k_1, j_1) in the "$\prec$" order. Observe that $Q_{j_1}^{k_1}$ is an output of a hash function H when evaluated on an input that contains $Q_{j_0}^{k_0}$ (with a convention that $Q_0^1 := 00 \,\|\, Z \,\|\, W$). But $i_{j_0}^{k_0} > i_{j_1}^{k_1}$ means that $Q_{j_1}^{k_1}$ was submitted to the oracle *before* the adversary learned $Q_{j_0}^{k_0}$. Since the outputs of a random oracle are uniform over $\{0,1\}^\kappa$, this happens with negligible probability. This finishes the proof of the claim. □

Claim 3. Suppose the number of fast W's is at most $\kappa \cdot 2^{\varsigma-3}$. Then the probability that $\mathcal{V}(1^\kappa, S)$ accepts on input S is negligible.

Proof (sketch). Recall that we assumed that $\sigma \leq \kappa \cdot 2^{\varsigma-3}$ and in Claim 1 we have shown that for distinct W and $\widehat{W}$ the S-scratches for W and $\widehat{W}$ are disjoint. Since $Z \in \{0,1\}^\kappa$ is sampled by the prover in the online phase, thus with overwhelming probability $(00 \parallel Z \parallel W)$ is sent to the oracle in the online phase. By Claim 2, this means that with overwhelming probability, all of the S-scratches on T for W contain only queries sent to the oracle in the online phase. Thus, the total number of slow W's is at most $\kappa \cdot 2^{\varsigma-3}$. Adding the fast ones, we get that the total number C of W's for which an S-scratch in T exists is at most $\kappa \cdot 2^{\varsigma-2}$. Let $W^1, \ldots, W^C$ be these nonces.

By Claim 2, with overwhelming probability, the adversary *first* needs to compute the entire S-scratch before learning whether it was successful or not. For each $i \in \{1, \ldots, C\}$ let $U_i \in \{0,1\}$ be equal to 1 if and only if $\mathsf{scratch}(S, Z, W^i)$ starts with ς zeros. Clearly, the U_i's are independent and $\Pr[U_i = 1] = 2^{-\varsigma}$. Let $U = U_1 + \cdots + U_C$. Using Lemma 2, we get that $\Pr[U \geq \kappa/2] \leq \mathsf{negl}(\kappa)$. Recall that $\mathcal{V}$ accepts only if she receives $(W^1, \ldots, W^\kappa)$ such that each $\mathsf{scratch}(S, Z, W^i)$ starts with ς zeros. From the analysis above, we get that with overwhelming probability, there exists $\kappa - \kappa/2 = \kappa/2$ values W_i such that the corresponding value $(10 \parallel S_n \parallel Q_n^d)$ is not in T, or, in other words, H was not evaluated on it. Clearly, the probability that $H(10 \parallel S_n \parallel Q_n^d)$ starts with ς zeros for all such W_i's is equal to $(2^{-\varsigma})^{\kappa/2} = 2^{-\varsigma \cdot \kappa/2} \leq \mathsf{negl}(\kappa)$. $\square$

Before presenting our extractor $\mathcal{E}$, consider the following natural construction idea. By Claim 3, if the adversary was successful, then T^{fast} needs to contain at least $\kappa \cdot 2^{\varsigma-3}$ S-scratches of a computation of $\mathsf{scratch}(S, Z, W)$ (for some W's). Each such an S-scratch contains $d = \rho + 1$ traces for S, where ρ is the maximal number of communication rounds. Therefore every S-scratch contains a trace computed in a single round. As we show formally later (see Claim 4), all the queries corresponding to such a trace had to come from a single adversary. Hence, it should be possible to find it by scanning all T_b^{fast}'s.

More concretely, consider an extractor that scans the transcript T_b^{fast} in order to find elements of a form $(01 \parallel \widehat{S}_1 \parallel \widehat{Q}_1)$ (for some $\widehat{S}_1$ and $\widehat{Q}_1$). Each such element is potentially part of an attempt by $\mathcal{A}_b$ to compute a scratch path on a message starting with $\widehat{S}_1$. The extractor stores $\widehat{S}_1$ and $\widehat{Q}_2 := H(01 \parallel \widehat{S}_1 \parallel \widehat{Q}_1)$. It then continues scanning the transcript to find elements of a form $(10 \parallel \widehat{S}_2 \parallel \widehat{Q}_2)$. Suppose $\mathcal{E}$ found such an element, and let $Q_3 := H(10 \parallel \widehat{S}_2 \parallel \widehat{Q}_2)$. It then looks for elements of a form $(10 \parallel \widehat{S}_2 \parallel \widehat{Q}_3)$, and so on, until it finds n strings: $(\widehat{S}^1, \ldots, \widehat{S}^n)$. It then outputs $(\widehat{S}^1 \parallel \cdots \parallel \widehat{S}^n)$.

The above approach essentially works, although it needs some modifications. The main challenge is that the adversary can make "fake" calls to Ω_H, whose goal would be just to mislead the extractor. Hence, a hash transcript can contain S-scratches for some other $\widehat{S}$'s (possibly sharing a prefix with S). We deal with these problems by exploiting the fact that in a successful execution, the adversary still needs to perform a large number $(\kappa \cdot 2^{\varsigma-3})$ of scratch executions on real S. Our solution is presented in Fig. 3. The $\mathcal{E}$ procedure maintains a set $\mathcal{F}$ containing information that can lead to finding the solution S. The values are added to this set only with a certain probability $(2^{-\varsigma})$. This probability is chosen so that the most likely *some* S-scratch is included in $\mathcal{F}$, yet, it reduces the size of $\mathcal{F}$ significantly, leading to better parameters. In particular, it prevents the size of $\mathcal{F}$ from becoming too large if the adversary makes lots of "fake" hash queries described above.

Knowledge extractor $\mathcal{E}(\mathcal{T}_b^{\mathsf{fast}})$

1. Let $\ell_b := |\mathcal{T}_b^{\mathsf{fast}}|$.
2. Let $\mathcal{F}$ be a set that is initially empty. Set $\mathcal{F}$ contains pairs of a form $(\widehat{Q}, \widehat{S})$, where $\widehat{Q} \in \{0,1\}^{\kappa}$ is a hash output, and $\widehat{S} \in \{0,1\}^*$.
3. For each $i = 1, \ldots, \ell_b$ do
   (a) If $\mathcal{T}_b^{\mathsf{fast}}[i]$ is of a form $(01||\widehat{S}||\widehat{Q})$ (for some $\widehat{S}$ and $\widehat{Q}$) then with probability $2^{-\varsigma}$ add a pair $(H(01 || \widehat{S} || \widehat{Q}), \widehat{S})$ to $\mathcal{F}$ (if it is not stored there yet). Note that $(01 || \widehat{S} || \widehat{Q})$ can appear more than once in $\mathcal{T}_b^{\mathsf{fast}}$. Since we want the probability of being added to $\mathcal{F}$ to be the same for every string $(01||\widehat{S}||\widehat{Q})$ (no matter how often it appears in $\mathcal{T}_b^{\mathsf{fast}}$), we perform this random choice by evaluating some function $\varphi : \{0,1\}^* \to \{0,1\}$ (treated as a random oracle) such that $\Pr[\varphi(x) = 1] = 2^{-\varsigma}$. We add $(H(01 || \widehat{S} || \widehat{Q}), \widehat{S})$ to $\mathcal{F}$ if and only it $\varphi(01 || \widehat{S} || \widehat{Q}) = 1$.
   (b) If $\mathcal{T}_b^{\mathsf{fast}}[i]$ is of a form $(10||\widehat{S}||\widehat{Q})$ (for some $\widehat{S}$ and $\widehat{Q}$) and that there exists a pair $(\widehat{Q}, \widehat{S}') \in \mathcal{F}$ (for some $\widehat{S}' \in \{0,1\}^*$) then add $(H(10||\widehat{S}||\widehat{Q}), (\widehat{S}'||\widehat{S}))$ to $\mathcal{F}$.
   Additionally, if $|(\widehat{S}'||\widehat{S})| = n$ then **output** $(\widehat{S}'||\widehat{S})$ (but do not terminate),

---

Fig. 3. The knowledge extractor for our PIK protocol. It preoceeds in an online fashion, reading $\mathcal{T}_b^{\mathsf{fast}}$ and outputting during the execution the "candidate" values for S. The output of $\mathcal{E}(\mathcal{T}_b^{\mathsf{fast}})$ is the set of all values that were output during the execution of $\mathcal{E}$.

Claim 4. Consider an execution of $\mathcal{A} = (\mathcal{A}_1, \ldots, \mathcal{A}_a)$ against an honest verifier $\mathcal{V}$ on input $(1^{\kappa}, S)$. For each b, let $\mathcal{T}_b^{\mathsf{fast}}$ be the fast-hash transcript of $\mathcal{A}_b$. Suppose $\mathcal{V}(1^{\kappa}, S)$ accepts. Then with overwhelming probability for some b, the string S is among the values output by the knowledge extractor $\mathcal{E}(\mathcal{T}_b^{\mathsf{fast}})$.

Proof. Consider a global hash transcript $\mathcal{T}^{\mathsf{fast}}$. Let W be a fast W (see Definition 3). Recall that, since the adversary can evaluate H on the same value multiple times, there can be multiple S-scratches on $\mathcal{T}^{\mathsf{fast}}$ for W. Let first-scratch$(W, \mathcal{T})$ denote the S-scratch composed of the *first* positions on $\mathcal{T}^{\mathsf{fast}}$ for W where the given value appears on $\mathcal{T}^{\mathsf{fast}}$. More formally, let first-scratch(W) be the S-scratch $(i_1, \ldots, i_m)$ for W such that for every i_j is the least index i such that $\mathcal{T}^{\mathsf{fast}}[i_j] = \mathcal{T}^{\mathsf{fast}}[i]$, i.e., we have:

$$\forall_{j \in \{1,\ldots,m\}} \; \forall_{i < i_j} \; \mathcal{T}^{\mathsf{fast}}[i] \neq \mathcal{T}^{\mathsf{fast}}[i_j]. \tag{4}$$

Recall that ρ is the number of rounds, and we assumed that $\rho \leq d-1$. Therefore for every fast W and first-scratch(W) of form as in Eq. (2), there needs to exist a round and an index k such that hashes of values $T[i_1^k], \ldots, T[i_n^k]$ were all sent to Ω_H in a single round. Observe that the knowledge of each $T[i_j^k]$ is needed to compute the next value $T[i_{j+1}^k]$ and, because of Eq. (4) $H(T[i_j^k])$ was not computed in the previous round. Since the output of a hash can be guessed with probability $2^{-\kappa}$, thus with overwhelming probability, all the values $T[i_1^k], \ldots, T[i_n^k]$ had to be submitted to Ω_H by single sub-adversary $\mathcal{A}_b$. Hence there must exist a trace $i_1^k, \ldots, i_n^k$ in first-scratch(W) that was computed by a single sub-adversary $\mathcal{A}_b$.

By Claim 3, with overwhelming probability, the total number of fast W's is greater than $\kappa \cdot 2^{\varsigma-3}$. Hence, at least $\kappa \cdot 2^{\varsigma-3}$ traces for S were computed by a single $\mathcal{A}_b$. The probability that each trace is added to $\mathcal{F}$ is $2^{-\varsigma}$. Hence, the probability that at least one trace for S is output by *some* $\mathcal{A}_b$ is at least $1 - (1 - 2^{-\varsigma})^{\kappa \cdot 2^{\varsigma-3}}$, which, by Lemma 1, is at least $1 - e^{-\kappa/8} \geq 1 - \mathsf{negl}\,(\kappa)$. □

It remains to analyze the extraction efficiency of the extractor. Consider a run on $\mathcal{E}$ on input T_b. We first show the following bound on the expected output size of $\mathcal{F}$:

$$\mathbb{E}\left[|\mathcal{F}|\right] \leq 2^{-\varsigma} \cdot \ell_b \tag{5}$$

(where ℓ_b is the number of fast hash queries of $\mathcal{A}_b$). Recall that new values are added to $\mathcal{F}$ by scanning all ℓ_b positions on T_b^{fast} in the following way:

1. if $T_b^{\mathsf{fast}}[i]$ is of a form $(01 \,\|\, \widehat{S} \,\|\, \widehat{Q})$ then a new value is added to $\mathcal{F}$ with probability at most $2^{-\varsigma}$ and
2. if $T_b^{\mathsf{fast}}[i]$ is of a form $(10 \,\|\, \widehat{S} \,\|\, \widehat{Q})$ then a new value is added if $\widehat{Q}$ is a result of a chain of hashes that started with hashing some $(01 \,\|\, \widehat{S} \,\|\, \widehat{Q}')$ and $\varphi(01 \,\|\, \widehat{S} \,\|\, \widehat{Q}') = 1$. Since this happens with probability 2^{ς} we get that the probability that $(10 \,\|\, \widehat{S} \,\|\, \widehat{Q})$ is added to $\mathcal{F}$ is $2^{-\varsigma}$.

This proves (5). Since the values that are output by the extractor are a subset of $\mathcal{F}$, and $\ell = \ell_1 + \cdots + \ell_b$, thus we get that $\mathbb{E}\left[\alpha_{\mathsf{O}}\right] = \mathbb{E}\left[\mathcal{E}_1(T_b^{\mathsf{fast}}) \cup \cdots \cup \mathcal{E}_a(T_b^{\mathsf{fast}})\right] \leq 2^{-\varsigma} \cdot \ell$.

To analyze the time and space complexity of $\mathcal{E}$ observe that $\mathcal{E}$ is an online algorithm that reads T_b^{fast} once. Assume that $\mathcal{F}$ is maintained using Cuckoo Hashing [28], where in every pair $(\widehat{Q}, \widehat{S})$, the element $\widehat{Q}$ is treated as the key, and $\widehat{S}$ is the stored value. Thanks to this, looking up and inserting the values in $\mathcal{F}$ takes constant time. Thus, the expected time complexity α_{T} of each $\mathcal{E}$ is $O(\ell_b)$, and the expected space complexity α_{S} is $O(2^{-\varsigma} \cdot \ell_b \cdot |S|)$. This concludes the proof. □

4.4   Extensions

This section describes possible extensions of the basic PIK protocol from Sect. 4. We leave the formalization of these extensions for future work as formally modeling attacks in the network settings is often highly non-trivial. For example, it requires us to consider different attack scenarios (e.g., man-in-the-middle, replay attacks, etc.) and typically involves a detailed description of the attack model (including modeling the network and the environment).

PIK as Building Block. As mentioned in Sect. 1, PIK is a primitive that will usually not be used in a "standalone" way but rather as a part of a more extensive system. The main reason for this is that the messages sent by the prover may provide some information about S. Indeed, the definition of PIK does not mention any privacy guarantees for the prover, neither against an external attacker nor against the verifier (who actually, in our setting from Definition 1, knows S entirely). In this section, we describe two extensions of PIK that address this problem. The first one ("Encrypted and Authenticated PIK") answers the issue of security against an external adversary, and the second one provides a version of PIK ("zero-knowledge PIK") that works against a verifier that does *not* know S. This version of PIK does not reveal any information about S to the verifier (or any other party).

Encrypted and Authenticated PIK (eaPIK). *Encrypted and Authenticated PIK (eaPIK)* is a version of PIK where the communication between the prover and the verifier is secured using a symmetric key K. Let us describe this solution as a general transformation of any PIK protocol $\pi_{\mathsf{PIK}}^{\rho;\sigma}$. The main idea is quite straightforward: we let every message[3] in the protocol $\pi_{\mathsf{PIK}}^{\rho;\sigma}$ be encrypted and authenticated with a fresh key K that is shared between the prover and the verifier, sampled independently from S. Note that since we have a setup phase (for establishing S), thus assuming that in this phase, we also generate K is very mild. To summarize: the client and the server share the following:

- key K for encrypting messages during the execution of the PIK protocol and
- secret S that is used as the input of both parties in PIK.

Of course, as long as the prover is honest (and hence: she stores S on a single machine), she easily convinces the verifier that she knows S. On the other hand, by the PIK properties, a dishonest prover cannot distribute S among different sub-adversaries. It is important to note that the PIK protocol only guarantees that S cannot be distributed, and K is not protected similarly. Hence, any potential application accessing the server should require the knowledge of S only, and it should not be assumed that K is stored on a single machine.

ZK-Proofs of Individual Knowledge. Let us now describe a solution for a setting where S is known only to the prover. In this case, PIK makes sense only if some publicly-available information on S is known. We model this in the following standard way. Suppose L is an NP-language characterized by some

---

[3] It is easy to see that in case of our protocol $\pi_{\mathsf{PIK}}^{\rho;\sigma}$ (see Fig. 1) the only message that may contain sensitive information about S is $(W^1, \ldots, W^\kappa)$ sent by the prover to the verifier in Step 3. Hence, it is enough if only this message is encrypted.

NP-relation $\varphi : \{0,1\}^* \times \{0,1\}^* \to \{0,1\}$. The verifier holds some public information $pub \in \{0,1\}^*$, while the prover has an NP-witness $S \in \{0,1\}^*$ such that $(S, pub) \in L$. A natural example of L is the language of all secret keys in some public-key encryption scheme, with pub being the public key and S being the corresponding private key. The goal of the prover is to convince the verifier that she knows S such that $\varphi(S, pub) = 1$ and that this S is stored on an individual machine. Moreover, this should be done in zero-knowledge, i.e., without revealing additional information to the verifier about S. We call a protocol that satisfies these requirements a *ZK-proof of individual knowledge (zkPIK)* for relation φ.

Let us now outline how to transform a public-coin PIK protocol $\pi_{\text{PIK}}^{\rho,\sigma}$ into a zkPIK, where by "public-coin PIK" we mean protocols where the messages of the verifier are drawn at random, independently from S. It is easy to see that our $\pi_{\text{PIK}}^{\rho,\sigma}$ protocol (see Fig. 1) is public-coin since the only message that the verifier sends is the random challenge Z in Step 1. Our protocol works as follows. The prover and the verifier execute $\pi_{\text{PIK}}^{\rho,\sigma}$ with the following modification: the prover, instead of sending her messages in clear, commits to them using a cryptographic commitment scheme [9], and later proves in zero-knowledge [21] that she committed to messages that would make the verifier in protocol $\pi_{\text{PIK}}^{\rho,\sigma}$ accept. Note that the zero-knowledge proof can be executed after the message exchange is finished; hence, the time needed to execute it does not influence the time bounds of the original PIK protocol. Clearly, this proof can also be executed in a non-interactive way [8], e.g., using one of the Zero-Knowledge Succinct Non-Interactive Argument of Knowledge (zkSNARK) schemes (see, e.g., [7]). Note that this solution assumes a generic use of zero-knowledge protocols.

Reducing the Number of Candidate Messages. Recall that one of the parameters in PIK is the maximal size α_O of the set of "candidate secrets $\widehat{S}$", that besides the real value, S contains a lot of "false positives". Moreover, α_O can be quite large in our construction. A simple technique for eliminating the false positives is to let the verifier publish a hash $h = H'(S)$ (where H' is some hash function different from the one used in constructing PIK). Once h is known, everyone (including the prover) can check for every candidate $\widehat{S}$ if $H'(\widehat{S}) = h$, and if it does not hold, eliminate this $\widehat{S}$ from the candidate set. It is easy to see that $\widehat{S} = S$ passes this test, while (assuming no collisions in H are found) all $\widehat{S}$'s such that $\widehat{S} \neq S$ get eliminated. This solution can be proven secure in the random oracle model as long as the entropy of S (from the point of view of an external adversary) is large enough to guarantee that the adversary cannot guess S. This is the case, e.g., if S is a uniform random key.

Let us also discuss how h can be published. One option is to let h be sent to the verifier by the prover during the execution of the protocol. In the case of the eaPIK protocol, h would be encrypted by key K. Note that we do not even need the assumption that S has high entropy since it remains hidden from the external attacker. In the case of zkPIK, h could just be a part of the public key.

5   Individual Secret Sharing

In this section, we define and construct a secret sharing scheme that is "individually secure" in the following sense. Any secret S shared between the parties can be either reconstructed entirely by a single individual party or it remains completely hidden. In other words: it is impossible to reconstruct the secret "partly" or to convert its shares to some shares from a standard secret sharing scheme (so that the parties could, e.g., perform some MPC computation on such standard shares). We call our scheme *individual secret sharing* (for a formal definition, see Definition 4). It is constructed using another primitive that we also define and construct, called individual *random* secret sharing scheme (IRSS, see Definition 5). The difference between ISS and IRSS is that in the latter, the shared secret is chosen randomly by the sharing procedure. Our schemes are passively secure, i.e., we do not address the problem of secure reconstruction in case some of the parties are actively cheating. A scheme that addresses this in the blockchain settings has been recently proposed in [17].

5.1   Standard Secret Sharing

Recall that secret sharing [30] is a protocol that allows a *dealer* to share a secret S between a group of parties. Let $a, t \in \mathbb{N}$ be such that $t \leq a$. A (t, a)-*secret sharing* ((t, a)-SS) is a pair of poly-time algorithms (share, rec) such that share is a randomized algorithm that takes as input $(S, 1^\kappa)$ (where $S \in \{0, 1\}^*$ and 1^κ is a security parameter), and outputs a sequence $(S_1, \ldots, S_a, pub) \in (\{0, 1\}^*)^{a+1}$ and rec takes as input a subset $\{S_{i_1}, \ldots, S_{i_t}\} \subseteq \{S_1, \ldots, S_a\}$ of size t and pub and outputs $\widehat{S} \in \{0, 1\}^* \cup \{\bot\}$. Each S_i is called a *share of S*. The value pub is not a part of the standard secret sharing definition. We will use it to denote a public value (in our case: a ciphertext encrypted with a shared key) known to every party (think of it as included in every share or published by the dealer on some public bulletin board).

We require that if $\{S_{i_1}, \ldots, S_{i_t}\}$ and pub come from the output of share(S), then rec($\{S_{i_1}, \ldots, S_{i_t}, pub\}$) = S. The security of a (t, a)-SS is defined as follows. Let a *distinguisher* be a pair $(\mathcal{D}_1, \mathcal{D}_2)$ of poly-time machines such that:

- machine $\mathcal{D}_1$ takes as input 1^κ and outputs $S^0, S^1, Y \in \{0, 1\}^*$ (with $|S^0| = |S^1|$) and
- machine $\mathcal{D}_2$ takes as input $Y \in \{0, 1\}^*$, a subset of shares, and $pub \in \{0, 1\}^*$ and outputs a bit.

We require that for every subset $\{i_1, \ldots, i_{t-1}\} \subseteq \{1, \ldots, a\}$ and every distinguisher $(\mathcal{D}_1, \mathcal{D}_2)$ it holds that

$$
\Pr\left[\mathcal{D}_2(Y, \{S^0_{i_1}, \ldots, S^0_{i_{t-1}}\}, pub) = 1\right]
$$
$$
- \Pr\left[\mathcal{D}_2(Y, \{S^1_{i_1}, \ldots, S^1_{i_{t-1}}\}, pub) = 1\right] \leq \mathsf{negl}\,(\kappa), \tag{6}
$$

where for $b \in \{0, 1\}$ we have $(S^b_1, \ldots, S^b_a, pub) \leftarrow_\$ \mathsf{share}(S^b, 1^\kappa)$. Note that the machine $\mathcal{D}_2$ learns pub "for free". The role of Y is to "pass" the information from $\mathcal{D}_1$ to $\mathcal{D}_2$ — one can think of $(\mathcal{D}_1, \mathcal{D}_2)$ as a single entity operating in two phases, and Y as the state of this entity between these phases.

We also define a *random* secret sharing to be a secret sharing scheme where the secret S is not chosen by the dealer but is selected randomly by the share algorithm together with the shares of S. Formally, a (t, a)-*random secret sharing ((t, a)-RSS)* is a pair of poly-time algorithms (share, rec) such that share is a randomized algorithm that takes as input 1^κ and outputs a sequence $(S, (S_1, \ldots, S_a))$, where $S \in \{0, 1\}^\kappa$ and rec is the same as rec in the SS definition (except that there is no "*pub*" input). We require for $(S, (S_1, \ldots, S_a)) \leftarrow_\$ \mathsf{share}(1^\kappa)$ we always have $\mathsf{rec}(\{S_{i_1}, \ldots, S_{i_t}\}) = S$ and that for every $\{i_1, \ldots, i_{t-1}\} \subseteq \{1, \ldots, a\}$ and every poly-time distinguisher $\mathcal{D}$ that takes as input a secret S and a set of $t - 1$ shares and outputs a bit, it holds that

$$\left| \Pr\left[\mathcal{D}(S^0, \{(S_{i_1}^0, \ldots, S_{i_1}^0\}) = 1\right] - \Pr\left[\mathcal{D}(S^1, \{S_{i_1}^0, \ldots, S_{i_1}^0\}) = 1\right] \right| \leq \mathsf{negl}(\kappa), \tag{7}$$

where $(S^0, (S_1^0, \ldots, S_a^0)) \leftarrow_\$ \mathsf{share}(1^\kappa)$ and $S^1 \leftarrow_\$ \{0, 1\}^\kappa$. It is easy to see that every random secret sharing scheme can be converted into a standard secret sharing by using the random key S to encrypt the shared messages and making *pub* equal to the resulting ciphertext. We will use this technique is Sect. 5.4.

Examples. Let $(\mathbb{F}, \oplus, \times)$ be a finite field and let t, a be some parameter with $t \leq a$. The following is an (a, a)-random secret sharing: $\mathsf{share}_\oplus(1^\kappa) := (S_1, \ldots, S_a)$, and $\mathsf{rec}_\oplus(S_1, \ldots, S_a) := S_1 + \cdots + S_a$. Another standard example is the Shamir's (t, a)-random secret sharing [30] ($\mathsf{share}_{\mathsf{Shamir}}, \mathsf{rec}_{\mathsf{Shamir}}$) defined as follows. Let $1, \ldots, a$ be some distinct elements of $\mathbb{F}$. Then $\mathsf{share}_{\mathsf{Shamir}}(1^\kappa) := ((1, P(1)), \ldots, (a, P(a)))$, where P is a random polynomial over $\mathbb{F}$ with degree at most $t - 1$ and $\mathsf{rec}_{\mathsf{Shamir}}((i_1, X_1), \ldots, (i_t, X_t)) := P(0)$, where P is the polynomial of degree at most t interpolated at points $(i_1, X_1), \ldots, (i_t, X_t)$. It is easy to see that both of these schemes satisfy our definition in a very strong sense, namely Eq. (7) holds even if we substitute "$\mathsf{negl}(\kappa)$" with 0 (note that this also explains why the share algorithms do not depend on 1^κ).

5.2   ISS and IRSS Definitions

In this section, we present the definition of our main primitive, individual secret sharing (ISS), as well as the auxiliary notion of individual random secret sharing (where the shared secret is chosen randomly by the sharing algorithm). The main idea of the ISS definition is that we require that the scheme should be secure in the standard sense (in the random oracle model), and additionally, we require that for any distributed adversary $(\mathcal{A}_1, \ldots, \mathcal{A}_a)$ (with each poly-time machine $\mathcal{A}_b$ holding a share S_i of a secret S) that learns some information about the shared secret at least one $\mathcal{A}_b$'s learns the secret S entirely. As in Sect. 4, we consider an distributed adversary that operates in a *pre-processing phase*, and then in the *main phase*. The adversary interacts with an oracle Ω_H. She is σ-bounded, meaning that she can send at most σ slow queries to the oracle in the online phase. Unlike, in Sect. 4, in this definition, we do not make any restriction on the number of rounds in which the distributed adversary operates.

More concretely, suppose that $(\mathcal{A}_1, \ldots, \mathcal{A}_a)$ can distinguish between the shares of two secrets S^0 and S^1 with advantage $p_{\mathcal{A}}$. We then require that there exists an extractor $\mathcal{E}$ that extracts S entirely from the fast hash transcript of one of the $\mathcal{A}_i$'s with probability proportional to $p_{\mathcal{A}}$ (i.e., $\xi \cdot p_{\mathcal{A}}$, where ξ is the parameter of the scheme). Additionally, $\mathcal{E}$ gets as input string pub, which is assumed to be public according to the secret sharing definition (see Sect. 5.1). The "distinguishing game" is denoted as ISS and presented in Fig. 4 (a). Similarly to what we had in the PIK definition (see Definition 1), we can assume that the game is played by one of the adversaries, say $\mathcal{A}_1$. Our definition uses the notion of "extraction efficiency" in the same way as it was done in the PIK definition.

Definition 4. *For $\xi \in [0,1]$ a (t,a,σ,ξ)-individual secret sharing $((t,a,\sigma,\xi)$-ISS) is a (t,a)-SS scheme with both* share *and* rec *having access to a random oracle $\Omega_{H:\{0,1\}^\lambda \to \{0,1\}^\kappa}$, and security holding against $(\mathcal{D}_1, \mathcal{D}_2)$ that have access to Ω_H. Consider a distributed adversary $\mathcal{A} = (\mathcal{A}_1, \ldots, \mathcal{A}_a)$ and the $\mathsf{ISS}(\sigma, b, \mathcal{A})$ experiment from Fig. 4 (a). Let*

$$p_{\mathcal{A}} := |\Pr\left[\mathsf{ISS}(\sigma, 0, \mathcal{A}) = 1\right] - \Pr\left[\mathsf{ISS}(\sigma, 1, \mathcal{A}) = 1\right]|. \tag{8}$$

We require that for every $\mathcal{A}$ there exists a poly-time extractor $\mathcal{E}$ such that for both $b \in \{0,1\}$

$$\Pr\left[S^b \in \mathcal{E}(T_1^{\mathsf{fast}}, pub) \cup \cdots \cup \mathcal{E}(T_a^{\mathsf{fast}}, pub)\right] \geq \xi \cdot p_{\mathcal{A}} - \mathsf{negl}\,(\kappa), \tag{9}$$

where pub comes from the $\mathsf{ISS}(\sigma, b, \mathcal{A})$ experiment and $T_1^{\mathsf{fast}}, \ldots, T_a^{\mathsf{fast}}$ are the fast hash transcripts of $\mathcal{A}_1, \ldots, \mathcal{A}_a$ (respectively) in this experiment. We say that $(\mathsf{share}, \mathsf{rec})$ has extraction efficiency $(\alpha_O, \alpha_T, \alpha_S)$ if $|\mathcal{E}_1(T_1^{\mathsf{fast}}, pub) \cup \cdots \cup \mathcal{E}_a(T_a^{\mathsf{fast}}, pub)| \leq \alpha_O$, and $\mathcal{E}$ operates in time at most α_T and uses space at most α_S. The parameters α_O, α_T and α_S can be functions of some other parameters in the system.

We also have the following.

Definition 5. *A (t,a,σ)-random individual secret sharing $((t,a,\sigma)$-ISS) is a (t,a)-RSS scheme with both* share *and* rec *having access to a random oracle $\Omega_{H:\{0,1\}^\lambda \to \{0,1\}^\kappa}$, and security holding against $\mathcal{D}$ that has access to Ω_H. Consider a distributed adversary $\mathcal{A} = (\mathcal{A}_1, \ldots, \mathcal{A}_a)$ and the $\mathsf{IRSS}(\sigma, b, \mathcal{A})$ experiment from Fig. 4 (b). Let*

$$p_{\mathcal{A}} := |\Pr\left[\mathsf{IRSS}(\sigma, 0, \mathcal{A}) = 1\right] - \Pr\left[\mathsf{IRSS}(\sigma, 1, \mathcal{A}) = 1\right]|. \tag{10}$$

We require that for every $\mathcal{A}$ there exists an extractor $\mathcal{E}$ such that

$$\Pr\left[S^0 \in \mathcal{E}(T_1^{\mathsf{fast}}) \cup \cdots \cup \mathcal{E}(T_a^{\mathsf{fast}})\right] \geq p_{\mathcal{A}} - \mathsf{negl}\,(\kappa), \tag{11}$$

where $T_1^{\mathsf{fast}}, \ldots, T_a^{\mathsf{fast}}$ are the fast hash transcripts of $\mathcal{A}_1, \ldots, \mathcal{A}_a$ (respectively) in the $\mathsf{IRSS}(\sigma, b, \mathcal{A})$ experiment. The extraction efficiency is defined as in Definition 4.

Note that unlike Deinition 4, this definition does not use the ξ parameter. This is done for the sake of simplicity, since, as it turns out, our construction (see Sect. 5.3) works without the need for this parameter. The extractors do not take *pub* as input, as in the *random* secret sharing definition this value does not exist.

ISS$(\sigma, b, \mathcal{A})$

1. The sub-adversaries perform the pre-computation phase in which they can send an unbounded number of queries (including the slow ones) to the oracle Ω_H.
2. $\mathcal{A}_1$ chooses (S^0, S^1) (with $|S^0| = |S^1|$)
3. For $b \in \{0,1\}$ let $(S_1^b, \ldots, S_a^b, pub) \leftarrow_\$ \mathsf{share}(S^b, 1^\kappa)$.
4. Each $\mathcal{A}_i$ receives (S_i^b, pub),
5. The sub-adversaries $\mathcal{A}_i$ engage in an interactive protocol with access to σ-bounded oracle Ω_H, at the end of which, $\mathcal{A}_1$ outputs $\widehat{b} \in \{0,1\}$. The experiment outputs $\widehat{b}$.

(a)

IRSS$(\sigma, b, \mathcal{A})$

1. The sub-adversaries perform the pre-computation phase in which they can send an unbounded number of queries (including the slow ones) to the oracle Ω_H.
2. Let $(S^0, (S_1^0, \ldots, S_a^0)) \leftarrow_\$ \mathsf{share}(S^0, 1^\kappa)$ and let $S^1 \leftarrow_\$ \{0,1\}^\kappa$.
3. Each $\mathcal{A}_i$ receives S_i^0.
4. Proceed as in Step 5. in the ISS$(\sigma, b, \mathcal{A})$ experiment above.

(b)

Fig. 4. (a) The ISS experiment and (b) the IRSS experiment. Above, $\mathcal{A}$ is a distributed adversary consisting of sub-adversaries $\mathcal{A}_1, \ldots, \mathcal{A}_a$.

5.3 IRSS Construction

In this section, we construct an IRSS scheme (share, rec). Our scheme is presented in Fig. 5. It uses an arbitrary (standard) (t, a)-random secret sharing scheme (share$_\mathsf{std}$, rec$_\mathsf{std}$) as a building block. It is parameterized by the maximal number σ of slow queries available to the distributed adversary and a parameter $\eta > 2 \cdot \max(\kappa, \sigma)$. Its main idea is fairly simple: we first use a standard random secret sharing (RSS) scheme to share a random secret X. The shares in our individual random secret sharing are the same as those in the RSS, while the shared secret is equal to $\mathsf{iter}^{1 \mapsto \eta}(X)$. Here, $\mathsf{iter}^{1 \mapsto \eta}(X)$ is a procedure that simply applies H to itself η times, adding the index j to each hash (see Fig. 4 (a)). Intuitively, the security of our scheme is based on the fact that computing iter in a reasonable amount of time is impossible without one of the parties learning one of the intermediate values used in this computation. This is formalized in Lemma 3 below.

Procedure $\text{iter}^{\alpha \mapsto \eta}(X)$

1. Let $X^{a-1} := X$.
2. For $j = \alpha$ to β let $X^j := H((j-1) \,\|\, X^{j-1})$.
3. Output X^η.

(a)

Protocol $(\text{share}, \text{rec})$

The protocol is parameterized by a parameter σ denoting the maximal number of slow queries available to the distributed adversary and a parameter $\eta > 2 \cdot \max(\kappa, \sigma)$.

$\text{share}(1^\kappa)$:
1. Let $(X, (S_1, \ldots, S_a)) \leftarrow_\$ \text{share}_{\text{std}}(1^\kappa)$.
2. Output $(S, (S_1, \ldots, S_a))$, where $S = \text{iter}^{1 \mapsto \eta}(X)$.
$\text{rec}(\{S_{i_1}, \ldots, S_{i_t}\})$:

1. Let $X := \text{rec}_{\text{std}}(\{S_{i_1}, \ldots, S_{i_t}\})$.
2. Output $S := \text{iter}^{1 \mapsto \eta}(X)$.

(b)

Fig. 5. The IRSS protocol $(\text{share}, \text{rec})$ that satisfies Def. 5 (see Lemma 3 for the proof). The main procedure is depicted in point (b). It is based on an RSS scheme $(\text{share}_{\text{std}}, \text{rec}_{\text{std}})$ it uses a sub-routine iter, see point (a).

Lemma 3. *For any* (t, a) *suppose* $(\text{share}_{\text{std}}, \text{rec}_{\text{std}})$ *is a* (t, a)-*random secret sharing scheme. Then for any* σ *the scheme* $(\text{share}, \text{rec})$ *from Fig. 5 is a* (t, a, σ)-*individual random secret sharing with extraction efficiency* $(\alpha_O, \alpha_T, \alpha_S)$, *where* $\mathbb{E}[\alpha_O] \leq \kappa \cdot \ell/\eta$, $\mathbb{E}[\alpha_T] \leq \ell$ *(where ell is the number of fast hashes computed by* A *and time complexity is measured in the number of* H *evaluations), and* $\alpha_S = O(\kappa)$.

Proof (sketch). We first show that $(\text{share}, \text{rec})$ is a (t, a)-RSS, i.e., that for any poly-time distinguisher $\mathcal{D}$ (having access to Ω_H) Eq. (6) holds. From the security of the underlying RSS scheme $(\text{share}_{\text{rnd}}, \text{rec}_{\text{rnd}})$ we know that X is computationally indistinguishable from random, given the knowledge of $t - 1$ shares. Hence the probability that $\mathcal{A}$ queries the oracle on X is negligible, and thus X^1 is uniform from $\mathcal{A}$'s point of view. By induction, the same is true for each X^j (for $j = 1, \ldots, \eta - 1$) and for $S_\eta = H((\eta - 1) \,\|\, X^{j-1})$. Therefore (share, rec) is a (t, a)-RSS.

To finish the proof we construct a knowledge extractor $\mathcal{E}$ that satisfies the security definition of IRSS. The extractor is presented in Fig. 6. Let $\mathcal{Z}$ denote the event that all the values $(0\|X^0), (1\|X^1), \ldots, ((\eta-1)\|X^{\eta-1})$ in the computation of $\mathrm{iter}^{1\mapsto\eta}(X)$ (see Fig. 5 (a)) appear the global hash transcript $\mathcal{T}$.

Knowledge extractor $\mathcal{E}(\mathcal{T}_b^{\mathrm{fast}})$

1. Let $\ell_n = |\mathcal{T}_b^{\mathrm{fast}}|$.
2. For each $i = 1, \ldots, \ell_b$:
    if $\mathcal{T}_b^{\mathrm{fast}}[i]$ is of a form $(j \,\|\, \widehat{X}^{j-1})$ (for some $j \in \{1, \ldots, \ell\}$ and some $\widehat{X}^{j-1} \in \{0,1\}^\kappa$) then with probability κ/η:
       output $\mathrm{iter}^{j\mapsto\eta}(\widehat{X})$ (but do not terminate)
       and call such $(j \,\|\, \widehat{X}^{j-1})$ *selected*.

Fig. 6. Our knowledge extractor for IRSS. For its analysis see proof of Lemma 3.

Claim 5. For $\mathcal{Z}$ defined above we have that

$$|\Pr\left[\mathsf{IRSS}(\sigma, 0, \mathcal{A}) = 1 | \neg\mathcal{Z}\right] - \Pr\left[\mathsf{IRSS}(\sigma, 1, \mathcal{A}) = 1 | \neg\mathcal{Z}\right]| \leq \mathsf{negl}\,(\kappa). \qquad (12)$$

Proof. The argument is similar to the one from the proof of Lemma 3. Suppose $\mathcal{Z}$ did not happen. This means that there exists j such that the adversary never queried Ω_H on $(j \,\|\, X^j)$. Since $X^{j+1} = H(j \,\|\, X^j)$ is uniform over $\{0,1\}^\kappa$ from $\mathcal{A}$'s point of view, thus the probability that $\mathcal{A}$ queries Ω_H on $(j + 1, X^{j+1})$ is negligible. By induction, the same is true for each $(j' + 1, X^{j'+1})$ (for $j' \geq j$) and for $S_b = H((\eta - 1) \,\|\, X^{j-1})$. Therefore S_0 is indistinguishable from S_1 and hence Eq. (10) holds. $\qquad \square$

Claim 6. For $\mathcal{Z}$ defined above we have that

$$\Pr\left[S_b \in \mathcal{E}(\mathcal{T}_1) \cup \cdots \cup \mathcal{E}(\mathcal{T}_a) | \mathcal{Z}\right] \geq 1 - \mathsf{negl}\,(\kappa), \qquad (13)$$

Proof (sketch). First, observe that since S and X^j's are random strings of length κ, thus, by an argument similar to the one in the proof of Theorem 1, Ω^H is queried on any of them in the pre-processing phase with negligible probability. Thus, we can assume that no hash query was computed in Step. 1. Assume that $\mathcal{Z}$ occurred. We have to show that with overwhelming probability $S \in \mathcal{E}(\mathcal{T}_1) \cup \cdots \cup \mathcal{E}(\mathcal{T}_a)$. For $S \in \mathcal{E}(\mathcal{T}_1) \cup \cdots \cup \mathcal{E}(\mathcal{T}_a)$ to happen, it suffices that at least one (j, X^j) was selected by the extractor (since $\mathrm{iter}^{1\mapsto\eta}(X) = \mathrm{iter}^{(j+1)\mapsto\eta}(X_j)$).

Since we assumed that $\mathcal{Z}$ occurred, thus there are at least $\eta - \sigma$ fast queries containing (j, X^j)'s (note that $\eta - \sigma > 0$, since we assumed that $\eta > 2\sigma$). Each of them is selected with probability κ/η by some $\mathcal{E}(\mathcal{T}_b)$ (note that $\kappa/\eta < 1$, since we assumed that $\eta > 2\kappa$). Therefore the probability that at least one of them is selected is at least $1 - (1 - \kappa/\eta)^{\eta-\sigma} = 1 - (1 - \kappa/\eta)^{(\eta/\kappa) \cdot (\eta-\sigma) \cdot \kappa/\eta}$, which, by Lemma 1 is at least $1 - e^{-(\eta-\sigma) \cdot \kappa/\eta} = 1 - e^{-\kappa \cdot (1-\sigma/\eta)}$, which is overwhelming, since we assumed that $\eta > 2 \cdot \sigma$.   □

Now, denote $q := \Pr[\mathcal{Z}]$. We have

$$p_{\mathcal{A}} = |\Pr[\mathsf{IRSS}(\sigma, 0, \mathcal{A}) = 1] - \Pr[\mathsf{IRSS}(\sigma, 1, \mathcal{A}) = 1]| \tag{14}$$

$$= |\Pr[\mathsf{IRSS}(\sigma, 0, \mathcal{A}) = 1|\neg\mathcal{Z}] \cdot (1 - q) + \Pr[\mathsf{IRSS}(\sigma, 0, \mathcal{A}) = 1|\mathcal{Z}] \cdot q$$

$$- \Pr[\mathsf{IRSS}(\sigma, 1, \mathcal{A}) = 1|\neg\mathcal{Z}] \cdot (1 - q) - \Pr[\mathsf{IRSS}(\sigma, 1, \mathcal{A}) = 1|\mathcal{Z}] \cdot q|$$

$$\leq |(1 - q) \cdot (\Pr[\mathsf{IRSS}(\sigma, 0, \mathcal{A}) = 1|\neg\mathcal{Z}] - \Pr[\mathsf{IRSS}(\sigma, 1, \mathcal{A}) = 1|\neg\mathcal{Z}])| \tag{15}$$

$$+ |q \cdot (\Pr[\mathsf{IRSS}(\sigma, 0, \mathcal{A}) = 1|\mathcal{Z}] - \Pr[\mathsf{IRSS}(\sigma, 1, \mathcal{A}) = 1|\mathcal{Z}])|$$

$$\leq |(\Pr[\mathsf{IRSS}(\sigma, 0, \mathcal{A}) = 1|\neg\mathcal{Z}] - \Pr[\mathsf{IRSS}(\sigma, 1, \mathcal{A}) = 1|\neg\mathcal{Z}])| + q$$

$$\leq \mathsf{negl}(\kappa) + q, \tag{16}$$

where Eq. (14) comes from the definition of $p_{\mathcal{A}}$ (see Eq. (10)), Eq. (15) comes from rearranging the terms and from the triangle inequality, and Eq. (16) comes from Claim 5. Hence

$$q \geq p_{\mathcal{A}} - \mathsf{negl}(\kappa) \tag{17}$$

By Claim 6 we have

$$1 - \mathsf{negl}(\kappa) \leq \Pr[S_b \in \mathcal{E}(\mathcal{T}_1) \cup \cdots \cup \mathcal{E}(\mathcal{T}_a)|\mathcal{Z}]$$

$$= \Pr[S_b \in \mathcal{E}(\mathcal{T}_1) \cup \cdots \cup \mathcal{E}(\mathcal{T}_a) \wedge \mathcal{Z}]/\Pr[\mathcal{Z}]$$

$$\leq \Pr[S_b \in \mathcal{E}(\mathcal{T}_1) \cup \cdots \cup \mathcal{E}(\mathcal{T}_a)]/q,$$

which implies that

$$q \cdot (1 - \mathsf{negl}(\kappa)) \leq \Pr[S_b \in \mathcal{E}(\mathcal{T}_1) \cup \cdots \cup \mathcal{E}(\mathcal{T}_a)]. \tag{18}$$

The last inequality, together with Eq. (17) implies that Eq. (11) holds. Hence, the only thing that remains to finish the proof of the lemma is to analyze the efficiency of the extractor. Let ℓ denote the total number of hashes computed by the adversary. First observe that the expected number of values selected by $\mathcal{E}(\mathcal{T}_b^{\mathsf{fast}})$ is at most $\ell_b \cdot \kappa/\nu$, and therefore $\mathbb{E}[\alpha_O] = \mathbb{E}[|\mathcal{E}(\mathcal{T}_1^{\mathsf{fast}}) \cup \cdots \cup \mathcal{E}(\mathcal{T}_a^{\mathsf{fast}})|] \leq \kappa \cdot \ell/\eta$.

To analyze the time and space complexity of $\mathcal{E}$ observe that $\mathcal{E}$ is an online algorithm that reads $\mathcal{T}_b^{\mathsf{fast}}$ once. Each iter operation takes at most η hash computations, and therefore $\mathbb{E}[\alpha_T] \leq \eta \cdot \ell/\eta = \ell$. Clearly, this computation can be done in constant space (in the number of hash output blocks), and therefore $\alpha_S = O(\kappa)$. This concludes the proof.   □

5.4   ISS Construction

Let $(\mathsf{Enc}, \mathsf{Dec})$ a CPA-secure symmetric encryption scheme (see Sect. 2). Let $(\mathsf{share}^{\mathsf{rnd}}, \mathsf{rec}^{\mathsf{rnd}})$ be a (t, a, σ)-IRSS. Our ISS scheme is constructed on top of $(\mathsf{share}^{\mathsf{rnd}}, \mathsf{rec}^{\mathsf{rnd}})$ by using the random shared secret as a key for $(\mathsf{Enc}, \mathsf{Dec})$ and letting pub be equal to the ciphertext C. Our $(t, a, \sigma, 1/2)$-ISS scheme is presented in Fig. 7 its security is proven below. Its security is stated in the following theorem whose proof appears in the extended version of this paper [18].

Theorem 2. *The protocol* $(\mathsf{share}, \mathsf{rec})$ *is a* $(t, a, \sigma, 1/2)$-*ISS scheme. Moreover, suppose the extraction efficiency of* $(\mathsf{share}_{\mathsf{IRSS}}, \mathsf{rec}_{\mathsf{IRSS}})$ *is* $\alpha_{\mathsf{O}}, \alpha_{\mathsf{T}}$, *and* α_{S}. *Then the extraction efficiency of* $(\mathsf{share}, \mathsf{rec})$ *is* $\alpha_{\mathsf{O}}, \alpha_{\mathsf{T}}$, *and* $\alpha_{\mathsf{S}} = O(\kappa) + \mathcal{S}(\mathsf{Dec})$, *where* $\mathcal{S}(\mathsf{Dec})$ *denotes the space needed for running the* Dec *algorithm.*

ISS scheme $(\mathsf{share}, \mathsf{rec})$

$\mathsf{share}(1^\kappa, S)$:
   1. Let $(K, (S_1, \ldots, S_a)) \leftarrow_{\$} \mathsf{share}_{\mathsf{IRSS}}(1^\kappa)$.
   2. Let $pub := \mathsf{Enc}(K, S)$.
   3. Output $(S_1, \ldots, S_a, pub)$.
$\mathsf{rec}(\{S_{i_1}, \ldots, S_{i_t}\}, pub)$:

   1. Let $K := \mathsf{rec}_{\mathsf{IRSS}}(\{S_{i_1}, \ldots, S_{i_t}\})$.
   2. Output $\mathsf{Dec}(K, pub)$

Fig. 7. Our ISS scheme that satisfies Def. 4 (see Thm. 2 for the analysis).

5.5   Concrete Examples

Concrete examples of ISS schemes are presented on Fig. 8. Their security is stated in the following lemma, whose proof appears in [18].

Lemma 4. *Suppose* $(\mathsf{Enc}, \mathsf{Dec})$ *is a CPA-secure symmetric encryption scheme such that* Dec *works in space* $O(\kappa)$. *Then for any* a, t, σ, *and* $\eta \cdot \max(\kappa, \sigma)$ *we have that (a)* $(\mathsf{share}_{\oplus}^{\mathsf{ISS}}, \mathsf{rec}_{\oplus}^{\mathsf{ISS}})$ *is an* $(a, a, \sigma, 1/2)$-*ISS and (b)* $(\mathsf{share}_{\mathsf{Shamir}}^{\mathsf{ISS}}, \mathsf{rec}_{\mathsf{Shamir}}^{\mathsf{ISS}})$ *is an* $(t, a, \sigma, 1/2)$-*ISS and with extraction efficiency* $(\alpha_{\mathsf{O}}, \alpha_{\mathsf{T}}, \alpha_{\mathsf{S}})$, *where* $\mathbb{E}[\alpha_{\mathsf{O}}] \leq \kappa \cdot \ell / \eta$, $\mathbb{E}[\alpha_{\mathsf{T}}] \leq \ell$ *and* $\alpha_{\mathsf{S}} = O(\kappa) + \mathcal{S}(\mathsf{Dec})$ *with* $\mathcal{S}(\mathsf{Dec})$ *denoting space needed for running the* Dec *algorithm and* ℓ *denoting the number of fast hashes computed by* $\mathcal{A}$.

ISS scheme $(\text{share}_\oplus^{\text{ISS}}, \text{rec}_\oplus^{\text{ISS}})$

$\text{share}(1^\kappa, S)$:
1. Let $(S_1, \ldots, S_n) \leftarrow_\$ \mathbb{F}^n$.
2. Let $K := \text{iter}^{1 \mapsto \eta}(S_1 + \cdots + S_n)$.
3. Let $pub := \text{Enc}(K, S)$.
4. Output $(S_1, \ldots, S_n, pub)$.
$\text{rec}(1^\kappa, (S_1, \ldots, S_n, pub))$:

1. Let $K := \text{iter}^{1 \mapsto \eta}(S_1 + \cdots + S_n)$.
2. Output $\text{Dec}(K, pub)$.

(a)

ISS scheme $(\text{share}_{\text{Shamir}}^{\text{ISS}}, \text{rec}_{\text{Shamir}}^{\text{ISS}})$

$\text{share}(1^\kappa, S)$:
1. Let $((1, P(1)), \ldots, (a, P(a)))$, where P is a random polynomial over $\mathbb{F}$ with degree at most $t - 1$.
2. Let $K := \text{iter}^{1 \mapsto \eta}(P(0))$.
3. Let $pub := \text{Enc}(K, S)$.
4. Output $(S_1, \ldots, S_n, pub)$.
$\text{rec}(1^\kappa, (S_{1_1}, \ldots, S_{i_t}, pub))$:

1. Let P be the polynomial of degree at most t interpolated at points $(i_1, X_1), \ldots, (i_t, X_t)$.
2. Let $K := \text{iter}^{1 \mapsto \eta}(P(0))$.
3. Output $\text{Dec}(K, pub)$.

(b)

Fig. 8. Two concrete examples of ISS schemes: (a) an (a, a) scheme based on $(\text{share}_\oplus, \text{rec}_\oplus)$ and (b) a (t, a) scheme based on $(\text{share}_{\text{Shamir}}, \text{rec}_{\text{Shamir}})$ (see Sect. 5.1). Above $\mathbb{F}$ is a finite field and (Enc, Dec) is a CPA-secure symmetric encryption scheme. Procedure iter is defined on Fig. 5 (a).

6 Conclusion

In this paper, we initiated the formal study of individual cryptography. It would be exciting to search for particular computational problems that are MPC- or TEE-hard in practice (one good candidate would be functions that require many memory lookups), and to improve the practical parameters that we achieve. This would be, in a sense, a complementary effort to the search for "MPC-friendly primitives" (see, e.g., [23]).

Acknowledgments. We would like to thank the anonymous Crypto reviewers for their helpful comments, especially for pointing out to use the fact the need to model the pre-processing attacks.

References

1. Alwen, J., Chen, B., Pietrzak, K., Reyzin, L., Tessaro, S.: Scrypt is maximally memory-hard. In: Coron, J.-S., Nielsen, J.B. (eds.) EUROCRYPT 2017, Part III. LNCS, vol. 10212, pp. 33–62. Springer, Cham (2017). https://doi.org/10.1007/978-3-319-56617-7_2
2. Bahmani, R., et al.: Secure multiparty computation from SGX. In: Kiayias, A. (ed.) FC 2017. LNCS, vol. 10322, pp. 477–497. Springer, Cham (2017). https://doi.org/10.1007/978-3-319-70972-7_27
3. Bellare, M., Goldreich, O.: On defining proofs of knowledge. In: Brickell, E.F. (ed.) CRYPTO 1992. LNCS, vol. 740, pp. 390–420. Springer, Heidelberg (1993). https://doi.org/10.1007/3-540-48071-4_28
4. Bellare, M., Rogaway, P.: Random oracles are practical: A paradigm for designing efficient protocols. In: Denning, D.E., Pyle, R., Ganesan, R., Sandhu, R.S., Ashby, V. (eds.) CCS 1993, Proceedings of the 1st ACM Conference on Computer and Communications Security, Fairfax, Virginia, USA, 3–5 November 1993, pp. 62–73. ACM (1993). https://doi.org/10.1145/168588.168596
5. Bellare, M., Rogaway, P.: Optimal asymmetric encryption. In: De Santis, A. (ed.) EUROCRYPT 1994. LNCS, vol. 950, pp. 92–111. Springer, Heidelberg (1995). https://doi.org/10.1007/BFb0053428
6. Ben-Or, M., Goldwasser, S., Wigderson, A.: Completeness theorems for non-cryptographic fault-tolerant distributed computation (extended abstract). In: Simon, J. (ed.) Proceedings of the 20th Annual ACM Symposium on Theory of Computing, May 2–4, 1988, Chicago, Illinois, USA. pp. 1–10. ACM (1988). https://doi.org/10.1145/62212.62213
7. Bitansky, N., et al.: The Hunting of the SNARK. J. Cryptology **30**(4), 989–1066 (2016). https://doi.org/10.1007/s00145-016-9241-9
8. Blum, M., Feldman, P., Micali, S.: Non-interactive zero-knowledge and its applications (extended abstract). In: Simon, J. (ed.) Proceedings of the 20th Annual ACM Symposium on Theory of Computing, May 2–4, 1988, Chicago, Illinois, USA. pp. 103–112. ACM (1988). https://doi.org/10.1145/62212.62222
9. Brassard, G., Chaum, D., Crépeau, C.: Minimum disclosure proofs of knowledge. J. Comput. Syst. Sci. **37**(2), 156–189 (1988). https://doi.org/10.1016/0022-0000(88)90005-0
10. Campanelli, M., David, B., Khoshakhlagh, H., Konring, A., Nielsen, J.B.: Encryption to the future: A paradigm for sending secret messages to future (anonymous) committees. Cryptology ePrint Archive, Paper 2021/1423 (2021). https://eprint.iacr.org/2021/1423
11. Chandran, N., Goyal, V., Moriarty, R., Ostrovsky, R.: Position-based cryptography. SIAM J. Comput. **43**(4), 1291–1341 (2014). https://doi.org/10.1137/100805005
12. Chaum, D., Crépeau, C., Damgård, I.: Multiparty unconditionally secure protocols (extended abstract). In: Simon, J. (ed.) Proceedings of the 20th Annual ACM Symposium on Theory of Computing, May 2–4, 1988, Chicago, Illinois, USA, pp. 11–19. ACM (1988). https://doi.org/10.1145/62212.62214
13. Chor, B., Fiat, A., Naor, M., Pinkas, B.: Tracing traitors. IEEE Trans. Inf. Theory **46**(3), 893–910 (2000). https://doi.org/10.1109/18.841169

14. Damgård, I.: Towards practical public key systems secure against chosen ciphertext attacks. In: Feigenbaum, J. (ed.) CRYPTO 1991. LNCS, vol. 576, pp. 445–456. Springer, Heidelberg (1992). https://doi.org/10.1007/3-540-46766-1_36

15. Dwork, C., Naor, M., Wee, H.: Pebbling and proofs of work. In: Shoup, V. (ed.) CRYPTO 2005. LNCS, vol. 3621, pp. 37–54. Springer, Heidelberg (2005). https://doi.org/10.1007/11535218_3

16. Dziembowski, S., Faust, S., Kolmogorov, V., Pietrzak, K.: Proofs of space. In: Gennaro, R., Robshaw, M. (eds.) CRYPTO 2015, Part II. LNCS, vol. 9216, pp. 585–605. Springer, Heidelberg (2015). https://doi.org/10.1007/978-3-662-48000-7_29

17. Dziembowski, S., Faust, S., Lizurej, T.: Secret sharing with snitching, manuscript

18. Dziembowski, S., Faust, S., Lizurej, T.: Individual cryptography. IACR Cryptol. ePrint Arch. p. 88 (2023). https://eprint.iacr.org/2023/088

19. Dziembowski, S., Kazana, T., Wichs, D.: One-time computable self-erasing functions. In: Ishai, Y. (ed.) TCC 2011. LNCS, vol. 6597, pp. 125–143. Springer, Heidelberg (2011). https://doi.org/10.1007/978-3-642-19571-6_9

20. Goldreich, O., Micali, S., Wigderson, A.: How to play any mental game or A completeness theorem for protocols with honest majority. In: Aho, A.V. (ed.) Proceedings of the 19th Annual ACM Symposium on Theory of Computing, 1987, New York, New York, USA, pp. 218–229. ACM (1987). https://doi.org/10.1145/28395.28420

21. Goldwasser, S., Micali, S., Rackoff, C.: The knowledge complexity of interactive proof systems. SIAM J. Comput. **18**(1), 186–208 (1989). https://doi.org/10.1137/0218012

22. Goyal, V., Kothapalli, A., Masserova, E., Parno, B., Song, Y.: Storing and retrieving secrets on a blockchain. In: Hanaoka, G., Shikata, J., Watanabe, Y. (eds.) Public-Key Cryptography - PKC 2022, Part I. LNCS, vol. 13177, pp. 252–282. Springer, Cham (2022). https://doi.org/10.1007/978-3-030-97121-2_10

23. Grassi, L., Rechberger, C., Rotaru, D., Scholl, P., Smart, N.P.: MPC-friendly symmetric key primitives. In: Weippl, E.R., Katzenbeisser, S., Kruegel, C., Myers, A.C., Halevi, S. (eds.) Proceedings of the 2016 ACM SIGSAC Conference on Computer and Communications Security, Vienna, Austria, 24–28 October 2016, pp. 430–443. ACM (2016). https://doi.org/10.1145/2976749.2978332

24. Katz, J., Lindell, Y.: Introduction to Modern Cryptography, 2nd edn. CRC Press (2014). https://www.crcpress.com/Introduction-to-Modern-Cryptography-Second-Edition/Katz-Lindell/p/book/9781466570269

25. Kelkar, M., Babel, K., Daian, P., Austgen, J., Buterin, V., Juels, A.: Complete knowledge: Preventing encumbrance of cryptographic secrets. Cryptology ePrint Archive, Paper 2023/044 (2023). https://eprint.iacr.org/2023/044

26. Kiayias, A., Tang, Q.: How to keep a secret: leakage deterring public-key cryptosystems. In: Sadeghi, A., Gligor, V.D., Yung, M. (eds.) 2013 ACM SIGSAC Conference on Computer and Communications Security, CCS 2013, Berlin, Germany, 4–8 November 2013. pp. 943–954. ACM (2013). https://doi.org/10.1145/2508859.2516691

27. Mangipudi, E.V., Lu, D., Kate, A.: Collusion-deterrent threshold information escrow. IACR Cryptol. ePrint Arch, p. 95 (2021). https://eprint.iacr.org/2021/095

28. Pagh, R., Rodler, F.F.: Cuckoo hashing. J. Algorithms **51**(2), 122–144 (2004). https://doi.org/10.1016/j.jalgor.2003.12.002

29. Puddu, I., Lain, D., Schneider, M., Tretiakova, E., Matetic, S., Capkun, S.: Teevil: identity lease via trusted execution environments. CoRR abs/1903.00449 (2019). https://arxiv.org/1903.00449
30. Shamir, A.: How to share a secret. Commun. ACM **22**(11), 612–613 (1979). https://doi.org/10.1145/359168.359176
31. Young, A.L., Yung, M.: Cryptovirology: Extortion-based security threats and countermeasures. In: 1996 IEEE Symposium on Security and Privacy, 6–8 May 1996, Oakland, CA, USA, pp. 129–140. IEEE Computer Society (1996). https://doi.org/10.1109/SECPRI.1996.502676

Extractors: Low Entropy Requirements Colliding with Non-malleability

Divesh Aggarwal[1](✉)(iD), Eldon Chung[2](iD), and Maciej Obremski[1](iD)

[1] National University of Singapore, Singapore, Singapore
`divesh@comp.nus.edu.sg`
[2] Centre for Quantum Technologies, Singapore, Singapore
`eldon.chung@u.nus.edu`

Abstract. Two-source extractors are deterministic functions that, given two independent weak sources of randomness, output a (close to) uniformly random string of bits. Cheraghchi and Guruswami (TCC 2015) introduced two-source non-malleable extractors that combine the properties of randomness extraction with tamper resilience. Two-source non-malleable extractors have since then attracted a lot of attention, and have very quickly become fundamental objects in cryptosystems involving communication channels that cannot be fully trusted. Various applications of two-source non-malleable extractors include in particular non-malleable codes, non-malleable commitments, non-malleable secret sharing, network extraction, and privacy amplification with tamperable memory.

The best known constructions of two-source non-malleable extractors are due to Chattopadhyay, Goyal, and Li (STOC 2016), Li (STOC 2017), and Li (CCC 2019). All of these constructions require both sources to have min-entropy at least $0.99n$, where n is the bit-length of each source.

In this work, we introduce collision-resistant randomness extractors. This allows us to design a compiler that, given a two-source non-malleable extractor, and a collision-resistant extractor, outputs a two-source non-malleable extractor that inherits the non-malleability property from the non-malleable extractor, and the entropy requirement from the collision-resistant extractor. Nested application of this compiler leads to a dramatic improvement of the state-of-the-art mentioned above. We obtain a construction of a two-source non-malleable extractor where one source is required to have min-entropy greater than $0.8n$, and the other source is required to have only polylog(n) min-entropy. Moreover, the other parameters of our construction, i.e., the output length, and the error remain comparable to prior constructions.

Keywords: Two-Source Non-Malleable Extractors · Privacy Amplification

1 Introduction

Two-source Extractors. The problem of constructing efficient two-source extractors for low min-entropy sources with negligible error has been an important

© International Association for Cryptologic Research 2023
H. Handschuh and A. Lysyanskaya (Eds.): CRYPTO 2023, LNCS 14082, pp. 580–610, 2023.
https://doi.org/10.1007/978-3-031-38545-2_19

focus of research in pseudorandomness for more than 30 years, with fundamental connections to combinatorics and many applications in computer science. The first non-trivial construction was given by Chor and Goldreich [16] who showed that the inner product function is a low-error two-source extractor for n-bit sources with min-entropy $(1/2 + \gamma)n$, where $\gamma > 0$ is an arbitrarily small constant. A standard application of the probabilistic method shows that (inefficient) low-error two-source extractors exist for polylogarithmic min-entropy. While several attempts were made to improve the construction of [16] to allow for sources with smaller min-entropy, the major breakthrough results were obtained after almost two decades. Raz [38] gave an explicit low-error two-source extractor where one of the sources must have min-entropy $(1/2 + \gamma)n$ for an arbitrarily small constant $\gamma > 0$, while the other source is allowed to have logarithmic min-entropy. In an incomparable result, Bourgain [11] gave an explicit low-error two-source extractor for sources with min-entropy $(1/2 - \gamma)n$, where $\gamma > 0$ is a small constant. An improved analysis by Lewko [29] shows that Bourgain's extractor can handle sources with min-entropy $4n/9$.

(Seeded) Non-malleable Extractors. The problem of privacy amplification against active adversaries was first considered by Maurer and Wolf [35]. In a breakthrough result, Dodis and Wichs [22] introduced the notion of seeded non-malleable extractors as a natural tool towards achieving a privacy amplification protocol in a minimal number of rounds, and with minimal entropy loss. Roughly speaking, the output of a seeded non-malleable extractor with a uniformly random seed Y, and a source X with some min-entropy independent of Y, should look uniformly random to an adversary who can tamper the seed, and obtain the output of the non-malleable extractor on a tampered seed.

More precisely, we require that

$$\mathbf{nmExt}(X, Y), \mathbf{nmExt}(X, g(Y)), Y \approx_\varepsilon U_m, \mathbf{nmExt}(X, g(Y)), Y \,,$$

where X and Y are independent sources with X having sufficient min-entropy and Y uniformly random, g is an arbitrary tampering function with no fixed points, U_m is uniform over $\{0, 1\}^m$ and independent of X, Y, and $\approx_\varepsilon$ denotes the fact that the two distributions are ε-close in statistical distance (for small ε).

Prior works have also studied seeded extractors with weaker non-malleability guarantees such as look-ahead extractors [22] or affine-malleable extractors [4], and used these to construct privacy amplification protocols.

Non-malleable Two-Source Extractors. A natural strengthening of both seeded non-malleable extractors, and two-source extractors are two-source *non-malleable* extractors. Two-source non-malleable extractors were introduced by Cheraghchi and Guruswami [15]. Roughly speaking, a function $\mathbf{2NMExt}$: $\{0, 1\}^n \times \{0, 1\}^n \to \{0, 1\}^m$ is said to be a non-malleable extractor if the output of the extractor remains close to uniform (in statistical distance), even conditioned on the output of the extractor inputs correlated with the original sources. In other words, we require that

$$\mathbf{2NMExt}(X,Y), \mathbf{2NMExt}(f(X), g(Y)), Y \approx_\varepsilon U_m, \mathbf{2NMExt}(f(X), g(Y)), Y .$$

where X and Y are independent sources with enough min-entropy, f, g are arbitrary tampering functions such that one of f, g has no fixed points.

The original motivation for studying efficient two-source non-malleable extractors stems from the fact that they directly yield explicit split-state non-malleable codes [24] (provided the extractor also supports efficient preimage sampling).

The first constructions of non-malleable codes [3,23] relied heavily on the (limited) non-malleability of the inner-product two-source extractor. Subsequent improved constructions of non-malleable codes in the split-state model relied on both the inner-product two-source extractor [2,6], and on more sophisticated constructions of the two-source non-malleable extractors [12,32,33]. Soon after they were introduced, non-malleable extractors have found other applications such as non-malleable secret sharing [1,25].

Connections, and State-of-the-Art Constructions. As one might expect, the various notions of extractors mentioned above are closely connected to each other. Li [30] obtained the first connection between seeded non-malleable extractors and two-source extractors based on inner products. This result shows that an improvement of Bourgain's result would immediately lead to better seeded non-malleable extractors, and a novel construction of seeded non-malleable extractors with a small enough min-entropy requirement and a small enough seed size would immediately lead to two-source extractors that only require small min-entropy. However, [30] could only obtain seeded non-malleable extractors for entropy rate above $1/2$.

In yet another breakthrough result, [12] obtained a sophisticated construction of seeded non-malleable extractors for polylogarithmic min-entropy. Additionally, they showed that similar techniques can also be used to obtain two-source non-malleable extractors. This immediately led to improved privacy amplification protocols and improved constructions of non-malleable codes in the split-state model. Building on this result, in a groundbreaking work, Chattopadhyay and Zuckerman [14] gave a construction of two-source extractors with polylogarithmic min-entropy and polynomiallly small error. All of these results have subsequently been improved in [10,17,31–33]. We summarize the parameters of the best known constructions of seeded extractors, two-source extractors, seeded non-malleable extractors, and two-source non-malleable extractors alongside those of our construction in Table 1. We note here that all prior constructions of two-source non-malleable extractors required both sources to have almost full min-entropy. A recent result [27] has not been included in this table since it constructs a weaker variant of a non-malleable two-source extractor (that does not fulfil the standard definition) that is sufficient for their application to network extraction. Even if one is willing to relax the definition to that in [27], the final parameters of our two-source non-malleable extractor are better!

The research over the past few years has shown that non-malleable two-source extractors, seeded non-malleable extractors, two-source extractors, non-malleable codes, and privacy amplification protocols are strongly connected to each other in the sense that improved construction of one of these objects has led to improvements in the construction of others. Some results have made these connections formal by transforming a construction of one object into a construction of another object. For instance, in addition to the connections already mentioned, Ben-Aroya et al. [9] adapt the approach of [14] to show explicit *seeded* non-malleable extractors with improved seed length lead to explicit low-error two-source extractors for low min-entropy.

Also, [7] showed that some improvement in the parameters of non-malleable two-source extractor constructions from [12,32,33] leads to explicit low-error two-source extractors for min-entropy δn with a very small constant $\delta > 0$.

Table 1. In the table, we assume that the left source has length n, and γ is a very small universal constant that has a different value for different results. Most of the constructions two-source non-malleable extractors including ours allow for t-time tampering at the cost of a higher min-entropy requirement. In particular (as described in Remark 1, 2, and 3), for our extractor we require the left source to have min-entropy rate $\mathrm{polylog}(n)/n$, and the right source has min-entropy rate $(1 - \frac{1}{2t+3})$.

Citation	Left Rate	Right Rate	Non-malleability
Seeded			
[39] Theorem 1	$\mathrm{polylog}(n)/n$	1	None
[28] Theorem 4.17	$\log(n)/n$	1	None
Seeded, Non-malleable			
[30]	$1/2 - \gamma$	1	Right source
[18]	$1/2 + \gamma$	1	Right source
[20] Theorem 1.4	$1/2 + \gamma$	1	Right source
[12]	$\log^2 n/n$	1	Right-source
[32] Theorem 6.2	$\log(n)/n$	1	Right source
[33]	$\log(n)/n$	1	Right-source
Two-source			
[16]	$1/2$	$1/2$	None
[11]	$1/2 - \gamma$	$1/2 - \gamma$	None
[38]	$\log(n)/n$	$1/2 + \gamma$	None
Two-source, Non-malleable			
[12]	$1 - \frac{1}{n^\gamma}$	$1 - \frac{1}{n^\gamma}$	Two-sided
[32]	$(1 - \gamma)$	$(1 - \gamma)$	Two-sided
[33] Theorem 1.11	$(1 - \gamma)$	$(1 - \gamma)$	Two-sided
This Work	$\mathrm{polylog}(n)/n$	$4/5 + \gamma$	Two-sided

Parameters for each extractor were chosen such that the error is $2^{-\kappa^c}$ and the output length is $\Omega(\kappa)$ for some constant c, where κ is the amount of entropy in the left source.

Best of all Worlds. Notice that the seeded non-malleable extractor, and the two-source extractors can be seen as special case of a two-source non-malleable extractor. With this view, the known constructions of negligible error (non-malleable) two-source extractors can be broadly classified in three categories:

- Constructions where one source has min-entropy rate about 1/2, the other source can have small min-entropy rate, but the extractor doesn't guarantee non-malleability.
- Constructions where one source is uniform, and the other can have small min-entropy rate, and the extractor guarantees non-malleability when the uniform source is tampered.
- Constructions where both sources have entropy rate very close to 1 and the extractor guarantees non-malleability against the tampering of both sources.

The main focus of this work is the question whether we can have one construction that subsumes all the above constructions.

Question 1. Is there an explicit construction of a two-source non-malleable extractor which requires two sources of length n_1 and n_2, and min-entropy requirement cn_1 (for some constant $c < 1$), and $\text{poly} \log n_2$, respectively, that guarantees non-malleability against the tampering of both sources, and for which the error is negligible? In particular, can we obtain a construction with parameters suitable for application to privacy amplification with tamperable memory [7]?

In this work, we make progress towards answering this question.

Applications of Two-Source Non-malleable Extractors. Two-source non-malleable extractors have in the recent years attracted a lot of attention, and have very quickly become fundamental objects in cryptosystems involving communication channels that cannot be fully trusted. As we discussed earlier, two-source non-malleable extractors have applications in the construction of non-malleable codes, and in constructing two-source extractors. The other primary applications of two-source non-malleable extractors include non-malleable secret sharing [1,25], non-malleable commitments [26], network extractors [27], and privacy amplification [7,13].

In particular, in [7], the authors introduce an extension of privacy amplification (PA) against active adversaries where, Eve as the active adversary is additionally allowed to *fully corrupt* the internal memory of one of the honest parties, Alice and Bob, before the execution of the protocol. Their construction required two-source non-malleable extractors with one source having a small entropy rate δ (where δ is a constant close to 0). Since no prior construction of two-source non-malleable extractor satisfied these requirements, the authors constructed such extractors under computational assumptions and left the construction of the information-theoretic extractor with the desired parameters as an open problem. Our construction in this work resolves this open problem. We do not include here the details of the PA protocol due to space constraints. We refer the reader to [7] for the PA protocol.

Subsequent Work. Li, inspired by our work and that of [27], in [34] gives a two-source non-malleable extractor construction with $\frac{2}{3}$-rate entropy in one source and $\frac{\log(n)}{n}$-rate entropy in the other. Based on the proof sketch in [34], the key idea of the construction and proof seems similar, the fundamental difference being the use of an correlation breaker with advice instead of a collision resistant extractor.

Our Contributions and Roadmap of the Paper. We build two-source non-malleable extractors, with one source having polylogarithmic min-entropy, and the other source having min-entropy rate 0.81. We introduce collision-resistant extractors, and extend and improve efficiency of the privacy amplification protocol from [7]. The following is a roadmap of the paper.

- In Sect. 2, we give an overview of our technical details.
- In Sect. 3, we give mathematical preliminaries needed in the paper.
- In Sect. 4, we give a generic transformation that, takes in (1) a non-malleable two-source extractor which requires sources with high min-entropy, and (2) a two-source extractor which requires sources with smaller min-entropy and an additional collision-resistance property, and constructs a two-source non-malleable extractor with min-entropy requirement comparable to (but slightly worse) that of the two-source extractor used by the construction.
- In Sect. 5.1, we give a generic transformation that converts any seeded extractor (two-source extractor where one of the source is uniformly distributed) to a collision-resistant seeded extractor with essentially the same parameters.
- In Sect. 5.2, we show that the two-source extractor from [38] is collision resistant.
- In Sect. 6, we apply our generic transformation from Sect. 5.1 to the seeded extractor from [39] to obtain a collision-resistant seeded extractor. We then use the generic transformation from Sect. 4 along with the non-malleable extractor from [33] to obtain a two-source non-malleable extractor, where one of the source is uniform and the other has min-entropy polylogarithmic in the length of the sources.
- In Sect. 7, we apply the generic transformation from Sect. 4 to the non-malleable extractor from Sect. 6, and the two-source extractor from [38] to obtain a two-source non-malleable extractor where one source is required to have polylogarithmic min-entropy and the source is required to have min-entropy rate greater than 0.8.
- In Sect. 8, we use a generic transformation from [5] to obtain a non-malleable two-source extractor where the length of the output is $1/2 - o(1)$ times the length of the input. Notice that via the probabilistic method, it can be shown that the output length of this construction is optimal.[1]

---

[1] The main drawback of this construction compared to the construction from Sect. 7 is that this is not a strong two-source non-malleable extractor, and hence cannot be used in most applications.

2   Technical Overview

2.1   Collision Resistant Extractors

At the core of our non-malleable extractor compiler is a new object we call a *collision resistant extractor*. An extractor is an object that takes as input two sources of randomness X and Y (in case of the seeded extractors Y but uniform) and guarantees that, as long as X and Y are independent and have sufficient min-entropy, the output $\mathsf{ext}(X, Y)$ will be uniform (even given Y^2). A *collision resistant extractor* $\mathbf{C}$ has the added property that for all fixed-point-free functions f (i.e. $f(x) \neq x$ for all x) the probability that $\mathbf{C}(X, Y) = \mathbf{C}(f(X), Y)$ is negligible[3].

Readers might notice the resemblance to the collision resistant hashing families and the leftover hash lemma. The leftover hash lemma states that if the probability that $h(x_0, Y) = h(x_1, Y)$ is sufficiently small then $h(., .)$ is an extractor. Obremski and Skorski ([37]) showed that the inverse is almost true — there exists a 'core' of inputs on which every extractor has to fulfill the small collision probability property. This inverse leftover hash lemma is sadly not constructive and not efficient (the description of the core might be exponential), and thus we are unable to use it to obtain an efficient *collision resistant extractor*.

We show that Raz's extractor ([38]) is a *collision resistant extractor* with essentially the same parameters. We obtain this result by carefully modifying the original proof. The proof techniques are similar and we do not discuss the details in this section.

We also show a generic transform that turns any seeded extractor (a two-source extractor where one source is uniform) into a *collision resistant extractor* with a slight increase in the size of the seed.

General Compiler for Seeded Extractors. We first construct a collision-resistant extractor h with a short output based on the Nisan-Widgerson generator [36] or Trevisan's extractor [39]. Given the input X and the seed Z, function h will output $\hat{X}(Z_1) \circ \hat{X}(Z_2) \circ \cdots \circ \hat{X}(Z_t)$ where EC is an error-correcting code of appropriate minimum distance, and $a \circ b$ denotes the concatenation of a and b, $\hat{X} = \mathsf{EC}(X)$, and $Z = Z_1 \circ Z_2 \circ \cdots \circ Z_t$, and $\hat{X}(Z_i)$ denotes Z_i-th bit of $\hat{X}$. Proof that this is an extractor follows directly from Nisan-Widgerson generator properties, while the collision resistance follows from the large distance of the error-correcting code.

We can now use any seeded extractor and the collision resistant extractor mentioned above to obtain a collision resistant seeded extractor with output size comparable to the seeded extractor. Consider seeded extractors that take as input a random source X and a short but uniform source S and output

---

[2] This property is often referred to as strong extraction.

[3] This notion might somewhat resemble various non-malleability notions, however in case of the non-malleability one would expect $\mathbf{C}(f(X), Y)$ to be independent of $\mathbf{C}(X, Y)$, here we only expect that those two outputs don't collide.

$\mathsf{ext}(X, S)$ which is uniform (even given S (See footnote 2)). Let us require on input a slightly longer uniform seed $S \circ Z$ (where $\circ$ denotes concatenation), and consider the following extractor: $\mathbf{C}(X, S \circ Z) = \mathsf{ext}(X, S) \circ h(X, Z)$, where h is either a collision resistant hash function or a collision resistant extractor.

The proof follows quite easily. Function h ensures that collisions indeed happen with negligible probability, the only thing left to show is that $\mathbf{C}(X, S \circ Z)$ is uniform. First notice that by the definition the seeded extractor $\mathsf{ext}(X, S)$ is uniform, so we only have to show that $h(X, Z)$ is uniform even given $\mathsf{ext}(X, S)$. Observe that Z is uniform and independent given X, S, so it suffices to show that X has some remaining entropy given $\mathsf{ext}(X, S), S$, then $h(X, Z)$ will be uniform (either by leftover hash lemma, if h is a collision resistant hash function, or by the definition of collision resistant extractor). This last step can be ensured simply by setting ext to extract fewer bits than the entropy of X, thus a slight penalty in the parameters. Also notice that h above can be a fairly bad extractor in terms of the rate or the output size and seed size. We can make the output and the seed of h very small and thus the parameters of $\mathbf{C}$ will be dominated by the parameters of ext.

2.2 Our Non-malleable Extractor Compiler

Our compiler takes as an input two objects, one is a collision resistant extractor (as discussed in the previous section), the other object is a strong two-source non-malleable extractor. A right-strong[4] non-malleable extractor gives the guarantee that $\mathsf{ext}(X, Y)$ is uniform even given $\mathsf{ext}(f(X), g(Y))$ and Y (or X in case of a left-strong non-malleable extractor) for any tampering functions f, g where at least one of them are fixed-point-free. When we refer to a non-malleable extractor as strong without specifying if it's left-strong or right-strong we mean that the non-malleable extractor is both left-strong and right-strong. The construction is as follows: For a collision resistant extractor $\mathbf{C}$, and a strong non-malleable extractor $\mathbf{E}$ we consider following extractor:

$$\mathbf{2NMExt}(X, Y_\ell \circ Y_r) := \mathbf{E}(Y_\ell \circ Y_r, \mathbf{C}(X, Y_\ell)). \tag{1}$$

We will show that $\mathbf{2NMExt}$ inherits the best of both worlds — strong non-malleability of $\mathbf{E}$ and the good entropy requirements of $\mathbf{C}$.

There are two main issues to handle:

Issue of the Independent Tampering. Notice that the definition of the non-malleable extractor guarantees that $\mathsf{ext}(X, Y)$ is uniform given $\mathsf{ext}(X', Y')$ only if the sources are tampered independently (i.e. X' is a function of only X, and Y' is a function of only Y).

To leverage the non-malleability of $\mathbf{E}$, we need to ensure that the tampering $X \to X'$ and $Y_\ell \circ Y_r \to Y'_\ell \circ Y'_r$ translates to the independent tampering of $Y_\ell \circ$

---

[4] Notice that unlike many results in the literature, we need to distinguish between left strong and right strong for our extractor since the construction is inherently not symmetric.

$Y_r \to Y'_\ell \circ Y'_r$ and $\mathbf{C}(X, Y_\ell) \to \mathbf{C}(X', Y'_\ell)$. The problem is that both tamperings depend on Y_ℓ. To alleviate this issue we will simply reveal Y_ℓ and Y'_ℓ (notice that Y'_ℓ can depend on Y_r thus revealing Y_ℓ alone is not sufficient). Once $Y_\ell = y_\ell$ and $Y'_\ell = y'_\ell$ are revealed (and therefore fixed) the tampering $y_\ell \circ Y_r \to y'_\ell \circ Y'_r$ and $\mathbf{C}(X, y_\ell) \to \mathbf{C}(X', y'_\ell)$ becomes independent since right tampering depends only on X, which is independent of $Y_\ell \circ Y_r$ and remains independent of Y_r even after we reveal Y_ℓ and Y'_ℓ (this extra information only lowers the entropy of Y_r).

Issue of the Fixed Points (or Why We Need Collision Resistance). Non-malleable extractors guarantee that $\mathtt{ext}(X, Y)$ is uniform given $\mathtt{ext}(X', Y')$ if and only if $(X, Y) \neq (X', Y')$.

The issue in our compiler is clear: If $Y_\ell \circ Y_r$ do not change, and X is tampered to be $X' \neq X$ but $\mathbf{C}(X', Y_\ell) = \mathbf{C}(X, Y_\ell)$ then

$$\begin{aligned} \mathbf{2NMExt}(X, Y_\ell \circ Y_r) &= \mathbf{E}(Y_\ell \circ Y_r, \mathbf{C}(X, Y_\ell)) \\ &= \mathbf{E}(Y_\ell \circ Y_r, \mathbf{C}(X', Y_\ell)) = \mathbf{2NMExt}(X', Y_\ell \circ Y_r) \ . \end{aligned}$$

To mitigate this problem, we require $\mathbf{C}$ to be collision resistant, which means the probability that $\mathbf{C}(X, Y_\ell) = \mathbf{C}(X', Y_\ell)$ is negligible thereby resolving this issue. It is also possible to use $\mathbf{C}$ without the collision resilience property, this gives a weaker notion of non-malleable extractor as was done in [27].

Is $\mathbf{2NMExt}$ *strong?* Here we briefly argue that if $\mathbf{E}$ is strong (i.e. both left and right strong) then $\mathbf{2NMExt}$ will also be strong. To argue that compiled extractor is left-strong, we notice that revealing X on top of Y_ℓ and Y'_ℓ (which we had to reveal to maintain independence of tampering) translates to revealing $\mathbf{C}(X, Y_\ell)$ which reveals right input of $\mathbf{E}$ (revealing of Y_ℓ and Y'_ℓ is irrelevant since Y_r maintains high enough entropy). As for the right-strongness, revealing Y_r on top of Y_ℓ and Y'_ℓ translates to revealing of the left input of $\mathbf{E}$, notice that $\mathbf{C}(X, Y_\ell)$ remains uniform given Y_ℓ by the strong extraction property of $\mathbf{C}$.

For our construction, we will apply the compiler twice. First, we will use a collision resistant seeded extractor and the Li's extractor [33]. This gives us a strong non-malleable extractor $\mathbf{FNMExt}$ for the first source with poly-logarithmic entropy, and the second source being uniform. We will refer to this object as a *fully non-malleable seeded extractor.* We emphasize that this object is stronger than the seeded non-malleable extractor since it guarantees non-malleability for both sources. Then, we will then apply our compiler to Raz's extractor [38] and $\mathbf{FNMExt}$ which will produce an extractor $\mathbf{nmRaz}$ that is a strong non-malleable extractor for the first source with poly-logarithmic entropy and the second source with entropy rate[5] 0.8.

Compiling Seeded Extractor with Li's Extractor. In this section we will apply our compiler to the collision resistant seeded extractor $\mathbf{crTre}$ and strong non-malleable extractor $\mathbf{Li}$ from [33], yielding the following construction:

$$\mathbf{FNMExt}(X, Y_\ell \circ Y_r) = \mathbf{Li}(Y_\ell \circ Y_r, \mathbf{crTre}(X, Y_\ell)). \tag{2}$$

---

[5] Entropy rate is a ratio of min-entropy of the random variable to its length: $\frac{H_\infty(X)}{|X|}$.

The extractor $\mathbf{Li}(0.99, 0.99)$ requires both sources to have a high entropy rate of $99\%^6$, while the extractor $\mathbf{crTre}(\text{poly-log}, \text{uniform})$ requires first source to have poly-logarithmic entropy, and the second source to be uniform. Let us analyse the entropy requirements of the extractor $\mathbf{FNMExt}$: Since part of the construction is $\mathbf{crTre}(X, Y_\ell)$ we require Y_ℓ to be uniform, which means that whole $Y_\ell \circ Y_r$ has to be uniform. On the other hand X has to only have a poly-logarithmic entropy. The output of $\mathbf{crTre}(X, Y_\ell)$ will be uniform which will fulfill the 0.99 entropy rate requirement of $\mathbf{Li}$. There is a small caveat: While $Y_\ell \circ Y_r$ is uniform one has to remember that we had to reveal Y_ℓ and Y'_ℓ to ensure independent tampering, therefore we only have to make sure that Y_ℓ is very short so $Y_\ell \circ Y_r$ will have over 0.99 entropy rate even given Y_ℓ and Y'_ℓ. This is possible since $\mathbf{crTre}$ requires only a very short seed length. Thus we get that $\mathbf{FNMExt}(\text{poly-log}, \text{uniform})$ requires first source to have poly-logarithmic entropy, while the second source is uniform, and non-malleability is guaranteed for both sources.

Compiling Raz's Extractor with the Above. Now we will compile Raz's extractor [38] with above obtained $\mathbf{FNMExt}$. The result will be:

$$\mathbf{nmRaz}(X, Y_\ell \circ Y_r) = \mathbf{FNMExt}(Y_\ell \circ Y_r, \mathbf{Raz}(X, Y_\ell)). \tag{3}$$

As we discussed above $\mathbf{FNMExt}(\text{poly-log}, \text{uniform})$ requires first source to have poly-logarithmic entropy, while the second source has to be uniform, $\mathbf{Raz}(\text{poly-log}, 0.5)$ requires first source to have poly-logarithmic entropy while the second source has to have over 0.5 entropy rate. Therefore we require Y_ℓ to have an entropy rate above 0.5 and it is sufficient if X has poly-logarithmic entropy. As for requirements enforced by $\mathbf{FNMExt}$, since the output of $\mathbf{Raz}$ will be uniform we only have check if $Y_\ell \circ Y_r$ has poly-logarithmic entropy given Y_ℓ and Y'_ℓ. Given that Y'_ℓ can not lower the entropy of Y_r by more than its size $|Y'_\ell|$ we have two equations:

$$H_\infty(Y_r) > |Y_\ell|$$
$$H_\infty(Y_\ell) > 0.5|Y_\ell|$$

which implies

$$H_\infty(Y_\ell \circ Y_r) > 2|Y_\ell|$$
$$H_\infty(Y_\ell \circ Y_r) > |Y_r| + 0.5|Y_\ell|$$

which asserts that $\frac{H_\infty(Y_\ell \circ Y_r)}{|Y_\ell \circ Y_r|} > 0.8$. Therefore $\mathbf{nmRaz}(\text{poly-log}, 0.8)$ requires first source to have poly-logarithmic entropy, while second source has to have entropy rate above 0.8.

Finally notice that $\mathbf{Raz}$ has a relatively short output (shorter than both inputs) but that is not a problem since $\mathbf{FNMExt}$ can have its first input much

---

^{6} This is a simplification, formally speaking there exist a constant δ such that sources are required to have entropy rate above $1 - \delta$. The reader may think of $\delta = 0.01$.

longer than the second input. We can adjust the output size of **crTre** to accommodate the input size requirements of **Li** (this extractor requires both inputs to have the same length). We stress however that taking into consideration all inputs requirements both in terms of entropy and in terms of sizes is not trivial and our construction is tuned towards seeded-extractors and the Raz's extractor.

3   Preliminaries

3.1   Random Variables, Statistical Distance and Entropy

For any set S, we denote by U_S the uniform distribution over the set S. For any positive integer m, we shorthand $U_{\{0,1\}^m}$ by U_m. For any random variable X, we denote the support of X by $\mathbf{supp}(X)$. Also, for any random variable X and event E, we denote by $X|_E$ the random variable X' such that for all $x \in \mathbf{supp}(X)$, $\Pr[X' = x] = \Pr[X = x|E]$.

Definition 1 (Statistical Distance). *Let $X, Y \in S$ be random variables. The statistical distance between X and Y is defined by*

$$\Delta(X;Y) := \frac{1}{2} \sum_{a \in S} |\Pr[X = a] - \Pr[Y = a]|$$

or equivalently,

$$\Delta(X;Y) := \max_{A \subseteq S} |\Pr[X \in S] - \Pr[Y \in S]|.$$

We shorthand the statement $\Delta(X;Y) \le \varepsilon$ by $X \approx_\varepsilon Y$ and we sometimes write this as X is ε-close to Y.

For any random variables A, B, C, and event E, we shorthand $\Delta(A, C; B, C)$ by $\Delta(A; B\,|C)$, and $\Delta(A|_E; B|_E)$ by $\Delta(A; B\,|E)$ i.e.,

$$\Delta(A; B\,|C) = \Delta(A, C; B, C)\ ,$$

and

$$\Delta(A; B\,|E) = \Delta(A|_E; B|_E)\ .$$

The following lemma is immediate from the definitions and triangle inequality.

Lemma 1. *Let A, B, C be random variables such that $A, B \in S$ and $\mathbf{supp}(C) = T$ with $T = T_1 \cup T_2, T_1 \cap T_2 = \emptyset$. Then:*

1. $\Delta(A; B\,|C) \le \sum_{c \in T} \Pr[C = c]\Delta(A; B\,|C = c)$
2. $\Delta(A; B\,|C) \le \Pr[C \in T_1]\Delta(A; B\,|C \in T_1) + \Pr[C \in T_2]\Delta(A; B\,|C \in T_2)$

We will need the following standard lemmas.

Lemma 2 (Lemma 10 of [2]). *Let* $X_1, \ldots, X_m$ *be binary random variables and for any non-empty* $\tau \subseteq [m]$, $|\Pr[\bigoplus_{i \in \tau} X_i = 0] - \frac{1}{2}| \leq \varepsilon$, *then* $\Delta(X_1, \ldots, X_m; U_m) \leq \varepsilon \cdot 2^{\frac{m}{2}}$.

Lemma 3. *Let* X, Y *be random variables. Further let* f_I *be a family of functions* f *indexed by set* I *and let* S *be a random variable supported on* I *that is independent of both* X *and* Y. *Then* f_S *can be thought of as a randomised function such that* $f_S(x) = f_s(x)$ *with probability* $\Pr[S = s]$.
Then it holds that:

$$\Delta(f_S(X); f_S(Y)) \leq \Delta(X; Y).$$

Lemma 4 (Lemma 4 of [19], Lemma 9 of [2]). *Let* A, B *be independent random variables and consider a sequence* $V_1, \ldots, V_i$ *of random variables, where for some function* ϕ, $V_i = \phi_i(C_i) = \phi(V_1, \ldots, V_{i-1}, C_i)$ *with each* $C_i \in \{A, B\}$. *Then* A *and* B *are independent conditioned on* $V_1, \ldots, V_i$. *That is,* $I(A; B | V_1, \ldots, V_i) = 0$.

Definition 2. *Call a sequence of variables* $Z_1, \ldots, Z_N$ (k, ε)*-biased against linear tests if for any non-empty* $\tau \subseteq [N]$ *such that* $|\tau| \leq k$, $|\Pr[\bigoplus_{i \in \tau} Z_i = 0] - \frac{1}{2}| \leq \varepsilon$.

Lemma 5 (Theorem 2 of [8]). *Let* $N = 2^t - 1$ *and let* k *be an odd integer. Then it is possible to construct* N *random variables* Z_i *with* $i \in [N]$ *which are* (k, ε)*-biased against linear tests using a seed of size at most* $2\lceil \log(1/\varepsilon) + \log \log N + \log k \rceil + 1$ *bits.*

3.2 Min-Entropy

Definition 3 (Min-entropy). *Given a distribution* X *over* $\mathcal{X}$, *the* min-entropy *of* X, *denoted by* $H_\infty(X)$, *is defined as*

$$H_\infty(X) = -\log\left(\max_{x \in \mathcal{X}} \Pr[X = x]\right).$$

Definition 4 (Average min-entropy). *Given distributions* X *and* Z, *the* average min-entropy *of* X *given* Z, *denoted by* $\tilde{H}_\infty(X|Z)$, *is defined as*

$$\tilde{H}_\infty(X|Z) = -\log\left(\mathbb{E}_{z \leftarrow Z}\left[\max_{x \in \mathcal{X}} \Pr[X = x | Z = z]\right]\right).$$

Lemma 6 ([21]). *Given arbitrary distributions* X *and* Z *such that* $|\mathsf{supp}(Z)| \leq 2^\lambda$, *we have*
$$\tilde{H}_\infty(X|Z) \geq H_\infty(X, Z) - \lambda \geq H_\infty(X) - \lambda.$$

Lemma 7 ([35]). *For arbitrary distributions* X *and* Z, *it holds that*

$$\Pr_{z \leftarrow Z}[H_\infty(X|Z = z) \geq \tilde{H}_\infty(X|Z) - s] \geq 1 - 2^{-s}.$$

Definition 5 ((n,k)-sources). *We say that a random variable X is an (n,k)-source if $\text{supp}(X) \subseteq \{0,1\}^n$ and $H_\infty(X) \geq k$. Additionally, we say that X is a flat (n,k)-source if for any $a \in \text{supp}(X)$, $\Pr[X = a] = 2^{-k}$, i.e., X is uniform over its support.*

$X \sim (n,k)$ denotes the fact that X is an (n,k)-source. Further, we call X (n,k)-flat if $X \sim (n,k)$ and is flat. We say that X is ε-close to a flat distribution if there exists a set S such that $X \approx_\varepsilon U_S$.

Definition 6 (ε-smooth min-entropy). *A random variable X is said to have ε-smooth min-entropy at least k if there exists Y such that $\Delta(X;Y) \leq \varepsilon$, and*

$$H_\infty(Y) \geq k \,.$$

3.3   Extractors

Definition 7 ((Strong) Two-Source Extractor, Collision Resistance). *Call $E : \{0,1\}^{n_1} \times \{0,1\}^{n_2} \to \{0,1\}^m$ a two-source extractor for input lengths n_1, n_2, min-entropy k_1, k_2, output length m, and error ε if for any two independent sources X, Y with $X \sim (n_1, k_1)$, $Y \sim (n_2, k_2)$, the following holds:*

$$\Delta(E(X,Y); U_m) \leq \varepsilon$$

If $n_2 = k_2$, we call such an extractor seeded. We use $E : [(n_1, k_1), (n_2, k_2) \mapsto m \sim \varepsilon]$ to denote the fact that E is such an extractor.
Additionally, we call the extractor E right strong, if:

$$\Delta(E(X,Y); U_m \,|\, Y) \leq \varepsilon \,,$$

and we call the extractor E left strong, if:

$$\Delta(E(X,Y); U_m \,|\, X) \leq \varepsilon \,.$$

We call an extractor E strong if it is both left strong and right strong.
The extractor is said to be $\varepsilon_{Collision}$-collision resistant if $\Pr_{X,Y}[E(X,Y) = E(f(X), Y)] \leq \varepsilon_{Collision}$ for all fixed-point-free functions f.

Definition 8 (Two Source Non-malleable Extractor). *Call $E : [(n_1, k_1), (n_2, k_2) \mapsto m \sim \varepsilon]$ a two source non-malleable extractor if additionally for any pair of functions $f : \{0,1\}^{n_1} \to \{0,1\}^{n_1}$, $g : \{0,1\}^{n_2} \to \{0,1\}^{n_2}$ such at least one of f, g is fixed-point-free[7], the following holds:*

$$\Delta(E(X,Y); U_m \,|\, E(f(X), g(Y))) \leq \varepsilon$$

Additionally, we call the extractor E a right strong non-malleable two-source extractor if:

$$\Delta(E(X,Y); U_m \,|\, E(f(X), g(Y)), Y) \leq \varepsilon \,,$$

and we call the extractor E a left strong non-malleable two-source extractor if:

$$\Delta(E(X,Y); U_m \,|\, E(f(X), g(Y)), X) \leq \varepsilon \,,$$

---

[7] A function f is said to be fixed-point-free if for any x, $f(x) \neq x$.

Definition 9 ((Fully) Non-malleable Seeded Extractor). *Call* E : $[(n_1, k_1), (n_2, n_2) \mapsto m \sim \varepsilon]$ *a non-malleable seeded extractor if additionally for some fixed-point-free function* $g : \{0,1\}^{n_2} \to \{0,1\}^{n_2}$, *the following holds:*

$$\Delta\left(E(X,Y); U_m \mid E(X, g(Y))\right) \leq \varepsilon$$

A natural strengthening of a non-malleable seeded extractor is to consider a pair of tampering functions on both its inputs rather than on just the seed. Thus call a E *a fully non-malleable seeded extractor if additionally for some pair of fixed-point-free functions* $g : \{0,1\}^{n_2} \to \{0,1\}^{n_2}$, *and* $f : \{0,1\}^{n_1} \to \{0,1\}^{n_1}$, *the following holds:*

$$\Delta\left(E(X,Y); U_m \mid E(f(X), g(Y))\right) \leq \varepsilon .$$

One useful thing to note is that the extractor remains non-malleable even if the functions f, g are randomised with shared coins (independent of X and Y).

Lemma 8. *Let* E *be a two source non-malleable extractor for* (n, k)-*sources* X, Y *with output length* m *and error* ε. *Let* f_S, g_S *random functions over the shared randomness of* S *independent of* X *and* Y *such that for all* $s \in \mathbf{supp}(S)$, *at at least one of* f_s *or* g_s *is fixed-point-free. Then*

$$\Delta\left(E(X,Y); U_m \mid E(f_S(X), g_S(Y))\right) \leq \varepsilon .$$

Proof. Deferred to the full version on arXiv.

Lemma 9. *If* $\mathsf{ext} : [(n, k), (d, d) \mapsto m \sim \varepsilon]$ *is a strong seeded extractor, then for any* X, W *such that* $\mathbf{supp}(X) \subseteq \{0,1\}^n$ *and* $\tilde{H}_\infty(X|W) \geq k + \log(1/\eta)$ *with* $\eta > 0$, *it holds that*

$$\Delta\left(\mathsf{ext}(X, U_d); U_m \mid U_d, W\right) \leq \varepsilon + \eta .$$

Proof. Deferred to the full version on arXiv.

We will need the following constructions of extractors.

Lemma 10 (Theorem 6.9 of [33]). *There exists a constant* $0 < \gamma < 1$ *and an explicit two-source non-malleable extractor* $\mathbf{Li} : [(n, (1-\gamma)n), (n, (1-\gamma)n) \mapsto \Omega(n) \sim \varepsilon_L]$ *such that* $\varepsilon_L = 2^{-\Omega(n \frac{\log \log n}{\log n})}$.

Lemma 11 (Theorem 2 of [39]). *For every* n, k *there exists an explicit strong seeded extractor* $\mathbf{Tre} : [(n, k), (d, d) \mapsto \Omega(k) \sim \varepsilon]$ *such that* $d = O(\log^2(n) \log(1/\varepsilon))$.

Lemma 12 (Theorem 1 of [38]). *For any* n_1, n_2, k_1, k_2, m *and any* $0 < \delta < \frac{1}{2}$ *such that:*

1. $k_1 \geq 5 \log(n_2 - k_2)$
2. $n_2 \geq 6 \log n_2 + 2 \log n_1$,

3. $k_2 \geq (\frac{1}{2} + \delta) \cdot n_2 + 3 \log n_2 + \log n_1$,
4. $m = \Omega(\min\{n_2, k_1\})$,

there exists a strong two-source extractor **Raz** $: [(n_1, k_1), (n_2, k_2) \mapsto m \sim \varepsilon]$, such that $\varepsilon = 2^{-\frac{3m}{2}}$.

Rejection Sampling for Extractors. In this section we present two lemmas that use rejection sampling to lower the entropy requirement for strong two-source extractors and their collision resistance.

We first define a sampling algorithm $\mathtt{samp}$ that given a flat distribution $Y' \sim (n, k)$, tries to approximate some distribution $Y \sim (n, k - \delta)$ (with $supp(Y) \subseteq supp(Y')$). Letting $d = \max_{y \in supp(Y)} \left\{ \frac{\Pr[Y=y]}{\Pr[Y'=y]} \right\}$:

$$\mathtt{samp}(y) = \begin{cases} y, & w.p. \ \frac{\Pr[Y=y]}{d \cdot \Pr[Y'=y]} \\ \perp, & else \end{cases}$$

Lemma 13. The probability $\mathtt{samp}(Y') = y$ is $\frac{\Pr[Y=y]}{d}$ and furthermore, the probability that $\mathtt{samp}(Y') \neq \perp$ is $\frac{1}{d}$. Consequently, the distribution $\mathtt{samp}(Y')$ conditioned on the event that $\mathtt{samp}(Y') \neq \perp$ is identical to Y.

Proof. Letting $\mathtt{samp}$ and d be defined as above, then:

$$\Pr[\mathtt{samp}(Y') = y] = \frac{1}{d} \frac{\Pr[Y = y]}{\Pr[Y' = y]} \cdot \Pr[Y' = y] = \frac{\Pr[Y = y]}{d}$$

Then it follows that:

$$\Pr[\mathtt{samp}(Y') \neq \perp] = \sum_y \Pr[\mathtt{samp}(Y) = y] = \sum_y \frac{\Pr[Y = y]}{d} = \frac{1}{d}$$

Thus, conditioned on the event that $\mathtt{samp}(Y') \neq \perp$, $\mathtt{samp}(Y')$ is the distribution Y.

$$\Pr[\mathtt{samp}(Y') = y | \mathtt{samp}(Y') \neq \perp] = \frac{\Pr[\mathtt{samp}(Y') \neq \perp | \mathtt{samp}(Y') = y] \Pr[\mathtt{samp}(Y') = y]}{\Pr[\mathtt{samp}(Y') \neq \perp]}$$

$$= \Pr[Y = y]$$

$\square$

Lowering the Entropy Requirement for Strong Two-Source Extractors.

Lemma 14. Let $\mathtt{ext} : [(n_1, k_1), (n_2, k_2) \mapsto m \sim \varepsilon]$ be a strong two-source extractor using input distributions X and Y'. Then letting $Y \sim (n_2, k_2 - \delta)$:

$$\Delta \left(\mathtt{ext}(X, Y); U_m | Y \right) \leq 2^\delta \varepsilon$$

Proof. Assume by contradiction that there exists a distribution $Y \sim (n, k-\delta)$ for which $\Delta(\texttt{ext}(X,Y); U_m | Y) > 2^\delta \varepsilon$, i.e. there exists a distinguisher $A : \{0,1\}^m \to \{0,1\}$ such that $|\Pr[A(\texttt{ext}(X,Y),Y) = 1] - \Pr[A(U_m,Y) = 1]| > 2^\delta \varepsilon$. We want to use this fact to create a distinguisher D that distinguishes $\texttt{ext}(X,Y')$ from U_m *for some distribution* $Y' \sim (n,k)$. Note that Y can be expressed as a convex combination of $(n, k - \delta)$ flat distributions, i.e. $Y = \sum_i \alpha_i Y_i$. We define Y' in the following way: Y' is a convex combination of flat distributions Y_i' where each Y_i' is some (n,k) flat distribution such that $supp(Y_i) \subseteq supp(Y_i')$. We first note that for all $y \in supp(Y)$:

$$\frac{Pr[Y = y]}{Pr[Y' = y]} = \frac{\sum_i \alpha_i Pr[Y_i = y]}{\sum_i \alpha_i Pr[Y_i' = y]} \le \frac{2^{-k+\delta}}{2^{-k}} \le 2^\delta$$

Furthermore, note that Y' has min-entropy k. To see this, note that for any $y \in supp(Y)$:

$$\Pr[Y' = y] = \sum_i \alpha_i \Pr[Y_i' = y] \le \sum_i \alpha_i 2^{-k} \le 2^{-k}$$

Let $\texttt{samp}$ be a rejection sampler that on input distribution Y, samples for Y'. Now, D is defined as follows:

$$D(Z, Y') = \begin{cases} A(Z, Y') & \text{, if } \texttt{samp}(Y') \ne \bot \\ 1 & \text{, } w.p. \; \frac{1}{2}, \text{ if } \texttt{samp}(Y') = \bot \\ 0 & \text{, } else \end{cases}$$

Note that by Lemma 13, $\Pr[\texttt{samp}(Y') \ne \bot] \ge \frac{1}{2^\delta}$ and $\texttt{samp}(Y')$ is identical to Y conditioned on the event that $\texttt{samp}(Y') = \bot$. Then the advantage that D distinguishes between $\texttt{ext}(X,Y')$ and U_m given Y' is given as:

$$|\Pr[D(\texttt{ext}(X,Y'),Y') = 1] - \Pr[D(U_m,Y') = 1]|$$
$$\ge \Pr[\texttt{samp}(Y) \ne \bot] |\Pr[A(\texttt{ext}(X,Y),Y) = 1] - \Pr[A(U_m,Y) = 1]|$$
$$> \frac{1}{2^\delta} 2^\delta \varepsilon = \varepsilon$$

Which in turn implies that $\Delta(\texttt{ext}(X,Y'); U_m | Y') > \varepsilon$, which implies the desired contradiction.

Lowering the Entropy Requirement for Collision Resistance in Extractors.

Lemma 15. *Let* $\texttt{ext} : [(n_1, k_1), (n_2, k_2) \mapsto m \sim \varepsilon]$ *be a strong two-source extractor using input distributions* X *and* Y' *that has collision probability* $\varepsilon_{Collision}$. *Then letting* $Y \sim (n_2, k_2 - \delta)$ *and* f *be any fixed-point-free function:*

$$\Pr[\texttt{ext}(X,Y) = \texttt{ext}(f(X),Y)] \le 2^\delta \varepsilon_{Collision}$$

Proof. For the sake of contradiction, Y be any $(n, k - \delta)$ distribution for which the collision probability is at least $2^\delta \cdot \varepsilon_{Collision}$.

Note that Y can be expressed as a convex combination of $(n, k - \delta)$ flat distributions, i.e. $Y = \sum_i \alpha_i Y_i$. We define Y' in the following way: Y' is a convex combination of flat distributions Y_i' where each Y_i' is some (n, k) flat distribution such that $supp(Y_i) \subseteq supp(Y_i')$. We first note that for all $y \in supp(Y)$:

$$\frac{Pr[Y = y]}{Pr[Y' = y]} = \frac{\sum_i \alpha_i Pr[Y_i = y]}{\sum_i \alpha_i Pr[Y_i' = y]}$$
$$\leq \frac{2^{-k+\delta}}{2^{-k}} \leq 2^\delta$$

Furthermore, note that Y' has min-entropy k. To see this, note that for any $y \in supp(Y)$:

$$Pr[Y' = y] = \sum_i \alpha_i Pr[Y_i' = y] \leq \sum_i \alpha_i 2^{-k} \leq 2^{-k}$$

Let `samp` be a rejection sampler that on input distribution Y', samples for Y. By the collision resilience property of `ext`, it follows that:

$$\varepsilon_{Collision} \geq Pr[\text{ext}(X, Y') = \text{ext}(f(X), Y')]$$
$$\geq Pr[\text{ext}(X, Y) = \text{ext}(f(X), Y) | \text{samp}(Y) \neq \bot] \, Pr[\text{samp}(Y) \neq \bot]$$
$$= Pr[\text{ext}(X, Y) = \text{ext}(f(X), Y)] 2^{-\delta}$$

$\square$

4   A Generic Construction of a Two-Source Non-malleable Extractor

In this section we present a generic construction that transforms a non-malleable two-source extractor $\mathbf{E}$ into another non-malleable two-source extractor with a much smaller entropy rate requirement via a two-source extractor.

Theorem 1. *For any integers* $n_1, n_2, n_3, n_4, k_1, k_2, k_3, k_4, m$ *and* $\delta_\mathbf{E}, \delta_\mathbf{C}$, $\varepsilon_{Collision} > 0$, $n_4 < n_1$, *given an efficient construction of*

- *a strong non-malleable extractor* $\mathbf{E} : [(n_1, k_1), (n_2, k_2) \mapsto m \sim \delta_\mathbf{E}]$,
- *a right strong two-source extractor* $\mathbf{C} : [(n_3, k_3), (n_4, k_4) \mapsto n_2 \sim \delta_\mathbf{C}]$ *that is* $\varepsilon_{Collision}$-*collision resistant,*

then for any integers $k_1^*, k_2^*, \varepsilon, \tau > 0$ *that satisfy the following conditions, there is an efficient construction of a left and right strong non-malleable two-source extractor* $\mathbf{2NMExt} : [(n_3, k_1^*), (n_1, k_2^*) \mapsto m \sim \varepsilon]$.

$$k_1^* \geq k_3 \,,$$

$$k_2^* \geq \log 1/\tau + \max\left(k_4 + (n_1 - n_4), k_1 + 2n_4\right) \, ,$$

and

$$\varepsilon \leq 3\tau + 3\delta_{\mathbf{E}} + 2\delta_{\mathbf{C}} + 2\sqrt{\varepsilon_{Collision}} \, .$$

Proof. Our construction is as follows: Given inputs $x \in \{0,1\}^{n_3}$ and $y = y_\ell \circ y_r$, where $y_\ell \in \{0,1\}^{n_4}$, and $y_r \in \{0,1\}^{n_1 - n_4}$ our extractor is defined as:

$$\mathbf{2NMExt}(x, y) := \mathbf{E}(y_\ell \circ y_r, \mathbf{C}(x, y_\ell)) \, . \tag{4}$$

Let $f : \{0,1\}^{n_3} \to \{0,1\}^{n_3}$ and $g : \{0,1\}^{n_1} \to \{0,1\}^{n_1}$. For any $y \in \{0,1\}^{n_1}$, by $g(y)_\ell$ we denote the n_4 bit prefix of $g(y)$. We assume that f does not have any fixed points. The proof for the case when g not having any fixed points is similar (in fact, simpler) as we explain later.

Right Strongness. We first prove that our non-malleable extractor is right strong.

Claim. Let $\widetilde{Y}$ be a random variable with min-entropy $k_2^* - \log 1/\tau$ and is independent of X. Consider the randomized function $T_{f,g}$ that given a, b, c, samples $\mathbf{C}(f(X), c)$ conditioned on $\mathbf{C}(X, b) = a$, i.e.,

$$T_{f,g} : a, b, c \mapsto \mathbf{C}(f(X), c)_{|\mathbf{C}(X,b)=a} \, .$$

Then:

$$\Delta \left(\begin{matrix} \mathbf{C}(X, \widetilde{Y}_\ell) & U_d \\ \mathbf{E}(\widetilde{Y}_\ell \circ \widetilde{Y}_r, \mathbf{C}(X, \widetilde{Y}_\ell)) \; ; & \mathbf{E}(\widetilde{Y}_\ell \circ \widetilde{Y}_r, U_d) \\ \mathbf{E}(g(\widetilde{Y}), \mathbf{C}(f(X), g(\widetilde{Y})_\ell)) & \mathbf{E}(g(\widetilde{Y}), T_{f,g}(U_d, \widetilde{Y}_\ell, g(\widetilde{Y})_\ell)) \end{matrix} \; \middle| \begin{matrix} \widetilde{Y}_r \\ \widetilde{Y}_\ell \\ g(\widetilde{Y})_\ell \end{matrix} \right) \leq \delta_{\mathbf{C}} \, . \tag{5}$$

Proof. We have that $H_\infty(X) \geq k_1^* \geq k_3$ and $H_\infty(\widetilde{Y}_\ell) \geq k_2^* - \log 1/\tau - |\widetilde{Y}_r| = k_2^* - \log 1/\tau - (n_1 - n_4) \geq k_4$, and $X, \widetilde{Y}_\ell$ are independently distributed. It follows that $\Delta\left(\mathbf{C}(X, \widetilde{Y}_\ell); U_d \middle| \widetilde{Y}_\ell\right) \leq \delta_{\mathbf{C}}$. Then, Lemma 3 implies that

$$\Delta\left(\mathbf{C}(X, \widetilde{Y}_\ell); U_d \middle| \widetilde{Y}_\ell, \widetilde{Y}_r, g(\widetilde{Y})_\ell\right) \leq \delta_{\mathbf{C}} \, .$$

Observing that since $\widetilde{Y}_r$ is independent of $\mathbf{C}(f(X), g(\widetilde{Y})_\ell), \mathbf{C}(X, \widetilde{Y}_\ell)$ given $\widetilde{Y}_\ell, g(\widetilde{Y})_\ell$, we have that the tuple $\mathbf{C}(X, \widetilde{Y}_\ell), \widetilde{Y}_\ell, \widetilde{Y}_r, T_{f,g}(\mathbf{C}(X, \widetilde{Y}_\ell), \widetilde{Y}_\ell, g(\widetilde{Y})_\ell)$ is identically distributed as $\mathbf{C}(X, \widetilde{Y}_\ell), \widetilde{Y}_\ell, \widetilde{Y}_r, \mathbf{C}(f(X), g(\widetilde{Y})_\ell)$. Again applying Lemma 3, we get the desired statement. $\square$

Now, let $\mathcal{Y}_0$ be the set of y such that $g(y)_\ell = y_\ell$, and $\mathcal{Y}_1$ be the set of all y such that $g(y)_\ell \neq y_\ell$ (in other words, $\mathcal{Y}_0$ contains all the fixed-points of g, and $\mathcal{Y}_1$ is the complement set). Also, let $\mathcal{Y}_{0,0}$ be the set of all $y \in \mathcal{Y}_0$ such that $\Pr[\mathbf{C}(X, y_\ell) = \mathbf{C}(f(X), y_\ell)] \leq \sqrt{\varepsilon_{Collision}}$, and $\mathcal{Y}_{0,1} = \mathcal{Y}_0 \setminus \mathcal{Y}_{0,0}$.

Claim. If $\Pr[Y \in \mathcal{Y}_1] \geq \tau$, then

$$\Delta\left(\begin{array}{cc} \mathbf{E}(\widetilde{Y}_\ell \circ \widetilde{Y}_r, \mathbf{C}(X, \widetilde{Y}_\ell)) & U_m \\ \mathbf{E}(g(\widetilde{Y}), \mathbf{C}(f(X), g(\widetilde{Y})_\ell)) & \mathbf{E}(g(\widetilde{Y}), \mathbf{C}(f(X), g(\widetilde{Y})_\ell)) \end{array} \middle| \begin{array}{c} \widetilde{Y}_\ell \\ \widetilde{Y}_r \end{array}\right) \leq \delta_{\mathbf{C}} + \delta_{\mathbf{E}}, \quad (6)$$

where $\widetilde{Y} = Y|_{Y \in \mathcal{Y}_1}$.

Proof. Notice that conditioned on Y being in $\mathcal{Y}_1$, g does not have a fixed point. Thus, since U_{n_2} is independent of $\widetilde{Y}_r$ given $\widetilde{Y}_\ell, g(\widetilde{Y})_\ell$, and $H_\infty(U_{n_2}) = n_2 \geq k_2$, $H_\infty(\widetilde{Y}_r | \widetilde{Y}_\ell, g(\widetilde{Y}_r)) \geq k_2^* - \log 1/\tau - 2n_4 \geq k_1$, by the definition of a strong non-malleable extractor, we have that

$$\Delta\left(\begin{array}{cc} \mathbf{E}(\widetilde{Y}_\ell \circ \widetilde{Y}_r, U_{n_2}) & U_m \\ \mathbf{E}(g(\widetilde{Y}), T_{f,g}(U_{n_2}, \widetilde{Y}_\ell, g(\widetilde{Y})_\ell)) & \mathbf{E}(g(\widetilde{Y}), T_{f,g}(U_{n_2}, \widetilde{Y}_\ell, g(\widetilde{Y})_\ell)) \end{array} \middle| \begin{array}{c} \widetilde{Y}_\ell \\ \widetilde{Y}_r \end{array}\right) \leq \delta_{\mathbf{E}}.$$

Furthermore, from Claim 4 and Lemma 3, we get that

$$\Delta\left(\begin{array}{cc} \mathbf{E}(\widetilde{Y}_\ell \circ \widetilde{Y}_r, U_{n_2}) & \mathbf{E}(\widetilde{Y}_\ell \circ \widetilde{Y}_r, \mathbf{C}(X, \widetilde{Y}_\ell)) \\ \mathbf{E}(g(\widetilde{Y}), T_{f,g}(U_{n_2}, \widetilde{Y}_\ell, g(\widetilde{Y})_\ell)) & \mathbf{E}(g(\widetilde{Y}), \mathbf{C}(f(X), g(\widetilde{Y})_\ell)) \end{array} \middle| \begin{array}{c} \widetilde{Y}_\ell \\ \widetilde{Y}_r \end{array}\right) \leq \delta_{\mathbf{C}}.$$

The desired statement follows from triangle inequality. $\qquad\square$

Similarly, we prove the following claim.

Claim. If $\Pr[Y \in \mathcal{Y}_{0,0}] \geq \tau$, then

$$\Delta\left(\begin{array}{cc} \mathbf{E}(\widetilde{Y}_\ell \circ \widetilde{Y}_r, \mathbf{C}(X, \widetilde{Y}_\ell)) & U_m \\ \mathbf{E}(g(\widetilde{Y}), \mathbf{C}(f(X), g(\widetilde{Y})_\ell)), & \mathbf{E}(g(\widetilde{Y}), \mathbf{C}(f(X), g(\widetilde{Y})_\ell)) \end{array} \middle| \begin{array}{c} \widetilde{Y}_\ell \\ \widetilde{Y}_r \end{array}\right) \leq \delta_{\mathbf{E}} + 2\delta_{\mathbf{C}} + \sqrt{\varepsilon_{Collision}},$$

$$(7)$$

where $\widetilde{Y} = Y|_{Y \in \mathcal{Y}_{0,0}}$.

Proof. Notice that the probability that $\mathbf{C}(X, \widetilde{Y}) = \mathbf{C}(f(X), g(\widetilde{Y})_\ell)$ is at most $\sqrt{\varepsilon_{Collision}}$. Thus, by Claim 4, the probability that $U_{n_2} = T_{f,g}(U_{n_2}, \widetilde{Y}_\ell, g(\widetilde{Y})_\ell)$ is at most $\sqrt{\varepsilon_{Collision}} + \delta_{\mathbf{C}}$. Also, since U_{n_2} is independent of $\widetilde{Y}_r$ given $\widetilde{Y}_\ell, g(\widetilde{Y})_\ell$, and $H_\infty(U_{n_2}) = n_2 \geq k_2$, $H_\infty(\widetilde{Y}_r | \widetilde{Y}_\ell, g(\widetilde{Y}_r)) \geq k^* - \log 1/\tau - 2n_4 \geq k_2$, by the definition of a strong non-malleable extractor, we have that

$$\Delta\left(\begin{array}{cc} \mathbf{E}(\widetilde{Y}_\ell \circ \widetilde{Y}_r, U_{n_2}) & U_m \\ \mathbf{E}(g(\widetilde{Y}), T_{f,g}(U_{n_2}, \widetilde{Y}_\ell, g(\widetilde{Y})_\ell)) & \mathbf{E}(g(\widetilde{Y}), T_{f,g}(U_{n_2}, \widetilde{Y}_\ell, g(\widetilde{Y})_\ell)) \end{array} \middle| \begin{array}{c} \widetilde{Y}_\ell \\ \widetilde{Y}_r \end{array}\right) \leq \begin{array}{c} \delta_{\mathbf{E}} + \\ \delta_{\mathbf{C}} + \\ \sqrt{\varepsilon_{Collision}} \end{array}.$$

Furthermore, from Claim 4 and Lemma 3, we get that

$$\Delta\left(\begin{array}{cc} \mathbf{E}(\widetilde{Y}_\ell \circ \widetilde{Y}_r, U_{n_2}) & \mathbf{E}(\widetilde{Y}_\ell \circ \widetilde{Y}_r, \mathbf{C}(X, \widetilde{Y}_\ell)) \\ \mathbf{E}(g(\widetilde{Y}), T_{f,g}(U_{n_2}, \widetilde{Y}_\ell, g(\widetilde{Y})_\ell)) & \mathbf{E}(g(\widetilde{Y}), \mathbf{C}(f(X), g(\widetilde{Y})_\ell)) \end{array} \middle| \begin{array}{c} \widetilde{Y}_\ell \\ \widetilde{Y}_r \end{array}\right) \leq \delta_{\mathbf{C}}.$$

The desired statement follows from triangle inequality. $\qquad\square$

We now show that $Y \in \mathcal{Y}_{0,1}$ with small probability.

Claim.
$$\Pr[Y \in \mathcal{Y}_{0,1}] \leq \tau + \sqrt{\varepsilon_{Collision}} \, .$$

Proof. If $\Pr[Y \in \mathcal{Y}_0] < \tau$, then the statement trivially holds. So, we assume $\Pr[Y \in \mathcal{Y}_0] \geq \tau$. Let $\widetilde{Y} = Y|_{Y \in \mathcal{Y}_0}$ Then $H_\infty(\widetilde{Y}) \geq k_2^* - \log 1/\tau - (n_1 - n_4) \geq k_4$. Since $\mathbf{C}$ is collision-resistant, we have that

$$\varepsilon_{Collision} \geq \Pr[\mathbf{C}(X, \widetilde{Y}_\ell) = \mathbf{C}(f(X), g(\widetilde{Y})_\ell)] \Pr[\widetilde{Y} \in \mathcal{Y}_{0,1}] \cdot \sqrt{\varepsilon_{Collision}}$$
$$\geq \Pr[Y \in \mathcal{Y}_{0,1}] \cdot \sqrt{\varepsilon_{Collision}} \, .$$
$\square$

We now conclude the proof of right strongness of our non-malleable extractor as follows. We shorthand $\mathbf{2NMExt}(X,Y), Y, \mathbf{2NMExt}(f(X), g(Y))$ by $\phi(X,Y)$, and $U_m, Y, \mathbf{2NMExt}(f(X), g(Y))$ by $\psi(X,Y)$.

$$\Delta\left(\phi(X,Y); \psi(X,Y)\right) \leq \Pr[Y \in \mathcal{Y}_{0,1}] + \Pr[Y \in \mathcal{Y}_1] \cdot \Delta\left(\phi(X,Y)|_{Y \in \mathcal{Y}_1}; \psi(X,Y)|_{Y \in \mathcal{Y}_1}\right)$$
$$+ \Pr[Y \in \mathcal{Y}_{0,0}] \cdot \Delta\left(\phi(X,Y)|_{Y \in \mathcal{Y}_{0,0}}; \psi(X,Y)|_{Y \in \mathcal{Y}_{0,0}}\right)$$
$$\leq (\tau + \delta_\mathbf{E} + \delta_\mathbf{C}) + (\tau + 2\delta_\mathbf{E} + \delta_\mathbf{C} + \sqrt{\varepsilon_{Collision}}) + (\tau + \sqrt{\varepsilon_{Collision}})$$
$$= 3\tau + 3\delta_\mathbf{E} + 2\delta_\mathbf{C} + 2\sqrt{\varepsilon_{Collision}} \, .$$

Note that we assumed that f does not have fixed points. On the other hand, if g does not have fixed points then a simpler proof works that does not need to partition the domain into $\mathcal{Y}_{0,0}, \mathcal{Y}_{0,1}, \mathcal{Y}_1$. Since the first source for the non-malleable extractor $\mathbf{E}$, we can conclude the statement similar to Claim 4 with Y instead of $\widetilde{Y}$.

Left Strongness. The proof of left strongness is nearly the same (the statistical distance statements include X instead of Y_r), but we include it here for completeness.

Claim. Let $\widetilde{Y}$ be a random variable with min-entropy $k^* - \log 1/\tau$ and is independent of X. Consider the randomized function S that given a, b, samples X conditioned on $\mathbf{C}(X, b) = a$, i.e.,

$$S : a, b \mapsto X|_{\mathbf{C}(X,b)=a} \, .$$

Then:

$$\Delta\left(\begin{matrix} \mathbf{C}(X, \widetilde{Y}_\ell), & U_d, \\ X & S(U_{n_2}, \widetilde{Y}_\ell) \end{matrix} \, \middle| \, \begin{matrix} \widetilde{Y}_\ell \\ \widetilde{Y}_r \end{matrix} \right) \leq \delta_\mathbf{C} \, . \tag{8}$$

Proof. We have that $H_\infty(X) \geq k_1^* \geq k_3$ and $H_\infty(\widetilde{Y}_\ell) \geq k_2^* - \log 1/\tau - |\widetilde{Y}_r| = k_2^* - \log 1/\tau - (n_1 - n_4) \geq k_4$, and $X, \widetilde{Y}_\ell$ are independently distributed. It follows that $\Delta\left(\mathbf{C}(X, \widetilde{Y}_\ell); U_d \middle| \widetilde{Y}_\ell\right) \leq \delta_\mathbf{C}$. Then, using Lemma 3 and observing that since $\widetilde{Y}_r$ is independent of X given $\widetilde{Y}_\ell$, we have that $\mathbf{C}(X, \widetilde{Y}_\ell), \widetilde{Y}_\ell, \widetilde{Y}_r, S(\mathbf{C}(X, \widetilde{Y}_\ell), \widetilde{Y}_\ell)$ is identically distributed as $\mathbf{C}(X, \widetilde{Y}_\ell), \widetilde{Y}_\ell, \widetilde{Y}_r, X$, we get the desired statement. $\square$

Now, let $\mathcal{Y}_0$ be the set of y such that $g(y)_\ell = y_\ell$, and $\mathcal{Y}_1$ be the set of all y such that $g(y)_\ell \neq y_\ell$. Also, let $\mathcal{Y}_{0,0}$ be the set of all $y \in \mathcal{Y}_0$ such that $\Pr[C(X, y_\ell) = C(f(X), y_\ell)] \leq \sqrt{\varepsilon_{Collision}}$, and $\mathcal{Y}_{0,1} = \mathcal{Y}_0 \setminus \mathcal{Y}_{0,0}$.

Claim. If $\Pr[Y \in \mathcal{Y}_1] \geq \tau$, then

$$\Delta \left(\mathbf{E}(\widetilde{Y}_\ell \circ \widetilde{Y}_r, \mathbf{C}(X, \widetilde{Y}_\ell)) ; U_m \left| \begin{array}{c} \widetilde{Y}_\ell \\ g(\widetilde{Y})_\ell \\ X \\ \mathbf{E}(g(\widetilde{Y}), \mathbf{C}(f(X), g(\widetilde{Y})_\ell)) \end{array} \right. \right) \leq 2\delta_{\mathbf{C}} + \delta_{\mathbf{E}} , \quad (9)$$

where $\widetilde{Y} = Y|_{Y \in \mathcal{Y}_1}$.

Proof. Notice that conditioned on Y being in $\mathcal{Y}_1$, g does not have a fixed point. Thus, since U_{n_2} is independent of $\widetilde{Y}_r$ given $\widetilde{Y}_\ell, g(\widetilde{Y})_\ell$, and $H_\infty(U_{n_2}) = n_2 \geq k_2$, $H_\infty(\widetilde{Y}_r | \widetilde{Y}_\ell, g(\widetilde{Y})) \geq k^* - \log 1/\tau - 2n_4 \geq k_1$, by the definition of a strong non-malleable extractor, we have that

$$\Delta \left(\mathbf{E}(\widetilde{Y}_\ell \circ \widetilde{Y}_r, U_{n_2}) ; U_m \left| U_{n_2}, \mathbf{E}(g(\widetilde{Y}), \mathbf{C}(f(S(U_{n_2}, \widetilde{Y}_\ell)), g(\widetilde{Y})_\ell)), \widetilde{Y}_\ell, g(\widetilde{Y})_\ell \right. \right) \leq \delta_{\mathbf{E}} ,$$

Furthermore, by applying Claim 4 and Lemma 3 twice, we get that

$$\Delta \left(\begin{array}{cc} U_m, S(U_{n_2}, \widetilde{Y}_\ell) & U_m, X \\ \mathbf{E}(g(\widetilde{Y}), \mathbf{C}(f(S(U_{n_2}, \widetilde{Y}_\ell)), g(\widetilde{Y})_\ell)) & \mathbf{E}(g(\widetilde{Y}), \mathbf{C}(f(X), g(\widetilde{Y})_\ell)) \end{array} \left| \begin{array}{c} \widetilde{Y}_\ell \\ g(\widetilde{Y})_\ell \end{array} \right. \right) \leq \delta_{\mathbf{C}} .$$

and

$$\Delta \left(\begin{array}{cc} \mathbf{E}(\widetilde{Y}_\ell \circ \widetilde{Y}_r, U_{n_2}), S(U_{n_2}, \widetilde{Y}_\ell) & \mathbf{E}(\widetilde{Y}_\ell \circ \widetilde{Y}_r, \mathbf{C}(X, \widetilde{Y}_\ell)), X \\ \mathbf{E}(g(\widetilde{Y}), \mathbf{C}(f(S(U_{n_2}, \widetilde{Y}_\ell)), g(\widetilde{Y})_\ell)) & \mathbf{E}(g(\widetilde{Y}), \mathbf{C}(f(X), g(\widetilde{Y})_\ell)) \end{array} \left| \begin{array}{c} \widetilde{Y}_\ell \\ g(\widetilde{Y})_\ell \end{array} \right. \right) \leq \delta_{\mathbf{C}} .$$

The desired statement follows from triangle inequality. $\square$

Similarly, we prove the following claim.

Claim. If $\Pr[Y \in \mathcal{Y}_{0,0}] \geq \tau$, then

$$\Delta \left(\mathbf{E}(\widetilde{Y}_\ell \circ \widetilde{Y}_r, \mathbf{C}(X, \widetilde{Y}_\ell)) ; U_m \left| \begin{array}{c} \widetilde{Y}_\ell \\ g(\widetilde{Y})_\ell \\ X \\ \mathbf{E}(g(\widetilde{Y}) \mathbf{C}(f(X), g(\widetilde{Y})_\ell)) \end{array} \right. \right) \leq \delta_{\mathbf{E}} + 3\delta_{\mathbf{C}} + \sqrt{\varepsilon_{Collision}} , \quad (10)$$

where $\widetilde{Y} = Y|_{Y \in \mathcal{Y}_{0,0}}$.

Proof. Notice that the probability that $\mathbf{C}(X, \widetilde{Y}) = \mathbf{C}(f(X), g(\widetilde{Y})_\ell)$ is at most $\sqrt{\varepsilon_{Collision}}$. Thus, by Claim 4, the probability that $U_{n_2} = \mathbf{C}(S(U_{n_2}, \widetilde{Y}_\ell), g(\widetilde{Y})_\ell)$ is at most $\sqrt{\varepsilon_{Collision}} + \delta_{\mathbf{C}}$. Also, since U_{n_2} is independent of $\widetilde{Y}_r$ given $\widetilde{Y}_\ell, g(\widetilde{Y})_\ell$, and $H_\infty(U_{n_2}) = n_2 \geq k_2$, $H_\infty(\widetilde{Y}_r | \widetilde{Y}_\ell, g(\widetilde{Y}_r)) \geq k^* - \log 1/\tau - 2n_4 \geq k_1$, by the definition of a strong non-malleable extractor, we have that

$$\Delta \left(\mathbf{E}(\widetilde{Y}_\ell \circ \widetilde{Y}_r, U_{n_2}) \, ; \, U_m \, \middle| \, \begin{matrix} U_{n_2} \\ \mathbf{E}(g(\widetilde{Y}), \mathbf{C}(f(S(U_{n_2}, \widetilde{Y}_\ell)), g(\widetilde{Y})_\ell)) \\ \widetilde{Y}_\ell \\ g(\widetilde{Y})_\ell \end{matrix} \right) \leq \delta_\mathbf{E} + \delta_\mathbf{C} + \sqrt{\varepsilon_{Collision}} \,.$$

Furthermore, by applying Claim 4 and Lemma 3 twice, we get that

$$\Delta \left(\begin{matrix} U_m & U_m \\ S(U_{n_2}, \widetilde{Y}_\ell) & X \\ \mathbf{E}(g(\widetilde{Y}), \mathbf{C}(f(S(U_{n_2}, \widetilde{Y}_\ell)), g(\widetilde{Y})_\ell)) & \mathbf{E}(g(\widetilde{Y}), \mathbf{C}(f(X), g(\widetilde{Y})_\ell)) \end{matrix} \, \middle| \, \widetilde{Y}_\ell, g(\widetilde{Y})_\ell \right) \leq \delta_\mathbf{C} \,.$$

and

$$\Delta \left(\begin{matrix} \mathbf{E}(\widetilde{Y}_\ell \circ \widetilde{Y}_r, U_{n_2}), S(U_{n_2}, \widetilde{Y}_\ell) & \mathbf{E}(\widetilde{Y}_\ell \circ \widetilde{Y}_r, \mathbf{C}(X, \widetilde{Y}_\ell)), X \\ \mathbf{E}(g(\widetilde{Y}), \mathbf{C}(f(S(U_{n_2}, \widetilde{Y}_\ell)), g(\widetilde{Y})_\ell)) & \mathbf{E}(g(\widetilde{Y}), \mathbf{C}(f(X), g(\widetilde{Y})_\ell)) \end{matrix} \, \middle| \, \begin{matrix} \widetilde{Y}_\ell \\ g(\widetilde{Y})_\ell \end{matrix} \right) \leq \delta_\mathbf{C} \,.$$

The desired statement follows from triangle inequality. □

We then conclude the proof of right strongness of our non-malleable extractor exactly as we obtained left strongness. □

Remark 1. We remark that one can apply the above compiler to multi-tampering non-malleable extractors as a **E**. Briefly speaking t-tampering non-malleable extractor guarantees that extraction output remains uniform even given not one but t tampering outputs:

$$\Delta \left(E(X, Y); U_m \, \middle| \, E(f_1(X), g_1(Y)), ..., E(f_t(X), g_t(Y)) \right) \leq \varepsilon.$$

As a result, compiled extractor will also be t-tamperable. The proof is almost identical, there are only two differences:

1. To ensure the reduction to split state tampering it is not sufficient to reveal $\widetilde{Y}_\ell$ and $g_1(\widetilde{Y})_\ell$, but also all other tamperings: $g_2(\widetilde{Y})_\ell, \ldots, g_t(\widetilde{Y})_\ell$. This will have an impact of the calculations of entropy requirement.
2. Notice that when considering the collision resistance adversary has now t chances instead of 1, but since the attempts are non-adaptive we can easily bound the collision probability by $t \cdot \varepsilon_{Collision}$, this impacts the error calculations.

5 Collision Resistance of Extractors

5.1 Generic Collision Resistance for Seeded Extractors

Lemma 16. *Let* $\mathsf{ext} : [(n, k), (d, d) \mapsto m \sim \varepsilon]$ *be a strong seeded extractor. Then there exists a strong seeded extractor* $\mathsf{crTre} : [(n, k), (d + z, d + z) \mapsto m - 2\log(1/\varepsilon_{Collision}) \sim \varepsilon + \varepsilon_T + \sqrt{\varepsilon_{Collision}}]$ *with collision probability* $\varepsilon_{Collision}$ *and* $z = O(\log(1/\varepsilon_{Collision}) \log^2(\log(1/\varepsilon_{Collision})) \log(1/\varepsilon_T))$.

Proof. We will first mention [39]'s construction of **Tre**. The aforementioned construction uses an error correcting code and a weak design, defined respectively as below:

Lemma 17 (Error Correcting Code, Lemma 35 of [39]). *For every $n \in \mathbb{N}$, and $\delta > 0$, there exists a code* $\mathsf{EC} : \{0,1\}^n \to \{0,1\}^{\hat{n}}$ *where $\hat{n} = poly(n, 1/\delta)$ such that for $x, x' \in \{0,1\}^n$ with $x \neq x'$, it is the case that $\mathsf{EC}(x)$ and $\mathsf{EC}(x')$ disagree in at least $(\frac{1}{2} - \delta)\hat{n}$ positions.*

Definition 10 (Weak Design, Definition 6 of [39]). *A family of sets $S_1, \ldots, S_m \subseteq [d]$ is a weak (ℓ, ρ)-design if:*

1. *For all i, $|S_i| = \ell$;*
2. *For all i,*

$$\sum_{j<i} 2^{|S_i \cap S_j|} \leq \rho \cdot (m-1).$$

In particular, any family of disjoint sets $S_1, \ldots, S_m \subseteq [d]$ with $|S_i| = \ell$ is trivially a weak design as well.

Extractor **Tre** operates in the following way: X is firstly evaluated on an error correcting code EC to obtain $\hat{X}$. Then viewing seed bits Z as $Z_1 \circ Z_2 \circ \ldots \circ Z_d$, then the ith bit of $\mathbf{Tre}(X, Z)$ is given as the $(Z_{|S_i})^{th}$ bit of $\hat{X}$ where $Z_{|S_i}$ is understood to specify an ℓ-bit index $Z_{j_1} \circ Z_{j_2} \circ \ldots \circ Z_{j_\ell}$ for $S_i = \{j_1, j_2, \ldots, j_\ell\}$. In short, the output is given as:

$$\mathbf{Tre}(X, Z) = \hat{X}(Z_{|S_1}) \circ \hat{X}(Z_{|S_2}) \circ \cdots \circ \hat{X}(Z_{|S_m}).$$

The modification is to truncate the output of $\mathsf{ext}(X, S)$ by $t = \frac{5}{2} \log(1/\varepsilon_{Collision})$ bits, and then treating Z as $\frac{4t}{5}$ blocks of $\ell = O(\log^2(t) \log(1/\varepsilon_T))$ many bits, we concatenate the output with $\frac{4t}{5}$ bits. In short, the output is given as:

$$\mathbf{crTre}(X, S \circ Z)_i = \begin{cases} \mathsf{ext}(X, S)_i & \text{, if } i \leq m - t \\ \hat{X}(Z_{i-(m-t)}) & \text{, if } i > m - t \end{cases}$$

where Z_j denotes the jth block of Z.

To show that **crTre** is indeed a strong extractor, note that S and Z are independent and furthermore by Lemma 6 $\tilde{H}_\infty(X | \mathsf{ext}(X, S), S) \geq k - m + t \geq t$. Instantiating **crTre** with a family of disjoint sets, an error correcting code EC with minimum distance $(\frac{1}{2} - \frac{\varepsilon_T}{4m})\hat{n}$ for inputs of min-entropy $(t, \frac{4t}{5})$ and seed length $O(\log(1/\varepsilon_{Collision}) \log^2(t) \log(1/\varepsilon_T))$, Lemma 9 implies that:

$$\Delta\left(\mathsf{ext}(X, S)\mathbf{Tre}(X, Z); \mathsf{ext}(X, S), U_{\Omega(t)} | S, Z\right) \leq \varepsilon_T + 2^{-\frac{t}{5}}$$

which in turn yields us:

$$\Delta\left(\mathsf{ext}(X, S) \circ \mathbf{Tre}(X, Z); U_{m-O(t)} | S, Z\right) \leq \varepsilon + \varepsilon_T + 2^{-\frac{t}{5}} = \varepsilon + \varepsilon_T + \sqrt{\varepsilon_{Collision}}$$

As for the collision probability, note that for any x and fixed-point-free function f:

$$\Pr[\mathbf{crTre}(x, S \circ Z) = \mathbf{crTre}(f(x), S \circ Z)] \leq \Pr\left[\forall i, \mathbf{EC}(x)(Z_i) = \mathbf{EC}(f(x))(Z_i)\right]$$

$$\leq \left(\frac{1}{2} + \frac{\varepsilon_T}{4m}\right)^{2\log(1/\varepsilon_{Collision})}$$

$$\leq \varepsilon_{Collision}$$

Since this bound holds for all possible values x, it follows that it holds for any random variable X as well. □

An instantiation that will suit our purpose will be to use Trevisan's extractor **Tre** as ext. Then for any n, k, we have $\mathbf{crTre} : [(n, k), (d, d) \mapsto \Omega(k) \sim 3\varepsilon_T]$ with $d = O(\log^2(n)\log(1/\varepsilon_T)) + O(\log(1/\varepsilon_T)\log^2(\log(1/\varepsilon_T))\log(1/\varepsilon_T)) = O(\log^2(n)\log^2(1/\varepsilon_T))$ such that $\varepsilon = \varepsilon_T$ andwith collision probability $\varepsilon_{Collision} = (\varepsilon_T)^2 < 2^{-\Omega(k)}$.

5.2 Collision Resistance of the Raz Extractor

Lemma 18. *For any n_1, n_2, k_1, k_2, m and any $0 < \delta < \frac{1}{2}$ such that:*

1. $k_1 \geq 12\log(n_2 - k_2) + 15$,
2. $n_2 \geq 6\log n_2 + 2\log n_1 + 4$,
3. $k_2 \geq (\frac{1}{2} + \delta) \cdot n_2 + 3\log n_2 + \log n_1 + 4$,
4. $m = \Omega(\min\{n_2, k_1\})$,

there exists a strong two-source extractor $\mathbf{Raz} : [(n_1, k_1), (n_2, k_2) \mapsto m \sim \varepsilon]$, *such that* $\varepsilon = 2^{-\frac{3m}{2}}$ *with collision probability* 2^{-m+1}.

Proof. Deferred to the full version on arXiv.

6 A Fully Non-malleable Seeded Extractor

In this section, we will use $\mathbf{crTre}$ as $\mathbf{C}$ and $\mathbf{Li}$ as $\mathbf{E}$ for Theorem 1 with the following instantiations:

1. $\mathbf{crTre}$ is an extractor given by $[(n_x, k_x), (s, s) \mapsto d \sim \varepsilon_T]$ for $s = O(\log^2(n_x)\log^2(1/\varepsilon_T))$, and $d = \Omega(k_x)$, with collision probability $\left(\frac{\varepsilon_T}{3}\right)^2$.
2. $\mathbf{Li}$ is an extractor given by $[(d, (1-\gamma)d), (d, (1-\gamma)d) \mapsto m \sim \varepsilon_L]$ for some constant γ, $m = \Omega(d)$, and $\varepsilon_L = 2^{-d\left(\frac{\log\log d}{\log d}\right)}$.

with $\varepsilon_{Collision} = 2^{-(k_x)^c}$ for some $c < \frac{1}{2}$. It follows that $s = o(d)$.

Theorem 2. *For any n_x, k_x, there exists a fully non-malleable seeded extractor* $\mathbf{FNMExt} : [(n_x, k_x), (s + d, s + d) \mapsto m \sim \varepsilon_{fnm}]$ *with* $m = \Omega(d)$, $d < k_x$, $s = O(\log^2(n_x)\log^2(\varepsilon_T))$, $\varepsilon_{fnm} < 10\varepsilon_T$ *with* $\varepsilon_T = 2^{-\left(\frac{k_x}{2}\right)^c}$ *for some* $c < \frac{1}{2}$.

Proof. It suffices to show that for our choice of parameters, the entropy requirements of **crTre** (from Lemma 16) and **Li** (from Lemma 10) are met for Theorem 1.

Setting input parameters $n_3 = n_x$, $k_1^* = k_x$, $n_4 = k_4 = s$, $k_2^* = s + d$, and extractor parameters $n_1 = n_2 = d$, $k_1 = k_2 = (1-\gamma)d$, $k_3 = k_x$, note that indeed $k_1^* \geq k_3$. Furthermore,

$$k_2^* = s + d = s + k_4 + n_1 - n_4$$
$$k_2^* = d + s \geq \left(\frac{\gamma}{2}\right)d + (1-\gamma)d + 2s .$$

And thus by our choice of s, $\varepsilon_{fnm} \leq 3 \cdot 2^{-(\frac{k_x}{2})^{2c}} + 7\varepsilon_T < 10\varepsilon_T$ with $\varepsilon_T = 2^{-(\frac{k_x}{2})^c}$ for some $c < \frac{1}{2}$.   □

It will also be useful in the subsequent subsection that we relax the entropy requirement of this extractor.

Theorem 3. *For any n_x, k_x, there exists a fully non-malleable seeded extractor* **FNMExt** : $[(n_x, k_x), (s + d, s + d - 1) \mapsto m \sim \varepsilon_{fnm}]$ *with* $m = \Omega(k_x)$, $d < k_x$, $s = O(\log^2(n_x)\log^2(\varepsilon_T))$, $\varepsilon_{fnm} < 12\varepsilon_T$ *with* $\varepsilon_T = 2^{-(\frac{k_x}{2})^c}$ *for some* $c < \frac{1}{2}$.

Proof. By Lemma 14 and Lemma 15, **crTre** can also be viewed as **crTre** : $[(n_x, k_x), (s, s - 1) \mapsto \Omega(k_x) \sim 2\varepsilon_T]$ with collision probability $2\varepsilon_{Collision} = 2\left(\frac{\varepsilon_T}{3}\right)^2 \leq \varepsilon_T^2$.

For a similar choice of parameters: $n_3 = n_x$, $k_1^* = k_x$, $n_4 = s$, $k_4 = s - 1$ $k_2^* = s + d$, and extractor parameters $n_1 = n_2 = d$, $k_1 = k_2 = (1-\gamma)d$, $k_3 = k_x$, note that indeed $k_1^* \geq k_3$. Furthermore,

$$k_2^* = s + d - 1 = s + s - 1 + d - s = s + k_4 + n_1 - n_4$$
$$k_2^* = s + d - 1 \geq \left(\frac{\gamma}{2}\right)d + (1-\gamma)d + 2s - 1$$

And thus by our choice of s, $\varepsilon_{fnm} \leq 3 \cdot 2^{-(\frac{k_x}{2})^{2c}} + 9\varepsilon_T < 12\varepsilon_T$ with $\varepsilon_T = 2^{-(\frac{k_x}{2})^c}$ for some $c < \frac{1}{2}$.   □

Remark 2. As we have already mentioned in the Remark 1, we can use t−tamperable extractor like [32]. As a result our **FNMExt** will be t-tamperable non-malleable extractor with negligible error. One only has to make sure that $|y_\ell| < \frac{\gamma \cdot n}{t+1}$, which follows from the first point in the Remark 1, where $(1-\gamma) \cdot n$ is the entropy requirement from [32] extractor. The error one obtains is therefore at least $2^{-\Omega(n/\log n)} + 2^{-\Omega(\frac{\gamma \cdot n}{t+1} - \log^2(n))} + t \cdot 2^{-\Omega(\frac{\gamma \cdot n}{t+1})} \geq 2^{-\Omega(n^c)}$, for $c < 1$ depending on t only. Please notice that the entropy requirements for this extractor do not change.

7 A Two-Source Non-malleable Extractor

In this section, we will use **Raz** as **C** and **FNMExt** as **E** from Theorem 3 with the following instantiations:

1. **Raz** : $[(n_x, k_x), (n_\ell, k_\ell) \mapsto d \sim 2^{-(1.5)d}]$ with $d = \Omega(\min\{k_x, k_\ell\})$ and collision probability 2^{-d+1}.
2. **FNMExt** : $[(n_y, \tau \cdot d), (d, d-1) \mapsto m \sim \varepsilon_{fnm}]$ is a two-source non-malleable extractor for some $0 < \tau < 1$, $m = \Omega(d)$, and $\varepsilon_{fnm} < 12 \cdot \varepsilon_T$ with $\varepsilon_T < 2^{-\Omega((m)^c)}$ for some $c < \frac{1}{2}$.

Theorem 4. *There exists a two source non-malleable seeded extractor* **2NMExt** : $[(n_x, k_x), (n_y, k_y) \mapsto m \sim \varepsilon_{tnm}]$, *and* $m = \Omega(\min\{n_y, k_x\})$, *such that:*

1. $k_x \geq 12 \log(n_y - k_y) + 15$,
2. $n_y \geq 30 \log(n_y) + 10 \log(n_x) + 20$,
3. $k_y \geq (\frac{4}{5} + \gamma)n_y + 3\log(n_y) + \log(n_x) + 4$,
4. $\varepsilon_{tnm} \leq 3 \cdot 2^{-\frac{9\gamma}{10} n_y} + 40 \cdot \varepsilon_T$ *where* $\varepsilon_T = 2^{-\Omega(d^c)}$ *with* $c < \frac{1}{2}$.

Proof. For any given $Y \sim (n_y, k_y)$, we treat it as $Y = Y_\ell \circ Y_r$ where $|Y_\ell| = n_\ell$ and $|Y_r| = n_r$.

The extractor **Raz** : $[(n_x, k_x), (n_\ell, k_\ell) \mapsto d \sim 2^{-(1.5)d}]$ from Lemma 18 requires the following conditions:

1. $k_x \geq 12 \log(n_\ell - k_\ell) + 15$
2. $n_\ell \geq 6 \log n_\ell + 2 \log n_x + 4$,
3. $k_\ell \geq (\frac{1}{2} + \gamma) \cdot n_\ell + 3 \log n_\ell + \log n_x + 4$,
4. $d \leq \gamma \min\{\frac{n_\ell}{4}, \frac{k_x}{16}\} - 1$

for some $0 < \gamma < \frac{1}{2}$.

Setting $n_\ell = (\frac{2}{5} - \gamma)n_y$ (and consequently $n_r = (\frac{3}{5} + \gamma)n_y$), we first show that indeed the input requirements for **Raz** are met. Note that

$$(n_y - k_y) - (n_\ell - k_\ell) = n_y - k_y - (n_\ell - (k_y - n_r)) = 0$$

which implies that:

$$k_x \geq 12 \log(n_y - k_y) + 15 = 12 \log(n_\ell - k_\ell) + 15$$

Next:

$$n_\ell \geq \frac{1}{5}n_y \geq 6 \log(n_y) + 2 \log(n_x) + 4 \geq 6 \log(n_\ell) + 2 \log(n_x) + 4$$

And lastly:

$$k_\ell \geq k_y - n_r = \left(\frac{4}{5} + \gamma\right) n_y + 3\log(n_\ell) + \log(n_x) + 4 - \left(\frac{3}{5} + \gamma\right) n_y$$

$$= \left(\frac{1}{5}\right) n_y + 3\log(n_\ell) + \log(n_x) + 4 = \left(\frac{1}{5}\right)\left(\frac{1}{0.4 - \gamma}\right) n_\ell + 3\log(n_\ell) + \log(n_x) + 4$$

$$\geq \left(\frac{1}{2} + \frac{5\gamma}{4}\right) n_\ell + 3\log(n_\ell) + \log(n_x) + 4$$

Setting input parameters $n_3 = n_x$, $k_1^* = k_x$, $n_1 = n_y$, $k_2^* = (\frac{4}{5} + \gamma)n_y$, and extractor parameters $n_4 = n_\ell$, $k_4 = k_\ell$, $n_1 = n_y$, $k_1 = \tau \cdot d$, $n_2 = d$, $k_2 = d - 1$ for some $0 < \tau < 1$, we get that $k_1^* \geq k_3$. Furthermore:

$$k_2^* - k_4 - n_1 + n_4 = k_y - k_\ell - n_y + n_\ell = k_y - k_\ell - \left(\frac{3}{4} + \gamma\right)n_y$$

$$\geq \left(\frac{1}{5} + \gamma\right)n_y - \left(\frac{1}{2} + \gamma\right)\left(\frac{2}{5} - \gamma\right)n_y$$

$$= \left(\frac{11}{10}\gamma + \gamma^2\right)n_y$$

and:

$$k_2^* - k_1 - 2n_4 = k_2^* - \tau \cdot d - 2n_\ell \geq \gamma n_y - \tau\gamma\frac{n_\ell}{4} \geq \frac{9\gamma}{10}n_y$$

Thus, by Theorem 1 it follows that $\mathbf{2NMExt} : [(n_3, k_1^*), (n_1, k_2^*) \mapsto m \sim \varepsilon_{tnm}]$ is a strong non-malleable extractor with error:

$$\varepsilon_{tnm} \leq 3 \cdot 2^{-\frac{9\gamma}{10}n_y} + 36 \cdot \varepsilon_T + 2 \cdot 2^{-\frac{3}{2}d} + 2\sqrt{2^{-d+1}}$$

$$\leq 3 \cdot 2^{-\frac{9\gamma}{10}n_y} + 40 \cdot \varepsilon_T$$

where $\varepsilon_T = 2^{-\Omega(d^c)}$ with $c < \frac{1}{2}$.   □

Remark 3. As we noted in Remark 1 we can use multi-tampering extractor from Remark 2, and obtain a t-tamperable non-malleable extractor. The error of such extractor remains negligible. Entropy requirements change due to first point from Remark 1: One source can have poly-logarithmic entropy, while the other requires entropy rate $(1 - \frac{1}{2t+3})$.

8   A Two-Source Non-malleable Extractor with Rate $\frac{1}{2}$

In [5] the authors give a compiler that turns any left-strong non-malleable extractor into a non-malleable extractor with optimal output rate of $\frac{1}{2}$. The construction looks as follows:

$$\mathbf{2NMExt}^*(X, Y) = \mathtt{SExt}(X, \mathbf{2NMExt}(X, Y)),$$

where $\mathtt{SExt}$ is a seeded extractor from [28] with output size equal $\frac{1}{2}H_\infty(X)$, and $\mathbf{2NMExt}$ is a left-strong non-malleable extractor.

We will briefly discuss the idea behind that construction. Let X' be a tampering of X, and Y' be a tampering of Y. We need to argue that if $X \neq X' \vee Y \neq Y'$ then $\mathbf{2NMExt}^*(X, Y)$ remains uniform even given $\mathbf{2NMExt}^*(X', Y')$. If $X \neq X' \vee Y \neq Y'$ then left-strong non-malleable extractor $\mathbf{2NMExt}(X, Y)$ is uniform even given $\mathbf{2NMExt}(X', Y'), X$. The final idea crucially relies on the fact that SExt extracts only half of the entropy of X: we can reveal $\mathbf{2NMExt}(X', Y')$ and then $\mathbf{SExt}(X', \mathbf{2NMExt}(X', Y'))$ becomes a leakage from X (i.e. it is just a deterministic function of X with a small output). We get that $\tilde{H}_\infty(X|\mathbf{2NMExt}(X', Y'), \mathbf{SExt}(X', \mathbf{2NMExt}(X', Y'))) \approx \frac{1}{2}H_\infty(X)$ (size of $\mathbf{2NMExt}(X', Y')$ is tiny so it's asymptotically irrelevant). Moreover by the left-strong property of $\mathbf{2NMExt}$ we get that X and $\mathbf{2NMExt}(X, Y)$ remain independent given $\mathbf{2NMExt}(X', Y'), \mathbf{SExt}(X', \mathbf{2NMExt}(X', Y'))$, this means that $\mathbf{SExt}(X, \mathbf{2NMExt}(X, Y))$ is uniform given $\mathbf{2NMExt}(X', Y')$, $\mathbf{SExt}(X', \mathbf{2NMExt}(X', Y'))$ which gives the result.

If we make use of $\mathbf{2NMExt}$ from the previous section we can obtain a two-source unbalanced non-malleable extractor with rate $\frac{1}{2}$.

Lemma 19 (Theorem 5 of [5]). *If $\mathbf{2NMExt} : [(n_1, k_1), (n_2, k_2) \mapsto d \sim \varepsilon_1]$ is a strong two-source unbalanced non-malleable extractor, with $n_2 = o(n_1)$ and* $\mathrm{ext} : [(n_1, k_1), (d, d) \mapsto \ell \sim \varepsilon_2]$ *is a strong seeded extractor, then there exists a two source non-malleable extractor $\mathbf{2NMExt}^* : [(n_1, k_1), (n_2, k_2) \mapsto \ell \sim \varepsilon_1 + \varepsilon_2]$. Furthermore, if $k_1, \ell < \frac{n_1}{2}$, then $\mathbf{2NMExt}^*$ has a rate of $\frac{1}{2}$.*

Theorem 5. *There exists an extractor $\mathbf{2NMExt}^* : [(n_1, k_1), (n_2, k_2) \mapsto \ell \sim \varepsilon_1 + \varepsilon_2]$ such that:*

1. $k_1 \geq \max\{12 \log(n_2 - k_2) + 15, \log^3(n_1) \log(1/\varepsilon_2)\}$
2. $n_2 \geq \max\{30 \log(n_2) + 10 \log(n_1) + 20, \log^3(n_1) \log(1/\varepsilon_2)\}$
3. $k_2 \geq (\frac{4}{5} + \gamma)n_2 + 3 \log(n_2) + \log(n_1) + 4$
4. $\varepsilon_1 \leq 3 \cdot 2^{-\frac{9\gamma}{10}n_2} + 40 \cdot \varepsilon_T$ *where* $\varepsilon_T = 2^{-\Omega(d^c)}$ *with* $c < \frac{1}{2}$
5. $\ell < \frac{k_1}{2}$

Furthermore, if $n_2 = o(n_1)$, $k_1, \ell < \frac{n_1}{2}$, then $\mathbf{2NMExt}^*$ has a rate of $\frac{1}{2}$.

Proof. By Theorem 4 there exists an extractor $\mathbf{2NMExt} : [(n_1, k_1), (n_2, k_2) \mapsto m \sim \varepsilon_1]$ such that:

1. $k_1 \geq 12 \log(n_2 - k_2) + 15$
2. $n_2 \geq 30 \log(n_2) + 10 \log(n_1) + 20$
3. $k_2 \geq (\frac{4}{5} + \gamma)n_2 + 3 \log(n_2) + \log(n_1) + 4$
4. $\varepsilon_1 \leq 3 \cdot 2^{-\frac{9\gamma}{10}n_2} + 40 \cdot \varepsilon_T$ *where* $\varepsilon_T = 2^{-\Omega(d^c)}$ *with* $c < \frac{1}{2}$
5. $m = \Omega(\min\{n_2, k_1\})$

Using Lemma 11, $\mathbf{Tre} : [(n_1, k_1), (m, m) \mapsto \Omega(k_1) \sim \varepsilon_2]$ is a strong seeded extractor with $m = O(\log^2(n_1) \log(1/\varepsilon_2))$. Thus by Lemma 19 there exists a two source non-malleable extractor $\mathbf{2NMExt}^* : [(n_1, k_1), (n_2, k_2) \mapsto \Omega(k_1) \sim \varepsilon_1 + \varepsilon_2]$.

Furthermore, with $n_2 = o(n_1)$ and $k_1, \ell < \frac{n_1}{2}$, we get that $\mathbf{2NMExt}^*$ has a rate of at most $\frac{n_1}{2(n_1 + n_2)} < \frac{1}{2}$. $\qquad\square$

References

1. Aggarwal, D., et al.: Stronger leakage-resilient and non-malleable secret sharing schemes for general access structures. In: Boldyreva, A., Micciancio, D. (eds.) CRYPTO 2019. LNCS, vol. 11693, pp. 510–539. Springer, Cham (2019). https://doi.org/10.1007/978-3-030-26951-7_18

2. Aggarwal, D., Dodis, Y., Kazana, T., Obremski, M.: Non-malleable reductions and applications. In: Proceedings of the Forty-Seventh Annual ACM Symposium on Theory of Computing, pp. 459–468. STOC 2015, Association for Computing Machinery, New York, NY, USA (2015). https://doi.org/10.1145/2746539.2746544

3. Aggarwal, D., Dodis, Y., Lovett, S.: Non-malleable codes from additive combinatorics. SIAM J. Comput. **47**(2), 524–546 (2018)

4. Aggarwal, D., Hosseini, K., Lovett, S.: Affine-malleable extractors, spectrum doubling, and application to privacy amplification. In: 2016 IEEE International Symposium on Information Theory (ISIT), pp. 2913–2917. IEEE (2016)

5. Aggarwal, D., Kanukurthi, B., Obbattu, S.L.B., Obremski, M., Sekar, S.: Rate one-third non-malleable codes. Cryptology ePrint Archive, Report 2021/1042 (2021)

6. Aggarwal, D., Obremski, M.: A constant rate non-malleable code in the split-state model. In: 2020 IEEE 61st Annual Symposium on Foundations of Computer Science (FOCS), pp. 1285–1294. IEEE (2020)

7. Aggarwal, D., Obremski, M., Ribeiro, J., Simkin, M., Siniscalchi, L.: Privacy amplification with tamperable memory via non-malleable two-source extractors. IEEE Transactions on Information Theory (2022)

8. Alon, N., Goldreich, O., Hastad, J., Peralta, R.: Simple construction of almost k-wise independent random variables. In: Proceedings [1990] 31st Annual Symposium on Foundations of Computer Science, vol. 2, pp. 544–553 (1990). https://doi.org/10.1109/FSCS.1990.89575

9. Ben-Aroya, A., Chattopadhyay, E., Doron, D., Li, X., Ta-Shma, A.: A new approach for constructing low-error, two-source extractors. In: Proceedings of the 33rd Computational Complexity Conference, pp. 1–19. CCC 2018, Schloss Dagstuhl-Leibniz-Zentrum fuer Informatik, Germany (2018)

10. Ben-Aroya, A., Doron, D., Ta-Shma, A.: An efficient reduction from two-source to non-malleable extractors: Achieving near-logarithmic min-entropy. In: Proceedings of the 49th Annual ACM SIGACT Symposium on Theory of Computing, pp. 1185–1194. STOC 2017, Association for Computing Machinery, New York, NY, USA (2017)

11. Bourgain, J.: More on the sum-product phenomenon in prime fields and its applications. Int. J. Number Theory **1**(01), 1–32 (2005)

12. Chattopadhyay, E., Goyal, V., Li, X.: Non-malleable extractors and codes, with their many tampered extensions. In: Proceedings of the Forty-Eighth annual ACM symposium on Theory of Computing, pp. 285–298. ACM (2016)

13. Chattopadhyay, E., Kanukurthi, B., Obbattu, S.L.B., Sekar, S.: Privacy amplification from non-malleable codes. In: Hao, F., Ruj, S., Sen Gupta, S. (eds.) INDOCRYPT 2019. LNCS, vol. 11898, pp. 318–337. Springer, Cham (2019). https://doi.org/10.1007/978-3-030-35423-7_16

14. Chattopadhyay, E., Zuckerman, D.: Explicit two-source extractors and resilient functions. Annal. Math. **189**(3), 653–705 (2019). https://www.jstor.org/stable/10.4007/annals.2019.189.3.1

15. Cheraghchi, M., Guruswami, V.: Non-malleable coding against bit-wise and split-state tampering. J. Cryptol. **30**(1), 191–241 (2017)

16. Chor, B., Goldreich, O.: Unbiased bits from sources of weak randomness and probabilistic communication complexity. SIAM J. Comput. **17**(2), 230–261 (1988)
17. Cohen, G.: Towards optimal two-source extractors and Ramsey graphs. In: Proceedings of the 49th Annual ACM SIGACT Symposium on Theory of Computing, pp. 1157–1170. STOC 2017, ACM, New York, NY, USA (2017)
18. Cohen, G., Raz, R., Segev, G.: Nonmalleable extractors with short seeds and applications to privacy amplification. SIAM J. Comput. **43**(2), 450–476 (2014)
19. Davì, F., Dziembowski, S., Venturi, D.: Leakage-resilient storage. In: Garay, J.A., De Prisco, R. (eds.) SCN 2010. LNCS, vol. 6280, pp. 121–137. Springer, Heidelberg (2010). https://doi.org/10.1007/978-3-642-15317-4_9
20. Dodis, Y., Li, X., Wooley, T.D., Zuckerman, D.: Privacy amplification and non-malleable extractors via character sums. SIAM J. Comput. **43**(2), 800–830 (2014). https://doi.org/10.1137/120868414
21. Dodis, Y., Ostrovsky, R., Reyzin, L., Smith, A.: Fuzzy extractors: how to generate strong keys from biometrics and other noisy data. SIAM J. Comput. **38**(1), 97–139 (2008)
22. Dodis, Y., Wichs, D.: Non-malleable extractors and symmetric key cryptography from weak secrets. In: Proceedings of the Forty-first Annual ACM Symposium on Theory of Computing, pp. 601–610. STOC 2009, ACM, New York, NY, USA (2009)
23. Dziembowski, S., Kazana, T., Obremski, M.: Non-malleable codes from two-source extractors. In: Canetti, R., Garay, J.A. (eds.) CRYPTO 2013. LNCS, vol. 8043, pp. 239–257. Springer, Heidelberg (2013). https://doi.org/10.1007/978-3-642-40084-1_14
24. Dziembowski, S., Pietrzak, K., Wichs, D.: Non-malleable codes. J. ACM **65**(4), 1–32 (2018)
25. Goyal, V., Kumar, A.: Non-malleable secret sharing. In: Proceedings of the 50th Annual ACM SIGACT Symposium on Theory of Computing, pp. 685–698. STOC 2018, Association for Computing Machinery, New York, NY, USA (2018)
26. Goyal, V., Pandey, O., Richelson, S.: Textbook non-malleable commitments. In: Proceedings of the Forty-Eighth Annual ACM Symposium on Theory of Computing, pp. 1128–1141 (2016)
27. Goyal, V., Srinivasan, A., Zhu, C.: Multi-source non-malleable extractors and applications. In: Eurocrypt (2021)
28. Guruswami, V., Umans, C., Vadhan, S.: Unbalanced expanders and randomness extractors from Parvaresh-Vardy codes. J. ACM **56**(4), 1–34 (2009)
29. Lewko, M.: An explicit two-source extractor with min-entropy rate near 4/9. Mathematika **65**(4), 950–957 (2019). https://doi.org/10.1112/S0025579319000238
30. Li, X.: Non-malleable extractors, two-source extractors and privacy amplification. In: 2012 IEEE 53rd Annual Symposium on Foundations of Computer Science, pp. 688–697. IEEE (2012)
31. Li, X.: Improved two-source extractors, and affine extractors for polylogarithmic entropy. In: 2016 IEEE 57th Annual Symposium on Foundations of Computer Science (FOCS), pp. 168–177 (2016). https://doi.org/10.1109/FOCS.2016.26
32. Li, X.: Improved non-malleable extractors, non-malleable codes and independent source extractors. In: Proceedings of the 49th Annual ACM SIGACT Symposium on Theory of Computing, pp. 1144–1156. ACM (2017)
33. Li, X.: Non-malleable extractors and non-malleable codes: partially optimal constructions. In: Proceedings of the 34th Computational Complexity Conference. CCC 2019, Schloss Dagstuhl-Leibniz-Zentrum fuer Informatik, Dagstuhl, DEU (2019). https://doi.org/10.4230/LIPIcs.CCC.2019.28

34. Li, X.: Two source extractors for asymptotically optimal entropy, and (many) more (2023)
35. Maurer, U., Wolf, S.: Privacy amplification secure against active adversaries. In: Kaliski, B.S. (ed.) CRYPTO 1997. LNCS, vol. 1294, pp. 307–321. Springer, Heidelberg (1997). https://doi.org/10.1007/BFb0052244
36. Nisan, N., Wigderson, A.: Hardness vs randomness. J. Comput. Syst. Sci. **49**(2), 149–167 (1994). https://doi.org/10.1016/S0022-0000(05)80043-1. https://www.sciencedirect.com/science/article/pii/S0022000005800431
37. Obremski, M., Skórski, M.: Inverted leftover hash lemma. ISIT (2018)
38. Raz, R.: Extractors with weak random seeds. In: Proceedings of the Thirty-seventh Annual ACM Symposium on Theory of Computing, pp. 11–20. STOC 2005, ACM, New York, NY, USA (2005)
39. Raz, R., Reingold, O., Vadhan, S.: Extracting all the randomness and reducing the error in Trevisan's extractors. In: Proceedings of the Thirty-First Annual ACM Symposium on Theory of Computing, pp. 149–158. STOC 1999, Association for Computing Machinery, New York, NY, USA (1999)

PAC Privacy: Automatic Privacy Measurement and Control of Data Processing

Hanshen Xiao$^{(\boxtimes)}$ and Srinivas Devadas

MIT, Cambridge, USA
{hsxiao,devadas}@mit.edu

Abstract. We propose and study a new privacy definition, termed Probably Approximately Correct (PAC) Privacy. PAC Privacy characterizes the information-theoretic hardness to recover sensitive data given arbitrary information disclosure/leakage during/after any processing. Unlike the classic cryptographic definition and Differential Privacy (DP), which consider the *adversarial (input-independent) worst case*, PAC Privacy is a simulatable metric that quantifies *the instance-based* impossibility of inference. A fully automatic analysis and proof generation framework is proposed: security parameters can be produced with arbitrarily high confidence via Monte-Carlo simulation for any black-box data processing oracle. This appealing automation property enables analysis of complicated data processing, where the worst-case proof in the classic privacy regime could be loose or even intractable. Moreover, we show that the produced PAC Privacy guarantees enjoy simple composition bounds and the automatic analysis framework can be implemented in an online fashion to analyze the composite PAC Privacy loss even under correlated randomness. On the utility side, the magnitude of (necessary) perturbation required in PAC Privacy is *not* lower bounded by $\Theta(\sqrt{d})$ for a d-dimensional release but could be $O(1)$ for many practical data processing tasks, which is in contrast to the input-independent worst-case information-theoretic lower bound. Example applications of PAC Privacy are included with comparisons to existing works.

Keywords: PAC Privacy · Automatic Security Proof · f-Divergence · Mutual Information · Instance-based Posterior Advantage · Reconstruction Hardness · Inference Hardness · Membership Attack

1 Introduction

Privacy concerns with information leakage from data processing are receiving increasing attention. Obtaining usable security which provides high utility, low implementation overhead and meaningful interpretation, is challenging. Theoretically, the underlying problem can be described by the following generic model. Assume some sensitive data X is processed by some mechanism $\mathcal{M}$ and the

© International Association for Cryptologic Research 2023
H. Handschuh and A. Lysyanskaya (Eds.): CRYPTO 2023, LNCS 14082, pp. 611–644, 2023.
https://doi.org/10.1007/978-3-031-38545-2_20

output $\mathcal{M}(X)$ is published. We want to characterize, given $\mathcal{M}(X)$, how much information an adversary can infer about X. In the applications of data analysis and machine learning, $\mathcal{M}(X)$ could be any statistics or model learned from X [1]; in encryption, $\mathcal{M}(X)$ could be ciphertexts of X [31]; in side channel attacks, $\mathcal{M}(X)$ could be any physical signal observed by the adversary, such as memory access pattern [49] or network traffic [19] when accessing or sending X.

To formalize and quantify the information leakage, a large number of security metrics have been proposed varying from the perfect secrecy [46] of Shannon, to computational indistinguishability [32], which forms the foundation of modern cryptography, to Differential Privacy (DP) [25] and its variants based on various statistical divergence metrics [41], and many other definitions based on information-theoretic quantities, such as Fisher-information privacy [27].

Most existing privacy or security definitions (including all above-mentioned examples) are rooted in indistinguishability likelihoods. They set out to quantify the difference between the likelihoods $\mathbb{P}(\mathcal{M}(X) = o | X = X_0)$ and $\mathbb{P}(\mathcal{M}(X) = o | X = X_0')$ for different input selections from various perspectives. For instance, perfect secrecy requires that for arbitrary input data X, the distribution of $\mathcal{M}(X)$ must be identical. Cryptographic security relaxes the statistical indistinguishability to that any polynomial-time adversary cannot distinguish the distributions of $\mathcal{M}(X_0)$ and $\mathcal{M}(X_0')$ for any input candidates X_0 and X_0'. Similarly, DP and its variants quantify the difference between $\mathcal{M}(X_0)$ and $\mathcal{M}(X_0')$ for any two *adjacent datasets*[1] by some divergence function $\mathcal{D}\big(\mathsf{P}_{\mathcal{M}(X_0)} \| \mathsf{P}_{\mathcal{M}(X_0')}\big)$. For example, classic ϵ-DP [25] is based on maximal divergence $\mathcal{D}_\infty(\mathsf{P}_{\mathcal{M}(X_0)} \| \mathsf{P}_{\mathcal{M}(X_0')}) = \sup_o \log\big(\mathbb{P}(\mathcal{M}(X_0) = o)/\mathbb{P}(\mathcal{M}(X_0') = o)\big)$.

The interested reader may wonder if there is an intuitive privacy interpretation of the limited likelihood difference? In particular, can likelihood indistinguishability tell us given $\mathcal{M}(X)$, how much of the sensitive data X an adversary can recover? Unfortunately, none of above-mentioned definitions can directly answer this question. This is *not* because those metrics are incomplete but because additional assumptions must be made. In general, to quantify reconstruction hardness, we have to specify the adversary's prior knowledge and the (conditional) entropy of objective X. In the extreme case where the adversary already has the full knowledge of X, or where X is simply a public constant, then no matter what kind of mechanism $\mathcal{M}$ is applied to encode X, the adversary can perfectly recover it, regardless of $\mathcal{M}(X)$. Thus, *the likelihood difference only partially captures the changes to the adversary's belief or the additional information regarding X after observing $\mathcal{M}(X)$.*

Compared to the extensive studies along the line of (in)distinguishability, formal characterization of reconstruction hardness is a long-standing, challenging problem. The estimation of the priors regarding sensitive data X and resultant output distribution of $\mathcal{M}(X)$ could already be intractable – this is especially likely in the high-dimensional scenario. Thus, as mentioned before, most security/privacy definitions only focus on the likelihood divergence and avoid

---

[1] Here, we say X_0 and X_0' are adjacent if they only differ in one datapoint, i.e., their Hamming distance is 1.

complicated, such as Bayesian, analysis to properly quantify the posterior inference hardness. As a consequence, to make a meaningful guarantee, most classic
definitions treat the sensitive input *deterministically* and consider the adversarial worst-case, i.e., the maximal distribution divergence between $\mathcal{M}(X_0)$ and
$\mathcal{M}(X_0')$ for two arbitrary input candidates X_0 and X_0'. Such worst-case indistinguishability is a very strong guarantee since it is independent of any particular
input distribution, but is also expensive, especially for statistical data processing.
At a high level, there are two key obstacles in the application of such indistinguishability measurement:

(a) **Adversarial Worst-case Proof is Hard**: It is, in general, non-trivial
    to tightly or analytically characterize the worst case and privatize an
    (adaptively-iterative) algorithm to ensure satisfied output divergence. For
    example, in DP, calculation of the sensitivity, the maximal possible change
    on the output by replacing a single datapoint, is, in general, NP-hard [55].
    Even in common applications such as to differentially privately train a neural
    network, the tight sensitivity bound of Stochastic Gradient Descent (SGD)
    remains open. The only known generic privatization approach, DP-SGD,
    restricts the sensitivity using clipped/normalized per-sample gradient, and
    adds noise step by step to derive an upper bound in a compositional fashion
    [1]. However, the tight composition bound calculation is also known to be
    #P hard [43]. Though many efforts have been devoted to obtaining efficient
    and tighter composition [41], the applications of DP-SGD in modern deep
    learning, and large-scale private database queries still encounter severe utility
    compromise. Therefore, an automatic and usable privacy analysis framework
    for arbitrary data processing is desirable.

(b) **Data Entropy Matters in Reconstruction**: Reconstruction (or infer-
    ence) of data is, in general, a harder problem for an adversary than simply
    distinguishing [33]. However, worst-case indistinguishability cannot capture
    the data entropy. We give a simple example. A dataset $X = \{x_1, x_2, \ldots, x_n\}$
    is generated as i.i.d. samples from some Gaussian distribution and we sim-
    ply publish its empirical average, i.e., $\mathcal{M}(X) = 1/n \cdot (\sum_{i=1}^{n} x_i)$. Even with-
    out any further obfuscation on $\mathcal{M}(X)$ like perturbation, intuitively, we see
    some potential hardness to reconstruct X from its average $\mathcal{M}(X)$. For an
    adversary who only knows the data distribution, it is impossible to perfectly
    reconstruct X deterministically due to ambiguity. But the data leakage of
    this trivial aggregation cannot be properly analyzed from a distinguishabil-
    ity angle, since one can always determine the true input from two datasets
    whose means are different. However, in practical processing even for a given
    data pool, many kinds of randomness can enforce data to be processed to
    enjoy entropy, for example, subsampling or data augmentation [48], where
    the participants are randomized. Therefore, a more generic security/privacy
    definition, which enables *instance-based analysis* in terms of both data priors
    and specific inference objective, is attractive.

In this paper, we tackle the fundamental problem of quantifying the relationship among data entropy, disclosure, and reconstruction hardness. Besides a

more meaningful interpretation via inference impossibility, to address the above two mentioned challenges in classic security/privacy regimes, we want a more generic definition, which enables (a) automatic security proof, and (b) instance-based worst-case analysis. To this end, a new privacy definition, termed Probably Approximately Correct (PAC) Privacy, is proposed, which enables a user to keep track of the data leakage of an arbitrary (black-box) processing mechanism with confidence, via simulation. At a high level, (δ, ρ, D) PAC Privacy characterizes the following reconstruction hardness:

For some sensitive data X distributed in D and a mechanism $\mathcal{M}$, given $\mathcal{M}(X)$, there does not exist an adversary (possibly computationally-unbounded) who can successfully return $\tilde{X}$ such that $\rho(\tilde{X}, X) = 1$ under measure function ρ with probability at least $(1 - \delta)$.

We use the notion *"PAC"* as we borrow the idea of well-known PAC learning theory [53] and describe the adversary's reconstruction/inference task as a generic learning problem. The difference compared to classic learning theory is that we study impossibility results. The $\rho(\cdot, \cdot)$ captures an arbitrary inference task of interest and $\rho(\tilde{X}, X) = 1$ if and only if adversary's inference $\tilde{X}$ satisfies the reconstruction criterion. For example, if we set out to prevent the adversary from recovering a single digital bit of data X, then we may select ρ such that $\rho(\tilde{X}, X)$ returns 1 only when $\tilde{X}$ and X collide in at least one coordinate. More discussions can be found below Definition 1.

Our presented PAC Privacy framework has the following appealing properties and important implications:

1. **Wide Applicability**: The PAC Privacy framework presented can theoretically be used to analyze any data processing. Via f-divergence, we present a simple quantification of the posterior advantage that the adversary gains by observing the disclosure $\mathcal{M}(X)$ for arbitrary inference problems. Thus, PAC Privacy can characterize very generic reconstruction/inference hardness under any selection of the measure function ρ, which captures classic attacks such as membership inference and identification. Through instance-based (Gaussian) perturbation, we show how to efficiently control PAC Privacy parameters. In contrast to the adversarial worst-case, the noise magnitude in PAC Privacy does not necessarily scale with dimensionality but can be $O(1)$ in high-dimensional release.

2. **Automatic Privacy Analysis**: To our knowledge, PAC Privacy is the first non-trivial automatic security definition. Theoretically, no worst-case proof is needed but one can determine a perturbation mechanism (if necessary) fully automatically in polynomial time to ensure desired security parameters with arbitrarily high confidence. More importantly, this universal framework only requires sufficient Monte-Carlo simulations while the underlying data processing mechanism could be a black-box oracle – no algorithmic analysis is required. This is very different from classic definitions such as cryptography and DP, where the key challenge is to derive the algorithmic worst-case proof.

3. **Connections to the Input-Independent Worst Case and Generalization Error**: We also connect PAC Privacy, DP and generalization error.

Given assumptions on priors, we show DP can produce PAC Privacy, and PAC Privacy can then provide a generalization error guarantee, while the reverse direction, in general, does not hold. However, in practical data applications, PAC Privacy could bring significant (empirical) perturbation improvement, and can characterize the optimal instance-based perturbation required. We show concrete examples in private release of local samples, mean estimation and deep learning models. Though the tools we apply to develop the foundation of PAC Privacy include f-divergence and mutual information, we stress that PAC Privacy is *not* defined using any existing information-theoretical metric or statistical divergence, but by the impossibility of inference described above. Therefore, PAC Privacy enjoys a very straightforward interpretation. More discussion can be found in Sect. 7.

Paper Organization: At a high level, the paper has two parts, i.e., the definition of PAC Privacy and the control of security parameters via automatic analysis. In Sect. 2, we formally present the definitions and interpretations of PAC Privacy. In Sect. 3, we show generic bounds of PAC Privacy parameters using f-divergence and mutual information in various setups. With these bounds, we move on to present automatic algorithms to determine proper perturbation (if necessary) to produce desired PAC Privacy. In Sect. 4.1, we present the methods for deterministic data processing, and in Sect. 4.2, we study the case of randomized mechanisms. In Sect. 4.3, we discuss how to approximate the optimal perturbation in general. In Sect. 5, we study the composition of PAC Privacy in various setups. In Sect. 6, we proceed to study and compare the adversarial and instance-based worst case. Practical applications of PAC Privacy are included. We summarize related works in Sect. 7, where we also discuss the relationship between PAC Privacy, Differential Privacy and generalization error. Finally, we conclude in Sect. 8. The generalization to local PAC Privacy via secure implementation of automatic privacy analysis in a decentralized setup can be found in the full version.

2   PAC Privacy

We assume each private datapoint x is defined over some domain $\mathcal{X}$, and the dataset $X \in \mathcal{X}^*$. Our goal is to formalize the privacy leakage from a data processing mechanism $\mathcal{M}$, where $\mathcal{M} : \mathcal{X}^* \rightarrow \mathcal{Y} \subset \mathbb{R}^d$. Both $\mathcal{X}$ and $\mathcal{Y}$ are measurable spaces. The data distribution D is defined over $\mathcal{X}^*$. $\mathcal{M}$ can be either deterministic or randomized. Different analyses will be provided later for these two cases. The formal definition of PAC Privacy is as follows.

Definition 1 ((δ, ρ, D) PAC Privacy). *For a data processing mechanism $\mathcal{M}$, given some data distribution D, and a measure function $\rho(\cdot, \cdot)$, we say $\mathcal{M}$ satisfies $(\delta, \rho, \mathsf{D})$-PAC Privacy if the following experiment is impossible:*

A user generates data X from distribution D and sends $\mathcal{M}(X)$ to an adversary. The adversary who knows D and $\mathcal{M}$ is asked to return an estimation $\tilde{X} \in \mathcal{X}^*$ on X such that with probability at least $(1 - \delta)$, $\rho(\tilde{X}, X) = 1$.

In Definition 1, we adopt a way to describe the reconstruction hardness as a game between the user and the adversary. The adversary sets out to learn something from the disclosure $\mathcal{M}(X)$. The measure function (on the adversary's learning performance) $\rho(\cdot, \cdot)$ can be arbitrarily selected according to the adversarial inference task of interest. For example, $\mathcal{X} \subset \mathbb{R}^{d'}$ for some dimension d' and a safe reconstruction error is set to be ϵ in the l_2 norm. Then, we can define $\rho(\tilde{X}, X) = 1$ if and only if $\|\tilde{X} - X\|_2 \leq \epsilon$ and Definition 1 suggests it is impossible for an adversary to recover private data X within ϵ error with probability at least $(1 - \delta)$. Another example, $\mathcal{X}^*$ is some finite set and $X \in \mathcal{X}^*$ contains n elements. Similarly, we define $\rho(\tilde{X}, X) = 1$ iff $\#(\tilde{X} \cap X) > (n - \epsilon)$. Then, Definition 1 implies that there does not exist an adversary who can identify more than $(n - \epsilon)$ elements/participants of X from $\mathcal{X}^*$ with probability at least $(1 - \delta)$. As a remark, a neat expression of ρ is not important or even necessary in PAC Privacy and we simply use ρ to indicate whether the adversary's reconstruction satisfies a certain criterion.

It is worthwhile to mention that in Definition 1 and results presented later, we do not put any specific restrictions on D or the adversary's strategy. D could be a generic joint distribution of datapoints generated, though with additional assumptions we may obtain tighter bounds (such as Theorem 2). Before proceeding, we augment the definition of PAC Privacy to incorporate (instance-based) additional *posterior advantage*, commonly adopted in classic privacy definitions. That is, for any specific priors given, we set out to quantify how much the disclosure of $\mathcal{M}(X)$ can help the adversary to implement successful inference. To measure such advantage, we first formally introduce the definition of f-divergence.

Definition 2 (f-Divergence). *Let $f : (0, +\infty) \to \mathbb{R}$ be a convex function with $f(1) = 0$. Let P and Q be two distributions on some measurable space, and the f-divergence $\mathcal{D}_f$ between P and Q is defined as*

$$\mathcal{D}_f(P\|Q) := \mathbb{E}_Q\left[f(\frac{dP}{dQ})\right].$$

Here, we use dP (dQ) to represent the probability density (or mass) function of the continuous (or discrete) probability distribution P (Q).

In Definition 2, when we select $f(x) = x \log(x)$, it becomes the Kullback-Leibler (KL) divergence; when we select $f(x) = \frac{1}{2}|x - 1|$, it becomes the total variation, where $\mathcal{D}_{TV}(P\|Q) = \frac{1}{2} \cdot \int |dP - dQ|$. In the following, we define $(1 - \delta_o^\rho)$ as the optimal *a priori* chance that an adversary who only knows the data distribution D can complete the objective reconstruction task *before* observing the release $\mathcal{M}(X)$.

Definition 3 (Optimal Prior Success Rate). *For given measure ρ and data distribution $\mathcal{D}$, we define $(1 - \delta_o^\rho)$ as*

$$1 - \delta_o^\rho := \sup_{\tilde{X} \in \mathcal{X}^*} \Pr_{X \sim D} \left(\rho(\tilde{X}, X) = 1\right),$$

which represents the optimal a priori success rate only based on adversary's prior knowledge on D *to recover* X *such that the reconstruction satisfies the criterion defined by* ρ.

Definition 4 $((\Delta_f \delta, \rho, \mathsf{D})$ PAC Advantage Privacy$)$. *A mechanism* $\mathcal{M}$ *is termed* $(\Delta_f \delta, \rho, \mathsf{D})$ *PAC-advantage private if it is* $(\delta, \rho, \mathsf{D})$ *PAC private and*

$$\Delta_f \delta := \mathcal{D}_f(\mathbf{1}_\delta \| \mathbf{1}_{\delta_o^\rho}) = \delta_o^\rho f(\frac{\delta}{\delta_o^\rho}) + (1 - \delta_o^\rho) f(\frac{1 - \delta}{1 - \delta_o^\rho}).$$

Here, $\mathbf{1}_\delta$ *and* $\mathbf{1}_{\delta_o^\rho}$ *represent two Bernoulli distributions of parameters* δ *and* δ_o^ρ, *respectively.*

In Definition 4, $\Delta_f \delta$ captures the additional (posterior) advantage gained by the adversary after observing $\mathcal{M}(X)$. When we select $\mathcal{D}_f$ to be total variation, $\Delta_{TV} \delta$ simply becomes the difference $\delta_o^\rho - \delta$, as commonly used in classic cryptographic analysis. Accordingly, once we have an upper bound on $\delta_o^\rho - \delta$, plugging in δ_o^ρ provides a lower bound on the posterior failure rate δ.

The seemingly artificial aspect of Definition 4 in using f-divergence as the measure is motivated by Theorem 1, where we give generic upper bounds on $\Delta_f \delta$. In particular, when $\mathcal{D}_f$ is selected to be KL-divergence, we can simply bound $\Delta_{KL} \delta$ via mutual information. In addition, it is not hard to see that when $\mathcal{M}$ satisfies perfect secrecy, $\Delta_f \delta$ is 0 for any f. Before the end of this section, we have the following important remarks on PAC Privacy.

Reconstruction Metric Selection: Definitions 1 and 4 provide a unified framework to capture generic inference hardness. Membership and identification attacks are now special cases by selecting a specific data generation and a specific measure ρ.

Definition 5 $((\delta, \rho, \mathsf{U}, \mathsf{D})$ PAC Membership Privacy$)$. *For a data processing mechanism* $\mathcal{M}$, *given some measure* ρ *and a data set* $\mathsf{U} = (u_1, u_2, \ldots, u_N)$, *we say* $\mathcal{M}$ *satisfies* $(\delta, \rho, \mathsf{U}, \mathsf{D})$*-PAC Membership Privacy if the following experiment is impossible:*

A user applies certain sampling (described by D*) on* U *to generate a dataset* $X \sim \mathsf{D}$, *and sends* $\mathcal{M}(X)$ *to an adversary. The adversary who knows* U, D *and* $\mathcal{M}$ *is asked to return an* N*-dimensional binary vector* $\tilde{\mathbf{1}}_\mathsf{U} = (\tilde{\mathbf{1}}_{u_1}, \ldots, \tilde{\mathbf{1}}_{u_N})$ *to predict the participation of each* u_i, *denote by* $\mathbf{1}_\mathsf{U} = (\mathbf{1}_{u_1}, \ldots, \mathbf{1}_{u_N})$, *where* $\mathbf{1}_{u_i}$ *is an indicator to represent the participation of* u_i, *such that with probability at least* $(1 - \delta)$, $\rho(\tilde{\mathbf{1}}_\mathsf{U}, \mathbf{1}_\mathsf{U}) = 1$.

One can imagine the distribution D could be Poisson (i.i.d.) sampling or random sampling with(out) replacement from U. From a DP angle, such privacy amplification from sampling has been studied in [4,54]. PAC Membership Privacy is a very important variant of PAC Privacy in practical applications, which can give a formal security proof against the well-known and fundamental *membership inference attack* problem [47].

We may consider the classic statistical query model, where there is some sensitive data set U, for example, medical records of N patients, held by a server.

The server is asked to answer some query, expressed as disclosing the results of $\mathcal{M}$. The server randomly samples a subset X of elements from U; for example, each datapoint in U will be independently selected with probability $1/2$, to participate in the computation of $\mathcal{M}(X)$. If we select $\rho(\tilde{1}_\mathsf{U}, 1_\mathsf{U}) = 1$ only when $\tilde{1}_\mathsf{U}$ and 1_U collide in at least one entry, then $(\delta, \rho, \mathsf{U}, \mathsf{D})$-PAC Membership Privacy suggests that *even if the adversary already knows the whole data pool* U, *he still cannot successfully infer any participants in the processing mechanism* $\mathcal{M}$. In other words, PAC Membership Privacy quantifies the *risk* incurred by any group of persons who allow their data to be processed through $\mathcal{M}$.

If, on the other hand, our privacy concern pertains to individuals, we simply consider the reconstruction hardness of each single datapoint in the set X, and similarly define PAC Individual Privacy as follows.

Definition 6 $((\delta, \rho, n, \mathsf{D})$ PAC Individual Privacy). *For a data processing mechanism* $\mathcal{M}$, *given some data distribution* D, *the total number* n *of datapoints, a measure* $\rho(\cdot, \cdot)$, *we say* $\mathcal{M}$ *satisfies* $(\delta, \rho, n, \mathsf{D})$-*PAC Individual Privacy if for any* $i \in [1 : n]$ *the following experiment is impossible:*

A user generates data $X = (x_1, x_2, \ldots, x_n)$ *from distribution* D *and sends* $\mathcal{M}(X)$ *to an adversary. The adversary who knows* D *and* $\mathcal{M}$ *is asked to return an estimation* $\tilde{x}_i$ *on* x_i *such that with probability at least* $(1 - \delta)$, $\rho(\tilde{x}_i, x_i) = 1$.

If the input domain $\mathcal{X}$ is some finite set and we want to measure how hard it is for an adversary to identify the true selection of x_i, we may set ρ to be $\rho(\tilde{x}_i, x_i) = 1$ iff $\tilde{x}_i = x_i$. Then, the reconstruction becomes the *identification problem*. We have to stress that a proper selection of measure ρ is important to make PAC Privacy meaningful in different scenarios. Different error metrics will capture different perspectives of data privacy. For biological or financial data, such as ages and incomes, l_p norm, such as l_1 and l_2, is usually meaningful. But for sensitive image or natural language data, l_p norm may not be able to fully characterize the leakage of contextual information, and membership and identification hardness are better options. PAC Privacy provides a unified framework for arbitrary inference tasks and privacy concerns.

Lack of Knowledge: In all the above definitions, we assume the adversary has full knowledge of the *a priori* data generation distribution D, or D is public. However, our current PAC Privacy framework cannot properly quantify the inference hardness due to the *lack/absence* of prior knowledge. For example, suppose the data X is generated from some distribution D, say a random picture selected from a pool of cat images. For an adversary who does not have full knowledge but only knows that the users' pictures could be selected from an image pool of cats or dogs, the inference would be harder compared to the full knowledge setup. Unfortunately, our techniques used in PAC Privacy rely on the entropy of data, which does not change conditional on such lack of knowledge. However, in the other direction, PAC Privacy *does* quantify the inference hardness in a more generic scenario when the adversary has more knowledge rather than simply knowing D. We refer the reader to Remark 1 in Sect. 3.

Although our current framework cannot exactly quantify the inference hardness amplification from the lack of knowledge, PAC Privacy enjoys strong and realistic privacy interpretation from this perspective. If a certain inference problem is already difficult for an adversary who has full knowledge, then it is even more difficult for an adversary who lacks knowledge. Suppose a user holds a set U of cat images and randomly samples, say, 1000 samples from them, to produce X and discloses $\mathcal{M}(X)$. If $\mathcal{M}(X)$ satisfies PAC Privacy such that even an adversary who knows U and the data generation D cannot identify or recover the 1000 participants, then it is even more difficult for an adversary to identify or recover the 1000 selected samples from the universe of cat images.

3   Foundation of PAC Privacy

In this section, we present our generic results to enable concrete PAC Privacy analysis. Before we state the theorems, we need the following additional notations to express the results.

Definition 7 (Entropy). *For a random variable x defined on a discrete set $\mathcal{X}$, the (Shannon) entropy $\mathcal{H}(x)$ of x is defined as $\mathcal{H}(x) = \sum_{x_0 \in \mathcal{X}} -\Pr(x = x_0) \log \Pr(x = x_0)$. If x is in a continuous distribution on some domain $\mathcal{X}$, then the (differential) entropy $h(x)$ of x is defined as $h(x) = \int_{x_0 \in \mathcal{X}} -\mathbb{P}(x = x_0) \log \mathbb{P}(x = x_0) dx_0$, where $\mathbb{P}$ represents the probability density function.*

With a slight abuse of notation, we simply apply $\mathcal{H}(x)$ to denote the (Shannon/differential) entropy of x depending on its distribution for simplicity. Accordingly, we can define the conditional entropy $\mathcal{H}(x|w)$ for two random variables x and w in some joint distribution, where $\mathcal{H}(x|w) = \sum_{w_0 \in \mathcal{W}} \mathcal{H}(x|w = w_0) \Pr(w = w_0)$. When w is in some continuous distribution, we can similarly define the conditional entropy in an integral form as differential entropy. In the following, we will use P_x to denote the distribution of a random variable x.

Definition 8 (Mutual Information). *For two random variables x and w in some joint distribution, the mutual information $\mathsf{MI}(x; w)$ is defined as*

$$\mathsf{MI}(x; w) := \mathcal{H}(x) - \mathcal{H}(x|w) = \mathcal{D}_{KL}(\mathsf{P}_{x,w} \| \mathsf{P}_x \otimes \mathsf{P}_w),$$

i.e., the KL-divergence between the joint distribution of (x, w) and the product of the marginal distributions of x and w, respectively.

Mutual information measures the dependence between x and w. $\mathsf{MI}(x; w) = \mathsf{MI}(w; x)$ is always non-negative and equals 0 if x is independent of w.

Theorem 1. *For any selected f-divergence $\mathcal{D}_f$, a mechanism $\mathcal{M} : \mathcal{X}^* \to \mathcal{Y}$ satisfies $(\delta, \rho, \mathsf{D})$ PAC Privacy where*

$$\Delta_f \delta = \mathcal{D}_f(\mathbf{1}_\delta \| \mathbf{1}_{\delta^\rho}) \leq \inf_{\mathsf{P}_W} \mathcal{D}_f(\mathsf{P}_{X, \mathcal{M}(X)} \| \mathsf{P}_X \otimes \mathsf{P}_W). \tag{1}$$

Here, $\mathbf{1}_\delta$ and $\mathbf{1}_{\delta_o^\rho}$ are two Bernoulli distributions of parameters δ and δ_o^ρ, respectively; $\mathsf{P}_{X,\mathcal{M}(X)}$ and P_X are the joint distribution and the marginal distribution of $(X, \mathcal{M}(X))$ and X, respectively; and P_W represents the distribution of an arbitrary random variable $W \in \mathcal{Y}$.

In particular, when we select $\mathcal{D}_f$ to be the KL-divergence and $\mathcal{P}_W = \mathcal{P}_{\mathcal{M}(X)}$, $\mathcal{M}$ satisfies $(\delta, \rho, \mathsf{D})$ PAC Privacy where

$$\Delta_{KL}\delta := \mathcal{D}_{KL}(\mathbf{1}_\delta \| \mathbf{1}_{\delta_o^\rho}) \leq \mathsf{MI}(X; \mathcal{M}(X)). \tag{2}$$

Here, $\mathcal{D}_{KL}(\mathbf{1}_\delta \| \mathbf{1}_{\delta_o^\rho}) = \delta \log(\frac{\delta}{\delta_o^\rho}) + (1 - \delta) \log(\frac{1-\delta}{1-\delta_o^\rho})$.

Remark 1. *In general, if the adversary has more prior knowledge (besides the data distribution D) on X, denoted by a variable Adv, we can obtain a corresponding PAC Privacy bound using Theorem 1, where the only difference is that in (2), $\mathsf{MI}(X; \mathcal{M}(X))$ and δ_o^ρ are changed to the conditional $\mathsf{MI}(X; \mathcal{M}(X)|Adv)$ and the corresponding failure probability of optimal a priori guessing on X conditional on Adv, respectively.*

Theorem 1 is rooted in the well-known data processing inequality of f-divergence (Lemma 2 in Appendix A in the full version). Roughly speaking, this inequality says postprocessing cannot increase information. Given priors, the adversary's reconstruction or decision is determined by (a postprocessing of) his observation on $\mathcal{M}(X)$. Therefore, to information-theoretically bound the posterior advantage, it suffices to quantify the correlation between X and $\mathcal{M}(X)$. Theorem 1 serves as the foundation of PAC Privacy analysis. From (1), we know that $\Delta_f \delta = \mathcal{D}_f(\mathbf{1}_\delta \| \mathbf{1}_{\delta_o^\rho})$, the change to the f-divergence between the optimal a priori and posterior reconstruction/inference performance, is bounded by the corresponding f-divergence between the distributions of $(X, \mathcal{M}(X))$ and (X, W), where W is an arbitrary random variable independent of X. With the freedom of the selections of both f and W, if we apply KL-divergence and set W to be distributed the same as $\mathcal{M}(X)$, we have $\Delta_{KL}\delta \leq \mathsf{MI}(X; \mathcal{M}(X))$, the mutual information between X and $\mathcal{M}(X)$.

It is noted that we are also free to select *arbitrary ρ* as the objective inference task and the success criterion in (1). Thus, another important implication from Theorem 1 is that once we have an upper bound on $\mathcal{D}_f(\mathsf{P}_{X,\mathcal{M}(X)} \| \mathsf{P}_X \otimes \mathsf{P}_{\mathcal{M}(X)})$, we indeed also control *the posterior advantage of all possible adversaries' inference tasks*. This is also the foundation of the automatic proof of PAC Privacy, where the *entirety of data generation and processing $\mathcal{M}$ could be a black-box oracle*; as shown in Sect. 4, we are able to control such f-divergence without any algorithmic analysis of $\mathcal{M}$. We can compute δ_o^ρ based on ρ and D for any given inference task. Given δ_o^ρ, once we have the upper bound on $\Delta_f \delta$, we can consequently lower bound the adversary's failure probability δ for inference since $\mathcal{D}_f$ is a deterministic function.

In the following, we will mainly focus on $\Delta_{KL}\delta$ to control PAC Privacy since mutual information is a well-studied quantity in information theory and has many nice properties to simplify our analysis. Intuitively, $\mathsf{MI}(X; \mathcal{M}(X))$ quantifies the dependence between X and $\mathcal{M}(X)$, and shows how much such instance-based information (in nats/bits by taking $\log_e/\log_2$ in KL-divergence) is provided by $\mathcal{M}(X)$ to support the adversary's inference. Especially, when we select $\mathcal{D}_f$ to be total variation and still $\mathsf{P}_W = \mathsf{P}_{\mathcal{M}(X)}$,

$$\Delta_{TV}\delta = \delta_o^\rho - \delta \leq \mathcal{D}_{TV}\big(\mathsf{P}_{X,\mathcal{M}(X)}\|\mathsf{P}_X \otimes \mathsf{P}_{\mathcal{M}(X)}\big).$$

By Pinsker's inequality, which states that for two distributions P and Q on the same measurable space, $\Delta_{TV}(\mathsf{P}\|\mathsf{Q}) \leq \sqrt{\frac{1}{2} \cdot \Delta_{KL}(\mathsf{P}\|\mathsf{Q})}$, we have the following corollary to give a quantification on the more intuitive and classic posterior advantage.

Corollary 1. *With the same setup as Theorem 1, the posterior advantage ($\delta_o^\rho - \delta$) for arbitrary ρ is upper bounded as*

$$\Delta_{TV}\delta = \delta_o^\rho - \delta \leq \sqrt{\frac{1}{2} \cdot \mathsf{MI}\big(X;\mathcal{M}(X)\big)}.$$

On the other hand, we can also apply Theorem 1 to interpret the classic worst-case security definitions. To derive the *data-independent* maximal leakage when exposing $\mathcal{M}(X)$, we may take a supremum on the right side of (2) and study $\sup_{\mathsf{D},X\sim\mathsf{D}} \mathsf{MI}(X;\mathcal{M}(X))$ instead. Thus, the adversarial worst-case analysis can be used to produce a (loose) upper bound of PAC Privacy. For example, if we know $\mathcal{M}$ is ϵ-DP, then $\sup_{\mathsf{D},X\sim\mathsf{D}} \mathsf{MI}(X;\mathcal{M}(X)) \leq 0.5\epsilon^2 n^2$ for an n-datapoint set X (Theorem 1.10 and Proposition 1.4 in [13]).

With Theorem 1, our goal for the remainder of this paper is clear, where we set out to determine or bound $\mathsf{MI}(X;\mathcal{M}(X))$ with high confidence. We first move on to analyze an important special case where x_i is i.i.d. generated and $\mathcal{M}(\cdot)$ is a symmetric mechanism. Here, we call $\mathcal{M}(x_1, x_2, \ldots, x_n)$ symmetric if for an arbitrary perturbation π on $[1:n]$, the distribution of $\mathcal{M}(x_{\pi(1)}, x_{\pi(2)}, \ldots, x_{\pi(n)})$ is identical, where each element x_i is treated equally. Many data processing tasks satisfy the symmetric property, for example mean/median estimation or empirical risk minimization (ERM) in machine learning, where the order of samples does not change the result. The main motivation to study this special case is that we can show tighter and simpler bounds to control the security parameter δ in many applications, especially when the mechanism $\mathcal{M}$ is deterministic with respect to X. This will become clear in Sect. 4. For notional clarity, we will use $X \sim \bar{\mathsf{D}}^n$ to denote that x_i is i.i.d. generated from some distribution $\bar{\mathsf{D}}$ to differentiate from the generic joint distribution case.

Theorem 2. *A mechanism $\mathcal{M}$ satisfies $(\delta, \rho, n, \mathsf{D})$ PAC Individual Privacy if there exist δ_i for $i = 1, 2, \ldots, n$, satisfying $\delta_i \geq \delta$ and*

$$\mathcal{D}_{KL}(\mathbf{1}_{\delta_i}\|\mathbf{1}_{\delta_{o,i}^\rho}) \leq \mathsf{MI}\big(x_i;\mathcal{M}(X)\big). \tag{3}$$

Here, $1 - \delta_{o,i}^\rho = \sup_{\tilde{x}_i \in \mathcal{X}} \Pr(\rho(\tilde{x}_i, x_i) = 1)$ represents the optimal prior success rate of recovering x_i.

In particular, when $X \sim \bar{\mathsf{D}}^n$ and $\mathcal{M}$ is a symmetric mechanism, then

$$\delta \geq \sum_{j=1}^{n} \frac{\tilde{\delta}^j}{n},$$

for any selection of $\tilde{\delta}^j$ satisfying $\mathcal{D}_{KL}(1_{\tilde{\delta}^j} \| 1_{\tilde{\delta}^{j,\rho}_o}) \leq \mathsf{MI}(X; \mathcal{M}(X))$, where

$$1 - \tilde{\delta}^{j,\rho}_o = \sum_{l=j}^{n} \binom{n}{l} (\bar{\delta}^\rho_o)^{n-l} \cdot (1 - \bar{\delta}^\rho_o)^l, \tag{4}$$

and $1 - \bar{\delta}^\rho_o = \sup_{\tilde{x} \in \mathcal{X}} \Pr_{x \sim \bar{D}}(\rho(\tilde{x}, x) = 1)$.

In Theorem 2, we point out that if our objective is individual privacy, we may get tighter bounds by applying $\mathsf{MI}(x_i; \mathcal{M}(X))$ rather than $\mathsf{MI}(X; \mathcal{M}(X))$. By the chain rule of mutual information [23], we know that $\mathsf{MI}(X; \mathcal{M}(X))$ is an upper bound for any $\mathsf{MI}(x_i; \mathcal{M}(X))$ since for any i,

$$\mathsf{MI}(X; \mathcal{M}(X)) = \mathsf{MI}(x_i; \mathcal{M}(X)) + \mathsf{MI}(X \backslash \{x_i\}; \mathcal{M}(X)|x_i) \geq \mathsf{MI}(x_i; \mathcal{M}(X)).$$

However, to analyze $\mathsf{MI}(x_i; \mathcal{M}(X))$, generally we need to take the other elements $X \backslash \{x_i\}$ as part of randomness seeds and enforce $\mathcal{M}$ to be randomized, which makes it more difficult to give tight bounds. Therefore, in the second part of Theorem 2, in the case of i.i.d. data with symmetric processing, we give a more fine-grained analysis but stick to $\mathsf{MI}(X, \mathcal{M}(X))$. The idea behind this is that we consider the chance, denoted by $(1 - \tilde{\delta}^j)$, that the adversary can successfully recover at least j many elements out of an n-sample set X, and use the symmetric property to bound the success rate of each individual x_i.

Example 1 (Applications of Theorems 1 and 2). *We consider a set X of n datapoints where each datapoint x_i is i.i.d. uniformly selected from a finite set of size N and $\mathcal{M}$ is some symmetric mechanism. Suppose $N = 100$ and for any given i, we know the optimal prior success rate $(1 - \delta^\rho_o)$ to identify the true selection of x_i is 0.01. When $\mathsf{MI}(X; \mathcal{M}(X)) = 1$, via Theorem 1, by numerically solving $\mathcal{D}_{KL}(1_{\delta_i} \| 1_{0.99}) \leq 1$, we have a global bound $(1 - \delta) \leq 0.36$ for any n.*

Applying Theorem 2, a larger n will produce a tighter bound of $(1 - \delta)$. Given $\mathsf{MI}(X; \mathcal{M}(X)) = 1$, we numerically solve $\mathcal{D}_{KL}(1_{\tilde{\delta}^j} \| 1_{\tilde{\delta}^{j,\rho}_o}) \leq 1$ to obtain the lower bound of $\tilde{\delta}_j$, the failure probability that an adversary can recover at least j elements for $j = 1, 2, \cdots, n$, and consequently obtain the lower bound of individual inference failure probability δ. When $n = 10$, we have $(1 - \delta) \leq 0.17$, and when $n = 50$, we have $(1 - \delta) \leq 0.06$.

So far, we have presented the generic bounds of PAC Privacy, and to ensure desired security parameters, the problem is reduced to controlling the mutual information $\mathsf{MI}(X; \mathcal{M}(X))$ $\big($or $\mathsf{MI}(x_i; \mathcal{M}(X))\big)$ with high confidence.

4   Automatic Control of Mutual Information

In this section, we present our main results on automatic privacy measurement and control. At a high level, we want an automatic protocol which takes security parameters as input and returns a privatization scheme on $\mathcal{M}$ to ensure required privacy guarantees with high confidence. In particular, we want the least assumptions on mechanism $\mathcal{M}$, which ideally could be a black-box oracle and no specific algorithmic analysis is needed to produce the security proof.

One natural idea to achieve information leakage control is perturbation: when $\mathsf{MI}(X; \mathcal{M}(X))$ is not small enough to produce satisfied PAC Privacy, we may add additional noise $\boldsymbol{B}$, say Gaussian, to produce smaller $\mathsf{MI}(X; \mathcal{M}(X) + \boldsymbol{B})$. In PAC Privacy, the role of noise is not simply perturbation but to also enforce the output of a black-box oracle into a class of parameterized distributions. As shown below for either deterministic or randomized algorithms, with Gaussian noise, the analysis is reduced to the study of divergences of Gaussian mixture models. The key question left is how to automatically determine the parameters of the noise $\boldsymbol{B}$. We give solutions in this section. In Sect. 4.1, we focus on the deterministic $\mathcal{M}(\cdot)$ w.r.t. X, while, in Sect. 4.2, we analyze generic randomized $\mathcal{M}(\cdot)$ w.r.t. either X or a single datapoint x_i. Finally, in Sect. 4.3, we discuss how to approximate the optimal perturbation.

4.1   Deterministic Mechanism

The estimation of mutual information is a long-standing open problem, though it enjoys a very simple expression via (conditional) entropy or KL-divergence. Practical mutual information estimations have been studied in many empirical works using deep learning [10,20] or kernel methods [42] with different motivations such as information bottleneck [52] and causality [14]. However, one key obstacle to use those heuristic estimations is that we cannot derive a high confidence bound and design necessary perturbation for rigorous security guarantees.

In this section, we assume that $\mathcal{M}$ is some deterministic function w.r.t. X, for example, $\mathcal{M}$ returns the average/median of X or the global optimum of some loss function determined by X. Beyond the deterministic assumption, the only other restriction is that the output $\mathcal{M}(X)$ is bounded. Without loss of generality, we assume the l_2 norm $\|\mathcal{M}(x)\|_2 \leq r$. Since the distribution of $\mathcal{M}(X)$ could be arbitrary over $\mathbb{B}_r^d$, the d-dimensional l_2 ball of radius r centered at zero, in general, there do not exist non-trivial upper bounds of $\mathsf{MI}(X; \mathcal{M}(X))$. Indeed, possibly counter-intuitively, we cannot even say that the aggregation of a larger sample set would incur less information leakage. For example, imagine a finite set U where the empirical means of its subsets are distinct. X represents a subset of U randomly selected and $\mathcal{M}(X)$ outputs the average of X. Since there is a bijection between X and $\mathcal{M}(X)$, $\mathsf{MI}(X; \mathcal{M}(X)) = \mathcal{H}(X) = O(\log 2^{|\mathsf{U}|})$, increasing with $|\mathsf{U}|$.

Fortunately, adding *continuous* noise, especially Gaussian noise, enables us to derive generic control of $\mathsf{MI}(X; \mathcal{M}(X) + \boldsymbol{B})$. Continuous noise $\boldsymbol{B}$ enforces the distribution of output $\mathcal{M}(X) + \boldsymbol{B}$ to be parameterized and continuous regardless of $\mathcal{M}$ and X. Below, we show how to apply covariance estimation to fully auto-matically determine a noise B to control $\mathsf{MI}(X; \mathcal{M}(X) + B)$ with confidence for any black-box oracle $\mathcal{M}$. In the following, we simply set B to be some multi-variate Gaussian in a form $\mathcal{N}(0, \Sigma_B)$, whose covariance is Σ_B. Similarly, $\Sigma_{\mathcal{M}(X)}$ represents the covariance matrix of $\mathcal{M}(X)$.

Theorem 3. *For an arbitrary deterministic mechanism $\mathcal{M}$ and a Gaussian noise of the form $B \sim \mathcal{N}(0, \Sigma_B)$,*

$$\mathsf{MI}(X; \mathcal{M}(X) + B) \le \frac{1}{2} \cdot \log \det\!\big(I_d + \Sigma_{\mathcal{M}(X)} \cdot \Sigma_B^{-1}\big). \tag{5}$$

In particular, let the eigenvalues of $\Sigma_{\mathcal{M}(X)}$ be $(\lambda_1, \dots, \lambda_d)$, then there exists some Σ_B such that $\mathbb{E}[\|B\|_2^2] = (\sum_{j=1}^d \sqrt{\lambda_j})^2$, and $\mathsf{MI}(X; \mathcal{M}(X) + B) \le 1/2$.

From Theorem 3, we have a simple upper bound on the mutual information after perturbation which only requires the knowledge of the covariance of $\mathcal{M}(X)$ when $\mathcal{M}$ is deterministic. Another important and appealing property is that the noise calibrated to ensure the target mutual information bound is *not* explicitly dependent on the output dimensionality d but instead on the square root sum of eigenvalues of $\Sigma_{\mathcal{M}(X)}$. When $\mathcal{M}(X)$ is largely distributed in a p-rank subspace

---

Algorithm 1. $(1 - \gamma)$-Confidence Noise Determination of Deterministic Mechanism $\mathcal{M}$

1: **Input:** A deterministic mechanism $\mathcal{M} : \mathcal{X}^* \to \mathbb{B}_r^d$, data distribution D, sampling complexity m, security parameter c, and mutual information quantities v and β.
2: **for** $k = 1, 2, \dots, m$ **do**
3:     Independently generate data $X^{(k)}$ from distribution D.
4:     Record $y^{(k)} = \mathcal{M}(X^{(k)})$.
5: **end for**
6: Calculate empirical mean $\hat{\mu} = \sum_{k=1}^m y^{(k)}/m$ and the empirical covariance estimation $\hat{\Sigma} = \sum_{k=1}^m (y^{(k)} - \hat{\mu})(y^{(k)} - \hat{\mu})^T/m$.
7: Apply singular value decomposition (SVD) on $\hat{\Sigma}$ and obtain the decomposition as $\hat{\Sigma} = \hat{U}\hat{\Lambda}\hat{U}^T$, where $\hat{\Lambda}$ is the diagonal matrix of eigenvalues $\hat{\lambda}_1 \ge \hat{\lambda}_2 \ge \dots \ge \hat{\lambda}_d$.
8: Determine the maximal index $j_0 = \arg\max_j \hat{\lambda}_j$, for those $\hat{\lambda}_j > c$.
9: **if** $\min_{1 \le j \le j_0, 1 \le l \le d} |\hat{\lambda}_j - \hat{\lambda}_l| > r\sqrt{dc} + 2c$ **then**
10:     **for** $j = 1, 2, \dots, d$ **do**
11:         Determine the j-th element of a diagonal matrix Λ_B as

$$\lambda_{B,j} = \frac{2v}{\sqrt{\hat{\lambda}_j + 10cv/\beta} \cdot \big(\sum_{j=1}^d \sqrt{\hat{\lambda}_j + 10cv/\beta}\big)}.$$

12:     **end for**
13:     Determine the Gaussian noise covariance as $\Sigma_B = \hat{U}\Lambda_B^{-1}\hat{U}^T$.
14: **else**
15:     Determine the Gaussian noise covariance as $\Sigma_B = (\sum_{j=1}^d \hat{\lambda}_j + dc)/(2v) \cdot I_d$.
16: **end if**
17: **Output:** Gaussian covariance matrix Σ_B.

---

of $\mathbb{R}^d$, Theorem 3 suggests that a noise of scale $O(\sqrt{p})$ is needed. This is different from DP where the expected l_2 norm of noise is in a scale of $\Theta(\sqrt{d})$ given constant l_2-norm sensitivity; we will present a comprehensive comparison in Sect. 6.

Based on Theorem 3, we now proceed to present an automatic protocol Algorithm 1 to determine Σ_B and produce an upper bound such that $\mathsf{MI}(X; \mathcal{M}(X) + B) \leq (v + \beta)$ with high confidence, where v and β are positive parameters selected as explained below. After sufficiently many simulations, the following theorem ensures that we can obtain accurate enough estimation with arbitrarily high probability. A characterization on the relationship among security parameter c, simulation complexity m and confidence parameter γ is given in (6).

Theorem 4. *Assume that $\mathcal{M}(X) \in \mathbb{R}^d$ and $\|\mathcal{M}(X)\|_2 \leq r$ for some constant r uniformly for any X, and apply Algorithm 1 to obtain the Gaussian noise covariance Σ_B for a specified mutual information bound $v + \beta$. v and β can be chosen independently, and c is a security parameter. Then, there exists a fixed and universal constant κ such that one can ensure $\mathsf{MI}(X; \mathcal{M}(X) + B) \leq v + \beta$ with confidence at least $(1 - \gamma)$ once the selections of c, m and γ satisfy,*

$$c \geq \kappa r \Big(\max\{ \sqrt{\frac{d + \log(4/\gamma)}{m}}, \frac{d + \log(4/\gamma)}{m} \} + \sqrt{\frac{d \log(4/\gamma)}{m}} \Big). \qquad (6)$$

At a high level, Algorithm 1 shows a way to estimate both the eigenvectors and the spectrum (eigenvalues) of the covariance matrix $\Sigma_{\mathcal{M}(X)}$ (lines 6–7), which afterwards determines the noise parameter Σ_B (lines 8–16) to ensure desired mutual information upper bound $(v + \beta)$. In the first part, we simply apply the eigenvalue and eigenvectors of the empirical covariance obtained by the results of m simulations as the estimations of those of the true covariance matrix $\Sigma_{\mathcal{M}(X)}$. In the second part to determine the noise B, depending on the eigenvalue gap (line 9), we present two different upper bounds of Σ_B as explained later.

Theorem 4 presents a generic tradeoff between noise, sampling complexity and confidence. The role of c in Algorithm 1 is a safe parameter that provides a lower bound on noise. From (6), in general, we may use a larger noise (larger c for looser noise estimation) to produce higher confidence (smaller γ) given limited computation power m for sampling and simulation; on the other hand, both c and β can also be arbitrarily small provided sufficiently many simulations m to produce accurate enough estimation.

The main reason for the need to estimate the eigenvectors of $\Sigma_{\mathcal{M}(X)}$ in Algorithm 1 is because we need the instance-based noise to fit the geometry of the eigenspace of $\Sigma_{\mathcal{M}(X)}$. This is different from the adversarial worst-case, such as DP, which only focuses on the magnitude of sensitivity and adds isometric noise; *in PAC Privacy, we add anisotropic noise, as much as needed in each direction.* The key intuition behind why we can ensure arbitrarily high confidence is because the output domain of $\mathcal{M}(X)$ is bounded and thus $\mathcal{M}(X)$ is in a certain sub-Gaussian distribution with concentration guarantees captured by bounded r. Therefore, provided sufficiently many simulations, we can approximate the true covariance matrix $\Sigma_{\mathcal{M}(X)}$ with arbitrary precision with a mild assumption on the eigenvalue gap.

It is noted that depending on the *eigenvalue gap* defined in line 9 of Algorithm 1, there are two cases of perturbation. When the *significant eigenvalues* of $\Sigma_{\mathcal{M}(X)}$ are distinct, then for arbitrary high confidence $(1 - \gamma)$, the determined noise covariance Σ_B matches that described in Theorem 3 given large enough m, which allows selection of small enough c. However, though the spectrum of $\Sigma_{\mathcal{M}(X)}$ can be estimated with arbitrary high precision, we cannot ensure a satisfied eigenvector space approximation in our current analysis framework without the assumption on the eigenvalue gap. To this end, in the special case without the eigenvalue gap guarantee, we have to switch to a more pessimistic perturbation (described in line 15 in Algorithm 1), where the l_2 norm of the noise is then explicitly dimension dependent, $\Theta(\sqrt{d})$. In practice, such a case is very rare, and we leave the improvement of Algorithm 1 or a tighter analysis as an open question.

4.2   Randomized Mechanism

We proceed to consider the more complicated case where the mechanism $\mathcal{M}$ is randomized, where to be specific we use the form $\mathcal{M}(X, \theta)$ and θ is the randomness seed. Given selection of θ, $\mathcal{M}(\cdot, \theta)$ becomes deterministic. As mentioned earlier, to analyze $\mathsf{MI}(x_i; \mathcal{M}(X))$, we can simply combine $X \backslash \{x_i\}$, the other elements in X without x_i, with θ as randomness seeds. Therefore, without loss of generality, we only focus on the control of $\mathsf{MI}(X; \mathcal{M}(X) + B)$. The randomness seed θ of mechanism $\mathcal{M}$ is randomly selected from a set $\Theta = \{\theta_1, \theta_2, \ldots, \theta_{|\Theta|}\}$. As a simple generalization of Theorem 3, we have the following bound.

Corollary 2.

$$\mathsf{MI}(X; \mathcal{M}(X, \theta) + B(\theta)) \leq \mathbb{E}_\theta \frac{\log det(I_d + \Sigma_{\mathcal{M}(X,\theta)} \cdot \Sigma_{B(\theta)}^{-1})}{2}. \tag{7}$$

Here, we assume a random-seed dependent Gaussian noise $B(\theta)$, where when $\theta = \theta_0$, $B \sim \mathcal{N}(0, \Sigma_{B(\theta_0)})$.

Corollary 2 utilizes the following properties of mutual information.

$$\mathsf{MI}(\theta, \mathcal{M}(X, \theta); X) = \mathsf{MI}(\theta; X) + \mathsf{MI}(\mathcal{M}(X, \theta); X|\theta) = \mathsf{MI}(\mathcal{M}(X, \theta); X|\theta);$$

$$\mathsf{MI}(\theta, \mathcal{M}(X, \theta); X) = \mathsf{MI}(\mathcal{M}(X, \theta); X) + \mathsf{MI}(\theta; X|\mathcal{M}(X; \theta)) \geq \mathsf{MI}(\mathcal{M}(X, \theta); X).$$

Therefore, $\mathsf{MI}(X; \mathcal{M}(X, \theta) + B(\theta))$ is upper bounded by $\mathsf{MI}(X; \mathcal{M}(X, \theta) + B(\theta)|\theta)$, where given θ, $\mathcal{M}$ is deterministic. Thus, we can apply the results of Sect. 4.1 to control each subcase dependent on the selection of θ, and Corollary 2 follows straightforwardly. However, there are two potential limitations of Corollary 2. First, there could be exponentially many possible selections of θ and

---

Algorithm 2. $(1 - \gamma)$-Confidence Noise Determination of Randomized Mechanism $\mathcal{M}(\cdot, \theta)$

1: **Input:** A randomized mechanism $\mathcal{M}(\cdot, \theta) : \mathcal{X}^* \to \mathbb{B}_r^d$, $\theta \in \Theta$, data distribution D, sampling complexity m, mutual information bound v, and security parameters c and τ.

2: **for** $k = 1, 2, \ldots, m$ **do**

3:    From distribution $\mathcal{D}$, independently sample $X_1^{(k)}$ and $X_2^{(k)}$.

4:    Randomly select τ seeds, denoted by $\mathcal{C}^{(k)} = \{\theta_1^{(k)}, \theta_2^{(k)}, \ldots, \theta_\tau^{(k)}\}$, from Θ.

5:    Compute and record

$$y^{(k,1)} = (\mathcal{M}(X_1^{(k)}, \theta_1^{(k)}), \ldots, \mathcal{M}(X_1^{(k)}, \theta_\tau^{(k)})),$$

$$y^{(k,2)} = (\mathcal{M}(X_2^{(k)}, \theta_1^{(k)}), \ldots, \mathcal{M}(X_2^{(k)}, \theta_\tau^{(k)})).$$

6:    Compute minimal-permutation distance $\psi^{(k)} = \mathsf{d}_\pi(y^{(k,1)}, y^{(k,2)})$.

7: **end for**

8: Calculate empirical mean $\bar{\psi} = \sum_{k=1}^m \psi_\tau^{(k)}/m$.

9: **Output:** Gaussian covariance $\Sigma_B = \frac{\bar{\psi}+c}{2v} \cdot I_d$.

---

estimations on all $\Sigma_{\mathcal{M}(X,\theta)}$ could be intractable. The other issue is that (7) is tight only if for given θ, $\mathcal{M}(X, \theta)$ is concentrated. However, in some applications this may not be true. One example is non-convex optimization, e.g., we run SGD in deep learning. If the generalization error is small, the global distributions of $\mathcal{M}(X, \theta)$ and $\mathcal{M}(X', \theta)$ for any two representative datasets X and X' could be very close, but different X with different randomness may converge to very different local minima. Therefore, we propose an alternative approach as Algorithm 2 and its security proof is shown in Theorem 5.

In Algorithm 2, we need the following definition of *minimal-permutation distance*. The minimal-permutation distance between two k-block vectors $\boldsymbol{a}$ and $\boldsymbol{b}$ is defined as $\mathsf{d}_\pi(\boldsymbol{a}, \boldsymbol{b}) = \min_\pi \sum_j \|\boldsymbol{a}(j) - \boldsymbol{b}(\pi(j))\|^2/k$, where $\boldsymbol{a}(j)$ and $\boldsymbol{b}(j)$ represent their j-th blocks, respectively, and π is some permutation on the block index $[1 : k]$.

Theorem 5. *Assume that $\mathcal{M}(X, \theta) \in \mathbb{R}^d$ and $\|\mathcal{M}(X, \theta)\|_2 \leq r$ for some constant r, and we apply Algorithm 2 to obtain the Gaussian noise covariance Σ_B for a specified mutual information bound v. Then, if $\frac{|\Theta|}{\tau}$ is an integer, where $|\Theta|$ is the total number of the randomness seeds of $\mathcal{M}(\cdot, \theta)$ and τ is the number of seeds selected in Algorithm 2, and c is a safe parameter in Algorithm 2, one can ensure that $\mathsf{MI}(X; \mathcal{M}(X, \theta) + \boldsymbol{B}) \leq v$ with confidence at least $1 - \gamma$ once*

$$m \geq \frac{8r^4 \log(1/\gamma)}{c^2}.$$

In Algorithm 2, our key idea is to do sampling on the randomness seeds across Θ rather than accessing all possible selections of θ. Similar to Algorithm 1, we set a safe parameter c, which could be arbitrarily small, to lower bound the magnitude of noise added. Given $c > 0$, combining the assumption that $\|\mathcal{M}(X, \theta)\| \leq r$, we have a very rough but uniform upper bound on $\text{MI}(X; \mathcal{M}(X, \theta))$ for any possible distributions of X and $\mathcal{M}(X, \theta)$. With this fact, in each iteration in Algorithm 2, we independently sample two data inputs $\bar{X}^k = \{X_1^{(k)}, X_2^{(k)}\}$, and $\mathcal{C}^{(k)} = \{\theta_1^{(k)}, \dots, \theta_\tau^{(k)}\}$ as a random τ-subset selection of θ. It can be proved that

$$\text{MI}(X; \mathcal{M}(X, \theta) + B) \leq \mathbb{E}_{\bar{X}^{(k)}, \mathcal{C}^{(k)}, \theta \in \mathcal{C}^{(k)}} \mathcal{D}_{KL}\left(\mathsf{P}_{\mathcal{M}(X_1^{(k)}, \theta) + B} \| \mathsf{P}_{\mathcal{M}(X_2^{(k)}, \theta) + B}\right), \quad (8)$$

Thus, it suffices to consider a conditional local distribution when θ is restricted to the τ-subset selected. τ does not influence the lower bound of sampling complexity m required. However, a larger τ, which also requires higher computational complexity to evaluate more $\mathcal{M}(X, \theta)$, will produce a tighter upper bound. The reason behind this is that the conditional sub-sampled distribution with $\theta \in \mathcal{C}^{(k)}$ gets closer to the global distribution with $\theta \in \Theta$ as τ increases. We assume $|\Theta|/\tau$ is an integer, i.e., we can split Θ into multiple τ-subsets, to enable the application of minimal-perturbation distance d_π (Lemma 6 in Appendix E in the full version) to give a tighter upper bound of the objective KL-divergence to estimate.

However, for any proper selection of τ, the upper bound (8) always holds. Thus, once we have a high-confidence estimation of the expectation on the right side of (8), we also obtain a high-confidence upper bound on the objective $\text{MI}(X; \mathcal{M}(X, \theta) + B)$. Further, recall that KL-divergence between $\mathsf{P}_{\mathcal{M}(X_1^{(k)}, \theta) + B}$ and $\mathsf{P}_{\mathcal{M}(X_2^{(k)}, \theta) + B}$ for $\theta \in \mathcal{C}^{(k)}$ is always bounded given $c > 0$ and bounded r. Therefore, through i.i.d. sampling, we can simply use the empirical mean to approximate the expectation with a high probability bound.

Before the end of this section, we have some comments on the computation complexity of Algorithms 1 and 2. As mentioned before, the deterministic $\mathcal{M}$ is a special case of the randomized processing and Algorithm 2 also applies to the deterministic $\mathcal{M}$ where we may view Θ as only containing a single randomness seed. As a comparison, Algorithm 1 requires $O(\frac{d + \log(1/\gamma)}{c^2})$ simulation trials, while Algorithm 2 only requires $O(\frac{\log(1/\gamma)}{c^2})$ simulation trials. Here, we assume the parameters r and β are all constants. The reason behind the dependence on the dimensionality d in Algorithm 1 is because to characterize the optimal Gaussian noise, we need to estimate the power of output distribution $\mathcal{M}(X)$ in each direction in $\mathbb{R}^d$, captured by the spectrum of $\Sigma_{\mathcal{M}(X)}$. Though the estimation on l_2-norm based (minimal-permutation) distance is more efficient, as a trade-off, the noise upper bound produced by Algorithm 2 is looser, $\Theta(\sqrt{d})$, with a strict dependence on d. We leave a more generic tradeoff between the simulation efficiency and noise control to future work.

4.3   Towards Optimal Perturbation

The algorithms presented so far all produce conservative bounds of perturbation. Indeed, even for mean estimation, we will show (Example 5 in Sect. 6) that the gap between the proposed and the optimal perturbation could be asymptotically large. Indeed, in both Algorithms 1 and 2, the proposal of perturbation distribution P_B of noise B is independent of the selections of input selection X and randomness seed θ, while the optimal perturbation could be dependent on both. Theoretically, we can define the optimal perturbation problem as follows.

Definition 9 (Optimal Perturbation). *Given a data generation distribution* D, *a mechanism* $\mathcal{M}(\cdot, \theta)$, *an objective mutual information bound* v, *and a perturbation scheme* B *in a form that* $B(X, \theta) \sim Q^*(X, \theta)$, *i.e.,* B *is generated from distribution* $Q^*(X, \theta)$ *given selections of* X *and* θ, *we call the noise distribution* $Q^*(X, \theta)$ *optimal w.r.t.* $(\mathsf{D}, \mathcal{M}, \mathcal{K})$ *for some loss function* $\mathcal{K}$, *if*

$$Q^*(X, \theta) = \arg\inf_{Q} \mathbb{E}_{X, \theta, B \sim Q} \mathcal{K}(B(X, \theta)),$$
$$s.t. \quad \mathsf{MI}(X; \mathcal{M}(X, \theta) + B(X, \theta)) \leq v. \tag{9}$$

Optimal perturbation characterizes the least noise (measured by loss function $\mathcal{K}$) that we have to add to achieve the required mutual information bound v. For example, in many applications, we are mainly concerned with the expected l_2 norm of perturbation, where $\mathcal{K}(\mathcal{B}(X, \theta)) = \|\mathcal{B}(X, \theta)\|_2$. Though a generic efficient solution to find the optimal perturbation may not exist, we present

---

Algorithm 3. $(1 - \gamma)$-Confidence Verification of Perturbation Proposal

1: **Input:** A randomized mechanism $\mathcal{M}(\cdot, \theta) : \mathcal{X}^* \rightarrow \mathbb{B}_r^d$, $\theta \in \Theta$, $\mathcal{X}^* = \{X_1, X_2, \ldots, X_N\}$, a perturbation proposal $B(X, \theta) \sim Q(X, \theta)$, sampling complexity m, security parameters c, τ_1, τ_2 and τ_3.

2: **for** $k = 1, 2, \ldots, m$ **do**

3:     Randomly sample τ_1 selections of X from $\mathcal{X}^*$, denoted by $\bar{X}^{(k,1)} = \{X_1^{(k,1)}, \ldots, X_{\tau_1}^{(k,1)}\}$, and independently sample another τ_2 selections of X, denoted by $\bar{X}^{(k,2)} = \{X_1^{(k,2)}, \ldots, X_{\tau_2}^{(k,2)}\}$.

4:     Randomly sample τ_3 selections of θ from Θ, denoted by $\mathcal{C}^{(k)} = \{\theta_1^{(k)}, \theta_2^{(k)}, \ldots, \theta_{\tau_3}^{(k)}\}$.

5:     Define two sets of distributions for independent $B_c \sim \mathcal{N}(0, c \cdot \mathbf{I}_d)$,

$$\mathsf{P}_i^{(k,1)} = \sum_{j=1}^{\tau_3} \frac{1}{\tau_3} \cdot \left(\mathsf{P}_{\mathcal{M}(X_i^{(k,1)}, \theta_j^{(k)}) + B(X_i^{(k,1)}, \theta_j^{(k)}) + B_c}\right), i = 1, 2, \ldots, \tau_1,$$

$$\mathsf{P}_l^{(k,2)} = \sum_{j=1}^{\tau_3} \frac{1}{\tau_3} \cdot \left(\mathsf{P}_{\mathcal{M}(X_l^{(k,2)}, \theta_j^{(k)}) + B(X_l^{(k,2)}, \theta_j^{(k)}) + B_c}\right), l = 1, 2, \ldots, \tau_2.$$

6:     Compute the average of KL-divergences,

$$\psi^{(k)} = \sum_{i=1}^{\tau_1} \left(\frac{1}{\tau_1} \cdot \mathcal{D}_{KL}(\mathsf{P}_i^{(k,1)} \| \sum_{l=1}^{\tau_2} \frac{1}{\tau_2} \cdot \mathsf{P}_l^{(k,2)})\right). \tag{10}$$

7: **end for**

8: Calculate empirical mean $\bar{\psi} = \sum_{k=1}^{m} \psi^{(k)}/m$.

9: **Output:** $\bar{\psi}$.

a *propose-then-verify* framework to approximate the optimal solution. Without loss of generality, we consider the generic setup where $\mathcal{M}(\cdot, \theta)$, $\theta \in \Theta$, could be randomized and we consider an equivalent discrete data generation procedure to randomly select X from a set $\mathcal{X}^* = \{X_1, X_2, \dots, X_N\}$ of size N, where the X_is are not necessarily all distinct.

Theorem 6. *Assume that $\mathcal{M}(X, \theta) \in \mathbb{R}^d$ and $\|\mathcal{M}(X, \theta)\|_2 \leq r$ for some constant r, and for any perturbation proposal $Q(X, \theta)$, $\boldsymbol{B}(X, \theta) \sim Q(X, \theta)$, we apply Algorithm 3 to obtain $\bar{\psi}$. Then, if $\frac{N}{\tau_2}$ and $\frac{|\Theta|}{\tau_3}$ are integers, one can ensure that $\mathsf{MI}\big(X; \mathcal{M}(X, \theta) + \boldsymbol{B}(X, \theta) + \boldsymbol{B}_c\big) \leq \bar{\psi} + \beta$ for an independent Gaussian noise of the form $\boldsymbol{B}_c \sim \mathcal{N}(0, c \cdot \boldsymbol{I}_d)$ with confidence at least $1 - \gamma$ where*

$$m \geq \frac{2\log(1/\gamma)}{\beta^2} \cdot \big((2r^2/c)^2/\tau_1 + \beta/3 \cdot (2r^2/c)\big).$$

In Algorithm 3, we can give a high-confidence claim on the security parameters produced by any perturbation proposal $Q(X, \theta)$. In practice, when input set X is large and representative enough, and the mechanism $\mathcal{M}$ can stably learn populational information from X, the distributions of $\mathcal{M}(X)$ would be close to each other for most selections of X. Therefore, an empirical approximation framework of optimal perturbation can be described as follows.

1. We follow Steps 3–5 in Algorithm 2 to sample and evaluate on some large enough sets with respect to the selections of X and θ, respectively, and optimize the noise distribution to minimize its $\mathcal{K}$ loss in (9) such that the estimated divergence defined in (10) is smaller than $(1/O(1)) \cdot v$. Here, v is the desired mutual information bound.
2. Provided the locally-optimized noise proposal $\hat{Q}$, we can apply Algorithm 3 to test $\hat{Q}$. If $\boldsymbol{B} \sim \hat{Q}$ does not produce the desired mutual information bound v, we adjust $\boldsymbol{B} \sim \hat{Q}$ in a form $\boldsymbol{B} + \boldsymbol{B}_\alpha$, where $\boldsymbol{B}_\alpha$ is an independent Gaussian noise of the form $\mathcal{N}(0, \alpha \cdot \boldsymbol{I}_d)$. We then perform binary search on α via Algorithm 3 until we find a proper value.

5   Composition

In this section, we study the composition of PAC Privacy. Composition is an important requirement of a practical security definition. Since the privacy loss of any release cannot be revoked, it is necessary to keep track of the accumulated leakage. Ideally, the respective privacy loss of multiple releases is expected to be analytically aggregated to produce an upper bound on the accumulated loss incurred. For example, it is well known that for two mechanisms $\mathcal{M}_1$ and $\mathcal{M}_2$, which each satisfy (ϵ_0, δ_0)-DP and use *independent* randomness, the composite mechanism $\bar{\mathcal{M}}(X) = \big(\mathcal{M}_1(X), \mathcal{M}_2(X)\big)$ then satisfies $(2\epsilon_0, 2\delta_0)$-DP. With advanced composition, one may obtain a sharpened bound $\tilde{O}(\sqrt{T \log \delta'}\epsilon_0, T\delta_0 + \delta')$-DP for a free parameter $\delta' > 0$ after a T-fold composition of mechanisms each satisfying (ϵ_0, δ_0)-DP.

Composition also plays an important role in a classic privacy regime, especially for DP, to analyze complicated algorithms. As mentioned before, since the worst-case sensitivity is hard to compute, in general, to enable non-trivial privacy analysis, a complex algorithm usually needs to be artificially decomposed into multiple, relatively simpler operations. Composition then provides a way to upper bound the entire leakage by aggregating per-operation privacy loss. DP-SGD, one of the most widely-applied DP optimization methods, is an example. The DP analysis is developed in a compositional fashion where it is pessimistically assumed that intermediate gradients across each iteration are released. The entire iterative optimization is thus decomposed into multiple per-sample gradient aggregations [1]. Accordingly, the DP composition result also shows a simple way to determine the scale of noise required, which increases as $\tilde{O}(\sqrt{T})$ to produce a fixed privacy guarantee.

However, we have to stress that in DP, the above described results only hold when the randomness in different mechanisms is independent. This limitation makes tight Differential Privacy in many applications intractable. For example, if $\mathcal{M}_{[1:T]}$ represent T sequential processings on subsampled data from the sensitive X set but the subsampling schemes in different $\mathcal{M}_{[1:T]}$ are correlated, then more involved compositional analysis is needed. In comparison, our PAC Privacy analysis framework can indeed handle composition of arbitrary (possibly correlated) mechanisms. Besides, PAC Privacy allows us to measure the end-to-end privacy leakage of the output from an arbitrary (black-box) $\mathcal{M}$. Therefore, there is no need to artificially decompose an algorithm and control leakage step-by-step. This is one key difference compared to DP: we use composition in PAC Privacy only when multiple releases are necessary.

We first consider the simplest case for T mechanisms $\mathcal{M}_{[1:T]}$ where the data generation and randomness are both independent. By the chain rule of mutual information, we then have the following equation,

$$\mathsf{MI}(X_{[1:T]}; \mathcal{M}_1(X_1, \theta_1), \ldots, \mathcal{M}_T(X_T, \theta_T)) = \sum_{t=1}^{T} \mathsf{MI}(X_t; \mathcal{M}_t(X_t, \theta_t)), \quad (11)$$

which states that mutual information can be simply summed. Therefore, by plugging $\sum_{k=1}^{T} \mathsf{MI}(X_k; \mathcal{M}_k(X_k))$ into (2) in Theorem 1, we can obtain an upper bound on the posterior advantage $\Delta_{KL}\delta$, and accordingly a lower bound of δ.

Now, we turn to consider the more generic scenario where $\mathcal{M}_{[1:T]}$ apply independent randomnesses but share the same input X generated from D. Unfortunately, (11) does not hold anymore in this setup and mutual information does *not* enjoy a triangle inequality: $\mathsf{MI}(X; \mathcal{M}_1(X), \mathcal{M}_2(X))$ is not upper bounded by $\mathsf{MI}(X; \mathcal{M}_1(X)) + \mathsf{MI}(X; \mathcal{M}_2(X))$ in general. This is also true for most other selections of f-divergence and thus PAC Privacy, in general, cannot be simply summed up to produce an upper bound. Fortunately, we will show below that the upper bound on mutual information studied in Algorithm 2 and Theorem 5 can be simply summed up to form a new bound under the composition. In other words, the PAC Privacy of privatized algorithms using the proposed automatic analysis framework *does* enjoy a simple summable composition bound.

Theorem 7. *For arbitrary T mechanisms $\mathcal{M}_t(X, \theta_t)$, $t = 1, 2, \ldots, T$, whose randomness seeds θ_t are independently selected, and data generation $X \sim \mathcal{D}$, if via Algorithm 2, for each $\mathcal{M}_t$ a noise B_t is determined and independently generated such that with confidence $(1 - \gamma_t)$, $\mathsf{MI}(X; \mathcal{M}_t(X, \theta_t)) \le v_t$, then with confidence $(1 - \sum_{t=1}^{T} \gamma_t)$, $\mathsf{MI}(X; \mathcal{M}_1(X, \theta_1), \ldots, \mathcal{M}_T(X, \theta_T)) \le \sum_{t=1}^{T} v_t$.*

From Theorem 7, when the mechanisms $M_{[1:T]}$ are identical, we need to increase the noise by a factor at most $\sqrt{T}$ to ensure the same bound of the T-composite mutual information compared to the case of a single mechanism. Before proceeding, we have several important remarks. Even if one does not know the mechanisms to be composed in advance, one can choose v_t for each $\mathcal{M}_t$ in an online fashion and use Algorithm 2 to determine appropriate noise for each exposure. Though the composition bound in Theorem 7 is simple, tighter analysis exists using the proposed automatic framework. It is noted that one can always build a new joint mechanism $\bar{\mathcal{M}}$ which outputs $(\mathcal{M}_1(X, \theta_1), \ldots, \mathcal{M}_T(X, \theta_T))$, and simply apply Algorithm 2 on $\bar{\mathcal{M}}$ (or Algorithm 1 in the deterministic case).

In the following, we move on to the even more generic case for adaptive composition with correlated randomness. We consider T mechanisms $\mathcal{M}_{[1:T]}$ which are implemented in a sequential manner with possibly correlated selection of randomness seeds. More formally, the output $\mathcal{M}_t(X, \theta_t, \mathcal{M}_j(X, \theta_j), j = 1, 2, \ldots, t - 1)$ is defined by X, the randomness θ_t, and the previous outputs $\mathcal{M}_j(X, \theta_j)$ for $j = 1, 2, \ldots, t - 1$. Without loss of generality, in the following, we use $\mathcal{M}_t(X, \bar{\theta}_t)$ to denote the t-th mechanism where $\bar{\theta}_t = (\theta_1, \ldots, \theta_t)$ represents the joint randomness seed and θ_t may be selected dependent on $\bar{\theta}_{t-1}$. On the other hand, we are given a sequence of privacy budgets $v_0 = 0 < v_1 < v_2 < \ldots < v_T$ and our goal is to ensure that for any $t = 1, 2, \ldots, T$, the accumulated privacy loss measured as mutual information is upper bounded by v_t with high confidence.

To this end, we propose an online implementation of Algorithm 2 described as Algorithm 4. The key idea is still to incrementally aggregate existing mechanisms to form a joint one, that we can apply similar techniques in Algorithm 2 to analyze. Algorithm 4 has an initialization step (lines 2–6) where m input pairs $(X_1^{(k)}, X_2^{(k)})$, $k = 1, 2, \ldots, m$, are randomly generated from D, and for each pair we select τ randomness seeds $\bar{\theta}_{1,l}^{(k)}$, $l = 1, 2, \ldots, \tau$, for $\mathcal{M}_1$ (lines 3–4). In the online phase, for steps $t > 1$, we generate new randomness seeds $\bar{\theta}_{t,l}^{(k)}$ conditional on $\bar{\theta}_{t-1,l}^{(k)}$ determined previously (line 9) and continue the simulations on newly-incoming $\mathcal{M}_t$ over the same m input pairs selected (line 11). This saves computation, avoiding reevaluating $\mathcal{M}_{[1:t-1]}$ on fresh samples and randomness. Given previous noise schemes $B_{[1:(t-1)]}$ determined by Algorithm 4 such that $\mathsf{MI}(X; \mathcal{M}_1(X, \bar{\theta}_1) + B_1, \ldots, \mathcal{M}_{t-1}(X, \bar{\theta}_{t-1}) + B_{t-1}) \le v_{t-1}$, we can always determine some independent Gaussian noise B_t such that

$$\mathsf{MI}(X; \mathcal{M}_1(X, \bar{\theta}_1) + B_1, \ldots, \mathcal{M}_{t-1}(X, \bar{\theta}_{t-1}) + B_{t-1}, \mathcal{M}_t(X, \bar{\theta}_t) + B_t) \le v_t,$$

for any $v_t > v_{t-1}$ with high confidence. The following theorem describes the tradeoff between the confidence level and sampling complexity.

Theorem 8. *Assume that $\mathcal{M}_t(X, \bar{\theta}_t) \in \mathcal{R}^d$ and $\|\mathcal{M}_t(X, \bar{\theta}_t)\|_2 \leq r$ uniformly for some constant r, for $t = 1, 2, \ldots, T$, and we apply Algorithm 4 which returns a sequence of Gaussian noise covariances Σ_{B_t} in an online setup. Then, one can ensure that $\mathsf{MI}(X; \mathcal{M}_1(X, \bar{\theta}_1) + B_1, \ldots, \mathcal{M}_t(X, \bar{\theta}_t) + B_t) \leq v_t$ for any $t = 1, 2, \ldots, T$, with confidence at least $1 - \gamma$ once $m \geq \frac{8r^4 \log(T/\gamma)}{c^2}$. c as before is a security parameter.*

As a final remark, though the deterministic algorithm is a special case of the randomized algorithm (with a single randomness seed as discussed earlier) and we can always use Algorithm 2 for privacy analysis, Algorithm 1 can usually produce tighter noise bounds. However, the composition of the PAC Privacy result derived from Algorithm 1 is more involved, which depends on the eigenspace estimated. We leave the generalization of Theorem 7 for Algorithm 1 as an open problem. However, with simulations on incrementally aggregated mechanisms to be composed, one can similarly build an online version of Algorithm 1 to determine the perturbation sequentially given increasing privacy budget for composition.

Algorithm 4. Online Noise Determination of Adaptively-Composed Randomized Mechanisms $\mathcal{M}_{[1:T]}$

1: **Input:** A set of randomized mechanisms $\mathcal{M}_t(\cdot, \bar{\theta}_t) : \mathcal{X}^* \times \Theta^* \to \mathbb{B}_r^d$, $\bar{\theta}_t \in \Theta_1 \times \ldots \times \Theta_t$, where $\mathcal{M}_t(\cdot, \bar{\theta}_t)$ is provided at time slot t for $t = 1, 2, \ldots, T$, data distribution D, sampling complexity m, security parameters c, τ, and privacy budget $\{v_0 = 0, v_1, v_2, \ldots, v_T\}$ such that $0 < v_1 < v_2 < \ldots < v_T$.

2: **for** $k = 1, 2, \ldots, m$ **do**

3:     From distribution $\mathcal{D}$, independently sample $X_1^{(k)}$ and $X_2^{(k)}$.

4:     Initially randomly select τ seeds, denoted by $\bar{\mathcal{C}}_1^{(k)} = \{\bar{\theta}_{1,1}^{(k)}, \bar{\theta}_{1,2}^{(k)}, \ldots, \bar{\theta}_{1,\tau}^{(k)}\}$, $\bar{\theta}_{1,l}^{(k)} \in \Theta_1$.

5: **end for**

6: **for** $t = 1, 2, \ldots, T$ **do**

7:     **for** $k = 1, 2, \ldots, m$ **do**

8:         **if** $t > 1$ **then**

9:             Conditional on $\bar{\theta}_{t-1,l}^{(k)}$, randomly select $\theta_{t,l}^{(k)} \in \Theta_t$ and form a new joint seed $\bar{\theta}_{t,l}^{(k)} = (\bar{\theta}_{t-1,l}^{(k)}, \theta_{t,l}^{(k)})$, for $l = 1, 2, \ldots, \tau$.

10:         **end if**

11:         Compute and record

$$y_t^{(k,1)} = \left(\mathcal{M}_t(X_1^{(k)}, \bar{\theta}_{t,1}^{(k)}), \ldots, \mathcal{M}_t(X_1^{(k)}, \bar{\theta}_{t,\tau}^{(k)})\right),$$

$$y_t^{(k,2)} = \left(\mathcal{M}_t(X_2^{(k)}, \bar{\theta}_{t,1}^{(k)}), \ldots, \mathcal{M}_t(X_2^{(k)}, \bar{\theta}_{t,\tau}^{(k)})\right).$$

12:         Compute averaged l_2-norm pairwise distance $\psi_t^{(k)} = \|y_t^{(k,1)} - y_t^{(k,2)}\|_2^2/\tau$.

13:     **end for**

14:     Calculate empirical mean $\bar{\psi}_t = \sum_{k=1}^m \psi_t^{(k)}/m$.

15:     **Output:** Gaussian covariance $\Sigma_{B_t} = \frac{\bar{\psi}_t + c}{2(v_t - v_{t-1})} \cdot I_d$.

16: **end for**

Example 2 (Composition). *We take the* Hospital *dataset from Mathworks Sample[2] as an example. This set contains the records of 100 patients and we consider two mechanisms $\mathcal{M}_1$ and $\mathcal{M}_2$ which return the average of ages, weight, and the average of blood pressure range, respectively. We consider randomly selecting 50 individual samples to form the input X and via Algorithm 2 we need Gaussian noises $\mathbb{E}[\|B_1\|_2] = 6.85$ and $\mathbb{E}[\|B_2\|_2] = 2.60$ to ensure that $\mathsf{MI}(X; \mathcal{M}_1(X) + B_1) \leq 0.5$ and $\mathsf{MI}(X; \mathcal{M}_2(X) + B_2) \leq 0.5$. With the simple composition bound, we have that $\mathsf{MI}(X; \mathcal{M}_1(X) + B_1, \mathcal{M}_2(X) + B_2) \leq 1$. As a comparison, by applying the automatic analysis on the joint mechanism $\bar{M} = (\mathcal{M}_1, \mathcal{M}_2)$, we obtain a tighter noise bound where there exists certain Gaussian noise $\bar{B}$ with $\mathbb{E}[\|\bar{B}\|_2] = 4.57$ to ensure $\mathsf{MI}(X; \bar{\mathcal{M}}(X) + \bar{B}) \leq 1$. Using the simple composition, it is noted that the noise magnitude $\mathbb{E}[\|(B_1, B_2)\|_2] = 7.32$, when we handle $\mathcal{M}_1$ and $\mathcal{M}_2$ separately with lower-complexity privacy analysis.*

6   Comparison Between Adversarial and Instance-based Worst Case

We start by a lower bound of the Gaussian noise if we want to ensure an input-independent upper bound of the mutual information.

Theorem 9 (Lower Bound of Adversarial Gaussian Mechanism). *Given that $\|\mathcal{M}(X)\|_2 \leq r$, for an arbitrary Gaussian perturbation mechanism $Q(y) = \mathcal{N}(0, \Sigma(y))$, i.e., when $\mathcal{M}(X) = y \in \mathbb{B}_r^d$, we generate $B \sim Q(y)$ and publish $\mathcal{M}(X) + B$. Given $v = o(1)$, if*

$$\sup_{\mathcal{M}, \mathsf{P}_X} \mathsf{MI}(X; \mathcal{M}(X) + B) \leq v,$$

then for any $y \in \mathbb{B}_r^d$ and $B \sim Q(y)$, $\mathbb{E}[\|\bar{B}\|_2] = \Omega(r\sqrt{d}/\sqrt{v})$.

From Theorem 9, we see that if we want a data-independent Gaussian perturbation to ensure bounded mutual information in the adversarial worst case, we must add a noise of magnitude of $\Omega(r\sqrt{d}/\sqrt{v})$ to *any possible output* $\mathcal{M}(X)$[3]. On the other hand, from Theorem 3, we know this bound is also tight where a Gaussian noise of magnitude $O(r\sqrt{d}/\sqrt{v})$ can universally ensure the mutual information is bounded by v. This matches our intuition that without any other assumptions if we want to hide arbitrary information disclosure (bounded by r in l_2 norm), we need noise on each direction in $\mathbb{R}^d$ in a scale of $\Omega(r)$, which finally produces the $\Omega(r\sqrt{d})$ magnitude. This, in general, makes the perturbed release useless. Therefore, for a particular processing mechanism $\mathcal{M}$, when the practical data is far away from the adversarial worst case or the data-independent worst-case proof cannot be tightly produced, there could be a huge utility compromise relative to the PAC Privacy measurement from an instance-based angle.

---

[2] https://www.mathworks.com/help/stats/sample-data-sets.html.
[3] In Theorem 9, we restrict the noise distribution to be Gaussian. We leave a generic lower bound for arbitrary noise distribution as an open problem.

Example 3 (Membership Inference from Mean Estimation). *We suppose* U *to be CIFAR10 [37], a canonical test dataset commonly used in computer vision, which consists of* $60,000$ 32×32 *color images. We normalize each pixel to within* $[0,1]$ *and take each sample as a 3072-dimensional vector. We suppose each of the* $60,000$ *3072-dimensional samples is i.i.d. randomly selected into the set* X, *where the expected cardinality of* $|X|$ *equals* $30,000$, *to conduct the mean estimation analysis, where* $\mathcal{M}(X)$ *simply returns the sum of* X *divided by* $30,000$, *as an unbiased mean estimator. Via Algorithm 1, we have that an independent Gaussian noise whose* $\mathbb{E}[\|\boldsymbol{B}\|_2] = 0.28$ *is sufficient to ensure* $\mathsf{MI}(X; \mathcal{M}(X) + \boldsymbol{B}) \leq 1$. *On the other hand, in the adversarial worst-case setup, the data of normalized pixel suggests that the* l_∞*-norm of the sensitivity is bounded by* 1. *The mutual information bound requires* $\xi = 1/60000$*-zCDP [13], in turn requiring a noise* $\mathbb{E}[\|\boldsymbol{B}\|_2] = 17.7$, *which is* $63\times$ *larger than the instance-based analysis.*

In Example 3, we already utilize the property that each data point is independently sampled and the individual sensitivity of the averaging operator has a closed form $O(1/n)$ to get a tighter bound for the adversarial worst case [13][4]. However, in general, when the sampling is not independent or the sensitivity is intractable, one may need to adopt the loose noise bound shown in Theorem 9, where a noise in a scale of 2.2×10^3 is needed. Below, we provide such an example where producing a non-trivial adversarial worst-case proof remains open.

Example 4 (Private Machine Learning). *We consider measuring data leakage of deep learning on practical data. In general, in machine learning, our goal is to optimize the weights/parameters* w *of some model, viewed as some function* $G(\cdot, w)$, *to minimize the loss* $\min_w \mathbb{E}_{(x,y)} \mathcal{L}(G(x, w), y)$. *Here,* $\mathcal{L}$ *represents some loss function, while* x *and* y *represent the feature and label of a sample, respectively. Ideally, we expect the trained out model* $G(x, w)$ *to predict the true label* y *well.*

In this example, we consider training a three-layer fully-connected neural network on the MNIST dataset [39]. MNIST contains $70,000$ 28×28 *handwritten-digit images. We consider a data generation* X *by randomly sampling* $35,000$ *samples out of the entire data set. The neural network has three layers, where the weights of the first layer are a* 784×30 *matrix, those of the second layer are a* 30×30 *matrix, and those of the last layer are a* 30×10 *matrix. We select the activation function between layers to be the Relu function and use cross-entropy as the loss function, as a common setup in deep learning [38]. The total number of parameters in this network is* $24,790$. *Let the mechanism* $\mathcal{M}$ *correspond to running full-batch gradient descent for* $1,500$ *iterations with step size* 0.05 *and outputting the final weight obtained. From Algorithm 1, we have that an independent Gaussian noise* $\mathbb{E}[\|\boldsymbol{B}\|_2] = 3.7$ *is sufficient to ensure* $\mathsf{MI}(X; \mathcal{M}(X) + \boldsymbol{B}) \leq 1$. *Non-privately, the trained-out neural network achieves* 94.8% *classification accuracy; under the perturbation to ensure PAC Privacy, we achieve an accuracy of* 93.5%, *i.e., a slight compromise. Unfortunately, for*

---

[4] If each entry of X is independently generated, and $\mathcal{M}$ satisfies ξ-Concentrated Differential Privacy (CDP), then $\mathsf{MI}(X; \mathcal{M}(X)) \leq n\xi$ [13].

the *adversarial data-independent worst case*, the sensitivity/stability of generic non-convex optimization remains open[5].

Before the end of this section, we want to point out that there could be an asymptotically large gap between our proposed conservative perturbation and the optimal noise required, in particular for the individual privacy case.

Example 5 (Gap to Optimal Perturbation). *We return to the problem of mean estimation of Gaussian distributions mentioned in Sect. 1, where we assume each $x_i \in \mathbb{R}^d \sim \mathcal{N}(\mu, \Sigma)$ and $\mathcal{M}(X) = 1/n \cdot \sum_{i=1}^n x_i$. We focus on the individual privacy $\mathsf{MI}(x_i; \mathcal{M}(X))$ and set out to quantify the least noise needed. For any independent Gaussian noise, $\boldsymbol{B}' \sim \mathcal{N}(0, \Sigma_{\boldsymbol{B}'})$, we have*

$$\mathsf{MI}(x_i; \mathcal{M}(X) + \boldsymbol{B}') = \frac{1}{2} \cdot \log\left(det\left((\frac{1}{n} \cdot \Sigma + \Sigma_{\boldsymbol{B}'}) \cdot (\frac{(n-1)}{n^2} \cdot \Sigma + \Sigma_{\boldsymbol{B}'})^{-1}\right)\right). \quad (12)$$

On the other hand, when we apply Algorithm 1 and measure $\mathsf{MI}(X; \mathcal{M}(X))$ as a uniform upper bound,

$$\mathsf{MI}(X; \mathcal{M}(X) + \boldsymbol{B}) = \frac{1}{2} \cdot \log\left(det\left((\frac{1}{n} \cdot \Sigma + \Sigma_{\boldsymbol{B}}) \cdot \Sigma_{\boldsymbol{B}}^{-1}\right)\right). \quad (13)$$

From (12) and (13), we can determine the corresponding Gaussian noises to ensure a mutual information bound v and their gap shows as a lower bound of the gap between $\boldsymbol{B}$ and the optimal perturbation $\boldsymbol{B}_o$, since in this example we already restrict the noises to be Gaussian. With some calculation, we have

$$\mathbb{E}[\|\boldsymbol{B}\|_2^2] - \mathbb{E}[\|\boldsymbol{B}_o\|_2^2] \geq \begin{cases} \mathbb{E}[\|\boldsymbol{B}\|_2^2] = \frac{1}{2v} \cdot (\sum_{j=1}^d \sqrt{\lambda_j})^2, & v \geq \frac{d}{n-1} \\ \sum_{j=1}^d \min\{\sqrt{\lambda_j}(\sum_{j=1}^d \sqrt{\lambda_j})/(2v), (n-1)\lambda_j\}, & v < \frac{d}{n-1}. \end{cases}$$
$$(14)$$

Here, $\lambda_{[1:d]}$ are the eigenvalues of Σ. From (14), when the privacy budget $v \geq d/(n-1)$, there is even no need to add noise; in the high privacy regime, such a gap could be $\Omega(n \operatorname{Tr}(\Sigma_{\mathcal{M}(X)}))$. Therefore, there is still much room to improve the current analysis.

7   Related Works

7.1   Differential Privacy

DP is the most successful and practical information-theoretic privacy notion over the last two decades. Lower bounds both in DP noise [29, 35] and Theorem 9 suggest that, in general, there is no free lunch for input-independent privacy guarantees – to produce meaningful security parameters, the perturbation could

---

[5] An upper bound on individual sensitivity of Empirical Risk Minimization is only known for strongly-convex optimization [17] with an additional Lipschitz assumption and the loss function needs to be a sum of individual losses on each sample.

be much larger than the objective disclosure and destroy the released information. This is especially true in the high-dimensional case, known as the curse of dimensionality. DP and our PAC Privacy propose two different solutions to overcome this challenge.

Differential Privacy (DP) can be most naturally interpreted in a binary hypothesis form. Consider two adjacent datasets S_0 and S_1 which only differ in one individual datapoint and two hypotheses: H_0 where the input set is S_0, and H_1 where the input set is S_1. A strong DP guarantee implies that the hypothesis testing error (a combination of Type I and II errors) is large [24]. In general, when the adversarial objective is specified to identify the secret from a class of candidates, such inference can be naturally characterized by a (multiple) hypothesis testing model, and one natural privacy definition is to measure the lower bound of the probability when the adversary outputs a wrong guess [16].

The beauty of DP in bridging meaningful privacy and tolerable utility compromise is to focus on an individual datapoint rather than the entire sensitive dataset. DP stays within the data-independent privacy regime. ϵ-DP for constant ϵ cannot make meaningful guarantees for the entire data, because the security parameter grows linearly with $n\epsilon$ for the privacy concern of n datapoints (group privacy). However, a noise of magnitude $O(\sqrt{d}/n)$ can hide any individual among the n-population if one can ensure an $O(1/n)$ sensitivity. Therefore, once the population size n is large enough and we can ensure the contribution from each individual to the output is limited enough, reasonably small perturbation can ensure good individual privacy, interpreted as some constant hypothesis test error [5]. However, as mentioned before, the worst-case sensitivity proof becomes the key step in DP, which is generally not easy beyond simple aggregation.

PAC Privacy tackles this challenge by enforcing the privacy measurement to be instance-based to get rid of the restriction from data-independent impossibilities. In terms of the objective to protect, PAC Privacy is stronger and more generic, where now the privacy of *the entire dataset* could be preserved once the processing mechanism $\mathcal{M}(X)$ learns or behaves stably based on some population property of the underlying distribution D, from which the sensitive data X is generated. Individual Privacy is only a special case in PAC Privacy. One can imagine that if the output of $\mathcal{M}$ is only dependent on the distribution D, X is then independent of $\mathcal{M}(X)$ and we achieve perfect secrecy with respect to the whole dataset. In particular, for applications in machine learning, PAC Privacy would benefit from strong learning algorithms $\mathcal{M}$ of good generalization. More details can be found in Sect. 7.2.

However, PAC Privacy also has limitations since it is not applicable when we cannot simulate or we don't have access to the data generation of X. In contrast, data-independent privacy (if it can be proven) can always work with meaningful interpretation regardless of any assumptions on priors. But for most statistical data processing, where we are allowed to conduct the analysis on subsampled data, this limitation can be overcome. Even for a given deterministic dataset, through sub-sampling we can enforce that the selected samples enjoy entropy and PAC Privacy provides a strong security interpretation: even the adversary, who has full knowledge of the data pool, cannot infer too much about selected samples in the processing mechanism $\mathcal{M}$.

7.2 Other Privacy Metrics and Learning Theory Quantities

Mutual Information (MI) based Attack and Privacy Definition: MI is a well-studied measure on the dependence between two random variables quantified in information bits. Naturally, one may consider the MI between the secret and the release/leakage for security purposes. A large number of existing works apply MI to construct side-channel attacks [9, 30] or even simply adopt MI as a privacy definition [15, 40]. For example, given known plaintexts, [30] built a distinguisher based on empirical MI estimation where the adversary proposes a guessing of the encryption key with the highest correlation score regarding the side-channel leakage. [15] showed further asymptotic analysis of empirical MI estimations under discrete randomness. Though we use f-divergence, where MI based on KL-divergence is a special case, to develop impossibility results as the foundation of PAC Privacy, our motivations and results are very different from those prior works. On one hand, PAC Privacy is rigorously resistant to arbitrary adversary attacks[6], without any restrictions on the adversary's inference strategy or the computation power. In addition, PAC Privacy does *not* use MI or other information metrics, such as Fisher information [27], discussed below, or anonymity set [45, 50], as the leakage measurement, which, in general, lack semantic security interpretation. Unfortunately, except DP, most of those metrics are not semantic. For example, recent work [22] argued that the concept of anonymity set does not resist singling-out attacks and does not produce desirable individual privacy guarantees. In contrast, the entire theory developed for PAC Privacy is devoted to answering the fundamental question of how to quantify the hardness of an arbitrary adversarial inference task.

DP Under Adversary Uncertainty: With a different motivation to add less noise, there is a line of works such as distributional DP [6] and noiseless privacy [11], which study the relaxation of DP and take the data entropy into account. As mentioned before, the original DP definition ensures indistinguishable likelihoods of any two adjacent datasets in the worst case. Instead, [6, 11] considered statistical adjacent datasets where both their common part and the differing datapoint are generated from some distributions. The goal of such relaxation is to exploit the data entropy to substitute (part of) the external perturbation for the release. However, since those works are still developed within the DP framework, [6, 11] encounter similar restrictions as those in generic DP analysis. First, analytical distributional DP [6] and noiseless privacy [11] bounds are only known for a limited number of applications with very specific assumptions on the underlying data distributions. Second, the privacy concern is still regarding the participation of an individual. In contrast, PAC Privacy can automatically

---

[6] Besides MI, there are many other efficient side-channel attacks based on different statistical tests such as Pearson correlation [12].

handle any black-box data generation and processing mechanism for arbitrary adversarial inference.

Empirical Membership Inference/Data Reconstruction: As a consequence of the loose/conservative worst-case privacy analysis such as DP [25] and maximal leakage [36], a large number of works are devoted to empirically measuring the actual information leakage [47,57] or the actual privacy guarantees produced by existing privatization methods [44,51] especially in machine learning. For example, [47] measured the influence of overfitting on the adversary's advantage of membership or attribute inference. The results in [47] suggest that without proper privacy preservation, many popular machine learning algorithms could have severe privacy risks. On the other hand, [44] empirically studied the actual privacy guarantee provided by DP-SGD and showed that there is a substantial gap between the best theoretical bound we can claim so far and the practical distinguishing advantage of the adversary. [51] studied DP-SGD from a different angle. [51] showed that compared to distinguishing individual participation, DP-SGD may provide a much stronger privacy guarantee against extraction of rare features in training data. In other words, certain data reconstruction tasks could be much harder than simply identifying the enrollment of an individual sample. This matches our earlier discussion on data reconstruction and distinguishing attack in the introduction section. Empirical works on overfitting and generalization control are complementary, and can instruct the design of more stable processing mechanisms with better privacy-utility tradeoff under PAC Privacy.

Fisher Privacy: A recently proposed privacy metric, which also measures the data reconstruction error, is rooted in the Fisher information and the Cramér-Rao bound, and is termed Fisher information leakage [27,33,34]. Given an upper bound of Fisher information, one can lower bound the expected l_2 norm of reconstruction error for an adversary with *given bias*. However, Fisher information leakage is still input-independent and based on likelihood difference. There are several essential differences compared to priors-based PAC Privacy. First, to apply the Cramér-Rao bound in data reconstruction, the bias of the adversary's reconstruction on each selection of X must be specified beforehand, while the optimal selection of such point-wise bias is, in general, unknown. In contrast, PAC Privacy does not put any restrictions or assumptions on the adversary's strategy. Second, Fisher information only measures the mean squared error whereas PAC Privacy handles impossibility of arbitrary inference tasks and criteria.

Generalization Error: In learning theory, generalization error is defined as the gap between the loss (prediction accuracy) by applying the trained model on local data (seen) and on the data population (unseen) [56]. To be formal, in our context, let $\mathcal{M}(X)$ represent the model learned via the (possibly randomized) algorithm $\mathcal{M}$ from a set of samples X, generated from some distribution D. Given some loss $\mathcal{L}$, the generalization error is defined as

$$\text{Gen}(\mathsf{D}, \mathcal{M}) = \mathbb{E}_{\bar{X} \perp X \sim \mathsf{D}, \mathcal{M}}\big(\mathcal{L}(\bar{X}, \mathcal{M}(X))\big) - \mathbb{E}_{X \sim \mathsf{D}, \mathcal{M}}\big(\mathcal{L}(X, \mathcal{M}(X))\big).$$

$\bar{X} \perp X \sim \mathsf{D}$ represents that $\bar{X}$ and X are i.i.d. in D. $\mathbb{E}_{\bar{X}\perp X\sim \mathsf{D},\mathcal{M}}(\mathcal{L}(\bar{X},\mathcal{M}(X)))$ captures the expected accuracy from the model $\mathcal{M}(X)$ on population data, while $\mathbb{E}_{X\sim \mathsf{D},\mathcal{M}}(\mathcal{L}(X,\mathcal{M}(X)))$ captures the expected training accuracy. It is well known that DP can control the generalization error [7]. Indeed, the relationship between DP, PAC Privacy and generalization error can be described as follows. As mentioned earlier, DP guarantees of $\mathcal{M}(X)$ can upper bound the mutual information $\mathsf{MI}(X;\mathcal{M}(X))$ [13], and from [56], $\mathsf{MI}(X;\mathcal{M}(X))$ can then upper bound the generalization error. In the following, we show that PAC Privacy can also control the generalization error. For simplicity, we assume that the distribution D of X is uniform over a finite set $\mathcal{X}^* = \{X_1, X_2, \ldots, X_N\}$ of N elements.

Theorem 10. *For any given* $\mathcal{M} : \mathcal{X}^* \to \mathcal{Y}$, *and loss function* $\mathcal{L} : (\mathcal{X}^*, \mathcal{Y}) \to (0,1)$, *suppose* D *is a uniform distribution over* $\mathcal{X}^*$. *If* $\mathcal{M}$ *satisfies* $\Delta_{KL}\delta \leq v$, *for the criterion* $\rho(\tilde{X}, X) = 1$ *if* $\tilde{X} = X$, *i.e., the identification problem, then we have* $Gen(\mathsf{D}, \mathcal{M}) \leq \sqrt{v/2}$.

However, we need to stress that the reverse direction does not hold in general. Recall the example of mutual information in mean estimation in Sect. 4.1: we can construct some discrete distribution where given sufficiently many samples one can learn the true mean arbitrarily accurately but the mean estimator $\mathcal{M}$ could be a bijective function, where $\mathcal{M}(X)$ essentially leaks everything about X. However, small generalization error does help PAC Privacy if the learning mechanism ensures the trained out model is close to the population optimum. Thus, even in a case that $\mathcal{M}(\cdot)$ is bijective, we only need small noise to satisfy a mutual information bound.

8   Conclusions and Prospects

In this paper, we propose and study a new instance-based information-theoretic privacy notion, termed PAC Privacy. PAC Privacy enjoys intuitive and meaningful interpretations: it enables concrete measurement on the adversary's success rate or the posterior advantage for arbitrary data inference/reconstruction task with the observation of disclosures. A simple quantification via generic f-divergence is presented. More importantly, based on data priors, we show an automatic privacy analysis and proof generation framework, where theoretically no algorithmic worst-case proof is needed. Data leakage control of black-box oracles becomes possible via PAC Privacy. Though the instance-based and adversarial setups are, in general, incomparable, PAC Privacy does have strong connections to cryptography and DP. Indeed, many problems or concerns in the research or applications of DP and cryptography have a corresponding version in PAC Privacy. The underlying technical challenges are not necessarily the same but motivations are very similar. We list some interesting problems here.

Gap Between the Local and Central: Collaboration of semi-honest users to amplify local DP via shuffling models has been recently proposed and studied in [21,26]. The key idea is to securely aggregate the local noisy response from each user, where the underlying locally added noises also aggregate to produce a more powerful perturbation with amplified privacy. As analyzed in Appendix K, via MPC, PAC Privacy analysis can be implemented in a decentralized setup and each user's local PAC Privacy would then also benefit from other people's data entropy, similar to a centralized case. However, local PAC Privacy puts more requirements on MPC, and cheap MPC implementation is a key challenge in making it practical in large-scale systems.

Optimal Perturbation: Minimal perturbation is another fundamental problem in both PAC Privacy and DP. In DP, the theoretical study of (asymptotically) optimal utility loss in different data processing remains very active. Many tight results are known for mean estimation [3], convex ERM optimization [8] with specific solution restrictions like on l_1 norm [2], stochastic optimization [28], and principal component analysis (PCA) [18]. All these problems can also be systemically studied under PAC Privacy. While in PAC Privacy, privacy at a certain level could come for free (see Example 5), our current automatic framework needs noise to produce generic high-confidence security parameters. Therefore, besides a theoretically tight perturbation bound, PAC Privacy also raises its own special research problem, i.e., how to efficiently implement privacy analysis protocols and produce perturbation schemes matching the optimal bound? For example, with assistance of public data, how can we properly truncate the output domain and reduce sampling/simulation complexity?

Acknowledgements. We gratefully acknowledge the support of DSTA Singapore, Cisco Systems, Capital One, and a MathWorks fellowship. We also thank the anonymous reviewers for their helpful comments.

References

1. Abadi, M., et al.: Deep learning with differential privacy. In: Proceedings of the 2016 ACM SIGSAC Conference on Computer and Communications Security, pp. 308–318 (2016)
2. Asi, H., Feldman, V., Koren, T., Talwar, K.: Private stochastic convex optimization: optimal rates in l1 geometry. In: International Conference on Machine Learning, pp. 393–403. PMLR (2021)
3. Asi, H., Feldman, V., Talwar, K.: Optimal algorithms for mean estimation under local differential privacy. arXiv preprint arXiv:2205.02466 (2022)
4. Balle, B., Barthe, G., Gaboardi, M.: Privacy amplification by subsampling: tight analyses via couplings and divergences. In: Advances in Neural Information Processing Systems, vol. 31 (2018)
5. Balle, B., Barthe, G., Gaboardi, M., Hsu, J., Sato, T.: Hypothesis testing interpretations and renyi differential privacy. In: International Conference on Artificial Intelligence and Statistics, pp. 2496–2506. PMLR (2020)
6. Bassily, R., Groce, A., Katz, J., Smith, A.: Coupled-worlds privacy: Exploiting adversarial uncertainty in statistical data privacy. In: 2013 IEEE 54th Annual Symposium on Foundations of Computer Science, pp. 439–448. IEEE (2013)
7. Bassily, R., Nissim, K., Smith, A., Steinke, T., Stemmer, U., Ullman, J.: Algorithmic stability for adaptive data analysis. In: Proceedings of the Forty-Eighth Annual ACM Symposium on Theory of Computing, pp. 1046–1059 (2016)

8. Bassily, R., Smith, A., Thakurta, A.: Private empirical risk minimization: efficient algorithms and tight error bounds. In: 2014 IEEE 55th Annual Symposium on Foundations of Computer science, pp. 464–473. IEEE (2014)

9. Batina, L., Gierlichs, B., Prouff, E., Rivain, M., Standaert, F.X., Veyrat-Charvillon, N.: Mutual information analysis: a comprehensive study. J. Cryptol. **24**(2), 269–291 (2011)

10. Belghazi, M.I., et al.: Mine: mutual information neural estimation. arXiv preprint arXiv:1801.04062 (2018)

11. Bhaskar, R., Bhowmick, A., Goyal, V., Laxman, S., Thakurta, A.: Noiseless database privacy. In: Lee, D.H., Wang, X. (eds.) ASIACRYPT 2011. LNCS, vol. 7073, pp. 215–232. Springer, Heidelberg (2011). https://doi.org/10.1007/978-3-642-25385-0_12

12. Brier, E., Clavier, C., Olivier, F.: Correlation power analysis with a leakage model. In: Joye, M., Quisquater, J.-J. (eds.) CHES 2004. LNCS, vol. 3156, pp. 16–29. Springer, Heidelberg (2004). https://doi.org/10.1007/978-3-540-28632-5_2

13. Bun, M., Steinke, T.: Concentrated differential privacy: simplifications, extensions, and lower bounds. In: Hirt, M., Smith, A. (eds.) TCC 2016. LNCS, vol. 9985, pp. 635–658. Springer, Heidelberg (2016). https://doi.org/10.1007/978-3-662-53641-4_24

14. Butte, A.J., Kohane, I.S.: Mutual information relevance networks: functional genomic clustering using pairwise entropy measurements. In: Biocomputing 2000, pp. 418–429. World Scientific (1999)

15. Chatzikokolakis, K., Chothia, T., Guha, A.: Statistical measurement of information leakage. In: Esparza, J., Majumdar, R. (eds.) TACAS 2010. LNCS, vol. 6015, pp. 390–404. Springer, Heidelberg (2010). https://doi.org/10.1007/978-3-642-12002-2_33

16. Chatzikokolakis, K., Palamidessi, C., Panangaden, P.: Probability of error in information-hiding protocols. In: 20th IEEE Computer Security Foundations Symposium (CSF 2007), pp. 341–354. IEEE (2007)

17. Chaudhuri, K., Monteleoni, C., Sarwate, A.D.: Differentially private empirical risk minimization. J. Mach. Learn. Res. **12**(3), 1069–1109 (2011)

18. Chaudhuri, K., Sarwate, A., Sinha, K.: Near-optimal differentially private principal components. In: Advances in Neural Information Processing Systems, vol. 25 (2012)

19. Chen, S., Wang, R., Wang, X., Zhang, K.: Side-channel leaks in web applications: a reality today, a challenge tomorrow. In: 2010 IEEE Symposium on Security and Privacy, pp. 191–206. IEEE (2010)

20. Cheng, P., Hao, W., Dai, S., Liu, J., Gan, Z., Carin, L.: Club: a contrastive log-ratio upper bound of mutual information. In: International Conference on Machine Learning, pp. 1779–1788. PMLR (2020)

21. Cheu, A., Smith, A., Ullman, J., Zeber, D., Zhilyaev, M.: Distributed differential privacy via shuffling. In: Ishai, Y., Rijmen, V. (eds.) EUROCRYPT 2019. LNCS, vol. 11476, pp. 375–403. Springer, Cham (2019). https://doi.org/10.1007/978-3-030-17653-2_13

22. Cohen, A., Nissim, K.: Towards formalizing the GDPR's notion of singling out. Proc. Natl. Acad. Sci. **117**(15), 8344–8352 (2020)

23. Cover, T.M.: Elements of Information Theory. Wiley, Hoboken (1999)

24. Dong, J., Roth, A., Su, W.J.: Gaussian differential privacy. arXiv preprint arXiv:1905.02383 (2019)

25. Dwork, C., McSherry, F., Nissim, K., Smith, A.: Calibrating noise to sensitivity in private data analysis. In: Halevi, S., Rabin, T. (eds.) TCC 2006. LNCS, vol. 3876, pp. 265–284. Springer, Heidelberg (2006). https://doi.org/10.1007/11681878_14

26. Erlingsson, Ú., Feldman, V., Mironov, I., Raghunathan, A., Talwar, K., Thakurta, A.: Amplification by shuffling: From local to central differential privacy via anonymity. In: Proceedings of the Thirtieth Annual ACM-SIAM Symposium on Discrete Algorithms, pp. 2468–2479. SIAM (2019)

27. Farokhi, F., Sandberg, H.: Fisher information as a measure of privacy: preserving privacy of households with smart meters using batteries. IEEE Trans. Smart Grid **9**(5), 4726–4734 (2017)

28. Feldman, V., Koren, T., Talwar, K.: Private stochastic convex optimization: optimal rates in linear time. In: Proceedings of the 52nd Annual ACM SIGACT Symposium on Theory of Computing, pp. 439–449 (2020)

29. Geng, Q., Viswanath, P.: Optimal noise adding mechanisms for approximate differential privacy. IEEE Trans. Inf. Theory **62**(2), 952–969 (2015)

30. Gierlichs, B., Batina, L., Tuyls, P., Preneel, B.: Mutual information analysis. In: Oswald, E., Rohatgi, P. (eds.) CHES 2008. LNCS, vol. 5154, pp. 426–442. Springer, Heidelberg (2008). https://doi.org/10.1007/978-3-540-85053-3_27

31. Goldwasser, S., Micali, S.: Probabilistic encryption & how to play mental poker keeping secret all partial information. In: Proceedings of the Fourteenth Annual ACM Symposium on Theory of Computing, pp. 365–377 (1982)

32. Goldwasser, S., Micali, S.: Probabilistic encryption. J. Comput. Syst. Sci. **28**(2), 270–299 (1984)

33. Guo, C., Karrer, B., Chaudhuri, K., van der Maaten, L.: Bounding training data reconstruction in private (deep) learning. arXiv preprint arXiv:2201.12383 (2022)

34. Hannun, A., Guo, C., van der Maaten, L.: Measuring data leakage in machine-learning models with fisher information. In: Uncertainty in Artificial Intelligence, pp. 760–770. PMLR (2021)

35. Hardt, M., Talwar, K.: On the geometry of differential privacy. In: Proceedings of the Forty-Second ACM Symposium on Theory of Computing, pp. 705–714 (2010)

36. Issa, I., Wagner, A.B., Kamath, S.: An operational approach to information leakage. IEEE Trans. Inf. Theory **66**(3), 1625–1657 (2019)

37. Krizhevsky, A., Hinton, G., et al.: Learning multiple layers of features from tiny images (2009)

38. LeCun, Y., Bengio, Y., Hinton, G.: Deep learning. Nature **521**(7553), 436–444 (2015)

39. LeCun, Y., Bottou, L., Bengio, Y., Haffner, P.: Gradient-based learning applied to document recognition. Proc. IEEE **86**(11), 2278–2324 (1998)

40. Makhdoumi, A., Salamatian, S., Fawaz, N., Médard, M.: From the information bottleneck to the privacy funnel. In: 2014 IEEE Information Theory Workshop (ITW 2014), pp. 501–505. IEEE (2014)

41. Mironov, I.: Rényi differential privacy. In: 2017 IEEE 30th Computer Security Foundations Symposium (CSF), pp. 263–275. IEEE (2017)

42. Moon, Y.I., Rajagopalan, B., Lall, U.: Estimation of mutual information using kernel density estimators. Phys. Rev. E **52**(3), 2318 (1995)

43. Murtagh, J., Vadhan, S.: The complexity of computing the optimal composition of differential privacy. In: Kushilevitz, E., Malkin, T. (eds.) TCC 2016. LNCS, vol. 9562, pp. 157–175. Springer, Heidelberg (2016). https://doi.org/10.1007/978-3-662-49096-9_7

44. Nasr, M., Songi, S., Thakurta, A., Papemoti, N., Carlin, N.: Adversary instantiation: lower bounds for differentially private machine learning. In: 2021 IEEE Symposium on Security and Privacy (SP), pp. 866–882. IEEE (2021)

45. Serjantov, A., Danezis, G.: Towards an information theoretic metric for anonymity. In: Dingledine, R., Syverson, P. (eds.) PET 2002. LNCS, vol. 2482, pp. 41–53. Springer, Heidelberg (2003). https://doi.org/10.1007/3-540-36467-6_4

46. Shannon, C.E.: Communication theory of secrecy systems. Bell Syst. Tech. J. **28**(4), 656–715 (1949)

47. Shokri, R., Stronati, M., Song, C., Shmatikov, V.: Membership inference attacks against machine learning models. In: 2017 IEEE Symposium on Security and Privacy (SP), pp. 3–18. IEEE (2017)

48. Shorten, C., Khoshgoftaar, T.M.: A survey on image data augmentation for deep learning. J. Big Data **6**(1), 1–48 (2019)

49. Stefanov, E., et al.: Path ORAM: an extremely simple oblivious RAM protocol. J. ACM (JACM) **65**(4), 1–26 (2018)

50. Steinbrecher, S., Köpsell, S.: Modelling unlinkability. In: Dingledine, R. (ed.) PET 2003. LNCS, vol. 2760, pp. 32–47. Springer, Heidelberg (2003). https://doi.org/10.1007/978-3-540-40956-4_3

51. Stock, P., Shilov, I., Mironov, I., Sablayrolles, A.: Defending against reconstruction attacks with r\'enyi differential privacy. arXiv preprint arXiv:2202.07623 (2022)

52. Tishby, N., Pereira, F.C., Bialek, W.: The information bottleneck method. arXiv preprint physics/0004057 (2000)

53. Valiant, L.G.: A theory of the learnable. Commun. ACM **27**(11), 1134–1142 (1984)

54. Wang, Y.X., Balle, B., Kasiviswanathan, S.P.: Subsampled rényi differential privacy and analytical moments accountant. In: The 22nd International Conference on Artificial Intelligence and Statistics, pp. 1226–1235. PMLR (2019)

55. Xiao, X., Tao, Y.: Output perturbation with query relaxation. Proc. VLDB Endowment **1**(1), 857–869 (2008)

56. Xu, A., Raginsky, M.: Information-theoretic analysis of generalization capability of learning algorithms. In: Advances in Neural Information Processing Systems, vol. 30 (2017)

57. Yeom, S., Giacomelli, I., Fredrikson, M., Jha, S.: Privacy risk in machine learning: analyzing the connection to overfitting. In: 2018 IEEE 31st Computer Security Foundations Symposium (CSF), pp. 268–282. IEEE (2018)

One-Way Functions and the Hardness of (Probabilistic) Time-Bounded Kolmogorov Complexity w.r.t. Samplable Distributions

Yanyi Liu[1(✉)] and Rafael Pass[2]

[1] Cornell Tech, New York, USA
yl2866@cornell.edu
[2] Tel-Aviv University & Cornell Tech, Tel Aviv, Israel
rafaelp@tau.ac.il

Abstract. Consider the recently introduced notion of *probabilistic time-bounded Kolmogorov Complexity*, pK^t (Goldberg et al., CCC'22), and let $\mathsf{MpK^tP}$ denote the language of pairs (x,k) such that $pK^t(x) \leq k$. We show the equivalence of the following:

- $\mathsf{MpK^{poly}P}$ is (mildly) hard-on-average w.r.t. *any* samplable distribution $\mathcal{D}$;
- $\mathsf{MpK^{poly}P}$ is (mildly) hard-on-average w.r.t. the *uniform* distribution;
- existence of one-way functions.

As far as we know, this yields the first natural class of problems where hardness with respect to any samplable distribution is equivalent to hardness with respect to the uniform distribution.

Under standard derandomization assumptions, we can show the same result also w.r.t. the standard notion of time-bounded Kolmogorov complexity, K^t.

1 Introduction

A *one-way function* [5] (OWF) is a function f that can be efficiently computed (in polynomial time), yet no probabilistic polynomial-time (PPT) algorithm can invert f with inverse polynomial probability for infinitely many input lengths n. Whether one-way functions exist is unequivocally the most important open problem in Cryptography (and arguably the most importantly open problem in

Y. Liu—Work done while visiting the Simons Institute during the Meta-complexity program. Supported by a JP Morgan fellowship.

R. Pass—Supported in part by NSF Award CNS 2149305, NSF Award CNS-2128519, NSF Award RI-1703846, AFOSR Award FA9550-18-1-0267, FA9550-23-1-0312, a JP Morgan Faculty Award, the Algorand Centres of Excellence programme managed by Algorand Foundation, and DARPA under Agreement No. HR00110C0086. Any opinions, findings and conclusions or recommendations expressed in this material are those of the author(s) and do not necessarily reflect the views of the United States Government, DARPA or the Algorand Foundation.

H. Handschuh and A. Lysyanskaya (Eds.): CRYPTO 2023, LNCS 14082, pp. 645–673, 2023.
https://doi.org/10.1007/978-3-031-38545-2_21

the theory of computation, see e.g., [19]): OWFs are both necessary [16] and sufficient for many of the most central cryptographic primitives and protocols (e.g., pseudorandom generators [2,12], pseudorandom functions [8], private-key encryption [9], digital signatures [28], commitment schemes [26], identification protocols [6], coin-flipping protocols [1], and more). These primitives and protocols are often referred to as *private-key primitives*, or "Minicrypt" primitives [14] as they exclude the notable task of public-key encryption [5,27]. Additionally, as observed by Impagliazzo [10,14], the existence of a OWF is equivalent to the existence of polynomial-time method for sampling hard *solved* instances for an NP language (i.e., hard instances together with their witnesses).

The Win-Win Paradigm, and OWFs from Average-case Hardness of NP? A central problem in the theory of Cryptography is whether the existence of OWFs can be based on some simple complexity-theoretic assumptions. Ideally, we would want an assumption that leads to a *win-win* scenario: either we have secure OWFs (and thus can securely implement all primitives in Minicrypt), or we get some algorithmic breakthroughs that are useful to society/the pursuit of knowledge etc. The ideal win-win scenario would be to get a construction of OWF based on worst-case hardness of NP (i.e., on the assumption that NP $\not\subseteq$ BPP)— the question of whether this is possible goes back to the original work by Diffie and Hellman [5] and is sometimes referred to as the "holy-grail" of Cryptography. A slightly less ambitious goal that still would yield a very strong win-win scenario would be to base the existence of OWF on the existence of an NP language that is *average-case hard* w.r.t. to some samplable distribution $\mathcal{D}$. (Note that the existence of OWF trivially implies this assumption.) If such a reduction were to be obtained (or in Impagliazzo's language, if we rule out "Pessiland"—a world where NP is hard on average but OWFs do not exist.), then either OWF exists, or we can solve all NP problems "in practice", whenever the instances are sampled by an "efficient world". Unfortunately, also obtaining such a reduction has remained an open problem for 5 decades:

> Does the average-case hardness (w.r.t. some efficiently samplable distribution) of some language in NP imply the existence of OWFs?

There has, however, been some recent progress towards this question based on connections between OWFs and Kolmogorov Complexity.

On OWFs and Kolmogorov Complexity. The notion of *Kolmogorov complexity* (*K*-complexity), introduced by Solomonoff [31], Kolmogorov [18] and Chaitin [4], provides an elegant method for measuring the amount of "randomness" in individual strings: The *K*-complexity of a string is the length of the shortest program (to be run on some fixed universal Turing machine U) that outputs the string x; the notion of $t(\cdot)$-*time-bounded Kolmogorov Complexity* (*K^t-complexity*) [11,17,18,30,32] considers a time-bounded version of this problem: $K^t(x)$ is defined as the length of the shortest program that outputs the string x within time $t(|x|)$.

A recent result by Liu and Pass [21] shows that "mild" average-case hardness[1] of the time-bounded Kolmogorov complexity problem (when the time-bound is some polynomial) is *equivalent* to the existence of OWFs. Additionally, [23] demonstrates that the same type of result also holds for the, so-called, *conditional time-bounded Kolmogorov Complexity problem* [20,24,32,34] (where $K^t(x|z)$ is defined as the length of the shortest program that within time $t(|x|)$ outputs x having access to z) that they also show is NP-complete. The problem, however, is that it is not known whether the problem is *average-case* complete with respect to the *uniform distribution*. In other words, if NP is average-case hard (with respect to some samplable distribution), then the (conditional) time-bounded Kolmogorov complexity problem is hard for *some* efficiently samplable distribution (by its NP-completeness), but the characterization of OWFs considers hardness of the problem with respect to the *uniform* distribution.

Hardness w.r.t. Samplable or the Uniform Distribution. Thus, resolving the above central open problem (of basing OWF on average-case hardness of NP) is *equivalent* to showing that average-case hardness of the time-bounded Kolmogorov complexity problem with respect to *any* samplable distribution implies average-case hardness with respect to the uniform distribution. More generally, we may ask:

For what classes of problems does average-case hardness with respect to **any samplable distributions** *imply average-case hardness with respect to the* **uniform distribution**?

Our focus here will be on time-bounded Kolmogorov complexity-style problem due to their connection with cryptography. As mentioned, showing this for the particular conditional time-bounded Kolmogorov complexity problem is equivalent to basing OWF on the average-case hardness of NP (i.e., ruling out Pessiland). But showing this for just the "plain" time-bounded Kolmogorov complexity problem would also yield a very natural win-win scenario: while there are many important applications to solving the time-bounded Kolmorogov complexity (e.g., optimal file-compression, inductive reasoning in science, optimal machine learning etc.[2]), we typically do not care much about solving it on random instances, but rather instances with structure. If one can base OWF on the hardness of this problem with respect to any samplable distribution, we would get non-existence of OWF implies that the K^t-complexity can be "solved in practice".

An elegant step in this direction was recently taken by Ilango, Ren and Santhanam [13]; they show that the existence of OWFs is equivalent to average-case hardness of a *Gap* version—with a $\omega(\log n)$ gap—of the Kolmogorov complexity

---

[1] By "mild" average-case hardness, we here mean that no PPT algorithm is able to solve the problem with probability $1 - \frac{1}{p(n)}$ on inputs of length n, for some polynomial $p(\cdot)$.

[2] Typically, one would actually like to solve a *search version* of this problem, where one not only finds the time-bounded K-complexity of a string but also the program that "witnesses" this complexity; as we shall see our results actually consider this.

problem w.r.t. any efficiently samplable distribution; Liu and Pass [22] extend this result to show that it suffices to assume that it is hard to *approximate* K-complexity within a term of $\omega(\log n)$ with respect to any samplable distribution. [13] also show that under standard derandomization assumption, it suffices to assume average-case hardness also of a Gap version (again with $\omega(\log n)$ gap) also of the time-bounded Kolmogorov complexity problem, and thus for a problem in NP, w.r.t. any samplable distribution. These results thus show that one can characterize OWFs through average-case hardness of some natural gap/approximation problem with respect to any samplable distribution. The problem, however, is that they all work in a gap/approximation regime where the problem is provably easy under the uniform distribution—It is trivial to provide a $\omega(\log n)$ approximation of K or K^t w.r.t. the uniform distribution: simply output the length of the string! Indeed, as these result show, in this regime, the sampler for the hard distribution must it self be a OWF. So in a sense, these result do not give us any insight into how to build a OWF "from scratch".

As far as we know, the only result that we are away of showing that hardness with respect to any samplable distributions implies hardness with respect to the uniform distribution is the seminal result of Impagliazzo and Levin [15]; their result however only shows average-case hardness of NP with respect to some samplable distribution implies average-case hardness of some (artificial) specially-constructed NP language with respect to the uniform distribution. As far as we known, no such reductions are not known for any "natural" classes of languages.

1.1   Our Results

Roughly speaking, our main result shows that for a *probabilistic version* of K^t, average-case hardness with respect to any samplable distribution (of the exact, as opposed to the approximate) problem is equivalent to the average-case hardness with respect to the uniform distribution, which in turn is equivalent to the existence of OWFs. This notion, called *probabilistic K^t* (denoted pK^t) was recently introduced by Goldberg et al [7]. Roughly speaking, this notion measures the length of the shortest program that outputs a string x if we get access to a random string (think of it as K^t in the "Common Random String" (CRS) model). More formally, let

$$pK^t_\delta(x) = \min\{w \in \mathbb{N} \mid \Pr[r \leftarrow \{0,1\}^{t(|x|)} : K^t(x \mid r) \leq w] \geq \delta\}$$

and let $\mathsf{MpK^tP}$ denote the promise problem $(\Pi_{\mathsf{YES}}, \Pi_{\mathsf{NO}})$ where Π_{YES} consists of (x, k), $|k| = \lceil \log |x| \rceil$, $pK^t_{2/3}(x) \leq k$ and Π_{NO} consists of (x, k), $|k| = \lceil \log |x| \rceil$, $pK^t_{1/3}(x) > k$.

Our main result shows:

Theorem 11 *The following are equivalent:*

- *There exists an efficiently samplable distribution $\mathcal{D}$ such $\mathsf{MpK^tP}$ is mildly hard-on-average on $\mathcal{D}$ for some (or every) sufficiently large polynomial $t(\cdot)$;*

– $\mathsf{MpK}^t\mathsf{P}$ *is mildly hard-on-average on the uniform distribution for some (or every) sufficiently large polynomial* $t(\cdot)$
– *OWF exists.*

In fact, our formal proof is even stronger; we show that it suffices to assume hardness of a search version of the pK^t problem where given any x sampled from an efficient distribution $\mathcal{D}$, and a random CRS r, the goal is to find the shortest program that generates x given r. This yields a strong and natural win-win scenario:

Either OWF exist, or we can (with probability $1 - 1/\mathsf{poly}(n)$) find the best way to compress any efficiently sampled string x, in the presence of a CRS.

We highlight that such compression is not just useful in its own; if ascribe to Occam's razor (i.e., "rule of parsimony"· that the simplost way to explain a phenomena is preferable to a more complex), then solving this search version of K^t (even in the presence of a CRS), yields a powerful tool for scientific discovery.

We next turn to considering the "standard" K^t problem; let $\mathsf{MK}^t\mathsf{P}$ denote the language of pairs of (x, k), $|k| = \lceil \log |x| \rceil$, $K^t(x) \leq k$. We show that under standard derandomization assumptions (used to show that $\mathsf{AM} \subset \mathsf{NP}$), hardness of $\mathsf{MK}^{\mathsf{poly}}\mathsf{P}$ w.r.t. some samplable distribution is equivalent to hardness w.r.t. the uniform distribution (which by [21] is equivalent to OWF).

Theorem 12. *Assume that* $\mathsf{E} \not\subseteq \mathsf{ioNSIZE}[2^{\Omega(n)}]$. *Then, the following are equivalent:*

– *There exists an efficiently samplable distribution* $\mathcal{D}$ *such that* $\mathsf{MK}^t\mathsf{P}$ *is mildly hard-on-average on* $\mathcal{D}$ *for some (or every) sufficiently large polynomial* $t(\cdot)$;
– $\mathsf{MK}^t\mathsf{P}$ *is mildly hard-on-average on the uniform distribution for some (or every) sufficiently large polynomial* $t(\cdot)$;
– *OWF exists.*

Again, we can strengthen the result and base it on the hardness of solving the search version of the K^t problem.

This final results is related to the recent result by [13], that shows equivalence of *infinitely-often* OWFs and the io-average-case hardness of a Gap K^t problem (with a $\omega(\log n)$ gap) under a derandomization assumption. First, their result does not extend to handle also "standard" OWFs (on the other hand, it uses a weaker derandomization assumptions).[3] More significantly, our result weakens the assumption to only require hardness of solving the *exact* (as opposed to Gap/approximate) version of the K^t problem. This difference is significant, and the results are different on a qualitative level: K^t seemingly is hard to compute on essentially any "well-spread" distribution (and in particular on the uniform distribution), but it seems very hard to (unconditionally) find a distribution on which it is hard to approximate within $\omega(\log n)$. Indeed, as mentioned above,

---

[3] It would seem that we can also use a weaker derandomization assumption in case we only want to deduce io-OWFs; we defer the details to the full version.

the proof in [13] essentially show that the Gap problem can only be hard on a samplable distribution $\mathcal{D}$ if the sampling procedure for the distribution itself is a OWF.

1.2   Proof Overview

We here provide some intuitions behind the proofs of Theorems 11 and 12. We will show that (1) hardness with respect to any samplable distribution implies OWF, and (2) OWFs imply hardness with respect to the uniform distribution. Step (2) will actually follow mostly using the techniques from [21]—they pass through the notion of an "entropy-preserving PRG" constructed in [21] from OWFs, and we next observe that just as [21] showed that such PRGs imply (mild) average-case hardness of $\mathsf{MK}^t\mathsf{P}$, we can also show (dealing just with some minor technical details) that they also imply mild average-case hardness of $\mathsf{MpK}^t\mathsf{P}$.

We here focus on (1); for simplicity of notation, let us start by considering the standard K^t problem. We aim to construct a OWF assuming K^t is mildly hard-on-average to compute with respect to some samplable distribution. Towards doing this, let us first recall the high-level idea behind the construction of [21], that was based on the average-case hardness of computing K^t with respect to the *uniform* distribution.

The LP20 OWF. [21] actually only constructs a so-called *weak* OWF[4]; a (strong) OWF can be be obtained by relying on Yao's hardness amplification theorem [33]. Their construction proceeds as follows. Let c be a constant such that every string x can be output by a program of length $|x| + c$ (running on the fixed Universal Turing machine U). Consider the function $f(\ell||\Pi')$, where ℓ is a bitstring of length $\log(n + c)$ and Π' is a bitstring of length $n + c$, that lets Π be the first ℓ bits of Π', and outputs $\ell||y$ where y is the output generated by running the program Π[5] for $t(n)$ steps.

We aim to show that if f can be inverted with high probability—significantly higher than $1 - 1/n$—then K^t-complexity of *random strings* $z \in \{0,1\}^n$ can be computed with high probability. The heuristic $\mathcal{H}$, given a string z, simply tries to invert f on $\ell||z$ for all $\ell \in [n + c]$, and outputs the smallest ℓ for which inversion succeeds.[6]

The key idea for arguing that this works is that for every string z with K^t-complexity w, there exists some program Π_z of length w that outputs it; furthermore, by our assumption on c, $w \leq n + c$. We thus have that $f(\mathcal{U}_{n+c+\log(n+c)})$ will output $w||z$ with probability at least

---

[4] Recall that an efficiently computable function f is a weak OWF if there exists some polynomial $q > 0$ such that f cannot be efficiently inverted with probability better than $1 - \frac{1}{q(n)}$ for sufficiently large n.

[5] Formally, the program/description Π is an encoding of a pair (M, w) where M is a Turing machine and w is some input, and we evaluate $M(w)$ on the Universal Turing machine U.

[6] Or, in case, we also want solve the search problem, we also output the ℓ-bit truncation of the program Π' output by the inverter.

$$\frac{1}{n+c} \cdot 2^{-w} \geq \frac{1}{n+c} \cdot 2^{-(n+c)} = \frac{2^{-n}}{O(n)}$$

(we need to pick the right length, and next the right program). So, if the heuristic fails with probability δ, then the one-way function inverter must fail with probability at least $\frac{\delta}{O(n)}$, which leads to the conclusion that δ must be small (as we assumed the inverter fails with probability significantly smaller than $\frac{1}{n}$).

Dealing with Samplable Distributions: Step 1. Our main insight is that the above proof idea actually works to solve K^t not only on the uniform distribution but in fact also on any distribution D that samples any string x with probability upperbounded by $\frac{\mathsf{poly}(n)}{2^{K^t(x)}}$—we refer to such a distribution as being *polynomially bounded by* K^t. To see why this holds, consider again a string z with K^t complexity w. As before, $f(\mathcal{U}_{n+c+\log(n+c)})$ will output $w||z$ with probability at least

$$\frac{1}{n+c} \cdot 2^{-w}$$

Given that this string z is sampled by D with probability $\leq \mathsf{poly}(n)2^{-w}$, we again have that if the heuristic fails for a set of string z with probability mass δ, then the OWF inverter must fail with probability $\delta/\mathsf{poly}(n)$ (since pointwise, the probabilities in the OWFs experiment "dominate" the probabilities assigned by D, except for a polynomial factor.) This concludes that the LP20 OWF actually is secure even if we simply assume that K^t is hard for any distribution that is polynomially bounded by K^t. (Note that it directly follows that the uniform distribution is polynomially bounded by K^t, by the observation that $K^t(x) \leq |x| + c$; so this condition already trivially generalizes the condition from [21].)

Dealing with Samplable Distributions: Step 2. In the second step of the proof we aim to show that if we take an efficiently samplable distribution, then it must be polynomially bounded by K^t. (As we shall discuss shortly, we will not quite be able to do this, but either turning to pK^t, or using derandomization, will help. But let's postpone this for a moment.)

The intuition for why this ought to be true is the following. Consider some efficient sampler D that is able to sample an element x s.t. $K^t(x) = w$ with probability $n^{\omega(1)} \cdot 2^{-w}$. We can have at most $2^w/n^{\omega(1)}$ such elements so intuitively, we can compress x into $\log(2^{w-\omega(1)\log n}) = w - \omega(1)\log n$ bits, which seems like a contradiction. The problem, however is that we cannot efficiently recover x from the list of these strings.

However, the very recently-established Coding Theorem of Lu, Oliviera and Zimand [25] essentially shows how to do this exactly with the caveat that we need to consider pK^t as opposed to just K^t. Their proof uses quite heavy machinery. As an independent contribution, we here provide an elementary proof.

In particular, to efficiently recover x, what if we had access to a universal hash function H, provided as a CRS? As we shall argue, we can indeed find a short ($< w$) representation of x that can be efficiently decoded. Let ℓ denote the number of random bits used by the sampler, and let S denote the set of random tapes that map x; note that $|S| \geq 2^{\ell} \cdot n^{\omega(1)} \cdot 2^{-w} = 2^{\ell-w-\omega(1)\log n}$. If we apply H to each of these random tapes, truncate the answer to $\log|S| - O(1)$ bits, then it follows from the Chebyshev's inequality that with some large constant probability, there will exist some random tape leading to x that gets mapped to the all 0 string. Furthermore, by the same Chebyshev's inequality-based argument, there are at most $2^{\ell-\log|S|} = 2^{w-\omega(1)\log n}$ strings in total that get mapped to the all 0 string. We can finally rely on the fact that universal hash functions can be constructed using a linear mapping, and we can leverage this structure to efficiently index each of these pre-images to the all 0 string of the hash function. Essentially, we can simply use a basis for the kernel of the matrix describing the hash function. Since the space contains $2^{w-\omega(1)\log n}$ strings, we will have $w - \omega(1)\log n$ basis vectors, and each such string in the space can thus be specified by a binary vector of length $w - \omega(1)\log n$ bits.

This still does not contradict the assumption that $K^t(x) = w$ since the above compression uses an external hash function. However, if we instead switch to using pK^t, then we do get a contradiction. This, of course, requires redoing also Step 1 w.r.t to pK^t, which introduces some additional technicalities but we can essentially proceed in the same way.

Finally, we remark that if we rely on derandomization assumptions, we can actually derandomize the hashfunction and actually prove Step 2 also for K^t. (In fact, proving step 2 for K^t can be obtained as a direct corollary step 2 w.r.t. pK^t and a result from [7] that relates pK^t and K^t under derandomization assumption; for completeness, also provide a a simple direct proof based on derandomizing the hashfunction.)

2   Preliminaries

2.1   One-Way Functions

We recall the definition of one-way functions [5]. Roughly speaking, a function f is one-way if it is polynomial-time computable, but hard to invert for PPT attackers.

Definition 21. *Let* $f : \{0,1\}^* \to \{0,1\}^*$ *be a polynomial-time computable function.* f *is said to be a* one-way function *(OWF) if for every* PPT *algorithm* $\mathcal{A}$, *there exists a negligible function* μ *such that for all* $n \in \mathbb{N}$,

$$\Pr[x \leftarrow \{0,1\}^n; y = f(x) : A(1^n, y) \in f^{-1}(f(x))] \leq \mu(n)$$

We may also consider a weaker notion of a *weak one-way function* [33], where we only require all PPT attackers to fail with probability noticeably bounded away from 1:

Definition 22. *Let* $f : \{0,1\}^* \to \{0,1\}^*$ *be a polynomial-time computable function.* f *is said to be an* α-weak one-way function *(α-weak OWF) if for every* PPT *algorithm* $\mathcal{A}$, *for all sufficiently large* $n \in N$,

$$\Pr[x \leftarrow \{0,1\}^n; y = f(x) : A(1^n, y) \in f^{-1}(f(x))] < 1 - \alpha(n)$$

We say that f is simply a weak one-way function (weak OWF) if there exists some polynomial $q > 0$ such that f is a $\frac{1}{q(\cdot)}$-weak OWF.

Yao's hardness amplification theorem [33] shows that any weak OWF can be turned into a (strong) OWF.

Theorem 23 ([33]). *Assume there exists a weak one-way function. Then there exists a one-way function.*

2.2   Time-Bounded Kolmogorov Complexity

We introduce the notion of time-bounded conditional Kolmogorov complexity. Roughly speaking, the *t-time-bounded Kolmogorov complexity*, $K^t(x \mid z)$, of a string $x \in \{0,1\}^*$ conditioned on a string $z \in \{0,1\}^*$ is the length of the shortest program $\Pi = (M, y)$ such that $\Pi(z)$ outputs x in $t(|x|)$ steps.

Formally, fix some universal RAM machine U (with only polynomial overhead), and let $t(\cdot)$ be a running time bound. For any string $x, z \in \{0,1\}^*$, we define

$$K^t(x \mid z) = \min\{w \in \mathbb{N} \mid \exists \Pi \in \{0,1\}^w, U(\Pi(z), 1^{t(|x|)}) = x\}$$

When z is an empty string, we simply denote the quantity by $K^t(x)$. We consider RAM machines (as in [7,23]) since it allows z to be as long as (or even longer than) the running time of the machine Π.

Very recently, Goldberg et al [7] introduced a probabilistic variant of time-bounded Kolmogorov complexity, denoted as pK^t. Let us recall the notion here. Roughly speaking, in the probabilistic version, the program is allowed to be picked after a uniform random string. And a string will have small pK^t-complexity if a short program exists over a large fraction of random strings. We proceed to the formal definition. Let $\delta(n)$ be a probability threshold function. For any string $x \in \{0,1\}^*$, the δ-probabilistic t-bounded Kolmogorov complexity of x [7], $pK_\delta^t(x)$, is defined to be

$$pK_\delta^t(x) = \min\{w \in \mathbb{N} \mid \Pr[r \leftarrow \{0,1\}^{t(|x|)} : K^t(x \mid r) \leq w] \geq \delta(n)\}$$

We usually consider δ as being a constant. We omit the subscript δ if $\delta = 2/3$.

We rely on the following decisional/search problems about time-bound Kolmogorov complexity (and its probabilistic variant).

Decisional. We turn to defining the decisional version of the minimum time-bounded Kolmogorov complexity problem. Let $\mathsf{MK^tP}$ denote the language of pairs of (x, k), $|k| = \lceil \log |x| \rceil$, $K^t(x) \leq k$. For its probabilistic version, let $\mathsf{MpK^tP}$ denote the promise problem $(\Pi_{\mathsf{YES}}, \Pi_{\mathsf{NO}})$ where Π_{YES} consists of (x, k), $|k| = \lceil \log |x| \rceil$, $pK_{2/3}^t(x) \leq k$ and Π_{NO} consists of (x, k), $|k| = \lceil \log |x| \rceil$, $pK_{1/3}^t(x) > k$.

Search. We will rely on the search version of the minimum time-bounded Kolmogorov complexity problem. In our search problem, an instance is a single string $x \in \{0,1\}^*$ (as opposed to a pair of string x and threshold k, as in the decisional version). A witness of a string x is the shortest program that outputs x within $t(|x|)$ steps. We turn to the formal definition. Let Search-K^t denote the binary relation $R_{\text{search-}K^t} \subseteq \{0,1\}^n \times \{0,1\}^*$ where $(x, \Pi) \in R_{\text{search-}K^t}$ iff $|\Pi| = K^t(x)$, and $U(\Pi, 1^{t(|x|)}) = x$.

We will also define the search version of the minimum conditional time-bounded Kolmogorov complexity problem. In this problem, an instance is a pair of a target string x and an auxiliary input z. And its witness is just the "K^t-witness" of x conditioned on z. More formally, let Search-cK^t denote the binary relation $R_{\text{search-}cK^t} \subseteq \{0,1\}^{n+t(n)} \times \{0,1\}^*$ where $((x, z), \Pi) \in R_{\text{search-}cK^t}$ iff $z \in \{0,1\}^{t(|x|)}, |\Pi| = K^t(x \mid z)$, and $U(\Pi(z), 1^{t(|x|)}) = x$.

Finally, we recall two useful properties with respect to K^t: (1) The K^t-complexity of x is always bounded by its length (plus a universal constant); and (2) random strings will have high K^t-complexity with high probability. We notice that these two properties are also satisfied if we focus on its probabilistic variant pK^t.

Fact 24 ([7]). *The following statements hold.*

1. *There exists a constant c such that for all polynomials $t(n) \geq n$, all functions $\delta(n) \leq 1$, for all strings $x \in \{0,1\}^*$ it holds that $pK_\delta^t(x) \leq K^t(x) \leq |x| + c$.*
2. *For any $n \in \mathbb{N}, m < n$, $\Pr[x \leftarrow \{0,1\}^n : pK_\delta^t(x) \leq m] \geq 1 - \frac{1}{\delta(n)2^{n-m+1}}$*

2.3   Average-Case Complexity

We turn to defining what it means for complexity problems to be average-case hard (for PPT algorithms). We will be considering problems that are only defined on some input lengths (such as MK^{t}P). We say that a language L is *defined over inputs lengths* $s(\cdot)$ if $L \subseteq \cup_{n \in \mathbb{N}} \{0,1\}^{s(n)}$. (For promise problems or search problems, this can also be done analogously.) For concreteness, note that MK^{t}P is defined on input lengths $s(n) = n + \lceil \log n \rceil$.

We will also consider ensembles that are only defined on some input lengths. We say that $\mathcal{D} = \{D_n\}_{n \in \mathbb{N}}$ is an *ensemble* defined over input lengths $s(\cdot)$ if for all $n \in \mathbb{N}$, D_n is a probability distribution over $\{0,1\}^{s(n)}$. (In this work, we will only consider ensembles that are defined only over $s(n) = n + \lceil \log n \rceil$.) We say that an ensemble $\mathcal{D} = \{D_n\}_{n \in \mathbb{N}}$ is *samplable* if there exists a probabilistic polynomial-time Turing machine S such that $S(1^n)$ samples D_n; we use the notation $S(1^n; r)$ to denote the algorithm S with randomness fixed to r. We say that $\mathcal{D}$ is $t_D(\cdot)$-time samplable if for all $n \in \mathbb{N}$, $S(1^n)$ terminates in $t_D(n)$ steps. One example of an ensemble defined over input lengths $s(\cdot)$ is the uniform distribution, which samples each $x \in \{0,1\}^{s(n)}$ with equal probability for each $n \in \mathbb{N}$.

Definition 25 (Average-case Complexity). *We say that a problem P defined over input lengths $s(\cdot)$ is* mildly hard-on-average (mildly HoA) *with respect to an ensemble $\mathcal{D}$ (also defined over input lengths $s(\cdot)$) if there exists a polynomial p such that for all PPT heuristic $\mathcal{H}$, for all sufficiently large $n \in \mathbb{N}$,*

$$\Pr[x \leftarrow D_n : \mathcal{H}(x) \text{ fails to solve } P \text{ on } x] \geq \frac{1}{p(n)}$$

where

- *if P is a language L, $\mathcal{H}(x)$ fails to solve L on x iff $\mathcal{H}(x) \neq L(x)$;*
- *if P is a promise problem $\Pi = (\Pi_{\mathsf{YES}}, \Pi_{\mathsf{NO}})$, $\mathcal{H}(x)$ fails to solve Π on x iff $x \in \Pi_{\mathsf{YES}} \land \mathcal{H}(x) = 0$ or $x \in \Pi_{\mathsf{NO}} \land \mathcal{H}(x) = 1$;*
- *if P is a search problem $R \subseteq \{0,1\}^* \times \{0,1\}^*$, $\mathcal{H}(x)$ fails to solve R on x iff $(x, \mathcal{H}(x)) \notin R$;*

We next show some search-to-decision reductions for the Kolmogorov complexity problems we considered. These reductions are easy to see in the worst-case setting, we now prove them in the average-case setting. Let $\mathcal{D}$ be a distribution ensemble for $\mathsf{MK}^t\mathsf{P}$ (or $\mathsf{MpK}^t\mathsf{P}$). Recall that D_n will sample a pair of a string $x \in \{0,1\}^n$ and a threshold $k \in \{0,1\}^{\lceil \log n \rceil}$. We consider the *projected distribution*, $\mathcal{D}'$, of $\mathcal{D}$, where each D'_n is just D_n but only samples x from D_n.

Lemma 26. *Let t be a polynomial.*

- *If there exists an ensemble $\mathcal{D}$ under which $\mathsf{MpK}^t\mathsf{P}$ is mildly HoA, then Search-cK^t is mildly HoA w.r.t. $(\mathcal{D}', \mathcal{U})$ where $\mathcal{D}'$ is the projected distribution of $\mathcal{D}$.*
- *If there exists an ensemble $\mathcal{D}$ under which $\mathsf{MK}^t\mathsf{P}$ is mildly HoA, then Search-K^t is mildly HoA w.r.t. the projected distribution of $\mathcal{D}$.*

Proof. We sketch the proof for the former statement, and the latter statement will follow from essentially the same proof with minor adjustments.

For any polynomial p, we will show that if there is an algorithm $\mathcal{A}$ that solves Search-cK^t with probability at least $1 - \frac{1}{2p(n)^2}$ over $(\mathcal{D}', \mathcal{U})$ for infinitely many n, then there exists an algorithm $\mathcal{H}$ that decides $\mathsf{MpK}^t\mathsf{P}$ with probability $\geq 1 - \frac{1}{p(n)}$ w.r.t. $\mathcal{D}$ for infinitely many n. Fix some n on which $\mathcal{A}$ succeeds over $x \leftarrow D'_n$, $r \leftarrow \{0,1\}^{t(n)}$.

Consider the algorithm $\mathcal{H}$ that acts as follows. On input $(x, k) \leftarrow D_n$, $\mathcal{H}$ repeats the following procedure for at least n times. In each iteration, $\mathcal{H}$ samples random $r \leftarrow \{0,1\}^{t(n)}$, and invokes $\mathcal{A}(x, r)$. Finally, $\mathcal{H}$ outputs 1 if in at least a half fraction of iterations, $\mathcal{A}$ returns a program of length at most k.

By a standard averaging argument, with probability at least $1 - \frac{1}{2p(n)}$ over $x \leftarrow D'_n$, $\mathcal{A}(x, r)$ will output a $K^t(x \mid r)$-witness with probability at least $1 - \frac{1}{p(n)}$. We refer to such x as being "good". We argue that on input a good x, $\mathcal{H}(x)$ fails to decide $\mathsf{MpK}^t\mathsf{P} = (\Pi_{\mathsf{YES}}, \Pi_{\mathsf{NO}})$ with probability at most $\frac{1}{2p(n)}$: If $(x, k) \in \Pi_{\mathsf{YES}}$, it follows that $K^t(x \mid r) \leq k$ with probability at least $2/3$, and $\mathcal{A}(x, r)$ will output a program with length $\leq k$ with probability $2/3 - \frac{1}{p(n)}$. By a standard Chernoff-type argument, if follows that $\mathcal{H}(x)$ will output 0 with probability at most $\frac{1}{2p(n)}$. If $(x, k) \in \Pi_{\mathsf{NO}}$, the same argument can be made and $\mathcal{H}(x)$ will output 1 with probability at most $\frac{1}{2p(n)}$. Combining this with the fact that x is "bad" with probability at most $\frac{1}{2p(n)}$, we conclude that the heuristic $\mathcal{H}$ fails with probability at most $\frac{1}{p(n)}$. Finally, note that this holds for infinitely many n, which is a contradiction.

3   Theorems

We state our main results in this section.

Theorem 31. *There exists a polynomial γ such that the following are equivalent:*

1. *The existence of a $t_D(\cdot)$-time samplable ensemble $\mathcal{D}$, a polynomial $t(\cdot)$, $t(n) \geq \gamma(t_D(n))$ such that Search-cK^t is mildly hard-on-average w.r.t. $(\mathcal{D}, \mathcal{U})$.*
2. *The existence of a $t_D(\cdot)$-time samplable ensemble $\mathcal{D}$, a polynomial $t(\cdot)$, $t(n) \geq \gamma(t_D(n))$ such that $\mathsf{MpK^t P}$ is mildly hard-on-average w.r.t. $\mathcal{D}$.*
3. *The existence of one-way functions.*
4. *For all polynomials $t(n)$, $t(n) > (1+\varepsilon)n$ for some $\varepsilon > 0$, $\mathsf{MpK^t P}$ is mildly hard-on-average w.r.t. the uniform distribution.*

Proof. (2) $\Rightarrow$ (1) is proved in Lemma 26. The implication (1) $\Rightarrow$ (3) follows from Theorem 41 (stated and proved in Sect. 4). By Theorem 51 (stated and proved in Sect. 5), (3) implies (4). Finally, (4) trivially implies (2).

Theorem 32. *Assume that $\mathsf{E} \not\subseteq \mathsf{ioNSIZE}[2^{\Omega(n)}]$. There exists a polynomial γ such that the following are equivalent.*

1. *The existence of a $t_D(\cdot)$-time samplable ensemble $\mathcal{D}$, and a polynomial $t(\cdot)$, $t(n) \geq \gamma(t_D(n))$, such that Search-K^t is mildly hard-on-average w.r.t. $\mathcal{D}$.*
2. *The existence of one-way functions.*
3. *For all polynomials $t(n)$, $t(n) > (1+\varepsilon)n$ for some $\varepsilon > 0$, $\mathsf{MK^t P}$ is mildly hard-on-average w.r.t. the uniform distribution.*

Proof. (1) $\Rightarrow$ (2) follows from Theorem 42 (stated and proved in Sect. 4). By Theorem 52, (2) implies (3). Finally, the implication (3) $\Rightarrow$ (1) is proved in Lemma 26.

4   OWFs from Hardness of $\mathsf{MpK^{poly} P}$ w.r.t. Any Samplable Distribution

In this section, we show that if there exists a samplable distribution under which Search-cK^{poly} is mildly hard-on-average, then one-way functions exist. In addition, this result can be extend to assuming mild average-case hardness of Search-K^{poly} under a derandomization assumption. Note that by Lemma 26, hardness of $\mathsf{MpK^{poly} P}$ (resp $\mathsf{MK^{poly} P}$) implies hardness of Search-cK^{poly} (resp Search-K^t). Therefore, we obtained OWFs assuming mild average-case hardness of $\mathsf{MpK^{poly} P}$ (resp of $\mathsf{MK^{poly} P}$).

Theorem 41. *There exists a polynomial γ such that the following holds. Assume that there exist a $t_D(\cdot)$-time samplable ensemble $\mathcal{D}$, and a polynomial $t(\cdot)$, $t(n) \geq \gamma(t_D(n))$, such that Search-cK^t is mildly HoA w.r.t. $(\mathcal{D}, \mathcal{U})$. Then, one-way functions exist.*

Proof. This theorem follows from Lemma 43 (stated and proved in Sect. 4.1) and Lemma 46 (stated and proved in Sect. 4.2).

Theorem 42. *Assume that* $E \not\subseteq ioNSIZE[2^{\Omega(n)}]$. *There exists a polynomial* γ *such that the following holds. Assume that there exist a* $t_D(\cdot)$-*time samplable ensemble* D, *and a polynomial* $t(\cdot)$, $t(n) \geq \gamma(t_D(n))$, *such that Search-K^t is mildly HoA w.r.t.* D. *Then, one-way functions exist.*

Proof. This theorem follows from Lemma 44 (stated and proved in Sect. 4.1) and Lemma 48 (stated and proved in Sect. 4.2).

The above theorems are proved in two steps. We first show that if we only consider distributions that are "polynomially bounded by the complexity measure" (defined blow), we can deduce OWFs from average-case hardness of Search-cK^{poly} (if the complexity measure is cK^{poly}) or Search-K^{poly} (if K^{poly}). Then we show that any samplable distribution will be polynomial bounded by pK^{poly}, and by K^{poly} under derandomization assumption.

We turn to defining what it means for a distribution to be polynomially bounded by a complexity measure. For a distribution ensemble D, we say that D is *polynomially bounded* by pK^t (resp by K^t) if there exists a polynomial $\delta(\cdot)$ such that for all string $x \in \{0,1\}^*$, $n = |x|$, $\Pr[x' \leftarrow D_n : x' = x] \leq \delta(n)2^{-pK^t(x)}$ (resp $\leq \delta(n)2^{-K^t(x)}$).

4.1   When D Is Polynomially Bounded

Lemma 43. *Assume that there exist a polynomial t and an ensemble D such that D is polynomially bounded by pK^t and Search-cK^t is mildly HoA w.r.t. D. Then, weak one-way functions exist.*

Proof. Let c be the constant from Fact 24, and t be the polynomial as in the lemma statement. We consider the function $f : \{0,1\}^{\lceil \log(n+c) \rceil + n + c + t(n)} \rightarrow \{0,1\}^*$, which takes an input $\ell||\Pi'||r$ where $|\ell| = \lceil \log(n+c) \rceil$, $|\Pi'| = n + c$ and $|r| = t(n)$, outputs

$$f(\ell||\Pi'||r) = \ell||r||U(\Pi(r), 1^{t(n)})$$

where Π is a prefix of Π' and Π is of length ℓ (where the bit-string ℓ is interpreted as an integer $\in [n+c]$).

This function is only defined over some input lengths, but by an easy padding trick, it can be transformed into a function f' defined over all input lengths, such that if f is weakly one-way (over the restricted input lengths), then f' will be weakly one-way (over all input lengths): $f'(x')$ simply truncates its input x' (as little as possible) so that the (truncated) input x now becomes of length $n' = \lceil \log(n+c) \rceil + n + c + t(n)$ for some n and outputs $f(x)$. This will decrease the input length by a polynomial factor (since t is a polynomial) so the padding trick can be applied here.

We now show that f is a weak OWF (over the restricted input length) assuming that Search-cK^t is mildly HoA w.r.t. $(\mathcal{D}, \mathcal{U})$. Since the search problem is mildly HoA and the distribution $\mathcal{D}$ is polynomially bounded by $pK^t_{1-2^{-n}}$, let p be the polynomial in the mild average-case hardness and δ be the polynomial in the bound where pK^t bounds $\mathcal{D}$. Let $q(n) = 16n\delta(n)p(n)^2$. We assume for contradiction that f is not $\frac{1}{q}$-weak one-way. (In the later proof, although the input length of f we consider is $m = \lceil \log(n + c) \rceil + n + c + t(n)$ for some n, we will view n as a "security parameter" and analyze the one-wayness of f on input length m with respect to n. Since n and m are polynomially related, we can still conclude that f is weak one-way.) Then, there exists a PPT attacker $\mathcal{A}$ that inverts f with probability at least $1 - \frac{1}{q(n)}$ on infinitely many n. We will use $\mathcal{A}$ to solve the cK^t search problem over $(\mathcal{D}, \mathcal{U})$ with probability at least $1 - \frac{1}{p(n)}$ (and thus a contradiction).

Our search algorithm, $\mathcal{H}$, proceeds as follows. On input $z \leftarrow D_n, r \leftarrow \mathcal{U}_{t(n)}$, the search algorithm enumerates over all possible $i \in [n + c]$, and for each i, $\mathcal{H}$ will invoke the attacker $\mathcal{A}$ to invert f on the string $i||r||z$. And $\mathcal{H}$ will also check if the inversion succeeds. If the inverter succeeds, it will output a pre-image of $i||r||z$. By the definition of f, this string will be of the form $i||\Pi'||r$, and from which we can obtain a program Π of length i. Finally, $\mathcal{H}$ outputs the shortest program it obtains.

We turn to proving that $\mathcal{H}$ is a good search algorithm that succeeds with probability $1 - \frac{1}{p(n)}$. Fix some $n \in \mathbb{N}$ such that the inverter $\mathcal{A}$ succeeds on security parameter n. It is helpful here to introduce what it means for a string z to be "good": Let $\alpha = \frac{1}{2p(n)}$. For each string $z \in \{0,1\}^n$, $r \in \{0,1\}^{t(n)}$, we let $w_{z,r} = K^t(z \,|\, r)$ denote the length of the shortest program that outputs z on input r within $t(n)$ steps. We refer to a string $z \in \{0,1\}^n$ as being good if

$$\Pr[r \leftarrow \{0,1\}^{t(n)} : \mathcal{A}(w_{z,r}||r||z) \text{ succeeds}] \geq 1 - \alpha(n)$$

where the probability is also taken over the internal randomness of $\mathcal{A}$, and the inverter $\mathcal{A}$ succeeds on $w_{z,r}||r||z$ if it returns a valid pre-image. Notice that by our choice of $w_{z,r}$, it is guaranteed that a pre-image must exist. Let G denote the set of all good strings $z \in \{0,1\}^n$. We first claim that heuristic $\mathcal{H}$ will succeeds with high probability on any good z.

Claim 1. *For any $z \in \{0,1\}^n$, if z is good, then $\mathcal{H}(z,r)$ fails with probability at most $\frac{1}{2p(n)}$ over random $r \leftarrow \{0,1\}^{t(n)}$.*

Proof. Notice that for any z, r, if the inverter succeeds in inverting f on $w_{z,r}||r||z$, it will obtain a program Π of length $w_{z,r}$ that on input r, outputs z within $t(n)$ steps. By our choice of $w_{z,r}$, this will be the shortest such program, $\mathcal{H}(z,r)$ will finally output it as a witness. Therefore, if z is good, then $\mathcal{H}(z,r)$ will output a valid $K^t(z \,|\, r)$-witness with probability at least $1 - \alpha(n) = 1 - \frac{1}{2p(n)}$ over r.

On the other hand, since our inverter $\mathcal{A}$ succeeds with high probability, there should be only "a few" bad strings. We assume for contradiction that the total probability weight of bad strings (w.r.t. D_n) is $\geq \frac{1}{2p(n)}$. That is,

$$\sum_{z \notin G} \Pr[z' \leftarrow D_n : z' = z] \geq \frac{1}{2p(n)}$$

Recall that the distribution $\mathcal{D}$ is polynomial bounded by pK^t. So for any string $z \notin G$, the probability that z is sampled by D_n is at most $\delta(n)2^{-pK^t(z)}$. It follows that

$$\sum_{z \notin G} \delta(n)2^{-pK^t(z)} \geq \sum_{z \notin G} \Pr[z' \leftarrow D_n : z' = z] \geq \frac{1}{2p(n)} \tag{1}$$

However, z will be sampled with probability at least

$$\frac{1}{2t(n)} \sum_{r \in \{0,1\}^{\ell(n)}} \frac{1}{n+c} \frac{1}{2^{w_{z,r}}}$$

in the one-way function experiment, since for each randomness r, there exists a program of length $w_{z,r} = K^t(z \mid r)$ that outputs z (on input r) within $t(n)$ steps, and the OWF will output z if the program is picked. By the definition of pK^t, it follows that z will be sampled with probability at least

$$\frac{1}{n+c} \left(2^{-pK^t(z)} \cdot 2/3\right) \geq \frac{1}{2(n+c)}2^{-pK^t(z)} \geq \frac{1}{4n}2^{-pK^t(z)}$$

When a bad string z is sampled, the inverter $\mathcal{A}$ will fail with probability at least $\frac{1}{\alpha(n)}$. Thus, $\mathcal{A}$ will fail with probability at least

$$\sum_{z \notin G} \frac{1}{4n\alpha(n)}2^{-pK^t(z)}$$

By Eq. 1, this is at least

$$\frac{1}{4n\alpha(n)} \cdot \frac{1}{2p(n)\delta(n)} > \frac{1}{q(n)}$$

which is a contradiction (since $\mathcal{A}$ is a good inverter). We thus conclude that the total probability weight of bad strings (w.r.t. D_n) is $\leq \frac{1}{2p(n)}$. Finally, by a Union bound (also taking into account good strings) and Claim 1, the probability that the heuristic fails w.r.t. D_n is at most $\frac{1}{p(n)}$.

Combining the above argument with the fact that the attacker $\mathcal{A}$ succeeds on infinitely many input lengths n, we conclude that $\mathcal{H}$ fails with probability at most $\frac{1}{p(n)}$ on infinitely many n, which is a contradiction.

We can prove that Lemma 43 also holds for K^t analogously.

Lemma 44. *Assume that there exist a polynomial t and an ensemble $\mathcal{D}$ such that $\mathcal{D}$ is polynomially bounded by K^t and Search-K^t is mildly HoA w.r.t. $\mathcal{D}$. Then, weak one-way functions exist.*

Proof. This lemma will be proved using similar ideas in the proof of Lemma 43, so the proof is presented based on the proof of Lemma 43. We assume familiarity of the proof of Lemma 43.

We will consider roughly the same OWF construction as in Lemma 43, except that we no longer need to sample a random string r in the construct. We consider the function $f : \{0,1\}^{\lceil \log(n+c) \rceil + n + c} \to \{0,1\}^*$, which takes an input $\ell || \Pi'$ where $|\ell| = \lceil \log(n + c) \rceil$, and $|\Pi'| = n + c$, outputs

$$f(\ell || \Pi') = \ell || U(\Pi(r), 1^{t(n)})$$

where Π is a prefix of Π' and Π is of length ℓ (where the bit-string ℓ is interpreted as an integer $\in [n + c]$).

This function is also only defined over some input lengths, but it suffices to show that f is a weak OWF over input lengths on which f is well defined. As showed in Lemma 43, by using a padding trick, we can transform this function f to a standard OWF.

In this lemma, we will show that f is a weak OWF (over the restricted input length) assuming that K^t is mildly HoA to search w.r.t. $\mathcal{D}$. Since Search-K^t is mildly HoA and $\mathcal{D}$ is polynomially bounded by K^t, let p be the polynomial in the mild average-case hardness and δ be the polynomial in the bound where K^t bounds $\mathcal{D}$. Let $q(n) = 8n\delta(n)p(n)^2$. We assume for contradiction that f is not $\frac{1}{q}$-weak one-way. (In the later proof, although the input length of f we consider is $m = \lceil \log(n + c) \rceil + n + c + t(n)$ for some n, we will view n as a "security parameter", as in Lemma 43.) Then, there exists a PPT attacker $\mathcal{A}$ that inverts f with probability at least $1 - \frac{1}{q(n)}$ on infinitely many n. We will use $\mathcal{A}$ to solve the Search-K^t problem over $\mathcal{D}$ with probability at least $1 - \frac{1}{p(n)}$ (and thus a contradiction).

Our search algorithm for K^t, $\mathcal{H}$, proceeds as follows. On input $z \leftarrow D_n$, $\mathcal{H}$ will enumerate over all possible $i \in [n + c]$, and for each i, the heuristic will invoke the attacker $\mathcal{A}$ to invert f on the string $i || z$. And $\mathcal{H}$ will also check if the inversion succeeds. If the inverter succeeds, it will output a pre-image of $i || z$. By the definition of f, this string will be of the form $i || \Pi'$, and from which we can obtain a program Π of length i. Finally, $\mathcal{H}$ outputs the shortest program it obtains.

We turn to proving that $\mathcal{H}$ is a good search algorithm that succeeds with probability $1 - \frac{1}{p(n)}$. Fix some $n \in \mathbb{N}$ such that the inverter $\mathcal{A}$ succeeds on security parameter n. As in Lemma 43, it is also helpful here to introduce what it means for a string z to be "good": Let $\alpha(n) = \frac{1}{2p(n)}$. For each string $z \in \{0,1\}^n$, we let $w_z = K^t(z)$ denote the length of the shortest program that outputs z within $t(n)$ steps. We refer to a string $z \in \{0,1\}^n$ as being *good* if

$$\Pr[\mathcal{A}(w_z || z) \text{ succeeds}] \geq 1 - \alpha(n)$$

where the probability is taken over the internal randomness of $\mathcal{A}$. Notice that by our choice of w_z, it is guaranteed that a pre-image must exist. Let G denote the set of all good strings $z \in \{0,1\}^n$. We first claim that heuristic $\mathcal{H}$ will succeeds with high probability on any good z (similar to the proof of Lemma 43).

Claim 2. *For any $z \in \{0,1\}^n$, if z is good, $\mathcal{H}(z)$ fails with probability at most $\frac{1}{2p(n)}$.*

Proof. Note that if the inverter $\mathcal{A}$ succeeds on $w_z\|z$, it will obtain a program Π which is a K^t-witness of z – Π will output z within time $t(n)$ and it's of length $K^t(z)$. Therefore, $\mathcal{H}(z)$ will eventually output this program. This implies that if z is good, $\mathcal{H}(z)$ will find a correct witness with probability at least $1 - \alpha(n) = 1 - \frac{1}{2p(n)}$

On the other hand, since our inverter $\mathcal{A}$ succeeds with high probability, there should be only "a few" bad strings. We assume for contradiction that the total probability weight of bad strings (w.r.t. D_n) is $\geq \frac{1}{2p(n)}$. That is,

$$\sum_{z \notin G} \Pr[z' \leftarrow D_n : z' = z] \geq \frac{1}{2p(n)}$$

Recall that the distribution $\mathcal{D}$ is polynomial bounded by K^t. So for any string $z \notin G$, the probability that z is sampled by D_n is at most $\delta(n)2^{-K^t(z)}$. It follows that

$$\sum_{z \notin G} \delta(n)2^{-K^t(z)} \geq \sum_{z \notin G} \Pr[z' \leftarrow D_n : z' = z] \geq \frac{1}{2p(n)} \tag{2}$$

However, z will be sampled with probability at least

$$\frac{1}{n+c}\frac{1}{2^{w_z}} = \frac{1}{n+c}\frac{1}{2^{K^t(z)}}$$

in the one-way function experiment, since there exists a program of length $w_z = K^t(z)$ that outputs z within $t(n)$ steps, and the OWF will output z if the program is picked. When a bad string z is sampled, the inverter $\mathcal{A}$ will fail with probability at least $\frac{1}{\alpha(n)}$. Thus, $\mathcal{A}$ will fail with probability at least

$$\sum_{z \notin G} \frac{1}{2n\alpha(n)}2^{-K^t(z)}$$

By Eq. 2, this is at least

$$\frac{1}{2n\alpha(n)} \cdot \frac{1}{2p(n)\delta(n)} > \frac{1}{q(n)}$$

which is a contradiction (since $\mathcal{A}$ is a good inverter). We thus conclude that the total probability weight of bad strings (w.r.t. D_n) is $\leq \frac{1}{2p(n)}$. Finally, by a Union bound (to take into account good strings) and Claim 2, the probability that the heuristic fails w.r.t. D_n is at most $\frac{1}{p(n)}$.

4.2 Bounding Any Samplable Distribution

We proceed to showing that samplable distributions are bounded by the complexity measures we consider. We first focus our attention to pK^{poly}. Towards this, let us recall the Coding Theorem for pK^{poly}.

Theorem 45. ([25, Theorem 30]) *There exists a polynomial γ such that for any t_D-time samplable ensemble $\mathcal{D}$, any string $x \in \{0,1\}^n$ such that D_n samples x with probability $\delta > 0$, for any polynomial t such that $t(n) \geq \gamma(t_D(n))$, it holds that*

$$pK^t(x) \leq \log(1/\delta) + O(\log t_D(n))$$

The coding theorem roughly says that if a (samplable) distribution assign too much weight to an individual string, we will be able to find a short description of that string. We next use the coding theorem to show that any samplable distribution can be bounded by pK^{poly}.

Lemma 46. *There exists a polynomial γ such that for all polynomial t, any t_D-time samplable ensemble $\mathcal{D}$ is polynomially bounded by pK^t if $t(n) \geq \gamma(t_D(n))$.*

Proof. Let γ be the polynomial in Theorem 45. It follows that for any t_D-time $\mathcal{D}$, any $x, \delta = \Pr[D_n = x]$, and any polynomial $t(n) \geq \gamma(t_D(n))$, it holds that

$$1/\delta \cdot t_D(n)^{O(1)} \geq 2^{pK^t(x)}$$

which implies that $\delta \leq t_D(n)^{O(1)} \cdot 2^{-pK^t(x)}$. Notice that $t_D(n)^{O(1)}$ is a polynomial, and the above equation holds for any x in the support of $\mathcal{D}$, we thus conclude that $\mathcal{D}$ is polynomially bounded by pK^t. ∎

The above proof relies on Theorem 45, whose proof uses tools from complexity theory (unconditional PRGs that fool constant-depth circuits). As a result of independent interest, in Appendix A, we present an alternative direct proof of Lemma 46 (which implicitly also proves Theorem 45) using only elementary machinery (in particular, simply universal hash functions).

We move on to considering K^{poly}. As observed by [7], K^{poly} is at most pK^{poly} up to an additive $O(\log n)$ factor under a derandomization assumption.

Proposition 47 ([7, Proposition 66]). *Assume that $\mathsf{E} \not\subseteq \mathsf{ioNSIZE}[2^{\Omega(n)}]$. It holds that there exists a polynomial p such that for every polynomial $t, t', t'(n) \geq p(t(n))$, for every $x \in \{0,1\}^n$, it holds that*

$$K^{t'}(x) \leq pK^t(x) + \log(t(n))$$

Combining the above Proposition and Lemma 46, we prove that any samplable distribution will also be bounded by K^{poly}. (In addition, we also give another proof of this statement (see the Lemma below for a formal version) in Appendix A without using Proposition 47, for concreteness.)

Lemma 48. *Assume that* $\mathsf{E} \not\subseteq \mathsf{ioNSIZE}[2^{\Omega(n)}]$. *There exists a polynomial* γ' *such that for all polynomial* t', *any* t_D-*time samplable ensemble* $\mathcal{D}$ *is polynomially bounded by* $K^{t'}$ *if* $t'(n) \geq \gamma'(t_D(n))$.

Proof. The proof of Lemma 48 relies on the proof of Lemma 46, and we refer the reader to the proof of Lemma 46 for notations used in this proof. Let p be the polynomial in Proposition 47. Recall that the proof of Lemma 46 showed that $\delta \leq t_D(n)^{O(1)} \cdot 2^{-pK^t(x)}$. We now consider any polynomial t' such that $t'(n) \geq p(t(n))$. By Proposition 47, it follows that

$$\delta \leq t_D(n)^{O(1)} \cdot 2^{-pK^t(x)} \leq t_D(n)^{O(1)} \cdot 2^{-K^{t'}(x) + \log(t(n))} = t_D(n)^{O(1)} t(n) \cdot 2^{-K^{t'}(x)}$$

Thus, we conclude that $\mathcal{D}$ is polynomially bounded by $K^{t'}$. ∎

5   Hardness of $\mathsf{MpK^{poly}P}$ w.r.t. Uniform from OWFs

We here show that that for every polynomial $t(n) \geq 1.1n$, the existence of OWFs implies mild average-case hardness of $\mathsf{MpK^{poly}P}$ and mild average-case hardness of $\mathsf{MK^{poly}P}$. Our proof closely follows the proof in [21] with only minor modifications to deal with the fact that we now consider the probabilistic variant of Kolmogorov complexity and we focus on languages/promise problems.

Theorem 51. *Assume that one-way functions exist. Then,* $\mathsf{MpK^tP}$ *is mildly hard-on-average with respect to the uniform distribution.*

Proof. This theorem follows from Theorem 55 and Theorem 56. ∎

Theorem 52. *Assume that one-way functions exist. Then,* $\mathsf{MK^tP}$ *is mildly hard-on-average with respect to the uniform distribution.*

Proof. This theorem follows from Theorem 55 and Theorem 57. ∎

5.1   Some Additional Preliminaries

Let us first recall some additional standard preliminaries.

Computational Indistinguishability. We recall the definition of (computational) indistinguishability [9].

Definition 53. *Two ensembles* $\{A_n\}_{n \in \mathbb{N}}$ *and* $\{B_n\}_{n \in \mathbb{N}}$ *are said to be* $\mu(\cdot)$- *indistinguishable, if for every probabilistic machine* D *(the "distinguisher") whose running time is polynomial in the length of its first input, there exists some* $n_0 \in \mathbb{N}$ *so that for every* $n \geq n_0$:

$$|\Pr[D(1^n, A_n) = 1] - \Pr[D(1^n, B_n) = 1]| < \mu(n)$$

We say that are $\{A_n\}_{n \in \mathbb{N}}$ *and* $\{B_n\}_{n \in \mathbb{N}}$ *simply indistinguishable if they are* $\frac{1}{p(\cdot)}$-*indistinguishable for every polynomial* $p(\cdot)$.

Statistical Distance and Entropy. For any two random variables X and Y defined over some set $\mathcal{V}$, we let $\mathsf{SD}(X,Y) = \frac{1}{2}\sum_{v\in\mathcal{V}}|\Pr[X=v] - \Pr[Y=v]|$ denote the *statistical distance* between X and Y. For a random variable X, let $H(X) = \mathsf{E}[\log\frac{1}{\Pr[X=x]}]$ denote the (Shannon) entropy of X, and let $H_\infty(X) = \min_{x\in Supp(X)}\log\frac{1}{\Pr[X=x]}$ denote the *min-entropy* of X.

5.2 Entropy-Preserving PRGs

Liu and Pass [21] defined a notion of a *conditionally-secure entropy-preserving pseudorandom generator (cond EP-PRG)*. Roughly speaking, a cond EP-PRG is a function where the output is indistinguishable from the uniform distribution and also preserves the entropy in the input only when *conditioned on* some event E.

Definition 54. *An efficiently computable function $G : \{0,1\}^n \to \{0,1\}^{n+\gamma\log n}$ is a $\mu(\cdot)$-conditionally secure entropy-preserving pseudorandom generator (μ-cond EP-PRG) if there exist a sequence of events $= \{E_n\}_{n\in\mathbb{N}}$ and a constant α (referred to as the entropy-loss constant) such that the following conditions hold:*

- **(pseudorandomness):** $\{G(\mathcal{U}_n \mid E_n)\}_{n\in\mathbb{N}}$ *and* $\{\mathcal{U}_{n+\gamma\log n}\}_{n\in\mathbb{N}}$ *are* $\mu(n)$-*indistinguishable;*
- **(entropy-preserving):** *For all sufficiently large* $n \in \mathbb{N}$, $H(G(\mathcal{U}_n \mid E_n)) \geq n - \alpha\log n$.

We say that G has *rate-1 efficiency* if its running time on inputs of length n is bounded by $n + O(n^\varepsilon)$ for some constant $\varepsilon < 1$.

Theorem 55. ([21]) *Assume that OWFs exist. Then, for every $\gamma > 1$, there exists a rate-1 efficient μ-cond-EP PRG $G_\gamma : \{0,1\}^n \to \{0,1\}^{n+\gamma\log n}$, where $\mu = \frac{1}{n^2}$.*

Though in [21], running time was counted in terms of execution on Turing machines, as noted in [23], the PRG is also rate-1 efficient when run on a RAM.

5.3 Hardness of MpK^{t}P and MK^{t}P from Cond EP-PRG

Theorem 56. *Assume that for some $\gamma \geq 4$, there exists a rate-1 efficient μ-cond EP-PRG $G : \{0,1\}^n \to \{0,1\}^{n+\gamma\log n}$ where $\mu(n) = 1/n^2$. Then, for every $\epsilon > 0$, all $t(n) \geq (1+\epsilon)n$, MpK^{t}P is mildly HoA w.r.t. the uniform distribution.*

Proof. The proof follows exactly the same structure as the proof [21] with only minor adjustments to deal with the fact that we now consider probabilistic Kolmogorov complexity and MpK^{t}P, a promise problem. Essentially, the key observation is that random strings have high probabilistic Kolmogorov complexity, and due to this observation, essentially the proof in [21] can still be applied. We proceed to the full details.

Let $\gamma \geq 4$, and let $G' : \{0,1\}^n \to \{0,1\}^{m'(n)}$ where $m'(n) = n + \gamma \log n$ be a rate-1 efficient μ-cond EP-PRG, where $\mu = 1/n^2$. For any constant c, let $G^c(x)$ be a function that computes $G'(x)$ and truncates the last c bits. It directly follows that G^c is also a rate-1 efficient μ-cond EP-PRG (since G' is so). Consider any $\varepsilon > 0$ and any polynomial $t(n) \geq (1+\varepsilon)n$ and let $p(n) = 2n^{2(\alpha+\gamma+1)}$.

Assume for contradiction that there exists some PPT $\mathcal{H}(x,k)$ that decides MpK^{t}P with probability $1 - \frac{1}{p(m)}$ over random $x \in \{0,1\}^m, k \in \{0,1\}^{\lceil \log m \rceil}$ for infinitely many $m \in \mathbb{N}$. Since $m'(n+1) - m'(n) \leq \gamma + 1$, there must exist some constant $\dot{c} \leq \gamma + 1$ such that $\mathcal{H}$ succeeds (to decide MpK^{t}P) with probability $1 - \frac{1}{p(m)}$ for infinitely many m of the form $m = m(n) = n + \gamma \log n - c$. Let $G(x) = G^c(x)$; recall that G is a rate-1 efficient μ-cond EP-PRG (trivially, since G^c is so), and let $\alpha, \{E_n\}$, respectively, be the entropy loss constant and sequence of events, associated with it.

We next show that $\mathcal{H}$ can be used to break the cond EP-PRG G. Towards this, note that a random string still has high pK^t-complexity with high probability: for $m = m(n)$, by Fact 24, we have,

$$\Pr_{x \in \{0,1\}^m}[pK^t_{1/3}(x) > m - \frac{\gamma}{2} \log n] \geq 1 - \frac{3}{n^{\gamma/2}}, \tag{3}$$

However, any string output by G, must have "low" pK^t complexity : For every sufficiently large $n, m = m(n)$, we have that,

$$\Pr_{x \in \{0,1\}^n}[pK^t_1(G(x)) > m - \frac{\gamma}{2} \log n] = 0, \tag{4}$$

since for every string $r \in \{0,1\}^{t(m)}$, $G(x)$ can be produced by a program Π with the seed x of length n and the code of G (of constant length) hardwired in it (and the string r is skipped). The running time of Π is bounded by $t(m)$ for all sufficiently large n (since G is rate-1 efficient) , so $K^t(G(x)) = n + O(1) \leq m - \gamma/2 \log n$ for sufficiently large n (since recall that $\gamma \geq 4$).

Based on these observations, we now construct a PPT distinguisher $\mathcal{A}$ breaking G. On input $1^n, x$, where $x \in \{0,1\}^{m(n)}$, $\mathcal{A}(1^n, x)$ picks $k = m - \frac{\gamma}{2} \log n$. $\mathcal{A}$ outputs 1 if $\mathcal{H}(x,k)$ outputs 1 and 0 otherwise. Fix some $n, m = m(n)$ for which $\mathcal{H}$ succeeds to decide MpK^{t}P with probability $\frac{1}{p(m)}$. The following two claims conclude that $\mathcal{A}$ distinguishes $\mathcal{U}_{m(n)}$ and $G(\mathcal{U}_n \mid E_n)$ with probability at least $\frac{1}{n^2}$.

Claim 3. $\mathcal{A}(1^n, \mathcal{U}_m)$ outputs 0 with probability at least $1 - \frac{4}{n^{\gamma/2}}$.

Proof. Note that $\mathcal{A}(1^n, x)$ will output 0 if (1) x is a string with $pK^t_{1/3}$-complexity larger than $m - \gamma/2 \log n$ and (2) $\mathcal{H}$ succeeds on input (x, k). (Note that if (1) holds, (x, k) is guaranteed to be a NO instance in $\mathsf{MpK^tP}$.) Thus,

$$
\begin{aligned}
&\Pr[\mathcal{A}(1^n, x) = 0] \\
&\geq \Pr[pK_{1/3}^t(x) > m - \gamma/2\log n \wedge \mathcal{H} \text{ succeeds on } (x, k)] \\
&\geq 1 - \Pr[pK_{1/3}^t(x) \leq m - \gamma/2\log n] - \Pr[\mathcal{H} \text{ fails on } (x, k)] \\
&\geq 1 - \frac{3}{n^{\gamma/2}} - \frac{1}{p(m)} \\
&\geq 1 - \frac{4}{n^{\gamma/2}}.
\end{aligned}
$$

where the probability is over a random $x \leftarrow \mathcal{U}_m$, $k \leftarrow \lceil \log m \rceil$ and the randomness of $\mathcal{A}$ and $\mathcal{H}$.

Claim 4. $\mathcal{A}(1^n, G(\mathcal{U}_n \mid E_n))$ *outputs 0 with probability at most* $1 - \frac{1}{n} + \frac{2}{n^2}$

Proof. Recall that by assumption, $\mathcal{H}(x, k)$ fails to decide whether $(x, k) \in \mathsf{MpK^tP}$ for a random $x \in \{0, 1\}^m, k \in \{0, 1\}^{\lceil \log m \rceil}$ with probability at most $\frac{1}{p(m)}$.

By an averaging argument, for at least a $1 - \frac{1}{n^2}$ fraction of random tapes r for $\mathcal{H}$, the deterministic machine $\mathcal{H}_r$ fails to decide $\mathsf{MpK^tP}$ with probability at most $\frac{n^2}{p(m)}$. Fix some "good" randomness r such that $\mathcal{H}_r$ decides $\mathsf{MpK^tP}$ with probability at least $1 - \frac{n^2}{p(m)}$.

We next analyze the success probability of $\mathcal{A}_r$. Assume for contradiction that $\mathcal{A}_r$ outputs 1 with probability at least $1 - \frac{1}{n} + \frac{1}{n^{\alpha+\gamma}}$ on input $G(\mathcal{U}_n \mid E_n)$. Recall that (1) the entropy of $G(\mathcal{U}_n \mid E_n)$ is at least $n - \alpha \log n$ and (2) the quantity $-\log \Pr[G(\mathcal{U}_n \mid E_n) = y]$ is upper bounded by n for all $y \in G(\mathcal{U}_n \mid E_n)$. By an averaging argument, with probability at least $\frac{1}{n}$, a random $y \in G(\mathcal{U}_n \mid E_n)$ will satisfy

$$-\log \Pr[G(\mathcal{U}_n \mid E_n) = y] \geq (n - \alpha \log n) - 1.$$

We refer to an output y satisfying the above condition as being "good" and other y's as being "bad". Let $S = \{y \in G(\mathcal{U}_n \mid E_n) : \mathcal{A}_r(1^n, y) = 0 \wedge y \text{ is good}\}$, and let $S' = \{y \in G(\mathcal{U}_n \mid E_n) : \mathcal{A}_r(1^n, y) = 0 \wedge y \text{ is bad}\}$. Since

$$\Pr[\mathcal{A}_r(1^n, G(\mathcal{U}_n \mid E_n)) = 0] = \Pr[G(\mathcal{U}_n \mid E_n) \in S] + \Pr[G(\mathcal{U}_n \mid E_n) \in S'],$$

and $\Pr[G(\mathcal{U}_n \mid E_n) \in S']$ is at most the probability that $G(\mathcal{U}_n \mid E_n)$ is "bad" (which as argued above is at most $1 - \frac{1}{n}$), we have that

$$\Pr[G(\mathcal{U}_n \mid E_n) \in S] \geq \left(1 - \frac{1}{n} + \frac{1}{n^{\alpha+\gamma}}\right) - \left(1 - \frac{1}{n}\right) = \frac{1}{n^{\alpha+\gamma}}.$$

Furthermore, since for every $y \in S$, $\Pr[G(\mathcal{U}_n \mid E_n) = y] \leq 2^{-n+\alpha \log n+1}$, we also have,

$$\Pr[G(\mathcal{U}_n \mid E_n) \in S] \leq |S| 2^{-n+\alpha \log n+1}$$

So,
$$|S| \geq \frac{2^{n-\alpha \log n - 1}}{n^{\alpha + \gamma}} = 2^{n - (2\alpha + \gamma) \log n - 1}$$

However, for any $y \in G(\mathcal{U}_n \mid E_n)$, if $\mathcal{A}_r(1^n, y)$ outputs 0, then by Eq. 4, $pK_1^t(y) \leq m - \gamma/2 \log n = k$ (and therefore a YES instance in $\mathsf{MpK}^t\mathsf{P}$), so $\mathcal{H}_r$ fails to decide $\mathsf{MpK}^t\mathsf{P}$ on input $(y, m - \gamma/2 \log n)$.

Thus, the probability that $\mathcal{H}_r$ fails (to decide $\mathsf{MpK}^t\mathsf{P}$) on a random input (y, k) (where y and k are uniformly sampled in $\{0,1\}^m$ and $\{0,1\}^{\lceil \log m \rceil}$) is at least
$$|S|/2^{m + \lceil \log m \rceil} = \frac{2^{n - (2\alpha + \gamma) \log n - 1}}{2^{n + \gamma \log n + \lceil \log m \rceil}} \geq \frac{1}{2n^{2(\alpha + \gamma + 1)}}$$

which contradicts the fact that $\mathcal{H}_r$ fails to decide $\mathsf{MpK}^t\mathsf{P}$ with probability at most $\frac{n^2}{p(m)} < \frac{1}{2n^{2(\alpha + \gamma + 1)}}$ (since $n < m$).

We conclude that for every good randomness r, $\mathcal{A}_r$ outputs 0 with probability at most $1 - \frac{1}{n} + \frac{1}{n^{\alpha + \gamma}}$. Finally, by union bound (and since a random tape is bad with probability $\leq \frac{1}{n^2}$), we have that the probability that $\mathcal{A}(G(\mathcal{U}_n \mid E_n))$ outputs 1 is at most
$$\frac{1}{n^2} + \left(1 - \frac{1}{n} + \frac{1}{n^{\alpha + \gamma}}\right) \leq 1 - \frac{1}{n} + \frac{2}{n^2},$$

since $\gamma \geq 2$.

We conclude, recalling that $\gamma \geq 4$, that $\mathcal{A}$ distinguishes $\mathcal{U}_m$ and $G(\mathcal{U}_n \mid E_n)$ with probability of at least
$$\left(1 - \frac{4}{n^{\gamma/2}}\right) - \left(1 - \frac{1}{n} + \frac{2}{n^2}\right) \geq \left(1 - \frac{4}{n^2}\right) - \left(1 - \frac{1}{n} + \frac{2}{n^2}\right) = \frac{1}{n} - \frac{6}{n^2} \geq \frac{1}{n^2}$$

for infinitely many $n \in \mathbb{N}$.

Theorem 57. *Assume that for some $\gamma \geq 4$, there exists a rate-1 efficient μ-cond EP-PRG $G : \{0,1\}^n \rightarrow \{0,1\}^{n + \gamma \log n}$ where $\mu(n) = 1/n^2$. Then, for every $\epsilon > 0$, all $t(n) \geq (1 + \epsilon)n$, $\mathsf{MK}^t\mathsf{P}$ is mildly HoA w.r.t. the uniform distribution.*

Proof. The proof of Theorem 56 can also prove this theorem by replacing pK^t with K^t, and $\mathsf{MpK}^t\mathsf{P}$ with $\mathsf{MK}^t\mathsf{P}$.

A An Alternative Proof of Lemma 46 and Lemma 48

As mentioned in Sect. 4.2, we provide direct proofs for Lemma 46 and Lemma 48. Let us start by a reminder of the statement of Lemma 46.

Lemma A1. (Lemma 46, restated). *There exists a polynomial γ such that for all polynomial t, any t_D-time samplable ensemble $\mathcal{D}$ is polynomially bounded by pK^t if $t(n) \geq \gamma(t_D(n))$.*

We recall the notion of a universal hash function [3].

Definition A2. *Let $\mathcal{H}_m^\ell$ be a family of functions where $m < \ell$ and each function $h \in \mathcal{H}_m^\ell$ maps $\{0,1\}^\ell$ to $\{0,1\}^m$. We say that $\mathcal{H}_m^\ell$ is a* universal hash family *if (i) the functions $h_\sigma \in \mathcal{H}_m^\ell$ can be described by a string σ of ℓ^c bits where c is a universal constant that does not depend on ℓ; (ii) for all $x \neq x' \in \{0,1\}^\ell$, and for all $y, y' \in \{0,1\}^m$*

$$\Pr[h_\sigma \leftarrow \mathcal{H}_m^\ell : h_\sigma(x) = y \ \text{ and } \ h_\sigma(x') = y'] = 2^{-2m}$$

We will rely on the following properties of universal hash functions.

Proposition A3. *Let $\ell \in \mathbb{N}$, $S \subseteq \{0,1\}^\ell$ be a set, $\mathcal{H}_m^\ell$ be a universal hash family such that $m \leq \log|S|$. The following statements hold:*

- *With probability at least $1 - 2^{-\log|S|+m+3}$ over $h_\sigma \leftarrow \mathcal{H}_m^\ell$, there exists $s \in S$ such that $h_\sigma(s) = 0^m$.*
- *With probability at least $1 - 2^{-\ell+m+3}$ over $h_\sigma \leftarrow \mathcal{H}_m^\ell$, $|h_\sigma^{-1}(0^m)| \leq 2 \cdot 2^{\ell-m}$.*

For completeness, we provide the proof of Proposition A3 here.

Proof. We first prove the former statement. We consider picking a random hash function $h_\sigma \leftarrow \mathcal{H}_m^\ell$. For each element $s \in S$, let X_s denote the random variable such that $X_s = 1$ iff $h_\sigma(s) = 0^m$. Let X denote the random variable $X = \sum_{s \in S} X_s$. Note that $\mathsf{E}[X] = |S|/2^m$ and the variance of X is

$$\mathsf{V}(X) = \mathsf{E}[X^2 - \mathsf{E}[X]^2] = |S|(\frac{1}{2^m} - \frac{1}{2^{2m}}) \leq \mathsf{E}[X]$$

since $\mathcal{H}_m^\ell$ is a universal hash family and all $s_1, s_2 \in S$, X_{s_1} and X_{s_2} are independent. Therefore the variance of X is very small and we can apply Chebyshev's Inequality to show that

$$\Pr[X = 0] \leq \Pr[|X - \mathsf{E}[X]| \geq \mathsf{E}[X] - 1]$$
$$\leq \Pr[|X - \mathsf{E}[X]| \geq (\sqrt{\mathsf{V}(X)}/2)\sqrt{\mathsf{V}(X)}]$$
$$\leq \frac{1}{\mathsf{V}(X)/4} \leq 2^{-\log|S|+m+3}$$

So we conclude that with probability at least $1 - \Pr[X = 0] \geq 1 - 2^{-\log|S|+m+3}$, there exists $s \in S$ such that $h_\sigma(s) = 0^m$.

The latter statement follows from essentially the same proof. For each element $z \in \{0,1\}^\ell$, let Y_z denote the random variable such that $Y_z = 1$ iff $h_\sigma(z) = 0^m$. Let Y denote the random variable $Y = \sum_{z \in \{0,1\}^\ell} Y_z$. Note that $\mathsf{E}[Y] = 2^\ell/2^m$ and the variance of Y is

$$\mathsf{V}(Y) = \mathsf{E}[Y^2 - \mathsf{E}[Y]^2] = 2^\ell(\frac{1}{2^m} - \frac{1}{2^{2m}})$$

since $\mathcal{H}_m^\ell$ is a universal hash family and all $z_1, z_2 \in \{0,1\}^\ell$, Y_{z_1} and Y_{z_2} are independent.. Notice that by Chebyshev's inequality,

$$\Pr[Y \geq 2 \cdot 2^{\ell-m}] \leq \Pr[|Y - \mathsf{E}[Y]| \geq (\sqrt{\mathsf{V}(Y)}/2)\sqrt{\mathsf{V}(Y)}] \leq \frac{1}{\mathsf{V}(Y)/4} \leq 2^{-\ell+m+3}$$

So we conclude that with probability at least $1 - 2^{-\ell+m+3}$, $|h_\sigma^{-1}(0^m)| \leq 2 \cdot 2^{\ell-m}$.

We turn to introducing the linear universal hash family construction [3].

Proposition A4 ([3]). *Let $\ell, m \in \mathbb{N}, m < \ell$. For each $\sigma \in \{0,1\}^{\ell m + m}$, define h_σ to be the function such that for each $x \in \{0,1\}^\ell$, $h_\sigma(x) = Ax + b$ where $\sigma = (A, b)$, A is a binary matrix of $m \times \ell$, and b is a binary vector of length m. Let $\mathcal{H}_m^\ell = \{h_\sigma \mid \sigma \in \{0,1\}^{\ell m + m}\}$. Then, it holds that $\mathcal{H}_m^\ell$ is a universal hash family.*

We are now ready to prove Lemma A1.

Proof. Consider any polynomial t, and any t_D-time samplable ensemble $\mathcal{D}$. Let M be the PPT sampler such that $M(1^n, r)$ uses $r \in \{0,1\}^{t_D(n)}$ as random coins and samples D_n for each $n \in \mathbb{N}$.

We will show that $\mathcal{D}$ is polynomially bounded by pK_{1-2-n}^t. Consider any string $x \in \{0,1\}^*$, $n = |x|$. Let $\ell = t_D(n)$ be the length of the random tape of M. Let $p_x = \Pr[r \leftarrow \{0,1\}^\ell, x' = M(1^n, r) : x' = x]$ denote the probability mass of x in D_n. Our goal is to show that there exists a polynomial δ such that $p_x \leq \delta(n) 2^{-pK^t(x)}$ holds for all x.

Let $S = \{r \in \{0,1\}^\ell : M(1^n, r) = x\}$ be the set of random tapes on which M will output x. (Note that $|S| = 2^\ell p_x$.) Let $m = \lceil \log |S| \rceil - 5$. Let $\mathcal{H}_m^\ell$ be the universal hash family defined in Proposition A4.

For any hash function $h_\sigma \in \mathcal{H}_m^\ell$, we refer to a hash function h_σ as being *good* if (1) $\exists s \in S, h_\sigma(s) = 0^m$ and (2) $|h^{-1}(0^m)| \leq 2 \cdot 2^{\ell - m}$. We first claim that with high probability over $h_\sigma \leftarrow \mathcal{H}_m^\ell$, h_σ will be good.

Claim 5. *h_σ is good with probability at least $1/2$ over $h_\sigma \leftarrow \mathcal{H}_m^\ell$.*

Proof. By Proposition A3 and a Union Bound, a random h_σ is good with probability at least $1 - 2^{-\log|S| + m + 3} - 2^{-\ell + m - 3} \geq \frac{1}{2}$.

We next claim that given a good hash function h_σ, there exists a short program of size roughly $\log |S|$ that produce the string x.

Claim 6. *For any good hash function $h_\sigma \in \mathcal{H}_m^\ell$, there exists a program Π of length at most*

$$O(\log \ell) + \lceil \log 1/p_x \rceil$$

that, given h_σ as input, outputs the string x within time $O(\ell^3)$.

Proof. Since h_σ is good, and let s be an string $\in S$ such that $h_\sigma(s) = 0^m$. Note that if s can be produced using a short program, x can be generated by running $M(1^n, s)$, which adds $|M| = c$ bits to the description and can be done in time $t_D(n)$.

Finally, we show how to produce s using linear algebra. Recall that the hash function $h_\sigma(x)$ is defined to be $Ax + b$ where $\sigma = (A, b)$, A, b are a binary matrix and a binary vector. We can use the Gaussian Elimination algorithm to find an vector $v \in \{0,1\}^\ell$ such that $Av + b = 0^m$ and a basis $(b_1, \ldots, b_d)$ for the kernel of A. Note that each $y \in h^{-1}(0^m)$ can be represented by a d-bit coordinate vector (under the basis $(b_1, \ldots, b_d)$ and with respect to the offset vector v). So $d \leq \ell - m + 1$ and s can also be represented a coordinate vector of $\ell - m + 1$ bits (and let e denote this vector). We then use this fact to construct a program Π with length $\leq 4 \log \ell + \ell - m + O(1)$ bits to produce the string x. Π has the integers n, ℓ, the coordinate vector, and the code of M hardcoded ($\leq 4 \log \ell + \ell - m + 1 + O(1)$ bits). On input a hash function description σ, it computes v and $(b_1, \ldots, b_d)$ using Gaussian Elimination and Gram Schmidt, and computes $s = \sum_{i \in [d]} b_i \cdot e_i + v$. Finally, Π outputs $M_1(1^n, s)$. Notice that Π runs in time $O(\ell^3) + t_D(n) = O(t_D(n)^3) \leq t(n)$. Also notice that Π can be described by $4 \log \ell + \ell - m + 1 + O(1)$, and we fix c to be the constant such that Π can be described using $4 \log \ell + \ell - m + c$ bits.

Finally, we are ready to show that $p_x \leq \delta(n) 2^{-pK^t(x)}$. Towards this, we will prove that

$$pK^t(x) \leq O(\log \ell) + \lceil \log 1/p_x \rceil$$

and the aforementioned inequality will follow if we set $\delta(n) = \ell^{O(1)} = t_D(n)^{O(1)}$ to be a large polynomial. Consider any random string $r \in \{0,1\}^{2n(\ell m + m)}$, and we view r as $r = \sigma_1 || \sigma_2 || \ldots || \sigma_{2n}$ where each σ_i is a description of a random hash function $h_{\sigma_i} \leftarrow \mathcal{H}_m^\ell$. By Claim 5, with probability at least $1 - 2^{-2n} \geq 2/3$, there exists $i \in [2n]$ such that h_{σ_i} is a good hash function. By Claim 6, there exists a program Π' that on input h_{σ_i}, outputs the string x. Thus, let Π be a program with the index i and Π' hardcoded, and Π on input r simply outputs $\Pi'(h_{\sigma_i})$. Note that Π can be implemented using $O(\log \ell) + \lceil \log 1/p_x \rceil$ bits, and it terminates within time $O(\ell^3)$. By picking $\gamma(n) = O(n^3)$, it follows that Π runs in $O(\ell^3) \leq \gamma(\ell) \leq \gamma(t_D(n)) \leq t(n)$.

We below prove Lemma 48. We first recall the statement.

Lemma A5 (Lemma 48, restated). *Assume that* $\mathsf{E} \not\subseteq \mathsf{ioNSIZE}[2^{\Omega(n)}]$. *There exists a polynomial γ' such that for all polynomial t', any t_D-time samplable ensemble $\mathcal{D}$ is polynomially bounded by $K^{t'}$ if $t'(n) \geq \gamma'(t_D(n))$.*

Proof. The idea behind our proof is to derandomize the hash function used in Lemma A1. Therefore, this proof will rely on the proof of Lemma A1 heavily and we assume familiarity of Lemma A1.

Let $t, t_D, \mathcal{D}, M, x, n, \ell, p_x, S, m, \mathcal{H}_m^\ell, h_\sigma$ be as in Lemma A1. The proof of Lemma A1 shows that (1) with probability at least 0.5, a random hash function is "good" (as defined in Lemma A1) and (2) if a hash function is good, there exists a small program Π that produces x on input the hash function within time $\mathsf{poly}(\ell)$. Note that for the purpose of derandomization, the probability 0.5 is good enough for us and we don't need the parallel repetition performed in the end of Lemma A1.

Towards derandomizing h_σ, we first show that whether h_σ is good can be verified by a non-deterministic circuit. Consider a non-deterministic circuit N_x with the string x hardcoded in it. Recall that a hash function h_σ is good if (1) $\exists s \in S$ such that $h_\sigma(s) = 0^m$ and (2) $|h^{-1}(0^m)| \leq 2 \cdot 2^{\ell - m}$. (1) can be checked by guessing a string $w \in \{0,1\}^\ell$, verifying if $h_\sigma(w) = 0^m$ and if $M(1^n, w)$

outputs x. (2) can be checked deterministically. Recall that h_σ is a linear hash function defined to be $h_\sigma(x) = Ax + b$ where $\sigma = (A, b)$. By facts in linear algebra, $|h_\sigma^{-1}(0^m)| = 2^d$ where d is the dimension of the kernel for A. And d can be computed using Gram Schmidt. Therefore, we can implement a non-deterministic circuit N_x such that $N_x(\sigma) = 1$ iff h_σ is good (so N_x accepts with probability at least 0.5), and N_x is of size $\leq O(|\sigma|^2)$.

Shaltiel and Umas [29] showed that under the assumption that $\mathsf{E} \not\subseteq$ ioNSIZE$[2^{\Omega(n)}]$, there exists a PRG $G : \{0,1\}^{O(\log l)} \to \{0,1\}^l$ running in time poly(l) such that for all $l \in \mathbb{N}$, for all non-deterministic circuits C of size $\leq O(l^2)$, it holds that

$$| \Pr[C(G(\mathcal{U}_{O(\log l)})) = 1] - \Pr[C(\mathcal{U}_l) = 1]| \leq \frac{1}{6}$$

It follows that G also fools N_x. Thus, there exists a seed $z \in \{0,1\}^{O(\log |\sigma|)}$ such that $h_{G(z)}$ is a good hash function.

We are now ready to show that x has a deterministic short description. We consider a program Π with the seed z hardcoded in it. Π first compute $\sigma = G(z)$. Since h_σ is a good hash function, as shown in the proof of Lemma 46, there exists a program Π' of length at most

$$O(\log \ell) + \lceil \log 1/p_x \rceil$$

that produces the string x on input the hash function description σ within time $O(\ell^3)$. Π also hardcodes the program Π', and Π just runs it on σ to obtain x. Note that Π's running time is bounded by the PRG's running time ($\leq$ poly$|\sigma|$) plus the running time of Π' ($\leq O(\ell^3)$). So there exists a polynomial γ' such that Π runs in time $\gamma'(\ell) \leq \gamma'(t_D(n))$. Consider any polynomial $t'(n) \geq \gamma'(t_D(n))$. It follows that

$$K^{t'}(x) \leq |z| + O(1) + O(\log \ell) + \lceil \log 1/p_x \rceil \leq -\lceil \log 1/p_x \rceil + O(\log n)$$

which implies that there exists a polynomial δ such that for all x, $p_x \leq \delta(n)2^{-K^{t'}(x)}$. Note that this holds for any t_D-time ensemble if $t'(n) \geq \gamma'(t_D(n))$, which concludes our proof.

References

1. Blum, M.: Coin flipping by telephone - A protocol for solving impossible problems. In: COMPCON1982, Digest of Papers, Twenty-Fourth IEEE Computer Society International Conference, San Francisco, California, USA, 22–25 February 1982, pp. 133–137. IEEE Computer Society (1982)
2. Blum, M., Micali, S.: How to generate cryptographically strong sequences of pseudo-random bits. SIAM J. Comput. 13(4), 850–864 (1984)
3. Carter, L., Wegman, M.: Universal classes of hash functions. J. Comput. Syst. Sci. 18(2), 143–154 (1979)
4. Chaitin, G.J.: On the simplicity and speed of programs for computing infinite sets of natural numbers. J. ACM 16(3), 407–422 (1969)

5. Diffie, W., Hellman, M.: New directions in cryptography. IEEE Trans. Inf. Theory **22**(6), 644–654 (1976)
6. Feige, U., Shamir, A.: Witness indistinguishable and witness hiding protocols. In: STOC 1990, pp. 416–426 (1990). http://doi.acm.org/10.1145/100216.100272
7. Goldberg, H., Kabanets, V., Lu, Z., Oliveira, I.C.: Probabilistic Kolmogorov complexity with applications to average-case complexity. In: 37th Computational Complexity Conference (CCC 2022). Schloss Dagstuhl-Leibniz-Zentrum für Informatik (2022)
8. Goldreich, O., Goldwasser, S., Micali, S.: On the cryptographic applications of random functions. In: CRYPTO, pp. 276–288 (1984)
9. Goldwasser, S., Micali, S.: Probabilistic encryption. J. Comput. Syst. Sci. **28**(2), 270–299 (1984)
10. Gurevich, Y.: The challenger-solver game: variations on the theme of p=np. In: Logic in Computer Science Column, The Bulletin of EATCS (1989)
11. Hartmanis, J.: Generalized Kolmogorov complexity and the structure of feasible computations. In: 24th Annual Symposium on Foundations of Computer Science (SFCS 1983), pp. 439–445 (1983). https://doi.org/10.1109/SFCS.1983.21
12. Håstad, J., Impagliazzo, R., Levin, L.A., Luby, M.: A pseudorandom generator from any one-way function. SIAM J. Comput. **28**(4), 1364–1396 (1999)
13. Ilango, R., Ren, H., Santhanam, R.: Robustness of average-case meta-complexity via pseudorandomness. In: Proceedings of the 54th Annual ACM SIGACT Symposium on Theory of Computing, pp. 1575–1583 (2022)
14. Impagliazzo, R.: A personal view of average-case complexity. In: Structure in Complexity Theory 1995, pp. 134–147 (1995)
15. Impagliazzo, R., LA, L.: No better ways to generate hard np instances than picking uniformly at random. In: Proceedings [1990] 31st Annual Symposium on Foundations of Computer Science, pp. 812–821. IEEE (1990)
16. Impagliazzo, R., Luby, M.: One-way functions are essential for complexity based cryptography (extended abstract). In: 30th Annual Symposium on Foundations of Computer Science, Research Triangle Park, North Carolina, USA, 30 October - 1 November 1989, pp. 230–235 (1989)
17. Ko, K.: On the notion of infinite pseudorandom sequences. Theor. Comput. Sci. **48**(3), 9–33 (1986). https://doi.org/10.1016/0304-3975(86)90081-2
18. Kolmogorov, A.N.: Three approaches to the quantitative definition of information. Int. J. Comput. Math. **2**(1–4), 157–168 (1968)
19. Levin, L.A.: The tale of one-way functions. Prob. Inf. Trans. **39**(1), 92–103 (2003). https://doi.org/10.1023/A:1023634616182
20. Levin, L.A.: Universal search problems (Russian), translated into English by BA Trakhtenbrot in [32]. Prob. Inf. Transmission **9**(3), 265–266 (1973)
21. Liu, Y., Pass, R.: On one-way functions and Kolmogorov complexity. In: 61st IEEE Annual Symposium on Foundations of Computer Science, FOCS 2020, Durham, NC, USA, 16–19 November 2020, pp. 1243–1254. IEEE (2020)
22. Liu, Y., Pass, R.: A note on one-way functions and sparse languages. Cryptology ePrint Archive (2021)
23. Liu, Y., Pass, R.: On one-way functions from np-complete problems. In: Proceedings of the 37th Computational Complexity Conference, pp. 1–24 (2022)
24. Longpré, L., Mocas, S.: Symmetry of information and one-way functions. In: Hsu, W.-L., Lee, R.C.T. (eds.) ISA 1991. LNCS, vol. 557, pp. 308–315. Springer, Heidelberg (1991). https://doi.org/10.1007/3-540-54945-5_75

25. Lu, Z., Oliveira, I.C., Zimand, M.: Optimal coding theorems in time-bounded Kolmogorov complexity. In: 49th International Colloquium on Automata, Languages, and Programming (ICALP 2022). Schloss Dagstuhl-Leibniz-Zentrum für Informatik (2022)
26. Naor, M.: Bit commitment using pseudorandomness. J. Cryptol. **4**(2), 151–158 (1991). https://doi.org/10.1007/BF00196774
27. Rivest, R.L., Shamir, A., Adleman, L.M.: A method for obtaining digital signatures and public-key cryptosystems (reprint). Commun. ACM **26**(1), 96–99 (1983). https://doi.org/10.1145/357980.358017
28. Rompel, J.: One-way functions are necessary and sufficient for secure signatures. In: STOC, pp. 387–394 (1990)
29. Shaltiel, R., Umans, C.: Simple extractors for all min-entropies and a new pseudo-random generator. J. ACM (JACM) **52**(2), 172–216 (2005)
30. Sipser, M.: A complexity theoretic approach to randomness. In: Proceedings of the 15th Annual ACM Symposium on Theory of Computing, 25–27 April 1983, Boston, Massachusetts, USA, pp. 330–335. ACM (1983)
31. Solomonoff, R.: A formal theory of inductive inference, part I. Inf. Control **7**(1), 1–22 (1964). https://doi.org/10.1016/S0019-9958(64)90223-2
32. Trakhtenbrot, B.A.: A survey of Russian approaches to Perebor (brute-force searches) algorithms. Annal. History Comput. **6**(4), 384–400 (1984)
33. Yao, A.C.: Theory and applications of trapdoor functions (extended abstract). In: 23rd Annual Symposium on Foundations of Computer Science, Chicago, Illinois, USA, 3–5 November 1982, pp. 80–91 (1982)
34. Zvonkin, A.K., Levin, L.A.: The complexity of finite objects and the development of the concepts of information and randomness by means of the theory of algorithms. Russ. Math. Surv. **25**(6), 83–124 (1970). https://doi.org/10.1070/RM1970v025n06ABEH001269

Universal Amplification of KDM Security: From 1-Key Circular to Multi-Key KDM

Brent Waters[1,2(✉)] and Daniel Wichs[2,3]

[1] University of Texas at Austin, Austin, TX, USA
[2] NTT Research, Sunnyvale, CA, USA
bwaters@cs.utexas.edu
[3] Northeastern University, Boston, MA, USA

Abstract. An encryption scheme is *Key Dependent Message* (KDM) secure if it is safe to encrypt messages that can arbitrarily depend on the secret keys themselves. In this work, we show how to upgrade essentially the weakest form of KDM security into the strongest one. In particular, we assume the existence of a *symmetric-key bit-encryption* that is *circular-secure* in the *1-key* setting, meaning that it maintains security even if one can encrypt individual bits of a single secret key under itself. We also rely on a standard CPA-secure public-key encryption. We construct a *public-key* encryption scheme that is *KDM secure for general functions* (of a-priori bounded circuit size) in the *multi-key* setting, meaning that it maintains security even if one can encrypt arbitrary functions of arbitrarily many secret keys under each of the public keys. As a special case, the latter guarantees security in the presence of arbitrary length key cycles. Prior work already showed how to amplify n-key circular to n-key KDM security for general functions. Therefore, the main novelty of our work is to upgrade from 1-key to n-key security for arbitrary n.

As an independently interesting feature of our result, our construction does not need to know the actual *specification* of the underlying 1-key circular secure scheme, and we only rely on the *existence* of some such scheme in the proof of security. In particular, we present a *universal* construction of a multi-key KDM-secure encryption that is secure as long as some 1-key circular-secure scheme exists. While this feature is similar in spirit to Levin's universal construction of one-way functions, the way we achieve it is quite different technically, and does not come with the same "galactic inefficiency".

1 Introduction

An encryption system is Key Dependent Message (KDM) secure if it maintains security even if the messages can arbitrarily depend on the secret key.

Supported by NSF CNS-1908611 and Simons Investigator award.
Research supported by NSF grant CNS-1750795, CNS-2055510, and the JP Morgan faculty research award.

H. Handschuh and A. Lysyanskaya (Eds.): CRYPTO 2023, LNCS 14082, pp. 674–693, 2023.
https://doi.org/10.1007/978-3-031-38545-2_22

KDM security has several interesting connections to both the application and theory of cryptography. For instance, the Bitlocker encryption utility will sometimes encrypt its own secret key resulting in a KDM ciphertext. The anonymous credential system of Camenisch and Lysyanskaya [CL01] requires users encrypt their own secret keys in an effort to deter users from delegating their keys. More recently the work of Koppula and Waters [KW19] showed how to build chosen ciphertext security [RS92] PKE via a key dependent type primitive they called hinting PRG. Their methods were subsequently adapted [KMT19] to apply a similar transformation using KDM secure encryption. Following this [LQR+19, KM19] showed how to leverage these techniques to build reusable designated verifier zero knowledge proofs. In addition, earlier connections to CCA were made [HK15], but using an additional reproducibility property.

On the flipside one can gain many insights from the technically challenging problem of creating cryptosystems that meet the traditional notion of CPA security [GM82], but are *not* KDM secure. Multiple works [ABBC10, CGH12, Rot13, BHW15, KRW15, KW16, AP16, GKW17b, GKW17c] have explored such questions employing a variety of number theoretic assumptions. Notably, the KDM insecure bit encryption system of [GKW17c] forms the machinery upon which lockable or compute and compare obfuscation is built [GKW17a, WZ17].

Initially, the only provably KDM secure constructions of encryption systems relied on the random oracle heuristic [BRS03]. In a breakthrough result Boneh, Halevi, Hamburg and Ostrovsky [BHHO08] showed how to achieve public key encryption system that were n-key KDM secure for affine functions under the Decisional Diffie-Hellman (DDH) assumption. At a very high level their solution consisted to two core ideas. First, they manipulated algebraic properties of DDH hard groups to allow for the creation of a ciphertext with a message that depended on a chosen affine function of a secret key, but without knowing the secret key. Second, they created a proof technique that allowed for a reduction to (undetectably) derive several public keys from one "master" public key. This second idea is what allowed them to get KDM security for n keys. It also relied on the underlying algebraic properties of the groups. Subsequently, [ACPS09] showed how these concepts applied in domains beyond DDH hard groups. They achieved n-KDM security for affine functions from the Learning with Errors (LWE) assumption for public key encryption and from the Learning Parity with Noise (LPN) assumption for secret key encryption. The work of [BLSV18] showed how to construct 1-KDM security for affine functions generically from a building block called *batch encryption* (a variant of chameleon encryption [DG17] and laconic OT [CDG+17]), which can be instantiated from the CDH assumption, the LWE assumption, or LPN with extremely small noise.

At first glance having KDM security for just affine functions seems limited as one would ideally like to achieve security for arbitrary functions of the secret key. To this end a second set of works [BHHI10, BGK11, App11, KM20] looked to amplify security from weak to more expressive functions. Barak et al. [BHHI10] first showed how to get n-key KDM security for functions of bounded circuit-size from the DDH or LWE assumptions. Applebaum [App11] then showed a generic technique for amplifying *any* n-key KDM security for *projection functions* to n-key KDM security to arbitrary functions of bounded circuit-size using garbled circuits.[1] Projection functions are intuitively functions where every output bit depends on at most a single bit from the secret keys. That is an output bit can be a constant 0 or 1 bit, one that copies a key bit, or one that flips it. Critically, projections are captured by the class of affine functions from the work of [BHHO08, ACPS09]. Kitagawa and Matsuda [KM20] later employed garbling to amplify from an even weaker class of functionality, which allowed for constant functions or copying a secret key bit, but not flipping it, which they call *circular security*. (We note in the KDM literature the term "circular security" can also refer a different notion of just encrypting key cycles.)

The most recent works give an eloquent and generic way to move from a scheme supporting a very weak form of KDM queries to an expressive over a given number of keys. However, there do not exist techniques that allow for amplification of the *number of keys* a KDM supports. These techniques are essentially "stuck with" whatever number of keys are supported in the base scheme leaving fundamental questions.[2] For example, if we start with a 1-KDM secure scheme can we achieve KDM security for n-key cycles for $n > 1$? Or arbitrary functions on n keys?

Our Results. In this work we answer these questions in the affirmative. Starting with any standard CPA-secure public key encryption (PKE), we create a PKE that is n-key KDM secure for arbitrary n and for any functions of a-priori bounded circuit size, as long as there exists some symmetric-key encryption scheme that is 1-key circular secure. As a concrete corollary of our work, by relying on the existence of 1-key circular secure encryption from the CDH assumption [BLSV18], we get the first n-key KDM secure scheme under CDH.

Like prior works [BHHI10, App11, KM20] our construction leverages garbled circuits, but with a different twist. Remarkably, our construction does need to know the specification of any 1-key circular secure scheme. Instead the 1-key circular scheme only manifests in our proof of security. Thus we are able to achieve a form of *universal security*, where our concrete scheme is secure so long as there exists some 1-key circular secure scheme, without needing to know which one.[3] Even though our construction is universal, it does not employ any "algorithm enumeration" style techniques associated with most other universal constructions starting with [Lev85]. It also avoids the "galactic inefficiency" tied to such approaches, where huge constant factors in the resulting schemes imply

---

[1] Applebaum [App11] describes his transformation using the terminology of randomized encodings; however, we refer to it in terms of garbled circuits to simplify comparisons.

[2] We note that there are some trivial amplifications one can do by scaling the security parameter. For example, if we had a scheme that supported $n = \lambda$ keys, then for any constant c we could achieve KDM security for $n = \lambda^c$ keys. The transformation is to simply let $\lambda' = \lambda^c$ and then run the same scheme with security parameter λ'.

[3] While our construction does not need to know the 1-key circular secure scheme, it does need to know the specification of the CPA secure PKE.

that they likely cannot be executed in the lifetime of the universe if we want reasonable concrete security. Interestingly, our proof would still work even if the underlying 1-key circular scheme only had a non-uniform instantiation, meaning that the description of the algorithms themselves could depend on λ but their specification could take superpolynomial time to generate. This is in contrast to other prior universal constructions based on "algorithm enumeration", which crucially rely on the underlying secure scheme having a uniform (constant-sized) algorithmic description.

A core contribution is that we devise a proof method to link several disparate secret keys to a single master key. At the beginning of the proof all n secret keys are independently generated, but at the end they can all be viewed as being derived from an introduced master key. This matches in spirit the key linking concept pioneered by [BHHO08], but with the difference that we generically utilize 1-key circular security to achieve the linking as opposed to algebraic properties of a particular number theoretic domain.

1.1 Overview

We now give an overview of our construction and proof of security. A feature of our construction is its simplicity and we begin by describing the algorithms. We will utilize a CPA-secure public-key encryption scheme CPA = (CPA.KeyGen, CPA.Enc, CPA.Dec) that is not necessarily KDM secure and a garbled circuit scheme (Garble, Eval). In the security proof, we will further assume the existence of some symmetric-key encryption scheme that is 1-key KDM secure for projection functions (this is implied by 1-key circular security via [KM20]), denoted by PRJ = (PRJ.KeyGen, PRJ.Enc, PRJ.Dec), but we do not need to know this scheme for our construction.

Our key generation algorithm KDM.KeyGen(1^λ) begins by randomly sampling an "indicator value" $u \leftarrow \{0,1\}^\lambda$. Next it samples 2λ public secret key pairs as $(\mathsf{pk}_{i,b}, \mathsf{sk}_{i,b}) \leftarrow$ CPA.KeyGen(1^λ) for $i \in [\lambda]$, $b \in \{0,1\}$. The public key and secret key is set as $\overline{\mathsf{pk}} = \{\mathsf{pk}_{i,b}\}_{i\in[\lambda],b\in\{0,1\}}$, $\overline{\mathsf{sk}} = (u, \{sk_{i,u_i}\}_{i\in[\lambda]})$. Intuitively, all 2λ public keys are published, while only half of the secret keys as chosen by u are kept. This means that for all i any value which is later encrypted to pk_{i,u_i} can be recovered by the secret key and any value encrypted to $\mathsf{pk}_{i,1-u_i}$ cannot.

Our encryption algorithm KDM.Enc($\overline{\mathsf{pk}}, \mu$) takes as input the public key and a message μ. It begins by first constructing a circuit C_μ that is a constant circuit of λ input bits that outputs μ on any input. (We pad it to an appropriate size, but leave details of padding to the main body description.) Next we created a garbling of C_μ as $(\widetilde{C}, \{\mathsf{lab}_{i,b}\}_{i\in[\lambda],b\in\{0,1\}}) \leftarrow$ Garble($1^\lambda, C_\mu$). Finally, we encrypt each label to the corresponding public key component as $\mathsf{ct}_{i,b} \leftarrow$ CPA.Enc($\mathsf{pk}_{i,b}, \mathsf{lab}_{i,b}$). And output the ciphertext as $\overline{\mathsf{ct}} = (\widetilde{C}, \{\mathsf{ct}_{i,b}\}_{i\in[\lambda],b\in\{0,1\}})$. The ciphertext consists of the garbled circuit $\widetilde{C}$ plus an encryption of each label.

The decryption algorithm utilizes the indicator value u to guide it to which labels it should attempt to recover. The algorithm recovers lab_{i,u_i} by decrypting ct_{i,u_i} with sk_{i,u_i} to for each i. At this point it has a label for each input and can recover the message by evaluating the garbled circuit. Since $\widetilde{C}$ is a garbling of the constant circuit C_μ it will output the message μ regardless of what set of label are recovered.

One can easily observe that our construction uses plain PKE and does not use any KDM scheme whatsoever. We also observe that our decryption process communicates the indicator value u to the garbled circuit. This doesn't matter much for the correctness of the construction since C_μ is a constant circuit; however, this feature will come into play further along in the proof.

Security for n-keys by Key Linking. We consider KDM security for n-keys where the attacker will get a single challenge ciphertext under the public key of the t-th user of some function f applied to the secret keys of all the users. The adversary chooses t, f, where the function f can be an arbitrary function of some a-prior bounded circuit size.[4] The general case of multiple challenge ciphertexts is handled almost as easily, but we restrict ourselves to a single one here for ease of exposition. Our proof proceeds over multiple steps.

In the first step we begin by linking the indicator values of these keys as follows. First, we introduce a 1-key KDM scheme PRJ for projection functions and sample $k \leftarrow \mathsf{PRJ.KeyGen}(1^\lambda)$. Without loss of generality, we can assume $|k| = \lambda$. Next choose random $v^j \leftarrow \{0,1\}^\lambda$ and set $u^j := k \oplus v^j$ for all $j \in [n]$ where u^j is the indicator component of the j-th key. This concludes the first step where we can now view the indicator components of the j-th key as being derived from a single k by XORing with v^j. Arguing indistinguishability of this step is immediate as it only involves a syntatic change and the distribution is the same as the prior hybrid. At this point the secret key of user j is only partly derived (in the indicator component) from k.

In the second step of the proof we let $\mathsf{ct}_{i,1-u_i^t} \leftarrow \mathsf{CPA.Enc}(\mathsf{pk}_{i,1-u_i^t}^t, 0^\lambda))\}_{i \in [\lambda]}$. That is replace the encryption of lab_{i,u_i^t} with the all 0's string, which effectively erases lab_{i,u_i^t} from the ciphertext. Indistinguishability of this step follows immediately from CPA security coupled with the fact that $\mathsf{sk}_{i,1-u_i^t}^t$ is *not* part of user t's secret key as it was discarded during key generation.

In the third step, we now move to fully derive the all the secret keys from k when creating our ciphertext. To do this, we first encrypt all the secret keys $\overline{\mathsf{sk}}^j$ under k to derive ciphertexts $\widehat{\mathsf{ct}}^j \leftarrow \mathsf{PRJ.Enc}(k, \overline{\mathsf{sk}}^j)$ for $j \in [n]$. We then change from garbling the constant circuit C_μ to garbling a new circuit $\widehat{C}$ that has the ciphertext $\widehat{\mathsf{ct}}^j$ hard-coded and performs the following steps:

1. Takes in an input x, which should be u^t when decrypting properly with the t-th secret key.
2. Computes $x \oplus v^j$. Under the presumption $x = u^t$, this is equal to k.

---

[4] The bound on the circuit size affects the size of the padding we need to add to the circuit C_μ in the construction.

3. Derives from k the secret keys $\overline{\mathsf{sk}}^j$ for all n users by decrypting $\overline{\mathsf{sk}}^j = \mathsf{PRJ.Dec}(k, \widehat{\mathsf{ct}}^j)$.[5]

4. Evaluate the function $f(\overline{\mathsf{sk}}^1, \ldots, \overline{\mathsf{sk}}^n)$ on the secret keys obtained from the previous step where f is the KDM query supplied by the attacker.

This proof step can be fulfilled by garbled circuit security. We can employ this argument since at this stage only one label per input bit is contained in the ciphertext.

At this point the keys are fully derived from the "master key" k. Before we can apply KDM security to erase the message we must first erase knowledge of k from the challenge ciphertext. Currently, k is indirectly embedded in the challenge ciphertext by the fact that labels are only encrypted in ct_{i,u_i^t} and not $\mathsf{ct}_{i,1-u_i^t}$. To remedy this we reverse an earlier step and add labels $\mathsf{lab}_{i,1-u_i^t}$ back to $\mathsf{ct}_{i,1-u_i^t}$.

With this modification the only information regarding k is inside the KDM ciphertexts $\widehat{\mathsf{ct}}^j$ contained within the garbled circuit. But now that k is gone elsewhere we can (finally) leverage KDM security to change $\widehat{\mathsf{ct}}^j$ to each be encryptions of the all 0's strings. Finally, now that all information regarding $\overline{\mathsf{sk}}^j$ is gone we can apply CPA security to remove *all* labels by changing both $\mathsf{ct}_{i,0}$ and $\mathsf{ct}_{i,1}$ to be encryptions of the all 0's string. And follow this by changing $\widetilde{C}$ to be a garbling of the constant function encrypting outputing the all 0's string.

1.2 Extensions and Comparisons

We conclude by mentioning a few extensions to our work as well as exploring technique comparisons.

Symmetric-Key KDM. The scheme described above shows how to go from 1-key KDM security to n-key KDM security for public key encryption, by additionally using standard CPA-secure PKE. We can also achieve the same results for secret key encryption without the additional assumption via a small modifications to our approach. One might try to achieve this by running the same system and simply replacing the use of a CPA secure public key encryption with CPA secure secret key encryption. This runs into the issue of how the encryption algorithm generates the values $\mathsf{ct}_{i,1-u_i}$ without a public key. One possibility is to add the components $\mathsf{sk}_{i,1-u_i}$ to the secret key; however, doing this will break our security argument. Instead, we will use a symmetric key encryption scheme with pseudorandom ciphertexts. (This is known from pseudorandom functions.) Then we can encrypt by setting $\mathsf{ct}_{i,1-u_i}$ to be a random string. The proof of security then proceeds in a mostly similar way to before. We give further details in the

---

[5] We actually only need to derive the secret keys j that are used in the computation of f. For a bounded size function f this may be considerably fewer than all n. However, for this overview we act as though all keys are derived here.

main body. Note that the resulting scheme depends on the symmetric-key CPA-secure encryption, but not on the 1-key KDM secure one – we only assume the latter exists, without knowing what it is.

In many applications it will be desirable to have KDM security with respect to an adversary that can also make chosen ciphertext attacks. As mentioned at the beginning starting with [KW19] several recent works have explored ways of achieving CCA security from key dependent type primitives. After applying our transformation for CPA security one can apply a theorem statement from [KM20] to then make the scheme CCA secure while maintaining KDM security for n-keys.

Given that prior schemes (e.g. [BHHI10, App11, KM20]) applied garbled circuits for function amplification, it is instructive to take a slightly closer look into the similarities and differences with our construction. We focus on the work of Applebaum [App11]. The construction of Applebaum is fairly straightforward. A user's public and secret key is created by calling the key generation algorithm for a scheme that is KDM secure for some weak functionality. To encrypt, one first simulates a garbled circuit that outputs the message μ—the simulation includes a simulated circuit and a single label for each input. These are all encrypted under the public key. To obtain the message the algorithm first decrypts the KDM ciphertext to get the garbled circuit and labels and then performs an evaluation which produces the message.

To prove security the challenge ciphertext is modified so that it is a garbling of a circuit which KDM function query f provided by the attacker and the labels given out correspond the secret key of the underlying KDM scheme. The properties of the garbling construction imply that this garbling itself can be viewed as a projection function of the secret key. Security then follows from the fact that the underlying scheme was KDM with respect to projection functions.

One critical structural difference between our approach and the above is that in [App11] the starting KDM scheme is exposed on the outside. If we run an n-key KDM experiment the attacker will see all n keys. If the underlying scheme were only 1-key KDM secure, it is unclear how one would argue n-key security from an attacker that sees many 1-key secure schemes. In contrast our proof starts with a 1-key secure scheme, but it is hidden within the garbled circuit and not exposed to the outside. Moreover, the security proof only uses a single 1-KDM secure key. If there are multiple KDM ciphertexts, it will be under the *same* key over and over again. Interestingly, the structure of our key amplification is arguably closer to the structure used by [KMT19] in showing that hinting PRGs implied a encryption system that was one time KDM secure.

Another interesting comparison point is the construction of Kitagawa and Tanaka [KT18] for realizing KDM secure public key encryption from KDM secure secret key encryption and standard IND-CPA secure public key encryption. Their construction shares some stylistic features similar to ours in that λ pairs of public keys are generated and a symmetric key k is used to select which of each pair to keep in the secret key and which one to drop. Likewise, encryption will communicate a set of labels and the decryptor gets a set corresponding to the key k.

There are also some crucial differences in the approaches. First, in the Kitagawa and Tanaka scheme the evaluation of the garbled circuit during decryption produces a symmetric key KDM which must be then decrypted by k to get the message. In contrast our scheme never exposes the symmetric key ciphertext outside the garbled circuit during decryption. In fact (as mentioned before) no such scheme is actually used in the main construction and the value u is simply a random value and not a KDM secret key. This distinction allows us to instead link u to a single KDM key in our proof. And during the proof the symmetric key KDM ciphertexts are used within the garbled circuit giving us our universal property.

2   Preliminaries

For any integer $n \geq 1$, define $[n] = \{1, \ldots, n\}$. A function $\nu : \mathbb{N} \to \mathbb{N}$ is said to be negligible, denoted $\nu(n) = \mathsf{negl}(n)$, if for every positive polynomial $p(\cdot)$ and all sufficiently large n it holds that $\nu(n) < 1/p(n)$. We use the abbreviation PPT for probabilistic polynomial time. For a finite set S, we write $a \leftarrow S$ to mean a is sampled uniformly randomly from S. For a randomized algorithm A, we let $a \leftarrow A(\cdot)$ denote the process of running $A(\cdot)$ and assigning the outcome to a; when A is deterministic, we write $a := A(\cdot)$ instead. We denote the security parameter by λ. For two distributions X, Y parameterized by λ we say that they are computationally indistinguishable, denoted by $X \approx_c Y$ if for every PPT distinguisher D we have $|\Pr[D(X) = 1] - \Pr[D(Y) = 1]| = \mathsf{negl}(\lambda)$.

2.1   Garbled Circuits

Definition 1 (Garbling Scheme). *A garbling scheme* (Garble, Eval) *has the following syntax:*

- $(\widetilde{C}, \{\mathsf{lab}_{i,b}\}_{i \in [n], b \in \{0,1\}}) \leftarrow \mathsf{Garble}(1^\lambda, C)$*: Takes as input a circuit C having n input wires and m output wires, and outputs the garbled circuit $\widetilde{C}$ along with $2n$ labels $\mathsf{lab}_{i,b} \in \{0,1\}^\lambda$.*
- $y = \mathsf{Eval}(\widetilde{C}, \{\mathsf{lab}_{i,x_i}\})$*: Given a garbled circuit $\widetilde{C}$ and n labels $\{\mathsf{lab}_{i,x_i}\}_{i \in [n]}$ for some input $x \in \{0,1\}^n$, outputs $y = C(x)$.*

Correctness: *For all circuits C with n input wires, for all $x \in \{0,1\}^n$, we have:*

$$\Pr[\mathsf{Eval}(\widetilde{C}, \{\mathsf{lab}_{i,x_i}\}_{i \in [n]}) = C(x)] = 1 - \mathsf{negl}(\lambda),$$

where the probability is over $(\widetilde{C}, \{\mathsf{lab}_{i,b}\}_{i \in [n], b \in \{0,1\}}) \leftarrow \mathsf{Garble}(1^\lambda, C)$.

Security: *There exists a PPT simulator* Sim *such that, for all circuits C with n input wires and m output wires, for all $x \in \{0,1\}^n$ we have*

$$(\widetilde{C}, \{\mathsf{lab}_{i,x_i}\}_{i \in [n]}) \approx_c \mathsf{Sim}(1^\lambda, 1^n, 1^m, 1^{|C|}, C(x))$$

where $(\widetilde{C}, \{\mathsf{lab}_{i,b}\}_{i \in [n], b \in \{0,1\}}) \leftarrow \mathsf{Garble}(1^\lambda, C)$.

Claim 1 (Indistinguishability Security). *Assume* (Garble, Eval) *is a garbling scheme. Then for any circuits* C_0, C_1 *with* n *input wires,* m *output wires and equal circuit size* $|C_0| = |C_1|$, *for any input* $x \in \{0,1\}^n$ *such that* $C_0(x) = C_1(x)$ *and we have:*

$$(\widetilde{C}^0, \{\mathsf{lab}_{i,x_i}^0\}_{i\in[n]}) \approx_c (\widetilde{C}^1, \{\mathsf{lab}_{i,x_i}^1\}_{i\in[n]})$$

where $(\widetilde{C}^\beta, \{\mathsf{lab}_{i,b}^\beta\}_{i\in[n],b\in\{0,1\}}) \leftarrow \mathsf{Garble}(1^\lambda, C_\beta)$.

Proof. Follows via a hybrid argument. By the definition of garbled circuit security, there is a simulator Sim such that the following holds. Let $s := |C_0| = |C_1|$ and $y = C_0(x) = C_1(x)$. Then:

$$(\widetilde{C}^0, \{\mathsf{lab}_{i,x_i}^0\}_{i\in[n]}) \approx_c \mathsf{Sim}(1^\lambda, 1^n, 1^m, 1^s, y) \approx_c (\widetilde{C}^1, \{\mathsf{lab}_{i,x_i}^1\}_{i\in[n]}).$$

Claim 2 (No-Label Security). *Assume* (Garble, Eval) *is a garbling scheme. Then for any circuits* C_0, C_1 *with* n *input wires,* m *output wires and equal circuit size* $|C_0| = |C_1|$ *we have*

$$\widetilde{C}^0 \approx_c \widetilde{C}^1$$

where $(\widetilde{C}^\beta, \{\mathsf{lab}_{i,b}^\beta\}_{i\in[n],b\in\{0,1\}}) \leftarrow \mathsf{Garble}(1^\lambda, C_\beta)$.

Proof. Let $y_0 = C_0(0^n)$ and $y_1 = C_1(0^n)$. Define the circuits

$$C_{alt(b)}(x) = \begin{cases} y_b & \text{if } x = 0^n \\ 0^m & \text{else} \end{cases}$$

and pad these circuits to be the same size as C_0, C_1.[6]

Let $(\widetilde{C}^\beta, \{\mathsf{lab}_{i,b}^\beta\}_{i\in[n],b\in\{0,1\}}) \leftarrow \mathsf{Garble}(1^\lambda, C_\beta)$ for $\beta \in \{0, 1, alt(0), alt(1)\}$. Then

$$(\widetilde{C}^0, \{\mathsf{lab}_{i,0}^0\}_{i\in[n]}) \approx_c (\widetilde{C}^{alt(0)}, \{\mathsf{lab}_{i,0}^{alt(0)}\}_{i\in[n]})$$

by Claim 1 and the fact that $C_0(0^n) = C_{alt(0)}(0^n)$. Therefore $\widetilde{C}^0 \approx_c \widetilde{C}^{alt(0)}$.

Also,

$$(\widetilde{C}^{alt(0)}, \{\mathsf{lab}_{i,1}^{alt(0)}\}_{i\in[n]}) \approx_c (\widetilde{C}^{alt(1)}, \{\mathsf{lab}_{i,1}^{alt(1)}\}_{i\in[n]})$$

by Claim 1 and the fact that $C_{alt(0)}(1^n) = C_{alt(1)}(1^n) = 0^m$. Therefore $\widetilde{C}^{alt(0)} \approx_c \widetilde{C}^{alt(1)}$.

Lastly,

$$(\widetilde{C}^{alt(1)}, \{\mathsf{lab}_{i,0}^{alt(1)}\}_{i\in[n]}) \approx_c (\widetilde{C}^1, \{\mathsf{lab}_{i,0}^1\}_{i\in[n]})$$

by Claim 1 and the fact that $C_{alt(1)}(0^n) = C_1(1^n)$. Therefore $\widetilde{C}^{alt(1)} \approx_c \widetilde{C}^1$.

By a hybrid argument, we therefore get $\widetilde{C}^0 \approx_c \widetilde{C}^1$.

---

[6] We assume that $|C_b|$ is at least as large as $C_{alt(b)}$, which is of some fixed size $O(n+m)$. We can make this hold without loss of generality by always padding all circuits to be at least of that size before garbling them.

2.2 KDM Security Definitions

Definition 2 (KDM Security [BRS03]). *Let* (KeyGen, Enc, Dec) *be a public-key encryption scheme with the usual correctness property. Let* $n = n(\lambda)$ *be some polynomial and let* $\mathcal{F} = \{\mathcal{F}_\lambda\}$ *be some family of functions. We say that the scheme is* $(n, \mathcal{F})$-*KDM if for all PPT adversary* $\mathcal{A}$ *we have*

$$|\Pr[\mathsf{KDMGame}^0_\mathcal{A}(1^\lambda) = 1] - \Pr[\mathsf{KDMGame}^1_\mathcal{A}(1^\lambda)]| = \mathrm{negl}(\lambda)$$

where $\mathsf{KDMGame}^\beta_\mathcal{A}(1^\lambda)$ *is defined as the output of* $\mathcal{A}$ *in the following game:*

- *For* $j \in [n]$, *the challenger chooses* $(\mathsf{pk}^j, \mathsf{sk}^j) \leftarrow \mathsf{KeyGen}(1^\lambda)$ *and gives* $\mathsf{pk}^1, \ldots, \mathsf{pk}^n$ *to* $\mathcal{A}$.
- *The adversary* $\mathcal{A}$ *makes arbitrary many KDM encryption queries:*
  - *The adversary* $\mathcal{A}$ *chooses a pair* (t, f) *where* $t \in [n]$ *and* $f \in \mathcal{F}_\lambda$.
  - *The challenger replies with* $\mathsf{ct} \leftarrow \mathsf{Enc}(\mathsf{pk}^t, \mu)$ *were* μ *is defined as:*
    - *If* $\beta = 0$, *then* $\mu := 0^\ell$ *where* ℓ *is the output length of* f.
    - *If* $\beta = 1$ *then* $\mu := f(\mathsf{sk}^1, \ldots, \mathsf{sk}^n)$.

By default, we only consider bit-encryption schemes whose native message space is 1-bit. However, we will abuse notation and write $\mathsf{Enc}(\mathsf{sk}, \mu)$ for longer messages μ to denote encrypting μ bitwise, one bit at a time. Also, we always allow the adversary to choose the constant-0 or constant-1 functions, which corresponds to encrypting 0 or 1, even when we do not explicitly define these as part of the class $\mathcal{F}$. Lastly, we note that the definition of $(n, \mathcal{F})$ security only makes sense syntactically when $\mathcal{F}_\lambda$ contains functions f whose inputs consist of $n(\lambda)$ secret keys. We specify some classes of interest below.

(n, s)-*circuit-KDM.* For a polynomial $s = s(\lambda)$, we say that an encryption scheme is (n, s)-circuit-KDM secure if it is $(n, \mathcal{F})$-KDM secure, where $\mathcal{F} = \{\mathcal{F}_\lambda\}$ is the class of circuits having size $s(\lambda)$. Although we think of functions $f \in \mathcal{F}$ as taking the input $\mathsf{sk}^1, \ldots, \mathsf{sk}^n$, it will be meaningful to talk about (n, s)-KDM security for $s \ll n$. In this case, the function's circuit size is too small for it to even read the entire input. Instead, we think of the circuit f as specifying, for each input wire, a pair of indices (i, j) indicating that this input wire reads the j'th bit of the i'th secret key sk^i. We let $\mathsf{inp}(f) \subseteq [n]$ denote the subset of the secret keys that the input wires of f depend on, and we can write $f(\{\mathsf{sk}^i\}_{i \in \mathsf{inp}(f)})$ in place of $f(\mathsf{sk}^1, \ldots, \mathsf{sk}^n)$.

n-*circular.* We say that a scheme is n-*circular secure* if it is $(n, \mathcal{F})$-KDM secure where $\mathcal{F}$ consists of the class of functions $f_{i,j}(\mathsf{sk}^1, \ldots, \mathsf{sk}^n)$ that output the j'th bit of the i'th secret key sk^i for some (i, j).

n-*projection-KDM.* We say that a scheme is n-projection-KDM secure if it is $(n, \mathcal{F})$-KDM secure where $\mathcal{F}$ consists of the class of functions $f_{i,j,b}(\mathsf{sk}^1, \ldots, \mathsf{sk}^n) = f_{i,j}(\mathsf{sk}^1, \ldots, \mathsf{sk}^n) \oplus b$ for arbitrary (i, j, b) and for $f_{i,j}$ as defined above. When extended to multi-bit messages encrypted bit-wise, n-projection-KDM implies security for the class of functions $\mathcal{F}$ where each output bit can depend arbitrarily on any single bit of $\mathsf{sk}^1, \ldots, \mathsf{sk}^n$.

$(\infty, \mathcal{F})$-*KDM*. We say that a scheme is $(\infty, \mathcal{F})$-KDM secure if it $(n, \mathcal{F})$-KDM secure for all polynomial $n = n(\lambda)$. The notions of (∞, s)-circuit-KDM security and ∞-circular-security are defined analogously.

Symmetric-Key KDM. We define KDM security for symmetric-key encryption analogously to the above definition for public key encryption. In particular, $\mathsf{sk} \leftarrow \mathsf{KeyGen}(1^\lambda)$ now only outputs a secret key (and no public key), and $\mathsf{ct} \leftarrow \mathsf{Enc}(\mathsf{sk}, \mu)$ now takes a secret key as an input instead of the public key. Security is defined analogously by modifying the KDM security so that (i) the adversary does not get any $\mathsf{pk}^1, \ldots, \mathsf{pk}^n$, (ii) the KDM encryption queries are now answered via a symmetric-key encryption $\mathsf{ct} \leftarrow \mathsf{Enc}(\mathsf{sk}^t, u)$.

3 Amplifying KDM

Let $\mathsf{CPA} = (\mathsf{CPA.KeyGen}, \mathsf{CPA.Enc}, \mathsf{CPA.Dec})$ be a CPA-secure public-key encryption scheme. Let $(\mathsf{Garble}, \mathsf{Eval})$ be a garbled circuit scheme (Definition 1). We construct a public-key encryption scheme $\mathsf{KDM} = (\mathsf{KDM.KeyGen}, \mathsf{KDM.}$ $\mathsf{Enc}, \mathsf{KDM.Dec})$, parameterized by some padding parameter $p = p(\lambda)$ to be specified later, as follows:

$(\overline{\mathsf{pk}}, \overline{\mathsf{sk}}) \leftarrow \mathsf{KDM.KeyGen}(1^\lambda)$: For $i \in [\lambda]$, $b \in \{0,1\}$, sample $(\mathsf{pk}_{i,b}, \mathsf{sk}_{i,b}) \leftarrow$ $\mathsf{CPA.KeyGen}(1^\lambda)$. Sample $u \leftarrow \{0,1\}^\lambda$. Let $\overline{\mathsf{pk}} = \{\mathsf{pk}_{i,b}\}_{i\in[\lambda], b\in\{0,1\}}$, $\overline{\mathsf{sk}} = (u, \{sk_{i,u_i}\}_{i\in[\lambda]})$.

$\overline{\mathsf{ct}} \leftarrow \mathsf{KDM.Enc}(\overline{\mathsf{pk}}, \mu)$: Let C_μ be the constant circuit that takes any input $x \in \{0,1\}^\lambda$ and always outputs μ. We pad C_μ to be of size $p(\lambda)$ for the padding parameter p. Let

$$(\widetilde{C}, \{\mathsf{lab}_{i,b}\}_{i\in[\lambda], b\in\{0,1\}}) \leftarrow \mathsf{Garble}(1^\lambda, C_\mu).$$

For $i \in [\lambda]$, $b \in \{0,1\}$, sample $\mathsf{ct}_{i,b} \leftarrow \mathsf{CPA.Enc}(\mathsf{pk}_{i,b}, \mathsf{lab}_{i,b})$. Output $\overline{\mathsf{ct}} = (\widetilde{C}, \{\mathsf{ct}_{i,b}\}_{i\in[\lambda], b\in\{0,1\}})$.

$\mu := \mathsf{KDM.Dec}(\overline{\mathsf{sk}}, \overline{\mathsf{ct}})$: For $i \in [\lambda]$, let $\mathsf{lab}_{i,u_i} := \mathsf{CPA.Dec}(\mathsf{sk}_{i,u_i}, \mathsf{ct}_{i,u_i})$. Output $\mu := \mathsf{Eval}(\widetilde{C}, \{\mathsf{lab}_{i,u_i}\})$.

Correctness. Let $\overline{\mathsf{pk}} = \{\mathsf{pk}_{i,b}\}_{i\in[\lambda], b\in\{0,1\}}$, $\overline{\mathsf{sk}} = (u, \{sk_{i,u_i}\}_{i\in[\lambda]})$ be a key pair output by the KDM.KeyGen algorithm. And let $\overline{\mathsf{ct}} = (\widetilde{C}, \{\mathsf{ct}_{i,b}\}_{i\in[\lambda], b\in\{0,1\}})$ be a ciphertext produced from $\mathsf{KDM.Enc}(\overline{\mathsf{pk}}, \mu)$ for some μ. When the algorithm $\mathsf{KDM.Dec}(\overline{\mathsf{sk}}, \overline{\mathsf{ct}})$ is run it first produces $\mathsf{lab}_{i,u_i} := \mathsf{CPA.Dec}(\mathsf{sk}_{i,u_i}, \mathsf{ct}_{i,u_i})$. By the correctness of the underlying CPA secure encryption scheme $\mathsf{lab}_{i,u_i} = \mathsf{lab}'_{i,u_i}$ for all i where lab'_{i,u_i} are the labels generated during the encryption procedure. Next, we have that $\mathsf{Eval}(\widetilde{C}, \{\mathsf{lab}_{i,u_i}\}) = C_\mu(u)$ by the correctness of the garbling scheme where μ is the message encrypted. Finally, $C_\mu(u) = \mu$ since C_μ is the constant function and correctness holds.

3.1   Security

Theorem 1. *Let* CPA *be a CPA-secure public-key encryption scheme and let* (Garble, Eval) *be a secure garbling scheme. Then for any polynomial $s(\lambda)$ there exists some polynomial padding parameter $p(\lambda)$ such that the following holds. Assume that there exists some 1-circular symmetric-key encryption scheme. Then the above* KDM *scheme with padding parameter p is an $(\infty, s(\lambda))$-circuit-KDM secure public-key encryption.*

Proof. We define the polynomial $p(\lambda)$ further below. Assume there exists some symmetric-key 1-circular secure bit-encryption scheme. Then by [KM20] there also exists 1-projection-KDM secure symmetric-key encryption denoted by PRJ = (PRJ.KeyGen, PRJ.Enc, PRJ.Dec).

By rescaling the security parameter, we can assume without loss of generality that: (i) the secret key size of $k \leftarrow$ PRJ.KeyGen(1^λ) is of size $|k| \leq \lambda$ and (ii) the circuit size of the decryption function PRJ.Dec($\cdot$, ct) (which has a hard-coded bit-ciphertext ct, takes as input the key k, and outputs PRJ.Dec(k, ct)) is bounded by $|$PRJ.Dec($\cdot$, ct)$| \leq \lambda$. In particular, assume we have some scheme PRJ' where the maximum of the keys size $|k|$ and the circuit size of PRJ'.Dec are bounded by some potentially large polynomial $q(\lambda) \leq c_1 \cdot \lambda^{c_2}$ for some constants c_1, c_2. We can define the scheme PRJ by taking PRJ.KeyGen(1^λ) = PRJ'.KeyGen($1^{\lambda'}$) where $\lambda' = \lambda^{1/c_2}/c_1$ to satisfy (ii) and ensure $|k| \leq \lambda$. It is easy to see that asymptotic security is preserved, although exact security degrades. Furthermore, we can strengthen (i) to require that the key size is exactly $|k| = \lambda$ while preserving (ii). We do this by padding the key with dummy bits, which the decryption circuit ignores (this allows us to have a potentially smaller decryption circuit than key size).

For any polynomial $n = n(\lambda)$, we prove the (n, s)-circuit-KDM security of the KDM scheme via the following sequence of hybrids:

Hybrid 0. This is (n, s)-KDM security game of the scheme KDM with the challenge bit $\beta = 1$, which proceeds as follows:
- For $j \in [n]$, the challenger chooses $(\overline{\mathsf{pk}}^j, \overline{\mathsf{sk}}^j) \leftarrow$ KDM.KeyGen(1^λ) and gives $\overline{\mathsf{pk}}^1, \ldots, \overline{\mathsf{pk}}^n$ to $\mathcal{A}$.
- The adversary $\mathcal{A}$ makes arbitrary many KDM encryption queries:
  - The adversary $\mathcal{A}$ chooses a pair (t, f) where $t \in [n]$ and f is a circuit of size $|f| \leq s$.
  - The challenger sets $\mu := f(\{\overline{\mathsf{sk}}^j\}_{j \in \mathsf{inp}(f)})$ and replies with $\overline{\mathsf{ct}} \leftarrow$ KDM.Enc($\overline{\mathsf{pk}}^t, \mu$).

Hybrid 1. We modify how the values $(\overline{\mathsf{pk}}^j, \overline{\mathsf{sk}}^j)$ are chosen by the challenger. In Hybrid 0, the challenger chooses $(\overline{\mathsf{pk}}^j, \overline{\mathsf{sk}}^j) \leftarrow$ KDM.KeyGen(1^λ) as follows:
- Sample $u^j \leftarrow \{0, 1\}^\lambda$.
- Sample $(\mathsf{pk}^j_{i,b}, \mathsf{sk}^j_{i,b}) \leftarrow$ CPA.KeyGen(1^λ). Let $\overline{\mathsf{pk}}^j := \{\mathsf{pk}^j_{i,b}\}_{i \in [\lambda], b \in \{0,1\}}$, $\overline{\mathsf{sk}} := (u^j, \{sk^j_{i,u^j_i}\}_{i \in [\lambda]})$.

In Hybrid 1, the challenger first samples $k \leftarrow \mathsf{PRJ.KeyGen}(1^\lambda)$. The challenger sets $(\overline{\mathsf{pk}}^j, \overline{\mathsf{sk}}^j)$ as:

- Sample $v^j \leftarrow \{0,1\}^\lambda$ and set $u^j := k \oplus v^j$.
- Sample $(\mathsf{pk}_{i,b}^j, \mathsf{sk}_{i,b}^j) \leftarrow \mathsf{CPA.KeyGen}(1^\lambda)$. Let $\overline{\mathsf{pk}}^j := \{\mathsf{pk}_{i,b}^j\}_{i\in[\lambda], b\in\{0,1\}}$, $\overline{\mathsf{sk}}^j := (u^j, \{sk_{i,u_i^j}^j\}_{i\in[\lambda]})$.

The challenger uses the PRJ scheme to encrypt all the secret keys:

$\widehat{\mathsf{ct}}^j \leftarrow \mathsf{PRJ.Enc}(k, \overline{\mathsf{sk}}^j)$ for $j \in [n]$. It stores the ciphertexts $\widehat{\mathsf{ct}}^j$, but does not do anything with them yet in this hybrid.

It is easy to see that the above only introduces a syntactical difference, but the distribution of hybrids 0 and 1 is identical since $u^j = k \oplus v^j$ is uniform over the choice of v^j. Note that the ciphertexts $\widehat{\mathsf{ct}}^j$ do not appear in the view of the adversary.

Hybrid 2. We now modify how KDM encryption queries (t, f) are answered.

In Hybrid 1, the challenger chooses $\overline{\mathsf{ct}} \leftarrow \mathsf{KDM.Enc}(\overline{\mathsf{pk}}^t, \mu)$, where $\overline{\mathsf{ct}} = (\widetilde{C}, \{\mathsf{ct}_{i,b}\}_{i\in[\lambda], b\in\{0,1\}})$ with $(\widetilde{C}, \{\mathsf{lab}_{i,b}\}_{i\in[\lambda], b\in\{0,1\}}) \leftarrow \mathsf{Garble}(1^\lambda, C_\mu)$, and $\{\mathsf{ct}_{i,b} \leftarrow \mathsf{CPA.Enc}(\mathsf{pk}_{i,b}^t, \mathsf{lab}_{i,b})\}_{i\in[\lambda], b\in\{0,1\}}$.

In Hybrid 2, the challenger replaces $\mathsf{ct}_{i,b}$ with a dummy encryption of 0's when $b = 1 - u_i^t$. That is, the challenger chooses $\overline{\mathsf{ct}} = (\widetilde{C}, \{\mathsf{ct}_{i,b}\}_{i\in[\lambda], b\in\{0,1\}})$ with $(\widetilde{C}, \{\mathsf{lab}_{i,b}\}_{i\in[\lambda], b\in\{0,1\}}) \leftarrow \mathsf{Garble}(1^\lambda, C_\mu)$, and $\{\mathsf{ct}_{i,u_i^t} \leftarrow \mathsf{CPA.Enc}(\mathsf{pk}_{i,u_i^t}^t, \mathsf{lab}_{i,u_i^t}), \mathsf{ct}_{i,1-u_i^t} \leftarrow \mathsf{CPA.Enc}(\mathsf{pk}_{i,1-u_i^t}^t, 0^\lambda)\}_{i\in[\lambda]}$.

These hybrids are computationally indistinguishable by the CPA security of the encryption scheme CPA. In particular, the secret keys $\{sk_{i,1-u_i^t}^t\}_{i\in[\lambda]}$ are not used anywhere in the game and are not a part of $\overline{\mathsf{sk}}^t$. Therefore, CPA security allows us to replace $\mathsf{ct}_{i,1-u_i^t} \leftarrow \mathsf{CPA.Enc}(\mathsf{pk}_{i,1-u_i^t}^t, \mathsf{lab}_{i,1-u_i^t})$ by $\mathsf{ct}_{i,1-u_i^t} \leftarrow \mathsf{CPA.Enc}(\mathsf{pk}_{i,1-u_i^t}^t, 0^\lambda)$. Formally, proving indistinguishability of Hybrid 1 and 2 requires an internal hybrid argument over all the encryption queries and all the indices $i \in [\lambda]$, where we replace each such ciphertext $\mathsf{ct}_{i,1-u_i^t}$ one by one.

Hybrid 3. We modify how the KDM encryption queries (t, f) are answered once more. This time we change how the garbled circuit is sampled.

In Hybrid 2, we set $\overline{\mathsf{ct}} := (\widetilde{C}, \{\mathsf{ct}_{i,b}\}_{i\in[\lambda], b\in\{0,1\}})$ where $(\widetilde{C}, \{\mathsf{lab}_{i,b}\}_{i\in[\lambda], b\in\{0,1\}}) \leftarrow \mathsf{Garble}(1^\lambda, C_\mu)$, and $\{\mathsf{ct}_{i,u_i^t} \leftarrow \mathsf{CPA.Enc}(\mathsf{pk}_{i,u_i^t}^t, \mathsf{lab}_{i,u_i^t}), \mathsf{ct}_{i,1-u_i^t} \leftarrow \mathsf{CPA.Enc}(\mathsf{pk}_{i,1-u_i^t}^t, 0^\lambda)\}_{i\in[\lambda]}$.

In Hybrid 3, for each KDM encryption query (t, f) the challenger constructs a circuit $\widehat{C}$ that contains hard-coded values $f, v^t, \{\widehat{\mathsf{ct}}^j\}_{j\in[\mathsf{inp}(f)]}$ and is defined as follows:

$\widehat{C}(x)$ {
- Compute $k' := v^t \oplus x$.
- For $j \in \mathsf{inp}(f)$: compute $\overline{\mathsf{sk}}^j \leftarrow \mathsf{PRJ.Dec}(k', \widehat{\mathsf{ct}}^j)$.

– Output $f(\{\overline{\mathsf{sk}}^j\}_{j\in\mathsf{inp}(f)})$
}

The challenger sets $\overline{\mathsf{ct}} := (\widetilde{C}, \{\mathsf{ct}_{i,b}\}_{i\in[\lambda], b\in\{0,1\}})$,

where $(\widetilde{C}, \{\mathsf{lab}_{i,b}\}_{i\in[\lambda], b\in\{0,1\}}) \leftarrow \mathsf{Garble}(1^\lambda, \widehat{C})$, and

$$\{\mathsf{ct}_{i,u_i^t} \leftarrow \mathsf{CPA.Enc}(\mathsf{pk}_{i,u_i^t}^t, \mathsf{lab}_{i,u_i^t}) \ , \ \mathsf{ct}_{i,1-u_i^t} \leftarrow \mathsf{CPA.Enc}(\mathsf{pk}_{i,1-u_i^t}^t, 0^\lambda))\}_{i\in[\lambda]}.$$

We also now define the padding parameter $p(\lambda)$ to be the circuit size of the circuit $\widehat{C}$. Note that $p(\lambda)$ only depends on $s(\lambda)$ but is independent of n. It is also independent of the exact parameters of the 1-circular secure bit-encryption, since no matter which such encryption we started with, we ensured the PRJ decryption circuit has size $\le \lambda$ to decrypt each bit.

These hybrids are computationally indistinguishable by the indistinguishability security of garbled circuits (see Claim 1). In particular, recall that $v^t = u^t \oplus k$ and therefore, on input $x = u^t$ we have $k' = k$ during the computation of $\widehat{C}(x)$ and hence $\widehat{C}(u^t) = f(\{\overline{\mathsf{sk}}^j\}_{j\in\mathsf{inp}(f)}) = C_\mu(u^t)$. Furthermore, in both hybrids, the adversary's view only depends on the garbled circuit $\widetilde{C}$ and the labels $\{\mathsf{lab}_{i,u_i^t}\}_{i\in[\lambda]}$, but not on the other labels $\{\mathsf{lab}_{i,1-u_i^t}\}_{i\in[\lambda]}$. Therefore, we can rely on indistinguishability security of garbled circuits to replace the circuit being garbled from C_μ to $\widehat{C}$. Formally, proving indistinguishability of Hybrids 2 and 3 requires an internal hybrid argument over all the KDM encryption queries, where we replace the circuit being garbled in each query one by one.

Hybrid 4. We modify how the KDM encryption queries are answered once again.

In Hybrid 3, we set $\overline{\mathsf{ct}} = (\widetilde{C}, \{\mathsf{ct}_{i,b}\}_{i\in[\lambda], b\in\{0,1\}})$ where $(\widetilde{C}, \{\mathsf{lab}_{i,b}\}_{i\in[\lambda], b\in\{0,1\}}) \leftarrow \mathsf{Garble}(1^\lambda, \widehat{C})$ and

$$\left\{\mathsf{ct}_{i,u_i^t} \leftarrow \mathsf{CPA.Enc}(\mathsf{pk}_{i,u_i^t}^t, \mathsf{lab}_{i,u_i^t}), \mathsf{ct}_{i,1-u_i^t} \leftarrow \mathsf{CPA.Enc}(\mathsf{pk}_{i,1-u_i^t}^t, 0^\lambda)\right\}_{i\in[\lambda]}.$$

In Hybrid 4, we set $\overline{\mathsf{ct}} = (\widetilde{C}, \{\mathsf{ct}_{i,b}\}_{i\in[\lambda], b\in\{0,1\}})$ where $(\widetilde{C}, \{\mathsf{lab}_{i,b}\}_{i\in[\lambda], b\in\{0,1\}}) \leftarrow \mathsf{Garble}(1^\lambda, \widehat{C})$ and

$$\left\{\mathsf{ct}_{i,b} \leftarrow \mathsf{CPA.Enc}(\mathsf{pk}_{i,b}^t, \mathsf{lab}_{i,b})\right\}_{i\in[\lambda], b\in\{0,1\}}.$$

These hybrids are computationally indistinguishable by the CPA security of the encryption scheme CPA. In particular, the secret keys $\{sk_{i,1-u_i^t}^t\}_{i\in[\lambda]}$ are not used anywhere in the game and are not a part of $\overline{\mathsf{sk}}^t$. Therefore, we can replace $\mathsf{ct}_{i,1-u_i^t} \leftarrow \mathsf{CPA.Enc}(\mathsf{pk}_{i,1-u_i^t}^t, 0^\lambda)$ by $\mathsf{ct}_{i,1-u_i^t} \leftarrow \mathsf{CPA.Enc}(\mathsf{pk}_{i,1-u_i^t}^t, \mathsf{lab}_{i,1-u_i^t})$. Formally, proving indistinguishability of Hybrid 3 and 4 requires an internal hybrid argument over all the encryption queries and all the indices $i \in [\lambda]$, where we replace how we sample each such ciphertext $\mathsf{ct}_{i,1-u_i^t}$ one by one.

Hybrid 5. We now change how the ciphertexts $\widehat{\mathsf{ct}}^j$ are chosen during key generation. Recall that these ciphertexts are hard-coded in the circuits $\widehat{C}$ used to answer KDM encryption queries.

In Hybrid 4, the challenger chooses $\widehat{\mathsf{ct}}^j \leftarrow \mathsf{PRJ.Enc}(k, \overline{\mathsf{sk}}^j)$ for $j \in [n]$.

In Hybrid 5, the challenger chooses $\widehat{\mathsf{ct}}^j \leftarrow \mathsf{PRJ.Enc}(k, 0^\alpha)$ for $j \in [n]$, where $\alpha = \left|\overline{\mathsf{sk}}^j\right|$.

These hybrids are computationally indistinguishable by the 1-projection-KDM security of the scheme PRJ. *To see this at a high level, note that we can think of* $\overline{\mathsf{sk}}^j = \{\mathsf{sk}^j_{i,u^j_i}\}$ *as being defined by the function* $\overline{\mathsf{sk}}^j = \phi^j(k)$, *where* ϕ^j *knows the values* v^j *and* $\{\mathsf{sk}^j_{i,b}\}$, *computes* $u^j = k \oplus v^j$ *and sets* $\overline{\mathsf{sk}}^j = \{\mathsf{sk}^j_{i,u^j_i}\}$; *each bit of* $\overline{\mathsf{sk}}^j$ *depends on a single bit of* u^j, *which in tun depends on a single bit of* k, *making* ϕ^j *a projection function.*

Formally, we give a reduction showing the indistinguishability of Hybrid 4 and 5. The reduction samples:

- $v^j \leftarrow \{0,1\}^\lambda$ *for* $j \in [n]$.
- $(\mathsf{pk}^j_{i,b}, \mathsf{sk}^j_{i,b}) \leftarrow \mathsf{CPA.KeyGen}(1^\lambda)$ *for* $j \in [n], i \in [\lambda], b \in \{0,1\}$. *Let* $\overline{\mathsf{pk}}^j := \{\mathsf{pk}^j_{i,b}\}_{i\in[\lambda],b\in\{0,1\}}$.

  Define the functions $\phi^j(k)$ *where* ϕ^j *has the values* v^j *and* $\{\mathsf{sk}^j_{i,b}\}$ *hard-coded, computes* $u^j = k \oplus v^j$ *and sets* $\overline{\mathsf{sk}}^j = \{\mathsf{sk}^j_{i,u^j_i}\}$. *This is a projection function. The reduction makes encryption queries to the* PRJ *scheme with the function* ϕ^j *and gets back ciphertexts* $\widehat{\mathsf{ct}}^j$ *for* $j \in [n]$. *The reduction then runs the adversary* $\mathcal{A}$ *by giving it the public keys* $\overline{\mathsf{pk}}^j$ *and answering KDM encryption queries exactly as the challenger in Hybrid 4 using the values* $v^j, \{\widehat{\mathsf{ct}}^j\}$. *It outputs whatever* $\mathcal{A}$ *outputs at the end.*

  If the reduction received ciphertexts $\widehat{\mathsf{ct}}^j \leftarrow \mathsf{PRJ.Enc}(k, \phi^j(k))$ *then the above matches the distribution of Hybrid 4, and if the reduction received ciphertexts* $\widehat{\mathsf{ct}}^j \leftarrow \mathsf{PRJ.Enc}(k, 0^\alpha)$ *then the above matches the distribution of Hybrid 5. Therefore, the reduction break the projection-KDM security of the* PRJ *scheme with the same advantage as that of* $\mathcal{A}$ *in distinguishing Hybrids 4 and 5.*

Hybrid 6. We modify how the KDM encryption queries (t, f) are answered.

In Hybrid 5, we set $\overline{\mathsf{ct}} = (\widetilde{C}, \{\mathsf{ct}_{i,b}\}_{i\in[\lambda],b\in\{0,1\}})$ where $(\widetilde{C}, \{\mathsf{lab}_{i,b}\}_{i\in[\lambda],b\in\{0,1\}}) \leftarrow \mathsf{Garble}(1^\lambda, \widehat{C})$ and

$$\left\{\mathsf{ct}_{i,b} \leftarrow \mathsf{CPA.Enc}(\mathsf{pk}^t_{i,b}, \mathsf{lab}_{i,b})\right\}_{i\in[\lambda],b\in\{0,1\}}.$$

In Hybrid 6, we set $\overline{\mathsf{ct}} = (\widetilde{C}, \{\mathsf{ct}_{i,b}\}_{i\in[\lambda],b\in\{0,1\}})$ where $(\widetilde{C}, \{\mathsf{lab}_{i,b}\}_{i\in[\lambda],b\in\{0,1\}}) \leftarrow \mathsf{Garble}(1^\lambda, \widehat{C})$ and

$$\left\{\mathsf{ct}_{i,b} \leftarrow \mathsf{CPA.Enc}(\mathsf{pk}^t_{i,b}, 0^\lambda))\right\}_{i\in[\lambda],b\in\{0,1\}}.$$

These hybrids are computationally indistinguishable by the CPA security of the encryption scheme CPA. *In particular, now the secret keys* $\{\mathsf{sk}^t_{i,b}\}$ *are not used anywhere in the game after they are generated! Formally, proving* *indistinguishability of Hybrid 5 and 6 requires an internal hybrid argument over all the encryption queries and all the indices $i \in [\lambda], b \in \{0,1\}$, where we replace how we sample each such ciphertext $\mathsf{ct}_{i,b}$ one by one.*

Hybrid 7. We modify how the KDM encryption queries are answered again. In Hybrid 6, we set $\overline{\mathsf{ct}} = (\widetilde{C}, \{\mathsf{ct}_{i,b}\}_{i \in [\lambda], b \in \{0,1\}})$ where

$$(\widetilde{C}, \{\mathsf{lab}_{i,b}\}_{i \in [\lambda], b \in \{0,1\}}) \leftarrow \mathsf{Garble}(1^\lambda, \widehat{C}) \text{ and } \mathsf{ct}_{i,b} \leftarrow \mathsf{CPA.Enc}(\mathsf{pk}_{i,b}^t, 0^\lambda).$$

In Hybrid 7, we set $\overline{\mathsf{ct}} = (\widetilde{C}, \{\mathsf{ct}_{i,b}\}_{i \in [\lambda], b \in \{0,1\}})$ where

$$(\widetilde{C}, \{\mathsf{lab}_{i,b}\}_{i \in [\lambda], b \in \{0,1\}}) \leftarrow \mathsf{Garble}(1^\lambda, C_{0^\ell}), \text{ for } \ell \text{ being the output size of } f,$$

and $\mathsf{ct}_{i,b} \leftarrow \mathsf{CPA.Enc}(\mathsf{pk}_{i,b}^t, 0^\lambda)$. The circuit $C_{0^\ell}(x)$ always outputs the constant 0^ℓ on every input x, but we pad the circuit to be of size $p(\lambda)$.

These hybrids are computationally indistinguishable by the garbled circuit security with no labels (Claim 2). In particular, the labels $\mathsf{lab}_{i,b}$ are not used anywhere else in game after they are generated. Formally, proving indistinguishability of Hybrids 6 and 7 requires an internal hybrid argument over all the KDM encryption queries, where we replace the circuit being garbled in each query one by one.

Hybrid 8. We modify how the KDM encryption queries are answered once more.

In Hybrid 7, we set $\overline{\mathsf{ct}} = (\widetilde{C}, \{\mathsf{ct}_{i,b}\}_{i \in [\lambda], b \in \{0,1\}})$ where

$(\widetilde{C}, \{\mathsf{lab}_{i,b}\}_{i \in [\lambda], b \in \{0,1\}}) \leftarrow \mathsf{Garble}(1^\lambda, C_{0^\ell})$, for ℓ being the output size of f, and $\mathsf{ct}_{i,b} \leftarrow \mathsf{CPA.Enc}(\mathsf{pk}_{i,b}^t, 0^\lambda)$.

In Hybrid 8, we set $\overline{\mathsf{ct}} = (\widetilde{C}, \{\mathsf{ct}_{i,b}\}_{i \in [\lambda], b \in \{0,1\}})$ where

$(\widetilde{C}, \{\mathsf{lab}_{i,b}\}_{i \in [\lambda], b \in \{0,1\}}) \leftarrow \mathsf{Garble}(1^\lambda, C_{0^\ell})$, for ℓ being the output size of f, and $\mathsf{ct}_{i,b} \leftarrow \mathsf{CPA.Enc}(\mathsf{pk}_{i,b}^t, \mathsf{lab}_{i,b})$.

These hybrids are computationally indistinguishable by the CPA security of the encryption scheme CPA. In particular, the secret keys $\{\mathsf{sk}_{i,b}^t\}$ are not used anywhere in the game after they are generated. Formally, proving indistinguishability of Hybrids 7 and 8 requires an internal hybrid argument over all the encryption queries and all the indices $i \in [\lambda], b \in \{0,1\}$, where we replace how we sample each such ciphertext $\mathsf{ct}_{i,b}$ one by one.

Note that Hybrid 8 is equivalent to the (n, s)-KDM security game of the scheme KDM with the challenge bit $\beta = 0$, which proceeds as follows:

- For $j \in [n]$, the challenger chooses $(\overline{\mathsf{pk}}^j, \overline{\mathsf{sk}}^j) \leftarrow \mathsf{KDM.KeyGen}(1^\lambda)$ and gives $\overline{\mathsf{pk}}^1, \ldots, \overline{\mathsf{pk}}^n$ to $\mathcal{A}$.
- The adversary $\mathcal{A}$ makes arbitrary many KDM encryption queries:
  - The adversary $\mathcal{A}$ chooses a pair (t, f) where $t \in [n]$ and f is a circuit of size $|f| \leq s$.
  - The challenger set $\mu = 0^\ell$ where ℓ is the output size of f and replies with $\overline{\mathsf{ct}} \leftarrow \mathsf{KDM.Enc}(\overline{\mathsf{pk}}^t, \mu)$.

Therefore, the indistinguishability of Hybrid 0 and Hybrid 8 as shows above implies the security of the scheme KDM as claimed.

3.2 Symmetric-Key Setting

We show the same amplification from 1-circular to KDM security also holds in the symmetric-key setting. Let $\mathsf{CPA} = (\mathsf{CPA.KeyGen}, \mathsf{CPA.Enc}, \mathsf{CPA.Dec})$ be a CPA-secure symmetric-key encryption scheme with pseudorandom ciphertexts and ciphertext space $\mathcal{C}_\lambda$. Let $(\mathsf{Garble}, \mathsf{Eval})$ be a garbled circuit scheme (Definition 1). We construct a symmetric-key encryption scheme $\mathsf{KDM} = (\mathsf{KDM.KeyGen}, \mathsf{KDM.Enc}, \mathsf{KDM.Dec})$, parameterized by some padding parameter $p = p(\lambda)$ to be specified later, as follows:

$\overline{\mathsf{sk}} \leftarrow \mathsf{KDM.KeyGen}(1^\lambda)$: For $i \in [\lambda]$, $b \in \{0,1\}$, sample $\mathsf{sk}_{i,b} \leftarrow \mathsf{CPA.KeyGen}(1^\lambda)$. Sample $u \leftarrow \{0,1\}^\lambda$. Let $\overline{\mathsf{sk}} = (u, \{sk_{i,u_i}\}_{i\in[\lambda]})$.

$\overline{\mathsf{ct}} \leftarrow \mathsf{KDM.Enc}(\overline{\mathsf{sk}}, \mu)$: Let C_μ be the constant circuit that takes any input $x \in \{0,1\}^\lambda$ and always outputs μ. We pad C_μ to be of size $p(\lambda)$ for the padding parameter p. Let

$$(\widetilde{C}, \{\mathsf{lab}_{i,b}\}_{i\in[\lambda], b\in\{0,1\}}) \leftarrow \mathsf{Garble}(1^\lambda, C_\mu).$$

For $i \in [\lambda]$:
  – Sample $\mathsf{ct}_{i,u_i} \leftarrow \mathsf{CPA.Enc}(\mathsf{sk}_{i,u_i}, \mathsf{lab}_{i,u_i})$.
  – Sample $\mathsf{ct}_{i,1-u_i} \leftarrow \mathcal{C}_\lambda$.
Output $\overline{\mathsf{ct}} = (\widetilde{C}, \{\mathsf{ct}_{i,b}\}_{i\in[\lambda], b\in\{0,1\}})$.

$\mu := \mathsf{KDM.Dec}(\overline{\mathsf{sk}}, \overline{\mathsf{ct}})$: For $i \in [\lambda]$, let $\mathsf{lab}_{i,u_i} := \mathsf{CPA.Dec}(\mathsf{sk}_{i,u_i}, \mathsf{ct}_{i,u_i})$. Output $\mu := \mathsf{Eval}(\widetilde{C}, \{\mathsf{lab}_{i,u_i}\})$.

Theorem 2. *Let* CPA *be a CPA-secure symmetric-key encryption scheme with pseudorandom ciphertexts and let* $(\mathsf{Garble}, \mathsf{Eval})$ *be a secure garbling scheme, both of which follow from one-way function. Then for any polynomial* $s(\lambda)$ *there exists some polynomial padding parameter* $p(\lambda)$ *such that the following holds. Assume that there exists some 1-circular symmetric-key encryption scheme. Then the above* KDM *scheme with padding parameter* p *is an* $(\infty, s(\lambda))$*-circuit-KDM secure secret-key encryption scheme.*

The proof of correctness and security are essentially the same as in the public-key scheme, with the following minor changes. Firstly, we can skip hybrid 2 since, already in the actual scheme, we choose $\mathsf{ct}_{i,1-u_i} \leftarrow \mathcal{C}_\lambda$ as dummy ciphertexts that don't contain any information about the label lab_{i,u_i}. All other hybrids are defined analogously with all occurrences of $\mathsf{ct}_{i,b} \leftarrow \mathsf{CPA.Enc}(\mathsf{pk}_{i,b}^t, \mathsf{lab}_{i,b})$ replaced by $\mathsf{ct}_{i,b} \leftarrow \mathsf{CPA.Enc}(\mathsf{sk}_{i,b}^t, \mathsf{lab}_{i,b})$ and all occurrences of $\mathsf{ct}_{i,b} \leftarrow \mathsf{CPA.Enc}(\mathsf{pk}_{i,b}^t, 0^\ell)$ replaced by $\mathsf{ct}_{i,b} \leftarrow \mathcal{C}_\lambda$. Lastly, we can again skip hybrid 8 for the same reason as why we skipped hybrid 2.

References

ABBC10. Acar, T., Belenkiy, M., Bellare, M., Cash, D.: Cryptographic agility and its relation to circular encryption. In: Gilbert, H. (ed.) EUROCRYPT 2010. LNCS, vol. 6110, pp. 403–422. Springer, Heidelberg (2010). https://doi.org/ 10.1007/978-3-642-13190-5_21

ACPS09. Applebaum, B., Cash, D., Peikert, C., Sahai, A.: Fast cryptographic primitives and circular-secure encryption based on hard learning problems. In: Halevi, S. (ed.) CRYPTO 2009. LNCS, vol. 5677, pp. 595–618. Springer, Heidelberg (2009). https://doi.org/10.1007/978-3-642-03356-8_35

AP16. Alamati, N., Peikert, C.: Three's compromised too: circular insecurity for any cycle length from (ring-)LWE. In: Robshaw, M., Katz, J. (eds.) CRYPTO 2016, Part II. LNCS, vol. 9815, pp. 659–680. Springer, Heidelberg (2016). https://doi.org/10.1007/978-3-662-53008-5_23

App11. Applebaum, B.: Key-dependent message security: generic amplification and completeness. In: Paterson, K.G. (ed.) EUROCRYPT 2011. LNCS, vol. 6632, pp. 527–546. Springer, Heidelberg (2011). https://doi.org/10.1007/ 978-3-642-20465-4_29

BGK11. Brakerski, Z., Goldwasser, S., Kalai, Y.T.: Black-box circular-secure encryption beyond affine functions. In: Ishai, Y. (ed.) TCC 2011. LNCS, vol. 6597, pp. 201–218. Springer, Heidelberg (2011). https://doi.org/10.1007/978-3-642-19571-6_13

BHHI10. Barak, B., Haitner, I., Hofheinz, D., Ishai, Y.: Bounded key-dependent message security. In: Gilbert, H. (ed.) EUROCRYPT 2010. LNCS, vol. 6110, pp. 423–444. Springer, Heidelberg (2010). https://doi.org/10.1007/978-3-642-13190-5_22

BHHO08. Boneh, D., Halevi, S., Hamburg, M., Ostrovsky, R.: Circular-secure encryption from decision Diffie-Hellman. In: Wagner, D. (ed.) CRYPTO 2008. LNCS, vol. 5157, pp. 108–125. Springer, Heidelberg (2008). https://doi.org/10.1007/978-3-540-85174-5_7

BHW15. Bishop, A., Hohenberger, S., Waters, B.: New circular security counterexamples from decision linear and learning with errors. In: Iwata, T., Cheon, J.H. (eds.) ASIACRYPT 2015, Part II. LNCS, vol. 9453, pp. 776–800. Springer, Heidelberg (2015). https://doi.org/10.1007/978-3-662-48800-3_32

BLSV18. Brakerski, Z., Lombardi, A., Segev, G., Vaikuntanathan, V.: Anonymous IBE, leakage resilience and circular security from new assumptions. In: Nielsen, J.B., Rijmen, V. (eds.) EUROCRYPT 2018, Part I. LNCS, vol. 10820, pp. 535–564. Springer, Cham (2018). https://doi.org/10.1007/978-3-319-78381-9_20

BRS03. Black, J., Rogaway, P., Shrimpton, T.: Encryption-scheme security in the presence of key-dependent messages. In: Nyberg, K., Heys, H. (eds.) SAC 2002. LNCS, vol. 2595, pp. 62–75. Springer, Heidelberg (2003). https://doi.org/10.1007/3-540-36492-7_6

CDG+17. Cho, C., Döttling, N., Garg, S., Gupta, D., Miao, P., Polychroniadou, A.: Laconic oblivious transfer and its applications. In: Katz, J., Shacham, H. (eds.) CRYPTO 2017, Part II. LNCS, vol. 10402, pp. 33–65. Springer, Cham (2017). https://doi.org/10.1007/978-3-319-63715-0_2

CGH12. Cash, D., Green, M., Hohenberger, S.: New definitions and separations for circular security. In: Fischlin, M., Buchmann, J., Manulis, M. (eds.) PKC 2012. LNCS, vol. 7293, pp. 540–557. Springer, Heidelberg (2012). https://doi.org/10.1007/978-3-642-30057-8_32

CL01. Camenisch, J., Lysyanskaya, A.: An efficient system for non-transferable anonymous credentials with optional anonymity revocation. In: Pfitzmann, B. (ed.) EUROCRYPT 2001. LNCS, vol. 2045, pp. 93–118. Springer, Heidelberg (2001). https://doi.org/10.1007/3-540-44987-6_7

DG17. Döttling, N., Garg, S.: Identity-based encryption from the Diffie-Hellman assumption. In: Katz, J., Shacham, H. (eds.) CRYPTO 2017, Part I. LNCS, vol. 10401, pp. 537–569. Springer, Cham (2017). https://doi.org/10.1007/978-3-319-63688-7_18

GKW17a. Goyal, R., Koppula, V., Waters, B.: Lockable obfuscation. In: Umans, C. (ed.) 58th Annual Symposium on Foundations of Computer Science, pp. 612–621. IEEE Computer Society Press, October 2017

GKW17b. Goyal, R., Koppula, V., Waters, B.: Separating IND-CPA and circular security for unbounded length key cycles. In: Fehr, S. (ed.) PKC 2017, Part I. LNCS, vol. 10174, pp. 232–246. Springer, Heidelberg (2017). https://doi.org/10.1007/978-3-662-54365-8_10

GKW17c. Goyal, R., Koppula, V., Waters, B.: Separating semantic and circular security for symmetric-key bit encryption from the learning with errors assumption. In: Coron, J.-S., Nielsen, J.B. (eds.) EUROCRYPT 2017, Part II. LNCS, vol. 10211, pp. 528–557. Springer, Cham (2017). https://doi.org/10.1007/978-3-319-56614-6_18

GM82. Goldwasser, S., Micali, S.: Probabilistic encryption and how to play mental poker keeping secret all partial information. In: 14th Annual ACM Symposium on Theory of Computing, pp. 365–377. ACM Press, May 1982

HK15. Hajiabadi, M., Kapron, B.M.: Reproducible circularly-secure bit encryption: applications and realizations. In: Gennaro, R., Robshaw, M. (eds.) CRYPTO 2015, Part I. LNCS, vol. 9215, pp. 224–243. Springer, Heidelberg (2015). https://doi.org/10.1007/978-3-662-47989-6_11

KM19. Kitagawa, F., Matsuda, T.: CPA-to-CCA transformation for KDM security. In: Hofheinz, D., Rosen, A. (eds.) TCC 2019, Part II. LNCS, vol. 11892, pp. 118–148. Springer, Cham (2019). https://doi.org/10.1007/978-3-030-36033-7_5

KM20. Kitagawa, F., Matsuda, T.: Circular security is complete for KDM security. In: Moriai, S., Wang, H. (eds.) ASIACRYPT 2020, Part I. LNCS, vol. 12491, pp. 253–285. Springer, Cham (2020). https://doi.org/10.1007/978-3-030-64837-4_9

KMT19. Kitagawa, F., Matsuda, T., Tanaka, K.: CCA security and trapdoor functions via key-dependent-message security. In: Boldyreva, A., Micciancio, D. (eds.) CRYPTO 2019, Part III. LNCS, vol. 11694, pp. 33–64. Springer, Cham (2019). https://doi.org/10.1007/978-3-030-26954-8_2

KRW15. Koppula, V., Ramchen, K., Waters, B.: Separations in circular security for arbitrary length key cycles. In: Dodis, Y., Nielsen, J.B. (eds.) TCC 2015, Part II. LNCS, vol. 9015, pp. 378–400. Springer, Heidelberg (2015). https://doi.org/10.1007/978-3-662-46497-7_15

KT18. Kitagawa, F., Tanaka, K.: Key dependent message security and receiver selective opening security for identity-based encryption. In: Abdalla, M., Dahab, R. (eds.) PKC 2018, Part I. LNCS, vol. 10769, pp. 32–61. Springer, Cham (2018). https://doi.org/10.1007/978-3-319-76578-5_2

KW16. Koppula, V., Waters, B.: Circular security separations for arbitrary length cycles from LWE. In: Robshaw, M., Katz, J. (eds.) CRYPTO 2016, Part II. LNCS, vol. 9815, pp. 681–700. Springer, Heidelberg (2016). https://doi.org/10.1007/978-3-662-53008-5_24

KW19. Koppula, V., Waters, B.: Realizing chosen ciphertext security generically in attribute-based encryption and predicate encryption. In: Boldyreva, A., Micciancio, D. (eds.) CRYPTO 2019, Part II. LNCS, vol. 11693, pp. 671–700. Springer, Cham (2019). https://doi.org/10.1007/978-3-030-26951-7_23

Lev85. Levin, L.A.: One-way functions and pseudorandom generators. In: 17th Annual ACM Symposium on Theory of Computing, pp. 363–365. ACM Press, May 1985

LQR+19. Lombardi, A., Quach, W., Rothblum, R.D., Wichs, D., Wu, D.J.: New constructions of reusable designated-verifier NIZKs. In: Boldyreva, A., Micciancio, D. (eds.) CRYPTO 2019, Part III. LNCS, vol. 11694, pp. 670–700. Springer, Cham (2019). https://doi.org/10.1007/978-3-030-26954-8_22

Rot13. Rothblum, R.D.: On the circular security of bit-encryption. In: Sahai, A. (ed.) TCC 2013. LNCS, vol. 7785, pp. 579–598. Springer, Heidelberg (2013). https://doi.org/10.1007/978-3-642-36594-2_32

RS92. Rackoff, C., Simon, D.R.: Non-interactive zero-knowledge proof of knowledge and chosen ciphertext attack. In: Feigenbaum, J. (ed.) CRYPTO 1991. LNCS, vol. 576, pp. 433–444. Springer, Heidelberg (1992). https://doi.org/10.1007/3-540-46766-1_35

WZ17. Wichs, D., Zirdelis, G.: Obfuscating compute-and-compare programs under LWE. In: Umans, C. (ed.) 58th Annual Symposium on Foundations of Computer Science, pp. 600–611. IEEE Computer Society Press, October 2017

Improved Multi-user Security Using the Squared-Ratio Method

Yu Long Chen[1], Wonseok Choi[2(✉)], and Changmin Lee[3]

[1] imec-COSIC, KU Leuven, Leuven, Belgium
yulong.chen@kuleuven.be
[2] Purdue University, West Lafayette, IN, USA
wonseok@purdue.edu
[3] KIAS, Seoul, Korea
changminlee@kias.re.kr

Abstract. Proving security bounds in contexts with a large number of users is one of the central problems in symmetric-key cryptography today. This paper introduces a new method for information-theoretic multi-user security proofs, called "the Squared-Ratio method". At its core, the method requires the expectation of the square of the ratio of observing the so-called good transcripts (from Patarin's H-coefficient technique) in the real and the ideal world. Central to the method is the observation that for information-theoretic adversaries, the KL-divergence for the multi-user security bound can be written as a summation of the KL-divergence of every single user.

We showcase the Squared-Ratio method on three examples: the Xor of two Permutations by Bellare et al. (EUROCRYPT '98) and Hall et al. (CRYPTO '98), the Encrypted Davies-Mayer by Cogliati and Seurin (CRYPTO '16), and the two permutation variant of the nEHtM MAC algorithm by Dutta et al. (EUROCRYPT '19). With this new tool, we provide improved bounds for the *multi-user* security of these constructions. Our approach is modular in the sense that the multi-user security can be obtained directly from single-user results.

Keywords: symmetric-key cryptography · provable security · multi-user security · pseudorandom function

1 Introduction

Commonly used cryptographic constructions in practice are usually deployed in contexts with a large number of users. An obvious question is to what extent the number of users will affect the security bound of these cryptographic constructions, this question leads to consider adversaries that may try to analyze the mode of operation with multiple independent keys at the same time. This setting is known as multi-user security and has been attracting more and more attention from researchers in recent years.

© International Association for Cryptologic Research 2023
H. Handschuh and A. Lysyanskaya (Eds.): CRYPTO 2023, LNCS 14082, pp. 694–724, 2023.
https://doi.org/10.1007/978-3-031-38545-2_23

From a cryptographic perspective, a potential weakness of the multi-user security can be interpreted as the following. Let $\mathbf{Adv}(\mathcal{A})$ and $\mathbf{Adv}^u(\mathcal{A})$ be an advantage of single-user security and u-user security with an adversary $\mathcal{A}$, respectively. Under an assumption that each user exploits independent keys, it gives an obvious relation $\mathbf{Adv}^u(\mathcal{A}) \leq u \cdot \mathbf{Adv}(\mathcal{A})$ by the hybrid argument (for short, the factor u is called security loss). If the worst-case bound holds, the multi-user settings would not be as secure as the cryptographic scheme requires for a sufficiently large security loss, even if the single-user security is provably guaranteed. On the one hand, this worst-case loss is unfortunately unavoidable in the case of key-recovery attacks against block ciphers [9]. On the other hand, in some cases, it is shown that the gap between single-user and u-user security is relatively small [8, 14]. These results indicate that there is no general relationship between currently known single-user security and multi-user security. It simultaneously gives a natural question of how known single-user security results can be rearranged into multi-user security

Multi-user Security. The multi-user security was first considered in the provable security setting by Mouha and Luykx [33], by proving the multi-user security of the Even-Mansour cipher. Since then, various constructions have been analyzed in the multi-user setting [10, 25, 26, 37, 38]. These works show that evaluating how security degrades as the number of users grows is a challenging technical problem. Firstly, a dedicated proof is required for each construction that we want to consider, even when the security is known in the single-user setting. Secondly, the security analysis of all the aforementioned work is performed in the ideal cipher model. Assuming that a construction is based on perfectly random primitives can be too strong, which can lead to an overly optimistic security bound that does not cover practical attacks. Recently at ASIACRYPT 2022, Chen [12] proposed a modular approach to proving the multi-user security of permutation-based constructions that satisfy certain properties. Unfortunately, as the author himself mentioned in the paper, his technique is not extendable to the block cipher-based setting. This is because his technique is based on the mirror theory in the ideal permutation model and therefore cannot be easily extended to the ideal cipher model.

A Different Avenue. We revisit the multi-user provable security suggested by Bhattacharya and Nandi [8]. To be precise, they have shown that a mu-prf advantage of multi-user security for bitwise-xor of three n-bit pseudorandom permutations (for short, XORP[3]) is bounded by $< \sqrt{u \cdot q_{max}}/2^n$, where u is the number of users and q_{max} is the allowed number of queries the adversary can make to each user. It implies that XORP[3] for $O(2^n)$ users with $O(2^n)$ queries to each user still guarantees the mu-prf security. For this purpose, the authors leverage the chi-squared method described by Dai et al. [21].

Subsequently, Choi et al. [14] have proposed two variants of truncated xor of two n-bit pseudorandom permutations, named SaT1 and SaT2 respectively. Here SaT1 uses a single n-bit pseudorandom permutation with domain separation, while SaT2 employs two independent permutations. At the same time, the authors state that both SaT constructions also satisfy a multi-user security with the advanced techniques.

While this proof regime has the advantage that it proves a tighter security bound rather than the naive one for the multi-user security, it seems that this proof technique is not easily extendable to the other constructions. This obstacle arises from the characteristic that for the chi-square method, it is not easy to compute an expectation of chi-square divergence when responses adaptively depend on the adversary's queries.

Our Contribution. This paper aims at investigating generic techniques that are applicable to more constructions in the case of *multi-user* security.

Technically, we describe two novel inequalities to achieve the goal. We assume that adversary $\mathcal{A}$ can access to one of two systems S_0 or S_1, where S_0 is an "ideal" system and S_1 is a real one. A common way to see if two systems are indistinguishable is to bound the statistical distance of $\|\mathsf{p}_{\mathcal{S}_1}(\cdot) - \mathsf{p}_{\mathcal{S}_0}(\cdot)\|$, where $\mathsf{p}_{\mathcal{S}_i}(\cdot)$ is the probability distributions of the responses of the q queries when $\mathcal{A}$ interacts with system $\mathcal{S}_i$. In the prior work by Dai et al. [21], the authors suggested using well-known relations to bound the statistical distance:

$$\|\mathsf{p}_{\mathcal{S}_1}(\cdot) - \mathsf{p}_{\mathcal{S}_0}(\cdot)\| \leq \left(\frac{1}{2}\Delta_{KL}\left(\mathsf{p}_{\mathcal{S}_1}(\cdot), \mathsf{p}_{\mathcal{S}_0}(\cdot)\right)\right)^{\frac{1}{2}}$$

$$\Delta_{KL}\left(\mathsf{p}_{\mathcal{S}_1}(\cdot), \mathsf{p}_{\mathcal{S}_0}(\cdot)\right) \stackrel{\text{def}}{=} \sum_{z \in \Omega} \mathsf{p}_{\mathcal{S}_1}(z) \ln\left(\frac{\mathsf{p}_{\mathcal{S}_1(z)}}{\mathsf{p}_{\mathcal{S}_0(z)}}\right),$$

$$\Delta_{KL}\left(\mathsf{p}_{\mathcal{S}_1}(\cdot), \mathsf{p}_{\mathcal{S}_0}(\cdot)\right) \leq \sum_{z \in \Omega} \frac{(\mathsf{p}_{\mathcal{S}_1}(z) - \mathsf{p}_{\mathcal{S}_0}(z))^2}{\mathsf{p}_{\mathcal{S}_0}(z)}.$$

where Ω is the support of $\mathsf{p}_{\mathcal{S}_0}(\cdot)$.

In this work, we follow similar inequalities as above. Because we consider the multi-user security, we have the u-system $(\mathcal{S}_{i,1}, \ldots, \mathcal{S}_{i,u})$ for $i \in \{0, 1\}$. For simplicity, we let $\mathcal{S}_i$ denote the u-system and $\mathbf{z}$ be a set of u-strings $\{z_1, \ldots, z_u\}$. We assume that the adversary gets u responses simultaneously from each query. Let $\mathsf{p}_{\mathcal{S}_i}(\mathbf{z})$ (resp. $\mathsf{p}_{\mathcal{S}_{i,j}}(z_j)$) be a probability that the j-th system answers z_j for all $1 \leq j \leq u$ (resp. for index j). Following the footsteps of [8,14], we assume that in the standard model, an information-theoretic adversary $\mathcal{D}$ makes distinct queries to individual user interfaces. Since those interfaces have identical distribution (for the same transcript), previous interactions with other interfaces do not impact subsequent user interactions,, which means the systems are mutually independent. It gives one more relation:

$$\mathsf{p}_{\mathcal{S}_i}(\mathbf{z}) = \prod_{j=1}^{u} \mathsf{p}_{\mathcal{S}_{i,j}}(z_j).$$

Combining it together, this auxiliary relation enables to hold that

$$\Delta_{KL}\left(\mathsf{p}_{\mathcal{S}_1}(\cdot),\mathsf{p}_{\mathcal{S}_0}(\cdot)\right) = \sum_{z\in\Omega}\mathsf{p}_{\mathcal{S}_1}(z)\ln\left(\frac{\mathsf{p}_{\mathcal{S}_1}(z)}{\mathsf{p}_{\mathcal{S}_0}(z)}\right)$$

$$= \sum_{z\in\Omega}\sum_{j=1}^{u}\mathsf{p}_{\mathcal{S}_1}(z)\ln\left(\frac{\mathsf{p}_{\mathcal{S}_{1,j}}(z_j)}{\mathsf{p}_{\mathcal{S}_{0,j}}(z_j)}\right) = \sum_{j=1}^{u}\sum_{z\in\Omega}\mathsf{p}_{\mathcal{S}_1}(z)\ln\left(\frac{\mathsf{p}_{\mathcal{S}_{1,j}}(z_j)}{\mathsf{p}_{\mathcal{S}_{0,j}}(z_j)}\right)$$

$$= \sum_{j=1}^{u}\sum_{z_j\in\Omega_j}\mathsf{p}_{\mathcal{S}_{1,j}}(z_j)\ln\left(\frac{\mathsf{p}_{\mathcal{S}_{1,j}}(z_j)}{\mathsf{p}_{\mathcal{S}_{0,j}}(z_j)}\right) = u\cdot\Delta_{KL}\left(\mathsf{p}_{\mathcal{S}_{1,j}}(\cdot),\mathsf{p}_{\mathcal{S}_{0,j}}(\cdot)\right),$$

where the first equality comes from the properties of logarithm and the other equalities are trivially derived.

It can be interpreted as for information-theoretic adversaries, the KL-divergence for the multi-user security bound can be written as a summation of each security bound. It means that to guarantee the multi-user security it is sufficient to bound the KL-divergence for a single user. For this purpose, we mimic a standard proof based on Patarin's H-coefficient technique [35]. Patarin's H-coefficient shows that

$$\frac{P_{S_1,1}(z)}{P_{S_0,1}(z)} \geq 1 - \epsilon. \tag{1}$$

In addition to this, we aim at proving that

$$\frac{P_{S_1,1}(z)}{P_{S_0,1}(z)} \leq 1 + \epsilon,$$

except for bad cases. Combining it together, it holds that

$$\left|\frac{P_{S_1,1}(z)}{P_{S_0,1}(z)} - 1\right| \leq \epsilon. \tag{2}$$

It allows bounding the KL-divergence in a function of ϵ, which eventually gives a bound for the statistical distance between two systems.

Our approach, called the Squared-Ratio method, combines the chi-squared method with the H-coefficient technique. Here, we employed the notion of transcripts and good/bad partitioning. For $u = 1$, it appears more similar to the expectation-method [25,26]. The requirement of our method is the same to that of expectation-method, but an upper bound of good ratio instead of a lower bound. This allows our method to be applicable to most constructions. Note that we utilize "each user's transcript" rather than "each query (chi-squared method)" or "entire transcript (H-coefficient technique)". We refer to Sect. 3 for more details.

From the explanation above, we see that the Squared-Ratio method allows us to get the multi-user security directly from the single-user bound, where Patarin's Mirror theory [36] is used for the counting arguments in the single-user case. Mirror theory allows one to sharply lower bound the number of solutions to a certain type of system of equations and non-equations. In our security proof, we will consider the following system of equations; for two sets of unknowns $\mathcal{V}_P = \{P_1, \ldots, P_{q_P}\}$ and $\mathcal{V}_Q = \{Q_1, \ldots, Q_{q_Q}\}$, and for constants λ_i, $i = 1, \ldots, q$,

$$\Gamma : \begin{cases} P_{I_1} \oplus Q_{I_1} = \lambda_1, \\ P_{I_2} \oplus Q_{I_2} = \lambda_2, \\ \quad\vdots \\ P_{I_q} \oplus Q_{I_q} = \lambda_q. \end{cases}$$

This system of equations can be represented by a simple graph $\mathcal{G} = (\mathcal{V}, \mathcal{E})$, where $\mathcal{V} = \mathcal{V}_P \sqcup \mathcal{V}_Q$. The unknowns P_{I_i} and Q_{I_i} are connected by a λ_i-weighted edge for $i = 1, \ldots, q$ and are mapped to $\mathcal{V}_P$ and $\mathcal{V}_Q$ using two surjective index mappings. This graph consists of q edges, and the size of the largest component in this graph is denoted by $\xi_{\max}$. This system of equations has been studied in [36], and later revisited with more complete and detailed arguments [19,22].

To apply our Squared-Ratio method here, we want an upper bound on the ratio of observing the good transcripts in the form as given in equation (2), instead of a lower bound in the form of $1 - \epsilon$ (as in (1)) given in the traditional mirror theory. We prove the result both when there are large components ($q_c > 0$) and when there are only isolated edges ($q_c = 0$), where q_c refers to the number of edges in the large components. We refer to Sect. 4 for more details.

We then illustrate the Squared-Ratio method by applying it to prove the *multi-user* prf security of Xor of Permutation (XoP), Encrypted Davies-Mayer (EDM), and nonce-based Enhance Hash-then-Mask (nEHtM). These three constructions have been chosen because of their practical relevance and a large amount of attention they have received in recent years. In the rest of this paper, we will use $q_{\max}$ to indicate the maximum number of queries the adversary can make against each of its u users in the *multi-user* setting, while q indicates the *total number of queries* that the adversary can execute in the *single-user* setting. Depending on the context, we have $q_{\max} \leq q \leq u q_{\max}$.

Applications: Xor of Permutations. Block ciphers are usually considered to be pseudorandom permutations (PRPs) under a uniform random key. That means someone cannot distinguish a secure block cipher from a random permutation before performing a specific number of encryption and decryption queries in a black-box manner. On the other hand, various cryptographic constructions such as encryption modes [2], MAC algorithms [3,7] and authenticated encryption schemes [15] need pseudorandom functions (PRFs) to achieve beyond-birthday-bound security. When such PRFs are replaced with block ciphers, it may degrade security up to the birthday bound [4,6,11,24,27]. To solve the problem of security degradation, Bellare et al. [5] and Hall et al. [24] initiated the study of constructing a good PRF from block ciphers with security beyond the birthday-bound barrier, i.e., above $2^{n/2}$. Given two n-bit (keyed) PRPs P and Q, their sum, denoted as the Xor of Permutations (XoP), maps $x \in \{0, 1\}^n$ to

$$\mathsf{XoP}[\mathsf{P}, \mathsf{Q}](x) \overset{\text{def}}{=} \mathsf{P}(x) \oplus \mathsf{Q}(x).$$

Subsequently, after the introduction of this XoP construction, a series of works improved this seminal result [1,18,30,34], culminating with the proof by Dai et al. [21] and Dutta et al. [22] that the sum of two n-bit random permutations is (fully) secure up to $O(2^n)$ queries, using the chi-squared method and a verifiable version of the mirror theory respectively. Recently, Choi et al. [14] showed for the first time that the XoP construction achieves a multi-user security of $O(\sqrt{u}q_{max}^{1.5}/2^{1.5n})$. As the first application of our Squared-Ratio method, we give a fairly simple proof giving us a multi-user security bound of $O(\sqrt{u}q_{max}^2/2^{2n})$. One can argue that the improvement is small. However, we believe the analysis of the XoP construction is fundamental, and a tight security bound has been sought for nearly two decades. On the other hand, the result of Choi et al. requires a dedicated proof, while our approach is modular in that we can obtain the multi-user bound directly from the single-user result using our Squared-Ratio method. We refer to Sect. 5 for more details.

Application: The EDM Construction. As another application of the Squared-Ratio method, we consider the Encrypted Davis-Meyer (EDM) construction, proposed by Cogliati and Seurin [20], defined as

$$\mathsf{EDM}[\mathsf{P}, \mathsf{Q}](x) \stackrel{\text{def}}{=} \mathsf{Q}(\mathsf{P}(x) \oplus x).$$

They proved PRF-security of EDM up to $O(2^{\frac{2n}{3}})$ queries. The best known multi-user security bound for EDM is $O\left(uq^2/2^{1.5n}\right)$, obtained from the combination of hybrid argument with the result of Dai et al. via the Chi-squared method [21]. Using our Squared-Ratio method, we show a significant improvement that achieves a multi-user security of $O\left(n\sqrt{u}q_{max}^4/2^{3n}\right)$. We refer to Sect. 6 for more details. We note that in the work of Mennink and Neves [31], they proved that EDM achieves a single-user security of $O(q/2^n)$ for $q \leq 2^n/\xi_{max}$. However, their result uses an unverified version of Patarin's mirror theory, while we aim for a simpler-to-use framework for multi-user security with verifiable proofs. Whether the multi-user security of EDM can be improved by improving the mirror theory result for the single-user security is an interesting future research direction.

Application: The nEHtM MAC Algorithm. As our final application, we consider the two-permutation variant of the nonce-based Enhanced Hash-then-Mask (nEHtM) construction, proposed by Dutta et al. [23], defined as

$$\mathsf{nEHtM}[\mathsf{P}, \mathsf{Q}](x) \stackrel{\text{def}}{=} \mathsf{P}(N) \oplus \mathsf{Q}(H_{K_h}(M) \oplus N).$$

Note that nEHtM is structurally similar to the Enhanced Hash-then-Mask (EHtM) construction first proposed by Minematsu [32], except that the random salt is used instead of a nonce and a PRF instead of a block cipher. We also note this two permutation variant was the $F_{B_2}^{\mathsf{SoP}}$ construction considered in the work of Chen et al. [13]. For the original single permutation variant, Dutta et al. [23] proved that the single-user security of nEHtM is up to $2^{2n/3}$ MAC queries and 2^n verification queries in a nonce-respecting setting. Later, Choi et al. [16] improved this result, and showed that nEHtM is secure up to $2^{3n/4}$

MAC queries and 2^n verification queries. Chen et al. [13] considered the single-user PRF security of this two-permutation variant and showed that it is secure up to $O(2^{3n/4})$ queries.

Indeed the original construction was defined as the form:

$$\mathsf{nEHtM}[\mathsf{P}](x) \overset{\text{def}}{=} P(0 \parallel N) \oplus P(1 \parallel H_{K_h}(M) \oplus N).$$

It is obvious that this construction cannot yield a n-bit zero value. That is why this construction has a naive and tight advantage bound $uq/2^n$ for the mu-prf security. On the other hand, we show $\mathsf{nEHtM}[\mathsf{P}, \mathsf{Q}]$ can achieve better security than $\mathsf{nEHtM}[\mathsf{P}]$ in the nonce-respecting setting. Our application serves the evidence that there is a security gap between them in the case of multi-user security. As a result of our new Squared-Ratio method, we end up with a multi-user security bound that improves significantly over the previously best-known result when the number of users is large. When the number of users is $O(2^{n/2})$, previous results [13,16] on nEHtM are totally insecure for the case $q = uq_{\max}$, and only reached $O(2^{n/2})$ birthday bound security for the case $q = q_{\max}$. While our new result shows that nEHtM achieves beyond birthday bound security for $u = O(2^{n/2})$, and is still birthday bound secure even when the number of users is close to $O(2^n)$. We refer to Sect. 7 and Fig. 1 for more details.

We believe that a similar approach also works on the nonce-misuse setting, however, the combinatorics will be very complex. We emphasize that our contribution is providing a new hybrid method to prove better mu-security which can be applied to most constructions including hash-based ones. Note that the expectation of chi-squared divergence should be taken over the real world. We can handle hash-based constructions like nEHtM thanks to expectation over ideal world. To the best of our knowledge, there is no proof via the chi-squared-method for MAC or AEAD security (hash-based). In this regard, our method is more versatile and can be applied to all constructions if they can be proven via the coefficient-H technique/expectation-method.

2   Preliminaries

NOTATION. Throughout this paper, we fix positive integers n and u to denote the block size and the number of users, respectively. For a non-empty finite set $\mathcal{X}$, we let $\mathcal{X}^{*\ell}$ denote a set $\{(x_1, \ldots, x_\ell) \in \mathcal{X}^\ell \mid x_i \neq x_j \text{ for } i \neq j\}$. For an integer A and b, we denote $(A)_b = A(A-1)\ldots(A-b+1)$. A notation $x \leftarrow_\$ \mathcal{X}$ means that x is chosen uniformly at random from $\mathcal{X}$. $|\mathcal{X}|$ means the number of elements in $\mathcal{X}$. The set of all permutations of $\{0,1\}^n$ is simply denoted $\mathsf{Perm}(n)$. The set of all functions with domain $\{0,1\}^n$ and codomain $\{0,1\}^m$ is simply denoted by $\mathsf{Func}(n,m)$. For a keyed function $F : \mathcal{K} \times \mathcal{X} \to \mathcal{Y}$ with key space $\mathcal{K}$ and non-empty sets $\mathcal{X}$ and $\mathcal{Y}$, we will denote $F(K, \cdot)$ by $F_K(\cdot)$ for $K \in \mathcal{K}$. When two sets $\mathcal{X}$ and $\mathcal{Y}$ are disjoint, their (disjoint) union is denoted $\mathcal{X} \sqcup \mathcal{Y}$. We write T_{re} and T_{id} as random variables following the distribution of the transcripts in the real world and the ideal world, respectively. For any positive integer i, and $a_1, \ldots, a_i, b \in \{0,1\}^n$, We denote $\{a_1, \ldots, a_i\} \oplus b \overset{\text{def}}{=} \{a_1 \oplus b, \ldots, a_i \oplus b\}$.

2.1   Security Notions

PSEUDORANDOM PERMUTATIONS. Let $E : \mathcal{K} \times \{0,1\}^n \to \{0,1\}^n$ be a keyed permutation with key space $\mathcal{K}$, where $E(K, \cdot)$ is a permutation for each $K \in \mathcal{K}$. We will denote $E_K(X)$ for $E(K, X)$. A (q, t)-distinguisher against E is an algorithm $\mathcal{D}$ with oracle access to an n-bit permutation and its inverse, making at most q oracle queries, running in time at most t, and outputting a single bit. The advantage of $\mathcal{D}$ in breaking the PRP-security of E, i.e., in distinguishing E from a uniform random permutation $\pi \leftarrow_\$ \mathsf{Perm}(n)$, is defined as

$$\mathsf{Adv}_E^{\mathsf{prp}}(\mathcal{D}) = \left| \Pr\left[K \leftarrow_\$ \mathcal{K} : \mathcal{D}^{E_K, E_K^{-1}} = 1 \right] - \Pr\left[\pi \leftarrow_\$ \mathsf{Perm}(n) : \mathcal{D}^{\pi, \pi^{-1}} = 1 \right] \right|.$$

We define $\mathsf{Adv}_E^{\mathsf{prp}}(q, t)$ as the maximum of $\mathsf{Adv}_E^{\mathsf{prp}}(\mathcal{D})$ over all (q, t)-distinguishers against E. When we consider information-theoretic security, we will drop the parameter t. In the following analyses, we will consider PRP-based constructions, such as XoP, EDM, or nEHtM. Those constructions can be built upon a block cipher, and in this case, one can obtain a security bound by simply adding PRP-security of the given block cipher.

MULTI-USER PSEUDORANDOM FUNCTION. Let $\mathsf{C} : \mathcal{K} \times \{0,1\}^n \to \{0,1\}^m$ be a keyed function with key space $\mathcal{K}$. We will consider an information-theoretic distinguisher $\mathcal{A}$ that makes oracle queries to C and returns a single bit. The advantage of $\mathcal{A}$ in breaking the mu-prf security of C, i.e., in distinguishing $\mathsf{C}(K_1, \cdot), \ldots, \mathsf{C}(K_u, \cdot)$ where $K_1, \ldots, K_u \leftarrow_\$ \mathcal{K}$ from uniformly chosen functions $\mathsf{F}_1, \ldots, \mathsf{F}_u \leftarrow_\$ \mathsf{Func}(n, m)$, is defined as

$$\mathbf{Adv}_\mathsf{C}^{\mathsf{mu\text{-}prf}}(\mathcal{A}) = \left| \Pr\left[K_1, \ldots, K_u \leftarrow_\$ \mathcal{K} : \mathcal{A}^{\mathsf{C}_{K_1}(\cdot), \ldots, \mathsf{C}_{K_u}(\cdot)} = 1 \right] \right.$$
$$\left. - \Pr\left[\mathsf{F}_1, \ldots, \mathsf{F}_u \leftarrow_\$ \mathsf{Func}(n, m) : \mathcal{A}^{\mathsf{F}_1(\cdot), \ldots, \mathsf{F}_u(\cdot)} = 1 \right] \right|.$$

We define $\mathbf{Adv}_\mathsf{C}^{\mathsf{mu\text{-}prf}}(u, q_{\max}, t)$ as the maximum of $\mathbf{Adv}_\mathsf{C}^{\mathsf{mu\text{-}prf}}(\mathcal{A})$ over all the distinguishers against C for u users making at most $q_{\max}$ queries to each user and running in time at most t. When we consider information-theoretic security, we will drop the parameter t.

ALMOST XOR UNIVERSAL HASH FUNCTIONS. Let $\delta > 0$, and let $H : \mathcal{K}_h \times \mathcal{M} \to \mathcal{X}$ be a keyed function for three non-empty sets $\mathcal{K}_h$, $\mathcal{M}$, and $\mathcal{X}$. H is said to be δ-XOR almost universal (δ-XAU) if for any distinct $M, M' \in \mathcal{M}$ and $X \in \mathcal{X}$,

$$\Pr\left[K_h \leftarrow_\$ \mathcal{K}_h : H_{K_h}(M) \oplus H_{K_h}(M') = X \right] \leq \delta.$$

2.2   Total Variation Distance, KL Divergence and Chi-Squared Divergence in a Subspace

Let P and Q be two probability distributions over discrete set Γ. The *total variation distance* of P and Q is denoted by

$$\|P(x) - Q(x)\| \stackrel{\text{def}}{=} \sum_{x \in \Gamma} \max\{P(x) - Q(x), 0\} = \frac{1}{2} \sum_{x \in \Gamma} |P(x) - Q(x)|.$$

This total variation distance is related to the Kullback-Leibler (KL) divergence by Pinsker's inequality, where the KL divergence is

$$\Delta_{KL}(P, Q) \stackrel{\text{def}}{=} \sum_{x \in \Gamma} P(x) \ln \left(\frac{P(x)}{Q(x)} \right)$$

and Pinsker's inequality says that

$$\|P - Q\| \leq \left(\frac{1}{2} \Delta_{KL}(P, Q) \right)^{\frac{1}{2}}.$$

Note that Q should have full support to define KL-divergence well. On the other hand, there is well-known inequality between KL divergence and χ^2 divergence.

$$\Delta_{KL}(P, Q) \leq \chi^2(P, Q) \stackrel{\text{def}}{=} \sum_{x \in \Gamma} \frac{(P(x) - Q(x))^2}{Q(x)}.$$

We modify these inequalities over a subset $\Gamma' \subset \Gamma$. In other words, we define the quantity

$$\Delta_{KL,\Gamma'}(P, Q) \stackrel{\text{def}}{=} \sum_{x \in \Gamma'} P(x) \ln \left(\frac{P(x)}{Q(x)} \right)$$

and prove the following lemmas:

Lemma 1. *For any subset $\Gamma' \subset \Gamma$, one has*

$$\sum_{x \in \Gamma'} |P(x) - Q(x)| \leq \left(2\Delta_{KL,\Gamma'}(P, Q) + 2 \sum_{x \in \Gamma \backslash \Gamma'} P(x) - Q(x) \right)^{\frac{1}{2}}.$$

Lemma 2. *For any subset $\Gamma' \subset \Gamma$, one has*

$$\Delta_{KL,\Gamma'}(P, Q) \leq \sum_{x \in \Gamma'} \frac{(P(x) - Q(x))^2}{Q(x)} - \sum_{x \in \Gamma \backslash \Gamma'} P(x) - Q(x).$$

The proofs of these Lemmas are given in the full version of the paper.

2.3   Useful Lemma

Lemma 3. *If $(\lambda_1, \ldots, \lambda_q) \in (\{0,1\}^n)^q$ are uniformly randomly distributed and $C = \left| \{(i,j) \in [q]^{*2} \mid (i < j) \wedge (\lambda_i = \lambda_j)\} \right|$, for any $A > 0$, one has*

$$\mathbf{Ex}\,[C] \leq \frac{q^2}{2^{n+1}},$$

$$\mathbf{Ex}\,[C^2] \leq \frac{q^2}{2^{n+1}} + \frac{q^4}{2^{2n+2}},$$

$$\Pr\left[C \geq \frac{q^2}{2^{n+1}} + A\right] \leq \frac{q^2}{2^{n+1}A^2} + \frac{q^4}{2^{2n+2}A^2}.$$

The proof of this Lemma is given in the full version of the paper.

This lemma will be used for the computation of $\mathbf{Ex}\left[\epsilon_1(z)^2\right]$ and ϵ_2 in Theorem 1. The expectation can be identified to an expectation taken over the distribution of all transcripts in the ideal world (and so, regardless of what is a real construction).

3   The Squared-Ratio Method

We fix a set of random systems and a deterministic distinguisher $\mathcal{A}$ that makes exactly $q(= uq_{\max})$ oracle queries to one of the random systems. Each random system has u interfaces with independent random but identical distribution, and $\mathcal{A}$ makes $q_{\max}$ queries to each interface in order. We also fix a set Ω that contains all possible transcripts for oracle queries to an interface of random systems. For a random system $\mathcal{S} = (\mathcal{S}^1, \ldots, \mathcal{S}^u)$ and $i \in \{1, \ldots, u\}$, let $Z_{\mathcal{S}^i}$ be the random variable over Ω that follows the distribution of the transcripts obtained by $\mathcal{A}$ interacting with $\mathcal{S}^i$. Let

$$\mathbf{Z}_{\mathcal{S}} \stackrel{\text{def}}{=} (Z_{\mathcal{S}^1}, \ldots, Z_{\mathcal{S}^u}),$$

$$\mathsf{p}_{\mathcal{S}^i}(z) \stackrel{\text{def}}{=} \Pr\left[Z_{\mathcal{S}^i} = z\right]$$

and

$$\mathsf{p}_{\mathcal{S}}(\mathbf{z}) \stackrel{\text{def}}{=} \Pr\left[\mathbf{Z}_{\mathcal{S}} = \mathbf{z}\right]$$

for $z \in \Omega$ and $\mathbf{z} \in \Omega^u$. $\mathcal{A}$'s distinguishing advantage is upper bounded by the total variation distance of $\mathsf{p}_{\mathcal{S}_0}(\cdot)$ and $\mathsf{p}_{\mathcal{S}_1}(\cdot)$. In the following, we aim to show that

$$\|\mathsf{p}_{\mathcal{S}_1}(\cdot) - \mathsf{p}_{\mathcal{S}_0}(\cdot)\| \leq O\left(\sqrt{u \cdot \mathbf{Ex}\,[\epsilon(z)^2]}\right),$$

where $\epsilon(z)$ is a function such that $\left|\frac{\mathsf{p}_{\mathcal{S}_1^i}(z)}{\mathsf{p}_{\mathcal{S}_0^i}(z)} - 1\right| \leq \epsilon(z)$. However, such a function $\epsilon(z)$ may not exist over Ω. Therefore, we try to show a similar upper bound under some constraints. To do this, we split the set Ω into two distinct sets $\Gamma_{\mathsf{good}} \sqcup \Gamma_{\mathsf{bad}} = \Omega$ in a way inspired by Patarin's H-Coefficient technique [35]. The sets satisfy following conditions:

1. For all $z \in \Gamma_{\text{good}}$, there exists a function $\epsilon_1(z)$ such that

$$\left| \frac{\mathsf{p}_{\mathcal{S}_1^1}(z)}{\mathsf{p}_{\mathcal{S}_0^1}(z)} - 1 \right| \le \epsilon_1(z)$$

2. and there exists a constant ϵ_2 such that

$$\Pr\left[Z_{\mathcal{S}_0^1} \in \Gamma_{\text{bad}} \right] \le \epsilon_2.$$

Since we consider a multi-user case, the target set is multi-set Ω^u, not Ω. Whereas $\Omega \setminus \Gamma_{\text{good}} = \Gamma_{\text{bad}}$ by the definition, $\Omega^u \setminus \Gamma_{\text{good}}^u \neq \Gamma_{\text{bad}}^u$ for any $u \ge 2$. We thus rearrange the set $\Omega^u \setminus \Gamma_{\text{good}}^u$. Let $\Gamma_{\text{bad}\,i}$ denote an event $\{z_i \in \Gamma_{\text{bad}}\}$. On the one hand, the event $\{\mathbf{z} \in \Omega^u \setminus \Gamma_{\text{good}}^u\}$ can be interpreted as $\cup_{i=1}^u \Gamma_{\text{bad}\,i}$. On the other hand, thanks to the inclusion-exclusion principle, the set includes a set $\Omega' \overset{def}{=} \cup_{i=1}^u \Gamma_{\text{bad}\,i} \setminus \cup_{(i,j)} \left(\Gamma_{\text{bad}\,i} \cap \Gamma_{\text{bad}\,j} \right)$.

An adversary can adaptively choose queries on $\mathcal{S}^i$ after the end of the interaction with $\mathcal{S}^j$ for $i > j$; however, we assume that an information-theoretic adversary $\mathcal{D}$ makes distinct queries to individual user interfaces, and previous interactions with other interfaces do not impact interactions with next users. We are allowed to make this assumption since our work focuses on standard model proofs for information-theoretic adversaries. In the standard model, we assume an independent random distribution for each user (but the opponent already knows what the distribution is). In the information-theory setting, block-ciphers based on independent uniform keys will be replaced by independent random permutations. Each user in our construction uses independent keys based on random primitives, hence the other users' queries cannot increase the power of the adversary. This implies that the query-response pairs of one user cannot affect the selection of queries for other users. Therefore, querying all users simultaneously is equivalent to querying each user separately without loss of generality. The same assumption was previously used in [8,14].

Since $Z_{\mathcal{S}^i}$ are mutually independent, for $\mathbf{z} = (z_1, \ldots, z_u)$, it holds that

$$\mathsf{p}_{\mathcal{S}}(\mathbf{z}) = \prod_{i=u}^n \mathsf{p}_{\mathcal{S}^i}(z_i).$$

Combining this equality and the set identity, it holds that

$$\sum_{i=1}^u \sum_{z_i \in \Gamma_{\text{bad}}} \mathsf{p}_{\mathcal{S}_1^i}(z_i) - \sum_{i,j=1}^u \sum_{z_i, z_j \in \Gamma_{\text{bad}}} \mathsf{p}_{\mathcal{S}^i}(z_i) \cdot \mathsf{p}_{\mathcal{S}^j}(z_j)$$

$$\le \sum_{\mathbf{z} \in \Omega^u \setminus \Gamma_{\text{good}}^u} \mathsf{p}_{\mathcal{S}_1}(\mathbf{z}) \le \sum_{i=1}^u \sum_{z_i \in \Gamma_{\text{bad}}} \mathsf{p}_{\mathcal{S}_1^i}(z_i)$$

Putting it together, we are now ready to bound the total variation of $\mathsf{p}_{\mathcal{S}_0}(\cdot)$ and $\mathsf{p}_{\mathcal{S}_1}(\cdot)$ using Lemma 1:

$$\|\mathsf{p}_{\mathcal{S}_1}(\cdot) - \mathsf{p}_{\mathcal{S}_0}(\cdot)\| = \sum_{\mathbf{z} \in \Omega^u} \max\{\mathsf{p}_{\mathcal{S}_0}(\mathbf{z}) - \mathsf{p}_{\mathcal{S}_1}(\mathbf{z}), 0\}$$

$$= \sum_{\mathbf{z} \in \Gamma^u_{\text{good}}} \max\{\mathsf{p}_{\mathcal{S}_0}(\mathbf{z}) - \mathsf{p}_{\mathcal{S}_1}(\mathbf{z}), 0\} + \sum_{\mathbf{z} \in \Omega^u \setminus \Gamma^u_{\text{good}}} \max\{\mathsf{p}_{\mathcal{S}_0}(\mathbf{z}) - \mathsf{p}_{\mathcal{S}_1}(\mathbf{z}), 0\}$$

$$\leq \sum_{\mathbf{z} \in \Gamma^u_{\text{good}}} |\mathsf{p}_{\mathcal{S}_1}(\mathbf{z}) - \mathsf{p}_{\mathcal{S}_0}(\mathbf{z})| + u\epsilon_2$$

$$\leq \sqrt{2\Delta_{KL, \Gamma^u_{\text{good}}}\left(\mathsf{p}_{\mathcal{S}_1}(\cdot), \mathsf{p}_{\mathcal{S}_0}(\cdot)\right) + 2 \sum_{\mathbf{z} \in \Omega^u \setminus \Gamma^u_{\text{good}}} \mathsf{p}_{\mathcal{S}_1}(\mathbf{z}) - \mathsf{p}_{\mathcal{S}_0}(\mathbf{z})} + u\epsilon_2$$

$$\leq \sqrt{2\Delta_{KL, \Gamma^u_{\text{good}}}\left(\mathsf{p}_{\mathcal{S}_1}(\cdot), \mathsf{p}_{\mathcal{S}_0}(\cdot)\right) + 2u\left(\sum_{u \in \Gamma_{\text{bad}}} \mathsf{p}_{\mathcal{S}_1^1}(z) - \mathsf{p}_{\mathcal{S}_0^1}(z)\right) + 2\binom{u}{2} \sum_{z \in \Gamma_{\text{bad}}} \mathsf{p}_{\mathcal{S}_0^1}(z)^2} + u\epsilon_2$$

$$\leq \sqrt{2\Delta_{KL, \Gamma^u_{\text{good}}}\left(\mathsf{p}_{\mathcal{S}_1}(\cdot), \mathsf{p}_{\mathcal{S}_0}(\cdot)\right) + 2u\left(\sum_{z \in \Gamma_{\text{bad}}} \mathsf{p}_{\mathcal{S}_1^1}(z) - \mathsf{p}_{\mathcal{S}_0^1}(z)\right) + u^2\epsilon_2^2} + u\epsilon_2$$

$$\leq \sqrt{2\Delta_{KL, \Gamma^u_{\text{good}}}\left(\mathsf{p}_{\mathcal{S}_1}(\cdot), \mathsf{p}_{\mathcal{S}_0}(\cdot)\right) + 2u\left(\sum_{z \in \Gamma_{\text{bad}}} \mathsf{p}_{\mathcal{S}_1^1}(z) - \mathsf{p}_{\mathcal{S}_0^1}(z)\right)} + 2u\epsilon_2$$

We next rearrange the (partial) KL-divergence term with respect to one random system $\mathcal{S}^1$. It follows that

$$\Delta_{KL, \Gamma^u_{\text{good}}}\left(\mathsf{p}_{\mathcal{S}_1}(\cdot), \mathsf{p}_{\mathcal{S}_0}(\cdot)\right) = \sum_{\mathbf{z} \in \Gamma^u_{\text{good}}} \mathsf{p}_{\mathcal{S}_1}(\mathbf{z}) \ln\left(\frac{\mathsf{p}_{\mathcal{S}_1}(\mathbf{z})}{\mathsf{p}_{\mathcal{S}_0}(\mathbf{z})}\right)$$

$$= \sum_{\mathbf{z} = (z_1, \ldots, z_u) \in \Gamma^u_{\text{good}}} \mathsf{p}_{\mathcal{S}_1}(\mathbf{z}) \ln\left(\prod_{i=1}^{u} \frac{\mathsf{p}_{\mathcal{S}_1^i}(z_i)}{\mathsf{p}_{\mathcal{S}_0^i}(z_i)}\right)$$

$$= \sum_{\mathbf{z} = (z_1, \ldots, z_u) \in \Gamma^u_{\text{good}}} \sum_{i=1}^{u} \mathsf{p}_{\mathcal{S}_1}(\mathbf{z}) \ln\left(\frac{\mathsf{p}_{\mathcal{S}_1^i}(z_i)}{\mathsf{p}_{\mathcal{S}_0^i}(z_i)}\right)$$

$$\leq \sum_{i=1}^{u} \sum_{\mathbf{z} = (z_1, \ldots, z_u) \in \Gamma^u_{\text{good}}} \mathsf{p}_{\mathcal{S}_1}(\mathbf{z}) \ln\left(\frac{\mathsf{p}_{\mathcal{S}_1^i}(z_i)}{\mathsf{p}_{\mathcal{S}_0^i}(z_i)}\right)$$

$$= \sum_{i=1}^{u} \sum_{z_i \in \Gamma_{\text{good}}} \mathsf{p}_{\mathcal{S}_1^i}(z_i) \ln\left(\frac{\mathsf{p}_{\mathcal{S}_1^i}(z_i)}{\mathsf{p}_{\mathcal{S}_0^i}(z_i)}\right)$$

$$= \sum_{i=1}^{u} \Delta_{KL, \Gamma_{\text{good}}}\left(\mathsf{p}_{\mathcal{S}_1^i}(\cdot), \mathsf{p}_{\mathcal{S}_0^i}(\cdot)\right)$$

$$= u \cdot \Delta_{KL, \Gamma_{\text{good}}}\left(\mathsf{p}_{\mathcal{S}_1^1}(\cdot), \mathsf{p}_{\mathcal{S}_0^1}(\cdot)\right).$$

where the last equality comes from the fact that the distributions of $\mathcal{S}^i$ are the same. A remarkable property is that this conversion replaces the u-product term with the u-summation term. This rearrangement is quite helpful in understanding the security of multiple systems. From Lemma 2, we have

$$
\Delta_{KL,\Gamma_{\text{good}}}\left(\mathsf{p}_{\mathcal{S}_1^1}(\cdot),\mathsf{p}_{\mathcal{S}_0^1}(\cdot)\right) \leq \sum_{z\in\Gamma_{\text{good}}} \frac{\left(\mathsf{p}_{\mathcal{S}_1^1}(z) - \mathsf{p}_{\mathcal{S}_0^1}(z)\right)^2}{\mathsf{p}_{\mathcal{S}_0^1}(z)} - \sum_{z\in\Gamma_{\text{bad}}}\left(\mathsf{p}_{\mathcal{S}_1^1}(z) - \mathsf{p}_{\mathcal{S}_0^1}(z)\right)
$$

$$
\leq \sum_{z\in\Gamma_{\text{good}}} \mathsf{p}_{\mathcal{S}_0^1}(z)\epsilon_1(z)^2 - \sum_{z\in\Gamma_{\text{bad}}}\left(\mathsf{p}_{\mathcal{S}_1^1}(z) - \mathsf{p}_{\mathcal{S}_0^1}(z)\right)
$$

$$
\leq \mathbf{Ex}\left[\epsilon_1(z)^2\right] - \sum_{z\in\Gamma_{\text{bad}}}\left(\mathsf{p}_{\mathcal{S}_1^1}(z) - \mathsf{p}_{\mathcal{S}_0^1}(z)\right).
$$

Putting it together, we have

$$
\|\mathsf{p}_{\mathcal{S}_1}(\cdot) - \mathsf{p}_{\mathcal{S}_0}(\cdot)\| \leq \sqrt{2u\mathbf{Ex}\left[\epsilon_1(z)^2\right]} + 2u\epsilon_2.
$$

where the expectation is taken over the distribution of $Z_{\mathcal{S}_0^1}$. In summary, we can prove the following theorem.

Theorem 1. *Suppose whenever* $\mathsf{p}_{\mathcal{S}_1^1}(\cdot) > 0$ *then* $\mathsf{p}_{\mathcal{S}_0^1}(\cdot) > 0$. *Let* $\Omega = \Gamma_{\text{good}} \sqcup \Gamma_{\text{bad}}$. *If a function* $\epsilon_1(z)$ *and a constant* ϵ_2 *holds the following constraints*

$$
\left|\frac{\mathsf{p}_{\mathcal{S}_1^1}(z)}{\mathsf{p}_{\mathcal{S}_0^1}(z)} - 1\right| \leq \epsilon_1(z)
$$

for all attainable $z \in \Gamma_{\text{good}}$ *and*

$$
\Pr\left[Z_{\mathcal{S}_0^1} \in \Gamma_{\text{bad}}\right] \leq \epsilon_2,
$$

one has

$$
\|\mathsf{p}_{\mathcal{S}_1}(\cdot) - \mathsf{p}_{\mathcal{S}_0}(\cdot)\| \leq \sqrt{2u\mathbf{Ex}\left[\epsilon_1(z)^2\right]} + 2u\epsilon_2
$$

where the expectation is taken over the distribution of $Z_{\mathcal{S}_0^1}$.

Remark. Many typical proofs based on Patarin's H-Coefficient technique shows

$$
\frac{\mathsf{p}_{\mathcal{S}_1^1}(z)}{\mathsf{p}_{\mathcal{S}_0^1}(z)} \geq 1 - \epsilon(z)
$$

for almost all z as good transcripts. Compared to the prior one, we need one step more to apply our method:

$$
\frac{\mathsf{p}_{\mathcal{S}_1^1}(z)}{\mathsf{p}_{\mathcal{S}_0^1}(z)} \leq 1 + \epsilon(z).
$$

Indeed, there is a lack of such analysis due to no requirement for the previous proofs. In the following section, we show that the $\epsilon(z)$ is well bounded for highly secure constructions.

4   Upper Bounds from Mirror Theory

For any two systems $\mathcal{S}_0$ and $\mathcal{S}_1$ except for $\mathsf{p}_{\mathcal{S}_0^1}(z) = 0$, it is obvious that there exists $\epsilon(z)$ such that

$$\left| \frac{\mathsf{p}_{\mathcal{S}_1^1}(z)}{\mathsf{p}_{\mathcal{S}_0^1}(z)} - 1 \right| \leq \epsilon(z).$$

From the result of the Sect. 3, it is desirable to show that the $\epsilon(z)$ function is as small as possible so that the two systems are indistinguishable. In this section, we aim to serve a useful theorem to sharply bound the ratio of the probabilities when $\mathcal{S}_0$ is an ideal world and $\mathcal{S}_1$ is a real world via revisiting the Mirror theory.

DEFINITIONS AND NOTATIONS. For fixed positive integers q, q_P, q_Q, let $\mathcal{P} = \{P_1, \ldots, P_{q_P}\}$ and $\mathcal{Q} = \{Q_1, \ldots, Q_{q_Q}\}$ be sets of *unknowns* such that $P_i, Q_j \in \{0, 1\}^n$ for $i \in [q_P]$ and $j \in [q_Q]$. For a sequence of constants $(\lambda_1, \ldots, \lambda_q) \in (\{0, 1\}^n)^q$, consider a system of equations

$$\Gamma : \begin{cases} P_{\varphi_P(1)} \oplus Q_{\varphi_Q(1)} = \lambda_1, \\ P_{\varphi_P(2)} \oplus Q_{\varphi_Q(2)} = \lambda_2, \\ \quad\vdots \\ P_{\varphi_P(q)} \oplus Q_{\varphi_Q(q)} = \lambda_q, \end{cases}$$

where φ_P and φ_Q are two surjective index mappings such that

$$\varphi_P \colon \{1, \ldots, q\} \to \{1, \ldots, q_P\},$$
$$\varphi_Q \colon \{1, \ldots, q\} \to \{1, \ldots, q_Q\},$$

for $q_P, q_Q \leq q$. This equation system Γ is then uniquely determined by $(\varphi_P, \varphi_Q, (\lambda_1, \ldots, \lambda_q))$.

We will represent this system of equations Γ by a simple graph containing no loops or multiple edges. Let $\mathcal{G}(\Gamma) = (\mathcal{V}, \mathcal{E})$ be a graph where $\mathcal{V} = \mathcal{P} \sqcup \mathcal{Q}$, and let $\overline{PQ} \in \mathcal{E}$ be an edge for $P, Q \in \mathcal{V}$. If this edge is labeled with λ_i for $i = 1, \ldots, q$, then it represents the equation $P \oplus Q = \lambda_i$. We will sometimes write $P \overset{\star}{-} Q$ when an edge $\overline{PQ}$ is labeled with $\star \in \{\lambda_1, \ldots, \lambda_q\}$. Here, $\mathcal{G}(\Gamma)$ contains no isolated vertex; every vertex is incident with at least one edge.

As a natural extension of the label over an edge, we consider a trail of ℓ-length

$$\mathcal{L} : V_0 \overset{\lambda_1}{-} V_1 \overset{\lambda_2}{-} \cdots \overset{\lambda_\ell}{-} V_\ell$$

in $\mathcal{G}(\Gamma)$, its label is defined as

$$\lambda(\mathcal{L}) \overset{\text{def}}{=} \lambda_1 \oplus \lambda_2 \oplus \cdots \oplus \lambda_\ell.$$

Since we only consider acyclic graphs, the label between two vertices is uniquely determined, and thus the following definition is well-defined: $\lambda(V_0, V_\ell) \overset{\text{def}}{=} \lambda(\mathcal{L})$.

When there is no trail between V and V', we denote $\lambda(V, V') \overset{\text{def}}{=} \perp$. Additionally, a connected path is called a component. For a component $\mathcal{C}$, we let $\xi(\mathcal{C})$ denote the number of vertices in $\mathcal{C}$. We then define the maximum component size $\xi_{\max} \overset{\text{def}}{=} \max\{\xi(\mathcal{C}) \mid \mathcal{C} \in \mathcal{G}(\Gamma)\}$. We also define two notions related to the graph:

Definition 1 (acyclic). *In case $\mathcal{G}$ contains no cycle, we call the graph acyclic.*

Definition 2 (non-degenerate). $\lambda(\mathcal{L}) \neq \mathbf{0}$ *for any trails $\mathcal{L}$ of even length in $\mathcal{G}$.*

Any graph $\mathcal{G}(\Gamma)$ which is acyclic and non-degenerate will be called a *nice graph* [16, 29]. For a nice graph $\mathcal{G}(\Gamma)$, $\mathcal{G}$ is a bipartite graph with no cycle, where every edge connects a vertex in $\mathcal{P}$ to one in $\mathcal{Q}$. So $\mathcal{G}$ is decomposed into its connected components, all of which are trees; let

$$\mathcal{G} = \mathcal{C}_1 \sqcup \mathcal{C}_2 \sqcup \cdots \sqcup \mathcal{C}_\alpha \sqcup \mathcal{C}_{\alpha+1} \sqcup \mathcal{C}_{\alpha+2} \sqcup \cdots \sqcup \mathcal{C}_{\alpha+\beta}$$

for some $\alpha, \beta \geq 0$, where $\mathcal{C}_1, \ldots, \mathcal{C}_\alpha$ denote the components of size greater than 2, and $\mathcal{C}_{\alpha+1}, \ldots, \mathcal{C}_{\alpha+\beta}$ denote the components of size 2. We also define the following sets for $i \in [\alpha + \beta]$ to state our theorem.

$$\mathcal{R}_i \overset{\text{def}}{=} \left\{ (\{V_1, V_1'\}, \{V_2, V_2'\}) \in \mathcal{C}_i^{*2} \times \mathcal{C}_j^{*2} \mid j < i \text{ and } \lambda(V_1, V_1') = \lambda(V_2, V_2') \right\}.$$

Any solution to $\mathcal{G}(\Gamma)$ (identifying $\mathcal{G}(\Gamma)$ with its corresponding system of equations) should satisfy all the equations in Γ, while all the variables in $\mathcal{P}$ (resp. $\mathcal{Q}$) should take on different values. The number of solutions to $\mathcal{G}(\Gamma)$ will be denoted $h(\mathcal{G}(\Gamma))$. We remark that if we assign any value to a vertex P, then the labeled edges determine the values of all the other vertices in the component containing P, where the assignment is unique since $\mathcal{G}(\Gamma)$ contains no cycle. The values in the same part are all distinct since $\lambda(\mathcal{L}) \neq \mathbf{0}$ for any trail $\mathcal{L}$ of even length. For any nice graph, we can then bound the term $\frac{h(\mathcal{G})N^q}{(N)_{q_P}(N)_{q_Q}}$, which will be appeared in computing the ratio $\frac{\mathsf{p}_{S_1^1}(z)}{\mathsf{p}_{S_0^1}(z)}$. To be precise, we have the following:

Theorem 2. *Let $\mathcal{G}$ be a nice graph, let q denote the number of edges of $\mathcal{G}$, and let q_c denote the number of edges of $\mathcal{C}_1 \sqcup \cdots \sqcup \mathcal{C}_\alpha$ of size > 2. We then have*

(a) When $q \leq \frac{2^n}{4\xi_{\max}}$ and $0 < q_c \leq q$, it holds that

$$\left| \frac{h(\mathcal{G})N^q}{(N)_{q_P}(N)_{q_Q}} - 1 \right| \leq \exp\left(\frac{2\sum_{i=1}^{\alpha+\beta} |\mathcal{R}_i| + 2\xi_{\max}q_c}{N} + \frac{4\xi_{\max}q_cq^2}{N^2} + \frac{20\xi_{\max}q^4}{N^3} \right) - 1,$$

(b) When $q \leq \frac{2^n}{13}$ and $q_c = 0$, it holds that

$$\left| \frac{h(\mathcal{G})N^q}{(N)_{q_P}(N)_{q_Q}} - 1 \right| \leq \exp\left(\frac{3\sum_{i=1}^{\alpha+\beta} |\mathcal{R}_i|}{N} + \frac{2q^2}{N^2} + \frac{6(n+1)^2}{N} \right) - 1.$$

The full proof is given in the full version of the paper. From Theorem 2, the below corollary immediately follows from the fact $e^X - 1 \leq 2X$ for $X \leq 1$.

Corollary 1. *With the same notation of Theorem 2, we have*

(a) When $q \leq \frac{2^n}{4\xi_{max}}$, $0 < q_c \leq q$, *and*

$$\frac{2\sum_{i=1}^{\alpha+\beta}|\mathcal{R}_i| + 2\xi_{max}q_c}{N} + \frac{4\xi_{max}q_cq^2}{N^2} + \frac{20\xi_{max}q^4}{N^3} \leq 1,$$

it holds that

$$\left|\frac{h(\mathcal{G})N^q}{(N)_{q_P}(N)_{q_Q}} - 1\right| \leq \frac{4\sum_{i=1}^{\alpha+\beta}|\mathcal{R}_i| + 4\xi_{max}q_c}{N} + \frac{8\xi_{max}q_cq^2}{N^2} + \frac{40\xi_{max}q^4}{N^3};$$

(b) When $q \leq \frac{2^n}{13}$, $q_c = 0$, *and*

$$\frac{3\sum_{i=1}^{\alpha+\beta}|\mathcal{R}_i|}{N} + \frac{2q^2}{N^2} + \frac{6(n+1)^2}{N} \leq 1,$$

it holds that

$$\left|\frac{h(\mathcal{G})N^q}{(N)_{q_P}(N)_{q_Q}} - 1\right| \leq \frac{6\sum_{i=1}^{\alpha+\beta}|\mathcal{R}_i|}{N} + \frac{4q^2}{N^2} + \frac{12(n+1)^2}{N}.$$

Proof Overview (of Theorem 2). We give here a brief overview of the proof. The proof is almost similar to that of the existing Mirror theory. To be precise, the former proof shows that $\frac{h(\mathcal{G})N^q}{(N)_{q_P}(N)_{q_Q}} - 1$ has a lower bound. We complete the proof by showing that $\frac{h(\mathcal{G})N^q}{(N)_{q_P}(N)_{q_Q}} - 1$ has an upper bound in the same vein. To prove it, we count the number of solutions in each component involved in $\mathcal{G} = \sqcup_{i=1}^{\alpha+\beta}\mathcal{C}_i$ as shown by the lower bound. We do that first for the part consisting of components of size greater than two and then for the part of components of size two. We abuse the aforementioned notation $h(\cdot)$ for ease of description. Let $h(i)$ be the number of solutions to $\sqcup_{j=1}^{i}\mathcal{C}_j$ and $h(0) = 1$. Under this notation, it holds that $h(\alpha+\beta) = h(\mathcal{G})$. The key strategy is to show that $h(i+1)$ is bounded by a function of $h(i)$. Then the term $h(\mathcal{G}) = h(\alpha + \beta)$ can be computed by the recursive relation between $h(i)$ and $h(i+1)$.

In order to perform a sharp estimation, we also need to bound a term, namely $h'(P, Q)$, that appeared in the recursive relation tightly. Depending on whether there are large components (whether $q_c > 0$), we can distinguish the analysis of $h'(P, Q)$ into two cases, namely for $q_c > 0$ and $q_c = 0$. For the case $q_c = 0$, we reuse some results of [17] to obtain optimal bound.   □

5   Multi-user Security of XoP

In this section, we consider the XoP construction that was first proposed by Bellare et al. [5]. This construction is used to obtain a secure pseudorandom function from a block cipher. Here, in particular, we consider a version that involves two independent permutations.

Let $n \in \mathbb{N}$ and $\mathsf{P}, \mathsf{Q} \leftarrow_\$ \mathrm{Perm}(n)$. One can define $\mathsf{XoP} : \mathrm{Perm}(n) \times \mathrm{Perm}(n) \times \{0,1\}^n \to \{0,1\}^n$ as the generic construction that takes permutations $\mathsf{P}, \mathsf{Q} \in \mathrm{Perm}(n)$ as keys, and on input X it returns

$$\mathsf{XoP}(X) \stackrel{\text{def}}{=} \mathsf{P}(X) \oplus \mathsf{Q}(X).$$

Theorem 3 below gives the new mu-prf security of XoP.

Theorem 3. *Let n, u and q_{max} be positive integers such that $n > 10$ and $q_{max} \leq \frac{2^n}{4n}$. Then one has*

$$\mathbf{Adv}_{\mathsf{XoP}}^{\text{mu-prf}}(u, q_{max}) \leq \frac{10 u^{\frac{1}{2}} q_{max}{}^2}{2^{2n}} + \frac{17 u^{\frac{1}{2}} (n+1)^2}{2^n}.$$

The upper bound of adversarial advantage to distinguish between (multi-user) XoP and the uniformly random function in terms of the threshold number of queries is given by $O\left(\sqrt{u} q_{max}{}^2/2^{2n}\right)$. This is strictly better bound to compare with the previous result of Choi et al. [14] by setting $m = n$ for $\mathsf{SaT2}$ at ASIACRYPT 2022, where the result is $O\left(\sqrt{u} q_{max}{}^{1.5}/2^{1.5n}\right)$. The difference between the above bounds comes from the difference between single-user bounds obtained by the Mirror theory and the χ^2 method. This way, the Squared-Ratio method can prove multi-user security tighter than previous analyses.

Proof. Suppose that a distinguisher $\mathcal{D}$ makes q_{max} queries $X_i \in \{0,1\}^n$, obtaining the corresponding responses $Z_i \in \{0,1\}^n$ for $i = 1, \ldots, q_{max}$. In this way, $\mathcal{D}$ obtains a transcript

$$\tau = ((X_1, Z_1), \ldots, (X_{q_{max}}, Z_{q_{max}})).$$

In the real world, $P_i \stackrel{\text{def}}{=} \mathsf{P}(X_i)$ and $Q_i \stackrel{\text{def}}{=} \mathsf{Q}(X_i)$ should be a solution to the following system of equations.

$$\begin{cases} P_1 \oplus Q_1 = Z_1, \\ P_2 \oplus Q_2 = Z_2, \\ \quad \vdots \\ P_{q_{max}} \oplus Q_{q_{max}} = Z_{q_{max}}. \end{cases}$$

"Bad" Transcript Analysis. To upper-bound $|\mathcal{R}_i|$ corresponding to this system of equations for any $i \in [q_{max}]$, we define a bad event as follows:

– bad $\Leftrightarrow \exists (i_1, i_2 \ldots, i_n) \in [q_{max}]^{*n}$ such that $Z_{i_1} = Z_{i_2} = \cdots = Z_{i_n}$.

For this bad event, we have

$$\Pr\left[\text{bad}\right] = \frac{\binom{q_{max}}{n}}{2^{n(n-1)}} \leq \frac{q_{max}{}^n}{2^{n^2}} = \left(\frac{q_{max}}{2^n}\right)^n. \tag{3}$$

"GOOD" TRANSCRIPT ANALYSIS. Let T_{re} and T_{id} be random variables following the distribution of the transcripts in the real world and the ideal world, respectively. Then we have

$$\frac{\Pr\left[\mathsf{T}_{re} = \tau\right]}{\Pr\left[\mathsf{T}_{id} = \tau\right]} = \frac{h(\mathcal{G}(\tau))2^{nq_{max}}}{(2^n)_{q_{max}}(2^n)_{q_{max}}}.$$

Furthermore, since we ignore the "Bad" transcript, it holds that $|\mathcal{R}_i| \leq n$ for all indices i. It then implies that

$$\frac{3\sum_{i=1}^{q_{max}}|\mathcal{R}_i|}{2^n} + \frac{2q_{max}{}^2}{2^{2n}} + \frac{6(n+1)^2}{2^n} \leq \frac{3nq_{max}}{2^n} + \frac{2q_{max}{}^2}{2^{2n}} + \frac{6(n+1)^2}{2^n} \leq 1$$

for $n > 10$ and $q_{max} \leq \frac{2^n}{4n}$. Therefore, by Corollary 1,

$$\left|\frac{h(\mathcal{G})2^{nq_{max}}}{(2^n)_{|\mathcal{P}|}(2^n)_{|\mathcal{Q}|}} - 1\right| \leq \frac{6\sum_{i=1}^{q_{max}}|\mathcal{R}_i|}{2^n} + \frac{4q_{max}{}^2}{2^{2n}} + \frac{12(n+1)^2}{2^n}.$$

CONCLUDING THE PROOF. Therefore, we can define

$$\epsilon_1(\tau) = \frac{6\sum_{i=1}^{q_{max}}|\mathcal{R}_i|}{2^n} + \frac{4q_{max}{}^2}{2^{2n}} + \frac{12(n+1)^2}{2^n},$$

and $\epsilon_2 = \left(\frac{q_{max}}{2^n}\right)^n$. To apply the Theorem 1, we need to bound the expectation of $\epsilon_1(\tau)^2$ where the expectation is taken over the distribution of the ideal world. To be precise, we have

$$\mathbf{Ex}\left[\epsilon_1(\tau)^2\right] = \frac{36}{2^{2n}}\mathbf{Ex}\left[\left(\sum_{i=1}^{q_{max}}|\mathcal{R}_i|\right)^2\right] + \left(\frac{4q_{max}{}^2}{2^{2n}} + \frac{12(n+1)^2}{2^n}\right)^2$$

$$+ \frac{12}{2^n}\cdot\left(\frac{4q_{max}{}^2}{2^{2n}} + \frac{12(n+1)^2}{2^n}\right)\cdot\mathbf{Ex}\left[\sum_{i=1}^{q_{max}}|\mathcal{R}_i|\right]. \tag{4}$$

On the other hand, by Lemma 3, we have

$$\mathbf{Ex}\left[\sum_{i=1}^{q_{max}}|\mathcal{R}_i|\right] \leq \frac{q_{max}{}^2}{2^{n+1}},$$

$$\mathbf{Ex}\left[\left(\sum_{i=1}^{q_{max}}|\mathcal{R}_i|\right)^2\right] \leq \frac{q_{max}{}^2}{2^{n+1}} + \frac{q_{max}{}^4}{2^{2n+2}}.$$

Using the derived bounds in (4), we obtain

$$\mathbf{Ex}\left[\epsilon_1(\tau)^2\right] \le \frac{49q_{max}^4}{2^{4n}} + \frac{18q_{max}^2}{2^{3n}} + \frac{168q_{max}^2(n+1)^2}{2^{3n}} + \frac{144(n+1)^4}{2^{2n}}$$
$$\le \frac{49q_{max}^4}{2^{4n}} + \frac{169q_{max}^2(n+1)^2}{2^{3n}} + \frac{144(n+1)^4}{2^{2n}}. \tag{5}$$

By utilizing (5) and (3) in the Theorem 1, we have

$$\mathbf{Adv}_{\mathsf{XoP}}^{\mathsf{mu\text{-}prf}}(u, q_{max}) \le \sqrt{2u\mathbf{Ex}\left[\epsilon_1(\tau)^2\right]} + 2u\epsilon_2(\tau)$$
$$\le \sqrt{2u\left(\frac{49q_{max}^4}{2^{4n}} + \frac{169q_{max}^2(n+1)^2}{2^{3n}} + \frac{144(n+1)^4}{2^{2n}}\right)} + 2u\left(\frac{q_{max}}{2^n}\right)^n$$
$$\le \sqrt{\frac{98uq_{max}^4}{2^{4n}}} + \sqrt{\frac{288u(n+1)^4}{2^{2n}}} + 2u\left(\frac{q_{max}}{2^n}\right)^n$$
$$\le \frac{10u^{\frac{1}{2}}q_{max}^2}{2^{2n}} + \frac{17u^{\frac{1}{2}}(n+1)^2}{2^n}.$$

This completes the proof. □

6   Multi-user Security of EDM

In this section, we consider the EDM construction proposed by Cogliati and Seurin [20]. Let $n \in \mathbb{N}$ and $\mathsf{P}, \mathsf{Q} \leftarrow_\$ \mathsf{Perm}(n)$. One can define $\mathsf{EDM} : \mathsf{Perm}(n) \times \mathsf{Perm}(n) \times \{0,1\}^n \to \{0,1\}^n$ as the generic construction that takes permutations $\mathsf{P}, \mathsf{Q} \in \mathsf{Perm}(n)$ as keys, and on input X it returns

$$\mathsf{EDM}(X) \stackrel{\mathrm{def}}{=} \mathsf{Q}(\mathsf{P}(X) \oplus X).$$

Theorem 4 below gives the new mu-prf security of EDM.

Theorem 4. *Let n, u and q_{max} be positive integers such that $n > 5$ and $q_{max} \le \frac{2^{3n/4}}{4n}$. Then one has*

$$\mathbf{Adv}_{\mathsf{EDM}}^{\mathsf{mu\text{-}prf}}(u, q_{max}) \le \frac{9u^{1/2}nq_{max}^3}{2^{2.5n}} + \frac{122u^{1/2}nq_{max}^4}{2^{3n}}.$$

Therefore, the upper bound of adversarial advantage to distinguish between (multi-user) EDM and the uniformly random function in terms of the threshold number of queries is given by $O\left(n\sqrt{u}q_{max}^4/2^{3n}\right)$, significantly better than the result of Dai et al. [21] at CRYPTO 2017 with the hybrid argument: $O\left(uq^2/2^{1.5n}\right)$. Note that for the case where $q = uq_{max}$, the result of Dai et al. only gives us $O\left(u^3q_{max}^2/2^{1.5n}\right)$, which makes EDM insecure even for $q_{max} = O(1)$ when the number of users is $u = O(2^{\frac{n}{2}})$. On the other hand, our bound ensures that EDM is still beyond birthday-bound secure with the same u.

Proof. Suppose that a distinguisher $\mathcal{D}$ makes $q_{\max}$ queries $X_i \in \{0,1\}^n$, obtaining the corresponding responses $Z_i \in \{0,1\}^n$ for $i = 1, \ldots, q_{\max}$. In this way, $\mathcal{D}$ obtains a transcript

$$\tau = ((X_1, Z_1), \ldots, (X_{q_{\max}}, Z_{q_{\max}})).$$

In the real world, $P_i \overset{\text{def}}{=} \mathsf{P}(X_i)$ and $Q_i \overset{\text{def}}{=} \mathsf{Q}^{-1}(Z_i)$ should be a solution to the following system of equations while regarding Q^{-1} as a permutation.

$$\begin{cases} P_1 \oplus Q_1 = X_1, \\ P_2 \oplus Q_2 = X_2, \\ \quad \vdots \\ P_{q_{\max}} \oplus Q_{q_{\max}} = X_{q_{\max}}. \end{cases}$$

"Bad" Transcript Analysis. To upper-bound $\xi_{\max}$ (bad$_1$), $\sum_{i=1}^{\alpha+\beta} |\mathcal{R}_i|$ (bad$_2$), and q_c (bad$_3$), for a fixed $A > 0$, we define bad events as follows:

- bad$_1 \Leftrightarrow \exists (i_1, i_2 \ldots, i_n) \in [q_{\max}]^{*n}$ such that $Z_{i_1} = Z_{i_2} = \cdots = Z_{i_n}$,
- bad$_2 \Leftrightarrow \exists (i_1, i_1', i_2, i_2' \ldots, i_{n-1}, i_{n-1}') \in [q_{\max}]^{*(2n-2)}$ such that $X_{i_1} \oplus X_{i_1'} = X_{i_j} \oplus X_{i_j'}$ and $Z_{i_j} = Z_{i_j'}$ for all $j \in [n-1]$,
- bad$_3 \Leftrightarrow q_c \geq \frac{q_{\max}^2}{2^{n+1}} + \frac{2^{2n}}{8n q_{\max}^2}$.

1. We have

$$\Pr[\mathsf{bad}_1] = \frac{\binom{q_{\max}}{n}}{2^{n(n-1)}} \leq \frac{q_{\max}^n}{2^{n^2}} = \left(\frac{q_{\max}}{2^n}\right)^n.$$

2. Let $\mathcal{B} = \{(i_1, i_1', i_2, i_2' \ldots, i_{n-1}, i_{n-1}') \in [q_{\max}]^{*(2n-2)} \mid X_{i_1} \oplus X_{i_1'} = X_{i_j} \oplus X_{i_j'}$ for all $j \in [n-1]\}$, we have

$$\Pr[\mathsf{bad}_2] = \frac{|\mathcal{B}|}{2^{n(n-2)}} \leq \frac{2^n \binom{q_{\max}/2}{n-1}}{2^{n(n-2)}} \leq \left(\frac{q_{\max}}{2^n}\right)^{n-1}.$$

3. By Lemma 3 with $A = \frac{2^{2n}}{8n q_{\max}^2}$, we have

$$\Pr[\mathsf{bad}_3] \leq \frac{32n^2 q_{\max}^6}{2^{5n}} + \frac{16n^2 q_{\max}^8}{2^{6n}}.$$

In conclusion, we have

$$\Pr[\mathsf{bad}_1 \vee \mathsf{bad}_2 \vee \mathsf{bad}_3] \leq 2\left(\frac{q_{\max}}{2^n}\right)^{n-1} + \frac{32n^2 q_{\max}^6}{2^{5n}} + \frac{16n^2 q_{\max}^8}{2^{6n}}.$$

"Good" Transcript Analysis. Note that

$$\frac{\Pr[\mathsf{T}_{\mathrm{re}} = \tau]}{\Pr[\mathsf{T}_{\mathrm{id}} = \tau]} = \frac{h(\mathcal{G}(\tau)) 2^{n q_{\max}}}{(2^n)_{|\mathcal{P}|}(2^n)_{|\mathcal{Q}|}}$$

and $\sum_{i=1}^{\alpha} (\xi(\mathcal{C}_i) - 1) = q_c$. In order to upper-bound $|\mathcal{R}_i|$, we distinguish into following two cases, namely when $i \in [\alpha]$ and $i \in [\alpha+1, \alpha+\beta]$. We first consider $i \in [\alpha]$, note that we have $\xi_{\max} \leq n$ by $\neg\mathsf{bad}_1$, hence there are at most

$$\binom{\xi(\mathcal{C}_i)+1}{2} \leq \frac{(n+1)\xi(\mathcal{C}_i)}{2}$$

ways to choose trails of i-th component. For each of those trails, there can be at most $n-1$ trails with the same label by $\neg\mathsf{bad}_2$. So we have

$$|\mathcal{R}_i| \leq \frac{(n+1)\xi(\mathcal{C}_i)}{2} \cdot (n-1) \leq \frac{n^2\xi(\mathcal{C}_i)}{2}.$$

Now we consider $i \in [\alpha+1, \alpha+\beta]$, note that since we are considering the nonce-respecting adversary, two nonces can never collide, therefore the label values of two single-edge trails cannot be the same. Hence there are at most

$$\sum_{k=1}^{\alpha} \binom{\xi(\mathcal{C}_k)}{2} \leq \frac{nq_c}{2}$$

trails of two joint edges (in the first α components) of which the label can be the same as the unique label of the i-th component (consists of one edge). Also, a label of any trail of two joint edges cannot simultaneously collide with the labels of two different components i and j, for any $j \neq i \in [\alpha+1, \alpha+\beta]$. Since that means the unique label values of components i and j are the same, which contradicts the nonce-respecting assumption. This observation makes us have

$$\sum_{i=\alpha+1}^{\alpha+\beta} |\mathcal{R}_i| \leq \frac{nq_c}{2}.$$

It follows that

$$\sum_{i=1}^{\alpha+\beta} |\mathcal{R}_i| \leq \left(\sum_{i=1}^{\alpha} \frac{n^2\xi(\mathcal{C}_i)}{2}\right) + \frac{nq_c}{2} \leq \frac{3n^2q_c}{4} + \frac{nq_c}{2}.$$

Furthermore, by $\neg\mathsf{bad}_3$ and $n > 5$, we also have

$$\frac{2\sum_{i=1}^{\alpha+\beta} |\mathcal{R}_i| + 2nq_c}{2^n} + \frac{4nq_cq_{\max}^2}{2^{2n}} + \frac{20nq_{\max}^4}{2^{3n}}$$
$$\leq \frac{2n^2q_c}{2^n} + \frac{4nq_cq_{\max}^2}{2^{2n}} + \frac{20nq_{\max}^4}{2^{3n}} \leq 1.$$

By Corollary 1 and the above, we have

$$\left| \frac{h(\mathcal{G})2^{nq}}{(2^n)_{|\mathcal{P}|}(2^n)_{|\mathcal{Q}|}} - 1 \right| \leq \frac{4n^2q_c}{2^n} + \frac{8nq_cq_{\max}^2}{2^{2n}} + \frac{40nq_{\max}^4}{2^{3n}}.$$

CONCLUDING THE PROOF. Hence we can set

$$\epsilon_1(\tau) = \frac{4n^2 q_c}{2^n} + \frac{8n q_c q_{max}^2}{2^{2n}} + \frac{40 n q_{max}^4}{2^{3n}},$$

and

$$\epsilon_2 = 2\left(\frac{q_{max}}{2^n}\right)^{n-1} + \frac{32 n^2 q_{max}^6}{2^{5n}} + \frac{16 n^2 q_{max}^8}{2^{6n}}$$

for Theorem 1. We need to compute the expectation of $\epsilon_1(\tau)^2$ where the expectation is taken over the distribution of the ideal world. It gives an identity:

$$\mathbf{Ex}\left[\epsilon_1(\tau)^2\right] = \left(\frac{4n^2}{2^n} + \frac{8n q_{max}^2}{2^{2n}}\right)^2 \mathbf{Ex}\left[q_c^2\right] + \frac{1600 n^2 q_{max}^8}{2^{6n}}$$
$$+ 2\left(\frac{4n^2}{2^n} + \frac{8n q_{max}^2}{2^{2n}}\right)\frac{40 n q_{max}^4}{2^{3n}}\mathbf{Ex}\left[q_c\right].$$

By Lemma 3, we have

$$\mathbf{Ex}\left[q_c\right] \le \frac{q_{max}^2}{2^{n+1}},$$

$$\mathbf{Ex}\left[q_c^2\right] \le \frac{q_{max}^2}{2^{n+1}} + \frac{q_{max}^4}{2^{2n+2}}.$$

Combining it together, it implies that:

$$\mathbf{Ex}\left[\epsilon_1(\tau)^2\right] = \left(\frac{q_{max}^2}{2^{n+1}} + \frac{q_{max}^4}{2^{2n+2}}\right)\left(\frac{4n^2}{2^n} + \frac{8n q_{max}^2}{2^{2n}}\right)^2 + \frac{1600 n^2 q_{max}^8}{2^{6n}}$$
$$+ \frac{q_{max}^2}{2^{n+1}}\left(\frac{4n^2}{2^n} + \frac{8n q_{max}^2}{2^{2n}}\right)\frac{80 n q_{max}^4}{2^{3n}}. \tag{6}$$

Under the constraint $q_{max} \le \frac{2^{3n/4}}{4n}$, it holds that $\frac{4n^2}{2^n} + \frac{8n q_{max}^2}{2^{2n}} \le \frac{9n q_{max}^2}{2^{2n}} \le 1$. Using the inequality, the equality (6) can be bounded by:

$$\mathbf{Ex}\left[\epsilon_1(\tau)^2\right] \le \left(\frac{q_{max}^2}{2^{n+1}} + \frac{q_{max}^4}{2^{2n+2}}\right)\frac{81 n^2 q_{max}^4}{2^{4n}} + \frac{360 n^2 q_{max}^8}{2^{6n}} + \frac{1600 n^2 q_{max}^8}{2^{6n}}.$$

The Theorem 1 then gives

$$\mathbf{Adv}_{EDM}^{mu\text{-}prf}(u, q_{max}) \le \left(\frac{q_{max}}{2^{n/2}} + \frac{q_{max}^2}{2^{n+1}}\right)\frac{9\sqrt{2}u n q_{max}^2}{2^{2n}} + \frac{\sqrt{720}u n q_{max}^4}{2^{3n}}$$
$$+ \frac{\sqrt{3200}u n q_{max}^4}{2^{3n}} + 4u\left(\frac{q_{max}}{2^n}\right)^{n-1} + \frac{64 u n^2 q_{max}^6}{2^{5n}} + \frac{32 u n^2 q_{max}^8}{2^{6n}}.$$

When $q_{max} \le \frac{2^{3n/4}}{4n}$, it can be bounded by

$$\frac{9 u^{1/2} n q_{max}^3}{2^{2.5n}} + \frac{122 u^{1/2} n q_{max}^4}{2^{3n}}.$$

This completes the proof.   □

7   Multi-user Security of a Variant of nEHtM in the Nonce-Respecting Setting

In this section, we consider mu-prf security of a variant of nEHtM proposed by Dutta et al. [23], based on an n-bit δ-AXU hash function H with a hash key K_h and two random permutations P and Q. A tag T is an output of nEHtM generated by a message M with an n-bit nonce N:

$$T = P(N) \oplus Q(H_{K_h}(M) \oplus N).$$

We will consider a nonce-respecting setting that assumes nonces never repeat. we have the following theorem.

Theorem 5. *Let $\delta > 0$, and let $H : \mathcal{K} \times \mathcal{M} \to \{0,1\}^n$ be a δ-almost AXU hash function. For positive integers u, q_{max}, and L such that $4 \leq n \leq L \leq \min\left\{\frac{2^n}{4q_{max}}, \frac{2^{3n}}{20q_{max}{}^4}\right\}$, we have*

$$\mathbf{Adv}_{nEHtM}^{mu\text{-}prf}(u, q_{max}) \leq \frac{4(2u)^{1/2}}{2^n}\left(\frac{q_{max}}{2^{n/2}} + \frac{q_{max}{}^2}{2^{n+1}}\right) + \frac{3u^{1/2}(n+1)Lq_{max}{}^2\delta}{2^n}$$

$$+ \frac{6u^{1/2}Lq_{max}{}^4\delta}{2^{2n}} + \frac{2uq_{max}{}^2\delta}{2^n} + \frac{4uq_{max}^2\delta}{L^2} + 2u\left(\frac{q_{max}L}{2^n}\right)^{n-1} + \frac{65u^{1/2}Lq_{max}{}^4}{2^{3n}}.$$

Suppose that $\delta = O\left(\frac{\ell}{2^n}\right)$ for a constant ℓ. We can now optimize the advantage over L in the Theorem 5 via arithmetic-geometric mean inequality. In other words, we can set the L to $\left(\frac{2^n\sqrt{u}}{n}\right)^{1/3}$ and $\left(\frac{2^{2n}\sqrt{u}}{q_{max}^2}\right)^{1/3}$ for sufficiently small u, respectively. We thus have the following corollary:

Corollary 2. *Assume $\delta = O\left(\frac{\ell}{2^n}\right)$ for a constant ℓ. Then one has*

$$\mathbf{Adv}_{nEHtM}^{mu\text{-}prf}(u, q_{max}) \leq \begin{cases} O\left(\frac{\ell uq_{max}{}^2}{2^{2n}} + \frac{\ell(un)^{\frac{2}{3}}q_{max}{}^2}{2^{\frac{5n}{3}}}\right) & \text{if } q_{max} \leq O(2^{\frac{n}{2}}) \\ O\left(\frac{\ell uq_{max}{}^2}{2^{2n}} + \frac{\ell u^{\frac{2}{3}}q_{max}^{\frac{10}{3}}}{2^{\frac{7n}{3}}}\right) & \text{if } q_{max} \geq O(2^{\frac{n}{2}}) \end{cases}.$$

Since the previous bound of two permutations case [13] is slightly worst than that of a single permutation [16] in the multi-user setting, we will recall the result by Choi et al. [16] for comparison (by ignoring the nonce-misuse terms):

$$\frac{uq}{2^n} + \frac{u\ell^{\frac{1}{2}}q^2}{2^{\frac{3n}{2}}},$$

where $q_{max} \leq q \leq u \cdot q_{max}$ in our notation. Figure 1 shows the results of graphing our bounds and the previous bounds as functions of $\log_2(u)$: the level of security given by Choi et al. is in the shaded area of Fig. 1 and depends on the value of q. For example, fixing $\log_2(u) = n/2$, the security bound of Choi et al. lies between $O(1)$ (for $q = u \cdot q_{max}$) and $O(2^{\frac{n}{2}})$ (for $q = q_{max}$). We see that our new bound improves over the result of Choi et al. [16] when the number of users becomes large, and is superior for $u \geq O\left(2^{\frac{n}{26}}\right)$ and $2^{\frac{n}{26}} \approx 30.3$ if $n = 128$ and $q = u \cdot q_{max}$.

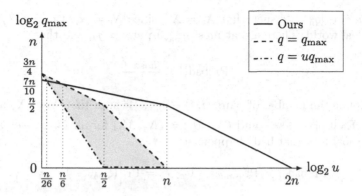

Fig. 1. Comparison of the security bounds (in terms of the threshold number of queries per user) as functions of $\log_2 u$. The solid line represents our bounds, and the dashed line (resp. the dash-dotted line) represents the previous bound by the hybrid argument where $q = q_{max}$ (resp. $q = u \cdot q_{max}$). We neglect the logarithmic term n.

Proof (of Theorem 5). Suppose that a distinguisher $\mathcal{D}$ makes q_{max} queries (N_i, M_i), obtaining the corresponding responses $T_i \in \{0,1\}^n$ for $i = 1, \ldots, q_{max}$. Recall that $N_i \neq N_j$ if $i \neq j$ for all $i, j \in [q_{max}]$ by the nonce-respecting assumption. $\mathcal{D}$ obtains a transcript

$$\tau = ((N_1, M_1, T_1), \ldots, (N_{q_{max}}, M_{q_{max}}, T_{q_{max}}), K_h),$$

where K_h is given for free at the end of the attack. From τ, one can fix $X_i \overset{\text{def}}{=} H_{K_h}(M_i) \oplus N_i$ for $i = 1, \ldots, q_{max}$. In the real world, $P_i \overset{\text{def}}{=} \mathsf{P}(N_i)$ and $Q_i \overset{\text{def}}{=} \mathsf{Q}(X_i)$ should be a solution to the following system of equations.

$$\begin{cases} P_1 \oplus Q_1 = T_1, \\ P_2 \oplus Q_2 = T_2, \\ \quad \vdots \\ P_{q_{max}} \oplus Q_{q_{max}} = T_{q_{max}}. \end{cases}$$

"BAD" TRANSCRIPT ANALYSIS. Let L be an arbitrary number such that $4 \leq n \leq L \leq \min\left\{\frac{2^n}{4q_{max}}, \frac{2^{3n}}{20q_{max}^4}\right\}$. To satisfy the non-degeneracy property (bad_1) and to upper-bound ξ_{max} (bad_2), $\sum_{i=1}^{\alpha+\beta} |\mathcal{R}_i|$ (bad_3 and bad_4) and q_c (bad_5), we define bad events as follows:

- $\mathsf{bad}_1 \Leftrightarrow$ there exists $(i,j) \in [q_{max}]^{*2}$ such that $X_i = X_j$ and $T_i = T_j$;
- $\mathsf{bad}_2 \Leftrightarrow \exists (i_1, i_2 \ldots, i_L) \in [q_{max}]^{*L}$ such that $X_{i_1} = X_{i_2} = \cdots = X_{i_L}$,
- $\mathsf{bad}_3 \Leftrightarrow \exists (i_1, i_2, \ldots, i_n) \in [q_{max}]^{*n}$ such that $T_{i_1} = T_{i_2} = \cdots = T_{i_n}$,
- $\mathsf{bad}_4 \Leftrightarrow \exists (i_1, i'_1, i_2, i'_2 \ldots, i_{n-1}, i'_{n-1}) \in [q_{max}]^{*2n-2}$ such that $T_{i_j} \oplus T_{i'_j} = T_{i_1} \oplus T_{i'_1}$ and $X_{i_j} = X_{i'_j}$ for all $j \in [n-1]$.
- $\mathsf{bad}_5 \Leftrightarrow q_c \geq \frac{q_{max}^2}{2^{n+1}} + \frac{2^{2n}}{4Lq_{max}^2}$.

1. For $(i, j) \in [q_{\max}]^{*2}$ such that $X_i = X_j$, since $N_i \neq N_j$, $\Pr[T_i = T_j] = \frac{1}{2^n}$ in the ideal world. There are at most $q_{\max}^2 \delta$ pairs (i, j), and thus

$$\Pr[\mathsf{bad}_1] \leq \frac{q_{\max}^2 \delta}{2^n}.$$

2. Let Col be the number of pairs $(i, j) \in [q_{\max}]^{*2}$ such that $X_i = X_j$ and $i < j$. Since $\mathbf{Ex}[\mathsf{Col}] \leq \frac{q_{\max}^2 \delta}{2}$ and $(N_i, M_i) \neq (N_j, M_j)$ for all $i \neq j$, we can bound the probability that bad_2 happens as

$$\Pr[\mathsf{bad}_2] = \Pr[\xi_{\max} - 1 \geq L] = \Pr\left[(\xi_{\max} - 1)^2 \geq L^2\right]$$

$$\leq \Pr\left[\sum_{i=1}^{\alpha} (\xi(C_i) - 1)^2 \geq L^2\right]$$

$$\leq \Pr\left[2\mathsf{Col} + \sum_{i=1}^{\alpha} (\xi(C_i) - 1) \geq L^2\right]$$

$$\leq \Pr[4\mathsf{Col} \geq L^2] \leq \frac{2q_{\max}^2 \delta}{L^2}.$$

Note that this is the same technique as Corollary 4.1. in Jha and Nandi [28], where our result relies on the δ-AXU property instead of the almost universal property.

3. We have

$$\Pr[\mathsf{bad}_3] = \frac{\binom{q_{\max}}{n}}{2^{n(n-1)}} \leq \frac{q_{\max}^n}{2^{n^2}} = \left(\frac{q_{\max}}{2^n}\right)^n.$$

4. We will bound the probability of bad_4 under the condition of $\neg\mathsf{bad}_2$. Let $\mathcal{B} = \{(i_1, i_1', i_2, i_2' \ldots, i_{n-1}, i_{n-1}') \in [q_{\max}]^{*(2n-2)} \mid X_{i_j} = X_{i_j'} \text{ for all } j \in [n-1]\}$. By $\neg\mathsf{bad}_2$, we have

$$|\mathcal{B}| \leq \binom{q_{\max}}{n-1}(L-1)^{n-1} \leq \frac{(q_{\max}(L-1))^{n-1}}{2^n}.$$

Thus we have

$$\Pr\left[T_{i_1} \oplus T_{i_1'} = T_{i_j} \oplus T_{i_j'}\right] = \frac{1}{2^n}$$

and

$$\Pr[\mathsf{bad}_4 \mid \neg\mathsf{bad}_2] = \frac{|\mathcal{B}|}{2^{n(n-2)}} \leq \left(\frac{q_{\max}(L-1)}{2^n}\right)^{n-1}.$$

5. By Lemma 3 with $A = \frac{2^{2n}}{4Lq_{\max}^2}$, we have

$$\Pr[\mathsf{bad}_5] \leq \frac{2L^2 q_{\max}^6}{2^{5n}} + \frac{64L^2 q_{\max}^8}{2^{6n}}.$$

In conclusion, we have

$$\Pr[\mathsf{bad}_1 \vee \mathsf{bad}_2 \vee \mathsf{bad}_3 \vee \mathsf{bad}_4 \vee \mathsf{bad}_5]$$
$$\leq \Pr[\mathsf{bad}_1] + \Pr[\mathsf{bad}_2] + \Pr[\mathsf{bad}_3] + \Pr[\mathsf{bad}_4 \mid \neg\mathsf{bad}_2] + \Pr[\mathsf{bad}_5]$$
$$\leq \frac{q_{\max}^2 \delta}{2n} + \frac{2q_{\max}^2 \delta}{L^2} + \left(\frac{q_{\max}}{2n}\right)^n + \left(\frac{q_{\max}(L-1)}{2n}\right)^{n-1} + \frac{2Lq_{\max}^6}{2^{5n}} + \frac{4L^2 q_{\max}^8}{2^{6n}}$$
$$\leq \frac{q_{\max}^2 \delta}{2n} + \frac{2q_{\max}^2 \delta}{L^2} + \left(\frac{q_{\max}L}{2n}\right)^{n-1} + \frac{2L^2 q_{\max}^6}{2^{5n}} + \frac{4L^2 q_{\max}^8}{2^{6n}} .$$

"GOOD" TRANSCRIPT ANALYSIS. Note that

$$\frac{\Pr\left[\mathsf{T}_{\mathrm{re}} = \tau\right]}{\Pr\left[\mathsf{T}_{\mathrm{id}} = \tau\right]} = \frac{h(\mathcal{G}(\tau))N^{q_{\max}}}{(N)_{|\mathcal{P}|}(N)_{|\mathcal{Q}|}}$$

and we denote the transcript graph $\mathcal{G}(\tau) = (\mathcal{V}, \mathcal{E})$. We define the following sets

$$\mathcal{S}_i = \left\{ (\{V_1, V_1'\}, \{V_2, V_2'\}) \in \mathcal{R}_i \,\middle|\, \overline{V_1 V_1'}, \overline{V_2 V_2'} \in \mathcal{E} \right\},$$
$$\mathcal{D}_i = \mathcal{R}_i \setminus \mathcal{S}_i .$$

Since $|\mathcal{R}_i| = |\mathcal{S}_i| + |\mathcal{D}_i|$, we will first focus on upper-bounding $|\mathcal{D}_i|$. Recall that $\sum_{i=1}^{\alpha} (\xi(\mathcal{C}_i) - 1) = q_c$. In order to upper-bound $|\mathcal{D}_i|$, we distinguish into following two cases, namely when $i \in [\alpha]$ and $i \in [\alpha+1, \alpha+\beta]$. We first consider $i \in [\alpha]$, note that we have $\xi_{\max} \leq L$ by $\neg\mathsf{bad}_2$, hence there are at most

$$\binom{\xi(\mathcal{C}_i) + 1}{2} \leq \frac{(L+1)\xi(\mathcal{C}_i)}{2}$$

ways to choose trails of i-th component. By $\neg\mathsf{bad}_3$ and $\neg\mathsf{bad}_4$, if the chosen trail consists of two edges, there are at most n trails of a single edge and $(n-2)$ trails of two joint edges with the same label to the chosen trail. Similarly, if the chosen trail consists of a single edge, there are at most $(n-1)$ trails of two joint edges. For each case, there can be at most $(2n-2)$ trails with the same label. So we have

$$|\mathcal{D}_i| \leq \frac{(L+1)\xi(\mathcal{C}_i)}{2} \cdot (2n-2) \leq nL\xi(\mathcal{C}_i)$$

since $L \geq n$. Now we consider $i \in [\alpha+1, \alpha+\beta]$, note that there are at most

$$\sum_{k=1}^{\alpha} \binom{\xi(\mathcal{C}_k)}{2} \leq \frac{Lq_c}{2}$$

trails of two joint edges (in the first α components) of which the label can be the same as the unique label of the i-th component (consists of one edge). Also, by $\neg\mathsf{bad}_3$, there are at most n different components in $[\alpha+1, \alpha+\beta]$ that share the same label value (single edge components) with the label of i-th component. This observation makes us have

$$\sum_{i=\alpha+1}^{\alpha+\beta} |\mathcal{D}_i| \leq \frac{nLq_c}{2} .$$

It follows that

$$\sum_{i=1}^{\alpha+\beta} |\mathcal{D}_i| \le \left(\sum_{i=1}^{\alpha} nL\xi(\mathcal{C}_i)\right) + \frac{nLq_c}{2} \le \frac{3nLq_c}{2} + \frac{nLq_c}{2} \le 2nLq_c.$$

Furthermore, by $\neg\mathsf{bad}_3$ and $\neg\mathsf{bad}_5$, we also have $4 \le n \le L \le \min\left\{\frac{2^n}{4q_{max}}, \frac{2^{3n}}{20q_{max}^4}\right\}$

$$\frac{2\sum_{i=1}^{\alpha+\beta}|\mathcal{S}_i|}{2^n} + \frac{2(n+1)Lq_c}{2^n} + \frac{4Lq_cq_{max}^2}{2^{2n}} + \frac{20\,Lq_{max}^4}{2^{3n}}$$

$$\le \frac{2nq_{max}}{2^n} + \frac{2(n+1)Lq_c}{2^n} + \frac{4Lq_cq_{max}^2}{2^{2n}} + \frac{20\,Lq_{max}^4}{2^{3n}} \le 1.$$

By Corollary 1 and the above, we have

$$\left|\frac{h(\mathcal{G})2^{nq_{max}}}{(2^n)_{|\mathcal{P}|}(2^n)_{|\mathcal{Q}|}} - 1\right| \le \frac{4\sum_{i=1}^{\alpha+\beta}|\mathcal{S}_i|}{2^n} + \frac{4(n+1)Lq_c}{2^n} + \frac{8Lq_cq_{max}^2}{2^{2n}} + \frac{40\,Lq_{max}^4}{2^{3n}}.$$

CONCLUDING THE PROOF. Now we can set

$$\epsilon_1(\tau) = \frac{4\sum_{i=1}^{\alpha+\beta}|\mathcal{S}_i|}{2^n} + \frac{4(n+1)Lq_c}{2^n} + \frac{8Lq_cq_{max}^2}{2^{2n}} + \frac{40\,Lq_{max}^4}{2^{3n}},$$

and

$$\epsilon_2 = \frac{q_{max}^2\delta}{2^n} + \frac{2q^2\delta}{L^2} + \left(\frac{q_{max}L}{2^n}\right)^{n-1} + \frac{2L^2q_{max}^6}{2^{5n}} + \frac{4L^2q_{max}^8}{2^{6n}}$$

for Theorem 1. We need to compute the expectation of $\epsilon_1(\tau)^2$ where the expectation is taken over the distribution of the ideal world. To be precise, we have

$$\mathbf{Ex}\left[\epsilon_1(\tau)^2\right] = \frac{16}{2^{2n}}\mathbf{Ex}\left[\left(\sum_{i=1}^{\alpha+\beta}|\mathcal{S}_i|\right)^2\right] + \left(\frac{4(n+1)L}{2^n} + \frac{8Lq_{max}^2}{2^{2n}}\right)^2\mathbf{Ex}\left[q_c^2\right]$$

$$+ \frac{8}{2^n}\left(\frac{4(n+1)L}{2^n} + \frac{8Lq_{max}^2}{2^{2n}}\right)\mathbf{Ex}\left[q_c\sum_{i=1}^{\alpha+\beta}|\mathcal{S}_i|\right] + \frac{1600L^2q_{max}^8}{2^{6n}}$$

$$+ \frac{8}{2^n}\cdot\frac{40\,Lq_{max}^4}{2^{3n}}\mathbf{Ex}\left[\sum_{i=1}^{\alpha+\beta}|\mathcal{S}_i|\right] + \left(\frac{4(n+1)L}{2^n} + \frac{8Lq_{max}^2}{2^{2n}}\right)\frac{80\,Lq_{max}^4}{2^{3n}}\mathbf{Ex}\left[q_c\right],$$

By Lemma 3, we have

$$\mathbf{Ex}\left[\sum_{i=1}^{\alpha+\beta}|\mathcal{S}_i|\right] \le \frac{q_{max}^2}{2^{n+1}},$$

$$\mathbf{Ex}\left[\left(\sum_{i=1}^{\alpha+\beta}|\mathcal{S}_i|\right)^2\right] \le \frac{q_{max}^2}{2^{n+1}} + \frac{q_{max}^4}{2^{2n+2}},$$

$$\mathbf{Ex}[q_c] \le \frac{q_{max}^2\delta}{2},$$

$$\mathbf{Ex}\left[q_c^2\right] \le \frac{q_{max}^2\delta}{2} + \frac{q_{max}^4\delta^2}{4}.$$

Note that

$$\mathbf{Ex}\left[q_c \sum_{i=1}^{\alpha+\beta} |\mathcal{S}_i|\right] = \mathbf{Ex}\left[q_c\right] \mathbf{Ex}\left[\sum_{i=1}^{\alpha+\beta} |\mathcal{S}_i|\right] \le \frac{q_{max}^4 \delta}{2^{n+2}},$$

since q_c and $\mathcal{S}_i$ are independent in the ideal world. Combining it together, it implies that:

$$\mathbf{Ex}\left[\epsilon_1(\tau)^2\right] \le \frac{16}{2^{2n}}\left(\frac{q_{max}^2}{2^{n+1}} + \frac{q_{max}^4}{2^{2n+2}}\right) + \left(\frac{4(n+1)L}{2^n} + \frac{8Lq_{max}^2}{2^{2n}}\right)\frac{2q_{max}^4\delta}{2^{2n}}$$

$$+ \left(\frac{4(n+1)L}{2^n} + \frac{8Lq_{max}^2}{2^{2n}}\right)^2\left(\frac{q_{max}^2\delta}{2} + \frac{q_{max}^4\delta^2}{4}\right) + \frac{160\,Lq_{max}^6}{2^{5n}}$$

$$+ \left(\frac{4(n+1)L}{2^n} + \frac{8Lq_{max}^2}{2^{2n}}\right)\frac{40\,Lq_{max}^6\delta}{2^{3n}} + \frac{1600L^2q_{max}^8}{2^{6n}},$$

and Theorem 1 then gives

$$\mathbf{Adv}_{\mathsf{nEHtM}}^{\mathsf{mu\text{-}prf}}(u, q_{max}) \le \frac{4\sqrt{2u}}{2^n}\left(\frac{q_{max}}{2^{n/2}} + \frac{q_{max}^2}{2^{n+1}}\right) + \frac{4\sqrt{u(n+1)L\delta}q_{max}^2}{2^{1.5n}} + \frac{\sqrt{32uL\delta}q_{max}^3}{2^{2n}}$$

$$+ \left(\frac{4\sqrt{2u}(n+1)L}{2^n} + \frac{8\sqrt{2u}Lq_{max}^2}{2^{2n}}\right)\left(q_{max}\delta^{1/2} + \frac{q_{max}^2\delta}{2}\right)$$

$$+ \frac{\sqrt{320uL}q_{max}^3}{2^{2.5n}} + \frac{\sqrt{320u(n+1)\delta L}q_{max}^3}{2^{2n}} + \frac{\sqrt{640u\delta L}q_{max}^4}{2^{2.5n}} + \frac{\sqrt{3200uL}q_{max}^4}{2^{3n}}$$

$$+ \frac{2uq_{max}^2\delta}{2^n} + \frac{4uq_{max}^2\delta}{L^2} + 2u\left(\frac{q_{max}L}{2^n}\right)^{n-1} + \frac{4uL^2q_{max}^6}{2^{5n}} + \frac{8uL^2q_{max}^8}{2^{6n}}.$$

When $L \le \min\left\{\frac{2^n}{4q_{max}}, \frac{2^{3n}}{20q_{max}^4}\right\}$, it can be bounded by

$$\frac{4(2u)^{1/2}}{2^n}\left(\frac{q_{max}}{2^{n/2}} + \frac{q_{max}^2}{2^{n+1}}\right) + \frac{3u^{1/2}(n+1)Lq_{max}^2\delta}{2^n} + \frac{6u^{1/2}Lq_{max}^4\delta}{2^{2n}}$$

$$+ \frac{2uq_{max}^2\delta}{2^n} + \frac{4uq_{max}^2\delta}{L^2} + 2u\left(\frac{q_{max}L}{2^n}\right)^{n-1} + \frac{65u^{1/2}Lq_{max}^4}{2^{3n}}.$$

This completes the proof.   □

Acknowledgement. Yu Long Chen was supported by in part by the Research Council KU Leuven: GOA TENSE (C16/15/058). Wonseok Choi was Supported in part by the Sunday Group and the Algorand Centres of Excellence program managed by the Algorand Foundation. Changmin Lee was supported by a KIAS Individual Grant CG080601 at the Korea Institute for Advanced Study. Any opinions, findings, and conclusions or recommendations expressed in this material are those of the author(s) and do not necessarily reflect the views of the Algorand Foundation. We would like to express our appreciation to the anonymous reviewers of CRYPTO 2023 for their valuable feedback and insightful suggestions. Special thanks are extended to Jooyoung Lee, Byeonghak Lee, and Minki Hhan for their assistance and fruitful discussions, which greatly contributed to the development of this research paper.

References

1. Bellare, M., Impagliazzo, R.: A tool for obtaining tighter security analyses of pseudorandom function based constructions, with applications to PRP to PRF conversion. Cryptology ePrint Archive, Report 1999/024 (1999). https://eprint.iacr.org/1999/024
2. Bellare, M., Desai, A., Jokipii, E., Rogaway, P.: A concrete security treatment of symmetric encryption. In: 38th FOCS, pp. 394–403
3. Bellare, M., Guérin, R., Rogaway, P.: XOR MACs: new methods for message authentication using finite pseudorandom functions. In: Coppersmith, D. (ed.) CRYPTO 1995. LNCS, vol. 963, pp. 15–28. Springer, Heidelberg (1995). https://doi.org/10.1007/3-540-44750-4_2
4. Bellare, M., Kilian, J., Rogaway, P.: The security of cipher block chaining. In: Desmedt, Y.G. (ed.) CRYPTO 1994. LNCS, vol. 839, pp. 341–358. Springer, Heidelberg (1994). https://doi.org/10.1007/3-540-48658-5_32
5. Bellare, M., Krovetz, T., Rogaway, P.: Luby-Rackoff backwards: Increasing security by making block ciphers non-invertible. In: Nyberg, K. (ed.) EUROCRYPT 1998. LNCS, vol. 1403, pp. 266–280. Springer, Heidelberg (1998). https://doi.org/10.1007/BFb0054132
6. Bellare, M., Rogaway, P.: The security of triple encryption and a framework for code-based game-playing proofs. In: Vaudenay, S. (ed.) EUROCRYPT 2006. LNCS, vol. 4004, pp. 409–426. Springer, Heidelberg (2006). https://doi.org/10.1007/11761679_25
7. Bernstein, D.J.: How to stretch random functions: the security of protected counter sums. Journal of Cryptology **12**(3), 185–192 (1999). https://doi.org/10.1007/s001459900051
8. Bhattacharya, S., Nandi, M.: Luby-Rackoff backwards with more users and more security. In: Tibouchi, M., Wang, H. (eds.) ASIACRYPT 2021. LNCS, vol. 13092, pp. 345–375. Springer, Cham (2021). https://doi.org/10.1007/978-3-030-92078-4_12
9. Biham, E.: How to decrypt or even substitute des-encrypted messages in 2^{28} steps. Inf. Process. Lett. **84**(3), 117–124 (2002)
10. Bose, P., Hoang, V.T., Tessaro, S.: Revisiting AES-GCM-SIV: multi-user security, faster key derivation, and better bounds. In: Nielsen, J.B., Rijmen, V. (eds.) EUROCRYPT 2018. LNCS, vol. 10820, pp. 468–499. Springer, Cham (2018). https://doi.org/10.1007/978-3-319-78381-9_18
11. Chang, D., Nandi, M.: A short proof of the PRP/PRF switching lemma. Cryptology ePrint Archive, Report 2008/078 (2008). https://eprint.iacr.org/2008/078
12. Chen, Y.L.: A modular approach to the security analysis of two-permutation constructions. In: Agrawal, S., Lin, D. (eds.) Advances in Cryptology – ASIACRYPT 2022. ASIACRYPT 2022. Lecture Notes in Computer Science, vol. 13791. Springer, Cham (2022). https://doi.org/10.1007/978-3-031-22963-3_13
13. Chen, Y.L., Mennink, B., Preneel, B.: Categorization of faulty nonce misuse resistant message authentication. In: Tibouchi, M., Wang, H. (eds.) ASIACRYPT 2021. LNCS, vol. 13092, pp. 520–550. Springer, Cham (2021). https://doi.org/10.1007/978-3-030-92078-4_18
14. Choi, W., Kim, H., Lee, J., Lee, Y.: Multi-user security of the sum of truncated random permutations. In: Agrawal, S., Lin, D. (eds.) Advances in Cryptology – ASIACRYPT 2022. ASIACRYPT 2022. Lecture Notes in Computer Science, vol. 13792. Springer, Cham (2022). https://doi.org/10.1007/978-3-031-22966-4_23

15. Choi, W., Lee, B., Lee, J., Lee, Y.: Toward a fully secure authenticated encryption scheme from a pseudorandom permutation. In: Tibouchi, M., Wang, H. (eds.) Advances in Cryptology – ASIACRYPT 2021. ASIACRYPT 2021. Lecture Notes in Computer Science, vol. 13092. Springer, Cham (2021). https://doi.org/10.1007/978-3-030-92078-4_14

16. Choi, W., Lee, B., Lee, Y., Lee, J.: Improved security analysis for nonce-based enhanced hash-then-mask MACs. In: Moriai, S., Wang, H. (eds.) ASIACRYPT 2020. LNCS, vol. 12491, pp. 697–723. Springer, Cham (2020). https://doi.org/10.1007/978-3-030-64837-4_23

17. Choi, W., Lee, J., Lee, Y.: Building PRFs from TPRPs: beyond the block and the tweak length bounds. Cryptology ePrint Archive, Paper 2022/918 (2022). https://eprint.iacr.org/2022/918

18. Cogliati, B., Lampe, R., Patarin, J.: The indistinguishability of the XOR of k permutations. In: Cid, C., Rechberger, C. (eds.) FSE 2014. LNCS, vol. 8540, pp. 285–302. Springer, Heidelberg (2015). https://doi.org/10.1007/978-3-662-46706-0_15

19. Cogliati, B., Patarin, J.: Mirror theory: A simple proof of the pi+pj theorem with $\xi_{max} = 2$. Cryptology ePrint Archive, Report 2020/734 (2020). https://eprint.iacr.org/2020/734

20. Cogliati, B., Seurin, Y.: EWCDM: an efficient, beyond-birthday secure, nonce-misuse resistant MAC. In: Robshaw, M., Katz, J. (eds.) CRYPTO 2016. LNCS, vol. 9814, pp. 121–149. Springer, Heidelberg (2016). https://doi.org/10.1007/978-3-662-53018-4_5

21. Dai, W., Hoang, V.T., Tessaro, S.: Information-theoretic indistinguishability via the chi-squared method. In: Katz, J., Shacham, H. (eds.) CRYPTO 2017. LNCS, vol. 10403, pp. 497–523. Springer, Cham (2017). https://doi.org/10.1007/978-3-319-63697-9_17

22. Dutta, A., Nandi, M., Saha, A.: Proof of mirror theory for $\xi_{max} = 2$. IEEE Trans. Inf. Theory **68**(9), 6218–6232 (2022)

23. Dutta, A., Nandi, M., Talnikar, S.: Beyond birthday bound secure MAC in faulty nonce model. In: Ishai, Y., Rijmen, V. (eds.) EUROCRYPT 2019. LNCS, vol. 11476, pp. 437–466. Springer, Cham (2019). https://doi.org/10.1007/978-3-030-17653-2_15

24. Hall, C., Wagner, D., Kelsey, J., Schneier, B.: Building PRFs from PRPs. In: Krawczyk, H. (ed.) CRYPTO 1998. LNCS, vol. 1462, pp. 370–389. Springer, Heidelberg (1998). https://doi.org/10.1007/BFb0055742

25. Hoang, V.T., Tessaro, S.: Key-alternating ciphers and key-length extension: exact bounds and multi-user security. In: Robshaw, M., Katz, J. (eds.) CRYPTO 2016. LNCS, vol. 9814, pp. 3–32. Springer, Heidelberg (2016). https://doi.org/10.1007/978-3-662-53018-4_1

26. Hoang, V.T., Tessaro, S.: The multi-user security of double encryption. In: Coron, J.-S., Nielsen, J.B. (eds.) EUROCRYPT 2017. LNCS, vol. 10211, pp. 381–411. Springer, Cham (2017). https://doi.org/10.1007/978-3-319-56614-6_13

27. Impagliazzo, R., Rudich, S.: Limits on the provable consequences of one-way permutations. In: Goldwasser, S. (ed.) CRYPTO 1988. LNCS, vol. 403, pp. 8–26. Springer, New York (1990). https://doi.org/10.1007/0-387-34799-2_2

28. Jha, A., Nandi, M.: Tight security of cascaded LRW2. J. Cryptol. **33**(3), 1272–1317 (2020). https://doi.org/10.1007/s00145-020-09347-y

29. Kim, S., Lee, B., Lee, J.: Tight security bounds for double-block hash-then-sum MACs. In: Canteaut, A., Ishai, Y. (eds.) EUROCRYPT 2020. LNCS, vol. 12105, pp. 435–465. Springer, Cham (2020). https://doi.org/10.1007/978-3-030-45721-1_16

30. Lucks, S.: The sum of PRPs is a secure PRF. In: Preneel, B. (ed.) EUROCRYPT 2000. LNCS, vol. 1807, pp. 470–484. Springer, Heidelberg (2000). https://doi.org/10.1007/3-540-45539-6_34

31. Mennink, B., Neves, S.: Encrypted Davies-Meyer and its dual: towards optimal security using mirror theory. In: Katz, J., Shacham, H. (eds.) CRYPTO 2017. LNCS, vol. 10403, pp. 556–583. Springer, Cham (2017). https://doi.org/10.1007/978-3-319-63697-9_19

32. Minematsu, K.: How to thwart birthday attacks against MACs via small randomness. In: Hong, S., Iwata, T. (eds.) FSE 2010. LNCS, vol. 6147, pp. 230–249. Springer, Heidelberg (2010). https://doi.org/10.1007/978-3-642-13858-4_13

33. Mouha, N., Luykx, A.: Multi-key security: the even-Mansour construction revisited. In: Gennaro, R., Robshaw, M. (eds.) CRYPTO 2015. LNCS, vol. 9215, pp. 209–223. Springer, Heidelberg (2015). https://doi.org/10.1007/978-3-662-47989-6_10

34. Patarin, J.: A proof of security in $O(2^n)$ for the Xor of two random permutations. In: Safavi-Naini, R. (ed.) ICITS 2008. LNCS, vol. 5155, pp. 232–248. Springer, Heidelberg (2008). https://doi.org/10.1007/978-3-540-85093-9_22

35. Patarin, J.: The "Coefficients H" technique. In: Avanzi, R.M., Keliher, L., Sica, F. (eds.) SAC 2008. LNCS, vol. 5381, pp. 328–345. Springer, Heidelberg (2009). https://doi.org/10.1007/978-3-642-04159-4_21

36. Patarin, J.: Mirror theory and cryptography. Appl. Algebra Eng. Commun. Comput. **28**(4), 321–338 (2017). https://doi.org/10.1007/s00200-017-0326-y

37. Shen, Y., Wang, L., Gu, D., Weng, J.: Revisiting the security of DbHtS MACs: beyond-birthday-bound in the multi-user setting. In: Malkin, T., Peikert, C. (eds.) CRYPTO 2021. LNCS, vol. 12827, pp. 309–336. Springer, Cham (2021). https://doi.org/10.1007/978-3-030-84252-9_11

38. Tessaro, S.: Optimally secure block ciphers from ideal primitives. In: Iwata, T., Cheon, J.H. (eds.) ASIACRYPT 2015. LNCS, vol. 9453, pp. 437–462. Springer, Heidelberg (2015). https://doi.org/10.1007/978-3-662-48800-3_18

The Power of Undirected Rewindings for Adaptive Security

Dennis Hofheinz[✉], Julia Kastner[iD], and Karen Klein

Department of Computer Science, ETH Zurich, Zürich, Switzerland
{hofheinz,julia.kastner,karen.klein}@inf.ethz.ch

Abstract. Existing proofs of adaptive security (e.g., in settings in which decryption keys are adaptively revealed) often rely on guessing arguments. Such guessing arguments can be simple (and, e.g., just involve guessing which keys are revealed), or more complex "partitioning" arguments. Since guessing directly and negatively impacts the loss of the corresponding security reduction, this leads to black-box lower bounds for a number of cryptographic scenarios that involve adaptive security.

In this work, we provide an alternative to such guessing arguments: instead of guessing in a security reduction which adaptive choices an adversary $\mathcal{A}$ makes, we *rewind* $\mathcal{A}$ many times until we can successfully embed a given computational challenge. The main benefit of using rewindings is that these rewindings can be arranged sequentially, and the corresponding reduction loss only accumulates additively (instead of multiplicatively, as with guessing). The main technical challenge is to show that $\mathcal{A}$'s success is not negatively affected after (potentially many) rewindings. To this end, we develop a machinery for "undirected" rewindings that preserve $\mathcal{A}$'s success across (potentially many) rewindings.

We use this strategy to show
- security of the "Logical Key Hierarchy" protocol underlying the popular TreeKEM key management protocol, and
- security of the Goldreich-Goldwasser-Micali (GGM) pseudorandom function (PRF) as a prefix-constrained PRF.

In both cases, we provide the first polynomial reductions to standard assumptions (i.e., to IND-CPA and PRG security, respectively), and in case of the GGM PRF, we also circumvent an existing lower bound.

1 Introduction

Security Reductions. The security of most cryptographic primitives implies $P \neq NP$, and hence we cannot expect to simply prove them secure. Instead, we typically rely on *security reductions* that transform a given adversary $\mathcal{A}$ on the primitive into a problem solver $\mathcal{S}$ for a given computational problem.[1] For convincing security guarantees, we often desire reductions to very simple and "static" problems like integer factorization or the discrete logarithm problem in a given group. On the other hand, certain security notions are complex and may

---

[1] Often, $\mathcal{S}$ itself is also denoted as the reduction.

© International Association for Cryptologic Research 2023
H. Handschuh and A. Lysyanskaya (Eds.): CRYPTO 2023, LNCS 14082, pp. 725–758, 2023.
https://doi.org/10.1007/978-3-031-38545-2_24

give $\mathcal{A}$ a lot of freedom to adaptively influence what information is available during an attack.

Adaptive Security Example: Signatures. As a concrete example, the standard notion of security for digital signatures, "EUF-CMA security" [18], allows an adversary $\mathcal{A}$ to receive signatures for arbitrarily and adaptively chosen (by $\mathcal{A}$) messages before expecting $\mathcal{A}$ to actually forge a new signature. Hence, if we view a signature scheme as a collection of "signature generation" problem instances (one for each message m), then $\mathcal{A}$ first expects to see many solutions to adaptively chosen instances before generating a solution to a new instance by itself. Now a security reduction must find a way to embed its own computational challenge X^* into this signature setting, in a way such that all instance solutions requested by $\mathcal{A}$ can be solved, but $\mathcal{A}$'s final forgery implies a solution to X^*.

For signatures, several strategies were found to overcome this difficulty. For instance, "partitioning reductions" (explicitly investigated in [10,20,34], but implicit in many earlier works) embed a given computational challenge X^* in a certain fraction ρ of all signature generation instances (i.e., messages). The hope is that if we choose ρ right, then with small but significant probability, X^* is embedded only in the message on which $\mathcal{A}$ finally forges, but not in any message that needs to be signed by the reduction. This leads to a successful reduction that however fails with a high probability.

Abstraction: Guessing Strategies. We might (informally, and only for the purpose of this exposition) call such reduction strategies "guessing strategies". These reductions make certain random guesses about $\mathcal{A}$'s behavior, and fail if those guesses are not accurate. For certain types of primitives, constructions, or reductions it is often possible to show that there are no better strategies (in terms of reduction loss) than guessing strategies:

- For unique [10] or rerandomizable [19] signature schemes, a certain[2] class of reductions must have a loss that is linear in the number of signature queries.
- For the security of secret-key encryption under adaptive corruptions (as formalized by the "generalized selective decryption" notion, which was introduced to prove adaptive security of the "logical key hierarchy" protocol [30,35]), a similar class of "straight-line" reductions must have a *superpolynomial* reduction loss [23].
- Similar superpolynomial lower bounds [23] affect the related "TreeKEM" protocol [3] for continuous group key agreement, and the GGM pseudorandom function [15] when viewed as a prefix-constrained PRF [5,6,25].

More examples of such lower bounds include specific signature schemes [13], certain types of encryption schemes [1,23,28], non-interactive key exchange [1], and even (composable) zero-knowledge protocols [9].

---

[2] These reductions must use $\mathcal{A}$ in a black-box way and the corresponding computational problem must be non-interactive. This covers a large class of existing reductions.

The intuition for these lower bounds is that the reduction can be forced to guess many of $\mathcal{A}$'s choices simultaneously and early in the security experiment. This induces a reduction loss that is related to the *product* of the probabilities that each guess (for each of $\mathcal{A}$'s choices) is correct. As a consequence, most (although not all) of the above bounds only consider non-rewinding reductions, i.e., reductions that run an adversary $\mathcal{A}$ in a black-box and straightline manner.[3]

Our Contribution. In this work, we consider *rewinding* as an alternative to *guessing* $\mathcal{A}$'s choices. Hence, we design reductions that do not guess, e.g., which parties $\mathcal{A}$ corrupts, but instead (a) run $\mathcal{A}$ in a setting without any embedded challenges, and then (b) rewind and rerun $\mathcal{A}$ in a setting in which challenges have been embedded based on $\mathcal{A}$'s choices in the first run. Of course, it is not clear a priori why this might work (since $\mathcal{A}$'s choices might depend on concrete values that have changed during the runs), and we give details on our concrete strategy and necessary technical conditions below.

The benefit of the use of rewindings over guesses is that guessing n choices of $\mathcal{A}$ simultaneously leads to a reduction loss *exponential* in n. In contrast, with our strategy, the corresponding number of rewindings (when arranged carefully) and thus the reduction loss is only *polynomial* in n.

We apply this idea to two of the above settings. We show

- security of the "logical key hierarchy" (LKH) protocol assuming IND-CPA security of the underlying secret-key encryption scheme, and
- security of the GGM PRF as a prefix-constrained PRF, assuming pseudorandomness of the underlying pseudorandom generator.

The corresponding security reductions have a polynomial loss, and thus circumvent the above-mentioned lower bounds.[4] We believe that these results hint at the potential of using rewindings instead of guessing strategies.

More Related Work on Rewindings. Rewindings have already numerous applications in cryptography, including zero-knowledge simulators [17], signature [31] and even encryption schemes [27]. In some cases, even complex *nested* rewinding strategies have proved useful [9,32]. Jumping ahead, one key difference to our approach is that existing works rewind to a *particular point* in a previous run. For instance, [31] analyze a Fiat-Shamir-based [12] signature scheme in the random oracle model, and rewind an adversary $\mathcal{A}$ to the point where a particular random oracle query (related to $\mathcal{A}$'s eventual forgery) is made. As we will explain below, this means that the second run (after $\mathcal{A}$'s rewinding) may not have the same distribution as the first run (before the rewinding). In other words, such

---

[3] An interesting exception is the work of [10] that does consider rewinding reductions. This is possible because the corresponding signature setting and adversary $\mathcal{A}$ is particularly simple (so that rewinding $\mathcal{A}$ is of little use).

[4] Strictly speaking, in case of LKH, lower bounds are only known for the (very related) "TreeKEM" protocol [23].

"directed rewindings" may change $\mathcal{A}$'s success probability, and complex technical tools like the "forking lemma" [31] may be necessary to analyze such scenarios.

As a consequence, "directed rewindings" may not scale well to settings in which we want to rewind very liberally to replace complex guessing strategies. In contrast, we develop a very different, "undirected" rewinding machinery that will preserve $\mathcal{A}$'s output distribution across rewindings.

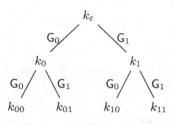

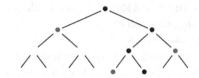

(b) GGM PRF tree with randomized keys along the path (blue •) and co-path (red •) to k_{101}, as desirable when $x^* = 101$ is selected as challenge.

(a) The GGM PRF evaluation.

Fig. 1. The GGM PRF evaluation (Fig. 1a) and tree (Fig. 1b).

1.1 Technical Overview

Example: The GGM PRF. Our approach is perhaps easiest to showcase with the pseudorandom function of Goldreich, Goldwasser, and Micali [15] (henceforth "GGM PRF"). Recall that the GGM PRF starts from a length-doubling pseudorandom generator $G : \{0,1\}^\lambda \to \{0,1\}^{2\lambda}$ written as $G(s) = G_0(s)\|G_1(s)$ for $G_0, G_1 : \{0,1\}^\lambda \to \{0,1\}^\lambda$. The PRF output $F(k, x^*)$, for a PRF key $k \in \{0,1\}^\lambda$ and an input $x^* \in \{0,1\}^d$ (for some fixed input length d) is defined as k_{x^*}, which is iteratively given through

$$k_\varepsilon := k, \quad \forall x \in \{0,1\}^{<d}, b \in \{0,1\} : \ k_{x\|b} := G_b(k_x). \tag{1}$$

This evaluation process is illustrated in Fig. 1a.

The GGM PRF as a Prefix-Constrained PRF. The GGM PRF is known to have a very nice key delegation feature [5,6,25]. Namely, observe that an "intermediate key" $k_{x'}$ (for $0 < |x'| < d$) as defined in (1) allows to compute precisely those outputs k_x that start with x'. Furthermore, $k_{x'}$ can be efficiently computed from k_ε, or even any intermediate key $k_{x''}$ for an x'' that is a prefix of x'. Of course, for security we would also hope that $k_{x'}$ does not reveal anything about outputs k_{x^*} for x^* that do *not* start with x'.

This type of delegation property is called "prefix-constrainability". The corresponding security experiment requires pseudorandomness of a single output $F(k, x^*) = k_{x^*}$ for an adversarially chosen x^*, *even* when that adversary has adaptive access to many constrained keys $k_{x'}$ (where of course no x' may be a prefix of x^*).

Selective Security. To set the stage, we first observe that it is relatively easy to prove a *selective* version of prefix-constrainability, in which the adversary $\mathcal{A}$ has to commit in advance to x^*. Namely, if x^* is known, a reduction could proceed in a hybrid argument and successively embed G-challenges along the path from k_ε to k_{x^*}. This embedding is possible, since $\mathcal{A}$ may not ask for constrained keys $k_{x'}$ that are ancestors of k_{x^*}, and thus no G-preimage will ever have to be revealed. Furthermore, this way, gradually all keys on the path (and co-path) to k_{x^*} will be randomized (see Fig. 1b). Once k_{x^*} itself is independently random, $\mathcal{A}$ cannot win the security game anymore.

The Difficulty. Interestingly, the situation is completely different in the adaptive setting, when $\mathcal{A}$ may ask for constrained keys $k_{x'}$ *before* committing to x^*. The difficulty lies in the fact that $\mathcal{A}$ can force a security reduction to "commit" to a large part of the evaluation tree from Fig. 1a by asking for constrained keys $k_{x'}$, but without finally committing itself to the challenge x^*. This forces a reduction (to the pseudorandomness of G) to decide early on where challenge G-images are to be embedded, and in essence guess (parts of) x^* in advance.

Viewed from a different angle, trying to proceed as in the selective case will require to randomize k_{x^*} and thus, at least in parts, intermediate keys $k_{x'}$ for prefixes x' of x^*, all while being able to (for constrained key queries) explain the rest of the evaluation tree as being pseudorandom. Since $\mathcal{A}$ may choose x^* very late, however, it is not at all clear how to suitably embed G-challenges for this randomization.

In fact, [23] formally prove that no black-box, non-rewinding reduction with polynomial security loss exists in this setting for the GGM PRF. (The hardness of achieving adaptive prefix-constrainability even with more powerful tools and more complex PRF constructions is also explicitly mentioned in [11].) Notwithstanding, [14] do manage to give a black-box, non-rewinding reduction for the GGM PRF with only slightly superpolynomial loss. Their argument is a clever "pebbling strategy" that manages to, informally, guess x^* not all at once, but only in parts. Still, even with this clever strategy, there will be times when several parts of x^* have to be guessed simultaneously, which leads to a superpolynomial security loss.

Our Solution. Our approach is not to guess x^* at all, but to *rewind* an adversary $\mathcal{A}$ in the above setting many times, embedding more and more G-values along the challenge path to k_{x^*} (as in Fig. 1b). Of course, when changing $\mathcal{A}$'s view in any way (and in particular when embedding G-values), the challenge preimage x^* chosen by $\mathcal{A}$ may change completely. Thus, we will have to ensure that during those rewindings, already embedded G-values remain on that challenge path.

To make things clearer, let us first describe a strategy that only *almost* works, but demonstrates the basic ideas. Concretely, consider an adversary $\mathcal{A}$ attacking the GGM PRF of depth $d = 3$, as in Fig. 1b. Without loss of generality, we may assume that $\mathcal{A}$ eventually asks for all keys $k_{x'}$ for x' on the co-path of the challenge path to x^*. (That is, if $\mathcal{A}$ eventually nominates $x^* = 101$ as challenge, we assume that $\mathcal{A}$ will have asked for $k_{x'}$ for all $x' \in \{0, 11, 100\}$.) Intuitively, this means that $\mathcal{A}$ eventually knows the whole evaluation tree except for the challenge path.

Our (preliminary) reduction proceeds as follows:

1. First, run $\mathcal{A}$ on an evaluation tree with fully known keys k_x (for all $x \in \{0, 1\}^{\leq d}$). For concreteness, let us say that the challenge input that $\mathcal{A}$ eventually chooses is $x^* = 101$, as in Fig. 1b.
2. Next, rewind $\mathcal{A}$ back to the point in time t_1 at that k_1, the first intermediate key on the challenge path to k_{101}, is computed. (Since *every* constrained key query requires to commit to k_ε, and hence also compute k_1, this means we rewind to the first constrained key query.) Then, rerun $\mathcal{A}$ from this point t_1 onwards with a fresh G-challenge embedded for (the image of) k_ε.
3. Continue with the rewound run that includes an embedded G-challenge for (the image of) k_ε, and may now feature a new $x^* = 001 \neq 101$. Rewind to the point t_2 in time when the second key $k_{x'}$ along the new challenge path, i.e. a key for the length-2 prefix x' of the new x^*, is computed. Rerun $\mathcal{A}$ from this point t_2 onwards with a fresh G-challenge embedded for (the image of) k_0. This embedding is possible since k_0 is already uniformly random (as it is the output of the first embedded G-challenge), and since this is the first query in which k_0 is used. Unfortunately, this embedding also requires that at no point, any ancestor of $k_{x'}$ will have to be revealed, even when later constrained key queries and even x^* may change after the rewinding. Hence, rewind repeatedly[5], until that particular query at time t_2 is the first one to explicitly use the key for the length-1 prefix of (the now potentially different) x^*.[6] Note that by definition, $t_2 > t_1$, so the new rewindings will not replace the previously embedded G-challenge.
4. Continue with this process for longer prefixes of x^*, eventually embedding the output of a G-challenge into $\mathcal{A}$'s own challenge k_{x^*}. In the resulting run, G-challenges are embedded exactly along the evaluation tree path to the PRF challenge input x^*, as depicted in Fig. 1b for $x^* = 101$. Hence, $\mathcal{A}$'s final output in this run can be used to break the pseudorandomness of G.

We remark that the choice of queries that involve *prefixes* of x^* resembles similar techniques in the signature setting [7,21,29] (and has also been used as an ingredient in the context of the GGM PRF [14]).

A Technical Complication... While the previous description is largely accurate, it glosses over one crucial detail. Namely, recall that we make liberal use of rewindings. Moreover, our final argument implicitly uses that runs generated

---

[5] Polynomially many rewindings will suffice (with high probability), since the condition we require to be preserved is not overly specific.

[6] We are simplifying here. In particular, this step assumes that k_1 is already random, not only a G-challenge. Our actual proof uses a hybrid argument, much like the one for selective security from above.

through rewindings have (at least computationally) the same distribution as non-rewound ones. In particular, $\mathcal{A}$'s success probability must be preserved across rewindings. But this is not guaranteed with "directed rewindings" as above, where the choice of the point in time to rewind to is chosen adaptively, based on what happened pre-rewinding.

To explain the issue, consider the toy example of a one-dimensional random walk

$$T := \sum_{i=1}^{n} t_i \quad \text{for independently uniformly random } t_i \in \{-1, 1\}$$

of length n. Clearly, the expected value of T is 0. On the other hand, if we

1. sample T (and all t_i) as above,
2. then fix the smallest m of a local maximum (such that $t_m = 1$ and $t_{m+1} = -1$), and
3. resample T conditioned on $(t_1, \ldots, t_m)$ (i.e., keeping the values of $(t_1, \ldots, t_m)$),

then the resulting T has a positive expected value. A similar situation may arise in our reduction above: we resample runs with $\mathcal{A}$ conditioned on run prefixes, where the prefix length is based on $\mathcal{A}$'s behavior up to that point. We cannot guarantee that this resampling does not bias, e.g., $\mathcal{A}$'s success probability.

. . . resolved. We will overcome this obstacle with "undirected" rewindings, that rewind to a pre-determined point in time, independently of what happened in the run prior to rewinding. Going back to the toy example of a random walk T, observe that when sampling T and then conditioning on $(t_1, \ldots, t_m)$ for any a-priori fixed prefix length m does not change T's distribution. (Since all t_i are independently random, this is just a complicated way of sampling a single T.) More generally, we will show that rewindings as in our reduction do not change run distributions if the condition itself that we seek to be preserved during rewindings does not depend on the initial run.

Recall that for us, the conditions to be preserved across rewindings are of the form "the query at time t_1 is the first one to explicitly use $k_{x'}$ for a prefix x' of x^*". The problem with this formulation is that this time t_1 depends on the previously sampled run. Our actual solution is hence a bit more complex: we rewind (repeatedly) at *every* time index t, and preserve a function on runs across rewindings. This function is of the form "output the length of the longest prefix x' of x^* such that a key $k_{x'}$ was explicitly computed/defined before or at time t". Preserving this function value across rewindings allows to implement the above reduction strategy, although at the cost of a higher (but still polynomial) number of rewindings.

Second Application: Encryption Security Under Adaptive Corruptions. Our second application concerns the "Logical Key Hierarchy" (LKH) protocol [35] (in the "fixed version" [30]) and the related "TreeKEM" protocol [3] for continuous group key agreement. In these protocols, a binary tree of decryption keys k_x (for $x \in \{0,1\}^{\le d}$) is arranged as in Fig. 1a. Unlike with the GGM PRF setting, the keys k_x themselves are independently chosen. However, for every $x \in \{0,1\}^{<d}$ and $b \in \{0,1\}$, a ciphertext $c_{x\|b}$ that encrypts k_x under key $k_{x\|b}$ is publicly available.[7]

This setup enables the owner of any leaf key k_x to compute the root key k_ε, which can then be used for group communication. We also consider a dynamic setting, in which users leave or join this group. When user x (i.e., the user who owns k_x) leaves, the shared key k_ε and all keys on the path to k_x are refreshed, along with all ciphertexts that encrypt these keys. This requires an update of only $O(|x|)$ many ciphertexts and keys. Similarly, a join only requires the generation of $O(|x|)$ new ciphertexts.

For security, we desire that an adversary who may adaptively initiate leaves and joins, and who learns the corresponding keys k_x of leaving users, cannot distinguish the eventual refreshed root key k_ε from a random key. We will seek to prove security based on the semantic (or IND-CPA) security of the underlying encryption scheme.

Our overall strategy will be similar to the GGM PRF case. However, we will also need to embed challenge ciphertexts (and not only challenge keys) into runs. Besides, one key difference is that in the LKH security experiment, there is no single challenge leaf x^* (as with the GGM PRF). Instead, we will build upon the intricate "pebbling" strategy of [22] to randomize k_ε, only with guesses replaced by rewindings. This will translate into a more complex property to be preserved across rewindings, which also causes a more complex runtime analysis. Concretely, we will have to switch between games with a bounded number of rewindings (to be able to use a reduction to a computational assumption), and ones without such a bound (to be able to switch equivalent preserved properties).

1.2 Roadmap

We recall some relevant preliminaries about probability theory and cryptographic primitives in Sect. 2. In Sect. 3, we give an abstract and application-independent version of our rewinding analysis. In the following sections, we consider the GGM PRF (in Sect. 4) and adaptive encryption security (in Sect. 5) applications.

2   Preliminaries

2.1   Notation

Security Parameter. Throughout the paper, $\lambda \in \mathbb{N}$ denotes the security parameter. Many other variables (such as parameters or distributions) may depend on λ. A function $\delta = \delta(\lambda)$ is *negligible* (in λ) if $\forall c \in \mathbb{N} \; \exists \lambda_0 \; \forall \lambda > \lambda_0 : |\delta(\lambda)| < 1/\lambda^c$.

---

[7] The LKH and TreeKEM protocols are very similar, with one key difference being that the former uses secret-key encryption, while latter employs public-key encryption. Our results are formulated in the secret-key setting and thus directly apply only to LKH (although we are confident that our strategy can also be used for TreeKEM).

Sets and Bitstrings. We write $[n] := \{1, \ldots, n\}$ and $[n]_0 := \{0, 1, \ldots, n\}$. For two sets $\mathcal{X}$, $\mathcal{Y}$ we denote the symmetric difference between $\mathcal{X}$ and $\mathcal{Y}$ as $\mathcal{X} \Delta \mathcal{Y} := (\mathcal{X} \setminus \mathcal{Y}) \cup (\mathcal{Y} \setminus \mathcal{X})$. With $\{0, 1\}^n$, $\{0, 1\}^{\leq n}$, and $\{0, 1\}^{<n}$, we mean all bitstrings of length exactly n, at most n, and less than n, respectively. The lexicographic ordering upon bitstrings x is denoted with $\leq_{\mathsf{lex}}$. If x is a prefix of x', we write $x \leq_{\mathsf{pfx}} x'$, for a proper pefix we write $x <_{\mathsf{pfx}} x'$. For a finite vector $x = (x_1, \ldots, x_n) \in \Sigma^n$ over an alphabet Σ, we denote by $\mathsf{pfx}_j(x)$ the prefix $(x_1, \ldots, x_j)$ of x. The symbol $\|$ denotes string or sequence concatenation.

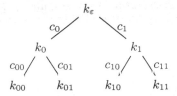

Fig. 2. A depth-2 binary tree with node and edge names.

Tree Notation. For our applications, we will consider complete binary trees whose depth we generally denote by d. We derive generic names for nodes and edges from our applications: concretely, we denote the root node as k_ε (where ε is the empty bitstring), and the two child nodes of each node k_x as $k_{x\|0}$ and $k_{x\|1}$. For each $x \in \{0, 1\}^{<d}$ and $b \in \{0, 1\}$, there is an edge $c_{x\|b}$ between k_x and $k_{x\|b}$. (See Fig. 2 for an example with $d = 2$.) For a binary tree of depth d and a path $P = (k_x, \ldots, k_\varepsilon)$ from a leaf $x \in \{0, 1\}^d$ to the root, the *co-path* of P consists of the sibling vertices of the vertices on P. More formally, writing $x = (x_1, \ldots, x_d)$, the co-path consists of the vertices $(k_{\mathsf{pfx}_{d-1}(x)\|(1-x_d)}, k_{\mathsf{pfx}_{d-2}(x)\|(1-x_{d-1})}, \ldots, k_{1-x_1})$.

Probabilities, Distributions, and Predicates. If $\mathcal{D}$ is a distribution over some set $\mathcal{X}$, then
$$\rho_{\mathcal{D}}(x) := \Pr_{X \leftarrow \mathcal{D}}[X = x].$$

Furthermore, if $f : \mathcal{X} \to \mathcal{Y}$ is a function, then $f(\mathcal{D})$ denotes the distribution over $\mathcal{Y}$ that arises by applying f to values sampled from $\mathcal{D}$. If $\mathrm{P} : \mathcal{X} \to \{\texttt{true}, \texttt{false}\}$ is a predicate, then $\mathcal{D} \mid \mathrm{P}$ denotes the conditional distribution of $\mathcal{D}$ conditioned on $\mathrm{P}(\cdot) = \texttt{true}$. As a special case, we consider equalities as predicates P in the above sense, and may write, e.g., $\mathcal{D} \mid [f(\cdot) = y]$.

For two random variables X, Y (which may depend on the security parameter λ), we write $X \equiv Y$ if they are identically distributed, $X \stackrel{\mathrm{s}}{\approx}_\delta Y$ if their statistical distance is at most δ, and $X \stackrel{\mathrm{c}}{\approx} Y$ if they are computationally indistinguishable.

2.2   Probability Theory

We will need a special Chernoff bound. We state without proof:

Lemma 1. *Let $E_1, \ldots, E_\ell$ be independent events that each occur with probability p. Then*

$$\Pr\left[\bigvee_{t=1}^{\ell} E_t \right] \geq 1 - 1/e^{\ell p/2}.$$

The following lemma is straightforward:

Lemma 2. *Let $\mathcal{D}$ be a distribution over $\mathcal{X}$, and $f : \mathcal{X} \to \mathcal{Y}$ be a function. Consider random variables X, X_0 with*

$$X_0 \leftarrow \mathcal{D} \qquad\qquad X \leftarrow \mathcal{D} \mid [f(\cdot) = f(X_0)].$$

Then X is distributed according to $\mathcal{D}$, i.e., we have $\forall x \in \mathcal{X} : \Pr[X = x] = \Pr[X_0 = x] = \rho_{\mathcal{D}}(x)$.

Intuitively, Lemma 2 states that resampling conditioned on a "current value" $f(X_0)$ does not change the distribution. We defer the proof to the full version.

The next lemma is a probabilistic version of the "bucket lemma" of Kastner, Loss, and Xu [24], which in turn generalizes the "forking lemma" of Pointcheval and Stern [31].

Lemma 3. *Let $\mathcal{D}$ be a distribution over $\mathcal{X}$, and $f : \mathcal{X} \to \mathcal{Y}$ be a function with finite range $\mathcal{Y}$. For any $\alpha \in [0, 1]$,*

$$\Pr_{X \leftarrow \mathcal{D}}\left[\rho_{f(\mathcal{D})}(f(X)) \geq \alpha \right] \geq 1 - \alpha \cdot |\mathcal{Y}|.$$

Intuitively, Lemma 3 states that it is likely that an $X \leftarrow \mathcal{D}$ has a "somewhat common" value of $f(X)$. We defer the proof to the full version.

2.3   Cryptographic Primitives

For convenience, we define pseudorandom number generators (PRGs) with a multi-instance security notion (that is however easily seen to be polynomially equivalent to the ordinary one-instance notion using a hybrid argument):

Definition 1 (($\mathcal{Q}, t, \delta$)-hard pseudorandom generator (PRG)). *An efficiently computable function $\mathsf{G} : \{0,1\}^n \mapsto \{0,1\}^m$ with $m > n$ is a $(\mathcal{Q}, t, \delta)$-hard pseudo-random generator (PRG) if every probabilistic adversary $\mathcal{A}$ that makes at most $\mathcal{Q}$ oracle queries and runs in time at most t satisfies $|\mathrm{Adv}^{\mathrm{PR}}_{\mathsf{G}, \mathcal{A}}(\lambda)| \leq \delta$, where*

$$\mathrm{Adv}^{\mathrm{PR}}_{\mathsf{G}, \mathcal{A}}(\lambda) := \Pr[\mathsf{MI\text{-}PRG}^{\mathcal{A}}_{\mathsf{G}}(\lambda) = 1] - 1/2$$

for the experiment $\mathsf{MI\text{-}PRG}^{\mathcal{A}}_{\mathsf{G}}$ defined in Fig. 3.

Asymptotically, we say that G is a secure PRG if for all polynomials $\mathcal{Q}, t$ in λ, there is a negligible $\delta = \delta(\lambda)$, so that G is a $(\mathcal{Q}, t, \delta)$-hard PRG.

Algorithm 1: MI-PRG$_{\mathsf{F}}^{\mathcal{A}}(\lambda)$	**Algorithm 2:** challenge()
1 $b \leftarrow \{0,1\}$	1 $s \leftarrow \{0,1\}^n$
2 $b' \leftarrow \mathcal{A}^{\text{challenge}}(1^\lambda)$	2 $y_0 := \mathsf{G}(s); y_1 \leftarrow \{0,1\}^m$
3 **return** $[b = b']$	3 **return** y_b

Fig. 3. Multi-instance PRG indistinguishability game

In our setting, we will only be interested in PRGs with $n = \lambda$ and $m = 2\lambda$.

Definition 2 (Prefix-constrained pseudorandom functions). *Consider an efficiently computable function* $\mathsf{F} : \{0,1\}^\lambda \times \{0,1\}^n \rightarrow \{0,1\}^m$ *that takes as input a key* $k \in \{0,1\}^\lambda$ *and an input* $x \in \{0,1\}^n$, *and outputs an image* $y \in \{0,1\}^m$.

We say that F *is a* prefix-constrained pseudorandom function *(PC-PRF) if there are polynomial-time algorithms* constrain *and* ceval *with the following properties:* constrain *may be probabilistic, takes as input a key* $k \in \{0,1\}^\lambda$ *and a prefix* $x' \in \{0,1\}^{\leq n}$, *and outputs a constrained key* $k_{x'}$. ceval *is deterministic, takes as input such a constrained key* $k_{x'}$ *and an input* $x \in \{0,1\}^n$, *and outputs an image* $y \in \{0,1\}^m$. *We require that for all* λ, $k \in \{0,1\}^\lambda$, $k_{x'} \leftarrow$ constrain(k, x'), *and* $x \in \{0,1\}^n$ *with* $x' \leq_{\mathsf{pfx}} x$, *we have*

$$\mathsf{ceval}(k_{x'}, x) = \mathsf{F}(k, x).$$

The main security property of PC-PRFs is indistinguishability:

Definition 3 ($(\mathcal{Q}, t, \delta)$-indistinguishability for PC-PRFs). *Let* F *be a PC-PRF as in Definition 2. We say that* F *is* $(\mathcal{Q}, t, \delta)$-indistinguishable *if for every probabilistic adversary* $\mathcal{A}$ *that runs in time at most* t, *makes at most* $\mathcal{Q}$ *queries to the* constrain *oracle and at most one query to the* challenge *oracle in the* PC-PRF$_{\mathsf{F}, \mathcal{A}}$ *experiment, we have* $|\mathrm{Adv}_{\mathsf{F}, \mathcal{A}}^{\text{PC-PRF}}(\lambda)| \leq \delta$, *where*

$$\mathrm{Adv}_{\mathsf{F}, \mathcal{A}}^{\text{PC-PRF}}(\lambda) := \Pr[\mathsf{PC\text{-}PRF}_{\mathsf{F}}^{\mathcal{A}}(\lambda) = 1] - 1/2$$

for the experiment PC-PRF$_{\mathsf{F}}^{\mathcal{A}}$ *defined in Fig. 4.*

Asymptotically, we say that F *is an* indistinguishable PC-PRF *if for all polynomials* $\mathcal{Q}, t$ *in* λ, *there is a negligible* $\delta = \delta(\lambda)$, *so that* F *is* $(\mathcal{Q}, t, \delta)$-*indistinguishable.*

Algorithm 3: PC-PRF$_F^A(\lambda)$	**Algorithm 4:** constrain(x')
1 $b \leftarrow \{0,1\}$	1 **if** $x' \leq_{\mathsf{pfx}} x^*$ **then return** $\perp$
2 $k \leftarrow \{0,1\}^\lambda$	2 $X := X \cup \{x'\}$
3 $X := \emptyset$	3 $k_{x'} \leftarrow$ constrain(k, x')
4 $x^* := \varepsilon$	4 **return** $k_{x'}$
5 $b' \leftarrow \mathcal{A}^{\text{constrain,challenge}}(1^\lambda)$	
6 **return** $[b = b']$	**Algorithm 5:** challenge(x)
	1 **if** $\exists x' \in X : x' \leq_{\mathsf{pfx}} x$ **then return** $\perp$
	2 $x^* := x$
	3 $y_0^* := F(k, x); y_1^* \leftarrow \{0,1\}^m$
	4 **return** y_b^*

Fig. 4. CP-PRF indistinguishability game

Definition 4 (Secret-key encryption). *A secret-key encryption scheme consists of the following algorithms* SKE = (**Gen, Enc, Dec**):

Gen(1^λ) *takes as input the security parameter encoded in unary, and outputs a key k.*

Algorithm 6: IND-CPA$_{\mathsf{SKE}}^A(\lambda)$	**Algorithm 7:** NU
1 $b \leftarrow \{0,1\}$	1 $k \leftarrow$ **Gen**(1^λ)
2 $U := [\,]$ // empty array	2 $U[\text{len}(U) + 1] := k$ // append to array
3 $b' \leftarrow \mathcal{A}^{LoR,NU}(1^\lambda)$	
4 **return** $[b = b']$	**Algorithm 8:** $LoR(i, m_0, m_1)$
	1 $c \leftarrow$ **Enc**$(U[i], m_b)$ // $\perp$ if $U[i]$ undef'd
	2 **return** c

Fig. 5. Many-user, many-challenge IND-CPA game

Enc(k, m) *takes as input a key k and a message* $m \in \mathcal{M}$, *and outputs a ciphertext c.*

Dec(k, c) *takes as input a key k and a ciphertext c and outputs either a message* $m \in \mathcal{M}$ *or an error symbol* $\perp$.

We require correctness, *i.e.,* $\forall \lambda$, *and* $m \in \mathcal{M}$, *we have*

$$\Pr[\mathbf{Dec}(k, c) = m \mid k \leftarrow \mathbf{Gen}(1^\lambda), c \leftarrow \mathbf{Enc}(k, m)] = 1.$$

Definition 5 (Many-user, many-ciphertext SKE indistinguishability).
A secret-key encryption scheme SKE *is* $(\mathcal{Q}_{\mathsf{LoR}}, \mathcal{Q}_{\mathsf{NU}}, t, \delta)$-*indistinguishable under chosen-plaintext attacks (short:* $(\mathcal{Q}_{\mathsf{ctxt}}, \mathcal{Q}_{\mathsf{NU}}, t, \delta)$-IND-CPA *secure) if every probabilistic adversary* $\mathcal{A}$ *that runs in time at most* t, *and makes at most* $\mathcal{Q}_{\mathsf{LoR}}$ *and* $\mathcal{Q}_{\mathsf{NU}}$

queries to the LoR and NU oracles below, respectively, satisfies $|\mathrm{Adv}_{\mathsf{SKE},\mathcal{A}}^{\mathsf{IND\text{-}CPA}}(\lambda)| \leq$
δ, *where*

$$\mathrm{Adv}_{\mathsf{SKE},\mathcal{A}}^{\mathsf{IND\text{-}CPA}}(\lambda) := \Pr[\mathsf{IND\text{-}CPA}_{\mathsf{SKE}}^{\mathcal{A}}(\lambda) = 1] - 1/2$$

for the $\mathsf{IND\text{-}CPA}_{\mathsf{SKE}}^{\mathcal{A}}$ *experiment defined in Fig. 5.*

Asymptotically, we say that SKE *is* IND-CPA *secure if for all polynomials* $\mathcal{Q}_{\mathsf{LoR}}, \mathcal{Q}_{\mathsf{NU}}, t$ *in* λ, *there is a negligible* $\delta = \delta(\lambda)$, *so that* SKE *is* $(\mathcal{Q}_{\mathsf{LoR}}, \mathcal{Q}_{\mathsf{NU}}, t, \delta)$-IND-CPA *secure.*

We remark that this many-user, many-ciphertext formulation of IND-CPA security is polynomially equivalent (using a standard hybrid argument) to the traditional one-user, one-ciphertext formulation (as in, e.g., [2]).

3 Analysis of a Repeated Resampling Algorithm

Overview. In this section, we will provide a few helper results for our upcoming applications. Specifically, we will investigate what happens when we first sample some X_0 from a distribution (which can be a run with an adversary $\mathcal{A}$), and then resample conditioned on parts of X_0. (This latter operation corresponds to rewinding and rerunning $\mathcal{A}$ until a certain property of the full run is preserved.)

As explained in the introduction, the main difference to previous rewinding treatments is that we consider "undirected" rewindings, which translates to resampling conditioned on a-priori fixed properties of X_0. This will enable us to deduce that this resampling does not change the output distribution, and that resampling is likely to preserve any "sufficiently common" property of the initial X_0 in the process.

Algorithm 9: Repeated resampling, generic

Input: $\mathcal{D}, f_1, \ldots, f_{\mathcal{T}}$
1 $X_0 \leftarrow \mathcal{D}$
2 **for** $t := 1$ **to** $\mathcal{T}$ **do**
3 $\quad \mid \quad X_t \leftarrow \mathcal{D} \mid [f_t(\cdot) = f_t(X_{t-1})]$
4 **end**
5 **return** $X_{\mathcal{T}}$

Generic Framework. In the following, let $\mathcal{D}$ be a distribution over some set $\mathcal{X}$, and assume functions $f_1, \ldots, f_{\mathcal{T}} : \mathcal{X} \to \mathcal{Y}$ for a finite set $\mathcal{Y}$. Now consider Algorithm 9. Algorithm 9 starts with a fresh $\mathcal{D}$-sample, and then repeatedly resamples while preserving the value of the functions f_t on those samples. We have:

Lemma 4. *All X_t defined through Algorithm 9 are distributed according to $\mathcal{D}$, i.e.,* $\forall t, x : \Pr[X_t = x] = \rho_{\mathcal{D}}(x)$.

Proof. For X_0, this is clear. For $X_{t-1} \leftarrow \mathcal{D}$, we obtain $\forall x : \Pr[X_t = x] = \rho_{\mathcal{D}}(x)$ by applying Lemma 2. $\qquad\square$

This in particular holds for Algothim 9's output $X_{\mathcal{T}}$. Hence, Algorithm 9 would seem like an unnecessarily complicated way to sample from $\mathcal{D}$. However, in the following, we will refine Algorithm 9 to better capture our upcoming rewinding process.

Algorithm 10: Repeated resampling, split

    Input: $\mathcal{D}, g_1, \ldots, g_{\mathcal{T}}, h_1, \ldots, h_{\mathcal{T}}$

1 $X_0 \leftarrow \mathcal{D}$

2 for $t := 1$ **to** $\mathcal{T}$ **do**

3   **repeat**

4 | $X_t \leftarrow \mathcal{D} \mid [h_t(\cdot) = h_t(X_{t-1})]$

5   **until** $g_t(X_t) = g_t(X_{t-1})$

6 end

7 return $X_{\mathcal{T}}$

Split Resampling. Now Algorithm 10 performs the generation of the X_t through a different, yet conceptually equivalent form of resampling. More concretely, Algorithm 10 conditions not only on one function value $f_t(X_{t-1})$, but on two function values $g_t(X_{t-1})$ and $h_t(X_{t-1})$. Here, we assume functions $g_t : \mathcal{X} \rightarrow \mathcal{Y}$ and $h_t : \mathcal{X} \rightarrow \mathcal{Z}$ for a finite set $\mathcal{Y}$ and a set $\mathcal{Z}$. This "double resampling" is done in a somewhat peculiar way: the distribution already conditioned on $h_t(X_{t-1})$ is sampled until a value X_t with $g_t(X_t) = g_t(X_{t-1})$ appears. Still, we obtain as before:

Lemma 5. *All X_t defined through Algorithm 10 are distributed according to $\mathcal{D}$, i.e., $\forall t, x : \Pr[X_t = x] = \rho_{\mathcal{D}}(x)$.*

Proof. For any $t \in [\mathcal{T}]$, the **repeat** loop samples X_t from

$$\left(\mathcal{D} \mid [h_t(\cdot) = h_t(X_{t-1})]\right) \mid [g_t(\cdot) = g_t(X_{t-1})] \;=\; \mathcal{D} \mid [f_t(\cdot) = f_t(X_{t-1})]$$

for the function $f_t(X) = (g_t(X), h_t(X))$. Hence, Algorithm 10 is equivalent to Algorithm 9 (for these f_t), and Lemma 4 yields the statement. $\qquad\square$

Additionally, we can bound the runtime of Algorithm 10:

Lemma 6. *Let T_t^{rep} be the number of all iterations of the **repeat** loop for this value of t in Algorithm 10. For any $\gamma \in (0, 1]$, we have*

$$\Pr[\,\forall t \in [\mathcal{T}] : T_t^{\mathsf{rep}} \leq \underbrace{2\mathcal{T} \cdot \ln(2\mathcal{T}/\gamma) \cdot |\mathcal{Y}|/\gamma}_{=:T_{\mathbf{max}}(\mathcal{T}, |\mathcal{Y}|, \gamma)}\,] \;\geq\; 1 - \gamma, \qquad (2)$$

where $\mathcal{Y}$ is the (finite) domain of the g_t.

Proof. First fix a $t \in [\mathcal{T}]$. By Lemma 5, X_{t-1} is distributed according to $\mathcal{D}$. Hence, using Lemma 2, X_{t-1} is also distributed according to

$$\mathcal{D}' := \mathcal{D} \mid [h_t(\cdot) = h_t(X^*)]$$

for some independently chosen $X^* \leftarrow \mathcal{D}$. Since $h_t(X_t) = h_t(X^*)$ by definition, in each iteration of Line 4, X_t is also distributed according to $\mathcal{D}'$. Now invoke Lemma 3 with $\alpha := \gamma/(2\mathcal{T} \cdot |\mathcal{Y}|)$, distribution $\mathcal{D}'$, and function g_t. This yields

$$\Pr_{X_t \leftarrow \mathcal{D}'}[g_t(X_t) = g_t(X_{t-1})] \geq \alpha, \tag{3}$$

except with probability $\gamma/(2\mathcal{T})$ (over X_{t-1}).

Recall that T_t^{rep} is the number of iterations of the **repeat** loop for this t. Conditioned on (3), Lemma 1 (instantiated with E_t as the event that the t-th iteration succeeds, $p := \alpha$, and $\ell := 2\ln(2\mathcal{T}/\gamma)/\alpha$) shows

$$\Pr\left[T_t^{\mathsf{rep}} \leq \frac{2\ln(2\mathcal{T}/\gamma)}{\alpha}\right] \geq 1 - \frac{\gamma}{2\mathcal{T}}, \tag{4}$$

where the probability is taken (only) over the resamplings in the loop. Now a union bound shows that (3) and the bound from (4) hold for all t, except with probability γ. This finally yields (2). $\qquad\qquad\square$

The split approach of Algorithm 10 reflects our upcoming rewinding scenario. In particular, conditioning on a "common partial history" $h_t(X_t) = h_t(X_{t-1})$ will correspond to rewinding a simulation up to the t-th "branching point", while $g_t(X_t) = g_t(X_{t-1})$ is a condition we hope the rewound simulation to fulfill. We will be able to sample from $\mathcal{D} \mid [h_t(\cdot) = h_t(X_{t-1})]$ directly through rewinding, but will then have to condition on $g_t(\cdot) = g_t(X_{t-1})$ by a brute-force **repeat** loop.

4   Adaptive Security for the GGM PC-PRF

In this section we use the results on repeated resampling from Sect. 3 to prove that the PRF construction by Goldreich, Goldwasser and Micali [16] is adaptively secure as a prefix-constrained pseudorandom function (PC-PRF), based on the security of the underlying PRG.

Definition 6 (GGM PRF). *Given a length-doubling PRG* $\mathsf{G} : \{0,1\}^\lambda \to \{0,1\}^{2\lambda}$ *and an input length* $d = d(\lambda)$, *the GGM PRF* $\mathsf{F}_d : \{0,1\}^\lambda \times \{0,1\}^d \to \{0,1\}^\lambda$ *with key space* $\{0,1\}^\lambda$ *is defined as*

$$\mathsf{F}_d(k, x) = k_x \text{ where } k_\varepsilon = k \text{ and } \forall x' \in \{0,1\}^{<d} : k_{x'\|0}\|k_{x'\|1} = \mathsf{G}(k_{x'}).$$

It was noted independently in [5,25], and [6] that the above PRF construction allows for the use as a prefix-constrained PRF (PC-PRF), with

$$\mathsf{constrain}(k, x') := (x', \mathsf{F}_{|x'|}(k, x')) = (x', k_{x'}) \text{ for } x' \in \{0,1\}^{<d}.$$

For ease of presentation, in the following we will often refer to $k_{x'}$ as the constrained key for x'. The algorithm ceval, on input a constrained key $(x', k_{x'})$ for a prefix x' of x and the string $x = x'\|x'' \in \{0,1\}^d$, then computes k_x as

$$\mathsf{ceval}((x', k_{x'}), x) := \mathsf{constrain}(k_{x'}, x'').$$

4.1 Proving Security from PR

We now define the security experiment $\mathrm{Exp}_{G,\mathcal{A},d}^{\mathsf{GGMPRF}}$. Security in the sense of the following definition immediately implies adaptive security of the GGM PC-PRF (see also Remark 1).

Definition 7 (GGMPRFsecurity experiment). *Let* $G : \{0,1\}^\lambda \to \{0,1\}^{2\lambda}$ *be a length-doubling PRG, let* $d = d(\lambda)$ *an input length, and let* $\mathcal{A}$ *be a probabilistic adversary. We denote the first half of the output of* G *on input* k *by* $G_0(k)$, *the second half by* $G_1(k)$. *The experiment* $\mathrm{Exp}_{G,\mathcal{A},d}^{\mathsf{GGMPRF}}$ *initially samples uniformly at random a challenge bit* $b_{\mathsf{ggmprf}} \leftarrow \{0,1\}$ *and a key* $k_\varepsilon \leftarrow \{0,1\}^\lambda$. *The adversary* $\mathcal{A}$ *can then make the following queries:*

- *$\mathcal{A}$ can adaptively make corruption queries for strings $x \in \{0,1\}^{\leq d}$. This initiates the computation of all so far undefined keys $k_{x'b}$ with $x' <_{\mathsf{pfx}} x$ and $b \in \{0,1\}$ as $k_{x'b} := G_b(k_{x'})$, and exposes k_x to $\mathcal{A}$.*
- *At any point, $\mathcal{A}$ may stop the game and ask to be challenged on $x^* \in \{0,1\}^d$, and then has to distinguish the real key k_{x^*} (case $b_{\mathsf{ggmprf}} = 0$) from a random key (case $b_{\mathsf{ggmprf}} = 1$). To make the game non-trivial, for the challenge x^* it must hold that no corruption of any prefix of x^* was made throughout the game.*

The output of the experiment is 1 if $\mathcal{A}$ correctly guesses the bit b_{ggmprf}, and 0 otherwise. We define the advantage of $\mathcal{A}$ in this game as

$$\mathrm{Adv}_{G,\mathcal{A},d}^{\mathsf{GGMPRF}}(\lambda) := \Pr[\mathrm{Exp}_{G,\mathcal{A},d}^{\mathsf{GGMPRF}}(\lambda) = 1] - 1/2.$$

We say that GGMPRF *security holds (for* G *and* d*) if* $\mathrm{Adv}_{G,\mathcal{A},d}^{\mathsf{GGMPRF}}(\lambda)$ *is negligible for every probabilistic polynomial-time* $\mathcal{A}$.

One can view this security experiment as a game on a binary tree of depth d as defined in Sect. 2.1, where the adversary can adaptively compromise labels k_x. For security, we require that keys that cannot be computed trivially from compromised keys should remain pseudorandom.

Remark 1. We note that we consider adversaries that make their challenge query as the last query. This is not a restriction as any adaptive adversary can be transformed into such an adversary with only d additional constrained key queries, using the following reduction: All queries and responses until the challenge query are forwarded. Once the adversary submits the challenge query, the reduction queries all constrained keys on the co-path before forwarding the challenge query and its response. To answer any future constrained key queries, the reduction uses the previously queried constrained keys on the co-path.

To see that security of the GGM PRF as a PC-PRF follows from our results on the GGMPRF security experiment, note that a reduction can answer adversarial constrained key queries and PRF evaluation queries in the PC-PRF security experiment for the GGM PRF by making corresponding corruption queries in the GGMPRF security experiment. In particular, this means that for any adversary $\mathcal{A}$ that has advantage $\mathrm{Adv}_{G,\mathcal{A},d}^{\mathsf{GGMPRF}}(\lambda)$, runs in time $t_{\mathcal{A}}$, and makes $\mathcal{Q}_{\mathsf{corrupt}}$ constrained key queries, there exists an adversary $\mathcal{B}$ that runs in time $t_{\mathcal{B}}$ roughly equal[8] to $t_{\mathcal{A}}$ with

$$\mathrm{Adv}_{F_d,\mathcal{A}}^{\mathsf{PC\text{-}PRF}}(\lambda) = \mathrm{Adv}_{G,\mathcal{A},d}^{\mathsf{GGMPRF}}(\lambda)$$

and makes $\mathcal{Q}'_{\mathsf{corrupt}} \leq \mathcal{Q}_{\mathsf{corrupt}} + d$ constrained key queries.

Our Strategy. Let us fix a length-doubling PRG G and a depth/input length $d = d(\lambda)$. Let us first consider a *selective* setting where an adversary $\mathcal{A}$ has to commit to the challenge x^* in the beginning of the game. For this setting, we can bound the success probability of any PPT adversary $\mathcal{A}$ by a sequence of $d + 1$ hybrid games where in the ith hybrid game, the first i PRG evaluations on the path from the root to x^* are replaced by random sampling, i.e. the keys $k_{x\|0}, k_{x\|1}$ for all $x \preceq_{\mathsf{pfx}} x^*$ with $|x| < l$ are sampled uniformly at random instead of computing $G(k_x)$. For each $i \in [d]$, one can then prove that games $i-1$ and i are indistinguishable based on the security of the PRG G. Furthermore, since in game d, the key k_{x^*} is sampled independently and uniformly at random, the cases $b_{\mathsf{ggmprf}} = 0$ and $b_{\mathsf{ggmprf}} = 1$ are information-theoretically indistinguishable, hence the advantage of $\mathcal{A}$ is 0 in this game. We thus obtain an upper bound on $\mathcal{A}$'s advantage in the selective GGMPRF experiment in terms of PR security of the PRG G, with a security loss linear in d.

Also in the adaptive setting, where $\mathcal{A}$ can make its choices on the fly, we will bound $\mathcal{A}$'s advantage to win the GGMPRF game through a similar hybrid argument. Again, we will start with the original GGMPRF game above and apply a number of successive changes until finally $\mathcal{A}$'s view is independent of the challenge bit b_{ggmprf}. Since we make a liberal use of rewindings, it will be helpful to formalize $\mathcal{A}$'s view:

Definition 8 (Adversarial view). *In a run of the experiment* $\mathrm{Exp}_{G,\mathcal{A},d}^{\mathsf{GGMPRF}}$ *from Definition 7, we define $\mathcal{A}$'s view* $\mathsf{view}_{\mathcal{A}}$ *in this run as a sequence* $(\mathsf{ev}_1, \ldots, \mathsf{ev}_\ell)$ *of events, where each* ev_i *can be one of the following:*

Query. *One of $\mathcal{A}$'s queries (without reply), either of the form* $(\mathsf{corrupt}, x)$ *for a corruption query, or* $(\mathsf{challenge}, x^*)$.

New keys. *Every time new keys* $k_{x\|0}, k_{x\|1}$ *are defined, right before that, a corresponding* (PRG, x) *event is appended to* view. *Concretely, a query* $(\mathsf{corrupt}, x)$ *or* $(\mathsf{challenge}, x^*)$ *in* view *automatically causes also entries* (PRG, x') *for all proper prefixes x' of x for which no* PRG *query has been issued yet, to be appended immediately after that* $(\mathsf{corrupt}, x)$ *entry. Entries* (PRG, x) *defined at the same time are ordered in* view *with keys closer to the root (i.e., with shorter x) first.*

Corrupted key. *A key* (key, x, k_x) *as a response to a corruption query.*

---

[8] By "roughly equal", we mean that $\mathcal{B}$ runs $\mathcal{A}$ only once, but as discussed with up to d added oracle queries and some additional constrain operations.

Challenge key. *The response to the final challenge query, in the form* (challenge, x^*, k) *(i.e., depending on* b_{ggmprf} *with either* k *being the real key* k_{x^*} *or a random value). This event comes after the corresponding* (PRG, x) *events which are triggered by the challenge query.*

Decision bit. *The final output bit* $b_{\mathcal{A}}$ *of* $\mathcal{A}$, *in the form* (guess, $b_{\mathcal{A}}$). *This event is the last in* view, *and we may write* $\text{out}_{\mathcal{A}}(\text{view})$ *to denote that bit* $b_{\mathcal{A}}$.

We are now ready to formulate and prove our main result:

Theorem 1. *Let* $G : \{0,1\}^\lambda \to \{0,1\}^{2\lambda}$ *be a PRG. Then*

- *for every* GGMPRF *adversary* $\mathcal{A}$ *that runs in time* $t_{\mathcal{A}}$ *and makes at most* $\mathcal{Q}_{\text{corrupt}}$ *corrupt queries,*
- *for every* GGMPRF *depth* d *and every* $\gamma \in (0,1]$,

there is a PR *adversary* $\mathcal{B}$ *that runs in time* $t_{\mathcal{B}}$, *makes at most* $\mathcal{Q}_{\mathcal{B}}$ *oracle queries, and for which*

$$\text{Adv}_{G,\mathcal{B}}^{\text{PR}}(\lambda) \geq \frac{1}{2d} \cdot \left(\text{Adv}_{G,\mathcal{A},d}^{\text{GGMPRF}}(\lambda) - \gamma \right), \tag{5}$$

where

$$t_{\mathcal{B}} \lessapprox \left(2 \cdot \ln\left(2 \cdot \mathcal{T}/\gamma\right) \cdot \mathcal{T}^4/\gamma \right) \cdot t_{\mathcal{A}} \quad and \quad \mathcal{Q}_{\mathcal{B}} \leq 2 \cdot \ln\left(2 \cdot \mathcal{T}/\gamma\right) \cdot \mathcal{T}^3/\gamma \tag{6}$$

with $\mathcal{T} \leq ((d+2) \cdot \mathcal{Q}_{\text{corrupt}} + 2)$.

Before we proceed to a proof, we notice that Theorem 1 implies asymptotic security when setting γ accordingly:

Corollary 1 (G secure $\Rightarrow$ GGM PRF secure PC-PRF). *If* G *is a secure PRG (as in Definition 1) and* $d = d(\lambda)$ *is a polynomial, then the GGM PRF* F_d *is an indistinguishable PC-PRF (as in Definition 3).*

Proof of Corollary 1. Assume for contradiction that there is a polynomial-time adversary $\mathcal{A}'$ against the PC-PRF indistinguishability with non-negligible advantage. By Remark 1, this immediately yields a polynomial-time GGMPRF adversary $\mathcal{A}$ with (the same) non-negligible advantage $\varepsilon_{\mathcal{A}} := \text{Adv}_{G,\mathcal{A},d}^{\text{GGMPRF}}(\lambda)$. Since $\varepsilon_{\mathcal{A}}$ is non-negligible, there exists a polynomial p such that for infinitely many values of λ, we have $\varepsilon_{\mathcal{A}} \geq 1/p(\lambda)$.

Now set $\gamma = 1/(2p(\lambda))$ and invoke Theorem 1. We obtain a PR adversary $\mathcal{B}$ with (by (6)) polynomial runtime and non-negligible advantage

$$\text{Adv}_{G,\mathcal{B}}^{\text{PR}}(\lambda) \overset{(5)}{\geq} \frac{1}{2d} \cdot (\varepsilon_{\mathcal{A}} - \gamma) \overset{(*)}{\geq} \frac{1}{2d} \cdot \left(\frac{1}{p(\lambda)} - \gamma \right) = \frac{1}{4d \cdot p(\lambda)},$$

where $(*)$ holds (only) for infinitely many λ. $\qquad\qquad\square$

Proof of Theorem 1. Fix $\mathcal{A}$ and d. In the following, we will consider a number of hybrid games, with Game ggmprf being the original GGMPRF experiment. Denoting with out_i the output of Game i, we trivially get

$$\Pr[\text{out}_{\text{ggmprf}} = 1] = \text{Adv}_{G,\mathcal{A},d}^{\text{GGMPRF}}(\lambda) + 1/2. \tag{7}$$

Moving on, we will formulate Game i (for $0 \leq i \leq d$) in a (for us) convenient way, see Algorithm 11. This formulation outsources the bulk of the game into the sampling of $\mathcal{A}$'s view view from a suitable distribution $\mathcal{D}^{\text{view}}_{i,b_{\text{ggmprf}}}$. In our upcoming refinements, we will only change $\mathcal{D}^{\text{view}}_{i,b_{\text{ggmprf}}}$ and investigate the effects on out_i.

Algorithm 11: Game i, with the bulk of the work outsourced into the sampling from $\mathcal{D}^{\text{view}}_{i,b_{\text{ggmprf}}}$.

---

1 $b_{\text{ggmprf}} \leftarrow \{0,1\}$
2 view $\leftarrow \mathcal{D}^{\text{view}}_{i,b_{\text{ggmprf}}}$ // view has the format from Definition 8
3 **return** $[b_{\text{ggmprf}} = \text{out}_\mathcal{A}(\text{view})]$ // returns 1 iff $b_{\text{ggmprf}} = \text{out}_\mathcal{A}(\text{view})$

The Distributions $\mathcal{D}^{\text{view}}_{i,b_{\text{ggmprf}}}$. To define the distribution $\mathcal{D}^{\text{view}}_{i,b_{\text{ggmprf}}}$ for Game i with $i \in [d]_0$, we use the following notation:

- $\mathcal{D}^{\text{view}}_{\text{ggmprf},b_{\text{ggmprf}}}$ is the distribution of $\mathcal{A}$-views (as in Definition 8) that is induced by running the GGMPRF experiment with challenge bit b_{ggmprf} (that decides whether $\mathcal{A}$ is challenged with k_{x^*} or a random key).
- $\text{len}(\text{view})$ is the length of a given $\mathcal{A}$-view view (measured in events).
- $\text{pfx}_t(\text{view})$ outputs the prefix of view up to (and including) the t-th event (as defined in Sect. 2.1).
- $\text{lastpre}_t(\text{view})$ on input view $= (\text{ev}_1, \ldots, \text{ev}_\mathcal{T})$ outputs the largest index $t' \leq t$ such that event $\text{ev}_{t'}$ defines a key on the path from the root to x^*, i.e.,

$$\text{lastpre}_t(\text{view}) := \max\left(\left\{ t' \;\middle|\; \begin{array}{c} \text{ev}_{t'} = (\text{PRG}, x) \\ \wedge\, t' \leq t \,\wedge\, x <_{\text{pfx}} x^* \end{array} \right\} \cup \{0\}\right).$$

- $B \in \mathbb{N}$ is a bound on the number of repetitions of Lines 6 to 13 in Algorithm 12 for each t. In case of B unsuccessful repetitions for one t, the whole algorithm outputs $\perp$. We will fix a suitable value for B later.

Now consider Algorithm 12. Our distribution $\mathcal{D}^{\text{view}}_{i,b_{\text{ggmprf}}}$ will be defined almost like $\mathcal{D}^{\text{view}}_{\text{ggmprf},b_{\text{ggmprf}}}$ (i.e., like $\mathcal{A}$'s view in a GGMPRF run), but will additionally replace PRG evaluations by random sampling as indicated by index i and use rewindings at every step. Concretely, fix an i and consider Algorithm 12, which programmatically defines $\mathcal{D}^{\text{view}}_{i,b_{\text{ggmprf}}}$ as its output.

For an adversary $\mathcal{A}$ with view view $= (\text{ev}_1, \ldots, \text{ev}_\mathcal{T})$ we denote by *rewinding* the adversary to time t the cutting-off of the view at point $t - 1$, i.e. $(\text{ev}_1, \ldots, \text{ev}_{t-1})$ and resetting the adversary to the state it had directly before ev_t. (By keeping track of $\mathcal{A}$'s state throughout our rewindings, this will always be possible.)

We say we *resample* from point t (after rewinding $\mathcal{A}$ to t) if we rerun $\mathcal{A}$ from t onwards, using fresh challenger random coins from that point onwards. In some cases, we will also rerun $\mathcal{A}$ with a specific replacement (e.g., an embedded computational challenge) in ev_t (if ev_t contains an answer to one of $\mathcal{A}$'s previous queries). The view resulting from rewinding to t and then resampling from point t is $\mathsf{view}' = (\mathsf{ev}_1, \ldots, \mathsf{ev}_{t-1}, \mathsf{ev}'_t, \ldots, \mathsf{ev}'_{\mathcal{T}'})$.

Algorithm 12: Sampler for $\mathcal{D}^{\mathsf{view}}_{i,b_{\mathsf{ggmprf}}}$

Input: $i \in \{0, \ldots, d\}, b_{\mathsf{ggmprf}} \in \{0,1\}, B \in \mathbb{N}$ // $\mathsf{len}, \mathsf{lastpre}_{i,t}, B$ described in proof

1 $\mathsf{view}_0 \leftarrow \mathcal{D}^{\mathsf{view}}_{\mathsf{ggmprf}, b_{\mathsf{ggmprf}}}$
2 $\mathcal{T} := \mathsf{len}(\mathsf{view}_{\mathsf{GGMPRF}})$ // Length of $\mathsf{view}_{\mathsf{GGMPRF}}$ (in entries)
3 **for** $t := 1$ **to** $\mathcal{T}$ **do**
4   Write $\mathsf{view}_{t-1} = (\mathsf{ev}_{t-1,1}, \ldots, \mathsf{ev}_{t-1,\mathcal{T}})$
5   **repeat**   // Output $\bot$ if B repetitions fail for this t
6   Rewind adversary to point t
7   **if** $\mathsf{ev}_{t-1,t} = (\mathsf{PRG}, x)$ *with* $|x| \le i$ *and* $\mathsf{lastpre}_t(\mathsf{view}_{t-1}) = t$ **then**
          // Checks if $\mathsf{ev}_{t-1,t}$ defines a PRG evaluation to be replaced
          by random
8   Sample fresh $k_{x\|0}, k_{x\|1} \leftarrow \{0,1\}^\lambda$ // Fresh independent keys
9   Resample from point $t+1$ to obtain
             $\mathsf{view}_t = (\mathsf{ev}_{t-1,0}, \ldots, \mathsf{ev}_{t-1,t-1}, \mathsf{ev}_{t-1,t}, \mathsf{ev}_{t,t+1}, \ldots, \mathsf{ev}_{t,\tau})$
10   **else**
11   Resample from point t to obtain
             $\mathsf{view}_t = (\mathsf{ev}_{t-1,0}, \ldots, \mathsf{ev}_{t-1,t-1}, \mathsf{ev}_{t,t}, \ldots, \mathsf{ev}_{t,\tau})$
12   **end**
13   **until** $\mathsf{lastpre}_t(\mathsf{view}_t) = \mathsf{lastpre}_t(\mathsf{view}_{t-1})$ *and* $\mathsf{len}(\mathsf{view}_t) = \mathsf{len}(\mathsf{view}_{t-1})$
14 **end**
15 **return** $\mathsf{view}_{\mathcal{T}}$

Game ggmprf $\overset{\equiv}{\rule{1.5em}{0pt}}$ $\mathcal{D}^{\mathsf{view}}_{0,b_{\mathsf{ggmprf}}}$

$$\Big\downarrow \approx_\gamma^s$$

$$\mathcal{D}^{\mathsf{view}}_{0,b_{\mathsf{ggmprf}}} \overset{c}{\approx} \mathcal{D}^{\mathsf{view}}_{1,b_{\mathsf{ggmprf}}} \overset{c}{\approx} \mathcal{D}^{\mathsf{view}}_{2,b_{\mathsf{ggmprf}}} \overset{c}{\approx} \cdots \overset{c}{\approx} \mathcal{D}^{\mathsf{view}}_{d,b_{\mathsf{ggmprf}}}$$

Fig. 6. Sequence of hybrids. Perfect indistinguishability ($\equiv$) is shown in Proposition 1, statistical distance ($\approx_\gamma^s$) is shown in Proposition 2, and computational indistinguishability ($\overset{c}{\approx}$) is shown in proposition 3.

Having defined our hybrid distributions $\mathcal{D}^{\mathsf{view}}_{i,b_{\mathsf{ggmprf}}}$, we will additionally consider the distribution $\widetilde{\mathcal{D}}^{\mathsf{view}}_{0,b_{\mathsf{ggmprf}}}$ which is defined as the output of a variant of Algorithm 12 for $i = 0$ without a bound B on the runtime. (Hence, $\widetilde{\mathcal{D}}^{\mathsf{view}}_{0,b_{\mathsf{ggmprf}}}$ will not be efficiently sampleable in general.) We will first show that the distribution $\widetilde{\mathcal{D}}^{\mathsf{view}}_{0,b_{\mathsf{ggmprf}}}$ coincides with the distribution of views in Game ggmprf. Here we will use our results from Sect. 3, namely Lemma 5, for the distribution $\mathcal{D} = \mathcal{D}^{\text{view}}_{\text{ggmprf}, b_{\text{ggmprf}}}$ where functions h_t on input view will output the $(t-1)$-sized prefix of view, and resampling conditioned on $h_t(\text{view})$ simply means rewinding and rerunning from point t. The stopping conditions $g_t(\text{view})$ will preserve (1) the value of $\text{lastpre}_t(\text{view})$, and (2) the length of view. Intuitively, preserving $\text{lastpre}_t(\text{view})$ implies that "PRG embedding slots" along the path to the challenge x^* defined prior to point t remain the same. This implies that no preimages of previously embedded PRG images have to be revealed, and the rewinding did not "undo" any of the progress made so far.

Again using our results from Sect. 3, namely Lemma 6 with similar interpretation as above, we will then choose the bound B such that the probability of an abort in $\mathcal{D}^{\text{view}}_{0, b_{\text{ggmprf}}}$ can be bounded by γ. Then we will show that $\mathcal{A}$ has no advantage in Game d since the view sampled according to $\mathcal{D}^{\text{view}}_{d, b_{\text{ggmprf}}}$ is independent of b_{ggmprf}. Finally, we will argue that $\mathcal{D}^{\text{view}}_{0, b_{\text{ggmprf}}}$ is computationally indistinguishable from $\mathcal{D}^{\text{view}}_{d, b_{\text{ggmprf}}}$ by the pseudorandomness of G. Combining these results will allow us to conclude the proof. Our path along this sequence of hybrids can be seen in Fig. 6. □

Proposition 1. $\mathcal{D}^{\text{view}}_{\text{ggmprf}, b_{\text{ggmprf}}} \equiv \widetilde{\mathcal{D}^{\text{view}}_{0, b_{\text{ggmprf}}}}.$

Proof. This follows from Lemma 5, where $\mathcal{D} = \mathcal{D}^{\text{view}}_{\text{ggmprf}, b_{\text{ggmprf}}}$, $h_t(\text{view}_s) = (\text{ev}_{s,1}, \ldots, \text{ev}_{s,t-1})$, and $g_t(\text{view}_s) = (\text{lastpre}_t(\text{view}_s), \text{len}(\text{view}_s))$. We note that for $i = 0$, the **if** on Line 7 never returns true, and thus the sampling procedure always enters the **else** branch which behaves just as in Lemma 5. □

Proposition 2 (Abort probability). *For*

$$B := 2 \cdot \ln\left(2 \cdot ((d+2) \cdot \mathcal{Q}_{\text{corrupt}} + 2)/\gamma\right) \cdot ((d+2) \cdot \mathcal{Q}_{\text{corrupt}} + 2)^3 / \gamma,$$

we have $\Pr[\perp \leftarrow \mathcal{D}^{\text{view}}_{0, b_{\text{lkh}}}] \leq \gamma.$

Proof. To prove this claim, we consider the process of sampling from $\mathcal{D}^{\text{view}}_{0, b_{\text{lkh}}}$ according to Algorithm 12 and bound the probability that any of the iterations in the "**for**" loop runs the "**repeat**" loop more than B times.

By Lemma 6, with $g_t(\text{view}) = (\text{lastpre}_t(\text{view}), \text{len}(\text{view}))$ and $h_t(\text{view}) = (\text{ev}_1, \ldots, \text{ev}_t)$ for $\text{view} = (\text{ev}_1, \ldots, \text{ev}_{\text{len}(\text{view})})$, it holds that for any $\gamma \in (0, 1]$ (thus in particular the γ from the theorem statement)

$$\Pr[\forall t \in [T] : T_t^{\text{rep}} \leq 2T \cdot \ln(2T/\gamma) \cdot |\mathcal{Y}|/\gamma] \geq 1 - \gamma \tag{8}$$

where T_t^{rep} denotes the number of runs of the "**repeat**" loop in the t-th iteration of the "**for**" loop. We note that

$$\text{len}(\text{view}) \leq \underbrace{\mathcal{Q}_{\text{corrupt}} + 1}_{\text{Query Events}} + \underbrace{d \cdot \mathcal{Q}_{\text{corrupt}} +}_{\text{PRG Events}} \underbrace{\mathcal{Q}_{\text{corrupt}} + 1}_{\text{Corr./Chal. Key Events}}$$

for any view resulting from a run of an adversary that makes at most $\mathcal{Q}_{\text{corrupt}}$ constrained key queries. This means that $\text{len}(\text{view})$ can take values up to

$\mathcal{T}_{\max} = (d+2) \cdot \mathcal{Q}_{\mathsf{corrupt}} + 2$. Furthermore, $\mathsf{lastpre}_t(\mathsf{view})$ takes values from 0 to $\mathsf{len}(\mathsf{view})$. Thus, we can bound the size of the range $\mathcal{Y}$ of the g_t with $|\mathcal{Y}| \leq ((d+2) \cdot \mathcal{Q}_{\mathsf{corrupt}} + 2)^2$.

Plugging this into (8) yields

$$\Pr\left[\forall t \in [\mathcal{T}] : T_t^{\mathsf{rep}} \leq 2\mathcal{T} \cdot \ln(2\mathcal{T}/\gamma) \cdot ((d+2) \cdot \mathcal{Q}_{\mathsf{corrupt}} + 2)^2 /\gamma \right] \geq 1 - \gamma. \quad (9)$$

Thus, using the bound for $\mathsf{len}(\mathsf{view})$ for $\mathcal{T}$ again, i.e. $\mathcal{T} \leq (d+2) \cdot \mathcal{Q}_{\mathsf{corrupt}} + 2$, gives $\Pr\left[\forall t \in [\mathcal{T}] : T_t^{\mathsf{rep}} \leq B \right] \geq 1 - \gamma$. which yields the claim.   □

Proposition 3 (PR $\Rightarrow \mathcal{D}_{0,b_{\mathsf{ggmprf}}}^{\mathsf{view}} \overset{c}{\approx} \mathcal{D}_{d,b_{\mathsf{ggmprf}}}^{\mathsf{view}}$). *Let B be as in Claim 2. If G is PR secure, then the distributions $\mathcal{D}_{0,b_{\mathsf{ggmprf}}}^{\mathsf{view}}$ and $\mathcal{D}_{d,b_{\mathsf{ggmprf}}}^{\mathsf{view}}$ are computationally indistinguishable. More precisely, there exists a PR adversary $\mathcal{C}$ that runs in time $t_{\mathcal{C}}$ and makes $\mathcal{Q}_{\mathcal{C}}$ oracle queries, such that*

$$\mathsf{Adv}_{\mathsf{G},\mathcal{C}}^{\mathsf{PR}}(\lambda) = \frac{1}{2d} \cdot \left(\mathsf{Adv}_{\mathsf{G},\mathcal{A},d}^{\mathsf{GGMPRF},0}(\lambda) - \mathsf{Adv}_{\mathsf{G},\mathcal{A},d}^{\mathsf{GGMPRF},d}(\lambda) \right) \quad (10)$$

$$t_{\mathcal{C}} \lesssim (2 \cdot \ln(2 \cdot \mathcal{T}_{\max}/\gamma) \cdot \mathcal{T}_{\max}^4/\gamma) \cdot t_{\mathcal{A}} \quad and \quad \mathcal{Q}_{\mathcal{C}} \leq 2 \cdot \ln(2 \cdot \mathcal{T}/\gamma) \cdot \mathcal{T}^3/\gamma \quad (11)$$

with $\mathcal{T} \leq \mathcal{T}_{\max} = (d+2) \cdot \mathcal{Q}_{\mathsf{corrupt}} + 2$.

Proof. To generate a sample $\mathsf{view}_{\mathcal{T}}$, our PR adversary $\mathcal{C}$ modifies the procedure of Algorithm 12 by first sampling an index $i^* \leftarrow [d]$ and a bit $b_{\mathsf{pr}} \leftarrow \{0,1\}$ uniformly at random, and then embedding a PR challenge in the "**if**" clause in the "**repeat**" loop, see Algorithm 13. $\mathcal{C}$ outputs 0 if $\mathcal{A}$ succeeds and 1 else.

Note that the key for node $\mathsf{pfx}_{i^*-1}(x^*)$ is sampled freshly and uniformly at random. Thus, we have that for $b_{\mathsf{pr}} = 0$ and $i^* = i$ the modified algorithm samples from exactly the same distribution as Algorithm 12 on input $i-1$ (and same $b_{\mathsf{ggmprf}} \in \{0,1\}, B \in \mathbb{N}$), and for $b_{\mathsf{pr}} = 1$ and $i^* = i$ from the same distribution as Algorithm 12 on input i (and same $b_{\mathsf{ggmprf}} \in \{0,1\}, B \in \mathbb{N}$). We obtain for the advantage of $\mathcal{C}$:

$$\mathsf{Adv}_{\mathsf{G},\mathcal{C}}^{\mathsf{PR}}(\lambda) = \Pr[b_{\mathcal{C}} = b_{\mathsf{pr}}] - \frac{1}{2}$$

$$= \frac{1}{2} \cdot (\Pr[b_{\mathcal{C}} = 0 \mid b_{\mathsf{pr}} = 0] - \Pr[b_{\mathcal{C}} = 0 \mid b_{\mathsf{pr}} = 1])$$

$$= \frac{1}{2} \cdot \frac{1}{d} \cdot \sum_{i \in [d]} \left(\Pr\left[b_{\mathcal{C}} = 0 \;\middle|\; \begin{matrix} b_{\mathsf{pr}} = 0 \\ \wedge \; i^* = i \end{matrix} \right] - \Pr\left[b_{\mathcal{C}} = 0 \;\middle|\; \begin{matrix} b_{\mathsf{pr}} = 1 \\ \wedge \; i^* = i \end{matrix} \right] \right)$$

$$= \frac{1}{2d} \cdot \sum_{i \in [d]} (\Pr[\mathbf{out}_{i-1} = 1] - \Pr[\mathbf{out}_i = 1])$$

$$= \frac{1}{2d} \cdot \left(\mathsf{Adv}_{\mathsf{G},\mathcal{A},d}^{\mathsf{GGMPRF},0}(\lambda) - \mathsf{Adv}_{\mathsf{G},\mathcal{A},d}^{\mathsf{GGMPRF},d}(\lambda) \right).$$

$\mathcal{C}$ runs $\mathcal{A}$ at most $\mathcal{T} \cdot B$ times. Bounding $\mathcal{T} = \mathsf{len}(\mathsf{view}_0)$ by $\mathcal{T}_{\max} = (d+2) \cdot \mathcal{Q}_{\mathsf{corrupt}} + 2$ (see proof of Claim 2) and plugging in $B = \frac{2\mathcal{T} \cdot \ln(2\mathcal{T}/\gamma) \cdot ((d+2) \cdot \mathcal{Q}_{\mathsf{corrupt}} + 2)^2}{\gamma}$

Algorithm 13: Variant of Algorithm 12 for sampling from $\mathcal{D}^{\text{view}}_{i^*-1+b_{\text{pr}},b_{\text{ggmprf}}}$ given oracle access to a PR challenger with challenge bit b_{pr}. The functions $\text{len}, \text{lastpre}_t$ are as described in the proof, $B \in \mathbb{N}$ is as in Proposition 2.

1   $i^* \leftarrow \{1, \ldots, d\}, b_{\text{ggmprf}} \leftarrow \{0, 1\}$

2   $\text{view}_0 \leftarrow \mathcal{D}^{\text{view}}_{\text{ggmprf},b_{\text{ggmprf}}}$

3   $\mathcal{T} := \text{len}(\text{view}_0)$ // Length of $\text{view}_{\text{GGMPRF}}$ (in entries)

4   **for** $t := 1$ **to** $\mathcal{T}$ **do**

5   Write $\text{view}_{t-1} = (\text{ev}_{t-1,1}, \ldots, \text{ev}_{t-1,\mathcal{T}})$

6   **repeat**   // Output $\bot$ if B repetitions fail for this t

7   Rewind adversary to point t

8   **if** $\text{ev}_{t-1,t} = (\text{PRG}, x)$ *with* $|x| \le i^*$ *and* $\text{lastpre}_t(\text{view}_{t-1}) = t$ **then**
           // Checks if $\text{ev}_{t,t}$ defines a PRG evaluation to be replaced
           by random

9   **if** $|x| = i^*$ **then**

10   Request fresh PR challenge (k_0^*, k_1^*) from PR challenger
             // Fresh PR challenge

11   Set $(k_{x\|0}, k_{x\|1}) := (k_0^*, k_1^*)$

12   **else**

13   Sample fresh $k_{x\|0}, k_{x\|1} \leftarrow \{0, 1\}^\lambda$ // Fresh independent keys

14   **end**

15   Resample from point $t+1$ to obtain
           $\text{view}_t = (\text{ev}_{t-1,0}, \ldots, \text{ev}_{t-1,t-1}, \text{ev}_{t-1,t}, \text{ev}_{t,t+1} \ldots, \text{ev}_{t,\tau})$

16   **else**

17   Resample from point t to obtain
           $\text{view}_t = (\text{ev}_{t-1,0}, \ldots, \text{ev}_{t-1,t-1}, \text{ev}_{t,t}, \ldots, \text{ev}_{t,\tau})$

18   **end**

19   **until** $\text{lastpre}_t(\text{view}_t) = \text{lastpre}_t(\text{view}_{t-1})$ *and* $\text{len}(\text{view}_t) = \text{len}(\text{view}_{t-1})$

20   **end**

21   **return** $\text{view}_\mathcal{T}$

---

leads to the claimed bound on $t_\mathcal{C}$. (We assume the time complexity of random sampling, PR oracle calls and PRG evaluations to be significantly smaller than $t_\mathcal{A}$ and thus neglect the corresponding terms in our bound.)

For the upper bound on the number of oracle calls $\mathcal{Q}_\mathcal{C}$, note that for each possible choice of i^* there is only one t such that $\text{ev}_{t-1,t} = (\text{PRG}, x)$ with $|x| = i^*$ and $\text{lastpre}_t(\text{view}_{t-1}) = t$. Thus, the inner **if** clause will apply only in one of the **for** iterations, which implies that there are as many PR calls as there are iterations of the **repeat** loop for that t. Hence, the reduction makes at most B calls to the PR oracle. $\square$

Proposition 4. $\mathcal{D}^{\text{view}}_{d,b_{\text{ggmprf}}}$ *and* b_{ggmprf} *are independent, so* $\text{Adv}^{\text{GGMPRF},d}_{G,\mathcal{A},d}(\lambda) = 0$.

Proof. Recall that b_{ggmprf} is only used when responding to the challenge query, which by assumption is the last query the adversary makes. Hence, neither the abort probability nor any of the events in $\text{view}_\mathcal{T}$ before the very last events $(\text{challenge}, x^*, k)$ and $(\text{guess}, b_\mathcal{A})$ depend on b_{ggmprf}. The latter also implies that the values for lastpre and len are independent of b_{ggmprf} for all t. As the last two events of the view (that are the only ones carrying information about b_{ggmprf}) are cut off when rewinding and resampling, no information about b_{ggmprf} is carried from view_{t-1} to view_t for any t. Furthermore, in the final view view_T the challenge key k_{x^*} is sampled independently and uniformly at random, hence k has the same distribution for both cases $b_{\mathsf{ggmprf}} = 0$ and $b_{\mathsf{ggmprf}} = 0$. Thus, $\mathcal{A}$ has no advantage in distinguishing k_{x^*} from a random independent key.   □

To finish the proof of the theorem, it only remains to combine the above claims. In particular, we define the adversary $\mathcal{B}$ exactly as $\mathcal{C}$ from Proposition 3. The bound on the runtime of $\mathcal{B}$ follows immediately and for the advantage of $\mathcal{B}$ we have

$$
\begin{aligned}
\mathrm{Adv}_{\mathsf{G},\mathcal{B}}^{\mathsf{PR}}(\lambda) &= \frac{1}{2d} \cdot \left(\mathrm{Adv}_{\mathsf{G},\mathcal{A},d}^{\mathsf{GGMPRF},\,0}(\lambda) - \mathrm{Adv}_{\mathsf{G},\mathcal{A},d}^{\mathsf{GGMPRF},\,d}(\lambda) \right) \\
&\geq \frac{1}{2d} \cdot \left(\widetilde{\mathrm{Adv}_{\mathsf{G},\mathcal{A},d}^{\mathsf{GGMPRF},\,0}}(\lambda) - \mathrm{Adv}_{\mathsf{G},\mathcal{A},d}^{\mathsf{GGMPRF},\,d}(\lambda) - \gamma \right) \\
&\geq \frac{1}{2d} \cdot \left(\mathrm{Adv}_{\mathsf{G},\mathcal{A},d}^{\mathsf{GGMPRF}}(\lambda) - \mathrm{Adv}_{\mathsf{G},\mathcal{A},d}^{\mathsf{GGMPRF},\,d}(\lambda) - \gamma \right) \\
&\geq \frac{1}{2d} \cdot \left(\mathrm{Adv}_{\mathsf{G},\mathcal{A},d}^{\mathsf{GGMPRF}}(\lambda) - \gamma \right).
\end{aligned}
$$

5   Adaptive Security for LKH

Overview. The main application we have in mind in this section is a multicast key distribution protocol called the Logical Key Hierarchy (LKH) [8,33,35]; more precisely, we consider the rectified version by Panjwani [30]. Our strategy can easily be generalized to minor modifications of LKH and therefore we do not focus on specific implementation details. Rather, we provide a very brief high-level description of the protocol as well as the security guarantees we aim to guarantee. More broadly, we believe that our results provide the core techniques to prove adaptive security also for multicast key agreement as defined in [4], as well as (various versions of) the related "TreeKEM" protocol [3,26] for (public-key) continuous group key agreement (CGKA).

Multicast Key Distribution (MKD). A protocol for multicast key distribution (MKD, see [30]) is a server-aided secret-key protocol that enables a dynamically changing group of users to securely communicate over a broadcast channel. In an initial registration step, it is assumed that each user establishes a secret key with the server; this key infrastructure setup is however outside the protocol specification. The server then uses these shared secret keys to communicate a group key to the current set of user. Upon a join/leave request, the server refreshes the group key and sends rekey messages to the new set of users, which allow each user to derive the new group key. In the security experiment, the adversary can request join and leave operations for arbitrary users fully adaptively and learns all keys of removed users. Finally, it can request a challenge and in return obtains either the real group key or a random independent key.

Logical Key Hierarchy (LKH). A trivial MKD protocol would be to simply encrypt a freshly sampled group key to all current users after each membership change. However, for large groups this does not scale well, as it requires a linear number of encryptions. A smarter approach is taken in the Logical Key Hierarchy (LKH) protocol, as proposed in [8,33,35]. We will consider the rectified version of LKH by Panjwani [30]: LKH is based on a binary tree structure, where each node is associated with a secret key k_x and edges represent secret-key encryptions $c_{x\|b}$ of the parent key k_x under the child key $k_{x\|b}$ (see binary tree notation in Sect. 2.1). The keys associated to leaves in the tree belong to members participating in the multicast key distribution, the key k_ε associated to the root is used as the group key. Users can be added to or removed from the group, which leads to a state update where all the keys and ciphertexts associated with nodes and edges on the path from the user's leaf to the root are refreshed (except for the edge attached to the leaf in case of a remove), and also the edges connecting these nodes to co-path nodes are refreshed (see Fig. 7a). Note that in contrast to the trivial protocol, each remove or add operation only requires an update of a logarithmic (in the size of the group) number of ciphertexts.

5.1   Pebbling for LKH

Similarly to the case of GGM, the graphs that occur in the security game of LKH are trees. But now, we are interested in randomizing the key at the root of the binary tree structure. This root key can be derived from any of the leaf keys (and publicly available ciphertexts). Hence, there are now many paths to

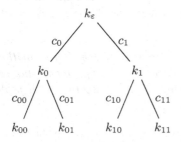

(a) Adding user 4 to a group of 3 users. The keys and ciphertexts that got refreshed in this process are denoted in blue.

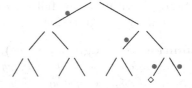

(b) A depth-3 binary tree with red pebbles (•) at the edges c_0, c_{10}, c_{110}, and c_{111}. This configuration occurs when pebbling this graph with the pebbling algorithm (see the full version) at some step i^*. The node leaf_{3,i^*} is marked with a blue diamond (◇).

Fig. 7. (a) Adding a user in LKH. (b) A pebbling configuration occuring in the recursive pebbling strategy from the full version.

the root which we need to take into account in order to randomize the root key. We therefore will build upon the intricate "edge pebbling" strategy of [22] to randomize k_ε, only with guesses replaced by rewindings.

Edge pebbling is a multi-round game on a graph—in our case a binary tree—, where in each step a pebble can be placed on or removed from an edge. The goal is to "pebble" the tree, which means to reach a pebbling configuration where all edges incident on the root are pebbled. The rule is the following.

Edge-pebbling rule. We can at any point add or remove a pebble on an edge c_x when all of k_x's incoming edges (i.e., edges $c_{x\|0}$ and $c_{x\|1}$, if exist) are pebbled.

In particular, we can pebble or unpebble leaf edges at any point. It is easy to see that we can pebble a binary tree in $2^{d+1} - 2$ steps (by pebbling all edges of the tree, level by level from the leaves to the root).

Aiming to reduce the number of pebbles (i.e., the maximum number of pebbled edges at any given point in time), one can observe that a binary tree of depth d can be pebbled in $\Theta(2^{2d})$ steps with only $2d$ pebbles, essentially by a straightforward recursion and removing all used pebbles after pebbling upwards (see the full version, adapted from [22, Algorithm 5]). While for our approach the number of pebbles is not that relevant, this recursive strategy will nevertheless turn out useful. In the following we will derive some useful properties of this strategy.

Definition 9 (Pebbling time). *For $d \in \mathbb{N}$, let T_d be the pebbling time for depth-d binary trees, i.e., the runtime (measured in the number of times a basic pebbling rule is applied) of the pebbling algorithm in the full version on a depth-d binary tree.*

Lemma 7. *We have $T_d = (2/3) \cdot (2^{2d} - 1)$.*

Proof. $T_{d+1} = 4T_d + 2$ and $T_1 = 2$ follow immediately from the structure of pebbling algorithm in the full version . The claimed closed form of T_d can then be proven, e.g., by induction. □

Definition 10 (Edge index set). *For a given run of pebbling algorithm in the full version on a depth-d binary tree as above, let $\mathsf{edges}_{d,i}$ denote the set of indices x of edges c_x pebbled after the i-th step (i.e., application of a pebbling rule).*

Hence, $\mathsf{edges}_{d,0} = \emptyset$ and $\mathsf{edges}_{d,T_d} = \{0,1\}$. A related observation to the following was already used in [22].

Lemma 8. *For each $i \in [T_d]_0$, there is a leaf node k_x (for $x \in \{0,1\}^d$) such that both sets $\mathsf{edges}_{d,i-1}$ and $\mathsf{edges}_{d,i}$ (where we set $\mathsf{edges}_{d,-1} := \emptyset$) consist only of edge indices on the path from k_x to k_ε, or its co-path. Formally, for each i, there is an $x \in \{0,1\}^d$, such that for each $x'\|b \in \mathsf{edges}_{d,i-1} \cup \mathsf{edges}_{d,i}$ (for $x' \in \{0,1\}^{<d}$ and $b \in \{0,1\}$), we have $x' \leq_{\mathsf{pfx}} x$.*

We defer the proof to the full version.

Definition 11. *In the situation of Lemma 8, let* $\mathsf{leaf}_{d,i}$ *be the lexicographically smallest such* $x \in \{0,1\}^d$.

See Fig. 7b for an example of a state that occurs when recursively pebbling a depth-3 binary tree. We provide further properties of the pebbling algorithm relevant for the proof of Theorem 2 in the full version.

5.2 Proving Security from IND-CPA

We now define the LKH security experiment $\mathrm{Exp}_{\mathsf{SKE},\mathcal{A},d}^{\mathsf{LKH}}$. This game models the security of LKH as an MKD protocol.

Definition 12 (LKHsecurity experiment). *Let* $\mathsf{SKE} = (\mathbf{Gen}, \mathbf{Enc}, \mathbf{Dec})$ *be a secret-key encryption scheme and* $d = d(\lambda)$ *some depth. The* LKH *experiment* $\mathrm{Exp}_{\mathsf{SKE},\mathcal{A},d}^{\mathsf{LKH}}$ *initially samples uniformly at random a challenge bit* $b_{\mathsf{lkh}} \leftarrow \{0,1\}$ *and keys* $k_x \leftarrow \{0,1\}^\lambda$ *for each* $x \in \{0,1\}^{\leq d}$. *It then computes ciphertexts* $c_{x\|b}$ *for all* $x \in \{0,1\}^{<d}$ *and* $b \in \{0,1\}$, *which encrypt key* k_x *under key* $k_{x\|b}$. *The adversary* $\mathcal{A}$ *receives the ciphertexts* $c_{x\|b}$ *and can then make the following queries:*

– $\mathcal{A}$ *can adaptively corrupt "leaf" keys* k_x *(for* $x \in \{0,1\}^d$). *This exposes* k_x *to* $\mathcal{A}$, *and results in a refresh of not only* k_x, *but also all* $k_{x'}$ *for proper prefixes* x' *of* x. *Furthermore, fresh encryptions of those* $k_{x'}$ *under keys* $k_{x'\|0}$ *and* $k_{x'\|1}$ *are generated and exposed to* $\mathcal{A}$.
– *At any point,* $\mathcal{A}$ *may stop the game by asking to be challenged to distinguish the then-current key* k_ε *(case* $b_{\mathsf{lkh}} = 0$) *from a random key (case* $b_{\mathsf{lkh}} = 1$).

The output of the experiment is 1 if $\mathcal{A}$ *correctly guesses the bit* b_{lkh}, *and 0 otherwise. We define the advantage of* $\mathcal{A}$ *in this game as*

$$\mathrm{Adv}_{\mathsf{SKE},\mathcal{A},d}^{\mathsf{LKH}}(\lambda) := \Pr[\mathrm{Exp}_{\mathsf{SKE},\mathcal{A},d}^{\mathsf{LKH}}(\lambda) = 1] - 1/2.$$

Asymptotically, we say that LKH *is secure (with* SKE*) if for every polynomial-time* $\mathcal{A}$ *and every constant* $c \in \mathbb{N}$, *the advantage* $\mathrm{Adv}_{\mathsf{SKE},\mathcal{A},c\cdot\log(\lambda)}^{\mathsf{LKH}}(\lambda)$ *is negligible.*[9]

Our Strategy. We will prove that $\mathcal{A}$ has a negligible advantage to win the game $\mathrm{Exp}_{\mathsf{SKE},\mathcal{A},d}^{\mathsf{LKH}}$ through a large hybrid argument. We will start with the game above and apply a number of successive changes until finally $\mathcal{A}$'s view is independent of the real final key k_ε. Similar to Sect. 4, we make a liberal use of rewindings, thus, it will be helpful to formalize $\mathcal{A}$'s view:

Definition 13 (Adversarial view). *In a run of the* LKH *experiment* $\mathrm{Exp}_{\mathsf{SKE},\mathcal{A},d}^{\mathsf{LKH}}$ *from Definition 12, we define* $\mathcal{A}$'s *view* $\mathsf{view}_\mathcal{A}$ *in this run as a sequence* $(\mathsf{ev}_1, \ldots, \mathsf{ev}_T)$ *of events, where each* ev_i *can be one of the following:*

---

[9] Like previous works, we focus on a logarithmic depth and thus to polynomially many users.

Query. *One of $\mathcal{A}$'s queries (without reply), either of the form* (corrupt, x), *or* challenge.

New key. *Every time a new key k_x is defined, right before that, a corresponding* (newkey, x) *event is appended to* view. *Concretely,* view *starts with* (newkey, x) *events for $x \in \{0,1\}^{\leq d}$. Furthermore, a query* (corrupt, x) *automatically causes also entries* (newkey, x') *for a prefix x' of x to be appended immediately after that* corrupt *entry. Entries* (newkey, x) *defined at the same time are ordered in* view *with keys further from the root (i.e., with longer x) first.*

Ciphertext. *An event* (ctxt, $x\|b, c_{x\|b}$) *for a ciphertext $c_{x\|b} = \mathbf{Enc}(k_{x\|b}, k_x)$, either as part of $\mathcal{A}$'s initial input, or as a side effect of a corruption query.* ctxt *entries defined at the same time are ordered with ciphertexts furthest from the root (i.e., with longer x) first, and lexicographically (according to $x\|b$) for x of the same length.*

Corrupted key. *A key* (key, x, k_x) *as a result of a corruption query. We assume that this key appears before the corresponding new key events and the ciphertexts that are sent to $\mathcal{A}$ in the same reply.*

Challenge key. *The result of the final challenge query, in the form* (challenge, k) *(i.e., depending on $b_\mathcal{B}$ with either k being a key k_ε or a random value).*

Decision bit. *The final output bit $b_\mathcal{A}$ of $\mathcal{A}$, in the form* (guess, $b_\mathcal{A}$). *This event is the last in* view, *and we may write* $\mathbf{out}_\mathcal{A}$(view) *for the output bit $b_\mathcal{A}$.*

Remark 2. Note that the ordering of events above implies for an event (corrupt, x) that it is followed by an event (key, x, k_x), then a sequence of events (newkey, x') for all prefixes x' of x, in decreasing length, and then a sequence (ctxt, $x'\|b, c_{x'\|b}$) for all strict prefixes x' of x and bits $b \in \{0,1\}$, again ordered by decreasing length, and siblings ordered alphabetically. For example, for depth $d = 3$, a (corrupt, 010) event causes the following sequence of events: (key, 010, k_{010}), (newkey, 010), (newkey, 01), (newkey, 0), (newkey, ε), (ctxt, 010, c_{010}), (ctxt, 011, c_{011}), (ctxt, 00, c_{00}), (ctxt, 01, c_{01}), (ctxt, 0, c_0), and (ctxt, 1, c_1).

We are now ready to formulate and prove our main result:

Algorithm 14: Game i, with the bulk of the work outsourced into the sampling from $\mathcal{D}_{i,b_{\mathsf{lkh}}}^{\mathsf{view}}$.

---

1 $b_{\mathsf{lkh}} \leftarrow \{0,1\}$
2 view $\leftarrow \mathcal{D}_{i,b_{\mathsf{lkh}}}^{\mathsf{view}}$ // view has the format from Definition 13
3 **return** $[b_{\mathsf{lkh}} = \mathbf{out}_\mathcal{A}(\text{view})]$ // returns 1 iff $b_{\mathsf{lkh}} = \mathbf{out}_\mathcal{A}(\text{view})$

Theorem 2. *Let* SKE $= (\mathbf{Gen}, \mathbf{Enc}, \mathbf{Dec})$ *be an SKE scheme. Then*

- *for every* LKH *adversary $\mathcal{A}$ that runs in time $t_\mathcal{A}$ and places at most $\mathcal{Q}_{\mathsf{corrupt}}$ corruption queries,*
- *for every* LKH *depth d and every $\gamma \in (0,1]$,*

there is an IND-CPA *adversary* $\mathcal{B}$ *that makes at most* $\mathcal{Q}_{\text{LoR}} \leq 2 \cdot \ln(2\mathcal{T}/\gamma) \cdot \mathcal{T}^4 \cdot (d+1)/\gamma$ *LoR queries,* $\mathcal{Q}_{\text{NU}} \leq 2 \cdot \ln(2\mathcal{T}/\gamma) \cdot \mathcal{T}^3 \cdot (d+1)/\gamma$ *new user queries, and runs in time* $t_{\mathcal{B}}$ *and for which*

$$\text{Adv}_{\text{SKE},\mathcal{B}}^{\text{IND-CPA}}(\lambda) \geq \frac{1}{2} \cdot \frac{1}{T_d} \cdot \text{Adv}_{\text{SKE},\mathcal{A},d}^{\text{LKH}}(\lambda) - \frac{\gamma}{2}. \tag{12}$$

where

$$t_{\mathcal{B}} \lessapprox 2 \cdot \ln(2\mathcal{T}/\gamma) \cdot \mathcal{T}^4 \cdot (d+1)/\gamma \cdot t_{\mathcal{A}}. \tag{13}$$

where $\mathcal{T} \leq 2^{d+2} + (3d+1) \cdot \mathcal{Q}_{\text{corrupt}}$.

Again, before proceeding to a proof, we remark that Theorem 2 implies asymptotic security when setting γ suitably:

Corollary 2 (SKE IND-CPA $\Rightarrow$ LKHsecure). *If* SKE *is* IND-CPA *secure (as in Definition 5), then* LKH *is secure with* SKE *(in the sense of Definition 12).*

The proof is similar to the one for Corollary 1. We provide it in the full version.

Proof sketch for Theoorem 2. Fix SKE, $\mathcal{A}$, and d. In the following, we will consider a number of hybrid games, with Game lkh being the original LKH experiment. Denoting with out_i the output of Game i, we trivially get

$$\Pr[\text{out}_{\text{lkh}} = 1] = \text{Adv}_{\text{SKE},\mathcal{A},d}^{\text{LKH}}(\lambda) + 1/2. \tag{14}$$

To move on, we will formulate Game i (for $0 \leq i \leq T_d$) in a (for us) convenient way, see Algorithm 14. This formulation outsources the bulk of the game into the sampling of $\mathcal{A}$'s view view from a suitable distribution $\mathcal{D}_{i,b_{\text{lkh}}}^{\text{view}}$. In our upcoming refinements, we will only change $\mathcal{D}_{i,b_{\text{lkh}}}^{\text{view}}$ and investigate the effects on out_i.

The distributions $\mathcal{D}_{i,b_{\text{lkh}}}^{\text{view}}$. To define the distribution $\mathcal{D}_{i,b_{\text{lkh}}}^{\text{view}}$ for Game i, we use the following notation:

- $\mathcal{D}_{\text{lkh},b_{\text{lkh}}}^{\text{view}}$ is the distribution of $\mathcal{A}$-views (as in Definition 13) that is induced by running the LKH experiment with challenge bit b_{lkh} (that decides whether $\mathcal{A}$ is challenged with k_ε or a random key).
- $\text{edges}_{d,i}$ is the edge index set from Definition 10 that arises out of pebbling a depth-d binary tree.
- $\text{len}(\text{view})$ is the length of a given $\mathcal{A}$-view view (measured in events).
- $\text{pfx}_t(\text{view})$ outputs the prefix of view up to (and including) the t-th event (see Sect. 2.1).
- $\text{maxcor}_{i,t}(\text{view})$ on input $\text{view} = (\text{ev}_1, \ldots, \text{ev}_\mathcal{T})$ outputs

$$\max\left(\left\{ |x| \mid \text{ev}_{t'} = (\text{ctxt}, x, c_x) \text{ for some } t' > t \text{ and } x \leq_{\text{pfx}} \text{leaf}_{d,i} \right\} \cup \{0\}\right).$$

– lastkey$_i$(view) on input view $= (\mathsf{ev}_1, \ldots, \mathsf{ev}_{\mathcal{T}})$ outputs

$$\max\{\, t' \mid \mathsf{ev}_{t'} = (\mathsf{newkey}, x_i^*)\},$$

where $x_i^* := \mathsf{edges}_{d,i-1} \Delta \mathsf{edges}_{d,i}$ for $i \geq 1$ and $x_0^* := \mathsf{edges}_{d,0} \Delta \mathsf{edges}_{d,1}$.
– $B \in \mathbb{N}$ is a bound on the number of repetitions of Lines 6 to 14 for each t. In case of B unsuccessful repetitions for one t, the whole algorithm outputs $\bot$. We will fix a suitable value for B later.

We prove some properties of maxcor and lastkey in the full version

We are now ready to define the distributions $\mathcal{D}_{i,b_{\mathsf{lkh}}}^{\mathsf{view}}$; see Algorithm 15. Our distribution $\mathcal{D}_{i,b_{\mathsf{lkh}}}^{\mathsf{view}}$ will be defined like $\mathcal{D}_{\mathsf{lkh},b_{\mathsf{lkh}}}^{\mathsf{view}}$ (i.e., like a LKH run with $\mathcal{A}$), but will use rewinding and resampling at every step. Additionally, we will replace certain ciphertexts c_x as indicated by $x \in \mathsf{edges}_{d,i}$ during the rewindings. Concretely, fix an i and consider Algorithm 15, which programmatically describes sampling view$_{\mathcal{T}}$ according to $\mathcal{D}_{i,b_{\mathsf{lkh}}}^{\mathsf{view}}$.

We use the same notion of resampling and rewinding as in Sect. 4.

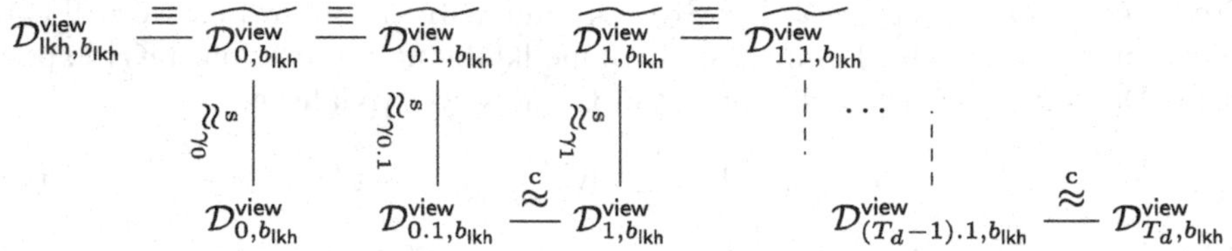

Fig. 8. Sequence of hybrids from the proof of Theorem 2. Perfect indistinguishabilities are denoted by $\equiv$, statistical indistinguishabilities by $\overset{s}{\approx}$, and computational indistinguishabilities by $\overset{c}{\approx}$. See the full version for detail.

Proof Overview. Having defined our hybrid distributions $\mathcal{D}_{i,b_{\mathsf{lkh}}}^{\mathsf{view}}$, we will additionally consider potentially inefficient procedures $\widetilde{\mathcal{D}_{i,b_{\mathsf{lkh}}}^{\mathsf{view}}}$ which are defined similar to Algorithm 15 but without a bound B on the runtime. We will first show that the distribution $\widetilde{\mathcal{D}_{0,b_{\mathsf{lkh}}}^{\mathsf{view}}}$ coincides with the distribution of views in Game lkh. Next, we will consider the intermediate distributions $\mathcal{D}_{i.1,b_{\mathsf{lkh}}}^{\mathsf{view}}$ (the difference to $\mathcal{D}_{i,b_{\mathsf{lkh}}}^{\mathsf{view}}$ being marked gray in Algorithm 15) and show that for all $i \in [T_d - 1]_0$ it holds that $\widetilde{\mathcal{D}_{i,b_{\mathsf{lkh}}}^{\mathsf{view}}}$ and $\widetilde{\mathcal{D}_{i.1,b_{\mathsf{lkh}}}^{\mathsf{view}}}$ have the same distribution.

Algorithm 15: Sampler for $\mathcal{D}^{\text{view}}_{i.1,b_{\text{lkh}}}$

Input: $i \in \{0, \ldots, T_d\}, b_{\text{lkh}} \in \{0,1\}, B \in \mathbb{N}$ // len, pfx_t, $\text{maxcor}_{i,t}$, lastkey_i, B
         described in proof

1 $\text{view}_0 \leftarrow \mathcal{D}^{\text{view}}_{\text{lkh},b_{\text{lkh}}}$

2 $\mathcal{T} := \text{len}(\text{view}_{\text{lkh}})$ // Length of view_{lkh} (in entries)

3 **for** $t := 1$ **to** $\mathcal{T}$ **do**

4 $\quad$ Write $\text{view}_{t-1} = (\text{ev}_{t-1,1}, \ldots, \text{ev}_{t-1,\mathcal{T}})$

5 $\quad$ **repeat**   // Output $\perp$ if B repetitions fail for this t

6 $\quad\quad$ Rewind adversary to point t // Checks if $\text{ev}_{t,t}$ defines a
        $\quad\quad$ ciphertext to be pebbled

7 $\quad\quad$ **if** $\text{ev}_{t-1,t} = (\text{ctxt}, x, c_x)$ *with* $x \in \text{edges}_{d,i}$ *and*
        $\quad\quad$ $\text{maxcor}_{i+1,t+1}(\text{view}_{t-1}) < |x|$ **then**

8 $\quad\quad\quad$ Sample fresh $c_x^{\perp} \leftarrow \text{Enc}(l_{0_x}, \perp)$ // Fresh dummy ciphertext

9 $\quad\quad\quad$ Set $\text{ev}_{t,t} := (\text{ctxt}, x, c_x^{\perp})$ in view_t // Replace c_x with $c_w^{\perp}$ in
        $\quad\quad\quad$ view_{t-1}

10 $\quad\quad\quad$ Resample from point $t+1$ to obtain
        $\quad\quad\quad$ $\text{view}_t = (\text{ev}_{t-1,0}, \ldots, \text{ev}_{t-1,t-1}, \text{ev}_{t,t}, \text{ev}_{t,t+1}, \ldots, \text{ev}_{t,\tau})$

11 $\quad\quad$ **else**

12 $\quad\quad\quad$ Resample from point t to obtain
        $\quad\quad\quad$ $\text{view}_t = (\text{ev}_{t-1,0}, \ldots, \text{ev}_{t-1,t-1}, \text{ev}_{t,t}, \ldots, \text{ev}_{t,\tau})$

13 $\quad\quad$ **end**

14 $\quad$ **until** $\text{maxcor}_{i+1,t+1}(\text{view}_t) = \text{maxcor}_{i+1,t+1}(\text{view}_{t-1})$ *and*
        $\quad$ $\text{len}(\text{view}_t) = \text{len}(\text{view}_{t-1})$ *and* $\text{lastkey}_{i+1}(\text{view}_t) = \text{lastkey}_{i+1}(\text{view}_{t-1})$

15 **end**

16 **return** $\text{view}_{\mathcal{T}}$

We will then bound the difference in the probability of an abort in the games $\mathcal{D}^{\text{view}}_{i,b_{\text{lkh}}}$ and $\mathcal{D}^{\text{view}}_{i.1,b_{\text{lkh}}}$. To prove this we will need an additional technical lemma about the abort probability in such mixed sampling procedures and this is the main difference to Sect. 4 in which such a mixed resampling procedure does not occur. Setting the bound B appropriately we will be able to bound the probability of an abort in $\mathcal{D}^{\text{view}}_{0,b_{\text{lkh}}}$ by γ. In the subsequent claim we will show that $\mathcal{A}$ has no advantage in Game T_d since the view sampled according to $\mathcal{D}^{\text{view}}_{T_d,b_{\text{lkh}}}$ is independent of b_{lkh}. Finally, we will conclude the proof by arguing that for all $i \in [T_d-1]_0$ the distributions $\mathcal{D}^{\text{view}}_{i.1,b_{\text{lkh}}}$ and $\mathcal{D}^{\text{view}}_{i+1,b_{\text{lkh}}}$ are computationally indistinguishable by IND-CPA security of the SKE scheme SKE. See Fig. 8 for an overview of this sequence of arguments. We defer the full proof to the full version.

$\square$

References

1. Bader, C., Jager, T., Li, Y., Schäge, S.: On the impossibility of tight cryptographic reductions. In: Fischlin, M., Coron, J.-S. (eds.) EUROCRYPT 2016. LNCS, vol. 9666, pp. 273–304. Springer, Heidelberg (2016). https://doi.org/10.1007/978-3-662-49896-5_10

2. Bellare, M., Desai, A., Jokipii, E., Rogaway, P.: A concrete security treatment of symmetric encryption. In: 38th FOCS, pp. 394–403. IEEE Computer Society Press (Oct 1997). https://doi.org/10.1109/SFCS.1997.646128

3. Bhargavan, K., Barnes, R., Rescorla, E.: TreeKEM: asynchronous decentralized key management for large dynamic groups a protocol proposal for messaging layer security (MLS). Research report, Inria Paris (May 2018). https://hal.inria.fr/hal-02425247

4. Bienstock, A., Dodis, Y., Tang, Y.: Multicast key agreement, revisited. In: Galbraith, S.D. (ed.) CT-RSA 2022. LNCS, vol. 13161, pp. 1–25. Springer, Cham (2022). https://doi.org/10.1007/978-3-030-95312-6_1

5. Boneh, D., Waters, B.: Constrained pseudorandom functions and their applications. In: Sako, K., Sarkar, P. (eds.) ASIACRYPT 2013. LNCS, vol. 8270, pp. 280–300. Springer, Heidelberg (2013). https://doi.org/10.1007/978-3-642-42045-0_15

6. Boyle, E., Goldwasser, S., Ivan, I.: Functional signatures and pseudorandom functions. In: Krawczyk, H. (ed.) PKC 2014. LNCS, vol. 8383, pp. 501–519. Springer, Heidelberg (2014). https://doi.org/10.1007/978-3-642-54631-0_29

7. Brakerski, Z., Kalai, Y.T.: A framework for efficient signatures, ring signatures and identity based encryption in the standard model. Cryptology ePrint Archive, Report 2010/086 (2010). https://eprint.iacr.org/2010/086

8. Canetti, R., Garay, J.A., Itkis, G., Micciancio, D., Naor, M., Pinkas, B.: Multicast security: a taxonomy and some efficient constructions. In: IEEE INFOCOM'99, pp. 708–716. New York, NY, USA (Mar 21–25, 1999)

9. Canetti, R., Kilian, J., Petrank, E., Rosen, A.: Black-box concurrent zero-knowledge requires omega (log n) rounds. In: 33rd ACM STOC, pp. 570–579. ACM Press (Jul 2001). https://doi.org/10.1145/380752.380852

10. Coron, J.-S.: Optimal security proofs for PSS and other signature schemes. In: Knudsen, L.R. (ed.) EUROCRYPT 2002. LNCS, vol. 2332, pp. 272–287. Springer, Heidelberg (2002). https://doi.org/10.1007/3-540-46035-7_18

11. Davidson, A., Katsumata, S., Nishimaki, R., Yamada, S., Yamakawa, T.: Adaptively secure constrained pseudorandom functions in the standard model. In: Micciancio, D., Ristenpart, T. (eds.) CRYPTO 2020. LNCS, vol. 12170, pp. 559–589. Springer, Cham (2020). https://doi.org/10.1007/978-3-030-56784-2_19

12. Fiat, A., Shamir, A.: How to prove yourself: practical solutions to identification and signature problems. In: Odlyzko, A.M. (ed.) CRYPTO 1986. LNCS, vol. 263, pp. 186–194. Springer, Heidelberg (1987). https://doi.org/10.1007/3-540-47721-7_12

13. Fischlin, M., Fleischhacker, N.: Limitations of the meta-reduction technique: the case of schnorr signatures. In: Johansson, T., Nguyen, P.Q. (eds.) EUROCRYPT 2013. LNCS, vol. 7881, pp. 444–460. Springer, Heidelberg (2013). https://doi.org/10.1007/978-3-642-38348-9_27

14. Fuchsbauer, G., Konstantinov, M., Pietrzak, K., Rao, V.: Adaptive security of constrained PRFs. In: Sarkar, P., Iwata, T. (eds.) ASIACRYPT 2014. LNCS, vol. 8874, pp. 82–101. Springer, Heidelberg (2014). https://doi.org/10.1007/978-3-662-45608-8_5

15. Goldreich, O., Goldwasser, S., Micali, S.: How to construct random functions (extended abstract). In: 25th FOCS, pp. 464–479. IEEE Computer Society Press (Oct 1984). https://doi.org/10.1109/SFCS.1984.715949

16. Goldreich, O., Goldwasser, S., Micali, S.: On the cryptographic applications of random functions. In: Blakley, G.R., Chaum, D. (eds.) CRYPTO'84. LNCS, vol. 196, pp. 276–288. Springer, Heidelberg (1984). https://doi.org/10.1007/3-540-39568-7_22

17. Goldreich, O., Micali, S., Wigderson, A.: How to prove all NP Statements in zero-knowledge and a methodology of cryptographic protocol design (extended abstract). In: Odlyzko, A.M. (ed.) CRYPTO 1986. LNCS, vol. 263, pp. 171–185. Springer, Heidelberg (1987). https://doi.org/10.1007/3-540-47721-7_11

18. Goldwasser, S., Micali, S., Rivest, R.L.: A digital signature scheme secure against adaptive chosen-message attacks. SIAM J. Comput. 17(2), 281–308 (1988)

19. Hofheinz, D., Jager, T., Knapp, E.: Waters signatures with optimal security reduction. In: Fischlin, M., Buchmann, J., Manulis, M. (eds.) PKC 2012. LNCS, vol. 7293, pp. 66–83. Springer, Heidelberg (2012). https://doi.org/10.1007/978-3-642-30057-8_5

20. Hofheinz, D., Kiltz, E.: Programmable hash functions and their applications. In: Wagner, D. (ed.) CRYPTO 2008. LNCS, vol. 5157, pp. 21–38. Springer, Heidelberg (2008). https://doi.org/10.1007/978-3-540-85174-5_2

21. Hohenberger, S., Waters, B.: Short and stateless signatures from the RSA assumption. In: Halevi, S. (ed.) CRYPTO 2009. LNCS, vol. 5677, pp. 654–670. Springer, Heidelberg (2009). https://doi.org/10.1007/978-3-642-03356-8_38

22. Jafargholi, Z., Kamath, C., Klein, K., Komargodski, I., Pietrzak, K., Wichs, D.: Be adaptive, avoid overcommitting. In: Katz, J., Shacham, H. (eds.) CRYPTO 2017. LNCS, vol. 10401, pp. 133–163. Springer, Cham (2017). https://doi.org/10.1007/978-3-319-63688-7_5

23. Kamath, C., Klein, K., Pietrzak, K., Walter, M.: The cost of adaptivity in security games on graphs. In: Nissim, K., Waters, B. (eds.) TCC 2021. LNCS, vol. 13043, pp. 550–581. Springer, Cham (2021). https://doi.org/10.1007/978-3-030-90453-1_19

24. Kastner, J., Loss, J., Xu, J.: The abe-okamoto partially blind signature scheme revisited. In: Agrawal, S., Lin, D. (eds.) Advances in Cryptology - ASIACRYPT 2022, pp. 279–309. Springer Nature Switzerland, Cham (2022). https://doi.org/10.1007/978-3-031-22972-5_10

25. Kiayias, A., Papadopoulos, S., Triandopoulos, N., Zacharias, T.: Delegatable pseudorandom functions and applications. In: Sadeghi, A.R., Gligor, V.D., Yung, M. (eds.) ACM CCS 2013, pp. 669–684. ACM Press (Nov 2013). https://doi.org/10.1145/2508859.2516668

26. Klein, K., et al.: Keep the dirt: tainted TreeKEM, adaptively and actively secure continuous group key agreement. In: 2021 IEEE Symposium on Security and Privacy, pp. 268–284. IEEE Computer Society Press (May 2021). https://doi.org/10.1109/SP40001.2021.00035

27. Kuchta, V., Sakzad, A., Stehlé, D., Steinfeld, R., Sun, S.-F.: Measure-rewind-measure: tighter quantum random oracle model proofs for one-way to hiding and CCA security. In: Canteaut, A., Ishai, Y. (eds.) EUROCRYPT 2020. LNCS, vol. 12107, pp. 703–728. Springer, Cham (2020). https://doi.org/10.1007/978-3-030-45727-3_24

28. Lewko, A., Waters, B.: Why proving HIBE systems secure is difficult. In: Nguyen, P.Q., Oswald, E. (eds.) EUROCRYPT 2014. LNCS, vol. 8441, pp. 58–76. Springer, Heidelberg (2014). https://doi.org/10.1007/978-3-642-55220-5_4

29. Naor, M., Yung, M.: Universal one-way hash functions and their cryptographic applications. In: 21st ACM STOC, pp. 33–43. ACM Press (May 1989). https://doi.org/10.1145/73007.73011

30. Panjwani, S.: Tackling adaptive corruptions in multicast encryption protocols. In: Vadhan, S.P. (ed.) TCC 2007. LNCS, vol. 4392, pp. 21–40. Springer, Heidelberg (2007). https://doi.org/10.1007/978-3-540-70936-7_2

31. Pointcheval, D., Stern, J.: Security proofs for signature schemes. In: Maurer, U. (ed.) EUROCRYPT 1996. LNCS, vol. 1070, pp. 387–398. Springer, Heidelberg (1996). https://doi.org/10.1007/3-540-68339-9_33

32. Richardson, R., Kilian, J.: On the concurrent composition of zero-knowledge proofs. In: Stern, J. (ed.) EUROCRYPT 1999. LNCS, vol. 1592, pp. 415–431. Springer, Heidelberg (1999). https://doi.org/10.1007/3-540-48910-X_29

33. Wallner, D.M., Harder, E.J., Agee, R.C.: Key management for multicast: issues and architectures. Internet Draft (Sep 1998). http://www.ietf.org/ID.html

34. Waters, B.: Efficient identity-based encryption without random oracles. In: Cramer, R. (ed.) EUROCRYPT 2005. LNCS, vol. 3494, pp. 114–127. Springer, Heidelberg (2005). https://doi.org/10.1007/11426639_7

35. Wong, C.K., Gouda, M.G., Lam, S.S.: Secure group communications using key graphs. IEEE/ACM Trans. Netw. **8**(1), 16–30 (2000). https://doi.org/10.1109/90.836475

Anamorphic Signatures: Secrecy from a Dictator Who Only Permits Authentication!

Mirosław Kutyłowski[1,6](✉), Giuseppe Persiano[2,3], Duong Hieu Phan[4], Moti Yung[3,5], and Marcin Zawada[1]

[1] Wrocław University of Science and Technology, Wrocław, Poland
marcin.zawada@pwr.edu.pl
[2] Università di Salerno, Fisciano, Italy
giuper@gmail.com
[3] Google LLC, New York City, USA
motiyung@gmail.com
[4] Telecom Paris, Institut Polytechnique de Paris, Palaiseau, France
[5] Columbia University, New York, USA
[6] NASK -National Research Institute, Warsaw, Poland
miroslaw.kutylowski@nask.pl

Abstract. The goal of this research is to raise technical doubts regarding the usefulness of the repeated attempts by governments to curb Cryptography (aka the "Crypto Wars"), and argue that they, in fact, cause more damage than adding effective control. The notion of *Anamorphic Encryption* was presented in Eurocrypt'22 for a similar aim. There, despite the presence of a Dictator who possesses all keys and knows all messages, parties can arrange a hidden *"anamorphic"* message in an otherwise indistinguishable from regular ciphertexts (wrt the Dictator).

In this work, we postulate a stronger cryptographic control setting where encryption does not exist (or is neutralized) since all communication is passed through the Dictator in, essentially, cleartext mode (or otherwise, when secure channels to and from the Dictator are the only confidentiality mechanism). Messages are only authenticated to assure recipients of the identity of the sender. We ask whether security against the Dictator still exists, even under such a strict regime which allows only authentication (i.e., authenticated/ signed messages) to pass end-to-end, and where received messages are determined by/ known to the Dictator, and the Dictator also eventually gets all keys to verify compliance of past signing. To frustrate the Dictator, this authenticated message setting gives rise to the possible notion of anamorphic channels inside signature and authentication schemes, where parties attempt to send undetectable secure messages (or other values) using signature tags which are indistinguishable from regular tags. We define and present implementation of schemes for anamorphic signature and authentication; these are applicable to existing and standardized signature and authentication schemes which were designed independently of the notion of anamorphic messages. Further, some cornerstone constructions of the foundations of signatures, in fact, introduce anamorphism.

© International Association for Cryptologic Research 2023
H. Handschuh and A. Lysyanskaya (Eds.): CRYPTO 2023, LNCS 14082, pp. 759–790, 2023.
https://doi.org/10.1007/978-3-031-38545-2_25

The extended version of this paper, including extra results and proofs, is available as [17].

1 Introduction

The notion of *anamorphic encryption* [23] was introduced recently to deal with a very restricted cryptographic setting, where the dictatorial government requests to know all the keys. Yet, the notion allows parties to exploit the existing (and so severely debilitated) encrypted communication to exchange secret messages that remain hidden from the dictator while keeping the dictator's constraints.

Whereas in the above, parties are authorized to employ encryption, in this paper we consider a dictator who is much more restrictive with respect to encryption. In fact, in this new setting the use of encryption is totally prohibited except for private channels to and from the dictator.

The scenario we envision here assumes that all messages that are exchanged are sent via a central clearing house (i.e., through the dictator itself), which gets the message from the sender over a secure channel and forwards the message to the receiver on another secure channel. In this configuration encryption is completely neutralized, and, depending on the implementation of secure channels, may essentially not exist. Specifically, if the secure channel is physically protected (e.g., via quantum communication) there is no encryption indeed. If instead the secure channel is implemented with cryptographic tools, the ciphertext sent by the sender to the dictator is first decrypted and thus the plaintext is revealed, and the dictator and effectively re-encrypts it and eventually sends it to the receiver, who recovers the message. The two ciphertexts from the sender to the dictator and from the dictator to the receiver are completely independent, but for the fact that they conceal the same plaintext. Note that this configuration kills any steganographic channel or any anamorphic channel which the sender might have employed; simply, what the receiver gets is independent of the sender's ciphertext randomness, and this very restrictive configuration essentially overcomes the anamorphic encryption of [23].

We note that in many configurations `https` communication is broken by a middlebox which inspects plaintext (for various safety purposes) away from the final user, so having intermediate channels between sender and receiver is not a completely outrageous and unusual configuration (see, for example, [9]).

Note, however, that if we simply trust the dictator as a built-in man-in-the-middle, then it has absolute power to control the messages sent, as he can send any message at anytime to anyone on behalf of anyone else. Of course, no one and certainly not a dictator can be trusted to not employ such an unlimited power, hence the above configuration on its own does not make sense. To minimally make sense, authenticity of the messages (against the dictator) must be assured. Then, if messages (even those re-encrypted by the dictator) are authenticated (signed) by the sender, then a message can include a header which includes: *"the sender name," "the receiver name," "time and date,"* and even the *"hash of all prior messages in this exchange."* Using this extended message, the dictator is forced to send all messages from sender to receiver and the receiver can check the authenticity of a stream of messages. Now, secrecy (with respect to the dictator) is lost, but the dictator has to be faithful due to the authenticity assured by signing the stream of messages with a key they do not possess. So, in case we need to give up privacy, to have a minimal level of trust we need authenticated enhanced messages as above.

Assume we are then interested in reintroducing anamorphic communication that is hidden for the dictator, in spite of the loss of privacy in this scenario. Namely, we are interested in people obeying the dictator's rules while still interested in having an additional secret channel for communication that remains hidden from the dictator. In the above system, where the dictator is the clearing house for ciphertexts, signature schemes (or authentication and identification procedures) are the only remaining cryptographic tool shared end-to-end between senders and receivers used to keep the dictator from impersonating users and creating fake messages. This gives rise to the question we tackle in this work:

- Can we have anamorphic channels inside signature schemes? and
- Can we implement such schemes and employ them in existing established signature and authentication mechanisms?

Further, when the dictator needs to analyze compliance of the parties with his demands, he gets to know (or even dictates) the messages, and he gets the signing key to check the validity of the messages regarding compliance. In fact, view this checking as done after the messaging is over (so the dictator cannot forge messages, but can eventually check the compliance of signed messages, say, when a new signing key is certified and the old key is revoked, and in any event these signing keys are merely for authentication and are not used for signing legally binding documents, etc.). It goes without saying that non-compliance has dire consequences for users who are caught!

This strict configuration is the subject of this work in which we answer the above in the *positive*; we further point at various issues of characterizing the anamorphic channels in this setting; and we develop methods to build such channels in various existing families of signature, authentication, and identification schemes. Moreover, we show how existing cornerstone method of the theory of signatures, which allow building signatures from basic simpler components also allow the introduction of anamorphism!

Obviously, the notion of *Anamorphic Cryptography* deals with possible abuses, misuses, and new uses of cryptosystems beyond their primary goals, which is an interesting take of cryptographic systems, after their primary goals are understood, formalized, and proved. Anamorphism is one way to view what side uses cryptographic systems enable (directly in the hands of the users themselves). This is a different way from and requires more than simply having a subliminal channel [30], and even different from kleptographic abuse of cryptosystems which exploit such channels in a way hidden from the user [32] and also different from countermeasures against them (e.g., [28]). Such unplanned readily available anamorphic uses constitute a note against controlling cryptography by governments attempting control of the primary use of cryptography. Next, we can see that anamorphic systems may further lead to other notions and applications.

An Implication: Watermarking and Anamorphic Signatures. Anamorphic channels obviously demonstrate the futility of direct control over encryption keys. Additionally, anamorphic methods have applications beyond subverting the dictator's limitations. In particular, let us concentrate on watermarking.

The aim of watermarking is to insert some information, a *mark*, in a digital object in order to be able to trace its origin. The marked object should be indistinguishable from an unmarked one and the mark should be difficult to remove. Hopper et al. [16] first formalized the goal, and further work has been done on this important concept (for more recent work, see e.g. [14]). We note that watermarking can be seen as an anamorphic message to oneself (or to a designated checker), thus in fact, watermarking can be reduced from anamorphism.

Consider the concept of an anamorphic signatures as proposed in this work, and suppose that one party signs and wants to distribute a confidential document to a set of users and to guarantee authenticity of the document which is digitally signed. The signer is also afraid that the document will be leaked in its signed version as it could not be denied. For this reason the signer decides to put in place a mechanism by which it would be possible to trace the leak. Anamorphic signatures come to help in this case. Indeed the party can sign the document for each receiver and insert a different anamorphic message in the signature. By extracting the anamorphic message from the leaked signed document, the signer can trace the leak. The leakage of the document without the signature is less dangerous as the document cannot be attributed to the signer with certainty (i.e., the document can be repudiated). As this example shows, watermarking is similar to an anamorphic message to oneself.

Using this method, one can insert different watermarking scheme (i.e., a different pseudorandom function to derive the mark and insert it in the anamorphic channel) to each of signing devices holding the same signing key, so the source of the signature can be determined from the inserted watermark.

We can employ the watermarking method to also protect the leakage or cryptanalysis of the signing key (since the one who gets/ cryptanalyzes the key cannot use a proper watermarking), hence the forgery will be caught.

Chaffing and Winnowing [26]. *Chaffing and Winnowing* is a technique that provides message confidentiality without using encryption or steganography. The two parties that want to establish a confidential channel share a secret *authentication* key. Each message is authenticated using the authentication key and then other fake messages (the *chaff*) are added with an incorrect authentication tag. In other words, the real messages (the *wheat*) are carried by correctly authenticated packets that can be winnowed by the legitimate receiver that knows the authentication key. A third party that sees all the messages flowing between the two parties cannot tell the wheat from the chaff without the authentication key. It is thus crucial for the confidentiality of the communication that dictator does not have the authentication key. The author of [26] justifies this assumption as he considers a dictator seeking "access to all authentication keys as well, a truly frightening prospect." In this paper, we consider the frightening prospect in which the dictator has access to the authentication keys (in our setting, the signing keys) and we show that anamorphic signatures comes to the rescue.

1.1 Our Contribution

As said, our work is primarily geared toward developing anamorphism as a tool for answering issues that are raised in the "crypto wars." In the setting considered, encryption is completely neutralized and only message authentication through signatures (like TLS signing) is allowed. We show that, even in this extremely restricted setting, existing digital signature schemes and design techniques allow for private communication, despite a dictator that has the power to request all signing keys. In other words, to pursue the futile goal of disallowing private communication, the dictator must disallow not only encryption but also digital signatures with obvious dire consequences for digital communication: not only all communication is public, but nobody knows whom they are talking to, and, in fact, the dictator can impersonate anyone!

Defining anamorphic signatures. In Sect. 2, we formally define the concept of an *anamorphic signature scheme*. This is a special type of signature scheme that allows the signer to embed an *anamorphic* message in a signature. The anamorphic message can only be read by a set of trusted parties that have received a special *double key* from the signer. To every other party, a signature carrying an anamorphic message, an *anamorphic signature*, is indistinguishable from a regular signature. And, this holds also w.r.t. parties, like the dictator, that can demand to see all secret material (including the signing keys).

Let us contrast anamorphic signatures with regular signatures. In the typical usage of a signature scheme, a signer Bob runs the *key generation* algorithm to obtain a *verification key* svk and a *signing key* ssk. Bob publishes the verification key svk in a public directory and keeps the signing key ssk private. Whenever Bob wants to sign a message msg, he runs the *signing* algorithm on input ssk and msg and obtains a signature that can be verified by running the *verification* algorithm on input the signature and msg and svk. An anamorphic signature scheme consists of three *anamorphic* algorithms: the *anamorphic key generation* algorithm, the *anamorphic signing* algorithm, and the *anamorphic decryption* algorithm. Their usage is slightly different. More specifically, the *anamorphic key generation* algorithm returns (svk, ssk), as in a regular signature scheme, and, additionally, a *double key* dkey. As before, svk is published and ssk is kept secret and the dkey is distributed by Bob to a trusted set of users with which Bob wants to establish an hidden communication channel. Whenever Bob wishes to secretly send a message amsg, the *anamorphic* message, to his trusted circle, Bob picks an innocent looking message msg, the *regular* message, and signs msg by running the *anamorphic signing* algorithm on input the two messages msg and amsg, the signing key ssk and the double key dkey. The signature sig produced has the following anamorphic property: it can be successfully verified using the verification key svk and the message msg; if instead it is given as input to the *anamorphic decryption* algorithm along with dkey, it returns the anamorphic message amsg. In other words, the same signature sig gives different results depending on the key used to operate on it. The security requirement posits that key pairs (svk, ssk) and signatures sig returned by the anamorphic algorithms are indistinguishable from those returned by the regular algorithms. And this holds also not only for parties that have access to the verification key svk but also for the dictator that has access to the signing key ssk.

Many-to-many vs. One-to-many. We consider two types of anamorphic signatures that implement two different types of communication channel hidden from the dictator: *many-to-many* and *one-to-many.*

By looking ahead, the formal definition of an anamorphic signature scheme (see Def. 2) does not make any claim about the unforgeability of the signature scheme by the parties that hold the double key (the circle of trusted users). Indeed, the possibility that every member of the circle is able produce an anamorphic signature by relying only on the double key is not ruled-out by the definition. If this is the case, that is if knowledge of the double key allows to produce valid signatures, then we call the anamorphic signature *symmetric.* The name *symmetric* indicates that the set of users holding the double key can all produce signatures carrying anamorphic message; in other words, symmetric anamorphic signatures implement a *many-to-many* communication channel hidden from the dictator. As we shall see, this is the case for the anamorphic ElGamal signature scheme in which the double key contains the signing key. We note that the signer shares his secret key with the members of the group which is interested in a clandestine many-to-many secret communication under the mask of non-repudiated authentication (analogous to TLS authentication keys not serving as contract signing keys!). Interestingly, Davies [7], already in 1983, was the first to consider giving up non-repudiation for other, more nefarious, reasons.

Another possible option is where the signature scheme remains unforgeable even if the double key is revealed. Such an anamorphic signature implements a *one-to-many* communication channel hidden from the dictator in which only the owner of the signing key can produce an anamorphic signature. All other members can read anamorphic messages that come with an implicit origin authentication as they are part of a signature that can only be produced by the owner of the signing key. We call this type of anamorphic signatures *private* because the privacy of the signing key is preserved.

Constructions. The main message of this paper is that anamorphic signatures do exist, both symmetric and private, and they do not exist by accident but they systematically emerge from central design techniques.

To start, in Sect. 3, we show that the ElGamal signature scheme is *symmetric* anamorphic. This signature scheme exemplifies our general technique to obtain anamorphism. Specifically, we show that some of the randomness used by the signer can be recovered by the verifier and it can be used to hide the anamorphic message by means of an encryption with pseudorandom ciphertexts. The encryption key is the *double key* that is shared by the signer with a restricted group of trusted users.

However, anamorphism is not simply a special property enjoyed by a sparse group of construction from the literature. Indeed, in this paper, we make the stronger point of showing that two cornerstone design techniques for signature schemes give anamorphic signature schemes (for all their widely used instantiations). More specifically, we prove the following.

1. In Sect. 4, we introduce the concept of an *anamorphic three-message public-coin* protocol and show that several instances of this important class of protocols are anamorphic. In other words, an anamorphic protocol can be used by the prover to send an hidden message to whomever has the double key and receives a transcript of the protocol. The message remnains hidden even with respect to a Dictator that has the secret information of the prover (i.e., the witness) and the dictator itself plays the role of the verifier.

   Having introduced the concept of an anamorphic three-message public-coin protocols, we give a sufficient condition for a protocol to be anamorphic and show that the most well-known protocols (e.g., the protocol for proving knowledge of discrete log and for graph isomorphism) do enjoy this property.

2. Then we look at the Fiat-Shamir heuristics that transforms three-message public-coin protocols into signature schemes that can be proved unforgeable in the Random Oracle Model. In Sect. 4.2, we prove that if the Fiat-Shamir heuristics is applied to an anamorphic three-message public-coin protocol the resulting signature scheme is *symmetric* anamorphic. In other words, Fiat-Shamir preserves anamorphism. This general result includes as a special case our warm-up examples, ElGamal.

3. In Sect. 5, we present the notion of *private* anamorphism. In a private anamorphic signature scheme we require that knowledge of the *double-key* does not give signing capabilities. Private anamorphism provides a one-to-many channel hidden from the dictator in which there is one designated sender, the one holding the signing key, that can send messages to the rest of the group.

4. In Sect. 7, we show that the Naor-Yung paradigm for constructing unforgeable many-time signature schemes from unforgeable one-time signature scheme gives private anamorphic signature schemes. More specifically, in Sect. 6 we introduce the notion of *weak anamorphism* for one-time signatures; we show that several well-known one-time signatures schemes, including Lamport's tagging system, enjoy weak anamorphism; and, finally, we prove that the Naor-Yung paradigm, when instantiated with a weakly anamorphic one-time signatures yields private anamorphic many-time signature schemes in the standard model. In the full version, we extend this to the tree-based extension of the NY paradigm.

   As a corollary, we obtain that private anamorphic signature schemes can be constructed in the standard model under the sole assumption of the existence of one-way functions.

Let us describe some additional results that can be found in the full version [17]. Since signature schemes are used as a component in encryption schemes, we show anamorphic channels in encryption schemes which contain a signature component. For example we show that the CCA encryption scheme of Canetti-Halevi-Katz [4] can be made anamorphic. In the full version, we also show private anamorphic schemes with standardized random-oracle based schemes (PSS RSA in particular). Morever, in the full version, we present an anamorphic scheme where the double key is generated jointly with the signing key (as it contains part of it) but still it cannot be used to forge signatures.

Bandwidth of the anamorphic channel. We stress that all our constructions have polynomial bandwidth. That is, the size of the anamorphic message is lower bounded by a polynomial in the size of the signature carrying it. The underlying technique of our construction is to replace the randomness that is used in the generation of the signing and verification keys (for the case of weak anamorphism) or in the generation of the signature (for the case of anamorphism) with a pseudorandom ciphertext encrypting the anamorphic message using the double key. The randomness must be extractable from the signature at verification, and depending on whether the signing key is needed for extraction or not the scheme gives rise to a different type of anamorphism.

Double-Key Distribution. As we have observed above, and as it will be made clear by our formal definitions, all security guarantees are void if the dictator obtains the double key. This is obvious as the double key allows to extract the anamorphic message from an anamorphic signature. In other words, an anamorphic signature symmetrically encrypts the anamorphic message.

Previous work on anamorphic encryption [23] also considered the setting in which parties do not share any prior information; that is, the sender and the receiver of an anamorphic ciphertext do not share any private information. In other words, the anamorphic message is asymmetrically encrypted. This seems to be a very natural and important setting as it dispenses of the need of a secure channel for the distribution of the double key. It is thus natural to ask if an equivalent notion could be considered for anamorphic signatures as well. Note, however, that for anamorphic signatures, the receiver of the anamorphic message coincides with the one with only the public information (the verification key). The fact that no double key is used in signatures would mean that everybody can read the anamorphic message, which is not what we want (as this will include the dictator!). In the context of encryption, things are different since the receiver of the anamorphic message is the owner of the secret information. In this case, having an anamorphic encryption scheme with no double key means that any user can send an anamorphic message exclusively to the owner of a public key.

2   Definitions and Models

In this section we introduce the notion of an *anamorphic signature* scheme and of a *symmetric anamorphic signature* scheme. We postpone the formal definition of a *private anamorphic signature* scheme to Sect. 5.

Informally, an unforgeable signature scheme is anamorphic if there exists an *anamorphic* triplet of algorithms that allows to generate a key pair of signing/verification key along with a *double key*. The double key is shared by the signer with one or more selected trusted verifiers and it allows the signer to embed a secret message, called the *anamorphic message*, into a signature. The correctness condition is that the anamorphic message is readable by verifiers that have the double key. The security condition requires that no PPT dictator is able to distinguish whether the keys and the signatures are produced by the normal triplet of algorithm or by the anamorphic triplet. This indistinguishability implies that the anamorphic message is indistinguishable from a random field (hence it has semantic security) and the signature is unforgeable (were it not, it would give a way to distinguish the anamorphic one from the regular signature which is unforgeable!). We make this intuition formal in Theorem 3 and Theorem 5 in Sect. 2.1.

Let us start by defining the concept of an *anamorphic triplet* which will be used to define the concept of an *anamorphic signature scheme*.

Definition 1 (Anamorphic Triplet). *An* anamorphic triplet $\mathsf{T} = (\mathsf{aKG}, \mathsf{aSig}, \mathsf{aDec})$ *consists of three PPT algorithms such that*

1. *the* anamorphic key generation algorithm aKG *on input security parameter* 1^λ *outputs the triplet* $(\mathsf{asvk}, \mathsf{assk}, \mathsf{dkey})$ *composed of the* anamorphic verification key asvk, *the* anamorphic signing key assk, *and the* double key dkey;
2. *the* anamorphic signing algorithm aSig *takes as input a* regular *message* msg, *an* anamorphic *message* amsg, *an anamorphic signing key* assk, *and a double key* dkey *and outputs an* anamorphic signature asig;
3. *the* anamorphic decryption algorithm aDec *takes as input an anamorphic signature* asig *and a* double key dkey *and outputs an anamorphic message* amsg;

and that satisfy the following correctness requirement

- *For every pair of messages* $(\mathsf{msg}, \mathsf{amsg})$, *the probability that* $\mathsf{aDec}(\mathsf{asig},$ $\mathsf{dkey}) \neq \mathsf{amsg}$ *is negligible, where* $(\mathsf{asvk}, \mathsf{assk}, \mathsf{dkey}) \leftarrow \mathsf{aKG}(1^\lambda)$ *and* $\mathsf{asig} \leftarrow$ $\mathsf{aSig}(\mathsf{msg}, \mathsf{amsg}, \mathsf{assk}, \mathsf{dkey})$, *and the probability is taken over the random coin tosses of* aKG *and* aSig.

The concept of an anamorphic signature is formalized by means of two games: the *real game*, in which the adversary receives keys and signatures generated by the signature scheme S, and the *anamorphic game*, in which keys and signatures are output by the anamorphic triplet T. The definition requires the two games to be indistinguishable.

Definition 2 (Anamorphic Signature Scheme). *An unforgeable signature scheme* $\mathsf{S} = (\mathsf{KG}, \mathsf{Sig}, \mathsf{Verify})$ *is anamorphic if there exists an anamorphic triplet* $\mathsf{T} = (\mathsf{aKG}, \mathsf{aSig}, \mathsf{aDec})$ *such that for every PPT dictator* $\mathcal{D}$ *there exists a negligible function* negl *such that*

$$\left| \mathrm{Prob}\left[\mathsf{RealG}_{\mathsf{S},\mathcal{D}}(\lambda) = 1 \right] - \mathrm{Prob}\left[\mathsf{AnamorphicG}_{\mathsf{T},\mathcal{D}}(\lambda) \right] \right| \leq \mathsf{negl}(\lambda),$$

where

$\mathsf{RealG}_{\mathsf{S},\mathcal{D}}(\lambda)$

1. $(\mathsf{svk}, \mathsf{ssk}) \leftarrow \mathsf{KG}(1^\lambda);$
2. return $\mathcal{D}^{\mathsf{Os}(\cdot,\cdot,\mathsf{ssk})}(\mathsf{svk}, \mathsf{ssk})$, where
   $\mathsf{Os}(\mathsf{msg}, \mathsf{amsg}, \mathsf{ssk}) = \mathsf{Sig}(\mathsf{msg}, \mathsf{ssk}).$

$\mathsf{AnamorphicG}_{\mathsf{T},\mathcal{D}}(\lambda)$

1. $(\mathsf{asvk}, \mathsf{assk}, \mathsf{dkey}) \leftarrow \mathsf{aKG}(1^\lambda);$
2. return $\mathcal{D}^{\mathsf{Oa}(\cdot,\cdot,\mathsf{assk},\mathsf{dkey})}(\mathsf{asvk}, \mathsf{assk})$, where
   $\mathsf{Oa}(\mathsf{msg}, \mathsf{amsg}, \mathsf{assk}, \mathsf{dkey}) = \mathsf{aSig}(\mathsf{msg}, \mathsf{amsg}, \mathsf{assk}, \mathsf{dkey}).$

In the next section, we consider two consequences of anamorphism. Specifically, the anamorphic message is IND-CPA secure with respect to a party, like the dictator, that does not have the double key; and that if the keys are generated anamorphically, the signature scheme is unforgeable with respect to parties that do not have the signing key and the double key. As we shall see, whether the signature scheme remains unforgeable with respect to parties that have the double key is independent from the security guarantee of anamorphism. In Sect. 2.2, we define the notion of a *symmetric anamorphic signature scheme*, an anamorphic signature scheme for which the double key enables signing. In Sect. 5, we define the notion of a *private anamorphic signature scheme*, an anamorphic signature scheme that remains unforgeable even if the double key is available.

2.1   Security of the Associated Schemes

An anamorphic signature scheme is naturally associated with two schemes: the signature scheme in which keys and signatures are anamorphic (that is, computed by the anamorphic triplet); and the symmetric encryption scheme that hides the anamorphic message by means of the double key. Quite obviously, one would like the signature to be unforgeable and the anamorphic message to be IND-CPA secure. Indeed, the purpose of an anamorphic scheme is to hide the anamorphic message. The formal definition of anamorphic signatures (Definition 2) makes no explicit security guarantee neither about the IND-CPA security of the anamorphic message nor about the security of the signature scheme when the verification key is anamorphic. Note though that the indistinguishability of the two games as required by Definition 2 means in particular that the mere existence of an anamorphic message is indistinguishable from its non-existence which, intuitively, should be sufficient for semantic security of the anamorphic message. Also, anamorphism should imply that forging with respect to an anamorphic verification key is as hard as forging messages in the original signature (as forging in both cases is without the key(s) and if it becomes easy for the anamorphic version, due to the indistinguishability it is easy for the original scheme (a contradiction)). We next give formal proofs for the two intuitions above.

We start by proving that for an anamorphic signature scheme the anamorphic message is hidden from a party that has access to the signing and verification keys but not, obviously, to the double key. This is made formal by means of the IND-CPA game for anamorphic messages, that we call AcpaG. This game is the adaptation of the IND-CPA game to the anamorphic signature setting in which the anamorphic message is "encrypted" by computing a signature of the regular message. This is reflected in the working of the encryption oracle Oe and of the challenge oracle Oc. In game AcpaG the adversary $\mathcal{A}$ has access to the anamorphic keys, both verification and signing, and can ask to see anamorphic signatures for pairs (msg, amsg) of regular/anamorphic messages of their choice; that is, $\mathcal{A}$ can ask for "encryptions" of anamorphic messages of their choice just as in chosen plaintext attack. Once ready, $\mathcal{A}$ outputs the regular message msg and the pair of anamorphic messages $(\mathrm{amsg}_0, \mathrm{amsg}_1)$ on which they want to be tested. Finally, one of the two anamorphic messages is encrypted and $\mathcal{A}$ should not be able to distinguish which one has been used to produce the anamorphic signature. Below we define the anamorphic IND-CPA game AcpaG for an anamorphic triplet $\mathsf{T} = (\mathsf{aKG}, \mathsf{aSig}, \mathsf{aDec})$, PPT adversary $\mathcal{A}$, and bit $\beta \in \{0, 1\}$.

$\mathsf{AcpaG}^{\beta}_{\mathsf{T}, \mathcal{A}}(\lambda)$

1. $(\mathrm{asvk}, \mathrm{assk}, \mathrm{dkey}) \leftarrow \mathsf{aKG}(1^{\lambda})$;
2. $(\mathrm{msg}, \mathrm{amsg}_0, \mathrm{amsg}_1, \mathrm{st}) \leftarrow \mathcal{A}^{\mathsf{Oe}(\cdot, \cdot, \mathrm{assk}, \mathrm{dkey})}(\mathrm{asvk}, \mathrm{assk})$;
3. $\mathrm{asig} = \mathsf{Oc}^{\beta}(\mathrm{msg}, \mathrm{amsg}_0, \mathrm{amsg}_1, \mathrm{assk}, \mathrm{dkey})$;
4. return $\mathcal{A}^{\mathsf{Oe}(\cdot, \cdot, \mathrm{assk}, \mathrm{dkey})}(\mathrm{asig}, \mathrm{st})$;

where

- $\mathsf{Oe}(\mathrm{msg}, \mathrm{amsg}, \mathrm{assk}, \mathrm{dkey}) = \mathsf{aSig}(\mathrm{msg}, \mathrm{amsg}, \mathrm{assk}, \mathrm{dkey})$;
- $\mathsf{Oc}^{\beta}(\mathrm{msg}, \mathrm{amsg}_0, \mathrm{amsg}_1, \mathrm{assk}, \mathrm{dkey}) = \mathsf{aSig}(\mathrm{msg}, \mathrm{amsg}_{\beta}, \mathrm{assk}, \mathrm{dkey})$;

The following theorem holds.

Theorem 3. *Let* S *be anamorphic signature scheme and let* T *be the associated anamorphic triplet. Then for all PPT adversaries* $\mathcal{A}$ *we have*

$$\left| \mathrm{Prob}\left[\mathsf{AcpaG}^0_{\mathsf{T}, \mathcal{A}}(\lambda) = 1\right] - \mathrm{Prob}\left[\mathsf{AcpaG}^1_{\mathsf{T}, \mathcal{A}}(\lambda) = 1\right] \right| \leq \mathsf{negl}(\lambda).$$

Proof. Towards a contradiction, suppose there exists a PPT adversary $\mathcal{A}$ such that

$$\mathrm{Prob}\left[\mathsf{AcpaG}^1_{\mathsf{T}, \mathcal{A}}(\lambda) = 1\right] \geq \mathrm{Prob}\left[\mathsf{AcpaG}^0_{\mathsf{T}, \mathcal{A}}(\lambda) = 1\right] + 1/\mathsf{poly}(\lambda)$$

for some polynomial $\mathsf{poly}(\cdot)$. We construct the following dictator $\mathcal{D}$ that distinguishes games RealG and AnamorphicG. Dictator $\mathcal{D}$ receives a pair of keys (svk, ssk) (that is either regular or anamorphic) and has access to an oracle $O(\cdot, \cdot)$ (that is either Os or Oa) and uses $\mathcal{A}$ in the following way. $\mathcal{D}$ runs $\mathcal{A}$ on input (svk, ssk) and replies to queries (msg, amsg) by returning $O(\mathrm{msg}, \mathrm{amsg})$. When $\mathcal{A}$ return $(\mathrm{msg}, \mathrm{amsg}_0, \mathrm{amsg}_1)$, $\mathcal{D}$ randomly selects β from $\{0, 1\}$ and sets

$\mathtt{ct} = O(\mathtt{msg}, \mathtt{amsg}_\beta)$. Then $\mathcal{D}$ runs $\mathcal{A}$ on input $\mathtt{ct}$ and replies to $\mathcal{A}$'s oracle queries as before. Finally, $\mathcal{A}$ returns bit η and $\mathcal{D}$ outputs 1 iff $\beta = \eta$.

Let us denote by $p_{\alpha,\beta}$ the probability that $\mathcal{A}$ outputs α in game AcpaG^β. By hypothesis we have that $p_{11} \geq p_{10} + 1/\mathsf{poly}(\lambda)$. Suppose that $\mathcal{D}$ is playing the anamorphic game and thus the pair of keys received in input is anamorphic (i.e., output by aKG) and $O = \mathsf{Oa}$. Then observe that $\mathcal{D}$ is providing $\mathcal{A}$ with a view from AcpaG^β and therefore the probability that $\mathcal{D}$ outputs 1 is

$$\frac{1}{2}(p_{11} + p_{00}) = \frac{1}{2}(p_{11} + 1 - p_{10}) \geq \frac{1}{2} + \frac{1}{2 \cdot \mathsf{poly}(\lambda)}.$$

Suppose instead that $\mathcal{D}$ is playing the real game and thus the pair of keys receives in input is regular (i.e., output by KG) and $O = \mathsf{Os}$. Then in this case, the view of $\mathcal{A}$ is independent of β as Os ignores its second argument. Therefore in this case $\mathcal{D}$ outputs 1 with at most probability $1/2$.

We can thus conclude that $\mathcal{D}$ violates the anamorphism of S. Contradiction.

Next we define the concept of the *associated* signature scheme. In the associated signature scheme, the pair of signing and verification keys are anamorphically generated and the regular signing and verifying algorithms are used for the other operations. Then we show that the associated signature scheme is unforgeable as well.

Definition 4. *Let* $\mathsf{S} = (\mathsf{KG}, \mathsf{Sig}, \mathsf{Verify})$ *be an* anamorphic *signature scheme and let* $(\mathsf{aKG}, \mathsf{aSig}, \mathsf{aDec})$ *be the associated anamorphic triplet. The signature scheme associated with* S *is* $\mathsf{S}^\star = (\mathsf{aKG}^\star, \mathsf{aSig}, \mathsf{Verify})$, *where* $\mathsf{aKG}^\star(1^\lambda)$ *is the algorithm that obtains* $(\mathtt{asvk}, \mathtt{assk}, \mathtt{dkey}) \leftarrow \mathsf{aKG}(1^\lambda)$ *and outputs* $(\mathtt{asvk}, \mathtt{assk})$.

Theorem 5. *Let* $\mathsf{S} = (\mathsf{KG}, \mathsf{Sig}, \mathsf{Verify})$ *an* anamorphic *signature scheme and let* $(\mathsf{aKG}, \mathsf{aSig}, \mathsf{aDec})$ *be its anamorphic triplet. Then the associated signature scheme* $\mathsf{S}^\star = (\mathsf{aKG}^\star, \mathsf{aSig}, \mathsf{Verify})$ *is a secure signature scheme.*

Proof. For sake of contradiction, suppose that there exists a PPT adversary $\mathcal{A}$ such that game $\mathsf{sigG}_{\mathsf{S}^\star}$ has a non-negligible probability of outputting 1 and consider the following dictator $\mathcal{D}$ that receives as input a pair of keys $(\mathtt{svk}, \mathtt{ssk})$ and runs $\mathcal{A}$ on input $\mathtt{svk}$. Whenever $\mathcal{A}$ issues a query for message m, $\mathcal{D}$ replies by returning the pair $(m, \mathsf{Sig}(m, \mathtt{ssk}))$. $\mathcal{D}$ outputs 1 if and only if $\mathcal{A}$ outputs a pair $(\mathtt{msg}, \mathtt{sig})$ that is accepted by Verify and that was not returned as a reply to one of $\mathcal{A}$'s queries.

Now observe that if the input pair $(\mathtt{svk}, \mathtt{ssk})$ is anamorphic, that is it is output by $\mathsf{aKG}^\star$, then $\mathcal{D}$ is actually playing game $\mathsf{AnamorphicG}$ while simulating game $\mathsf{sigG}_{\mathsf{S}^\star}$ for $\mathcal{A}$. Thus, by our assumption, the probability that $\mathcal{D}$ outputs 1 is non-negligible. On the other hand, if the input pair $(\mathtt{svk}, \mathtt{ssk})$ is output by KG, then $\mathcal{D}$ is actually playing game RealG while simulating game $\mathsf{sigG}_{\mathsf{S}}$ for $\mathcal{A}$. Since S is secure the probability that $\mathcal{D}$ outputs 1 is negligible.

Therefore, dictator $\mathcal{D}$ described above contradicts the anamorphism of S.

2.2 Symmetric Anamorphism

We next define the concept of a *symmetric* anamorphic signature scheme. As we discussed in the introduction, in a symmetric anamorphic scheme, the double key allows to produce signatures and not just to extract the anamorphic message from a signature. This implies that every user that has the double key can send anamorphic messages that will be read by all other members of the trusted circle, thus implementing a many-to-many communication channel hidden from the dictator. The definition we present below requires the existence of an extraction algorithm that extracts the signing key from the double. This is not the most general definition but all symmetric schemes we present satisfy this definition.

Definition 6 (Symmetric Anamorphic Triplet). *An anamorphic triplet* $T = (aKG, aSig, aDec)$ *is symmetric if there exists an efficient extraction algorithm* Extract *such that, for* $(svk, ssk, dkey) \leftarrow aKG(1^\lambda)$, *we have that* Extract($svk, dkey$) = ssk *except with probability negligible in* λ, *over the coin tosses of* aKG.

Definition 7 (Symmetric Anamorphic Signature Scheme). *An anamorphic signature scheme* $S = (KG, Sig, Verify)$ *with anamorphic symmetric triplet* $T = (aKG, aSig, aDec)$ *is symmetric if* T *is symmetric.*

3 A First Example

In this section we give the first concrete example of an anamorphic signature scheme by showing that the ElGamal signature scheme is symmetric anamorphic.

We start by reviewing the concept of a symmetric encryption scheme with pseudo-random ciphertexts.

In Fig. 1, we describe the ElGamal [10] signature scheme EIS = (EIKG, EISig, ElVerify) as modified by [25]. The signature scheme is proved secure in the Random Oracle Model under the assumption of hardness of the discrete logarithm problem. A variation of this scheme, called the DSA, constitutes the Digital

---

1. The key generation algorithm EIKG, on input security parameter 1^λ, randomly selects (the description of) a cyclic group $\mathbb{G}$ of prime order p, for p of length $\Theta(\lambda)$, a generator g for $\mathbb{G}$, and a hash function $H : \{0,1\}^* \times \mathbb{G} \rightarrow \mathbb{Z}_p$. In addition the algorithm randomly selects $x \leftarrow \mathbb{Z}_p^*$ and sets $y = g^x$.
   Finally, the algorithm outputs the verification key $svk := (\mathbb{G}, g, H, y)$ and the signing key $ssk := (\mathbb{G}, g, H, x)$.
2. The signing algorithm EISig, on input message m and signing key $ssk = (\mathbb{G}, g, H, x)$, outputs $sig = (r, s)$ computed as follows.
   Randomly select $\kappa \leftarrow \mathbb{Z}_p$, set $r := g^\kappa$ and $s := (H(m, r) - x \cdot r)/\kappa \mod (p - 1)$.
3. The verification algorithm ElVerify, on input message m, signature (r, s), and verification key svk, checks if $g^{H(m,r)} = y^r \cdot r^s$.

Fig. 1. The ElGamal signature scheme EIS.

Signature Standard [8] and adapting our proof of anamorphism for ElGamal to DSA is straightforward.

To show that the ElGamal signature scheme is anamorphic, we use the technique of hiding the anamorphic message in the randomness used to produce the signature by means of an encryption scheme with pseudorandom ciphertexts. These are special IND-CPA symmetric encryption schemes whose ciphertexts are pseudorandom; that is, indistinguishable from truly random strings of the same length. Specifically, instead of being selected at random, κ is set equal to an encryption of the anamorphic message computed using an encryption scheme with pseudorandom ciphertexts. The encryption key K used to compute the ciphertext constitutes the double key. To construct a valid signature, we observe that the ElGamal signature scheme imposes the following relation:

$$H(m, r) = x \cdot r + s \cdot \kappa.$$

Therefore, if κ and, consequently, $r = g^\kappa$ are fixed and x is the secret key, then the above equation can be solved for s so to produce a legal signature (r, s).

Let us proceed more formally and denote by prE = (prKG, prEnc, prDec) an IND-CPA secure encryption scheme with pseudorandom ciphertexts. Consider the following anamorphic triplet EIT = (aKG, aSig, aDec).

1. The anamorphic key-generation algorithm aKG on input 1^λ runs EIKG to obtain (asvk := $(\mathbb{G}, g, H, y)$, assk := $(\mathbb{G}, g, H, x)$). In addition, the algorithm randomly selects $K \leftarrow$ prKG(1^λ) and sets dkey := (K, x). Finally, the algorithm outputs (asvk, assk, dkey).
2. The anamorphic signing algorithm aSig, on input messages (msg, amsg), signing key assk = (p, h, H, x) and double key K, computes ciphertext prct = prEnc$(K,$ amsg$)$, and sets $\kappa :=$ prct and $r = g^\kappa$. Finally, s is computed as $s = (H($msg$, r) - x \cdot r) \cdot \kappa^{-1}$ and the pair (r, s) is output.
3. The anamorphic decryption algorithm aDec receives a signature (r, s) for normal message msg and double key (K, x) and computes act as prct = $(H($msg$, r) - x \cdot r) \cdot s^{-1}$ and amsg as amsg = prDec$(K,$ prct$)$.

The proof of the following theorem can be found in the full version.

Theorem 8. *Given that the ElGamal signature is unforgeable in the Random Oracle Model, the ElGamal signature scheme is a symmetric anamorphic signature scheme in the Random Oracle Model.*

Remark. In the construction of the anamorphic triplet for ElGamal we have made the implicit assumption that the ciphertexts of prE are randomly distributed in $\mathbb{Z}_p$. Indeed, the anamorphic signing algorithm should sample ciphertexts until one in $\mathbb{Z}_p$ is obtained and this on average will require at most 2 trials. Similar considerations apply to other constructions prensented in this paper.

4   Three-Message Public-Coin Protocols

In this section, we study the Fiat-Shamir heuristics [11] that constructs signature schemes from three-message public-coin protocols. If the protocol enjoys a specific security property (see Theorem 11 below), the resulting signature scheme is unforgeable in the Random Oracle Model. We show that this general technique preserves anamorphism; that is, if the starting protocol is anamorphic (in a sense that will be formally defined below) then the resulting signature scheme is also anamorphic. We then give a simple sufficient condition for anamorphism of a protocol and use it to show that several well known three-message public-coin protocols are anamorphic and thus so are the signature schemes obtained from them via Fiat-Shamir heuristics.

Let us set up our terminology. Let (P, V) be two PPT machines playing a three round protocol for a polynomial relation $\mathcal{R}$. If $(x, w) \in \mathcal{R}$ we say that x is the *instance* and w is the *witness*. Following the notation used for Sigma protocols [6], we let $(a, \mathsf{st}) \leftarrow P(x, w)$ be the pair of the first message a of the interaction and P's state. Message a is sent to V which responds with a random string e of length $r(\lambda)$, for some polynomially bounded function $r(\cdot)$. P concludes the interaction by computing and sending message $z \leftarrow P(x, w, \mathsf{st}, e)$. Finally, V outputs a bit $b \leftarrow V(x, a, e, z)$. We denote by $[P(x, w) \leftrightarrow V(x)]$ the distribution of the transcripts (a, e, z) of interactions between P and V over random coin tosses of P and V. We say that a transcript $(a, e, z) \leftarrow [P(x, w) \leftrightarrow V(x)]$ is accepting for x if $V(x, a, e, z)$.

In the next section, we define the notion of an anamorphic three-message public-coin protocol.

4.1   Anamorphic Three-Message Public-Coin Protocols

Roughly speaking, a *prover-to-verifier anamorphic* three-message public-coin protocol for relation $\mathcal{R}$ is a protocol in which prover and verifier have access to a private input called the *double key* dkey. Like in a regular protocol (P, V), (x, w) is sampled from $\mathcal{R}$ and the prover has (x, w) and the verifier has x. In addition, both prover and verifier share a *double key* and the prover has an *anamorphic message* amsg that would like to send the verifier in a secure way. At the end of an execution, in which the anamorphic prover runs on input $(x, w, \mathsf{amsg}, \mathsf{dkey})$ and the anamorphic verifier on input (x, dkey), the verifier extracts amsg from the transcript. The security property requires that the dictator that has access to (x, w, amsg), but not to dkey, cannot tell whether it is interacting with a real prover or with an anamorphic prover. Let us proceed more formally.

Definition 9. *Let* 3Prot $= (P, V)$ *be a three-message public-coin protocol for relation* $\mathcal{R}$. *We say that* RRT $= (\mathsf{dKG}, \mathsf{aP}, \mathsf{aDec})$ *is an anamorphic triplet for* 3Prot *if*

1. *The* double-key *generation algorithm* dKG, *on input security parameter* 1^λ *and* (x, w) *in the support of* $\mathcal{R}(\lambda)$, *returns* double key dkey.
2. aP *is the* anamorphic prover *algorithm that, on input a pair instance-witness* (x, w), *an anamorphic message* amsg, *and a double key* dkey, *plays the protocol with a verifier. That is,* $\mathsf{aP}(x, w, \mathsf{amsg}, \mathsf{dkey})$ *outputs* (a, st) *and* $\mathsf{aP}(x, w, \mathsf{amsg}, \mathsf{dkey}, a, \mathsf{st}, e)$ *outputs* z.

and the following correctness *condition is satisfied:* $\mathsf{aDec}(x, \mathsf{dkey}, \mathsf{tx}) = \mathsf{amsg}$, *except with negligible probability, where* $(x, w) \leftarrow \mathcal{R}(\lambda)$, $\mathsf{dkey} \leftarrow \mathsf{dKG}(1^\lambda, x, w)$ *and* $\mathsf{tx} \leftarrow [\mathsf{aP}(x, w, \mathsf{amsg}, \mathsf{dkey}) \leftrightarrow V(x)]$.

We are now ready for the definition of a *prover-to-verifier anamorphic three-message public-coin protocol*.

Definition 10. *We say that three-message public-coin protocol* $\mathsf{3Prot} = (P, V)$ *is* prover-to-verifier anamorphic *(or simply,* anamorphic*) if there exists an anamorphic triplet* $\mathsf{T} = (\mathsf{dKG}, \mathsf{aP}, \mathsf{aDec})$ *such that, for all PPT dictators* $\mathcal{D}$,

$$\left|\mathrm{Prob}\left[\mathsf{ProtG}^0_{\mathsf{3Prot},\mathsf{T},\mathcal{D}}(\lambda) = 1\right] - \mathrm{Prob}\left[\mathsf{ProtG}^1_{\mathsf{3Prot},\mathsf{T},\mathcal{D}}(\lambda) = 1\right]\right| \leq \mathsf{negl}(\lambda),$$

where

$\mathsf{ProtG}^\beta_{\mathsf{3Prot},\mathsf{T},\mathcal{D}}(\lambda)$

1. Set $(x, w) \leftarrow \mathcal{R}(\lambda)$ and $\mathbf{dkey} \leftarrow \mathsf{dKG}(1^\lambda, x, w)$;
2. return $\mathcal{D}(x, w)^{O^\beta(\mathbf{amsg})}$, where
   $O^0(\mathbf{amsg})$ samples a transcript from $[P(x, w) \leftrightarrow \mathcal{D}(x, w, \mathbf{amsg})]$; and
   $O^1(\mathbf{amsg})$ samples a transcript from $[\mathsf{aP}(x, w, \mathbf{amsg}, \mathbf{dkey}) \leftrightarrow \mathcal{D}(x, \mathbf{amsg})]$.

Two remarks are in order. First of all, we let the dictator $\mathcal{D}$ pick the anamorphic message $\mathbf{amsg}$ and the challenge e, and have access to the witness w for x. This in the spirit of anamorphism that requires the dictator to have access to any secret information related to a public information they are aware of. Moreover, we also stress that the double key depends on the pair (x, w) and thus they must be generated and securely shared for each different pair (x, w). This does not affect the applicability of the notion. Indeed, we note that in the two main applications to identifications protocols and to signature schemes, the prover's input (x, w) is fixed as they constitute the id and the authentication key in the case of identification protocols, and the verification and the signing keys in the case of signature schemes.

4.2   Fiat-Shamir Gives Symmetric Anamorphic Signatures

The Fiat-Shamir heuristics [11] constructs a signature scheme from any three-message public-coin protocol for a relation $\mathcal{R}$ satisfying a specific security condition. See Theorem 11 below.

Before proceeding further, let us fix a three-message public-coin protocols $\mathsf{3Prot} = (P, V)$ for a relation $\mathcal{R}$ and describe the signature scheme $\mathsf{FS} = (\mathsf{fsKG}, \mathsf{fsSig}, \mathsf{fsVerify})$ obtained by applying the Fiat-Shamir heuristics to $\mathsf{3Prot}$. Below, with a slight abuse of notation, we identify the relation $\mathcal{R}$ with the sampling algorithm $\mathcal{R}$ that on input 1^λ returns a pair $(x, w) \in \mathcal{R}$ with $|x| = \lambda$. The transform uses hash function H.

1. The key-generation algorithm $\mathsf{fsKG}(1^\lambda)$ samples a pair $(x, w) \leftarrow \mathcal{R}(1^\lambda)$. The instance x is the verification key $\mathtt{fsvk} = x$ and the pair (x, w) is the signing key $\mathtt{fssk} = (x, w)$.

2. The signing algorithm fsSig, on input message msg and signing key fssk = (x, w), runs the prover P on input (x, w) and produces the first message a along with state st. Then, it sets $e = H(a, \text{msg})$ and computes message $z = P(x, w, a, \text{st})$. The signature of msg is the transcript sig = (a, e, z).
3. The verification algorithm fsVerify on input signature verification key fsvk = x, message msg and signature sig = (a, e, z) checks if $V(x, a, e, z) = 1$ and if $e = H(a, \text{msg})$.

There is a long series of results starting from [11] that establish the security of the transform. The minimal conditions for the security of FS were given by [1] and are motivated by the use of three-message public-coin protocols as identification protocols. Here the prover picks a pair $(x, w) \in \mathcal{R}$ and x will be the prover's identity and w their secret key. The prover successfully manages to identify themselves if the verifier accepts. A possible security notion for identification schemes is *security against under passive attacks*, where an *impersonator* tries to convince the verifier without the knowledge of the secret key. The impersonator is allowed to obtain any (polynomial) number of of transcripts of honest executions of the protocol, after which he can try to impersonate the legitimate prover. The attack is passive as only honest executions of the protocol are made available to the impersonator. If any PPT impersonator has only negligible probability of success, then we say that the protocol is secure against passive attacks (see [1] for a formal definition).

Theorem 11 ([1]). *If* 3Prot = (P, V) *is secure against passive attacks, then the signature scheme obtained by applying the Fiat-Shamir heuristics is secure against chosen-message attacks in the ROM.*

Next, we show that if 3Prot is anamorphic, then the signature resulting from applying Fiat-Shamir is anamorphic.

Theorem 12. *Suppose that* 3Prot *is anamorphic and secure against passive attacks. Then the signature scheme* FS = (fsKG, fsSig, fsVerify) *obtained by applying the Fiat-Shamir transform to* 3Prot *is symmetric anamorphic.*

Proof. First of all observe that if 3Prot is secure against passive attacks then, by Theorem 11, FS is unforgeable. Consider now the following anamorphic triplet afsT = (afsKG, afsSig, afsDec) that is, essentially, the Fiat-Shamir transform applied to the anamorphic prover. More precisely, let T = (dKG, aP, aDec) be the anamorphic triplet associated with 3Prot.

1. The anamorphic key generation algorithm afsKG(1^λ) runs fsKG(1^λ) to get verification key svk := x and signing key ssk := (x, w), and it then selects $d \leftarrow$ dKG($1^\lambda, x, w$) and sets dkey := (d, x, w).
   Note that dkey contains the signing key ssk and thus the scheme is symmetrically anamorphic.
2. The anamorphic signing algorithm afsSig takes as input message msg, anamorphic message amsg, signing key ssk = (x, w), and double key dkey = (d, x, w) and computes the anamorphic signature in the following way. Set $(a, \text{st}) \leftarrow$

$\mathsf{aP}(x, w, \mathsf{amsg}, d)$, $e = H(a, \mathsf{msg})$, and $z \leftarrow \mathsf{aP}(x, w, \mathsf{amsg}, d, a, \mathsf{st}, e)$. Finally, $\mathsf{asig} = (a, e, z)$ is the anamorphic signature produced.

3. The anamorphic decryption algorithm afsDec receives anamorphic signature $\mathsf{asig} = (a, e, z)$ and double key $\mathsf{dkey} = (d, x, w)$ and runs algorithm $\mathsf{aDec}(\mathsf{asig}, d)$ to obtain amsg.

Correctness follows from the correctness property of the anamorphic triplet of (P, V). Let us now assume for the sake of contradiction that there exists a dictator $\mathcal{D}$ that breaks anamorphism of FS and consider the following adversary $\mathcal{A}$ that breaks the anamorphism of (P, V) and of the triplet T.

$\mathcal{A}$ receives a pair $(x, w) \leftarrow \mathcal{R}(1^\lambda)$ and interacts with an oracle O that is either prover P or anamorphic prover aP. Upon receiving (x, w) as input, $\mathcal{A}$ prepares $(\mathsf{svk}, \mathsf{ssk}) = (x, (x, w))$ and runs $\mathcal{D}$ on input $(\mathsf{svk}, \mathsf{ssk})$. When $\mathcal{D}$ issues query $(\mathsf{msg}, \mathsf{amsg})$, $\mathcal{A}$ interacts with the oracle O on input (x, w, amsg) and in the interaction $\mathcal{A}$ sets $e = H(a, \mathsf{msg})$. Finally, $\mathcal{A}$ returns the transcript of the interaction as a response to $\mathcal{D}$'s query $(\mathsf{msg}, \mathsf{amsg})$. When $\mathcal{D}$ stops, $\mathcal{A}$ returns $\mathcal{D}$'s output has its own output.

Now observe that if $\mathcal{A}$ plays ProtG^0, and thus $\mathcal{A}$ interacts with prover P, then every query by $\mathcal{D}$ is answered with a regular signature. Therefore, the probability that $\mathcal{A}$ returns 1 in game ProtG^0 is equal to the probability that $\mathcal{D}$ returns 1 in game RealG. On the other hand, if $\mathcal{A}$ plays ProtG^1, and thus $\mathcal{A}$ interacts with anamorphic prover aP, then every query by $\mathcal{D}$ is answered with an anamorphic signature. Therefore, the probability that $\mathcal{A}$ returns 1 in game ProtG^1 is equal to the probability that $\mathcal{D}$ returns 1 in game $\mathsf{AnamorphicG}$. Therefore

$$\left| \mathrm{Prob}\left[\mathsf{ProtG}^0_{\mathsf{3Prot}, \mathsf{T}, \mathcal{A}}(\lambda) = 1\right] - \mathrm{Prob}\left[\mathsf{ProtG}^1_{\mathsf{3Prot}, \mathsf{T}, \mathcal{A}}(\lambda) = 1\right]\right|$$

$$= \left| \mathrm{Prob}\left[\mathsf{RealG}_{\mathsf{FS}, \mathcal{D}}(\lambda) = 1\right] - \mathrm{Prob}\left[\mathsf{AnamorphicG}_{\mathsf{afsT}, \mathcal{D}}(\lambda) = 1\right]\right| \geq 1/\mathsf{poly}(\lambda).$$

We thus reached a contradiction since we had assumed that 3Prot was anamorphic.

4.3   A Sufficient Condition for Anamorphism

In this section we give a sufficient condition for a three-message public-coin protocol to be anamorphic. Roughly speaking, we say that a prover P is *randomness recovering*, if there exists a way to recover the randomness used by P to produce the first message a. As we shall see, randomness recovering are easily proved to be anamorphic. Let us now proceed more formally.

Definition 13 (Randomness Recovering Protocol.). *We say that a prover P of a three-message public-coin protocol is* randomness recovering, *if there exists a recovering algorithm* RRecov *that, on input $(x, w) \in \mathcal{R}$ and a transcript (a, e, z) for (x, w), outputs the randomness used to create a.*

We next show that a protocol $\mathsf{3Prot} = (P, V)$ with randomness recovering prover is (prover-to-verifier) anamorphic by using an encryption scheme $\mathsf{prE} = (\mathsf{prKG}, \mathsf{prEnc}, \mathsf{prDec})$ with pseudorandom ciphertexts. More precisely, consider the following "randomness-recovering" anamorphic triplet RRT = (dKG, aP, aDec).

1. The *double-key generation* algorithm dKG on input (x, w), randomly selects $K \leftarrow \mathsf{prKG}(1^\lambda)$ and outputs $\mathsf{dkey} := (x, w, K)$.
2. The *anamorphic prover* aP on input (x, w, K, amsg), computes act equal to $\mathsf{prEnc}(K, \mathsf{amsg})$ and then aP runs the code of P by using act as a random tape.
3. The *anamorphic decryption* algorithm aDec, on input a transcript $\mathsf{tx} = (a, e, z)$ and $\mathsf{dkey} = (x, w, K)$, runs the recovering algorithm $\mathsf{RRecov}(x, w, \mathsf{tx})$ to obtain act and gets amsg by decrypting act using K.

We have the following theorem.

Theorem 14. *Any Randomness Recovering protocol is (prover-to-verifier) anamorphic.*

Proof. We observe that the only difference between the games AnamorphicG and RealG is in the randomness used to construct the first message as in the former true randomness is used, whereas in the latter a pseudorandom ciphertext is employed. Any adversary that distinguishes the two games can be used to distinguish a ciphertext of prE from true randomness thus breaking the pseudo-randomness property of prE.

4.4 Examples of Three-Message Protocols with Randomness Recovering

Several 3-message protocols can be shown to be *randomness recovering* (see, for example, [2,3,11,12,15,19,21,22,24,29,31]). In this section, we give two explicit examples, one from the number theoretic domain that can be used to derive the ElGamal signature scheme via the Fiat-Shamir transform (see Sect. 4.2) and one from the graph theoretic domain.

Discrete Log. Consider the protocol for Discrete Log by Chaum and Pedersen [5]. In this protocol, the common input consists of a group $\mathbb{G}$ of a prime order p, a generator g and $x \in \mathbb{G}$. The prover holds a the discrete w such that $x = g^w$. He produces a commitment a by picking r at random and setting $a = g^r$. After receiving a random challenge e from the verifier, the prover replies with $z = r + ew$. Finally, the verifier accepts the proof if $g^z = a \cdot x^e$.

To see that the protocol is randomness extracting, we observe that the randomness r used to produce first message a can be obtained from z. Indeed, $r = z - ew$ and the value of e is in the transcript and w is the witness. This is very similar to how we proved that ElGamal and Schnorr signatures and this is no coincidence as the ElGamal and Schnorr signatures derive from the protocol above through the Fiat-Shamir transform. In the next section we show that this general technique that derives signature schemes from three-message public-coin protocols when applied to protocol with randomness recovery yield anamorphic signature schemes.

Graph Isomorphism. This is a classical proof system by [13] that is not used as part of the Fiat-Shamir heuristic as the resulting signature scheme would be inefficient. This is mainly due to the fact that a hard instance would require very large graphs and that the verifier's challenge is only 1-bit long and thus several instances must be executed in parallel to achieve a small error probability. Nonetheless, we give it as an example of a proof system that is not number-theoretic in nature.

Here the common input is a pair of graphs (G_0, G_1) and the prover holds as a witness an isomorphism π such that $\pi(G_0) = G_1$. To produce the first message, the prover picks a random permutation σ and sends the graph $H = \sigma(G_0)$ to the verifier. The verifier's challenge is a random bit e and the final prover's message is an isomorphism $\tau : G_e \to H$.

To see that the protocol is randomness extracting, we observe that the randomness σ used to produce the first message H is equal to τ if $e = 0$; otherwise, $\sigma = \tau \circ \pi$. Note that τ is part of the transcript and π is the witness for the common input.

5   Private Anamorphic Signatures

In this section we introduce the notion of a *private* anamorphic signature scheme, that captures the idea that the anamorphic signing key remains *private*, even if the double key is released. More precisely, the signature scheme remains unforgeable even by an adversary that has access to the double key. Whereas symmetric anamorphic signatures can be used to implement a many-to-many communication channel hidden from the dictator, private anamorphic signatures yield one-to-many channels in which the owner of the signer key is the designated sender and the parties with the double key are the receivers. Of course, every private anamorphic signature can be made symmetric by appending the signing key to the double key.

Requiring that the signature scheme remains unforgeable even if the double key is released is similar to the requirements studied in Theorem 5 that proved that the anamorphic verification keys do not weaken the unforgeability of the signature scheme and this latter property is a direct consequence of the anamorphism property. A *private* anamorphic signature makes the same requirement with respect to adversaries that have access to the *double key* but, of course, not to the anamorphic signing key.

We formally define this concept by strengthening experiment sigG used to formalize unforgeability by letting the adversary also receive the double key; then we present a simple condition (that we call *separability*) on the anamorphic key generation algorithm that is readily seen to be sufficient for private anamorphism. This will allow us to simplify the proof of private anamorphism for our constructions. In Sect. 7, we show that the Naor-Yung paradigm [20] that lifts one-time signatures to many-time signatures gives private anamorphic signature schemes when instantiated with one-time signature schemes that enjoy a weaker form of anamorphism. As a special case, NY instantiated with Lamport's tagging systems [18] gives private anamorphic signature schemes under the sole assumption of existence of one-way functions.

5.1   Formal Definition of Private Anamorphism

To formalize the concept of a private anamorphic signature, we consider the following game DsigG for an anamorphic signature scheme $\mathsf{S} = (\mathsf{KG}, \mathsf{Sig}, \mathsf{Verify})$, associated triplet $\mathsf{T} = (\mathsf{aKG}, \mathsf{aSig}, \mathsf{aDec})$ and PPT adversary $\mathcal{A}$. The game is similar to the game used to define unforgeability and the goal of the adversary is to produce a new signature that has not been returned by the signature oracle. However, here we consider a stronger adversary that has access to the double key dkey.

$\mathsf{DsigG}_{\mathsf{S},\mathsf{T}}^{\mathcal{A}}(\lambda)$

1. $(\mathsf{asvk}, \mathsf{assk}, \mathsf{dkey}) \leftarrow \mathsf{aKG}(1^{\lambda})$;
2. $(\mathsf{msg}, \mathsf{sig}) \leftarrow \mathcal{A}^{\mathsf{Os}(\cdot, \mathsf{assk})}(\mathsf{asvk}, \mathsf{dkey})$,
   where $\mathsf{Os}(m, \mathsf{assk}) = (m, \mathsf{Sig}(m, \mathsf{assk}))$;
3. if $\mathsf{Verify}(\mathsf{sig}, \mathsf{msg}, \mathsf{asvk}) = 1$ and $(\mathsf{msg}, \mathsf{sig})$ has not been returned by Os then return 1; else return 0.

Definition 15. *An anamorphic signature scheme* $\mathsf{S} = (\mathsf{KG}, \mathsf{Sig}, \mathsf{Verify})$ *with anamorphic triplet* $\mathsf{T} = (\mathsf{aKG}, \mathsf{aSig}, \mathsf{aDec})$ *is* private anamorphic *if, for every PPT adversary* $\mathcal{A}$, *the probability that* $\mathsf{DsigG}_{\mathsf{S},\mathsf{T}}^{\mathcal{A}}(\lambda)$ *returns 1 is negligible in* λ.

The ElGamal Signature Scheme. It is not difficult to see that the anamorphic triplet presented in Sect. 3 for ElGamal is not private as it contains the signing key x. We want to briefly describe how to make it private by using the *rejection sampling technique*, that has been used in the context of anamorphic encryption by [23]. The double key is the seed K of a pseudorandom function F with one-bit output. To embed a one-bit anamorphic message, the signer samples signatures (r, s) until they obtain a signature with $F(K, r) = b$. On average two samples suffice. This technique can be extended for any message with $O(\log \lambda)$ bits. In this section we will give private schemes with polynomial bandwidth.

5.2   A Sufficient Condition for Private Anamorphism

In the definition of anamorphic triplet, we allow the anamorphic key generation algorithm to jointly generate the anamorphic verification and signing keys, and the double key. This means that the double key and the signing key could share random coin tosses used in their generation and in this case it is not clear whether unforgeability still holds if an adversary has access to the double key. We consider a special case of anamorphic key generation algorithms that can be seen as the parallel (and independent) composition of the normal key-generation algorithm KG and of the *double-key* generation algorithm dKG that are run on fresh and independent randomness. We call these algorithms and the anamorphic triplets with such key generation algorithms *separable*. Since separable anamorphic key generation algorithms unlink the generation of signing and double key, the same double key can be used across multiple signing keys. This is crucial for anamorphic signature schemes that update the signing (and the verification) key as new signatures are produced (e.g., the Naor-Yung construction discussed in Sect. 7).

Definition 16 (Separable Anamorphic Key Generation.). *Let* S *be an anamorphic signature scheme with anamorphic triplet* T = (aKG, aSig, aDec). *We say that the* T *is separable if* aKG *is the parallel and independent composition of algorithm* KG, *that outputs the signing and verification keys, and of PPT algorithm* dKG *that outputs the double key.*

We have the following theorem whose proof is straightforward and is found in the full version.

Theorem 17. *Let* S *be an anamorphic signature scheme with anamorphic triplet* T. *If* T *is separable then* S *is private anamorphic.*

6 One-Time Signature Schemes

In this section we look at one-time signature schemes and define the notion of a *weakly anamorphic* one-time signature where the anamorphic message must be available at key-generation time and not at signature time like in anamorphic signatures. From a technical point of view, this is due to the fact that one-time signature schemes have often deterministic signature algorithms and randomization is only used in the selection of the signing and verification keys. On the positive side, as we shall see below, weak anamorphism allows for a limited decoupling of the generation of the double key and of the pair of anamorphic signing and verification key and thus the same double key can be used in conjuction with more than one anamorphic pair of keys.

Clearly, weakly anamorphic signatures have limited interest *per se*. The reason for studying this concept is in its applications. We shall see, in Sect. 7, that weakly anamorphic one-time signatures give full private anamorphism when lifted to many-time signatures by the Naor-Yung paradigm. In addition, in the full version we show that weakly anamorphic one-time signature can be used in the context of the CHK [4] CCA encryption scheme to make the resulting encryption scheme anamorphic. Let us now proceed in order.

Syntax for One-Time Signature Schemes. We modify slightly the syntax of a one-time signature OneTSig = (oKG, oSig, oVerify) by having the key-generation algorithm oKG accept as input the security parameter 1^λ as well as the length parameter 1^ℓ that determines the length of the one message that will be signed. Also, the security game sigG is modified to reflect the one-time nature of the scheme by allowing the adversary $\mathcal{A}$ at most one query to the signature oracle Os.

We have the following definition.

Definition 18 (Weakly Anamorphic Triplet). *A* weakly anamorphic triplet T = (odKG, oaKG, oaDec) *for one-time signature scheme* OneTSig = (oKG, oSig, oVerify) *consists of three PPT algorithms such that*

1. *the double-key generation algorithm* odKG *that, on input security parameter* 1^λ, *outputs the double-key* odkey*;*
2. *the anamorphic key-generation algorithm* oaKG *that, on input security parameter* 1^λ, *length parameter* 1^ℓ, *double-key* odkey, *and anamorphic message* amsg *outputs the pair* (asvk, assk) *composed of the anamorphic verification key* asvk *and the anamorphic signing key* assk*;*
3. *the anamorphic decryption algorithm* oaDec *takes as input a signature* asig *and a double key* odkey *and outputs an anamorphic message* amsg*;*

and that satisfy the following correctness requirement

– *For every pair of ℓ-bit messages* (msg, amsg) *the probability that* oaDec(sig, dkey) $\neq$ amsg *is negligible, where* odkey $\leftarrow$ odKG(1^λ), (asvk, assk) $\leftarrow$ oaKG(1^λ, 1^ℓ, dkey, amsg), *and* sig = Sig(msg, assk) *and the probability is taken over the random coin tosses of* odKG *and* oaKG.

We next present the definition of a weakly anamorphic signature scheme.

Definition 19. *An unforgeable one-time signature scheme* OneTSig = (oKG, oSig, oVerify) *is weakly anamorphic with weakly anamorphic triplet* T = (odKG, oaKG, oaDec) *if for every PPT dictator* $\mathcal{D}$, *and for every* ℓ = poly(λ), *there exists a negligible function* negl *such that*

$$\left| \text{Prob}\left[\text{WeakG}^0_{\text{S,T},\mathcal{D}}(\lambda, \ell) = 1\right] - \text{Prob}\left[\text{WeakG}^1_{\text{S,T},\mathcal{D}}(\lambda, \ell) = 1\right] \right| \leq \text{negl}(\lambda)$$

where

$\text{WeakG}^\beta_{\text{S,T},\mathcal{D}}(\lambda, \ell)$

1. odkey $\leftarrow$ odKG(1^λ);
2. return $\mathcal{D}^{\text{OracleKG}^\beta(1^\lambda, 1^\ell, \text{odkey}, \cdot)}(1^\lambda)$;
   where $\text{OracleKG}^0(1^\lambda, 1^\ell, \text{odkey}, \text{amsg}) = \text{oKG}(1^\lambda, 1^\ell)$
   and $\text{OracleKG}^1(1^\lambda, 1^\ell, \text{odkey}, \text{amsg}) = \text{oaKG}(1^\lambda, 1^\ell, \text{odkey}, \text{amsg})$.

In the game above the dictator has access to an oracle that returns pairs of verification and signing keys that are generated either regularly by oKG or anamorphically by oaKG. We note that if keys are generated anamorphically they are with respect to the same double key odkey. Also note that the dictator can compute all signatures of their choice since the signing key is provided by the oracle. At the end the dictator outputs its guess to whether the keys received are anamorphic or regular.

6.1 Lamport's Tagging Systems

We describe Lamport's tagging system $\mathsf{L} = (\mathsf{LKG}, \mathsf{LSig}, \mathsf{LVerify})$, a one-time signature scheme that uses a one-way function $f : \{0,1\}^* \to \{0,1\}^*$ (see [18]). For sake of compactness and without loss of generality, we assume that f is length preserving. The idea behind Lamport's tagging system is to select a secret $x_{b,j}$ for each bit position j and for each bit-value b of the message and then hide it by means of a one-way function f by computing $y_{b,j} = f(x_{b,j})$. The $y_{b,j}$'s constitute the verification key and to sign a message one reveals the secrets for each bit position j and value m_j of the message m in that position. Verification then just consists in re-applying the function f to the revealed secrets and checking that the value obtained appears in the verification key. See Fig. 2 for a formal description of L.

---

1. $\mathsf{LKG}(1^\lambda, 1^\ell)$ randomly selects $x_{0,j}, x_{1,j} \leftarrow \{0,1\}^\lambda$ and sets $y_{0,j} = f(x_{0,j})$ and $y_{1,j} = f(x_{1,j})$, for $j = 1, \ldots, \ell$. The verification key is the sequence $\mathsf{Lvk} = ((y_{0,j}, y_{1,j}))_{j=1}^\ell$ and the signing key is the sequence $\mathsf{Lsk} = ((x_{0,j}, x_{1,j}))_{j=1}^\ell$.
2. LSig on input message $\mathsf{msg} = m_1, \ldots, m_\ell$ and signing key $\mathsf{Lsk} = ((x_{0,j}, x_{1,j}))_{j=1}^\ell$ computes the signature by setting $\mathsf{sig} = (x_{m_j,j})_{j=1}^\ell$.
3. To verify signature $\mathsf{sig} = (s_j)_{j=1}^\ell$ of message $\mathsf{msg} = m_1, \ldots, m_\ell$ against verification key $\mathsf{Lvk} = ((y_{0,j}, y_{1,j}))_{j=1}^\ell$, the $\mathsf{LVerify}$ algorithm checks that $f(s_j) = y_{m_j,j}$ for $j = 1, \ldots, \ell$.

Fig. 2. Lamport's tagging system L [18]

We have the following theorem.

Theorem 20 ([18]). *Assuming existence of one-way functions, Lamport's tagging system is an unforgeable one-time signature scheme.*

Note that for one-time signatures the PPT adversary $\mathcal{A}$ is allowed to make at most one call to oracle Os in game sigG.

How to make Lamport's tagging system weakly anamorphic? Essentially, instead of picking $x_{0,1}$ and $x_{1,1}$ at random, the anamorphic key generation algorithm picks them as the ciphertext of the anamorphic message amsg computed with respect to an encryption scheme with pseudorandom ciphertexts (message randomized and then encrypted, each time randomized differently). Note that every signature will include exactly one of $x_{0,1}$ and $x_{1,1}$. This embeds the anamorphic message in the verification and signing key. We also note that the encryption key K used to encrypt the anamorphic message in the $x_{0,1}$ and $x_{1,1}$ can be chosen prior and independently from the anamorphic keys. On the other hand the anamorphic keys do depend on K as they contain ciphertexts encrypted with K.

More formally, let $\mathsf{prE} = (\mathsf{prKG}, \mathsf{prEnc}, \mathsf{prDec})$ be a symmetric encryption scheme with pseudorandom ciphertexts. We assume that prE for security parameter λ encrypts $n(\lambda)$-bit plaintexts into λ-bit ciphertexts and that $\ell = n(\lambda)$. Consider the following weakly anamorphic triplet $\mathsf{T} = (\mathsf{LdKG}, \mathsf{LaKG}, \mathsf{LaDec})$.

1. Algorithm $\mathsf{LdKG}(1^\lambda)$ randomly samples a key $K \leftarrow \mathsf{prKG}(1^\lambda)$. The key K is the double key.
2. Algorithm LaKG, on input security parameter 1^λ, length parameter 1^ℓ, double key K, and anamorphic amsg, constructs the signing and verification key just as $\mathsf{LKG}(1^\lambda, 1^\ell)$ with the only exceptions that $x_{0,1} \leftarrow \mathsf{prEnc}(K, \mathsf{amsg})$ and $x_{1,1} \leftarrow \mathsf{prEnc}(K, \mathsf{amsg})$. The algorithm returns $(\mathsf{asvk}, \mathsf{assk})$ so computed.
3. Algorithm LaDec receives a signature $(x_1, \ldots, x_\ell)$ for message msg and double key K and returns the anamorphic message computed by decrypting x_1 with key K. That is, aDec returns $\mathsf{prDec}(K, x_1)$.

Theorem 21. *Assuming existence of one-way functions, Lamport's tagging system is weakly anamorphic.*

The proof is found in the full version where we also discuss other one-time signatures.

7   The Naor-Yung Paradigm for Signatures

The Naor-Yung paradigm [20] is a general paradigm to lift one-time signatures to many-time signatures in the standard model and it relies on the notion of a *Universal One-Way Hash functions (UOWHF)*. We show that when instantiated with weakly anamorphic one-time signature schemes, the NY paradigm yields many-time private anamorphic signature schemes. Specifically, the NY paradigm instantiated with Lamport's tagging systems [18] and Rompel's UOWHF based on one-way functions [27] gives a private anamorphic signature scheme based on the minimal assumption of one-way functions.

Roughly speaking, the NY paradigm upgrades a one-time signature scheme to many-time signature by updating the verification key and, consequently, the signing key before each use of the signing algorithm. The i-th key is used to sign the hash of two new keys: one will be used to sign the $(i + 1)$-st message and the other is the $(i + 1)$-st key. In this way, a one-time key is only used once. A positive side effect of this is that, even if the one-time signature scheme is only weakly anamorphic, NY can be shown to be anamorphic (that is, without the limitation that the anamorphic message is fixed at key-generation time): key-generation time for the one-time signature coincides with the signature time of the many-time signature. In the full version we will show that the extensions to a tree-based approach of the NY paradigm can give stateless private anamorphic signature schemes.

Going into more details, let us fix a weakly anamorphic one-time signature $\mathsf{OneTSig} = (\mathsf{oKG}, \mathsf{oSig}, \mathsf{oVerify})$. The many-time scheme obtained from applying the NY paradigm to $\mathsf{OneTSig}$ will have, at any give time, a public state $\mathsf{st} = (H, \mathsf{Svk})$, consisting of (the description of) a UOWHF H and of a one-time *state* verification key Svk; and a private state consisting of the *state* signing key Ssk

- The *key-generation* algorithm NYKG(1^λ) runs oKG($1^\lambda, 1^\ell$) and let Svk$_0$ and Ssk$_0$ be the verification and the signing key obtained.
  NYKG then randomly selects a UOWHF $H_0 : \{0,1\}^{2\ell+h(\lambda)} \to \{0,1\}^\ell$ from $\mathbb{H}_\lambda$ and outputs initial st$_0 = (H_0, \text{Svk}_0)$ and signing key Ssk$_0$. (Here, $h(\lambda)$ is the length of the description of a UOWHF.)
- The *signing algorithm* NYSig takes as input the i-th ℓ-bit message msg$_i$, the current state st$_{i-1} = (H_{i-1}, \text{Svk}_{i-1})$ and the current signing key Ssk$_{i-1}$ and proceeds as follows.
  1. Randomly select a UOWHF $H_i \leftarrow \mathbb{H}_\lambda$ and construct the following pairs of keys
     - (Svk$_i$, Ssk$_i$) $\leftarrow$ oKG($1^\lambda, 1^\ell$);
     - (Mvk$_i$, Msk$_i$) $\leftarrow$ oKG($1^\lambda, 1^\ell$);
     The new state and signing key are st$_i = (H_i, \text{Svk}_i)$ and Ssk$_i$.
  2. Construct the following two signatures:
     - signature stSig$_i$ of $H_{i-1}(\text{st}_i, \text{Mvk}_i)$ by running oSig on input signing key Ssk$_{i-1}$;
     - signature mSig$_i$ of msg$_i$ by running oSig on input signing key Msk$_i$.
  3. Signature sig$_i = (\text{st}_i, \text{Mvk}_i, \text{stSig}_i, \text{mSig}_i)$ is output.
- The *verification algorithm* NYVerify takes as input signature sig$_i =$ (st$_i$, Mvk$_i$, stSig$_i$, mSig$_i$) of msg$_i$ and the current state st$_{i-1} = (H_{i-1}, \text{Svk}_{i-1})$. First it checks stSig$_i$ by running oVerify on input message $H_{i-1}(\text{st}_i, \text{Mvk}_i)$ and Svk$_{i-1}$. Then it checks mSig$_i$ by running oVerify on input message msg$_i$ and Mvk$_i$.

Fig. 3. The NY signature scheme NYS = (NYKG, NYSig, NYVerify) obtained from one-time signature OneTSig = (oKG, oSig, oVerify) .

associated with Svk. Now let st$_{i-1} = (H_{i-1}, \text{Svk}_{i-1})$ be the public state after the $(i-1)$-st message has been signed and let Ssk$_{i-1}$ be the associated signing key. To sign the next message msg$_i$, the signing algorithm selects a new UOWHF H_i and runs oKG twice to select two pairs of one-time verification and signing keys: the new *state* pair (Svk$_i$, Ssk$_i$) $\leftarrow$ oKG(1^λ) and an ephemeral *message* pair (Mvk$_i$, Msk$_i$) $\leftarrow$ oKG(1^λ). The oSig algorithm is then run twice. The first time on input the message signing key Msk$_i$ to compute a signature of msg$_i$ and the second time on input the current state signing key Ssk$_{i-1}$ to sign a hash computed with respect to H_{i-1} of the new state st$_i = (H_i, \text{Svk}_i)$ and of the ephemeral message verification key Mvk$_i$. A formal description is found in Fig. 3.

Let T $=$ (odKG, oaKG, oaDec) be the weakly anamorphic triplet associated with OneTSig and let us describe the *separable* anamorphic triplet (aNYKG, aNYSig, aNYDec). The anamorphic key-generation aNYKG consists of the parallel execution of algorithm odKG that returns dkey and of NYKG that returns the initial public state (H_0, Svk$_0$) with initial signing key Ssk$_0$. To encrypt the i-th anamorphic message amsg$_i$ as part of the signature of the i-th regular message msg$_i$, the anamorphic signing algorithm aNYSig first runs oaKG on input dkey and amsg$_i$ and obtains the ephemeral message pair (Mvk$_i$, Msk$_i$) and then runs oKG to generate the new state pair (Svk$_i$, Ssk$_i$). The rest of the

- The *anamorphic key-generation* algorithm aNYKG($1^\lambda, 1^\ell$) runs the normal key-generation NYKG algorithm and let $\mathtt{st}_0$ and $\mathtt{Ssk}_0$ be the initial verification and signing key, respectively. In addition the algorithm runs odKG to obtain double key dkey.
- The *anamorphic signing* algorithm aNYSig takes as input the i-th ℓ-bit normal message $\mathtt{msg}_i$, the i-th anamorphic message $\mathtt{amsg}_i$, the current state $\mathtt{st}_{i-1} = (H_{i-1}, \mathtt{Svk}_{i-1})$, the current state signing key $\mathtt{Ssk}_{i-1}$ and the double key dkey and proceeds as follows.
  1. Randomly selects a UOWHF H_i;
  2. The algorithm selects the following key pairs:
     - Message pair ($\mathtt{Mvk}_i, \mathtt{Msk}_i$) is obtained by running oaKG on input dkey and $\mathtt{amsg}_i$;
     - State pair ($\mathtt{Svk}_i, \mathtt{Ssk}_i$) is obtained by running oKG.
  3. The algorithm constructs the following two signatures:
     - signature $\mathtt{stSig}_i$ of $H_{i-1}(\mathtt{st}_i, \mathtt{Mvk}_i)$ by running oSig on input signing key $\mathtt{Ssk}_{i-1}$;
     - signature $\mathtt{mSig}_i$ of $\mathtt{msg}_i$ by running oSig on input signing key $\mathtt{Msk}_i$.
  4. return $\mathtt{sig}_i = (\mathtt{st}_i, \mathtt{Mvk}_i, \mathtt{stSig}_i, \mathtt{mSig}_i)$.
- The *anamorphic decryption* algorithm aNYDec takes as input the anamorphic signature $\mathtt{sig}_i = (\mathtt{st}_i, \mathtt{Mvk}_i, \mathtt{stSig}_i, \mathtt{mSig}_i)$ of $\mathtt{msg}_i$ and the double key dkey. It extracts the first component act of $\mathtt{mSig}_i$ and returns $\mathtt{amsg} = \mathtt{oaDec}(\mathtt{dkey}, \mathtt{act})$.

Fig. 4. The anamorphic triplet aNY = (aNYKG, aNYSig, aNYDec) of the NY signature scheme NYS.

signature algorithm stays unchanged; that is, oSig is used with key $\mathtt{Msk}_i$ to sign $\mathtt{msg}_i$ and with key $\mathtt{Ssk}_{i-1}$ to sign $H_{i-1}(H_i, \mathtt{Svk}_i, \mathtt{Mvk}_i)$. Algorithm aNYDec, on input the signature of $\mathtt{msg}_i$, runs aDec to extract the anamorphic message $\mathtt{amsg}_i$. A formal description is found in Fig. 4. The following theorem is due to [20].

Theorem 22 ([20])**.** *If Universal One-Way Hash functions exist then* NYS *is an unforgeable signature scheme.*

Let us now convince ourselves that the Naor-Yung paradigm yields a private anamorphic many-time signature scheme whenever OneTSig is weakly anamorphic. First of all, observe that in the NY paradigm a new key pair is generated before each signature is produced and this allows to embed the anamorphic message into the verification key. In other words the signature time for the many-time signature scheme produced by NY coincides with the key-generation time of the one-time signature scheme and this allows us to upgrade from weak anamorphism to anamorphism. Moreover, observe that the anamorphic key-generation algorithm is indeed separable as the anamorphic keys are obtained by the regular key-generation algorithm and the double key by an independent execution of algorithm odKG that is guaranteed to exist by weak anamorphism. This guarantees private anamorphism.

We have the following theorem.

Theorem 23. *If universal one-way hash functions exist, the NY signature scheme* NYS = (NYKG, NYSig, NYVerify) *of Fig. 3 is private anamorphic whenever* OneTSig *is weakly anamorphic.*

Proof. First of all, note that if universal one-way hash functions exist then, by Theorem 22, NYS is an unforgeable signature scheme. Next, note that the triplet aNY is separable as aNYKG generates the double-key and the pair of verification and signing key by independent and parallel execution of odKG and of NYKG. See Fig. 4.

To finish the proof, let us assume, for sake of contradiction, that there exists a PPT dictator $\mathcal{D}$ that breaks the anamorphism of NY = (NYKG, NYSig, NYVerify) and its triplet aNY and we show existence of PPT dictator $\mathcal{A}$ that breaks the weak anamorphism of OneTSig = (oKG, oSig, oVerify) and of its weakly anamorphic triplet T = (odKG, oaKG, oaDec)

For clarity, in Fig. 5 and 6, we instantiate the real game for NY and the anamorphic game for aNY by describing NYKG and NYSig in terms of the underlying one-time signature scheme OneTSig and the algorithms of the anamorphic triplet aNY = (aNYSig, NYVerify, aNYDec) in terms of the algorithms of the weakly anamorphic triplet T = (odKG, oaKG, oaDec) for the one-time signature scheme.

$\mathsf{RealG}^{\mathcal{D}}_{\mathsf{NY}}(\lambda)$

- $(\mathbf{svk}_0, \mathbf{ssk}_0) \leftarrow \mathsf{oKG}(1^\lambda)$ and $H_0 \leftarrow \mathbb{H}_\lambda$;
- return $\mathcal{D}^{\mathsf{Os}(\cdot,\cdot,\mathbf{ssk}_0)}((H_0, \mathbf{svk}_0), \mathbf{ssk}_0)$.

where $\mathsf{Os}(\mathbf{msg}_i, \mathbf{amsg}_i, \mathbf{ssk}_0)$ computes its reply using NYSig and precisely as follows:

1. Let $\mathbf{st}_{i-1} = (H_{i-1}, \mathsf{Svk}_{i-1})$ be the current state and let Ssk_{i-1} be the current signing key.
2. Randomly select a UOWHF $H_i \leftarrow \mathbb{H}_\lambda$ and construct the following pairs of keys
   - $(\mathsf{Svk}_i, \mathsf{Ssk}_i) \leftarrow \mathsf{oKG}(1^\lambda, 1^\ell)$;
   - $(\mathsf{Mvk}_i, \mathsf{Msk}_i) \leftarrow \mathsf{oKG}(1^\lambda, 1^\ell)$;
   The new state and signing key are $\mathbf{st}_i = (H_i, \mathsf{Svk}_i)$ and Ssk_i.
3. Construct the following two signatures:
   - signature $\mathbf{stSig}_i$ of $H_{i-1}(\mathbf{st}_i, \mathsf{Mvk}_i)$ by running oSig on input signing key Ssk_{i-1};
   - signature $\mathbf{mSig}_i$ of $\mathbf{msg}_i$ by running oSig on input signing key Msk_i.
4. Signature $\mathbf{sig}_i = (\mathbf{st}_i, \mathsf{Mvk}_i, \mathbf{stSig}_i, \mathbf{mSig}_i)$ is returned.

Fig. 5. The real game

Simple inspection of the description of the two games shows that the only difference between the two games is in the way the message pair of keys $(\mathsf{Mvk}_i, \mathsf{Msk}_i)$

$\text{AnamorphicG}_{\text{aNY}}^{\mathcal{D}}(\lambda)$

  - $(\text{svk}_0, \text{ssk}_0) \leftarrow \text{oKG}(1^\lambda)$ and $H_0 \leftarrow \mathbb{H}_\lambda$;
  - $\text{dkey} \leftarrow \text{odKG}(1^\lambda)$.
  - return $\mathcal{D}^{\text{Oa}(\cdot, \cdot, \text{assk}_0, \text{dkey})}(\text{svk}_0, \text{ssk}_0)$.

where $\text{Oa}(\text{msg}_i, \text{amsg}_i, \text{assk}_0, \text{dkey})$ computes its reply using aNYSig and precisely as follows:

1. Randomly select a UOWHF $H_i \leftarrow \mathbb{H}_\lambda$ and construct the following pairs of keys
   - $(\text{Svk}_i, \text{Ssk}_i) \leftarrow \text{oKG}(1^\lambda, 1^\ell)$;
   - $(\text{Mvk}_i, \text{Msk}_i) \leftarrow \text{oaKG}(1^\lambda, 1^\ell, \text{dkey}, \text{amsg}_i)$;
   The new state and signing key are $\text{st}_i = (H_i, \text{Svk}_i)$ and Ssk_i.
2. Construct the following two signatures:
   - signature stSig_i of $H_{i-1}(\text{st}_i, \text{Mvk}_i)$ by running oSig on input signing key Ssk_{i-1};
   - signature mSig_i of msg_i by running oSig on input signing key Msk_i.
3. Signature $\text{sig}_i = (\text{st}_i, \text{Mvk}_i, \text{stSig}_i, \text{mSig}_i)$ is returned.

Fig. 6. The anamorphic game

is computed. Now suppose that that there exists a PPT dictator $\mathcal{D}$ that distinguishes the two games. That is, there exists a polynomial poly such that

$$\left| \text{Prob}\left[\text{RealG}_{\text{NY},\mathcal{D}}(\lambda) = 1\right] - \text{Prob}\left[\text{AnamorphicG}_{\text{aNY},\mathcal{D}}(\lambda) = 1\right] \right| \geq 1/\text{poly}(\lambda).$$

We construct an adversary $\mathcal{A}$ that contradicts the weak anamorphism of OneTSig and of its triplet T. $\mathcal{A}$ constructs $(\text{svk}_0, \text{ssk}_0)$ by running oKG, picks H_0 at random and runs $\mathcal{D}$ on input $((H_0, \text{svk}_0), \text{ssk}_0)$. $\mathcal{A}$ has access to an oracle $O(\cdot)$ that takes an anamorphic message amsg and returns either a regular pair of one-time verification and signing key or an anamorphic pair with amsg embedded in it. $\mathcal{A}$ uses O to compute the reply to $\mathcal{D}$ oracle queries for anamorphic message amsg. Specifically, $\mathcal{A}$ computes the reply just as in RealG (or AnamorphicG) with the only exception that the pair (Mvk, Msk) is computed by querying O on amsg.

Now observe that if $\mathcal{A}$ is playing $\text{WeakG}_{\text{S,T},\mathcal{A}}^0$ then the oracle computes its output by running oKG and thus $\mathcal{A}$ is providing $\mathcal{D}$ with a view from $\text{RealG}_{\text{NY},\mathcal{D}}$. Therefore we have that

$$\text{Prob}\left[\text{WeakG}_{\text{S,T},\mathcal{A}}^0(1^\lambda)\right] = \text{Prob}\left[\text{RealG}_{\text{NY},\mathcal{D}}(1^\lambda) = 1\right].$$

On the other hand, if $\mathcal{A}$ is playing $\text{WeakG}_{\text{S,T},\mathcal{A}}^1$ then the oracle computes its output by running oaKG and thus $\mathcal{A}$ is providing $\mathcal{D}$ with a view from $\text{AnamorphicG}_{\text{aNY},\mathcal{D}}$. Therefore we have that

$$\text{Prob}\left[\text{WeakG}_{\text{S,T},\mathcal{A}}^1(1^\lambda) = 1\right] = \text{Prob}\left[\text{AnamorphicG}_{\text{aNY},\mathcal{D}}(1^\lambda) = 1\right].$$

By our assumption on $\mathcal{D}$, we obtain that $\mathcal{A}$ breaks the weak anamorphism of OneTSig. Contradiction.

We observe, but do not elaborate further as optimizing efficiency is not a goal of this paper, that one NY signature can accommodate l anamorphic messages making the anamorphic communication very efficient. By instantiating the NY paradigm [20] with Lamport's tagging system [27] and by using Rompel's construction for UOWHF [27], we obtain the Naor-Yung-Lamport-Rompel private anamorphic signature scheme, whose security can be based on the existence of one-way functions.

Theorem 24. *If one-way functions exist, then there exists a private anamorphic signature scheme.*

8 Conclusions

Naturally, when the primary reason(s) for designing a cryptosystem are well motivated, formalized, and understood, the next issues to think about are abuse and misuse of such systems in the overall systems security ecosystem. Anamorphic Cryptography is one concrete tool (in the user hand) to review such steps.

We demonstrated that even in scenarios where only authentication/ signatures are allowed and encryption is neutralized, there is a direct way to implement anamorphic channels between a signer and a receiver of the signed message (while employing already designed, existing, or standardized methods and systems). We formulated the conditions under which hidden anamorphic channels are possible, primarily to demonstrate some of the futility of restrictions imposed by governments on cryptographic systems, and we hope others will build on this initial study. However, we also noted that anamorphic signature schemes have other uses, and we showed that they can contribute to other cryptosystems being anamorphic, and be used to design watermarking of signature schemes in order to serve various protective purposes. More applications of the notion are expected to be discovered in future work.

Acknowledgment. The first and the last author have been supported by the National Centre for Research and Development (Warsaw), project ESCAPE PL-TW/VII/5/2020.

References

1. Abdalla, M., An, J.H., Bellare, M., Namprempre, C.: From identification to signatures via the Fiat-Shamir transform: minimizing assumptions for security and forward-security. In: Knudsen, L.R. (ed.) EUROCRYPT 2002. LNCS, vol. 2332, pp. 418–433. Springer, Heidelberg (2002). https://doi.org/10.1007/3-540-46035-7_28
2. Beth, T.: Efficient zero-knowledge identification scheme for smart cards. In: Günther, C.G. (ed.) EUROCRYPT'88. LNCS, vol. 330, pp. 77–84. Springer, Heidelberg (1988)

3. Brickell, E.F., McCurley, K.S.: An interactive identification scheme based on discrete logarithms and factoring. In: Damgård, I.B. (ed.) EUROCRYPT 1990. LNCS, vol. 473, pp. 63–71. Springer, Heidelberg (1991). https://doi.org/10.1007/3-540-46877-3_6

4. Canetti, R., Halevi, S., Katz, J.: Chosen-ciphertext security from identity-based encryption. In: Cachin, C., Camenisch, J. (eds.) EUROCRYPT 2004. LNCS, vol. 3027, pp. 207–222. Springer, Heidelberg (2004). https://doi.org/10.1007/978-3-540-24676-3_13

5. Chaum, D., Pedersen, T.P.: Wallet databases with observers. In: Brickell, E.F. (ed.) CRYPTO 1992. LNCS, vol. 740, pp. 89–105. Springer, Heidelberg (1993). https://doi.org/10.1007/3-540-48071-4_7

6. Cramer, R., Damgård, I., Schoenmakers, B.: Proofs of partial knowledge and simplified design of witness hiding protocols. In: Desmedt, Y.G. (ed.) CRYPTO 1994. LNCS, vol. 839, pp. 174–187. Springer, Heidelberg (1994). https://doi.org/10.1007/3-540-48658-5_19

7. Davies, D.W.: Applying the RSA digital signature to electronic mail. Computer 16(2), 55–62 (1983)

8. Digital Signature Standard (DSS). National Institute of Standards and Technology (NIST), FIPS PUB 186-4, U.S. Department of Commerce, July (2013)

9. Durumeric, Z., et al.: The security impact of HTTPS interception. In: NDSS 2017. The Internet Society, February/March (2017)

10. ElGamal, T.: A public key cryptosystem and a signature scheme based on discrete logarithms. In: Blakley, G.R., Chaum, D. (eds.) CRYPTO 1984. LNCS, vol. 196, pp. 10–18. Springer, Heidelberg (1985). https://doi.org/10.1007/3-540-39568-7_2

11. Fiat, A., Shamir, A.: How to prove yourself: practical solutions to identification and signature problems. In: Odlyzko, A.M. (ed.) CRYPTO'86. LNCS, vol. 263, pp. 186–194. Springer, Heidelberg (1987)

12. Girault, M.: An identity-based identification scheme based on discrete logarithms modulo a composite number (rump session). In: Damgård, I. (ed.) EUROCRYPT'90. LNCS, vol. 473, pp. 481–486. Springer, Heidelberg (1991)

13. Goldreich, O., Micali, S., Wigderson, A.: Proofs that yield nothing but their validity and a methodology of cryptographic protocol design (extended abstract). In: 27th FOCS, pages 174–187. IEEE Computer Society Press, October (1986)

14. Goyal, R., Kim, S., Manohar, N., Waters, B., David, J.W.: Watermarking public-key cryptographic primitives. In: Boldyreva, A., Micciancio, D. (eds.) CRYPTO 2019. Part III, volume 11694 of LNCS, pp. 367–398. Springer, Heidelberg (2019). https://doi.org/10.1007/978-3-030-26954-8_12

15. Guillou, L.C., Quisquater, J.-J.: A "Paradoxical" indentity-based signature scheme resulting from zero-knowledge. In: Goldwasser, S. (ed.) CRYPTO 1988. LNCS, vol. 403, pp. 216–231. Springer, New York (1990). https://doi.org/10.1007/0-387-34799-2_16

16. Hopper, N., Molnar, D., Wagner, D.: From weak to strong watermarking. In: Vadhan, S.P. (ed.) TCC 2007. LNCS, vol. 4392, pp. 362–382. Springer, Heidelberg (2007). https://doi.org/10.1007/978-3-540-70936-7_20

17. Kutyłowski, M., Persiano, G., Hieu Phan, D., Yung, M., Zawada, M.: Anamorphic signatures: secrecy from a dictator who only permits authentication! Cryptology ePrint Archive, Report 2023/356 (2023). https://eprint.iacr.org/2023/356

18. Lamport, L.: Constructing digital signatures from a one-way function. Technical Report SRI-CSL-98, SRI International Computer Science Laboratory, October (1979)

19. Micali, S., Shamir, A.: An improvement of the Fiat-Shamir identification and signature scheme. In: Goldwasser, S. (ed.) CRYPTO'88. LNCS, vol. 403, pp. 244–247. Springer, Heidelberg (1990)
20. Naor, M., Yung, M.: Universal one-way hash functions and their cryptographic applications. In: 21st ACM STOC, pp. 33–43. ACM Press, May (1989)
21. Okamoto, T.: Provably secure and practical identification schemes and corresponding signature schemes. In: Brickell, E.F. (ed.) CRYPTO'92. LNCS, vol. 740, pp. 31–53. Springer, Heidelberg (1993). https://doi.org/10.1007/3-540-48071-4_3
22. Ong, H., Schnorr, C.P.: Fast signature generation with a Fiat Shamir — like scheme. In: Damgård, I.B. (ed.) EUROCRYPT 1990. LNCS, vol. 473, pp. 432–440. Springer, Heidelberg (1991). https://doi.org/10.1007/3-540-46877-3_38
23. Persiano, G., Hieu Phan, D., Yung, M.: Anamorphic encryption: private communication against a dictator. In: Dunkelman, O., Dziembowski, S., editors, EUROCRYPT 2022, Part II, volume 13276 of LNCS, pp. 34–63. Springer, Heidelberg, May/June (2022). https://doi.org/10.1007/978-3-031-07085-3_2
24. Pointcheval, D.: A new identification scheme based on the perceptrons problem. In: Guillou, L.C., Quisquater, J.-J. (eds.) EUROCRYPT'95. LNCS, vol. 921, pp. 319–328. Springer, Heidelberg (1995). https://doi.org/10.1007/3-540-49264-X_26
25. Pointcheval, D., Stern, J.: Security proofs for signature schemes. In: Maurer, U.M. (ed.) EUROCRYPT'96. LNCS, vol. 1070, pp. 387–398. Springer, Heidelberg (1996). https://doi.org/10.1007/3-540-68339-9_33
26. Rivest, R.L.: Chaffing and Winnowing: confidentiality without encryption (1998). https://people.csail.mit.edu/rivest/pubs/Riv98a.prepub.txt
27. Rompel, J.: One-way functions are necessary and sufficient for secure signatures. In: 22nd ACM STOC, pp. 387–394. ACM Press, May (1990)
28. Russell, A., Tang, Q., Yung, M., Zhou, H.-S.: Cliptography: clipping the power of kleptographic attacks. In: Cheon, J.H., Takagi, T. (eds.) ASIACRYPT 2016. LNCS, vol. 10032, pp. 34–64. Springer, Heidelberg (2016). https://doi.org/10.1007/978-3-662-53890-6_2
29. Schnorr, C.-P.: Efficient signature generation by smart cards. J. Cryptol. 4(3), 161–174 (1991)
30. Simmons, G.J.: The prisoners' problem and the subliminal channel. In: Chaum, D., editor, CRYPTO'83, pp. 51–67. Plenum Press, New York, USA (1983)
31. Stern, J.: A new identification scheme based on syndrome decoding. In: Stinson, D.R. (ed.) CRYPTO 1993. LNCS, vol. 773, pp. 13–21. Springer, Heidelberg (1994). https://doi.org/10.1007/3-540-48329-2_2
32. Young, A., Yung, M.: The dark side of "Black-Box" cryptography or: should we trust capstone? In: Koblitz, N. (ed.) CRYPTO 1996. LNCS, vol. 1109, pp. 89–103. Springer, Heidelberg (1996). https://doi.org/10.1007/3-540-68697-5_8

Author Index

A

Aggarwal, Divesh   580

B

Bellés-Muñoz, Marta   3
Bitansky, Nir   132
Bootle, Jonathan   227, 384
Brakerski, Zvika   252
Brodsky, Maya Farber   252

C

Champion, Jeffrey   38
Chase, Melissa   418
Chen, Yu Long   694
Chiesa, Alessandro   227
Choi, Wonseok   694
Chung, Eldon   580
Cini, Valerio   72

D

Dao, Quang   315
Devadas, Srinivas   611
Dodis, Yevgeniy   514
Durak, F. Betül   418
Dziembowski, Stefan   547

F

Faust, Sebastian   547
Ferguson, Niels   514
Fisch, Ben   106

G

Ghoshal, Ashrujit   482
Goldin, Eli   514
Golovnev, Alexander   193, 453
Guo, Siyao   453

H

Hall, Peter   514
Hofheinz, Dennis   725

I

Ishai, Yuval   159, 315

J

Jain, Aayush   315
Jeudy, Corentin   351
Jiménez Urroz, Jorge   3

K

Kalai, Yael Tauman   252
Kastner, Julia   725
Klein, Karen   725
Kutyłowski, Mirosław   759

L

Lai, Russell W. F.   72
Lazzaretti, Arthur   284
Lee, Changmin   694
Lee, Jonathan   193
Lin, Huijia   315
Liu, Yanyi   645
Liu, Zeyu   106
Lizurej, Tomasz   547
Lombardi, Alex   252
Lyubashevsky, Vadim   384

M

Malavolta, Giulio   72

N

Nguyen, Ngoc Khanh   384

O

Obremski, Maciej   580
Ostrovsky, Rafail   159

P

Paneth, Omer   132, 252
Papamanthou, Charalampos   284
Pass, Rafael   645
Persiano, Giuseppe   759
Peters, Spencer   453

Phan, Duong Hieu   759
Pietrzak, Krzysztof   514

R

Roux-Langlois, Adeline   351

S

Sanders, Olivier   351
Setty, Srinath   193
Shah, Akash   159
Shamir, Dana   132
Silva, Javier   3
Solomon, Tomer   132
Sorniotti, Alessandro   384
Sotiraki, Katerina   227
Stephens-Davidowitz, Noah   453

T

Tessaro, Stefano   482
Thaler, Justin   193

V

Vaudenay, Serge   418
Vesely, Psi   106

W

Wahby, Riad S.   193
Waters, Brent   674
Wichs, Daniel   674
Wu, David J.   38

X

Xiao, Hanshen   611

Y

Yung, Moti   759

Z

Zawada, Marcin   759

Printed in the United States
by Baker & Taylor Publisher Services